1952 First edition of DSM published by the American Psychiatric Association. *p. 108*

1952 Sex-change operation performed on Christine Jorgensen. *p. 447*

1955 The Los Angeles Suicide Prevention Center founded. *p. 333*

1956 Family systems theory and therapy launched. *pp. 76, 79*

1958 Joseph Wolpe develops desensitization. *p. 66*

1961 Thomas Szasz publishes *The Myth of Mental Illness*. *p. 5*

1962 Albert Ellis proposes rational-emotive therapy. *pp. 68, 127*

1963 The Community Mental Health Act helps trigger deinstitutionalization in the United States. *p. 497*

1963 Antianxiety drug Valium introduced in the United States. *p. 132*

1964 U.S. Surgeon General warns that smoking can be dangerous to human health. *p. 374*

1965 Norepinephrine and serotonin theories of depression proposed. *p. 249*

1967 Aaron Beck publishes cognitive theory and therapy for depression. *pp. 257, 282*

1967 Methadone maintenance treatment begins. *p. 382*

1970 Masters and Johnson publish *Human Sexual Inadequacy* and launch sex therapy. *p. 428*

1972 CAT scan introduced. *p. 102*

1973 DSM stops listing homosexuality as a mental disorder. *p. 444*

1973 David Rosenhan conducts study *On Being Sane in Insane Places*. *pp. 76, 475*

1975 Endorphins—natural opioids—discovered in human brain. *p. 384*

1975 U.S. Supreme Court declares that patients in institutions have right to adequate treatment. *p. 634*

1981 MRI first used as diagnostic tool. *p. 102*

1982 John Hinckley found not guilty by reason of insanity of the attempted murder of President Reagan. *p. 619*

1987 Antidepressant Prozac approved in the United States. *p. 294*

1988 American Psychological Society founded. *p. 23*

1990 Dr. Jack Kevorkian performs his first assisted suicide. *p. 334*

1990 FDA approves first atypical antipsychotic drug, *clozapine*. *p. 491*

1994 DSM-IV published. *p. 444*

1995 APA task force begins search to identify empirically supported (evidence-based) treatments. *p. 144*

1998 Viagra goes on sale in the United States. *p. 421*

1999 Killing rampage at Columbine High School stirs public concern about dangerousness in children. *p. 563*

2000 DSM-IV-TR is published and changes criteria for pedophilia, exhibitionism, voyeurism, frotteurism, and sexual sadism. *pp. 107, 441*

2000 Scientists finish mapping (i.e., sequencing) the human genome—spelling out the chemical "letters" that make up human DNA. *p. 53*

2001 Around 1,600 mental health workers mobilize to help 57,000 victims in wake of 9/11 terrorist attacks. *pp. 172, 181*

2002 New Mexico grants prescription privileges to specially trained psychologists. *p. 637*

2004 FDA orders *black box* warnings on all antidepressant drug containers, stating that the drugs "increase the risk of suicidal thinking and behavior in children." *p. 329*

2006 U.S. Supreme Court upholds Oregon's "Death with Dignity" Act, allowing doctors to assist suicides by terminally ill individuals under certain conditions. *p. 334*

2006 Andrea Yates, who drowned her five children while suffering from postpartum psychosis, is retried and found not guilty by reason of insanity. *p. 625*

2007 Thirteen work groups begin meeting to produce DSM-V by 2012. *p. 111*

2008 U.S. Congress passes "parity" bill, requiring insurance companies to provide equal (parity) coverage for mental and physical problems. *p. 20*

2008 The American Psychological Association votes to ban members from participating in all forms of interrogation at U.S. detention centers, including Guantanamo Bay. *p. 172*

Abnormal Psychology

Abnormal Psychology

SEVENTH EDITION

Ronald J. Comer

Princeton University

Worth Publishers

New York

Senior Publisher: Catherine Woods
Senior Acquisitions Editor: Kevin Feyen
Senior Development Editor: Mimi Melek
Marketing Manager: Amy Shefferd
Associate Managing Editor: Tracey Kuehn
Media Editor: Peter Twickler
Project Editor: Jane O'Neill
Photo Editor: Ted Szczepanski
Art Director and Cover/Text Designer: Barbara Reingold
Art Researcher and Production Designer: Lyndall Culbertson
Layout Designer: Paul Lacy
Cover Illustrator: Wieslaw Walkuski
Production Manager: Sarah Segal
Composition: Northeastern Graphic, Inc.
Printing and Binding: RR Donnelley

We are grateful to the following artists for providing the illustrations on the chapter opening pages: Wieslaw Walkuski, pp. xxviii, 202, 508; Elizabeth Lada, p. 26; Phillipe Lardy, p. 48; Brian Stauffe, p. 88; Jean Francois Podevin, p. 120; James Steinberg, p. 162; Jordin Isip, p. 240; John Dinser, p. 274; Anthony Tremmaglia, p. 306; Diane Fenster, p. 340; Simon G. Phelipot, p. 372; Thomas Ehretsmann, p. 414; Anita Kunz, pp. 452, 618; Richard Hess, p. 480; Greg Spalenka, p. 548; James Fryer, p. 592.

Credits for timeline photos, inside front cover (by date): 1893, Sigmund Freud Copyrights/Everett Collection; 1901, W. H. Freeman and Company; 1907, Stephane Audras/REA/Redux; 1929, Joe McNally, Sygma; 1964, Greg Baker/AP Photo; 1981, Pallava Bagla/Corbis; 2001, AP Photo/Ernesto Mora; 2006, Pool photo by Getty Images.

Credits for miscellaneous text excerpts: p. 307, Dennis Yusko, "At Home, but Locked in War," *Times Union* (Albany) Online. Copyright © 2008 by *Times Union*/Albany. Reproduced with permission via Copyright Clearance Center; p. 513, case study excerpt from Bernstein et al., *Personality Disorders*. Copyright © 2007 by Sage Publications Inc. Books. Reproduced with permission via Copyright Clearance Center; pp. 529–530, case study excerpts from Meyer and Osborne, *Case Studies in Abnormal Behavior,* 2nd edition. Copyright © 2002. Reprinted by permission of Pearson Education, Inc.; pp. 537–538, case study excerpt reprinted with permission from the DSM IV-TR Casebook. Copyright © 2002 American Psychiatric Association.

Library of Congress Control Number: 2008911149

ISBN-13 978-1-4292-1631-9
ISBN-10 1-4292-1631-X

Printed in the United States of America
Third Printing

Worth Publishers
41 Madison Avenue
New York, NY 10010
www.worthpublishers.com

To the remarkable Kevin Feyen
Thank you for your wisdom,
guidance, and friendship

ABOUT THE AUTHOR

Ronald J. Comer has been a professor in Princeton University's Department of Psychology for the past 35 years and has served as Director of Clinical Psychology Studies for most of that time. His courses—Abnormal Psychology, Theories of Psychotherapy, Childhood Psychopathology, Experimental Psychopathology, and Controversies in Clinical Psychology—have been among the university's most popular offerings.

Professor Comer has received the President's Award for Distinguished Teaching at the university. He is also a practicing clinical psychologist and serves as a consultant to the Eden Institute for Persons with Autism and to hospitals and family practice residency programs throughout New Jersey.

In addition to writing *Abnormal Psychology,* Professor Comer is the author of the textbook *Fundamentals of Abnormal Psychology,* now in its fifth edition, and the co-author of *Case Studies in Abnormal Psychology.* He is the producer of a range of educational videos, including *The Higher Education Video Library Series, Video Segments in Abnormal Psychology, Video Segments in Neuroscience, Introduction to Psychology Video Clipboard,* and

Developmental Psychology Video Clipboard. He also has published numerous journal articles in clinical psychology, social psychology, and family medicine.

Professor Comer completed his undergraduate studies at the University of Pennsylvania and his graduate work at Clark University. He lives in Lawrenceville, New Jersey, with his wife, Marlene. From there he can keep an eye on his sons, Greg and Jon, and his daughter-in-law, Jami, who live in New York City, and on the Philadelphia sports teams with which he grew up. Frustrated for years by the latter, he was shaken to the core by the 2008 World Series success of the Philadelphia Phillies and currently is trying his best to adjust to the new world order.

CONTENTS IN BRIEF

CONTENTS

CHAPTER :9

⚙ Treatments for Mood Disorders 275

CHAPTER :10

⚙ Suicide 307

CHAPTER :11

⚙ Eating Disorders 341

CHAPTER :14

Schizophrenia 453

CHAPTER :15

Treatments for Schizophrenia and Other Severe Mental Disorders 481

CHAPTER :16

Personality Disorders 509

CHAPTER :**17**

Disorders of Childhood and Adolescence **549**

CHAPTER :**18**

Disorders of Aging and Cognition **593**

CHAPTER :19

Law, Society, and the Mental Health Profession 619

PREFACE

I have been writing my textbooks, *Abnormal Psychology* and *Fundamentals of Abnormal Psychology*, for close to three decades—almost half of my life. The current version, *Abnormal Psychology*, Seventh Edition, represents the twelfth edition of one or the other of the textbooks. The journey truly has been a labor of love, but I also must admit that each edition has required enormous effort, ridiculous pressure, and too many sleepless nights to count.

I do not mention these labors to complain. To the contrary, I feel deeply appreciative and privileged to have had the opportunity to help educate more than a half-million readers over the years. Instead, I mention them to help emphasize that I have approached each edition as a totally new undertaking rather than as a cut-and-paste update of past editions. My goal each time has been that the new edition is a fresh, comprehensive, and exciting presentation of the current state of this ever-changing field and that it includes state-of-the-art pedagogical techniques and insights. This "new book" approach to each edition is, I believe, the key reason for the continuing success of the textbooks, and the current edition has been written in this same tradition.

In fact, the current edition includes even more changes than in any of the textbook's previous editions. This was done for several reasons: (1) The field of abnormal psychology has had a dramatic growth spurt over the past several years; (2) the field of education has produced a wide range of new pedagogical tools; (3) the world of publishing has developed new, striking ways of presenting material to readers; and (4) the world at large has changed dramatically, featuring a monumental rise in the Internet's impact on our lives, growing influence by the media, near unthinkable economic and political events, and a changing world order. All such changes should find their way into a book about the current state of human functioning, and I have worked hard to include them here in a profound and integrated way.

That said, I believe I have produced a new edition of *Abnormal Psychology* that will once again excite readers, open the field of abnormal psychology to them, and speak to them and their times, while at the same time demonstrating that behavior, including abnormal behavior, pervades their lives and their world. Throughout the book I have again sought to convey my passion for the field, and I have built on the generous feedback of my colleagues in this enterprise—the students and professors who have used this textbook over the years. At the risk of sounding even more grandiose than I actually am, let me describe what I believe to be special about this edition.

Changes and Features New to This Edition

As I just noted, enormous changes have taken place over the past several years both in the fields of abnormal psychology, education, and publishing and in the world. Keeping such developments in mind, I have brought the following changes and new features to the current edition.

EXPANDED MULTICULTURAL COVERAGE Over the past 25 years, clinical theorists and researchers increasingly have become interested in ethnic, racial, gender, and other cultural factors, and my previous editions of *Abnormal Psychology* certainly have included these important factors. In the twenty-first century, however, the study of such factors has, appropriately, been elevated to a broad perspective—the *multicultural perspective*, a theoretical and treatment approach to abnormal behavior that is, or should be, considered across all forms of psychopathology and treatment. Consistent with this clinical movement, the current edition includes the following:

1. Broad *multicultural perspective* sections within each chapter of the textbook, each examining in depth the impact of cultural issues on the diagnosis, development, and treatment of the abnormal pattern in question. Chapter 3, *Models of Abnormality,* for example, includes sections on culture-sensitive therapies and gender-sensitive therapies (pages 82–83); Chapter 5, *Anxiety Disorders,* examines the ties between race, culture, and posttraumatic stress disorder (pages 178–179); Chapter 8, *Mood Disorders,* discusses the links between gender, culture, and depression (pages 261–263); and Chapter 11, *Eating Disorders,* probes the relationships between race, gender, and eating disorders (pages 360–362).

2. Numerous boxes, collectively titled *Eye on Culture* boxes, appear throughout the text, further emphasizing multicultural issues. These include boxes such as "Culture-Bound Abnormality" (Chapter 4), "First Dibs on Antidepressant Drugs?" (Chapter 9), "Eating Disorders across the World" (Chapter 11), and "First Dibs on Atypical Antipsychotic Drugs?" (Chapter 15).

3. *Multicultural photography, figures, and cases.* If our society is indeed multicultural and the clinical field has increasingly appreciated this, then photographs, art, and case presentations throughout the textbook should reflect such diversity. Even a quick look through the pages of this textbook will reveal that it truly reflects the cultural diversity of our society and of the field of abnormal psychology.

"NEW-WAVE" COGNITIVE AND COGNITIVE-BEHAVIORAL THEORIES AND TREATMENTS Beginning in the 1960s, cognitive and cognitive-behavioral therapists sought to help clients undo the maladaptive attitudes and thought processes that contribute to their psychological dysfunctioning. This, of course, remains a key thrust of the cognitive and cognitive-behavioral models, but it also has been joined in recent years by a major new focus, "new-wave" cognitive and cognitive-behavioral theories and therapies that help clients "accept" and objectify those maladaptive thoughts and perspectives that are resistant to change. The current edition of *Abnormal Psychology* fully covers these "new-wave" theories and therapies, including *mindfulness-based cognitive therapy* and *Acceptance and Commitment Therapy* (ACT), presenting their propositions, techniques, and research in chapters throughout the text (for example, pages 69, 130, 283, and 492).

EXPANDED NEUROSCIENCE COVERAGE The twenty-first century has witnessed the continued growth and impact of remarkable brain-imaging techniques, genetic mapping strategies, and other neuroscience approaches, all of which are expanding our understanding of the brain. Correspondingly, biological theories and treatments for abnormal behavior have taken unprecedented leaps forward during the past several years. The current edition brings these leaps to life—fully and in all their splendor. In addition to the biochemical view of abnormal behavior on display in previous editions, the current edition includes detailed coverage of the following:

1. Broader discussions of the genetic underpinnings of abnormal behavior (for example, pages 52–53, 173–176, 247–248, and 464–466).

2. Detailed explanations of both the brain structures and brain functions at the root of abnormal behavior, including, for example, presentations of how various *neural networks* operate and contribute to panic disorder (pages 146–147), obsessive-compulsive disorder (page 157), depression (pages 250–251), and other forms of psychopathology.

3. More revealing descriptions of the neuroimaging techniques themselves and their role in the study of abnormal psychology (for example, pages 100–102).

4. *Neuroscience photography and art.* This edition is filled with photos of exciting *brain scans* that reveal the brain structures and activities at work in abnormal-

ity (for example, pages 157, 250, 267, 401, and 470). Similarly, numerous pieces of new, current, and enlightening anatomical art fill each chapter of the book to help readers better appreciate the locations and interactions of various brain structures as they work together to help produce both normal and abnormal behavior (for example, pages 146, 147, 157, and 470).

5. Analyses of how genetic factors and brain chemicals and structures interact with psychosocial factors to produce abnormal behavior. Abnormality is rarely a matter of biological versus psychosocial factors, and this edition repeatedly clarifies that point (for example, pages 84–85, 158–159, and 369–370).

•NEW• *THE MEDIA SPEAKS* The media is, of course, an extraordinary force in our society, both reflecting and affecting events that occur all around us. And, indeed, its role has become even more powerful and confusing in the twenty-first century as use of the Internet has exploded, countless blogs have emerged, and ordinary people now are able to communicate with masses of unknown others at the click of a mouse. Given the media's profound impact on our behaviors, thoughts, and knowledge, I have added an important recurring feature throughout the text—boxes called *The Media Speaks* in which news and magazine writers offer pieces on subjects and movements in abnormal psychology (for example, "How Well Do Colleges Treat Depression?" on page 277), individuals write firsthand about their experiences with psychological disorders (for example, "Self-Cutting: The Wound That Will Not Heal" on pages 526–527), and editorial writers consider the clinical implications of pop culture (for example, "In Real Time, Amy Winehouse's Deeper Descent" on page 408).

EXPANDED COVERAGE OF KEY DISORDERS AND TOPICS In line with the field's (and society's) increased interest in certain psychological problems and treatments, I have added or greatly expanded the coverage of topics such as torture, terrorism, and psychopathology (pages 172–173); methamphetamine use (pages 387–388); transgender issues (pages 443, 445, and 448); childhood bipolar disorders (pages 556–557); self-cutting (pages 524–527); dialectical behavior therapy (pages 528–529); antidepressant drugs and suicide risk (page 329); music and suicide attempts (pages 318–319); brain interventions such as vagus nerve stimulation, transcranial magnetic stimulation, and deep brain stimulation (pages 293–295); meta-worry explanations of generalized anxiety disorder (pages 128–129); and more.

EXPANDED COVERAGE OF PREVENTION AND OF THE PROMOTION OF MENTAL HEALTH In accord with the clinical field's growing emphasis on prevention, positive psychology, and psychological wellness, I have increased significantly the textbook's attention to these important approaches.

RESTRUCTURED CHAPTER ON CHILDHOOD AND ADOLESCENT DISORDERS To reflect current directions in the clinical field, I have made key changes to Chapter 17, "Disorders of Childhood and Adolescence." Those childhood disorders that parallel adult disorders—particularly anxiety and mood disorders—are now covered in depth within this chapter (rather than spread throughout the book), along with the disorders that are more narrowly tied to young age, such as conduct disorder, ADHD, and enuresis.

SPECIAL FOCUS ON TODAY'S WORLD Abnormal psychology has a long history, affects people of all ages, emerges across many different cultures and societies, has ties to all kinds of events—past and present—and grows from a wide range of factors. And, of course, these elements are all on display throughout the textbook. At the same time, however, one element often is neglected in textbooks—the modern world! We live in an ever-changing world that has, in fact, undergone a major facelift over the past decade. If a textbook is to speak to today's readers—especially student readers—the book's topics, examples, cases, photos, and more must also represent the world in which students live. With this in mind, I also have included throughout the book relevant discussions about "now" factors, such as Facebook, MySpace, YouTube, ecoanxiety, cell phone use, transgender issues, pop culture, emo music, Internet addiction, club drugs, and more. The finished product is, in turn, a more complete book about abnormal psychology—past and present—that is relevant to all.

NEW BOXES In this edition, I have grouped the various boxes into four categories to orient the reader better. In addition to *The Media Speaks* boxes and *Eye on Culture* boxes mentioned earlier, the seventh edition contains *A Closer Look* boxes (ones that examine text topics in more depth) and *PsychWatch* boxes (ones that look at examples of abnormal psychology in movies, the news, and the world around us). I have, of course, updated all of the boxes retained from the last edition, and I have also added 21 completely new boxes, including boxes such as:

- *The Media Speaks:* "Can You Live with the Voices in Your Head?" (Chapter 15)
- *PsychWatch:* "Dark Sites on the Internet" (Chapter 4)
- *A Closer Look:* "The Black Box Controversy: Do Antidepressants Cause Suicide?" (Chapter 10)
- *Eye on Culture:* "Eating Disorders across the World" (Chapter 11)
- *The Media Speaks:* "Mad Pride Fights a Stigma" (Chapter 19)
- *PsychWatch:* "Surfing for Help" (Chapter 3)

NEW, CURRENT, AND INNOVATIVE DESIGN The seventh edition of *Abnormal Psychology* has been redesigned strikingly to give it an eye-catching and modern look—one that builds on new trends in publishing and pedagogy, speaks to the reader, and leads the way for new textbook designs. In one feature of this design, for example, figures and photos *pop* with captions that literally "grab" the reader's attention. At the same time, the design retains a feature from past editions that has been very popular among students and professors—the use of a single text column along with a wide margin that provides space for reader-friendly elements called "Between the Lines"—text-relevant tidbits, surprising facts, current events, historical notes, interesting trends, fun lists, and provocative quotes.

THOROUGH UPDATE In this edition I present recent theories, research, and events, including more than 2,000 new references from the years 2006–2009, as well as hundreds of new photos, tables, and figures.

Continuing Strengths

In this edition I have also been careful to retain the themes, material, and techniques that have worked successfully and been embraced enthusiastically by past readers.

BREADTH AND BALANCE The field's many theories, studies, disorders, and treatments are presented completely and accurately. All major models—psychological, biological, and sociocultural—receive objective, balanced, up-to-date coverage, without bias toward any single approach.

INTEGRATION OF MODELS Discussions throughout the text, particularly those headed "Putting It Together," help students better understand where and how the various models work together and how they differ.

EMPATHY The subject of abnormal psychology is people—very often people in great pain. I have tried therefore to write always with empathy and to impart this awareness to students.

INTEGRATED COVERAGE OF TREATMENT Discussions of treatment are presented throughout the book. In addition to a complete overview of treatment in the opening chapters, each of the pathology chapters includes a full discussion of relevant treatment approaches.

RICH CASE MATERIAL I integrate numerous and culturally diverse clinical examples to bring theoretical and clinical issues to life. More than 25 percent of the clinical material in this edition is new or revised significantly.

TOPICS OF SPECIAL INTEREST I devote full chapters to important subjects that are of special interest to college-age readers, such as eating disorders and suicide, and I also cover controversial issues that currently are receiving considerable public attention, including the impact of managed care, direct-to-consumer advertising, the rise in use of Ritalin, virtual reality treatments, and the right to commit suicide.

DSM CHECKLISTS The discussion of each disorder is accompanied by a detailed checklist of the DSM-IV-TR criteria used to diagnose the disorder.

MARGIN GLOSSARY Hundreds of key words are defined in the margins of pages on which the words appear. In addition, a traditional glossary is available at the back of the book.

"PUTTING IT TOGETHER" A section toward the end of each chapter, "Putting It Together," asks whether competing models can work together in a more integrated approach and also summarizes where the field now stands and where it may be going.

FOCUS ON CRITICAL THINKING The textbook provides tools for thinking critically about abnormal psychology. In particular, toward the end of each chapter a section called "Critical Thoughts" poses questions that help students to analyze and apply the material they have just read. Twenty-five percent of these questions are new to the seventh edition.

"CYBERSTUDY" Each chapter ends with a "CyberStudy" section, a guide to integrating the chapter material with videos and other features found on the *Abnormal Psychology* Student Tool Kit.

STIMULATING ILLUSTRATIONS Chapters illustrate concepts, disorders, treatments, and applications with stunning photographs, diagrams, graphs, and anatomical figures. All of the figures, graphs, and tables, many new to this edition, reflect the most up-to-date data available.

ADAPTABILITY Chapters are self-contained, so they can be assigned in any order that makes sense to the professor.

Supplements

I have been delighted by the enthusiastic responses of both professors and students to the supplements that accompany my textbooks. This edition offers those supplements once again, revised and enhanced, and adds a number of exciting new ones.

FOR PROFESSORS

•NEW• VIDEO SEGMENTS FOR *ABNORMAL PSYCHOLOGY, NEW EDITION Produced and edited by Ronald J. Comer, Princeton University, and Gregory Comer, Princeton Academic Resources. Faculty Guide* included. This incomparable video series offers 125 clips—half of them new to this edition—that depict disorders, show historical footage, and illustrate clinical topics, pathologies, treatments, experiments, and dilemmas. Videos are available on DVD, VHS, or CD-ROM. I also have written an accompanying guide that fully describes and discusses each video clip, so that professors can make informed decisions about the use of the segments in lectures.

In addition, Nicholas Greco, College of Lake County, has written a completely new set of questions to accompany each video segment in the series. The questions have been added to the *Faculty Guide* (now available in the *Instructor's Resource Manual*) and are also available in PowerPoint® on the companion Web site or the Instructor's Resource CD-ROM (for use with Worth Publishers' iClicker Classroom Response System).

CLINICAL VIDEO CASE FILE FOR *ABNORMAL PSYCHOLOGY* *Produced and edited by Ronald J. Comer and Gregory Comer. Faculty Guide included.* To accompany this edition, I have also pulled together a set of 10 longer *video case studies* that bring to life particularly interesting forms of psychopathology and treatment. These in-depth and authentic videos provide students with a critical window into the world of abnormal psychology and the people who suffer from the disorders. The videos are available on DVD, VHS, or CD-ROM.

POWERPOINT® SLIDES *Available at www.worthpublishers.com/comer or on the Instructor's Resource CD-ROM.* These PowerPoint® slides can be used directly or customized to fit a professor's needs. There are two customizable slide sets for each chapter of the book—one featuring chapter text, the other featuring all chapter art and illustrations.

POWERPOINT® PRESENTATION SLIDES *by Karen Clay Rhines, Northampton Community College, available at www.worthpublishers.com/comer or on the Instructor's Resource CD-ROM.* These customized slides focus on key text terms and themes, reflect the main points in significant detail, and feature tables, graphs, and figures from the book. Each set of chapter slides is accompanied by a set of handouts, which can be distributed to students for use during lectures. The handouts are based on the instructor slides, with key points replaced by "fill-in" items. Answer keys and suggestions for use are also provided.

STEP UP TO *ABNORMAL PSYCHOLOGY*: A POWERPOINT® REVIEW GAME *by John Schulte, Cape Fear Community College and University of North Carolina, available at www.worthpublishers.com/comer or on the Instructor's Resource CD-ROM.* This PowerPoint®-based review adopts a game-show approach: students divide into teams to compete to climb the pyramid by answering questions related to chapter material.

DIGITAL PHOTO LIBRARY *Available at www.worthpublishers.com/comer or on the Instructor's Resource CD-ROM.* This collection gives you access to all of the photographs from *Abnormal Psychology,* Seventh Edition.

IMAGE AND LECTURE GALLERY *Available at www.worthpublishers.com/ILG.* The Image and Lecture Gallery is a convenient way to access electronic versions of lecture materials. Users can browse, search, and download text art, illustrations, and prebuilt PowerPoint® presentation files for all Worth titles. Users also can create personal folders for easy organization of the materials.

INSTRUCTOR'S RESOURCE MANUAL *by Karen Clay Rhines, Northampton Community College.* This comprehensive guide ties together the ancillary package for professors and teaching assistants. The manual includes detailed chapter outlines, lists of principal learning objectives, ideas for lectures, discussion launchers, classroom activities, extra credit projects, word search and crossword puzzles, transparency masters for every table in the text, and precise DSM-IV-TR criteria for each of the disorders discussed in the text. It also offers strategies for using the accompanying media, including the video segments series, the CD-ROM, the companion Web site, and the transparencies. Finally, it includes a comprehensive set of valuable materials that can be obtained from outside sources—items such as relevant feature films, documentaries, teaching references, and Internet sites related to abnormal psychology.

ASSESSMENT TOOLS

PRINTED TEST BANK *by John H. Hull, Bethany College, and Debra B. Hull, Wheeling Jesuit University.* A comprehensive test bank offers more than 2,200 multiple-choice, fill-in-the-blank, and essay questions. Each question is graded according to difficulty, identified as factual or applied, and keyed to the topic and page in the text where the source information appears.

DIPLOMA COMPUTERIZED TEST BANK This *Windows and Macintosh dual-platform CD-ROM* guides professors step by step through the process of creating a test and allows them to add an unlimited number of questions, edit or scramble questions, format a test, and include pictures, equations, and multimedia links. The accompanying grade book enables them to record students' grades throughout the course and includes the capacity to sort student records and view detailed analyses of test items, curve tests, generate reports, add weights to grades, and more. The CD-ROM also provides the access point for Diploma Online Testing, as well as Blackboard- and WebCT-formatted versions of the Test Bank for *Abnormal Psychology*, Seventh Edition.

ONLINE TESTING, POWERED BY DIPLOMA *Available at www.brownstone.net.* With Diploma, professors can create and administer secure exams over a network and over the Internet, with questions that incorporate multimedia and interactive exercises. The program also allows them to restrict tests to specific computers or time blocks and includes a suite of grade-book and result-analysis features.

ONLINE QUIZZING, POWERED BY QUESTIONMARK *Accessed via the companion Web site at www.worthpublishers.com/comer.* Professors can quiz students online easily and securely using provided multiple-choice questions for each chapter (note that questions are not from the Test Bank). Students receive instant feedback and can take the quizzes multiple times. Professors can view results by quiz, student, or question or can get weekly results via e-mail.

FOR STUDENTS

***ABNORMAL PSYCHOLOGY* STUDENT TOOL KIT** *Produced and edited by Ronald J. Comer, Princeton University, and Gregory Comer, Princeton Academic Resources.* Tied directly to the CyberStudy sections in the text, this Student Tool Kit offers 57 intriguing video cases running three to seven minutes each. The video cases focus on persons affected by disorders discussed in the text. Students first view the video and then answer a series of thought-provoking questions about it. Additionally, the Student Tool Kit contains multiple-choice practice test questions with built-in instructional feedback for every option.

STUDENT WORKBOOK *by Ronald J. Comer, Princeton University, and Gregory Comer, Princeton Academic Resources.* The engaging exercises in this student guide actively involve students in the text material. Each chapter includes a selection of practice tests and exercises, as well as key concepts, guided study questions, and section reviews.

***ABNORMAL PSYCHOLOGY* COMPANION WEB SITE** *by Nicholas Greco, College of Lake County, and Jason Spiegelman, Community College of Baltimore County, accessible at www.worthpublishers.com/comer.* This Web site provides students with a virtual study guide, 24 hours a day, seven days a week. These resources are free and do not require any special access codes or passwords. The tools on the site include chapter outlines, annotated Web links, quizzes, interactive flash cards, research exercises, frequently asked questions about clinical psychology, and interactive crossword puzzles (also included in the *Instructor's Resource Manual*).

In addition, the site includes nine case studies by Elaine Cassel, Marymount University and Lord Fairfax Community College; Danae L. Hudson, Missouri State University; and Brooke L. Whisenhunt, Missouri State University. Each case describes an individual's history and symptoms and is accompanied by a set of guided questions that point to the precise DSM-IV-TR criteria for the disorder and suggest a course of treatment.

CASE STUDIES IN ABNORMAL PSYCHOLOGY by Ethan E. Gorenstein, Behavioral Medicine Program, New York–Presbyterian Hospital, and Ronald J. Comer, Princeton University. This casebook provides 20 case histories, each going beyond DSM-IV-TR diagnoses to describe the individual's history and symptoms, a theoretical discussion of treatment, a specific treatment plan, and the actual treatment conducted. The casebook also provides three cases without diagnoses or treatment, so that students can identify disorders and suggest appropriate therapies. In addition, case study evaluations by Ann Brandt-Williams, Glendale Community College, are available at www.worthpublishers.com/comer. Each evaluation accompanies a specific case and can be assigned to students to assess their understanding as they work through the text.

THE *SCIENTIFIC AMERICAN READER* TO ACCOMPANY *ABNORMAL PSYCHOLOGY* Edited by Ronald J. Comer, Princeton University. Upon request, this reader is free when packaged with the text. Drawn from *Scientific American*, this full-color collection of articles enhances coverage of important topics covered by the course. Keyed to specific chapters, the selections provide a preview of and discussion questions for each article.

SCIENTIFIC AMERICAN EXPLORES THE HIDDEN MIND: A COLLECTOR'S EDITION Upon request, this reader is free when packaged with the text. In this special edition, *Scientific American* provides a compilation of updated articles that explore and reveal the mysterious inner workings of our wondrous minds and brains.

iCLICKER RADIO FREQUENCY CLASSROOM RESPONSE SYSTEM *Offered by Worth Publishers in partnership with iClicker.* iClicker is Worth's new polling system, created by educators for educators. This radio frequency system is the hassle-free way to make your class time more interactive. The system allows you to pause to ask questions and instantly record responses, as well as take attendance, direct students through lectures, gauge your students' understanding of the material, and much more.

COURSE MANAGEMENT

•ENHANCED• COURSE MANAGEMENT SOLUTIONS: SUPERIOR CONTENT, ALL IN ONE PLACE *Available for WebCT, Blackboard, Desire2Learn, and Angel at www.bfwpub.com/lms.* As a service for adopters, Worth Publishers is offering an enhanced turnkey course for *Abnormal Psychology*, Seventh Edition. The enhanced course includes a suite of robust teaching and learning materials in one location, organized so you can customize content for your needs quickly, eliminating hours of work. For instructors, our enhanced course cartridge includes the complete Test Bank and all PowerPoint® slides. For students, we offer interactive flash cards, quizzes, crossword puzzles, chapter outlines, annotated Web links, research exercises, case studies, and more.

Acknowledgments

I am very grateful to the many people who have contributed to writing and producing this book. I particularly thank Marlene Comer and Marion Kowalewski for their outstanding work on the manuscript and their constant good cheer.

In addition, I am indebted to Marlene Catania and Sharon Kraus for their fine work on the references. And I sincerely appreciate the superb work of the book's research assistants, including Dina Altshuler, Linda Chamberlin, Jon Comer, Greg Comer, Lindsay Downs, Jami Furr, and Jamie Hambrick.

I am indebted greatly to those outstanding academicians and clinicians who have reviewed the manuscript of this new edition of *Abnormal Psychology*, along with that of its partner, *Fundamentals of Abnormal Psychology*, and have commented with great insight and wisdom on its clarity, accuracy, and completeness. Their collective knowledge has in large part shaped the seventh edition: Dave W. Alfano, Community College of Rhode Island; Jillian Bennett, University of Massachusetts Boston; Jeffrey A. Buchanan, Minnesota State University; Miriam Ehrenberg, John Jay College of Criminal Justice; Carlos A. Escoto, Eastern Connecticut State University; David M. Fresco, Kent State University; Alan J. Fridlund, University of California, Santa Barbara; Jinni A. Harrigan, California State University, Fullerton; Lynn M. Kemen, Hunter College; Audrey Kim, University of California, Santa Cruz; Barbara Lewis, University of West Florida; Regina Miranda, Hunter College; Linda M. Montgomery, University of Texas, Permian Basin; Crystal Park, University of Connecticut; Julie C. Piercy, Central Virginia Community College; Lloyd R. Pilkington, Midlands Technical College; Laura A. Rabin, Brooklyn College; Susan J. Simonian, College of Charleston; Joanne H. Stohs, California State University, Fullerton; and Mitchell Sudolsky, University of Texas at Austin.

I also thank the professors and clinicians around the country who offered special counsel during the writing of the text: Jeffrey Cohn, University of Pittsburgh; Elizabeth Lindner, Madison Area Technical College; Professor Joni Mihura, University of Toledo; Professor David Mrad, Missouri State University; Salma Osmani, University of Leicester, United Kingdom; and Irving Weiner, president, Society of Personality Assessment.

Earlier I also received valuable feedback from academicians and clinicians who reviewed portions of the first six editions of *Abnormal Psychology*. Certainly their collective knowledge has also helped shape the seventh edition, and I gratefully acknowledge their important contributions: Kent G. Bailey, Virginia Commonwealth University; Sonja Barcus, Rochester College; Marna S. Barnett, Indiana University of Pennsylvania; Otto A. Berliner, Alfred State College; Allan Berman, University of Rhode Island; Douglas Bernstein, University of Toronto, Mississauga; Greg Bolich, Cleveland Community College; Barbara Brown, Georgia Perimeter College; Jeffrey A. Buchanan, Minnesota State University, Mankato; Gregory M. Buchanan, Beloit College; Laura Burlingame-Lee, Colorado State University; Loretta Butehorn, Boston College; Glenn M. Callaghan, San Jose State University; E. Allen Campbell, University of St. Francis; Julie Carboni, San Jose College and National University; David N. Carpenter, Southwest Texas University; Sarah Cirese, College of Marin; June Madsen Clausen, University of San Francisco; Victor B. Cline, University of Utah; E. M. Coles, Simon Fraser University; Michael Connor, California State University, Long Beach; Frederick L. Coolidge, University of Colorado, Colorado Springs; Timothy K. Daugherty, Winthrop University; Mary Dozier, University of Delaware; S. Wayne Duncan, University of Washington, Seattle; Morris N. Eagle, York University; Anne Fisher, University of Southern Florida; William F. Flack Jr., Bucknell University; John Forsyth, State University of New York, Albany; Alan Fridlund, University of California, Santa Barbara; Stan Friedman, Southwest Texas State University;

Dale Fryxell, Chaminade University; Lawrence L. Galant, Gaston College; Karla Gingerich, Colorado State University; Nicholas Greco, College of Lake County; Jane Halonen, James Madison University; James Hansell, University of Michigan; Neth Hansjoerg, Rensselaer Polytechnic Institute; Morton G. Harmatz, University of Massachusetts; Anthony Hermann, Kalamazoo College; Paul Hewitt, University of British Columbia; David A. Hoffman, University of California, Santa Cruz; Danae Hudson, Missouri State University; William G. Iacono, University of Minnesota; Guadalupe Vasquez King, Milwaukee Area Technical College; Bernard Kleinman, University of Missouri, Kansas City; Futoshi Kobayashi, Northern State University; Alan G. Krasnoff, University of Missouri, St. Louis; Robert D. Langston, University of Texas, Austin; Kimberlyn Leary, University of Michigan; Harvey R. Lerner, Kaiser-Permanente Medical Group; Arnold D. LeUnes, Texas A&M University; Michael P. Levin, Kenyon College; Mary Margaret Livingston, Louisiana Technical University; Karsten Look, Columbus State Community College; Joseph LoPiccolo, University of Missouri, Columbia; L. F. Lowenstein, Southern England Psychological Services; Jerald J. Marshall, University of Central Florida; Janet R. Matthews, Loyola University; Robert J. McCaffrey, State University of New York, Albany; F. Dudley McGlynn, Auburn University; Lily D. McNair, University of Georgia; Mary W. Meagher, Texas A&M University; Dorothy Mercer, Eastern Kentucky University; Joni L. Mihura, University of Toledo; Robin Mogul, Queens University; Karen Mottarella, University of Central Florida; Karla Klein Murdock, University of Massachusetts, Boston; Sandy Naumann, Delaware Technical & Community College; Paul Neunuebel, Sam Houston State University; Ryan Newell, Oklahoma Christian University; Katherine M. Nicolai, Rockhurst University; Fabian Novello, Purdue University; Mary Ann M. Pagaduan, American Osteopathic Association; Daniel Paulson, Carthage College; Paul A. Payne, University of Cincinnati; David V. Perkins, Ball State University; Harold A. Pincus, chair, DSM-IV, University of Pittsburgh, Western Psychiatric Institute and Clinic; Chris Piotrowski, University of West Florida; Norman Poppel, Middlesex County College; David E. Powley, University of Mobile; Max W. Rardin, University of Wyoming, Laramie; Lynn P. Rehm, University of Houston; Leslie A. Rescorla, Bryn Mawr College; R. W. Rieber, John Jay College, CUNY; George Esther Rothblum, University of Vermont; Vic Ryan, University of Colorado, Boulder; Randall Salekin, Florida International University; A. A. Sappington, University of Alabama, Birmingham; Martha Sauter, McLennon Community College; Laura Scaletta, Niagara County Community College; George W. Shardlow, City College of San Francisco; Roberta S. Sherman, Bloomington Center for Counseling and Human Development; Wendy E. Shields, University of Montana; Sandra T. Sigmon, University of Maine, Orono; Janet A. Simons, Central Iowa Psychological Services; Jay R. Skidmore, Utah State University; Rachel Sligar, James Madison University; Robert Sommer, University of California, Davis; Jason S. Spiegelman, Community College of Baltimore County; John M. Spores, Purdue University, South Central; Amit Steinberg, Tel Aviv University; B. D. Stillion, Clayton College and State University; John Suler, Rider University; Thomas A. Tutko, San Jose State University; Norris D. Vestre, Arizona State University; Lance L. Weinmann, Canyon College; Doug Wessel, Black Hills State University; Laura Westen, Emory University; Brook Whisenhunt, Missouri State University; Joseph L. White, University of California, Irvine; Amy C. Willis, Veterans Administration Medical Center, Washington, DC; James M. Wood, University of Texas, El Paso; Lisa Wood, University of Puget Sound; David Yells, Utah Valley State College; and Carlos Zalaquett, University of South Florida.

A special thank you to the authors of the book's supplements package for doing splendid jobs with their respective supplements: Debra B. Hull, Wheeling Jesuit University, and John H. Hull, Bethany College (Test Bank); Karen Clay Rhines, Northampton Community College (*Instructor's Resource Manual*); Gregory Comer, Princeton Academic Resources (*Student Workbook*); Nicholas Greco, College of Lake County, and Jason Spiegelman, Community College of Baltimore County (Web site); and Ann Brandt-Williams, Glendale Community College; Elaine Cassel,

Marymount University and Lord Fairfax Community College; Danae L. Hudson, Missouri State University; John Schulte, Cape Fear Community College and University of North Carolina; and Brooke L. Whisenhunt, Missouri State University (additional Web site materials).

I also extend my deep appreciation to the core team of professionals at Worth Publishers and W. H. Freeman and Company who have worked so closely with me to produce this edition. This team consists of truly extraordinary people—each extremely talented, each committed to excellence, each dedicated to the education of readers, each bound by a remarkable work ethic, and each a wonderful person. It is accurate to say that they were my co-authors and co-teachers in this enterprise, and I am in their debt. They are Kevin Feyen, senior acquisitions editor; Tracey Kuehn, associate managing editor; Paul Lacy, layout designer; Mimi Melek, senior development editor; Jane O'Neill, project editor; Barbara Reingold, art director; Sarah Segal, production manager; Ted Szczepanski, photo editor; and Catherine Woods, senior publisher.

Elizabeth Widdicombe, president of Worth and Freeman, has continued to lead the companies superbly, to create a very supportive environment for my books, and to be a good friend. I also am indebted to Peter Twickler, Worth's media editor, who, along with Stacey Alexander and Jenny Chiu, has so skillfully developed and guided the production of the extraordinary and innovative supplements package that accompanies the text. Still other professionals at Worth and at Freeman to whom I am indebted are Todd Elder, director of advertising; Michele Kornegay, copy editor; Ellen Brennan and Sharon Kraus, indexers; Lorraine Klimowich, assistant editor; Nancy Giraldo Walker, rights and permissions manager; Eric Dorger, intern; and John Philp for his outstanding work on the video supplements for professors and students.

Not to be overlooked are the superb professionals at Worth and at Freeman who continuously work with great passion, skill, and judgment to bring my books to the attention of professors across the world: Kate Nurre, executive marketing manager; Amy Shefferd, marketing manager; Tom Scotty, vice president of sales and operations; and the company's wonderful sales representatives. Thank you so much.

One final note. With each passing year, I become increasingly aware of just how fortunate I am. At the risk of sounding like a walking cliché, let me say, with a clarity that, at the age of 61, is sharper and better informed than at earlier points in my life, how appreciative I am that I have the opportunity each day to work with so many interesting and stimulating students during this important and exciting stage of their lives. Similarly, I am grateful beyond words that I have a number of wonderful friends and an extraordinary family, particularly my terrific and accomplished sons, Greg and Jon; my wonderful new daughter-in-law, Jami; and my magnificent wife, Marlene, whose generosity, strength, and grace are always present.

Ron Comer
Princeton University

ABNORMAL PSYCHOLOGY: PAST AND PRESENT

Alisha cries herself to sleep every night. She is certain that the future holds nothing but misery. Indeed, this is the only thing she does feel certain about. "I'm going to suffer and suffer and suffer, and my daughters will suffer as well. We're doomed. The world is ugly. I hate every moment of my life." She has great trouble sleeping. She is afraid to close her eyes. When she does, the hopelessness of her life—and the ugly future that awaits her daughters—becomes all the clearer to her. When she drifts off to sleep, her dreams are nightmares filled with terrible images—bodies, flooding, decay, death, destruction.

Some mornings Alisha even has trouble getting out of bed. The thought of facing another day overwhelms her. She wishes that she and her daughters were dead. "Get it over with. We'd all be better off." She feels paralyzed by her depression and anxiety, overwhelmed by her sense of hopelessness, too tired to move, too negative to try anymore. On such mornings, she huddles her daughters close to her, makes sure that the shades of her trailer home are drawn and the door locked, and sits away the day in the darkened room. She feels she has been assaulted by society and then deserted by the world and left to rot. She is both furious at life and afraid of it at the same time.

During the past year Brad has been hearing mysterious voices that tell him to quit his job, leave his family, and prepare for the coming invasion. These voices have brought tremendous confusion and emotional turmoil to Brad's life. He believes that they come from beings in distant parts of the universe who are somehow wired to him. Although it gives him a sense of purpose and specialness to be the chosen target of their communications, they also make him tense and anxious. He dreads the coming invasion. When he refuses an order, the voices insult and threaten him and turn his days into a waking nightmare.

Brad has put himself on a sparse diet against the possibility that his enemies may be contaminating his food. He has found a quiet apartment far from his old haunts where he has laid in a good stock of arms and ammunition. His family and friends have tried to reach out to Brad, to understand his problems, and to dissuade him from the disturbing course he is taking. Every day, however, he retreats further into his world of mysterious voices and imagined dangers.

Most of us would probably consider Alisha's and Brad's emotions, thoughts, and behavior psychologically abnormal, the result of a state sometimes called *psychopathology, maladjustment, emotional disturbance,* or *mental illness* (see *Psych Watch* on the next page). These terms have been applied to the many problems that seem closely tied to the human brain or mind. Psychological abnormality affects the famous and the obscure, the rich and the poor. Actors, writers, politicians, and other public figures of the present and the past have struggled with it. Psychological problems can bring great suffering, but they can also be the source of inspiration and energy.

Because they are so common and so personal, these problems capture the interest of us all. Hundreds of novels, plays, films, and television programs have explored what many people see as the dark side of human nature, and self-help books flood the market. Mental health experts are popular guests on both television and radio, and some even have their own shows.

Verbal Debuts

We use words like "abnormal" and "mental disorder" so often that it is easy to forget that there was a time not that long ago when these terms did not exist. When did these and similar words (including slang terms) make their debut in print as expressions of psychological dysfunctioning? The *Oxford English Dictionary* offers the following dates.

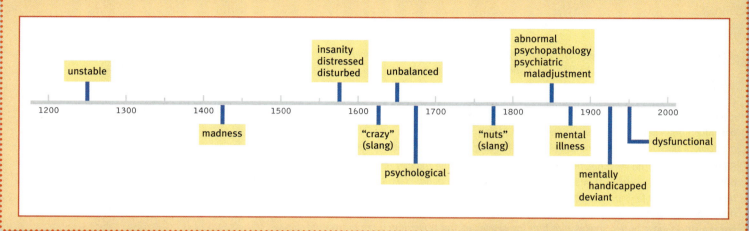

The field devoted to the scientific study of the problems we find so fascinating is usually called **abnormal psychology.** As in any science, workers in this field, called *clinical scientists,* gather information systematically so that they may describe, predict, and explain the phenomena they study. The knowledge that they acquire is then used by *clinical practitioners,* whose role is to detect, assess, and treat abnormal patterns of functioning.

What Is Psychological Abnormality?

Although their general goals are similar to those of other scientific professionals, clinical scientists and practitioners face problems that make their work especially difficult. One of the most troubling is that psychological abnormality is very hard to define. Consider once again Alisha and Brad. Why are we so ready to call their responses abnormal?

While many definitions of abnormality have been proposed over the years, none is universally accepted (Boysen, 2007). Still, most of the definitions have certain features in common, often called "the four Ds": deviance, distress, dysfunction, and danger. That is, patterns of psychological abnormality are typically *deviant* (different, extreme, unusual, perhaps even bizarre), *distressing* (unpleasant and upsetting to the person), *dysfunctional* (interfering with the person's ability to conduct daily activities in a constructive way), and possibly *dangerous.* These criteria offer a useful starting point from which to explore the phenomena of psychological abnormality. As you will see, however, they have key limitations.

Deviance

Abnormal psychological functioning is *deviant,* but deviant from what? Alisha's and Brad's behaviors, thoughts, and emotions are different from those that are considered normal in our place and time. We do not expect people

Deviance and abnormality
Along the Niger River, men of the Wodaabe tribe put on elaborate makeup and costumes to attract women. In Western society, the same behavior would break behavioral norms and probably be judged abnormal.

to cry themselves to sleep each night, hate the world, wish themselves dead, or obey voices that no one else hears.

In short, behavior, thoughts, and emotions are deemed abnormal when they differ markedly from a society's ideas about proper functioning. Each society establishes **norms**—explicit and implicit rules for proper conduct. Behavior that breaks legal norms is considered to be criminal. Behavior, thoughts, and emotions that break norms of psychological functioning are considered to be abnormal.

Judgments of abnormality vary from society to society. A society's norms grow from its particular **culture**—its history, values, institutions, habits, skills, technology, and arts. A society that values competition and assertiveness may accept aggressive behavior, whereas one that emphasizes cooperation and gentleness may consider aggressive behavior unacceptable and even abnormal. A society's values may also change over time, causing its views of what is psychologically abnormal to change as well. In Western society, for example, a woman's participation in the business world was widely considered inappropriate and strange a hundred years ago. Today the same behavior is valued.

Judgments of abnormality depend on *specific circumstances* as well as on cultural norms. What if, for example, we were to learn that the hopelessness and desperate unhappiness of Alisha were in fact occurring in the days, weeks, and months following Hurricane Katrina, the deadly storm that struck New Orleans in the summer of 2005—a storm whose aftermath destroyed her home, deprived her of all of her earthly possessions, and shattered her community, scattering neighbors, friends, and family members who had lived together for generations. The flood and its immediate impact had been a nightmare, but the weeks and months that followed were even worse, as Alisha came to appreciate that help was not coming, that she and her daughters would never be returning to their home in their old community, and that she would probably not be reunited with the friends and neighbors who had once given her life so much meaning. As she and her daughters moved from one temporary run-down location to another throughout Louisiana and Mississippi, Alisha gradually gave up all hope that her life would ever return to normal. The modest but happy life she and her daughters had once known was now gone, seemingly forever. In this light, Alisha's reactions do not seem quite so inappropriate. If anything is abnormal here, it is her situation. Many human experiences produce intense reactions—large-scale catastrophes and disasters, rape, child abuse, war, terminal illness, chronic pain (Miller, 2007). Is there an "appropriate" way to react to such things? Should we ever call reactions to such experiences abnormal?

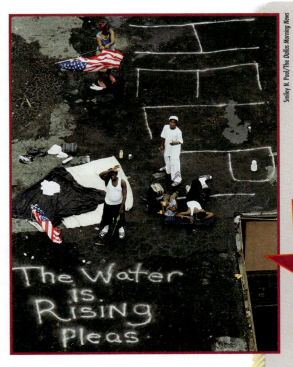

Smiley N. Pool/The Dallas Morning News

Context is key
On the morning after Hurricane Katrina, desperate residents stand fearfully on the roof of an apartment house hoping to be evacuated from the floodwaters. Panic, anxiety, and even profound depression were common, seemingly normal reactions in the wake of this extraordinary disaster, rather than being clear symptoms of psychopathology.

Distress

Even functioning that is considered unusual does not necessarily qualify as abnormal. According to many clinical theorists, behavior, ideas, or emotions usually have to cause *distress* before they can be labeled abnormal. Consider the Ice Breakers, a group of people in Michigan who go swimming in lakes throughout the state every weekend from November through February. The colder the weather, the better they like it. One man, a member of the group for 17 years, says he loves the challenge of man against the elements. A 37-year-old lawyer believes that the weekly shock is good for her health.

•**abnormal psychology**•The scientific study of abnormal behavior in an effort to describe, predict, explain, and change abnormal patterns of functioning.

•**norms**•A society's stated and unstated rules for proper conduct.

•**culture**•A people's common history, values, institutions, habits, skills, technology, and arts.

A spiritual experience
In the Val d'Isère, France, students bury themselves in snow up to their necks. Far from experiencing distress or displaying abnormality, they are engaging in a Japanese practice designed to open their hearts and enlarge their spirits.

BETWEEN THE LINES

Deviant

39% People who confess to snooping in their hosts' medicine cabinets ‹‹

30% Those who refuse to sit on a public toilet seat ‹‹

27% Those who admit taking more than the maximum number of items through a supermarket express line ‹‹

23% Those who confess to not flushing the toilet all the time ‹‹

10% Those who believe they have seen a ghost ‹‹

(Kanner, 2004, 1995)

"It cleanses me," she says. "It perks me up and gives me strength." Another Ice Breaker likes the special bond the group members share. "When we get together, we know we've done something special, something no one else understands. I can't even tell most of the people I know that I'm an Ice Breaker."

Certainly these people are different from most of us, but is their behavior abnormal? Far from experiencing distress, they feel energized and challenged. Their positive feelings must cause us to hesitate before we decide that they are functioning abnormally.

Should we conclude, then, that feelings of distress must always be present before a person's functioning can be considered abnormal? Not necessarily. Some people who function abnormally maintain a positive frame of mind. Consider once again Brad, the young man who hears mysterious voices. Brad does experience distress over the coming invasion and the life changes he feels forced to make. But what if he enjoyed listening to the voices, felt honored to be chosen, and looked forward to saving the world? Shouldn't we still regard his functioning as abnormal? As you will read in Chapter 8, people whose behaviors are described as manic often feel just wonderful, yet still they are diagnosed as psychologically disturbed. Indeed, in many cases it is their euphoria and disproportionate sense of well-being that make them candidates for this diagnosis.

Dysfunction

Abnormal behavior tends to be *dysfunctional;* that is, it interferes with daily functioning. It so upsets, distracts, or confuses people that they cannot care for themselves properly, participate in ordinary social interactions, or work productively. Brad, for example, has quit his job, left his family, and prepared to withdraw from the productive life he once led.

Here again one's culture plays a role in the definition of abnormality. Our society holds that it is important to carry out daily activities in an effective, self-enhancing manner. Thus Brad's behavior is likely to be regarded as abnormal and undesirable, whereas that of the Ice Breakers, who continue to perform well in their jobs and enjoy fulfilling relationships, would probably be considered simply unusual.

Then again, dysfunction alone does not necessarily indicate psychological abnormality. Some people (Gandhi or César Chávez, for example) fast or in other ways deprive themselves of things they need as a means of protesting social injustice. Far from receiving a clinical label of some kind, they are widely viewed as admirable people—caring, sacrificing, even heroic.

Danger

Perhaps the ultimate in psychological dysfunctioning is behavior that becomes *dangerous* to oneself or others. Individuals whose behavior is consistently careless, hostile, or confused may be placing themselves or those around them at risk. Brad, for example, seems to be endangering both himself, with his diet, and others, with his buildup of arms and ammunition.

Although danger is often cited as a feature of abnormal psychological functioning, research suggests that it is actually the exception rather than the rule (Freedman et al., 2007; Fazel & Grann, 2006). Despite popular misconceptions, most people struggling with anxiety, depression, and even bizarre thinking pose no immediate danger to themselves or to anyone else.

The Elusive Nature of Abnormality

If the concept of abnormality depends so heavily on social norms and values, it is no wonder that efforts to define psychological abnormality typically raise as many questions as they answer. Ultimately, each society selects general criteria for defining abnormality and then uses those criteria to judge particular cases.

Noting society's role in this process, one clinical theorist, Thomas Szasz (2006, 2005, 1997, 1960), argues that the whole concept of mental illness is invalid, a myth of sorts. According to Szasz, the deviations that society calls abnormal are simply "problems in living," not signs of something wrong within the person. Societies, he is convinced, invent the concept of mental illness so that they can better control or change people whose unusual patterns of functioning upset or threaten the social order.

Even if we assume that psychological abnormality is a valid concept and that it can indeed be defined, we may be unable to apply our definition consistently. If a behavior—excessive use of alcohol among college students, say—is familiar enough, the society may fail to recognize that it is deviant, distressful, dysfunctional, and dangerous. Thousands of college students throughout the United States are so dependent on alcohol that it interferes with their personal and academic lives, causes them great discomfort, jeopardizes their health, and often endangers them and the people around them. Yet their problem often goes unnoticed, certainly undiagnosed, by college administrators, other students, and health professionals. Alcohol is so much a part of the college subculture that it is easy to overlook drinking behavior that has become abnormal.

Conversely, a society may have trouble distinguishing between an abnormality that requires intervention and an *eccentricity,* or marked individuality, with which others have no right to interfere. From time to time we see or hear about people who behave in ways we consider strange, such as a man who lives alone with two dozen cats and rarely talks to other people. The behavior of such people is deviant, and it may well be distressful and dysfunctional, yet many professionals think of it as eccentric rather than abnormal (see *A Closer Look* on page 7).

In short, while we may agree to define psychological abnormalities as patterns of functioning that are deviant, distressful, dysfunctional, and sometimes dangerous, we should be clear that these criteria are often vague and subjective. In turn, few of the current categories of abnormality that you will meet in this book are as clear-cut as they may seem, and most continue to be debated by clinicians.

❁What Is Treatment?

Once clinicians decide that a person is indeed suffering from some form of psychological abnormality, they seek to treat it. *Treatment,* or *therapy,* is a procedure designed to change abnormal behavior into more normal behavior; it, too, requires careful definition. For clinical scientists, the problem is closely related to defining abnormality. Consider the case of Bill:

February: *He cannot leave the house; Bill knows that for a fact. Home is the only place where he feels safe—safe from humiliation, danger, even ruin. If he were to go to work, his co-workers would somehow reveal their contempt for him. A pointed remark, a quizzical look—that's all it would take for him to get the message. If he were to go shopping at the store, before long everyone would be staring at him. Surely others would see his dark mood and thoughts; he wouldn't be able to hide them. He dare not even go for a walk alone in the woods—his heart would probably start racing again, bringing him to his knees and leaving him breathless, incoherent, and unable to get home. No, he's much better off staying in his room, trying to get through another evening of this curse called life.*

July: *Bill's life revolves around his circle of friends: Bob and Jack, whom he knows from the office, where he was recently promoted to director of customer relations, and Frank and Tim, his weekend tennis partners. The gang meets for dinner every week at someone's house, and they chat about life, politics, and their jobs. Particularly special in Bill's life is Janice. They go to movies, restaurants, and shows together. She thinks Bill's just*

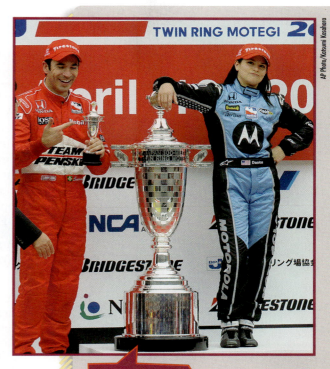

Changing times
Just decades ago, a woman's love for race car driving would have been considered strange, perhaps even abnormal. Today, Danica Patrick (right) is one of America's finest race car drivers. The size difference between her first-place trophy at the Indy Japan 300 auto race and that of second-place male driver Helio Castroneves symbolizes just how far women have come in this sport.

Therapy . . . not
In 2007 a hotel in Spain that was about to undergo major renovations invited members of the public to relieve their stress by destroying the rooms on one floor of the hotel. This activity may indeed have been therapeutic for some, but it was not *therapy*. It lacked, among other things, a "trained healer" and a series of systematic contacts between healer and sufferer.

BETWEEN THE LINES

Mental Dysfunction

"Insanity: doing the same thing over and over again and expecting different results." ‹‹
Albert Einstein

"Insanity—a perfectly rational adjustment to an insane world." ‹‹
R. D. Laing

"The distance between insanity and genius is measured only by success." ‹‹
James Bond in *Tomorrow Never Dies*

terrific, and Bill finds himself beaming whenever she's around. Bill looks forward to work each day and his one-on-one dealings with customers. He is enjoying life and basking in the glow of his many activities and relationships.

Bill's thoughts, feelings, and behavior interfered with all aspects of his life in February. Yet most of his symptoms had disappeared by July. All sorts of factors may have contributed to Bill's improvement—advice from friends and family members, a new job or vacation, perhaps a big change in his diet or exercise regimen. Any or all of these things may have been useful to Bill, but they could not be considered treatment, or therapy. Those terms are usually reserved for special, systematic procedures for helping people overcome their psychological difficulties. According to the clinical theorist Jerome Frank, all forms of therapy have three essential features:

1. A *sufferer* who seeks relief from the healer.
2. A trained, socially accepted *healer,* whose expertise is accepted by the sufferer and his or her social group.
3. A *series of contacts* between the healer and the sufferer, through which the healer, often with the aid of a group, tries to produce certain changes in the sufferer's emotional state, attitudes, and behavior.

(Frank, 1973, pp. 2–3)

Despite this straightforward definition, clinical treatment is surrounded by conflict and confusion. Carl Rogers, a pioneer in the modern clinical field (you will meet him in Chapter 3), noted that "therapists are not in agreement as to their goals or aims. . . . They are not in agreement as to what constitutes a successful outcome of their work. They cannot agree as to what constitutes a failure. It seems as though the field is completely chaotic and divided."

Some clinicians view abnormality as an illness and so consider therapy a procedure that helps *cure* the illness. Others see abnormality as a problem in living and therapists as *teachers* of more functional behavior and thought. Clinicians even differ on what to call the person who receives therapy: those who see abnormality as an illness speak of the "patient," while those who view it as a problem in living refer to the "client." Because both terms are so common, this book will use them interchangeably.

Despite their differences, most clinicians do agree that large numbers of people need therapy of one kind or another. Later we shall encounter evidence that therapy is indeed often helpful (Hofmann & Weinberger, 2007).

How Was Abnormality Viewed and Treated in the Past?

In any given year as many as 30 percent of the adults and 19 percent of the children and adolescents in the United States display serious psychological disturbances and are in need of clinical treatment (Kessler et al., 2007, 2005, 1994; Kazdin, 2003, 2000; Narrow et al., 2002). The rates in other countries are similarly high. Furthermore, most people have difficulty coping at various times and go through periods of extreme tension, dejection, or other forms of psychological discomfort in their lives.

It is tempting to conclude that something about the modern world is responsible for these many emotional problems—perhaps rapid technological change, the growing threat of terrorism, or a decline in religious, family, or other support systems (Comer & Kendall, 2007; Schumaker, 2001) (see *Psych Watch* on page 9). Although the pressures of modern life probably do contribute to psychological dysfunctioning, they are hardly its primary cause. Every society, past and present, has witnessed psychological abnormality. Perhaps, then, the proper place to begin our examination of abnormal behavior and treatment is in the past.

Marching to a Different Drummer: Eccentrics

- Writer **James Joyce** always carried a tiny pair of lady's bloomers, which he waved in the air to show approval.
- **Emily Dickinson** always wore white, never left her room, and hid her poems in tiny boxes.
- **Benjamin Franklin** took "air baths" for his health, sitting naked in front of an open window.
- **President John Quincy Adams** swam nude in the Potomac River each morning.
- **Alexander Graham Bell** covered the windows of his house to keep out the rays of the full moon. He also tried to teach his dog how to talk.
- Writer **D. H. Lawrence** enjoyed removing his clothes and climbing mulberry trees.

(ASIMOV, 1997; WEEKS & JAMES, 1995)

John Maier/The New York Times/Redux

Musical eccentric Called the "mad genius of Brazilian pop music," composer and instrumentalist Hermeto Pascoal is as famous for his odd musical ways as he is for his special talent. He regularly uses alternative musical instruments such as bicycle pumps, toys, and gum wrappers.

These famous and accomplished persons have been called eccentrics. The dictionary defines an *eccentric* as a person who deviates from common behavior patterns or displays odd or whimsical behavior. But how can we separate a psychologically healthy person who has unusual habits from a person whose oddness is a symptom of psychopathology? For years, little research was done on eccentrics, but some studies conducted over the past decade seem to have started the ball rolling (Pickover, 1999; Weeks & James, 1995).

For example, researcher David Weeks studied 1,000 eccentrics over a 10-year period and estimated that as many as 1 in 5,000 persons may be "classic, full-time eccentrics." Men and women seem equally prone to such patterns. Weeks pinpointed 15 characteristics common to the eccentrics in his study: *nonconformity, creativity, strong curiosity, idealism, extreme interests and hobbies, lifelong awareness of being different, high intelligence, outspokenness, noncompetitiveness, unusual eating and living habits, disinterest in others' opinions or company, mischievous sense of humor, nonmarriage, eldest or only child,* and *poor spelling skills.*

Weeks suggests that eccentrics do not typically suffer from mental disorders. Whereas the unusual behavior of persons with mental disorders is thrust upon them and usually causes them suffering, eccentricity is chosen freely and provides pleasure. In short, "Eccentrics know they're different and glory in it" (Weeks & James, 1995, p. 14). Similarly, the thought processes of eccentrics are not severely disrupted and do not leave these persons dysfunctional. In fact, Weeks found that eccentrics in his study actually had fewer emotional problems than individuals in the general population. Perhaps being an "original" is good for mental health.

As we look back, we can see how each society has struggled to understand and treat psychological problems, and we can observe that many present-day ideas and treatments have roots in the past. A look backward makes it clear that progress in the understanding and treatment of mental disorders has hardly been a steady movement forward. In fact, many of the inadequacies and controversies that mark the clinical field today parallel those of the past. At the same time, looking back can help us to appreciate the significance of recent breakthroughs and the importance of the journey that lies ahead.

Ancient Views and Treatments

Historians who have examined the unearthed bones, artwork, and other remnants of ancient societies have concluded that these societies probably regarded abnormal behavior as the work of evil spirits. People in prehistoric societies apparently believed that all events around and within them resulted from the actions of magical, sometimes sinister, beings who controlled the world. In particular, they viewed the human body and mind as a battleground between external forces of good and evil. Abnormal behavior was

•**trephination**•An ancient operation in which a stone instrument was used to cut away a circular section of the skull, perhaps to treat abnormal behavior.

•**humors**•According to the Greeks and Romans, bodily chemicals that influence mental and physical functioning.

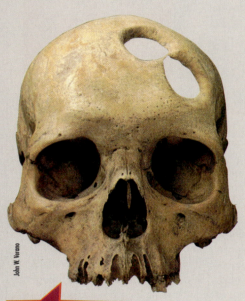

John W. Verano

Expelling evil spirits
The two holes in this skull recovered from ancient times indicate that the person underwent trephination, possibly for the purpose of releasing evil spirits and curing mental dysfunctioning.

Humors in action
Hippocrates believed that imbalances of the four humors affected personality. In these depictions of two of the humors, yellow bile (left) drives a husband to beat his wife, and black bile (right) leaves a man melancholic and sends him to bed.

typically interpreted as a victory by evil spirits, and the cure for such behavior was to force the demons from a victim's body.

This supernatural view of abnormality may have begun as far back as the Stone Age, a half-million years ago. Some skulls from that period recovered in Europe and South America show evidence of an operation called **trephination,** in which a stone instrument, or *trephine,* was used to cut away a circular section of the skull. Some historians have concluded that this early operation was performed as a treatment for severe abnormal behavior—either hallucinations, in which people saw or heard things not actually present, or melancholia, characterized by extreme sadness and immobility. The purpose of opening the skull was to release the evil spirits that were supposedly causing the problem (Selling, 1940).

In recent decades, some historians have questioned whether Stone Age people actually believed that evil spirits caused abnormal behavior. Trephination may instead have been used to remove bone splinters or blood clots caused by stone weapons during tribal warfare (Maher & Maher, 2003, 1985). Either way, later societies clearly did attribute abnormal behavior to possession by demons. Egyptian, Chinese, and Hebrew writings all account for psychological deviance this way. The Bible, for example, describes how an evil spirit from the Lord affected King Saul and how David feigned madness to convince his enemies that he was visited by divine forces.

The treatment for abnormality in these early societies was often *exorcism.* The idea was to coax the evil spirits to leave or to make the person's body an uncomfortable place in which to live. A *shaman,* or priest, might recite prayers, plead with the evil spirits, insult the spirits, perform magic, make loud noises, or have the person drink bitter potions. If these techniques failed, the shaman performed a more extreme form of exorcism, such as whipping or starving the person.

Greek and Roman Views and Treatments

In the years from roughly 500 B.C. to 500 A.D., when the Greek and Roman civilizations thrived, philosophers and physicians often offered different explanations and treatments for abnormal behaviors. Hippocrates (460–377 B.C.), often called the father of modern medicine, taught that illnesses had *natural* causes. He saw abnormal behavior as a disease arising from internal physical problems. Specifically, he believed that some form of brain pathology was the culprit and that it resulted—like all other forms of disease, in his view—from an imbalance of four fluids, or **humors,** that flowed through the body: *yellow bile, black bile, blood,* and *phlegm* (Arikha, 2007). An excess of yellow bile, for example, caused *mania,* a state of frenzied activity; an excess of black bile was the source of *melancholia,* a condition marked by unshakable sadness.

Modern Pressures: Modern Problems

Do the fast pace, multiple roles, economic uncertainties, and other pressures of modern life explain today's high rate of psychological disorders? No, say most clinical theorists. Such factors may *contribute* to psychological dysfunctions, but they do not fully account for the high rates of anxiety, depression, and other psychological problems.

At the same time, the twenty-first century, like each of the centuries before it, has spawned new fears and concerns that are tied to its unique technological advances, community threats, and environmental dangers. These new fears have received little study. They may or may not reflect abnormal functioning. Indeed, we could argue that some of them represent appropriate, although painful, concerns about very real problems. Either way, they have caught the attention of the media and some clinical observers and, perhaps most important, have received catchy names.

Eco-threat The ancient Parthenon temple in Athens is seen before a storm in 2006. This and other European monuments, such as the Colosseum in Rome, have withstood earthquakes, fire, and plundering for centuries, but some studies suggest that climate changes over the next half century may damage their marble and limestone bases and cause cracks and breaks throughout the monuments.

"Eco-Anxiety" People who suffer from this problem are tormented by concern and a sense of doom over our polluted and endangered environment. They often complain of panic attacks, loss of appetite, irritability, and unexplained bouts of weakness and sleeplessness. These fears are fueled by abundant media coverage of crises such as global warming, collapsed fisheries, and food shortages (Nobel, 2007). A treatment approach called *ecopsychology* is now practiced by hundreds of therapists to help reduce the anxiety of such individuals (Glaser, 2008).

"Terrorism Terror" Global terrorism is a major source of anxiety in contemporary society, particularly since the September 11, 2001, attacks on the World Trade Center in New York City and the Pentagon in Washington, DC. This fear increasingly has expanded to cover almost all aspects of modern life. Everyday hassles of the past have been turned into potential threats by their association with the actions of terrorists (Furedi, 2007).

When boarding planes, subway cars, or buses, for example, travelers who formerly worried only about the low risks of flying, the possibility of being late for work, or the repercussions of missing an appointment may now find themselves worrying that the transporting vehicles are about to become targets or tools of terrorist actions. Indeed, for some individuals, such concerns have become a terrifying and obsessive preoccupation that transforms normal travel into a truly anxiety-provoking experience.

"Crime Phobia" People today have become increasingly anxious about crime. Some observers note that the fear of crime—predominantly armed violence—has increasingly restructured the lives of Americans and its institutions. "The fear of crime can have a more powerful effect on people and neighborhoods than crime itself," says political scientist Jonathan Simon. "Fear of crime governs us in our choices of where to live, where to work, where to send our children to school. And these choices are made with increasing reference to crime" (quoted in Bergquist, 2002). Many theorists point to disproportionate media coverage of violent crimes as a major cause of crime phobia, particu-

larly given that crime anxiety seems to keep rising even while actual crime rates are falling (Stearns, 2006).

"Cyber Fear" Some people, particularly individuals in the workplace, are literally afraid of their computers. Such persons fear that they will inadvertently break their computers or be unable to learn new computer tasks. Among more sophisticated computer users, many live in fear of computer crashes, server overloads, or computer viruses. And some, stricken by a combination of crime phobia and cyber fear, worry constantly about *e-crimes*, such as computer hoaxes or scams, computer-identity theft, or cyberterrorism. Several treatment programs have, in fact, been developed to help people deal with such anxieties and return to carefree keyboarding. Still another Internet-linked problem is *information anxiety*, a sense of being intimidated and overwhelmed by the ever-growing influx of information currently bombarding us from the Internet and other mass media vehicles (Wurman et al., 2000). The flip side of cyber fear, information anxiety, and the like is *Internet addiction*, the uncontrollable need to be online—yet another technology-driven problem that you'll be coming across in Chapter 16.

To treat psychological dysfunctioning, Hippocrates sought to correct the underlying physical pathology. He believed, for instance, that the excess of black bile underlying melancholia could be reduced by a quiet life, a diet of vegetables, temperance, exercise, celibacy, and even bleeding. Hippocrates' focus on internal causes for abnormal behavior was shared by the great Greek philosophers Plato (427–347 B.C.) and Aristotle (384–322 B.C.) and by influential Greek and Roman physicians.

Europe in the Middle Ages: Demonology Returns

The enlightened views of Greek and Roman physicians and scholars were not enough to shake ordinary people's belief in demons. And with the decline of Rome, demonological views and practices became popular once again. A growing distrust of science spread throughout Europe.

From 500 to 1350 A.D., the period known as the Middle Ages, the power of the clergy increased greatly throughout Europe. In those days the church rejected scientific forms of investigation, and it controlled all education. Religious beliefs, which were highly superstitious and demonological, came to dominate all aspects of life. Once again behavior was usually interpreted as a conflict between good and evil, God and the devil. Deviant behavior, particularly psychological dysfunctioning, was seen as evidence of Satan's influence. Although some scientists and physicians still insisted on medical explanations and treatments, their views carried little weight in this atmosphere.

The Middle Ages were a time of great stress and anxiety—of war, urban uprisings, and plagues. People blamed the devil for these troubles and feared being possessed by him. Abnormal behavior apparently increased greatly during this period (Henley & Thorne, 2005). In addition, there were outbreaks of *mass madness,* in which large numbers of people apparently shared *delusions* (blatantly false beliefs) and *hallucinations* (imagined sights or sounds). In one such disorder, *tarantism* (also known as *Saint Vitus' dance*), groups of people would suddenly start to jump, dance, and go into convulsions (Sigerist, 1943). Some dressed oddly; others tore off their clothing. All were convinced that they had been bitten and possessed by a wolf spider, now called a tarantula, and they sought to cure their disorder by performing a dance called a tarantella. In another form of mass madness, *lycanthropy,* people thought they were possessed by wolves or other animals. They acted wolflike and imagined that fur was growing all over their bodies. Stories of lycanthropes, more popularly known as *werewolves,* have been passed down to us and continue to fire the imagination of writers, moviemakers, and their audiences.

Not surprisingly, some of the earlier demonological treatments for psychological abnormality reemerged during the Middle Ages. Once again the key to the cure was to rid the person's body of the devil that possessed it. Exorcisms were revived, and clergymen, who generally were in charge of treatment during this period, would plead, chant, or pray to the devil or evil spirit (Sluhovsky, 2007). If these techniques did not work, they had others to try, some indistinguishable from torture.

It was not until the Middle Ages drew to a close that demonology and its methods began to lose favor (Magherini & Biotti, 1998). Towns throughout Europe grew into cities, and government authorities gained more power and took over nonreligious activities. Among their other responsibilities, they began to run hospitals and direct the care of people suffering from mental disorders. Medical views of abnormality gained favor once again. When *lunacy trials* were held in late thirteenth-century England to determine the sanity of certain persons, it was not unusual for natural causes, such as a "blow to the head" or "fear of one's father," to be held responsible for an individual's unusual behavior (Neugebauer, 1979, 1978). During these same years, many people with psychological disturbances received treatment in medical hospitals, such as the Trinity Hospital in England (Allderidge, 1979, p. 322).

Exorcism at the movies

In the 1973 movie *The Exorcist,* an exorcist offers prayers and administers holy water to try to force the devil to leave the body of a troubled teenage girl. This popular horror movie has spurred a rash of books and movies on demonic possession and a number of attempted modern-day exorcisms.

Photofest

The Renaissance and the Rise of Asylums

During the early part of the Renaissance, a period of flourishing cultural and scientific activity (about 1400–1700), demonological views of abnormality continued to decline. German physician Johann Weyer (1515–1588), the first physician to specialize in mental illness, believed that the mind was as susceptible to sickness as the body was. He is now considered the founder of the modern study of psychopathology.

The care of people with mental disorders continued to improve in this atmosphere. In England such individuals might be kept at home while their families were aided financially by the local parish. Across Europe religious shrines were devoted to the humane and loving treatment of people with mental disorders. Perhaps the best known of these shrines was at Gheel in Belgium. Beginning in the fifteenth century, people came to it from all over the world for psychic healing. Local residents welcomed these pilgrims into their homes, and many stayed on to form the world's first "colony" of mental patients. Gheel was the forerunner of today's *community mental health programs,* and it continues to demonstrate that people with psychological disorders can respond to loving care and respectful treatment (van Walsum, 2004; Aring, 1975, 1974). Many patients still live in foster homes there, interacting with other residents, until they recover.

Unfortunately, these improvements in care began to fade by the mid-sixteenth century. Government officials discovered that private homes and community residences could house only a small percentage of those with severe mental disorders and that medical hospitals were too few and too small. More and more, they converted hospitals and monasteries into **asylums,** institutions whose primary purpose was to care for people with mental illness. These institutions began with every intention of providing good care. Once the asylums started to overflow, however, they became virtual prisons where patients were held in filthy conditions and treated with unspeakable cruelty.

The first asylum had been founded in Muslim Spain in the early fifteenth century, but the idea did not gain full momentum until the 1500s. In 1547, Bethlehem Hospital was given to the city of London by Henry VIII for the sole purpose of confining the mentally ill. In this asylum patients bound in chains cried out for all to hear. During

Bewitched or bewildered?
A great fear of witchcraft swept Europe even during the "enlightened" Renaissance. Tens of thousands of people, mostly women, were thought to have made a pact with the devil. Some appear to have had mental disorders, which caused them to act strangely (Zilboorg & Henry, 1941). This individual is being "dunked" repeatedly until she confesses to witchery.

Bedlam
In this eighteenth-century work from *The Rake's Progress,* William Hogarth depicted London's Bethlehem Hospital, or Bedlam, as a chaotic asylum where people of fashion came to marvel at the strange behavior of the inmates.

•asylum•A type of institution that first became popular in the sixteenth century to provide care for persons with mental disorders. Most became virtual prisons.

The Moon and the Mind

Primitive societies believed that the moon had magical, mystical powers and that its changes portended events of many kinds. The moon supposedly had the power to impregnate women, to make plants grow, and to drive people crazy. Later societies also credited the power of the moon to affect behavior—the so-called Transylvania Effect—and applied the terms "lunatic" and "lunacy" to certain persons and behaviors to capture their lunar, or

moonlike, qualities. Even today, many institutions and people believe that behavior is affected by the phases of the moon (Wells et al., 2007; Owens & McGowan, 2006; Kung & Mrazek, 2005).

A number of scientists have advanced theories to explain a possible lunar effect on human behavior. Some, for example, say that since the phases of the moon affect the tides of the oceans, they may have similar effects on the bodily fluids of

Silvia Otte/Photonica/Getty Images

human beings, whose composition is more than 80 percent water (Thakur & Sharma, 1984). The increase in births might therefore be explained by the force of the moon on the expectant mother's amniotic fluid. Similar tidal and gravitational effects have been used to explain the apparent increase in bizarre behavior when the moon is full. But skeptics have noted that even if a small association does exist between lunar cycles and behavior, it may simply be caused by people's expectations. That is, because certain persons expect to be influenced by a full moon, they may be more attentive and responsive to their internal sensations or desires at that time.

A number of researchers have tried to determine whether the activity of the moon is in fact related to human behavior by calculating the precise numbers of births, crimes, and unusual behaviors that occur when the moon is full. A few such investigators have indeed found an association between a full moon and unintentional poisonings (Oderda & Klein-Schwartz, 1983), aggression (Lieber, 1978), absenteeism (Sands & Miller, 1991), and crime (Thakur & Sharma, 1984). More often, however, researchers have found no relationship between lunar cycles and human biology or behavior (McLay et al., 2006; Owen & McGowan, 2006; Arliss et al., 2005; Kung & Mrazek, 2005).

Despite so little research support, many people continue to believe in the power of the moon. And so the debate continues, as scientists and philosophers alike try to clarify whether the cause of lunacy does indeed lie in the heavens or in our minds.

certain phases of the moon in particular, they might be chained and whipped to prevent violence (Asimov, 1997) (see *A Closer Look* above). The hospital even became a popular tourist attraction; people were eager to pay to look at the howling and gibbering inmates. The hospital's name, pronounced "Bedlam" by the local people, has come to mean a chaotic uproar. Similarly, in the Lunatics' Tower in Vienna, patients were herded into narrow hallways by the outer walls so that tourists outside could look up and see them. In La Bicêtre, an asylum in Paris for male patients, patients were shackled to the walls of cold, dark, dirty cells with iron collars and given spoiled food that could be sold nowhere else (Selling, 1940). Such asylums remained a widely used form of "care" until the late 1700s.

The Nineteenth Century: Reform and Moral Treatment

As 1800 approached, the treatment of people with mental disorders began to improve once again (Maher & Maher, 2003). Historians usually point to La Bicêtre as the first site of asylum reform. In 1793, during the French Revolution, Philippe Pinel (1745–1826) was named the chief physician there. He argued that the patients were sick people whose illnesses should be treated with sympathy and kindness rather than chains and beatings (van Walsum, 2004). He unchained the patients and allowed them to move freely about the hospital grounds; replaced the dark dungeons with sunny, well-ventilated rooms; and offered support and advice. Pinel's approach proved remarkably successful. Many patients who had been shut away for decades improved greatly over a short period of time and were released. Pinel later brought similar reforms to a mental hospital in Paris for female patients, La Salpetrière.

Meanwhile an English Quaker named William Tuke (1732–1819) was bringing similar reforms to northern England. In 1796 he founded the York Retreat, a rural estate where about 30 mental patients lived as guests in quiet country houses and were treated with a combination of rest, talk, prayer, and manual work (Charland, 2007; Borthwick et al., 2001).

George Wesley Bellows, *Dance in a Madhouse*, 1907. Photograph ©1997 The Art Institute of Chicago.

Dance in a madhouse
A popular feature of moral treatment was the "lunatic ball." Hospital officials would bring patients together to dance and enjoy themselves. One such ball is shown in this painting, *Dance in a Madhouse*, by George Bellows.

The Spread of Moral Treatment

The methods of Pinel and Tuke, called **moral treatment** because they emphasized moral guidance and humane and respectful techniques, caught on throughout Europe and the United States. Patients with psychological problems were increasingly perceived as potentially productive human beings whose mental functioning had broken down under stress. They were considered deserving of individual care, including discussions of their problems, useful activities, work, companionship, and quiet.

The person most responsible for the early spread of moral treatment in the United States was Benjamin Rush (1745–1813), an eminent physician at Pennsylvania Hospital who is now considered the father of American psychiatry. Limiting his practice to mental illness, Rush developed innovative, humane approaches to treatment (Whitaker, 2002). For example, he required that the hospital hire intelligent and sensitive attendants to work closely with patients, reading and talking to them and taking them on regular walks. He also suggested that it would be therapeutic for doctors to give small gifts to their patients now and then.

Rush's work was influential, but it was a Boston schoolteacher named Dorothea Dix (1802–1887) who made humane care a public and political concern in the United States. In 1841 Dix had gone to teach Sunday school at a local prison and been shocked by the conditions she saw there. Before long, her interest in prison conditions broadened to include the plight of poor and mentally ill people throughout the country. From 1841 to 1881, Dix went from state legislature to state legislature and to Congress speaking of the horrors she had observed at asylums and calling for reform. Dix's campaign led to new laws and greater government funding to improve the treatment of people with mental disorders (Zilboorg & Henry, 1941). Each state was made responsible for developing effective public mental hospitals. Dix personally helped establish 32 of these **state hospitals,** all intended to offer moral treatment (Boardman & Makari, 2007; Pomerantz, 2003; Viney, 2000). Similar hospitals were established throughout Europe.

The Decline of Moral Treatment

By the 1850s, a number of mental hospitals throughout Europe and America reported success using moral approaches. By the end of that century, however, several factors led to a reversal of the moral treatment movement

•**moral treatment**•A nineteenth-century approach to treating people with mental dysfunction that emphasized moral guidance and humane and respectful treatment.

•**state hospitals**•State-run public mental institutions in the United States.

The "crib"
Outrageous devices and techniques, such as the "crib," were used in asylums, and some continued to be used even during the reforms of the nineteenth century.

(Bockoven, 1963). One factor was the speed with which the movement had spread. As mental hospitals multiplied, severe money and staffing shortages developed, recovery rates declined, and overcrowding in the hospitals became a major problem. Another factor was the assumption behind moral treatment that all patients could be cured if treated with humanity and dignity. For some, this was indeed sufficient. Others, however, needed more effective treatments than any that had yet been developed. An additional factor contributing to the decline of moral treatment was the emergence of a new wave of prejudice against people with mental disorders. As more and more patients disappeared into large, distant mental hospitals, the public came to view them as strange and dangerous. In turn, people were less open-handed when it came to making donations or allocating government funds. Moreover, many of the patients entering public mental hospitals in the United States in the late nineteenth century were poor foreign immigrants, whom the public had little interest in helping.

By the early years of the twentieth century, the moral treatment movement had ground to a halt in both the United States and Europe. Public mental hospitals were providing only custodial care and ineffective medical treatments and were becoming more overcrowded every year. Long-term hospitalization became the rule once again.

The Early Twentieth Century: The Somatogenic and Psychogenic Perspectives

As the moral movement was declining in the late 1800s, two opposing perspectives emerged and began to vie for the attention of clinicians: the **somatogenic perspective,** the view that abnormal psychological functioning has physical causes, and the **psychogenic perspective,** the view that the chief causes of abnormal functioning are psychological. These perspectives came into full bloom during the twentieth century.

The Somatogenic Perspective
The somatogenic perspective has at least a 2,400-year history—remember Hippocrates' view that abnormal behavior resulted from brain disease and an imbalance of humors? Not until the late nineteenth century, however, did this perspective make a triumphant return and begin to gain wide acceptance.

Two factors were responsible for this rebirth. One was the work of an eminent German researcher, Emil Kraepelin (1856–1926). In 1883 Kraepelin published an influential textbook arguing that physical factors, such as fatigue, are responsible for mental dysfunction. In addition, as you will see in Chapter 4, he also constructed the first modern system for classifying abnormal behavior. He identified various syndromes, or clusters of symptoms; listed their physical causes; and discussed their expected course (Engstrom et al., 2006; Decker, 2004; Kihlstrom, 2002).

New biological discoveries also triggered the rise of the somatogenic perspective. One of the most important discoveries was that an organic disease, *syphilis,* led to *general paresis,* an irreversible disorder with both physical and mental symptoms, including paralysis and delusions of grandeur. In 1897 Richard von Krafft-Ebing (1840–1902), a German neurologist, injected matter from syphilis sores into patients suffering from general paresis and found that none of the patients developed symptoms of syphilis. Their immunity could have been caused only by an earlier case of syphilis. Since all patients with general paresis were now immune to syphilis, Krafft-Ebing theorized that syphilis had been the cause of their general paresis. Finally, in 1905, Fritz Schaudinn (1871–1906), a German zoologist, discovered that the microorganism *Treponema pallida* was responsible for syphilis, which in turn was responsible for general paresis.

The more things change . . .
Patients at a modern-day mental hospital in Bangladesh eat their lunch off of the floor of their ward. Such conditions are similar to those that existed in some state hospitals throughout the United States well into the twentieth century.

table: 1-1

Eugenics and Mental Disorders

Year	Event
1896	Connecticut became the first state in the United States to prohibit persons with mental disorders from marrying.
1896–1933	Every state in the United States passed a law prohibiting marriage by persons with mental disorders.
1907	Indiana became the first state to pass a bill calling for people with mental disorders, as well as criminals and other "defectives," to undergo sterilization.
1927	The U.S. Supreme Court ruled that eugenic sterilization was constitutional.
1907–1945	Around 45,000 Americans were sterilized under eugenic sterilization laws; 21,000 of them were patients in state mental hospitals.
1929–1932	Denmark, Norway, Sweden, Finland, and Iceland passed eugenic sterilization laws.
1933	Germany passed a eugenic sterilization law, under which 375,000 people were sterilized by 1940.
1940	Nazi Germany began to use "proper gases" to kill people with mental disorders; 70,000 or more people were killed in less than two years.

Source: Whitaker, 2002.

•**somatogenic perspective**•The view that abnormal psychological functioning has physical causes.

•**psychogenic perspective**•The view that the chief causes of abnormal functioning are psychological.

The work of Kraepelin and the new understanding of general paresis led many researchers and practitioners to suspect that physical factors were responsible for many mental disorders, perhaps all of them. These theories and the possibility of quick and effective medical solutions for mental disorders were especially welcomed by those who worked in mental hospitals, where patient populations were now growing at an alarming rate.

Despite the general optimism, biological approaches yielded mostly disappointing results throughout the first half of the twentieth century. Although many medical treatments were developed for patients in mental hospitals during that time, most of the techniques failed to work. Physicians tried tooth extraction, tonsillectomy, hydrotherapy (alternating hot and cold baths), and lobotomy, a surgical cutting of certain nerve fibers in the brain. Even worse, biological views and claims led, in some circles, to proposals for immoral solutions such as *eugenic sterilization,* the elimination (through medical or other means) of individuals' ability to reproduce (see Table 1–1). Not until the 1950s, when a number of effective medications were finally discovered, did the somatogenic perspective truly begin to pay off for patients.

The Psychogenic Perspective The late nineteenth century also saw the emergence of the psychogenic perspective, the view that the chief causes of abnormal functioning are often psychological. This view, too, had a long history. The Roman statesman and orator Cicero (106–43 B.C.) held that psychological disturbances could cause bodily ailments, and the Greek physician Galen (c. 129–c. 200) believed that many mental disorders are caused by fear, disappointment in love, and other psychological events. However, the psychogenic perspective did not gain much of a following until studies of *hypnotism* demonstrated its potential.

Hypnotism is a procedure that places people in a trancelike mental state during which they become extremely suggestible. It was used to help treat psychological disorders as far back as 1778, when an Austrian physician named Friedrich Anton Mesmer (1734–1815) established a clinic in Paris. His patients suffered from *hysterical disorders,* mysterious bodily ailments that had no apparent physical basis. Mesmer had his

BETWEEN THE LINES

Literature and Abnormal Psychology

In 1586 Dr. Timothie Bright wrote *Treatise on Melancholia,* the first English-language book on mental disorders. William Shakespeare borrowed many of the portrayals of madness in his plays from Bright's book (Street, 1994). ‹‹

Writing during the Renaissance, Shakespeare speculated on the nature and causes of abnormal behavior in 20 of his 38 plays and in many of his sonnets (Dalby, 1997). ‹‹

Although controversial in professional circles, Anton Mesmer's work attracted many persons outside the clinical field. Charles Dickens, the nineteenth-century English novelist, so strongly believed in mesmerism that he considered himself to be a doctor in this method of healing the sick (Asimov, 1997). ‹‹

Oscar Sosa/AP Photo

Hypnotism update
Hypnotism, the procedure that opened the door for the psychogenic perspective, continues to influence many areas of modern life, including the fields of psychotherapy, entertainment, and law enforcement. Here a forensic clinician uses hypnosis to help a witness recall the details of a crime. Recent research has clarified, however, that hypnotic procedures are as capable of creating false memories as they are of uncovering real memories.

•**psychoanalysis**•Either the theory or the treatment of abnormal mental functioning that emphasizes unconscious psychological forces as the cause of psychopathology.

•**psychotropic medications**•Drugs that mainly affect the brain and reduce many symptoms of mental dysfunctioning.

•**deinstitutionalization**•The practice, begun in the 1960s, of releasing hundreds of thousands of patients from public mental hospitals.

patients sit in a darkened room filled with music; then he appeared, dressed in a colorful costume, and touched the troubled area of each patient's body with a special rod. A surprising number of patients seemed to be helped by this treatment, called *mesmerism.* Their pain, numbness, or paralysis disappeared. Several scientists believed that Mesmer was inducing a trancelike state in his patients and that this state was causing their symptoms to disappear (Lynn & Kirsch, 2006). The treatment was so controversial, however, that eventually Mesmer was banished from Paris (Spiegel, 2002).

It was not until years after Mesmer died that many researchers had the courage to investigate his procedure, later called *hypnotism* (from *hypnos,* the Greek word for "sleep"), and its effects on hysterical disorders. The experiments of two physicians practicing in the city of Nancy in France, Hippolyte-Marie Bernheim (1840–1919) and Ambroise-Auguste Liébault (1823–1904), showed that hysterical disorders could actually be induced in otherwise normal people while they were under the influence of hypnosis. That is, the physicians could make normal people experience deafness, paralysis, blindness, or numbness by means of hypnotic suggestion—and they could remove these artificial symptoms by the same means. Thus they established that a *mental* process—hypnotic suggestion—could both cause and cure even a physical dysfunction. Leading scientists concluded that hysterical disorders were largely psychological in origin, and the psychogenic perspective rose in popularity.

Among those who studied the effects of hypnotism on hysterical disorders was Josef Breuer (1842–1925) of Vienna. This physician discovered that his patients sometimes awoke free of hysterical symptoms after speaking candidly under hypnosis about past upsetting events. During the 1890s Breuer was joined in his work by another Viennese physician, Sigmund Freud (1856–1939). As you will see in Chapter 3, Freud's work eventually led him to develop the theory of **psychoanalysis,** which holds that many forms of abnormal and normal psychological functioning are psychogenic. In particular, he believed that *unconscious* psychological processes are at the root of such functioning.

Freud also developed the *technique* of psychoanalysis, a form of discussion in which clinicians help troubled people gain insight into their unconscious psychological processes. He believed that such insight, even without hypnotic procedures, would help the patients overcome their psychological problems.

Freud and his followers applied the psychoanalytic treatment approach primarily to patients suffering from anxiety or depression, problems that did not typically require hospitalization. These patients visited therapists in their offices for sessions of approximately an hour and then went about their daily activities—a format of treatment now known as *outpatient therapy.* By the early twentieth century, psychoanalytic theory and treatment were widely accepted throughout the Western world.

The psychoanalytic approach had little effect on the treatment of severely disturbed patients in mental hospitals, however. This type of therapy requires levels of clarity, insight, and verbal skill beyond the capabilities of most such patients. Moreover, psychoanalysis often takes years to be effective, and the overcrowded and understaffed public mental hospitals could not accommodate such a leisurely pace.

✿Current Trends

It would hardly be accurate to say that we now live in a period of great enlightenment about or dependable treatment of mental disorders. In fact, surveys conducted during the past decade have found that 43 percent of respondents believe that people bring mental disorders on themselves, 30 percent consider such disorders to be caused by sinful behavior, and 19 percent point to a lack of willpower or self-discipline as a cause (Stanford, 2007; NMHA, 1999; Murray, 1993). Nevertheless, the past 50 years have brought major changes in the ways clinicians understand and treat abnormal functioning. More theories and types of treatment exist, as do more research studies, more information, and, perhaps for these reasons, more disagreements about abnormal functioning today than at any time in the past. In some ways the study and treatment of psychological disorders have made great strides, but in other respects clinical scientists and practitioners are still struggling to make a difference.

How Are People with Severe Disturbances Cared For?

In the 1950s researchers discovered a number of new **psychotropic medications**—drugs that primarily affect the brain and alleviate many symptoms of mental dysfunctioning. They included the first *antipsychotic drugs,* which correct extremely confused and distorted thinking; *antidepressant drugs,* which lift the mood of depressed people; and *antianxiety drugs,* which reduce tension and worry.

When given these drugs, many patients who had spent years in mental hospitals began to show signs of improvement. Hospital administrators, encouraged by these results and pressured by a growing public outcry over the terrible conditions in public mental hospitals, began to discharge patients almost immediately.

Since the discovery of these medications, mental health professionals in most of the developed nations of the world have followed a policy of **deinstitutionalization,** releasing hundreds of thousands of patients from public mental hospitals. On any given day in 1955, close to 600,000 people were confined in public mental institutions across the United States (see Figure 1-1). Today the daily patient population in the same kinds of hospitals is around 60,000 (Torrey, 2006, 2001).

In short, outpatient care has now become the primary mode of treatment for people with severe psychological disturbances as well as for those with more moderate problems. Today when severely impaired people do need institutionalization, they are usually given *short-term* hospitalization. Ideally, they are then given outpatient psychotherapy and medication in community programs and residences (McEvoy & Richards, 2007).

Chapters 3 and 15 will look more closely at this recent emphasis on community care for people with severe psychological disturbances—a philosophy called the *community mental health approach.* The approach has been helpful for many patients, but too few community programs are available to address current needs in the United States (Rosenberg & Rosenberg, 2006; Talbott, 2004). As a result, hundreds of thousands of persons with severe disturbances fail to make lasting recoveries, and they shuttle back and forth between the mental hospital and the community. After release from the hospital, they at

Alternative treatment?
Tens of thousands of people with severe mental disorders are currently homeless. They receive no treatment or guidance and wind up on the streets, much like this man, who sleeps beneath a mural in the "skid row" area of downtown Los Angeles.

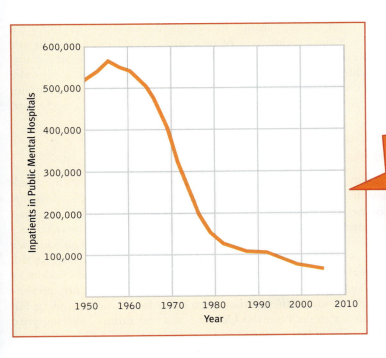

Figure 1-1

The impact of deinstitutionalization The number of patients (60,000) now hospitalized in public mental hospitals in the United States is a small fraction of the number hospitalized in 1955. (Adapted from Torrey, 2006, 2001; Lang, 1999.)

best receive minimal care and often wind up living in decrepit rooming houses or on the streets. In fact, only 40 percent of persons with severe psychological disturbances currently receive treatment of any kind (Wang et al., 2007, 2005, 2002). At least 100,000 individuals with such disturbances are homeless on any given day; another 135,000 or more are inmates of jails and prisons (Rosenberg & Rosenberg, 2006; Cutler et al., 2002; Torrey, 2001). Their abandonment is truly a national disgrace.

How Are People with Less Severe Disturbances Treated?

The treatment picture for people with moderate psychological disturbances has been more positive than that for people with severe disorders. Since the 1950s, outpatient care has continued to be the preferred mode of treatment for them, and the number and types of facilities that offer such care have expanded to meet the need.

Before the 1950s, almost all outpatient care took the form of **private psychotherapy,** an arrangement by which an individual directly pays a psychotherapist for counseling services. This tended to be an expensive form of treatment, available only to the wealthy. Since the 1950s, however, most health insurance plans have expanded coverage to include private psychotherapy, so that it is now also widely available to people with more modest incomes. In addition, outpatient therapy is now offered in a number of less expensive settings, such as community mental health centers, crisis intervention centers, family service centers, and other social service agencies. The new settings have spurred a dramatic increase in the number of persons seeking outpatient care for psychological problems. Nationwide surveys suggest that nearly one of every five adults in the United States receives treatment for psychological disorders in the course of a year (Wang et al., 2007, 2005). The majority of clients are seen for fewer than five sessions during the year.

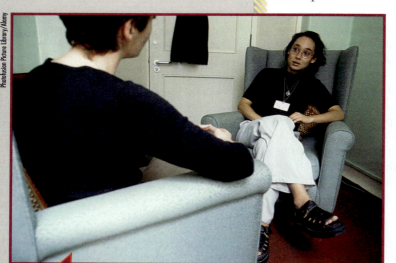

The availability of therapy
Therapy for people with mild to severe psychological disturbances is widely available in individual, group, and family formats.

Outpatient treatments are also becoming available for more and more kinds of problems. When Freud and his colleagues first began to practice, most of their patients suffered from anxiety or depression. These problems still dominate therapy today; almost half of all clients suffer from them. However, people with other kinds of disorders are also receiving therapy. In addition, at least 20 percent of clients enter therapy because of milder problems in living—problems with marital, family, job, peer, school, or community relationships (Druss et al., 2007; Wang et al., 2005).

Yet another change in outpatient care since the 1950s has been the development of programs devoted exclusively to one kind of psychological problem. We now have, for example, suicide prevention centers, substance abuse programs, eating disorder programs, phobia clinics, and sexual dysfunction programs. Clinicians in these programs have the kind of expertise that can be acquired only by concentration in a single area.

A Growing Emphasis on Preventing Disorders and Promoting Mental Health

Although the community mental health approach has often failed to address the needs of people with severe disorders, it has given rise to an important principle of mental health care—**prevention** (Bond & Hauf, 2007; Reese & Vera, 2007). Rather than wait for psychological disorders to occur, many of today's community programs try to correct the social conditions that underlie psychological problems (poverty or violence in the community, for example) and to identify and help individuals who are at risk for developing emotional problems (for example, teenage mothers or the children of people with severe psychological disorders). As you will see later, community prevention programs are not always successful and they often suffer from limited funding, but they have grown in number throughout the United States and Europe, offering great promise as the ultimate form of intervention.

Positive Psychology: Happiness Is All Around Us

Judging from TV news shows, news Web sites, and the spread of self-help books, you might think that happiness is rare. But there's good news. Research indicates that people's lives are, in general, more upbeat than we think. In fact, most people around the world say they're happy—including most of those who are poor, unemployed, elderly, and disabled (Becchetti & Santoro, 2007; Pugno, 2007; Wallis, 2005). Over 90 percent of people with quadriplegia say they're glad to be alive, and, overall, people with spinal cord injuries report feeling only slightly less happy than other people (Diener & Diener, 1996). Men and women are equally likely to declare themselves satisfied or very happy. Wealthy people appear only slightly happier than those of modest means (Easterbrook, 2005; Diener et al., 1993). Overall, only 1 person in 10 reports being "not too happy" (Myers, 2000; Myers & Diener, 1996), and only 1 in 7 reports waking up unhappy (Wallis, 2005).

Of course, some people are indeed happier than others. Particularly happy people seem to remain happy from decade to decade, regardless of job changes, moves, and family changes (Becchetti & Santoro, 2007; Myers & Diener, 1996). Such people adjust to negative events and return to their usual cheerful state within a few months (Diener et al., 2006, 1992). Conversely, unhappy people are not cheered in the long term even by positive events.

Some research indicates that happiness is linked to personality characteristics and interpretive styles (Diener et al., 2006; Stewart et al., 2005; Diener, 2000). Happy people are, for example, generally optimistic, outgoing, curious, and tender-minded; they also tend to persevere, have several close friends, possess high self-esteem, be spiritual, and have a sense of control over their lives (Peterson et al., 2007; Sahoo et al., 2005; Diener & Seligman, 2002). Some theorists also believe that people have a "happiness set point" to which they consistently return, despite life's ups and downs, although this notion is not always supported by research (Diener et al., 2007; Lucas, 2007). Some studies suggest that one's sense of happiness may have a genetic component (Roysamb, 2006; Lykken & Tellegen, 1996).

A better understanding of the roots of happiness is likely to emerge from the current flurry of research. In the meantime, we can take comfort in the knowledge that the human condition isn't quite as unhappy as news stories (and textbooks on abnormal psychology) may make it seem.

Happiness is everywhere As the joy in the faces of these Tibetan women illustrates, happiness is tied to factors beyond a person's economic plight, age, residence, or health.

© Azim Pamahpour

Prevention programs have been further energized in the past few years by the field of psychology's growing interest in **positive psychology** (Seligman, 2007; Seligman & Steen, 2005). Positive psychology is the study and enhancement of positive feelings such as optimism and happiness; positive traits like perseverance and wisdom; positive abilities such as interpersonal skill and other talents; and group-directed virtues, including altruism and tolerance (see *Psych Watch* above).

In the clinical arena, positive psychology suggests that practitioners can help people best by *promoting* positive development and psychological wellness. While researchers study and learn more about positive psychology in the laboratory, a growing number of clinicians are already beginning to apply its principles in their work. They are teaching people coping skills that may help protect them from stress and adversity and encouraging them to become more involved in personally meaningful activities and relationships (Bond & Hauf, 2007). In this way, the clinicians are trying to promote mental health and prevent mental disorders.

•**multicultural psychology**•The field of psychology that examines the impact of culture, race, ethnicity, gender, and similar factors on our behaviors and thoughts and focuses on how such factors may influence the origin, nature, and treatment of abnormal behavior.

•**managed care program**•A system of health care coverage in which the insurance company largely controls the nature, scope, and cost of medical or psychological services.

Multicultural Psychology

We are, without question, a society of multiple cultures, races, and languages. Indeed, in the coming decades, members of racial and ethnic minority groups in the United States will, collectively, outnumber white Americans (Gordon, 2005; U.S. Census Bureau, 2000). This change in our society's racial and ethnic composition is partly because of shifts in immigration trends and partly because of higher birth rates among minority groups in the United States. The majority of new immigrants to this country are Hispanic (34 percent) or Asian (34 percent). Moreover, while the average number of children born to white Americans is 1.7, the number born to African Americans and Hispanic Americans is 2.4 and 2.9, respectively.

In response to this growing diversity, a new area of study called **multicultural psychology** has emerged (Jackson, 2006). Multicultural psychologists seek to understand how culture, race, ethnicity, gender, and similar factors affect behavior and thought and how people of different cultures, races, and genders may differ psychologically (Alegria et al., 2007, 2004). As you will see throughout this book, the field of multicultural psychology has begun to have a profound effect on our understanding and treatment of abnormal behavior.

The Growing Influence of Insurance Coverage

So many people now seek therapy that private insurance companies have changed their coverage for mental health patients. Today the dominant form of coverage is the **managed care program**—a program in which the insurance company determines such key issues as which therapists its clients may choose, the cost of sessions, and the number of sessions for which a client may be reimbursed (Shore, 2007; Reed & Eisman, 2006; Corcoran, Gorin, & Moniz, 2005).

At least 75 percent of all privately insured persons in the United States are currently enrolled in managed care programs (Deb et al., 2006; Kiesler, 2000). The coverage for mental health treatment under such programs follows the same basic principles as coverage for medical treatment, including a limited pool of practitioners from which patients can choose, preapproval of treatment by the insurance company, strict standards for judging whether problems and treatments qualify for reimbursement, and ongoing reviews and assessments. In the mental health realm, both therapists and clients typically dislike managed care programs (Cutler, 2007). They fear that the programs inevitably shorten therapy (often for the worse), unfairly favor treatments whose results are not always lasting (for example, drug therapy), pose a special hardship for those with severe mental disorders, and result in treatments determined by insurance companies rather than by therapists (Whitaker, 2007; Reed & Eisman, 2006; Mowbray et al., 2002).

A key problem with insurance coverage—both managed care and other kinds of insurance programs—is that reimbursements for mental disorders tend to be lower than those for medical disorders. This disparity places persons with psychological difficulties at a distinct disadvantage in their efforts to overcome their problems and inevitably affects the quality and quantity of the treatment they seek. Recently the federal government and 35 states passed so-called *parity laws* that direct insurance companies to provide equal

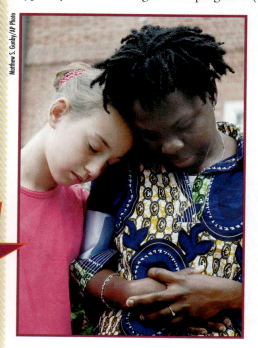

Matthew S. Gunby/AP Photo

Positive psychology in action
Often positive psychology and multicultural psychology work together. Here, for example, two young girls come together as one at the end of a "slave reconciliation" walk by 400 people in Maryland. The walk was intended to promote racial understanding and to help Americans overcome the lasting psychological effects of slavery.

"Wow! You need professional help."

coverage for mental and medical problems (Pear, 2008; Steverman, 2007). It is not yet clear, however, whether these laws are indeed leading to better coverage and whether they will improve the treatment picture for people with psychological problems (Busch et al., 2006; Harris et al., 2006).

What Are Today's Leading Theories and Professions?

One of the most important developments in the modern understanding and treatment of abnormal psychological functioning has been the growth of numerous theoretical perspectives that now coexist in the clinical field. Before the 1950s, the *psychoanalytic* perspective, with its emphasis on unconscious psychological problems as the cause of abnormal behavior, was dominant. Then the discovery of effective psychotropic drugs inspired new respect for the somatogenic, or *biological,* view. As you will see in Chapter 3, other influential perspectives that have emerged since the 1950s are the *behavioral, cognitive, humanistic-existential,* and *sociocultural* schools of thought. At present no single viewpoint dominates the clinical field as the psychoanalytic perspective once did. In fact, the perspectives often conflict and compete with one another, yet in some instances they complement each other and together provide more complete explanations and treatments for psychological disorders.

An ounce of prevention
The clinical field's growing emphasis on prevention has affected how employers address the problem of stress in the workplace. About 20 percent of corporate employers now offer some kind of stress reduction program, such as this regular yoga class at Armani (the fashion company) in New York City. Corporate spending has helped fuel the $12 billion stress-management industry.

table: 1-2

Profiles of Mental Health Professionals in the United States

	Degree	Began to Practice	Current Number	Percent Female
Psychiatrists	M.D., D.O.	1840s	33,000	25
Psychologists	Ph.D., Psy.D., Ed.D.	Late 1940s	152,000	52
Social workers	M.S.W., D.S.W.	Early 1950s	405,000	77
Counselors	Various	Early 1950s	375,000	50

Source: U.S. Bureau of Labor Statistics, 2008, 2002; AMA, 2007; APA, 2005; Weissman, 2000.

In addition, a variety of professionals now offer help to people with psychological problems (Wang et al., 2006). Before the 1950s, psychotherapy was offered only by *psychiatrists,* physicians who complete three to four additional years of training after medical school (a *residency*) in the treatment of abnormal mental functioning. After World War II, however, with millions of soldiers returning home to countries throughout North America and Europe, the demand for mental health services expanded so rapidly that other professional groups had to step in to fill the need (Humphreys, 1996).

Among those other groups are *clinical psychologists*—professionals who earn a doctorate in clinical psychology by completing four years of graduate training in abnormal functioning and its treatment and also complete a one-year internship at a mental hospital or mental health agency. Before their professional responsibilities expanded into the area of treatment, clinical psychologists were principally assessors and researchers of abnormal functioning. Some of them still specialize in those activities.

Psychotherapy and related services are also provided by *counseling psychologists, educational* and *school psychologists, psychiatric nurses, marriage therapists, family therapists,* and—the largest group—*psychiatric social workers* (see Table 1-2). Each of these specialties has its own graduate training program. Theoretically, each conducts therapy in a distinctive way, but in reality clinicians from the various specialties often use similar techniques. In fact, the individual differences within a professional group are sometimes greater than the general differences between groups.

One final key development in the study and treatment of mental disorders since World War II has been a growing appreciation of the need for effective research (Goodwin, 2007, 2002). As theories and forms of treatment have increased, *clinical researchers* have tried to determine which concepts best explain and predict abnormal behavior, which treatments are most effective, and what kinds of changes may be required. Today well-trained clinical researchers conduct studies in universities, medical schools, laboratories, mental hospitals, mental health centers, and other clinical settings throughout the world. Their work has produced important discoveries and has changed many of our ideas about abnormal psychological functioning.

PUTTING IT... together

A Work in Progress

Since ancient times, people have tried to explain, treat, and study abnormal behavior. By examining the responses of past societies to such behaviors, we can better understand the roots of our present views and treatments. In addition, a look backward helps us appreciate just how far we have come—how humane our present views are, how impressive our recent discoveries are, and how important our current emphasis on research is.

Phoenix Police Department Bureau of Records and ID

The more things change . . . part II
A surveillance camera shows Carol Anne Gotbaum, a 45-year-old mother of three, being led away by two Phoenix Sky Harbor Airport security guards in September 2007. After missing a connecting flight to Tucson, where she was to receive inpatient treatment for alcoholism and depression, Ms. Gotbaum became extremely upset, ran up and down the airport gate area, and was arrested and led screaming to a holding cell at the airport. While alone in the cell, she tried to move her handcuffs from behind her to the front of her and apparently was strangled by them. Her tragic death, and the events leading to it, remind us once again that we still have far to go in our understanding of, treatment for, and humanity toward people suffering from severe mental disorders.

At the same time we must recognize the many problems in abnormal psychology today. The field has yet to agree on one definition of abnormality. It is currently made up of conflicting schools of thought and treatment whose members are often unimpressed by the claims and accomplishments of the others. And clinical practice is carried out by a variety of professionals trained in different ways.

As you proceed through the topics in this book and look at the nature, treatment, and study of abnormal functioning, keep in mind the field's current strengths and weaknesses, the progress that has been made, and the journey that lies ahead. Perhaps the most important lesson to be learned from our look at the history of this field is that our current understanding of abnormal behavior represents a work in progress. The clinical field stands at a crossroads, with some of the most important insights, investigations, and changes yet to come.

How, then, should you proceed in your examination of abnormal psychology? To begin with, you need to learn about the basic tools and perspectives that today's scientists and practitioners find most useful. This is the task we turn to in the next several chapters. Chapter 2 describes the research strategies that are currently informing our knowledge of abnormal functioning. Chapter 3 then examines the range of views that influence today's clinical theorists and practitioners. Finally, Chapter 4 examines how abnormal behaviors are currently being assessed, diagnosed, and treated. Later chapters present the major categories of psychological abnormality as well as the leading explanations and treatments for each of them. In the final chapter you will see how the science of abnormal psychology and its professionals address current social issues and interact with legal, social, and other institutions in our world.

‹‹‹(SUMMING UP)›››

○ **What Is Psychological Abnormality?** Abnormal functioning is generally considered to be *deviant, distressful, dysfunctional,* and *dangerous.* Behavior must also be considered in the context in which it occurs, however, and the concept of abnormality depends on the *norms* and *values* of the society in question. *pp. 2–5*

○ **What Is Treatment?** *Therapy* is a systematic process for helping people overcome their psychological difficulties. It typically requires a *patient,* a *therapist,* and a *series of therapeutic contacts. pp. 5–6*

continued

○ **How Was Abnormality Viewed and Treated in the Past?** The history of psychological disorders stretches back to ancient times.

PREHISTORIC SOCIETIES Prehistoric societies apparently viewed abnormal behavior as the work of evil spirits. There is evidence that Stone Age cultures used *trephination,* a primitive form of brain surgery, to treat abnormal behavior. People of early societies also sought to drive out evil spirits by *exorcism. pp. 7–8*

GREEKS AND ROMANS Physicians of the Greek and Roman empires offered more enlightened explanations of mental disorders. Hippocrates believed that abnormal behavior was caused by an imbalance of the four bodily fluids, or *humors:* black bile, yellow bile, blood, and phlegm. Treatment consisted of correcting the underlying physical pathology through diet and lifestyle. *pp. 8–10*

THE MIDDLE AGES In the Middle Ages, Europeans returned to demonological explanations of abnormal behavior. The clergy was very influential and held that mental disorders were the work of the devil. As the Middle Ages drew to a close, such explanations and treatments began to decline, and people with mental disorders were increasingly treated in hospitals instead of by the clergy. *p. 10*

THE RENAISSANCE Care of people with mental disorders continued to improve during the early part of the Renaissance. Certain religious shrines became dedicated to the humane treatment of such individuals. By the middle of the sixteenth century, however, persons with mental disorders were being warehoused in *asylums. pp. 11–12*

THE NINETEENTH CENTURY Care of those with mental disorders started to improve again in the nineteenth century. In Paris, Philippe Pinel started the movement toward *moral treatment.* Similar reforms were brought to England by William Tuke. In the United States Dorothea Dix spearheaded a movement to ensure legal rights and protection for people with mental disorders and to establish state hospitals for their care. Unfortunately, the moral treatment movement disintegrated by the late nineteenth century, and mental hospitals again became warehouses where inmates received minimal care. *pp. 13–14*

THE EARLY TWENTIETH CENTURY The turn of the twentieth century saw the return of the *somatogenic perspective,* the view that abnormal psychological functioning is caused primarily by physical factors. Key to this development were the work of Emil Kraepelin in the late 1800s and the finding that *general paresis* was caused by the organic disease syphilis. The same period saw the rise of the *psychogenic perspective,* the view that the chief causes of abnormal functioning are psychological. An important factor in its rise was the use of *hypnotism* to treat patients with *hysterical disorders.* Sigmund Freud's psychogenic approach, *psychoanalysis,* eventually gained wide acceptance and influenced future generations of clinicians. *pp. 14–16*

○ **Current Trends** The past 50 years have brought significant changes in the understanding and treatment of abnormal functioning. In the 1950s, researchers discovered a number of new *psychotropic medications,* drugs that mainly affect the brain and reduce many symptoms of mental dysfunctioning. Their success contributed to a policy of *deinstitutionalization,* under which hundreds of thousands of patients were released from public mental hospitals. In addition, *outpatient treatment* has become the primary approach for most persons with mental disorders, both mild and severe; *prevention programs* are growing in number and influence; the field of *multicultural psychology* has begun to influence how clinicians view and treat abnormality; and *insurance coverage* is having a significant impact on the way treatment is conducted. Finally, a variety of *perspectives* and *professionals* have come to operate in the field of abnormal psychology, and many well-trained *clinical researchers* now investigate the field's theories and treatments. *pp. 16–22*

⫸ CRITICAL THOUGHTS ⫷

1. Why are movies and novels with themes of abnormal functioning so popular? Why do actresses and actors who portray characters with psychological disorders tend to receive more awards for their performances? *pp. 1, 22, 24*

2. What behaviors might fit the criteria of deviant, distressful, dysfunctional, or dangerous but would not be considered abnormal by most people? *pp. 2–5, 7*

3. In addition to exorcism, what other demonological explanations or treatments are still around today? Why do they persist? *pp. 8, 10*

4. Have episodes of "mass madness" occurred in recent times? Might the Internet, cable television, or other forms of modern technology pose a special danger in the emergence and spread of new forms of mass madness? *p. 10*

5. Clearly, positive behaviors have been around as long as negative ones, and multiple cultures and races have characterized Western society for centuries. Yet psychology's focus on positive psychology and on multicultural psychology is a relatively new phenomenon. Why do you think it took so long for psychologists to pay serious attention to these perspectives? *pp. 19–20*

cyberstudy

SEARCH

Search the *Abnormal Psychology* Video Tool Kit

www.worthpublishers.com/apvtk

▲ Chapter 1 Video Cases
   Benjamin Rush's Moral Treatments
   Early Hospital Treatments for Severe Mental Disorders
   Shameful Past Institutions for Persons with Developmental Disabilities

▲ Video case discussions, study guides, and questions

Log on to the Comer Web Page

www.worthpublishers.com/comer

▲ Chapter 1 outline, learning objectives, research exercises, study tools, and practice test questions

▲ Additional Chapter 1 case studies, Web links, and FAQs

RESEARCH IN ABNORMAL PSYCHOLOGY

"The brain is an organ of minor importance."

Aristotle, Greek philosopher, fourth century B.C.

"Woman may be said to be an inferior man."

Aristotle

"[Louis Pasteur's] theory of germs is a ridiculous fiction."

Pierre Pochet, professor of physiology, 1872

"Everything that can be invented has been invented."

Charles Duell, U.S. Patent Office, 1899

"If excessive smoking actually plays a role in the production of lung cancer, it seems to be a minor one."

W. C. Heuper, National Cancer Institute, 1954

"Space travel is utter bilge."

Richard van der Riet Wooley, British Astronomer Royal, 1956

"Guitar music is on the way out."

Decca Recording Company, 1962

"There is no reason for any individual to have a computer in their home."

Ken Olson, Digital Equipment Corp., 1977

"640K ought to be enough for anybody."

Bill Gates, 1981

"The cloning of mammals . . . is biologically impossible."

James McGrath and Davor Solter, genetic researchers, 1984

Each of these statements was once accepted as gospel. Had their validity not been tested, had they been judged on the basis of conventional wisdom alone, had new ideas not been proposed and investigated, human knowledge and progress would have been severely limited. What enabled thinkers to move beyond such misperceptions? The answer, quite simply, is research, the systematic search for facts through the use of careful observations and investigations.

Research is as important to the field of abnormal psychology as it is to any other field of study. Consider, for example, schizophrenia and the treatment procedure known as the lobotomy. *Schizophrenia* is a severe disorder that causes people to lose contact with reality. Their thoughts, perceptions, and emotions become distorted and disorganized, and their behavior may be bizarre and withdrawn. For the first half of the twentieth century, this condition was attributed to poor parenting. Clinicians blamed *schizophrenogenic* ("schizophrenia-causing") mothers for the disorder—women they described as cold, domineering, and unresponsive to their children's needs. As you will see in Chapter 14, this widely held belief turned out to be wrong.

During the same era, practitioners developed a surgical procedure that supposedly cured schizophrenia. In this procedure, called a *lobotomy*, a pointed instrument was inserted into the frontal lobe of the brain and rotated, destroying a considerable amount of brain tissue. Early clinical reports described lobotomized patients as showing near-miraculous improvement. This impression, too, turned out to be wrong, although the mistake wasn't discovered until tens of thousands of persons had been lobotomized. Far from curing schizophrenia, lobotomies caused irreversible brain damage that left many patients withdrawn and even stuporous.

These errors underscore the importance of scientific research in abnormal psychology. Theories and treatments that seem effective in individual instances may prove disastrous to other people in different situations. Only by rigorously testing a theory or technique on representative groups of individuals can clinicians evaluate the accuracy, effectiveness, and safety of their ideas and techniques. Until clinical researchers conducted properly designed studies, millions of parents, already heartbroken by their children's schizophrenia, were additionally stigmatized as the primary cause of the disorder; and countless people with schizophrenia, already debilitated by their symptoms, were made permanently apathetic and spiritless by a lobotomy.

Clinical researchers face certain challenges that make their investigations particularly difficult. They must, for example, figure out how to measure such elusive concepts as unconscious motives, private thoughts, mood changes, and human potential (Kazdin, 2003). They must consider the different cultural backgrounds, races, and genders of the people they choose to study. And, as we are reminded in *A Closer Look* on the facing page, they must always ensure that the rights of their research participants, both human and animal, are not violated (Barnard 2007; Joy, 2005). Despite such difficulties, research in abnormal psychology has taken giant steps forward, especially during the past 35 years. In the past, most clinical researchers were limited by a lack of training and a paucity of useful techniques. Now graduate clinical programs train large numbers of students to design and conduct proper studies on clinical topics. Moreover, the development of new research methods has greatly improved our understanding and treatment of psychological dysfunction. It may even help to prevent psychological disorders.

✿What Do Clinical Researchers Do?

Clinical researchers, also called clinical scientists, try to discover universal laws, or principles, of abnormal psychological functioning. They search for general, or *nomothetic,* truths about the nature, causes, and treatments of abnormality ("nomothetic" is derived from the Greek *nomothetis,* "lawgiver") (Harris, 2003). They do not typically assess, diagnose, or treat individual clients; that is the job of clinical practitioners, who seek an *idiographic,* or individualistic, understanding of abnormal behavior (Hurlburt & Knapp, 2006). We shall explore the work of practitioners in later chapters.

To gain a **nomothetic understanding** of abnormal psychology, clinical researchers, like scientists in other fields, rely primarily on the **scientific method**—that is, they systematically collect and evaluate information through careful observations. These observations in turn enable them to pinpoint and explain relationships between *variables.* Simply stated, a variable is any characteristic or event that can vary, whether from time to time, from place to place, or from person to person. Age, sex, and race are human variables. So are eye color, occupation, and social status. Clinical researchers are interested in variables such as childhood upsets, present life experiences, moods, social and occupational functioning, and responses to treatment. They try to determine whether two or more such variables change together and whether a change in one variable causes a change in another. Will the death of a parent cause a child to become depressed? If so, will a given treatment reduce that depression?

Such questions cannot be answered by logic alone because scientists, like all human beings, frequently make errors in thinking. Thus clinical researchers must depend mainly on three methods of investigation: the *case study,* which typically focuses on one individual, and the *correlational method* and *experimental method,* approaches that usually gather information about many individuals. Each is best suited to certain kinds of circumstances and questions (Martin & Hull, 2007; Beutler et al., 1995). Collectively, these methods

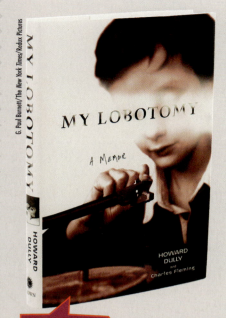

My lobotomy
After undergoing a lobotomy at age 12 to "cure" his psychological problems, Howard Dully experienced decades of misery and psychological pain—a journey that he recounts in his recent memoir *My Lobotomy.* Only after Dully and tens of thousands of other people received lobotomies did properly conducted research reveal that this form of brain surgery caused irreversible brain damage that left many patients withdrawn and even stuporous.

•**nomothetic understanding**•A general understanding of the nature, causes, and treatments of abnormal psychological functioning in the form of laws or principles.

•**scientific method**•The process of systematically gathering and evaluating information through careful observations to gain an understanding of a phenomenon.

•**hypothesis**•A hunch or prediction that certain variables are related in certain ways.

•**case study**•A detailed account of a person's life and psychological problems.

Animals Have Rights

For years researchers have learned about abnormal human behavior from experiments with animals. Animals have been shocked, prematurely separated from their parents, and starved. They have had their brains surgically changed and have even been killed, or "sacrificed," so that researchers could autopsy them. It is estimated that medical animal research (for example, cardiovascular research) has helped increase the life expectancy of humans by almost 24 years. Similarly, animal research has been key to the development of many medications for psychological disorders, leading to a savings of hundreds of billions of dollars every year in the United States alone (Lasker Foundation, 2000). Nevertheless, concerns remain: Are such actions always ethically acceptable?

Animal rights activists say no (Fellenz, 2007; Sunstein & Nussbaum, 2004). They have called such undertakings cruel and unnecessary and have fought many forms of animal research with legal protests and demonstrations. Some have even harassed scientists and vandalized their labs. In turn, some researchers have accused activists of caring more about animals than about human beings. In response to this controversy, a number of state courts, government agencies, and the American Psychological Association have issued rules and guidelines for animal research (Akins et al., 2005). But the battle still goes on.

Where does the public stand on this issue? In surveys of British citizens, 64 percent of the respondents said that they dislike animal research, but 75 percent said they can "accept" it as long as it is for medical purposes (MORI, 2005, 1999). People in such surveys tend to approve of experiments that use mice or rats more than those that use monkeys. Most of them disapprove of experiments that bring pain to animals, except when the investigations are seeking a cure for childhood leukemia, AIDS, or other life-threatening problems.

Paul Sakuma/AP Photo

Making a point Members of an organization called *In Defense of Animals* wear monkey outfits and sit in locked cages in front of the University of California, San Francisco, to protest the use of monkeys in research.

enable scientists to form and test **hypotheses,** or hunches, that certain variables are related in certain ways—and to draw broad conclusions as to why. More properly, a hypothesis is a tentative explanation offered to provide a basis for an investigation.

The Case Study

A **case study** is a detailed and often interpretive description of a person's life and psychological problems. It describes the person's history, present circumstances, and symptoms. It may also speculate about why the problems developed, and it may describe the application and results of a particular treatment.

In his famous case study of Little Hans (1909), Sigmund Freud discusses a 4-year-old boy who has developed a fear of horses. Freud gathered his material from detailed letters sent to him by Hans's father, a physician who had attended lectures on psychoanalysis, and from his own limited interviews with the child. Freud's study runs 140 pages in his *Collected Papers,* so only key excerpts are presented here.

One day while Hans was in the street he was seized with an attack of morbid anxiety. . . . [Hans's father wrote:] "He began to cry and asked to be taken home. . . . In the evening he grew visibly frightened; he cried and could not be separated from his mother. . . . [When taken for a walk the next day], again he began to cry, did not want to start, and was frightened. . . . On the way back from Schönbrunn he said to his mother, after much internal struggling: 'I was afraid a horse would bite me.' . . . In the evening he . . . had another attack similar to that of the previous evening. . . ."

But the beginnings of this psychological situation go back further still. . . . The first reports of Hans date from a period when he was not quite three years old. At that time, by means of various remarks and questions, he was showing a quite peculiarly lively interest in that portion of his body which he used to describe as his "widdler" [his word for penis]. . . .

When he was three and a half his mother found him with his hand to his penis. She threatened him in these words: "If you do that, I shall send for Dr. A. to cut off your widdler. And then what'll you widdle with?" . . . This was the occasion of his acquiring [a] "castration complex." . . .

[At the age of four, Hans entered] a state of intensified sexual excitement, the object of which was his mother. The intensity of this excitement was shown by . . . two attempts at seducing his mother. [One such attempt, occurring just before the outbreak of his anxiety, was described by his father:] "This morning Hans was given his usual daily bath by his mother and afterwards dried and powdered. As his mother was powdering round his penis and taking care not to touch it, Hans said: 'Why don't you put your finger there?' . . ."

. . . The father and son visited me during my consulting hours. . . . Certain details which I now learnt—to the effect that [Hans] was particularly bothered by what horses wear in front of their eyes and by the black round their mouths—were certainly not to be explained from what we knew. But as I saw the two of them sitting in front of me and at the same time heard Hans's description of his anxiety-horses, a further piece of the solution shot through my mind. . . . I asked Hans jokingly whether his horses wore eyeglasses, to which he replied that they did not. I then asked him whether his father wore eyeglasses, to which, against all the evidence, he once more said no. Finally I asked him whether by "the black round the mouth" he meant a moustache; and I then disclosed to him that he was afraid of his father, precisely because he was so fond of his mother. It must be, I told him, that he thought his father was angry with him on that account; but this was not so, his father was fond of him in spite of it, and he might admit everything to him without any fear. Long before he was in the world, I went on, I had known that a little Hans would come who would be so fond of his mother that he would be bound to feel afraid of his father because of it. . . .

By enlightening Hans on this subject I had cleared away his most powerful resistance. . . . [T]he little patient summoned up courage to describe the details of his phobia, and soon began to take an active share in the conduct of the analysis.

. . . It was only then that we learnt [that Hans] was not only afraid of horses biting him—he was soon silent upon that point—but also of carts, of furniture-vans, and of buses . . . , of horses that started moving, of horses that looked big and heavy, and of horses that drove quickly. The meaning of these specifications was explained by Hans himself: he was afraid of horses falling down, and consequently incorporated in his phobia everything that seemed likely to facilitate their falling down.

It was at this stage of the analysis that he recalled the event, insignificant in itself, which immediately preceded the outbreak of the illness and may no doubt be regarded as the exciting cause of the outbreak. He went for a walk with his mother, and saw a bus-horse fall down and kick about with its feet. This made a great impression on him. He was terrified, and thought the horse was dead; and from that time on he thought that all horses would fall down. His father pointed out to him that when he saw the horse fall down he must have thought of him, his father, and have wished that he might fall down in the same way and be dead. Hans did not dispute this interpretation. . . . From that time forward his behavior to his father was unconstrained and fearless, and in fact a trifle overbearing.

It is especially interesting . . . to observe the way in which the transformation of Hans's libido into anxiety was projected on to the principal object of his phobia, on to horses. Horses interested him the most of all the large animals; playing at horses was his favorite game with the older children. I had a suspicion—and this was confirmed by Hans's father *when I asked him—that the first person who had served Hans as a horse must have been his father. . . . When repression had set in and brought a revulsion of feeling along with it, horses, which had till then been associated with so much pleasure, were necessarily turned into objects of fear.*

[Hans later reported] two concluding phantasies, with which his recovery was rounded off. One of them, that of [a] plumber giving him a new and . . . bigger widdler, was . . . a triumphant wish-phantasy, and with it he overcame his fear of castration. . . . His other phantasy, which confessed to the wish to be married to his mother and to have many children by her . . . corrected that portion of those thoughts which was entirely unacceptable; for, instead of killing his father, it made him innocuous by promoting him to a marriage with Hans's grandmother. With this phantasy both the illness and the analysis came to an appropriate end.

(Freud, 1909)

Case study, Hollywood style
Case studies often find their way into the arts or media and capture the public's attention. Unfortunately, as this movie poster of *The Three Faces of Eve* illustrates, the studies may be trivialized or sensationalized in those venues.

Most clinicians take notes and keep records in the course of treating their patients, and some, like Freud, further organize such notes into a formal case study to be shared with other professionals. The clues offered by a case study may help a clinician better understand or treat the person under discussion (Stricker & Trierweiler, 1995). In addition, case studies may play nomothetic roles that go far beyond the individual clinical case (Goodwin, 2007; Martin & Hull, 2007).

How Are Case Studies Helpful?

Case studies can be a source of *new ideas* about behavior and "open the way for discoveries" (Bolgar, 1965). Freud's theory of psychoanalysis was based mainly on the patients he saw in private practice. He pored over their case studies, such as the one he wrote about Little Hans, to find what he believed to be universal psychological processes and principles of development. In addition, a case study may offer *tentative support* for a theory. Freud used case studies in this way as well, regarding them as evidence for the accuracy of his ideas. Conversely, case studies may serve to *challenge a theory's assumptions* (Elms, 2007; Kratochwill, 1992).

Case studies may also inspire *new therapeutic techniques* or describe unique applications of existing techniques. The psychoanalytic principle that says patients may benefit from discussing their problems and discovering underlying psychological causes, for example, has roots in the famous case study of Anna O., presented by Freud's collaborator Josef Breuer, a case you will read about in Chapter 3. Similarly, Freud believed that the case study of Little Hans demonstrated the therapeutic potential of a verbal approach for children as well as for adults.

Finally, case studies may offer opportunities to study *unusual problems* that do not occur often enough to permit a large number of observations (Goodwin, 2007; Martin & Hull, 2007). For years information about multiple personality disorders was based almost exclusively on case studies, such as the famous *The Three Faces of Eve*, a clinical account of a woman who displayed three alternating personalities, each having a distinct set of memories, preferences, and personal habits (Thigpen & Cleckley, 1957).

What Are the Limitations of Case Studies?

Case studies, although useful in many ways, also have limitations. First, they are reported by *biased observers,* that is, by therapists who have a personal stake in seeing their treatments succeed (Markin & Kivlighan, 2007; Stricker & Trierweiler, 1995). These observers must choose what to include in a case study, and their choices may at times be self-serving. Second, case studies rely upon *subjective evidence.* Are a client's dysfunction and improvement really caused by the events that the therapist or client says are responsible for them? In fact, these are only a small subset of the events that may be

Does mental dysfunctioning run in families? One of the most celebrated case studies in abnormal psychology is a study of identical quadruplets dubbed the "Genain" sisters by researchers (after the Greek term for "dire birth"). All of the sisters developed schizophrenia in their twenties.

contributing to the situation. When investigators are able to rule out all possible causes except one, a study is said to have internal accuracy, or **internal validity** (Wampold, 2006). Obviously, case studies rate low on that score.

Another problem with case studies is that they provide *little basis for generalization*. Even if we agree that Little Hans developed a dread of horses because he was terrified of castration and feared his father, how can we be confident that other people's phobias are rooted in the same kinds of causes? Events or treatments that seem important in one case may be of no help at all in efforts to understand or treat others. When the findings of an investigation can be generalized beyond the immediate study, the investigation is said to have external accuracy, or **external validity** (Wampold, 2006). Case studies rate low on external validity, too (Goodwin, 2007).

The limitations of the case study are largely addressed by two other methods of investigation: the *correlational method* and the *experimental method*. They do not offer the richness of detail that makes case studies so interesting, but they do help investigators draw broad conclusions about abnormality in the population at large. Thus they are now the preferred methods of clinical investigation. Three features of these methods enable clinical investigators to gain nomothetic insights: (1) The researchers typically observe many individuals (see *The Media Speaks* on the facing page). That way, they can collect enough information, or data, to support a conclusion. (2) The researchers apply procedures uniformly. Other researchers can thus repeat, or *replicate,* a particular study to see whether it consistently gives the same findings. (3) The researchers use *statistical tests* to analyze the results of a study. These tests can help indicate whether broad conclusions are justified.

⚙The Correlational Method

Correlation is the degree to which events or characteristics vary with each other. The **correlational method** is a research procedure used to determine this "co-relationship" between variables. This method can, for example, answer the question, "Is there a correlation between the amount of stress in people's lives and the degree of depression they experience?" That is, as people keep experiencing stressful events, are they increasingly likely to become depressed? To test this question, researchers have collected life stress scores (for example, the number of threatening events experienced during a certain period of time) and depression scores (for example, scores on a depression survey) from individuals and have correlated these scores.

The people who are chosen for a study are its subjects, or *participants,* the term preferred by today's investigators. The participants in a given study are collectively called its *sample.* A sample must be representative of the larger population that the researchers wish to understand. Otherwise the relationship found in the study may not apply elsewhere in the real world—it may not have external validity. If researchers were to find a correlation between life stress and depression in a sample consisting entirely of children, for example, they could not draw clear conclusions about what, if any, correlation exists among adults.

Describing a Correlation

Suppose you were to use the correlational method to conduct a study of depression. You would collect life stress scores and depression scores for 10 people and plot the scores on a graph, as shown in Figure 2-1 on page 34. As you can see, the participant named Jim has a recent life stress score of 7, meaning seven threatening events over the past three months; he also has a depression score of 25. Thus he is "located" at the point on the graph where these two scores meet. The graph provides a visual representation of your

•**internal validity**•The accuracy with which a study can pinpoint one of various possible factors as the cause of a phenomenon.

•**external validity**•The degree to which the results of a study may be generalized beyond that study.

•**correlation**•The degree to which events or characteristics vary along with each other.

•**correlational method**•A research procedure used to determine how much events or characteristics vary along with each other.

The Media SPEAKS

HOME   SEND   EXPLORE

SEARCH

On Facebook, Scholars Link Up with Data

BY STEPHANIE ROSENBLOOM, THE *NEW YORK TIMES*, DECEMBER 17, 2007

Photo Illustration by Chris Jackson/Getty Images

Each day about 1,700 juniors at an East Coast college log on to Facebook.com to accumulate "friends," compare movie preferences, share videos and exchange cybercocktails and kisses. Unwittingly, these students have become the subjects of academic research.

To study how personal tastes, habits and values affect the formation of social relationships (and how social relationships affect tastes, habits and values), a team of researchers from Harvard and the University of California, Los Angeles, are monitoring the Facebook profiles of an entire class of students at one college, which they declined to name because it could compromise the integrity of their research. . . .

In other words, Facebook—where users rate one another as "hot or not," play games like "Pirates vs. Ninjas" and throw virtual sheep at one another—is helping scholars explore fundamental social science questions.

"We're on the cusp of a new way of doing social science," said Nicholas Christakis, a Harvard sociology professor who is also part of the research. "Our predecessors could only dream of the kind of data we now have."

Facebook's network of 58 million active users and its status as the sixth-most-trafficked Web site in the United States have made it an irresistible subject for many types of academic research. . . .

Social scientists at Indiana, Northwestern, Pennsylvania State, Tufts, the University of Texas and other institutions are mining Facebook to test traditional theories in their fields about relationships, identity, self-esteem, popularity, collective action, race and political engagement. . . . In a few studies, the Facebook users do not know they are being examined. A spokeswoman for Facebook says the site has no policy prohibiting scholars from studying profiles of users who have not activated certain privacy settings. . . .

S. Shyam Sundar, a professor . . . at Penn State, has led students in several Facebook studies exploring identity. One involved the creation of mock Facebook profiles. Researchers learned that while people perceive someone who has a high number of friends as popular, attractive and self-confident, people who accumulate "too many" friends (about 800 or more) are seen as insecure.

[Another study] found that Facebook use could have a positive impact on students' well-being. . . . An important finding [in this research] was that students who reported low satisfaction with life and low self-esteem, and who used Facebook intensively, accumulated a form of social capital linked to what sociologists call "weak ties." A weak tie is a fellow classmate or someone you meet at a party, not a friend or family member. Weak ties are significant, scholars say, because they are likely to provide people with new perspectives and opportunities that they might not get from close friends and family. . . . .

But some scholars point out that Facebook is not representative of the ethnicity, educational background or income of the population at large, and its membership is self-selecting, so there are limits to research using the site. [A] professor at Northwestern . . . found in a study that Hispanic students were significantly less likely to use Facebook, and much more likely to use MySpace. White, Asian and Asian-American students, the study found, were much more likely to use Facebook and significantly less likely to use MySpace. . . .

. . . The site's users have mixed feelings about being put under the microscope. [One student] said she found it "fascinating that professors are using [Facebook]," but [another] said, "I don't feel like academic research has a place on a Web site like Facebook." He added that if that if it was going to happen, professors should ask students' permission.

Although federal rules govern academic study of human subjects, universities, which approve professors' research methods, have different interpretations of the guidelines. "The rules were made for a different world, a pre-Facebook world," said Samuel D. Gosling, an associate professor of psychology at the University of Texas, Austin, who uses Facebook to explore perception and identity. "There is a rule that you are allowed to observe public behavior, but it's not clear if online behavior is public or not." . . .

Dr. Christakis of Harvard said he and his colleagues were studying the profiles of the East Coast college class with the approval of Harvard's Institutional Review Board, and with the knowledge of the unnamed college's administration—but unknown to the students being studied. . . . "Employers are looking at people's online postings and Googling information about them, and I think researchers are right behind them."

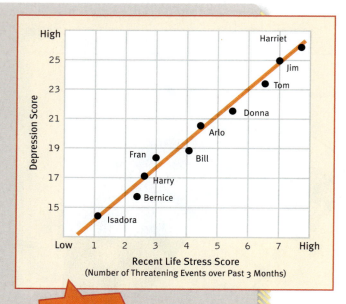

Figure 2-1

Positive correlation The relationship between amount of recent stress and feelings of depression shown by this hypothetical sample of 10 participants is a near-perfect "positive" correlation.

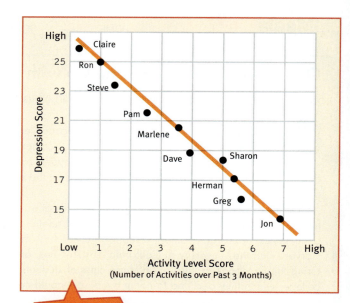

Figure 2-2

Negative correlation The relationship between number of activities and feelings of depression shown by this hypothetical sample is a near-perfect "negative" correlation.

BETWEEN THE LINES

Psychological Disorders Linked to Life Stress

Depression ‹‹

Anxiety disorders ‹‹

Eating disorders ‹‹

Posttraumatic stress disorder ‹‹

Substance abuse ‹‹

Dissociative disorder ‹‹

Sleep disorders ‹‹

Sexual dysfunction ‹‹

Suicide ‹‹

(Bernert et al., 2007; Bremner, 2007, 2002; Hartley et al., 2007; Fink, 2000)

data. Here, notice that the data points all fall roughly along a straight line that slopes upward. You would draw the line so that the data points are as close to it as possible. This line is called the *line of best fit.*

The line of best fit in Figure 2–1 slopes upward and to the right, indicating that the variables under examination are increasing or decreasing together. That is, the greater someone's life stress score, the higher his or her score on the depression scale. When variables change the same way, their correlation is said to have a positive *direction* and is referred to as a *positive correlation.* Most studies of recent life stress and depression have indeed found a positive correlation between those two variables (Monroe et al., 2007; Andrews & Wilding, 2004).

Correlations can have a negative rather than a positive direction. In a *negative correlation,* the value of one variable increases as the value of the other variable decreases. Researchers have found, for example, a negative correlation between depression and activity level. The greater one's depression, the lower the number of one's activities. When the scores of a negative correlation are plotted, they produce a downward-sloping graph, like the one shown in Figure 2-2.

There is yet a third possible outcome for a correlational study. The variables under study may be *unrelated,* meaning that there is no consistent relationship between them. As the measures of one variable increase, those of the other variable sometimes increase and sometimes decrease. The graph of this outcome looks like Figure 2-3. Here the line of best fit is horizontal, with no slope at all. Studies have found that depression and intelligence are unrelated, for example.

In addition to knowing the direction of a correlation, researchers need to know its *magnitude,* or strength (see Figure 2-4). That is, how closely do the two variables correspond? Does one always vary along with the other, or is their relationship less exact? When two variables are found to vary together very closely in subject after subject, the correlation is said to be high, or strong.

Look again at Figure 2-1. In this graph of a positive correlation between depression and life stress, the data points all fall very close to the line of best fit. Researchers can predict each person's score on one variable with a high degree of confidence if they know his or her score on the other. But what if the graph of the correlation between

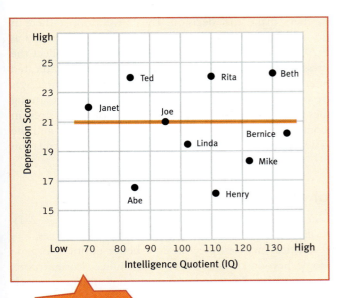

Figure 2-3
No correlation The relationship between intelligence and feelings of depression shown by this hypothetical sample is a "near-zero" correlation.

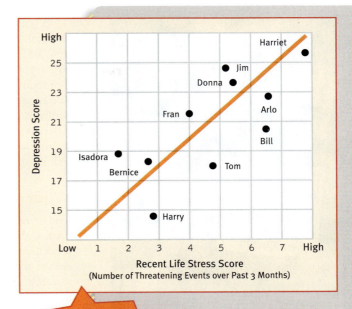

Figure 2-4
Magnitude of correlation The relationship between amount of recent stress and feelings of depression shown by this hypothetical sample is a "moderately positive" correlation.

depression and life stress looked more like Figure 2-4? In this figure the data points are loosely scattered around the line of best fit rather than hugging it closely. In this case, researchers could not predict with as much accuracy an individual's score on one variable from his or her score on the other variable. The correlation in Figure 2-1 is stronger, or greater in magnitude, than that in Figure 2-4.

The direction and magnitude of a correlation are often calculated numerically and expressed by a statistical term called the *correlation coefficient,* symbolized by the letter *r.* The correlation coefficient can vary from +1.00, which indicates a perfect positive correlation between two variables, down to −1.00, which represents a perfect negative correlation. The *sign* of the coefficient (+ or −) signifies the direction of the correlation; the *number* represents its magnitude. An *r* of .00 reflects a zero correlation, or no relationship between variables. The closer *r* is to .00, the weaker, or lower in magnitude, the correlation. Thus correlations of +.75 and −.75 are of equal magnitude and equally strong, whereas a correlation of +.25 is weaker than either.

Everyone's behavior is changeable, and many human responses can be measured only approximately. Most correlations found in psychological research, therefore, fall short of a perfect positive or negative correlation. For example, one study of life stress and depression, with a sample of 68 adults, found a correlation of +.53 (Miller, Ingham, & Davidson, 1976). Although hardly perfect, a correlation of this magnitude is considered large in psychological research.

When Can Correlations Be Trusted?

Scientists must decide whether the correlation they find in a given sample of participants accurately reflects a real correlation in the general population. Could the observed correlation have occurred by mere chance? Scientists can never know for certain, but they can test their conclusions with a *statistical analysis* of their data, using principles of probability. In essence, they ask how likely it is that the study's particular findings have occurred by chance. If the statistical analysis indicates that chance is unlikely to account for the correlation they found, researchers may conclude that their findings reflect a real correlation in the general population.

BETWEEN THE LINES

Most Investigated Correlations in Clinical Research

Stress and onset of mental disorders ‹‹

Culture (or gender or race) and mental disorders ‹‹

Wealth and mental disorders ‹‹

Social skills and mental disorders ‹‹

Social support and mental disorders ‹‹

Family conflict and mental disorders ‹‹

Culture and treatment responsiveness ‹‹

Which symptoms of a disorder appear together? ‹‹

How common is a disorder in a particular population? ‹‹

A cutoff point helps researchers make this decision. By convention, if there is less than a 5 percent probability that a study's findings are due to chance (signified as $p < .05$), the findings are said to be *statistically significant* and are thought to reflect the larger population. In the life stress study described earlier, a statistical analysis indicated a probability of less than 5 percent that the +.53 correlation found in the sample was due to chance. Therefore, the researchers concluded with some confidence that among adults in general, depression does tend to rise along with the amount of recent stress in a person's life. Generally, our confidence increases with the size of the sample and the magnitude of the correlation. The larger they are, the more likely it is that a correlation will be statistically significant.

What Are the Merits of the Correlational Method?

The correlational method has certain advantages over the case study (see Table 2-1). First, it possesses high *external validity*. Because researchers measure their variables, observe large samples, and apply statistical analyses, they are in a better position to generalize their correlations to people beyond the ones they have studied. Furthermore, researchers can easily repeat correlational studies using new samples of subjects to check the results of earlier studies.

On the other hand, correlational studies, like case studies, lack *internal validity* (Proctor & Capaldi, 2006; Field & Davey, 2005). Although correlations allow researchers to describe the relationship between two variables, they do not *explain* the relationship. When we look at the positive correlation found in many life stress studies, we may be tempted to conclude that increases in recent life stress cause people to feel more depressed. In fact, however, the two variables may be correlated for any one of three reasons: (1) Life stress may cause depression. (2) Depression may cause people to experience more life stress (for example, a depressive approach to life may cause people to mismanage their money or may interfere with social relationships). (3) Depression and life stress may each be caused by a third variable, such as financial problems (Mascaro et al., 2007; Andrews & Wilding, 2004).

Although correlations say nothing about causation, they can still be of great use to clinicians. Clinicians know, for example, that suicide attempts increase as people become more depressed. Thus, when they work with severely depressed clients, they stay on the lookout for signs of suicidal thinking. Perhaps depression directly causes suicidal behavior, or perhaps a third variable, such as a sense of hopelessness, causes both depression and suicidal thoughts. Whatever the cause, just knowing that there is a correlation may enable clinicians to take measures (such as hospitalization) to help save lives.

Of course, in other instances, clinicians do need to know whether one variable causes another. Do parents' marital conflicts cause their children to be more anxious? Does job dissatisfaction lead to feelings of depression? Will a given treatment help people to cope more effectively in life? Questions about causality call for the experimental method, as you will see later.

The impact of stress
In November 2007, these victims of home foreclosures protested outside Countrywide Financial, the largest mortgage lender in the United States. Researchers have found that the stress produced by the loss of one's home—an increasingly common event during the subprime loan crisis of recent years—is often accompanied by the onset of depression and other psychological symptoms.

table: 2-1

Relative Strengths and Weaknesses of Research Methods

	Provides Individual Information	Provides General Information (External Validity)	Provides Causal Information (Internal Validity)	Statistical Analysis Possible	Replicable
Case study	Yes	No	No	No	No
Correlational method	No	Yes	No	Yes	Yes
Experimental method	No	Yes	Yes	Yes	Yes

Special Forms of Correlational Research

Epidemiological studies and longitudinal studies are two kinds of correlational research used widely by clinical investigators. **Epidemiological studies** reveal the incidence and prevalence of a disorder in a particular population. **Incidence** is the number of new cases that emerge during a given period of time. **Prevalence** is the total number of cases in the population during a given time period; prevalence includes both existing and new cases. Many researchers also refer to epidemiological studies as "descriptive studies" because the goal of such investigations is largely to *describe* the incidence or prevalence of a disorder "without trying to predict or explain when or why it occurs" (Compas & Gotlib, 2002, p. 69).

Over the past 30 years clinical researchers throughout the United States have worked on the largest epidemiological study ever conducted, called the Epidemiologic Catchment Area Study. They have interviewed more than 20,000 people in five cities to determine the prevalence of many psychological disorders and the treatment programs used (Eaton et al., 2007; Narrow et al., 2002; Regier et al., 1993). Two other large-scale epidemiological studies in the United States, the National Comorbidity Survey and the National Comorbidity Survey Replication, have questioned more than 9,000 individuals (Druss et al., 2007; Kessler et al., 2007, 2005, 2003). These studies have been further compared with epidemiological studies of specific groups, such as Hispanic and Asian American populations, or with epidemiological studies conducted in other countries, to see how rates of mental disorders and treatment programs vary from group to group and from country to country (Alegria et al., 2007, 2004, 2000; Kessler et al., 2006).

Such epidemiological studies have helped researchers identify groups at risk for particular disorders. Women, it turns out, have a higher rate of anxiety disorders and depression than men, while men have a higher rate of alcoholism than women. Elderly people have a higher rate of suicide than young people. Hispanic Americans experience posttraumatic stress disorder more than other racial and ethnic groups in the United States. And persons in some countries have higher rates of certain mental disorders than those in other countries. Eating disorders such as anorexia nervosa, for example, appear to be more common in Western countries than in non-Western ones. These trends may lead researchers to suspect that something unique about certain groups or settings is helping to cause particular disorders. Declining health in elderly people, for example, may make them more likely to commit suicide. Similarly, the pressures or attitudes common in one country may be responsible for a rate of mental dysfunctioning that differs from the rate found in another. Yet, like other forms of correlational research, epidemiological studies alone cannot confirm such suspicions.

In **longitudinal studies** (also called *high-risk* or *developmental studies*), researchers observe the same individuals on many occasions over a long period of time (Donnellan & Conger, 2007). In one such study, investigators have observed the progress over the years of normally functioning children whose mothers or fathers suffered from schizophrenia (Schiffman et al., 2006, 2005, 2004; Mednick, 1971). The researchers have found, among other things, that the children of the parents with the most severe cases of schizophrenia were particularly likely to develop a psychological disorder and to commit crimes at later points in their development. Because longitudinal studies document the order of events, their correlations provide clues about which events are more likely to be causes and which are more likely to be consequences. Certainly, for example, the children's problems did not cause their parents' schizophrenia. But longitudinal studies still cannot pinpoint causation. Did the children who developed psychological problems inherit

David Young-Wolff/Photo Edit

•epidemiological study• A study that measures the incidence and prevalence of a disorder in a given population.

•incidence• The number of new cases of a disorder occurring in a population over a specific period of time.

•prevalence• The total number of cases of a disorder occurring in a population over a specific period of time.

•longitudinal study• A study that observes the same participants on many occasions over a long period of time.

Twins, correlation, and inheritance
Correlational studies of many pairs of twins have suggested a link between genetic factors and certain psychological disorders. Identical twins (who have identical genes) display a higher correlation for some disorders than do fraternal twins (whose genetic makeup is not identical).

•**experiment**•A research procedure in which a variable is manipulated and the effect of the manipulation is observed.

•**independent variable**•The variable in an experiment that is manipulated to determine whether it has an effect on another variable.

•**dependent variable**•The variable in an experiment that is expected to change as the independent variable is manipulated.

•**confound**•In an experiment, a variable other than the independent variable that is also acting on the dependent variable.

•**control group**•In an experiment, a group of participants who are not exposed to the independent variable.

•**experimental group**•In an experiment, the participants who are exposed to the independent variable under investigation.

BETWEEN THE LINES

Most Investigated Causal Questions in Clinical Research

Does factor X cause a disorder? ‹‹

Is cause A more influential than cause B? ‹‹

How does family communication and structure affect family members? ‹‹

How does a disorder affect the quality of a person's life? ‹‹

Does treatment X alleviate a disorder? ‹‹

Is treatment A more helpful than treatment B? ‹‹

Why does treatment X work? ‹‹

Can an intervention prevent abnormal functioning? ‹‹

a genetic factor? Or did their problems result from their parents' inadequate coping behaviors, the parents' long absences because of hospitalization, or some other factor? Only experimental studies can supply an answer.

The Experimental Method

An **experiment** is a research procedure in which a variable is manipulated and the manipulation's effect on another variable is observed. In fact, most of us perform experiments throughout our lives without knowing that we are behaving so scientifically. Suppose that you go to a party on campus to celebrate the end of midterm exams. As you mix with people at the party, you begin to notice many of them becoming quiet and depressed. It seems the more you talk, the more subdued the other guests become. As the party deteriorates before your eyes, you decide you have to do something, but what? Before you can eliminate the problem, you need to know what's causing it.

Your first hunch may be that something you're doing is responsible. Perhaps your remarks about academic pressures have been upsetting everyone. You decide to change the topic to skiing in the mountains of Colorado and to watch for signs of depression in the next round of conversations. The problem seems to clear up; most people now smile and laugh as they chat with you. As a final check of your suspicions, you could go back to talking about school with the next several people you meet. Their dark and dismal reaction would probably convince you that your propensity to talk about school was indeed the cause of the problem.

You have just performed an experiment, testing your hypothesis about a causal relationship between your conversational gambits and the depressed mood of the people around you. You manipulated the variable that you suspected to be the cause (the topic of discussion) and then observed the effect of that manipulation on the other variable (the mood of the people around you). In scientific experiments, the manipulated variable is called the **independent variable** and the variable being observed is called the **dependent variable.**

To examine the experimental method more fully, let's consider a question that is often asked by clinicians (Nathan, 2007): "Does a particular therapy relieve the symptoms of a particular disorder?" Because this question is about a causal relationship, it can be answered only by an experiment. That is, experimenters must give the therapy in question to people who are suffering from a disorder and then observe whether they improve. Here the therapy is the independent variable, and psychological improvement is the dependent variable.

If the true, or primary, cause of changes in the dependent variable cannot be separated from other possible causes, then an experiment gives very little information. Thus, experimenters must try to eliminate all **confounds** from their studies—variables other than the independent variable that may also be affecting the dependent variable. When there are confounds in an experiment, they, rather than the independent variable, may be causing the observed changes.

For example, situational variables, such as the location of the therapy office (say, a quiet country setting) or soothing music piped into the office, may have a therapeutic effect on participants in a therapy study. Or perhaps the participants are unusually motivated or have high expectations that the therapy will work, factors that thus account for their improvement. To guard against confounds, researchers include three important features in their experiments—a *control group, random assignment,* and a *blind design* (Wampold, 2006).

The Control Group

A **control group** is a group of research participants who are not exposed to the independent variable under investigation but whose experience is similar to that of the **experimental group,** the participants who are exposed to the independent variable. By comparing the two groups, an experimenter can better determine the effect of the independent variable.

PSYCH WATCH

Clear as a Bell?

To ensure that research participants know what they are getting into when they sign up for a study and to guarantee that participants feel free to leave the study at any time, researchers must inform them about the nature of the study and about their rights. This principle of "informed consent," the foundation of all human research, is usually implemented with a form that spells out everything the research participants need to know.

But how clear are informed consent forms? Not very, according to some studies (Christopher et al., 2007; Mathew & McGrath, 2002; Uretsky, 1999).

Many such forms are written at an advanced college level, making them incomprehensible to a large percentage of participants. When investigators used a readability scale to compare various writing samples (with higher scores indicating greater reading difficulty), they discovered the following:

- An old Ann Landers column earned a score of 7.67 (75 percent of the population can understand it).
- *Reader's Digest* magazine earned a score of 9.95 (69 percent can understand it).
- *The New Yorker* magazine earned a score of 13.3 (43 percent can understand it).
- Typical informed consent forms earned a score of 15.03 (37 percent can understand them).

To study the effectiveness of a particular therapy, for example, experimenters typically divide participants into two groups after obtaining their consent to participate in the experiment (see *Psych Watch* above). The experimental group may come into an office and receive the therapy for an hour, while the control group may simply come into the office for an hour. If the experimenters find later that the people in the experimental group improve more than the people in the control group, they may conclude that the therapy was effective, above and beyond the effects of time, the office setting, and any other confounds. To guard against confounds, experimenters try to provide all participants, both control and experimental, with experiences that are identical in every way—except for the independent variable.

Of course, it is possible that the differences observed between an experimental group and control group have occurred simply by chance. Thus, as with correlational studies, investigators who conduct experiments must do a statistical analysis on their data and find out how likely it is that the observed differences are due to chance. If the likelihood is very low—less than 5 percent ($p < .05$)—the differences between the two groups are considered to be statistically significant, and the experimenter may conclude with some confidence that they are due to the independent variable. As a general rule, if the sample of participants is large, if the difference observed between groups is great, and if the range of scores within each group is small, the findings of an experiment are likely to be statistically significant.

Ajay Verma/Reuters

Is laughter a good medicine?
Members of this laughter club in Chandigarh, India, practice therapeutic laughing, or *Hasyayog*, a relatively new group treatment based on the belief that laughing at least 15 minutes each day will drive away depression and other ills. As many as 400 kinds of therapies are currently used for psychological problems. An experimental design is needed to determine whether this or any other form of treatment actively causes clients to improve.

•**random assignment**•A selection procedure that ensures that participants are randomly placed either in the control group or in the experimental group.

•**blind design**•An experiment in which participants do not know whether they are in the experimental or the control condition.

•**placebo therapy**•A sham treatment that the participant in an experiment believes to be genuine.

•**double-blind design**•Experimental procedure in which neither the participant nor the experimenter knows whether the participant has received the experimental treatment or a placebo.

Random Assignment

Researchers must also watch out for differences in the makeup of the experimental and control groups, since those differences may also confound a study's results. In a therapy study, for example, the experimenter may unintentionally put wealthier participants in the experimental group and poorer ones in the control group. This difference, rather than their therapy, may be the cause of the greater improvement later found among the experimental participants. To reduce the effects of preexisting differences, experimenters typically use **random assignment.** This is the general term for any selection procedure that ensures that every subject in the experiment is as likely to be placed in one group as the other. Researchers might, for example, select people by flipping a coin or picking names out of a hat.

Blind Design

A final confound problem is *bias.* Participants may bias an experiment's results by trying to please or help the experimenter (Fritsche & Linneweber, 2007; Goodwin, 2007). In a therapy experiment, for example, if those participants who receive the treatment know the purpose of the study and which group they are in, they might actually work harder to feel better or fulfill the experimenter's expectations. If so, *subject,* or *participant, bias* rather than therapy could be causing their improvement.

To avoid this bias, experimenters can prevent participants from finding out which group they are in. This experimental strategy is called a **blind design** because the individuals are blind as to their assigned group. In a therapy study, for example, control participants could be given a *placebo* (Latin for "I shall please"), something that looks or tastes like real therapy but has none of its key ingredients. This "imitation" therapy is called **placebo therapy.** If the experimental (true therapy) participants then improve more than the control (placebo therapy) participants, experimenters have more confidence that the true therapy has caused their improvement.

An experiment may also be confounded by *experimenter bias* (Kazdin, 2003; Margraf et al., 1991)—that is, experimenters may have expectations that they unintentionally transmit to the participants in their studies. In a drug therapy study, for example, the experimenter might smile and act confident while providing real medications to the experimental participants but frown and appear hesitant while offering placebo drugs to the control participants. This kind of bias is sometimes referred to as the *Rosenthal effect,* after the psychologist who first identified it (Rosenthal, 1966). Experimenters can eliminate their own bias by arranging to be blind themselves. In a drug therapy study, for example, an aide could make sure that the real medication and the placebo drug look identical. The experimenter could then administer treatment without knowing which participants were receiving true medications and which were receiving false medications.

While either the participants or the experimenter may be kept blind in an experiment, it is best that both be blind—a research strategy called a **double-blind design.** In fact, most medication experiments now use double-blind designs to test promising drugs (Marder et al., 2007). Many experimenters also arrange for judges to assess the patients' improvement independently, and the judges, too, are blind to group assignments. This strategy is called a *triple-blind design* (Wheatley, 2004).

✿Alternative Experimental Designs

It is not easy to devise an experiment that is both well controlled and enlightening. Control of every possible confound is rarely attained in practice. Moreover, because psychological experiments typically use living beings, ethical and practical considerations limit the kinds of manipulations one can do (Taylor, 2007) (see *A Closer Look* on the facing page). Thus clinical researchers must often settle for experimental designs that are less than ideal. The most common such variations are the *quasi-experimental design,* the *natural experiment,* the *analogue experiment,* and the *single-subject experiment.*

A CLOSER LOOK

Humans Have Rights, Too

Soon after the Project MK-ULTRA, Willowbrook, and other scandalous studies came to light in the 1970s (see page 40), regulations were established to ensure that the rights of human participants, particularly those with psychological disorders, are protected in research. In the United States, for example, Congress passed a law requiring every research institute to set up a review board—an Institutional Review Board—to monitor and protect patients' well-being in all federally funded studies (Bankert & Madur, 2006; De Vries et al., 2004).

These efforts have greatly improved the ethics of clinical research, but some serious problems remain (Taylor, 2007; Emanuel et al., 2003). In fact, the clinical field was rocked just a few years ago by a series of reports that revealed that during the 1980s and 1990s, many patients with severe mental disorders had been harmed by or placed at risk in clinical studies (Emanuel et al., 2003; Kong, 1998). The studies in question typically involved antipsychotic drug treatments for patients with psychosis (loss of contact with reality). It appears that many patients in these studies had agreed to receive drug treatments (or not to receive them) without fully understanding the risks involved. In addition, the drugs used in these studies left some of the participants with more intense psychotic symptoms. Four types of studies were cited:

- **New Drug Studies** Patients are administered an experimental drug to see whether it reduces their symptoms. The new drug is being tested for effectiveness, safety, undesired effects, and dosage, meaning that the patients may be helped, unaffected, or damaged by the drug.

- **Placebo Studies** When a new drug is being tested on a group of experimental participants, researchers may administer a placebo drug to a group of control participants. The improvement of the experimental participants is then compared with that of the placebo control participants to determine

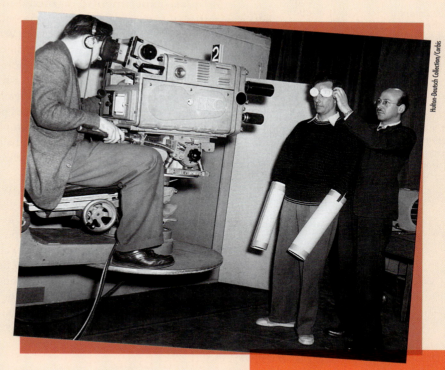

the new drug's effectiveness. Unfortunately, in such studies, the placebo control participants—often people with severe disorders—are receiving no treatment at all.

- **Symptom-Exacerbation Studies** Patients are given drugs designed to intensify their symptoms so that researchers may learn more about the biology of their disorder. For example, people suffering from psychotic disorders have been given apomorphine, amphetamine, ketamine, and other drugs that lead to more delusions, hallucinations, and the like.

- **Medication-Withdrawal Studies** Researchers prematurely stop medications for patients who have been symptom-free while taking the medications. The researchers then follow the patients as they relapse, in the hope of learning more about how and when patients can be taken off particular medications.

Each of these kinds of studies seeks to increase understanding of the biology of certain disorders and to improve treatment. Yet at what risk? When does the benefit to many outweigh the suffering

How times have changed In a 1957 study of the psychological effects of complete isolation, participants were placed in a sound-proof box wearing dark goggles, gloves, and cardboard tubes over their hands to deprive them of hearing, sight, and touch. The 25-hour study was actually televised live throughout England, an event that probably would not be permitted today, given current human research safeguards, such as participant confidentiality, informed consent, and research review board approval and monitoring.

of a few? As the clinical community and the public have grown more aware of the risks involved in these studies, they have called for still better safeguards to protect research participants with mental disorders. In 1999 the National Institute of Mental Health suspended some of its symptom-exacerbation studies. Moreover, the Office for Human Research Protection has, in recent years, become much more aggressive in its protection of human participants. Despite such initiatives, it is clear to most clinical theorists and policy makers that this important issue is far from resolved.

Hulton-Deutsch Collection/Corbis

•**quasi-experiment**•An experiment in which investigators make use of control and experimental groups that already exist in the world at large. Also called a mixed design.

•**natural experiment**•An experiment in which nature, rather than an experimenter, manipulates an independent variable.

•**analogue experiment**•A research method in which the experimenter produces abnormal-like behavior in laboratory participants and then conducts experiments on the participants.

Quasi-Experimental Design

In **quasi-experiments,** or **mixed designs,** investigators do not randomly assign participants to control and experimental groups but instead make use of groups that already exist in the world at large (Wampold, 2006). Consider, for example, research into the impact of child abuse. Because it would be highly unethical for investigators of this issue to actually abuse a randomly chosen group of children, they must instead compare children who already have a history of abuse with children who do not. Such a humane strategy is, of course, preferable, but, at the same time, it violates the rule of random assignment and so introduces possible confounds into the study. Children who receive physical punishment, for example, usually come from poorer and larger families than children who are punished verbally. Any differences found later in the moods or self-concepts of the two groups of children may be the result of differences in wealth or family size rather than abuse.

Child-abuse researchers often try to address the confound problems of quasi-experiments by using *matched control participants.* That is, they match the experimental participants with control participants who are similar in age, sex, race, number of children in the family, socioeconomic status, type of neighborhood, or other characteristics. For every abused child in the experimental group, they choose a child who is not abused but who has similar characteristics to be included in the control group. When the data from studies of this kind show that abused children are typically sadder and have lower self-esteem than matched control participants who have not been abused, the investigators can conclude with some confidence that abuse is causing the differences (Widom et al., 2007).

Natural Experiment

In **natural experiments** nature itself manipulates the independent variable, and the experimenter observes the effects. Natural experiments must be used for studying the psychological effects of unusual and unpredictable events, such as floods, earthquakes, plane crashes, and fires. Because the participants in these studies are selected by an accident of fate rather than by conscious design, natural experiments are actually a kind of quasi-experiment.

On December 26, 2004, an earthquake occurred beneath the Indian Ocean off the coast of Sumatra, Indonesia. The earthquake in turn triggered a series of massive tsunamis that inundated the ocean's coastal communities and killed more than 225,000 people in 11 countries, particularly Indonesia, Sri Lanka, India, and Thailand. It was one of the deadliest natural disasters in history. The Indian Ocean tsunami further injured and left millions of survivors homeless. Within months of this disaster, several teams of researchers collected data from several hundred survivors and from control groups of people who lived in areas not directly affected by the tsunami. The disaster survivors scored significantly higher on anxiety and depression measures (dependent variables) than the controls did. The survivors also experienced more nightmares and other sleep problems, feelings of detachment, symptoms of hyperalertness, difficulties concentrating, startle responses, and guilt feelings than the controls did (Bhushan & Kumar, 2007; Tang, 2007, 2006; van Griensven et al., 2006).

Because natural experiments rely on unexpected occurrences in nature, they cannot be repeated at will. Also, because each natural event is unique in certain ways, broad generalizations drawn from a single study could be incorrect. Nevertheless, catastrophes have provided opportunities for hundreds of natural experiments over the years, and certain findings have been obtained

Natural experiments

A man surveys the damage wrought by a hurricane upon his home and belongings. Natural experiments conducted in the aftermath of such catastrophes have found that many survivors experience lingering feelings of anxiety and depression.

Christopher Brown/Stock Boston

Similar enough? Chimpanzees and human beings share more than 90 percent of their genetic material, but their brains and bodies are very different, as are their perceptions and experiences. Thus, abnormal-like behavior produced in animal analogue experiments may differ from the human abnormality under investigation.

repeatedly. As a result, clinical scientists have identified patterns of reactions that often occur in such situations. You will read about these patterns—acute stress disorders and posttraumatic stress disorders—in Chapter 6.

Analogue Experiment

There is one way in which investigators can manipulate independent variables relatively freely while avoiding many of the ethical and practical limitations of clinical research. They can induce laboratory participants to behave in ways that seem to resemble real-life abnormal behavior and then conduct experiments on the participants in the hope of shedding light on the real-life abnormality. This is called an **analogue experiment.**

Analogue studies often use animals as participants. Animals are easier to gather and manipulate than humans, and their use poses fewer ethical problems. While the needs and rights of animal subjects must be considered, most experimenters are willing to subject animals to more discomfort than humans. They believe that the insights gained from such experimentation outweigh the discomfort of the animals, as long as their distress is not excessive (Barnard, 2007; Gluck & Bell, 2003). In addition, experimenters can, and often do, use human participants in analogue experiments.

As you'll see in Chapter 8, investigator Martin Seligman has used analogue studies with great success to investigate the causes of human depression. Seligman has theorized that depression results when people believe they no longer have any control over the good and bad things that happen in their lives. To test this theory, he has produced depression-like symptoms in laboratory participants—both animals and humans—by repeatedly giving them negative reinforcements (shocks, loud noises, task failures) over which they have no control. In these "learned helplessness" studies, the participants seem to give up, lose their initiative, and become sad—suggesting to some clinicians that human depression itself may indeed be caused by loss of control over the events in one's life.

It is important to remember that the laboratory-induced learned helplessness produced in Seligman's analogue experiments is not known with certainty to be analogous to human depression. If this laboratory phenomenon is actually only superficially similar to depression, then the clinical inferences drawn from such experiments may be misleading. This, in fact, is the major limitation of all analogue research: researchers can never be certain that the phenomena they see in the laboratory are the same as the psychological disorders they are investigating.

Tsunami analogue Harindra Joseph Fernando, a researcher at Arizona State University, stands in his *wave tank* on campus. Using this tank to mimic the water activity at work during tsunamis, such as the deadly Indian Ocean tsunami of 2004, Fernando and his colleagues have been able to study the properties of such massive waves and to develop effective warning systems for them. Still other researchers suggest that such wave tanks may also be useful in the study of human reactions during and after tsunamis.

•single-subject experimental design•
A research method in which a single participant is observed and measured both before and after the manipulation of an independent variable.

Single-Subject Experiment

Sometimes scientists do not have the luxury of experimenting on many participants. They may, for example, be investigating a disorder so rare that few participants are available. Experimentation is still possible, however, with a **single-subject experimental design.** Here a single participant is observed both before and after the manipulation of an independent variable.

Single-subject experiments first rely on baseline data—information gathered prior to any manipulations. These data set a standard with which later changes may be compared. The experimenter next introduces the independent variable and again observes the participant's behavior. Any changes in behavior are attributed to the effects of the independent variable. Common single-subject experimental designs are the *ABAB design* and the *multiple-baseline design* (Dolezal et al., 2007; McKee et al., 2007; Newman & Wong, 2004).

ABAB Design

In an *ABAB,* or *reversal, design,* a participant's reactions are measured and compared not only during a baseline period (condition A) and after the introduction of the independent variable (condition B) but also after the independent variable has been removed (condition A) and yet again after it has been reintroduced (condition B). If the individual's responses change back and forth along with changes in the independent variable, the experimenter may conclude that the independent variable is causing the shifting responses. Essentially, in an ABAB design a participant is compared with himself or herself under different conditions rather than with control participants. The individuals, therefore, serve as their own controls.

One researcher used an ABAB design to determine whether the systematic use of rewards was helping to reduce a teenage boy's habit of disrupting his special education class with loud talk (Deitz, 1977). The treatment program consisted of rewarding the boy, who suffered from mental retardation, with extra teacher time whenever he went 55 minutes without interrupting the class more than three times. When observed during a baseline period, the student was found to disrupt the class frequently with loud talk. Next the boy was given a series of teacher reward sessions (the independent variable); as expected, his loud talk decreased dramatically. Then the rewards from the teacher were stopped; the student's loud talk increased once again. Apparently the independent variable had indeed been the cause of the improvement. To be still more confident about this conclusion, the researcher had the teacher apply reward sessions yet again. Once again the student's behavior improved.

Multiple-Baseline Design

A *multiple-baseline design* does not employ the reversals found in an ABAB design. Instead, the experimenter selects two or more behaviors (two dependent variables) displayed by a participant and observes the effect that the manipulation of an independent variable has on each behavior (Bock, 2007; Winn et al., 2004). Let's say that the teenage boy in the ABAB study displayed two kinds of inappropriate behavior—the disruptive talk during class and odd grimaces. In a multiple-baseline design, the experimenter would first collect baseline data on both the frequency of the boy's disruptive talk and the frequency of his facial grimaces during a 55-minute period. In the next phase of the experiment, the experimenter would reward the boy with extra teacher time whenever he cut down his verbalizations but not when he cut down his grimaces. The experimenter would then measure changes in the boy's verbal and grimacing behaviors, expecting the verbal interruptions to decrease but the grimacing to remain about the same as before. In the final phase of the experiment, the experimenter would also reward the boy with extra teacher attention whenever he reduced his grimacing, expecting that this manipulation would now reduce the grimacing as well. If the expected pattern of changes was observed, it would be reasonable to conclude that the manipulation of the independent variable (attention from the teacher), rather than some other factor, was responsible for the changes in the two behaviors.

Obviously, single-subject experiments—both ABAB and multiple-baseline designs—are similar to individual case studies in their focus on one participant. In single-subject experiments, however, the independent variable is manipulated systematically so that the investigator can confidently draw conclusions about the cause of an observed effect (Compas & Gotlib, 2002). The single-subject experiment therefore has greater internal validity than the case study. At the same time, single-subject experiments, like case studies, have only limited external validity. Because only one person is studied, the experimenter cannot be sure that the participant's reaction to the independent variable is typical of people in general (Goodwin, 2007).

PUTTING IT... together

The Use of Multiple Research Methods

We began this discussion by noting that clinical scientists look for general laws that will help them understand, treat, and prevent psychological disorders. Various obstacles interfere with their progress, however. We have already observed some of them. The most fundamental are summarized here.

1. *Clinical scientists must respect the rights of both human and animal subjects.* Ethical considerations greatly limit the kinds of investigations that clinical scientists can conduct.

2. *The causes of human functioning are very complex.* Because human behavior generally results from multiple factors working together, it is difficult to pinpoint specific causes. So many factors can influence human functioning that it has actually been easier to unravel the complexities of energy and matter than to understand human sadness, stress, and anxiety.

3. *Human beings are changeable.* Moods, behaviors, and thoughts fluctuate. Is the person under study today truly the same as he or she was yesterday? Variability in a single person, let alone from person to person, limits the kinds of conclusions researchers can draw about abnormal functioning.

4. *Human self-awareness may influence the results of clinical investigations.* When human participants know they are being studied, that knowledge influences their behavior. They may try to respond as they think researchers expect them to or to present themselves in a favorable light. Similarly, the attention they receive from investigators may itself increase their optimism and improve their mood. It is an axiom of science that the very act of measuring an object distorts the object to some degree. Nowhere is this more true than in the study of human beings.

5. *Clinical investigators have a special link to their subjects.* Clinical scientists, too, experience mood changes, troubling thoughts, and family problems. They may identify with the pain of the participants in their studies or have personal opinions about their problems. These feelings can bias an investigator's attempts to understand abnormality.

In short, human behavior is so complex that clinical scientists must use a variety of methods to study it. Each method addresses some of the inherent problems, but no one approach overcomes them all. Case studies allow investigators to consider a broader range of causes, but experiments pinpoint causes more precisely. Similarly, correlational studies allow broad generalizations, but case studies are richer in detail. It is best to view each research method as part of a team of approaches that together may shed considerable light on abnormal human functioning. When more than one method has been used to investigate a disorder, it is important to ask whether all the results seem to

"Oh, if only it were so simple."

point in the same direction. If they do, clinical scientists are probably making progress toward understanding and treating that disorder. Conversely, if the various methods seem to produce conflicting results, the scientists must admit that knowledge in that particular area is still tentative.

Before accepting any research findings, however, students in the clinical field must review the details of these studies with a very critical eye. Were the variables properly controlled? Was the choice of participants representative, was the sample large enough to be meaningful, and has bias been eliminated? Are the investigator's conclusions justified? How else might the results be interpreted? Only after painstaking scrutiny can we conclude that a truly informative investigation has taken place.

‹‹‹(SUMMING UP)›››

○ **What Do Clinical Researchers Do?** Researchers use the *scientific method* to uncover *nomothetic* principles of abnormal psychological functioning. They attempt to identify and examine relationships between variables and depend primarily on three methods of investigation: the case study, the correlational method, and the experimental method. *pp. 28–29*

○ **The Case Study** A *case study* is a detailed account of a person's life and psychological problems. It can serve as a source of ideas about behavior, provide support for theories, challenge theories, clarify new treatment techniques, or offer an opportunity to study an unusual problem. Yet case studies may be reported by biased observers and rely on subjective evidence. In addition, they tend to have low *internal validity* and low *external validity. pp. 29–32*

○ **The Correlational Method** Correlational studies systematically observe the degree to which events or characteristics vary together. This method allows researchers to draw broad conclusions about abnormality in the population at large.

A *correlation* may have a *positive* or *negative direction* and may be high or low in *magnitude*. It can be calculated numerically and is expressed by the *correlation coefficient* (r). Researchers perform a *statistical analysis* to determine whether the correlation found in a study is truly characteristic of the larger population or due to chance. Correlational studies generally have high external validity but lack internal validity. Two widely used forms of the correlation method are *epidemiological studies* and *longitudinal studies. pp. 32–38*

○ **The Experimental Method** In *experiments*, researchers manipulate suspected causes to see whether expected effects will result. The variable that is manipulated is called the *independent variable*, and the variable that is expected to change as a result is called the *dependent variable*.

Confounds are variables other than the independent variable that are also acting on the dependent variable. To minimize their possible influence, experimenters use *control groups, random assignment*, and *blind designs*. The findings of experiments, like those of correlational studies, must be analyzed statistically. *pp. 38–40*

○ **Alternative Experimental Designs** Clinical experimenters must often settle for experimental designs that are less than ideal, including the *quasi-experiment*, the *natural experiment*, the *analogue experiment*, and the *single-subject experiment. pp. 40–45*

○ **The Use of Multiple Research Methods** Because research participants have rights that must be respected, because the origins of behavior are complex, because behavior varies, and because the very act of observing an individual's behavior influences that behavior, it can be difficult to assess the findings of clinical research. Also, researchers must take into account their own biases as well as a study's unintended impact on participants' usual behavior. To help address such obstacles, clinical investigators must use multiple research approaches. *pp. 45–46*

⫸ CRITICAL THOUGHTS ⫷

1. Can you think of beliefs, beyond those stated on page 27, that were once accepted as gospel but are now considered false?

2. Even when there are credible, well-known research findings to the contrary, many people hold on to false beliefs about human behavior, particularly abnormal behavior. Why does research fail to change their views? *pp. 27–28, 45–46*

3. Which are you more likely to be influenced by in your life—a case study (or similar anecdotal offering) or a research write-up? What fea-

tures of anecdotal presentations make them particularly influential? *pp. 29–32*

4. Do outside restrictions on research—either animal or human—interfere with necessary investigations and thus limit potential gains for human beings? *pp. 29, 33, 40, 41*

5. Prior to taking this course, you probably had heard about at least a few famous studies on stress, psychopathology, or treatment. Looking back, try to identify each of those studies as a case study, correlational study, or experimental study. *pp. 29–45*

6. The correlation found between life stress and depression does not necessarily indicate that stressors *cause* depression. Can you think of other correlations in life that are often interpreted as causal but that may actually reflect a different relationship between the variables? *pp. 32–36*

7. In drug therapy studies, some control participants who receive placebo pills actually show improvement. Why might sugar pills or other kinds of placebo treatments help people feel better? *p. 40*

❧❧ cyberstudy ❧❧

SEARCH

Search the *Abnormal Psychology* Video Tool Kit
www.worthpublishers.com/apvtk

▲ Chapter 2 Video Cases
   Experimental Design in Action
   Genetic Research: Violating One's Privacy?
   A Tragic Consequence of Research Misconduct

▲ Video case discussions, study guides, and questions

Log on to the Comer Web Page
www.worthpublishers.com/comer

▲ Chapter 2 outline, learning objectives, research exercises, study tools, and practice test questions

▲ Additional Chapter 2 case studies, Web links, and FAQs

MODELS OF ABNORMALITY

*P*hilip Berman, a 25-year-old single unemployed former copy editor for a large publishing house, . . . had been hospitalized after a suicide attempt in which he deeply gashed his wrist with a razor blade. He described [to the therapist] how he had sat on the bathroom floor and watched the blood drip into the bathtub for some time before he telephoned his father at work for help. He and his father went to the hospital emergency room to have the gash stitched, but he convinced himself and the hospital physician that he did not need hospitalization. The next day when his father suggested he needed help, he knocked his dinner to the floor and angrily stormed to his room. When he was calm again, he allowed his father to take him back to the hospital.

The immediate precipitant for his suicide attempt was that he had run into one of his former girlfriends with her new boyfriend. The patient stated that they had a drink together, but all the while he was with them he could not help thinking that "they were dying to run off and jump in bed." He experienced jealous rage, got up from the table, and walked out of the restaurant. He began to think about how he could "pay her back."

Mr. Berman had felt frequently depressed for brief periods during the previous several years. He was especially critical of himself for his limited social life and his inability to have managed to have sexual intercourse with a woman even once in his life. As he related this to the therapist, he lifted his eyes from the floor and with a sarcastic smirk said, "I'm a 25-year-old virgin. Go ahead, you can laugh now." He has had several girlfriends to date, whom he described as very attractive, but who he said had lost interest in him. On further questioning, however, it became apparent that Mr. Berman soon became very critical of them and demanded that they always meet his every need, often to their own detriment. The women then found the relationship very unrewarding and would soon find someone else.

During the past two years Mr. Berman had seen three psychiatrists briefly, one of whom had given him a drug, the name of which he could not remember, but that had precipitated some sort of unusual reaction for which he had to stay in a hospital overnight. . . . Concerning his hospitalization, the patient said that "It was a dump," that the staff refused to listen to what he had to say or to respond to his needs, and that they, in fact, treated all the patients "sadistically." The referring doctor corroborated that Mr. Berman was a difficult patient who demanded that he be treated as special, and yet was hostile to most staff members throughout his stay. After one angry exchange with an aide, he left the hospital without leave, and subsequently signed out against medical advice.

Mr. Berman is one of two children of a middle-class family. His father is 55 years old and employed in a managerial position for an insurance company. He perceives his father as weak and ineffectual, completely dominated by the patient's overbearing and cruel mother. He states that he hates his mother with "a passion I can barely control." He claims that his mother used to call him names like "pervert" and "sissy" when he was growing up, and that in an argument she once "kicked me in the balls." Together, he sees his parents as rich, powerful, and selfish, and, in turn, thinks that they see him as lazy, irresponsible, and a behavior problem. When his parents called the therapist to discuss their son's treatment, they stated that his problem began with the birth of his younger brother, Arnold, when Philip was 10 years old. After Arnold's birth Philip apparently became an "ornery" child who cursed a lot and was difficult to discipline. Philip recalls this period only vaguely. He reports that his mother once was hospitalized for depression, but that now "she doesn't believe in psychiatry."

Mr. Berman had graduated from college with average grades. Since graduating he had worked at three different publishing houses, but at none of them for more than one year. He always found some justification for quitting. He usually sat around his house doing very little for two or three months after quitting a job, until his parents prodded him into getting a new one. He described innumerable interactions in his life with teachers, friends, and employers in which he felt offended or unfairly treated, . . . and frequent arguments that left him feeling bitter . . . and spent most of his time alone, "bored." He was unable to commit himself to any person, he held no strong convictions, and he felt no allegiance to any group.

The patient appeared as a very thin, bearded, and bespectacled young man with pale skin who maintained little eye contact with the therapist and who had an air of angry bitterness about him. Although he complained of depression, he denied other symptoms of the depressive syndrome. He seemed preoccupied with his rage at his parents, and seemed particularly invested in conveying a despicable image of himself. . . .

(Spitzer et al., 1983, pp. 59–61)

Philip Berman is clearly a troubled person, but how did he come to be that way? How do we explain and correct his many problems? In confronting these questions, we must first look at the wide range of complaints we are trying to understand: Philip's depression and anger, his social failures, his lack of employment, his distrust of those around him, and the problems within his family. Then we must sort through all kinds of potential causes—internal and external, biological and interpersonal, past and present.

Although we may not realize it, we all use theoretical frameworks as we read about Philip. Over the course of our lives, each of us has developed a perspective that helps us make sense of the things other people say and do. In science, the perspectives used to explain events are known as **models,** or **paradigms.** Each model spells out the scientist's basic assumptions, gives order to the field under study, and sets guidelines for its investigation (Kuhn, 1962). It influences what the investigators observe as well as the questions they ask, the information they seek, and how they interpret this information (Sharf, 2008). To understand how a clinician explains or treats a specific set of symptoms, such as Philip's, we must know which model shapes his or her view of abnormal functioning.

Until recently, clinical scientists of a given place and time tended to agree on a single model of abnormality—a model greatly influenced by the beliefs of their culture. The demonological model that was used to explain abnormal functioning during the Middle Ages, for example, borrowed heavily from medieval society's concerns with religion, superstition, and warfare. Medieval practitioners would have seen the devil's guiding hand in Philip Berman's efforts to commit suicide and his feelings of depression, rage, jealousy, and hatred. Similarly, their treatments for him—from prayers to whippings—would have sought to drive foreign spirits from his body.

Today several models are used to explain and treat abnormal functioning. This variety has resulted from shifts in values and beliefs over the past half-century, as well as improvements in clinical research. At one end of the spectrum is the *biological model,* which sees physical processes as key to human behavior. In the middle are four models that focus on more psychological and personal aspects of human functioning: the *psychodynamic model* looks at people's unconscious internal processes and conflicts, the *behavioral model* emphasizes behavior and the ways in which it is learned, the *cognitive model* concentrates on the thinking that underlies behavior, and the *humanistic-existential model* stresses the role of values and choices. At the far end of the spectrum is the sociocultural model, which looks to social and cultural forces as the keys to human functioning. This model includes the *family-social perspective,* which focuses on an individual's family and social interactions, and the *multicultural perspective,* which emphasizes an individual's culture and the shared attitudes, beliefs, values, and history of that culture.

Given their different assumptions and concepts, the models are sometimes in conflict. Those who follow one perspective often scoff at the "naive" interpretations, investigations, and treatment efforts of the others. Yet none of the models is complete in itself. Each focuses mainly on one aspect of human functioning, and none can explain all aspects of abnormality.

•**model**•A set of assumptions and concepts that help scientists explain and interpret observations. Also called a *paradigm.*

•**neuron**•A nerve cell.

⚙The Biological Model

Philip Berman is a biological being. His thoughts and feelings are the results of bio-chemical and bioelectrical processes throughout his brain and body. Proponents of the *biological model* believe that a full understanding of Philip's thoughts, emotions, and behavior must therefore include an understanding of their biological basis. Not surprisingly, then, they believe that the most effective treatments for Philip's problems will be biological ones.

How Do Biological Theorists Explain Abnormal Behavior?

Adopting a medical perspective, biological theorists view abnormal behavior as an illness brought about by malfunctioning parts of the organism. Typically, they point to a malfunctioning brain as the cause of abnormal behavior, focusing particularly on problems in brain anatomy or brain chemistry (Lambert & Kinsley, 2005).

Brain Anatomy and Abnormal Behavior The brain is made up of approximately 100 billion nerve cells, called **neurons,** and thousands of billions of support cells, called *glia* (from the Greek meaning "glue"). Within the brain large groups of neurons form distinct areas, or *brain regions*. To identify the regions of the brain more easily, let's imagine them as continents, countries, and states.

At the bottom of the brain is the "continent" known as the *hindbrain,* which is in turn made up of countrylike regions called the *medulla, pons,* and *cerebellum* (see Figure 3-1). In the middle of the brain is the "continent" called the *midbrain*. And at the top is the "continent" called the *forebrain,* which consists of countrylike regions called the *cerebrum* (the two cerebral hemispheres), the *thalamus,* and the *hypothalamus,* each in turn made up of statelike regions. The cerebrum, for instance, includes structures such as the *cortex, corpus callosum, basal ganglia, hippocampus,* and *amygdala* (see Figure 3-2). The neurons in each of these brain regions control important functions. The cortex is the outer later of the brain; the corpus callosum connects the two cerebral hemispheres; the basal ganglia plays a crucial role in planning and producing movement; the hippocampus helps control

Figure 3-1
The human brain A slice through the center of the brain reveals its major divisions and regions. Each region, composed of numerous neurons, is responsible for certain functions.

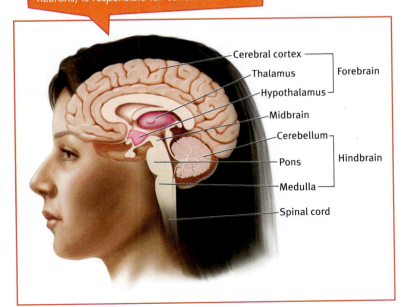

Figure 3-2
The cerebrum Some psychological disorders can be traced to abnormal functioning of neurons in the cerebrum, which includes brain structures such as the basal ganglia, hippocampus, amygdala, corpus callosum, and cortex.

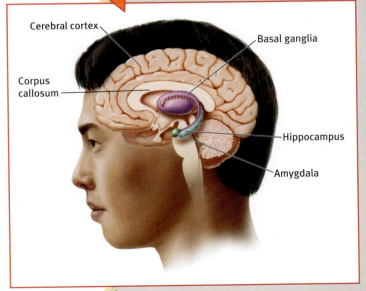

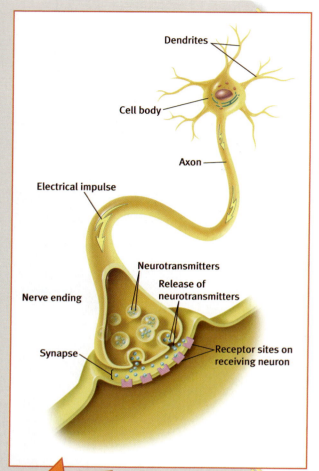

Figure 3-3
A neuron communicating information A message in the form of an electrical impulse travels down the sending neuron's axon to its nerve ending, where neurotransmitters are released and carry the message across the synaptic space to the dendrites of a receiving neuron.

emotions and memory; and the amygdala plays a key role in emotional memory. Clinical researchers have discovered connections between certain psychological disorders and problems in specific areas of the brain. One such disorder is *Huntington's disease,* a disorder marked by violent emotional outbursts, memory loss, suicidal thinking, involuntary body movements, and absurd beliefs. This disease has been traced to a loss of cells in the basal ganglia.

Brain Chemistry and Abnormal Behavior Biological researchers have also learned that psychological disorders can be related to problems in the transmission of messages between neurons. Information is communicated throughout the brain in the form of electrical impulses that travel from one neuron to one or more others. An impulse is first received by a neuron's *dendrites,* antenna-like extensions located at one end of the neuron. From there it travels through the neuron's body and down the neuron's *axon,* a long fiber extending from the neuron's body. Finally, it is transmitted through the nerve ending at the end of the axon to the dendrites of other neurons (see Figure 3-3).

But how do messages get from the axons of one neuron to the dendrites of another? After all, the neurons do not actually touch each other. A tiny space, called the **synapse,** separates one neuron from the next, and the message must somehow traverse that space. When an electrical impulse reaches the end of a neuron's axon, the ending is stimulated to release a chemical, called a **neurotransmitter,** that travels across the synaptic space to **receptors** on the dendrites of the neighboring neurons. After binding to the receiving neuron's receptors, some neurotransmitters tell the receiving neurons to "fire," that is, to trigger their own electrical impulse. Other neurotransmitters carry an inhibitory message; they tell receiving neurons to stop all firing. Clearly, neurotransmitters play a key role in moving information through the brain.

Researchers have identified dozens of neurotransmitters in the brain, and they have learned that each neuron uses only certain kinds. Studies indicate that abnormal activity by certain neurotransmitters can lead to specific mental disorders (Sarter, Bruno, & Parikh, 2007). Certain anxiety disorders, for example, have been linked to low activity of the neurotransmitter *gamma-aminobutyric acid* (*GABA*), schizophrenia has been linked to excessive activity of the neurotransmitter *dopamine,* and depression has been linked to low activity of the neurotransmitters *serotonin* and *norepinephrine.* Perhaps low serotonin activity is partly responsible for Philip Berman's pattern of depression and rage.

In addition to focusing on neurons and neurotransmitters, individuals have learned that mental disorders are sometimes related to abnormal chemical activity in the body's *endocrine system.* Endocrine glands, located throughout the body, work along with neurons to control such vital activities as growth, reproduction, sexual activity, heart rate, body temperature, energy, and responses to stress. The endocrine glands release chemicals called **hormones** into the bloodstream, and these chemicals then propel body organs into action. During times of stress, for example, the *adrenal glands,* located on top of the kidneys, secrete the hormone *cortisol.* Abnormal secretions of this chemical have been tied to anxiety and mood disorders.

Sources of Biological Abnormalities Why do some people have brain structures or biochemical activities that differ from the norm? Three factors have received particular attention in recent years—*genetics, evolution,* and *viral infections.*

GENETICS AND ABNORMAL BEHAVIOR Abnormalities in brain anatomy or chemistry are sometimes the result of genetic inheritance. Each cell in the human brain and body contains 23 pairs of *chromosomes,* with each chromosome in a pair inherited from one of the person's parents. Every chromosome contains numerous **genes**—segments that control the characteristics and traits a person inherits. Altogether, each cell contains between 30,000 and 40,000 genes (Andreasen, 2005, 2001). Scientists have known for years that genes help determine such physical characteristics as hair color, height, and eyesight. Genes can make people more prone to heart disease, cancer, or diabetes, and perhaps to possessing artistic or musical skill.

Studies suggest that inheritance also plays a part in mood disorders, schizophrenia, Alzheimer's disease, and other mental disorders. Yet, with few exceptions, researchers have not been able to identify the specific genes that are the culprits (Joseph, 2006). Nor do they yet know the extent to which genetic factors contribute to various mental disorders. It appears that in most cases several genes combine to help produce our actions and reactions, both functional and dysfunctional.

The precise contributions of various genes to mental disorders have become clearer in recent years, thanks in part to the completion of the *Human Genome Project* in 2000. In this major undertaking, scientists used the tools of molecular biology to *map,* or *sequence,* all of the genes in the human body in great detail. With this information in hand, researchers hope eventually to be able to prevent or change genes that help cause medical or psychological disorders (DeLisi & Fleischhaker, 2007; Holman et al., 2007).

EVOLUTION AND ABNORMAL BEHAVIOR Genes that contribute to mental disorders are typically viewed as unfortunate occurrences—almost mistakes of inheritance. The responsible gene may be a *mutation,* an abnormal form of the appropriate gene that emerges by accident. Or the problematic gene may be inherited by an individual after it has initially entered the family line as a mutation. According to some theorists, however, many of the genes that contribute to abnormal functioning are actually the result of normal *evolutionary* principles (Fábrega, 2007, 2006, 2004, 2002).

In general, evolutionary theorists argue that human reactions and the genes responsible for them have survived over the course of time because they have helped individuals to thrive and adapt. Ancestors who had the ability to run fast, for example, or the craftiness to hide were most able to escape their enemies and to reproduce. Thus, the genes responsible for effective walking, running, or problem solving were particularly likely to be passed on from generation to generation to the present day.

The evolutionary position with regard to abnormal functioning follows a similar logic. According to evolutionary theorists, the capacity to experience fear was, and in many instances still is, adaptive. Fear alerted individuals to dangers, threats, and losses, so that persons could avoid or escape potential problems. People who were particularly sensitive to danger—those with greater fear responses—were more likely to survive catastrophes, battles, and the like and to reproduce, and so to pass on their fear genes. Of course, in today's world pressures are more numerous, subtle, and complex than they were in the past, condemning many individuals with such genes to a near-endless stream of fear and arousal. That is, the very genes that helped their ancestors to survive and reproduce might now leave these individuals particularly prone to fear reactions and anxiety disorders.

Actually, today's evolutionary theorists are interested in a combination of variables—adaptive behaviors of the past, genes, and the interaction between genes and current environmental events (Fábrega, 2007, 2006, 2004, 2002). Despite this broad scope, the evolutionary perspective is controversial in the clinical field and has been rejected by many biological and nonbiological theorists. Imprecise and at times impossible to research, this explanation requires leaps of faith that many scientists find unacceptable. Nevertheless, as genetic discoveries and insights have grown, interest in the possible causes of genetic differences and how they relate to current circumstances has grown as well, and evolutionary theories have received considerable attention.

VIRAL INFECTIONS AND ABNORMAL BEHAVIOR Another possible source of abnormal brain structure or biochemical dysfunctioning is *viral infections.* As you will see in Chapter 14, for example, research suggests that *schizophrenia,* a disorder marked by delusions, hallucinations, or other departures from reality, may be related to exposure to certain viruses

More than coincidence?
Studies of twins suggest that some aspects of behavior and personality are influenced by genetic factors. Many identical twins, like these musicians, are found to have similar tastes, behave in similar ways, and make similar life choices. Some even develop similar abnormal behaviors.

•**synapse**•The tiny space between the nerve ending of one neuron and the dendrite of another.

•**neurotransmitter**•A chemical that, released by one neuron, crosses the synaptic space to be received at receptors on the dendrites of neighboring neurons.

•**receptor**•A site on a neuron that receives a neurotransmitter.

•**hormones**•The chemicals released by endocrine glands into the bloodstream.

•**gene**•Chromosome segments that control the characteristics and traits we inherit.

The brain bank

At Cornell University's "brain bank," researcher Barbara Finlay holds the brain of a person who had schizophrenia. There are currently more than 100 brain banks, each preserving between 50 and several hundred brains for study by researchers around the world (Kennedy, 2004). Thirty-five years ago there were none.

during childhood or *in utero,* before birth (Meyer et al., 2008; Shirts et al., 2007; Koponen et al., 2004). Studies have found that the mothers of many individuals with this disorder contracted influenza or related viruses during their pregnancy. This and related pieces of circumstantial evidence suggest that a damaging virus may enter the fetus's brain and remain dormant there until the individual reaches puberty or young adulthood. At that time, activated by hormone changes or by another infection, the virus may produce the symptoms of schizophrenia. During the past decade, researchers have sometimes linked viruses to anxiety and mood disorders, as well as to psychotic disorders (Dale et al., 2004; Kim et al., 2004).

Biological Treatments

Biological practitioners look for certain kinds of clues when they try to understand abnormal behavior. Does the person's family have a history of that behavior, and hence a possible genetic predisposition to it? (Philip Berman's case history mentions that his mother was once hospitalized for depression.) Is the behavior produced by events that could have had a physiological effect? (Philip was having a drink when he flew into a jealous rage at the restaurant.)

Once the clinicians have pinpointed physical sources of dysfunctioning, they are in a better position to choose a biological course of treatment. The three leading kinds of biological treatments used today are *drug therapy, electroconvulsive therapy,* and *neurosurgery.* Drug therapy is by far the most common of these approaches.

In the 1950s, researchers discovered several effective **psychotropic medications,** drugs that mainly affect emotions and thought processes (see Figure 3-4 on page 56). These drugs have greatly changed the outlook for a number of mental disorders and today are used widely, either alone or with other forms of therapy. However, the psychotropic drug revolution has also produced some major problems. Many people believe, for example, that the drugs are overused. Moreover, while drugs are effective in many cases, they do not help everyone.

Four major psychotropic drug groups are used in therapy: antianxiety, antidepressant, antibipolar, and antipsychotic drugs. **Antianxiety drugs,** also called **minor tranquilizers** or **anxiolytics,** help reduce tension and anxiety. These drugs include *lorazopam* (trade name Atavan), *alprazolam* (Xanax), and *diazepam* (Valium). **Antidepressant drugs**

BETWEEN THE LINES

How Do Genetic Defects Differ from Congenital Defects?

Genetic defects are inherited, are determined at the moment of conception, and can be passed down to future generations. Congenital defects—defects with which a child is born—are not inherited; they develop after conception, during the gestation period. ‹‹

"Don't judge me until you've walked a mile on my medication."

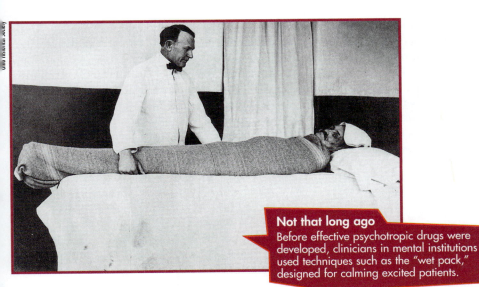

Not that long ago
Before effective psychotropic drugs were developed, clinicians in mental institutions used techniques such as the "wet pack," designed for calming excited patients.

help improve the mood of people who are depressed. They include *sertraline* (Zoloft), *fluoxetine* (Prozac), and *escitalopram* (Lexapro). **Antibipolar drugs,** also called **mood stabilizers,** help stabilize the moods of those with a bipolar disorder, a condition marked by mood swings from mania to depression. One of the most widely used of these drugs is *lithium.* And **antipsychotic drugs** help reduce the confusion, halluci-nations, and delusions of *psychotic disorders,* disorders marked by a loss of contact with reality. Common antipsychotic drugs are *quetiapine* (Seroquel), *risperidone* (Risperdal), and *haloperidol* (Haldol).

The second form of biological treatment, used primarily on depressed patients, is **electroconvulsive therapy (ECT).** Two electrodes are attached to a patient's forehead and an electrical current of 65 to 140 volts is passed briefly through the brain. The current causes a brain seizure that lasts up to a few minutes. After seven to nine ECT sessions, spaced two or three days apart, many patients feel considerably less depressed. The treatment is used on tens of thousands of depressed persons annually, particularly those whose depression fails to respond to other treatments (Eschweiler et al., 2007; Pagnin et al., 2004).

A third form of biological treatment is **neurosurgery,** or **psychosurgery,** brain surgery for mental disorders. It is thought to have roots as far back as trephining, the prehistoric practice of chipping a hole in the skull of a person who behaved strangely. Modern procedures are derived from a technique first developed in the late 1930s by a Portuguese neuropsychiatrist, Antonio de Egas Moniz. In that procedure, known as a *lobotomy,* a surgeon would cut the connections between the brain's frontal lobes and the lower centers of the brain. Today's psychosurgery procedures are much more precise than the lobotomies of the past (Aouizerate el al., 2006). Even so, they are considered experimental and are used only after certain severe disorders have continued for years without responding to any other form of treatment.

Assessing the Biological Model

Today the biological model enjoys considerable respect. Biological research constantly produces valuable new information. And biological treatments often bring great relief when other approaches have failed. At the same time, this model has its shortcomings. Some of its proponents seem to expect that all human behavior can be explained in biological terms and treated with biological methods. This view can limit rather than enhance our understanding of abnormal functioning. Our mental life is an interplay of biological and nonbiological factors, and it is important to understand that interplay rather than to focus on biological variables alone.

•**psychotropic medications**•Drugs that primarily affect the brain and reduce many symptoms of mental dysfunctioning.

•**antianxiety drugs**•Psychotropic drugs that help reduce tension and anxi-ety. Also called *minor tranquilizers* or *anxiolytics.*

•**antidepressant drugs**•Psychotropic drugs that improve the moods of people with depression.

•**antibipolar drugs**•Psychotropic drugs that help stabilize the moods of people suffering from a bipolar mood disorder. Also called *mood stabilizers.*

•**antipsychotic drugs**•Psychotropic drugs that help correct the confusion, hallucinations, and delusions found in psychotic disorders.

•**electroconvulsive therapy (ECT)**•A form of biological treatment, used pri-marily on depressed patients, in which a brain seizure is triggered as an elec-tric current passes through electrodes attached to the patient's forehead.

•**neurosurgery**•Brain surgery for men-tal disorders. Also called *psychosurgery.*

BETWEEN THE LINES

Whose Brain Has the Most Neurons?

Human	100,000,000,000 neurons	‹‹
Octopus	300,000,000 neurons	‹‹
Rat	21,000,000 neurons	‹‹
Frog	16,000,000 neurons	‹‹
Cockroach	1,000,000 neurons	‹‹
Honey bee	850,000 neurons	‹‹
Fruit fly	100,000 neurons	‹‹
Ant	10,000 neurons	‹‹

Figure 3-4

How does a new drug reach the market-place? It takes an average of 14 years and tens of millions of dollars for a pharmaceutical company in the United States to bring a newly discovered drug to market. The company must carefully follow steps that are mandated by law. (Adapted from Lemonick & Goldstein, 2002; Andreasen, 2001; Zivin, 2000.)

Preclinical Phase (5 years)
New drug is developed and identified. Drug is tested on animals, usually rats, to help determine its safety and efficacy.

Clinical Phase I:
Safety Screening (1.5 years)
Investigators test drug on human subjects to determine its safety.
- Number of subjects: 10–100
- Typical cost: $10 million

Clinical Phase II:
Preliminary Testing (2 years)
Investigators conduct studies with human subjects to determine how drug can best be evaluated and to obtain preliminary estimates of correct dosage and treatment procedures.
- Number of subjects: 50–500
- Typical cost: $20 million

Clinical Phase III:
Final Testing (3.5 years)
Investigators conduct controlled studies to fully determine drug's efficacy and important side effects.
- Number of subjects: 300–30,000
- Typical cost: $45 million

Review by FDA (1.5 years)
Research is reviewed by FDA, and drug is approved or disapproved.

Postmarketing Surveillance (10 years)
Long after the drug is on the market-place, testing continues and doctors' reports are gathered. Manufacturer must report any unexpected long-term effects and side effects.

A second shortcoming is that much of the evidence for biological explanations is incomplete or inconclusive. Many brain studies, for example, are conducted on animals in whom symptoms of depression, anxiety, or some other abnormality have been produced by drugs, surgery, or experimental manipulation. Researchers can never be certain that the animals are experiencing the human disorder under investigation.

Finally, several of today's biological treatments are capable of producing significant undesirable effects. Certain antipsychotic drugs, for example, may produce movement problems such as severe shaking, bizarre-looking contractions of the face and body, and extreme restlessness. Clearly such costs must be addressed and weighed against the drug's benefits.

❂ The Psychodynamic Model

The *psychodynamic model* is the oldest and most famous of the modern psychological models. Psychodynamic theorists believe that a person's behavior, whether normal or abnormal, is determined largely by underlying psychological forces of which he or she is not consciously aware. These internal forces are described as *dynamic*—that is, they interact with one another; and their interaction gives rise to behavior, thoughts, and emotions. Abnormal symptoms are viewed as the result of conflicts between these forces (Luborsky, O'Reilly-Landry, & Arlow, 2008).

Psychodynamic theorists would view Philip Berman as a person in conflict. They would want to explore his past experiences because, in their view, psychological conflicts are tied to early relationships and to traumatic experiences that occurred during childhood. Psychodynamic theories rest on the *deterministic* assumption that no symptom or behavior is "accidental": all behavior is determined by past experiences. Thus Philip's hatred for his mother, his memories of her as cruel and overbearing, the weakness and ineffectiveness of his father, and the birth of a younger brother when Philip was 10 may all be important to the understanding of his current problems.

The psychodynamic model was first formulated by Viennese neurologist Sigmund Freud (1856–1939) at the turn of the twentieth century. First, Freud worked with physician Josef Breuer (1842–1925), conducting experiments on hypnosis and hysterical illnesses—mysterious physical ailments with no apparent medical cause. In a famous case, Breuer had treated a woman he called "Anna O.," whose hysterical symptoms included paralysis of the legs and right arm, deafness, and disorganized speech. Breuer placed the woman under hypnosis, expecting that suggestions made to her in that state would help rid her of her hysterical symptoms. While she was under hypnosis, however, she began to talk about traumatic past events and to express deeply felt emotions. This venting of repressed memories seemed to enhance the effectiveness of the treatment. Anna referred to it as her "talking cure."

Building on this early work, Freud developed the theory of *psychoanalysis* to explain both normal and abnormal psychological functioning as well as a corresponding method of treatment, a conversational approach also called psychoanalysis. During the early 1900s, Freud and several of his colleagues in the Vienna Psychoanalytic Society—including Carl Gustav Jung (1875–1961) and Alfred Adler (1870–1937)—became the most influential clinical theorists in the Western world.

How Did Freud Explain Normal and Abnormal Functioning?

Freud believed that three central forces shape the personality—instinctual needs, rational thinking, and moral standards. All of these forces, he believed, operate at the unconscious level, unavailable to immediate awareness, and he further believed them to be dynamic, or interactive. Freud called the forces the *id,* the *ego,* and the *superego.*

The Id Freud used the term **id** to denote instinctual needs, drives, and impulses. The id operates in accordance with the *pleasure principle;* that is, it always seeks gratification. Freud also believed that all id instincts tend to be sexual, noting that from the very earli-

Lucasfilm/20th Century Fox/The Kobal Collection

"Luke, I am your father."
This light-saber fight between Luke Skywalker and Darth Vader highlights the most famous, and contentious, father-son relationship in movie history. According to Sigmund Freud, however, all fathers and sons experience significant tensions and conflicts that they must work through, even in the absence of the special pressures faced by Luke and his father in the *Star Wars* series.

est stages of life a child's pleasure is obtained from nursing, defecating, masturbating, or engaging in other activities that he considered to have sexual overtones. He further suggested that a person's *libido,* or sexual energy, fuels the id.

The Ego During our early years we come to recognize that our environment will not meet every instinctual need. Our mother, for example, is not always available to do our bidding. A part of the id separates off and becomes the **ego.** Like the id, the ego unconsciously seeks gratification, but it does so in accordance with the *reality principle,* the knowledge we acquire through experience that it can be unacceptable to express our id impulses outright. The ego, employing reason, guides us to know when we can and cannot express those impulses.

The ego develops basic strategies, called **ego defense mechanisms,** to control unacceptable id impulses and avoid or reduce the anxiety they arouse. The most basic defense mechanism, *repression,* prevents unacceptable impulses from ever reaching consciousness. There are many other ego defense mechanisms, and each of us tends to favor some over others (see Table 3-1 on the next page).

The Superego The **superego** grows from the ego, just as the ego grows out of the id. As we learn from our parents that many of our id impulses are unacceptable, we unconsciously adopt, or *introject,* our parents' values. Judging ourselves by their standards, we feel good when we uphold their values; conversely, when we go against them, we feel guilty. In short, we develop a *conscience.*

According to Freud, these three parts of the personality—the id, the ego, and the superego—are often in some degree of conflict. A healthy personality is one in which an effective working relationship, an acceptable compromise, has formed among the three forces. If the id, ego, and superego are in excessive conflict, the person's behavior may show signs of dysfunction.

Freudians would therefore view Philip Berman as someone whose personality forces have a poor working relationship. His ego and superego are unable to control his id impulses, which lead him repeatedly to act in impulsive and often dangerous ways—suicide gestures, jealous rages, job resignations, outbursts of temper, frequent arguments.

Developmental Stages Freud proposed that at each stage of development, from infancy to maturity, new events and pressures challenge individuals and require adjustments in their id, ego, and superego. If the adjustments are successful, they lead to personal growth. If not, the person may become **fixated,** or stuck, in an early stage of development. Then all subsequent development suffers, and the individual may well be headed for abnormal functioning in the future. Because parents are the key environmental figures during the early years of life, they are often seen as the cause of improper development.

•**id**•According to Freud, the psychological force that produces instinctual needs, drives, and impulses.

•**ego**•According to Freud, the psychological force that employs reason and operates in accordance with the reality principle.

•**ego defense mechanisms**•According to psychoanalytic theory, strategies developed by the ego to control unacceptable id impulses and to avoid or reduce the anxiety they arouse.

•**superego**•According to Freud, the psychological force that represents a person's values and ideals.

•**fixation**•According to Freud, a condition in which the id, ego, and superego do not mature properly and are frozen at an early stage of development.

Freud named each stage of development after the body area, or erogenous zone, that he considered most important to the child at that time. For example, he referred to the first 18 months of life as the *oral stage*. During this stage, children fear that the mother who feeds and comforts them will disappear. Children whose mothers consistently fail to gratify their oral needs may become fixated at the oral stage and display an "oral character" throughout their lives, one marked by extreme dependence or extreme mistrust. Such persons are particularly prone to develop depression. As you will see in later chapters, Freud linked fixations at the other stages of development—*anal* (18 months to 3 years of age), *phallic* (3 to 5 years), *latency* (5 to 12 years), and *genital* (12 years to adulthood)—to yet other kinds of psychological dysfunction.

How Do Other Psychodynamic Explanations Differ from Freud's?

Personal and professional differences between Freud and his colleagues led to a split in the Vienna Psychoanalytic Society early in the twentieth century. Carl Jung, Alfred Adler, and others developed new theories. Although the new theories departed from Freud's ideas in important ways, each held on to Freud's belief that human functioning is shaped by dynamic (interacting) psychological forces. Thus all such theories, including Freud's, are referred to as *psychodynamic*.

table: 3-1

Defense Mechanisms to the Rescue

Defense	Operation	Example
Repression	Person avoids anxiety by simply not allowing painful or dangerous thoughts to become conscious.	An executive's desire to run amok and attack his boss and colleagues at a board meeting is denied access to his awareness.
Denial	Person simply refuses to acknowledge the existence of an external source of anxiety.	You are not prepared for tomorrow's final exam, but you tell yourself that it's not actually an important exam and that there's no good reason not to go to a movie tonight.
Projection	Person attributes own unacceptable impulses, motives, or desires to other individuals.	The executive who repressed his destructive desires may project his anger onto his boss and claim that it is actually the boss who is hostile.
Rationalization	Person creates a socially acceptable reason for an action that actually reflects unacceptable motives.	A student explains away poor grades by citing the importance of the "total experience" of going to college and claiming that too much emphasis on grades would actually interfere with a well-rounded education.
Reaction formation	Person adopts behavior that is the exact opposite of impulses he or she is afraid to acknowledge.	A man experiences homosexual feelings and responds by taking a strong antihomosexual stance.
Displacement	Person displaces hostility away from a dangerous object and onto a safer substitute.	After your parking spot is taken, you release your pent-up anger by starting an argument with your roommate.
Intellectualization	Person represses emotional reactions in favor of overly logical response to a problem.	A woman who has been beaten and raped gives a detached, methodical description of the effects that such attacks may have on victims.
Regression	Person retreats from an upsetting conflict to an early developmental stage at which no one is expected to behave maturely or responsibly.	A boy who cannot cope with the anger he feels toward his rejecting mother regresses to infantile behavior, soiling his clothes and no longer taking care of his basic needs.
Sublimation	Person expresses sexual and aggressive energy in ways that are acceptable to society.	Athletes, artists, surgeons, and other highly dedicated and skilled people may be reaching their high levels of accomplishment by directing otherwise potentially harmful energies into their work.

Three of today's most influential psychodynamic theories are ego theory, self theory, and object relations theory. **Ego theorists** emphasize the role of the ego and consider it a more independent and powerful force than Freud did (Sharf, 2008). **Self theorists,** in contrast, emphasize the importance of developing a healthy self-interest and give the greatest attention to the role of the *self*—the unified personality. They believe that the basic human motive is to strengthen the wholeness of the self (Luborsky et al., 2008; Kohut, 2001, 1984, 1977). **Object relations theorists** propose that people are motivated mainly by a need to have relationships with others and that severe problems in the relationships between children and their caregivers may lead to abnormal development (Luborsky et al., 2008; Kernberg, 2005, 2001, 1997).

Psychodynamic Therapies

Psychodynamic therapies range from Freudian psychoanalysis to modern therapies based on self theory or object relations theory. All seek to uncover past traumas and the inner conflicts that have resulted from them. All try to help clients resolve, or settle, those conflicts and to resume personal development.

According to most psychodynamic therapists, the search for insight cannot be rushed or imposed. Therapists must subtly guide the explorations so that the patients discover their underlying problems for themselves. To aid in the process, the therapists rely on such techniques as *free association, therapist interpretation, catharsis,* and *working through.*

Free Association
In psychodynamic therapies, the patient is responsible for starting and leading each discussion. The therapist tells the patient to describe any thought, feeling, or image that comes to mind, even if it seems unimportant or irrelevant. This practice is known as **free association.** The therapist expects that the patient's associations will eventually uncover unconscious events and underlying dynamics. Notice how free association helps this New Yorker to discover threatening impulses and conflicts within herself:

Patient: So I started walking, and walking, and decided to go behind the museum and walk through Central Park. So I walked and went through a back field and felt very excited and wonderful. I saw a park bench next to a clump of bushes and sat down. There was a rustle behind me and I got frightened. I thought of men concealing themselves in the bushes. I thought of the sex perverts I read about in Central Park. I wondered if there was someone behind me exposing himself. The idea is repulsive, but exciting too. I think of father now and feel excited. I think of an erect penis. This is connected with my father. There is something about this pushing in my mind. I don't know what it is, like on the border of my memory. *(Pause)*

Therapist: Mm-hmm. *(Pause)* On the border of your memory?

Patient: *(The patient breathes rapidly and seems to be under great tension.)* As a little girl, I slept with my father. I get a funny feeling. I get a funny feeling over my skin, tingly-like. It's a strange feeling, like a blindness, like not seeing something. My mind blurs and spreads over anything I look at. I've had this feeling off and on since I walked in the park. My mind seems to blank off like I can't think or absorb anything.

(Wolberg, 1967, p. 662)

Therapist Interpretation
Psychodynamic therapists listen carefully as patients talk, looking for clues, drawing tentative conclusions, and sharing interpretations when they think the patient is ready to hear them. Interpretations of three phenomena are particularly important—*resistance, transference,* and *dreams.*

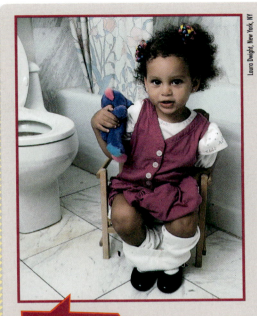

Laura Dwight, New York, NY

Critical training
Freud believed that toilet training is a critical developmental experience. Children whose training is too harsh may become "fixated" at the anal stage and develop an "anal character"—stubborn, contrary, stingy, or controlling.

•**ego theory**•The psychodynamic theory that emphasizes the role of the ego and considers it an independent force.

•**self theory**•The psychodynamic theory that emphasizes the role of the self—our unified personality.

•**object relations theory**•The psychodynamic theory that views the desire for relationships as the key motivating force in human behavior.

•**free association**•A psychodnamic technique in which the patient describes any thought, feeling, or image that comes to mind, even if it seems unimportant.

BETWEEN THE LINES

Does the Unconscious Differ from the Subconscious?

Yes. The unconscious consists of deep-seated, sometimes repressed, thoughts, needs, or desires that are not organized into conscious awareness. The subconscious consists of thoughts and needs that lie much closer to conscious awareness. They are unnoticed, rather than repressed, and can be brought to the surface relatively easily (Padwa, 1996). ‹‹

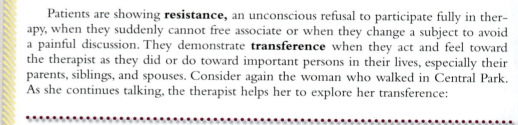

"Look, call it denial if you like, but I think what goes on in my personal life is none of my own damn business."

•**resistance**•An unconscious refusal to participate fully in therapy.

•**transference**•According to psychodynamic theorists, the redirection toward the psychotherapist of feelings associated with important figures in a patient's life, now or in the past.

•**dream**•A series of ideas and images that form during sleep.

•**catharsis**•The reliving of past repressed feelings in order to settle internal conflicts and overcome problems.

•**working through**•The psychoanalytic process of facing conflicts, reinterpreting feelings, and overcoming one's problems.

Patients are showing **resistance,** an unconscious refusal to participate fully in therapy, when they suddenly cannot free associate or when they change a subject to avoid a painful discussion. They demonstrate **transference** when they act and feel toward the therapist as they did or do toward important persons in their lives, especially their parents, siblings, and spouses. Consider again the woman who walked in Central Park. As she continues talking, the therapist helps her to explore her transference:

Patient: I get so excited by what is happening here. I feel I'm being held back by needing to be nice. I'd like to blast loose sometimes, but I don't dare.

Therapist: Because you fear my reaction?

Patient: The worst thing would be that you wouldn't like me. You wouldn't speak to me friendly; you wouldn't smile; you'd feel you can't treat me and discharge me from treatment. But I know this isn't so, I know it.

Therapist: Where do you think these attitudes come from?

Patient: When I was nine years old, I read a lot about great men in history. I'd quote them and be dramatic. I'd want a sword at my side; I'd dress like an Indian. Mother would scold me. Don't frown, don't talk so much. Sit on your hands, over and over again. I did all kinds of things. I was a naughty child. She told me I'd be hurt. Then at fourteen I fell off a horse and broke my back. I had to be in bed. Mother told me on the day I went riding not to, that I'd get hurt because the ground was frozen. I was a stubborn, self-willed child. Then I went against her will and suffered an accident that changed my life, a fractured back. Her attitude was, "I told you so." I was put in a cast and kept in bed for months.

(Wolberg, 1967, p. 662)

Finally, many psychodynamic therapists try to help patients interpret their **dreams** (see Figure 3-5 and Table 3-2). Freud (1924) called dreams the "royal road to the unconscious." He believed that repression and other defense mechanisms operate less completely during sleep and that dreams, if correctly recalled and interpreted, can reveal unconscious instincts, needs, and wishes. Freud identified two kinds of dream content—manifest and latent. *Manifest content* is the consciously remembered dream; *latent content,* its symbolic meaning. To interpret a dream, therapists must translate its manifest content into its latent content.

Catharsis
Insight must be an emotional as well as an intellectual process. Psychodynamic therapists believe that patients must experience **catharsis,** a reliving of past repressed feelings, if they are to settle internal conflicts and overcome their problems.

Working Through
A single episode of interpretation and catharsis will not change the way a person functions. The patient and therapist must examine the same issues over and over in the course of many sessions, each time with greater clarity. This process, called **working through,** usually takes a long time, often years. When psychodynamic treatment is scheduled once a week—as most forms of it now are—it is properly known as *psychodynamic,* or *psychoanalytic, therapy.* The term *psychoanalysis,* or simply *analysis,* is reserved for therapy given on a daily basis.

Contemporary Trends in Psychodynamic Therapy
The nature of psychodynamic therapy has continued to evolve. The past 30 years have witnessed substantial changes, especially in the way a large number of psychodynamic therapists conduct sessions. An increased demand for focused, time-limited psychotherapies has resulted in efforts to make psychodynamic therapy more efficient and cost-effective. Two contemporary psychodynamic approaches that illustrate this trend are *short-term psychodynamic therapies* and *relational psychoanalytic therapy.*

SHORT-TERM PSYCHODYNAMIC THERAPIES In several short versions of psychodynamic therapy, patients choose a single problem—a *dynamic focus*—to work on, such as difficulty getting along with other people (Charman, 2004). The therapist and patient focus on this problem throughout the treatment and work only on the psychodynamic issues that relate to it (such as unresolved oral needs). Only a limited number of studies have tested the effectiveness of these short-term psychodynamic therapies, but their findings do suggest that the approaches are sometimes quite helpful to patients (Present et al., 2008; Crits-Christoph et al., 2005).

table: 3-2

Percent of Research Participants Who Have Had Common Dreams

	Men	Women
Being chased or pursued, not injured	78%	83%
Sexual experiences	85	73
Falling	73	74
School, teachers, studying	57	71
Arriving too late, e.g., for a train	55	62
On the verge of falling	53	60
Trying to do something repeatedly	55	53
A person living as dead	43	59
Flying or soaring through the air	58	44
Sensing a presence vividly	44	50
Failing an examination	37	48
Being physically attacked	40	44
Being frozen with fright	32	44
A person now dead as living	37	39
Being a child again	33	38

Source: Kantrowitz & Springen, 2004.

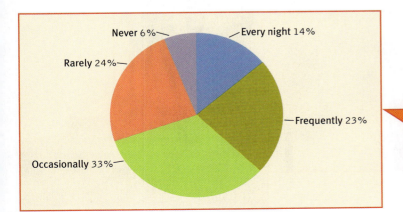

Figure 3-5
Remembering our dreams Although most adults dream several times each night, only 14 percent of them are able to remember their dreams every night. In contrast, 30 percent rarely or never recall any of their dreams. Children recall dreams even less frequently. (Adapted from Kantrowitz & Springen, 2004; Strauch, 2004.)

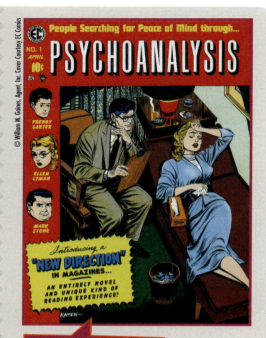

A cultural phenomenon
The psychodynamic model's impact has extended far beyond the clinical field. In 1955 a comic book series named *Psychoanalysis* hit the marketplace. Its first caption read, "This is a psychiatrist! Into his peaceful, tastefully-decorated, subdued office come the tormented and the driven."

RELATIONAL PSYCHOANALYTIC THERAPY Whereas Freud believed that psychodynamic therapists should take on the role of a neutral, distant expert during a treatment session, a contemporary school of psychodynamic therapy referred to as **relational psychoanalytic therapy** argues that therapists are key figures in the lives of patients—figures whose reactions and beliefs should be included in the therapy process (Luborsky et al., 2008; Reis, 2005; Levenson, 1982). In relational therapy, patients' feelings about what's happening in therapy are thought to reveal their long-standing relational problems, so both the patient and therapist can gain valuable insights by focusing on the treatment relationship. A key principle of relational therapy is that therapists should also disclose things about themselves, particularly their own reactions to patients, and try to establish more egalitarian relationships with patients.

Assessing the Psychodynamic Model

Freud and his followers have helped change the way abnormal functioning is understood (Corey, 2008). Largely because of their work, a wide range of theorists today look for answers and explanations outside of biological processes. Psychodynamic theorists have also helped us to understand that abnormal functioning may be rooted in the same processes as normal functioning (see *Psych Watch* on the facing page). Psychological conflict is a common experience; it leads to abnormal functioning only if the conflict becomes excessive.

Freud and his many followers have also had a monumental impact on treatment. They were the first to apply theory and techniques systematically to treatment. They were also the first to demonstrate the potential of psychological, as opposed to biological, treatment, and their ideas have served as starting points for many other psychological treatments.

At the same time, the psychodynamic model has its shortcomings. Its concepts are hard to research (Nietzel et al., 2003). Because processes such as id drives, ego defenses, and fixation are abstract and supposedly operate at an unconscious level, there is no way of knowing for certain if they are occurring. Not surprisingly, then, psychodynamic explanations and treatments have received limited research support traditionally, and psychodynamic theorists rely largely on evidence provided by individual case studies. Nevertheless, recent evidence suggests that long-term psychodynamic therapy may be helpful for many persons with chronic complex disorders (Leichsenring & Rabung, 2008), and 15 percent of today's clinical psychologists identify themselves as psychodynamic therapists (Prochaska & Norcross, 2007).

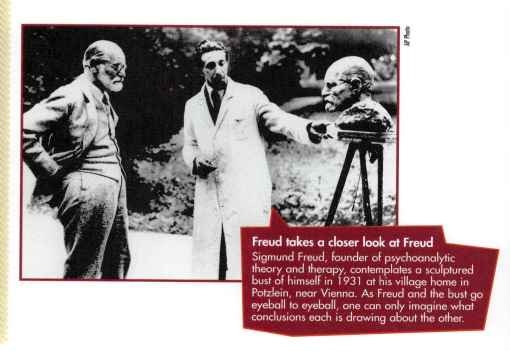

Freud takes a closer look at Freud
Sigmund Freud, founder of psychoanalytic theory and therapy, contemplates a sculptured bust of himself in 1931 at his village home in Potzlein, near Vienna. As Freud and the bust go eyeball to eyeball, one can only imagine what conclusions each is drawing about the other.

Maternal Instincts

On an August day in 1996, a 3-year-old boy climbed over a barrier at the Brookfield Zoo in Illinois and fell 24 feet onto the cement floor of the gorilla compound. An 8-year-old 160-pound gorilla named Binti-Jua picked up the child and cradled his limp body in her arms. The child's mother, fearing the worst, screamed out, "The gorilla's got my baby!" But Binti protected the boy as if he were her own. She held off the other gorillas, rocked him gently, and carried him to the entrance of the gorilla area, where rescue workers were waiting. Within hours, the incident was seen on videotape replays around the world, and Binti was being hailed for her maternal instincts.

When Binti was herself an infant, she had been removed from her mother, Lulu, who did not have enough milk. To make up for this loss, keepers at the zoo worked around the clock to nurture Binti; she was always being held in someone's arms. When Binti became pregnant at age 6, trainers were afraid that the early separation from her mother would leave her ill prepared to raise an infant of her own. So they gave her mothering lessons and taught her to nurse and carry around a stuffed doll.

After the incident at the zoo, clinical theorists had a field day interpreting the gorilla's gentle and nurturing care for the child, each within his or her preferred theory. Many *evolutionary theorists,* for example, viewed the behavior as an expression of the maternal instincts that have helped the gorilla species to survive and evolve. *Object relations theorists* suggested that the gorilla was expressing feelings of attachment and bonding, already experienced with her own 17-month-old daughter. And *behaviorists* held that the gorilla may have been imitating the nurturing behavior that she had observed in human models during her own infancy or enacting the parenting training that she had received during her pregnancy. While the clinical field tried frantically to sort out this issue, Binti-Jua, the heroic gorilla, returned to her relatively quiet and predictable life at the zoo.

Robert Allison/Contact Press Images

The Behavioral Model

Like psychodynamic theorists, behavioral theorists believe that our actions are determined largely by our experiences in life. However, the *behavioral model* concentrates wholly on *behaviors,* the responses an organism makes to its environment. Behaviors can be external (going to work, say) or internal (having a feeling or thought). In the behavioral view, people are the sum total of their learned behaviors. Behavioral theorists, therefore, base their explanations and treatments on *principles of learning,* the processes by which these behaviors change in response to the environment.

Many learned behaviors help people to cope with daily challenges and to lead happy, productive lives. However, abnormal behaviors also can be learned. Behaviorists who try to explain Philip Berman's problems might view him as a man who has received improper training: he has learned behaviors that offend others and repeatedly work against him.

•relational psychoanalytic therapy•
A form of psychodynamic therapy that considers therapists active participants in the formation of patients' feelings and reactions, and therefore calls for therapists to disclose their own experiences and feelings in discussions with patients.

Whereas the psychodynamic model had its beginnings in the clinical work of physicians, the behavioral model began in laboratories where psychologists were running experiments on **conditioning,** simple forms of learning. The researchers manipulated *stimuli* and *rewards,* then observed how their manipulations affected the responses of their research participants.

During the 1950s, many clinicians became frustrated with what they viewed as the vagueness and slowness of the psychodynamic model. Some of them began to apply the principles of learning to the study and treatment of psychological problems. Their efforts gave rise to the behavioral model of abnormality.

How Do Behaviorists Explain Abnormal Functioning?

Learning theorists have identified several forms of conditioning, and each may produce abnormal behavior as well as normal behavior. In **operant conditioning,** for example, humans and animals learn to behave in certain ways as a result of receiving *rewards*—any satisfying consequences—whenever they do so. In **modeling,** individuals learn responses simply by observing other individuals and repeating their behaviors.

In a third form of conditioning, **classical conditioning,** learning occurs by *temporal association.* When two events repeatedly occur close together in time, they become fused in a person's mind, and before long the person responds in the same way to both events. If one event produces a response of joy, the other brings joy as well; if one event brings feelings of relief, so does the other. A closer look at this form of conditioning illustrates how the behavioral model can account for abnormal functioning.

Ivan Pavlov (1849–1936), a famous Russian physiologist, first demonstrated classical conditioning with animal studies. He placed a bowl of meat powder before a dog, producing the natural response that all dogs have to meat: they start to salivate (see Figure 3-6). Next Pavlov added a step: just before presenting the dog with meat powder, he sounded a bell. After several such pairings of bell tone and presentation of meat powder, Pavlov noted that the dog began to salivate as soon as it heard the bell. The dog had learned to salivate in response to a sound.

In the vocabulary of classical conditioning, the meat in this demonstration is an *unconditioned stimulus (US).* It elicits the *unconditioned response (UR)* of salivation, that is, a natural response with which the dog is born. The sound of the bell is a *conditioned stimulus (CS),* a previously neutral stimulus that comes to be linked with meat in the dog's mind. As such, it too produces a salivation response. When the salivation response is produced by the conditioned stimulus rather than by the unconditioned stimulus, it is called a *conditioned response (CR).*

BEFORE CONDITIONING	AFTER CONDITIONING
CS: Tone → No response	CS: Tone → CR: Salivation
US: Meat → UR: Salivation	US: Meat → UR: Salivation

Classical conditioning explains many familiar behaviors. The romantic feelings a young man experiences when he smells his girlfriend's perfume, say, may represent a conditioned response. Initially, this perfume may have had limited emotional effect on him, but because the fragrance was present during several romantic encounters, it too came to elicit a romantic response.

Abnormal behaviors, too, can be acquired by classical conditioning. Consider a young boy who is repeatedly frightened by a neighbor's large German shepherd dog. Whenever the child walks past the neighbor's front yard, the dog barks loudly and lunges at him, stopped only by a rope tied to the porch. In this unfortunate situation, the boy's parents are not surprised to discover that he develops a fear of dogs. They are stumped, however, by another intense fear the child displays, a fear of sand. They cannot understand why he cries whenever they take him to the beach and screams in fear if sand even touches his skin.

A. Bandura, Stanford University

See and do
Modeling may account for some forms of abnormal behavior. A well-known study by Albert Bandura and his colleagues (1963) demonstrated that children learned to abuse a doll by observing an adult hit it. Children who had not been exposed to the adult model did not mistreat the doll.

Where did this fear of sand come from? Classical conditioning. It turns out that a big sandbox is set up in the neighbor's front yard for the dog to play in. Every time the dog barks and lunges at the boy, the sandbox is there too. After repeated pairings of this kind, the child comes to fear sand as much as he fears the dog.

Behavioral Therapies

Behavioral therapy aims to identify the behaviors that are causing a person's problems and then tries to replace them with more appropriate ones by applying the principles of classical conditioning, operant conditioning, or modeling (Wilson, 2008). The therapist's attitude toward the client is that of teacher rather than healer.

Classical conditioning treatments, for example, may be used to change abnormal reactions to particular stimuli. **Systematic desensitization** is one such method, often applied in cases of *phobia*—a specific and unreasonable fear. In this step-by-step procedure, clients learn to react calmly instead of with intense fear to the objects or situations they dread (Wolpe, 1997, 1995, 1990). First, they are taught the skill of relaxation over the course of several sessions. Next, they construct a *fear hierarchy*, a list of feared objects or situations, starting with those that are less feared and ending with the ones that are most dreaded. Here is the hierarchy developed by a man who was afraid of criticism, especially about his mental stability:

1. Friend on the street: "Hi, how are you?"
2. Friend on the street: "How are you feeling these days?"
3. Sister: "You've got to be careful so they don't put you in the hospital."
4. Wife: "You shouldn't drink beer while you are taking medicine."
5. Mother: "What's the matter, don't you feel good?"
6. Wife: "It's just you yourself, it's all in your head."
7. Service station attendant: "What are you shaking for?"
8. Neighbor borrows rake: "Is there something wrong with your leg? Your knees are shaking."
9. Friend on the job: "Is your blood pressure okay?"
10. Service station attendant: "You are pretty shaky, are you crazy or something?"

(Marquis & Morgan, 1969, p. 28)

Desensitization therapists next have their clients either imagine or actually confront each item on the hierarchy while in a state of relaxation. In step-by-step pairings of feared items and relaxation, clients move up the hierarchy until at last they can face every one of the items without experiencing fear. As you will read in Chapter 5, research has shown systematic desensitization and other classical conditioning techniques to be effective in treating phobias (Buchanan & Houlihan, 2008; Coldwell et al., 2007).

Assessing the Behavioral Model

The number of behavioral clinicians has grown steadily since the 1950s, and the behavioral model has become a powerful force in the clinical field. Various behavioral theories have been proposed over the years, and many treatment techniques have been developed. As you can see in Figure 3-7 on the next page, approximately 10 percent of today's clinical psychologists report that their approach is mainly behavioral (Prochaska & Norcross, 2007).

Figure 3-6
Working for Pavlov In Ivan Pavlov's experimental device, the dog's saliva was collected in a tube as it was secreted, and the amount was recorded on a revolving cylinder called a kymograph. The experimenter observed the dog through a one-way glass window.

•**conditioning**•A simple form of learning.

•**operant conditioning**•A process of learning in which behavior that leads to satisfying consequences is likely to be repeated.

•**modeling**•A process of learning in which an individual acquires responses by observing and imitating others.

•**classical conditioning**•A process of learning by temporal association in which two events that repeatedly occur close together in time become fused in a person's mind and produce the same response.

•**systematic desensitization**•A behavioral treatment in which clients with phobias learn to react calmly instead of with intense fear to the objects or situations they dread.

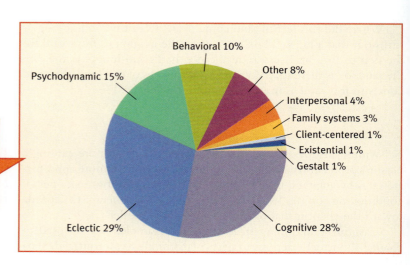

Figure 3-7
Theoretical orientations of today's clinical psychologists In one survey, 29 percent of clinical psychologists labeled themselves as "eclectic," 28 percent considered themselves "cognitive," and 15 percent called their orientation "psychodynamic." (Adapted from Prochaska & Norcross, 2007.)

Conditioning for fun and profit
Pet owners have discovered that they can teach animals a wide assortment of tricks by using the principles of conditioning. Only 3 percent of all dogs have learned to "sing," while 21 percent know how to sit, the most common dog trick (Pet Food Institute).

Perhaps the greatest appeal of the behavioral model is that it can be tested in the laboratory, whereas psychodynamic theories generally cannot. The behaviorists' basic concepts—stimulus, response, and reward—can be observed and measured. Even more important, the results of research have lent considerable support to the behavioral model. Experimenters have successfully used the principles of learning to create clinical symptoms in laboratory participants, suggesting that psychological disorders may indeed develop in the same way. In addition, research has found that behavioral treatments can be helpful to people with specific fears, compulsive behavior, social deficits, mental retardation, and other problems (Wilson, 2008).

At the same time, research has also revealed weaknesses in the model. Certainly behavioral researchers have produced specific symptoms in participants. But are these symptoms *ordinarily* acquired in this way? There is still no indisputable evidence that most people with psychological disorders are victims of improper conditioning. Similarly, behavioral therapies have limitations. The improvements noted in the therapist's office do not always extend to real life. Nor do they necessarily last without continued therapy.

Finally, some critics hold that the behavioral view is too simplistic, that its concepts fail to account for the complexity of behavior. In 1977 Albert Bandura, the behaviorist who earlier had identified modeling as a key conditioning process, argued that in order to feel happy and function effectively people must develop a positive sense of **self-efficacy.** That is, they must know that they can master and perform needed behaviors whenever necessary. Other behaviorists of the 1960s and 1970s similarly recognized that human beings engage in *cognitive behaviors,* such as anticipating or interpreting—ways of thinking that until then had been largely ignored in behavioral theory and therapy. These researchers developed *cognitive-behavioral* explanations that took unseen cognitive behaviors into greater account (Meichenbaum, 1993; Goldiamond, 1965) and **cognitive-behavioral therapies** that helped clients to change both their counterproductive behaviors and their dysfunctional ways of thinking.

Cognitive-behavioral theorists and therapists bridge the behavioral model and the cognitive model, the view to which we turn next. On the one hand, many parts of their explanations and treatments are based squarely on learning principles. A number of the theorists believe, for example, that cognitive processes are learned by classical conditioning, operant conditioning, and modeling. On the other hand, most cognitive-behavioral theorists share with other kinds of cognitive theorists a belief that the ability to think is the most important aspect of human functioning.

✿The Cognitive Model

Philip Berman, like the rest of us, has *cognitive* abilities—special intellectual capacities to think, remember, and anticipate. These abilities can help him accomplish a great deal in life. Yet they can also work against him. As he thinks about his experiences, Philip may develop false ideas. He may misinterpret experiences in ways that lead to poor decisions, maladaptive responses, and painful emotions.

In the early 1960s two clinicians, Albert Ellis (1962) and Aaron Beck (1967), proposed that cognitive processes are at the center of behaviors, thoughts, and emotions and that we can best understand abnormal functioning by looking to cognition—a perspective known as the *cognitive model*. Ellis and Beck claimed that clinicians must ask questions about the assumptions and attitudes that color a client's perceptions, the thoughts running through that person's mind, and the conclusions to which they are leading. Other theorists and therapists soon embraced and expanded their ideas and techniques.

How Do Cognitive Theorists Explain Abnormal Functioning?

According to cognitive theorists, abnormal functioning can result from several kinds of cognitive problems. Some people may make *assumptions* and adopt *attitudes* that are disturbing and inaccurate (Beck & Weishaar, 2008; Ellis, 2008). Philip Berman, for example, often seems to assume that his past history has locked him in his present situation. He believes that he was victimized by his parents and that he is now forever doomed by his past. He seems to approach all new experiences and relationships with expectations of failure and disaster.

Illogical thinking processes are another source of abnormal functioning, according to cognitive theorists. Beck, for example, has found that some people consistently think in illogical ways and keep arriving at self-defeating conclusions (Beck & Weishaar, 2008). As you will see in Chapter 8, Beck has identified a number of illogical thought processes regularly found in depression, such as *overgeneralization,* the drawing of broad negative conclusions on the basis of a single insignificant event. One depressed student couldn't remember the date of Columbus's third voyage to America during a history class. Overgeneralizing, she spent the rest of the day in despair over her invincible ignorance.

Cognitive Therapies

According to cognitive therapists, people with psychological disorders can overcome their problems by developing new, more functional ways of thinking. Because different forms of abnormality may involve different kinds of cognitive dysfunctioning, cognitive therapists have developed a number of strategies. Beck, for example, has developed an approach that is widely used in cases of depression (Beck & Weishaar, 2008; Beck, 2004, 2002, 1967).

In Beck's approach, called simply **cognitive therapy,** therapists help clients recognize the negative thoughts, biased interpretations, and errors in logic that dominate their thinking and, according to Beck, cause them to feel depressed. Therapists also guide clients to challenge their dysfunctional thoughts, try out new interpretations, and ultimately apply the new ways of thinking in their daily lives. As you will see in Chapter 9, people with depression who are treated with Beck's approach improve much more than those who receive no treatment.

In the excerpt that follows, a cognitive therapist guides a depressed 26-year-old graduate student to recognize the link between the way she interprets her experiences and the way she feels and to begin questioning the accuracy of her interpretations:

Therapist: How do you understand it?
   Patient: I get depressed when things go wrong. Like when I fail a test.
Therapist: How can failing a test make you depressed?

•**self-efficacy**•The belief that one can master and perform needed behaviors whenever necessary.

•**cognitive-behavioral therapies**• Therapy approaches that seek to help clients change both counterproductive behaviors and dysfunctional ways of thinking.

•**cognitive therapy**•A therapy developed by Aaron Beck that helps people recognize and change their faulty thinking processes.

BETWEEN THE LINES

Attitudes toward Therapy

19% People who believe that psychotherapy is primarily for "people with serious psychological difficulties" ‹‹

13% Those who think psychotherapy is "a waste of time" ‹‹

49% Those who have positive feelings when they find out that an acquaintance is seeing a therapist ‹‹

10% Those who have negative feelings when they find out that an acquaintance is seeing a therapist ‹‹

(Fetto, 2002)

Patient: Well, if I fail I'll never get into law school.

Therapist: So failing the test means a lot to you. But if failing a test could drive people into clinical depression, wouldn't you expect everyone who failed the test to have a depression? . . . Did everyone who failed get depressed enough to require treatment?

Patient: No, but it depends on how important the test was to the person.

Therapist: Right, and who decides the importance?

Patient: I do.

Therapist: And so, what we have to examine is your way of viewing the test (or the way that you think about the test) and how it affects your chances of getting into law school. Do you agree?

Patient: Right. . . .

Therapist: Now what did failing mean?

Patient: (Tearful) That I couldn't get into law school.

Therapist: And what does that mean to you?

Patient: That I'm just not smart enough.

Therapist: Anything else?

Patient: That I can never be happy.

Therapist: And how do these thoughts make you feel?

Patient: Very unhappy.

Therapist: So it is the meaning of failing a test that makes you very unhappy. In fact, believing that you can never be happy is a powerful factor in producing unhappiness. So, you get yourself into a trap—by definition, failure to get into law school equals "I can never be happy."

(Beck et al., 1979, pp. 145–146)

Assessing the Cognitive Model

The cognitive model has had very broad appeal. In addition to the large number of cognitive-behavioral clinicians who apply both cognitive and learning principles in their work, many cognitive practitioners concentrate exclusively on client interpretations, attitudes, assumptions, and other cognitive processes. Altogether approximately 28 percent of today's clinical psychologists identify their approach as cognitive (Prochaska & Norcross, 2007).

The cognitive model is popular for several reasons. First, it focuses on a process unique to human beings—the process of human thought—and many theorists from varied backgrounds find themselves drawn to a model that considers thought to be the primary cause of normal and abnormal behavior.

Cognitive theories also lend themselves to research. Investigators have found that people with psychological disorders often make the kinds of assumptions and errors in thinking the theorists claim (Ingram et al., 2007; Brown & Beck, 2002). Yet another reason for the popularity of this model is the impressive performance of cognitive and cognitive-behavioral therapies. They have proved very effective for treating depression, panic disorder, social phobia, and sexual dysfunctions, for example (Beck & Weishaar, 2008)

Nevertheless, the cognitive model, too, has its drawbacks. First, although disturbed cognitive processes are found in many forms of abnormality, their precise role has yet to be determined. The cognitions seen in psychologically troubled people could well be a result rather than a cause of their difficulties. Second, although cognitive and cognitive-behavioral therapies are clearly

of help to many people, they do not help everyone. Is it enough simply to change cognitions? Can such changes make a general and lasting difference in the way people feel and behave? A growing body of research suggests that the kinds of cognitive changes proposed by Beck and other cognitive therapists are not always possible to achieve (Sharf, 2008).

In response to such limitations, a new group of cognitive and cognitive-behavioral therapies, sometimes called the *new wave* of cognitive therapies, has emerged in recent years. These new approaches, such as the widely used *Acceptance and Commitment Therapy (ACT)*, help clients to *accept* many of their problematic thoughts rather than judge them, act on them, or try fruitlessly to change them (Hayes et al., 2004; Hayes, 2002). The hope is that by recognizing such thoughts for what they are—just thoughts—clients will eventually be able to let them pass through their awareness without being particularly troubled by them. As you will see in Chapter 5, ACT and other new-wave cognitive therapies often employ *mindfulness-based* techniques to help their clients achieve such acceptance. These techniques borrow heavily from a form of meditation called *mindfulness meditation,* which teaches individuals to pay attention to the thoughts and feelings that are flowing through their minds during meditation and to accept such thoughts in a nonjudgmental way. Early research indicates that ACT and other new-wave cognitive therapies are indeed often helpful in the treatment of anxiety and depression (Hayes et al., 2004).

A final drawback of the cognitive model is that, like the other models you have read about, it is narrow in certain ways. Although cognition is a very special human dimension, it is still only one part of human functioning. Aren't human beings more than the sum of their thoughts, emotions, and behaviors? Shouldn't explanations of human functioning also consider broader issues such as how people approach life, what value they extract from it, and how they deal with the question of life's meaning? This is the position of the humanistic-existential perspective.

A clinical pioneer
Aaron Beck proposes that many forms of abnormal behavior can be traced to cognitive factors, such as upsetting thoughts and illogical thinking.

⚙The Humanistic-Existential Model

Philip Berman is more than the sum of his psychological conflicts, learned behaviors, or cognitions. Being human, he also has the ability to pursue philosophical goals such as self-awareness, strong values, a sense of meaning in life, and freedom of choice. According to humanistic and existential theorists, Philip's problems can be understood only in the light of such complex goals. Humanistic and existential theorists are usually grouped together—in an approach known as the *humanistic-existential model*—because of their common focus on these broader dimensions of human existence. At the same time, there are important differences between them.

Humanists, the more optimistic of the two groups, believe that human beings are born with a natural tendency to be friendly, cooperative, and constructive. People, these theorists propose, are driven to **self-actualize**—that is, to fulfill this potential for goodness and growth. They can do so, however, only if they honestly recognize and accept their weaknesses as well as their strengths and establish satisfying personal values to live by. Humanists further suggest that self-actualization leads naturally to a concern for the welfare of others and to behavior that is loving, courageous, spontaneous, and independent (Maslow, 1970).

Existentialists agree that human beings must have an accurate awareness of themselves and live meaningful—they say "authentic"—lives in order to be psychologically well adjusted. These theorists do not believe, however, that people are naturally inclined to live constructively. They believe that from birth we have total freedom, either to face up to our existence and give meaning to our lives or to shrink from that responsibility. Those who choose to "hide" from responsibility and choice will view themselves as helpless and weak and may live empty, inauthentic, and dysfunctional lives as a result.

•self-actualization• The humanistic process by which people fulfill their potential for goodness and growth.

Actualizing the self
Humanists suggest that self-actualized people show concern for the welfare of humanity. This 89-year-old social services volunteer (right), for example, has participated for the past 20 years as a companion to elderly persons with mental retardation and developmental disabilities. The self-actualized are also thought to be highly creative, spontaneous, independent, and humorous.

Unconditional positive regard
Carl Rogers argued that clients must receive unconditional positive regard in order to overcome their psychological problems. In this spirit, a number of organizations now arrange for individuals to have close relationships with gentle and nonjudgmental animals. The Animal Welfare Foster Program of Virginia, for example, arranged for many dogs, including these two, to visit with students and staff at Virginia Tech in the days following the 2007 campus shooting that left 33 dead and many more injured.

The humanistic and existential views of abnormality both date back to the 1940s. At that time Carl Rogers (1902–1987), often considered the pioneer of the humanistic perspective, developed *client-centered therapy,* a warm and supportive approach that contrasted sharply with the psychodynamic techniques of the day. He also proposed a theory of personality that paid little attention to irrational instincts and conflicts.

The existential view of personality and abnormality appeared during this same period. Many of its principles came from the ideas of nineteenth-century European existential philosophers who held that human beings are constantly defining and so giving meaning to their existence through their actions (Mendelowitz & Schneider, 2008).

The humanistic and existential theories, and their uplifting and sometimes spiritual implications, were extremely popular during the 1960s and 1970s, years of considerable soul-searching and social upheaval in Western society. They have since lost some of their popularity, but they continue to influence the ideas and work of many clinicians.

Rogers's Humanistic Theory and Therapy

According to Carl Rogers (2000, 1987, 1951), the road to dysfunction begins in infancy. We all have a basic need to receive *positive regard* from the important people in our lives (primarily our parents). Those who receive *unconditional* (nonjudgmental) *positive regard* early in life are likely to develop *unconditional self-regard.* That is, they come to recognize their worth as persons, even while recognizing that they are not perfect. Such people are in a good position to actualize their positive potential.

Unfortunately, some children are repeatedly made to feel that they are not worthy of positive regard. As a result, they acquire *conditions of worth,* standards that tell them they are lovable and acceptable only when they conform to certain guidelines. To maintain positive self-regard, these people have to look at themselves very selectively, denying or distorting thoughts and actions that do not measure up to their conditions of worth. They thus acquire a distorted view of themselves and their experiences. They do not know what they are truly feeling, what they genuinely need, or what values and goals would be meaningful for them. Problems in functioning are then inevitable.

Rogers might view Philip Berman as a man who has gone astray. Rather than striving to fulfill his positive human potential, he drifts from job to job, relationship to relationship, and outburst to outburst. In every interaction he is defending himself, trying to interpret events in ways he can live with, usually blaming his problems on other people. Nevertheless, his basic negative self-image continually reveals itself. Rogers would probably link this problem to the critical ways Philip was treated by his mother throughout his childhood.

Clinicians who practice Rogers's **client-centered therapy** try to create a supportive climate in which clients feel able to look at themselves honestly and acceptingly (Raskin, Rogers, & Witty, 2008). The therapist must display three important qualities throughout the therapy—*unconditional positive regard* (full and warm acceptance for the client), *accurate empathy* (skillful listening and restatements), and *genuineness* (sincere communication). The following interaction shows the therapist using all these qualities to move the client toward greater self-awareness:

> *Client:* Yes, I know I shouldn't worry about it, but I do. Lots of things—money, people, clothes. In classes I feel that everyone's just waiting for a chance to jump on me. . . . When I meet somebody I wonder what he's actually thinking of me. Then later on I wonder how I match up to what he's come to think of me.
>
> *Therapist:* You feel that you're pretty responsive to the opinions of other people.
>
> *Client:* Yes, but it's things that shouldn't worry me.
>
> *Therapist:* You feel that it's the sort of thing that shouldn't be upsetting, but they do get you pretty much worried anyway.
>
> *Client:* Just some of them. Most of those things do worry me because they're true. The ones I told you, that is. But there are lots of little things that aren't true. . . . Things just seem to be piling up, piling up inside of me. . . . It's a feeling that things were crowding up and they were going to burst.
>
> *Therapist:* You feel that it's a sort of oppression with some frustration and that things are just unmanageable.
>
> *Client:* In a way, but some things just seem illogical. I'm afraid I'm not very clear here but that's the way it comes.
>
> *Therapist:* That's all right. You say just what you think.
>
> *(Snyder, 1947, pp. 2–24)*

In such an atmosphere, clients are expected to feel accepted by their therapists. They then may be able to look at themselves with honesty and acceptance—a process called *experiencing*. That is, they begin to value their own emotions, thoughts, and behaviors, and so they are freed from the insecurities and doubts that prevent self-actualization.

Client-centered therapy has not fared very well in research (Sharf, 2008; Greenberg et al., 1998, 1994). Although some studies show that participants who receive this therapy improve more than control participants, many other studies have failed to find any such advantage. All the same, Rogers's therapy has had a positive influence on clinical practice (Raskin et al., 2008; Kirschenbaum, 2004). It was one of the first major alternatives to psychodynamic therapy, and it helped open up the field to new approaches (see *Psych Watch* on the next page). Rogers also helped pave the way for *psychologists* to practice psychotherapy, which had previously been considered the exclusive territory of psychiatrists. And his commitment to clinical research helped promote the systematic study of treatment. Approximately 1 percent of today's clinical psychologists, 2 percent of social workers, and 4 percent of counseling psychologists report that they employ the client-centered approach (Prochasca & Norcross, 2007).

Gestalt Theory and Therapy

Gestalt therapy, another humanistic approach, was developed in the 1950s by a charismatic clinician named Frederick (Fritz) Perls (1893–1970). Gestalt therapists, like client-centered therapists, guide their clients toward self-recognition and self-acceptance (Yontef & Jacobs, 2008). But unlike client-centered therapists, they often try to achieve this goal by challenging and even frustrating their clients. Some of Perls's favorite techniques were skillful frustration, role playing, and numerous rules and exercises.

•**client-centered therapy**•The humanistic therapy developed by Carl Rogers in which clinicians try to help clients by conveying acceptance, accurate empathy, and genuineness.

•**gestalt therapy**•The humanistic therapy developed by Fritz Perls in which clinicians actively move clients toward self-recognition and self-acceptance by using techniques such as role playing and self-discovery exercises.

▌▌▌ BETWEEN THE LINES ▌▌▌

When Humanism and Neuroscience Cross Paths

When participants in a study conducted at the University of Oregon were led to believe that their research money was going to charity, the pleasure centers in their brains—the caudate nucleus and the nucleus accumbens—became more active. When the participants actually *chose* to give the money to charity, brain scans indicated that the pleasure centers were particularly active (Mayr, 2007). ‹‹

Surfing for Help

Today, computers and the Internet affect just about every area of life. Thus it is not surprising that many psychological counselors and marketers have tried to make use of digital technology. Over the past several decades, the growth of cybertherapy has closely paralleled developments in computer technology.

The clinical field's first excursion into the digital world took the form of *computer software therapy programs* (Mortley et al., 2004; Jacobs et al., 2001). These programs, which can be traced to the development of the famous computer program ELIZA in the mid-1960s, seek to reduce emotional distress by facilitating a typed conversation between a human user and a computer "therapist" (Tantam, 2006; Weizenbaum, 1966). Initially, these programs simulated *client-centered* therapy sessions. The individual seeking help would type a response to a question posed by the computer, and the computer program would then "ask" the next question on the basis of key words that appeared in the response. Eventually, as computer technology evolved to permit more complex exchanges, programs were developed that also captured the basic principles of other models of therapy. One program, for example, helped people articulate their problems in "if-then" statements, a basic technique used by cognitive therapists (Elias, 1995; Binik et al., 1988; Ghosh & Greist, 1988).

Advocates of computer therapy programs have argued that many people find it easier to disclose sensitive personal information to a computer than to a therapist. Computer programs offer them the freedom to express their thoughts and emotions without fear of being judged. Moreover, the programs are always available and their fees are modest—attractive attributes in a therapist. Research indicates that some of these programs are indeed helpful to at least a modest degree (Lange et al., 2004; Rochlen et al., 2004).

Computer therapy programs continue to enjoy some success in the marketplace (Tantam, 2006). Moreover, computer experts

AP Photo/Ron Heflin

are working to develop programs for recognizing clients' faces and emotions and programs that emulate emotion in computer-generated animation. Such sophisticated programming will undoubtedly bring about greater versatility and will increase the marketplace appeal of computer therapy programs. In the meantime, however, these programs have taken a back seat to another form of cybertherapy that has exploded in popularity—*on-line counseling.*

Over the past decade, thousands of therapists have set up on-line services that invite persons with problems to e-mail their questions and concerns (Chester & Glass, 2006; Rosen, 2005; Rochlen et al., 2004). Such services, often called *e-therapy,* can cost as much as $2 per minute. Although most of such exchanges are one-time e-sessions, some e-therapists offer an ongoing relationship. Services of this kind have raised concerns about the quality of care and about confidentiality. Many e-therapists do not even have advanced clinical training. Nevertheless, the use of e-therapy continues to grow by leaps and bounds.

Less common, but on the rise, is *audiovisual* e-therapy. This kind of offering more closely mimics the conventional therapy experience. A client sets up an appointment with a therapist, and, with the aid of a camera, microphone, and proper computer tools, the two proceed to have a face-to-face

session. The advantage? Clients can conveniently receive counseling while sitting at home or in their office, and they can have access to a counselor who is located even thousands of miles away. The key disadvantage? Once again, quality control.

Still more common than either e-mail or audiovisual e-therapies are Internet chat groups and "virtual" support groups. Tens of thousands of these groups are currently "in session" around the clock for everything from depression to substance abuse, anxiety, and eating disorders (Moskowitz, 2008, 2001). Like in-person self-help groups, the on-line chat groups provide opportunities for people with similar problems to communicate with each other, freely trading information, advice, and empathy (Griffiths & Christensen, 2006). Of course, unlike members of in-person self-help groups, people who choose chat group therapy do not know who is on the other end of the computer connection or whether the advice they receive is well-intentioned or at all appropriate.

Computers and on-line services may never substitute fully for the in-person judgment of a trained therapist or empathic hug of a fellow sufferer. Yet, as digital offerings increase in number and complexity, both computer and Internet services seem to be finding their place as adjuncts to conventional forms of treatment.

In the technique of *skillful frustration,* gestalt therapists refuse to meet their clients' expectations or demands. This use of frustration is meant to help people see how often they try to manipulate others into meeting their needs. In the technique of *role playing,* the therapists instruct clients to act out various roles. A person may be told to be another person, an object, an alternative self, or even a part of the body. Role playing can become intense, as individuals are encouraged to fully express emotions. Many cry out, scream, kick, or pound. Through this experience they may come to "own" (accept) feelings that previously made them uncomfortable.

Perls also developed a list of *rules* to ensure that clients will look at themselves more closely. In some versions of gestalt therapy, for example, clients may be required to use "I" language rather than "it" language. They must say, "I am frightened" rather than "The situation is frightening." Yet another common rule requires clients to stay in the *here and now.* They have needs now, are hiding their needs now, and must observe them now.

Approximately 1 percent of clinical psychologists and other kinds of clinicians describe themselves as gestalt therapists (Prochaska & Norcross, 2007). Because they believe that subjective experiences and self-awareness cannot be measured objectively, gestalt therapists have not often performed controlled research on their approach (Yontef & Jacobs, 2008; Strumpfel, 2006, 2004; Strumpfel & Goldman, 2001).

Spiritual Views and Interventions

For most of the twentieth century, clinical scientists viewed religion as a negative—or at best neutral—factor in mental health (Blanch, 2007; Richards & Bergin, 2005, 2004, 2000). In the early 1900s, for example, Freud argued that religious beliefs were defense mechanisms, "born from man's need to make his helplessness tolerable" (1961, p. 23). Subsequently, clinical theorists proposed that people with strong religious beliefs were more suspicious, irrational, guilt-ridden, and unstable than others and were less able to cope with life's difficulties. Correspondingly, spiritual principles and issues were considered a taboo topic in most forms of therapy.

The alienation between the clinical field and religion now seems to be ending. During the past decade, many articles and books linking spiritual issues to clinical treatment have been published, and the ethical codes of psychologists, psychiatrists, and counselors have each concluded that religion is a type of diversity that mental health professionals are obligated to respect (Richards & Bergin, 2005, 2004, 2000). Researchers have learned that spirituality can, in fact, be of psychological benefit to people. In particular, studies have examined the mental health of people who are devout and who view God as warm, caring, helpful, and dependable. Repeatedly, these individuals are found to be less lonely, pessimistic, depressed, or anxious than people without any religious beliefs or those who view God as cold and unresponsive (Loewenthal, 2007; Koenig, 2002; Bergin & Richards, 2001). Such individuals also seem to cope better with major life stressors—from illness to war—and to attempt suicide less often. In addition, they are less likely to abuse drugs. In line with such findings, many therapists now make a point of including spiritual issues when they treat religious clients (Raab, 2007; Helmeke & Sori, 2006; Serlin, 2005; Shafranske & Sperry, 2005), and some further encourage clients to use their spiritual resources to help them cope with current stresses and dysfunctioning.

Existential Theories and Therapy

Like humanists, existentialists believe that psychological dysfunctioning is caused by self-deception; existentialists, however, are referring to a kind of self-deception in which people hide from life's responsibilities and fail to recognize that it is up to them to give meaning to their lives. According to existentialists, many people become overwhelmed by the pressures of present-day society and so look to others for explanations, guidance, and authority. They overlook their personal freedom of choice and avoid responsibility for their lives and decisions (Mendelowitz & Schneider, 2008). Such people are left with empty, inauthentic lives. Their dominant emotions are anxiety, frustration, boredom, alienation, and depression.

Beating the blues
Gestalt therapists often guide clients to express their needs and feelings in their full intensity by banging on pillows, crying out, kicking, or pounding things. Building on these techniques, a new approach, *drum therapy,* teaches clients, such as this woman, how to beat drums in order to help release traumatic memories, change beliefs, and feel more liberated.

BETWEEN THE LINES

Prayer and Health

84% Percentage of Americans who believe that praying for the sick improves their chance of recovery ‹‹

65% Percentage of prayers about health that relate to mental health ‹‹

(Sheler, 2004; Kalb, 2003)

Religion and mental health
A Thai Buddhist monk speaks during a psychological session at a school in Bang Niang Camp. In Thailand, people recovering from personal problems often go to their local temple seeking consolation through prayer and meditation.

Existentialists might view Philip Berman as a man who feels overwhelmed by the forces of society. He sees his parents as "rich, powerful, and selfish," and he perceives teachers, acquaintances, and employers as abusive and oppressing. He fails to appreciate his choices in life and his capacity for finding meaning and direction. Quitting becomes a habit with him—he leaves job after job, ends every romantic relationship, and flees difficult situations.

In **existential therapy** people are encouraged to accept responsibility for their lives and for their problems. Therapists try to help clients recognize their freedom so that they may choose a different course and live with greater meaning and stronger values (Schneider, 2008, 2004, 2003). The precise techniques used in existential therapy vary from clinician to clinician. At the same time, most existential therapists place great emphasis on the *relationship* between therapist and client and try to create an atmosphere of candor, hard work, and shared learning and growth.

> *Patient:* I don't know why I keep coming here. All I do is tell you the same thing over and over. I'm not getting anywhere.
> *Doctor:* I'm getting tired of hearing the same thing over and over, too.
> *Patient:* Maybe I'll stop coming.
> *Doctor:* It's certainly your choice.
> *Patient:* What do you think I should do?
> *Doctor:* What do you want to do?
> *Patient:* I want to get better.
> *Doctor:* I don't blame you.
> *Patient:* If you think I should stay, ok, I will.
> *Doctor:* You want me to tell you to stay?
> *Patient:* You know what's best; you're the doctor.
> *Doctor:* Do I act like a doctor?
>
> *(Keen, 1970, p. 200)*

Existential therapists do not believe that experimental methods can adequately test the effectiveness of their treatments. To them, research dehumanizes individuals by reducing them to test measures. Not surprisingly, then, very little controlled research has been devoted to the effectiveness of this approach (Mendelowitz & Schneider, 2008;

BETWEEN THE LINES

Charitable Acts

$150 billion	Amount contributed to charity each year in the United States ‹‹
57%	Percentage of charitable donations contributed to religious organizations ‹‹
43%	Percentage of donations directed to education, human services, health, and the arts ‹‹
75%	Percentage of incoming college freshmen who have done volunteer work in the past year ‹‹

(Kate, 1998; Reese, 1998)

Schneider, 2008). Nevertheless, around 1 percent of today's therapists use an approach that is primarily existential (Prochaska & Norcross, 2007).

Assessing the Humanistic-Existential Model

The humanistic-existential model appeals to many people in and out of the clinical field. In recognizing the special challenges of human existence, humanistic and existential theorists tap into an aspect of psychological life that is typically missing from the other models (Cain, 2007; Wampold, 2007). Moreover, the factors that they say are essential to effective functioning—self-acceptance, personal values, personal meaning, and personal choice—are certainly lacking in many people with psychological disturbances.

The optimistic tone of the humanistic-existential model is also an attraction. Theorists who follow these principles offer great hope when they assert that, despite the often overwhelming pressures of modern society, we can make our own choices, determine our own destiny, and accomplish much. Still another attractive feature of the model is its emphasis on health. Unlike clinicians from some of the other models who see individuals as patients with psychological illnesses, humanists and existentialists view them simply as people who have yet to fulfill their potential.

At the same time, the humanistic-existential focus on abstract issues of human fulfillment gives rise to a major problem from a scientific point of view: these issues are difficult to research. In fact, with the notable exception of Rogers, who tried to investigate his clinical methods carefully, humanists and existentialists have traditionally rejected the use of empirical research. This anti-research position is just now beginning to change. Humanistic and existential researchers have conducted several recent studies that use appropriate control groups and statistical analyses, and they have found that their therapies can be beneficial in some cases (Schneider, 2008; Strumpfel, 2006; Elliott, 2002). This newfound interest in research should lead to important insights about the merits of this model in the coming years.

"Just remember, son, it doesn't matter whether you win or lose—unless you want Daddy's love."

✿The Sociocultural Model: The Family-Social and Multicultural Perspectives

Philip Berman is also a social being. He is surrounded by people and by institutions, he is a member of a family and a cultural group, he participates in social relationships, and he holds cultural values. Indeed, such sociocultural forces are always operating upon Philip, setting boundaries and expectations that guide and at times pressure him, helping to shape his behavior, thoughts, and emotions.

According to two *sociocultural perspectives*—the family-social perspective and the multicultural perspective—abnormal behavior is best understood in light of the broad forces that influence an individual. What are the norms of the individual's society and culture? What roles does the person play in the social environment? What kind of family structure or cultural background is the person a part of? And how do other people view and react to him or her?

How Do Family-Social Theorists Explain Abnormal Functioning?

Proponents of the family-social perspective argue that clinical theorists should concentrate on those broad forces that operate *directly* on an individual as he or she moves through life—that is, family relationships, social interactions, and community events. They believe that such forces help account for both normal and abnormal behavior, and they pay particular attention to three kinds of factors: *social labels and roles, social networks,* and *family structure and communication.*

•existential therapy•A therapy that encourages clients to accept responsibility for their lives and to live with greater meaning and values.

Social Labels and Roles Abnormal functioning can be influenced greatly by the labels and roles assigned to troubled people (Link & Phelan, 2006; Link et al., 2004, 2001). When people stray from the norms of their society, the society calls them deviant and, in many cases, "mentally ill." Such labels tend to stick. Moreover, when people are viewed in particular ways, reacted to as "crazy," and perhaps even encouraged to act sick, they gradually learn to accept and play the assigned social role. Ultimately the label seems appropriate.

A famous study by the clinical investigator David Rosenhan (1973) seems to support this position. Eight normal people presented themselves at various mental hospitals, complaining that they had been hearing voices say the words "empty," "hollow," and "thud." On the basis of this complaint alone, each was diagnosed as having schizophrenia and admitted. As this model would predict, the "pseudopatients" had a hard time convincing others that they were well once they had been given the diagnostic label. Their hospitalizations ranged from 7 to 52 days, even though they behaved normally as soon as they were admitted. In addition, the label kept influencing the way the staff viewed and dealt with them. For example, one pseudopatient who paced the corridor out of boredom was, in clinical notes, described as "nervous." Overall, the pseudopatients came to feel powerless, invisible, and bored.

Social Networks and Supports Family-social theorists are also concerned with the social networks in which people operate, including their social and professional relationships. How well do they communicate with others? What kind of signals do they send to or receive from others? Researchers have often found ties between deficiencies in social networks and a person's functioning (Yen et al., 2007; Paykel, 2006, 2003; Segrin et al., 2003). They have noted, for example, that people who are isolated and lack social support or intimacy in their lives are more likely to become depressed when under stress and to remain depressed longer than are people with supportive spouses or warm friendships.

Family Structure and Communication Of course, one of the important social networks for an individual is his or her family. According to **family systems theory,** the family is a system of interacting parts—the family members—who interact with one another in consistent ways and conform to rules unique to each family (Goldenberg & Goldenberg, 2008). The parts interact in ways that enable the system to maintain itself and survive—a state known as *homeostasis.* Family systems theorists believe that the *structure* and *communication* patterns of some families actually force individual members to behave in a way that otherwise seems abnormal. If the members were to behave normally,

Today's TV families
Unlike television viewers of the 1950s, when problem-free families like the Nelsons (of *Ozzie & Harriet*) ruled the airwaves, today's viewers prefer more complex, sometimes dysfunctional, families, like the Henricksons—Bill, his three wives, their eight children, and their extended family—whose trials and tribulations are on display in HBO's popular series *Big Love.*

HBO/The Kobal Collection

they would severely strain the family's homeostasis and usual manner of operation and would actually increase their own and their family's turmoil.

Family systems theory holds that certain family systems are particularly likely to produce abnormal functioning in individual members. Some families, for example, have an *enmeshed* structure in which the members are grossly overinvolved in each other's activities, thoughts, and feelings. Children from this kind of family may have great difficulty becoming independent in life (Santisteban et al., 2001). Some families display *disengagement,* which is marked by very rigid boundaries between the members. Children from these families may find it hard to function in a group or to give or request support (Corey, 2008, 2001).

Philip Berman's angry and impulsive personal style might be seen as the product of a disturbed family structure. According to family systems theorists, the whole family—mother, father, Philip, and his brother Arnold—relate in such a way as to maintain Philip's behavior. Family theorists might be particularly interested in the conflict between Philip's mother and father and the imbalance between their parental roles. They might see Philip's behavior as both a reaction to and stimulus for his parents' behaviors. With Philip acting out the role of the misbehaving child, or scapegoat, his parents may have little need or time to question their own relationship.

Family systems theorists would also seek to clarify the precise nature of Philip's relationship with each parent. Is he enmeshed with his mother and/or disengaged from his father? They would look too at the rules governing the sibling relationship in the family, the relationship between the parents and Philip's brother, and the nature of parent–child relationships in previous generations of the family.

The virtual family dinner
Many systems theorists are concerned that as family members spread out geographically, important family communications and dynamics are lost. To help maintain valuable family interactions and support systems, two researchers have developed "The Virtual Family Dinner," a video-conferencing device that enables family members to share meals and other experiences even from great distances.

Family-Social Treatments

The family-social perspective has helped spur the growth of several treatment approaches, including *group therapy, family* and *couple therapy,* and *community treatment.* Therapists of any orientation may work with clients in these various formats, applying the techniques and principles of their preferred models. However, more and more of the clinicians who use these formats believe that psychological problems emerge in family and social settings and are best treated in such settings, and they include special sociocultural strategies in their work.

Group Therapy Thousands of therapists specialize in **group therapy,** a format in which a therapist meets with a group of clients who have similar problems. Indeed, one survey of clinical psychologists revealed that almost one-third of them devoted some portion of their practice to group therapy (Norcross & Goldfried, 2005; Norcross et al., 1993). Typically, members of a therapy group meet together with a therapist and discuss the problems of one or more of the people in the group. Together they develop important insights, build social skills, strengthen feelings of self-worth, and share useful information or advice (Yalom & Leszcz, 2005). Many groups are created with particular client populations in mind; for example, there are groups for people with alcoholism, for those who are physically handicapped, and for people who are divorced, abused, or bereaved.

Research suggests that group therapy is of help to many clients, often as helpful as individual therapy (Shaughnessy et al., 2007; Kosters et al., 2006; Guimon, 2004; McDermut et al., 2001). The group format has also been used for purposes that are educational rather than therapeutic, such as "consciousness raising" and spiritual inspiration.

A format similar to group therapy is the **self-help group** (or **mutual help group**). Here people who have similar problems (for example, bereavement, substance abuse, illness, unemployment, divorce) come together to help and support one another without the direct leadership of a professional clinician (Mueller et al., 2007; Munn-Giddings & Borkman, 2005). According to estimates, there are now between 500,000 and 3 million

•**family systems theory**•A theory that views the family as a system of interacting parts whose interactions exhibit consistent patterns and unstated rules.

•**group therapy**•A therapy format in which a group of people with similar problems meet together with a therapist to work on those problems.

•**self-help group**•A group made up of people with similar problems who help and support one another without the direct leadership of a clinician. Also called a *mutual help group.*

Self-Help Groups: Too Much of a Good Thing?

Self-help groups are widely accepted in our society, by consumers and clinicians alike (Isenberg et al., 2004). Indeed, one survey of mental health professionals revealed that almost 90 percent of all therapists in the United States often recommend such groups to their clients as a supplement to therapy (Clifford et al., 1998).

Small wonder that the number, range, and appeal of such groups have grown rapidly over the past several decades and that 25 million people in the United States alone are estimated to attend self-help groups over the course of their lives. And this number does not even include the millions of chat group participants who seek on-line support, information, and help from fellow sufferers. The self-help group movement and its impact on our society are brought to life in the following notice that was posted in a Colorado church, listing support groups that would be meeting at the church during the coming week (Moskowitz, 2008, 2001):

Zigy Kaluzny/Stone/Getty Images

Sunday
12:00 noon	Cocaine Anonymous, main floor
5:30 p.m.	Survivors of Incest, main floor
6:00 p.m.	Al-Anon, 2nd floor
6:00 p.m.	Alcoholics Anonymous, basement

Monday
5:30 p.m.	Debtors Anonymous, basement
6:30 p.m.	Codependents of Sex Addicts Anonymous, 2nd floor
7:00 p.m.	Adult Children of Alcoholics, 2nd floor
8:00 p.m.	Alcoholics Anonymous, basement
8:00 p.m.	Al-Anon, 2nd floor
8:00 p.m.	Alateen, basement
8:00 p.m.	Cocaine Anonymous, main floor

Tuesday
8:00 p.m.	Survivors of Incest Anonymous, basement

Wednesday
5:30 p.m.	Sex & Love Addicts Anonymous, basement
7:30 p.m.	Adult Children of Alcoholics, 2nd floor
8:00 p.m.	Cocaine Anonymous, main floor

Thursday
7:00 p.m.	Codependents of Sex Addicts Anonymous, 2nd floor
7:00 p.m.	Women's Cocaine Anonymous, main floor

Friday
5:30 p.m.	Sex & Love Addicts Anonymous, basement
5:45 p.m.	Adult Overeaters Anonymous, 2nd floor
7:30 p.m.	Codependents Anonymous, basement
7:30 p.m.	Adult Children of Alcoholics, 2nd floor
8:00 p.m.	Cocaine Anonymous, main floor

Saturday
10:00 a.m.	Adult Children of Alcoholics, main floor
12:00 p.m.	Self-Abusers Anonymous, 2nd floor

such groups in the United States alone, attended each year by 3 to 4 percent of the population (see *Psych Watch* on the facing page). Self-help groups tend to offer more direct advice than is provided in group therapy and to encourage more exchange of information or "tips."

Family Therapy **Family therapy** was first introduced in the 1950s. A therapist meets with all members of a family, points out problem behaviors and interactions, and helps the whole family to change its ways (Goldenberg & Goldenberg, 2008; Bowen, 1960). Here, the entire family is viewed as the unit under treatment, even if only one of the members receives a clinical diagnosis. The following is a typical interaction between family members and a therapist:

Tommy sat motionless in a chair gazing out the window. He was fourteen and a bit small for his age. . . . Sissy was eleven. She was sitting on the couch between her Mom and Dad with a smile on her face. Across from them sat Ms. Fargo, the family therapist.

Ms. Fargo spoke. "Could you be a little more specific about the changes you have seen in Tommy and when they came about?"

Mrs. Davis answered first. "Well, I guess it was about two years ago. Tommy started getting in fights at school. When we talked to him at home he said it was none of our business. He became moody and disobedient. He wouldn't do anything that we wanted him to. He began to act mean to his sister and even hit her."

"What about the fights at school?" Ms. Fargo asked.

This time it was Mr. Davis who spoke first. "Ginny was more worried about them than I was. I used to fight a lot when I was in school and I think it is normal. . . . But I was very respectful to my parents, especially my Dad. If I ever got out of line he would smack me one."

"Have you ever had to hit Tommy?" Ms. Fargo inquired softly.

"Sure, a couple of times, but it didn't seem to do any good."

All at once Tommy seemed to be paying attention, his eyes riveted on his father. "Yeah, he hit me a lot, for no reason at all!"

"Now, that's not true, Thomas." Mrs. Davis has a scolding expression on her face. "If you behaved yourself a little better you wouldn't get hit. Ms. Fargo, I can't say that I am in favor of the hitting, but I understand sometimes how frustrating it may be for Bob."

"You don't know how frustrating it is for me, honey." Bob seemed upset. "You don't have to work all day at the office and then come home to contend with all of this. Sometimes I feel like I don't even want to come home."

Ginny gave him a hard stare. "You think things at home are easy all day? I could use some support from you. You think all you have to do is earn the money and I will do everything else. Well, I am not about to do that anymore." . . .

Mrs. Davis began to cry. "I just don't know what to do anymore. Things just seem so hopeless. Why can't people be nice in this family anymore? I don't think I am asking too much, am I?"

Ms. Fargo spoke thoughtfully. "I get the feeling that people in this family would like things to be different. Bob, I can see how frustrating it must be for you to work so hard and not be able to relax when you get home. And, Ginny, your job is not easy either. You have a lot to do at home and Bob can't be there to help because he has to earn a living. And you kids sound like you would like some things to be different too. It must be hard for you, Tommy, to be catching so much flack these days. I think this also makes it hard for you to have fun at home too, Sissy."

She looked at each person briefly and was sure to make eye contact. "There seems to be a lot going on. . . . I think we are going to need to understand a lot of things to see why this is happening. . . ."

(Sheras & Worchel, 1979, pp. 108–110)

BETWEEN THE LINES

Greater Father Involvement

57% Persons who believe that today's fathers bathe their children and change diapers more than fathers did 20 years ago. ‹‹

53% Those who believe that today's fathers play with their children more than fathers of the past. ‹‹

53% Those who believe that today's fathers help more with homework. ‹‹

53% Those who believe that today's fathers are more involved in caring for their sick children. ‹‹

(Fetto, 2002)

Family therapists may follow any of the major theoretical models, but more and more of them are adopting the principles of *family systems theory.* Today 3 percent of all clinical psychologists, 13 percent of social workers, and 1 percent of psychiatrists identify themselves mainly as family systems therapists (Prochaska & Norcross, 2007).

As you read earlier, family systems theory holds that each family has its own rules, structure, and communication patterns that shape the individual members' behavior. In one family systems approach, *structural family therapy,* therapists try to change the family power structure, the roles each person plays, and the relationships between members (Goldenberg & Goldenberg, 2008; Minuchin, 1997, 1987, 1974). In another, *conjoint family therapy,* therapists try to help members recognize and change harmful patterns of communication (Sharf, 2008; Innes, 2002; Satir, 1987, 1967, 1964).

Family therapies of various kinds are often helpful to individuals, although research has not yet clarified how helpful (Goldenberg & Goldenberg, 2008; Sexton & Alexander, 2002). Some studies have found that as many as 65 percent of individuals treated with family approaches improve, while other studies suggest much lower success rates. Nor has any one type of family therapy emerged as consistently more helpful than the others (Alexander et al., 2002; Diamond & Diamond, 2002).

Couple Therapy

In **couple therapy,** or **marital therapy,** the therapist works with two individuals who are in a long-term relationship. Often they are husband and wife, but the couple need not be married or even living together. Like family therapy, couple therapy often focuses on the structure and communication patterns occurring in the relationship (Baucom et al., 2006, 2005, 2000). A couple approach may also be used when a child's psychological problems are traced to problems in the parents' relationship.

Although some degree of conflict exists in any long-term relationship, many adults in our society experience serious marital discord. The divorce rate in Canada, the United States, and Europe is now close to 50 percent of the marriage rate (Marshall & Brown, 2008). Many couples who live together without marrying apparently have similar levels of difficulty (Harway, 2005).

"We're fighting like—well, we're fighting"

Couple therapy, like family and group therapy, may follow the principles of any of the major therapy orientations. *Behavioral couple therapy,* for example, uses many techniques from the behavioral perspective (Shadish & Baldwin, 2005; Gurman, 2003). Therapists help spouses recognize and change problem behaviors largely by teaching specific problem-solving and communication skills. A broader, more sociocultural version, called *integrative couple therapy,* further helps partners accept behaviors that they cannot change and embrace the whole relationship nevertheless (Christensen et al., 2006, 2004). Partners are asked to see such behaviors as an understandable result of basic differences between them.

Couples treated by couple therapy seem to show greater improvement in their relationships than couples with similar problems who fail to receive treatment (Fraser & Solovey, 2007), but no one form of couple therapy stands out as superior to others (Snyder, Castellani, & Whisman, 2006; Harway 2005; Gollan & Jacobson, 2002). Although two-thirds of treated couples experience improved marital functioning by the end of therapy, fewer than half of those who are treated achieve "distress-free" or "happy" relationships. Moreover, one-third of successfully treated couples may relapse within two years after therapy. Couples who are younger, well adjusted, and less rigid in their gender roles tend to have the best results.

Community Treatment

Community mental health treatment programs allow clients, particularly those with severe psychological difficulties, to receive treatment in familiar social surroundings as they try to recover. In 1963 President Kennedy called for such a "bold new approach" to the treatment of mental disorders—a community approach that would enable most people with psychological problems to receive services from nearby

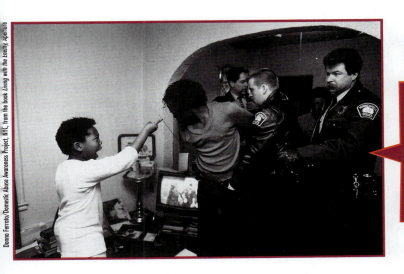

Donna Ferrato/Domestic Abuse Awareness Project, NYC, from the book *Living with the Enemy*, Aperture

Secondary prevention in action Community mental health professionals sometimes work with police and other public servants, teaching them how to address the psychological needs of people who are under extreme stress and upset. This 8-year-old had to call the police when he saw his father attacking his mother with a knife. The child's rage, frustration, and emotional pain are apparent.

agencies rather than distant facilities or institutions. Congress passed the Community Mental Health Act soon after, launching the community mental health movement across the United States. A number of other countries have launched similar movements.

As you read in Chapter 1, a key principle of community treatment is *prevention*. Here clinicians actively reach out to clients rather than wait for them to seek treatment. Research suggests that such efforts are often very successful (Hage et al., 2007; Harper & Dwivedi, 2004). Community workers recognize three types of prevention, which they call *primary*, *secondary*, and *tertiary*.

Primary prevention consists of efforts to improve community attitudes and policies. Its goal is to prevent psychological disorders altogether. Community workers may lobby for better community recreational programs, consult with a local school board, or offer public workshops on stress reduction (Bloom, 2008; LeCroy, 2005).

Secondary prevention consists of identifying and treating psychological disorders in the early stages, before they become serious. Community workers may work with school-teachers, ministers, or police to help them recognize the early signs of psychological dysfunction and teach them how to help people find treatment (Ervin et al., 2007; Molina et al., 2005).

The goal of *tertiary prevention* is to provide effective treatment as soon as it is needed so that moderate or severe disorders do not become long-term problems. Today community agencies across the United States do successfully offer tertiary care for millions of people with moderate psychological problems, but, as we also observed in Chapter 1, they often fail to provide the services needed by hundreds of thousands with severe disturbances. One of the reasons for this failure is lack of funding, an issue that you will read about in later chapters (Weisman, 2004; Humphreys & Rappaport, 1993).

How Do Multicultural Theorists Explain Abnormal Functioning?

Culture refers to the set of values, attitudes, beliefs, history, and behaviors shared by a group of people and communicated from one generation to the next (Matsumoto, 2007, 2001, 1994). We are, without question, a society of multiple cultures. Indeed, in the coming decades, members of racial and ethnic minority groups in the United States will, collectively, outnumber white Americans (Gordon, 2005; U.S. Census, 2000). This change in our society's racial and ethnic composition is partly because of shifts in immigration trends and partly because of higher birth rates among minority groups in the United States. The majority of new immigrants to this country are Hispanic (34 percent) or Asian (34 percent). Moreover, while the average number of children born to white Americans is 1.7, the number born to African Americans and Hispanic Americans is 2.4 and 2.9, respectively.

BETWEEN THE LINES

Cultural Oversight

Despite the growing cultural diversity throughout the United States, minority group members are remarkably underrepresented as participants in psychotropic drug treatment studies. A few years back, when UCLA researchers reviewed the best available studies of drugs for mood disorders, schizophrenia, and attention-deficit/hyperactivity disorder, they found that only 8 percent of the patients studied were members of minority groups. Of almost 44,000 patients in antidepressant studies, only 2 were Hispanic; of almost 3,000 patients with schizophrenia, 3 were Asian; and of 825 patients in bipolar disorder drug studies, none were Hispanic or Asian (Vedantam, 2005). «

Liss Sleve/Corbis Sygma

Victims of hate

This memorial service for Matthew Shepard, brutally beaten to death in 1998 because of his gay orientation, is a powerful reminder of the prejudice, discrimination, and even danger that members of minority groups can confront in our society. Culture-sensitive therapies seek to address the special impact of such stressors upon individuals, as well as other psychological issues.

BETWEEN THE LINES

Gender Issues in the Workplace

According to the Bureau of Labor Statistics, women today earn 76¢ for every $1 earned by a man. ‹‹

Around 42 percent of young adult women believe that women have to outperform men at work to get the same rewards; only 11 percent of young adult men agree. ‹‹

(Yin, 2002)

Partly in response to this growing diversity, the **multicultural perspective** has emerged (Jackson, 2006). Multicultural psychologists seek to understand how culture, race, ethnicity, gender, and similar factors affect behavior and thought and how people of different cultures, races, and genders differ psychologically (Alegria et al., 2007, 2004). Today's multicultural view is different from past—less enlightened—cultural perspectives: it does not imply that members of racial, ethnic, and other minority groups are in some way inferior or culturally deprived in comparison with a majority population (Sue & Sue, 2003). Rather, the model holds that an individual's behavior, whether normal or abnormal, is best understood when examined in the light of that individual's unique cultural context, from the values of that culture to the special external pressures faced by members of the culture.

The groups in the United States that have received the most attention from multicultural researchers are ethnic and racial minority groups (African American, Hispanic American, Native American, and Asian American groups) and groups such as economically disadvantaged persons, homosexual individuals, and women (although women are not technically a minority group). Each of these groups is subjected to special pressures in American society that may contribute to feelings of stress and, in some cases, to abnormal functioning. Researchers have learned, for example, that psychological abnormality, especially severe psychological abnormality, is indeed more common among poorer people than among wealthier people (Byrne et al., 2004; Draine et al., 2002). Perhaps the pressures of poverty explain this relationship. Of course, membership in these various groups overlaps. Many members of minority groups, for example, also live in poverty. The higher rates of crime, unemployment, overcrowding, and homelessness; the inferior medical care; and the limited educational opportunities typically experienced by poor persons may place great stress on many members of such minority groups.

Multicultural researchers have also noted that the prejudice and discrimination faced by many minority groups may contribute to certain forms of abnormal functioning (Nelson, 2006; Jackson et al., 2004). Women in Western society receive diagnoses of anxiety and depressive disorders at least twice as often as men (McSweeney, 2004). Similarly, African Americans experience unusually high rates of anxiety disorders (Blazer et al., 1991). Hispanic Americans, particularly young men, have higher rates of alcoholism than members of most other ethnic groups (Helzer, Burnman, & McEvoy, 1991). And Native Americans display exceptionally high alcoholism and suicide rates (Beals et al., 2005). Although many factors may combine to produce these differences, racial and sexual prejudice and the problems they pose may contribute to abnormal patterns of tension, unhappiness, low self-esteem, and escape (Nelson, 2006; Winston, 2004).

Of course, significant cultural differences occur not only *within* countries but *across* countries, and multicultural researchers have examined these differences as well. Indeed, they have learned that some of the disorders you will be reading about in this textbook—anorexia nervosa, agoraphobia, borderline personality disorder—are much less common in non–Western countries (Anderson-Fye, 2004; Cooper, 2001; Paris, 2001). It may be that key Western values—such as the importance of a young and thin appearance, emphasis on high mobility, and endorsement of emotional expression—help set the stage for such disorders.

Multicultural Treatments

Studies have found that members of ethnic and racial minority groups tend to show less improvement in clinical treatment than members of majority groups (Ward, 2007; Comas-Diaz, 2006; Mark et al., 2003; Lee & Sue, 2001). Similarly, studies conducted throughout the world have found that minority clients make less use of mental health services than members of majority groups (Wang et al., 2006; Stevens et al., 2005). In some cases, economic factors, cultural beliefs, language barriers, or lack of information about available services may prevent minority individuals from seeking help; in other cases, such persons may not trust the establishment, relying instead on traditional remedies that are available in their immediate social environment.

Research also indicates that members of minority groups stop therapy sooner than persons from majority groups. In the United States, African Americans, Native Americans, Asian Americans, and Hispanic Americans all have higher therapy dropout rates than white Americans (Lee & Sue, 2001). Members of these groups may stop treatment because they cannot afford to continue, do not feel they are benefiting from treatment, or have trouble developing a strong rapport with a therapist of a different ethnic or racial group (Richman et al., 2007; Gonzalez & Acevedo, 2006; Stevens et al., 2005).

How can clinicians be more helpful to people from minority cultures? A number of studies suggest that two features of treatment can increase a therapist's effectiveness with minority clients: (1) greater sensitivity to cultural issues and (2) inclusion of cultural morals and models in treatment, especially in therapies for children and adolescents (Castro, Holm-Denoma, & Buckner, 2007; Lee & Sue, 2001). Given such findings, some clinicians have developed **culture-sensitive therapies,** approaches that seek to address the unique issues faced by members of cultural minority groups (Carten, 2006; Comas-Diaz, 2006; Mio et al., 2006). Therapies geared to the pressures of being female in Western society, called **gender-sensitive,** or **feminist, therapies,** follow similar principles.

Culture-sensitive approaches typically include the following elements (Prochaska & Norcross, 2007; Wyatt & Parham, 2007):

1. Special cultural instruction of therapists in their graduate training programs
2. Awareness by the therapist of a client's cultural values
3. Awareness by the therapist of the stress, prejudices, and stereotypes that clients are exposed to as a consequence of their minority group status
4. Awareness by therapists of the hardships faced by the children of immigrants
5. Helping clients recognize the impact of both their own culture and the dominant culture on their self-views and behaviors
6. Helping clients identify and express suppressed anger and pain
7. Helping clients achieve a bicultural balance that feels right for them
8. Helping clients raise their self-esteem—a sense of self-worth that has often been damaged by generations of negative messages

Assessing the Sociocultural Model

The family-social and multicultural perspectives have added greatly to the understanding and treatment of abnormal functioning. Today most clinicians take family, cultural, social, and societal issues into account, factors that were overlooked just 35 years ago. In addition, clinicians have become more aware of the impact of clinical and social roles. Finally, the treatment formats offered by the sociocultural model sometimes succeed where traditional approaches have failed.

At the same time, the sociocultural model, like the biological and psychological models, has certain problems. To begin with, sociocultural research findings are often difficult to interpret. Indeed, research may reveal a relationship between certain family or cultural factors and a particular disorder yet fail to establish that they are its *cause*. Studies show a link between family conflict and schizophrenia, for example, but that finding does not necessarily mean that family dysfunction causes schizophrenia. It is equally possible that family functioning is disrupted by the tension and conflict created by the psychotic behavior of a family member.

Another limitation of the sociocultural model is its inability to predict abnormality in specific individuals. If, for example, social conditions such as prejudice and discrimination are key causes of anxiety and depression, why do only some of the people

•**multicultural perspective**•The view that each culture within a larger society has a particular set of values and beliefs, as well as special external pressures, that help account for the behavior and functioning of its members. Also called *culturally diverse perspective*.

•**culture-sensitive therapies**• Approaches that seek to address the unique issues faced by members of minority groups.

•**gender-sensitive therapies**• Approaches geared to the pressures of being a woman in Western society. Also called *feminist therapies*.

BETWEEN THE LINES

Couple Trouble

Annual marriage rate in the United States: 51 per 1,000 unmarried women ‹‹

Annual divorce rate: 20 per 1,000 married women ‹‹

Almost 40 percent of persons wish they could ask their spouse for more affection ‹‹

Almost 40 percent of persons report having kept a secret from their spouse ‹‹

Length of silent treatment after a spousal fight: one week (3 percent), one day (21 percent), one hour (31 percent), five minutes (19 percent) ‹‹

(Kanner, 2005, 1998, 1995; Henry & Miller, 2004; Yin, 2002)

table: 3-3

Comparing the Models

	Biological	Psychodynamic	Behavioral	Cognitive	Humanistic	Existential	Family-Social	Multicultural
Cause of dysfunction	Biological malfunction	Underlying conflicts	Maladaptive learning	Maladaptive thinking	Self-deceit	Avoidance of responsibility	Family or social stress	External pressures or cultural conflicts
Research support	Strong	Modest	Strong	Strong	Weak	Weak	Moderate	Moderate
Consumer designation	Patient	Patient	Client	Client	Patient or client	Patient or client	Client	Client
Therapist role	Doctor	Interpreter	Teacher	Persuader	Observer	Collaborator	Family/social facilitator	Cultural advocate/teacher
Key therapist technique	Biological intervention	Free association and interpretation	Conditioning	Reasoning	Reflection	Varied	Family/social intervention	Culture-sensitive intervention
Therapy goal	Biological repair	Broad psychological change	Functional behaviors	Adaptive thinking	Self-actualization	Authentic life	Effective family or social system	Cultural awareness and comfort

subjected to such forces experience psychological disorders? Are still other factors necessary for the development of the disorders?

Given these limitations, most clinicians view the family-social and multicultural explanations as operating in conjunction with the biological or psychological explanations. They agree that family, social, and cultural factors may create a climate favorable to the development of certain disorders. They believe, however, that biological or psychological conditions or both must also be present in order for the disorders to evolve.

PUTTING IT... together

Integration of the Models

Today's leading models vary widely (see Table 3-3). They look at behavior differently, begin with different assumptions, arrive at different conclusions, and apply different treatments. Yet none of the models has proved consistently superior. Each helps us appreciate a key aspect of human functioning, and each has important strengths as well as serious limitations.

With all their differences, the conclusions and techniques of the various models are often compatible. Certainly our understanding and treatment of abnormal behavior are more complete if we appreciate the biological, psychological, and sociocultural aspects of a person's problem rather than only one of them. Not surprisingly, then, a growing number of clinicians are formulating explanations of abnormal behavior that consider more than one kind of cause at a time. These explanations, sometimes called **biopsychosocial theories,** state that abnormality results from the interaction of genetic, biological, developmental, emotional, behavioral, cognitive, social, cultural, and societal influences (Gatchel et al., 2007; Gatchel, 2005; Suls & Rothman, 2004). If so, the task facing researchers and clinicians is to identify the relative importance of each factor and learn how the factors work together to produce abnormal functioning. A case of depression, for example, might best be explained by pointing collectively

•biopsychosocial theories•
Explanations that attribute the cause of abnormality to an interaction of genetic, biological, developmental, emotional, behavioral, cognitive, social, and societal influences.

to an individual's inheritance of unfavorable genes, traumatic losses during childhood, negative ways of thinking, and social isolation.

Some biopsychosocial theorists favor a *diathesis-stress* explanation of how the various factors work together to cause abnormal functioning ("diathesis" means a vulnerability or a predisposed tendency). According to this theory, people must first have a biological, psychological, or sociocultural predisposition to develop a disorder and must then be subjected to episodes of severe stress. In a case of depression, for example, we might find that unfavorable genes and related biochemical abnormalities predispose the individual to develop the disorder, while the loss of a loved one actually triggers its onset.

Other biopsychosocial theorists favor a *reciprocal effects* explanation of abnormal functioning. They believe that some key factors help produce abnormal functioning by influencing other key factors—that is, by increasing the likelihood or intensity of the other factors (Saudino et al., 2004, 1997; Kendler et al., 1995). Say, for example, a man inherits a genetic tendency to be timid and awkward. Because of his timidity and awkwardness, this individual may accept unpleasant partners in his life more readily than most other people would, thus increasing his chances of experiencing stressful relationships, breakups, or periods of isolation in his life—each a factor conducive to depression. In addition, his experiences of interpersonal stress may lower his serotonin activity, another factor conducive to depression. In short, by profoundly affecting each other, a variety of relevant factors may collectively drive an individual toward depression.

In a similar quest for integration, many therapists are now combining treatment techniques from several models. In fact, 29 percent of today's clinical psychologists, 34 percent of social workers, and 53 percent of psychiatrists describe their approach as "eclectic" or "integrative" (Prochaska & Norcross, 2007). Studies confirm that clinical problems often respond better to combined approaches than to any one therapy alone. For example, as you will see, drug therapy combined with cognitive therapy is sometimes the most effective treatment for depression (TADS, 2005, 2004).

Given the recent rise in biopsychosocial theories and combination treatments, the examination of abnormal behavior throughout this book will take two directions. As different disorders are presented, we will look at how today's models explain each disorder, how clinicians who endorse each model treat people with the disorder, and how well these explanations and treatments are supported by research. Just as important, however, we will also be observing how the explanations and treatments may build upon and strengthen each other, and we will examine current efforts toward integration of the models.

Community mental health: Argentine style
Staff members and patients from Buenos Aires's Neuropsychiatric Hospital set up a laptop and begin broadcasting on the popular radio station Radio La Colifata (*colifa* is slang for "crazy one"). The station was started 15 years ago to help patients pursue therapeutic activities and reach out to the community.

«‹‹[SUMMING UP]›››

○ **Models of Psychological Abnormality** Scientists and clinicians use *models,* or *paradigms,* to understand and treat abnormal behavior. The principles and techniques of treatment used by clinical practitioners correspond to their preferred models. *pp. 49–50*

○ **The Biological Model** Biological theorists look at the biological processes of human functioning to explain abnormal behavior, pointing to *anatomical* or

continued

biochemical problems in the brain and body. Such abnormalities are sometimes the result of *genetic inheritance of abnormalities, normal evolution,* or *viral infections.* Biological therapists use physical and chemical methods to help people overcome their psychological problems. The leading ones are *drug therapy, electroconvulsive therapy,* and, on rare occasions, *psychosurgery. pp. 51–56*

○ **The Psychodynamic Model** Psychodynamic theorists believe that an individual's behavior, whether normal or abnormal, is determined by underlying psychological forces. They consider psychological conflicts to be rooted in early parent–child relationships and traumatic experiences. The psychodynamic model was formulated by Sigmund Freud, who said that three dynamic forces—the *id, ego,* and *superego*—interact to produce thought, feeling, and behavior. Other psychodynamic theories are *ego theory, self theory,* and *object relations theory.* Psychodynamic therapists help people uncover past traumas and the inner conflicts that have resulted from them. They use a number of techniques, including *free association* and interpretations of psychological phenomena such as *resistance, transference,* and *dreams.* The leading contemporary psychodynamic approaches include short-term psychodynamic therapies and relational psychoanalytic therapy. *pp. 56–63*

○ **The Behavioral Model** Behaviorists concentrate on *behaviors* and propose that they develop in accordance with the *principles of learning.* These theorists hold that three types of conditioning—*classical conditioning, operant conditioning,* and *modeling*—account for all behavior, whether normal or dysfunctional. The goal of the behavioral therapies is to identify the client's problematic behaviors and replace them with more appropriate ones, using techniques based on one or more of the principles of learning. The classical conditioning approach of *systematic desensitization,* for example, has been effective in treating phobias. *pp. 63–66*

○ **The Cognitive Model** According to the cognitive model, we must understand human thought to understand human behavior. When people display abnormal patterns of functioning, cognitive theorists point to cognitive problems, such as *maladaptive assumptions* and *illogical thinking processes.* Cognitive therapists try to help people recognize and change their faulty ideas and thinking processes. Among the most widely used cognitive treatments is Beck's *cognitive therapy. pp. 67–69*

○ **The Humanistic-Existential Model** The humanistic-existential model focuses on the human need to confront philosophical issues such as self-awareness, values, meaning, and choice successfully to be satisfied in life.

Humanists believe that people are driven to *self-actualize.* When this drive is interfered with, abnormal behavior may result. One group of humanistic therapists, *client-centered therapists,* try to create a very supportive therapy climate in which people can look at themselves honestly and acceptingly, thus opening the door to self-actualization. Another group, *gestalt therapists,* use more active techniques to help people recognize and accept their needs. Recently the role of *religion* as an important factor in mental health and in psychotherapy has caught the attention of researchers and clinicians.

According to existentialists, abnormal behavior results from hiding from life's responsibilities. Existential therapists encourage people to accept *responsibility* for their lives, to recognize their *freedom to choose* a different course, and to choose to live with greater meaning. *pp. 69–75*

○ **The Sociocultural Model** The *family-social* perspective looks outward to three kinds of factors. Some proponents of this perspective focus on *social labels* and *roles;* they hold that society calls certain people "mentally ill" and that those individuals in turn follow the role implied by such a label. Others focus on *social networks and supports,* believing that isolation, poor social supports, and the like may contribute to psychological difficulties. Still others emphasize the *family system,* believing that a family's structure or communication patterns may force members to behave in abnormal ways. Practitioners from the family–social model may practice *group, family,* or *couple therapy* or *community treatment.*

The *multicultural* perspective holds that an individual's behavior, whether normal or abnormal, is best understood when examined in the light of his or her unique cultural context, including the values of that culture and the special external pressures faced by members of that culture. Practitioners of this model may practice *culture-sensitive therapies,* approaches that seek to address the unique issues faced by members of cultural minority groups. *pp. 75–84*

CRITICAL THOUGHTS

1. What might the enormous popularity of psychotropic drugs suggest about the needs and coping styles of individuals today and about problem solving in our technological society? *pp. 54–55*

2. In *Paradise Lost* Milton wrote, "The mind . . . can make a heaven of hell, a hell of heaven." Which model(s) of abnormal functioning would agree with this statement? *pp. 56–62, 67–75*

3. Freud's influence on Western society has extended beyond the clinical realm. Can you think of ways that his theory has affected literature, movies, child-rearing, philosophy, and education? *pp. 56–62*

4. Twenty-one percent of Americans say they are regularly "bored out of their mind" (Kanner, 2005, 1999). How might humanistic-existential theorists explain the phenomenon of severe boredom and such reactions to it? *pp. 69–75*

5. Why might positive religious beliefs be linked to mental health? Why have so many clinicians been suspicious of religious beliefs for so long? *p. 73*

6. In *Anna Karenina* writer Leo Tolstoy wrote, "All happy families resemble one another; every unhappy family is unhappy in its own fashion." Would family systems theorists agree with Tolstoy? *pp. 76–77, 79–80*

7. Group therapy was originally started to help with the overload of clients seeking treatment. However, it soon became clear that group sessions may offer special therapeutic features for clients. What might some of those features be? *pp. 77–79*

cyberstudy

SEARCH

Search the *Abnormal Psychology* Video Tool Kit
www.worthpublishers.com/apvtk

▲ Chapter 3 Video Cases
Separated at Birth: Nature versus Nurture
Bandura's Bobo Doll: Is Aggressive Behavior Learned?
The City of Gheel: Community Mental Health in Action
▲ Video case discussions, study guides, and questions

Log on to the Comer Web Page
www.worthpublishers.com/comer

▲ Chapter 3 outline, learning objectives, research exercises, study tools, and practice test questions
▲ Additional Chapter 3 case studies, Web links, and FAQs

CLINICAL ASSESSMENT, DIAGNOSIS, AND TREATMENT

A ngela Savanti was 22 years old, lived at home with her mother, and was employed as a secretary in a large insurance company. She . . . had had passing periods of "the blues" before, but her present feelings of despondency were of much greater proportion. She was troubled by a severe depression and frequent crying spells, which had not lessened over the past two months. Angela found it hard to concentrate on her job, had great difficulty falling asleep at night, and had a poor appetite. . . . Her depression had begun after she and her boyfriend Jerry broke up two months previously.

(Leon, 1984, p. 109)

Her feelings of despondency led Angela Savanti to make an appointment with a therapist at a local counseling center. The first step the clinician took was to learn as much as possible about Angela and her disturbance. Who is she, what is her life like, and what precisely are her symptoms? The answers might help to reveal the causes and probable course of her present dysfunction and suggest what kinds of strategies would be most likely to help her. Treatment could then be tailored to Angela's needs and particular pattern of abnormal functioning.

In Chapters 2 and 3 you read about how researchers in abnormal psychology build a *nomothetic,* or *general,* understanding of abnormal functioning. Clinical practitioners apply this general information in their work, but their main focus when faced with a new client is to gather **idiographic,** or individual, information about him or her (Bornstein, 2007). To help a particular client overcome his or her problems, a practitioner must have the fullest possible understanding of that person and must know the circumstances under which the problems arose. Only after thoroughly examining the person can the therapist effectively apply relevant nomothetic information. Clinicians use the procedures of *assessment* and *diagnosis* to gather individual information about a client. Then they are in a position to apply *treatment.*

⚙Clinical Assessment: How and Why Does the Client Behave Abnormally?

Assessment is simply the collecting of relevant information in an effort to reach a conclusion. It goes on in every realm of life. We make assessments when we decide what cereal to buy or which presidential candidate to vote for. College admissions officers, who have to select the "best" of the students applying to their college, depend on academic records, recommendations, achievement test scores, interviews, and application forms to help them decide (Sackett, Borneman, & Connelly, 2008). Employers, who have to predict which applicants are most likely to be effective workers, collect information from résumés, interviews, references, and perhaps on-the-job observations.

Clinical assessment is used to determine how and why a person is behaving abnormally and how that person may be helped. It also enables clinicians to evaluate people's progress after they have been in treatment for a while and decide whether the treatment should be changed. The specific tools that are used

•idiographic understanding• An understanding of the behavior of a particular individual.

•assessment• The process of collecting and interpreting relevant information about a client or research participant.

to do an assessment depend on the clinician's theoretical orientation. Psychodynamic clinicians, for example, use methods that assess a client's personality and probe for any unconscious conflicts he or she may be experiencing. This kind of assessment, called a *personality assessment,* enables them to piece together a clinical picture in accordance with the principles of their model. Behavioral and cognitive clinicians are more likely to use assessment methods that reveal specific dysfunctional behaviors and cognitions. The goal of this kind of assessment, called a *behavioral assessment,* is to produce a *functional analysis* of the person's behaviors—an analysis of how the behaviors are learned and reinforced (Kenny et al., 2008; Berg et al., 2007).

The hundreds of clinical assessment techniques and tools that have been developed fall into three categories: *clinical interviews, tests,* and *observations.* To be useful, these tools must be *standardized* and must have clear *reliability* and *validity.*

Characteristics of Assessment Tools

All clinicians must follow the same procedures when they use a particular technique of assessment. To **standardize** a technique is to set up common steps to be followed whenever it is administered. Similarly, clinicians must standardize the way they interpret the results of an assessment tool in order to be able to understand what a particular score means. They may standardize the scores of a test, for example, by first administering it to a group of research participants whose performance will then serve as a common standard, or norm, against which later individual scores can be measured. The group that initially takes the test is called the *standardization sample.* This sample must be typical of the larger population for whom the test is intended. If an aggressiveness test meant for the public at large were standardized on a group of marines, for example, the resulting "norm" might turn out to be misleadingly high.

Reliability refers to the *consistency* of assessment measures. A good assessment tool will always yield the same results in the same situation (Weiner & Greene, 2008; Allison et al., 2007). An assessment tool has high *test–retest reliability,* one kind of reliability, if it yields the same results every time it is given to the same people. If a woman's responses on a particular test indicate that she is generally a heavy drinker, the test should produce the same result when she takes it again a week later. To measure test–retest reliability, participants are tested on two occasions and the two scores are correlated. The higher the correlation, the greater the test's reliability (see Chapter 2).

An assessment tool shows high *interrater* (or *interjudge*) *reliability,* another kind of reliability, if different judges independently agree on how to score and interpret it. True–false and multiple-choice tests yield consistent scores no matter who evaluates them, but other tests require that the evaluator make a judgment. Consider a test that requires the person to draw a copy of a picture, which a judge then rates for accuracy. Different judges may give different ratings to the same drawing.

Finally, an assessment tool must have **validity:** it must *accurately* measure what it is supposed to measure (Weiner & Greene, 2008; Vieta & Phillips, 2007). Suppose a weight scale reads 12 pounds every time a 10-pound bag of sugar is placed on it. Although the scale is reliable because its readings are consistent, those readings are not valid, or accurate.

A given assessment tool may appear to be valid simply because it makes sense and seems reasonable. However, this sort of validity, called *face validity,* does not by itself mean that the instrument is trustworthy. A test for depression, for example, might include questions about how often a person cries. Because it makes sense that depressed people would cry, these test questions have face validity. It turns out, however, that many people cry a great deal for reasons other than depression, and some extremely depressed people fail to cry at all. Thus an assessment tool should not be used unless it meets more exacting criteria of validity, such as high *predictive* or *concurrent validity* (Sackett et al., 2008).

Unreliable assessments
On *American Idol,* the popular TV show, the performances of competing singers are assessed each week by judges Randy Jackson (left), Paula Abdul (center), and Simon Cowell. Typically, Cowell's assessment is negative (even insulting at times), Abdul's is positive, and Jackson's falls somewhere in between. Such low interrater reliability may reflect evaluator bias or defects in the scoring procedure.

Predictive validity is a tool's ability to predict future characteristics or behavior. Let's say that a test has been developed to identify elementary school children who are likely to take up cigarette smoking in junior high school. The test gathers information about the children's parents—their personal characteristics, smoking habits, and attitudes toward smoking—and on that basis identifies high-risk children. To establish the test's predictive validity, investigators could administer it to a group of elementary school students, wait until they were in junior high school, and then check to see which children actually did become smokers.

Concurrent validity is the degree to which the measures gathered from one tool agree with the measures gathered from other assessment techniques. Participants' scores on a new test designed to measure anxiety, for example, should correlate highly with their scores on other anxiety tests or with their behavior during clinical interviews.

Before any assessment technique can be fully useful, it must meet the requirements of standardization, reliability, and validity. No matter how insightful or clever a technique may be, clinicians cannot profitably use its results if they are uninterpretable, inconsistent, or inaccurate. Unfortunately, more than a few clinical assessment tools fall short, suggesting that at least some clinical assessments, too, miss their mark.

Clinical Interviews

Most of us feel instinctively that the best way to get to know people is to meet with them face to face. Under these circumstances, we can see them react to what we do and say, observe as well as listen as they answer, watch them observing us, and generally get a sense of who they are. A *clinical interview* is just such a face-to-face encounter (Sommers-Flanagan & Sommers-Flanagan, 2007, 2003). If during a clinical interview a man looks as happy as can be while describing his sadness over the recent death of his mother, the clinician may suspect that the man actually has conflicting emotions about this loss. Almost all practitioners use interviews as part of the assessment process.

Conducting the Interview
The interview is often the first contact between client and clinician. Clinicians use it to collect detailed information about the person's problems and feelings, lifestyle and relationships, and other personal history. They may also ask about the person's expectations of therapy and motives for seeking it. The clinician who worked with Angela Savanti began with a face-to-face interview:

Angela was dressed neatly when she appeared for her first interview. She was attractive, but her eyes were puffy and ringed with dark circles. She answered questions and related information about her life history in a slow, flat tone of voice, which had an impersonal quality to it. She sat stiffly in her chair. . . .

The client stated that the time period just before she and her boyfriend terminated their relationship had been one of extreme emotional turmoil. She was not sure whether she wanted to marry Jerry, and he began to demand that she decide either one way or the other. Mrs. Savanti [Angela's mother] did not seem to like Jerry and was very cold and aloof whenever he came to the house. Angela felt caught in the middle and unable to make a decision about her future. After several confrontations with Jerry over whether she would marry him or not, he told her he felt that she would never decide, so he was not going to see her anymore. . . .

Angela stated that her childhood was a very unhappy period. Her father was seldom home, and when he was present, her parents fought constantly. . . .

Angela recalled feeling very guilty when Mr. Savanti left. . . . She revealed that whenever she thought of her father, she always felt that she had been responsible in some way for his leaving the family. . . .

AP Photo/NASA, Orange County Sheriff

Failed assessment? U.S. astronaut Lisa Marie Nowak is shown at left in 2005 and again at right in a 2007 police photo after driving nonstop from Houston to Orlando to accost a woman whom she believed was romantically involved with a fellow astronaut. Although the National Aeronautics and Space Administration (NASA) subjects astronauts to extensive psychological testing, it was caught off guard by Nowak's psychological deterioration and bizarre behavior, leading the space agency to thoroughly reevaluate its psychological assessment tools and procedures.

•**standardization**•The process in which a test is administered to a large group of people whose performance then serves as a standard or norm against which any individual's score can be measured.

•**reliability**•A measure of the consistency of test or research results.

•**validity**•The accuracy of a test's or study's results; that is, the extent to which the test or study actually measures or shows what it claims.

•mental status exam• A set of interview questions and observations designed to reveal the degree and nature of a client's abnormal functioning.

•test• A device for gathering information about a few aspects of a person's psychological functioning from which broader information about the person can be inferred.

•projective test• A test consisting of ambiguous material that people interpret or respond to.

Angela described her mother as the "long-suffering type" who said that she had sacrificed her life to make her children happy, and the only thing she ever got in return was grief and unhappiness. . . . When Angela and [her sister] began dating, Mrs. Savanti . . . would make disparaging remarks about the boys they had been with and about men in general. . . .

Angela revealed that she had often been troubled with depressed moods. During high school, if she got a lower grade in a subject than she had expected, her initial response was one of anger, followed by depression. She began to think that she was not smart enough to get good grades, and she blamed herself for studying too little. Angela also became despondent when she got into an argument with her mother or felt that she was being taken advantage of at work. . . .

The intensity and duration of the [mood change] that she experienced when she broke up with Jerry were much more severe. She was not sure why she was so depressed, but she began to feel it was an effort to walk around and go out to work. Talking with others became difficult. Angela found it hard to concentrate, and she began to forget things she was supposed to do. . . . She preferred to lie in bed rather than be with anyone, and she often cried when alone.

(Leon, 1984, pp. 110–115)

Beyond gathering basic background data of this kind, clinical interviewers give special attention to whatever topics they consider most important (Wright & Truax, 2008). Psychodynamic interviewers try to learn about the person's needs and memories of past events and relationships. Behavioral interviewers try to pinpoint the precise nature of the abnormal responses, including information about the stimuli that trigger such responses and their consequences. Cognitive interviewers try to discover assumptions and interpretations that influence the person. Humanistic clinicians ask about the person's self-evaluation, self-concept, and values. Biological clinicians gather a family history from the individual to help uncover inherited tendencies and also look more directly for signs of biochemical or brain dysfunction. And sociocultural interviewers ask about the family, social, and cultural environments.

Interviews can be either unstructured or structured (O'Brien & Tabaczynski, 2007; Rabinowitz et al., 2007). In an *unstructured interview,* the clinician asks open-ended questions, perhaps as simple as "Would you tell me about yourself?" The lack of structure allows the interviewer to follow interesting leads and explore relevant topics that could not be anticipated before the interview.

In a *structured interview,* clinicians ask prepared questions. Sometimes they use a published *interview schedule*—a standard set of questions designed for all interviews. Many structured interviews include a **mental status exam,** a set of questions and observations that systematically evaluate the client's awareness, orientation with regard to time and place, attention span, memory, judgment and insight, thought content and processes, mood, and appearance (Palmer, Fiorito, & Tagliareni, 2007). A structured format ensures that clinicians will cover the same kinds of important issues in all of their interviews and enables them to compare the responses of different individuals.

Although most clinical interviews have both unstructured and structured portions, many clinicians favor one kind over the other. Unstructured interviews typically appeal to psychodynamic and humanistic clinicians, while structured formats are widely used by behavioral and cognitive clinicians, who need to pinpoint behaviors, attitudes, or thinking processes that may underlie abnormal behavior (Hersen, 2004; Thienemann, 2004).

"So, Mr. Fenton, . . . Let's begin with your mother."

What Are the Limitations of Clinical Interviews?

Although interviews often produce valuable information about people, there are limits to what they can accomplish (Hersen & Thomas, 2007). One problem is that they sometimes lack validity, or accuracy. Individuals may intentionally mislead in order to present themselves in a positive light or to avoid discussing embarrassing topics. Or people may be unable to give an accurate report in their interviews. Individuals who suffer from depression, for example, take a pessimistic view of themselves and may describe themselves as poor workers or inadequate parents when that isn't the case at all.

Interviewers too may make mistakes in judgments that slant the information they gather. They usually rely too heavily on first impressions, for example, and give too much weight to unfavorable information about a client (Wu & Shi, 2005; Meehl, 1996, 1960). Interviewer biases, including gender, race, and age biases, may also influence the interviewers' interpretations of what a client says (Ungar et al., 2006; McFarland et al., 2004).

Interviews, particularly unstructured ones, may also lack reliability (Wood et al., 2002; Wiens et al., 2001). People respond differently to different interviewers, providing, for example, less information to a cold interviewer than to a warm and supportive one (Quas et al., 2007; Black, 2005). Similarly, a clinician's race, sex, age, and appearance may influence a client's responses (Springman, Wherry, & Notaro, 2006; Caplan & Cosgrove, 2004).

Because different clinicians can obtain different answers and draw different conclusions, even when they ask the same questions of the same person, some researchers believe that interviewing should be discarded as a tool of clinical assessment. As you'll see, however, the two other kinds of clinical assessment methods also have serious limitations.

Clinical Tests

Tests are devices for gathering information about a few aspects of a person's psychological functioning, from which broader information about the person can be inferred (Gregory, 2004). On the surface, it may look easy to design an effective test. Every month, magazines and newspapers present new tests that supposedly tell us about our personalities, our relationships, our sex lives, our reactions to stress, or our ability to succeed. Such tests might sound convincing, but most of them lack reliability, validity, and standardization. That is, they do not yield consistent, accurate information or say anything meaningful about where we stand in comparison with others.

More than 500 clinical tests are currently in use throughout the United States. Clinicians use six kinds most often: projective tests, personality inventories, response inventories, psychophysiological tests, neurological and neuropsychological tests, and intelligence tests.

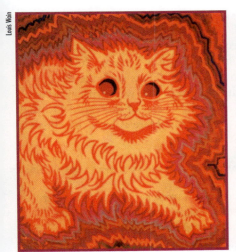

Louis Wain

The art of assessment
Clinicians often view works of art as informal projective tests in which artists reveal their conflicts and mental stability. The sometimes bizarre cat portraits of early-twentieth-century artist Louis Wain, for example, have been interpreted as reflections of the psychosis with which he struggled for many years. Others believe such interpretations are incorrect, however, and note that the decorative patterns in some of his later paintings were actually based on textile designs.

Figure 4-1
An inkblot similar to those used in the Rorschach

Projective Tests **Projective tests** require that clients interpret vague stimuli, such as inkblots or ambiguous pictures, or follow open-ended instructions such as "Draw a person." Theoretically, when clues and instructions are so vague, people will "project" aspects of their personality into the task. Projective tests are used primarily by psychodynamic clinicians to help assess the unconscious drives and conflicts they believe to be at the root of abnormal functioning (Hojnoski et al., 2006; Heydebrand & Wetzel, 2005). The most widely used projective tests are the *Rorschach test,* the *Thematic Apperception Test, sentence-completion tests,* and *drawings.*

RORSCHACH TEST In 1911 Hermann Rorschach, a Swiss psychiatrist, experimented with the use of inkblots in his clinical work. He made thousands of blots by dropping ink on paper and then folding the paper in half to create a symmetrical but wholly accidental design, such as the one shown in Figure 4-1. Rorschach found that everyone saw images in these blots. In addition, the images a viewer saw seemed to correspond in important ways with his or her psychological condition. People diagnosed with schizophrenia, for example, tended to see images that differed from those described by people suffering from depression.

Rorschach selected 10 inkblots and published them in 1921 with instructions for their use in assessment. This set was called the *Rorschach Psychodynamic Inkblot Test.* Rorschach died just eight months later, at the age of 37, but his work was continued by others, and his inkblots took their place among the most widely used projective tests of the twentieth century.

Clinicians administer the "Rorschach," as it is commonly called, by presenting one inkblot card at a time and asking respondents what they see, what the inkblot seems to be, or what it reminds them of. In the following exchange, a tense 32-year-old woman who complains of feeling unworthy and lacking in confidence responds to one Rorschach inkblot:

Subject: Oh, dear! My goodness! O.K. Just this [upper] part is a bug. Something like an ant—one of the social group which is a worker, trying to pull something. I think this is some kind of food for the rest of the ants. It's a bee because it has wings, a worker bee bringing up something edible for the rest of the clan. . . . Here is the bee, the mouth and the wings. I don't think bees eat leaves but it looks like a leaf or a piece of lettuce.
Clinician: What makes it look like a piece of lettuce?
Subject: Its shape and it has a vein up the middle. It is definitely a bee.

(Klopfer & Davidson, 1962, p. 164)

In the early years, Rorschach testers paid special attention to the themes and images that the inkblots evoked, called the *thematic content* (Weiner & Greene, 2008). Testers now also pay attention to the style of the responses: Do the clients view the design as a whole or see specific details? Do they focus on the blots or on the white spaces between them? Do they use or ignore the shadings and colors in several of the cards? Do they see human movement or animal movement in the designs? Here is how the clinician interpreted the bug responses of the woman just quoted:

The bee may reflect the image she has of herself as a hard worker (a fact noted by her supervisor). In addition, the "bee bringing up something edible for the rest of the clan" suggests that she feels an overwhelming sense of responsibility toward others.

(Klopfer & Davidson, 1962, pp. 182–183)

BETWEEN THE LINES

Believe It or Not

By a strange coincidence, Hermann Rorschach's young schoolmates gave him the nickname Klex, a variant of the German *Klecks,* which means "inkblot" (Schwartz, 1993). ‹‹

THEMATIC APPERCEPTION TEST The Thematic Apperception Test (TAT) is a pictorial projective test (Masling, 2004; Morgan & Murray, 1935). People who take the TAT are commonly shown 30 black-and-white pictures of individuals in vague situations and are asked to make up a dramatic story about each card. They must tell what is happening in the picture, what led up to it, what the characters are feeling and thinking, and what the outcome of the situation will be.

Clinicians who use the TAT believe that people always identify with one of the characters on each card, called the *hero*. The stories are thought to reflect the individuals' own circumstances, needs, emotions, and sense of reality and fantasy. For example, a female client seems to be revealing her own feelings in this story about the TAT picture shown in Figure 4-2, one of the few TAT pictures permitted for display in textbooks:

This is a woman who has been quite troubled by memories of a mother she was resentful toward. She has feelings of sorrow for the way she treated her mother, her memories of her mother plague her. These feelings seem to be increasing as she grows older and sees her children treating her the same way that she treated her mother.

(Aiken, 1985, p. 372)

SENTENCE-COMPLETION TEST The sentence-completion test, first developed in the 1920s (Payne, 1928), asks people to complete a series of unfinished sentences, such as "I wish . . ." or "My father . . ." The test is considered a good springboard for discussion and a quick and easy way to pinpoint topics to explore.

DRAWINGS On the assumption that a drawing tells us something about its creator, clinicians often ask clients to draw human figures and talk about them. Evaluations of these drawings are based on the details and shape of the drawing, solidity of the pencil line, location of the drawing on the paper, size of the figures, features of the figures, use of background, and comments made by the respondent during the drawing task. In the *Draw-a-Person (DAP) Test,* the most popular of the drawing tests, individuals are first told to draw "a person" and then are instructed to draw another person of the opposite sex.

Figure 4-2
A picture used in the Thematic Apperception Test

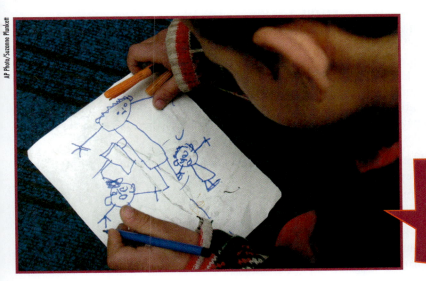

Drawing test
Drawing tests are commonly used to assess the functioning of children. A popular one is the Kinetic Family Drawing test, in which children draw their household members performing some activity ("kinetic" means "active").

"I'll say a normal word, then you say the first sick thing that pops into your head."

WHAT ARE THE MERITS OF PROJECTIVE TESTS? Until the 1950s, projective tests were the most common technique for assessing personality. In recent years, however, clinicians and researchers have relied on them largely to gain "supplementary" insights (Huprich, 2006; Westen et al., 1999). One reason for this shift is that practitioners who follow the newer models have less use for the tests than psychodynamic clinicians do. Even more important, the tests have not consistently demonstrated much reliability or validity (Wood et al., 2002).

In reliability studies, different clinicians have tended to score the same person's projective test quite differently. To address this problem and improve scoring consistency, several standardized procedures for administering and scoring the tests have been developed (Weiner & Greene, 2008). For example, the *Rorschach Comprehensive System* (Exner, 2007, 2003) is a highly regarded scoring system that has often yielded impressive reliability scores among clinicians who are trained in its use and application (Lis et al., 2007; SPA, 2005). However, only a minority of projective test administrators actually use such standardized procedures.

Research has also challenged the validity of projective tests. When clinicians try to describe a client's personality and feelings on the basis of responses to projective tests, their conclusions often fail to match the self-report of the client, the view of the psychotherapist, or the picture gathered from an extensive case history (Bornstein, 2007; Wood et al., 2002). Another validity problem is that projective tests are sometimes biased against minority ethnic groups (Costantino, Dana, & Malgady, 2007; Dana, 2005) (see Table 4–1). For example, people are supposed to identify with the characters in the Thematic Apperception Test (TAT) when they make up stories about them, yet no members of minority groups are in the TAT pictures. In response to this problem, some clinicians have developed other TAT-like tests with African American or Hispanic figures (Costantino et al., 2007).

Personality Inventories

An alternative way to collect information about individuals is to ask them to assess themselves. The **personality inventory** asks respondents a wide range of questions about their behavior, beliefs, and feelings. In the typical personality inventory, individuals indicate whether each of a long list of statements applies to them. Clinicians then use the responses to draw conclusions about the person's personality and psychological functioning.

By far the most widely used personality inventory is the *Minnesota Multiphasic Personality Inventory* (*MMPI*) (Weiner & Greene, 2008). Two adult versions are available—the original test, published in 1945, and the *MMPI-2,* a 1989 revision. A special version of the test for adolescents, the *MMPI-A,* is also used widely.

The MMPI consists of more than 500 self-statements, to be labeled "true," "false," or "cannot say." The statements describe physical concerns; mood; morale; attitudes toward religion, sex, and social activities; and psychological symptoms, such as fears or hallucinations. Altogether the statements make up 10 clinical scales, on each of which an individual can score from 0 to 120. When people score above 70 on a scale, their functioning on that scale is considered deviant. When the 10 scale scores are considered side by side, a pattern called a *profile* takes shape, indicating the person's general personality. The 10 scales on the MMPI measure the following:

Hypochondriasis (HS) Items showing abnormal concern with bodily functions ("I have chest pains several times a week.")

Depression (D) Items showing extreme pessimism and hopelessness ("I often feel hopeless about the future.")

Hysteria (Hy) Items suggesting that the person may use physical or mental symptoms as a way of unconsciously avoiding conflicts and responsibilities ("My heart frequently pounds so hard I can feel it.")

table: 4-1

Multicultural Hot Spots in Assessment and Diagnosis

Cultural Hot Spot	Effect on Assessment or Diagnosis
• Immigrant Client	**• Dominant-Culture Assessor**
Homeland culture may differ from current country's dominant culture	May misread culture-bound reactions as pathology
May have left homeland to escape war or oppression	May overlook client's vulnerability to posttraumatic stress
May have weak support systems in this country	May overlook client's heightened vulnerability to stressors
Lifestyle (wealth and occupation) in this country may fall below lifestyle in homeland	May overlook client's sense of loss and frustration
May refuse or be unable to learn dominant language	May misunderstand client's assessment responses, or may overlook or misdiagnose client's symptoms
• Ethnic-Minority Client	**• Dominant-Culture Assessor**
May reject or distrust members of dominant culture, including assessor	May experience little rapport with client, or may misinterpret client's distrust as pathology
May be uncomfortable with dominant culture's values (e.g., assertiveness, confrontation) and so find it difficult to apply clinician's recommendations	May view client as unmotivated
May manifest stress in culture-bound ways (e.g., somatic symptoms such as stomachaches)	May misinterpret symptom patterns
May hold cultural beliefs that seem strange to dominant culture (e.g., belief in communication with dead)	May misinterpret cultural responses as pathology (e.g., a delusion)
May be uncomfortable during assessment	May overlook and feed into client's discomfort
• Dominant-Culture Assessor	**• Ethnic-Minority Client**
May be unknowledgeable or biased about ethnic minority culture	Cultural differences may be pathologized, or symptoms may be overlooked
May nonverbally convey own discomfort to ethnic minority client	May become tense and anxious

Source: Dana, 2005, 2000; Westermeyer, 2004, 2001, 1993; López & Guarnaccia, 2005, 2000; Kirmayer, 2003, 2002, 2001; Sue & Sue, 2003; Tsai et al., 2001; Thakker & Ward, 1998.

Psychopathic deviate (PD) Items showing a repeated and gross disregard for social customs and an emotional shallowness ("My activities and interests are often criticized by others.")

Masculinity-femininity (Mf) Items that are thought to distinguish male and female respondents ("I like to arrange flowers.")

Paranoia (Pa) Items that show abnormal suspiciousness and delusions of grandeur or persecution ("There are evil people trying to influence my mind.")

Psychasthenia (Pt) Items that show obsessions, compulsions, abnormal fears, and guilt and indecisiveness ("I save nearly everything I buy, even after I have no use for it.")

Schizophrenia (Sc) Items that show bizarre or unusual thoughts or behavior, including extreme withdrawal, delusions, or hallucinations ("Things around me do not seem real.")

Hypomania (Ma) Items that show emotional excitement, overactivity, and flight of ideas ("At times I feel very 'high' or very 'low' for no apparent reason.")

Social introversion (Si) Items that show shyness, little interest in people, and insecurity ("I am easily embarrassed.")

•**personality inventory**•A test designed to measure broad personality characteristics, consisting of statements about behaviors, beliefs, and feelings that people evaluate as either characteristic or uncharacteristic of them.

In addition to the items that comprise these 10 scales, questions have been built into the MMPI to detect whether respondents are lying, defensive, or careless in their answers (Greene, 2006; Graham, 2006).

The MMPI-2, the newer version of the MMPI, contains 567 items—many identical to those in the original, some rewritten to reflect current language ("upset stomach," for instance, replaces "acid stomach"), and others that are new. This version was developed partly because the designers of the original MMPI had used a narrow standardization sample that did not represent the diverse populations that now mark Western societies. To better ensure the MMPI-2's validity and generalizability, the scale's designers sampled 2,600 persons who more properly represented various geographical regions; racial, cultural, and gender groups; occupations; educational levels; and treatment and nontreatment setttings. In turn, the MMPI-2 is a more valid indicator of personality and abnormal functioning than the original version (Butcher et al., 2007; Graham, 2006).

The MMPI and other personality inventories have several advantages over projective tests (Weiner & Greene, 2008; Wood et al., 2002). Because they are paper-and-pencil (or computerized) tests, they do not take much time to administer, and they are objectively scored. Like the MMPI, most personality inventories are standardized, so one person's scores can be compared to those of many others. Moreover, they often display greater test–retest reliability than projective tests. For example, people who take the MMPI a second time after a period of less than two weeks receive approximately the same scores (Graham, 2006).

Personality inventories also appear to have greater validity, or accuracy, than projective tests (Weiner & Greene, 2008; Lanyon, 2007). However, they can hardly be considered *highly* valid. When clinicians have used these tests alone, they have not typically been able to judge a respondent's personality accurately (Braxton et al., 2007; Johnson et al., 1996). One problem is that the personality traits that the tests seek to measure cannot be examined directly. How can we fully know a person's character, emotions, and needs from self-reports alone?

Another problem is that despite the more diverse sampling of standardization groups conducted by the MMPI-2 designers, this and other personality tests retain certain cultural limitations. In particular, they often fail to allow for cultural differences in people's responses (Chylinski & Wright, 1967; Dana, 2005). Responses indicative of a psychological disorder in one culture may be normal responses in another (Butcher et al., 2007). In Puerto Rico, for example, where it is common to practice spiritualism, it would be normal to answer "true" to the MMPI item "Evil spirits possess me at times." In other populations, that response could indicate psychopathology (Rogler, Malgady, & Rodriguez, 1989).

Despite their limited validity, personality inventories continue to be popular (Weiner & Greene, 2008; Butcher et al., 2007). Research indicates that they can help clinicians learn about people's personal styles and disorders as long as they are used in combination with interviews or other assessment tools.

Response Inventories Like personality inventories, **response inventories** ask people to provide detailed information about themselves, but these tests focus on one specific area of functioning. For example, one such test may measure affect (emotion), another social skills, and still another cognitive processes. Clinicians can use them to determine the role such factors play in a person's disorder.

Affective inventories measure the severity of such emotions as anxiety, depression, and anger (Osman et al., 2008; Wilson et al., 2004). In one of the most widely used affective inventories, the Beck Depression Inventory, shown in Table 4–2, people rate their level of sadness and its effect on their functioning. *Social skills inventories,* used particularly by behavioral and family-social clinicians, ask respondents to indicate how they would react in a variety of social situations (Wright & Truax, 2008; Deniz, Hamarta, & Ari, 2005). *Cognitive inventories* reveal a person's typical thoughts and assumptions and can uncover counterproductive patterns of thinking that may be at the root of abnormal functioning (Glass & Merluzzi, 2000). They are, not surprisingly, often used by cognitive therapists and researchers.

BETWEEN THE LINES

Popular Tests on the Web (Not Validated)

Accident Proneness Test
Are You an Optimist? Test
Mental Toughness (Hardiness) Test
Risk-Taking Test
Sensitivity to Criticism Test
Which Beatle Are You? Test
Arguing Style Test
Jealousy Test
Do You Believe in Yourself? Self-Esteem Test
Love Diagnostic Test
Relationship Satisfaction Test
Sensuality Test
Commitment Readiness Test
Romantic Personality Test
Roommate IQ Test
Maturity Test
How Do You Fight? Test
Lord of the Rings Personality Test
Eye Color Personality Test

table: 4-2

Sample Items from the Beck Depression Inventory

Items	Inventory	
Suicidal ideas	0	I don't have any thoughts of killing myself.
	1	I have thoughts of killing myself but I would not carry them out.
	2	I would like to kill myself.
	3	I would kill myself if I had the chance.
Work inhibition	0	I can work about as well as before.
	1	It takes extra effort to get started at doing something.
	2	I have to push myself very hard to do anything.
	3	I can't do any work at all.
Loss of libido	0	I have not noticed any recent change in my interest in sex.
	1	I am less interested in sex than I used to be.
	2	I am much less interested in sex now.
	3	I have lost interest in sex completely.

Because response inventories collect information directly from the clients themselves, they have strong face validity. Thus both the number of these tests and the number of clinicians who use them have increased steadily in the past 25 years (Black, 2005). At the same time, however, these inventories have major limitations. Unlike the personality inventories, they rarely include questions to indicate whether people are being careless or inaccurate in their accounts. Moreover, with the notable exceptions of the Beck Depression Inventory and a few others, response inventories generally have not been subjected to careful standardization, reliability, and validity procedures (Weis & Smenner, 2007; Kamphaus & Frick, 2002). Often they are improvised as a need arises, without being tested for accuracy and consistency.

Psychophysiological Tests Clinicians may also use **psychophysiological tests,** which measure physiological responses as possible indicators of psychological problems (Vershuere et al., 2006; Blanchard & Hickling, 2004). This practice began three decades ago after several studies suggested that states of anxiety are regularly accompanied by physiological changes, particularly increases in heart rate, body temperature, blood pressure, skin reactions (*galvanic skin response*), and muscle contraction. The measuring of physiological changes has since played a key role in the assessment of certain psychological disorders.

One psychophysiological test is the *polygraph,* popularly known as a *lie detector* (Verschuere et al., 2006; Vrij, 2004). Electrodes attached to various parts of a person's body detect changes in breathing, perspiration, and heart rate while the individual answers questions. The clinician observes these functions while the person answers "yes" to *control questions*—questions whose answers are known to be yes, such as "Are your parents both alive?" Then the clinician observes the same physiological functions while the person answers *test questions,* such as "Did you commit this robbery?" If breathing, perspiration, and heart rate suddenly increase, the person is suspected of lying.

Like other kinds of clinical tests, psychophysiological tests have their drawbacks. Many require expensive equipment that must be carefully tuned and maintained. In addition, psychophysiological measurements can be inaccurate and unreliable (see *A Closer Look* on the next page). The laboratory equipment itself—elaborate and sometimes frightening—

•**response inventories**•Tests designed to measure a person's responses in one specific area of functioning, such as affect, social skills, or cognitive processes.

•**psychophysiological test**•A test that measures physical responses (such as heart rate and muscle tension) as possible indicators of psychological problems.

The Truth, the Whole Truth, and Nothing but the Truth

In movies, criminals being grilled by the police reveal their guilt by sweating, shaking, cursing, or twitching. When they are hooked up to a *polygraph* (a lie detector), the needles bounce all over the paper. This image has been with us since World War I, when some clinicians developed the theory that people who are telling lies display systemic changes in their breathing, perspiration, and heart rate (Marston, 1917).

The danger of relying on polygraph tests is that, according to researchers, they do not work as well as we would like (Vrij, 2004; Raskin & Honts, 2002). The public did not pay much attention to this inconvenient fact until the mid-1980s, when the American Psychological Association officially reported that polygraphs were often inaccurate and the United States Congress voted to restrict their use in criminal prosecution and employment screening (Krapohl, 2002). Research clarifies that 8 out of 100 truths, on average, are called lies in polygraph testing (Raskin & Honts, 2002; MacLaren, 2001). Imagine, then, how many innocent people might be convicted of crimes if polygraph

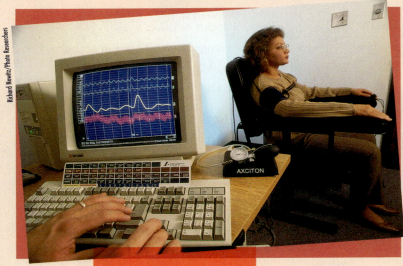

Polygraph, a test that lies?

findings were taken as valid evidence in criminal trials.

Given such findings, polygraphs are less trusted and less popular today than they once were. For example, few courts now admit results from such tests as evidence of criminal guilt (Daniels, 2002). Polygraph testing has by no means disappeared, however. The FBI uses it exten-

sively in counterintelligence work; parole boards and probation offices routinely use it to help evaluate sex offenders and to help decide whether to release convicted offenders; and in public-sector hiring (such as for police officers), the use of polygraph screening may actually be on the increase (Kokish et al., 2005; Krapohl, 2002).

•**neurological test**•A test that directly measures brain structure or activity.

•**neuroimaging techniques**•Neurological tests that provide images of brain structure or activity, such as CT scans, PET scans, and MRIs.

•**neuropsychological test**•A test that detects brain impairment by measuring a person's cognitive, perceptual, and motor performances.

may arouse a participant's nervous system and thus change his or her physical responses. Physiological responses may also change when they are measured repeatedly in a single session. Galvanic skin responses, for example, often decrease during repeated testing.

Neurological and Neuropsychological Tests Some problems in personality or behavior are caused primarily by damage to the brain or changes in brain activity. Head injury, brain tumors, brain malfunctions, alcoholism, infections, and other disorders can all cause such impairment. If a psychological dysfunction is to be treated effectively, it is important to know whether its primary cause is a physical abnormality in the brain.

A number of techniques may help pinpoint brain abnormalities. Some procedures, such as brain surgery, biopsy, and X ray, have been used for many years. More recently, scientists have developed a number of **neurological tests,** designed to measure brain structure and activity directly. One neurological test is the *electroencephalogram* (*EEG*), which records *brain waves,* the electrical activity taking place within the brain as a result of neurons firing. In this procedure, electrodes placed on the scalp transmit brain-wave impulses to an *oscillograph, a* machine that records them. When the electroencephalogram reveals an abnormal brain-wave pattern, or *dysrhythmia,* clinicians suspect the existence of brain injuries, tumors, seizures, or other brain abnormalities, and they turn to more precise and sophisticated techniques to determine the nature and scope of the problem. In particular, there are a group of other neurological tests that actually take "pictures" of brain structure or brain activity. These tests, called **neuroimaging techniques,** include *computerized axial tomography* (*CAT scan* or *CT scan*), *positron emission tomography* (*PET scan*), *magnetic resonance imaging* (*MRI*), and *functional magnetic resonance imaging* (*fMRI*).

A **CT scan** is a procedure in which X rays of the brain's *structure* are taken at different angles and then the images are combined by a computer. This kind of scan is considered superior to a conventional X ray because it yields a three-dimensional image of the brain's structure.

Rather than showing the structure of the brain, a **PET scan** reveals the *functioning* of different areas in the brain. A person who undergoes this procedure is administered a harmless radioactive compound, which travels to the brain. Then, as the individual experiences particular emotions or performs specific cognitive tasks (say, reading or speaking), his or her brain is scanned for radiation. Higher radioactivity in various brain areas reflects higher blood flow and neuron activity in those areas. The radioactivity readings are converted by a computer into a motion picture, revealing which brain areas are active during the individual's emotional experiences or cognitive behaviors.

An **MRI** is a procedure in which a computer gathers information about the magnetic properties of hydrogen atoms in the brain and then produces a very detailed picture of the brain's *structure* (Allen et al., 2008). An **fMRI** goes still further, producing a detailed picture of the *functioning* brain. In this procedure, an MRI scanner detects rapid changes in the flow or volume of blood in areas across the brain while an individual is experiencing emotions or performing specific cognitive tasks. By interpreting these blood changes as indications of neuron activity at sites throughout the brain, a computer then generates images of which brain areas are active during the individual's emotional experiences or cognitive behaviors, thus offering a picture of the functioning brain. Partly because fMRI-produced images of brain functioning are so much clearer than PET scan images, the fMRI has generated enormous enthusiasm among brain researchers since it was first developed in 1990.

Though widely used, these techniques are sometimes unable to detect subtle brain abnormalities. Clinicians have therefore developed less direct but sometimes more revealing **neuropsychological tests** that measure cognitive, perceptual, and motor performances on certain tasks and interpret abnormal performances as an indicator of underlying brain problems (Axelrod & Wall, 2007; Pelham & Lovell, 2005). Brain damage is especially likely to affect visual perception, memory, and visual-motor coordination, so neuropsychological tests focus particularly on these areas.

The *Bender Visual-Motor Gestalt Test* (Bender, 1938), one of the first neuropsychological tests, consists of nine cards, each displaying a simple design. Patients look at the designs one at a time and copy each one on a piece of paper. Later they try to redraw the designs from memory. By the age of 12, most people can remember and redraw the designs accurately. Notable errors in accuracy are thought to reflect organic brain impairment. Similar neuropsychological tests have since been developed and are often prefered by today's clinicians (see Figure 4-3 on page 103). To achieve greater precision

Joe McNally/Sygma

The EEG
Electrodes pasted to a person's scalp detect electrical impulses from the brain. The electroencephalogram (EEG), used here to measure the brain waves of a 4-month-old being stimulated with toys, is only a gross indicator of the brain's activity.

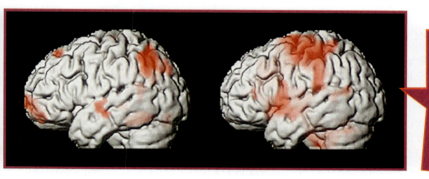

New kid on the block
The fMRI is a scanning procedure that has greatly enthused researchers in recent years because it produces extraordinarily clear images of both brain structure and brain function. The scans shown here reveal which areas of the brain are active when a person is thinking about performing a gesture (left) and which are active when the same person is actually performing the gesture (right).

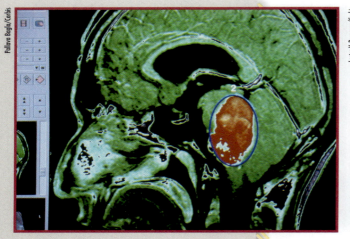

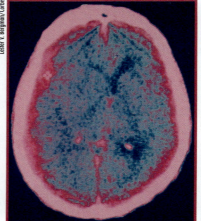

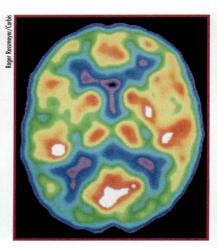

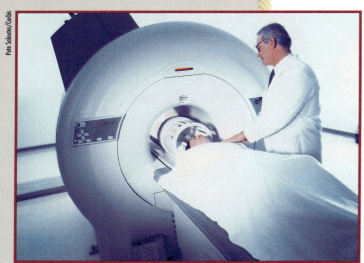

Traditional Scanning

The most widely used neuroimaging techniques in clinical practice—the MRI, CAT, and PET scans—take pictures of the living brain. The machinery for each of these techniques is bulky and imposing, much like the MRI machine shown at left. However, the scans produced by the machines are very different. Here, an MRI scan (above left) reveals a large tumor, colored in orange; a CAT scan (above center) reveals a subdural hemotoma, a mass of blood within the brain; and a PET scan (above right) shows which areas of the brain are active (those colored in red, orange, and yellow) when an individual is stimulated.

and accuracy in their assessments of brain abnormalities, clinicians often use a *battery,* or series, of neuropsychological tests, each targeting a specific skill area (Reitan & Wolfson, 2005, 2001, 1996).

Intelligence Tests An early definition of intelligence described it as "the capacity to judge well, to reason well, and to comprehend well" (Binet & Simon, 1916, p. 192). Because intelligence is an *inferred* quality rather than a specific physical process, it can be measured only indirectly. In 1905 the French psychologist Alfred Binet and his associate Theodore Simon produced an **intelligence test** consisting of a series of tasks requiring people to use various verbal and nonverbal skills. The general score derived from this and subsequent intelligence tests is termed an **intelligence quotient,** or **IQ,** so called because initially it represented the ratio of a person's "mental" age to his or her "chronological" age, multiplied by 100.

There are now more than 100 intelligence tests available, including the widely used *Wechsler Adult Intelligence Scale, Wechsler Intelligence Scale for Children,* and *Stanford-Binet Intelligence Scale.* As you will see in Chapter 17, intelligence tests play a key role in the diagnosis of mental retardation, but they can also help clinicians identify other problems.

Intelligence tests are among the most carefully produced of all clinical tests (Kellerman & Burry, 2007; Williams et al., 2007; Gottfredson, 2005). Because they have been standardized on large groups of people, clinicians have a good idea how each individual's score compares with the performance of the population at large. These tests have also shown very high reliability: people who repeat the same IQ test years later receive approximately the same score. Finally, the major IQ tests appear to have fairly high validity: children's IQ scores often correlate with their performance in school, for example.

Nevertheless, intelligence tests have some key shortcomings. Factors that have nothing to do with intelligence, such as low motivation and high anxiety, can greatly influence test performance (Gregory, 2004) (see *The Media Speaks* on the next page). In addition, IQ tests may contain cultural biases in their language or tasks that place people of one background at an advantage over those of another (Edwards & Oakland, 2006; Shuttleworth-Edwards et al., 2004). Similarly, members of some minority groups may have little experience with this kind of test, or they may be uncomfortable with test examiners of a majority ethnic background. Either way, their performances may suffer.

Clinical Observations

In addition to interviewing and testing people, clinicians may systematically observe their behavior. In one technique, called *naturalistic observation,* clinicians observe clients in their everyday environments. In another, *analog observation,* they observe them in an artificial setting, such as a clinical office or laboratory. Finally, in *self-monitoring,* clients are instructed to observe themselves.

Naturalistic and Analog Observations
Naturalistic clinical observations usually take place in homes, schools, institutions such as hospitals and prisons, or community settings. Most of them focus on parent-child, sibling-child, or teacher-child interactions and on fearful, aggressive, or disruptive behavior (Murdock et al., 2005). Often such observations are made by *participant observers,* key persons in the client's environment, and reported to the clinician.

When naturalistic observations are not practical, clinicians may resort to analog observations, often aided by special equipment such as a videotape recorder or one-way mirror (Haynes, 2001). Analog observations have often focused on children interacting with their parents, married couples attempting to settle a disagreement, speech-anxious people giving a speech, and fearful people approaching an object they find frightening.

Although much can be learned from actually witnessing behavior, clinical observations have certain disadvantages (Conner-Greene, 2007; Pine, 2005). For one thing, they are not always reliable. It is possible for various clinicians who observe the same person to focus on different aspects of behavior, assess the person differently, and arrive at different conclusions. Careful training of observers and the use of observer checklists can help reduce this problem.

Similarly, observers may make errors that affect the validity, or accuracy, of their observations (Aiken & Groth-Marnat, 2006; Pine, 2005). The observer may suffer from *overload* and be unable to see or record all of the important behaviors and events. Or the observer may experience *observer drift,* a steady decline in accuracy as a result of fatigue or of a gradual unintentional change in the standards used when an observation continues for a long period of time. Another possible problem is *observer bias*—the observer's judgments may be influenced by information and expectations he or she already has about the person (Markin & Kivlighan, 2007).

A client's *reactivity* may also limit the validity of clinical observations; that is, his or her behavior may be affected by the very presence of the observer (Kamphaus & Frick, 2002). If schoolchildren are aware that someone special is watching them, for example, they may change their usual classroom behavior, perhaps in the hope of creating a good impression.

Finally, clinical observations may lack *cross-situational,* or *external, validity.* A child who behaves aggressively in school is not necessarily aggressive at home or with friends after school. Because behavior is often specific to particular situations, observations in one setting cannot always be applied to other settings (Kagan, 2007; Haynes, 2001).

Self-Monitoring
As you saw earlier, personality and response inventories are tests in which persons report their own behaviors, feelings, or cognitions. In a related assessment procedure, *self-monitoring,* people observe themselves and carefully record the frequency

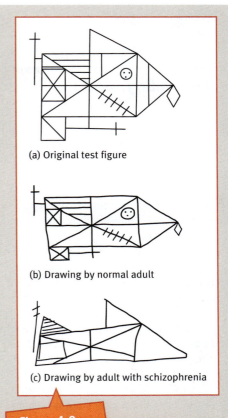

(a) Original test figure

(b) Drawing by normal adult

(c) Drawing by adult with schizophrenia

Figure 4-3
Impaired recall The Rey Complex Figure Test is a neuropsychological test in which individuals observe and then draw complex designs from memory. Here one figure from the test (a) is recalled and drawn by a normal adult (b) and by an adult with schizophrenia (c). The latter drawing contains unusually large errors, indicating visual memory defects and, perhaps, organic brain dysfunction. (Adapted from Sutherland et al., 1982.)

•**intelligence test**•A test designed to measure a person's intellectual ability.

•**intelligence quotient (IQ)**•A score derived from intelligence tests that is considered to represent a person's overall level of intelligence.

The Media SPEAKS

Tests, eBay, and the Public Good

BY MICHELLE ROBERTS, ASSOCIATED PRESS, DECEMBER 18, 2007

Intelligence tests . . . are for sale on eBay Inc.'s online auction site, and the test maker is worried they will be misused.

The series of Wechsler intelligence tests, made by San Antonio-based Harcourt Assessment, Inc., are supposed to be sold to and administered by only clinical psychologists and trained professionals.

Given more than a million times a year nationwide, according to Harcourt, the intelligence tests often are among numerous tests ordered by prosecutors and defense attorneys to determine the mental competence of criminal defendants. A low IQ, for example, can be used to argue leniency in sentencing.

Schools use the tests to determine whether to place a student in a special program, whether for gifted or struggling students. Harcourt officials say they fear the tests for sale on eBay will be misused for coaching by lawyers or parents.

But eBay has denied their request to restrict the sale of the tests. EBay officials say there is nothing illegal about selling the tests, and it cannot monitor every possible misuse of items sold through its network of 248 million buyers and sellers. Company spokesman Hani Durzy said eBay does prohibit the sale of items that are illegal in some states, even if they're legal in others. And it prohibits the sale of some legal items, like teacher editions of textbooks, as matter of public good. With regard to the Harcourt tests, he said, however, "at this point, this is our response."

Five of the tests were listed for sale . . . for about $175 to $900. The latest edition of the adult test, which retails for $939, was offered on eBay for $249.99.

"In order for it to maintain its integrity, there needs to be limited availability," said Harcourt spokesman Russell Schweiss. . . . "Misinterpreting the results [of questions and tasks on the tests], even without malicious intent, could lead to mistakes in assessing a child's intelligence," said Aurelio Prifitera, the president of Harcourt's clinical division. . . .

Schweiss said Harcourt was still considering how to respond to eBay's refusal. It has taken out a full-page ad in *The National Psychologist* magazine, asking clinicians and test publishers to contact eBay to express their concern, he said.

Jack King, communications director for the National Association of Criminal Defense Lawyers, said it would be very difficult to fake the results of an IQ test because cognitive and psychological tests are usually given as part of a battery of tests, and in most cases, there is a profile of scores that would be considered normal for certain disabilities or disorders. "Just flunking the test is not likely to be determinative of anything, and a person can always be tested again and again," he said. In any event, "it would be unethical to suggest to the client that they try to fudge a psychological test."

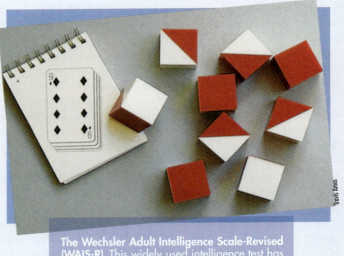

The Wechsler Adult Intelligence Scale-Revised (WAIS-R) This widely used intelligence test has 11 subtests, which cover such areas as factual information, memory, vocabulary, arithmetic, design, and eye-hand coordination.

Travis Amos

---

of certain behaviors, feelings, or cognitions as they occur over time (Wright & Truax, 2008; Cho, 2007). How frequently, for instance, does a drug user have an urge for drugs or a headache sufferer have a headache? What kinds of circumstances bring those feelings about?

Self-monitoring is especially useful in assessing behavior that occurs so infrequently that it is unlikely to be seen during other kinds of observations. It is also useful for behaviors that occur so frequently that any other method of observing them in detail would be impossible—for example, smoking, drinking, or other drug use (Tucker et al., 2007). Third, self-monitoring may be the only way to observe and measure private thoughts or perceptions.

•diagnosis• A determination that a person's problems reflect a particular disorder.

Like all other clinical assessment procedures, however, self-monitoring has drawbacks (Wright & Truax, 2008; Achenbach et al., 2005). Here too validity is often a problem. People do not always receive proper instruction in this form of observation, nor do they always try to record their observations accurately. Furthermore, when people monitor themselves, they may change their behaviors unintentionally (Otten, 2004; Plante, 1999). Smokers, for example, often smoke fewer cigarettes than usual when they are monitoring themselves, drug users take drugs less frequently, and teachers give more positive and fewer negative comments to their students.

✿Diagnosis: Does the Client's Syndrome Match a Known Disorder?

Clinicians use the information from interviews, tests, and observations to construct an integrated picture of the factors that are causing and maintaining a client's disturbance, a construction sometimes known as a *clinical picture* (Kellerman & Burry, 2007; Choca, 2004). Although research suggests that systematic statistical analyses of assessment data yield the most accurate clinical judgments, clinicians typically follow their own implicit rules of logic to form clinical pictures (Garb, 2006; Wood et al., 2002; Grove et al., 2000). Such pictures are also influenced by the clinicians' theoretical orientation. The psychologist who worked with Angela Savanti held a cognitive-behavioral view of abnormality and so produced a picture that emphasized modeling and reinforcement principles and Angela's expectations, assumptions, and interpretations:

An ideal observation
Using a one-way mirror, a clinical observer is able to view a mother interacting with her child without distracting the duo or influencing their behaviors.

> Angela was rarely reinforced for any of her accomplishments at school, but she gained her mother's negative attention for what Mrs. Savanti judged to be poor performance at school or at home. Mrs. Savanti repeatedly told her daughter that she was incompetent, and any mishaps that happened to her were her own fault. . . . When Mr. Savanti deserted the family, Angela's first response was that somehow she was responsible. From her mother's past behavior, Angela had learned to expect that in some way she would be blamed. At the time that Angela broke up with her boyfriend, she did not blame Jerry for his behavior, but interpreted this event as a failing solely on her part. As a result, her level of self-esteem was lowered still more.
>
> The type of marital relationship that Angela saw her mother and father model remained her concept of what married life is like. She generalized from her observations of her parents' discordant interactions to an expectation of the type of behavior that she and Jerry would ultimately engage in. . . .
>
> Angela's uncertainties intensified when she was deprived of the major source of gratification she had, her relationship with Jerry. Despite the fact that she was overwhelmed with doubts about whether to marry him or not, she had gained a great deal of pleasure through being with Jerry. Whatever feelings she had been able to express, she had shared with him and no one else. Angela labeled Jerry's termination of their relationship as proof that she was not worthy of another person's interest. She viewed her present unhappiness as likely to continue, and she attributed it to some failing on her part. As a result, she became quite depressed.
>
> (Leon, 1984, pp. 123–125)

BETWEEN THE LINES

What Is a Nervous Breakdown?

The term "nervous breakdown" is used by laypersons, not clinicians. Most people use it to refer to a *sudden* psychological disturbance that incapacitates a person, perhaps requiring hospitalization. Some people use the term simply to connote the onset of any psychological disorder (Padwa, 1996). ‹‹

With the assessment data and clinical picture in hand, clinicians are ready to make a **diagnosis** (from the Greek word for "a discrimination")—that is, a determination that a person's psychological problems constitute a particular disorder. When clinicians decide,

Culture-Bound Abnormality

Red Bear sits up wild-eyed, his body drenched in sweat, every muscle tensed. The horror of the dream is still with him; he is choked with fear. Fighting waves of nausea, he stares at his young wife lying asleep on the far side of the wigwam, illuminated by the dying embers.

His troubles began several days before, when he came back from a hunting expedition empty-handed. Ashamed of his failure, he fell prey to a deep, lingering depression. . . . The signs of windigo were all there: depression, lack of appetite, nausea, sleeplessness and, now, the dream. Indeed, there could be no mistake.

He had dreamed of the windigo—the monster with a heart of ice—and the dream sealed his doom. Coldness gripped his own heart. The ice monster had entered his body and possessed him. He himself had become a windigo, and he could do nothing to avert his fate.

Suddenly, the form of Red Bear's sleeping wife begins to change. He no longer sees a woman, but a deer. His eyes flame. Silently, he draws his knife from under the blanket and moves stealthily toward the motionless figure. . . . A powerful desire to eat raw flesh consumes him.

With the body of the "deer" at his feet, Red Bear raises the knife high, preparing the strike. Unexpectedly, the deer screams and twists away. But the knife flashes down, again and again. Too late, Red Bear's kinsmen rush into the wigwam. . . . [T]hey drag him outside into the cold night air and swiftly kill him. ////

(LINDHOLM & LINDHOLM, 1981, P. 52)

Red Bear was suffering from *windigo*, a disorder once common among Algonquin Indian hunters. They believed in a supernatural monster that ate human beings and had the power to bewitch them and turn them into cannibals. Red Bear was among the few afflicted hunters who actually did kill and eat members of their households.

Windigo is but one of numerous unusual mental disorders discovered around the world, each unique to a particular culture, each apparently growing from that culture's pressures, history, institutions, and ideas (Draguns, 2006; Glazer et al., 2004; Sarro & Sarro, 2004). Such disorders remind us that the classifications and diagnoses applied in one culture may not always be appropriate in another.

Susto, a disorder found among members of Indian tribes in Central and South America and Hispanic natives of the Andean highlands of Peru, Bolivia, and Colombia, is most likely to occur in infants and young children. The symptoms are extreme anxiety, excitability, and depression, along with loss of weight, weakness, and rapid heartbeat. The culture holds that this disorder is caused by contact with supernatural beings or with frightening strangers or by bad air from cemeteries.

People affected with *amok*, a disorder found in Malaysia, the Philippines, Java, and some parts of Africa, jump around violently, yell loudly, grab knives or other weapons, and attack any people and objects they encounter. Within the culture, amok is thought to be caused by stress, severe shortage of sleep, alcohol consumption, and extreme heat.

Koro is a pattern of anxiety found in Southeast Asia in which a man suddenly becomes intensely fearful that his penis will withdraw into his abdomen and that he will die as a result. Cultural lore holds that the disorder is caused by an imbalance of "yin" and "yang," two natural forces believed to be the fundamental components of life. Accepted forms of treatment include having the individual keep a firm hold on his penis until the fear passes, often with the assistance of family members or friends, and clamping the penis to a wooden box.

Latah is a disorder found in Malaysia, usually among uneducated middle-aged or elderly women. Certain circumstances

through diagnosis, that a client's pattern of dysfunction reflects a particular disorder, they are saying that the pattern is basically the same as one that has been displayed by many other people, has been observed and investigated in a variety of studies, and perhaps has responded to particular forms of treatment. They can then apply what is generally known about the disorder to the particular individual they are trying to help. They can, for example, better predict the future course of the person's problem and the treatments that are likely to be helpful.

Classification Systems

The principle behind diagnosis is straightforward. When certain symptoms regularly occur together—a cluster of symptoms is called a **syndrome**—and follow a particular course, clinicians agree that those symptoms make up a particular mental disorder. When people display this particular pattern of symptoms, diagnosticians assign them to that diagnostic category (see *Eye on Culture* above). A list of such categories, or disorders, with descriptions of the symptoms and guidelines for assigning individuals to the categories, is known as a **classification system.**

In 1883 Emil Kraepelin developed the first modern classification system for abnormal behavior (see Chapter 1). His categories have formed the foundation for the psychological part of the *International Classification of Diseases (ICD)*, the classification system

•**syndrome**•A cluster of symptoms that usually occur together.

•**classification system**•A list of disorders, along with descriptions of symptoms and guidelines for making appropriate diagnoses.

Do Western abnormalities follow? A culture clash is on display as this woman with a head scarf walks past a Western billboard upon leaving a metro stop in Turkey (religious Muslim women cover their hair). The spread of Western values, fashions, and ads to eastern European and Asian countries appears to have more than a political and cultural impact. According to research, such changes are often accompanied by a rise in the rates of anorexia nervosa and other psychological disorders that once seemed to be found strictly in Western society.

(hearing someone say "snake" or being tickled, for example) trigger a fright reaction that is marked by repeating the words and acts of other people, uttering obscenities, and doing the opposite of what others ask.

So how does DSM IV-TR, the most widely used classification manual in the United States, handle these and other culture-bound forms of abnormality? Largely, with an appendix. A section at the back of the manual offers information and guidance to clinicians about special issues and patterns they may encounter when making diagnoses in a multicultural environment.

In such cases, the appendix suggests, clinicians should supplement their DSM diagnosis with a *narrative* that describes (1) the cultural identity of the client, (2) cultural factors that may weigh into the individual's disorder and diagnosis, (3) cultural differences between the client and clinician, and (4) cultural considerations that may influence treatment. In addition, the appendix lists 25 of the best studied culture-bound syndromes, including those discussed here, particularly ones that are likely to be encountered in North America.

Many clinicians view this appendix as a poor compromise, one that "appears" to offer careful consideration to cultural-bound issues but that actually renders such issues a diagnostic afterthought. After all, the listed disorders are not themselves formal DSM categories, nor do the cultural narrative guidelines provide clinicians with an efficient system for taking into account the ethnic and cultural context of each client's problem. Others argue, however, that the appendix does at least underline the importance of multicultural factors in diagnosis and provides a first step toward properly incorporating these factors into the diagnostic process.

now used by the World Health Organization. They have also influenced the *Diagnostic and Statistical Manual of Mental Disorders* (*DSM*), a classification system developed by the American Psychiatric Association. The DSM, like the ICD, has been changed over time. First published in 1952, the DSM underwent major revisions in 1968 (DSM-II), 1980 (DSM-III), 1987 (DSM-IIIR), and 1994 (DSM-IV).

DSM-IV lists approximately 400 mental disorders (see Figure 4-4 on the next page). Each entry describes the criteria for diagnosing the disorder and its key clinical features. The system also describes related features, which are often but not always present. The classification system is further accompanied by *text information* (that is, background information) such as research indications; age, culture, or gender trends; and each disorder's prevalence, risk, course, complications, predisposing factors, and family patterns.

In 2000, the American Psychiatric Association published an update of the text information that accompanies DSM-IV. This update, called the *DSM-IV Text Revision* (*DSM-IV-TR*), also changed the *diagnostic criteria* for a few disorders (certain sexual disorders), as you'll see in Chapter 13. Because DSM-IV-TR did in fact make changes to the DSM-IV categories and criteria, few though they were, many clinicians cite DSM-IV-TR as the current edition of the DSM, a trend that will be followed throughout this textbook. Other clinicians continue to point to DSM-IV as the current edition. Either way, it is important to be clear that almost all of DSM-IV-TR's criteria were in fact introduced in 1994 with the publication of DSM-IV.

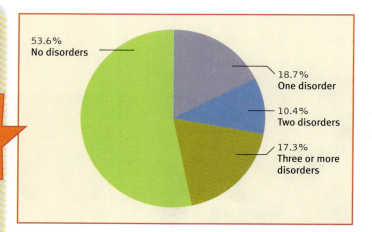

Figure 4-4

How many people in the United States qualify for a DSM diagnosis during their lives? Almost half, according to one survey. Some of them even experience two or more different disorders, an occurrence known as comorbidity. (Adapted from Kessler et al., 2005.)

53.6%
No disorders

18.7%
One disorder

10.4%
Two disorders

17.3%
Three or more disorders

DSM-IV-TR

DSM-IV-TR is the most widely used classification system in the United States (APA, 2000). It requires clinicians to evaluate a client's condition on five separate *axes,* or branches of information, when making a diagnosis. First, they must decide whether the person is displaying one or more of the disorders found on *Axis I,* an extensive list of clinical syndromes that typically cause significant impairment. Some of the most frequently diagnosed disorders listed on this axis are the anxiety disorders and mood disorders, problems you will read about later:

Anxiety disorders People with anxiety disorders may experience general feelings of anxiety and worry (*generalized anxiety disorder*), anxiety centered on a specific situation or object (*phobias*), periods of panic (*panic disorder*), persistent thoughts or repetitive behaviors or both (*obsessive-compulsive disorder*), or lingering anxiety reactions to unusually traumatic events (*acute stress disorder* and *posttraumatic stress disorder*).

Mood disorders People with mood disorders feel extremely sad or elated for long periods of time. These disorders include *major depressive disorder* and *bipolar disorders* (in which episodes of mania alternate with episodes of depression).

Next, diagnosticians must decide whether the person is displaying one of the disorders listed on *Axis II,* which includes long-standing problems that are frequently overlooked in the presence of the disorders on Axis I. There are only two groups of Axis II disorders, *mental retardation* and *personality disorders.* You will also read about these patterns in later chapters:

Mental retardation People with this disorder display significantly subaverage intellectual functioning and poor adaptive functioning by 18 years of age.

Personality disorders People with these disorders display a very rigid maladaptive pattern of inner experience and outward behavior that has continued for many years. People with *antisocial personality disorder,* for example, persistently disregard and violate the rights of others. People with *dependent personality disorder* are persistently dependent on others, clinging, obedient, and very afraid of separation.

Although people usually receive a diagnosis from *either* Axis I or Axis II, they may receive diagnoses from both axes. Angela Savanti would first receive a diagnosis of *major depressive disorder* from Axis I (a mood disorder). Let's suppose that the clinician judged that Angela also displayed a life history of dependent behavior. She might then also receive an Axis II diagnosis of *dependent personality disorder.*

The remaining axes of DSM-IV-TR guide diagnosticians in reporting other factors. *Axis III* asks for information concerning relevant general medical conditions from which the person is currently suffering. *Axis IV* asks about special psychosocial or environmental problems the person is facing, such as school or housing problems.

And *Axis V* requires the diagnostician to make a *global assessment of functioning (GAF)*, that is, to rate on a 100-point scale the person's psychological, social, and occupational functioning overall.

If Angela Savanti had diabetes, for example, the clinician might include that under Axis III information. Angela's recent breakup with her boyfriend would be noted on Axis IV. And because she seemed fairly dysfunctional at the time of diagnosis, Angela's GAF would probably be around 55 on Axis V, indicating a moderate level of dysfunction. The complete diagnosis for Angela Savanti would then be:

Axis I: Major depressive disorder

Axis II: Dependent personality disorder

Axis III: Diabetes

Axis IV: Problem related to the social environment (termination of engagement)

Axis V: GAF = 55 (current)

Because DSM-IV-TR uses several kinds of diagnostic information, each defined by a different "axis," it is known as a *multiaxial system*. The diagnoses arrived at under this classification system are thought to be more informative and more carefully considered than those derived from the early DSMs.

Is DSM-IV-TR an Effective Classification System?

A classification system, like an assessment method, is judged by its reliability and validity. Here *reliability* means that different clinicians are likely to agree on the diagnosis when they use the system to diagnose the same client. Early versions of the DSM were at best moderately reliable (Spiegel, 2005; Malik & Beutler, 2002; Kirk & Kutchins, 1992). In the early 1960s, for example, four clinicians, each relying on DSM-I, independently interviewed 153 patients (Beck et al., 1962). Only 54 percent of their diagnoses were in agreement. Because all four clinicians were experienced diagnosticians, their failure to agree suggested deficiencies in the classification system.

DSM-IV-TR appears to have greater reliability than the early DSMs (Keenan et al., 2007; Lyneham, Abbott, & Rapee, 2007; Black, 2005). The framers of DSM-IV conducted extensive reviews of research to pinpoint which categories in past DSMs had been too vague and unreliable. In turn, they developed a number of new diagnostic criteria and categories and then ran *field trials* to make sure that the new criteria and categories were in fact reliable. They had many clinicians and researchers use the new criteria in their work and found that, in most cases, the same clients or kinds of clients were receiving the same diagnoses.

When it was first published in 1994, DSM-IV was heralded as a *highly* reliable classification system. However, clinical use and research conducted over the past decade indicate that DSM-IV (and likewise DSM-IV-TR) does contain certain reliability problems (Black, 2005; Beutler & Malik, 2002). Many clinicians, for example, have difficulty distinguishing one kind of anxiety disorder from another. The disorder of a particular client may be classified as generalized anxiety disorder by one clinician, agoraphobia (fear of traveling outside of one's home) by another, and social phobia (fear of social situations) by yet another. Moreover, many anxious clients receive multiple (*comorbid*) diagnoses: they may receive, for example, a diagnosis of *both* agoraphobia *and* social phobia.

It may be that the criteria for certain categories overlap too much in the current DSM. For example, an excessive fear of embarrassment or humiliation is listed as a criterion for both agoraphobia and social phobia. Alternatively, it may simply be that people with one anxiety disorder are highly prone to develop

Phoning in

After initially receiving criticism for its slow responses to the psychological needs of combat veterans returning from Iraq, the U.S. military now employs active assessment programs to detect posttraumatic stress disorder and other problems among those veterans. Here, a spokesperson announces a new interactive automated phone-in mental health assessment program designed to reach out to soldiers and family members in need of psychological help.

AP Photo/Lawrence Jackson

The power of labeling
When looking at this late-nineteenth-century photograph of a baseball team at the State Homeopathic Asylum for the Insane in Middletown, New York, most observers assume that the players are patients. As a result, they tend to "see" depression or confusion in the players' faces and posture. In fact, the players are members of the asylum staff, some of whom even sought their jobs for the express purpose of playing for the hospital team.

another anxiety disorder as well. Either way, diagnostic confusion of this kind has spurred serious concerns about DSM-IV-TR's reliability.

The *validity* of a classification system is the accuracy of the information that its diagnostic categories provide. Categories are of most use to clinicians when they demonstrate *predictive validity*—that is, when they help predict future symptoms or events. A common symptom of major depressive disorder, for example, is either insomnia or excessive sleep. When clinicians give Angela Savanti a diagnosis of major depressive disorder, they expect that she may eventually develop sleep problems even if none are present now. In addition, they expect her to respond to treatments that are effective for other depressed persons. The more often such predictions are accurate, the greater a category's predictive validity.

The framers of DSM-IV tried to ensure the validity of their new version of the DSM by again conducting extensive reviews of research and running many field studies. As a result, its criteria and categories initially appeared to have stronger validity than those of the earlier versions of the DSM (Reeb, 2000; Nathan & Lagenbucher, 1999). Yet, again, since 1994 many clinical theorists have argued persuasively that at least some of the criteria and categories in DSM-IV (and carried over to DSM-IV-TR) are based on weak research and that others reflect gender or racial bias (Lowe et al., 2008; Vieta & Phillips, 2007; Cosgrove & Riddle, 2004).

Beyond these concerns about the reliability and validity of certain categories, a growing number of clinical theorists believe that two fundamental problems weaken the current edition of the DSM (Widiger, 2007; Widiger & Simonsen, 2005). One problem is DSM-IV-TR's basic assumption that clinical disorders are *qualitatively* different from normal behavior. Perhaps this assumption is incorrect. It may be, for example, that the feelings of dejection occasionally experienced by everyone differ from mild clinical depression in *degree* only and, similarly, that mild clinical depression differs from severe depression in degree rather than kind. In support of this notion, some studies find that the early features and predictors of mild depression are almost identical to those of severe depression (Akiskal & Benazzi, 2008; Akiskal, 2005; Judd et al., 2004, 2002, 1997). If certain psychological disorders actually differ from normal behavior and from each other in degree rather than kind, many of today's criteria and categories are, at the very least, misleading.

BETWEEN THE LINES

Bands with Psychological Labels

Bad Brains ‹‹

Clinic ‹‹

Placebo ‹‹

The Dissociatives ‹‹

Fear Factory ‹‹

Mood Elevator ‹‹

Neurosis ‹‹

Disturbed ‹‹

10,000 Maniacs ‹‹

Grupo Mania ‹‹

Suicidal Tendencies ‹‹

Xanax 25 ‹‹

The Insane Clown Posse ‹‹

Unsane ‹‹

Therapy? ‹‹

Another (related) criticism centers on DSM-IV-TR's use of *discrete* diagnostic categories, with each category of pathology considered to be separate from all the others. Some critics believe that certain of its categories reflect, in fact, variations of a single, fundamental *dimension* of functioning rather than separate disorders. Let's consider the dimension of *negative affect,* for example. Perhaps this dimension should be used when describing abnormal patterns. When an individual's negative affect is extreme and maladaptive and takes on a particular character, the person may appear highly anxious. Alternatively, a person with extreme negative affect may appear highly depressed or, indeed, may seem both anxious *and* depressed. In short, rather than distinguish two kinds of disorders—an anxiety disorder and a depressive disorder—the classification should list each pattern as a variation of a key dimension, negative affect. If this dimensional view is appropriate, the DSM-IV-TR is, once again, misleading clinicians when it asks them to determine whether persons are suffering from an anxiety disorder *or* a mood disorder. Small wonder that clinicians often find high anxiety levels among people with a major depressive disorder, or very depressed feelings among clients with an anxiety disorder. There is growing evidence that fundamental dimensions do indeed cut across different DSM categories and that this may be the reason that multiple diagnoses so often need to be assigned to the same client.

Given such concerns, there is no question that DSM-V, the next edition of DSM, will include some key changes, including at least some dimensional, rather than categorical, forms of classification. The DSM-V Task Force has now been assembled (Oldham, 2007). It consists of 12 Work Groups, each focusing on a particular set of disorders, and 4 additional Study Groups, each looking at overlapping features and issues across the various disorders. These groups are building upon the work that has already been conducted at numerous research planning conferences—conferences that have considered what kinds of changes might be appropriate for DSM-V. As you will see in Chapters 5 and 16, classifications of the anxiety disorders and the personality disorders are particularly likely to see changes. Nevertheless, the debut of DSM-V is not imminent. It will not be completed until 2012 or later (Garber, 2008). In the meantime, clinicians continue to rely on DSM-IV-TR, a classification system that is superior to its predecessors but, at the same time, filled with important limitations and questions.

Can Diagnosis and Labeling Cause Harm?

Even with trustworthy assessment data and reliable and valid classification categories, clinicians will sometimes arrive at a wrong conclusion (Rohrer, 2005; Wood et al., 2002). Like all human beings, they are flawed information processors. Studies show that they are influenced disproportionately by information gathered early in the assessment process (Dawes, Faust, & Meehl, 2002; Meehl, 1996, 1960). They sometimes pay too much attention to certain sources of information, such as a parent's report about a child, and too little to others, such as the child's point of view (McCoy, 1976). Finally, their judgments can be distorted by any number of personal biases—gender, age, race, and socioeconomic status, to name just a few (Vasquez, 2007; Winstead & Sanchez, 2005).

Given the limitations of assessment tools, assessors, and classification systems, it is small wonder that studies sometimes uncover shocking errors in diagnosis, especially in hospitals (Caetano & Babor, 2007; Chen, Swann, & Burt, 1996). In one study a clinical team was asked to reevaluate the records of 131 patients at a mental hospital in New York, conduct interviews with many of these persons, and arrive at a diagnosis for each one (Lipton & Simon, 1985). The researchers then compared the team's diagnoses with the original diagnoses for which the patients were hospitalized. Although 89 of the patients had originally received a diagnosis of schizophrenia, only 16 received it upon reevaluation. And whereas 15 patients originally had been given a diagnosis of mood disorder,

Insensitive labeling
Recognizing that glib labels can contribute to negative stereotypes and to the stigmatization of people with psychological disorders, a few years ago mental health advocacy groups protested the production and sale of "Crazy for You" bears, a new line of Vermont Teddy Bears. The teddy bear company subsequently agreed to cease the production and marketing of those bears.

Toby Talbot/AP Photo

EYE ON CULTURE

Oppression and Mental Health: The Politics of Labeling

Throughout history governments have applied the label of mental illness as a way of controlling or minimizing the influence of people whose views threaten the social order. This was a common practice in the former Soviet Union. There, political dissent was considered a symptom of abnormal mental functioning, and many dissidents were committed to mental hospitals.

In a more subtle process, a country's cultural values often influence the clinical assessments made by its practitioners. Historians Lynn Gamwell and Nancy Tomes (1995) have noted, for example, the widespread clinical belief in the nineteenth-century United States that freedom would drive "primitive" people such as Native Americans insane. Medical experts of that time went so far as to claim that the forcible movement of tribal groups onto reservations was in their best interest because it would save them from the madness that awaited them in free society. The medical officer who supervised the "removal" of the Cherokees from their homeland to Oklahoma was later pleased to report that during the whole time he oversaw the migration of 20,000 Cherokees (over 4,000 of whom died), he had not observed a single case of insanity.

Slave owners, too, liked to believe that slaves were psychologically comfortable with their subservience and that those who

Francis G. Meyer/Corbis

A ride for liberty Eastman Johnson's 1862 painting, *A Ride for Liberty—The Fugitive Slaves*, demonstrates the courage and clear-mindedness slaves needed to escape, in stark contrast to the mental instability of which they were accused.

tried to escape either were or would soon become insane. The work of clinicians at that time lent support to this belief. One specialist claimed that several kinds of mental disorders were unique to African Americans, including *drapetomania* (from the Latin *drapeta*, "fugitive")—an obsessive desire for freedom that drove some slaves to try to flee. Any slave who tried to run away more than twice was considered insane.

Drapetomania is long forgotten, but cultural views continue to influence psycho-

logical assessments and categories. Many clinicians have argued that categories such as "homosexuality," "sexual frigidity," and "masochistic personality"—each an established clinical category during much of the twentieth century—show all too well the impact of cultural beliefs on clinical categorizations and diagnoses.

50 received it now. It is obviously important for clinicians to be aware that such huge disagreements can occur.

Beyond the potential for misdiagnosis, the very act of classifying people can lead to unintended results (see *Eye on Culture* above). As you read in Chapter 3, for example, many family-social theorists believe that diagnostic labels can become self-fulfilling prophecies. When people are diagnosed as mentally disturbed, they may be viewed and reacted to correspondingly. If others expect them to take on a sick role, they may begin to consider themselves sick as well and act that way. Furthermore, our society attaches a stigma to abnormality (Spagnolo, Murphy, & Librera, 2008; Corrigan, 2007; Corrigan et al., 2007; Link et al., 2004, 2001). People labeled mentally ill may find it difficult to get a job, especially a position of responsibility, or to be welcomed into social relationships. Once a label has been applied, it may stick for a long time.

Because of these problems, some clinicians would like to do away with diagnoses. Others disagree. They believe we must simply work to increase what is known about psychological disorders and improve diagnostic techniques. They hold that classification and diagnosis are critical to understanding and treating people in distress.

✿Treatment: How Might the Client Be Helped?

Over the course of 10 months, Angela Savanti was treated for depression and related symptoms. She improved considerably during that time, as the following report describes:

Angela's depression eased as she began to make progress in therapy. A few months before the termination of treatment, she and Jerry resumed dating. Angela discussed with Jerry her greater comfort in expressing her feelings and her hope that Jerry would also become more expressive with her. They discussed the reasons why Angela was ambivalent about getting married, and they began to talk again about the possibility of marriage. Jerry, however, was not making demands for a decision by a certain date, and Angela felt that she was not as frightened about marriage as she previously had been. . . .

Psychotherapy provided Angela with the opportunity to learn to express her feelings to the persons she was interacting with, and this was quite helpful to her. Most important, she was able to generalize from some of the learning experiences in therapy and modify her behavior in her renewed relationship with Jerry. Angela still had much progress to make in terms of changing the characteristic ways she interacted with others, but she had already made a number of important steps in a potentially happier direction.

(Leon, 1984, pp. 118, 125)

Clearly, treatment helped Angela, and by its conclusion she was a happier, more functional person than the woman who had first sought help 10 months earlier. But how did her therapist decide on the treatment program that proved to be so helpful? And was the effectiveness of Angela's therapy typical of that offered by other therapists to other clients with other problems?

Treatment Decisions

Angela's therapist began, like all therapists, with assessment information and diagnostic decisions. Knowing the specific details and background of Angela's problem (*idiographic data*) and combining this information with established information about the nature and treatment of depression (*nomothetic data*), the clinician arrived at a treatment plan for her.

Yet therapists may be influenced by additional factors when they make treatment decisions. Their treatment plans typically reflect their theoretical orientations and how they have learned to conduct therapy (Sharf, 2008; Mahrer, 2003, 2000). As therapists apply a favored model in case after case, they become more and more familiar with its principles and treatment techniques and tend to use them in work with still other clients.

Current research may also play a role. Most clinicians say that they value research as a guide to practice (Beutler et al., 1995). However, not all of them actually read research articles, so they cannot be directly influenced by them (Stewart & Chambless, 2007). Research articles tend to be written for other researchers, in technical language that is not typically accessible to clinicians or other kinds of readers. In fact, according to surveys, therapists actually gather most of their information about the latest developments in the field from colleagues, professional newsletters, workshops, conferences, books, and the like (Corrie & Callanan, 2001; Goldfried & Wolfe, 1996). Unfortunately, the accuracy and usefulness of these sources vary widely.

To help clinicians become more familiar with and apply research findings, there is an ever-growing movement in the United States, the United Kingdom, and elsewhere called *empirically supported,* or *evidence-based, treatment* (Nathan & Gorman, 2007; Norcross, Beutler, & Levant, 2006; Ollendick, King, & Chorpita, 2006; Kazdin, 2004; Chambless, 2002). Proponents of this approach have formed task forces that seek to identify those therapies that have received clear research support, conduct new therapy research, develop treatment guidelines, and spread such information to clinicians. After carefully reviewing numerous treatment studies, for example, a task force on major depressive disorder, for example, has determined that this problem is most effectively treated by either cognitive or cognitive-behavioral therapy, antidepressant drug therapy, or interpersonal psychotherapy, a sociocultural approach that you will come across in Chapter 9 (Nemade, Reiss, & Dombeck, 2007). Critics of the empirically supported treatment approach worry that efforts to distinguish effective from ineffective treatments have thus far been simplistic, biased, and, at times, misleading (Weinberger & Rasco, 2007; Mahrer, 2005; Westen et al., 2005). However, the movement has been gaining momentum in recent years.

How much, in fact, do we currently know about treatment and treatment effectiveness? And how can researchers best examine such questions? Let's turn to this set of questions next.

The Effectiveness of Treatment

Altogether, more than 400 forms of therapy are currently practiced in the clinical field (Corsini, 2008). Naturally, the most important question to ask about each of them is whether it does what it is supposed to do. Does a particular treatment really help people overcome their psychological problems? If so, the practitioner has performed a significant service for the client (see *Psych Watch* on the facing page). On the surface, the question may seem simple. In fact, it is one of the most difficult questions for clinical researchers to answer.

The first problem is how to *define* "success." If, as Angela's therapist suggests, she still has much progress to make at the conclusion of therapy, should her recovery be considered successful? The second problem is how to *measure* improvement (Markin & Kivlighan, 2007; Luborsky, 2004; Luborsky et al., 2003, 2002, 1999). Should researchers give equal weight to the reports of clients, friends, relatives, therapists, and teachers? Should they use rating scales, inventories, therapy insights, observations, or some other measure?

Perhaps the biggest problem in determining the effectiveness of treatment is the *variety* and *complexity* of the treatments currently in use. People differ in their problems, personal styles, and motivations for therapy. Therapists differ in skill, experience, orientation, and personality. And therapies differ in theory, format, and setting. Because an individual's progress is influenced by all these factors and more, the findings of a particular study will not always apply to other clients and therapists.

"Are we there yet?"

PSYCH WATCH

Dark Sites

As you have seen in this chapter, it is the job of clinicians to help combat psychological disorders, either by preventive efforts or, if those fail, through assessment, diagnosis, and effective treatment. Unfortunately, today there are also other—more sinister—forces at work that counteract the work of mental health professionals. Among the most prominent are so-called dark sites on the Internet—sites with the goal of promoting behaviors and emotions that the clinical community, and most of society, consider abnormal and destructive. These sites commonly offer users help in concealing their disorders, forums for comparing their abnormal behaviors, and information about and tips for maintaining their symptoms. *Pro-anorexia sites* and *suicide sites* are two examples.

Pro-Anorexia Sites

The Eating Disorders Association reports that there are more than 500 pro-anorexia Internet sites with names such as "Dying to Be Thin" and "Starving for Perfection" (Catan, 2007). Users of these sites exchange tips on how they can starve themselves and disguise their weight loss from family, friends, and doctors. The sites also offer support and feedback about starvation diets. One such site sponsors a contest, "The Great Ana Competition," and awards a diploma to the girl who consumes the fewest calories in a two-week period (Catan, 2007). Another site, "Stick

James Filby/Image Zoo

Figures," endorses what it calls the *Pro-Anorexia Ten Commandments*—assertions such as "Being thin is more important than being healthy" and "Thou shall not eat without feeling guilty" (Barrett, 2000).

Suicide Sites

Suicide sites are another Internet phenomenon that has become the subject of criticism. Teens and young adults are at particularly high risk for imitative suicidal behavior, and they are also more likely to visit suicide chat rooms. Suicide forums and chat rooms vary in their messages, but they pose clear risks to impressionable users. Some pro-suicide Web sites celebrate former users who have committed suicide; others present opportunities to set up appointments for joint or partner suicides, and several offer specific instructions about suicide methods and locations and writing suicide notes (Becker & Schmidt, 2004).

During a two-month period in 2008, for example, 30 people committed suicide across Japan, all of them involving the use of detergent mixtures that produce a deadly hydrogen sulfide gas, a technique that had been repeatedly described and encouraged on Internet suicide sites (CNN, 2008). A 31-year-old man took his life in a car using a mixture of detergent and bath salts, a 42-year-old woman killed herself in her bathroom using toilet cleaner and bath powder, and a 14-year-old girl mixed laundry detergent with cleanser to commit suicide in her apartment. It is also worth noting that such detergent mixtures release powerful fumes that can endanger innocent bystanders. Indeed, 90 apartment house neighbors of the 14-year-old suicide victim were sickened by the fumes emitted during her self-inflicted death. Given such dangers, almost all of those who killed themselves by detergent mixtures in Japan hung warning signs at the locations of their suicide saying "Stay Away" or "Poisonous Gas Being Emitted," warnings apparently also suggested on the Internet suicide sites.

Many individuals, including clinicians, worry that Internet suicide sites place individuals who are depressed or impressionable at great risk, and they have called for the banning of these sites. Others argue, however, that despite their dangers, the sites represent fundamental freedoms that should not be violated—freedom of speech, for example, and perhaps even the freedom to do oneself harm.

Proper research procedures address some of these problems. By using control groups, random assignment, matched subjects, and the like, clinicians can draw certain conclusions about various therapies. Even in studies that are well designed, however, the variety and complexity of treatment limit the conclusions that can be reached (Kazdin, 2006, 2004, 1994).

Despite these difficulties, the job of evaluating therapies must be done, and clinical researchers have plowed ahead with it. Investigators have, in fact, conducted thousands of *therapy outcome studies,* studies that measure the effects of various treatments. The studies typically ask one of three questions:

1. Is therapy *in general* effective?
2. Are *particular* therapies generally effective?
3. Are *particular* therapies effective for *particular* problems?

Is Therapy Generally Effective?
Studies suggest that therapy is often more helpful than no treatment or than placebos. A pioneering review examined 375 controlled studies, covering a total of almost 25,000 people seen in a wide assortment of therapies (Smith, Glass, & Miller, 1980; Smith & Glass, 1977). The reviewers combined the findings of these studies by using a special statistical technique called *meta-analysis.* They rated the level of improvement in each treated research participant and in each untreated (control) participant and measured the average difference between the two groups. According to this statistical analysis, the average person who received treatment was better off than 75 percent of the untreated persons (see Figure 4-5). Other meta-analyses have found similar relationships between treatment and improvement (Bickman, 2005).

Some clinicians have concerned themselves with an important related question: Can therapy be harmful? In his book *My Analysis with Freud,* psychoanalyst Abraham Kardiner (1977) wrote, "Freud was always infuriated whenever I would say to him that you could not do harm with psychoanalysis. He said: 'When you say that, you also say it cannot do any good. Because if you cannot do any harm, how can you do good?'" In agreement with Freud, a number of studies have found that more than 5 percent of patients actually seem to get worse because of therapy (Nolan et al., 2004; Lambert & Bergin, 1994). Their symptoms may become more intense, or they may develop new ones, such as a sense of failure, guilt, reduced self-concept, or hopelessness, because of their inability to profit from therapy (Lambert, Shapiro, & Bergin, 1986; Hadley & Strupp, 1976).

Are Particular Therapies Generally Effective?
The studies you have read about so far have lumped all therapies together to consider their general effectiveness. Many researchers, however, consider it wrong to treat all therapies alike. Some critics suggest that these studies are operating under a *uniformity myth*—a false belief that all therapies are equivalent despite differences in the therapists' training, experience, theoretical orientations, and personalities (Good & Brooks, 2005; Kiesler, 1995, 1966).

Thus, an alternative approach examines the effectiveness of *particular* therapies (Bickman, 2005). Most research of this kind shows each of the major forms of therapy to be superior to no treatment or to placebo treatment (Prochaska & Norcross, 2006, 1999, 1994). A number of other studies have compared particular therapies with one another and found that no one form of therapy generally stands out over all others (Luborsky et al., 2003, 2002, 1975).

If different kinds of therapy have similar successes, might they have something in common? A **rapprochement movement** has tried to identify a set of common strategies that may run through the work of all effective therapists, regardless of the clinicians' particular orientation (Portnoy, 2008; Castonguay & Beutler, 2006; Luborsky et al., 2003, 2002; Korchin & Sands, 1983). Surveys of highly successful therapists suggest, for example, that most give feedback to patients, help patients focus on their own thoughts and behavior, pay attention to the way they and their patients are interacting, and try to promote self-mastery in their patients. In short, effective therapists of any type may practice more similarly than they preach.

Are Particular Therapies Effective for Particular Problems?
People with different disorders may respond differently to the various forms of therapy (Corsini, 2008). In an oft-quoted statement, influential clinical theorist Gordon Paul said more than 40 years ago that the most appropriate question regarding the effectiveness of

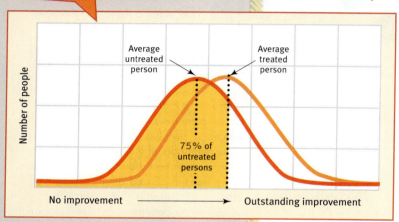

Figure 4-5
Does therapy help? Combining participants and results from hundreds of studies, investigators have determined that the average person who receives psychotherapy experiences greater improvement than do 75 percent of all untreated people with similar problems. (Adapted from Prochaska & Norcross, 2003; Lambert, Weber, & Sykes, 1993; Smith, Glass, & Miller, 1980.)

Average untreated person

Average treated person

Number of people

75% of untreated persons

No improvement → Outstanding improvement

therapy may be "_What_ specific treatment, by _whom,_ is most effective for _this_ individual with _that_ specific problem, and under _which_ set of circumstances?" (Paul, 1967, p. 111). Researchers have investigated how effective particular therapies are at treating particular disorders, and they have often found sizable differences among the various therapies. Behavioral therapies, for example, appear to be the most effective of all in treating phobias (Wilson, 2008), whereas drug therapy is the single most effective treatment for schizophrenia (Awad & Voruganti, 2007; Weiden & Kane, 2005).

As you read previously, studies also show that some clinical problems may respond better to _combined_ approaches (de Maat et al., 2007; Marder & Kane, 2005; TADS, 2004). Drug therapy is sometimes combined with certain forms of psychotherapy, for example, to treat depression. In fact, it is now common for clients to be seen by two therapists—one of them a **psychopharmacologist,** a psychiatrist who primarily prescribes medications, and the other a psychologist, social worker, or other therapist who conducts psychotherapy.

Obviously, knowledge of how particular therapies fare with particular disorders can help therapists and clients alike make better decisions about treatment (Clinton et al., 2007; Beutler, 2002, 2000, 1991) (see Figure 4-6). It can also lead researchers to a better understanding of why therapy works and ultimately of abnormal functioning. Thus this is a question to which this book shall keep returning as you examine the disorders the therapies have been devised to combat.

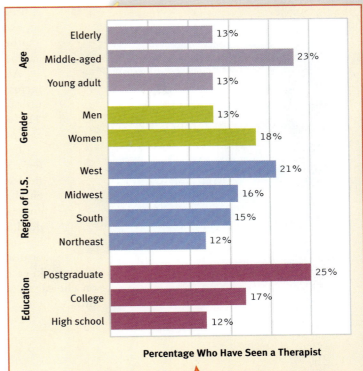

Percentage Who Have Seen a Therapist

Figure 4-6
Who seeks therapy? According to surveys conducted in the United States, people who are middle-aged, female, from Western states, and highly educated are the most likely to have been in therapy at some point in their lives. (Adapted from Fetto, 2002.)

PUTTING IT... together

Renewed Respect Collides with Economic Pressure

In Chapter 3 you read that today's leading models of abnormal behavior often differ widely in their assumptions, conclusions, and treatments. It should not surprise you, then, that clinicians also differ considerably in their approaches to assessment and diagnosis or that those who prefer certain assessment techniques sometimes scoff at those who use other approaches. Yet when all is said and done, no assessment technique stands out as superior to the rest. Each of the hundreds of available tools has significant limitations, and each produces at best an incomplete picture of how a person is functioning and why.

In short, even though some assessment procedures have received more research support than others (and clinicians should pay close attention to such findings when they are deciding which ones to use), the present state of assessment and diagnosis argues against relying exclusively on any one approach. As a result, more and more clinicians now use batteries of assessment tools in their work (Iverson et al., 2007; Meyer et al., 2003, 2001). Such batteries are already providing invaluable guidance in the assessment of Alzheimer's disease and certain other disorders that are particularly difficult to diagnose, as you shall see later.

Attitudes toward clinical assessment have shifted back and forth over the past several decades. Before the 1950s, assessment was a highly regarded part of clinical practice. As the number of clinical models grew during the 1960s and 1970s, however, followers of each model favored certain tools over others, and the practice of assessment became fragmented. Meanwhile, research began to reveal that a number of tools were inaccurate or inconsistent. In this atmosphere, many clinicians lost confidence in and abandoned systematic assessment and diagnosis.

Today, however, respect for assessment and diagnosis is on the rise once again. One reason for this renewal of interest is the development of more precise diagnostic criteria,

•**rapprochement movement**•An effort to identify a set of common strategies that run through the work of all effective therapists.

•**psychopharmacologist**•A psychiatrist who primarily prescribes medications. Also known as a pharmacotherapist.

as presented in DSM-IV-TR. Another is the drive by researchers for more rigorous tests to help them select appropriate participants for clinical studies. Still another factor is the clinical field's growing awareness that certain disorders can be properly identified only after careful assessment procedures.

Along with heightened respect for assessment and diagnosis has come increased research. Indeed, today's researchers are carefully scrutinizing every major kind of assessment tool—from projective tests to personality inventories. This work is helping many clinicians perform their work with more accuracy and consistency—welcome news for people with psychological problems.

Ironically, just as today's clinicians and researchers are rediscovering systematic assessment, rising costs and economic factors seem to be discouraging the use of assessment tools. In particular, managed care insurance plans, which emphasize cost containment and shorter treatments, often refuse to provide coverage for extensive clinical testing or observations (Wood et al., 2002). Indeed, in one survey of psychologists, half of the respondents reported spending less time giving clinical tests than they had done previously, using fewer tests, or discontinuing such tests altogether—all because of managed care policies (Piotrowski et al., 1998). Which of these forces will ultimately have a greater influence on clinical assessment and diagnosis—promising research or economic pressure? Only time will tell . . .

‹‹‹(SUMMING UP)›››

○ **The Practitioner's Task** Clinical practitioners are interested primarily in gathering *idiographic* information about their clients. They seek an understanding of the specific nature and origins of a client's problems through *clinical assessment* and *diagnosis. p. 89*

○ **Clinical Assessment** To be useful, assessment tools must be *standardized, reliable,* and *valid.* Most clinical assessment methods fall into three general categories: *clinical interviews, tests,* and *observations.* A clinical interview permits the practitioner to interact with a client and generally get a sense of who he or she is. It may be either *unstructured* or *structured.* Types of clinical tests include *projective, personality, response, psychophysiological, neurological, neuropsychological,* and *intelligence* tests. Types of observation include *naturalistic observation* and *analog observation.* Practitioners also employ *self-monitoring:* clients observe themselves and record designated behaviors, feelings, or cognitions as they occur. *pp. 89–105*

○ **Diagnosis** After collecting assessment information, clinicians form a *clinical picture* and decide upon a *diagnosis.* The diagnosis is chosen from a *classification system.* The system used most widely in the United States is the *Diagnostic and Statistical Manual of Mental Disorders (DSM). pp. 105–112*

○ **DSM-IV-TR** The most recent version of the DSM, known as *DSM-IV-TR,* lists approximately 400 disorders. Clinicians must evaluate a client's condition on five axes, or categories of information. The reliability and validity of DSM-IV-TR continue to receive broad clinical review and criticism. *pp. 108–111*

○ **Dangers of Diagnosis and Labeling** Even with trustworthy assessment data and reliable and valid classification categories, clinicians will not always arrive at the correct conclusion. They are human and so fall prey to various biases, misconceptions, and expectations. Another problem related to diagnosis is the prejudice that labels arouse, which may be damaging to the person who is diagnosed. *pp. 111–112*

○ **Treatment** The *treatment decisions* of therapists may be influenced by assessment information, the diagnosis, the clinician's theoretical orientation and familiarity with research, and the field's state of knowledge. Determining the *effectiveness of*

BETWEEN THE LINES

Smart Labels

In the 1960s, two psychologists told teachers which of their students had high IQs and low IQs (Rosenthal & Jacobson, 1968). Subsequently, the students identified as smart performed significantly better than the ones identified with a low IQ. The only problem was, the IQ scores told to the teachers had been faked. The students performed better strictly as a function of teacher expectations. ‹‹

treatment is difficult because therapists differ in their ways of defining and measuring success. The variety and complexity of today's treatments also present a problem. *Therapy outcome studies* have led to three general conclusions: (1) people in therapy are usually better off than people with similar problems who receive no treatment; (2) the various therapies do not appear to differ dramatically in their general effectiveness; and (3) certain therapies or combinations of therapies do appear to be more effective than others for certain disorders. Some therapists currently advocate *empirically supported treatment,* the active identification, promotion, and teaching of those interventions that have received clear research support. *pp. 113–117*

⫸ CRITICAL THOUGHTS ⫷

1. How would you grade the tests you take in school? That is, how reliable and valid are they? What about the tests you see in magazines? *pp. 90–91, 93–103*

2. Just about everybody has heard of and knows about the Rorschach, even though the test has limited reliability and validity. How might you explain the fame and popularity of this test throughout Western society? *pp. 94–96*

3. How might IQ scores be misused by school officials, parents, or other individuals? Why do you think our society is so preoccupied with the concept of intelligence and with IQ scores? *pp. 102–103*

4. Many people argue for a "people first" approach to clinical labeling. For example, they recommend using the phrase "a person with schizophrenia" rather than "a schizophrenic." Why might this approach to labeling be preferable? *pp. 105–112*

5. Few people question the value of diagnosis with regard to medical illnesses, yet many theorists worry that diagnosis may do more harm than good when applied to psychological dysfunctioning. Why is diagnosis viewed so differently in the two fields? *pp. 109–112*

6. A newspaper columnist has observed, "Newspapers usually take great care not to mention the race of those accused of violent crimes. But how many times have you seen the sentence, 'He had a history of mental illness'?" What does this double standard suggest about the status and rights of people with psychological disorders? *pp. 111–112*

7. How can persons make wise decisions about therapists and treatment approaches when they are seeking treatment? *pp. 113–117*

⬤ cyberstudy ⬤   SEARCH

Search the *Abnormal Psychology* Video Tool Kit
www.worthpublishers.com/apvtk
▲ Chapter 4 Video Cases
   DSM-IV-TR Categories: Bias against Females? Assessing Psychopathy
   "Brain Fingerprinting": Detecting Hidden Thoughts
▲ Video case discussions, study guides, and questions

Log on to the Comer Web Page
www.worthpublishers.com/comer
▲ Chapter 4 outline, learning objectives, research exercises, study tools, and practice test questions
▲ Additional Chapter 4 case studies, Web links, and FAQs

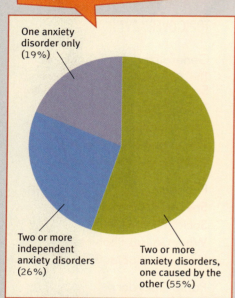

One anxiety disorder only (19%)

Two or more independent anxiety disorders (26%)

Two or more anxiety disorders, one caused by the other (55%)

as if you expected something unpleasant to happen. The vague sense of being in danger is usually called **anxiety,** and it has the same features—the same increase in breathing, muscular tension, perspiration, and so forth—as fear.

Although everyday experiences of fear and anxiety are not pleasant, they often have an adaptive function: they prepare us for action—for "fight or flight"—when danger threatens. They may lead us to drive more cautiously in a storm, keep up with our reading assignments, treat our dates more sensitively, and work harder at our jobs. Unfortunately, some people suffer such disabling fear and anxiety that they cannot lead normal lives (Koury & Rapaport, 2007). Their discomfort is too severe or too frequent, lasts too long, or is triggered too easily. These people are said to have an *anxiety disorder* or a related kind of disorder.

Anxiety disorders are the most common mental disorders in the United States. In any given year 18.1 percent of the adult population suffer from one or another of the six anxiety disorders identified by DSM-IV-TR, while close to 29 percent of all people develop one of the disorders at some point in their lives (Koury & Rapaport, 2007; Kessler et al., 2005). Only around one-fifth of these individuals seek treatment (Wang et al., 2005). The disorders cost society at least $42 billion each year in health care expenses, lost wages, and lost productivity (Dozois & Westra, 2004).

People with *generalized anxiety disorder* experience general and persistent feelings of worry and anxiety. People with *phobias* experience a persistent and irrational fear of a specific object, activity, or situation. Individuals with *panic disorder* have recurrent attacks of terror. Those with *obsessive-compulsive disorder* feel overrun by recurrent thoughts that cause anxiety or by the need to perform repetitive actions to reduce anxiety. And those with *acute stress disorder* and *posttraumatic stress disorder* are tormented by fear and related symptoms well after a traumatic event (for example, military combat, rape, torture) has ended. Most individuals with one anxiety disorder suffer from a second one as well (Angst et al., 2005) (see Figure 5-1). Bob Donaldson, for example, experiences the excessive worry found in generalized anxiety disorder and the repeated attacks of terror that mark panic disorder. In addition, more than than 90 percent of people with one of the anxiety disorders also experience a different kind of psychological disorder at some point in their lives (Garrett, 2009; Doughty et al., 2004; Kaufman & Charney, 2000). An overlap with mood disorders strongest. As many as 60 percent of people with major depression also experience an anxiety disorder during their lives, and 16 percent of individuals with bipolar disorder also display a panic disorder at some point.

This chapter looks at generalized anxiety disorder, phobias, panic disorder, and obsessive-compulsive disorder. The other anxiety disorders—acute and posttraumatic stress disorders—will be examined in the next chapter, which considers the effects that particularly intense or ongoing stress have on both our psychological and physical functioning.

✿Generalized Anxiety Disorder

People with **generalized anxiety disorder** experience excessive anxiety under most circumstances and worry about practically anything. In fact, their problem is sometimes described as *free-floating anxiety*. Like the young carpenter Bob Donaldson, they typically feel restless, keyed up, or on edge; tire easily; have difficulty concentrating; suffer from muscle tension; and have sleep problems (Neckelmann et al., 2007) (see Table 5-1). The symptoms last at least six months. Nevertheless, most people with the disorder are able, although with some difficulty, to carry on social relationships and job activities.

Generalized anxiety disorder is common in Western society. Surveys suggest that around 3 percent of the U.S. population have the symptoms of this disorder in any given year, a rate that holds across Canada, Britain, and other Western countries (Ruscio et al., 2007; Kessler et al., 2005). Altogether, close to 6 percent of all people develop generalized anxiety disorder sometime during their lives. It may emerge at any age, but usually it first appears in childhood or adolescence. Women diagnosed with the disorder

disorder can be traced to inadequacies in the early relationships between children and their parents (Scharf, 2008). Researchers have tested the psychodynamic explanations in various ways. In one strategy, they have tried to show that people with generalized anxiety disorder are particularly likely to use defense mechanisms. For example, one team of investigators examined the early therapy transcripts of patients with this diagnosis and found that the patients often reacted defensively. When asked by therapists to discuss upsetting experiences, they would quickly forget (*repress*) what they had just been talking about, change the direction of the discussion, or deny having negative feelings (Luborsky, 1973).

In another line of research, investigators have studied people who as children suffered extreme punishment for id impulses. As psychodynamic theorists would predict, these people have higher levels of anxiety later in life (Burijon, 2007; Chiu, 1971). In cultures where children are regularly punished and threatened, for example, adults seem to have more fears and anxieties (Whiting et al., 1966). In addition, several studies have supported the psychodynamic position that extreme protectiveness by parents may often lead to high levels of anxiety in their children (Hudson & Rapee, 2004; Jenkins, 1968).

Although these studies are consistent with psychodynamic explanations, some scientists question whether they show what they claim to show. When people have difficulty talking about upsetting events early in therapy, for example, they are not necessarily repressing those events. They may be focusing purposely on the positive aspects of their lives, or they may be too embarrassed to share personal negative events until they develop trust in the therapist.

Another problem is that some research studies and clinical reports have actually contradicted the psychodynamic explanations. In one, 16 people with generalized anxiety disorder were interviewed about their upbringing (Raskin et al., 1982). They reported relatively little of the excessive discipline or disturbed childhood environments that psychodynamic therapists might expect for people with this disorder.

Psychodynamic Therapies Psychodynamic therapists use the same general techniques to treat all psychological problems: *free association* and the therapist's interpretations of *transference, resistance,* and *dreams. Freudian psychodynamic therapists* use these methods to help clients with generalized anxiety disorder become less afraid of their id impulses and more successful in controlling them. Other psychodynamic therapists, particularly *object relations therapists,* use them to help anxious patients identify and settle the childhood relationship problems that continue to produce anxiety in adulthood (Lucas, 2006; Nolan, 2002).

Controlled studies have typically found psychodynamic treatments to be of only modest help to persons with generalized anxiety disorder (Goisman et al., 1999). An exception to this trend is *short-term psychodynamic therapy* (see Chapter 3), which has in some cases significantly reduced the levels of anxiety, worry, and social difficulty of patients with this disorder (Crits-Christoph et al., 2004).

The Humanistic Perspective

Humanistic theorists propose that generalized anxiety disorder, like other psychological disorders, arises when people stop looking at themselves honestly and acceptingly. Repeated denials of their true thoughts, emotions, and behavior make these people extremely anxious and unable to fulfill their potential as human beings.

The humanistic view of why people develop this disorder is best illustrated by Carl Rogers's explanation. As you saw in Chapter 3, Rogers believed that children who fail to receive *unconditional positive regard* from others may become overly critical of themselves and develop harsh self-standards, what Rogers called *conditions of worth.* They try to meet these standards by repeatedly distorting and denying their true thoughts and experiences. Despite such efforts, however, threatening self-judgments keep breaking through and causing them intense anxiety. This onslaught of anxiety sets the stage for generalized anxiety disorder or some other form of psychological dysfunctioning.

"*Dear Mom and Dad: Thanks for the happy childhood. You've destroyed any chance I had of becoming a writer.*"

•**client-centered therapy**•The human-istic therapy developed by Carl Rogers in which clinicians try to help clients by being accepting, empathizing accurately, and conveying genuineness.

•**basic irrational assumptions**•The inaccurate and inappropriate beliefs held by people with various psychologi-cal problems, according to Albert Ellis.

Practitioners of Rogers's treatment approach, **client–centered therapy,** try to show unconditional positive regard for their clients and to empathize with them. The therapists hope that an atmosphere of genuine acceptance and caring will help clients feel secure enough to recognize their true needs, thoughts, and emotions. When clients eventually are honest and comfortable with themselves, their anxiety or other symptoms will subside. In the following excerpt, Rogers describes the progress made by a client with anxiety and related symptoms:

Therapy was an experiencing of herself, in all its aspects, in a safe relationship. At first it was her guilt and her concern over being responsible for the maladjustments of others. Then it was her hatred and bitterness toward life for having cheated and frustrated her in so many different areas, particularly the sexual, and then it was the experiencing of her own hurt, of the sorrow she felt for herself for having been so wounded. But along with these went the experiencing of self as having a capacity for wholeness . . . a self that cared about others. This last followed . . . the realization that the therapist cared, that it really mattered to him how therapy turned out for her, that he really valued her. She ex-perienced the soundness of her basic directions. She gradually became aware of the fact that, though she had searched in every corner of herself, there was nothing fundamentally bad, but rather, at heart she was positive and sound.

(Rogers, 1954, pp. 261–264)

In spite of such optimistic case reports, controlled studies have failed to offer strong support for this approach. Although research does suggest that client-centered therapy is usually more helpful to anxious clients than no treatment, the approach is only sometimes superior to placebo therapy (Prochaska & Norcross, 2006, 2003). In addi-tion, researchers have found, at best, only limited support for Rogers's explanation of generalized anxiety disorder and other forms of abnormal behavior. Nor have other humanistic theories and treatment received much research support.

The Cognitive Perspective

Proponents of the cognitive model suggest that psychological problems are often caused by dysfunctional ways of thinking (see *A Closer Look* on the facing page). Given that excessive worry—a cognitive symptom—is a key characteristic of generalized anxiety disorder (see Figure 5-2), it is not surprising that cognitive theorists have had much to say about the causes of and treatments for this particular disorder (Holaway, Rodebaugh, & Heimberg, 2006).

Maladaptive Assumptions Initially, cognitive theorists suggested that generalized anxiety disorder is primarily caused by *maladaptive assumptions,* a notion that continues to be influential. Albert Ellis, for example, proposed that many people are guided by irratio-nal beliefs that lead them to act and react in inappropriate ways (Ellis, 2005, 2002, 1962). Ellis called these **basic irrational assumptions,** and he claimed that people with gen-eralized anxiety disorder often hold the following ones:

"It is a dire necessity for an adult human being to be loved or approved of by virtually every significant other person in his community."

"It is awful and catastrophic when things are not the way one would very much like them to be."

"If something is or may be dangerous or fearsome, one should be terribly con-cerned about it and should keep dwelling on the possibility of its occurring."

"One should be thoroughly competent, adequate, and achieving in all possible respects if one is to consider oneself worthwhile."

(Ellis, 1962)

Figure 5-2

How long do your worries last? In one survey, 62 percent of college students said they spend less than 10 minutes at a time worrying about something. In contrast, 20 percent worry for more than an hour. (Adapted from Tallis et al., 1994.)

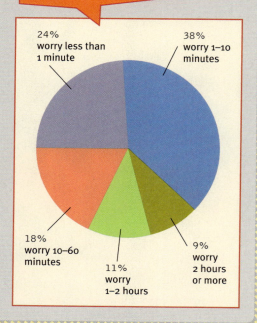

24% worry less than 1 minute

38% worry 1–10 minutes

18% worry 10–60 minutes

11% worry 1–2 hours

9% worry 2 hours or more

Fears, Shmears: The Odds Are Usually on Our Side

People with anxiety disorders have many unreasonable fears, but millions of other people, too, worry about disaster every day. Most of the catastrophes they fear are not probable. Perhaps the ability to live by laws of *probability* rather than *possibility* is what separates the fearless from the fearful. What are the odds, then, that commonly feared events will happen? The range of probability is wide, but the odds are usually heavily in our favor.

Build with care The chance of a construction worker being injured at work during the year is 1 in 27.

Jim Harrison/Stock Boston

A city resident will be a victim of a violent crime . . . 1 in 60

A suburbanite will be a victim of a violent crime . . . 1 in 1,000

A small-town resident will be a victim of a violent crime . . . 1 in 2,000

A child will suffer a high-chair injury this year . . . 1 in 6,000

The IRS will audit you this year . . . 1 in 100

You will be murdered this year . . . 1 in 12,000

You will be killed on your next bus ride . . . 1 in 500 million

You will be hit by a baseball at a major-league game . . . 1 in 300,000

You will drown in the tub this year . . . 1 in 685,000

Your house will have a fire this year . . . 1 in 200

Your carton will contain a broken egg . . . 1 in 10

You will develop a tooth cavity . . . 1 in 6

You will contract AIDS from a blood transfusion . . . 1 in 100,000

You will die in a tsunami . . . 1 in 500,000

You will be attacked by a shark . . . 1 in 4 million

You will receive a diagnosis of cancer this year . . . 1 in 8,000

A woman will develop breast cancer during her lifetime . . . 1 in 9

A piano player will eventually develop lower back pain . . . 1 in 3

You will be killed on your next automobile outing . . . 1 in 4 million

Condom use will eventually fail to prevent pregnancy . . . 1 in 10

An IUD will eventually fail to prevent pregnancy . . . 1 in 10

Coitus interruptus will eventually fail to prevent pregnancy . . . 1 in 5

You will die as a result of a collision between an asteroid and the earth . . . 1 in 500,000

You will die as a result of a lightning strike . . . 1 in 84,000

(ADAPTED FROM BRITT, 2005)

When people who make these assumptions are faced with a stressful event, such as an exam or a blind date, they are likely to interpret it as dangerous and threatening, to overreact, and to experience fear. As they apply the assumptions to more and more events, they may begin to develop generalized anxiety disorder (Warren, 1997).

Similarly, cognitive theorist Aaron Beck argued that people with generalized anxiety disorder constantly hold silent assumptions (for example, "A situation or a person is unsafe until proven to be safe" or "It is always best to assume the worst") that imply they are in imminent danger (Beck & Weishaar, 2008; Beck & Emery, 1985). Since the time of Ellis's and Beck's initial proposals, researchers have repeatedly found that people with generalized anxiety disorder do indeed hold maladaptive assumptions, particularly about dangerousness (Riskind & Williams, 2005).

table: 5-3

Worrying about Worrying: Items from the Meta-Worry Questionnaire

I am going crazy with worry.

My worrying will escalate and I'll cease to function.

I'm making myself ill with worry.

I'm abnormal for worrying.

My mind can't take the worrying.

I'm losing out in life because of worrying.

My body can't take the worrying.

Source: Wells, 2005.

What kinds of people are likely to have exaggerated expectations of danger? Some cognitive theorists point to those whose lives have been filled with *unpredictable negative events*. These individuals become generally fearful of the unknown and always wait for the boom to drop. To avoid being blindsided, they keep trying to predict negative events. They look everywhere for signs of danger, and they wind up seeing danger everywhere, thus setting up a life of anxiety. In support of this idea, studies have found that both animal and human research participants respond more fearfully to unpredictable negative events than to predictable ones and that people with generalized anxiety disorder are much more uncomfortable with uncertainty than other people are and worry more about the future (Mineka & Zinberg, 2006; Dugas et al., 2005, 2002).

New Wave Cognitive Explanations In recent years, three new explanations for generalized anxiety disorder, sometimes called the *new wave cognitive explanations,* have emerged. Each of them builds on the work of Ellis and Beck and their emphasis on danger.

The *metacognitive theory,* developed by the researcher Adrian Wells (2005), suggests that people with generalized anxiety disorder implicitly hold both positive and negative beliefs about worrying. On the positive side, they believe that worrying is a useful way of appraising and coping with threats in life. And so they look for and examine all possible signs of danger—that is, they worry constantly.

At the same time, Wells argues, individuals with generalized anxiety disorder also hold negative beliefs about worrying, and these negative attitudes are the ones that open the door to the disorder. Because society teaches them that worrying is a bad thing, the individuals come to believe that their repeated worrying is in fact harmful (mentally and physically) and uncontrollable. Now they further worry about the fact that they always seem to be worrying (so-called *metaworries*) (see Table 5-3). The net effect of all this worrying: generalized anxiety disorder.

This explanation has received considerable research support. Studies indicate, for example, that individuals who generally hold both positive and negative beliefs about worrying are particularly prone to developing generalized anxiety disorder (Khawaja & Chapman, 2007; Wells, 2005) and that repeated metaworrying is a powerful predictor of developing the disorder (Wells & Carter, 1999).

According to another new explanation for generalized anxiety disorder, the *intolerance of uncertainty theory,* certain individuals believe that any possibility of a negative event occurring, no matter how slim, means that the event is likely to occur. Given this intolerance of uncertainty, such persons are inclined to worry and are, in turn, more prone to develop generalized anxiety disorder (Dugas, Buhr, & Ladouceur, 2004). Think of when you meet someone you're attracted to and how you then feel prior to texting or calling call him or her for the first time—or how you feel while you're waiting for that person to contact you for the first time. The worry that you experience in such instances—the sense of sometimes unbearable uncertainty—is, according to this theory, how people with generalized anxiety disorder feel all the time.

A deep intolerance of uncertainty causes persons with the disorder to survey all situations—even mildly threatening ones—in order to help reduce potential terrible consequences. Even when faced with only modest problems, they cannot tolerate the uncertainty tied to the problems, and they keep worrying in an effort to find "correct" solutions. Because they cannot be sure that any given solution is a correct one, they are left to grapple with their intolerable level of uncertainty, and they continue to worry and to try to solve the problem at hand. They are stuck in a problem-solving loop.

Like the metacognitive theory of worry, considerable research supports this theory. Studies have found that people with generalized anxiety disorder do indeed display greater levels of intolerance of uncertainty than people with normal degrees of anxiety (Dugas et al., 1998). In fact, such individuals also experience higher levels of intolerance of uncertainty than people who experience other kinds of anxiety disorders (Dugas et al., 2001).

Finally, a third new explanation for generalized anxiety disorder, the *avoidance theory,* developed by researcher Thomas Borkovec, suggests that people with this disorder have greater bodily arousal (higher heart rate, perspiration, respiration) than other people and that worrying actually serves to *reduce* this arousal, perhaps by distracting the individuals from their unpleasant somatic feelings. In short, the avoidance theory holds that people with generalized anxiety disorder worry repeatedly in order to reduce or avoid uncomfortable states of bodily arousal. When, for example, they find themselves in an uncomfortable job situation or social relationship, they implicitly choose to intellectualize (that is, worry about) losing their job or losing their friend rather than having to stew in a state of intense negative arousal. The worrying serves as a quick, though ultimately maladaptive, way of coping with unpleasant bodily states.

Borkovec's explanation has also been supported in numerous studies. Research with laboratory participants has found, for example, that worrying does indeed temporarily reduce heart rate and other forms of bodily arousal. In addition, clinical studies reveal that people with generalized anxiety disorder experience particularly fast and intense bodily reactions, find such reactions overwhelming and unpleasant, worry more than other people upon becoming aroused, and successfully reduce their arousal whenever they worry (Mennin et al., 2005, 2004, 2002; Roemer et al., 2005; Turk et al., 2005).

Cognitive Therapies Two kinds of cognitive approaches are used in cases of generalized anxiety disorder. In one, based on the pioneering work of Ellis and Beck, therapists help clients change the maladaptive assumptions that characterize their disorder. In the other, new-wave cognitive therapists help clients to understand the special role that worrying may play in the disorder and to change their views about and reactions to worrying.

CHANGING MALADAPTIVE ASSUMPTIONS In Ellis's technique of **rational-emotive therapy**, therapists point out the irrational assumptions held by clients, suggest more appropriate assumptions, and assign homework that gives the individuals practice at challenging old assumptions and applying new ones (Ellis, 2005, 2002, 2001). Studies do suggest that this approach and similar cognitive approaches bring at least modest relief to persons suffering from generalized anxiety (Ellis, 2005; Tafet et al., 2005). Ellis's approach is illustrated in the following discussion between him and an anxious client who fears failure and disapproval at work, especially over a testing procedure that she has developed for her company:

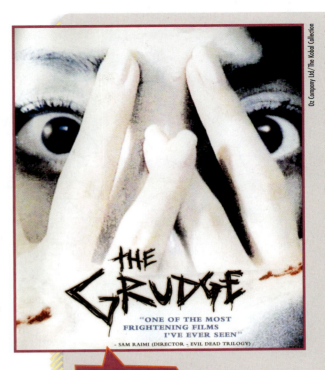

Fearful delights
Many people enjoy the feeling of fear as long as it occurs under controlled circumstances, as when they are safely watching the tension grow in the hugely popular series of movies *The Grudge 1, 2, and 3*. These films, American remakes of the Japanese movie *Ju-on*, have collectively grossed more than $200 million.

Client: I'm so distraught these days that I can hardly concentrate on anything for more than a minute or two at a time. My mind just keeps wandering to that damn testing procedure I devised, and that they've put so much money into; and whether it's going to work well or be just a waste of all that time and money. . . .

Ellis: Point one is that you must admit that you are telling yourself something to start your worrying going, and you must begin to look, and I mean really look, for the specific nonsense with which you keep reindoctrinating yourself. . . . The false statement is: "If, because my testing procedure doesn't work and I am functioning inefficiently on my job, my co-workers do not want me or approve of me, then I shall be a worthless person." . . .

Client: But if I want to do what my firm also wants me to do, and I am useless to them, aren't I also useless to me?

Ellis: No—not unless you think you are. You are frustrated, of course, if you want to set up a good testing procedure and you can't. But need you be desperately unhappy because you are frustrated? And need you deem yourself completely unworthwhile because you can't do one of the main things you want to do in life?

(Ellis, 1962, pp. 160–165)

•rational-emotive therapy• A cognitive therapy developed by Albert Ellis that helps clients identify and change the irrational assumptions and thinking that help cause their psychological disorder.

"No, no, that's not a sin, either. My goodness, you must have worried yourself to death."

Beck's similar but more systematic approach, called, simply, *cognitive therapy,* is an adaptation of his influential and very effective treatment for depression (which is discussed in Chapter 9). Researchers have found that, like Ellis's rational emotion therapy, it often helps reduce generalized anxiety to more tolerable levels (Tafet et al., 2005).

FOCUSING ON WORRYING Alternatively, some of today's new-wave cognitive therapists specifically guide clients with generalized anxiety disorder to recognize and change their dysfunctional use of worrying (Beck, 2008; Waters & Craske, 2005). They begin by educating the clients about the role of worrying in their disorder and have them observe their bodily arousal and cognitive responses across various life situations. In turn, the clients come to appreciate the triggers of their worrying, their misconceptions about worrying, and their misguided efforts to control and predict their emotions and their lives by worrying. As their insights grow, clients are expected to see the world as less threatening (and so less arousing), try out and adopt more constructive ways of dealing with arousal, and worry less about the fact that they worry so much. Research has begun to indicate that a concentrated focus on worrying is indeed a helpful addition to the traditional cognitive treatment for generalized anxiety disorder (Hollon et al., 2006; Waters & Craske, 2005; Mennin, 2004).

Treating individuals with generalized anxiety disorder by helping them to recognize their inclination to worry is similar to another cognitive approach that has gained popularity in recent years. The approach, *mindfulness-based cognitive therapy,* was developed by the psychologist Steven Hayes and his colleagues as part of their broader treatment approach called acceptance and commitment therapy (Hayes et al., 2004; Hayes, 2004, 2002). In mindfulness-based cognitive therapy, therapists help clients to become aware of their streams of thoughts, including their worries, as they are occurring and to *accept* such thinking as mere events of the mind. By accepting their thoughts rather than trying to eliminate them, the clients are expected to be less upset and affected by them.

Mindfulness-based cognitive therapy has also been applied to a range of other psychological problems such as depression, posttraumatic stress disorder, personality disorders, and substance abuse, often with promising results (Hayes et al., 2004). As you will see in the next chapter, this cognitive approach borrows heavily from a form of meditation called *mindfulness meditation,* which teaches individuals to pay attention to the thoughts and feelings that flow through their minds during meditation and to accept such thoughts in a nonjudgmental way.

The Biological Perspective

Biological theorists believe that generalized anxiety disorder is caused chiefly by biological factors. For years this claim was supported primarily by **family pedigree studies,** in which researchers determine how many and which relatives of a person with a disorder have the same disorder. If biological tendencies toward generalized anxiety disorder are inherited, people who are biologically related should have similar probabilities of developing this disorder. Studies have in fact found that biological relatives of persons with generalized anxiety disorder are more likely than nonrelatives to have the disorder also (Wetherell et al., 2006; Hettema et al., 2005, 2003, 2001). Approximately 15 percent of the relatives of people with the disorder display it themselves—much more than the 6 percent lifetime prevalence rate found in the general population. And the closer the relative (an identical twin, for example, as opposed to a fraternal twin or other sibling), the greater the likelihood that he or she will also have the disorder (APA, 2000).

Of course, investigators cannot have full confidence in biological interpretations of such findings. Because relatives are likely to share aspects of the same environment, their shared disorders may reflect similarities in environment and upbringing rather than similarities in biological makeup. And, indeed, the closer the relatives, the more similar their environmental experiences are likely to be. Because identical twins are more physically alike than fraternal twins, they may even experience more similarities in their upbringing.

Biological Explanations: GABA Inactivity

In recent decades important discoveries by brain researchers have offered clearer evidence that generalized anxiety disorder is related to biological factors. One of the first such discoveries occurred in the 1950s, when researchers determined that **benzodiazepines,** the family of drugs that includes *alprazolam* (Xanax), *lorazepam* (Ativan), and *diazepam* (Valium), provide relief from anxiety. At first, no one understood why benzodiazepines reduce anxiety. Eventually, however, the development of radioactive techniques enabled researchers to pinpoint the exact sites in the brain that are affected by benzodiazepines (Mohler & Okada, 1977). Apparently certain neurons have receptors that receive the benzodiazepines, just as a lock receives a key.

Investigators soon discovered that these benzodiazepine receptors ordinarily receive **gamma-aminobutyric acid (GABA),** a common and important neurotransmitter in the brain. As you read in Chapter 3, neurotransmitters are chemicals that carry messages from one neuron to another. GABA carries *inhibitory* messages: when GABA is received at a receptor, it causes the neuron to stop firing.

On the basis of such findings, biological researchers eventually pieced together several scenarios of how fear reactions may occur. One of the leading scenarios began with the notion that in normal fear reactions, key neurons throughout the brain fire more rapidly, triggering the firing of still more neurons and creating a general state of excitability throughout the brain and body. Perspiration, breathing, and muscle tension increase. This state is experienced as fear or anxiety. Continuous firing of neurons eventually triggers a feedback system—that is, brain and body activities that reduce the level of excitability. Some neurons throughout the brain release the neurotransmitter GABA, which then binds to GABA receptors on certain neurons and instructs those neurons to stop firing. The state of excitability ceases, and the experience of fear or anxiety subsides (Ator, 2005; Costa, 1985, 1983).

Some researchers concluded that a malfunction in this feedback system can cause fear or anxiety to go unchecked (Roy-Byrne, 2005). In fact, when investigators reduced GABA's ability to bind to GABA receptors, they found that animal subjects reacted with a rise in anxiety (Costa, 1985; Mohler, Richards, & Wu, 1981). This finding suggested that people with generalized anxiety disorder may have ongoing problems in their anxiety feedback system. Perhaps they have too few GABA receptors, or perhaps their GABA receptors do not readily capture the neurotransmitter.

This explanation was certainly promising, and it continues to have many supporters; but it is also problematic. The first problem is that recent biological discoveries have complicated the picture. It has been found, for example, that other neurotransmitters, such as serotonin and norepinephrine (neurotransmitters that you will read about in later sections), may also play important roles in anxiety and generalized anxiety disorder, acting alone or in conjunction with GABA (Garrett, 2009; Burijon, 2007). Another problem is that some of this research on the biology of anxiety has been done on laboratory animals. When researchers produce fear responses in animals, they assume that the animals are experiencing something similar to human anxiety, but it is impossible to be certain. The animals may be experiencing a high level of arousal that is quite different from human anxiety.

Finally, biological theorists are faced with the problem of establishing a causal relationship. Although studies have tied physiological functioning to generalized anxiety disorder, they have not established that the physiological events *cause* the disorder. The biological responses of anxious persons may be the result, rather than the cause, of their anxiety disorders. Perhaps long-term anxiety eventually leads to poorer GABA reception, for example.

•**family pedigree study**•A research design in which investigators determine how many and which relatives of a person with a disorder have the same disorder.

•**benzodiazepines**•The most common group of antianxiety drugs, which includes Valium and Xanax.

•**GABA**•The neurotransmitter gamma-aminobutyric acid, whose low activity has been linked to generalized anxiety disorder.

Do monkeys experience anxiety? Clinical researchers must be careful in interpreting the reactions of animal subjects. This infant monkey was considered "fearful" after being separated from its mother. But perhaps it was feeling depressed or experiencing a level of arousal that does not correspond to either fear or depression.

University of Wisconsin Primate Laboratory, Madison

table: 5-4

Drugs That Reduce Anxiety, by Class

Generic Name	Trade Name
Benzodiazepines	
Alprazolam	Xanax
Chlorazepate	Tranxene
Chlordiazepoxide	Librium
Clonazepam	Klonopin
Diazepam	Valium
Estazolam	ProSom
Halazepam	Paxipam
Lorazepam	Ativan
Midazolam	Versed
Oxazepam	Serax
Prazepam	Centrax
Temazepam	Rostoril
Others	
Buspirone	BuSpar
Propranolol	Inderal
Atenolol	Tenormin

Biological Treatments The leading biological approach to treating generalized anxiety disorder is drug therapy (see Table 5-4). Other biological interventions are *relaxation training,* which teaches people to relax the muscles throughout their bodies, and *biofeedback,* which trains clients to control underlying biological processes voluntarily.

ANTIANXIETY DRUG THERAPY In the late 1950s a group of drugs called *benzodiazopines* was marketed as **sedative-hypnotic drugs**—drugs that calm people in low doses and help them fall asleep in higher doses. These new antianxiety drugs seemed less addictive than previous sedative-hypnotic medications, such as *barbiturates,* and they appeared to produce less tiredness (Meyer & Quenzer, 2005). Thus, they were quickly embraced by both doctors and patients.

Only years later did investigators come to understand the reasons for the effectiveness of benzodiazepines. As you have read, researchers eventually learned that there are specific neuron sites in the brain that receive benzodiazepines (Mohler & Okada, 1977) and that these same receptor sites ordinarily receive the neurotransmitter GABA. Apparently, when benzodiazepines bind to these neuron receptor sites, particularly those receptors known as *GABA-A receptors,* they increase the ability of GABA to bind to them as well, and so improve GABA's ability to stop neuron firing and reduce anxiety (Dawson et al., 2005).

Studies indicate that benzodiazepines often provide temporary relief for people with generalized anxiety disorder (Burijon, 2007). However, clinicians have come to realize the potential dangers of these drugs. First, when the medications are stopped, many persons' anxieties return as strong as ever. Second, we now know that people who take benzodiazepines in large doses for an extended time can become physically dependent on them. Third, the drugs can produce undesirable effects such as drowsiness, lack of coordination, memory loss, depression, and aggressive behavior. Finally, the drugs mix badly with certain other drugs or substances. For example, if people on benzodiazepines drink even small amounts of alcohol, their breathing can slow down dangerously, sometimes fatally (Meyer & Quenzer, 2005).

In recent decades, still other kinds of drugs have become available for people with generalized anxiety disorder. In particular, it has been discovered that a number of *antidepressant* medications, drugs that are usually used to lift the moods of depressed persons, are also helpful to many people with generalized anxiety disorder. Only certain kinds of antidepressant drugs seem to reduce the symptoms of generalized anxiety disorder—namely, those that operate by increasing the activity of the neurotransmitter *serotonin.* Like GABA, serotonin is a neurotransmitter that carries messages between neurons. However, serotonin acts at different neurons and brain areas than GABA.

Based partly on this finding, some researchers believe that generalized anxiety may also be the result of low serotonin activity, and, in fact, a number of today's clinicians are more inclined to prescribe the serotonin-enhancing antidepressants to treat generalized anxiety disorder than the GABA-enhancing benzodiazepines (Burijon, 2007; Liebowitz et al., 2005).

If, as some clinical investigators suspect, low serotonin plays a key role in generalized anxiety disorder, why would benzodiazepine drugs be as helpful as they are to people with the disorder, especially since some research now suggests that benzodiazepines initially *reduce* serotonin activity in the brain? The answer to this question may lie in the *long-term* effects of benzodiazepines. Although these drugs do indeed initially suppress serotonin activity, they eventually seem to produce a compensatory increase in serotonin activity, just as they produce an increase in the activity of GABA (Garrett, 2009).

In short, at this point, research suggests that generalized anxiety disorder may be related to low GABA activity, low serotonin activity, or both and that drugs that increase GABA activity, serotonin activity, or both are helpful to individuals with the disorder.

RELAXATION TRAINING A nonchemical biological technique commonly used to treat generalized anxiety disorder is **relaxation training.** The notion behind this approach is that physical relaxation will lead to a state of psychological relaxation. In one version, therapists teach clients to identify individual muscle groups, tense them, release the tension, and ultimately relax the whole body. With continued practice, they can bring on a state of deep muscle relaxation at will, reducing their state of anxiety.

Research indicates that relaxation training is more effective than no treatment or placebo treatment in cases of generalized anxiety disorder. The improvement it produces, however, tends to be modest (Leahy, 2004; Butler et al., 1991), and other techniques that are known to relax people, such as *meditation,* often seem to be equally effective (Bourne et al., 2004; Kabat-Zinn et al., 1992). Relaxation training is of greatest help to people with generalized anxiety disorder when it is combined with cognitive therapy or with biofeedback (Lang, 2004; Brown et al., 2001).

BIOFEEDBACK In **biofeedback,** therapists use electrical signals from the body to train people to control physiological processes such as heart rate or muscle tension. Clients are connected to a monitor that gives them continuous information about their bodily activities. By attending to the therapist's instructions and the signals from the monitor, they may gradually learn to control even seemingly involuntary physiological processes.

The most widely applied method of biofeedback for the treatment of anxiety uses a device called an **electromyograph (EMG),** which provides feedback about the level of muscular tension in the body. Electrodes are attached to the client's muscles—usually the forehead muscles—where they detect the minute electrical activity that accompanies muscle tension (see Figure 5-3). The device then converts electric potentials coming from the muscles into an image, such as lines on a screen, or into a tone whose pitch changes along with changes in muscle tension. Thus clients "see" or "hear" when their muscles are becoming more or less tense. Through repeated trial and error, the individuals become skilled at voluntarily reducing muscle tension and, theoretically, at reducing tension and anxiety in everyday stressful situations.

Research finds that, in most cases, EMG biofeedback, like relaxation training, has only a modest effect on a person's anxiety level (Brambrink, 2004; Brown et al., 2001, 1992). As you will see in the next chapter, this and other forms of biofeedback have had their greatest impact when they play *adjunct* roles in the treatment of certain medical problems, including headaches, back pain, gastrointestinal disorders, seizure disorders, and neuromuscular disorders such as cerebral palsy (Astin, 2004; Engel et al., 2004).

Modern relaxation
At the Brain Mind Gym, business executives receive pulsations of light and sound from goggles and headphones, which are meant to lull their brains into deep relaxation.

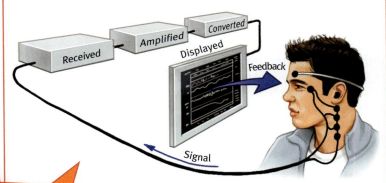

Figure 5-3
Biofeedback at work This biofeedback system records tension in the forehead muscles of an anxious person. The system receives, amplifies, converts, and displays information about the tension on a monitor, allowing the client to "observe" it and to try to reduce his tension responses.

•**sedative-hypnotic drugs**•Drugs that calm people at lower doses and help them to fall asleep at higher doses.

•**relaxation training**•A treatment procedure that teaches clients to relax at will so they can calm themselves in stressful situations.

•**biofeedback**•A treatment technique in which a client is given information about physiological reactions as they occur and learns to control the reactions voluntarily.

•**electromyograph (EMG)**•A device that provides feedback about the level of muscular tension in the body.

✿ Phobias

Most of us are none too eager to confront a spider or to be caught in a thunderstorm, but few of us have such dread as Marianne or Trisha:

Marianne *Seeing a spider makes me rigid with fear, hot, trembling and dizzy. I have occasionally vomited and once fainted in order to escape from the situation. These symptoms last three or four days after seeing a spider. Realistic pictures can cause the same effect, especially if I inadvertently place my hand on one.*

(Melville, 1978, p. 44)

Trisha *At the end of March each year, I start getting agitated because summer is coming and that means thunderstorms. I have been afraid since my early twenties, but the last three years have been the worst. I have such a heartbeat that for hours after a storm my whole left side is painful. . . . I say I will stay in the room, but when it comes I am a jelly, reduced to nothing. I have a little cupboard and I go there, I press my eyes so hard I can't see for about an hour, and if I sit in the cupboard over an hour my husband has to straighten me up.*

(Melville, 1978, p. 104)

A **phobia** (from the Greek word for "fear") is a persistent and unreasonable fear of a particular object, activity, or situation. People with a phobia become fearful if they even think about the object or situation they dread, but they usually remain comfortable as long as they avoid the object or thoughts about it.

We all have our areas of special fear, and it is normal for some things to upset us more than other things, perhaps even different things at different stages of our lives (Antony & Barlow, 2002). A survey of residents of a community in Burlington, Vermont, found that fears of crowds, death, injury, illness, and separation were more common among people in their sixties than in other age groups (Agras, Sylvester, & Oliveau, 1969). Among 20-year-olds, fears of snakes, heights, storms, enclosures, and social situations were much more common.

How do these common fears differ from phobias? DSM-IV-TR indicates that a phobia is more intense and persistent and the desire to avoid the object or situation is greater (APA, 2000). People with phobias often feel so much distress that their fears may interfere dramatically with their lives.

Most phobias technically fall under the category of *specific phobias,* DSM-IV-TR's label for a marked and persistent fear of a specific object or situation. In addition, there are two broader kinds of phobias: *social phobia,* a fear of social or performance situations in which embarrassment may occur, and *agoraphobia,* a fear of venturing into public places, especially when one is alone. Because agoraphobia is usually, perhaps always, experienced in conjunction with *panic attacks,* unpredictable attacks of terror, we shall examine that phobia later within our discussion of panic disorders.

Specific Phobias

A **specific phobia** is a persistent fear of a specific object or situation (see Table 5-5). When sufferers are exposed to the object or situation, they typically experience immediate fear. Common specific phobias are intense fears of specific animals or insects, heights, enclosed spaces, thunderstorms, and blood. Earlier, Marianne and Trisha described their specific phobias of spiders and thunderstorms. Here, Andrew talks about his phobic fear of flying:

table: 5-5

DSM Checklist

SPECIFIC PHOBIA

1. Marked and persistent fear of a specific object or situation that is excessive or unreasonable, lasting at least six months.

2. Immediate anxiety usually produced by exposure to the object.

3. Recognition that the fear is excessive or unreasonable.

4. Avoidance of the feared situation.

5. Significant distress or impairment.

Based on APA, 2000.

We got on board, and then there was the take-off. There it was again, that horrible feeling as we gathered speed. It was creeping over me again, that old feeling of panic. I kept seeing everyone as puppets, all strapped to their seats with no control over their destinies, me included. Every time the plane did a variation of speed or route, my heart would leap and I would hurriedly ask what was happening. When the plane started to lose height, I was terrified that we were about to crash.

(Melville, 1978, p. 59)

Each year 8.7 percent of all people in the United States have the symptoms of a specific phobia (Kessler et al., 2005). More than 12 percent of individuals develop such phobias at some point during their lives, and many people have more than one at a time. Women with the disorder outnumber men by at least 2 to 1. For reasons that are not clear, the prevalence of specific phobias also differs among racial and ethnic minority groups. In most, but not all, studies on this subject, African Americans and Hispanic Americans report having at least 50 percent more specific phobias than do white Americans, even when economic factors, education, and age are held steady across the groups (Hopko et al., 2008; Breslau et al., 2006; Antony & Barlow, 2002). At the same time, it is worth noting that these heightened rates are at work only among African and Hispanic Americans who were born in the United States, not those who emigrated to the United States at some point during their lives (Hopko et al., 2008).

The impact of a specific phobia on a person's life depends on what arouses the fear (Scher et al., 2006). People whose phobias center on dogs, insects, or water will keep encountering the objects they dread. Their efforts to avoid them must be elaborate and may greatly restrict their activities. Urban residents with snake phobias have a much easier time. The vast majority of people with a specific phobia do not seek treatment. They try instead to avoid the objects they fear (Roth & Fonagy, 2005; Wang et al., 2005).

Social Phobias

Many people worry about interacting with others or about talking or performing in front of others. A number of entertainers, from singer Barbra Streisand to actor Sir Laurence Olivier to football player Ricky Williams, have described major bouts of anxiety before performing. And others, such as actor Tom Hanks and talk show host David Letterman, report struggling with painful shyness at various points in their lives. Social fears of this kind are unpleasant and inconvenient, but usually the people who have them manage to function adequately, some at a very high level.

People with a **social phobia,** by contrast, have severe, persistent, and irrational fears of social or performance situations in which embarrassment may occur (see Table 5-6). A social phobia may be *narrow,* such as a fear of talking in public or writing in front of others, or it may be *broad,* such as a general fear of functioning poorly in front of others. In both forms, people repeatedly judge themselves as performing less adequately than they actually do.

A social phobia can interfere greatly with one's life (Koury & Rapaport, 2007). A person who is unable to interact with others or speak in public may fail to perform important responsibilities. One who cannot eat in public may reject dinner invitations and other social opportunities. Since most people with this phobia keep their fears secret, their social reluctance is often misinterpreted as snobbery, lack of interest, or hostility.

table: 5-6

DSM Checklist

SOCIAL PHOBIA

1. Marked and persistent fear of social or performance situations involving exposure to unfamiliar people or possible scrutiny by others, lasting at least six months. Concern about humiliating or embarrassing oneself.

2. Anxiety usually produced by exposure to the social situation.

3. Recognition that the fear is excessive or unreasonable.

4. Avoidance of feared situations.

5. Significant distress or impairment.

Based on APA, 2000.

Hidden fear
Miami Dolphins running back Ricky Williams has revealed that he experiences social anxiety, a disorder that led him to leave professional football from 2004 to 2005.

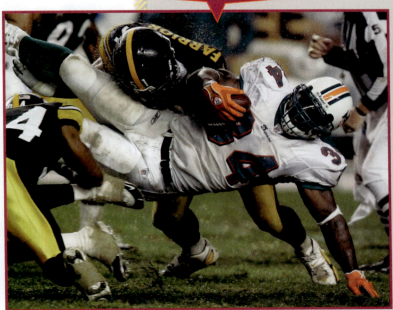

AP Photo/Gene J. Puskar

table: 5-7

Anxiety Disorders Profile

	One-Year Prevalence	Female to Male Ratio	Typical Age at Onset	Prevalence among Close Relatives	Percentage Currently Receiving Clinical Treatment
Generalized anxiety disorder	3.0%	2:1	0–20 years	Elevated	25.5%
Specific phobia	8.7%	2:1	Variable	Elevated	19.0%
Social phobia	7.1%	3:2	10–20 years	Elevated	24.7%
Panic disorder	2.8%	5:2	15–35 years	Elevated	34.7%
Obsessive-compulsive disorder	1.0%	1:1	4–25 years	Elevated	41.3%

Source: Ruscio et al., 2007; Kessler et al., 2005, 1999, 1994; Wang et al., 2005; Regier et al., 1993.

Surveys indicate that 7.1 percent of people in the United States and other Western countries—around three women for every two men—experience a social phobia in any given year (see Table 5-7). Around 12 percent develop this problem at some point in their lives (Ruscio et al., 2008; Kessler et al., 2005). It often begins in late childhood or adolescence and may continue into adulthood (APA, 2000).

There are some indications that social phobias may be more common among African Americans and Asian Americans than white Americans. In several studies, for example, African and Asian American participants have scored higher on surveys of social anxiety and social concerns (Schultz et al., 2008, 2006; Akazaki et al., 2002). In addition, a culture-bound disorder called *taijn kyofusho* seems to be particularly common in Asian countries such as Japan and Korea (Scultz et al., 2008; APA, 2000). Although this disorder is traditionally defined as a pervasive fear of making other people feel uncomfortable, a number of clinicians now suspect that its sufferers primarily fear being evaluated negatively by other people, a key feature of social phobias (Magee et al., 2006; Schultz et al., 2008; Suzuki et al., 2003).

Word limits

In 2004, Austrian author Elfriede Jelinek, the Nobel prize winner in literature, had to accept this prestigious honor and present her Nobel lecture by video transmission because she has a social phobia that prevented her from attending the festivities in Stockholm in person. She was the first literature winner in 40 years not to attend the prize ceremony.

AP Photo/Jonas Ekstromer

What Causes Phobias?

Each of the models offers explanations for phobias. Evidence tends to support the behavioral explanations. Behaviorists believe that people with phobias first learn to fear certain objects, situations, or events through conditioning (Wolfe, 2005; King et al., 2004). Once the fears are acquired, the individuals avoid the dreaded object or situation, permitting the fears to become all the more entrenched.

Behavioral Explanations: How Are Fears Learned?
Behaviorists propose **classical conditioning** as a common way of acquiring phobic reactions. Here, two events that occur close together in time become closely associated in a person's mind, and, as you saw in Chapter 3, the person then reacts similarly to both of them. If one event triggers a fear response, the other may also.

In the 1920s a clinician described the case of a young woman who apparently acquired a phobia of running water through classical conditioning (Bagby, 1922). As a child of 7 she went on a picnic with her mother and aunt and ran off by herself into the woods after lunch. While she was climbing over some large rocks, her feet were caught between two of them. The harder she tried to free herself, the more trapped she became. No one heard her screams, and she grew more and more terrified. In the language of behaviorists, the entrapment was eliciting a fear response.

Entrapment → Fear response

As she struggled to free her feet, the girl heard a waterfall nearby. The sound of the running water became linked in her mind to her terrifying battle with the rocks, and she developed a fear of running water as well.

Running water → Fear response

Eventually the aunt found the screaming child, freed her from the rocks, and comforted her; but the psychological damage had been done. From that day forward, the girl was terrified of running water. For years family members had to hold her down to bathe her. When she traveled on a train, friends had to cover the windows so that she would not have to look at any streams. The young woman had apparently acquired a phobia through classical conditioning.

In conditioning terms, the entrapment was an *unconditioned stimulus* (US) that understandably elicited an *unconditioned response* (UR) of fear. The running water represented a *conditioned stimulus* (CS), a formerly neutral stimulus that became associated with entrapment in the child's mind and came also to elicit a fear reaction. The newly acquired fear was a *conditioned response* (CR).

US: Entrapment → UR: Fear

CS: Running water → CR: Fear

Another way of acquiring a fear reaction is through **modeling,** that is, through observation and imitation (Bandura & Rosenthal, 1966). A person may observe that others are afraid of certain objects or events and develop fears of the same things. Consider a young boy whose mother is afraid of illnesses, doctors, and hospitals. If she frequently expresses those fears, before long the boy himself may fear illnesses, doctors, and hospitals.

Why should one upsetting experience develop into a long-term phobia? Shouldn't the trapped girl later have seen that running water would bring her no harm? Shouldn't the boy later see that illnesses are temporary and doctors and hospitals helpful? Behaviorists believe that after acquiring a fear response, people try to *avoid* what they fear. Whenever they find themselves near a fearsome object, they quickly move away. They may also plan ahead to ensure that such encounters will not occur. Remember that the girl had friends cover the windows on trains so that she could avoid looking at streams. People with phobias do not get close to the dreaded objects often enough to learn that they are really quite harmless.

Behaviorists also propose that specific learned fears will blossom into a generalized anxiety disorder when a person acquires a large number of them. This development is presumed to come about through **stimulus generalization:** responses to one stimulus

---

BETWEEN THE LINES

Famous People, Famous Fears

Napoleon Bonaparte	Cats ‹‹
Johnny Depp	Clowns, spiders, ghosts ‹‹
Justin Timberlake	Snakes ‹‹
Queen Elizabeth I	Roses ‹‹
Billy Bob Thornton	Antique furniture ‹‹
Edgar Allan Poe	Enclosed places ‹‹
Harry Houdini	Enclosed places ‹‹
Adolf Hitler	Enclosed places ‹‹
Nicole Kidman	Butterflies ‹‹
Howard Hughes	Germs ‹‹
Madonna	Thunder ‹‹
John Madden	Air travel ‹‹
Whoopi Goldberg	Air travel ‹‹
Aretha Franklin	Air travel ‹‹
Christina Ricci	Houseplants ‹‹
Cher	Air travel ‹‹

(abcnews.go.com, 2008; Szegedy-Maszak, 2004)

•**classical conditioning**•A process of learning in which two events that repeatedly occur close together in time become tied together in a person's mind and so produce the same response.

•**modeling**•A process of learning in which a person observes and then imitates others. Also, a therapy approach based on the same principle.

•**stimulus generalization**•A phenomenon in which responses to one stimulus are also produced by similar stimuli.

A CLOSER LOOK

Phobias, Familiar and Not So Familiar

Animals—zoophobia

Beards—pogonophobia

Being afraid—phobophobia

Blood—hematophobia

Books—bibliophobia

Churches—ecclesiaphobia

Corpses—necrophobia

Crossing a bridge—gephyrophobia

Crowds—ochlophobia

Darkness—achluophobia, nyctophobia

Demons or devils—demonophobia

Dogs—cynophobia

Dolls—pediophobia

Drugs—pharmacophobia

Enclosed spaces—claustrophobia

Eyes—ommatophobia

Feces—coprophobia

Fire—pyrophobia

Flood—antlophobia

Flowers—anthophobia

Flying—aerophobia

Fog—homichlophobia

Fur—doraphobia

Germs—spermophobia

Ghosts—phasmophobia

God—theophobia

Graves—taphophobia

Heat—thermophobia

Heights—acrophobia

Homosexuality—homophobia

Horses—hippophobia

Ice, frost—cryophobia

Insects—entomophobia

Michael Caulfield/AP Photo

Arachnophobia, not While many people experience arachnophobia, a fear of spiders, a hardy few actually enjoy these and other kinds of bugs. Here, Steve Kutcher, a bug wrangler, holds a Chilean rose tarantula (left) and an Emperor scorpion. He has turned his childhood fascination with bugs into a lucrative business, making his many creepy crawlers available to the movies.

Machinery—mechanophobia

Marriage—gamophobia

Meat—carnophobia

Mice—musophobia

Mirrors—eisoptrophobia

Money—chrometrophobia

Night—nyctophobia

Noise or loud talking—phonophobia

Odors—osmophobia

Pleasure—hedonophobia

Poison—toxiphobia

Poverty—peniaphobia

Pregnancy—maieusiophobia

Railways—siderodromophobia

Rain—ombrophobia

Rivers—potamophobia

Robbers—harpaxophobia

Satan—Satanophobia

Sexual intercourse—coitophobia, cypridophobia

Shadows—sciophobia

Sleep—hypnophobia

Snakes—ophidiophobia

Snow—chionophobia

Speed—tachophobia

Spiders—arachnophobia

Stings—cnidophobia

Strangers—xenophobia

Sun—heliophobia

Surgery—ergasiophobia

Teeth—odontophobia

Travel—hodophobia

Trees—dendrophobia

Wasps—spheksophobia

Water—hydrophobia

Wind—anemophobia

Worms—helminthophobia

Wounds, injury—traumatophobia

(VAN WAGNER, 2007; MELVILLE, 1978)

are also elicited by similar stimuli. The fear of running water acquired by the girl in the rocks could have generalized to such similar stimuli as milk being poured into a glass or even the sound of bubbly music. Perhaps a person experiences a series of upsetting events, each event produces one or more feared stimuli, and the person's reactions to each of these stimuli generalize to yet other stimuli. That person may then build up a large number of fears and eventually develop generalized anxiety disorder.

How Have Behavioral Explanations Fared in Research?

Some laboratory studies have found that animals and humans can indeed be taught to fear objects through classical conditioning (Miller, 1948; Mowrer, 1947, 1939). In one famous report, psychologists John B. Watson and Rosalie Rayner (1920) described how they taught a baby boy called Little Albert to fear white rats. For weeks Albert was allowed to play with a white rat and appeared to enjoy doing so. One time when Albert reached for the rat, however, the experimenter struck a steel bar with a hammer, making a very loud noise that upset and frightened Albert. The next several times that Albert reached for the rat, the experimenter again made the loud noise. Albert acquired a fear and avoidance response to the rat. As Watson (1930) described it, "The instant the rat was shown, the baby began to cry . . . and . . . crawl away" (p. 161). According to some reports, Albert's fear of white rats also generalized to such objects as a rabbit, human hair, cotton, and even a Santa Claus mask.

Research has also supported the behavioral position that fears can be acquired through modeling. Psychologists Albert Bandura and Theodore Rosenthal (1966), for example, had human research participants observe a person apparently being shocked by electricity whenever a buzzer sounded. The victim was actually the experimenter's accomplice—in research terminology, a *confederate*—who pretended to experience pain by twitching and yelling whenever the buzzer went on. After the unsuspecting participants had observed several such episodes, they themselves experienced a fear reaction whenever they heard the buzzer.

Although these studies support behaviorists' explanations of phobias, other research has called those explanations into question (Ressler & Davis, 2003). Several laboratory studies with children and adults have failed to condition fear reactions. In addition, although most case studies trace phobias to possible incidents of classical conditioning or modeling, quite a few fail to do so. So, although it appears that a phobia *can* be acquired by classical conditioning or modeling, researchers have not established that the disorder is *ordinarily* acquired in this way.

A Behavioral-Evolutionary Explanation

Some phobias are much more common than others (see *A Closer Look* on the facing page). Phobic reactions to animals, heights, and darkness are more common than phobic reactions to meat, grass, and houses. Theorists often account for these differences by proposing that human beings, as a species, have a predisposition to develop certain fears (Scher et al., 2006; Mineka & Ohman, 2002; Seligman, 1971). This idea is referred to as **preparedness** because human beings, theoretically, are "prepared" to acquire some phobias and not others. The following case makes the point:

A four-year-old girl was playing in the park. Thinking that she saw a snake, she ran to her parents' car and jumped inside, slamming the door behind her. Unfortunately, the girl's hand was caught by the closing car door, the results of which were severe pain and several visits to the doctor. Before this, she may have been afraid of snakes, but not phobic. After this experience, a phobia developed, not of cars or car doors, but of snakes. The snake phobia persisted into adulthood, at which time she sought treatment from me.

(Marks, 1977, p. 192)

In a series of studies on preparedness, psychologist Arne Ohman and his colleagues conditioned different kinds of fears in two groups of human participants (Lundqvist & Ohman, 2005; Ohman & Soares, 1993; Ohman et al., 1975). In one study they showed

Monkey see, monkey do? A chimpanzee interacts with and models behaviors for her young offspring. Although humans may acquire phobias by either classical conditioning or modeling, research indicates that chimpanzees are more likely to acquire such fears (or other kinds of behaviors and reactions) through modeling.

•**preparedness**•A predisposition to develop certain fears.

all participants slides of faces, houses, snakes, and spiders. One group received electric shocks whenever they observed the slides of faces and houses, while the other group received shocks when they looked at snakes and spiders. Were participants more prepared to fear snakes and spiders? Using skin reactions, or *galvanic skin responses (GSRs)*, as a measure of fear, the experimenters found that both groups learned to fear the intended objects after repeated shock pairings. But then they noted an interesting difference: after a short shock-free period, the persons who had learned to fear faces and houses stopped registering high GSRs in the presence of those objects, while the persons who had learned to fear snakes and spiders continued to show high GSRs in response to them for a long while. One interpretation is that animals and insects are stronger candidates for human phobias than faces or houses.

Researchers do not know whether human predispositions to fear are the result of evolutionary or environmental factors (Ohman & Mineka, 2003; Mineka & Ohman, 2002). Those who propose an *evolutionary* explanation argue that a predisposition to fear has been transmitted genetically through the evolutionary process. Among our ancestors, the ones who more readily acquired a fear of animals, darkness, heights, and the like were more likely to survive long enough to reproduce. Proponents of an *environmental* explanation argue instead that experiences teach us early in life that certain objects are legitimate sources of fear, and this training predisposes many people to acquire corresponding phobias.

How Are Phobias Treated?

Surveys reveal that 19 percent of individuals with specific phobias and 24.7 percent of those with social phobia are currently in treatment (Wang et al., 2005). Every theoretical model has its own approach to treating phobias, but behavioral techniques are more widely used than the rest, particularly for specific phobias. Research has shown such techniques to be highly effective and to fare better than other approaches in most head-to-head comparisons. Thus we shall focus primarily on the behavioral interventions.

Treatments for Specific Phobias Specific phobias were among the first anxiety disorders to be treated successfully in clinical practice. The major behavioral approaches to treating them are *desensitization, flooding,* and *modeling.* Together, these approaches are called **exposure treatments** because in all of them individuals are exposed to the objects or situations they dread.

People treated by **systematic desensitization,** a technique developed by Joseph Wolpe (1997, 1987, 1969), learn to relax while gradually facing the objects or situations they fear. Since relaxation and fear are incompatible, the new relaxation response is thought to substitute for the fear response. Desensitization therapists first offer *relaxation training* to clients, teaching them how to bring on a state of deep muscle relaxation at will. In addition, the therapists help clients create a **fear hierarchy,** a list of feared objects or situations, ordered from mildly to extremely upsetting.

Then clients learn how to pair relaxation with the objects or situations they fear. While the client is in a state of relaxation, the therapist has the client face the event at the bottom of his or her hierarchy. This may be an actual confrontation, a process called *in vivo desensitization.* A person who fears heights, for example, may stand on a chair or climb a stepladder. Or the confrontation may be imagined, a process called *covert desensitization.* In this case, the person imagines the frightening event while the therapist describes it. The client moves through the entire list, pairing his or her relaxation responses with each feared item. Because the first item is only mildly frightening, it is usually only a short while before the person is able to relax totally in its presence. Over the

Recovering lost revenues
These children scream out as they experience a sudden steep drop from the top of an amusement park ride called Super Shot. Missing out on thousands of dollars each year because many people are afraid of roller coasters and the new wave of horror rides, several parks offer behavioral programs to help customers overcome their fears. After "treatment," some clients are able to ride the rails with the best of them. For others, it's back to the relative calm of the Ferris wheel.

course of several sessions, clients move up the ladder of their fears until they reach and overcome the one that frightens them most of all.

Another behavioral treatment for specific phobias is **flooding.** Flooding therapists believe that people will stop fearing things when they are exposed to them repeatedly and made to see that they are actually quite harmless. Clients are forced to face their feared objects or situations without relaxation training and without a gradual buildup. The flooding procedure, like desensitization, can be either in vivo or covert.

When flooding therapists guide clients in imagining feared objects or situations, they often exaggerate the description so that the clients experience intense emotional arousal. In the case of a woman with a snake phobia, the therapist had her imagine the following scene, among others:

Close your eyes again. Picture the snake out in front of you, now make yourself pick it up. Reach down, pick it up, put it in your lap, feel it wiggling around in your lap, leave your hand on it, put your hand out and feel it wiggling around. Kind of explore its body with your fingers and hand. You don't like to do it, make yourself do it. Make yourself do it. Really grab onto the snake. Squeeze it a little bit, feel it. Feel it kind of start to wind around your hand. Let it. Leave your hand there, feel it touching your hand and winding around it, curling around your wrist.

(Hogan, 1968, p. 423)

In *modeling,* or *vicarious conditioning,* it is the therapist who confronts the feared object or situation while the fearful person observes (Bandura, 2004, 1977, 1971; Bandura, Adams, & Beyer, 1977). The behavioral therapist acts as a model to demonstrate that the person's fear is groundless. After several sessions many clients are able to approach the objects or situations calmly. In one version of modeling, *participant modeling,* the client is actively encouraged to join in with the therapist.

Clinical researchers have repeatedly found that each of the exposure treatments helps people with specific phobias (Pull, 2005; Wolfe, 2005). The key to success in all of these therapies appears to be *actual* contact with the feared object or situation (van Hout & Emmelkamp, 2002). In vivo desensitization is more effective than covert desensitization, in vivo flooding more effective than covert flooding, and participant modeling more helpful than strictly observational modeling. In addition, a growing number of therapists are using *virtual reality*—3D computer graphics that simulate real-world objects and situations—as a useful exposure tool (Winerman, 2005).

Treatments for Social Phobias
Only in recent years have clinicians been able to treat social phobias successfully (Ruscio et al., 2008; Cottraux, 2005; Kearney, 2005). Their newfound success is due in part to the growing recognition that social phobias have two distinct features that may feed upon each other: (1) people with the phobias may have overwhelming social fears, and (2) they may lack skill at starting conversations, communicating their needs, or meeting the needs of others. Armed with this insight, clinicians now treat social phobias by trying to reduce social fears, by providing training in social skills, or both.

HOW CAN SOCIAL FEARS BE REDUCED? Unlike specific phobias, which do not typically respond to psychotropic drugs, social fears are often reduced through medication (Julien, 2008). Somewhat surprisingly, it is *antidepressant medications* that seem to be the drugs of most help for this disorder, often more helpful than benzodiazepines or other kinds of antianxiety medications (Burijon, 2007; Davidson, 2004).

Participant modeling
Employing the exposure technique of participant modeling, therapist Pete Cohen treats clients who manifest *ophidiophobia* (fear of snakes) by first handling a snake himself, then encouraging the clients to handle it.

•**exposure treatments**•Behavioral treatments in which persons are exposed to the objects or situations they dread.

•**systematic desensitization**•A behavioral treatment that uses relaxation training and a fear hierarchy to help clients with phobias react calmly to the objects or situations they dread.

•**fear hierarchy**•A list of objects or situations that frighten a person, starting with those that are slightly feared and ending with those that are feared greatly.

•**flooding**•A treatment for phobias in which clients are exposed repeatedly and intensively to a feared object and made to see that it is actually harmless.

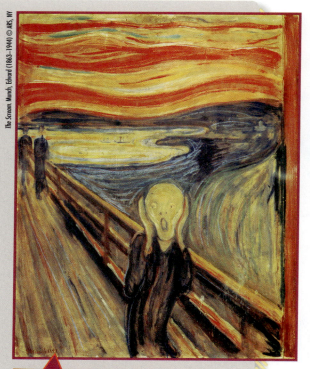

The Scream: Munch, Edvard (1863–1944) © ARS, NY

The Scream: The rest of the story

Edvard Munch's *The Scream* is one of the most famous paintings in the world, but few people know the story behind this work of art. While walking on a bridge at sunset with two friends, the artist stopped to admire the view. Munch's friends kept walking, however, and when he realized that they were gone, he experienced enormous anxiety, which he immortalized with the painting.

BETWEEN THE LINES

Young Dr. Ellis

Early in his career, in order to combat his own social anxiety (as well as test his theories), Albert Ellis sat on a park bench in Manhattan's Central Park day after day for a year, asking out every woman who passed by. ‹‹

At the same time, several types of psychotherapy have proved to be at least as effective as medication at reducing social fears, and people helped by such psychological treatments appear less likely to relapse than those treated with medications alone (Rodebaugh, Holaway, & Heimberg, 2004). This finding suggests to some clinicians that the psychological approaches should always be included in the treatment of social fears.

One psychological approach is *exposure therapy,* the behavioral intervention so effective with specific phobias. Exposure therapists guide, encourage, and persuade clients with social fears to expose themselves to the dreaded social situations and to remain until their fears subside (Rodebaugh et al., 2004). Usually the exposure is gradual, and it often includes homework assignments that are carried out in social situations. In addition, group therapy offers an ideal setting for exposure treatments by allowing people to face social situations in an atmosphere of support and caring (McEvoy, 2007; Turk et al., 2001). In one group, for example, a man who was afraid that his hands would tremble in the presence of other people had to write on a blackboard in front of the group and serve tea to the other members (Emmelkamp, 1982).

Cognitive therapies have also been widely used to treat social fears, often in combination with behavioral techniques (McEvoy, 2007; Hollon et al., 2006). In the following discussion, Albert Ellis uses rational-emotive therapy to help a man who fears he will be rejected if he speaks up at gatherings. The discussion took place after the man had done a homework assignment in which he was to observe his self-defeating social expectations and force himself to say anything he had on his mind in social situations, no matter how stupid it might seem to him:

After two weeks of this assignment, the patient came into his next session of therapy and reported: "I did what you told me to do. . . . [Every] time, just as you said, I found myself retreating from people, I said to myself: 'Now, even though you can't see it, there must be some sentences. What are they?' And I finally found them. And there were many of them! And they all seemed to say the same thing."

"What thing?"

"That I, uh, was going to be rejected. . . . [If] I related to them I was going to be rejected. And wouldn't that be perfectly awful if I was to be rejected. And there was no reason for me, uh, to take that, uh, sort of thing, and be rejected in that awful manner." . . .

"And did you do the second part of the homework assignment?"

"The forcing myself to speak up and express myself?"

"Yes, that part."

"That was worse. That was really hard. Much harder than I thought it would be. But I did it."

"And?"

"Oh, not bad at all. I spoke up several times; more than I've ever done before. Some people were very surprised. Phyllis was very surprised, too. But I spoke up." . . .

"And how did you feel after expressing yourself like that?"

"Remarkable! I don't remember when I last felt this way. I felt, uh, just remarkable—good, that is. It was really something to feel! But it was so hard. I almost didn't make it. And a couple of other times during the week I had to force myself again. But I did. And I was glad!"

(Ellis, 1962, pp. 202–203)

Studies show that rational-emotive therapy and other cognitive approaches do indeed help reduce social fears (McEvoy, 2007; Hollon et al., 2006). And these reductions typically persist for years. On the other hand, research also suggests that in most cases cognitive therapy, like drug therapy and exposure therapy, fails to eliminate social phobias fully.

It may reduce social fear, but it does not consistently help people perform effectively in social settings. This is where social skills training has come to the forefront.

HOW CAN SOCIAL SKILLS BE IMPROVED? In **social skills training,** therapists combine several behavioral techniques in order to help people improve their social skills. They usually *model* appropriate social behaviors for clients and encourage the individuals to try them out. The clients then *role-play* with the therapists, *rehearsing* their new behaviors until they become more effective. Throughout the process, therapists provide frank *feedback* and *reinforce* (praise) the clients for effective performances.

Reinforcement from other people with similar social difficulties is often more powerful than reinforcement from a therapist alone. In *social skills training groups* and *assertiveness training groups,* members try out and rehearse new social behavior with other group members. The group can also provide guidance on what is socially appropriate. According to research, social skills training, both individual and group formats, has helped many people perform better in social situations (Fisher et al., 2004).

✿Panic Disorder

Sometimes an anxiety reaction takes the form of a smothering, nightmarish panic in which people lose control of their behavior and, in fact, are practically unaware of what they are doing. Anyone can react with panic when a real threat looms up suddenly (see *Psych Watch* on page 145). Some people, however, experience **panic attacks**—periodic, short bouts of panic that occur suddenly, reach a peak within 10 minutes, and gradually pass.

The attacks feature at least four of the following symptoms of panic: palpitations of the heart, tingling in the hands or feet, shortness of breath, sweating, hot and cold flashes, trembling, chest pains, choking sensations, faintness, dizziness, and a feeling of unreality. Small wonder that during a panic attack many people fear they will die, go crazy, or lose control.

I was inside a very busy shopping precinct and all of a sudden it happened: in a matter of seconds I was like a mad woman. It was like a nightmare, only I was awake; everything went black and sweat poured out of me—my body, my hands and even my hair got wet through. All the blood seemed to drain out of me; I went as white as a ghost. I felt as if I were going to collapse; it was as if I had no control over my limbs; my back and legs were very weak and I felt as though it were impossible to move. It was as if I had been taken over by some stronger force. I saw all the people looking at me—just faces, no bodies, all merged into one. My heart started pounding in my head and in my ears; I thought my heart was going to stop. I could see black and yellow lights. I could hear the voices of the people but from a long way off. I could not think of anything except the way I was feeling and that now I had to get out and run quickly or I would die. I must escape and get into the fresh air.

(Hawkrigg, 1975)

Lots of people are capable of experiencing a panic attack when faced with something they dread. Indeed, more than one-quarter of all individuals have one or more panic attacks at some point in their lives (Kessler et al., 2006). Some people, however, have panic attacks repeatedly and unexpectedly without apparent reason. They may be suffering from **panic disorder.** In addition to the panic attacks, people who are diagnosed with panic disorder experience dysfunctional changes in their thinking or behavior as a result of the attacks for a period of a month or more (see Table 5-8). For example, they may worry persistently about having another attack, have concerns about what such an attack means ("Am I losing my mind?"), or plan their behavior around the possibility of a future attack.

•**social skills training**•A therapy approach that helps people learn or improve social skills and assertiveness through role playing and rehearsing of desirable behaviors.

•**panic attacks**•Periodic, short bouts of panic that occur suddenly, reach a peak within minutes, and gradually pass.

•**panic disorder**•An anxiety disorder marked by recurrent and unpredictable panic attacks.

table: **5-8**

DSM Checklist

PANIC DISORDER

1. Recurrent unexpected panic attacks.
2. A month or more of one of the following after at least one of the attacks.
   (a) Persistent concern about having additional attacks.
   (b) Worry about the implications or consequences of the attack.
   (c) Significant change in behavior related to the attacks.

Based on APA, 2000.

•**agoraphobia**•An anxiety disorder in which a person is afraid to be in places or situations from which escape might be difficult (or embarrassing) or help unavailable if panic-like symptoms were to occur.

Panic disorder is often accompanied by **agoraphobia,** one of the three categories of phobia mentioned earlier. People with agoraphobia (from the Greek word for "fear of the marketplace") are afraid to leave the house and travel to public places or other locations where escape might be difficult or help unavailable should panic symptoms develop. The intensity of agoraphobia may fluctuate. In severe cases, people become virtual prisoners in their own homes. Their social life dwindles, and they cannot hold a job.

Until recently, clinicians failed to recognize the close link between agoraphobia and panic attacks. They now realize that panic attacks, or at least some panic-like symptoms, typically set the stage for agoraphobia: after experiencing one or more unpredictable attacks, certain individuals become fearful of having new attacks in public places where help or escape might be difficult. Anne Watson's plight illustrates a typical onset of agoraphobia:

Ms. Watson reported that until the onset of her current problems two years ago, she had led a normal and happy life. At that time an uncle to whom she had been extremely close in her childhood died following a sudden unexpected heart attack. . . . Six months after his death she was returning home from work one evening when suddenly she felt that she couldn't catch her breath. Her heart began to pound, and she broke out into a cold sweat. Things began to seem unreal, her legs felt leaden, and she became sure she would die or faint before she reached home. She asked a passerby to help her get a taxi and went to a nearby hospital emergency room. The doctors there found her physical examination, blood count and chemistries, and electrocardiogram all completely normal. . . .

Four weeks later Ms. Watson had a second similar attack while preparing dinner at home. She made an appointment to see her family doctor, but again, all examinations were normal. She decided to put the episodes out of her mind and continue with her normal activities. Within the next several weeks, however, she had four attacks and noticed that she began to worry about when the next one would occur. . . .

She then found herself constantly thinking about her anxieties as attacks continued; she began to dread leaving the house alone for fear she would be stranded, helpless and alone, by an attack. She began to avoid going to movies, parties, and dinners with friends for fear she would have an attack and be embarrassed by her need to leave. When household chores necessitated driving she waited until it was possible to take her children or a friend along for the ride. She also began walking the twenty blocks to her office to avoid the possibility of being trapped in a subway car between stops when an attack occurred.

(Spitzer et al., 1983, pp. 7–8)

Not everyone with panic disorder develops agoraphobia, but many such persons do. Thus DSM-IV-TR distinguishes panic disorder without agoraphobia from panic disorder with agoraphobia. Around 2.8 percent of all people in the United States suffer from one or the other of these patterns in a given year; close to 5 percent develop one of the patterns at some point in their lives (Burijon, 2007; Kessler et al., 2006, 2005). Both kinds of panic disorder are likely to develop in late adolescence or early adulthood and are at least twice as common among women as among men (APA, 2000). The prevalence of panic disorder is the same across various cultural and racial groups in the United States. Moreover, the disorder seems to occur in equal numbers in cultures across the world, although its specific context and label differs from country to country—*ataque de nervios* ("attack of nerves") in Latin American and Carribbean countries, *kyol goeu* ("wind overload") in Cambodia, and "heart distress" in Iran (Nazarian & Craske, 2008; Nazemi et al., 2003; Hinton et al., 2001). Surveys indicate that around 35 percent of individuals with panic disorder in the United States are currently in treatment (Wang et al., 2005).

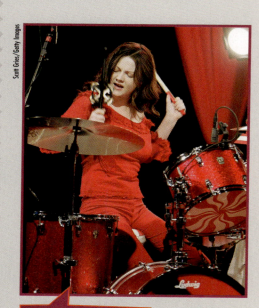

Scott Gries/Getty Images

The show can't go on
On September 12, 2007, the eclectic garage-rock duo The White Stripes had to announce to its many fans that it was canceling the remainder of its U.S. tour, saying that drummer Meg White was "suffering from acute anxiety and . . . unable to travel at this time."

PSYCH WATCH

Panic: Everyone Is Vulnerable

People with panic disorder are not the only ones to experience panic. In fact, many people panic when faced with a threat that unfolds very rapidly. The following news report describes the crowd reaction and human stampede that occurred at a trendy Chicago nightclub on February 17, 2003, after a security guard used pepper spray or mace to break up a fight between two women:

Panic's aftermath One year after the E2 nightclub stampede, friends and family members held a memorial at the site of the nightclub for the 21 people killed in the incident. Each victim was memorialized by a cross bearing his or her name and photograph.

Police and fire officials yesterday began an investigation into how a fight in a Chicago nightclub caused a stampede in which 21 people were crushed to death. Witnesses claimed a fight between two women led to security guards using a pepper spray or mace to separate them early yesterday morning. As the fumes caused a panic, the fleeing clubbers found the rear doors of the E2 club were chained shut, forcing an estimated 1,500 people inside to surge down a narrow stairwell as they attempted to flee.

About 150 people, including two firefighters involved in the rescue operation, were injured, at least ten of whom were in critical condition last night. Eyewitnesses described how a "mound of people" built up on the stairs as they fled towards an exit, with many trampled and suffocated in the panic. Others passed out from the effect of the chemical fumes, it was claimed.

Cory Thomas, 33, who was waiting outside to collect two friends, said: "People were stacking on top of each other screaming and gagging. The door got blocked because there were too many people stacked up against it. I saw at least ten lifeless bodies." Others staggered from the building breathless and incoherent. "Everybody smashed; people crying, couldn't breathe," said one clubber, Reggie Clark. "Two ladies next to me died. A guy under me passed out." Tonita Matthews, a young woman inside the club who tried to help the injured, said: "People just died in my arms." As the bodies of the dead and injured lay in the street outside, another woman who escaped described a young man fighting to breathe in a tangle of bodies, who had asked her to tell his mother he loved her. . . .

The incident occurred at about 2am local time on a busier than usual night at E2, a dance club above the upmarket Epitome restaurant in a predominantly black district on Chicago's south side, which is famed for its nightclubs. The dance club is a popular late-night party spot, known for attracting rock and rap stars. . . .

Most of those who died were killed at the bottom of the main front door stairwell. Kristy Mitchell, 22, was one of those rescued after falling on the stairway and being trampled as the crowd continued to pour over her. She said: "People were stomping my legs. When they pulled me up, I was dizzy and I couldn't breathe." Another of those rescued, Lamont James, said: "We heard the DJ say there was a fight and that caused a panic. People started heading for the corridor leading to the exit. There were people on top of me, people underneath me, people pressed up against the wall. I heard people screaming 'I can't breathe'." Ms Matthews blacked out but later managed to scramble out of the front door, turning back to see casualties pressed up against the glass.

It was by far the worst fatal incident of its kind in the US. In 1979, 11 people were killed in Cincinnati in a crush to get into a concert by The Who, and in 1991 nine young people were crushed to death in a gym stairwell while awaiting a celebrity basketball game in New York. . . .

Amishoov Blackwell, 30, who was knocked backwards down the stairs by the screaming crowd as he emerged from the cloakroom, lay on top of a pile of dead bodies for 30 minutes before he was freed by firefighters. "It wasn't anything but two girls fighting," he said. "Why did they have to spray mace?"

(From the article "Revellers Crushed to Death in Club," by Jacqui Goddard, February 18, 2003, The Scotsman)

Note: On February 20, 2003, just four days later, in a nightclub called The Station in Warwick, Rhode Island, 100 people were killed and 200 injured as a panicked crowd raced for the front door after the heavy metal band Great White set off fireworks that began burning out of control.

•norepinephrine• A neurotransmitter whose abnormal activity is linked to panic disorder and depression.

•locus ceruleus• A small area of the brain that seems to be active in the regulation of emotions. Many of its neurons use norepinephrine.

•amygdala• A small, almond-shaped structure in the brain that processes emotional information.

The Biological Perspective

In the 1960s, clinicians made the surprising discovery that panic disorder was helped more by certain *antidepressant drugs,* drugs that are usually used to reduce the symptoms of depression, than by most of the benzodiazepine drugs, the drugs useful in treating generalized anxiety disorder (Klein, 1964; Klein & Fink, 1962). This observation led to the first biological explanations and treatments for panic disorder.

What Biological Factors Contribute to Panic Disorder?

To understand the biology of panic disorder, researchers worked backward from their understanding of the antidepressant drugs that seemed to control it. They knew that the antidepressant drugs that alleviated panic disorder were those that operated in the brain primarily by changing the activity of **norepinephrine,** yet another one of the neurotransmitters that carry messages between neurons. If the drugs also eliminated panic attacks, researchers wondered, might panic disorder be caused in the first place by abnormal norepinephrine activity?

Several studies produced evidence that norepinephrine activity is indeed irregular in people who suffer from panic attacks. For example, the **locus ceruleus,** an area in the midbrain, is rich in neurons that use norepinephrine. When this area is electrically stimulated in monkeys, the monkeys have a panic-like reaction, suggesting that panic reactions may be related to increases in norepinephrine activity in the locus ceruleus (Redmond, 1981, 1979, 1977). Similarly, in another line of research, scientists were able to induce panic attacks in human beings by injecting them with chemicals known to increase the activity of norepinephrine (Bourin et al., 1995; Charney et al., 1990, 1987).

These findings strongly tied norepinephrine and the locus ceruleus to panic attacks. However, research conducted in recent years indicates that the root of panic attacks is probably more complicated than a single neurotransmitter or single brain area. Researchers have determined that emotional reactions of various kinds are tied to brain *circuits*—networks of brain structures that work together, triggering each other into action and producing a particular kind of emotional reaction. It turns out that the circuit that produces panic reactions includes brain areas such as the *amygdala, ventromedial nucleus of the hypothalamus, central gray matter,* and *locus ceruleus* (Ninan & Dunlop, 2005; Mezzasalma et al., 2004) (see Figure 5-4). When a person confronts a frightening object or situation, the **amygdala,** a small almond-shaped structure that processes emotional information, is stimulated. In turn, the amygdala stimulates the other brain areas in the circuit, setting into motion an "alarm-and-escape" response (increased heart rate, respiration, blood pressure, and the like) that is very similar to a panic reaction (Gray & McNaughton, 1996). Normally, such a reaction is countered by the activity of other brain regions so that the individual can calm down and cope with the situation at hand.

While most of today's researchers agree that this brain circuit probably functions improperly in people who experience panic disorder, they disagree as to where in the circuit the problem lies. Many researchers continue to believe that the locus ceruleus and the neurotransmitter norepinephrine are the key culprits (Burijon, 2007; Bailey et al., 2003). However, other investigators argue that dysfunctioning by other brain structures or neurotransmitters in the circuit is primarily responsible for panic disorder (Maron et al., 2005, 2004; Bellodi et al., 2003; Gorman, 2003).

It is worth noting that the brain circuit responsible for panic reactions appears to be different from the circuit responsible for *anxiety* reactions (reactions that are more diffuse, ongoing, and worry-dominated than panic reactions) (see Figure 5-5). The anxiety brain circuit, which functions improperly in people with generalized anxiety disorder, includes the *amygdala, prefrontal cortex,* and *anterior cingulate cortex* (McClure et al., 2007). Although some

Figure 5-4
The biology of panic The circuit in the brain that produces panic reactions includes areas such as the amygdala, ventromedial nucleus of the hypothalamus, central gray matter, and locus ceruleus.

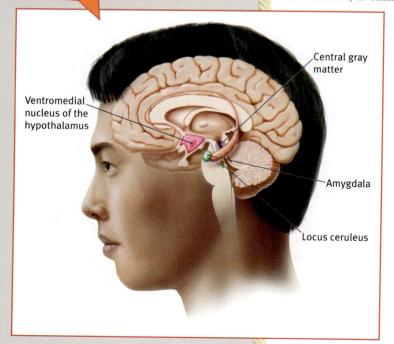

Ventromedial nucleus of the hypothalamus · Central gray matter · Amygdala · Locus ceruleus

of the brain areas and neurotransmitters in the two circuits obviously overlap—particularly the *amygdala,* which is at the center of each circuit—the finding that the panic brain circuit and the anxiety brain circuit are different has further convinced researchers that panic disorder is biologically different from generalized anxiety disorder—and, for that matter, from other kinds of anxiety disorders.

Why might some people have abnormalities in norepinephrine activity, locus ceruleus functioning, or other parts of their panic brain circuit? One possibility is that a predisposition to develop such abnormalities is inherited (Burijon, 2007; Maron et al., 2005; Torgersen, 1990, 1983). Once again, if a genetic factor is indeed at work, close relatives should have higher rates of panic disorder than more distant relatives. Studies do find that among identical twins (twins who share all of their genes), if one twin has panic disorder, the other twin has the same disorder in 24 to 31 percent of cases (Tsuang et al., 2004). Among fraternal twins (who share only some of their genes), if one twin has panic disorder, the other twin has the same disorder in only 11 percent of cases (Kendler et al., 1995, 1993).

Drug Therapies In 1962 researchers discovered that certain antidepressant drugs could prevent panic attacks or reduce their frequency. As you have read, this finding was a surprise at first. Since then, however, studies across the world have repeatedly confirmed this observation (Julien, 2008; Burijon, 2007; Pollack, 2005). In fact, these drugs seem to be helpful whether or not the panic disorder is accompanied by depressive symptoms.

It appears that any antidepressant drugs that restore proper activity of norepinephrine in the locus ceruleus and other parts of the panic brain circuit are able to help prevent or alleviate the symptoms of panic disorder (Pollack, 2005; Redmond, 1985). Such drugs bring at least some improvement to 80 percent of patients who have panic disorder. Approximately half recover markedly or fully, and the improvements can last indefinitely, as long as the drugs are continued (McNally, 2001). In recent years *alprazolam* (Xanax) and other powerful benzodiazepine drugs have also proved very effective (Julien, 2005; Pollack, 2005). Apparently, the benzodiazepines help people with panic disorder by indirectly reducing the activity of norepinephrine throughout the brain.

Clinicians have also found these antidepressant drugs or powerful benzodiazepines to be helpful in most cases of panic disorder with agoraphobia (Clum & Febbraro, 2001). As the drugs eliminate or reduce a sufferer's panic attacks, he or she becomes confident enough to journey out into public places once again. Some people with this disorder, however, need a combination of medication and behavioral exposure treatment to overcome their agoraphobic fears fully (Wolfe, 2005; Antony & Swinson, 2000).

The Cognitive Perspective

Cognitive theorists have come to recognize that biological factors are only part of the cause of panic attacks. In their view, full panic reactions are experienced only by people who further *misinterpret* the physiological events that are occurring within their bodies. Cognitive treatments are aimed at correcting such misinterpretations.

The Cognitive Explanation: Misinterpreting Bodily Sensations Cognitive theorists believe that panic-prone people may be very sensitive to certain bodily sensations; when they unexpectedly experience such sensations, they misinterpret them as signs of a medical catastrophe (Casey et al., 2004). Rather than understanding the probable cause of their sensations as "something I ate" or "a fight with the boss," the panic-prone grow increasingly upset about losing control, fear the worst, lose all perspective, and rapidly plunge into panic. For example, many people with panic disorder seem to "overbreathe," or hyperventilate, in stressful situations. The abnormal breathing makes

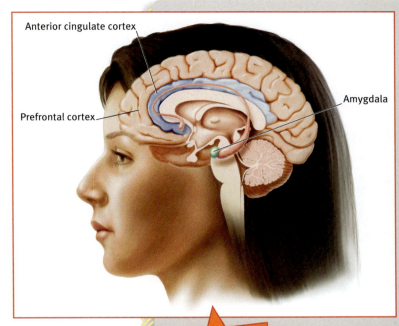

Anterior cingulate cortex

Prefrontal cortex

Amygdala

Figure 5-5
The biology of anxiety Researchers have found that the circuit in the brain linked to anxiety reactions may be different from the circuit linked to panic reactions, suggesting that generalized anxiety disorder is biologically distinct from panic disorder. While the anxiety circuit shares the amygdala with the panic circuit, it further includes brain areas such as the prefrontal cortex and the anterior cingulate cortex.

"I'm sorry, I didn't hear what you said. I was listening to my body."

them think that they are in danger of suffocation, so they panic (Dratcu, 2000). Such individuals further develop the belief that these and other "dangerous" sensations may return at any time and so set themselves up for future panic attacks.

In **biological challenge tests,** researchers produce hyperventilation or other biological sensations by administering drugs or by instructing clinical research participants to breathe, exercise, or simply think in certain ways. As you might expect, participants with panic disorder experience greater upset during these tests than participants without the disorder, particularly when they believe that their bodily sensations are dangerous or out of control (Masdrakis & Papaskostas, 2004).

Why might some people be prone to such misinterpretations? One possibility is that panic-prone individuals generally experience, through no fault of their own, more frequent or more intense bodily sensations than other people do (Nardi et al., 2001). In fact, the kinds of sensations that are most often misinterpreted in panic disorders seem to be carbon dioxide increases in the blood, shifts in blood pressure, and rises in heart rate—bodily events that are controlled in part by the locus ceruleus and other regions of the panic brain circuit.

Still other clinical theorists suggest that people are more prone to misinterpret bodily sensations (and, in turn, to experience panic attacks) if they have poor coping skills or lack social support. Perhaps their childhoods were filled with unpredictable events, lack of control, chronic illnesses in the family, or parental overreactions to their children's bodily symptoms (Stewart et al., 2001).

Whatever the precise causes, research suggests that panic-prone individuals generally have a high degree of what is called **anxiety sensitivity;** that is, they focus on their bodily sensations much of the time, are unable to assess them logically, and interpret them as potentially harmful (Wilson & Hayward, 2005). One study found that people who scored high on an anxiety sensitivity survey were five times more likely than other people to develop panic disorder (Maller & Reiss, 1992). Other studies have found that individuals with panic disorder typically earn higher anxiety sensitivity scores than other persons do (Dattilio, 2001; McNally, 2001).

Cognitive Therapy Cognitive therapists try to correct people's misinterpretations of their body sensations (McCabe & Antony, 2005). The first step is to educate clients about the general nature of panic attacks, the actual causes of bodily sensations, and the tendency of clients to misinterpret their sensations. The next step is to teach clients to apply more accurate interpretations during stressful situations, thus short-circuiting the panic sequence at an early point. Therapists may also teach clients to cope better with anxiety—for example, by applying relaxation and breathing techniques—and to distract themselves from their sensations, perhaps by striking up a conversation with someone.

Cognitive therapists may also use biological challenge procedures (called *interoceptive exposure* when applied in therapy) to induce panic sensations, so that clients can apply their new skills under watchful supervision (Meuret et al., 2005). Individuals whose attacks are typically triggered by a rapid heart rate, for example, may be told to jump up and down for several minutes or to run up a flight of stairs. They can then practice interpreting the resulting sensations appropriately and not dwelling on them.

According to research, cognitive treatments often help people with panic disorder (Hollon et al., 2006; Otto & Deveney, 2005). In international studies, 85 percent of participants given these treatments were free of panic for as long as two years or more, compared to only 13 percent of control participants. As with drug therapy, cognitive treatments are only sometimes sufficient for persons whose panic disorders are accompanied by agoraphobia. For many such individuals, therapists add exposure techniques to the cognitive treatment program—an addition that has produced high success rates.

•**biological challenge test**•A procedure used to produce panic in participants or clients by having them exercise vigorously or perform some other potentially panic-inducing task in the presence of a researcher or therapist.

•**anxiety sensitivity**•A tendency to focus on one's bodily sensations, assess them illogically, and interpret them as harmful.

•**obsession**•A persistent thought, idea, impulse, or image that is experienced repeatedly, feels intrusive, and causes anxiety.

•**compulsion**•A repetitive and rigid behavior or mental act that a person feels driven to perform in order to prevent or reduce anxiety.

•**obsessive-compulsive disorder**•A disorder in which a person has recurrent and unwanted thoughts, a need to perform repetitive and rigid actions, or both.

Cognitive therapy has proved to be at least as helpful as anti-depressant drugs or alprazolam in the treatment of panic disorder, sometimes even more so (McCabe & Antony, 2005). In view of the effectiveness of both cognitive and drug treatments, many clinicians have tried combining them (Julien, 2008; Baskin, 2007; Biondi & Picardi, 2003). It is not yet clear, however, whether this strategy is more effective than cognitive therapy alone.

✿Obsessive-Compulsive Disorder

Obsessions are persistent thoughts, ideas, impulses, or images that seem to invade a person's consciousness. **Compulsions** are repetitive and rigid behaviors or mental acts that people feel they must perform in order to prevent or reduce anxiety. As Figure 5-6 indicates, minor obsessions and compulsions are familiar to almost everyone. You may find yourself filled with thoughts about an upcoming performance or exam, or keep wondering whether you forgot to turn off the stove or lock the door. You may feel better when you avoid stepping on cracks, turn away from black cats, or arrange your closet in a particular manner.

Minor obsessions and compulsions can play a helpful role in life. Little rituals often calm us during times of stress. A person who repeatedly hums a tune or taps his or her fingers during a test may be releasing tension and thus improving performance. Many people find it comforting to repeat religious or cultural rituals, such as touching a mezuzah, sprinkling holy water, or fingering rosary beads.

According to DSM-IV-TR, a diagnosis of **obsessive-compulsive disorder** is called for when obsessions or compulsions feel excessive or unreasonable, cause great distress, take up much time, or interfere with daily functions (see Table 5-9 on the next page). The disorder is classified as an anxiety disorder because the obsessions cause intense anxiety, while the compulsions are aimed at preventing or reducing anxiety. In addition, anxiety rises if individuals try to resist their obsessions or compulsions.

Georgia, a woman with this disorder, observed: "I can't get to sleep unless I am sure everything in the house is in its proper place so that when I get up in the morning, the house is organized. I work like mad to set everything straight before I go to bed, but, when I get up in the morning, I can think of a thousand things that I ought to do. . . . I can't stand to know something needs doing and I haven't done it" (McNeil, 1967, pp. 26–28). Georgia's family was no less affected by her rigid pattern, as these comments by her husband indicate:

Sometimes I think she never sleeps. I got up one night at 4 a.m. and there she was doing the laundry downstairs. . . . If I forget to leave my dirty shoes outside the back door she gives me a look like I had just crapped in the middle of an operating room. I stay out of the house a lot and I'm about half-stoned when I do have to be home. She even made us get rid of the dog because she said he was always filthy. When we used to have people over for supper she would jitterbug around everybody till they couldn't digest their food. I hated to call them up and ask them over because I could always hear them hem and haw and make up excuses not to come over. Even the kids are walking down the street nervous about getting dirt on them. I'm going out of my mind but you can't talk to her. She just blows up and spends twice as much time cleaning things. We have guys in to wash the walls so often I think the house is going to fall down from being scrubbed all the time.

(McNeil, 1967, pp. 26–27)

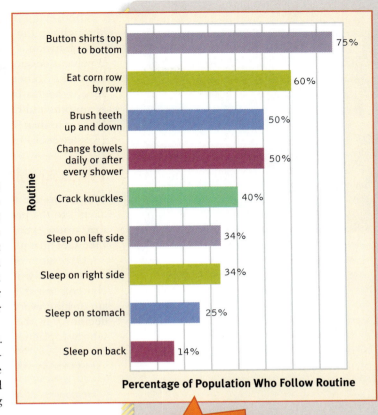

Percentage of Population Who Follow Routine

Figure 5-6
Normal routines Most people find it comforting to follow set routines when they carry out everyday activities, and, in fact, 40 percent become irritated if they are forced to depart from their routines. (Adapted from Kanner, 2005, 1998, 1995.)

table: 5-9

DSM Checklist

OBSESSIVE-COMPULSIVE DISORDER

1. Recurrent obsessions or compulsions.

2. Past or present recognition that the obsessions or compulsions are excessive or unreasonable.

3. Significant distress or impairment, or disruption by symptoms for more than one hour a day.

Based on APA, 2000.

Between 1 and 2 percent of the people in the United States and other countries throughout the world suffer from obsessive-compulsive disorder in any given year (Bjorgvinsson & Hart, 2008; Wetherell et al., 2006; Kessler et al., 2005). Between 2 and 3 percent develop the disorder at some point during their lives. It is equally common in men and women and among people of different races and ethnic groups. The disorder usually begins by young adulthood and typically persists for many years, although its symptoms and their severity may fluctuate over time (Angst et al., 2004). It is estimated that more than 40 percent of people with obsessive-compulsive disorder seek treatment (Kessler et al., 1999, 1994).

What Are the Features of Obsessions and Compulsions?

Obsessions are thoughts that feel both intrusive ("ego dystonic") and foreign ("ego alien") to the people who experience them. Attempts to ignore or resist these thoughts may arouse even more anxiety, and before long they come back more strongly than ever. Like Georgia, people with obsessions are quite aware that their thoughts are excessive.

Obsessions often take the form of obsessive *wishes* (for example, repeated wishes that one's spouse would die), *impulses* (repeated urges to yell out obscenities at work or in church), *images* (fleeting visions of forbidden sexual scenes), *ideas* (notions that germs are lurking everywhere), or *doubts* (concerns that one has made or will make a wrong decision). In the following excerpt, a clinician describes a 20-year-old college junior who was plagued by obsessive doubts.

He now spent hours each night "rehashing" the day's events, especially interactions with friends and teachers, endlessly making "right" in his mind any and all regrets. He likened the process to playing a videotape of each event over and over again in his mind, asking himself if he had behaved properly and telling himself that he had done his best, or had said the right thing every step of the way. He would do this while sitting at his desk, supposedly studying; and it was not unusual for him to look at the clock after such a period of rumination and note that, to his surprise, two or three hours had elapsed.

(Spitzer et al., 1981, pp. 20–21)

Certain basic themes run through the thoughts of most people troubled by obsessive thinking (Abramowitz, McKay, & Taylor, 2008; APA, 2000). The most common theme appears to be dirt or contamination (Tolin & Meunier, 2008) (see *The Media Speaks* on page 153). Other common ones are violence and aggression, orderliness, religion, and sexuality. The prevalence of such themes may vary from culture to culture. Religious obsessions, for example, seem to be more common in cultures or countries with strict moral codes and religious values (Bjorgvinsson & Hart, 2008; Rasmussen & Eisen, 1992).

Compulsions are similar to obsessions in many ways. For example, although compulsive behaviors are technically under voluntary control, the people who feel they must do them have little sense of choice in the matter. Most of these individuals recognize that their behavior is unreasonable, but they believe at the same time something terrible will happen if they don't perform the compulsions. After performing a compulsive act, they usually feel less anxious for a short while. For some people the compulsive acts develop into detailed *rituals*. They must go through the ritual in exactly the same way every time, according to certain rules.

Like obsessions, compulsions take various forms. *Cleaning compulsions* are very common. Like Georgia, people with these compulsions feel compelled to keep cleaning themselves, their clothing, or their homes. The cleaning may follow ritualistic rules and be repeated dozens or hundreds of times a day. People with *checking compulsions* check the same items over and over—door locks, gas taps, important papers—to make sure that all is as it should be (Radomsky et al., 2008). Another common compulsion is the constant effort to seek *order* or *balance* (Coles & Pietrefesa, 2008). People with this compulsion keep placing certain items (clothing, books, foods) in perfect order in accordance with strict rules.

Touching, verbal, and *counting* compulsions are also common. People with touching compulsions repeatedly touch or avoid touching certain items. Individuals with verbal rituals feel compelled to repeat expressions, phrases, or chants. And those with counting compulsions constantly count things they see around them.

Although some people with obsessive-compulsive disorder experience obsessions only or compulsions only, most of them experience both (Clark & Guyitt, 2008). In fact, compulsive acts are often a response to obsessive thoughts (Foa & Franklin, 2001). One study found that in most cases, compulsions seemed to represent a *yielding* to obsessive doubts, ideas, or urges (Akhtar et al., 1975). A woman who keeps doubting that her house is secure may yield to that obsessive doubt by repeatedly checking locks and gas jets. Or a man who obsessively fears contamination may yield to that fear by performing cleaning rituals. The study also found that compulsions sometimes serve to help *control* obsessions. A teenager describes how she tried to control her obsessive fears of contamination by performing counting and verbal rituals:

Cultural rituals
Rituals do not necessarily reflect compulsions. Indeed, cultural and religious rituals often give meaning and comfort to their practitioners. Here, for example, Buddhist monks splash water over themselves during their annual winter prayers at a temple in Tokyo. This cleansing ritual, performed to pray for good luck, is a far cry from the cleaning compulsions found in many cases of obsessive-compulsive disorder.

Patient:	*If I heard the word, like, something that had to do with germs or disease, it would be considered something bad, and so I had things that would go through my mind that were sort of like "cross that out and it'll make it okay" to hear that word.*
Interviewer:	*What sort of things?*
Patient:	*Like numbers or words that seemed to be sort of like a protector.*
Interviewer:	*What numbers and what words were they?*
Patient:	*It started out to be the number 3 and multiples of 3 and then words like "soap and water," something like that; and then the multiples of 3 got really high, and they'd end up to be 124 or something like that. It got real bad then.*

(Spitzer et al., 1981, p. 137)

Many people with obsessive-compulsive disorder worry that they will act out their obsessions. A man with obsessive images of wounded loved ones may worry that he is but a step away from committing murder; or a woman with obsessive urges to yell out in church may worry that she will one day give in to them and embarrass herself. Most such concerns are unfounded. Although many obsessions lead to compulsive acts—particularly to cleaning and checking compulsions—they do not usually lead to violence or immoral conduct.

Obsessive-compulsive disorder was once among the least understood of the psychological disorders. In recent decades, however, researchers have begun to learn more about it. The most influential explanations and treatments come from the psychodynamic, behavioral, cognitive, and biological models.

The Psychodynamic Perspective

As you have seen, psychodynamic theorists believe that an anxiety disorder develops when children come to fear their own id impulses and use ego defense mechanisms to lessen the resulting anxiety. What distinguishes obsessive-compulsive disorder from

BETWEEN THE LINES

Losing Battle
People who try to avoid all contamination and rid themselves and their world of all germs are fighting a losing battle. While talking, the average person sprays 300 microscopic saliva droplets per minute, or 2.5 per word. ◄◄

other anxiety disorders, in their view, is that here the battle between anxiety-provoking id impulses and anxiety-reducing defense mechanisms is not buried in the unconscious but is played out in dramatic thoughts and actions. The id impulses usually take the form of obsessive thoughts, and the ego defenses appear as counterthoughts or compulsive actions. A woman who keeps imagining her mother lying broken and bleeding, for example, may counter those thoughts with repeated safety checks throughout the house.

According to psychodynamic theorists, three ego defense mechanisms are particularly common in obsessive-compulsive disorder: *isolation, undoing,* and *reaction formation*. People who resort to **isolation** simply disown their unwanted thoughts and experience them as foreign intrusions. People who engage in **undoing** perform acts that are meant to cancel out their undesirable impulses. Those who wash their hands repeatedly, for example, may be symbolically undoing their unacceptable id impulses. People who develop a **reaction formation** take on a lifestyle that directly opposes their unacceptable impulses. A person may live a life of compulsive kindness and devotion to others in order to counter unacceptably aggressive impulses.

Sigmund Freud traced obsessive-compulsive disorder to the *anal stage* of development (occurring at about 2 years of age). He proposed that during this stage some children experience intense rage and shame as a result of negative toilet-training experiences. Other psychodynamic theorists have argued instead that such early rage reactions are rooted in feelings of insecurity (Erikson, 1963; Sullivan, 1953; Horney, 1937). Either way, these children repeatedly feel the need to express their strong aggressive id impulses while at the same time knowing they should try to restrain and control the impulses. If this conflict between the id and ego continues, it may eventually blossom into obsessive-compulsive disorder. Overall, research has not clearly supported the psychodynamic explanation (Fitz, 1990).

When treating patients with obsessive-compulsive disorder, psychodynamic therapists try to help the individuals uncover and overcome their underlying conflicts and defenses, using the customary techniques of free association and therapist interpretation. Research has offered little evidence, however, that a traditional psychodynamic approach is of much help (Bram & Bjorgvinsson, 2004; Foa & Franklin, 2004). Thus some psychodynamic therapists now prefer to treat these patients with short-term psychodynamic therapies, which, as you saw in Chapter 3, are more direct and action-oriented than the classical techniques.

The Behavioral Perspective

Behaviorists have concentrated on explaining and treating compulsions rather than obsessions. They propose that people happen upon their compulsions quite randomly. In a fearful situation, they happen just coincidentally to wash their hands, say, or dress a certain way. When the threat lifts, they link the improvement to that particular action. After repeated accidental associations, they believe that the action is bringing them good luck or actually changing the situation, and so they perform the same actions again and again in similar situations. The act becomes a key method of avoiding or reducing anxiety (Frost & Steketee, 2001).

The famous clinical scientist Stanley Rachman and his associates have shown that compulsions do appear to be rewarded by a reduction in anxiety. In one of their experiments, for example, 12 research participants with compulsive hand-washing rituals were placed in contact with objects that they considered contaminated (Hodgson & Rachman, 1972). As behaviorists would predict, the hand-washing rituals of these participants seemed to lower their anxiety.

If people keep performing compulsive behaviors in order to prevent bad outcomes and ensure positive outcomes, can't they be taught that such behaviors are not really serving this purpose? In a behavioral treatment called **exposure and response prevention** (or **exposure and ritual prevention**), first developed by psychiatrist Victor Meyer (1966), clients are repeatedly exposed to objects or situations that produce anxiety, obsessive fears, and compulsive behaviors, but they are told to *resist* performing the

HOME · SEND · EXPLORE

Dining Out: The Obsessive-Compulsive Experience

In this February 2008 *New York Times* article, Jeff Bell, a radio news anchor, describes the ordeal that he and other people with similar obsessive-compulsive disorders confront whenever they go to a restaurant for a "pleasurable" night out.

For some of us the trouble starts before we even step into a restaurant. . . . Some of us obsess about contamination, others about hurting people, and still others about symmetry. Almost all of us can find something to obsess about at a restaurant.

Sometimes the trouble is the element of public theater in the dining room, meaning we have to indulge in our often-embarrassing rituals under the eyes of so many strangers while trying not to get caught. Or it might be worrying about the safety of the food and the people who serve it.

Many of the situations that un-settle people with obsessive-compulsive disorder—driving, for instance—provoke at least some level of anxiety in just about everyone. But restaurants are designed to be calming and relaxing. That is one of the main reasons people like to eat out.

To many of us with obsessive-compulsive disorder, those pleasures are invisible. We walk into a calm and civilized dining room and see things we won't be able to control. . . .

Personally, I am fine with just about any table, although the wobbly ones can spell big trouble. I have harm obsessions, which means I am plagued by the fear that other people will be hurt by something I do, or don't do. Seated at a less-than-sturdy table, I conjure images of fellow diners being crushed or otherwise injured should I fail to notify the restaurant's management. This is called a re-porting compulsion in the vernacular of the disorder, and before I learned to fight these urges, many a manager heard from me.

One of them was the woman running a coffee house I frequent. One day while sipping my latte at a fake-marble table I leaned forward, and the far end of the tabletop lifted. This barely moved my coffee cup, but it sent my nerves right through the roof. Before I realized it I was crouched over, my head upside down beneath the table. The only responsible thing to do, I decided, was to ask the woman behind the counter to come over for a look. Her lack of concern only exacerbated my problems.

Forget the tabletop, my friend Matt S. tells me; it's what's on top of the table, and precisely where, that really matters. Mr. S. is a 39-year-old lawyer in Fort Worth with order compulsions. To enjoy a meal he needs to separate the salt and pepper shakers, and, ideally, place a napkin holder or other divider midway between them. . . .

Some of our other concerns may seem familiar. I imagine most diners, for example, have noticed and perhaps even struggled to remove white detergent spots that can sometimes be seen on silverware. But few, I suspect, have gone to the lengths Jared K. has to get rid of them. Mr. K. is a 24-year-old research assistant living outside of Boston who has obsessive fears of contamination. . . . Last year he visited a Chinese restaurant with several friends, one of whom pointed out that their silverware was spotted and seemed dirty. Mr. K. collected all the utensils at the table and attempted to sterilize them by holding them above a small flame at the center of a pu-pu platter, quickly attracting the attention of their waiter. . . .

As part of my harm obsession, one of my concerns is that germs from my mouth will hurt others. Although I try to keep my fingers away from my lips and their germs while I'm eating, I'm rarely successful (it's not as easy as it sounds). By the end of the meal I believe that my hands are contaminated. The problem is that I need them to scribble my signature on the check. If I'm lucky, I will have remembered to bring my own pen; if not, I may feel compelled to "table-wash" my hands, a little trick I developed over the years: I use the condensation on the outside of a cold water glass to rinse off the germs. (Forget drying my hands, by the way; my napkin would only re-contaminate them.)

Once the check is signed, I must be sure that it is really signed. At my worst, I have opened and closed the vinyl check holder again and again, seeing my signature each time, yet unable to feel certain. I've left the table, only to return to check again. And again. . . .

[*Postscript: After exposure and response prevention therapy*]
Today I travel extensively, sharing my recovery story and working with groups like the Obsessive Compulsive Foundation to raise awareness. In my job as a radio news anchor, I don't have to eat out much, but when I'm on the road for work related to the disorder, I wind up eating in a lot of restaurants. I can honestly say I'm starting to enjoy it. In fact, while I still like ice water with my meal, I often find myself drinking from the glass, not washing with it.

Now when I say check, please, I'm simply asking for my bill.

Bill Pugliano/Getty Images

Getting down and dirty
The principle behind *exposure and response prevention* is to place clients in anxiety-provoking situations while preventing them from performing their usual compulsive acts. Clients with cleaning compulsions, for example, might be instructed to do heavy-duty gardening and then resist washing their hands or taking a shower. They may never go so far as to participate in and enjoy mud wrestling, like these delight-fully filthy individuals at the annual Mud Day event in Westland, Michigan, but you get the point.

behaviors they feel so bound to perform. Because people find it very difficult to resist such behaviors, therapists may set an example first.

Many behavioral therapists now use exposure and response prevention in both individual and group therapy formats. Some of them also have people carry out *self-help* procedures at home (Foa et al., 2005). That is, they assign homework in exposure and response prevention, such as these assignments given to a woman with a cleaning compulsion:

- Do not mop the floor of your bathroom for a week. After this, clean it within three minutes, using an ordinary mop. Use this mop for other chores as well without cleaning it.
- Buy a fluffy mohair sweater and wear it for a week. When taking it off at night do not remove the bits of fluff. Do not clean your house for a week.
- You, your husband, and children all have to keep shoes on. Do not clean the house for a week.
- Drop a cookie on the contaminated floor, pick the cookie up and eat it.
- Leave the sheets and blankets on the floor and then put them on the beds. Do not change these for a week.

(Emmelkamp, 1982, pp. 299–300)

Eventually this woman was able to set up a reasonable routine for cleaning herself and her home.

Between 55 and 85 percent of clients with obsessive-compulsive disorder have been found to improve considerably with exposure and response prevention, improvements that often continue indefinitely (Abramowitz et al., 2008; Hollon et al., 2006; Franklin, Riggs, & Pai, 2005). The effectiveness of this approach suggests that people with obsessive-compulsive disorder are like the superstitious man in the old joke who keeps snapping his fingers to keep elephants away. When someone points out, "But there aren't any elephants around here," the man replies, "See? It works!" One review concludes, "With hindsight, it is possible to see that the obsessional individual has been snapping his fingers, and unless he stops (response prevention) and takes a look around at the same time (exposure), he isn't going to learn much of value about elephants" (Berk & Efran, 1983, p. 546).

At the same time, research has revealed certain limitations in exposure and response prevention. Few clients who receive the treatment overcome all their symptoms, and as many as one-quarter fail to improve at all (Foa et al., 2005; Frost & Steketee, 2001). In addition, many individuals drop out of or even refuse to enter into this kind of treatment because they consider it too demanding or threatening (Radomsky et al., 2008). And, finally, the approach is of limited help to those who have obsessions but no compulsions (Hohagen et al., 1998).

The Cognitive Perspective

Cognitive theorists begin their explanation of obsessive-compulsive disorder by pointing out that everyone has repetitive, unwanted, and intrusive thoughts. Anyone might have thoughts of harming others or being contaminated by germs, for example, but most people dismiss or ignore them with ease (Baer, 2001). Those who develop this disorder, however, typically blame themselves for such thoughts and expect that somehow terrible things will happen (Shafran, 2005; Salkovskis, 1999, 1985). To avoid such negative outcomes, they try to **neutralize** the thoughts—thinking or behaving in ways meant to put matters right or to make amends (Salkovskis et al., 2003).

Neutralizing acts might include requesting special reassurance from others, deliberately thinking "good" thoughts, washing one's hands, or checking for possible sources of danger. When a neutralizing effort brings about a temporary reduction in discomfort, it is reinforced and will likely be repeated. Eventually the neutralizing thought or act is used so often that it becomes, by definition, an obsession or compulsion. At the same time, the individual becomes more and more convinced that his or her unpleasant intrusive thoughts are dangerous. As the person's fear of such thoughts increases, the thoughts begin to occur more frequently and they, too, become obsessions.

In support of this explanation, studies have found that people who have obsessive-compulsive disorder experience intrusive thoughts more often than other people, resort to more elaborate neutralizing strategies, and experience reductions in anxiety after using neutralizing techniques (Shafran, 2005; Salkovskis et al., 2003).

Although everyone sometimes has undesired thoughts, only some people develop obsessive-compulsive disorder. Why do these individuals find such normal thoughts so disturbing to begin with? Researchers have found that this population tends (1) to be more depressed than other people (Hong et al., 2004), (2) to have exceptionally high standards of conduct and morality (Rachman, 1993), (3) to believe that their intrusive negative thoughts are equivalent to actions and capable of causing harm to themselves or

"Is the Itsy Bitsy Spider obsessive-compulsive?"

•neutralizing•A person's attempt to eliminate unwanted thoughts by thinking or behaving in ways that put matters right internally, making up for the unacceptable thoughts.

others (Steketee et al., 2003), and (4) generally to believe that they should have perfect control over all of their thoughts and behaviors (Coles et al., 2005; Frost & Steketee, 2002, 2001).

Cognitive therapists focus treatment on the cognitive processes that help produce and maintain obsessive thoughts and compulsive acts. Initially, they provide psychoeducation, teaching clients about their misinterpretations of unwanted thoughts, excessive sense of responsibility, and neutralizing acts. They then move on to help the clients identify, challenge, and change their distorted cognitions. Many cognitive therapists also include **habituation training** in their sessions, directing clients to call forth their obsessive thoughts again and again. The clinicians expect that with such repetitions, the obsessive thoughts will lose their power to frighten or threaten the clients, and thus will produce less anxiety and trigger fewer new obsessive thoughts and compulsive acts (Franklin et al., 2002; Salkovskis & Westbrook, 1989). It appears that such cognitive techniques often help reduce the number and impact of obsessions and compulsions (Rufer et al., 2005; Eddy et al., 2004).

While the behavioral approach (exposure and response prevention) and the cognitive approach have each been of help to clients with obsessive-compulsive disorder, some research suggests that a combination of the two approaches is often more effective than either intervention alone (Foa et al., 2005; Franklin et al., 2005; Clark, 2004). In *cognitive-behavioral treatments* of this kind, clients are taught to view their obsessive thoughts as inaccurate occurrences rather than as valid and dangerous cognitions for which they are responsible and upon which they must act. As they become better able to identify and understand such thoughts—to recognize them for what they are—they also become less inclined to act on them, more willing and able to subject themselves to the rigors of exposure and response prevention, and more likely to make gains in that behavioral technique.

The Biological Perspective

Family pedigree studies provided the earliest hints that obsessive-compulsive disorder may be linked in part to biological factors (Lambert & Kinsley, 2005). Studies of twins found that if one identical twin manifests obsessive-compulsive disorder, the other twin also develops it in at least 53 percent of cases. In contrast, among fraternal twins (twins who share half rather than all their genes) both twins manifest the disorder in only 23 percent of cases. In short, the more similar the gene composition of two individuals, the more likely both are to experience obsessive-compulsive disorder, if indeed one of them manifests the disorder. Currently, more direct genetic studies are being conducted to try to pinpoint the gene or combination of genes that may predispose some individuals to develop this disorder (Miguel et al., 2005, 1997; Delorme et al., 2004).

In recent years two lines of research have uncovered evidence that biological factors play a key role in obsessive-compulsive disorder, and promising biological treatments for the disorder have been developed as well. The research points to (1) abnormally low activity of the neurotransmitter *serotonin* and (2) abnormal functioning in key regions of the brain.

Abnormal Serotonin Activity
Serotonin, like GABA and norepinephrine, is a brain chemical that carries messages from neuron to neuron. The first clue to its role in obsessive-compulsive disorder was, once again, a surprising finding by clinical researchers—this time that two antidepressant drugs, *clomipramine* and *fluoxetine* (Anafranil and Prozac), reduce obsessive and compulsive symptoms (Stein & Fineberg, 2007). Since these particular drugs also increase serotonin activity, some researchers concluded that the disorder is caused by low serotonin activity. In fact, only those antidepressant drugs that increase serotonin activity help in cases of obsessive-compulsive disorder; antidepressants that mainly affect other neurotransmitters typically have no effect on it (Jenike, 1992).

Although serotonin is the neurotransmitter most often cited in explanations of obsessive-compulsive disorder, recent studies have suggested that other neurotransmitters, particularly *glutamate, GABA,* and *dopamine,* may also play important roles in the development of this disorder (Lambert & Kinsley, 2005). Some researchers even argue that, with regard to obsessive-compulsive disorder, serotonin may act largely as a **neuromodulator,** a chemical whose primary function is to increase or decrease the activity of other key neurotransmitters.

Abnormal Brain Structure and Functioning Another line of research has linked obsessive-compulsive disorder to abnormal functioning by specific regions of the brain, particularly the **orbitofrontal cortex** (just above each eye) and the **caudate nuclei** (structures located within the brain region known as the *basal ganglia*). These regions are part of a brain circuit that converts sensory information into thoughts and actions (Stein & Fineberg, 2007; Chamberlain et al., 2005; Szeszko et al., 2005). The circuit begins in the orbitofrontal cortex, where sexual, violent, and other primitive impulses normally arise. These impulses next move on to the caudate nuclei, which act as filters that send only the most powerful impulses on to the *thalamus,* the next stop on the circuit (see Figure 5-7). If impulses reach the thalamus, the person is driven to think further about them and perhaps to act. Many theorists now believe that either the orbitofrontal cortex or the caudate nuclei of some people are too active, leading to a constant eruption of troublesome thoughts and actions (Lambert & Kinsley, 2005). Additional parts of this brain circuit have also been identified in recent years, including the *cingulate cortex* and, once again, the *amygdala* (Stein & Fineberg, 2007). Of course, it may turn out that these regions also play key roles in obsessive-compulsive disorder.

In support of this brain circuit explanation, medical scientists have observed for years that obsessive-compulsive symptoms do sometimes arise or subside after the orbitofrontal cortex, caudate nuclei, or other regions in the circuit are damaged by accident or illness (Coetzer, 2004; Berthier et al., 2001). In one highly publicized case, a patient with obsessive-compulsive disorder tried to commit suicide by shooting himself in the head. Although he survived the shot, he did considerable damage to the brain areas in question. Perhaps as a result of the injury, his obsessive and compulsive symptoms declined dramatically. Similarly, neuroimaging studies, which offer pictures of brain functioning and structure, have shown that the caudate nuclei and the orbitofrontal cortex of research participants with obsessive-compulsive disorder are more active than those of control participants (Chamberlain et al., 2005; Baxter et al., 2001, 1990).

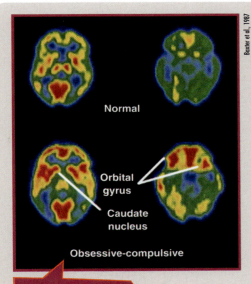

Normal

Orbital gyrus

Caudate nucleus

Obsessive-compulsive

Scanning for OCD
With the colors red and orange indicating high brain activity, these PET scans clarify that the caudate nucleus and orbitofrontal cortex are much more active in the brain of an obsessive-compulsive individual (below) than in the brain of a normal individual (above) (Baxter et al., 1987).

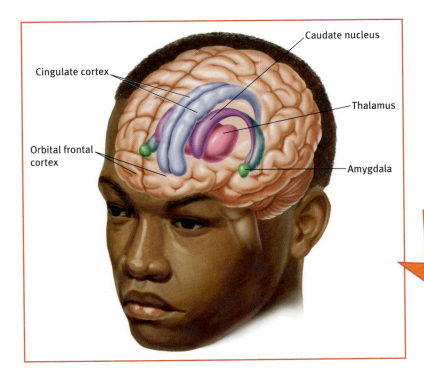

Cingulate cortex

Caudate nucleus

Thalamus

Orbital frontal cortex

Amygdala

Figure 5-7
The biology of obsessive-compulsive disorder Certain brain structures have been linked to obsessive-compulsive disorder, including the orbitofrontal cortex, caudate nucleus (in the basal ganglia), thalamus, amygdala, and cingulate cortex. The structures may be too active in people with the disorder. (Adapted from Rapoport, 1989, p. 85.)

Sprinkle lightly
In the early twentieth century, drug companies did not have to prove the safety or value of their products. Brain Salt, a patent medicine for anxiety and related difficulties, promised to cure nervous disability, headaches, indigestion, heart palpitations, and sleep problems.

•**stress management program**•An approach to treating generalized and other anxiety disorders that teaches clients techniques for reducing and controlling stress.

The serotonin and brain circuit explanations may themselves be linked. It turns out that serotonin—along with the neurotransmitters glutamate, GABA, and dopamine—plays a key role in the operation of the orbitofrontal cortex, caudate nuclei, and other parts of the brain circuit; certainly abnormal activity by one or more of these neurotransmitters could be contributing to the improper functioning of the circuit.

Biological Therapies Ever since researchers first discovered that certain antidepressant drugs help to reduce obsessions and compulsions, these drugs have been used to treat obsessive-compulsive disorder (Julien, 2008). We now know that the drugs not only increase brain serotonin activity but also help produce more normal activity in the orbitofrontal cortex and caudate nuclei (Stein & Fineberg, 2007; Baxter et al., 2000, 1992). Studies have found that clomipramine (Anafranil), fluoxetine (Prozac), fluvoxamine (Luvox), and similar antidepressant drugs bring improvement to between 50 and 80 percent of those with obsessive-compulsive disorder (Bareggi et al., 2004). The obsessions and compulsions do not usually disappear totally, but on average they are cut almost in half within eight weeks of treatment (DeVeaugh-Geiss et al., 1992). People who are treated with such drugs alone, however, tend to relapse if the medication is stopped. Thus, more and more individuals with obsessive-compulsive disorder are now being treated by a combination of behavioral, cognitive, and drug therapies. According to research, such combinations often yield higher levels of symptom reduction and bring relief to more clients than do each of the approaches alone—improvements that often last for years (Kordon et al., 2005; Rufer et al., 2005).

Obviously, the treatment picture for obsessive-compulsive disorder, like that for panic disorder, has improved greatly over the past 15 years. Once a very stubborn problem, this disorder is now helped by several forms of treatment, often used in combination. In fact, at least two studies suggest that the behavioral, cognitive, and biological approaches may ultimately have the same effect on the brain. In these investigations, both participants who responded to cognitive-behavioral treatments and those who responded to antidepressant drugs showed marked reductions in activity in the caudate nuclei (Stein & Fineberg, 2007; Schwartz & Begley, 2002; Baxter et al., 2000, 1992).

PUTTING IT... together

Diathesis-Stress in Action

Clinicians and researchers have developed many ideas about generalized anxiety disorder, phobias, panic disorder, and obsessive-compulsive disorder. At times, however, the sheer quantity of concepts and findings makes it difficult to grasp what is really known about the disorders.

Overall, it is fair to say that clinicians currently know more about the causes of phobias, panic disorder, and obsessive-compulsive disorder than about generalized anxiety disorder. It is worth noting that the insights about panic disorder and obsessive-compulsive disorder—once among the field's most puzzling patterns—did not emerge until clinical theorists took a look at the disorders from more than one perspective and integrated those views. Today's cognitive explanation of panic disorder, for example, builds squarely on the biological idea that the disorder begins with abnormal brain activity and unusual physical sensations. Similarly, the cognitive explanation of obsessive-compulsive disorder takes its lead from the biological position that some people are predisposed to experience more unwanted and intrusive thoughts than others.

It may be that a fuller understanding of generalized anxiety disorder awaits a similar integration of the various models. In fact, such an integration has already begun to unfold. Recall, for example, that one of the new cognitive explanations for generalized anxiety disorder links the cognitive process of worrying to heightened bodily arousal in individuals with the disorder.

Similarly, a growing number of theorists are adopting a *diathesis-stress* view of generalized anxiety disorder. They believe that certain individuals have a biological vulnerability toward developing the disorder—a vulnerability that is eventually brought to the surface by psychological and sociocultural factors. Indeed, genetic investigators have discovered that certain genes may determine whether a person reacts to life's stressors calmly or in a tense manner, and developmental researchers have found that even during the earliest stages of life some infants become particularly aroused when stimulated (Burijon, 2007; Lonigan et al., 2004; Kalin, 1993). Perhaps these easily aroused infants have inherited defects in GABA functioning or other biological characteristics that predispose them to generalized anxiety disorder. If, over the course of their lives, the individuals also face intense societal pressures, learn to interpret the world as a dangerous place, or come to regard worrying as a useful tool, they may indeed be candidates for developing generalized anxiety disorder.

Diathesis-stress principles may also be at work in the development of phobias. Several studies suggest, for example, that certain infants are born with a style of social inhibition or shyness that may increase their risk of developing a social phobia (Smoller et al., 2003; Kagan & Snidman, 1999, 1991). Perhaps people must have both a genetic predisposition and unfortunate conditioning experiences if they are to develop particular phobias.

In the treatment realm, integration of the models is already on display for each of the anxiety disorders. Therapists have discovered, for example, that treatment is at least sometimes more effective when medications are combined with cognitive techniques to treat panic disorder and when medications are combined with cognitive-behavioral techniques to treat obsessive-compulsive disorder. Similarly, cognitive techniques are now often combined with relaxation training or biofeedback in the treatment of generalized anxiety disorder—a package known as a **stress management program** (Taylor, 2006). And treatment programs for social phobias often include a combination of medications, exposure therapy, cognitive therapy, and social skills training. For the millions of people who suffer from these various anxiety disorders, such treatment combinations are a welcome development.

‹‹‹[SUMMING UP]›››

○ **Generalized anxiety disorder** People with *generalized anxiety disorder* experience excessive anxiety and worry about a wide range of events and activities. The various explanations and treatments for this anxiety disorder have received only limited research support, although recent cognitive and biological approaches seem to be promising.

According to the *sociocultural* view, *societal dangers, economic stress,* or related *racial and cultural pressures* may create a climate in which cases of generalized anxiety disorder are more likely to develop.

In the original *psychodynamic* explanation, Freud said that generalized anxiety disorder may develop when anxiety is excessive and defense mechanisms break down and function poorly. Psychodynamic therapists use free association, interpretation, and related psychodynamic techniques to help people overcome this problem.

Carl Rogers, the leading *humanistic* theorist, believed that people with generalized anxiety disorder fail to receive *unconditional positive regard* from significant others during their childhood and so become overly critical of themselves. He treated such individuals with *client-centered therapy.*

Cognitive theorists believe that generalized anxiety disorder is caused by *maladaptive assumptions* and *beliefs* that lead people to view most life situations as dangerous. Many cognitive theorists further believe that implicit beliefs about the power and value of *worrying* are particularly important in the development and maintenance of this disorder. Cognitive therapists help their clients to change such thinking and to find more effective ways of coping during stressful situations.

continued

continued

BETWEEN THE LINES

Young Dreams

Studies indicate that infants who are generally anxious or "difficult" are more likely than other infants to later experience nightmares throughout their childhood (Simard et al., 2008) ‹‹

BETWEEN THE LINES

Playlist Anxiety

Many individuals in today's digital music world share music playlists, so it may not be surprising that researchers have observed that a growing number of people are experiencing "playlist anxiety"— intense concern about the image they are projecting through the music they make available to others. The problem is particularly common among college students and office workers. A respondent in one study disclosed, "I just went through my playlist and said, 'I wonder what kind of image this is giving of me.' I went through it to see if there was stuff that I would not like people to know I had." ‹‹

(Conference on Human Factors in Computing Systems, 2005; ZDNET, 2005)

Biological theorists hold that generalized anxiety disorder results from low activity of the neurotransmitter *GABA*. Common biological treatments are *antianxiety drugs*, particularly *benzodiazepines*, and serotonin-enhancing *antidepressant drugs*. Relaxation training and *biofeedback* are also applied in many cases. *pp. 122–133*

○ **Phobias** A phobia is a severe, persistent, and unreasonable fear of a particular object, activity, or situation. There are three main categories of phobias: *specific phobias, social phobias,* and *agoraphobia*. Behavioral explanations of phobias, particularly specific phobias, are the most influential today. Behaviorists believe that phobias are learned from the environment through *classical conditioning* or through *modeling,* and then are maintained by avoidance behaviors.

Specific phobias have been treated most successfully with behavioral *exposure techniques* by which people are led to confront the objects they fear. The exposure may be gradual and relaxed (*desensitization*), intense (*flooding*), or vicarious (*modeling*).

Therapists who treat social phobias typically distinguish two components of this disorder: *social fears* and *poor social skills.* They try to reduce social fears by drug therapy, exposure techniques, group therapy, various cognitive approaches, or a combination of these interventions. They may try to improve social skills by *social skills training. pp. 134–143*

○ **Panic disorder** *Panic attacks* are periodic, discrete bouts of panic that occur suddenly. Sufferers of *panic disorder* experience panic attacks repeatedly and unexpectedly and without apparent reason. When panic disorder leads to *agoraphobia,* it is termed *panic disorder with agoraphobia.*

Some biological theorists believe that abnormal *norepinephrine* activity in the brain's *locus ceruleus* may be the key to panic disorder. Others believe that related neurotransmitters and brain regions may also play key roles. Biological therapists use certain *antidepressant drugs* or powerful *benzodiazepines* to treat people with this disorder. Patients whose panic disorder is accompanied by agoraphobia may need a combination of drug therapy and behavioral *exposure treatment.*

Cognitive theorists suggest that panic-prone people become preoccupied with some of their bodily sensations, misinterpret them as signs of medical catastrophe, panic, and in some cases develop panic disorder. Such persons have a high degree of *anxiety sensitivity* and also experience greater anxiety during *biological challenge tests.* Cognitive therapists teach patients to interpret their physical sensations more accurately and to cope better with anxiety. In cases of panic disorder with agoraphobia, practitioners may combine a cognitive approach with behavioral exposure techniques. *pp. 143–149*

○ **Obsessive-compulsive disorder** People with *obsessive-compulsive disorder* are beset by *obsessions,* perform *compulsions,* or display both. Common themes in obsessions are contamination and violence. Compulsions commonly center on cleaning or checking. Other common compulsions involve touching, verbal rituals, or counting. Compulsions are often a response to a person's obsessive thoughts.

According to the psychodynamic view, obsessive-compulsive disorder arises out of a battle between id impulses, which appear as obsessive thoughts, and ego defense mechanisms, which take the form of counterthoughts or compulsive actions. Behaviorists believe that compulsive behaviors develop through chance associations. The leading behavioral treatment combines prolonged *exposure* with *response prevention.* Cognitive theorists believe that obsessive-compulsive disorder grows from a normal human tendency to have *unwanted and unpleasant thoughts.* The efforts of some people to understand, eliminate, or avoid such thoughts actually lead to obsessions and compulsions. Cognitive therapy for this disorder includes psychoeducation and, at times, *habituation training.* While the behavioral and cognitive therapies are each helpful to clients with obsessive-compulsive disorder, research suggests that a combined *cognitive-behavioral approach* may be more effective than either therapy alone.

Biological researchers have tied obsessive-compulsive disorder to low *serotonin* activity and abnormal functioning in the *orbitofrontal cortex* and in the *caudate nuclei*. Antidepressant drugs that raise serotonin activity are a useful form of treatment. *pp. 149–159*

⫸ CRITICAL THOUGHTS ⫷

1. If fear is such an unpleasant experience, why do many people enjoy and even seek out the feelings of fear brought about by amusement park rides, scary movies, bungee jumping, and other such experiences? *pp. 121–122*

2. Why are antianxiety drugs so popular in today's world? *p. 132*

3. Why do so many professional performers seem particularly prone to social anxiety? Wouldn't their repeated exposure to audiences lead to a reduction in fear? *p. 135*

4. Today's human-participant review boards probably would not permit Watson and Rayner to conduct their study on Little Albert. What concerns might they raise about the procedure? Do these concerns outweigh the insights gained from this study? *p. 139*

5. Why might people whose childhoods were marked by unpredictable or uncontrollable events or by chronic family illnesses be inaccurate interpreters of their bodily sensations? *pp. 147–148*

6. Can you think of instances when you instinctively tried a simple version of exposure and response prevention in order to stop behaving in certain ways? Were your efforts successful? *pp. 152–155*

🌌 cyberstudy

SEARCH

Search the *Abnormal Psychology* Video Tool Kit
www.worthpublishers.com/apvtk

▲ Chapter 5 Video Cases
  Worrying: Key to Generalized Anxiety
  Overcoming a Fear of Flying
  The Impact of Obsessions and Compulsions

▲ Video case discussions, study guides, and questions

Log on to the Comer Web Page
www.worthpublishers.com/comer

▲ Chapter 5 outline, learning objectives, research exercises, study tools, and practice test questions

▲ Additional Chapter 5 case studies, Web links, and FAQs

STRESS DISORDERS

Specialist Latrell Robinson, a 25 year-old single African American man, was an activated National Guardsman [serving in the Iraq war]. He [had been] a full-time college student and competitive athlete raised by a single mother in public housing. . . .

Initially trained in transportation, he was called to active duty and retrained as a military policeman to serve with his unit in Baghdad. He described enjoying the high intensity of his deployment and [became] recognized by others as an informal leader because of his aggressiveness and self-confidence. He [had] numerous [combat] exposures while performing convoy escort and security details [and he came] under small arms fire on several occasions, witnessing dead and injured civilians and Iraqi soldiers and on occasion feeling powerless when forced to detour or take evasive action. He began to develop increasing mistrust of the [Iraq] environment as the situation "on the street" seemed to deteriorate. He often felt that he and his fellow soldiers were placed in harm's way needlessly.

On a routine convoy mission [in 2003], serving as driver for the lead HUMVEE, his vehicle was struck by an Improvised Explosive Device showering him with shrapnel in his neck, arm, and leg. Another member of his vehicle was even more seriously injured. . . . He denied feeling much pain at that time. He was evacuated to the Combat Support Hospital (CSH) where he was treated and returned to duty . . . after several days despite requiring crutches and suffering chronic pain from retained shrapnel in his neck. He began to become angry at his command and doctors for keeping him in [Iraq] while he was unable to perform his duties effectively. He began to develop insomnia, hypervigilance and a startle response. His initial dreams of the event became more intense and frequent and he suffered intrusive thoughts and flashbacks of the attack. He began to withdraw from his friends and suffered anhedonia, feeling detached from others, and he feared his future would be cut short. He was referred to a psychiatrist at the CSH. . . .

After two months of unsuccessful rehabilitation for his battle injuries and worsening depressive and anxiety symptoms, he was evacuated to a . . . military medical center [in the United States]. . . . He was screened for psychiatric symptoms and was referred for outpatient evaluation and management. He met DSM-IV criteria for acute PTSD and was offered medication management, supportive therapy, and group therapy. . . . He was ambivalent about taking passes or convalescent leave to his home because of fears of being "different, irritated, or aggressive" around his family or girlfriend. After three months at the military service center, he was [deactivated from service and] referred to his local VA Hospital to receive follow-up care.

National Center for PTSD, 2008

During the horror of combat, soldiers often become highly anxious and depressed and physically ill. Moreover, for many, like Latrell, these reactions to extraordinary stress continue well beyond the combat experience itself.

But it is not just combat soldiers who are affected by stress. Nor does stress have to rise to the level of combat trauma to have a profound effect on psychological and physical functioning. Stress comes in all sizes and shapes, and we are all greatly affected by it.

We feel some degree of stress whenever we are faced with demands or opportunities that require us to change in some manner. The state of stress has two components: a *stressor*, the event that creates the demands, and a *stress response*, the person's reactions to the demands. The stressors of life may include annoying

Different strokes for different folks
Some individuals are exhilarated by the opportunity to chase bulls through the streets of Pamplona, Spain, during the annual "running of the bulls" (left), while others are terrified by such a prospect. Conversely, certain individuals find it exciting to engage tamer animals, for example, ostriches, during the "running of the ostriches" fiesta (right) in Irurzun, Spain, while others are more than a little bored by such activities.

•**autonomic nervous system (ANS)**• The network of nerve fibers that connect the central nervous system to all the other organs of the body.

•**endocrine system**• The system of glands located throughout the body that help control important activities such as growth and sexual activity.

•**sympathetic nervous system**• The nerve fibers of the autonomic nervous system that quicken the heartbeat and produce other changes experienced as arousal and fear.

everyday hassles, such as rush-hour traffic or the appearance of unexpected company; turning-point events, such as college graduation or marriage; long-term problems, such as poverty, poor health, or overcrowded living conditions; or traumatic events, such as major accidents, assaults, tornadoes, or military combat. Our response to such stressors is influenced by the way we *appraise* both the events and our capacity to react to them in an effective way (Russo & Tartaro, 2008; Folkman & Moskowitz, 2004; Lazarus & Folkman, 1984). People who sense that they have the ability and the resources to cope are more likely to take stressors in stride and to respond constructively.

When we appraise a stressor as threatening, a natural reaction is arousal and a sense of fear—a response frequently on display in Chapter 5. As you saw in that chapter, fear is actually a package of responses that are *physical, emotional,* and *cognitive.* Physically, we perspire, our breathing quickens, our muscles tense, and our hearts beat faster. Turning pale, developing goose bumps, and feeling nauseated are other physical reactions. Emotional responses to extreme threats include horror, dread, and even panic, while in the cognitive realm fear can disturb our ability to concentrate and distort our view of the world. We may exaggerate the harm that actually threatens us or remember things incorrectly after the threat has passed.

Stress reactions, and the sense of fear they produce, are often at play in psychological disorders. People who experience a large number of stressful events are particularly vulnerable to the onset of the anxiety disorders that you read about in Chapter 5. Similarly, increases in stress have been linked to the onset of depression, schizophrenia, sexual dysfunctioning, and other psychological problems.

In addition, stress plays a more central role in certain psychological and physical disorders. In such disorders, the features of stress become severe and debilitating, linger for a long period of time, and may make it impossible for the individual to live a normal life. The key psychological stress disorders are *acute stress disorder* and *posttraumatic stress disorder (PTSD).* DSM-IV-TR technically lists these patterns as anxiety disorders, but as you will see, their features extend far beyond the symptoms of anxiety. The physical stress disorders are typically called *psychophysiological disorders,* problems that DSM-IV-TR now lists under the heading *psychological factors affecting medical condition.* These psychological and physical stress disorders are the focus of this chapter. Before examining them, however, you need to understand just how the brain and body react to stress.

Stress and Arousal: The Fight-or-Flight Response

The features of arousal and fear are set in motion by the brain area called the *hypothalamus.* When our brain interprets a situation as dangerous, neurotransmitters in the hypothalamus are released, triggering the firing of neurons throughout the brain and the release of chemicals throughout the body. In particular, the hypothalamus activates two important systems—the *autonomic nervous system* and the *endocrine system*. The **autonomic nervous system (ANS)** is the extensive network of nerve fibers that connect the *central nervous system* (the brain and spinal cord) to all the other organs of the body. These fibers help regulate the *involuntary* activities of the organs—breathing, heartbeat, blood pressure, perspiration, and the like (see Figure 6-1). The **endocrine system** is the network of *glands* located throughout the body. (As you read in Chapter 3, glands release *hormones* into the bloodstream and on to the various body organs.) The autonomic nervous system and the endocrine system often overlap in their responsibilities and activities. There are two pathways, or routes, by which these systems produce arousal and fear reactions—the *sympathetic nervous system* pathway and the *hypothalamic-pituitary-adrenal* pathway.

When we face a dangerous situation, the hypothalamus first excites the **sympathetic nervous system,** a group of autonomic nervous system fibers that work to quicken our heartbeat and produce the other changes that we experience as fear or

Jupiter Images/Thinkstock/Alamy

The stress of multitasking
The multiple—often conflicting—roles and tasks that people must perform in life can produce significant feelings of stress. Here a woman tries to conduct her professional business by computer and phone in her home office, while at the same time caring for her child, engaging him in play, and fending off the bites of his reptilian friend.

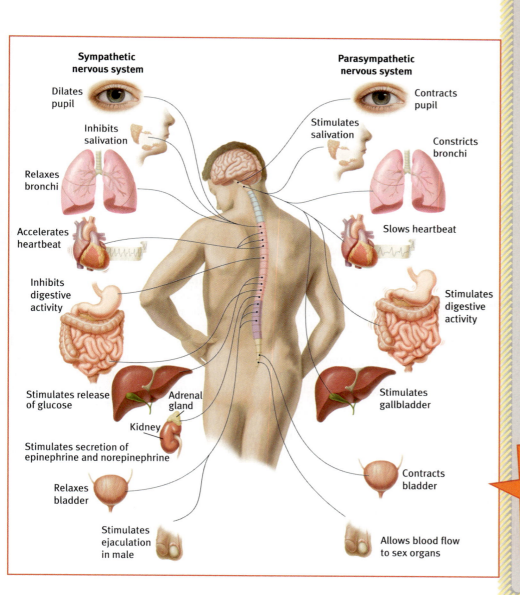

Sympathetic nervous system

- Dilates pupil
- Inhibits salivation
- Relaxes bronchi
- Accelerates heartbeat
- Inhibits digestive activity
- Stimulates release of glucose
- Adrenal gland
- Kidney
- Stimulates secretion of epinephrine and norepinephrine
- Relaxes bladder
- Stimulates ejaculation in male

Parasympathetic nervous system

- Contracts pupil
- Stimulates salivation
- Constricts bronchi
- Slows heartbeat
- Stimulates digestive activity
- Stimulates gallbladder
- Contracts bladder
- Allows blood flow to sex organs

Figure 6-1

The autonomic nervous system (ANS) When the sympathetic division of the ANS is activated, it stimulates some organs and inhibits others. The result is a state of general arousal. In contrast, activation of the parasympathetic division leads to an overall calming effect.

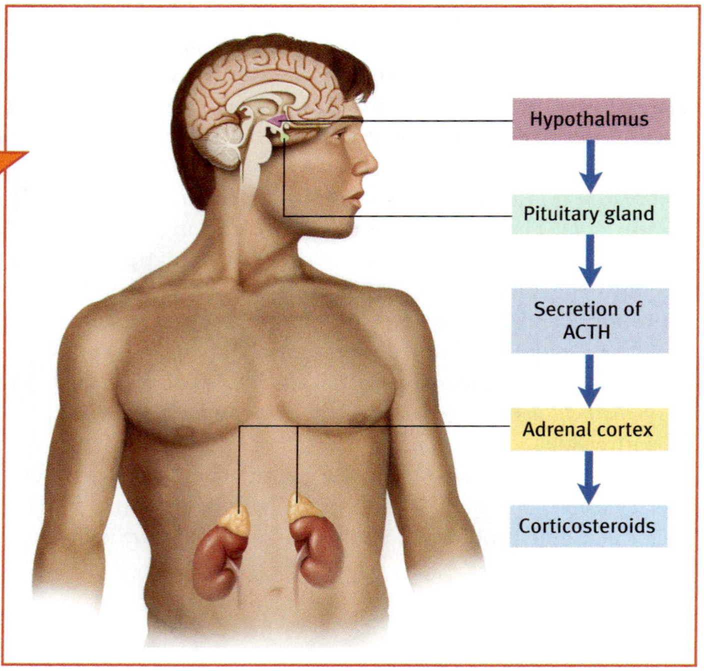

Figure 6-2
The endocrine system: The HPA pathway
When a person perceives a stressor, the hypothalamus activates the pituitary gland to secrete the adrenocorticotropic hormone, or ACTH, which stimulates the adrenal cortex. The adrenal cortex releases stress hormones called corticosteroids that act on other body organs to trigger arousal and fear reactions.

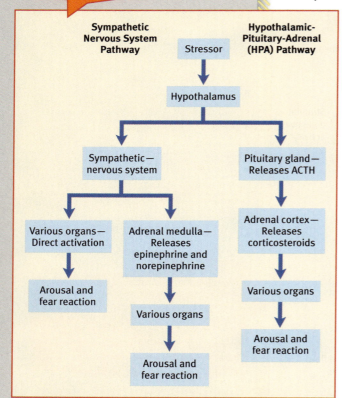

Figure 6-3
Pathways of arousal and fear When we are confronted by a stressor, our bodies produce arousal and fear reactions through two pathways. In one, the hypothalamus sends a message to the sympathetic nervous system, which then activates key body organs, either directly or by causing the adrenal medulla to release epinephrine and norepinephrine into the bloodstream. In the other pathway, the hypothalamus sends a message to the pituitary gland, which then signals the adrenal cortex to release corticosteroids—the stress hormones—into the bloodstream.

anxiety. These nerves may stimulate the organs of the body directly—for example, they may directly stimulate the heart and increase heart rate. The nerves may also influence the organs indirectly, by stimulating the *adrenal glands* (glands located on top of the kidneys), particularly the inner layer of these glands, an area called the *adrenal medulla*. When this layer of the adrenal glands is stimulated, the chemicals *epinephrine* (adrenaline) and *norepinephrine* (noradrenaline) are released. You have already seen that these chemicals are important neurotransmitters when they operate in the brain (pages 146–147). When released from the adrenal medulla, however, they act as hormones and travel through the bloodstream to various organs and muscles, further producing arousal and fear.

When the perceived danger passes, a second group of autonomic nervous system fibers, called the **parasympathetic nervous system,** helps return our heartbeat and other body processes to normal. Together the sympathetic and parasympathetic nervous systems help control our arousal and fear reactions.

The second pathway by which arousal and fear reactions are produced is the **hypothalamic-pituitary-adrenal (HPA) pathway** (see Figure 6-2). When we are confronted by stressors, the hypothalamus also signals the *pituitary gland,* which lies nearby, to secrete the *adrenocorticotropic hormone* (*ACTH*), sometimes called the body's "major stress hormone." ACTH, in turn, stimulates the outer layer of the adrenal glands, an area called the *adrenal cortex,* triggering the release of a group of stress hormones called **corticosteroids,** including the hormone *cortisol*. These corticosteroids travel to various body organs where they further generate arousal and fear reactions. Eventually the corticosteroids signal the *hippocampus,* the brain structure that seems to control memories, including emotional memories, and the hippocampus helps turn off the body's arousal.

The reactions on display in these two pathways are collectively referred to as the *fight-or-flight* response, precisely because they arouse our body and prepare us for a response to danger (see Figure 6-3). Each person has a particular pattern of autonomic and endocrine functioning and so a particular way of experiencing arousal and fear. Some people are almost always relaxed, while others typically feel tension, even when no threat is apparent. A person's general level of arousal and anxiety is sometimes called *trait anxiety* because it seems to be a general trait that each of us brings to the events in our lives (Spielberger, 1985, 1972, 1966). Psychologists have found that differences in trait anxiety appear soon after birth (Leonardo & Hen, 2006; Kagan, 2003).

People also differ in their sense of which situations are threatening (Fisher et al., 2004). Walking through a forest may be fearsome for one person but relaxing for another. Flying in an airplane may arouse terror in some people and boredom in others. Such variations are called differences in *situation,* or *state, anxiety.*

✿The Psychological Stress Disorders: Acute and Posttraumatic Stress Disorders

Of course when we actually confront stressful situations, we do not think to ourselves, "Oh, there goes my autonomic nervous system," or "My fight-or-flight seems to be kicking in." We just feel aroused psychologically and physically and experience a growing sense of fear. If the stressful situation is truly extraordinary and unusually dangerous, we may temporarily experience levels of arousal, anxiety, and depression that are beyond anything we have ever known. Consider, for example, the reaction of Mark to his first few weeks of combat in Vietnam.

Mark remembers his first "firefight" and encountering the VC [Viet Cong] for the first time. He lost all bladder and bowel control—in a matter of a few minutes. In his own words, "I was scared and literally shitless; I pissed all over myself, and shit all over myself too. Man, all hell broke loose. I tell you, I was so scared, I thought I would never make it out alive. I was convinced of that. Charlie had us pinned down and [was] hitting the shit out of us for hours. We had to call in the napalm and the bombing." During the first fight, Mark, an infantryman, experienced gruesome sights and strange sounds in battle. He witnessed headless bodies. "One guy said to me, 'Hey, Mark, new greenhorn boy, you saw that head go flying off that gook's shoulder. Isn't that something?'" Within 2 weeks Mark saw the head of a running comrade blown off his shoulders, the headless body moving for a few feet before falling to the ground. Mark, nauseous and vomiting for a long time, couldn't see himself surviving much longer: "I couldn't get that sight out of my head; it just kept on coming back to me in my dreams, nightmares. Like clockwork, I'd see R's head flying, and his headless body falling to the ground. I knew the guy. He was very good to me when I first got to the unit. Nobody else seemed to give a damn about me; he broke me in. It's like I would see his head and body, you know, man, wow!" Mark often found himself crying during his first weeks of combat. "I wanted to go home. I was so lonely, helpless, and really scared."

(Brende & Parson, 1985, pp. 23–24)

For Mark, these reactions subsided once he left the combat zone and certainly after he returned home. For some people, however, the symptoms of anxiety and depression, as well as other kinds of symptoms, persist well after the upsetting situation is over. These people may be suffering from *acute stress disorder* or *posttraumatic stress disorder,* patterns that arise in reaction to a psychologically traumatic event. The event usually involves actual or threatened serious injury to the person or to a family member or friend. Unlike the anxiety disorders that you read about in Chapter 5, which typically are triggered by situations that most people would not find threatening, the situations that cause acute

•**parasympathetic nervous system**• The nerve fibers of the autonomic nervous system that help maintain normal organ functioning. They also slow organ functioning after stimulation and return other bodily processes to normal.

•**hypothalamic-pituitary-adrenal (HPA) pathway**•One route by which the brain and body produce arousal and fear. At times of stress, the hypothalamus signals the pituitary gland, which in turn signals the adrenal glands. Stress hormones are then released to various body organs.

•**corticosteroids**•A group of hormones, including cortisol, released by the adrenal glands at times of stress.

table: 6-1

DSM Checklist

POSTTRAUMATIC STRESS DISORDER

1. A history of having experienced, witnessed, or confronted event(s) involving death, serious injury, or threat to the physical integrity of self or others. Reaction of intense fear, helplessness, or horror produced by event.

2. Event persistently reexperienced in at least one of the following ways:
   (a) Recurrent distressing recollections.
   (b) Recurrent distressing dreams, illusions, flashbacks, or a sense of reliving the experience.
   (c) Distress caused by reminders of event.
   (d) Physical arousal produced by reminders of event.

3. Persistent avoidance of reminders of the event and a subjective sense of numbing, detachment, or emotional unresponsiveness.

4. At least two marked symptoms of increased arousal:
   (a) Difficulty sleeping.
   (b) Irritability.
   (c) Poor concentration.
   (d) Hypervigilance.
   (e) Exaggerated startle response.

5. Significant distress or impairment, with symptoms lasting at least one month.

Based on APA, 2000.

•**acute stress disorder**•An anxiety disorder in which fear and related symptoms are experienced soon after a traumatic event and last less than a month.

•**posttraumatic stress disorder**•An anxiety disorder in which fear and related symptoms continue to be experienced long after a traumatic event.

stress disorder or posttraumatic stress disorder—combat, rape, an earthquake, an airplane crash—would be traumatic for anyone (Burijon, 2007).

If the symptoms begin within four weeks of the traumatic event and last for less than a month, DSM-IV-TR assigns a diagnosis of **acute stress disorder** (APA, 2000). If the symptoms continue longer than a month, a diagnosis of **posttraumatic stress disorder (PTSD)** is given. The symptoms of PTSD may begin either shortly after the traumatic event or months or years afterward (see Table 6-1).

Studies indicate that as many as 80 percent of all cases of acute stress disorder develop into posttraumatic stress disorder (Burijon, 2007; Bryant et al., 2005). Think back to Latrell, the soldier in Iraq whose case opened this chapter. As you'll recall, Latrell became consumed by anxiety, insomnia, worry, anger, depression, irritability, intrusive thoughts, flashback memories, and social detachment within days of the attack upon his convoy mission—thus qualifying him for a diagnosis of acute stress disorder. As his symptoms worsened and continued beyond one month—even long after his return to the United States—this diagnosis became PTSD. Aside from the differences in onset and duration, the symptoms of acute stress disorder and PTSD are almost identical:

Reexperiencing the traumatic event People may be battered by recurring thoughts, memories, dreams, or nightmares connected to the event (Clark, 2005; Michael et al., 2005). A few relive the event so vividly in their minds (flashbacks) that they think it is actually happening again.

Avoidance People will usually avoid activities that remind them of the traumatic event and will try to avoid related thoughts, feelings, or conversations (Marx & Sloan, 2005; Asmundson et al., 2004).

Reduced responsiveness People feel detached from other people or lose interest in activities that once brought enjoyment. Some experience symptoms of *dissociation*, or psychological separation (Marx & Sloan, 2005): they feel dazed, have trouble remembering things, have a sense of derealization (feeling that the environment is unreal or strange), or experience depersonalization (their thoughts or body feel unreal or foreign to them).

Increased arousal, anxiety, and guilt People with these disorders may feel overly alert (hyperalertness), be easily startled, have trouble concentrating, and develop sleep problems (Breslau et al., 2005; Feuer, Nishith, & Resick, 2005). They may feel extreme guilt because they survived the traumatic event while others did not. Some also feel guilty about what they may have had to do to survive.

You can see these symptoms in the recollections of a Vietnam combat veteran years after he returned home:

I can't get the memories out of my mind! The images come flooding back in vivid detail, triggered by the most inconsequential things, like a door slamming or the smell of stir-fried pork. Last night I went to bed, was having a good sleep for a change. Then in the early morning a storm-front passed through and there was a bolt of crackling thunder. I awoke instantly, frozen in fear. I am right back in Vietnam, in the middle of the monsoon season at my guard post. I am sure I'll get hit in the next volley and convinced I will die. My hands are freezing, yet sweat pours from my entire body. I feel each hair on the back of my neck standing on end. I can't catch my breath and my heart is pounding. I smell a damp sulfur smell.

(Davis, 1992)

What Triggers a Psychological Stress Disorder?

An acute or posttraumatic stress disorder can occur at any age, even in childhood, and can affect one's personal, family, social, or occupational life. People with these stress disorders may also experience depression, another anxiety disorder, or substance abuse or become suicidal (Koch & Haring, 2008). Surveys indicate that at least 3.5 percent of people in the United States experience one of the stress disorders in any given year; 7 to 9 percent suffer from one of them during their lifetimes (Burijon, 2007; Kessler et al., 2005). Around two-thirds of these individuals seek treatment at some point in their lives, but only 7 percent do so when they first develop the disorder (Wang et al., 2005). Women are at least twice as likely as men to develop stress disorders: around 20 percent of women who are exposed to a serious trauma may develop one, compared to 8 percent of men (Koch & Haring, 2008; Russo & Tartaro, 2008; Khouzam et al., 2005).

Any traumatic event can trigger a stress disorder; however, some are particularly likely to do so. Among the most common are combat, disasters, and abuse and victimization.

Combat and Stress Disorders

For years clinicians have recognized that many soldiers develop symptoms of severe anxiety and depression *during* combat. It was called "shell shock" during World War I and "combat fatigue" during World War II and the Korean War (Figley, 1978). Not until after the Vietnam War, however, did clinicians learn that a great many soldiers also experience serious psychological symptoms *after* combat (Koch & Haring, 2008).

By the late 1970s, it became apparent that many Vietnam combat veterans were still experiencing war-related psychological difficulties (Roy-Byrne et al., 2004). We now know that as many as 29 percent of all Vietnam veterans, male and female, suffered an acute or posttraumatic stress disorder, while another 22 percent experienced at least some stress symptoms (Weiss et al., 1992). In fact, 10 percent of the veterans of that war still experience posttraumatic stress symptoms, including flashbacks, night terrors, nightmares, and persistent images and thoughts.

A similar pattern is currently unfolding among veterans of the wars in Iraq and Afghanistan. In 2008, the RAND Corporation, a nonprofit research organization, completed the first large-scale, nongovernmental assessment of the psychological needs of military service members who have served in those two wars since 2001 (Gever, 2008; RAND Corporation, 2008). It found that of the 1.6 million Americans deployed to the wars, nearly 20 percent have so far reported symptoms of posttraumatic stress disorder. Given that not all of the individuals studied were in fact exposed to prolonged periods of combat-related stress, this is indeed a very large percentage. Moreover, only 53 percent of the individuals with such symptoms have sought treatment, and just half of those persons have received at least minimally adequate care. Half of the veterans interviewed in this extensive study described traumas in which they had seen friends seriously wounded or killed, 45 percent reported seeing dead or gravely wounded civilians, and 10 percent said they themselves had been injured and hospitalized. The report estimated that the psychological problems of the returning service members would cost the nation more than $6 billion during the two years following deployment, including both direct medical costs and costs of lost productivity.

It is also worth noting that the war in Iraq involves repeated deployments of many of the combat veterans and that those individuals who serve such multiple deployments are 50 percent more likely than those with one tour of service to experience acute combat stress, significantly raising their risk of developing posttraumatic stress disorder (Tyson, 2006).

Disasters and Stress Disorders

Acute and posttraumatic stress disorders may also follow natural and accidental disasters such as earthquakes, floods, tornadoes, fires, airplane crashes, and serious car accidents (see Table 6-2 on the next page). In fact, because they occur more often, civilian traumas have been implicated in stress disorders at least 10 times as often as combat traumas (Bremner, 2002). Studies have found, for

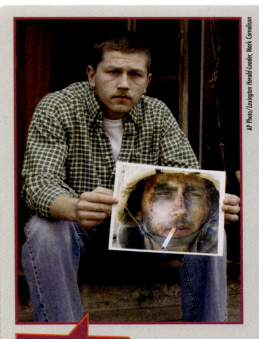

AP Photo/Lexington Herald-Leader, Mark Cornelison

"Marlboro Man"
One of the most famous photos to emerge from the war in Iraq was that of a U.S. marine, dubbed the "Marlboro Man" by the news media, taken during the battle for Fallujah in 2004. In it the soldier's face was smeared with blood and dirt and a cigarette dangled from his lips. Just two years after the photo was taken, however, 21-year-old James Blake Miller was sitting outside his home in Kentucky, holding the famous picture of himself and revealing that he had since received a diagnosis of posttraumatic stress disorder.

table: 6-2

Worst Natural Disasters of the Past 100 Years

Disaster	Year	Location	Number Killed
Flood	1931	Huang He River, China	3,700,000
Tsunami	2004	South Asia	280,000
Earthquake	1976	Tangshan, China	242,419
Heat wave	2003	Europe	35,000
Volcano	1985	Nevado del Ruiz, Colombia	23,000
Hurricane	1998	(Mitch) Central America	18,277
Landslide	1970	Yungay, Peru	17,500
Avalanche	1916	Italian Alps	10,000
Blizzard	1972	Iran	4,000
Tornado	1989	Shaturia, Bangladesh	1,300

Adapted from CBC, 2008; CNN, 2005; Ash, 2001, 1999, 1998.

example, that as many as 40 percent of victims of serious traffic accidents—adult or child—may develop PTSD within a year of the accident (Hickling & Blanchard, 2007; Wiederhold & Wiederhold, 2005).

Similarly, several studies found stress reactions among the survivors of Hurricane Andrew, a storm that ravaged Florida and other parts of the southeastern United States and Mexico in 1992 (Ibanez et al., 2004; Vernberg et al., 1996). By a month after the storm the number of calls received by the domestic violence hot line in Miami and the number of women applying for police protection had doubled (Treaster, 1992). By six months after the storm it was apparent that many elementary-school-age children were also victims of posttraumatic stress disorder; their symptoms ranged from misbehavior in school to failing grades and sleep problems (Vernberg et al., 1996).

Victimization and Stress Disorders
People who have been abused or victimized often experience lingering stress symptoms. Research suggests that more than one-third of all victims of physical or sexual assault develop posttraumatic stress disorder (Burijon, 2007; Brewin et al., 2003). Similarly, as many as half of all people who are directly exposed to terrorism or torture may develop this disorder (Basoglu et al., 2001).

SEXUAL ASSAULT A common form of victimization in our society today is sexual assault. **Rape** is forced sexual intercourse or another sexual act committed against a nonconsenting person or intercourse with an underage person. Surveys suggest that in the United States more than 300,000 persons are victims of rape or attempted rape each year (Ahrens et al., 2008; Rennison, 2002). Most rapists are men and most victims are women. Around one in six women is raped at some time during her life (Ahrens et al., 2008; Rozee, 2005). Surveys also suggest that most rape victims are young: 29 percent are under 11 years old, 32 percent are between the ages of 11 and 17, and 29 percent are between 18 and 29 years old. Approximately 70 percent of the victims are raped by acquaintances or relatives (Ahrens et al., 2008; Rennison, 2002).

The rates of rape appear to differ from race to race. In 2000, 46 percent of rape victims in the United States were white American, 27 percent were African American, and 19 percent were Hispanic American (Ahrens et al., 2008; Tjaden & Thoennes, 2000). These rates were in marked contrast to the 2000 general population distribution of 75 percent white American, 12 percent African American, and 13 percent Hispanic American.

The psychological impact of rape on a victim is immediate and may last a long time (Russo & Tartaro, 2008; Koss, 2005, 1993; Korinthenberg et al., 2004). Rape victims typically experience enormous distress during the week after the assault. Stress continues to rise for the next 3 weeks, maintains a peak level for another month or so, and then starts to improve. In one study, 94 percent of rape victims fully qualified for a clinical diagnosis of acute stress disorder when they were observed around 12 days after the assault (Rothbaum et al., 1992). Although most rape victims improve psychologically within 3 or 4 months, the effects may persist for up to 18 months or longer. Victims typically continue to have higher than average levels of anxiety, suspiciousness, depression, self-esteem problems, self-blame, flashbacks, sleep problems, and sexual dysfunction (Ahrens et al., 2008). The lingering psychological impact of rape is apparent in the following case description:

Mary Billings is a 33-year-old divorced nurse, referred to the Victim Clinic at Bedford Psychiatric Hospital for counseling by her supervisory head nurse. Mary had been raped two months ago. The assailant gained entry to her apartment while she was sleeping, and she awoke to find him on top of her. He was armed with a knife and threatened to kill her and her child (who was asleep in the next room) if she did not submit to his demands. He forced her to undress and repeatedly raped her vaginally over a period of 1 hour. He then admonished her that if she told anyone or reported the incident to the police he would return and assault her child.

After he left, she called her boyfriend, who came to her apartment right away. He helped her contact the Sex Crimes Unit of the Police Department, which is currently investigating the case. He then took her to a local hospital for a physical examination and collection of evidence for the police (traces of sperm, pubic hair samples, fingernail scrapings). She was given antibiotics as prophylaxis against venereal disease. Mary then returned home with a girlfriend who spent the remainder of the night with her.

Over the next few weeks Mary continued to be afraid of being alone and had her girlfriend move in with her. She became preoccupied with thoughts of what had happened to her and the possibility that it could happen again. Mary was frightened that the rapist might return to her apartment and therefore had additional locks installed on both the door and the windows. She was so upset and had such difficulty concentrating that she decided she could not yet return to work. When she did return to work several weeks later, she was still clearly upset, and her supervisor suggested that she might be helped by counseling.

During the clinic interview, Mary was coherent and spoke quite rationally in a hushed voice. She reported recurrent and intrusive thoughts about the sexual assault, to the extent that her concentration was impaired and she had difficulty doing chores such as making meals for herself and her daughter. She felt she was not able to be effective at work, still felt afraid to leave her home, to answer her phone, and had little interest in contacting friends or relatives.

. . . [Mary] talked in the same tone of voice whether discussing the assault or less emotionally charged topics, such as her work history. She was easily startled by an unexpected noise. She also was unable to fall asleep because she kept thinking about the assault. She had no desire to eat, and when she did attempt it, she felt nauseated. Mary was repelled by the thought of sex and stated that she did not want to have sex for a long time, although she was willing to be held and comforted by her boyfriend.

(Spitzer et al., 1983, pp. 20–21)

Preventing the trauma
In 2001, a Tokyo railway designated a "Women Only" rail car for female commuters who needed to travel late at night. Designation of special cars of this kind was spurred by a sharp increase in late-night sexual assaults in Japan's commuter trains.

BETWEEN THE LINES

Sexual Trafficking: Another Kind of Sexual Abuse

- Worldwide, hundreds of thousands of women are bought and sold each year for purposes of sexual slavery and prostitution.
- Around 30 million Asian women and children have been trafficked over the past 30 years.
- Between 16,000 and 20,000 Mexican and Central American children are trafficked for sexual purposes each year.
- Around 120,000 women and children are trafficked to Europe each year.
- Between 20,000 and 50,000 women and children are trafficked to the United States each year. ‹‹

(Dietrich, 2007; Huda, 2006; Cicero-Dominguez, 2005; Krug et al., 2002; Bremer, 2001; WHO, 2000)

BETWEEN THE LINES

Rape: Country by Country

The United States has the highest rate of rape of any industrialized nation— 4 times higher than Germany's, 12 times higher than England's, and 20 times higher than Japan's. (Rozee, 2005) ‹‹

No place for psychologists
California protesters rally in 2007 against participation by psychologists in military and CIA interrogations of suspected terrorists at Guantanamo Bay. In response to a public and professional uproar over this issue, the American Psychological Association voted in 2008 to ban its members from participating in all forms of interrogation at U.S. detention centers.

Although many rape victims are severely injured by their attacker or experience other physical problems as a result of their assault, only half receive the kind of formal medical care afforded Mary (Logan et al., 2006; Rennison, 2002). Between 4 and 30 percent of victims develop a sexually transmitted disease (Koss, 1993; Murphy, 1990) and 5 percent become pregnant (Beebe, 1991; Koss et al., 1991), yet surveys reveal that 60 percent of rape victims fail to receive pregnancy testing, preventive measures, or testing for exposure to HIV (National Victims Center, 1992).

Female victims of rape and other crimes are also much more likely than other women to suffer serious long-term health problems (Leibowitz, 2007; Koss & Heslet, 1992). Interviews with 390 women revealed that such victims had poorer physical well-being for at least five years after the crime and made twice as many visits to physicians.

As you will see in Chapter 17, ongoing victimization and abuse in the family—specifically child and spouse abuse—may also lead to psychological stress disorders. Because these forms of abuse may occur over the long term and violate family trust, many victims develop other symptoms and disorders as well (Dietrich, 2007; Woods, 2005).

TERRORISM People who are victims of terrorism or who live under the threat of terrorism often experience posttraumatic stress symptoms (Galea et al., 2007; Tramontin & Halpern, 2007; Hoven et al., 2005). Unfortunately, this source of traumatic stress is on the rise in our society. Few will ever forget the events of September 11, 2001, when hijacked airplanes crashed into and brought down the World Trade Center in New York City and partially destroyed the Pentagon in Washington, D.C., killing thousands of victims and rescue workers and forcing thousands more to desperately run, crawl, and even dig their way to safety. One of the many legacies of this infamous event is the lingering psychological effect that it has had on those people who were immediately affected and their family members and on tens of millions of others who were traumatized simply by watching images of the disaster on their television sets as the day unfolded. A number of studies clarify that stress reactions were common among victims and observers in the days following the terrorist attacks and that these posttraumatic symptoms have, in many cases, lingered for years (Tramontin & Halpern, 2007) (see *Psych Watch* on pages 174–175). Studies of subsequent acts of terrorism, such as the 2004 commuter train bombings in Madrid and the 2005 London subway and bus bombings, tell a similar story (Chacon & Vecina, 2007).

TORTURE Torture refers to the use of "brutal, degrading, and disorienting strategies in order to reduce victims to a state of utter helplessness" (Okawa & Hauss, 2007). Often, it is politically motivated—done on the orders of a government or another authority to force persons to yield information, make a confession, or the like (Gerrity, Keane, & Tuma, 2001). In fact, it is estimated that torture is currently practiced in more than 150 countries worldwide (AI, 2000).

The question of the morality of torturing prisoners who are considered suspects in the "war on terror" has been the subject of much discussion over the past few years. This discussion was triggered initially by claims that the U.S. government was subjecting such suspects to torture to extract information and was sending some suspected terrorists to other countries where they were being tortured, again in order to gain information (Okawa & Hauss, 2007; Danner, 2004).

It is hard to know how many people are in fact tortured around the world because such numbers are typically hidden by governments (Basoglu et al., 2001). It has been estimated, however, that between 5 and 35 percent of the world's 15 million refugees have suffered at least one episode of torture and that more than 400,000 torture survivors from around the world now live in the United States (ORR, 2006; AI, 2000; Baker, 1992). Of course, these numbers do not take into account the many thousands of victims who have remained in their countries even after being tortured.

People from all walks of life are subjected to torture worldwide—from suspected terrorists to student activists and members of religious, ethnic, and cultural minority groups. The techniques used on them may include *physical torture* (beatings, waterboarding, electrocution), *psychological torture* (threats of death, mock executions, verbal abuse, degradation), *sexual torture* (rape, violence to the genitals, sexual humiliation), or *torture through deprivation* (sleep, sensory, social, nutritional, medical, or hygiene deprivation).

Torture victims often experience physical and medical ailments as a result of their ordeal, from scarring and fractures to neurological problems and chronic pain. But many theorists believe that the lingering psychological effects of torture are even more problematic (Okawa & Hauss, 2007; Basoglu et al., 2001). Findings vary across studies, but it appears that between 30 and 50 percent of torture victims develop posttraumatic stress disorder (Basoglu et al., 2001). Even for those who do not develop a full-blown disorder, symptoms such as nightmares, flashbacks, repressed memories, depersonalization, poor concentration, anger outbursts, sadness, and suicidal thoughts are common (Okawa & Hauss, 2007; Okawa et al., 2003; Ortiz, 2001). In addition, torture can have a lingering impact on the families of victims. Families may have to split up as the torture victims seek asylum in other countries. Such separations may be so extended that marital relationships suffer or children fail to remember their parents in exile (Wenzel, 2002).

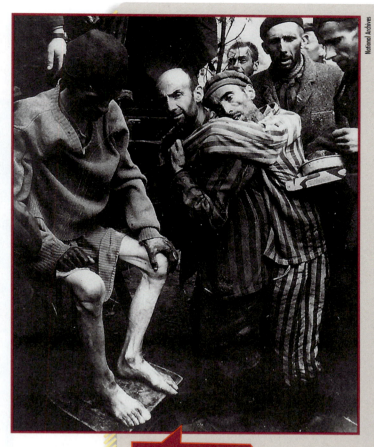

Victimization and posttraumatic stress disorder
Many survivors of Nazi concentration camps faced a long road back to psychological health (Joffe et al., 2003). However, because knowledge of posttraumatic stress disorder was nonexistent until recent years, most survivors had to find their way back without professional help.

Why Do People Develop a Psychological Stress Disorder?

Clearly, extraordinary trauma can cause a stress disorder. The stressful event alone, however, may not be the entire explanation. Certainly, anyone who experiences an unusual trauma will be affected by it, but only some people develop a stress disorder (Koch & Haring, 2008) (see *A Closer Look* on page 177). To understand the development of these disorders more fully, researchers have looked to the survivors' biological processes, personalities, childhood experiences, social support systems, and cultural backgrounds and to the severity of the traumas.

Biological and Genetic Factors Investigators have learned that traumatic events trigger physical changes in the brain and body that may lead to severe stress reactions and, in some cases, to stress disorders. They have, for example, found abnormal activity of the hormone *cortisol* and the neurotransmitter/hormone *norepinephrine* in the urine, blood, and saliva of combat soldiers, rape victims, concentration camp survivors, and survivors of other severe stresses (Burijon, 2007; Delahanty et al., 2005; Neylan et al., 2005).

Evidence from brain studies also shows that once a stress disorder sets in, individuals experience further biochemical arousal and this continuing arousal may eventually damage key brain areas (Carlson, 2008; Mirzaei et al., 2005; Pawlak et al., 2003). Two areas in particular seem to be affected—the *hippocampus* and the *amygdala*. Normally, the hippocampus plays a major role both in memory and in the regulation of the body's stress hormones. Clearly, a dysfunctional hippocampus may help produce the intrusive memories and ongoing arousal that characterize posttraumatic stress disorder (Bremner et al., 2004; Shin et al., 2005). Similarly, as you observed in Chapter 5, the amygdala helps control emotional responses, including anxiety and panic responses. The amygdala also works with the hippocampus to produce the emotional components of memory. A dysfunctional amygdala may help produce the repeated emotional symptoms and intense emotional memories experienced by persons with posttraumatic stress disorder (Protopopescu et al., 2005; Shin et al., 2005). In short, the excessive arousal generated by extraordinary traumatic events may lead to stress disorders in some people, and the stress disorders may produce yet further brain abnormalities, locking in the disorders all the more firmly.

It may also be that posttraumatic stress disorder leads to the transmission of biochemical abnormalities to the children of persons with the disorder. One team of

•**torture**•The use of brutal, degrading, and disorienting strategies to reduce victims to a state of utter helplessness.

September 11, 2001: The Psychological Aftermath

On September 11, 2001, the United States experienced the most catastrophic act of terrorism in history when four commercial airplanes were hijacked and three of them were crashed into the twin towers of the World Trade Center in New York City and the Pentagon in Washington, D.C. The attacks resulted in mass casualties and injuries, affecting not only the immediate victims and survivors but also the entire nation, as millions witnessed the resulting death and destruction on television. Studies conducted since that fateful day have confirmed what psychologists knew all too well would happen—that in the aftermath of September 11, many individuals experienced immediate and long-term psychological and physical effects, ranging from brief stress reactions, such as shock, fear, and anger, to enduring psychological disorders, such as posttraumatic stress disorder (Galea et al., 2007; Tramontin & Halpern, 2007; Blanchard et al., 2005; Hoven et al., 2005; Lengua et al., 2005).

In a survey conducted the week after the terrorist attacks, 560 randomly selected adults across the United States were interviewed. Forty-four percent of them reported substantial stress symptoms; 90 percent reported at least some increase in stress (Schuster et al., 2001). Moreover, individuals closest to the disaster site experienced the greatest stress reactions: 61 percent of adults living within 100 miles of the World Trade Center had substantial stress symptoms, compared to 36 percent of those living over 1,000 miles from the site.

Spencer Platt/Getty Images

AP Photo/Suzanne Plunkett

During the First Week

What percentage of the population had substantial stress reactions?

Adults	44
Children	35
Women	50
Men	37
Nonwhite Americans	62
White Americans	41
Residents within 100 miles of attack	61
Residents beyond 100 miles of attack	36

Schuster et al., 2001

A later survey of close to 2,000 individuals revealed that many Americans were still feeling the psychological effects of September 11 five months after the terrorist attacks (Bossolo & Lichtenstein, 2002). Nearly 25 percent of Americans reported that they continued to feel more depressed or anxious since the time of the attacks, and 77 percent said that they were still trying to gain perspective on their lives and to reprioritize their goals. A related study indicated that people who had experienced a greater number of traumas in the past were more likely than others to develop stress symptoms and disorders in the aftermath of September 11 (Pugh, 2003).

Research focusing specifically on New Yorkers indicated that they were almost twice as likely as those living elsewhere to develop depressive, anxiety, or posttraumatic stress disorders (Galea et al., 2007; Tramontin & Halpern, 2007; Bossolo & Lichtenstein, 2002). In addition, 40 percent of New York residents (twice the national average) reported extreme nervousness and anxiety at the sound of sirens or the sight of airplanes flying above.

Still other studies have been conducted in recent years, each looking at a particular aspect of the September 11 attack and its enormous psychological impact. Presented here are some notable findings from these studies, each serving in its own way to build a more complete understanding of this trauma and its lingering effects and each helping clinicians to serve better the victims of both this disaster and other kinds of disasters.

Six Months Later and Beyond

What percentage of the population continue to have terrorism-related concerns and problems?

Adults who report high terrorism fear	42
New Yorkers who report high terrorism fear	70
Adults who report drinking more alcohol	15
Adults who feel less safe in homes	23
U.S. adults with PTSD	4
New York adults with PTSD	9
Pentagon staff members with PTSD	23
U.S. college students with PTSD	7
New York college students with PTSD	8
U.S. children with PTSD	4
New York children with PTSD	11

Tramontin & Halpern, 2007; Adams & Boscarino, 2005; Blanchard et al., 2005; Hoven et al., 2005; Boscarino et al., 2004; Connelly & Dutton, 2002; Fetto, 2002; Gardyn, 2002; Lord, 2002; *Time* Poll, 2002

Two Months Later

What percentage of the population developed posttraumatic stress disorder?

Adults who live in New York City	11
Adults who live in Washington, D.C.	3
Adults who live in the United States	4
Children who live in the United States	8
College students in the United States	7
College students in New York State	11

Lengua et al., 2005; Blanchard et al., 2005; Schlenger et al., 2002

Gender and Posttraumatic Stress Disorder

Many researchers believe that women's higher rates of posttraumatic stress disorder are tied to the types of violent traumas they experience—namely, interpersonal assaults such as rape or sexual abuse (Russo & Tartaro, 2008; Olff et al., 2007). ‹‹

researchers examined the cortisol levels of women who had been pregnant during the September 11, 2001, terrorist attacks and had developed PTSD (Yehuda & Bierer, 2007). Not only did these women have higher-than-average cortisol levels, but the babies to whom they gave birth after the attacks also displayed higher cortisol levels, suggesting that the babies inherited a predisposition to develop the same disorder. The notion that a parent's PTSD may affect the biology and predisposition of their offspring has also received support from studies of the children of Holocaust survivors and from studies on rats (Yehuda & Bierer, 2007).

Many theorists believe that people whose biochemical reactions to stress are unusually strong are more likely than others to develop acute and posttraumatic stress disorders (Carlson, 2008; Burijon, 2007; Beck, 2004). But why would certain people be prone to such strong biological reactions? One possibility is that the propensity is inherited. Clearly, this is suggested by the mother–offspring studies just discussed. The notion of inheritance has also been suggested by studies that have been conducted on thousands of pairs of twins who have served in the military. These studies have found that if one twin develops stress symptoms after combat, an identical twin is more likely than a fraternal twin to develop the same problem (Koenen et al., 2003; True et al., 1993). We must remember, however, that the similarities seen in identical twins do not always reflect genetic influences: childhood experiences, personalities, and support systems may also be more similar in identical twins than in fraternal twins and thus may explain the greater similarity in their reactions to stress. More direct genetic studies are currently under way to determine whether a particular gene or combination of genes predisposes individuals to PTSD (Bachmann et al., 2005).

Personality Some studies suggest that people with certain personality profiles, attitudes, and coping styles are particularly likely to develop stress disorders (Burijon, 2007; Chung et al., 2005). In the aftermath of Hurricane Hugo in 1989, for example, children who had been highly anxious before the storm were more likely than other children to develop severe stress reactions (Hardin et al., 2002; Lonigan et al., 1994). Similarly, the victims who are most likely to develop stress disorders after being raped are the ones who had psychological problems before they were raped or who were struggling with stressful life situations (Darvres-Bornoz et al., 1995). The same is true of war veterans who had psychological problems before they went into combat (Dikel et al., 2005; Orsillo et al., 1996).

Research has also found that people who generally view life's negative events as beyond their control tend to develop more severe stress symptoms after sexual or other kinds of criminal assaults than people who feel greater control over their lives (Taylor, 2006; Bremner, 2002; Regehr et al., 1999). Similarly, individuals who generally find it difficult to derive anything positive from unpleasant situations adjust more poorly after traumatic events than people who find a way to greet aversive situations with positive emotions of one kind or another (gratitude, interest, love) (Bonanno, 2004; Fredrickson et al., 2003). These findings coincide with another discovery: many people respond to stress with a set of positive attitudes, collectively called *resiliency* or *hardiness,* that enables them to carry on their lives with a sense of fortitude, control, and commitment (Bonanno, 2004; Oulette, 1993).

Childhood Experiences Researchers have found that certain childhood experiences seem to leave some people at risk for later acute and posttraumatic stress disorders. People whose childhoods have been marked by poverty appear more likely to develop these disorders in the face of later trauma. So do people whose family members suffered from psychological disorders; who experienced assault, abuse, or catastrophe at an early age; or who were younger than 10 when their parents separated or divorced (Koch & Haring, 2008; Koopman et al., 2004; Ozer et al., 2003).

Building resiliency
Noting that a resilient, or "hardy," personality style may help protect people from developing stress disorders, many programs now claim to build resiliency. Here young South Korean schoolchildren fall on a mud flat at a five-day winter military camp designed to strengthen them mentally and physically.

AP Photo/Ahn Young-joon

A CLOSER LOOK

Adjustment Disorders: A Category of Compromise?

Some people react to a major stressor in their lives with extended and excessive feelings of anxiety, depressed mood, or antisocial behaviors. The symptoms do not quite add up to acute stress disorder or posttraumatic stress disorder, nor do they reflect an anxiety or mood disorder, but they do cause considerable distress or interfere with the person's job, schoolwork, or social life. Should we consider such reactions normal? No, says DSM-IV-TR. Somewhere between effective coping strategies and stress disorders lie the *adjustment disorders* (APA, 2000).

DSM-IV-TR lists several types of adjustment disorders, including *adjustment disorder with anxiety* and *adjustment disorder with depressed mood*. People receive such diagnoses if they develop their symptoms within three months of the onset of a stressor. If the stressor is long-term, such as

a medical condition, the adjustment disorder may last indefinitely.

Almost any kind of stressor may trigger an adjustment disorder. Common ones are the breakup of a relationship, marital problems, business difficulties, and living in a crime-ridden neighborhood. The disorder may also be triggered by developmental events such as going away to school, getting married, or retiring from a job.

Up to 30 percent of all people in outpatient therapy receive this diagnosis; it accounts for far more treatment claims submitted to insurance companies than any other (APA, 2000). However, some experts doubt that adjustment disorders are as common as this figure suggests. Rather, the diagnosis seems to be a favorite among clinicians—it can easily be applied to a range of problems yet is less stigmatizing than many other categories.

Candidates for dysfunction? A stock trader—exhausted, worried, and stunned—sits on the floor of the New York Stock Exchange after one of numerous bad financial days in 2007 and 2008. Business difficulties are among the most common stressors known to trigger adjustment disorders.

Such childhood experiences may help produce the personality styles or attitudes that have been linked to stress disorders. Perhaps their early situations teach children that the world is an unpredictable and dangerous place. In Chapter 5 you saw that such a worldview may help set the stage for generalized anxiety disorder. Similarly, it may lead people to react more hopelessly and fearfully to extraordinary trauma, and so increase their risk of developing a stress disorder.

Social Support It has been found that people whose social and family support systems are weak are also more likely to develop a stress disorder after a traumatic event (Charuvastra & Cloitre, 2008; Ozer, 2005; Simeon et al., 2005). Rape victims who feel loved, cared for, valued, and accepted by their friends and relatives recover more successfully. So do those treated with dignity and respect by the criminal justice system (Murphy, 2001; Davis et al., 1991; Sales et al., 1984). In contrast, clinical reports have suggested that poor social support contributes to the development of posttraumatic stress disorder in some combat veterans (Charuvastra & Cloitre, 2008; Dirkzwager, Bramsen, & van der Ploeg, 2005).

Multicultural Factors For years clinical theorists have anticipated that the rates of posttraumatic stress disorder would differ from ethnic group to ethnic group in the United States. After all, as you have just read, vulnerability to this disorder is related to factors such as a person's coping style, general attitudes, sense of control, childhood experiences, and social support system, and these factors frequently vary from culture to culture. However, the overall rate of PTSD has been surprisingly stable from group to group. Time and again, white Americans, African Americans, Hispanic Americans, and Asian Americans have seemed to display the same rate for PTSD—3.5 percent in any given year.

BETWEEN THE LINES

The Tsunami: Sociocultural Fallout

Since 2004, tourism in South Asia has been way down, largely because of fears about the occurrence of another tsunami. However, many Asian vacationers are also staying away from Asian beaches for another reason: they believe the Chinese superstition that if bodies are not recovered and buried properly, the spirits may wander the world restlessly and even drag living beings into their land of spiritual limbo (Foreman, 2005). 〈〈

Carolyn Cole / *Los Angeles Times*

Religious protection?
Jaquetta Banks, age 8, leads the way as a group of children enter the St. Joan of Arc Church in New Orleans for their first communion service, the first such ceremony held after Hurricane Katrina. Research indicates that children and adults with strong institutional, religious, and social ties often recover more readily from the effects of disasters and other traumatic events.

BETWEEN THE LINES

Stress and Coping: Eye on Culture

- 38 percent of Native Americans and African Americans feel stressed, compared to 34 percent of Hispanic Americans and Asian Americans and 30 percent of white Americans.
- 57 percent of Native Americans and African Americans feel stressed by finances, compared to 47 percent of the entire American population.
- 41 percent of Hispanic Americans feel stressed by employment issues, compared to 32 percent of the entire American population.
- 82 percent of African Americans turn to prayer and meditation when stressed, compared to 62 percent of the entire American population.
- 70 percent of Native Americans and Asian Americans turn to exercise when stressed, compared to 55 percent of the entire American population.

(MHA, 2008)

But now the wind is shifting. A more careful look at the research literature suggests that there may indeed be important cultural differences in the occurrence of posttraumatic stress disorder—differences that clinicians previously missed. In particular, Hispanic Americans may have a greater vulnerability to the disorder than other cultural groups (Koch & Haring, 2008; Galea et al., 2006; Pole et al., 2005).

Some cases in point: (1) Studies of combat veterans from the wars in Vietnam and Iraq have found higher rates of posttraumatic stress disorder among Hispanic American veterans than among white American and African American veterans (RAND Corporation, 2008; Kulka et al., 1990). (2) Research suggests that Hispanic American combat veterans with PTSD have, on average, more severe symptoms than veterans from other ethnic or racial groups (Rosenheck & Fontana, 1996). (3) In surveys of police officers, Hispanic officers typically report more severe duty-related stress symptoms than their non-Hispanic counterparts (Pole et al., 2001). (4) Data on hurricane victims reveal that after some hurricanes Hispanic victims have had a significantly higher rate of PTSD than victims from other ethnic groups (Perilla et al., 2002). (5) Surveys of New York City residents conducted in the months following the terrorist attacks of September 11, 2001, revealed that 14 percent of Hispanic American residents developed PTSD, compared to 9 percent of African American residents and 7 percent of white American residents (Galea et al., 2002).

Why might Hispanic Americans be more vulnerable to posttraumatic stress disorder than other racial or ethnic groups? Several explanations have been suggested. One centers on the initial reactions of Hispanic Americans to traumatic events. It appears that an early *dissociative* reaction (altered state of consciousness) is one of the strongest predictors that an individual will go on to develop PTSD (Ozer et al., 2003). At the same time, it is known from research in Latin America that dissociative symptoms are very common in a number of culture-bound Latin psychological disorders (Escobar, 1995). If Hispanic Americans are more likely than other individuals to react to traumatic events with dissociative symptoms, they may be particularly prone to develop PTSD (Pole et al., 2005).

Another explanation holds that as part of their cultural belief system, many Hispanic Americans tend to view traumatic events as inevitable and unalterable, a coping response that may heighten their risk for posttraumatic stress disorder (Perilla et al., 2002).

And still another explanation suggests that their culture's emphasis on social relationships and social support may place Hispanic American victims at special risk when traumatic events deprive them—temporarily or permanently—of important relationships and support systems. Indeed, a study conducted more than two decades ago found that among Hispanic American Vietnam combat veterans with stress disorders, those with poor family and social relationships suffered the most severe symptoms (Escobar et al., 1983).

Severity of Trauma As you might expect, the severity and nature of traumatic events help determine whether one will develop a stress disorder. Some events can override even a nurturing childhood, positive attitudes, and social support (Tramontin & Halpern, 2007). One study examined 253 Vietnam War prisoners five years after their release. Some 23 percent qualified for a clinical diagnosis, though all had been evaluated as well adjusted before their imprisonment (Ursano et al., 1981).

Generally, the more severe the trauma and the more direct one's exposure to it, the greater the likelihood of developing a stress disorder (Burijon, 2007). Among the Vietnam prisoners of war, for example, the men who had been imprisoned longest and treated most harshly had the highest percentage of disorders. Mutilation and severe physical injury in particular seem to increase the risk of stress reactions, as does witnessing the injury or death of other people (Koren et al., 2005; Ursano et al., 2003). It is, as a survivor of trauma once said, "hard to be a survivor" (Kolff & Doan, 1985, p. 45).

How Do Clinicians Treat the Psychological Stress Disorders?

Overall, about half of all cases of posttraumatic stress disorder improve within six months (Asnis et al., 2004). The remainder of cases may persist for years. Thus, treatment can be very important for persons who have been overwhelmed by traumatic events (DeAngelis, 2008; Bradley et al., 2005). One survey found that posttraumatic stress symptoms last an average of three years with treatment but five and a half years without it (Kessler & Zhao, 1999; Kessler et al., 1995). At the same time, more than one-third of people with PTSD fail to respond to treatment even after many years (Burijon, 2007; Cloitre et al., 2004).

Today's treatment procedures for troubled survivors typically vary from trauma to trauma. Was it combat, an act of terrorism, sexual molestation, or a major accident? Yet all the programs share basic goals: they try to help survivors put an end to their stress reactions, gain perspective on their painful experiences, and return to constructive living (Bryant et al., 2005; Ehlers et al., 2005). Programs for combat veterans who suffer from PTSD illustrate how these issues may be addressed.

Treatment for Combat Veterans Therapists have used a variety of techniques to reduce veterans' posttraumatic symptoms. Among the most common are *drug therapy, behavioral exposure techniques, insight therapy, family therapy,* and *group therapy.* Typically the approaches are combined, as no one of them successfully reduces all the symptoms (DeAngelis, 2008; Munsey, 2008).

Antianxiety drugs help control the tension that many veterans experience. In addition, antidepressant medications may reduce the occurrence of nightmares, panic attacks, flashbacks, and feelings of depression (Koch & Haring, 2008; Cooper et al., 2005; Davidson et al., 2005).

Behavioral exposure techniques, too, have helped reduce specific symptoms, and they have often led to improvements in overall adjustment (Koch & Haring, 2008). In fact, some studies indicate that exposure treatment is the single most helpful intervention for persons with stress disorders, irrespective of the precipitating trauma (Wiederhold & Wiederhold, 2005). This finding suggests to many clinical theorists that exposure of one kind or another should always be part of the treatment picture. In one case, the exposure technique of *flooding,* along with relaxation training, helped rid a 31-year-old veteran of frightening flashbacks and nightmares (Fairbank & Keane, 1982). The therapist and the veteran first singled out combat scenes that the man had been reexperiencing frequently. The therapist then helped the veteran to imagine one of these scenes in great detail and urged him to hold on to the image until his anxiety stopped. After each of these flooding exercises, the therapist had the veteran switch to a positive image and led him through relaxation exercises.

A widely applied form of exposure therapy is **eye movement desensitization and reprocessing (EMDR),** in which clients move their eyes in a *saccadic,* or rhythmic, manner from side to side while flooding their minds with images of the objects and situations they ordinarily try to avoid. Case studies and controlled studies suggest that this treatment can often be helpful to persons with posttraumatic stress disorder (Russell et al., 2007; Gonzalez-Brigmardello & Vasquez, 2004; Taylor et al., 2003). Many theorists argue that it is the exposure feature of EMDR, rather than the eye movement, that accounts for its success with the disorder (Lamprecht et al., 2004; Foa et al., 2003).

Although drug therapy and exposure techniques bring some relief, most clinicians believe that veterans with posttraumatic stress disorder cannot fully recover with these

•eye movement desensitization and reprocessing (EMDR)•A behavioral exposure treatment in which clients move their eyes in a saccadic (rhythmic) manner from side to side while flooding their minds with images of objects and situations they ordinarily avoid.

Combat stress relief
According to research, many U.S. troops experience significant psychological problems while fighting in Iraq, and many more develop stress symptoms and disorders within months after returning home from Iraq. Thus, the U.S. military has set up combat stress control teams that meet with soldiers throughout Iraq, talk with them soon after battles, and try to diagnose troops who have special mental health needs. Here, members of one such team give a class in stress relief to soldiers in Iraq in 2003.

Hiroko Masuike/The New York Times/Redux

"Virtual" exposure

Exposure therapy is a key element in the treatment of combat veterans with post-traumatic stress disorder. In recent years, this intervention has been enhanced by the use of reality software that enables clients to confront more vividly the objects and situations that continue to haunt them. Here an individual's virtual reality headset takes him to a battle scene in Iraq. The computer screen mirrors what he is seeing in his headset.

•**rap group**•A group that meets to talk about and explore members' problems in an atmosphere of mutual support.

•**psychological debriefing**•A form of crisis intervention in which victims are helped to talk about their feelings and reactions to traumatic incidents. Also called *critical incident stress debriefing*.

approaches alone: they must also come to grips in some way with their combat experiences and the impact those experiences continue to have (Burijon, 2007) (see *The Media Speaks* on page 183). Thus clinicians often try to help veterans bring out deep-seated feelings, accept what they have done and experienced, become less judgmental of themselves, and learn to trust and relate effectively with other people once again (Turner et al., 2005; Resick & Calhoun, 2001).

Similarly, cognitive therapists help individuals with posttraumatic stress disorder to systematically examine and change the dysfunctional attitudes and styles of interpretation that have emerged as a result of the traumatic event (DeAngelis, 2008; Ehlers et al., 2005; Taylor et al., 2005). In research along these lines, psychologist James Pennebaker has found that talking (or even writing) about traumatic experiences can reduce lingering anxiety and tension, particularly if individuals try to develop perspective and growth in their discussions or writings (Cohen et al., 2004; Smyth & Pennebaker, 2001).

People who have a psychological stress disorder may be further helped in a couple or family therapy format (DeAngelis, 2008; Johnson, 2005; Monson et al., 2005; Rodgers et al., 2005). The symptoms of posttraumatic stress disorder tend to be particularly apparent to family members, who may be directly affected by the client's anxieties, depressive mood, or angry outbursts. With the help and support of their family members, individuals may come to recognize their feelings, examine their impact on others, learn to communicate better, and improve their problem-solving skills.

Veterans may also benefit from group therapy, often provided in a form called **rap groups,** in which individuals meet with others like themselves to share experiences and feelings, develop insights, and give mutual support (Lifton, 2005; Ford & Stewart, 1999). One of the major issues rap groups deal with is *guilt*—guilt about things the members may have done to survive or about the very fact that they did survive while close friends died (Burijon, 2007). These groups may also focus on the rage many combat veterans feel.

Today hundreds of small *Veterans Outreach Centers* across the country, as well as treatment programs in Veterans Administration hospitals and mental health clinics, provide group treatments (Welch, 2007; Batres, 2003; Ford & Stewart, 1999). These agencies also offer individual therapy, counseling for spouses and children, family therapy, and aid in seeking jobs, education, and benefits. Clinical reports suggest that these programs offer a necessary, sometimes life-saving treatment opportunity. Julius's search for help upon his return from Vietnam was, unfortunately, an ordeal that many veterans of that war shared:

When I got back from the 'Nam, I knew I needed psychotherapy or something like that. I just knew that if I didn't get help I was going to kill myself or somebody else. . . . I went to see this doctor; he barely looked at me. I felt he "saw me coming" and knew all about my sickness. I was the "sicky" to him. He just kept on asking me all that bullshit about how many children I had killed and was I guilty and depressed about it. He asked how it felt to kill people. He also kept on asking me about my brothers and sisters. But he never asked me about what my experiences were like in Vietnam. He never did. I saw him for treatment for about a month—about three visits, but I quit because we weren't getting anywhere. . . . He just kept on giving me more and more medications. I could've set up my own pharmacy. I needed someone to talk to about my problems, my real problems, not some bullshit about my childhood. I needed someone who wanted to help. The clinic later referred me to another shrink. . . . I guess she thought she was being honest with me, by telling me that she was not a veteran, was not in Vietnam, and did not know what was wrong with me. She also told me that she had no experience working with Vietnam veterans, and that I should go to the Veterans Administration for help. . . .

It was only in the last 3 years when my wife made an important phone call to a local Veterans Outreach Center that I started feeling I had hope, that something could be done for me. I received the help that I have always needed. Finally, I found it easier to hold a job and take care of my family. My nightmares are not as frightening or as frequent as they used to be. Things are better now; I am learning to trust people and give more to my wife and children.

(Brende & Parson, 1985, pp. 206–208)

Psychological Debriefing: The Sociocultural Model in Action People who are traumatized by disasters, victimization, or accidents profit from many of the same treatments that are used to help survivors of combat. In addition, because their traumas occur in their own community, where mental health resources are close at hand, these individuals may, according to many clinicians, further benefit from immediate community interventions. The leading such approach is called **psychological debriefing, or critical incident stress debriefing.**

Psychological debriefing is actually a form of crisis intervention that has victims of trauma talk extensively—a session typically lasts three to four hours—about their feelings and reactions within days of the critical incident (Mitchell, 2003, 1983; Mitchell & Everly, 2000). Because such sessions are expected to prevent or reduce stress reactions, they are commonly applied to victims who have not yet manifested any symptoms at all, as well as those who have. During the sessions, often conducted in a group format, counselors guide the individuals to describe the details of the recent trauma and the thoughts that had accompanied the unfolding event vividly, to vent and relive the emotions provoked at the time of the event, and to express their lingering reactions. The clinicians then clarify to the victims that their reactions are perfectly normal responses to a terrible event, offer stress management tips, and, when necessary, refer the victims to professionals who can provide long-term counseling.

Thousands of counselors, both professionals and nonprofessionals, are now trained in psychological debriefing each year, and the intense approach has been applied in the aftermath of countless traumatic events (McNally, 2004). When the traumatic incident affects numerous individuals, debriefing-trained counselors may come from far and wide to gather at the scene of the incident and conduct debriefing sessions with the victims. For example, 1,600 counselors were mobilized to counsel people during the days and weeks following the World Trade Center attack in 2001 (Tramontin & Halpern, 2007; Pepe, 2002).

One of the largest mobilization programs of this kind is the *Disaster Response Network* (*DRN*), developed in 1991 by the American Psychological Association and the American Red Cross. The network is made up of more than 2,500 volunteer psychologists who offer free emergency mental health services at disaster sites throughout North America (APA, 2008). They have been mobilized for such disasters as earthquakes in California, the 1995 Oklahoma City bombing, the 1999 shooting of 23 persons at Columbine High School in Colorado, the 2001 World Trade Center attack, and the floods caused by Hurricane Katrina in 2005. In addition, some members of the DRN traveled to South Asia to work with victims of the devastating tsunami that occurred in late 2004 and to aid in the worldwide mobilization of counseling services for people in that area (APA, 2005).

In such community-wide mobilizations, the counselors may knock on doors or approach victims at shelters and service centers. Although victims from all socioeconomic

Psychological debriefing in action
A relief worker comforts the family member of a victim of Egypt Air Flight 990, a plane that crashed off Nantucket Island in 1999 under mysterious circumstances, killing all 217 aboard.

Paul Conner/AP Photo

groups may be engaged, some theorists argue that those who live in poverty are in particular need of such community-level interventions. These victims may experience more psychological distress after community traumas than survivors with higher incomes (Gibbs, 1989), partly because they cannot afford private counseling and are less likely to know where to seek counseling.

Relief workers, too, can become overwhelmed by the traumas they witness (Carll, 2007; Creamer & Liddle, 2005; Simons et al., 2005). During the 1992 Los Angeles riots, for example, a key responsibility of many community counselors was to help Red Cross workers vent and accept their own feelings as well as teach them about stress disorders and how to identify victims who needed further treatment. Many counselors who live in a disaster area may need counseling themselves, since they, too, are survivors.

Does Psychological Debriefing Work? Obviously, rapid mobilization programs for disaster victims personify the sociocultural model in action. Moreover, research and personal testimonials for these programs have often been favorable (Watson & Shalev, 2005; Mitchell, 2003; Raphael & Wilson, 2000). Nevertheless, a number of studies have called into question the effectiveness of these kinds of interventions (Tramontin & Halpern, 2007; McNally, 2004; McNally et al., 2003).

An investigation conducted in the early 1990s was among the first to raise concerns about disaster mental health programs (Bisson & Deahl, 1994). Crisis counselors offered debriefing sessions to 62 British soldiers whose job during the Gulf War was to handle and identify the bodies of individuals who had been killed. Despite such sessions, half of the soldiers displayed posttraumatic stress symptoms when interviewed nine months later, a finding that led some theorists to conclude that disaster intervention programs may not really make much difference.

In a properly controlled study conducted a few years later on hospitalized burn victims, researchers separated the victims into two groups (Bisson et al., 1997). One group received a single one-on-one debriefing session within 2 to 19 days of their burn accidents, while the other (control) group of burn victims received no such intervention. Three months later, it was found that the debriefed and the control patients had similar rates of posttraumatic stress disorder, suggesting once again that psychological debriefing may not prevent or reduce stress reactions.

A follow-up to this particular study was even more disturbing. Thirteen months after the debriefing sessions, the rate of posttraumatic stress disorder was, in fact, *higher* among the debriefed burn victims (26 percent) than among the control victims (9 percent). Several other studies, focusing on yet other kinds of disasters, have yielded similar patterns of findings (Van Emmerik et al., 2002; Rose et al., 2001). Obviously, these studies raise serious questions about this widespread and highly regarded approach. Some clinicians believe that the early intervention programs may encourage victims to dwell too long on the traumatic events that they have experienced. And a number worry that early disaster counseling may inadvertently "suggest" problems to victims, thus helping to produce stress disorders in the first place (McNally, 2004; McClelland, 1998).

Finally, questions have been raised about the *cultural competence* of the crisis counselors in these community interventions. When hundreds of clinicians were mobilized in New York City after the attacks of September 11, 2001, for example, many wound up working with residents of the Chinatown neighborhood, located near the World Trade Center (Tramontin & Halpern, 2007; Stoil, 2001). It is not clear that the counseling techniques of these clinicians were fully appropriate for a population that prefers to speak Cantonese and whose culture is often uncomfortable with the kinds of openness that characterize Western therapy.

The current clinical climate continues to favor disaster counseling, and research may indeed eventually clarify that such programs are as helpful as many clinicians believe. However, the concerns that have been raised merit serious consideration. We are reminded here, as elsewhere, of the constant need for careful research in the field of abnormal psychology.

certain receptor sites in the body and give *inhibitory messages,* which help calm down the overstressed body (Manuck et al., 1991). One such group of receptor sites is located on the lymphocytes. When the corticosteroids bind to these receptors, their inhibitory messages actually slow down the activity of the lymphocytes (Bauer, 2005; Bellinger et al., 1994). Thus, again, the very chemicals that initially help people to deal with stress eventually serve to slow the immune system.

Recent research has further indicated that one of the actions of the corticosteroids is to trigger an increase in the production of *cytokines,* proteins that bind to receptors throughout the body. At early and moderate levels of stress, the cytokines, another key player in the immune system, help combat infection. But as stress continues and more corticosteroids are released, the growing production and spread of cytokines lead to *chronic inflammation* throughout the body. Among other activities, the cytokines travel to the liver and induce increased production of *C-reactive protein,* or *CRP,* a protein that enters the bloodstream, spreads throughout the body, and, over time, contributes to heart disease, stroke, and other illnesses (Travis & Meltzer, 2008; Suarez, 2004; McEwen, 2002).

BEHAVIORAL CHANGES Stress may set in motion a series of behavioral changes that indirectly affect the immune system. Some people under stress may, for example, become anxious or depressed, perhaps even develop an anxiety or mood disorder. As a result, they may sleep badly, eat poorly, exercise less, or smoke or drink more—behaviors known to slow down the immune system (Irwin & Cole, 2005; Kiecolt-Glaser & Glaser, 2002, 1999).

PERSONALITY STYLE An individual's personality may also play a role in determining how much the immune system is slowed down by stress (Chung et al., 2005; Sarid et al., 2004). According to research, people who generally respond to life stress with optimism, constructive coping, and resilience—that is, people who welcome challenge and are willing to take control in their daily encounters—experience better immune system functioning and are better prepared to fight off illness (Taylor, 2006, 2004). Some studies find, for example, that people with "hardy" or resilient personalities remain healthy after stressful events, while those whose personalities are less hardy seem more susceptible to illness (Bonanno, 2004; Oulette & DiPlacido, 2001). One study even discovered that men with a general sense of hopelessness die at above-average rates from heart disease and other causes (Everson et al., 1996) (see Figure 6-7). Similarly, a growing body of research suggests that people who are spiritual tend to be healthier than individuals without spiritual beliefs, and a few studies have linked spirituality to better immune system functioning (Thoresen & Plante, 2005; Lutgendorf et al., 2004).

In related work, some studies have noted a relationship between certain personality characteristics and recovery from cancer (Hjerl et al., 2003; Greer, 1999). They have found that patients with certain forms of cancer who display a helpless coping style and who cannot easily express their feelings, particularly anger, tend to have less successful recoveries than patients who do express their emotions. Other studies, however, have found no relationship between personality and cancer outcome (Urcuyo et al., 2005; Garssen & Goodkin, 1999).

SOCIAL SUPPORT Finally, people who have few social supports and feel lonely seem to display poorer immune functioning in the face of stress than people who do not feel lonely (Curtis et al., 2004; Cohen, 2002). In a pioneering study, medical students were given the *UCLA Loneliness Scale* and then divided into "high" and "low" loneliness groups (Kiecolt-Glaser et al., 1984). The high-loneliness group showed lower lymphocyte responses during a final exam period.

Other studies have found that social support and affiliation may actually help protect people from stress, poor immune

Figure 6-7

Warning: psychological disorders may be dangerous to your health Psychological disorders are themselves a source of stress that can lead to medical problems. People with such disorders are twice as likely to die of natural causes (medical illnesses) as people without such difficulties. (Adapted from Harris & Barraclough, 1998.)

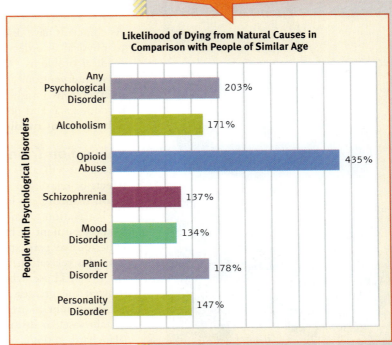

Likelihood of Dying from Natural Causes in Comparison with People of Similar Age

People with Psychological Disorders	
Any Psychological Disorder	203%
Alcoholism	171%
Opioid Abuse	435%
Schizophrenia	137%
Mood Disorder	134%
Panic Disorder	178%
Personality Disorder	147%

"You're not ill yet, Mr. Blendell, but you've got potential."

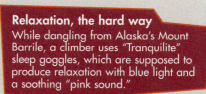

Relaxation, the hard way
While dangling from Alaska's Mount Barrile, a climber uses "Tranquilite" sleep goggles, which are supposed to produce relaxation with blue light and a soothing "pink sound."

system functioning, and subsequent illness or help speed up recovery from illness or surgery (Matsumoto & Juang, 2008; Taylor, 2006; Kiecolt-Glaser et al., 2002, 1998, 1991). Similarly, some studies have suggested that patients with certain forms of cancer who receive social support in their personal lives or supportive therapy often have better immune system functioning and, in turn, more successful recoveries than patients without such supports (Taylor, 2006; Spiegel & Fawzy, 2002) (see *The Media Speaks* on page 197).

Psychological Treatments for Physical Disorders

As clinicians have discovered that stress and related psychosocial factors may contribute to physical disorders, they have applied psychological treatments to more and more medical problems (Antoni, 2005; Gatchel & Maddrey, 2004). The most common of these interventions are relaxation training, biofeedback, meditation, hypnosis, cognitive interventions, insight therapy, and support groups. The field of treatment that combines psychological and physical approaches to treat or prevent medical problems is known as **behavioral medicine.**

Relaxation Training
As you saw in Chapter 5, people can be taught to relax their muscles at will, a process that sometimes reduces feelings of anxiety. Given the positive effects of relaxation on anxiety and the nervous system, clinicians believe that **relaxation training** can help prevent or treat medical illnesses that are related to stress.

Relaxation training, often in combination with medication, has been widely used in the treatment of high blood pressure (Stetter & Kupper, 2002). One study assigned hypertensive participants to one of three forms of treatment: medication, medication plus relaxation training, or medication plus supportive psychotherapy (Taylor et al., 1977). Those who received relaxation training in combination with medication showed the greatest reduction in blood pressure. Relaxation training has also been of some help in treating headaches, insomnia, asthma, diabetes, pain after surgery, certain vascular diseases, and the undesirable effects of cancer treatments (Devineni & Blanchard, 2005; Carmichael, 2004).

Biofeedback

As you also saw in Chapter 5, patients given **biofeedback training** are connected to machinery that gives them continuous readings about their involuntary body activities. This information enables them gradually to gain control over those activities. Somewhat helpful in the treatment of anxiety disorders, the procedure has also been applied to a growing number of physical disorders.

In a classic study, *electromyograph* (*EMG*) feedback was used to treat 16 patients who were experiencing facial pain caused in part by tension in their jaw muscles (Dohrmann & Laskin, 1978). In an EMG procedure, electrodes are attached to a person's muscles so that the muscle contractions are detected and converted into a tone for the individual to hear (see page 133). Changes in the pitch and volume of the tone indicate changes in muscle tension. After "listening" to EMG feedback repeatedly, the 16 patients in this study learned how to relax their jaw muscles at will and later reported a reduction in facial pain. In contrast, 8 people in the control group, who were wired to similar equipment but not given biofeedback training, showed little improvement in muscle tension or their experience of pain.

EMG feedback has also been used successfully in the treatment of headaches and muscular disabilities caused by strokes or accidents. Still other forms of biofeedback training have been of some help in the treatment of heartbeat irregularities, asthma, migraine headaches, high blood pressure, stuttering, and pain from burns (Martin, 2002; Moss, 2002; Gatchel, 2001).

Letting it all out
According to research, having multiple tests is the second most stressful life event for college students. These students at a dorm at Northwestern University tried to blow off steam by performing "primal screams" during the final exam period in 2007.

Meditation

Although meditation has been practiced since ancient times, Western health care professionals have only recently become aware of its effectiveness in relieving physical distress. **Meditation** is a technique of turning one's concentration inward, achieving a slightly changed state of consciousness, and temporarily ignoring all stressors. In the most common approach, meditators go to a quiet place, assume a comfortable posture, utter or think a particular sound (called a *mantra*) to help focus their attention, and allow their minds to turn away from all outside thoughts and concerns (Dass & Levine, 2002).

One form of meditation that has been applied in particular to patients suffering from severe pain is *mindfulness meditation* (Carey, 2008; Kabat-Zinn, 2005). In this form of meditation, people pay attention to the feelings, thoughts, and sensations that are flowing through their minds during meditation, but they do so with detachment and objectivity and, most important, without judgment. By just being mindful but not judgmental of their feelings and thoughts, including feelings of pain, they are less inclined to label them, fixate on them, or react negatively to them.

Many people who meditate regularly report feeling more peaceful, engaged, and creative. Meditation has been used to help manage pain to help treat high blood pressure, heart problems, asthma, skin disorders, diabetes, insomnia, and even viral infections (Stein, 2003; Andresen, 2000).

Hypnosis

As you saw in Chapter 1, individuals who undergo **hypnosis** are guided by a hypnotist into a sleeplike, suggestible state during which they can be directed to act in unusual ways, experience unusual sensations, remember seemingly forgotten events, or forget remembered events. With training some people are even able to induce their own hypnotic state (*self-hypnosis*). Hypnosis is now used as an aid to psychotherapy and to help treat many physical conditions (Shenefelt, 2003).

Hypnosis seems to be particularly helpful in the control of pain (Kiecolt-Glaser et al., 1998). One case study describes a patient who underwent dental surgery under

•**behavioral medicine**•A field that combines psychological and physical interventions to treat or prevent medical problems.

•**relaxation training**•A treatment procedure that teaches clients to relax at will.

•**biofeedback training**•A treatment technique in which a client is given information about physiological reactions as they occur and learns to control the reactions voluntarily.

•**meditation**•A technique of turning concentration inward and achieving a changed state of consciousness.

•**hypnosis**•A sleeplike suggestible state during which a person can be directed to act strangely, experience unusual sensations, and remember or forget events.

•**self-instruction training**•A cognitive treatment that teaches clients to use coping self-statements at times of stress or discomfort.

hypnotic suggestion: after a hypnotic state was induced, the dentist suggested to the patient that he was in a pleasant and relaxed setting listening to a friend describe his own success at undergoing similar dental surgery under hypnosis. The dentist then proceeded to perform a successful 25-minute operation (Gheorghiu & Orleanu, 1982). Although only some people are able to undergo surgery while anesthetized by hypnosis alone, hypnosis combined with chemical forms of anesthesia is apparently helpful to many patients (Fredericks, 2001). Beyond its use in the control of pain, hypnosis has been used successfully to help treat such problems as skin diseases, asthma, insomnia, high blood pressure, warts, and other forms of infection (Modlin, 2002; Hornyak & Green, 2000).

Cognitive Interventions People with physical ailments have sometimes been taught new attitudes or cognitive responses toward their ailments as part of treatment (Devineni & Blanchard, 2005; Kiecolt-Glaser et al., 2002, 1998). For example, an approach called **self-instruction training** has helped patients cope with severe pain (Allison & Friedman, 2004; Meichenbaum, 1997, 1993, 1977, 1975). In self-instruction training therapists teach people to identify and eventually rid themselves of unpleasant thoughts that keep emerging during pain episodes (so-called *negative self-statements* such as "Oh, no, I can't take this pain") and to replace them with *coping self-statements* instead ("When pain comes, just pause; keep focusing on what you have to do").

Insight Therapy and Support Groups If anxiety, depression, anger, and the like contribute to a person's physical ills, therapy to reduce these negative emotions should help reduce the ills (Antoni, 2005; Hawkins, 2004). In such cases, physicians may recommend insight therapy, support groups, or both to help patients overcome their medical difficulties (Antoni, 2005). Research suggests that the discussion of past and present upsets may indeed help improve a person's health, just as it may help one's psychological functioning (Leibowitz, 2007; Smyth & Pennebaker, 2001). In one study, asthma and arthritis patients who simply wrote down their thoughts and feelings about stressful events for a handful of days showed lasting improvements in their conditions. Similarly, stress-related writing was found to be beneficial for patients with HIV infections (Petrie et al., 2004). In addition, as we have seen, recovery from cancer and certain other illnesses is sometimes improved by participation in support groups (Antoni, 2005; Spiegel & Fawzy, 2002).

Combination Approaches Studies have found that the various psychological interventions for physical problems tend to be equal in effectiveness (Devineni & Blanchard, 2005; Brauer, 1999). Relaxation and biofeedback training, for example,

Fighting HIV on all fronts
As part of his treatment at the Wellness Center in San Francisco, this man meditates and writes letters to his HIV virus.

Empathy Goes a Long Way

BY DENISE GRADY, THE *NEW YORK TIMES*, JANUARY 8, 2008

Four years ago, my sister found out she had two types of cancer at the same time. It was like being hit by lightning—twice.

She needed chemotherapy and radiation, a huge operation, more chemotherapy and then a smaller operation. All in all, the treatment took about a year. Thin to begin with, she lost 30 pounds. The chemo caused cracks in her fingers, dry eyes, anemia and mouth sores so painful they kept her awake at night. A lot of her hair fell out. The radiation burned her skin. Bony, red-eyed, weak and frightfully pale, she tied scarves on her head, plastered her fingers with Band-Aids and somehow toughed it out.

She saw two doctors quite often. The radiation oncologist would sling her arm around my sister's frail shoulders and walk her down the corridor as if they were old friends. The medical oncologist kept a close watch on the side effects, suggested remedies, reminded my sister she had good odds of beating the cancer and reassured her that the hair would grow back. (It did.)

People in my family aren't huggy-kissy types, but my sister greatly appreciated the warmth and concern of those two women. She trusted them completely, and their advice. Now healthy, she says their compassion played a big part in helping her get through a difficult and frightening time.

Research supports the idea that a few kind words from an oncologist—what used to be called bedside manner—can go a long way toward helping people with cancer understand their treatment, stick with it, cope better and maybe even fare better medically. "It is absolutely the role of the oncologist" to provide a bit of emotional support, said Dr. James A. Tulsky, director of the Center for Palliative Care at Duke University Medical Center.

But in a study published last month in the *Journal of Clinical Oncology,* Dr. Tulsky and other researchers found that doctors and patients weren't communicating all that well about emotions. The researchers recorded 398 conversations between 51 oncologists and 270 patients with advanced cancer. They listened for moments when patients expressed negative emotions like fear, anger or sadness, and for the doctors' replies.

A response like "I can imagine how scary this must be for you" was considered empathetic—a "continuer" that would allow patients to keep expressing their emotions. But a comment like "Give us time; we are getting there" was labeled a "terminator" that could shut the patient down. The team found that doctors used continuers only 22 percent of the time. Male doctors were worse at it than female ones: 48 percent of the men never used continuers, as opposed to 20 percent of the women. . . .

One doctor who was especially good with patients, and who often consulted on very serious cases, opened discussions with new patients by saying, "Tell me what you understand about your illness," Dr. Tulsky said. And when patients wept, this doctor would pause and wait until they were ready to continue the discussion.

By contrast, with other doctors, Dr. Tulsky said, "There were a number of times when patients brought up emotional content and it went right by the doctors." For instance, a patient would say, "I'm scared," and the doctor would go off on a "scientific riff" about the disease. . . . The doctors don't lack empathy, he said. They just have trouble expressing it.

"Oncologists care deeply for their patients," said Kathryn I. Pollak, the first author of the study and a social psychologist at Duke. . . . Even so, oncologists sometimes miss signs of distress, particularly if those signs are indirect, she said. For example, a patient may ask how big the tumors are, and the doctor may answer in millimeters—when the patient really wants to know: "Is the cancer getting worse? Am I dying?"

The good news . . . is that most doctors can be taught to respond in more helpful ways. Brief, empathetic responses will suffice, the researchers said; they are not recommending extensive counseling or endless dialogue. Patients may benefit from some coaching, too. It's perfectly reasonable, Dr. Tulsky said, to talk to an oncologist about sadness or fears about treatment, and to ask for help. "You're vulnerable when you express your emotions," Dr. Pollak said. "But I would advise patients to be as direct as possible."

Tom & Dee Ann McCarthy/Corbis

are equally helpful (and more helpful than placebos) in the treatment of high blood pressure, headaches, and asthma. Psychological interventions are, in fact, often of greatest help when they are combined with other psychological interventions and with medical treatments (Suinn, 2001). In one study, ulcer patients who were given relaxation, self-instruction, and assertiveness training along with medication were found to be less anxious and more comfortable, have fewer symptoms, and have a better long-term outcome than patients who received medication only (Brooks & Richardson, 1980).

Combination interventions have also been helpful in changing Type A patterns and in reducing the risk of coronary heart disease among Type A people (Williams, 2001; Cohen et al., 1997). In a famous study, 862 patients who had suffered a heart attack within the previous six months were assigned to one of two groups (Friedman et al., 1984). The control group was given three years of cardiological counseling (diet, exercise, and medical advice). The experimental group received the same counseling *plus* Type A behavioral counseling. They were taught about the Type A personality style and to recognize their excessive physiological, cognitive, and behavioral responses in stressful situations. They were also trained in relaxation and taught to change counterproductive attitudes.

The addition of the Type A behavioral counseling led to major differences in lifestyle and health. Type A behavior was reduced in almost 80 percent of the patients who received both Type A counseling and cardiological counseling for three years, compared to only 50 percent of those who received cardiological counseling alone. Moreover, fewer of those who received the combined counseling suffered another heart attack—only 7 percent, compared to 13 percent of the subjects in the control group.

Clearly, the treatment picture for physical illnesses has been changing dramatically. While medical treatments continue to dominate, today's medical practitioners are traveling a course far removed from the mind-body dualism of centuries past.

PUTTING IT... together

Expanding the Boundaries of Abnormal Psychology

The concept of stress is familiar to everyone, yet only in recent decades have clinical scientists and practitioners had much success in understanding and treating it and recognizing its pervasive impact on our functioning. Now that the impact of stress has been identified, however, research efforts in this area are moving forward at near-lightning speed. What researchers once saw as a vague connection between stress and psychological dysfunctioning or between stress and physical illness is now understood as a complex interaction of many variables. Such factors as life changes, individual psychological and bodily reactions, social support, biochemical activity, and slowing of the immune system are all recognized as contributors to psychological and physical stress disorders.

Insights into the treatment of the various stress disorders have been accumulating just as rapidly. In recent years clinicians have learned that a combination of approaches—from drug therapy to behavioral techniques to community interventions—may be of help to people with acute and posttraumatic stress disorders. Similarly, psychological approaches such as relaxation training and cognitive therapy are being applied to various physical ills, usually in combination with traditional medical treatments. Small wonder that many practitioners are convinced that such treatment combinations will eventually be the norm in treating the majority of physical ailments.

One of the most exciting aspects of these recent developments is the field's growing emphasis on the *interrelationship* of the social environment, the brain, and the rest of the body. Researchers have observed repeatedly that mental disorders are often best understood and treated when sociocultural, psychological, and biological factors are all taken into consideration. They now know that this interaction also helps explain medical problems. We are reminded that the brain is part of the body and that both are part of a social context. For better and for worse, the three are inextricably linked.

AP Photo/Mike Derer

The power of distraction
Researchers at a medical center in New Jersey had this 10-year-old girl and other young presurgical patients play with handheld Game Boys while waiting for their anesthesia to take effect. It was found that such game-playing was more effective than antianxiety drugs or parent hand-holding at relaxing the young patients. Still other research suggests that patients who are more relaxed often have better surgical outcomes.

BETWEEN THE LINES

Room with a View
According to one hospital's records of individuals who underwent gallbladder surgery, those in rooms with a good view from their window had shorter hospitalizations and needed fewer pain medications than those in rooms without a good view (Ulrich, 1984).

Another exciting aspect of this work on stress and its wide-ranging impact is the interest it has sparked in *illness prevention* and *health promotion* (Compas & Gotlib, 2002; Kaplan, 2000). If stress is indeed key to the development of both psychological and physical disorders, perhaps such disorders can be prevented by eliminating or reducing stress—for example, by helping people to cope better generally or by better preparing their bodies for stress's impact. With this notion in mind, illness prevention and health promotion programs are now being developed around the world. Clinical theorists have, for example, designed school-curriculum programs to help promote *social competence* in children (Weissberg, 2000) and to teach children more *optimistic ways of thinking* (Gillham et al., 2000, 1995).

Similarly, prevention programs have been developed that teach *coping skills* to children whose parents are divorcing and *conflict-reduction skills* to the parents themselves (Wolchick et al., 2000). And in the realm of acute and posttraumatic stress disorders, one team of clinical researchers has developed a program that *immediately* offers rape victims a combination of relaxation training, exposure techniques, cognitive interventions, and education about rape's impact, all before the onset of psychological or physical symptoms (Muran, 2007; Foa et al., 2005, 1995). Research indicates that women who receive such preventive measures do indeed develop fewer stress symptoms in the months following their attacks than do other rape victims.

Amidst these exciting and rapidly unfolding developments also lies a cautionary tale. When problems are studied heavily, it is common for the public, as well as some researchers and clinicians, to draw conclusions that may be too bold. In the psychological realm, for example, many individuals—perhaps too many—are now receiving diagnoses of posttraumatic stress disorder partly because the symptoms of the disorder are many, a variety of life events can be considered traumatic, and the disorder has received so much attention. Similarly, given the growing body of work on psychophysiological disorders and psychoneuroimmunology, some people, including a number of clinicians, are all too quick to explain medical problems by pointing simplistically to psychosocial factors such as counterproductive attitudes, too little faith, or lack of social support. Explanations of this kind reflect a misapplication of the complex research that has been unfolding in the study of stress and health. We shall see such potential problems again when we look at other problems that are currently receiving great focus, such as attention-deficit/hyperactivity disorder, repressed memories of childhood abuse, and multiple personality disorder. The line between enlightenment and overenthusiasm is often thin.

BETWEEN THE LINES

Favorite Nights for Taking a Break from Stress

Monday	Most common night for "working out" ‹‹
Tuesday	Most popular night for attending a club meeting ‹‹
Friday	Most common night for staying at home and watching TV ‹‹
Saturday	Most popular night for going out to dinner and/or a movie ‹‹
Sunday	Most common night for catching up on correspondence ‹‹

(Fetto, 2001)

Everyone needs a break
Stress affects everyone, from humans to animals, and indeed everyone needs to find ways to overcome and cope with the pressures of their lives. These monkeys, who live in a valley in Yamanouchi, Japan, fight stress and find relaxation by bathing regularly in one of the valley's hot springs.

Michael Newman/Photo Edit

BETWEEN THE LINES

Traffic Stress

46 Average number of hours American motorists spend in rush-hour traffic each year ‹‹

93 Average number of hours that Los Angeles motorists spend in rush-hour traffic ‹‹

(Reuters, 2004)

Treating asthma
Children who suffer from asthma may use an aerochamber, or inhaler, to help them inhale helpful medications. With the aid of such devices, many asthmatic children are able to lead active and relatively normal lives.

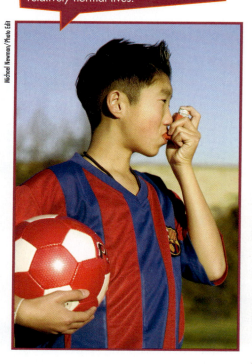

‹‹‹ [SUMMING UP] ›››

Effects of stress When we appraise a *stressor* as threatening, we often experience a *stress response* consisting of arousal and a sense of fear. The features of arousal and fear are set in motion by the *hypothalamus*, a brain area that activates the *autonomic nervous system* and the *endocrine system*. There are two pathways by which these systems produce arousal and fear—the *sympathetic nervous system* pathway and the *hypothalamic-pituitary-adrenal* pathway. *pp. 163–167*

Psychological stress disorders People with *acute stress disorder* or *posttraumatic stress disorder* react with anxiety and related symptoms after a traumatic event, including reexperiencing the traumatic event, avoiding related events, being markedly less responsive than normal, and experiencing increased arousal, anxiety, and guilt. The traumatic event may be *combat experience*, a *disaster*, or *victimization*. The symptoms of *acute stress disorder* begin soon after the trauma and last less than a month. Those of *posttraumatic stress disorder* may begin at any time (even years) after the trauma and may last for months or years.

In attempting to explain why some people develop a psychological stress disorder and others do not, researchers have focused on *biological factors, personality, childhood experiences, social support, multicultural factors,* and the *severity of the traumatic event.* Techniques used to treat the stress disorders include drug therapy and behavioral exposure techniques. Clinicians may also use insight therapy, family therapy, and group therapy (including *rap groups* for combat veterans) to help sufferers develop insight and perspective. Rapidly mobilized *community therapy,* such as that offered by the *Disaster Response Network,* follows the principles of *critical incident stress debriefing.* It often seems helpful after large-scale disasters; however, some studies have raised questions about the usefulness of this approach. *pp. 167–183*

Psychophysiological disorders *Psychophysiological disorders* are those in which psychosocial and physiological factors interact to cause a physical problem. Factors linked to these disorders are biological factors, such as defects in the autonomic nervous system or particular organs; psychological factors, such as particular needs, attitudes, or personality styles; and sociocultural factors, such as aversive social conditions and cultural pressures.

For years clinical researchers singled out a limited number of physical illnesses as psychophysiological. These traditional psychophysiological disorders include *ulcers, asthma, insomnia, chronic headaches, hypertension,* and *coronary heart disease.* Recently many other psychophysiological disorders have been identified. Scientists have linked many physical illnesses to stress and have developed a new area of study called *psychoneuroimmunology. pp. 184–191*

Psychoneuroimmunology The body's *immune system* consists of *lymphocytes* and other cells that fight off *antigens*—bacteria, viruses, and other foreign invaders—and cancer cells. Stress can slow *lymphocyte* activity, thereby interfering with the immune system's ability to protect against illness during times of stress. Factors that seem to affect immune functioning include *norepinephrine and corticosteroid activity, behavioral changes, personality style,* and *social support. pp. 191–194*

Psychological treatments for physical disorders *Behavioral medicine* combines psychological and physical interventions to treat or prevent medical problems. Psychological approaches such as *relaxation training, biofeedback training, meditation, hypnosis, cognitive techniques, insight therapy,* and *support groups* are increasingly being included in the treatment of various medical problems. *pp. 194–196*

Illness prevention and health promotion In recent years clinicians increasingly have designed programs that aim to eliminate or reduce stress by helping people generally to cope better or to prepare their bodies for stress's impact. The logic behind such programs is that the better people handle stress, the less likely they will be to develop the psychological and physical disorders that often result from stress. *pp. 196–198*

CRITICAL THOUGHTS

1. What types of events in modern society might trigger acute and post-traumatic stress disorders? What kinds of factors might serve to relieve the stresses of modern society? *pp. 167–173, 174–175*

2. Do you think the vivid images seen daily on television, in movies, in rock videos, and the like would make people more vulnerable to developing psychological stress disorders or less vulnerable? Why? *pp. 167–178*

3. How might physicians, police, the courts, and other agents better meet the psychological needs of rape victims? *pp. 170–172*

4. In order to help fend off terrorism attacks, the United States and other countries have instituted color-coded (threat-level) warning systems. How might such warning systems affect the psychological and physical health of citizens? *p. 172*

5. What jobs in our society might be particularly stressful and traumatizing? *pp. 183, 189*

6. Some observers fear that today there may be too much emphasis on psychosocial factors in explaining physical illness. What problems might result from an overemphasis on the role of psychosocial factors? *pp. 189–198*

 cyberstudy SEARCH

Search the *Abnormal Psychology* Video Tool Kit
www.worthpublishers.com/apvtk

▲ Chapter 6 Video Cases
  Fight-or-Flight: How Stress Affects Psychological and Bodily Functioning
  One Man's Return from Combat
  Caretaking: The Physical Toll

▲ Video case discussions, study guides, and questions

Log on to the Comer Web Page
www.worthpublishers.com/comer

▲ Chapter 6 outline, learning objectives, research exercises, study tools, and practice test questions

▲ Additional Chapter 6 case studies, Web links, and FAQs

SOMATOFORM AND DISSOCIATIVE DISORDERS

B rian was spending Saturday sailing with his wife, Helen. The water was rough but well within what they considered safe limits. They were having a wonderful time and really didn't notice that the sky was getting darker, the wind blowing harder, and the sailboat becoming more difficult to control. After a few hours of sailing, they found themselves far from shore in the middle of a powerful and dangerous storm.

The storm intensified very quickly. Brian had trouble controlling the sailboat amidst the high winds and wild waves. He and Helen tried to put on the safety jackets they had neglected to wear earlier, but the boat turned over before they were finished. Brian, the better swimmer of the two, was able to swim back to the overturned sailboat, grab the side, and hold on for dear life, but Helen simply could not overcome the rough waves and reach the boat. As Brian watched in horror and disbelief, his wife disappeared from view.

After a time, the storm began to lose its strength. Brian managed to right the sailboat and sail back to shore. Finally he reached safety, but the personal consequences of this storm were just beginning. The next days were filled with pain and further horror: the Coast Guard finding Helen's body . . . conversations with friends . . . self-blame . . . grief . . . and more.

Compounding this horror, the accident had left Brian with a severe physical impairment—he could not walk properly. He first noticed this terrible impairment when he sailed the boat back to shore, right after the accident. As he tried to run from the sailboat to get help, he could hardly make his legs work. By the time he reached the nearby beach restaurant, all he could do was crawl. Two patrons had to lift him to a chair, and after he told his story and the authorities were alerted, he had to be taken to a hospital.

At first Brian and the hospital physician assumed that he must have been hurt during the accident. One by one, however, the hospital tests revealed nothing—no broken bones, no spinal damage, nothing. Nothing that could explain such severe impairment.

By the following morning, the weakness in his legs had become near paralysis. Because the physicians could not pin down the nature of his injuries, they decided to keep his activities to a minimum. He was not allowed to talk long with the police. Someone else had to inform Helen's parents of her death. To his deep regret, he was not even permitted to attend Helen's funeral.

The mystery deepened over the following days and weeks. As Brian's paralysis continued, he became more and more withdrawn, unable to see more than a few friends and family members and unable to take care of the many unpleasant tasks attached to Helen's death. He could not bring himself to return to work or get on with his life. Almost from the beginning, Brian's paralysis had left him self-absorbed and drained of emotion, unable to look back and unable to move forward.

In the previous two chapters you saw how stress and anxiety can negatively affect functioning. Indeed, anxiety is the key feature of disorders such as generalized anxiety disorder, phobias, panic disorder, and obsessive–compulsive disorder. And stress can produce the lingering reactions seen in acute stress disorder, posttraumatic stress disorder, and psychophysiological disorders.

Two other kinds of disorders are commonly linked to stress and anxiety—somatoform disorders and dissociative disorders. *Somatoform disorders* are problems that appear to be medical but are actually caused by psychosocial factors. Unlike

Deliverance from danger
As a creek's wild waters rage around her, a young woman is saved from drowning. Unfortunately, for some people deliverance from a life-threatening event, such as a boating accident, combat, a flood, or a tornado, is the beginning rather than the end of their trauma. Somatoform disorders (particularly conversion disorders) and dissociative disorders may emerge during or shortly after such stressful events.

psychophysiological disorders, in which psychosocial factors interact with physical ailments, the somatoform disorders are psychological disorders masquerading as physical problems. Brian may have been suffering from a somatoform disorder. *Dissociative disorders* are patterns of memory loss and identity change that are caused almost entirely by psychosocial factors rather than physical ones.

The somatoform and dissociative disorders have much in common. Both, for example, may occur in response to severe stress, and both have traditionally been viewed as forms of escape from that stress. In addition, a number of individuals suffer from both a somatoform and a dissociative disorder (Brown et al., 2007; Sar et al., 2004). Indeed, theorists and clinicians often explain and treat the two groups of disorders in similar ways.

Somatoform Disorders

Think back to Brian, the young man whose tragic boating accident left him unable to walk. As medical test after test failed to explain his paralysis, physicians became convinced that the cause of his problem lay elsewhere.

When a physical ailment has no apparent medical cause, doctors may suspect a **somatoform disorder,** a pattern of physical complaints with largely psychosocial causes. People with such disorders do not consciously want or purposely produce their symptoms; like Brian, they almost always believe that their problems are genuinely medical (Phillips, Fallon, & King, 2008). In some somatoform disorders, known as *hysterical somatoform disorders,* there is an actual change in physical functioning. In others, the *preoccupation somatoform disorders,* people who are healthy mistakenly worry that there is something physically wrong with them.

What Are Hysterical Somatoform Disorders?

People with **hysterical somatoform disorders** suffer actual changes in their physical functioning. These somatoform disorders are often hard to distinguish from genuine medical problems (Phillips et al., 2008). In fact, it is always possible that a diagnosis of hysterical disorder is a mistake and that the patient's problem has an undetected organic cause (Merskey, 2004). DSM-IV-TR lists three hysterical somatoform disorders: *conversion disorder, somatization disorder,* and *pain disorder associated with psychological factors.*

Conversion Disorder In **conversion disorder,** a psychosocial conflict or need is converted into dramatic physical symptoms that affect voluntary motor or sensory functioning (see Table 7-1). Brian, the man with the unexplained paralysis, would probably receive this particular diagnosis. The symptoms often seem neurological, such as paralysis, blindness, or loss of feeling (*anesthesia*), and so may be called "pseudoneurological" (APA, 2000). One woman developed dizziness in apparent response to her unhappy marriage:

A 46-year-old married housewife . . . described being overcome with feelings of extreme dizziness, accompanied by slight nausea, four or five nights a week. During these attacks, the room around her would take on a "shimmering" appearance, and she would have the feeling that she was "floating" and unable to keep her balance. Inexplicably, the attacks almost always occurred at about 4:00 P.M. She usually had to lie down on the couch and often did not feel better until 7:00 or 8:00 P.M. After recovering, she generally spent the rest of the evening watching TV; and more often than not, she would fall asleep in the living room, not going to bed in the bedroom until 2:00 or 3:00 in the morning.

table: 7-1

DSM Checklist

CONVERSION DISORDER

1. One or more physical symptoms or deficits affecting voluntary motor or sensory function that suggest a neurological or other general medical condition.
2. Psychological factors judged to be associated with the symptom or deficit.
3. Symptom or deficit not intentionally produced or feigned.
4. Symptom or deficit not fully explained by a general medical condition or a substance.
5. Significant distress or impairment.

SOMATIZATION DISORDER

1. A history of many physical complaints, beginning before the age of 30, that occur over a period of several years and result in treatment being sought or in significant impairment.
2. Physical complaints over the period include all of the following:
   (a) Four different kinds of pain symptoms.
   (b) Two gastrointestinal symptoms.
   (c) One sexual symptom.
   (d) One neurological-type symptom.
3. Physical complaints not fully explained by a known general medical condition or a drug, or extending beyond the usual impact of such a condition.
4. Symptoms not intentionally produced or feigned.

PAIN DISORDER ASSOCIATED WITH PSYCHOLOGICAL FACTORS

1. Significant pain as the primary problem.
2. Psychological factors judged to have the major role in the onset, severity, exacerbation, or maintenance of the pain.
3. Symptom or deficit not intentionally produced or feigned.
4. Significant distress or impairment.

Based on APA, 2000.

•**somatoform disorder**•A physical illness or ailment that is explained largely by psychosocial causes, in which the patient experiences no sense of wanting or guiding the symptoms.

•**hysterical somatoform disorders**• Somatoform disorders in which people suffer actual changes in their physical functioning.

•**conversion disorder**•A somatoform disorder in which a psychosocial need or conflict is converted into dramatic physical symptoms that affect voluntary motor or sensory function.

The patient had been pronounced physically fit by her internist, a neurologist, and an ear, nose, and throat specialist on more than one occasion. Hypoglycemia had been ruled out by glucose tolerance tests.

When asked about her marriage, the patient described her husband as a tyrant, frequently demanding and verbally abusive of her and their four children. She admitted that she dreaded his arrival home from work each day, knowing that he would comment that the house was a mess and the dinner, if prepared, not to his liking. Recently, since the onset of her attacks, when she was unable to make dinner he and the four kids would go to McDonald's or the local pizza parlor. After that, he would settle in to watch a ballgame in the bedroom, and their conversation was minimal. In spite of their troubles, the patient claimed that she loved her husband and needed him very much.

(Spitzer et al., 1981, pp. 92–93)

Most conversion disorders begin between late childhood and young adulthood; they are diagnosed at least twice as often in women as in men (Abbey, 2005; APA, 2000). They usually appear suddenly, at times of extreme stress, and last a matter of weeks. Some research suggests that people who develop this disorder tend to be generally suggestible; many are highly susceptible to hypnotic procedures, for example (Roelofs et al., 2002). Conversion disorders are thought to be quite rare, occurring in at most 5 of every 1,000 persons.

BETWEEN THE LINES

Diagnostic Confusion

Many medical problems with vague or confusing symptoms—hyperparathyroidism, multiple sclerosis, lupus, and chronic fatigue syndrome are examples— are frequently misdiagnosed as hysterical somatoform disorders. In the past, whiplash was regularly diagnosed as hysteria (Ferrari, 2006; Nemecek, 1996; Merskey, 1986). ‹‹

•**somatization disorder**•A somatoform disorder marked by numerous recurring physical ailments without an organic basis. Also known as *Briquet's syndrome.*

•**pain disorder associated with psychological factors**•A somatoform disorder marked by pain, with psychosocial factors playing a central role in the onset, severity, or continuation of the pain.

Somatization Disorder Sheila baffled medical specialists with the wide range of her symptoms:

Sheila reported having abdominal pain since age 17, necessitating exploratory surgery that yielded no specific diagnosis. She had several pregnancies, each with severe nausea, vomiting, and abdominal pain; she ultimately had a hysterectomy for a "tipped uterus." Since age 40 she had experienced dizziness and "blackouts," which she eventually was told might be multiple sclerosis or a brain tumor. She continued to be bedridden for extended periods of time, with weakness, blurred vision, and difficulty urinating. At age 43 she was worked up for a hiatal hernia because of complaints of bloating and intolerance of a variety of foods. She also had additional hospitalizations for neurological, hypertensive, and renal workups, all of which failed to reveal a definitive diagnosis.

(Spitzer et al., 1981, pp. 185, 260)

Like Sheila, people with **somatization disorder** have many long-lasting physical ailments that have little or no organic basis (see again Table 7-1). This hysterical pattern, first described by Pierre Briquet in 1859, is also known as **Briquet's syndrome.** To receive this diagnosis, a person must have a range of ailments, including several pain symptoms (such as headaches and chest pain), gastrointestinal symptoms (such as nausea and diarrhea), a sexual symptom (such as erectile or menstrual difficulties), and a neurological symptom (such as double vision or paralysis) (APA, 2000). People with somatization disorder usually go from doctor to doctor in search of relief. They often describe their many symptoms in dramatic and exaggerated terms. Most also feel anxious and depressed (Fink et al., 2004; APA, 2000).

Between 0.2 and 2.0 percent of all women in the United States may experience a somatization disorder in any given year, compared to less than 0.2 percent of men (Eifer & Zvolensky, 2005; North, 2005; APA, 2000). The disorder often runs in families; 10 to 20 percent of the close female relatives of women with the disorder also develop it. It usually begins between adolescence and young adulthood.

Mind over matter
The opposite of hysterical disorders—although again demonstrating the power of psychological processes—are instances in which people "ignore" pain or other physical symptoms. Here a London performance artist manages to smile comfortably at onlookers while her skin is being pierced with sharp hooks that help suspend her from the ceiling above. Her action was part of a 2008 protest to end shark finning—the practice of cutting off a shark's fin and throwing its still living body back into the sea so that the fins can be used in the production of shark fin soup (a food delicacy) and other goods.

AP Photo/Lefteris Pitarakis

A somatization disorder lasts much longer than a conversion disorder, typically for many years (Yutzy, 2007). The symptoms may fluctuate over time but rarely disappear completely without therapy (Abbey, 2005; Smith, Rost, & Kashner, 1995). Two-thirds of individuals with this disorder in the United States receive treatment for their physical ailments from a medical or mental health professional in any given year (Regier et al., 1993).

Pain Disorder Associated with Psychological Factors When psychosocial factors play a central role in the onset, severity, or continuation of pain, patients may receive a diagnosis of **pain disorder associated with psychological factors** (see again Table 7-1). Patients with a conversion or somatization disorder may also experience pain, but it is the key symptom in this disorder.

Although the precise prevalence has not been determined, pain disorder associated with psychological factors appears to be fairly common (de Waal et al., 2004). The disorder may begin at any age, and women seem more likely than men to experience it (APA, 2000). Often it develops after an accident or during an illness that has caused genuine pain, which then takes on a life of its own. Laura, a 36-year-old woman, reported pains that went far beyond the usual symptoms of her tubercular disease, called sarcoidosis:

Before the operation I would have little joint pains, nothing that really bothered me that much. After the operation I was having severe pains in my chest and in my ribs, and those were the type of problems I'd been having after the operation, that I didn't have before. . . . I'd go to an emergency room at night, 11:00, 12:00, 1:00 or so. I'd take the medicine, and the next day it stopped hurting, and I'd go back again. In the meantime this is when I went to the other doctors, to complain about the same thing, to find out what was wrong; and they could never find out what was wrong with me either. . . .

. . . At certain points when I go out or my husband and I go out, we have to leave early because I start hurting. . . . A lot of times I just won't do things because my chest is hurting for one reason or another. . . . Two months ago when the doctor checked me and another doctor looked at the x-rays, he said he didn't see any signs of the sarcoid then and that they were doing a study now, on blood and various things, to see if it was connected to sarcoid. . . .

(Green, 1985, pp. 60–63)

Hysterical vs. Medical Symptoms As you have read, it can be difficult to distinguish hysterical somatoform disorders from "true" medical problems. Studies across the world suggest that as many as one-fifth of all patients who seek medical care from primary care physicians may actually suffer from somatoform disorders (Mergl et al., 2007; deWaal et al., 2004; Fink et al., 2004). Because hysterical somatoform disorders are so similar to "genuine" medical ailments, physicians sometimes rely on oddities in the patient's medical picture to help distinguish the two (Phillips et al., 2008; Kirmayer & Looper, 2007). The symptoms of a hysterical disorder may, for example, be at odds with the way the nervous system is known to work (APA, 2000). In a conversion symptom called *glove anesthesia,* numbness begins sharply at the wrist and extends evenly right to the fingertips. As Figure 7-1 shows, real neurological damage is rarely as abrupt or equally distributed.

The physical effects of a hysterical disorder may also differ from those of the corresponding medical problem. For example, when paralysis from the waist down, or paraplegia, is caused by damage to the spinal cord, a person's leg muscles may *atrophy,* or waste away, unless physical therapy is applied. People whose paralysis is the result of a conversion disorder, in contrast, do not usually experience atrophy. Perhaps they exercise their muscles without being aware that they are doing so. Similarly, people with conversion blindness have fewer accidents than people who are organically blind, an indication that they have at least some vision even if they are unaware of it.

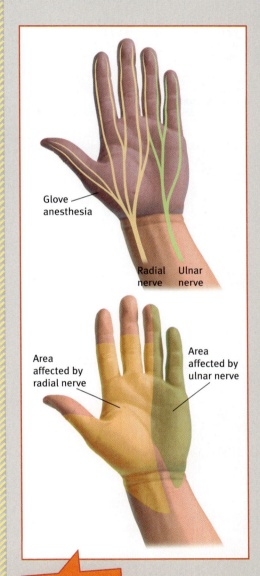

Figure 7-1

Glove anesthesia In this conversion symptom (upper figure) the entire hand, extending from the fingertips to the wrist, becomes numb. Actual physical damage (lower figure) to the ulnar nerve, in contrast, causes anesthesia in the ring finger and little finger and beyond the wrist partway up the arm; and damage to the radial nerve causes loss of feeling only in parts of the ring, middle, and index fingers and the thumb and partway up the arm. (Adapted from Gray, 1959.)

•**factitious disorder**•An illness with no identifiable physical cause, in which the patient is believed to be intentionally producing or faking symptoms in order to assume a sick role.

•**Munchausen syndrome**•The extreme and chronic form of factitious disorder.

•**Munchausen syndrome by proxy**•A factitious disorder in which parents make up or produce illnesses in their children. Also known as *factitious disorder by proxy*.

•**preoccupation somatoform disorders**•Disorders in which people misinterpret and overreact to minor, even normal, bodily symptoms or features.

•**hypochondriasis**•A disorder in which people mistakenly fear that minor changes in their physical functioning indicate a serious disease.

Hysterical vs. Factitious Symptoms Hysterical somatoform disorders are different from patterns in which individuals are purposefully producing or faking medical symptoms. A patient may, for example, *malinger*—intentionally fake illness to achieve some external gain, such as financial compensation or deferment from military service (Phillips et al., 2008). Or a patient may intentionally produce or fake physical symptoms simply out of a wish to be a patient; that is, the motivation for assuming the sick role may be the role itself. Physicians would then decide that the patient is displaying a **factitious disorder.**

A 29-year-old female laboratory technician was admitted to the medical service via the emergency room because of bloody urine. The patient said that she was being treated for lupus erythematosus by a physician in a different city. She also mentioned that she had had Von Willebrand's disease (a rare hereditary blood disorder) as a child. On the third day of her hospitalization, a medical student mentioned to the resident that she had seen this patient several weeks before at a different hospital in the area, where the patient had been admitted for the same problem. A search of the patient's belongings revealed a cache of anticoagulant medication. When confronted with this information she refused to discuss the matter and hurriedly signed out of the hospital against medical advice.

(Spitzer et al., 1981, p. 33)

People with a factitious disorder often go to extremes to create the appearance of illness (Phillips et al., 2008; Ford, 2005). Many give themselves medications secretly. Some, like the woman just described, inject drugs to cause bleeding. High fevers are especially easy to create. In one study of patients with prolonged mysterious fever, more than 9 percent were eventually diagnosed with factitious disorder (Feldman, Ford, & Reinhold, 1994). People with a factitious disorder often research their supposed ailments and are impressively knowledgeable about medicine. When confronted with evidence that their symptoms are factitious, they typically deny the charges and go to another doctor or hospital.

Factitious disorder seems to be most common among people who (1) as children received extensive medical treatment for a true physical disorder; (2) experienced family disruptions or physical or emotional abuse in childhood; (3) carry a grudge against the medical profession; (4) have worked as nurses, laboratory technicians, or medical aides; or (5) have an underlying personality problem such as extreme dependence (Ford, 2005; APA, 2000; Feldman et al., 1994). They often have limited social support, few enduring social relationships, and little family life.

Psychotherapists and medical practitioners often become angry at people with a factitious disorder, feeling that these individuals are, among other issues, wasting their time. Yet people with this disorder, like most persons with psychological disorders, feel they have no control over their problem, and they often experience great distress.

Munchausen syndrome is the extreme and long-term form of factitious disorder. It is named after Baron Munchausen, an eighteenth-century cavalry officer who journeyed from tavern to tavern in Europe telling fantastical tales about his supposed military adventures (Ford, 2005; Feldman, 2004). In a related disorder, **Munchausen syndrome by proxy,** or **factitious disorder by proxy,** parents make up or produce physical illnesses in their children, leading in some cases to repeated painful diagnostic tests, medication, and surgery (see *A Closer Look* on the next page).

What Are Preoccupation Somatoform Disorders?

Hypochondriasis and *body dysmorphic disorder* are **preoccupation somatoform disorders.** People with these problems misinterpret and overreact to bodily symptoms or features no matter what friends, relatives, and physicians may say. Although preoccupa-

BETWEEN THE LINES

Hypochondriasis through the Ages

Fourth Century B.C. Ancient Greeks used the term *hypochondria* to describe ailments such as melancholia and indigestion because they believed those problems to start in the *hypochondrium,* a section under the rib cage. ‹‹

Fifteenth Century A.D. Hypochondriasis was associated with witchcraft and treated with potions and chants. ‹‹

Eighteenth Century A.D. Hypochondriasis was called the "English malady" because it occurred mainly in the English aristocracy. ‹‹

Nineteenth Century A.D. Hypochondriasis was treated with fresh air, spas, and relaxation. ‹‹

(Mitchell, 2004)

Munchausen Syndrome by Proxy

[Jennifer] had been hospitalized 200 times and undergone 40 operations. Physicians removed her gallbladder, her appendix and part of her intestines, and inserted tubes into her chest, stomach and intestines. [The 9-year-old from Florida] was befriended by the Florida Marlins and served as a poster child for health care reform, posing with Hillary Rodham Clinton at a White House rally. Then police notified her mother that she was under investigation for child abuse. Suddenly, Jennifer's condition improved dramatically. In the next nine months, she was hospitalized only once, for a viral infection. . . . Experts said Jennifer's numerous baffling infections were "consistent with someone smearing fecal matter" into her feeding line and urinary catheter. ////

(KATEL & BECK, 1996)

Cases like Jennifer's have horrified the public and called attention to *Munchausen syndrome by proxy,* a pattern first identified in 1977. This disorder is caused by a caregiver who uses various techniques to induce symptoms in a child—giving the child drugs, tampering with medications, contaminating a feeding tube, or even smothering the child, for example. The illness can take almost any form, but the most common symptoms are bleeding, seizures, asthma, comas, diarrhea, vomiting, "accidental" poisonings, infections, fevers, and sudden infant death syndrome (Leamon et al., 2007; Ayoub, 2006; Feldman, 2004).

Between 6 and 30 percent of the victims of Munchausen syndrome by proxy die as a result of their symptoms, and 8 percent of those who survive are permanently disfigured or physically impaired (Ayoub, 2006; Mitchell, 2001). Psychological, educational, and physical development are also affected (Libow & Schreier, 1998; Libow, 1995). Jennifer missed so much school that at age 9 she could barely read or write.

The syndrome is very hard to diagnose and may be more common than clinicians once thought (Feldman, 2004; Rogers, 2004). The parent (usually the mother) seems to be so devoted and caring that others sympathize with and admire her (Abdulhamid, 2002). Yet the physical problems disappear when child and parent are separated. In many cases siblings of the sick child have also been victimized (Ayoub, 2006).

What kind of parent carefully inflicts pain and illness on her own child? The typical Munchausen mother is emotionally needy: she craves the attention and praise she receives for her devoted care of her sick child (Noeker, 2004). She may have little social support outside the medical system. Often the mothers have a medical background of some kind—perhaps having worked formerly in a doctor's office. Typically they deny their actions, even in the face of clear evidence, and refuse to undergo therapy. In fact, to date, successful treatment has been uncommon (Bluglass, 2001).

Law enforcement authorities are reluctant to consider Munchausen syndrome by proxy a psychological disorder and instead approach it as a crime—a carefully planned form of child abuse (Slovenko, 2006; Mart, 2004). They almost always require that the child be separated from the mother (Ayoub, 2006; Ayoub et al., 2000). At the same time, a parent who resorts to such actions is seriously disturbed and greatly in need of clinical help. Thus clinical researchers and practitioners must now work to develop clearer insights and more effective treatments for such parents and their young victims.

Convalescent, 1994, by Frank Holl

Christopher Wood Gallery, London, Bridgeman/Art Resource, NY

tion disorders also cause great distress, their impact on one's life differs from that of hysterical disorders.

Hypochondriasis People who suffer from **hypochondriasis** unrealistically interpret bodily symptoms as signs of a serious illness (see Table 7-2 on the next page). Often their symptoms are merely normal bodily changes, such as occasional coughing, sores, or sweating. Although some patients recognize that their concerns are excessive, many do not.

table: 7-2

DSM Checklist

HYPOCHONDRIASIS

1. Preoccupation with fears or beliefs that one has a serious disease, based on misinterpretation of bodily symptoms, lasting at least six months.
2. Persistence of preoccupation despite appropriate medical evaluation and reassurance.
3. Absence of delusions.
4. Significant distress or impairment.

BODY DYSMORPHIC DISORDER

1. Preoccupation with an imagined or exaggerated defect in appearance.
2. Significant distress or impairment.

Based on APA, 2000.

Extreme measures
As many as 15 percent of people who seek cosmetic surgery are believed to have body dysmorphic disorder. But that seems of little concern to Angela Bismarchi, Brazil's so-called Plastic Surgery Queen, who smiles as her surgeon explains how, for her forty-second plastic surgery procedure, he will implant nylon wires to give her eyes a more slanted look.

Hypochondriasis can present a picture very similar to that of somatization disorder (Noyes, 2008, 2003, 1999; Fink et al., 2004). Each typically involves numerous physical symptoms and frequent visits to doctors, and each causes considerable upset. If anxiety is great and bodily symptoms are relatively minor, a diagnosis of hypochondriasis is probably in order; if the symptoms overshadow the patient's anxiety, they may indicate somatization disorder.

Although hypochondriasis can begin at any age, it starts most often in early adulthood, among men and women in equal numbers. Between 1 and 5 percent of all people experience the disorder (Asmundson & Taylor, 2008; Bouman, 2008; APA, 2000). As with pain disorder associated with psychological factors, physicians report seeing many cases (Mitchell, 2004). As many as 7 percent of all patients seen by primary care physicians may display hypochondriasis (Asmundson & Taylor, 2008). For most patients, the symptoms rise and fall over the years (Bouman, 2008).

Body Dysmorphic Disorder People who experience **body dysmorphic disorder,** also known as **dysmorphophobia,** become deeply concerned about some imagined or minor defect in their appearance (see again Table 7-2). Most often they focus on wrinkles; spots on the skin; excessive facial hair; swelling of the face; or a misshapen nose, mouth, jaw, or eyebrow (McKay, Gosselin, & Gupta, 2008; Shapiro & Gavin, 2006; Veale, 2004). Some worry about the appearance of their feet, hands, breasts, penis, or other body parts (see *Eye on Culture* on page 212). Still others are concerned about bad odors coming from sweat, breath, genitals, or the rectum (Phillips & Castle, 2002). Here we see such a case:

A woman of 35 had for 16 years been worried that her sweat smelled terrible. The fear began just before her marriage when she was sharing a bed with a close friend who said that someone at work smelled badly, and the patient felt that the remark was directed at her. For fear that she smelled, for 5 years she had not gone out anywhere except when accompanied by her husband or mother. She had not spoken to her neighbors for 3 years because she thought she had overheard them speak about her to some friends. She avoided cinemas, dances, shops, cafes, and private homes. . . . Her husband was not allowed to invite any friends home; she constantly sought reassurance from him about her smell. . . . Her husband bought all her new clothes as she was afraid to try on clothes in front of shop assistants. She used vast quantities of deodorant and always bathed and changed her clothes before going out, up to 4 times daily.

(Marks, 1987, p. 371)

It is common in our society to worry about appearance (see Figure 7-2). Many teenagers and young adults worry about acne, for instance. The concerns of people with body dysmorphic disorder, however, are extreme. Sufferers may severely limit contact with other people, be unable to look others in the eye, or go to great lengths to conceal their "defects"—say, always wearing sunglasses to cover their supposedly misshapen eyes (Phillips, 2005). As many as half of people with this disorder seek plastic surgery or dermatology treatment, and often they feel worse rather than better afterward (McKay et al., 2008; Miller, 2005). One study found that 30 percent of participants with body dysmorphic disorder were housebound and 17 percent had attempted suicide (Phillips et al., 1993). Similarly, people with this disorder are more likely than others to be unemployed and to have limited academic success (Frare et al., 2004).

Most cases of body dysmorphic disorder begin during adolescence. Often, however, people don't reveal their concerns for many years (McKay et al., 2008; Phillips et al., 2005). Up to 5 percent of people in the United

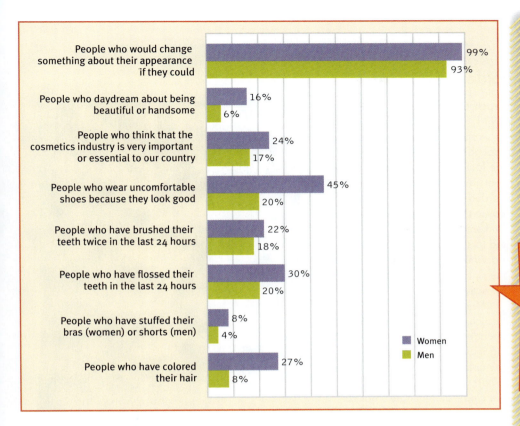

Figure 7-2
"Mirror, mirror, on the wall . . ." People with body dysmorphic disorder are not the only ones who have concerns about their appearance. Surveys find that in our appearance-conscious society, large percentages of people regularly think about and try to change the way they look (Noonan, 2003; Kimball, 1993; Poretz & Sinrod, 1991; Weiss, 1991; Simmon, 1990).

States—including many college students—suffer from the disorder (Ovsiew, 2006; Miller, 2005). Clinical reports suggest that it may be equally common among women and men (APA, 2000). Although both women and men with this disorder complain about their skin, hair, and nose, women are more likely to be concerned about their hips, buttocks, and breasts, while men are particularly likely to be preoccupied with their body build, genitals, and height (McKay et al., 2008).

What Causes Somatoform Disorders?

Theorists typically explain the preoccupation somatoform disorders much as they explain anxiety disorders (Asmundson & Taylor, 2008; Bouman, 2008; Noyes, 2008, 2003, 2001). Behaviorists, for example, believe that the fears found in hypochondriasis and body dysmorphic disorder are acquired through classical conditioning or modeling (Marshall et al., 2007). Cognitive theorists suggest that people with the disorders are so sensitive to and threatened by bodily cues that they come to misinterpret them (Williams, 2004).

In contrast, the hysterical somatoform disorders—conversion, somatization, and pain disorders—are widely considered unique and in need of special explanations. The ancient Greeks believed that only women had hysterical disorders. The uterus of a sexually ungratified woman was supposed to wander throughout her body in search of fulfillment, producing a physical symptom wherever it lodged. Thus Hippocrates suggested marriage as the most effective treatment for such disorders.

Work by Ambroise-Auguste Liébault and Hippolyte Bernheim in the late nineteenth century set the stage for today's prevailing opinion that psychosocial factors cause hysterical disorders. These researchers founded the Nancy School in Paris for the study and treatment of mental disorders. There they were able to produce hysterical symptoms in normal people—deafness, paralysis, blindness, and numbness—by hypnotic suggestion, and they could remove the symptoms by the same means (see Chapter 1). If hypnotic suggestion could both produce and reverse physical dysfunctioning, they concluded, hysterical disorders might themselves be caused by psychological processes.

•**body dysmorphic disorder**•A disorder marked by excessive worry that some aspect of one's physical appearance is defective. Also known as *dysmorphophobia*.

EYE ON CULTURE

Beauty Is in the Eye of the Beholder

People almost everywhere want to be attractive, and they tend to worry about how they appear in the eyes of others. At the same time, these concerns take different forms in different cultures.

Whereas people in Western society worry in particular about their body size and facial features, women of the Padaung tribe in Myanmar focus on the length of their neck and wear heavy stacks of brass rings to try to extend it. Many of them seek desperately to achieve what their culture has taught them is the perfect neck size. Said one, "It is most beautiful when the neck is really long. The longer it is, the more beautiful it is. I will never take off my rings. . . . I'll be buried in them" (Mydans, 1996).

Similarly, for centuries women of China, in response to the preferences and demands of men in that country, worried greatly about the size and appearance of their feet and practiced *foot binding* to stop the growth of these extremities (Wang Ping, 2000). In this procedure, which began in the year 900 and was widely

practiced until it was outlawed in 1911, young girls were instructed to wrap a long bandage tightly around their feet each day, forcing the four toes under the sole of the foot. The procedure, which was carried out for about two years, caused the feet to become narrower and smaller. Typically the practice led to serious medical problems and poor mobility, but it did produce the small feet that were considered attractive.

Western society also falls victim to such cultural influences. Recent decades have witnessed staggering increases in such procedures as *rhinoplasty* (reshaping of the nose), *breast augmentation,* and *body piercing*—all reminders that cultural values greatly influence each person's ideas and concerns about beauty, and in some cases may set the stage for body dysmorphic disorder.

Steve McCurry/Magnum Photos

Today's leading explanations for hysterical somatoform disorders come from the psychodynamic, behavioral, cognitive, and multicultural models. None has received much research support, however, and the disorders are still poorly understood (Kirmayer & Looper, 2007; Yutzy, 2007).

The Psychodynamic View As you read in Chapter 1, Freud's theory of psychoanalysis began with his efforts to explain hysterical symptoms. Indeed, he was one of the few clinicians of his day to treat patients with these symptoms seriously, as people with genuine problems. After studying hypnosis in Paris and becoming acquainted with the work of Liébault and Bernheim, Freud became interested in the work of an older physician, Josef Breuer (1842–1925). Breuer had successfully used hypnosis to treat a woman he called Anna O., who suffered from hysterical deafness, disorganized speech, and paralysis. Critics have since questioned whether Anna's ailments were entirely hysterical and whether Breuer's treatment helped her as much as he claimed (Ellenberger, 1972). But on the basis of this and similar cases, Freud (1894) came to believe that hysterical disorders represented a *conversion* of underlying emotional conflicts into physical symptoms.

Observing that most of his patients with hysterical disorders were women, Freud centered his explanation of hysterical disorders on the needs of girls during their *phallic stage* (ages 3 through 5). At that time in life, he believed, all girls develop a pattern of desires called the *Electra complex:* each girl experiences sexual feelings for her father and at the same time recognizes that she must compete with her mother for his affection. However, aware of her mother's more powerful position and of cultural taboos, the child typically represses her sexual feelings and rejects these early desires for her father.

Freud believed that if a child's parents overreact to her sexual feelings—with strong punishments, for example—the Electra conflict will be unresolved and the child may reexperience sexual anxiety throughout her life. Whenever events trigger sexual feelings, she may experience an unconscious need to hide them from both herself and others. Freud concluded that some women hide their sexual feelings by unconsciously converting them into physical symptoms.

Most of today's psychodynamic theorists take issue with Freud's explanation of hysterical disorders, particularly his notion that the disorders can always be traced to an unresolved Electra conflict (Verhaeghe, Vanheule, & de Rick, 2007; Hess, 1995). They continue to believe, however, that sufferers of these disorders have unconscious conflicts carried forth from childhood, that the conflicts arouse anxiety, and that the individuals convert this anxiety into "more tolerable" physical symptoms (Brown et al., 2005). Consistent with these beliefs, studies have found that people with the disorders often have childhood histories of trauma, abuse, or neglect (Sar et al., 2004; Noyes et al., 2002).

Psychodynamic theorists propose that two mechanisms are at work in hysterical somatoform disorders—primary gain and secondary gain (van Egmond, 2003). People achieve **primary gain** when their hysterical symptoms keep their internal conflicts out of awareness. During an argument, for example, a man who has underlying fears about expressing anger may develop a conversion paralysis of the arm, thus preventing his feelings of rage from reaching consciousness. People achieve **secondary gain** when their hysterical symptoms further enable them to avoid unpleasant activities or to receive sympathy from others. When, for example, a conversion paralysis allows a soldier to avoid combat duty or conversion blindness prevents the breakup of a relationship, secondary gain may be at work. Similarly, the conversion paralysis of Brian, the man who lost his wife in the boating accident, seemed to help him avoid many painful duties after the accident, from telling his wife's parents of her death to attending her funeral and returning to work. In short, primary gains initiate hysterical symptoms; secondary gains are by-products of the symptoms.

The Behavioral View Behavioral theorists propose that the physical symptoms of hysterical disorders bring *rewards* to sufferers (see Table 7-3). Perhaps the symptoms remove the individuals from an unpleasant relationship or bring attention from other people (Whitehead et al., 1994). In response to such rewards, the sufferers learn to display the symptoms more and more prominently. Behaviorists also hold that people who are familiar with an illness will more readily adopt its physical symptoms (Garralda, 1996). In

Electra complex goes awry
Freud argued that a hysterical disorder may result when parents overreact to their daughter's early displays of affection for her father. The child may go on to exhibit sexual repression in adulthood and convert sexual feelings into physical ailments.

•**primary gain**•In psychodynamic theory, the gain achieved when hysterical symptoms keep internal conflicts out of awareness.

•**secondary gain**•In psychodynamic theory, the gain achieved when hysterical symptoms elicit kindness from others or provide an excuse to avoid unpleasant activities.

table:

Disorders That Have Physical Symptoms

Disorder	Voluntary Control of Symptoms?	Symptoms Linked to Psychosocial Factor?	An Apparent Goal?
Malingering	Yes	Maybe	Yes
Factitious disorder	Yes	Yes	No*
Somatoform disorder	No	Yes	Maybe
Psychophysiological disorder	No	Yes	No
Physical illness	No	Maybe	No

*Except for medical attention.

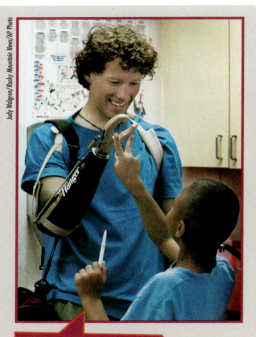

Phantom limb syndrome
While hiking in Utah, Aron Ralston's arm became pinned under a boulder and he had to amputate it himself. People who have lost their limbs often continue to feel pain and other sensations where their limbs used to be. Initially, such "phantom" pain was thought to reflect a somatoform pain disorder. However, neuroscientists have since discovered that even after amputation, brain areas that used to trigger sensations in the limbs remain intact and may sometimes produce sensations where the missing limbs used to be.

fact, studies find that many sufferers develop their hysterical symptoms after they or their close relatives or friends have had similar medical problems (Marshall et al., 2007).

The behavioral focus on rewards is similar to the psychodynamic idea of secondary gains. The key difference is that psychodynamic theorists view the gains as indeed secondary—that is, as rewards that come only after underlying conflicts produce the disorder. Behaviorists view them as the primary cause of the development of the disorder.

Like the psychodynamic explanation, the behavioral view of hysterical disorders has received little research support. Even clinical case reports only occasionally support this position. In many cases the pain and upset that surround the disorders seem to outweigh any rewards the symptoms may bring.

The Cognitive View Some cognitive theorists propose that hysterical disorders are forms of *communication,* providing a means for people to express emotions that would otherwise be difficult to convey (Mitchell, 2004). Like their psychodynamic colleagues, these theorists hold that the emotions of patients with hysterical disorders are being converted into physical symptoms. They suggest, however, that the purpose of the conversion is not to defend against anxiety but to communicate extreme feelings—anger, fear, depression, guilt, jealousy—in a "physical language" that is familiar and comfortable for the patient (Koh et al., 2005).

According to this view, people who find it particularly hard to recognize or express their emotions are candidates for a hysterical disorder. So are those who "know" the language of physical symptoms through firsthand experience with a genuine physical malady. Because children are less able to express their emotions verbally, they are particularly likely to develop physical symptoms as a form of communication (Dhossche et al., 2002). Like the other explanations, this cognitive view has not been widely tested or supported by research.

The Multicultural View As you have seen, the key feature of hysterical somatoform disorders is *somatization,* the development of somatic symptoms in response to personal distress. Whether somatization reaches the level of a full-blown disorder or is but an isolated symptom that an individual displays, it is considered inappropriate in most Western countries (Escobar, 2004). Some theorists believe that this attitude reflects a bias held by Western clinicians—a bias that sees somatic symptoms as an *inferior* way of dealing with emotions (Moldavsky, 2004; Fabrega, 1990).

In fact, the transformation of personal distress into somatic complaints is the norm in many non-Western cultures (Draguns, 2006; Kleinman, 1987). In such cultures, somatization is viewed as a socially and medically correct—and less stigmatizing—reaction to life's stressors.

Studies have found very high rates of somatization in non-Western medical settings throughout the world, including those in China, Japan, and Arab countries (Matsumoto & Juang, 2008). Individuals in Latin countries seem to display the greatest number of somatic symptoms (Escobar, 2004, 1995; Escobar et al., 1998, 1992). Even within the United States, people from Hispanic cultures display more somatic symptoms in the face of stress than do other populations.

In Chapter 6 you saw that posttraumatic stress disorder may be more common among Hispanic Americans than among other ethnic groups in the United States (see page 178). Interestingly, however, research clarifies that this trend exists only among Hispanic Americans who were born in the United States or have lived in the United States for a number of years (Escobar, 2004, 1998). Indeed, recent Latin immigrants display a *lower* rate of posttraumatic stress disorder than do other individuals throughout the country. It may be that recent immigrants, not yet influenced by the Western bias against somatization, react to traumatic events with familiar somatic symptoms and that those symptoms help prevent the onset of a full-blown posttraumatic stress disorder.

The lesson to be learned from such multicultural findings is not that somatic reactions to stress are superior to psychological ones or vice versa, but rather, once again, that reactions to life's stressors are often influenced by one's culture. Overlooking this point can lead to knee-jerk mislabels or misdiagnoses.

A Possible Role for Biology

Although hysterical somatoform disorders are, by definition, thought to result largely from psychological and sociocultural factors, the impact of biological processes should not be overlooked (Ovsiew, 2006). To understand this point, consider first what researchers have learned about *placebos* and the *placebo effect*.

For centuries physicians have observed that patients suffering from many kinds of illnesses, from seasickness to angina, often find relief from **placebos,** substances that have no known medicinal value (Price, Finniss, & Benedetti, 2008; Brody, 2000). Some studies have raised questions about the actual number of patients helped by placebos (Hrobjartsson & Goltzsche, 2006, 2004, 2001), but it is generally agreed that such "pretend" treatments do bring help to many people.

Why do placebos have a medicinal effect? Theorists used to believe that they operated in purely psychological ways—that the power of suggestion worked almost magically upon the body. More recently, however, researchers have found that a belief or expectation can trigger certain chemicals throughout the body into action, and these chemicals then may produce a medicinal effect (Price et al., 2008). The body chemicals most often implicated are *hormones* and *lymphocytes,* chemicals that you observed at work in Chapter 6, and *endorphins,* natural opioid substances that you will read about in Chapter 12. Howard Brody, a leading theorist on the subject, compares the placebo effect to visiting a pharmacy:

> Our bodies are capable of producing many substances that can heal a wide variety of illnesses, and make us feel generally healthier and more energized. When the body simply secretes these substances on its own, we have what is often termed "spontaneous healing." Some of the time, our bodies seem slow to react, and a message from outside can serve as a wake-up call to our inner pharmacy. The placebo response can thus be seen as the reaction of our inner pharmacies to that wake-up call.
>
> *(Brody, 2000, p. 61)*

If placebos can "wake up" our inner pharmacies in this way, perhaps traumatic events and related concerns or needs are doing the same thing (although in a negative way) in cases of conversion disorder, somatization disorder, or pain disorder associated with psychological factors. That is, such events and reactions may, in fact, be triggering our inner pharmacies and setting in motion the bodily symptoms of hysterical somatoform disorders.

"*If this doesn't help you don't worry, it's a placebo.*"

© 2003 The New Yorker Collection from Cartoonbank.com

•**placebo**•A sham treatment that a patient believes to be genuine.

Worldwide influence
A lingerie advertisement in a subway station in Shanghai, China, displays a woman in a push-up bra. As West meets East, Asian women have been bombarded by ads encouraging them to undergo Western-like cosmetic surgery, from facial changes (the most common procedures) to changes in other body parts. The number of Asian women who pursue cosmetic surgery has increased about sevenfold during the past 20 years, and over one-third of Asian women now say that they would like to have cosmetic surgery (Hakuhodo Institute of Life and Living, 2001).

How Are Somatoform Disorders Treated?

People with somatoform disorders usually seek psychotherapy only as a last resort. They fully believe that their problems are medical and at first reject all suggestions to the contrary (Asmundson & Taylor, 2008). When a physician tells them that their problems have no physical basis, they often go to another physician. Eventually, however, many patients with these disorders do consent to psychotherapy, psychotropic drug therapy, or both.

Individuals with preoccupation somatoform disorders—hypochondriasis and body dysmorphic disorder—typically receive the kinds of treatment that are applied to anxiety disorders, particularly obsessive-compulsive disorder (Bouman, 2008; Barksy & Ahern, 2004). Studies reveal, for example, that patients with either of the preoccupation disorders often improve considerably when treated with the same *antidepressant drugs* that are helpful in cases of obsessive-compulsive disorder (Bouman, 2008; Greeven et al., 2007; McKay et al., 2008).

Similarly, in one study, 17 patients with body dysmorphic disorder were treated with *exposure and response prevention*—the behavioral approach that often helps persons with obsessive-compulsive disorder. Over the course of four weeks, the clients were repeatedly reminded of their perceived physical defects and, at the same time, prevented from doing anything to help reduce their discomfort (for example, checking their appearance) (Neziroglu et al., 2004, 1996). By the end of treatment, these individuals were less concerned with their "defects" and spent less time checking their body parts, looking in the mirror, and avoiding social interactions. Increasingly, this behavioral approach is being successfully combined with a cognitive approach that also helps clients with body dysmorphic disorder identify, test, and change their distorted thoughts about their appearance and social impact (Sarwer, Gibbons, & Crerand, 2004; Geremia & Neziroglu, 2001).

Cognitive-behavioral therapies of this kind are also being applied to cases of hypochondriasis. Here, therapists repeatedly highlight bodily variations to clients while, at the same time, preventing them from seeking their usual medical attention. In addition, the therapists guide the clients to identify and change the illness-related cognitions that are helping to maintain their disorder (see Table 7-4). Once again, such approaches are receiving promising research support (Bouman, 2008; Greeven et al., 2007; Taylor et al., 2005).

An extreme case of hypochondriasis?
Not necessarily. After the 1918 flu epidemic killed 20 million people, people in Japan started wearing a *masuku* to protect them from stray germs. Some, like this commuter, continue the tradition during cold and flu season.

Treatments for hysterical somatoform disorders—conversion, somatization, and pain disorders—often focus on the *cause* of the disorder (the trauma or anxiety behind the physical symptoms) and apply the same kinds of techniques used in cases of posttraumatic stress disorder, particularly insight, exposure, and drug therapies. Psychodynamic therapists, for example, try to help individuals with hysterical disorders become conscious of and resolve their underlying fears, thus eliminating the need to convert anxiety into physical symptoms (Hawkins, 2004). Alternatively, behavioral therapists use exposure treatments: they expose clients to features of the horrific events that first triggered their physical symptoms, expecting that the individuals will become less anxious over the course of repeated exposures and, in turn, more able to face those upsetting events directly rather than through physical channels (Stuart et al., 2008; Ciano-Federoff & Sperry, 2005). And biological therapists use antianxiety drugs or certain antidepressant drugs to help reduce the anxiety of clients with hysterical disorders (Eifert et al., 2008; Han et al., 2008).

table: 7-4

Common Beliefs of People with Hypochondriasis

Beliefs about body	I'm healthy only when I don't have any bodily sensations.
	Bodily complaints are always a sign of disease.
	Red blotches are signs of skin cancer.
	Joint pain means that my bones are degenerating.
	Real symptoms aren't caused by anxiety.
Beliefs about disease	If I get sick I'll be in great pain and suffering.
	People will avoid or reject me if I get really ill.
	Serious diseases are everywhere.
	People don't recover from serious diseases.
Beliefs about vulnerability	My circulatory system is very sensitive.
	I need to avoid exertion because I'm physically frail.
	Illness is a sign of failure and inadequacy.
	If I'm ill people will abandon me.
Beliefs about doctors	Doctors should be able to explain all bodily complaints.
	Doctors can't be trusted because they often make mistakes.
	If a doctor refers me for further medical tests, then he or she must believe that there's something seriously wrong with me.
	Medical evaluations are unreliable if you don't give your doctor a complete and detailed description of your symptoms.
Beliefs about worrying	Worrying about my health will keep me safe.
	I need to frequently check my body to catch the first signs of illness.
	I need to carefully watch my health, otherwise something terrible will happen.

Adapted from Taylor and Asmundson, 2004.

BETWEEN THE LINES

Tanorexia

In his memoir *Me Talk Pretty One Day*, humorist David Sedaris (2000) dubbed his sun-worshiping sister "tanorexic." The label has stuck and is now used even by professionals to describe persons who addictively pursue a tan—both outdoors and in tanning salons. Half the adult population say they feel healthier with a tan and 30 million Americans visit tanning salons each year, despite the fact that the risk of developing melanoma (skin cancer) increases 75 percent if a person tans repeatedly indoors before age 35 (Flahive, 2008; Winterman, 2006). ‹‹

BETWEEN THE LINES

Strictly a Coincidence?

On February 17, 1673, French actor-playwright Molière collapsed onstage and died while performing in *Le Malade Imaginaire* (*The Hypochondriac*) (Ash, 1999). ‹‹

Influential Reading
The term *medical student's disease,*
or *hypochondriasis of medical students,*
refers to the tendency of medical students
to experience the symptoms of diseases
they are reading about and studying.

BETWEEN THE LINES

Most Common Forgotten Matters

- Where cell phone was left ‹‹
- Where keys were left ‹‹
- Where remote control was left ‹‹
- Phone numbers ‹‹
- Names ‹‹
- Dream content ‹‹
- Birthdays/anniversaries ‹‹
- Saving a computer document ‹‹
- Mathematical principles ‹‹
- Where reading glasses were left ‹‹
- Where a wallet was left ‹‹
- Details of TV shows, movies, or music ‹‹

Other therapists try to address the *physical symptoms* of the hysterical disorders rather than the causes, applying techniques such as *suggestion, reinforcement,* or *confrontation* (Yutzy, 2007). Those who employ *suggestion* offer emotional support to patients and tell them persuasively that their physical symptoms will soon disappear (Anooshian et al., 1999), or they suggest the same thing to them under hypnosis (Elkins & Perfect, 2007; Moene et al., 2002). Therapists who take a *reinforcement* approach arrange the removal of rewards for a client's "sick" behaviors and an increase of rewards for healthy behaviors (North, 2005). And therapists who take a *confrontational* approach try to force patients out of the sick role by straightforwardly telling them that their symptoms are without medical basis (Sjolie, 2002).

Researchers have not fully evaluated the effects of these particular approaches on hysterical disorders (Ciano-Federoff & Sperry, 2005). Case studies suggest, however, that conversion disorder and pain disorder respond better than somatization disorder to therapy and that approaches using a confrontational strategy are less helpful than suggestion and reinforcement interventions (Miller, 2004).

✿Dissociative Disorders

Most of us experience a sense of wholeness and continuity as we interact with the world. We perceive ourselves as being more than a random collection of isolated sensory experiences, feelings, and behaviors. In other words, we have an *identity,* a sense of who we are and where we fit in our environment. Others recognize us and expect certain things of us. But more important, we recognize ourselves and have our own expectations, values, and goals.

Memory is a key to this sense of identity, the link between our past, present, and future. Our recall of past experiences, although not always precisely accurate, helps us react to present events and guides us in making decisions about the future. We recognize our friends and relatives, teachers and employers, and respond to them in appropriate ways. Without a memory, we would always be starting over; with it, life moves forward.

People sometimes experience a major disruption of their memory, identity, or consciousness. They may, for example, lose their ability to remember new information they just learned or old information they once knew well. When such changes in memory lack a clear physical cause, they are called **dissociative disorders.** In such disorders, one part of the person's memory typically seems to be *dissociated,* or separated, from the rest.

There are several kinds of dissociative disorders. The primary symptom of *dissociative amnesia* is an inability to recall important personal events and information. A person with *dissociative fugue* not only forgets the past but also travels to a new location and may assume a new identity. Individuals with *dissociative identity disorder* (also known as *multiple personality disorder*) have two or more separate identities that may not always be aware of each other's thoughts, feelings, and behavior.

Several memorable books and movies have portrayed dissociative disorders. Two of the best known are *The Three Faces of Eve* and *Sybil,* each about a woman with multiple personalities. The topic is so fascinating that most television drama series seem to include at least one case of dissociation every season, creating the impression that the disorders are very common (Pope et al., 2007). Many clinicians, however, believe that they are rare.

DSM-IV-TR also lists *depersonalization disorder* as a dissociative disorder. People with this problem feel as though they have become detached from their own mental processes or body and are observing themselves from the outside. This listing is controversial because the memories and identities of people with depersonalization disorder seem to remain intact. It is their sense of self that changes: their mental processes or bodies feel unreal or foreign to them. You will read more about this disorder at the close of the chapter. Outside of that discussion, however, "dissociative disorders" will refer to those problems that involve clear changes in memory and identity: dissociative amnesia, dissociative fugue, and dissociative identity disorder.

As you read through the remainder of this chapter, keep in mind that dissociative symptoms are often found in cases of acute or posttraumatic stress disorder. Recall from Chapter 6 that sufferers of those disorders may feel dazed, have trouble remembering things, or experience a sense of unreality. When such symptoms occur as part of a stress disorder, they do not necessarily indicate a dissociative disorder, in which the dissociative symptoms dominate. On the other hand, research suggests that a number of people with one of these disorders also develop the other as well (Bremner, 2002).

Dissociative Amnesia

At the beginning of this chapter you met the unfortunate man named Brian. As you will recall, Brian developed a conversion disorder after a traumatic boating accident in which his wife was killed. To help examine dissociative amnesia, let us now revisit that case, changing the reactions and symptoms that Brian develops in the aftermath of the traumatic event.

Brian was spending Saturday sailing with his wife, Helen. The water was rough but well within what they considered safe limits. They were having a wonderful time and really didn't notice that the sky was getting darker, the wind blowing harder, and the sailboat becoming more difficult to control. After a few hours of sailing, they found themselves far from shore in the middle of a powerful and dangerous storm.

Reuters/Amir Cohen

At risk
The stunned look on the face of this Israeli soldier after a fierce battle in the Gaza Strip suggests confusion, shock, and exhaustion. Combat soldiers are particularly vulnerable to amnesia and other dissociative reactions. They may forget specific horrors, personal information, or even their identities.

•**memory**•The faculty for recalling past events and past learning.

•**dissociative disorders**•Disorders marked by major changes in memory that do not have clear physical causes.

The storm intensified very quickly. Brian had trouble controlling the sailboat amidst the high winds and wild waves. He and Helen tried to put on the safety jackets they had neglected to wear earlier, but the boat turned over before they were finished. Brian, the better swimmer of the two, was able to swim back to the overturned sailboat, grab the side, and hold on for dear life, but Helen simply could not overcome the rough waves and reach the boat. As Brian watched in horror and disbelief, his wife disappeared from view.

After a time, the storm began to lose its strength. Brian managed to right the sailboat and sail back to shore. Finally he reached safety, but the personal consequences of this storm were just beginning. The next days were filled with pain and further horror: the Coast Guard finding Helen's body . . . discussions with authorities . . . breaking the news to Helen's parents . . . conversations with friends . . . self-blame . . . grief . . . and more. On Wednesday, five days after that fateful afternoon, Brian collected himself and attended Helen's funeral and burial. It was the longest and most difficult day of his life. Most of the time, he felt as though he were in a trance.

Soon after awakening on Thursday morning, Brian realized that something was terribly wrong with him. Try though he might, he couldn't remember the events of the past few days. He remembered the accident, Helen's death, and the call from the Coast Guard after they had found her body. But just about everything else was gone, right up through the funeral. At first he had even thought that it was now Sunday, and that his discussions with family and friends and the funeral were all ahead of him. But the newspaper, the funeral guestbook, and a phone conversation with his brother soon convinced him that he had lost the past four days of his life.

In this revised scenario, Brian is reacting to his traumatic experience with symptoms of **dissociative amnesia.** People with this disorder are unable to recall important information, usually of an upsetting nature, about their lives (APA, 2000). The loss of memory is much more extensive than normal forgetting and is not caused by organic factors (see Table 7-5). Often an episode of amnesia is directly triggered by a specific upsetting event (McLeod, Byrne, & Aitken, 2004).

Dissociative amnesia may be *localized, selective, generalized,* or *continuous.* Any of these kinds of amnesia can be triggered by a traumatic experience such as Brian's, but each represents a particular pattern of forgetting. Brian was suffering from *localized,* or *circumscribed, amnesia,* the most common type of dissociative amnesia, in which a person loses all memory of events that took place within a limited period of time, almost always beginning with some very disturbing occurrence. Recall that Brian awakened on the day after the funeral and could not recall any of the events of the past difficult days, beginning after the boating tragedy. He remembered everything that happened up to and including the accident. He could also recall everything from the morning after the funeral onward, but the days in between remained a total blank. The forgotten period is called the *amnestic episode.* During an amnestic episode, people may appear confused; in some cases they wander about aimlessly. They are already experiencing memory difficulties but seem unaware of them. In the revised case, for example, Brian felt as though he were in a trance on the day of Helen's funeral.

People with *selective amnesia,* the second most common form of dissociative amnesia, remember some, but not all, events that occurred during a period of time. If Brian had selective amnesia, he might remember certain conversations with friends but perhaps not the funeral itself.

In some cases the loss of memory extends back to times long before the upsetting period. Brian might awaken after the funeral and find that, in addition to forgetting events of the past few days, he could not remember events that occurred earlier in his life. In this case, he would be experiencing *generalized amnesia.* In extreme cases, Brian might not even remember who he was and might fail to recognize relatives and friends.

In the forms of dissociative amnesia discussed so far, the period affected by the amnesia has an end. In *continuous amnesia,* however, forgetting continues into the present.

table: 7-5

DSM Checklist

DISSOCIATIVE AMNESIA

1. One or more episodes of inability to recall important personal information, usually of a traumatic or stressful nature, that is too extensive to be explained by ordinary forgetfulness.
2. Significant distress or impairment.

DISSOCIATIVE FUGUE

1. Sudden, unexpected travel away from home or one's customary place of work, with inability to recall one's past.
2. Confusion about personal identity, or the assumption of a new identity.
3. Significant distress or impairment.

DISSOCIATIVE IDENTITY DISORDER (MULTIPLE PERSONALITY DISORDER)

1. The presence of two or more distinct identities or personality states.
2. Control of the person's behavior recurrently taken by at least two of these identities or personality states.
3. An inability to recall important personal information that is too extensive to be explained by ordinary forgetfulness.

Based on APA, 2000.

Brian might forget new and ongoing experiences as well as what happened before and during the tragedy. Continuous forgetting of this kind is actually quite rare in cases of dissociative amnesia but not, as you will see in Chapter 18, in cases of organic amnesia.

All of these forms of dissociative amnesia are similar in that the amnesia interferes mostly with *episodic memory*—a person's memory of personal material. *Semantic memory*—memory for abstract or encyclopedic information—usually remains. People with dissociative amnesia are as likely as anyone else to know the name of the president of the United States and how to write, read, or drive a car.

Clinicians do not know how common dissociative amnesia is (Pope et al., 2007), but they do know that many cases seem to begin during serious threats to health and safety, as in wartime and natural disasters (Cardena & Gleaves, 2008; Witztum et al., 2002). Combat veterans often report memory gaps of hours or days, and some forget personal information, such as their names and addresses (Bremner, 2002). It appears that childhood abuse, particularly child sexual abuse, can also sometimes trigger dissociative amnesia; indeed, the 1990s witnessed many reports in which adults claimed to recall long-forgotten experiences of childhood abuse (see *A Closer Look* on page 223). In addition, dissociative amnesia may occur under more ordinary circumstances, such as the sudden loss of a loved one through rejection or death or guilt over certain actions (for example, an extramarital affair) (Koh et al., 2000).

The personal impact of dissociative amnesia depends on how much is forgotten. Obviously, an amnestic episode of two years is more of a problem than one of two hours. Similarly, an amnestic episode during which a person's life changes in major ways causes more difficulties than one that is quiet.

"*Are you going to trust your father's selective memory over mine?*"

Dissociative Fugue

People with a **dissociative fugue** not only forget their personal identities and details of their past lives but also flee to an entirely different location (see again Table 7-5). Some individuals travel but a short distance and make few social contacts in the new setting (APA, 2000). Their fugue may be brief—a matter of hours or days—and end suddenly. In other cases, however, the person may travel far from home, take a new name, and establish a new identity, new relationships, and even a new line of work. Such people may also display new personality characteristics; often they are more outgoing (APA, 2000). This pattern is seen in the case of the Reverend Ansel Bourne, described by famous psychologist William James at the end of the nineteenth century:

On January 17, 1887, [the Reverend Ansel Bourne, of Greene, R.I.] drew 551 dollars from a bank in Providence with which to pay for a certain lot of land in Greene, paid certain bills, and got into a Pawtucket horsecar. This is the last incident which he remembers. He did not return home that day, and nothing was heard of him for two months. He was published in the papers as missing, and foul play being suspected, the police sought in vain his whereabouts. On the morning of March 14th, however, at Norristown, Pennsylvania, a man calling himself A. J. Brown who had rented a small shop six weeks previously, stocked it with stationery, confectionery, fruit and small articles, and carried on his quiet trade without seeming to any one unnatural or eccentric, woke up in a fright and called in the people of the house to tell him where he was. He said that his name was Ansel Bourne, that he was entirely ignorant of Norristown, that he knew nothing of shop-keeping, and that the last thing he remembered—it seemed only yesterday—was drawing the money from the bank, etc. in Providence. . . . He was very weak, having lost apparently over twenty pounds of flesh during his escapade, and had such a horror of the idea of the candy-store that he refused to set foot in it again.

•**dissociative amnesia**•A dissociative disorder marked by an inability to recall important personal events and information.

•**dissociative fugue**•A dissociative disorder in which a person travels to a new location and may assume a new identity, simultaneously forgetting his or her past.

The first two weeks of the period remained unaccounted for, as he had no memory, after he had once resumed his normal personality, of any part of the time, and no one who knew him seems to have seen him after he left home. The remarkable part of the change is, of course, the peculiar occupation which the so-called Brown indulged in. Mr. Bourne has never in his life had the slightest contact with trade. "Brown" was described by the neighbors as taciturn, orderly in his habits, and in no way queer. He went to Philadelphia several times; replenished his stock; cooked for himself in the back shop, where he also slept; went regularly to church; and once at a prayer-meeting made what was considered by the hearers a good address, in the course of which he related an incident which he had witnessed in his natural state of Bourne.

(James, 1890, pp. 391–393)

Approximately 0.2 percent of the population experience dissociative fugue. Like dissociative amnesia, a fugue usually follows a severely stressful event (Cardena & Gleaves, 2008; APA, 2000). Some adolescent runaways may be in a state of fugue (Loewenstein, 1991). Like cases of dissociative amnesia, fugues usually affect personal (episodic) memories rather than encyclopedic or abstract (semantic) knowledge (Maldonado & Spiegel, 2007; Glisky et al., 2004; Kihlstrom, 2001).

Fugues tend to end abruptly. In some cases, as with Reverend Bourne, the person "awakens" in a strange place, surrounded by unfamiliar faces, and wonders how he or she got there. In other cases, the lack of personal history may arouse suspicion. Perhaps a traffic accident or legal problem leads police to discover the false identity; at other times friends search for and find the missing person. When people are found before their state of fugue has ended, therapists may find it necessary to ask them many questions about the details of their lives, repeatedly remind them who they are, and even initiate psychotherapy before they recover their memories. As these people recover their past, some forget the events of the fugue period (APA, 2000).

The majority of people who experience dissociative fugue regain most or all of their memories and never have a recurrence. Since fugues are usually brief and totally reversible, individuals tend to experience few aftereffects. People who have been away for months or years, however, often do have trouble adjusting to the changes that have occurred during their flights. In addition, some people commit illegal or violent acts in their fugue state and later must face the consequences.

Lost and found Cheryl Ann Barnes is helped off a plane by her grandmother and stepmother upon arrival in Florida in 1996. The 17-year-old high school honor student had disappeared from her Florida home and was found one month later in a New York City hospital listed as Jane Doe, apparently suffering from fugue.

Repressed Childhood Memories or False Memory Syndrome?

Throughout the 1990s, reports of *repressed childhood memory of abuse* attracted much public attention. Adults with this type of *dissociative amnesia* seemed to recover buried memories of sexual and physical abuse from their childhood. A woman might claim, for example, that her father had sexually molested her repeatedly between the ages of 5 and 7. Or a young man might remember that a family friend had made sexual advances on several occasions when he was very young. Often the repressed memories surfaced during therapy for another problem, perhaps for an eating disorder or depression.

Although the number of such claims has declined in recent years, experts remain split on this issue (Loftus & Cahill, 2007; McNally et al., 2005). Some believe that recovered memories are just what they appear to be—horrible memories of abuse that have been buried for years in the person's mind. Other experts believe that the memories are actually illusions—false images created by a mind that is confused. In fact, an organization called the False Memory Syndrome Foundation assists people who claim to be charged falsely with abuse.

Opponents of the repressed memory concept hold that the details of childhood sexual abuse are often remembered all too well, not completely wiped from memory (Loftus & Cahill, 2007; McNally et al., 2004; Loftus, 2000, 1993). They also point out that memory in general is hardly foolproof (Lindsay et al., 2004). Even when recalling events as dramatic as the 2001 terrorist attack on the World Trade Center, people give inaccurate accounts of where they were at the time of the event or who first told them about it. Moreover, false memories of various kinds can be created in the laboratory by tapping into research participants' imaginations (Brainerd, Reyna, & Ceci, 2008; Loftus & Cahill, 2007). If memory in general is so flawed, questions certainly can be raised about the accuracy of recovered memories.

If the alleged recovery of childhood memories is not what it appears to be, what is it? According to opponents of the concept, it may be a powerful case of suggestibility (Loftus & Cahill, 2007; Loftus, 2003, 2001, 1997). These theorists hold that the attention paid to the phenomenon by both clinicians and the public has led some therapists to make the diagnosis without sufficient evidence (Frankel, 1993). The therapists may actively search for signs of early sexual abuse in clients and even encourage clients to produce repressed memories (Gardner, 2004). Certain therapists in fact use special memory recovery techniques, including hypnosis, regression therapy, journal writing, dream interpretation, and interpretation of bodily symptoms (Madill & Holch, 2004; Lindsay, 1996, 1994). Perhaps some clients respond to the techniques by unknowingly forming false memories of abuse (Hyman & Loftus, 2002). The apparent memories may then become increasingly familiar to them as a result of repeated therapy discussions of the alleged incidents. In short, recovered memories may actually be *iatrogenic*—unintentionally caused by the therapist.

Of course, repressed memories of childhood sexual abuse do not emerge only in clinical settings (Loftus & Cahill, 2007; Leavitt, 2002, 2001). Many individuals come forward on their own. Opponents of the repressed memory concept explain these cases by pointing to various books, articles, and television shows that seem to validate repressed memories of childhood sexual abuse (Loftus, 1993). Several books even tell readers how to diagnose repression in themselves, often listing symptoms that are actually rather common and are not clinical symptoms at all (Tavris, 1993). Readers with a number of these symptoms may begin a search for repressed memories of childhood abuse. Still other opponents of the repressed memory concept believe that, for biological or other reasons, some individuals are more prone than others to experience false memories—either of childhood abuse or of other kinds of events (McNally et al., 2005).

It is important to recognize that the experts who question the recovery of repressed childhood memories do not in any way deny the problem of child sexual abuse. In fact, proponents and opponents alike are greatly concerned that the public may take this debate to mean that clinicians have doubts about the scope of the problem of child sexual abuse. Whatever may be the final outcome of the repressed memory debate, the problem of childhood sexual abuse is all too real and all too common.

Early recall Research suggests that our memories of early childhood may be influenced by the reminiscences of family members, our dreams, television and movie plots, and our present self-image.

M. Lerner/W. H. Freeman

•**dissociative identity disorder**•A dissociative disorder in which a person develops two or more distinct personalities. Also known as *multiple personality disorder.*

•**subpersonalities**•The two or more distinct personalities found in individuals suffering with dissociative identity disorder. Also known as *alternate personalities.*

Dissociative Identity Disorder (Multiple Personality Disorder)

Dissociative identity disorder is both dramatic and disabling, as we see in the case of Eric:

Dazed and bruised from a beating, Eric, 29, was discovered wandering around a Daytona Beach shopping mall on Feb. 9. . . . Transferred six weeks later to Daytona Beach's Human Resources Center, Eric began talking to doctors in two voices: the infantile rhythms of "young Eric," a dim and frightened child, and the measured tones of "older Eric," who told a tale of terror and child abuse. According to "older Eric," after his immigrant German parents died, a harsh stepfather and his mistress took Eric from his native South Carolina to a drug dealers' hideout in a Florida swamp. Eric said he was raped by several gang members and watched his stepfather murder two men.

*One day in late March an alarmed counselor watched Eric's face twist into a violent snarl. Eric let loose an unearthly growl and spat out a stream of obscenities. "It sounded like something out of **The Exorcist,**" says Malcolm Graham, the psychologist who directs the case at the center. "It was the most intense thing I've ever seen in a patient." That disclosure of a new personality, who insolently demanded to be called Mark, was the first indication that Graham had been dealing with a rare and serious emotional disorder: true multiple personality. . . .*

Eric's other manifestations emerged over the next weeks: quiet, middle-aged Dwight; the hysterically blind and mute Jeffrey; Michael, an arrogant jock; the coquettish Tian, whom Eric considered a whore; and argumentative Phillip, the lawyer. "Phillip was always asking about Eric's rights," says Graham. "He was kind of obnoxious. Actually, Phillip was a pain."

To Graham's astonishment, Eric gradually unfurled 27 different personalities, including three females. . . . They ranged in age from a fetus to a sordid old man who kept trying to persuade Eric to fight as a mercenary in Haiti. In one therapy session, reports Graham, Eric shifted personality nine times in an hour. "I felt I was losing control of the sessions," says the psychologist, who has eleven years of clinical experience. "Some personalities would not talk to me, and some of them were very insightful into my behavior as well as Eric's."

(Time, October 25, 1982, p. 70)

A person with **dissociative identity disorder,** or **multiple personality disorder,** develops two or more distinct personalities, often called **subpersonalities** or **alternate personalities,** each with a unique set of memories, behaviors, thoughts, and emotions (see again Table 7-5). At any given time, one of the subpersonalities takes center stage and dominates the person's functioning. Usually one subpersonality, called the *primary,* or *host,* personality, appears more often than the others.

The transition from one subpersonality to another, called *switching,* is usually sudden and may be dramatic (APA, 2000). Eric, for example, twisted his face, growled, and yelled obscenities while changing personalities. Switching is usually triggered by a stressful event, although clinicians can also bring about the change with hypnotic suggestion (APA, 2000).

Cases of dissociative identity disorder were first reported almost three centuries ago (Rieber, 2002). Many clinicians consider the disorder to be rare, but some reports suggest that it may be more common than was once thought (Sar et al., 2007; Lilienfeld & Lynn, 2003; APA, 2000). Most cases are first diagnosed in late adolescence or early adulthood, but, more often than not, the symptoms actually

"I'm Eve"
In 1975 Chris Sizemore revealed that she had been the subject of the book and the film *The Three Faces of Eve.* A fully integrated personality for more than 30 years, Ms. Sizemore is now an accomplished author, artist, and mental health spokesperson.

Lois Bernstein/Gamma Liaison

began in early childhood after episodes of abuse (often sexual abuse), perhaps even before the age of 5 (Maldonado & Spiegel, 2007; Roe-Sepowitz et al., 2007; Ross et al., 1991). Women receive this diagnosis at least three times as often as men (APA, 2000).

How Do Subpersonalities Interact?

How subpersonalities relate to or recall one another varies from case to case. Generally, however, there are three kinds of relationships. In *mutually amnesic relationships,* the subpersonalities have no awareness of one another (Ellenberger, 1970). Conversely, in *mutually cognizant patterns,* each subpersonality is well aware of the rest. They may hear one another's voices and even talk among themselves. Some are on good terms, while others do not get along at all.

In *one-way amnesic relationships,* the most common relationship pattern, some subpersonalities are aware of others, but the awareness is not mutual (Huntjens et al., 2005). Those who are aware, called *co-conscious subpersonalities,* are "quiet observers" who watch the actions and thoughts of the other subpersonalities but do not interact with them. Sometimes while another subpersonality is present, the co-conscious personality makes itself known through indirect means, such as auditory hallucinations (perhaps a voice giving commands) or "automatic writing" (the current personality may find itself writing down words over which it has no control).

Investigators used to believe that most cases of dissociative identity disorder involved two or three subpersonalities. Studies now suggest, however, that the average number of subpersonalities per patient is much higher—15 for women and 8 for men (APA, 2000). In fact, there have been cases in which 100 or more subpersonalities were observed (APA, 2000). Often the subpersonalities emerge in groups of two or three at a time.

In the case of "Eve White," made famous in the book and movie *The Three Faces of Eve,* a woman had three subpersonalities—Eve White, Eve Black, and Jane (Thigpen & Cleckley, 1957). Eve White, the primary personality, was quiet and serious; Eve Black was carefree and mischievous; and Jane was mature and intelligent. According to the book, these three subpersonalities eventually merged into Evelyn, a stable personality who was really an integration of the other three.

The book was mistaken, however; this was not to be the end of Eve's dissociation. In an autobiography 20 years later, she revealed that altogether 22 subpersonalities had come forth during her life, including 9 subpersonalities after Evelyn. Usually they appeared in groups of three, and so the authors of *The Three Faces of Eve* apparently never knew about her previous or subsequent subpersonalities. She has now overcome her disorder, achieving a single, stable identity, and has been known as Chris Sizemore for over 30 years (Sizemore, 1991).

How Do Subpersonalities Differ?

As in Chris Sizemore's case, subpersonalities often exhibit dramatically different characteristics. They may also have their own names and different *vital statistics, abilities and preferences,* and even *physiological responses.*

VITAL STATISTICS The subpersonalities may differ in features as basic as age, sex, race, and family history, as in the famous case of Sybil Dorsett. Sybil's dissociative identity disorder has been described in fictional form (in the novel *Sybil*) but is based on the real case of a patient named Shirley Ardell Mason, from the practice of the psychiatrist Cornelia Wilbur (Schreiber, 1973). Sybil displayed 17 subpersonalities, all with different identifying features. They included adults, a teenager, and a baby named Ruthie; two were male, named Mike and Sid. Sybil's subpersonalities each had particular images of themselves and of each other. The subpersonality named Vicky, for example, saw herself as an attractive blonde, while another, Peggy Lou, was described as a pixie with a pug nose. Mary was plump with dark hair, and Vanessa was a tall redhead with a willowy figure.

ABILITIES AND PREFERENCES Although memories of abstract or encyclopedic information are not usually affected in dissociative amnesia or fugue, they are often disturbed in dissociative identity disorder. It is not uncommon for the different subpersonalities to have

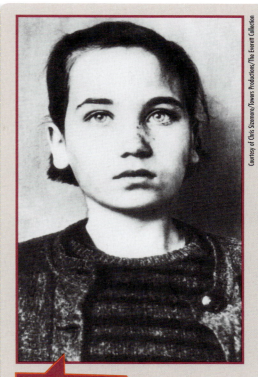

Courtesy of Chris Sizemore/Towers Productions/The Everett Collection

Early beginnings
Chris Sizemore's multiple personality disorder developed long before this photograph of her was taken at age 10. It emerged during her preschool years after she experienced several traumas (witnessing two deaths and a horrifying accident) within a three-month period.

BETWEEN THE LINES

Profit Distributions

Chris Sizemore received almost no revenues from the 1957 book and movie *The Three Faces of Eve.* In contrast, profits from *Sybil* were shared by the patient, her psychiatrist, and the book's author. Moreover, when the psychiatrist Cornelia Wilbur died in 1992, she left $25,000 and all *Sybil* royalties to the former patient (Miller & Kantrowitz, 1999). 〈〈

different abilities: one may be able to drive, speak a foreign language, or play a musical instrument, while the others cannot (Coons & Bowman, 2001; Coons et al., 1988). Their handwriting can also differ. In addition, the subpersonalities usually have different tastes in food, friends, music, and literature. Chris Sizemore ("Eve") later pointed out, "If I had learned to sew as one personality and then tried to sew as another, I couldn't do it. Driving a car was the same. Some of my personalities couldn't drive" (1977, p. 4).

PHYSIOLOGICAL RESPONSES Researchers have discovered that subpersonalities may have physiological differences, such as differences in autonomic nervous system activity, blood pressure levels, and allergies (Putnam, Zahn, & Post, 1990). One study looked at the brain activities of different subpersonalities by measuring their *evoked potentials*—that is, brain-response patterns recorded on an electroencephalograph (Putnam, 1984). The brain pattern a person produces in response to a specific stimulus (such as a flashing light) is usually unique and consistent. However, when an evoked potential test was administered to four subpersonalities of each of 10 people with dissociative identity disorder, the results were dramatic. The brain-activity pattern of each subpersonality was unique, showing the kinds of variations usually found in totally different people.

The evoked potential study also used control participants who pretended to have different subpersonalities. These normal individuals were instructed to create and rehearse alternate personalities. The brain-reaction patterns of these participants, in contrast to those of real patients, did not vary as they shifted from subpersonality to subpersonality, suggesting that simple faking cannot produce the variations in brain reaction found in cases of multiple personality.

How Common Is Dissociative Identity Disorder?

As you have seen, dissociative identity disorder has traditionally been thought of as rare. Some researchers even argue that many or all cases are *iatrogenic*—that is, unintentionally produced by practitioners (Loewenstein, 2007; Miller, 2005; Piper & Merskey, 2005, 2004). They believe that therapists create this disorder by subtly suggesting the existence of other personalities during therapy or by explicitly asking a patient to produce different personalities while under hypnosis. In addition, they believe, a therapist who is looking for multiple personalities may reinforce these patterns by displaying greater interest when a patient displays symptoms of dissociation.

These arguments seem to be supported by the fact that many cases of dissociative identity disorder first come to attention while the person is already in treatment for a less serious problem. But such is not true of all cases; many people seek treatment because they have noticed time lapses throughout their lives or because relatives and friends have observed their subpersonalities (Putnam, 2000, 1988, 1985).

The number of people diagnosed with dissociative identify disorder has been increasing (Sar et al., 2007; Casey, 2001). Although the disorder is still uncommon, thousands of cases have now been diagnosed in the United States and Canada alone. Two factors may account for this increase. First, a growing number of today's clinicians believe that the disorder does exist and are willing to diagnose it (Merenda, 2008; Lalonde et al., 2002, 2001). Second, diagnostic procedures tend to be more accurate today than in past years. For much of the twentieth century, schizophrenia was one of the clinical field's most commonly applied diagnoses. It was applied, often incorrectly, to a wide range of unusual behavioral patterns, perhaps including dissociative identity disorder (Turkington & Harris, 2001). Under the stricter criteria of recent editions of the DSM, clinicians are now more accurate in diagnosing schizophrenia, allowing more cases of dissociative identity disorder to be recognized (Welburn et al., 2003). In addition, several diagnostic tests have been developed to help detect dissociative identity disorder (Cardena, 2008). Despite such changes, however, many clinicians continue to question the legitimacy of this category (Lalonde et al., 2002, 2001).

Real or not real? False claims of dissociation are sometimes used to excuse bad deeds or cover up illegal acts. In 2007, former teacher John Darwin walked into a police station and said that he had no memory of the events that had taken place in his life since his disappearance five years earlier while canoeing off Britain's coast. An investigation revealed, however, that his disappearance was a case of life insurance fraud. Shortly after Darwin had been declared dead, he and his wife had collected the insurance money, paid off their debts, and moved to Panama. Here a police officer holds up the photo Darwin had used on a fake passport.

John Giles/PA Wire URN:5423846 (Press Association via AP Images)

How Do Theorists Explain Dissociative Disorders?

A variety of theories have been proposed to explain dissociative disorders. Older explanations, such as those offered by psychodynamic and behavioral theorists, have not received much investigation (Merenda, 2008). However, newer viewpoints, which combine cognitive, behavioral, and biological principles and highlight such factors as *state-dependent learning* and *self-hypnosis,* have captured the interest of clinical scientists.

The Psychodynamic View Psychodynamic theorists believe that dissociative disorders are caused by *repression,* the most basic ego defense mechanism: people fight off anxiety by unconsciously preventing painful memories, thoughts, or impulses from reaching awareness. Everyone uses repression to a degree, but people with dissociative disorders are thought to repress their memories excessively (Fayek, 2002).

In the psychodynamic view, dissociative amnesia and fugue are *single episodes* of massive repression. In each of these disorders, a person unconsciously blocks the memory of an extremely upsetting event to avoid the pain of facing it (Turkington & Harris, 2001). Repressing may be their only protection from overwhelming anxiety.

In contrast, dissociative identity disorder is thought to result from a *lifetime* of excessive repression (Wang & Jiang, 2007; Brenner, 1999; Reis, 1993). Psychodynamic theorists believe that continuous use of repression is motivated by traumatic childhood events, particularly abusive parenting. Young Sybil, for example, was repeatedly subjected to unspeakable tortures by her disturbed mother, Hattie:

A favorite ritual . . . was to separate Sybil's legs with a long wooden spoon, tie her feet to the spoon with dish towels, and then string her to the end of a light bulb cord, suspended from the ceiling. The child was left to swing in space while the mother proceeded to the water faucet to wait for the water to get cold. After muttering, "Well, it's not going to get any colder," she would fill the adult-sized enema bag to capacity and return with it to her daughter. As the child swung in space, the mother would insert the enema tip into the child's urethra and fill the bladder with cold water. "I did it," Hattie would scream triumphantly when her mission was accomplished. "I did it." The scream was followed by laughter, which went on and on.

(Schreiber, 1973, p. 160)

According to psychodynamic theorists, children who experience such traumas may come to fear the dangerous world they live in and take flight from it by pretending to be another person who is looking on safely from afar. Abused children may also come to fear the impulses that they believe are the reasons for their excessive punishments. Whenever they experience "bad" thoughts or impulses, they unconsciously try to disown and deny them by assigning them to other personalities.

Most of the support for the psychodynamic position is drawn from case histories, which report such brutal childhood experiences as beatings, cuttings, burnings with cigarettes, imprisonment in closets, rape, and extensive verbal abuse. Yet some individuals with dissociative identity disorder do not seem to have experiences of abuse in their background (Bliss, 1980). Moreover, child abuse appears to be far more common than dissociative identity disorder. Why might only a small fraction of abused children develop this disorder?

The Behavioral View Behaviorists believe that dissociation grows from normal memory processes such as drifting of the mind or forgetting (see *A Closer Look* on the next page). Specifically, they hold that dissociation is a response learned through *operant conditioning* (Casey, 2001). People who experience a horrifying event may later find temporary relief when their minds drift to other subjects. For some, this momentary

"Did you ever start to do something and then forget what the heck it was?"

A CLOSER LOOK

Peculiarities of Memory

Usually memory problems must interfere greatly with a person's functioning before they are considered a sign of a disorder. Peculiarities of memory, on the other hand, fill our daily lives. Memory investigators have identified a number of these peculiarities—some familiar, some useful, some problematic, but none abnormal (Mathews & Wang, 2007; Brown, 2004, 2003; Schacter, 2001; Turkington & Harris, 2001).

- **Absentmindedness** Often we fail to register information because our thoughts are focusing on other things. If we haven't absorbed the information in the first place, it is no surprise that later we can't recall it.

- **Déjà vu** Almost all of us have at some time had the strange sensation of recognizing a scene that we happen upon for the first time. We feel sure we have been there before.

- **Jamais vu** Sometimes we have the opposite experience: a situation or scene that is part of our daily life seems suddenly unfamiliar. "I knew it was my car, but I felt as if I'd never seen it before."

- **The tip-of-the-tongue phenomenon** To have something on the tip of the tongue is an acute "feeling of knowing": we are unable to recall some piece of information, but we know that we know it.

- **Eidetic images** Some people experience visual afterimages so vividly that they can describe a picture in detail after looking at it just once. The images may be memories of pictures, events, fantasies, or dreams.

- **Memory while under anesthesia** As many as two of every 1,000 anesthetized patients process enough of what is said in their presence during surgery to affect their recovery. In many such cases, the ability to understand language has continued under anesthesia, even though the patient cannot explicitly recall it.

- **Memory for music** Even as a small child, Mozart could memorize and reproduce a piece of music after having heard it only once. While no one yet has matched the genius of Mozart, many musicians can mentally hear whole pieces of music, so that they can rehearse anywhere, far from their instruments.

- **Visual memory** Most people recall visual information better than other kinds of information: they easily can bring to their mind the appearance of places, objects, faces, or the pages of a book. They almost never forget a face, yet they may well forget the name attached to it. Other people have stronger verbal memories: they remember sounds or words particularly well, and the memories that come to their minds are often puns or rhymes.

- **Prenatal memory** Some North American medicine men claim to remember parts of a prenatal existence, an ability they believe is lost to "common" people. Many practicing Buddhists also claim to remember past lives. A few—such as Buddha himself—claim to remember their very first existence.

•**state-dependent learning**•Learning that becomes associated with the conditions under which it occurred, so that it is best remembered under the same conditions.

forgetting, leading to a drop in anxiety, increases the likelihood of future forgetting. In short, they are reinforced for the act of forgetting and learn—without being aware that they are learning—that such acts help them escape anxiety. Thus, like psychodynamic theorists, behaviorists see dissociation as escape behavior. But behaviorists believe that a reinforcement process rather than a hardworking unconscious is keeping the individuals unaware that they are using dissociation as a means of escape.

Like psychodynamic theorists, behaviorists have relied largely on case histories to support their view of dissociative disorders. Such descriptions do often support this view, but they are equally consistent with other kinds of explanations as well: a case that seems to show reinforcement of forgetting can usually also be interpreted as an instance of unconscious repression. In addition, the behavioral explanation fails to explain precisely how temporary and normal escapes from painful memories grow into a complex disorder or why more people do not develop dissociative disorders.

State-Dependent Learning If people learn something when they are in a particular situation or state of mind, they are likely to remember it best when they are again in that same condition. If they are given a learning task while under the influence of alcohol, for example, their later recall of the information may be strongest under the influence of alcohol (Overton, 1966). Similarly, if they smoke cigarettes while learning, they may later have better recall when they are again smoking.

This link between state and recall is called **state-dependent learning.** It was initially observed in experimental animals who were given certain drugs and then taught to perform certain tasks. Researchers repeatedly found that the animals' subsequent test performances were best in the same drug states (Rezayof et al., 2008; Vakili et al., 2004; Overton, 1966, 1964). Research with human participants later showed that state-dependent learning can be associated with mood states as well: material learned during a happy mood is recalled best when the participant is again happy, and sad-state learning is recalled best during sad states (de l'Etoile, 2002; Bower, 1981) (see Figure 7-3).

What causes state-dependent learning? One possibility is that *arousal* levels are an important part of learning and memory. That is, a particular level of arousal will have a set of remembered events, thoughts, and skills attached to it. When a situation produces that particular level of arousal, the person is more likely to recall the memories linked to it.

Although people may remember certain events better in some arousal states than in others, most can recall events under a variety of states. However, perhaps people who are prone to develop dissociative disorders have state-to-memory links that are unusually rigid and narrow. Maybe each of their thoughts, memories, and skills is tied *exclusively* to a particular state of arousal, so that they recall a given event only when they experience an arousal state almost identical to the state in which the memory was first acquired. When such people are calm, for example, they may forget what occurred during stressful times, thus laying the groundwork for dissociative amnesia or fugue. Similarly, in dissociative identity disorder, different arousal levels may produce entirely different groups of memories, thoughts, and abilities—that is, different subpersonalities (Dorahy & Huntjens, 2007; Putnam, 1992). This could explain why personality transitions in dissociative identity disorder tend to be sudden and stress-related.

Self-Hypnosis As you first saw in Chapter 1, people who are *hypnotized* enter a sleep-like state in which they become very suggestible. While in this state, they can behave, perceive, and think in ways that would ordinarily seem impossible. They may, for example, become temporarily blind, deaf, or insensitive to pain. Hypnosis can also help people remember events that occurred and were forgotten years ago, a capability used by many

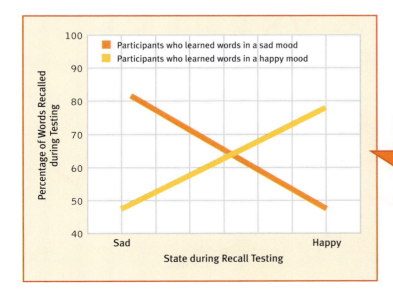

Figure 7-3

State-dependent learning In one study, participants who learned a list of words while in a hypnotically induced happy state remembered the words better if they were in a happy mood when tested later than if they were in a sad mood. Conversely, participants who learned the words when in a sad mood recalled them better if they were sad during testing than if they were happy (Bower, 1981).

psychotherapists. Conversely, it can make people forget facts, events, and even their personal identities—an effect called *hypnotic amnesia*.

Most studies of hypnotic amnesia follow similar formats. Participants are asked to study a word list or other material until they are able to repeat it correctly. Under hypnosis, they are then directed to forget the material until they receive a *cancellation signal* (such as the snap of a finger), at which time they will suddenly recall the learned material. Repeatedly these experiments have found the participants' memories to be poor during the period of hypnotic amnesia and then restored after the cancellation signal is given.

The parallels between hypnotic amnesia and dissociative disorders are striking. Both are conditions in which people forget certain material for a period of time yet later remember it. And in both, the people forget without any insight into why they are forgetting or any awareness that something is being forgotten. These parallels have led some theorists to conclude that dissociative disorders may be a form of **self-hypnosis** in which people hypnotize themselves to forget unpleasant events (Maldonado & Spiegel, 2007, 2003; Bryant et al., 2001). Dissociative amnesia may occur, for example, in people who, consciously or unconsciously, hypnotize themselves into forgetting horrifying experiences that have recently occurred in their lives. If the self-induced amnesia covers all memories of a person's past and identity, that person may undergo a dissociative fugue.

Self-hypnosis might also be used to explain dissociative identity disorder. On the basis of several investigations, some theorists believe that this disorder often begins between the ages of 4 and 6, a time when children are generally very suggestible and excellent hypnotic subjects (Kluft, 2001, 1987; Bliss, 1985, 1980) (see Figure 7-4). These theorists argue that some children who experience abuse or other horrifying events manage to escape their threatening world by self-hypnosis, mentally separating themselves from their bodies and fulfilling their wish to become some other person or persons. One patient with multiple personalities observed, "I was in a trance often [during my childhood]. There was a little place where I could sit, close my eyes and imagine, until I felt very relaxed just like hypnosis" (Bliss, 1980, p. 1392).

There are different schools of thought about the nature of hypnosis (Kihlstrom, 2007, 2005; Lynn et al., 2007; Hilgard, 1992, 1987, 1977; Spanos & Coe, 1992). Some theorists see hypnosis as a *special process,* an out-of-the-ordinary kind of functioning. Accordingly, these theorists contend that people with dissociative disorders place

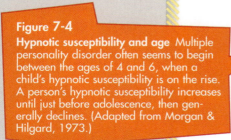

Figure 7-4

Hypnotic susceptibility and age Multiple personality disorder often seems to begin between the ages of 4 and 6, when a child's hypnotic susceptibility is on the rise. A person's hypnotic susceptibility increases until just before adolescence, then generally declines. (Adapted from Morgan & Hilgard, 1973.)

Columbia/The Kobal Collection

themselves in internal trances during which their conscious functioning is significantly altered. Other theorists believe that hypnotic behaviors, and hypnotic amnesia in particular, are produced by *common social and cognitive processes,* such as high motivation, focused attention, role enactment, and self-fulfilling expectations. According to this point of view, hypnotized people are simply highly motivated individuals performing tasks that are asked of them, while believing all along that the hypnotic state is doing the work for them. Common-process theorists hold that people with dissociative disorders provide themselves (or are provided by others) with powerful suggestions to forget and that social and cognitive mechanisms then put the suggestions into practice. Whether hypnosis consists of special or common processes, hypnosis research effectively demonstrates the power of our normal thought processes, and so renders the notion of dissociative disorders somewhat less remarkable.

How Are Dissociative Disorders Treated?

As you have seen, people with dissociative amnesia and fugue often recover on their own (see *The Media Speaks* on page 233). Only sometimes do their memory problems linger and require treatment. In contrast, people with dissociative identity disorder usually require treatment to regain their lost memories and develop an integrated personality. Treatments for dissociative amnesia and fugue tend to be more successful than those for dissociative identity disorder, probably because the former disorders are less complex.

How Do Therapists Help People with Dissociative Amnesia and Fugue?

The leading treatments for dissociative amnesia and fugue are *psychodynamic therapy, hypnotic therapy,* and *drug therapy,* although support for these interventions comes largely from case studies rather than controlled investigations (Maldonado & Spiegel, 2003). Psychodynamic therapists guide patients with these disorders to search their unconscious in the hope of bringing forgotten experiences back to consciousness (Bartholomew, 2000; Loewenstein, 1991). The focus of psychodynamic therapy seems particularly well suited to the needs of people with these disorders. After all, the patients need to recover lost memories, and the general approach of psychodynamic therapists is to try to uncover memories—as well as other psychological processes—that have been repressed. Thus many theorists, including some who do not ordinarily favor psychodynamic approaches, believe that psychodynamic therapy may be the most appropriate treatment for these disorders.

Another common treatment for dissociative amnesia and fugue is **hypnotic therapy,** or **hypnotherapy** (see Table 7-6 on the next page). Therapists hypnotize patients and then

•**self-hypnosis**•The process of hypnotizing oneself, sometimes for the purpose of forgetting unpleasant events.

•**hypnotic therapy**•A treatment in which the patient undergoes hypnosis and is then guided to recall forgotten events or perform other therapeutic activities. Also known as *hypnotherapy.*

guide them to recall forgotten events (Degun–Mather, 2002). Experiments have repeatedly indicated that hypnotic suggestion can help elicit forgotten memories, and experience has shown that people with dissociative disorders are usually highly susceptible to hypnosis (Maldonado & Spiegel, 2003). Given the possibility that dissociative amnesia and fugue may each be a form of self-hypnosis, hypnotherapy may be a particularly useful intervention. It has been applied both alone and in combination with other approaches.

Sometimes intravenous injections of barbiturates such as *sodium amobarbital* (Amytal) or *sodium pentobarbital* (Pentothal) are used to help patients with dissociative amnesia and fugue regain lost memories. These drugs are often called "truth serums," but the key to their success is their ability to sedate people and free their inhibitions, thus helping them to recall anxiety-producing events (Fraser, 1993; Kluft, 1988). These drugs do not always work, however, and if used at all, they are likely to be combined with other treatment approaches (Spiegel, 1994).

How Do Therapists Help Individuals with Dissociative Identity Disorder?
Unlike victims of amnesia and fugue, people with dissociative identity disorder do not typically recover without treatment (Maldonado & Spiegel, 2003; Spiegel, 1994). Treatment for this pattern is complex and difficult, much like the disorder itself. Therapists usually try to help the clients (1) recognize fully the nature of their disorder, (2) recover the gaps in their memory, and (3) integrate their subpersonalities into one functional personality (North & Yutzy, 2005; Kihlstrom, 2001).

RECOGNIZING THE DISORDER Once a diagnosis of dissociative identity disorder is made, therapists typically try to bond with the primary personality and with each of the subpersonalities (Kluft, 1999, 1992). As bonds are formed, therapists try to educate patients and help them to recognize fully the nature of their disorder (Krakauer, 2001; Allen, 1993). Some therapists actually introduce the subpersonalities to one another under hypnosis, and some have patients look at videotapes of their other personalities (Ross & Gahan, 1988; Sakheim, Hess, & Chivas, 1988). Many therapists have also found that

table: 7-6

Myths about Hypnosis

Myth	Reality
Hypnosis is all a matter of having a good imagination.	Ability to imagine vividly is unrelated to hypnotizability.
Relaxation is an important feature of hypnosis.	Hypnosis has been induced during vigorous exercise.
It's a matter of willful faking.	Physiological responses indicate that hypnotized subjects are not lying.
It is dangerous.	Standard hypnotic procedures are no more distressing than lectures.
It has something to do with a sleeplike state.	Hypnotized subjects are fully awake.
Responding to hypnosis is like responding to a placebo.	Placebo responsiveness and hypnotizability are not correlated.
People who are hypnotized lose control of themselves.	Subjects are perfectly capable of saying no or terminating hypnosis.
Hypnosis can enable people to "relive" the past.	Age-regressed adults behave like adults play-acting as children.
When hypnotized, people can remember more accurately.	Hypnosis may actually muddle the distinction between memory and fantasy and may artificially inflate confidence.
Hypnotized people can be led to do acts that conflict with usual values.	Hypnotized subjects fully adhere to their moral standards.
Hypnotized people spontaneously forget what happened during the session.	Posthypnotic amnesia does not occur spontaneously.
Hypnosis can enable people to perform otherwise impossible feats of strength, endurance, learning, and acuity.	Performance following hypnotic suggestions for increased sensory muscle strength, learning, and sensory activity does not exceed what can be accomplished by motivated subjects outside hypnosis.

Michael Nash (2006, 2005, 2004, 2001).

The
Media SPEAKS

HOME   SEND   EXPLORE

SEARCH

Homeward Hound: A Case of Dog Fugue?

BY SHERRY MORSE, *ANIMAL NEWS*, DECEMBER 13, 2003

The Flores family of Wichita, Kansas received an early Christmas present this year when their beloved dog Bear, who had disappeared in November of 1997, made it back home in time for Thanksgiving in 2003.

Jeanie Flores looked out the window of her house two days before Thanksgiving to see a dog that looked exactly like Bear standing outside. She recalls thinking, "Oh my God. I think that's my dog!" She called the dog; and he responded.

Jeanie burst into tears, then called her husband Frank and told him she thought Bear was really home. Frank Flores rushed home and, after seeing the dog, agreed with his wife that the brindle lab-chow mix was indeed their Bear. One of the family's neighbors told them she had spotted Bear a little earlier, walking around and carefully scrutinizing the houses.

A veterinarian who examined Bear said that although his paws were red and sore in spots, probably from pounding the pavement, he only weighed one pound less than when he disappeared. It appeared that someone had been taking care of him.

Bear had disappeared in 1997 about one month after the Flores family had moved to a new neighborhood. Jeanie let him out for exercise one night, and he never came back. "I waited up all night for him, and he never came home," she said.

At the time, Bear's ID tag had not yet been updated with his new address. The desperate family put up signs, canvassed their

Omar Torres/AFP/Getty Images

old neighborhood, ran ads in the paper, and visited shelters, but, tragically, the dog that Mr. Flores had brought home as a puppy in 1990 seemed to have disappeared without a trace.

Since his extraordinary return home six years later, Bear has been catching up on his sleep and getting reacquainted with his family, which includes a son who was not yet born when the dog disappeared.

The Flores family said they just wish that Bear could tell them where he's been all this time. "Where was he? We don't know how rough a life he's had," Frank Flores said.

---

group therapy helps to educate patients (Fine & Madden, 2000). Being with a group of people who all have multiple personalities helps relieve a person's feelings of isolation. Family therapy may also be used to help educate spouses and children about the disorder and to gather helpful information about the patient (Kluft, 2001, 2000; Porter et al., 1993).

RECOVERING MEMORIES To help patients recover the missing pieces of their past, therapists use many of the approaches applied in other dissociative disorders, including psychodynamic therapy, hypnotherapy, and drug treatment (Kluft, 2001, 1991, 1985). These techniques work slowly for patients with dissociative identity disorder, as some subpersonalities may keep denying experiences that the others recall (Lyon, 1992). One of the subpersonalities may even assume a "protector" role to prevent the primary personality from suffering the pain of recollecting traumatic experiences. Some patients become self-destructive and violent during this phase of treatment (Kelly, 1993).

INTEGRATING THE SUBPERSONALITIES The final goal of therapy is to merge the different subpersonalities into a single, integrated identity. Integration is a continuous process that occurs throughout treatment until patients "own" all of their behaviors, emotions, sensations, and knowledge. **Fusion** is the final merging of two or more subpersonalities. Many patients distrust this final treatment goal, and their subpersonalities are likely

•**fusion**•The final merging of two or more subpersonalities in multiple personality disorder.

Erin Painter/Midland Daily News/AP Photo

Hypnotic recall
Northwood University students react while under hypnosis to the suggestion of being on a beach in Hawaii and needing suntan lotion. Many clinicians use hypnotic procedures to help clients recall past events. Research reveals, however, that such procedures are as capable of creating false memories as they are of uncovering real memories.

to see integration as a form of death (Kluft, 2001, 1999, 1991). As one subpersonality said, "There are too many advantages to being multiple. Maybe we're being sold a bill of goods by therapists" (Hale, 1983). Therapists have used a range of approaches to help merge subpersonalities, including psychodynamic, supportive, cognitive, and drug therapies (Goldman, 1995; Fichtner et al., 1990).

Once the subpersonalities are integrated, further therapy is typically needed to maintain the complete personality and to teach social and coping skills that may help prevent later dissociations (Kihlstrom, 2001). In case reports, some therapists note high success rates (Coons & Bowman, 2001; Kluft, 2001, 1999, 1993), but others find that patients continue to resist full and final integration. A few therapists have in fact questioned the need for full integration. The limited number of reported cases generally prevents researchers from gathering samples that are large enough to conduct enlightening research on the treatment of this disorder.

In Sybil's case, the progress toward full integration was slow and halting and required 11 years of therapy. Her progress can be traced in the following excerpts from different stages of her treatment (Schreiber, 1973):

1957 *Integration? Far from it. As the past flooded back, there was all the more reason to regress into the other selves, defenses against the past. (p. 270)*

1958 *Peggy Lou's memories were becoming Sybil's. By responding to Peggy Lou's memory as if it were her own, . . . Sybil had been able to recall an incident from the childhood of the alternating self. And all at once Sybil realized that at that moment she felt not merely like Peggy Lou: she was **one** with her. (p. 272)*

1962 *"Am I going to die?" each of the selves asked Dr. Wilbur. For some of the selves integration seemed synonymous with death. The doctor's assurances that, although one with Sybil, the individual selves would not cease to be seemed at best only partly convincing. "There are many things I have to do," Vanessa told Marcia. "You see, I won't be here very long." (p. 316)*

1965 *Sybil's attitude toward these selves . . . had completely changed, from initial denial to hostility to acceptance—even to love. Having learned to love these parts of herself, she had in effect replaced self-derogation with self-love. This replacement was an important measure of her integration and restoration. . . . Dr. Wilbur hypnotized Sybil and called*

BETWEEN THE LINES

Major Impact Before the publication of *Sybil* in 1973, only 100 cases of multiple personality disorder had been published. Since then, an estimated 40,000 diagnoses have been made (Acocella, 1999; Miller & Kantrowitz, 1999). «

Author's License? Several colleagues who worked closely with the author of *Sybil* and with her therapist claim that Sybil was actually highly hypnotizable, suggestible, and eager to please her therapist and that her disorder was in fact induced by the treatment techniques of hypnosis and sodium pentothal (Rieber, 2002, 1999; Miller & Kantrowitz, 1999). «

for Vicky Antoinette. "How are things going, Vicky?" the doctor asked. "What progress is there underneath?" "I'm part of Sybil now, you know," Vicky replied. "She always wanted to be like me. Now we are one." (p. 337)

Depersonalization Disorder

As you read earlier, DSM-IV-TR categorizes **depersonalization disorder** as a dissociative disorder, even though it is quite different from the other dissociative patterns (Maldonado & Spiegel, 2007; APA, 2000). Its central symptom is persistent and recurrent episodes of *depersonalization,* a change in one's experience of the self in which one's mental functioning or body feels unreal or foreign.

A 24-year-old graduate student sought treatment because he felt he was losing his mind. He had begun to doubt his own reality. He felt he was living in a dream in which he saw himself from without, and did not feel connected to his body or his thoughts. When he saw himself through his own eyes, he perceived his body parts as distorted—his hands and feet seemed quite large. As he walked across campus, he often felt the people he saw might be robots; he began to ruminate about his dizzy spells—did this mean that he had a brain tumor? . . . He often noted that he spent so much time thinking about his situation that he lost contact with all feelings except a pervasive discomfort about his own predicament.

In his second session, he was preoccupied with his perception that his feet had grown too large for his shoes, and fretted over whether to break up with his girlfriend because he doubted the reality of his feelings for her, and had begun to perceive her in a distorted manner. He said he had hesitated before returning for his second appointment, because he wondered whether his therapist was really alive. He was very pessimistic that he could be helped, and had vague suicidal ideation. A thorough medical and neurological evaluation found no organic etiology.

(Kluft, 1988, p. 580)

Like this graduate student, people with depersonalization disorder feel as though they have become separated from their body and are observing themselves from outside. Occasionally their mind seems to be floating a few feet above them—a sensation known as *doubling.* Their body parts seem foreign to them, the hands and feet smaller or bigger than usual. Many sufferers describe their emotional state as "mechanical," "dreamlike," or "dizzy." Throughout the whole depersonalization experience, however, they are aware that their perceptions are distorted, and in that sense they remain in contact with reality.

In some cases this sense of unreality also extends to other sensory experiences and behavior. People may, for example, experience distortions in their sense of touch or smell or their judgments of time or space, or they may feel that they have lost control over their speech or actions.

Depersonalization is often accompanied by an experience of *derealization*—the feeling that the external world, too, is unreal and strange. Objects may seem to change shape or size; other persons may seem removed, mechanical, or even dead. The graduate student, for example, began to perceive his girlfriend in a distorted manner, and he hesitated to return for a second session of therapy because he wondered whether his therapist was really alive.

Depersonalization experiences by themselves do not indicate a depersonalization disorder. Transient depersonalization reactions are fairly common, while a depersonalization disorder is not (Maldonado & Spiegel, 2007; Miller, 2005; APA, 2000). One-third

•depersonalization disorder•A disorder marked by a persistent and recurrent feeling of being detached from one's own mental processes or body.

BETWEEN THE LINES

In the Zone: Depersonalization and Athletic Focus

"It is not a dreamlike state, but the somehow insulated state that a great musician achieves in a great performance. He's aware of where he is and what he's doing, but his mind is on the playing of the instrument with an internal sense of rightness. It is not merely mechanical, it is not only spiritual; it is something of both, on a different plane and a more remote one."

Arnold Palmer, golfer

Daniel Morel/Reuters/Corbis

Religious dissociations
Many people from around the world voluntarily enter into trances—states of depersonalization and derealization—as part of religious or cultural practices. Here, voodoo followers sing and flail about in trances inside a sacred pool at a temple in Souvenance, Haiti, part of an annual week-long celebration marked by song and dance rituals and offerings to voodoo spirits.

of all people say that on occasion they have felt as though they were watching themselves in a movie. Similarly, one-third of individuals who confront a life-threatening danger experience feelings of depersonalization or derealization. People sometimes have feelings of depersonalization after practicing meditation, and individuals who travel to new places often report a temporary sense of depersonalization. Young children may also experience depersonalization from time to time as they are developing their capacity for self-awareness. In most such cases, the individuals are able to compensate for the distortion and continue to function with reasonable effectiveness until the temporary episode eventually ends.

The symptoms of a depersonalization disorder, in contrast, are persistent or recurrent, cause considerable distress, and interfere with social relationships and job performance (Maldonado & Spiegel, 2007; Simeon et al., 2003). The disorder occurs most frequently in adolescents and young adults, hardly ever in people over 40 (APA, 2000). It usually comes on suddenly, triggered by experiences such as extreme fatigue, physical pain, intense stress, anxiety, depression, or recovery from substance abuse. Survivors of traumatic experiences or people caught in life-threatening situations, such as hostages or kidnap victims, seem to be particularly vulnerable (APA, 2000). The disorder tends to be long-lasting; the symptoms may improve and even disappear for a time, only to return or intensify during times of severe stress. Like the graduate student in our case discussion, many people with the disorder fear that they are losing their minds and become preoccupied with worry about their symptoms.

Like other dissociative symptoms, feelings of depersonalization and derealization may appear in other disorders. Sufferers of panic disorder, for example, commonly experience some feelings of unreality. Similarly, people with acute and posttraumatic stress disorders often have a sense of derealization.

Few theories have been offered to explain depersonalization disorder, and little research has been conducted on the problem. In recent times some investigators have used brain scan techniques, such as PET and fMRI scans, to determine whether the disorder is accompanied by particular changes in brain activity (Medford et al., 2006; Phillips et al., 2001). However, clear biological factors have yet to emerge. Similarly, treatments for this disorder have not received much study, although a range of approaches, including psychodynamic, cognitive, hypnotic, and drug therapies, have been tried (Maldonado & Spiegel, 2007; Sierra et al., 2001).

PUTTING IT... together

Disorders Rediscovered

Somatoform and dissociative disorders are among the clinical field's earliest identified psychological disorders. Indeed, as you read in Chapter 1, they were key to the development of the psychogenic perspective. Recall, for example, that Anton Mesmer developed the procedure of *hypnotism* (*mesmerism*) in the late eighteenth century by working with people who displayed hysterical somatoform disorders. Similarly, Freud's development of the psychoanalytic model in the late nineteenth century drew largely from his work with patients who displayed hysterical and dissociative disorders.

Despite this early impact, the clinical field stopped paying much attention to these disorders during the middle part of the twentieth century. The feeling among many clinical theorists was that the number of such cases was shrinking. And more than a few questioned the legitimacy of these diagnoses.

Much of that thinking has changed in the past two decades. The field's keen interest in the impact of stress upon health and physical illness has, by association, reawakened interest in somatoform disorders. Similarly, as you will see in Chapter 18, the field has greatly intensified its efforts to understand and treat Alzheimer's disease in recent years, and that work has sparked a broad interest in the operation of memory, including an interest in dissociative disorders.

Over the past 25 years there has been an explosion of research seeking to help clinicians recognize, understand, and treat unexplained physical and memory disorders. Although this research has yet to yield clear insights or highly effective treatments, it has already suggested that the disorders may be more common than clinical theorists had come to believe. Moreover, there is growing evidence that the disorders may be rooted in processes that are already well known from other areas of study, such as overattentiveness to bodily processes, cognitive misinterpretations, state-dependent learning, and self-hypnosis. Given this new wave of research enthusiasm, we may witness significant growth in our understanding and treatment of these disorders in the coming years.

Researchers' growing interest in these disorders has been accompanied by intense public interest as well. Moreover, it has sparked a greater belief in somatoform and dissociative disorders among many clinicians. More and more therapists are now identifying patients with multiple personalities, for example, and are trying to provide corresponding treatments.

With this heightened interest and work come new problems (Mayou et al., 2005). Many of today's clinicians worry that the focus on somatoform and dissociative disorders is swinging too far—that the high degree of interest in them may be creating a false impression of their prevalence or importance (Pope et al., 2007; Piper & Merskey, 2004). Some clinicians note, for example, that physicians are often quick to assign the label "somatoform" to elusive medical problems such as chronic fatigue syndrome and lupus—clearly a disservice to patients with such severe problems and to the progress of medical science. Similarly, a number of clinicians worry that at least some of the many legal defenses based on dissociative identity disorder or other dissociative disorders are contrived or inaccurate. Of course, such possibilities serve to highlight even further the importance of continued investigations into all aspects of the disorders.

«[SUMMING UP]»

○ **Somatoform disorders** *Patients with somatoform disorders* have physical complaints whose causes are largely psychosocial. Nevertheless, the individuals genuinely believe that their illnesses are organic.

Hysterical somatoform disorders involve an actual loss or change of physical functioning. They include *conversion disorder, somatization disorder* (or *Briquet's*

continued

BETWEEN THE LINES

Leading Cosmetic Procedures in the United States Annually

Nonsurgical procedures
- Botox injection (2,837,346 procedures)
- Laser hair removal (1,411,899)
- Chemical peel (1,110,401)
- Microdermabrasion (1,098,316)
- Hyaluronic acid (882,469) ‹‹

Surgical procedures
- Liposuction (478,251)
- Breast augmentation (334,052)
- Eyelid surgery (290,343)
- Rhinoplasty (reshape nose) (166,187)
- Facelift (157,061) ‹‹

(American Society for Aesthetic Plastic Surgery, 2004)

BETWEEN THE LINES

Why "A Memory Like an Elephant's"?

The popular belief that elephants have long memories is based on the observation that the animals effortlessly find their way back home even after traveling more than 30 miles to find water. ‹‹

syndrome), and *pain disorder associated with psychological factors.* Diagnosticians are sometimes able to distinguish hysterical somatoform disorders from "true" medical problems by observing oddities in the patient's medical picture. They must also distinguish hysterical somatoform disorders from *malingering* and *factitious disorders.*

Freud developed the initial *psychodynamic view* of hysterical somatoform disorders, proposing that the disorders represent a conversion of underlying emotional conflicts into physical symptoms. According to *behaviorists,* the physical symptoms of these disorders bring rewards to the sufferer, and such reinforcement helps maintain the symptoms. Some *cognitive theorists* propose that the disorders are forms of *communication* and that people express their emotions through their physical symptoms. *Biological factors* may also help explain these disorders, as we are reminded by recent studies of *placebos.* Treatments for hysterical disorders emphasize either *insight, suggestion, reinforcement,* or *confrontation.*

People with *preoccupation somatoform disorders* are preoccupied with the notion that something is wrong with them physically. In this category are *hypochodriasis* and *body dysmorphic disorder.* Theorists explain preoccupation somatoform disorders much as they do anxiety disorders. Treatment for the disorders includes medications, exposure and response prevention, and other treatments originally developed for anxiety disorders. *pp. 203–218*

○ **Dissociative disorders** Memory plays a key role in our functioning by linking our past, present, and future. People with *dissociative disorders* experience major changes in memory, consciousness, and identity that are not caused by clear physical factors. Typically, one part of the memory or identity is *dissociated,* or separated, from the rest. People with *dissociative amnesia* are suddenly unable to recall important personal information or past events in their lives. Those with *dissociative fugue* not only fail to remember their personal identities but also flee to a different location and may establish a new identity.

In another dissociative disorder, *dissociative identity disorder (multiple personality disorder),* people display two or more distinct *subpersonalities.* The subpersonalities often have complex relationships with one another and usually differ in *vital statistics, abilities and preferences,* and even *physiological responses.* A *primary personality* appears more often than the others. The number of people diagnosed with dissociative identity disorder has increased in recent years. *pp. 218–226*

○ **Explanations of dissociative disorders** The dissociative disorders are not well understood. Among the processes that have been cited to explain them are *extreme repression, operant conditioning, state-dependent learning,* and *self-hypnosis.* The latter two phenomena, in particular, have excited the interest of clinical scientists. The state-dependent learning explanation suggests that the thoughts, memories, and skills of people who develop dissociative disorders are tied exclusively to specific states of arousal, that is, to whatever mental state or emotion the people were experiencing when they first acquired the thoughts, memories, or skills. The self-hypnosis explanation proposes that people with these disorders have hypnotized themselves to forget horrifying experiences in their lives. *pp. 227–231*

○ **Treatments for dissociative disorders** Dissociative amnesia and fugue may end on their own or may require treatment. Dissociative identity disorder typically requires treatment. Approaches commonly used to help people with dissociative amnesia and fugue recover their lost memories are *psychodynamic therapy, hypnotic therapy,* and *sodium amobarbital* or *sodium pentobarbital.* Therapists who treat people with dissociative identity disorder use the same approaches but focus on trying to help the clients *recognize the nature and scope of their disorder, recover the gaps in their memory,* and *integrate their subpersonalities into one functional personality. pp. 231–235*

○ **Depersonalization disorder** People with *depersonalization disorder* feel as though they have become detached from their own mental processes or body and are observing themselves from the outside. Some also experience *derealization*. Transient depersonalization experiences seem to be relatively common, while depersonalization disorder is not. People who experience traumatic events seem particularly vulnerable to this disorder. *pp. 235–236*

⟩⟩ CRITICAL THOUGHTS ⟨⟨

1. Why do the terms "hysteria" and "hysterical" currently have such negative connotations in our society, as in "mass hysteria" and "hysterical personality"? *pp. 204–208*

2. If parents who harm their children are clearly disturbed, as in cases of Munchausen syndrome by proxy, how should society react to them? Which is more appropriate— treatment or punishment? *p. 209*

3. How might a culture help create individual cases of body dysmorphic disorder? Why do some people in a society carry a culture's aesthetic ideals to an extreme, while others stay within normal bounds? *pp. 210–212*

4. Periodically we read in the news about missing individuals who show up suddenly, claiming to have lost their memories while away. Although disorders such as dissociative amnesia and fugue are listed in DSM-IV-TR, many people greet such explanations with skepticism. Why? *pp. 218–222, 226*

5. Women are much more likely to receive a diagnosis of dissociative identity disorder than men. What might be some reasons for this difference? *pp. 224–231*

6. Some accused criminals claim that they have dissociative identity disorder and that their crimes were committed by one of their subpersonalities. If such claims are accurate, what would be an appropriate verdict? *pp. 224–231*

7. Have you ever experienced feelings of depersonalization and/or derealization? When? How did you explain such feelings at the time? How might you explain them now? *pp. 235–236*

⟨⟨ cyberstudy ⟩⟩

SEARCH

Search the *Abnormal Psychology* Video Tool Kit
www.worthpublishers.com/apvtk

▲ Chapter 7 Video Cases
   Beyond Perfection: Body Dysmorphic Disorder
   Repressed Memories or False Memories?
   Three Faces of Eve: The Real Patient

▲ Video case discussions, study guides, and questions

Log on to the Comer Web Page
www.worthpublishers.com/comer

▲ Chapter 7 outline, learning objectives, research exercises, study tools, and practice test questions

▲ Additional Chapter 7 case studies, Web links, and FAQs

MOOD DISORDERS

For . . . a six-month period, her irritability bordered on the irrational. She screamed in anger or sobbed in despair at every dirty dish left on the coffee table or on the bedroom floor. Each day the need to plan the dinner menu provoked agonizing indecision. How could all the virtues or, more likely, vices of hamburgers be accurately compared to those of spaghetti? . . . She had her whole family walking on eggs. She thought they would be better off if she were dead.

Beatrice could not cope with her job. As a branch manager of a large chain store, she had many decisions to make. Unable to make them herself, she would ask employees who were much less competent for advice, but then she could not decide whose advice to take. Each morning before going to work, she complained of nausea. . . .

Beatrice's husband loved her, but he did not understand what was wrong. He thought that she would improve if he made her life easier by taking over more housework, cooking, and child care. His attempt to help only made Beatrice feel more guilty and worthless. She wanted to make a contribution to her family. She wanted to do the chores "like normal people" did but broke down crying at the smallest impediment to a perfect job. . . . Months passed, and Beatrice's problem became more serious. Some days she was too upset to go to work. She stopped seeing her friends. She spent most of her time at home either yelling or crying. Finally, Beatrice's husband called the psychiatrist and insisted that something was seriously wrong.

Lickey & Gordon, 1991, p. 181

Most people's moods come and go. Their feelings of elation or sadness are understandable reactions to daily events and do not affect their lives greatly. The moods of people with mood disorders, in contrast, tend to last a long time. As in Beatrice's case, the mood colors all of their interactions with the world and interferes with normal functioning.

Depression and mania are the key emotions in mood disorders. **Depression** is a low, sad state in which life seems dark and its challenges overwhelming. **Mania,** the opposite of depression, is a state of breathless euphoria, or at least frenzied energy, in which people may have an exaggerated belief that the world is theirs for the taking. Most people with a mood disorder suffer only from depression, a pattern called **unipolar depression.** They have no history of mania and return to a normal or nearly normal mood when their depression lifts. Others experience periods of mania that alternate with periods of depression, a pattern called **bipolar disorder.** You might logically expect a third pattern of mood disorder, *unipolar mania,* in which people suffer from mania only, but this pattern is uncommon (APA, 2000).

Mood disorders have always captured people's interest, in part because so many famous people have suffered from them. The Bible speaks of the severe depressions of Nebuchadnezzar, Saul, and Moses. Queen Victoria of England and Abraham Lincoln seem to have experienced recurring depressions. Mood disorders also have plagued such writers as Ernest Hemingway, Eugene O'Neill, Virginia Woolf, and Sylvia Plath. Their mood problems have been shared by millions, and today the economic costs (work loss, treatment, hospitalization) amount to more than $80 billion each year (Sullivan et al., 2004; Greenberg et al., 2003). Of course, the human suffering that the disorders cause is beyond calculation.

•**depression**•A low, sad state marked by significant levels of sadness, lack of energy, low self-worth, guilt, or related symptoms.

•**mania**•A state or episode of euphoria or frenzied activity in which people may have an exaggerated belief that the world is theirs for the taking.

•**unipolar depression**•Depression without a history of mania.

•**bipolar disorder**•A disorder marked by alternating or intermixed periods of mania and depression.

⚙Unipolar Depression

Whenever we feel particularly unhappy, we are likely to describe ourselves as "depressed." In all likelihood, we are merely responding to sad events, fatigue, or unhappy thoughts (see *The Media Speaks* on page 245). This loose use of the term confuses a perfectly normal mood swing with a clinical syndrome. All of us experience dejection from time to time, but only some experience unipolar depression.

Normal dejection is seldom severe enough to influence daily functioning significantly or persist very long. Such downturns in mood can even be beneficial. Periods spent in contemplation can lead us to explore our inner selves, our values, and our way of life, and we often emerge with a sense of greater strength, clarity, and resolve.

Clinical depression, on the other hand, has no redeeming characteristics. It brings severe and long-lasting psychological pain that may intensify as time goes by. Those who suffer from it may lose their will to carry out the simplest of life's activities; some even lose their will to live.

How Common Is Unipolar Depression?

Almost 7 percent of adults in the United States suffer from a severe unipolar pattern of depression in any given year, while as many as 5 percent suffer from mild forms (Taube-Schiff & Lau, 2008; Kessler et al., 2005). Around 17 percent of all adults experience an episode of severe unipolar depression at some point in their lives. These prevalence rates are similar in Canada, England, France, and many other countries (Vasiliadis et al., 2007; WHO, 2004) (see Table 8-1).

People of any age may suffer from unipolar depression. In most countries, however, people in their forties are more likely than those in any other age group to have the disorder (Blanchflower & Oswald, 2007). The median age for its onset, now 34 in the United States, keeps dropping for each generation, and worldwide research projects suggest that the risk of experiencing this problem has increased steadily since 1915 (Drevets & Todd, 2005; Weissman et al., 1992, 1991).

Women are at least twice as likely as men to experience episodes of severe unipolar depression (Taube-Schiff & Lau, 2008; McSweeney, 2004). As many as 26 percent of women may have an episode at some time in their lives, compared with 12 percent of men. As you will see in Chapter 17, among children the prevalence of unipolar depression is similar for girls and boys (Avenevoli et al., 2008). All of these rates hold steady across the various socioeconomic classes and ethnic groups.

Approximately half of the people with unipolar depression recover within six weeks and 90 percent recover within a year, some without treatment (Kessler, 2002; Kendler et al., 1997). However, most of them have at least one other episode of depression later in their lives (Taube-Schiff & Lau, 2008).

What Are the Symptoms of Depression?

The picture of depression may vary from person to person. Earlier you saw how Beatrice's indecisiveness, uncontrollable sobbing, and feelings of despair, anger, and worthlessness brought her job and social life to a standstill. Other depressed people have symptoms that are less severe. They manage to function, although their depression typically robs them of much effectiveness or pleasure, as you can see in the case of Derek:

table: 8-1

Across the World: What Percentage of Adults Suffer from Mood Disorders Each Year?

United States	9.6%
France	8.5%
Colombia	6.8%
Lebanon	6.6%
Spain	4.9%
Mexico	4.8%
Italy	3.8%
Germany	3.6%
Japan	3.1%

Note: Mood disorders considered are major depressive disorder, dysthymic disorder, and bipolar disorder.
Source: WHO, 2004.

Derek has probably suffered from depression all of his adult life but was unaware of it for many years. Derek called himself a night person, claiming that he could not think clearly until after noon even though he was often awake by 4:00 A.M. He tried to schedule his work as editorial writer for a small town newspaper so that it was compatible with his depressed mood at the beginning of the day. Therefore, he scheduled meetings for the mornings; talking with people got him moving. He saved writing and decision making for later in the day.

. . . Derek's private thoughts were rarely cheerful and self-confident. He felt that his marriage was a mere business partnership. He provided the money, and she provided a home and children. Derek and his wife rarely expressed affection for each other. Occasionally, he had images of his own violent death in a bicycle crash, in a plane crash, or in a murder by an unidentified assailant.

Derek felt that he was constantly on the edge of job failure. He was disappointed that his editorials had not attracted the attention of larger papers. He was certain that several of the younger people on the paper had better ideas and wrote more skillfully than he did. He scolded himself for a bad editorial that he had written ten years earlier. Although that particular piece had not been up to his usual standards, everyone else on the paper had forgotten it a week after it appeared. But ten years later, Derek was still ruminating over that one editorial. . . .

Derek brushed off his morning confusion as a lack of quick intelligence. He had no way to know that it was a symptom of depression. He never realized that his death images might be suicidal thinking. People do not talk about such things. For all Derek knew, everyone had similar thoughts.

(Lickey & Gordon, 1991, pp. 183–185)

As the cases of Beatrice and Derek indicate, depression has many symptoms other than sadness. The symptoms, which often exacerbate one another, span five areas of functioning: emotional, motivational, behavioral, cognitive, and physical.

Emotional Symptoms Most people who are depressed feel sad and dejected. They describe themselves as feeling "miserable," "empty," and "humiliated." They tend to lose their sense of humor, report getting little pleasure from anything, and in some cases display *anhedonia,* an inability to experience any pleasure at all. A number also experience anxiety, anger, or agitation. This sea of misery may lead to crying spells. A successful writer and editor describes the agony she experienced each morning as her depression was unfolding:

Nights I could handle. I fell asleep easily, and sleep allowed me to forget. But my mornings were unmanageable. To wake up each morning was to remember once again that the world by which I defined myself was no more. Soon after opening my eyes, the crying bouts would start and I'd sit alone for hours, weeping and mourning my losses.

(Williams, 2008, p. 9)

Motivational Symptoms Depressed people typically lose the desire to pursue their usual activities. Almost all report a lack of drive, initiative, and spontaneity. They may have to force themselves to go to work, talk with friends, eat meals, or have sex. This state has been described as a "paralysis of will" (Beck, 1967). Terrie Williams, author of *Black Pain,* a book about depression in African Americans, describes her social withdrawal during a depressive episode:

I woke up one morning with a knot of fear in my stomach so crippling that I couldn't face light, much less day, and so intense that I stayed in bed for three days with the shades drawn and the lights out.

Three days. Three days not answering the phone. Three days not checking my e-mail. I was disconnected completely from the outside world, and I didn't care. Then on the

*morning of the fourth day there was a knock on my door. Since I hadn't ordered food I ig-
nored it. The knocking kept up and I kept ignoring it. I heard the sound of keys rattling in
my front door. Slowly the bedroom door opened and in the painful light from the doorway I
saw the figures of two old friends. "Terrie, are you in there?"*

(Williams, 2008, p. xxiv)

Suicide represents the ultimate escape from life's challenges. As you will see in Chapter 10, many depressed people become uninterested in life or wish to die; others wish they could kill themselves, and some actually do. It has been estimated that between 6 and 15 percent of people who suffer from severe depression commit suicide (Taube-Schiff & Lau, 2008; Stolberg et al., 2002).

Behavioral Symptoms Depressed people are usually less active and less productive. They spend more time alone and may stay in bed for long periods. One man recalls, "I'd awaken early, but I'd just lie there—what was the use of getting up to a miserable day?" (Kraines & Thetford, 1972, p. 21). Depressed people may also move and even speak more slowly (Joiner, 2002).

Dear diary, Sorry to bother you again.

LOW SELF-ESTEEM

Cognitive Symptoms Depressed people hold extremely negative views of themselves. They consider themselves inadequate, undesirable, inferior, perhaps evil. They also blame themselves for nearly every unfortunate event, even things that have nothing to do with them, and they rarely credit themselves for positive achievements.

Another cognitive symptom of depression is pessimism. Sufferers are usually convinced that nothing will ever improve, and they feel helpless to change any aspect of their lives. Because they expect the worst, they are likely to procrastinate. Their sense of hopelessness and helplessness makes them especially vulnerable to suicidal thinking (Taube-Schiff & Lau, 2008).

People with depression frequently complain that their intellectual ability is poor. They feel confused, unable to remember things, easily distracted, and unable to solve even the smallest problems. In laboratory studies, depressed individuals do perform more poorly than nondepressed persons on some tasks of memory, attention, and reasoning (Bremner et al., 2004). It may be, however, that these difficulties sometimes reflect motivational problems rather than cognitive ones.

Physical Symptoms People who are depressed frequently have such physical ailments as headaches, indigestion, constipation, dizzy spells, and general pain (Fishbain, 2000). In fact, many depressions are misdiagnosed as medical problems at first. Disturbances in appetite and sleep are particularly common (Neckelmann et al., 2007; Genchi et al., 2004). Most depressed people eat less, sleep less, and feel more fatigued than they did prior to the disorder. Some, however, eat and sleep excessively. Terrie Williams describes the changes in the pattern of her sleep:

*At first I didn't notice the change. Then things got worse. I always hated waking up, but
slowly it was turning into something deeper; it was less like I didn't want to wake up, and
more like I couldn't. I didn't feel tired, but I had no energy. I didn't feel sleepy, but I would
have welcomed sleep with open arms. I had the sensation of a huge weight, invisible but
gigantic, pressing down on me, almost crushing me into the bed and pinning me there.*

(Williams, 2008, p. xxii)

HOME | SEND | EXPLORE

SEARCH

The Crying Game: Male vs. Female Tears

BY JOCELYN NOVECK, THE ASSOCIATED PRESS, OCTOBER 24, 2007

"Please, please, please, just give the dog back," Ellen DeGeneres wept on national TV last week. It was a moment that quickly established itself in the pop-culture firmament, less for the plight of Iggy the adopted terrier than for the copious crying itself.

(To recap: DeGeneres had adopted Iggy from a rescue organization, then given it to her hairdresser's family when the dog didn't get along with her cats. That was against the rules, and the rescue group took the dog back.)

Setting aside the question of whether those sobs were 100 percent genuine, tears are a natural human response, and public figures are obviously not immune. But some who study this most basic expression of feeling will tell you that in this day and age, it can be easier for a crying man to be taken seriously than a crying woman.

In politics, it's a far cry from 1972, when Sen. Ed Muskie's presidential campaign was derailed by what were perceived to be tears in response to a newspaper attack on his wife. But decades later, an occasional Clintonesque tear is seen as a positive thing. Bill Clinton, that is.

"Bill could cry, and did, but Hillary can't," says Tom Lutz, a professor at the University of California, Riverside, who authored an exhaustive history of crying. The same tearful response that would be seen as sensitivity in Bill could be seen as a lack of control in his wife.

But there are additional rules for acceptable public crying. "We're talking about dropping a tear," Lutz notes, "no more than a tear or two." And it all depends on the perceived seriousness of the subject matter. Thus Jon Stewart or David Letterman could choke up with impunity just after Sept. 11. But a dog-adoption problem is another matter.

In a recently published study at Penn State, researchers sought to explore differing perceptions of crying in men and women, presenting their 284 subjects with a series of hypothetical vignettes. Reactions depended on the type of crying, and who was doing it. A moist eye was viewed much more positively than open crying, and males got the most positive responses.

"Women are not making it up when they say they're damned if they do, damned if they don't," said Stephanie Shields, the psychology professor who conducted the study. "If you don't express any emotion, you're seen as not human, like Mr. Spock on 'Star Trek,' " she said. "But too much crying, or the wrong kind, and you're labeled as overemotional, out of control and possibly irrational."

That comes as no surprise to Suzyn Waldman, a broadcaster of Yankee games on New York's WCBS Radio. Earlier this month, she choked up on live radio after the Yankees had just been eliminated from the playoffs. She was describing the scene as manager Joe Torre's coaches choked up themselves, watching him at the podium and foreseeing the end of an era. Her tearful report quickly became an Internet hit, and she was mocked far and wide, especially on radio. . . . "When men express anger they gain status, but when women express anger they lose status," Yale social psychologist Victoria Brescoll . . . said in an interview. . . .

For a little historical perspective, says Lutz, author of "Crying: The Natural and Cultural History of Tears," it's helpful to look back to the 19th century, when skillful politicians like Abraham Lincoln used tears as a natural part of their oratory.

The tide later shifted against male crying, but in the past 30 to 40 years male crying has gained in acceptability. "Every president since Ronald Reagan has used tears at some point," says Shields, the Penn State psychologist. . . . Military figures have cried at critical moments. Gen. Norman Schwarzkopf cried at a Christmas Eve ceremony in front of his troops, and when interviewed by Barbara Walters, Lutz notes. . . .

But in DeGeneres' case, along with the strong support from fans and many dog lovers, she also endured some criticism and mockery. . . .

Columbia/The Kobal Collection/Louis Goldman

"There's no crying in baseball!" In the 1992 film *A League of Their Own*, the cranky manager of a women's professional baseball team (Tom Hanks) and one of his players (Madonna) go at each other, leading to one of filmdom's most famous lines, "There's no crying in baseball." Apparently, when it comes to crying, the double standard between the sexes has continued to grow and expand in the twenty-first century.

•**major depressive disorder**•A severe pattern of depression that is disabling and is not caused by such factors as drugs or a general medical condition.

•**dysthymic disorder**•A mood disorder that is similar to but longer-lasting and less disabling than a major depressive disorder.

Diagnosing Unipolar Depression

According to DSM-IV-TR, a *major depressive episode* is a period marked by at least five symptoms of depression and lasting for two weeks or more (see Table 8-2). In extreme cases, the episode may include psychotic symptoms, ones marked by a loss of contact with reality, such as *delusions*—bizarre ideas without foundation—or *hallucinations*—perceptions of things that are not actually present. A depressed man with psychotic symptoms may imagine that he can't eat "because my intestines are deteriorating and will soon stop working," or he may believe that he sees his dead wife.

People who experience a major depressive episode without having any history of mania receive a diagnosis of **major depressive disorder.** The disorder may be additionally categorized as *recurrent* if it has been preceded by previous episodes; *seasonal* if it changes with the seasons (for example, if the depression recurs each winter); *catatonic* if it is marked by either immobility or excessive activity; *postpartum* if it occurs within four weeks of giving birth (see *Psych Watch* on page 248); or *melancholic* if the person is almost totally unaffected by pleasurable events (APA, 2000). It sometimes turns out that an apparent case of major depressive disorder is, in fact, a depressive episode occurring within a larger pattern of bipolar disorder—a pattern in which the individual's manic episode has not yet appeared. When the person experiences a manic episode at a later time, the diagnosis is changed to bipolar disorder (Angst et al., 2005; Bowden, 2005).

People who display a longer-lasting (at least two years) but less disabling pattern of unipolar depression may receive a diagnosis of **dysthymic disorder.** When dysthymic disorder leads to major depressive disorder, the sequence is called *double depression* (Taube-Schiff & Lau, 2008; Dunner, 2005).

table: 8-2

DSM Checklist

MAJOR DEPRESSIVE EPISODE
1. The presence of at least five of the following symptoms during the same two-week period: • depressed mood most of the day, nearly every day • markedly diminished interest or pleasure in almost all activities most of the day, nearly every day • significant weight loss or weight gain, or decrease or increase in appetite nearly every day • insomnia or hypersomnia nearly every day • psychomotor agitation or retardation nearly every day • fatigue or loss of energy nearly every day • feelings of worthlessness or excessive guilt nearly every day • reduced ability to think or concentrate, or indecisiveness, nearly every day • recurrent thoughts of death or suicide, a suicide attempt, or a specific plan for committing suicide.
2. Significant distress or impairment.

MAJOR DEPRESSIVE DISORDER
1. The presence of a major depressive episode.
2. No history of a manic or hypomanic episode.

DYSTHYMIC DISORDER
1. Depressed mood for most of the day, for more days than not, for at least two years.
2. Presence, while depressed, of at least two of the following: • poor appetite or overeating • insomnia or hypersomnia • low energy or fatigue • low self-esteem • poor concentration or difficulty making decisions • feelings of hopelessness.
3. During the two-year period, symptoms not absent for more than two months at a time.
4. No history of a manic or hypomanic episode.
5. Significant distress or impairment.

Based on APA, 2000.

BETWEEN THE LINES

World Count

Around 122,865,000 new cases of mood disorder emerge each year worldwide (World Health Organization, 2008). ‹‹

❖ What Causes Unipolar Depression?

Episodes of unipolar depression often seem to be triggered by stressful events (Henn & Vollmayr, 2005; Paykel, 2003). In fact, researchers have found that depressed people experience a greater number of stressful life events during the month just before the onset of their disorder than do other people during the same period of time (Kendler et al., 2004, 1999; Monroe & Hadjiyannakis, 2002). Of course, stressful life events also precede other psychological disorders, but depressed people report more such events than anybody else.

Some clinicians consider it important to distinguish a *reactive (exogenous) depression,* which follows clear-cut stressful events, from an *endogenous depression,* which seems to be a response to internal factors (Kessing, 2004). But can one ever know for certain whether a depression is reactive or not? Even if stressful events occurred before the onset of depression, that depression may not be reactive. The events could actually be a coincidence (Paykel, 2003). Thus, today's clinicians usually concentrate on recognizing both the situational and the internal aspects of any given case of unipolar depression.

The current explanations of unipolar depression point to biological, psychological, and sociocultural factors. Just as clinicians now recognize both internal and situational features in each case of depression, many believe that the various explanations should be viewed collectively for unipolar depression to be understood fully.

The Biological View

Medical researchers have been aware for years that certain diseases and drugs produce mood changes. Could unipolar depression itself have biological causes? Evidence from genetic, biochemical, and anatomical studies suggests that often it does.

Genetic Factors Four kinds of research—family pedigree, twin, adoption, and molecular biology gene studies—suggest that some people inherit a predisposition to unipolar depression. *Family pedigree studies* select people with unipolar depression as *probands* (the proband is the person who is the focus of a genetic study), examine their relatives, and see whether depression also afflicts other members of the family. If a predisposition to unipolar depression is inherited, a proband's relatives should have a higher rate of depression than the population at large. Researchers have in fact found that as many as 20 percent of those relatives are depressed (see Table 8-3), compared with fewer than 10 percent of the general population (Taube-Schiff & Lau, 2008; Berrettini, 2006).

If a predisposition to unipolar depression is inherited, you might also expect to find a particularly large number of cases among the close relatives of a proband. *Twin*

BETWEEN THE LINES

Overdiagnosis?

In 1999, a reporter asked two psychiatrists to diagnose Willy Loman, the beleaguered character in Arthur Miller's famous play *Death of a Salesman.* Both concluded that he suffers from clinical depression. Appalled, Miller said, "Loman is not a depressive. . . . He is weighed down by life. There are several reasons for why he is where he is" (Begley, 2008). ‹‹

table: **8-3**

Mood Disorders Profile

	One-year Prevalence (Percent)	Female to Male Ratio	Typical Age at Onset (Years)	Prevalence among First-Degree Relatives	Percentage Currently Receiving Treatment
Major depressive disorder	7.0%	2:1	24–29	Elevated	32.9%
Dysthymic disorder	1.5–5.0%	Between 3:2 and 2:1	10–25	Elevated	36.8%
Bipolar I disorder	1.6%	1:6	15–44	Elevated	33.8%
Bipolar II disorder	1.0%	1:1	15–44	Elevated	33.8%
Cyclothymic disorder	0.4%	1:1	15–25	Elevated	Unknown

Source: Taube-Schiff & Lau, 2008; Kessler et al., 2005, 1994; APA, 2000, 1994; Regier et al., 1993; Weissman et al., 1991.

PSYCH WATCH

Sadness at the Happiest of Times

Women usually expect the birth of a child to be a happy experience. But for 10 to 30 percent of new mothers, the weeks and months after childbirth bring clinical depression (Rubertsson et al., 2005; Grace et al., 2003; O'Hara, 2003). Postpartum depression typically begins within four weeks after the birth of a child (APA, 2000), and it is far more severe than simple "baby blues." It is also different from other postpartum syndromes such as *postpartum psychosis,* a problem that will be examined in Chapter 14.

The "baby blues" are so common—as many as 80 percent of women experience them—that most researchers consider them normal. As new mothers try to cope with the wakeful nights, rattled emotions, and other stresses that accompany the arrival of a new baby, they may experience crying spells, fatigue, anxiety, insomnia, and sadness. These symptoms usually disappear within days or weeks (Horowitz et al., 2005, 1995; Najman et al., 2000).

In postpartum depression, however, depressive symptoms continue and may last up to a year. The symptoms include extreme sadness, despair, tearfulness, insomnia, anxiety, intrusive thoughts, compulsions, panic attacks, feelings of inability to cope, and suicidal thoughts (Lindahl et al., 2005; Stevens et al., 2002). The mother-infant relationship and the health of the child may suffer as a result (Monti et al., 2004; Weinberg et al., 2001). Women who experience postpartum depression have a 25 to 50 percent chance of developing it again with a subsequent birth (Stevens et al., 2002; Wisner et al., 2001).

Many clinicians believe that the hormonal changes accompanying childbirth trigger postpartum depression. All women experience a kind of hormone "withdrawal" after delivery, as estrogen and progesterone levels, which rise as much as 50 times above normal during pregnancy, now drop sharply to levels far below normal (Horowitz et al., 2005, 1995). The levels of thyroid hormones, prolactin, and cortisol also change (Abou-Saleh et al., 1999). Perhaps some women are particularly influenced by these dramatic hormone changes. Still other theorists suggest a genetic predisposition to postpartum depression. A woman with a family history of mood disorders appears to be at high risk, even if she herself has not previously had a mood disorder (APA, 2000; Steiner & Tam, 1999).

At the same time, psychological and sociocultural factors may play important roles in the disorder. The birth of a baby brings enormous psychological and social change (Gjerdingen & Center, 2005; Nicolson, 1999). A woman typically faces changes in her marital relationship, daily routines, and social roles. Sleep and relaxation are likely to decrease, and financial pressures may increase. Perhaps she feels the added stress of giving up a career—or of trying to maintain one. This pileup of stress may heighten the risk of depression (Horowitz et al., 2005; Swendsen & Mazure, 2000; Terry et al., 1996). Mothers whose infants are sick or temperamentally "difficult" may experience yet additional pressure.

Fortunately, treatment can make a big difference for most women with postpartum depression. Self-help support groups have proved extremely helpful for many women with the disorder (O'Hara, 2003; Stevens et al., 2002; Honikman, 1999). In addition, many respond well to the same approaches that are applied to other forms of depression—antidepressant medications, cognitive therapy, interpersonal psychotherapy, or a combination of these approaches (O'Hara, 2003; Stuart et al., 2003).

However, many women who would benefit from treatment do not seek help because they feel ashamed about being sad at a time that is supposed to be joyous and are concerned about being judged harshly (APA, 2000). For them, and for the spouses and family members close to them, a large dose of education is in order. Even positive events, such as the birth of a child, can be stressful if they also bring major change to one's life. Recognizing and addressing such feelings are in everyone's best interest.

Dancing away depression Performer Marie Osmond, dancing here with professional partner Jonathan Roberts on the show *Dancing with the Stars,* recently revealed that she suffered from postpartum depression after giving birth in 1999. With support and treatment, she was able to overcome this disorder, continue raising her eight children, and resume her career, including advancing to the semifinal round of the popular dance show and contest in 2007 at the age of 48.

AP Photo/ABC Inc., Carol Kaelson

studies have supported this expectation (Richard & Lyness, 2006; Kalidindi & McGuffin, 2003). One study looked at nearly 200 pairs of twins. When a monozygotic (identical) twin had unipolar depression, there was a 46 percent chance that the other twin would have the same disorder. In contrast, when a dizygotic (fraternal) twin had unipolar depression, the other twin had only a 20 percent chance of developing the disorder (McGuffin et al., 1996).

Adoption studies have also implicated a genetic factor, at least in cases of severe unipolar depression. One study looked at the families of adopted persons who had been hospitalized for this disorder in Denmark. The biological parents of these adoptees turned out to have a higher incidence of severe depression (but not mild depression) than did the biological parents of a control group of nondepressed adoptees (Wender et al., 1986). Some theorists interpret these findings to mean that severe depression is more likely than mild depression to be caused by genetic factors.

Finally, today's scientists have at their disposal techniques from the field of molecular biology to help them directly identify genes and determine whether certain gene abnormalities are related to depression. Using such techniques, researchers have found evidence that unipolar depression may be tied to genes on chromosomes 1, 4, 9, 10, 11, 12, 13, 14, 17, 18, 20, 21, 22, and X (Carlson, 2008). For example, a number of researchers have found that individuals who are depressed often have an abnormality of their *5-HTT* gene, a gene located on chromosome 17. This gene is responsible for the brain's production of *serotonin transporters,* or *5-HTTs,* proteins that help the neurotransmitter serotonin carry messages from one neuron to another (Hecimovic & Gilliam, 2006). As you will read in the next section, low activity of serotonin is closely tied to depression (Brody et al., 2005; Murphy et al., 2004). People with an abnormality of the serotonin transporter gene are more likely than others to display low serotonin activity in their brains and may in turn be more prone to experience depression.

Biochemical Factors Low activity of two neurotransmitter chemicals, **norepinephrine** and **serotonin,** has been strongly linked to unipolar depression. In the 1950s, several pieces of evidence began to point to this relationship (Carlson, 2008). First, medical researchers discovered that *reserpine* and other medications for high blood pressure often caused depression (Ayd, 1956). As it turned out, some of these medications lowered norepinephrine activity and others lowered serotonin. A second piece of evidence was the discovery of the first truly effective antidepressant drugs. Although these drugs were discovered by accident, researchers soon learned that they relieve depression by increasing either norepinephrine or serotonin activity.

For years it was thought that low activity of *either* norepinephrine or serotonin was capable of producing depression, but investigators now believe that their relation to depression is more complicated (Carlson, 2008; Drevets & Todd, 2005). Research suggests that interactions between serotonin and norepinephrine activity, or between these neurotransmitters and other kinds of neurotransmitters in the brain, rather than the operation of any one neurotransmitter alone, may account for unipolar depression. Some studies hint, for example, that depressed people have an overall imbalance in the activity of the neurotransmitters serotonin, norepinephrine, dopamine, and acetylcholine (Thase et al., 2002). In a variation of this theory, some researchers believe that serotonin is actually a *neuromodulator,* a chemical whose primary function is to increase or decrease the activity of other key neurotransmitters. If so, perhaps low serotonin activity serves to disrupt the activity of the other neurotransmitters, resulting in depression.

Biological researchers have also learned that the body's *endocrine system* may play a role in unipolar depression. As you have seen, endocrine glands throughout the body release *hormones,* chemicals that in turn spur body organs into action (see Chapter 6). People with unipolar depression have been found to have abnormally high levels of

George P. A. Healy, 1887, The National Portrait Gallery, Smithsonian Institution

Lincoln's private war
In 1841 Abraham Lincoln wrote to a friend, "I am now the most miserable man living. If what I feel were equally distributed to the whole human family, there would be not one cheerful face on earth."

•**norepinephrine**•A neurotransmitter whose abnormal activity is linked to depression and panic disorder.

•**serotonin**•A neurotransmitter whose abnormal activity is linked to depression, obsessive-compulsive disorder, and eating disorders.

cortisol, one of the hormones released by the adrenal glands during times of stress (Neumeister et al., 2005). This relationship is not all that surprising, given that stressful events often seem to trigger depression. Another hormone that has been tied to depression is *melatonin,* sometimes called the "Dracula hormone" because it is released only in the dark (see *A Closer Look* on pages 252–253).

Still other biological researchers are starting to believe that unipolar depression is tied more closely to what happens *within* neurons than to the chemicals that carry messages between neurons (Julien, 2008). They believe that activity by key neurotransmitters or hormones ultimately leads to deficiencies of certain proteins and other chemicals within neurons, particularly to deficiencies of *brain-derived neurotrophic factor (BDNF),* a chemical that promotes the growth and survival of neurons (Higgins & George, 2007; Duman, 2004; Wallace et al., 2004). Such deficiencies within neurons may impair the health of the neurons and lead, in turn, to depression.

The biochemical explanations of unipolar depression have produced much enthusiasm, but research in this area has certain limitations. Some of it has relied on *analogue studies,* which create depression-like symptoms in laboratory animals. Researchers cannot be certain that these symptoms do in fact reflect the human disorder. Similarly, until recent years, technology was limited, and studies of human depression had to measure brain biochemical activity indirectly. As a result, investigators could never be certain of the biochemical events that were occurring in the brain. Current studies using newer technology, such as PET and MRI scans, are helping to eliminate such uncertainties about such brain activity.

Brain Anatomy and Brain Circuits In Chapter 5, you read that many biological researchers now believe that the root of psychological disorders is more complicated than a single neurotransmitter or single brain area (see pages 146–147). They have determined that emotional reactions of various kinds are tied to brain *circuits*—networks of brain structures that work together, triggering each other into action and producing a particular kind of emotional reaction. It appears that one brain circuit is tied largely to generalized anxiety disorder, another to panic disorder, and yet another to obsessive-compulsive disorder. Although research is far from complete, a brain circuit responsible for unipolar depression has also begun to emerge (Insel, 2007). An array of brain-imaging studies point to several brain areas that are likely members of this circuit, particularly the *prefrontal cortex,* the *hippocampus,* the *amygdala,* and *Brodmann Area 25,* an area located just under the brain part called the *cingulate cortex* (see Figure 8-1).

The *prefrontal cortex* is located within the frontal cortex of the brain. Because it receives information from a number of other brain areas, the prefrontal cortex is involved in many important functions, including mood, attention, and immune functioning (Lambert & Kinsley, 2005). Several imaging studies have found lower activity and blood flow in the prefrontal cortex of depressed research participants than in the prefrontal cortex of nondepressed individuals (Lambert & Kinsley, 2005; Rajkowska, 2000). However, other studies, focusing on select areas of the prefrontal cortex, have found increases in activity during depression (Carlson, 2008; Drevets, 2001, 2000). Correspondingly, research finds that the prefrontal cortex activity of depressed individuals increases after successful treatment by some antidepressant drugs, but decreases after successful treatment by other kinds of antidepressant drugs (Cook & Leuchter, 2001). Given these varied findings, researchers currently believe that the prefrontal cortex plays a critical role in depression but that the specific nature of this role has yet to be clearly defined (Higgins & George, 2007; Goldapple et al., 2004).

The prefrontal cortex has strong neural connections with another part of the depression brain circuit, the *hippocampus.* Indeed, messages are both sent and received between the two brain areas. The hippocampus is one of the few brain areas to produce new neurons throughout adulthood, an

Figure 8-1
The biology of depression Researchers believe that the brain circuit involved in unipolar depression includes the prefrontal cortex, hippocampus, amygdala, and Brodmann Area 25.

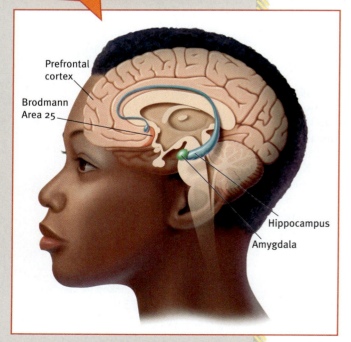

Prefrontal cortex

Brodmann Area 25

Hippocampus

Amygdala

activity known as *neurogenesis* (Carlson, 2008). Several studies indicate that such hippocampal neurogenesis decreases dramatically when individuals become depressed (Airan et al., 2007; Sapolsky, 2004, 2000). Correspondingly, when depressed individuals are successfully treated by antidepressant drugs, neurogenesis in the hippocampus returns to normal (Malberg & Schechter, 2005; Duman, 2004). Moreover, some imaging studies have detected a reduction in the size of the hippocampus among depressed persons (Campbell et al., 2004; Frodl et al., 2004). Recall from Chapter 6 that the hippocampus helps to control the brain's and body's reactions to stress and plays a role in the formation and recall of emotional memories. Thus, its role in depression is not surprising.

You may also recall from Chapters 5 and 6 that the *amygdala* is a brain area that repeatedly seems to be involved in the expression of negative emotions and memories. It has been found to be a key area in each of the brain circuits tied to generalized anxiety disorder, panic disorder, and posttraumatic stress disorder. Apparently, it also plays a role in depression. PET and fMRI scans indicate that activity and blood flow in the amygdala is 50 percent greater among depressed persons than nondepressed persons (Drevets, 2001; Links et al., 1996; Drevets et al., 1992). In fact, one study suggests that as a patient's depression increases in severity, the activity in his or her amygdala increases proportionately (Abercrombie et al., 1998). Moreover, among nondepressed research participants, activity in the amygdala increases as they are looking at pictures of sad faces; and among depressed participants, amygdala activity increases when they recall sad moments in their lives (Carlson, 2008; Liotti et al., 2002; Drevets, 2000).

The fourth part of the depression brain circuit, *Brodmann Area 25,* has received enormous attention in recent years (Insel, 2007; Mayberg, 2006, 2003; Mayberg et al., 2005, 2000, 1997; Drevets et al., 1997). This area, located just under the cingulate cortex, tends to be smaller in depressed people than nondepressed people. Moreover, like the amygdala, it is significantly more active among depressed people than among nondepressed people. In fact, brain scans reveal that when a person's depression subsides, the activity in his or her Area 25 decreases significantly. Because activation of Area 25 comes and goes with episodes of depression, some theorists believe that it may in fact be a "depression switch," a kind of junction box whose malfunction might be necessary and sufficient for depression to occur.

Area 25 is also of interest to depression researchers because this brain area is filled with serotonin transporters, or 5-HTTs, those proteins that help serotonin to carry messages from one neuron to another. Earlier you read that people with an abnormal 5-HTT gene are more prone to develop depression. It turns out that such individuals typically have a smaller and more active Area 25 than other people (Pezawas et al., 2005).

Psychological Views

The psychological models that have been most widely applied to unipolar depression are the psychodynamic, behavioral, and cognitive models. The psychodynamic explanation has not been strongly supported by research, and the behavioral view has received only modest support. In contrast, cognitive explanations have received considerable research support and have gained a large following.

The Psychodynamic View Sigmund Freud (1917) and his student Karl Abraham (1916, 1911) developed the first psychodynamic explanation of depression. They began by noting the similarity between clinical depression and grief in people who lose loved ones: constant weeping, loss of appetite, difficulty sleeping, loss of pleasure in life, and general withdrawal.

According to Freud and Abraham, a series of unconscious processes is set in motion when a loved one dies. Unable to accept the loss, mourners at first regress to the *oral stage* of development, the period of total dependency when infants cannot distinguish themselves from their parents. By

Early loss The young daughter of a policewoman killed during the September 11, 2001, terrorist attacks stands onstage holding her father's hand while the names of attack victims are read during ceremonies at Ground Zero marking the fifth anniversary of the event. Research has found that individuals who lose their parents as children have an increased likelihood of experiencing depression as adults.

The Rhythms of Depression

Our lives are structured by cycles and rhythms—daily, monthly, seasonal, and yearly. The 24-hour day provides the cycle to which we adapt our most common activities—sleeping, eating, working, and socializing. Although our daily rhythms are affected by our environment, they are also driven by a kind of internal clock consisting of recurrent biological fluctuations, called *circadian rhythms,* which must be coordinated with one another and with changes in the environment (Loros et al., 2004).

One of these circadian rhythms is strong and consistent, and it rigidly controls regular changes in body temperature, hormone secretions, and *rapid eye movement* (*REM*) sleep—the near-awake phase of sleep during which we dream.

Another, more flexible rhythm controls the sleep-wake cycle and activity-rest cycle. Most people can go to sleep late one night and early the next and have no trouble falling asleep quickly and sleeping soundly; but during this period their body temperature will rigidly follow its usual pattern,

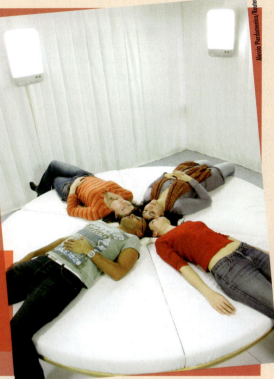

The Light Lounge These visitors to the Science Museum in London make themselves comfortable in the Light Lounge, a white enclosure containing four light boxes where individuals can relax and have light therapy to help beat the winter blues.

peaking at the same time each afternoon and bottoming out each morning.

Sleep and Depression

A series of revealing studies begun in the 1980s suggests that depression is often the result of an imbalance, or *desynchronization,* between the body's circadian rhythms and the rhythms of the environment (Bunney & Bunney, 2000). For example, the sleep cycle, the most basic rhythm in our lives, apparently is reversed in depressed people (Garrett, 2008; Thase et al., 2002). They move into REM sleep more quickly than nondepressed people after falling asleep, experience longer stretches of REM sleep during the early parts of the sleep cycle and shorter stretches toward the morning, display more frequent rapid eye movements during REM sleep, and enjoy less deep sleep overall (Taube-Schiff & Lau, 2008; Wichniak et al., 2000). Thus some theorists think that the body's circadian rhythms, the rigid one that is in control of REM sleep and the flexible one in control of the sleep-wake cycle, may be out of harmony for depressed people.

If the sleep-wake cycle is disturbed for depressed people, and if their body rhythms are indeed out of harmony,

regressing to this stage, the mourners merge their own identity with that of the person they have lost, and so symbolically regain the lost person. In this process, called *introjection,* they direct all their feelings for the loved one, including sadness and anger, toward themselves.

For most mourners, introjection is temporary. For some, however, grief worsens over time. They feel empty, they continue to avoid social relationships, and their sense of loss increases. They become depressed. Freud and Abraham believed that two kinds of people are particularly likely to become clinically depressed in the face of loss: those whose parents failed to nurture them and meet their needs during the oral stage and those whose parents gratified those needs excessively. Infants whose needs are inadequately met remain overly dependent on others throughout their lives, feel unworthy of love, and have low self-esteem. Those whose needs are excessively gratified find the oral stage so pleasant that they resist moving on to subsequent stages. Either way, the individuals may devote their lives to others, desperately searching for love and approval.

might it not be helpful to change their sleep patterns? This is, in fact, a strategy sometimes used on depressed people who do not respond to more conventional forms of treatment. In a number of sleep laboratories, clinicians have deprived depressed patients of partial or full episodes of sleep. Their findings? The moods and functioning of many such patients improve markedly (Garrett, 2008; Danilenko & Putilov, 2005).

Putting a Good Light on Depression

The hormone *melatonin* plays a major role in the operation of our circadian rhythms. For animals and humans alike, this hormone is released by the brain's *pineal gland* when environmental surroundings are dark, but not when they are light. In animals the hormone helps to control hibernation, activity levels, and the reproductive cycle. As nights grow longer during the fall, animals release more and more melatonin, which has the effect of slowing them down and preparing them for an extended rest over the winter. When daylight hours lengthen in the spring, melatonin secretions decline, raising energy levels.

Although they do not produce hibernation in humans, the heightened melatonin

secretions of winter do apparently cause us to slow down, have less energy, and need more rest (Wetterberg, 1999). While most people adjust to such changes, some individuals seem so sensitive to winter's heightened secretions that they find it impossible to carry on with business as usual. Their slowdown takes the form of depression each winter, a pattern called *seasonal affective disorder,* or *SAD* (Neto et al., 2004; Rosenthal & Blehar, 1989). SAD is less common in locations closer to the equator—that is, in areas where daylight hours vary little throughout the year and melatonin secretions do not increase appreciably in the winter months (Teng et al., 1995; Ito et al., 1992). The prevalence of this disorder is, for example, 1.4 percent in Florida, compared to 9.7 percent in New Hampshire (Friedman, 2007). Certain people with SAD are also very sensitive to the drop in melatonin secretions that occurs during the longer days of summer; some even become overenergized and manic every summer (Garrett, 2008; Faedda et al., 1993).

If in fact darkness is the problem in SAD, the answer may be light. One of the most effective treatments for SAD turns out to be *light therapy,* or *phototherapy,* exposure to extra amounts of artificial light throughout the winter. When seasonally

depressed patients sit under special lights for several hours every winter day, their depression is often reduced or eliminated (Garrett, 2008; Golden et al., 2005).

Of course, there are more natural ways to get extra light. Some researchers have found that SAD patients are helped by morning walks outside (Wirz-Justice et al., 1996). Similarly, clinicians often recommend taking a winter vacation in a sunny place. Some go so far as to suggest that people with wintertime blues, and certainly those with SAD, should spend a week or two just before winter begins in a location approximately 3 to 4 degrees north or south of the equator, where 70 percent more sunlight is available each day. The effectiveness of this form of "treatment" has yet to be investigated systematically.

Clinicians are also searching for simpler ways to change the melatonin levels of people with SAD. One possibility is the enormously popular *melatonin pills.* Research suggests that melatonin pills, given at key times in the day, might help readjust patients' secretions of their own melatonin and reduce depression (Leppamaki et al., 2003; Hätönen, Alila, & Laakso, 1996). Thus far, however, the optimal dosage and timing of such pills have proved elusive.

They are likely to feel a greater sense of loss when a loved one dies (Busch et al., 2004; Bemporad, 1992).

Of course, many people become depressed without losing a loved one. To explain why, Freud proposed the concept of **symbolic, or imagined, loss,** in which persons equate other kinds of events with loss of a loved one. A college student may, for example, experience failure in a calculus course as the loss of her parents, believing that they love her only when she excels academically.

Although many psychodynamic theorists have parted company with Freud and Abraham's theory of depression, it continues to influence current psychodynamic thinking (Busch et al., 2004). For example, *object relations theorists,* the psychodynamic theorists who emphasize relationships, propose that depression results when people's relationships leave them feeling unsafe and insecure (Allen et al., 2004; Blatt, 2004). People whose parents pushed them toward either excessive dependence or excessive self-reliance are more likely to become depressed when they later lose important relationships.

•**symbolic loss**•According to Freudian theory, the loss of a valued object (for example, a loss of employment) that is unconsciously interpreted as the loss of a loved one. Also called *imagined loss.*

•**anaclitic depression**•A pattern of depressed behavior found among very young children that is caused by separation from one's mother.

The following therapist description of a depressed middle-aged woman illustrates the psychodynamic concepts of dependence, loss of a loved one, symbolic loss, and introjection:

Marie Carls . . . had always felt very attached to her mother. As a matter of fact, they used to call her "Stamp" because she stuck to her mother as a stamp to a letter. She always tried to placate her volcanic mother, to please her in every possible way. . . .

After marriage [to Julius], she continued her pattern of submission and compliance. Before her marriage she had difficulty in complying with a volcanic mother, and after her marriage she almost automatically assumed a submissive role. . . .

[W]hen she was thirty years old . . . [Marie] and her husband invited Ignatius, who was single, to come and live with them. Ignatius and the patient soon discovered that they had an attraction for each other. They both tried to fight that feeling; but when Julius had to go to another city for a few days, the so-called infatuation became much more than that. There were a few physical contacts. . . . There was an intense spiritual affinity. . . . A few months later everybody had to leave the city. . . . Nothing was done to maintain contact. Two years later. . . . Marie heard that Ignatius had married. She felt terribly alone and despondent. . . .

Her suffering had become more acute as she realized that old age was approaching and she had lost all her chances. Ignatius remained as the memory of lost opportunities. . . . Her life of compliance and obedience had not permitted her to reach her goal. . . . When she became aware of these ideas, she felt even more depressed. . . . She felt that everything she had built in her life was false or based on a false premise.

(Arieti & Bemporad, 1978, pp. 275–284)

Studies have offered general support for the psychodynamic idea that depression may be triggered by a major loss. In a famous study of 123 infants who were placed in a nursery after being separated from their mothers, René Spitz (1946, 1945) found that 19 of the infants became very weepy and sad upon separation and withdrew from their surroundings—a pattern called **anaclitic depression.** Studies of infant monkeys who are separated from their mothers have noted a similar pattern of apparent depression (Harlow & Zimmermann, 1996; Harlow & Harlow, 1965).

Other research, involving both human participants and animal subjects, suggests that losses suffered early in life may set the stage for later depression (Pryce et al., 2005; Lara & Klein, 1999). When, for example, a depression scale was administered to 1,250 medical patients during visits to their family physicians, the patients whose fathers had died during their childhood scored higher on depression (Barnes & Prosen, 1985).

Related research supports the psychodynamic idea that people whose childhood needs were improperly met are particularly likely to become depressed after experiencing loss (Goodman, 2002). In some studies, depressed patients have filled out a scale called the Parental Bonding Instrument, which indicates how much care and protection people feel they received as children. Many have identified their parents' child-rearing style as "affectionless control," consisting of a mixture of low care and high protection (Martin et al., 2004; Parker et al., 1995).

These studies offer some support for the psychodynamic view of unipolar depression, but this support has key limitations. First, although the findings indicate that losses and inadequate parenting *sometimes* relate to depression, they do not establish that such factors are *typically* responsible for the disorder. In the studies of young children and young monkeys, for example, only some of the research participants who were separated from their mothers showed depressive reactions. In fact, it is estimated that less than 10 percent of all people who

Across the species
Researcher Harry Harlow and his colleagues found that infant monkeys reacted with apparent despair to separation from their mothers. Even monkeys raised with surrogate mothers—wire cylinders wrapped with foam rubber and covered with terry cloth—formed an attachment to them and mourned their absence.

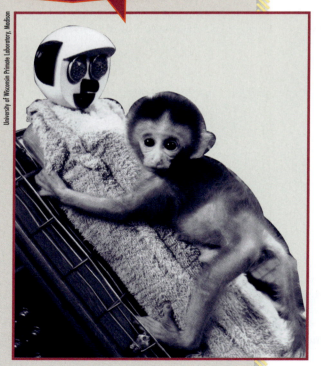

University of Wisconsin Primate Laboratory, Madison

experience major losses in life actually become depressed (Bonanno, 2004; Paykel & Cooper, 1992). Second, many findings are inconsistent. Though some studies find evidence of a relationship between childhood loss and later depression, others do not (Parker, 1992). Finally, certain features of the psychodynamic explanation are nearly impossible to test. Because symbolic loss is said to operate at an unconscious level, for example, it is difficult for researchers to determine if and when it is occurring.

The Behavioral View Behaviorists believe that unipolar depression results from significant changes in the number of rewards and punishments people receive in their lives (Farmer & Chapman, 2008). Clinical researcher Peter Lewinsohn has developed one of the leading behavioral explanations (Lewinsohn et al., 1990, 1984). He suggests that the positive rewards in life dwindle for some persons, leading them to perform fewer and fewer constructive behaviors. The rewards of campus life, for example, disappear when a young woman graduates from college and takes a job; and an aging baseball player loses the rewards of high salary and adulation when his skills deteriorate. Although many people manage to fill their lives with other forms of gratification, some become particularly disheartened. The positive features of their lives decrease even more, and the decline in rewards leads them to perform still fewer constructive behaviors. In this manner, the individuals spiral toward depression.

In a series of studies, Lewinsohn and his colleagues have found that the number of rewards people receive in life is indeed related to the presence or absence of depression. In some of their early studies, not only did depressed participants report fewer positive rewards than nondepressed participants, but when their rewards began to increase, their mood improved as well (Lewinsohn, Youngren, & Grosscup, 1979). Similarly, more recent investigations have found a strong relationship between positive life events and feelings of life satisfaction and happiness (Lu, 1999).

Lewinsohn and other behaviorists have further proposed that *social* rewards are particularly important in the downward spiral of depression (Farmer & Chapman, 2008; Lewinsohn et al., 1984). This claim has been supported by research showing that depressed persons experience fewer social rewards than nondepressed persons and that as their mood improves, their social rewards increase. Although depressed people are sometimes the victims of social circumstances, it may also be that their dark mood and flat behaviors help produce a decline in social rewards (Joiner, 2002; Coyne, 2001).

Behaviorists have done an admirable job of compiling data to support this theory, but this research, too, has limitations. It has relied heavily on the self-reports of depressed individuals, and, as you saw in Chapter 4, measures of this kind can be biased and inaccurate; reports by depressed persons may be influenced heavily by a gloomy mood and negative outlook. Moreover, the behavioral studies have been largely correlational and do not establish that decreases in rewarding events are the initial cause of depression. As you have just read, for example, a depressed mood in itself may lead to negative behaviors and decreases in activities and hence to fewer rewards.

Cognitive Views

Cognitive theorists believe that people with unipolar depression persistently view events in negative ways and that such perceptions lead to their disorder. The two most influential cognitive explanations are the *theory of negative thinking* and the *theory of learned helplessness.*

NEGATIVE THINKING Aaron Beck believes that negative thinking, rather than underlying conflicts or a reduction in positive rewards, lies at the heart of depression (Beck & Weishaar, 2008; Beck, 2002, 1991, 1967). Other cognitive theorists—Albert Ellis, for one—also point to maladaptive thinking as a key to depression, but Beck's theory is the one most often associated with the disorder. According to Beck, *maladaptive attitudes,* a *cognitive triad, errors in thinking,* and *automatic thoughts* combine to produce unipolar depression.

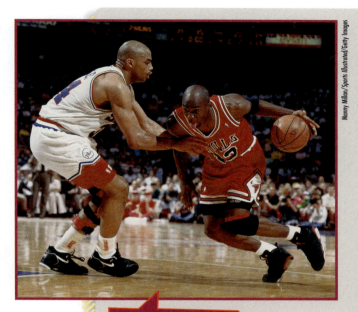

Finding new rewards
According to behaviorists, the reduction in rewards brought about by retirement places sports stars and other high achievers at risk for depression unless they can add new sources of gratification to their lives. Charles Barkley and Michael Jordan, two of the National Basketball Association's greatest players throughout the 1980s and 1990s, have indeed each found new rewards and achieved enormous success since leaving the court—Jordan as co-owner of the Charlotte Bobcats (an NBA team) and Barkley as a popular and outspoken TV commentator.

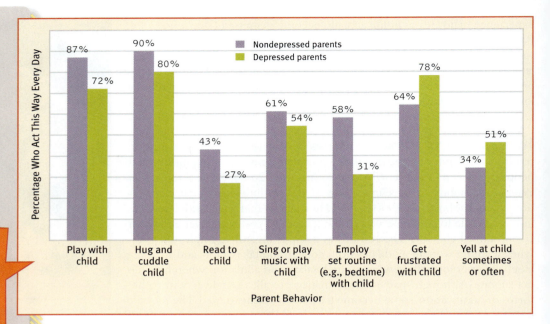

Figure 8-2
How depressed parents and their children interact Depressed parents are less likely than nondepressed parents to play with, hug, read to, or sing to their young children each day or to employ the same routine each day. They are also more likely to get frustrated with their children on a daily basis. (Adapted from Princeton Survey Research Associates, 1996.)

Beck believes that some people develop *maladaptive attitudes* as children, such as "My general worth is tied to every task I perform" or "If I fail, others will feel repelled by me." The attitudes result from their own experiences, their family relationships, and the judgments of the people around them (see Figure 8-2). Many failures are inevitable in a full, active life, so such attitudes are inaccurate and set the stage for all kinds of negative thoughts and reactions. Beck suggests that later in these people's lives, upsetting situations may trigger an extended round of negative thinking. That thinking typically takes three forms, which he calls the **cognitive triad:** the individuals repeatedly interpret (1) their *experiences,* (2) *themselves,* and (3) their *futures* in negative ways that lead them to feel depressed. The cognitive triad is at work in the thinking of this depressed person:

I can't bear it. I can't stand the humiliating fact that I'm the only woman in the world who can't take care of her family, take her place as a real wife and mother, and be respected in her community. When I speak to my young son Billy, I know I can't let him down, but I feel so ill-equipped to take care of him; that's what frightens me. I don't know what to do or where to turn; the whole thing is too overwhelming. . . . I must be a laughing stock. It's more than I can do to go out and meet people and have the fact pointed up to me so clearly.

(Fieve, 1975)

According to Beck, depressed people also make errors in their thinking. In one common error of logic, they draw arbitrary inferences—negative conclusions based on little evidence. A man walking through the park, for example, passes a woman who is looking at nearby flowers and concludes, "She's avoiding looking at me." Similarly, depressed people often minimize the significance of positive experiences or magnify that of negative ones. A college student receives an A on a difficult English exam, for example, but concludes that the grade reflects the professor's generosity rather than her own ability (minimization). Later in the week the same student must miss an English class and is convinced that she will be unable to keep up the rest of the semester (magnification).

Finally, depressed people experience **automatic thoughts,** a steady train of unpleasant thoughts that keep suggesting to them that they are inadequate and that their situation is hopeless. Beck labels these thoughts "automatic" because they seem to just happen, as if by reflex. In the course of only a few hours, depressed people may be visited

•cognitive triad•The three forms of negative thinking that Aaron Beck theorizes lead people to feel depressed. The triad consists of a negative view of one's experiences, oneself, and the future.

•automatic thoughts•Numerous unpleasant thoughts that help to cause or maintain depression, anxiety, or other forms of psychological dysfunction.

by hundreds of such thoughts: "I'm worthless. . . . I'll never amount to anything. . . . I let everyone down. . . . Everyone hates me. . . . My responsibilities are overwhelming. . . . I've failed as a parent. . . . I'm stupid. . . . Everything is difficult for me. . . . Things will never change." One therapist said of a depressed client, "By the end of the day, she is worn out, she has lived a thousand painful accidents, participated in a thousand deaths, mourned a thousand mistakes" (Mendels, 1970).

Many studies have produced evidence in support of Beck's explanation. Several of them confirm that depressed people hold maladaptive attitudes and that the more of these maladaptive attitudes they hold, the more depressed they tend to be (Evans et al., 2005; Whisman & McGarvey, 1995). Still other research has found the cognitive triad at work in depressed people (Ridout et al., 2003). In various studies, depressed individuals seem to recall unpleasant experiences more readily than positive ones, rate their performances on laboratory tasks lower than nondepressed people do, and select pessimistic statements in storytelling tests (for example, "I expect my plans will fail").

Beck's claims about errors in logic have also received research support (Cole & Turner, 1993). In one study, female participants—some depressed, some not—were asked to read and interpret paragraphs about women in difficult situations. Depressed participants made more errors in logic (such as arbitrary inference) in their interpretations than nondepressed women did (Hammen & Krantz, 1976).

Finally, research has supported Beck's claim that automatic thoughts are tied to depression. In several studies, nondepressed participants who are tricked into reading negative automatic-thought-like statements about themselves become increasingly depressed (Bates, Thompson, & Flanagan, 1999; Strickland, Hale, & Anderson, 1975). In a related line of research, it has been found that people who generally make *ruminative responses* during their depressed moods—that is, repeatedly dwell mentally on their mood without acting to change it—experience dejection longer and are more likely to develop clinical depression later in life than people who avoid such ruminations (Nolen-Hoeksema & Corte, 2004; Nolen-Hoeksema, 2002, 1998, 1995).

This body of research shows that negative thinking is indeed linked to depression, but it fails to show that such patterns of thought are the cause and core of unipolar depression. It could be that a central mood problem leads to thinking difficulties that then take a further toll on mood, behavior, and physiology.

LEARNED HELPLESSNESS Feelings of helplessness fill this account of a young woman's depression:

Mary was 25 years old and had just begun her senior year in college. . . . Asked to recount how her life had been going recently, Mary began to weep. Sobbing, she said that for the last year or so she felt she was losing control of her life and that recent stresses (starting school again, friction with her boyfriend) had left her feeling worthless and frightened. Because of a gradual deterioration in her vision, she was now forced to wear glasses all day. "The glasses make me look terrible," she said, and "I don't look people in the eye much any more." Also, to her dismay, Mary had gained 20 pounds in the past year. She viewed herself as overweight and unattractive. At times she was convinced that with enough money to buy contact lenses and enough time to exercise she could cast off her depression; at other times she believed nothing would help. . . . Mary saw her life deteriorating in other spheres, as well. She felt overwhelmed by schoolwork and, for the first time in her life, was on academic probation. . . . In addition to her dissatisfaction with her appearance and her fears about her academic future, Mary complained of a lack of friends. Her social network consisted solely of her boyfriend, with whom she was living. Although there were times she experienced this relationship as almost unbearably frustrating, she felt helpless to change it and was pessimistic about its permanence. . . .

(Spitzer et al., 1983, pp. 122–123)

Tracking those thoughts
The brain waves of this college student are measured with an EEG to help detect what happens in her brain while her mind is wandering. Researchers have discovered that people who make ruminative responses during their unhappy moods are more likely to develop clinical depression, but little is known about why some people are particularly prone to ruminate.

BETWEEN THE LINES

Loss of Confidants
Intimate social contact has been declining over the past two decades. When research participants were asked in 1985 how many confidants they turned to for discussion of important matters, most answered 3. In 2004, the most common response to the same question was 0 (Matsumoto & Juang, 2008; McPherson, Smith-Lovin, & Brashears, 2006). ‹‹

Figure 8-3
Jumping to safety Experimental animals learn to escape or avoid shocks that are administered on one side of a shuttle box by jumping to the other (safe) side.

Mary feels that she is "losing control of her life." According to psychologist Martin Seligman (1975), such feelings of helplessness are at the center of her depression. Since the mid-1960s Seligman has developed the **learned helplessness** theory of depression. It holds that people become depressed when they think (1) that they no longer have control over the reinforcements (the rewards and punishments) in their lives and (2) that they themselves are responsible for this helpless state.

Seligman's theory first began to take shape when he was working with laboratory dogs. In one procedure, he strapped dogs into an apparatus called a hammock, in which they received shocks periodically no matter what they would do. The next day each dog was placed in a *shuttle box,* a box divided in half by a barrier over which the animal could jump to reach the other side (see Figure 8-3). Seligman applied shocks to the dogs in the box, expecting that they, like other dogs in this situation, would soon learn to escape by jumping over the barrier. However, most of these dogs failed to learn anything in the shuttle box. After a flurry of activity, they simply "lay down and quietly whined" and accepted the shock.

Seligman decided that while receiving inescapable shocks in the hammock the day before, the dogs had learned that they had no control over unpleasant events (shocks) in their lives. That is, they had learned that they were helpless to do anything to change negative situations. Thus, when later they were placed in a new situation (the shuttle box) where they could in fact control their fate, they continued to believe that they were generally helpless. Seligman noted that the effects of learned helplessness greatly resemble the symptoms of human depression, and he proposed that people in fact become depressed after developing a general belief that they have no control over reinforcements in their lives.

In numerous human and animal studies, participants who undergo helplessness training have displayed reactions similar to depressive symptoms. When, for example, human participants are exposed to uncontrollable negative events, they later score higher than other individuals on a depressive mood survey (Miller & Seligman, 1975). Similarly, helplessness-trained animal subjects lose interest in sexual and social activities—a common symptom of human depression (Lindner, 1968). Finally, uncontrollable negative events result in lower norepinephrine and serotonin activity in rats (Wu et al., 1999). This, of course, is similar to the neurotransmitter activity found in the brains of people with unipolar depression.

The learned helplessness explanation of depression has been revised somewhat over the past two decades. According to a new version of the theory, the *attribution-helplessness theory,* when people view events as beyond their control, they ask themselves why this is so (Taube-Schiff & Lau, 2008; Abramson et al., 2002, 1989, 1978) (see Table 8-4). If they attribute their present lack of control to some *internal* cause that is both *global* and *stable*

table: 8-4

Internal and External Attributions
Event: "I failed my psych test today."

	INTERNAL		EXTERNAL	
	Stable	**Unstable**	**Stable**	**Unstable**
Global	"I have a problem with test anxiety."	"Getting into an argument with my roommate threw my whole day off."	"Written tests are an unfair way to assess knowledge."	"No one does well on tests that are given the day after vacation."
Specific	"I just have no grasp of psychology."	"I got upset and froze when I couldn't answer the first two questions."	"Everyone knows that this professor enjoys giving unfair tests."	"This professor didn't put much thought into the test because of the pressure of her book deadline."

("I am inadequate at everything and I always will be"), they may well feel helpless to prevent future negative outcomes and they may experience depression. If they make other kinds of attributions, this reaction is unlikely.

Consider a college student whose girlfriend breaks up with him. If he attributes this loss of control to an internal cause that is both global and stable—"It's my fault [internal], I ruin everything I touch [global], and I always will [stable]"—he then has reason to expect similar losses of control in the future and may generally experience a sense of helplessness. According to the learned helplessness view, he is a prime candidate for depression. If the student had instead attributed the breakup to causes that were more *specific* ("The way I've behaved the past couple of weeks blew this relationship"), *unstable* ("I don't know what got into me—I don't usually act like that"), or *external* ("She never did know what she wanted"), he might not expect to lose control again and would probably not experience helplessness and depression.

Hundreds of studies have supported the relationship between styles of attribution, helplessness, and depression (Taube-Schiff & Lau, 2008; Yu & Seligman, 2002). In one, depressed persons were asked to fill out an *Attributional Style Questionnaire* both before and after successful therapy. Before therapy, their depression was accompanied by the internal/global/stable pattern of attribution. At the end of therapy and again one year later, their depression was improved and their attribution styles were less likely to be limited to internal, global, and stable ones (Seligman et al., 1988).

Some theorists have refined the helplessness model yet again in recent years. They suggest that attributions are likely to cause depression only when they further produce a sense of *hopelessness* in an individual (Abela et al., 2004; Abramson et al., 2002, 1989). By taking this factor into consideration, clinicians are often able to predict depression with still greater precision (Robinson & Alloy, 2003).

Although the learned helplessness theory of unipolar depression has been very influential, it too has imperfections. First, laboratory helplessness does not parallel depression in every respect. Uncontrollable shocks in the laboratory, for example, almost always produce anxiety along with the helplessness effects (Seligman, 1975), but human depression is not always accompanied by anxiety. Second, much of the learned helplessness research relies on animal subjects (Henn & Vollmayr, 2005). It is impossible to know whether the animals' symptoms do in fact reflect the clinical depression found in humans. Third, the attributional feature of the theory raises difficult questions. What about the dogs and rats who learn helplessness? Can animals make attributions, even implicitly?

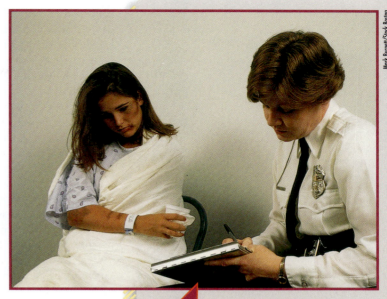

Spouse abuse: victimization and learned helplessness
According to the National Crime Victimization Survey, spouse abuse occurs in at least 4 million American homes each year. Psychologists believe that many victims of spouse abuse develop feelings of helplessness over the course of their ordeal, thus explaining their "decision" to stay with their abusive husbands. Many such women come to believe that nothing they can do will stop the repeated episodes of violence, that they have no economic alternatives, and that the criminal justice system will be unable to protect them. In turn, they typically develop feelings of depression, low self-esteem, and self-blame.

Sociocultural Views

Sociocultural theorists propose that unipolar depression is greatly influenced by the social context that surrounds people. Their belief is supported by the finding, discussed earlier, that this disorder is often triggered by outside stressors. Once again, there are two kinds of sociocultural views—the *family-social perspective,* which looks at the role played by interpersonal factors in the development of depression, and the *multicultural perspective,* which ties depression to factors such as gender, race, and economic status.

The Family-Social Perspective Earlier you read that some behaviorists believe that a decline in social rewards is particularly important in the development of depression. Although presented as part of their behavioral explanation, this view is consistent with the family-social perspective.

The connection between declining social rewards and depression is a two-way street. On the one hand, researchers have found that depressed persons often display weak social

•**learned helplessness**•The perception, based on past experiences, that one has no control over one's reinforcements.

José Azel/Aurora

Special companionship
Social support of various kinds helps reduce or prevent depression. Indeed, the companionship and warmth of dogs and other pets have been found to prevent loneliness and isolation and, in turn, to help alleviate or prevent depression.

skills and communicate poorly (Joiner, 2002; Segrin, 2001, 1990). They typically speak more slowly and quietly and in more of a monotone than nondepressed persons, pause longer between words and sentences, and take longer to respond to others (Taube-Shiff & Lau, 2008; Talavera et al., 1994). They also seek repeated reassurances from others (Joiner & Metalsky, 2001, 1995). Such social deficits make other people uncomfortable and may cause them to avoid the depressed individuals. As a result, the social contacts and rewards of depressed persons decrease, and, as they participate in fewer and fewer social interactions, their social skills deteriorate still further. Not surprisingly, over time depressed people, particularly those who have experienced repeated episodes of depression, seem to lower their expectations of what they can get from social relationships and scale back their social ambitions (Coyne & Calarco, 1995).

Consistent with these findings, depression has been tied repeatedly to the unavailability of social support such as that found in a happy marriage (Doss et al., 2008; Kendler et al., 2005). As you can see in Figure 8-4, across the United States, people who are separated or divorced display three times the depression rate of married or widowed persons and double the rate of people who have never been married (Weissman et al., 1991). In some cases, the spouse's depression may contribute to marital discord, a separation, or divorce, but often the interpersonal conflicts and low social support found in troubled relationships seem to lead to depression (Highet et al., 2005; Franchi, 2004; Whisman, 2001).

Generally, there is a high correlation between level of marital conflict and degree of sadness: .37 for men and .42 for women (Whisman, 2001). Among those who are clinically depressed, the correlation rises to .66. In one study, researchers first assessed how satisfying the marital relationships of research participants were. They then discovered that over the next 12 months, participants who were in an unsatisfying relationship were three times more likely to experience a major depressive episode than those in a satisfying relationship (Whisman & Bruce, 1999). Such findings led the experimenters to estimate that one-third of cases of major depression could be prevented if marital stress were eliminated.

Finally, it appears that people whose lives are isolated and without intimacy are particularly likely to become depressed at times of stress (Kendler et al., 2005; Nezlek et al., 2000). Some highly publicized studies conducted in England several decades ago showed that women who had three or more young children, lacked a close confidante, and had no outside employment were more likely than other women to become depressed after experiencing stressful events (Brown et al., 1995; Brown & Harris, 1978). Studies have also found that depressed people who lack social support remain depressed longer than those who have a supportive spouse or warm friendships (Moos & Cronkite, 1999).

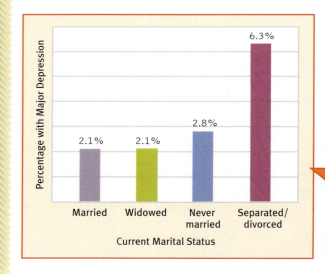

Figure 8-4
Marital status and major depressive disorder Currently separated or divorced people are three times more likely to be depressed than people who currently are married. (Adapted from Weissman et al., 1991.)

The Multicultural Perspective Two kinds of relationships have captured the interest of multicultural theorists: (1) links between *gender and depression* and (2) ties between *cultural and ethnic background and depression*. In the case of gender, a strong relationship has been found, but a clear explanation for that relationship has yet to emerge. The clinical field is still sorting out whether and what ties exist between cultural factors and depression.

GENDER AND DEPRESSION As you have read, a strong link exists between gender and depression. Women in places as far apart as Paris, Sweden, Lebanon, New Zealand, and the United States are at least twice as likely as men to receive a diagnosis of unipolar depression (Whiffen & Demidenko, 2006; McSweeney, 2004; Pajer, 1995). Women also appear to be younger when depression strikes, to have more frequent and longer-lasting bouts, and to respond less successfully to treatment. Why the huge difference between the sexes? A variety of theories have been offered (Russo & Tartaro, 2008; Nolen-Hoeksema, 2002, 1995, 1990, 1987).

The *artifact theory* holds that women and men are equally prone to depression but that clinicians often fail to detect depression in men (Brommelhoff et al., 2004). Perhaps men find it less socially acceptable to admit feeling depressed or to seek treatment. Perhaps depressed women display more emotional symptoms, such as sadness and crying, which are easily diagnosed, while depressed men mask their depression behind traditionally "masculine" symptoms such as anger. Although a popular explanation, this view has failed to receive consistent research support (McSweeney, 2004). It turns out that women are actually no more willing or able than men to identify their depressive symptoms and to seek treatment (Nolen-Hoeksema, 1990).

The *hormone explanation* holds that hormone changes trigger depression in many women (Parker & Brotchie, 2004; Dunn & Steiner, 2000). A woman's biological life from her early teens to middle age is marked by frequent changes in hormone levels. Gender differences in rates of depression also span these same years. Research suggests, however, that hormone changes alone are not responsible for the high levels of depression in women (Kessler et al., 2006; Whiffen & Demidenko, 2006). Important social and life events that occur at puberty, pregnancy, and menopause could likewise have an effect. Hormone explanations have also been criticized as sexist, since they imply that a woman's normal biology is flawed.

The *life stress theory* suggests that women in our society experience more stress than men (Kessler et al., 2006; Keyes & Goodman, 2006; Hankin & Abramson, 2001). On average they face more poverty, more menial jobs, less adequate housing, and more discrimination than men—all factors that have been linked to depression. And in many homes, women bear a disproportionate share of responsibility for child care and housework.

The *body dissatisfaction explanation* states that females in Western society are taught, almost from birth, to seek a low body weight and slender body shape—goals that are unreasonable, unhealthy, and often unattainable. As you will observe in Chapter 11, the cultural standard for males is much more lenient. As girls approach adolescence, peer pressure may produce greater and greater dissatisfaction with their weight and body, increasing the likelihood of depression. Consistent with this theory, gender differences in depression do indeed first appear during adolescence (Avenevoli et al., 2008; Nolen-Hoeksema & Girgus, 1995), and persons with eating disorders often experience high levels of depression (Stewart & Williamson, 2008). However, it is not clear that eating and weight concerns actually cause depression; they may instead be the result of depression.

The *lack-of-control theory* picks up on the learned helplessness research and argues that women may be more prone to depression because they feel less control than men over their lives. Some studies have, in fact, suggested that women are more prone than men to develop learned helplessness in the laboratory (Le Unes, Nation, & Turley, 1980). In addition, it has been found that victimization of any kind, from burglary to rape,

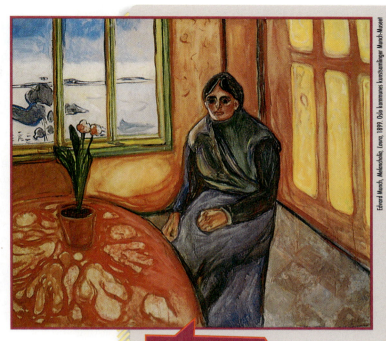
Edvard Munch, *Melancholia, Laura*, 1899. Oslo kommunes kunstsamlinger Munch-Museet

Female melancholy
Edvard Munch's painting *Melancholy, Laura* was inspired by his sister's bouts of severe depression.

BETWEEN THE LINES

Single ≠ Lonely in Germany

80% Unmarried German women who say they are perfectly content to live alone ‹‹

36% German women who say they opt to stay single because it is more fun ‹‹

36% German women who say they like single life because they do not have to endure watching sports on television with a male spouse ‹‹

2% Single German women who report that they do not enjoy their solitary lifestyle ‹‹

(Stern, 2004)

Non-Western depression
Depressed people in non-Western countries tend to have fewer cognitive symptoms, such as self-blame, and more physical symptoms, such as fatigue, weakness, and sleep disturbances.

Mimi Forsyth/Monkmeyer

often produces a general sense of helplessness and increases the symptoms of depression. Women in our society are more likely than men to be victims, particularly of sexual assault and child abuse (Whiffen & Demidenko, 2006; Nolen-Hoeksema, 2002).

The *self-blame explanation* holds that women are more likely than men to blame their failures on lack of ability and to attribute their successes to luck—an attribution style that, you'll recall, has been linked to depression by the attribution-helplessness theorists (Abramson et al., 2002). However, studies suggest that today's women and men may not differ as much as they used to in their levels of self-esteem and self-blame (Kling et al., 1999).

A final explanation for the gender differences found in depression is the *rumination theory.* As you read earlier, *rumination* is the tendency to keep focusing on one's feelings when depressed and to consider repeatedly the causes and consequences of that depression ("Why am I so down? . . . I won't be able to finish my work if I keep going like this. . . ."). Research shows that people who ruminate whenever they feel sad are more likely to become depressed and stay depressed longer. It turns out that women are more likely than men to ruminate when their moods darken, perhaps making them more vulnerable to the onset of clinical depression (Nolen-Hoeksema & Corte, 2004; Nolen-Hoeksema, 2002, 2000).

Each of these explanations for the gender difference in unipolar depression offers food for thought. Each has gathered just enough supporting evidence to make it interesting and just enough evidence to the contrary to raise questions about its usefulness (Russo & Tartaro, 2008). Thus, at present, the gender difference in depression remains one of the most talked-about but least understood phenomena in the clinical field.

CULTURAL BACKGROUND AND DEPRESSION Depression is a worldwide phenomenon, and certain symptoms of this disorder seem to be constant across all countries. A landmark study of four countries—Canada, Switzerland, Iran, and Japan—found that the great majority of depressed people in those very different countries reported symptoms of sadness, joylessness, anxiety, tension, lack of energy, loss of interest, loss of ability to concentrate, ideas of insufficiency, and thoughts of suicide (Matsumoto & Juang, 2008; WHO, 1983). Beyond such core symptoms, however, research suggests that the precise picture of depression varies from country to country (Kleinman, 2004; Tsai & Chentsova-Dutton, 2002). Depressed people in non-Western countries—China and Nigeria, for example—are more likely to be troubled by physical symptoms such as fatigue, weakness, sleep disturbances, and weight loss. Depression in those countries is less often marked by cognitive symptoms such as self-blame, low self-esteem, and guilt. As countries become more Westernized, depression seems to take on the more cognitive character it has in the West (Matsumoto & Juang, 2008; Okello & Ekblad, 2006).

Within the United States, researchers have found few differences in the symptoms of depression among members of different ethnic or racial groups. Nor have they found differences in the *overall* rates of depression between such minority groups. Investigators do, however, sometimes find striking differences when they look at specific ethnic populations living under special circumstances (Matsumoto & Juang, 2008; Ayalon & Young, 2003). A study of one Native American community in the United States, for example, showed that the lifetime risk of developing depression was 37 percent among women, 19 percent among men, and 28 percent overall, much higher than the risk in the general United States population (Kinzie et al., 1992). High prevalence rates of this kind may be linked to the terrible social and economic pressures faced by the people who live on Native American reservations. Similarly, in a survey of Hispanic and African Americans residing in public housing, almost half of the respondents reported that they were suffering from depression (Bazargan et al., 2005). Within these minority populations, the likelihood of being depressed rose along with the individual's degree of poverty, family size, and number of health problems.

Of course, each minority group itself comprises persons of varied backgrounds and cultural values. Thus, it is not surprising that depression is distributed unevenly across some of the groups. As with certain anxiety disorders (see page 214), depression is much more common among Hispanic Americans and African Americans born in the United States than among Hispanic and African American immigrants (Matsumoto & Juang, 2008; Miranda et al., 2005). Moreover, within the Hispanic American population, Puerto Ricans display a significantly higher rate of depression than do Mexican Americans or Cuban Americans (Matsumoto & Juang, 2008; Oquendo et al., 2004; Cho et al., 1993), while among African Americans, individuals whose families originally arrived in the United States directly from Africa and those whose families came by way of a Caribbean island experience similar rates of depression (Miranda et al., 2005).

(see page 214)

Bipolar Disorders

People with a *bipolar disorder* experience both the lows of depression and the highs of mania. Many describe their life as an emotional roller coaster, as they shift back and forth between extreme moods. A number of sufferers eventually become suicidal. Their roller-coaster ride and its impact on relatives and friends are seen in the following case study:

In his early school years he had been a remarkable student and had shown a gift for watercolor and oils. Later he had studied art in Paris and married an English girl he had met there. Eventually they had settled in London.

Ten years later, when he was thirty-four years old, he had persuaded his wife and only son to accompany him to Honolulu, where, he assured them, he would be considered famous. He felt he would be able to sell his paintings at many times the prices he could get in London. According to his wife, he had been in an accelerated state, but at that time the family had left, unsuspecting, believing with the patient in their imminent good fortune. When they arrived they found almost no one in the art world that he was supposed to know. There were no connections for sales and deals in Hawaii that he had anticipated. Settling down, the patient began to behave more peculiarly than ever. After enduring several months of the patient's exhilaration, overactivity, weight loss, constant talking, and unbelievably little sleep, the young wife and child began to fear for his sanity. None of his plans materialized. After five months in the Pacific, with finances growing thin, the patient's overactivity subsided and he fell into a depression.

During that period he refused to move, paint, or leave the house. He lost twenty pounds, became utterly dependent on his wife, and insisted on seeing none of the friends he had accumulated in his manic state. His despondency became so severe that several doctors came to the house and advised psychiatric hospitalization. He quickly agreed and received twelve electroshock treatments, which relieved his depressed state. Soon afterward he began to paint again and to sell his work modestly. Recognition began to come from galleries and critics in the Far East. Several reviews acclaimed his work as exceptionally brilliant.

This was the beginning of the lifelong career of his moodswing. While still in Honolulu, he once again became severely depressed. . . . Four years later he returned to London in a high. . . . When this manic period subsided and he surveyed the wreckage of his life, an eight-month interval of normal mood followed, after which he again switched into a profound depression.

(Fieve, 1975, pp. 64–65)

What Are the Symptoms of Mania?

Unlike people sunk in the gloom of depression, those in a state of mania typically experience dramatic and inappropriate rises in mood. The symptoms of mania span the same areas of functioning—*emotional, motivational, behavioral, cognitive,* and *physical*—as those of depression, but mania affects those areas in an opposite way.

War of a different kind
While starring as Princess Leia, the invincible heroine in the *Star Wars* movies from 1977 to 1983, actress Carrie Fisher received a diagnosis of bipolar disorder. The disorder is now under control with the help of medication, and Fisher says, "I don't want peace [in my life], I just don't want war" (Epstein, 2001, p. 36).

•**bipolar I disorder**•A type of bipolar disorder marked by full manic and major depressive episodes.

•**bipolar II disorder**•A type of bipolar disorder marked by mildly manic (hypomanic) episodes and major depressive episodes.

A person in the throes of mania has active, powerful emotions in search of an outlet. The mood of euphoric joy and well-being is out of all proportion to the actual happenings in the person's life. One person with mania explained, "I feel no sense of restriction or censorship whatsoever. I am afraid of nothing and no one" (Fieve, 1975, p. 68). Not every person with mania is a picture of happiness, however. Some instead become very irritable and angry, especially when others get in the way of their exaggerated ambitions.

In the motivational realm, people with mania seem to want constant excitement, involvement, and companionship. They enthusiastically seek out new friends and old, new interests and old, and have little awareness that their social style is overwhelming, domineering, and excessive.

The behavior of people with mania is usually very active. They move quickly, as though there were not enough time to do everything they want to do. They may talk rapidly and loudly, their conversations filled with jokes and efforts to be clever or, conversely, with complaints and verbal outbursts. Flamboyance is not uncommon: dressing in flashy clothes, giving large sums of money to strangers, or even getting involved in dangerous activities.

In the cognitive realm, people with mania usually show poor judgment and planning, as if they feel too good or move too fast to consider possible pitfalls. Filled with optimism, they rarely listen when others try to slow them down, interrupt their buying sprees, or prevent them from investing money unwisely. They may also hold an inflated opinion of themselves, and sometimes their self-esteem approaches grandiosity. During severe episodes of mania, some have trouble remaining coherent or in touch with reality.

Finally, in the physical realm, people with mania feel remarkably energetic. They typically get little sleep yet feel and act wide awake. Even if they miss a night or two of sleep, their energy level may remain high.

Diagnosing Bipolar Disorders

People are considered to be in a full *manic episode* when for at least one week they display an abnormally high or irritable mood, along with at least three other symptoms of mania (see Table 8-5). The episode may even include psychotic features such as delusions or hallucinations. When the symptoms of mania are less severe (causing little impairment), the person is said to be experiencing a *hypomanic episode* (APA, 2000).

DSM-IV-TR distinguishes two kinds of bipolar disorders—bipolar I and bipolar II. People with **bipolar I disorder** have full manic and major depressive episodes. Most of them experience an *alternation* of the episodes; for example, weeks of mania followed by a period of wellness, followed, in turn, by an episode of depression. Some people, however, have *mixed* episodes, in which they swing from manic to depressive symptoms and back again on the same day. In **bipolar II disorder,** hypomanic—that is, mildly manic—episodes alternate with major depressive episodes over the course of time. Some people with this pattern accomplish huge amounts of work during their mild manic periods (see *Psych Watch* on page 268).

Without treatment, the mood episodes tend to recur for people with either type of bipolar disorder (Julien, 2008). If people experience four or more episodes within a one-year period, their disorder is further classified as *rapid cycling*. Terri Cheney, author of the autobiography *Manic: A Memoir,* describes her rapid cycling in the following excerpt.

"Those? Oh, just a few souvenirs from my bipolar-disorder days."

table: 8-5

DSM Checklist

MANIC EPISODE

1. A period of abnormally and persistently elevated, expansive, or irritable mood, lasting at least one week.
2. Persistence of at least three of the following: • inflated self-esteem or grandiosity • decreased need for sleep • more talkativeness than usual, or pressure to keep talking • flight of ideas or the experience that thoughts are racing • distractibility • increase in activity or psychomotor agitation • excessive involvement in pleasurable activities that have a high potential for painful consequences.
3. Significant distress or impairment.

BIPOLAR I DISORDER

1. The presence of a manic, hypomanic, or major depressive episode.
2. If currently in a hypomanic or major depressive episode, history of a manic episode.
3. Significant distress or impairment.

BIPOLAR II DISORDER

1. The presence of a hypomanic or major depressive episode.
2. If currently in a major depressive episode, history of a hypomanic episode. If currently in a hypomanic episode, history of a major depressive episode. No history of a manic episode.
3. Significant distress or impairment.

Based on APA, 2000.

The precise term for my disorder is "ultraradian rapid cycler," which means that without medication I am at the mercy of my own spectacular mood swings: "up" for days (charming, talkative, effusive, funny and productive, but never sleeping and ultimately hard to be around), then "down," and essentially immobile, for weeks at a time. . . .

. . . In love there's no hiding: You have to let someone know who you are, but I didn't have a clue who I was from one moment to the next. When dating me, you might go to bed with Madame Bovary and wake up with Hester Prynne. Worst of all, my manic, charming self was constantly putting me into situations that my down self couldn't handle.

For example: One morning I met a man in the supermarket produce aisle. I hadn't slept for three days, but you wouldn't have known it to look at me. My eyes glowed green, my strawberry blond hair put the strawberries to shame, and I literally sparkled (I'd worn a gold sequined shirt to the supermarket—manic taste is always bad). I was hungry, but not for produce. I was hungry for him, in his well-worn jeans, Yankees cap slightly askew.

I pulled my cart alongside his and started lasciviously squeezing a peach. . . . That's all I needed, an opening, and I was off. I told him my name, asked him his likes and dislikes in fruit, sports, presidential candidates and women. I talked so quickly I barely had time to hear his answers. I didn't buy any peaches, but I left with a dinner date on Saturday, two nights away, leaving plenty of time to rest, shave my legs and pick out the perfect outfit.

But by the time I got home, the darkness had already descended. I didn't feel like plowing through my closet or unpacking the groceries. I just left them on the counter to rot or not rot—what did it matter? I didn't even change my sequined shirt. I tumbled into bed as I was, and stayed there. My body felt as if I had been dipped in slow-drying concrete. It was all I could do to draw a breath in and push it back out, over and over. I would have cried from the sheer monotony of it, but tears were too much effort.

On Saturday afternoon the phone rang. I was still in bed, and had to force myself to roll over, pick it up and mutter hello. "It's Jeff, from the peaches. Just calling to confirm your address." Jeff? Peaches? I vaguely remembered talking to someone who fit that description, but it seemed a lifetime ago. And that wasn't me doing the talking then, or at least not this me—I'd never wear sequins in the morning. But my conscience knew better. "Get up, get dressed!" it hissed in my ear. "It doesn't matter if she made the date, you've got to see it through."

When Jeff showed up at 7, I was dressed and ready, but more for a funeral than a date. I was swathed in black and hadn't put on any makeup, so my naturally fair skin looked ghostly and wan. But I opened the door, and even held up my cheek to be kissed. I took no pleasure in the feel of his lips on my skin. Pleasure was for the living.

I had nothing to say, not then or at dinner. So Jeff talked, a lot at first, then less and less until finally, during dessert, he asked, "You don't by any chance have a twin, do you?" And yet I was crushed when he didn't call.

A couple of weeks later, I awoke to a world gone Disney: daffodil sunshine, robin's egg sky. Birds were trilling outside my window, a song no doubt created especially for me. I couldn't stand it a minute longer. I flung back the covers and danced in my nightie—my gray flannel prison-issue nightie. I caught one glimpse of it in the mirror, shuddered, and flung it off, too.

I rifled through my closet for something decent to wear, but everything I put my hands on was wrong, wrong, wrong. For starters, it was all black. I hated black, even more than I hated gray. Redheads should be true to their colors, whatever the cost. I dug deeper, and there, shoved way in the back, was a pair of skin-tight jeans and something silky and sparkly and just what I needed: an exquisite gold sequined shirt.

I slipped it on and preened for a minute. Damn, I looked good. . . .

Jeff?

Jeff! I kicked the nightie out of my way and grabbed the bedside phone. Was 6:30 a.m. too early to call? No, not for good old Jeff! It rang and rang. I was about to give up when a thick, sleepy voice said "Hello?"

"It's me! Why haven't you called?"

It took a while to establish who "me" was, but eventually he remembered. "You sound different," he said. "Or no, maybe you sound more like yourself. I'm not sure. It's so early." Soon I had him laughing so hard he got the hiccups and had to get off the phone. But before he did, he asked me out for Friday, three nights away. No, I insisted, it had to be tonight, or even this afternoon. . . . We compromised on dinner that evening at 8. I spent the afternoon ridding my house of all evidence of depression. I soaped and scoured and dusted and vacuumed, using every attachment, even the ones that frightened me. . . .

When the house looked perfect, I turned on myself with the same fury. I buffed and polished and creamed and plucked. . . . As I was shadowing my eyes, . . . my hand started trembling and I couldn't finish applying my mascara. Suddenly I didn't look radiant. There were lines around my mouth and a hollowness to my eyes that aged me 10 years. My skin, despite the carefully applied foundation and blush, was so deathly pale I recoiled from my reflection.

I sat on the toilet and started to cry. I had met the enemy enough times to know it by sight. Not now, I prayed. Please not now. Globs of mascara ran down my cheeks, and I wiped them away, heedless of the streaks they left. It was 7:57. I had three minutes to wrestle my brain chemistry into submission. . . .

Maybe he would understand. Maybe I would find the courage. Maybe they would invent a cure. Maybe, but not tonight. As the doorbell rang and rang, I huddled in the bathroom, shivering. . . . When it was finally quiet, I rinsed off the rest of my mascara and tossed my cocktail dress into the hamper. Then I buttoned up my gray flannel nightie, and settled in for the long night to come.

I never heard from Jeff again.

(Cheney, 2008)

Regardless of their particular pattern, individuals with a bipolar disorder tend to experience depression more than mania over the years (Julien, 2008). In most cases, their depressive episodes occur three times as often as manic ones, and the depressive episodes also last longer.

Surveys from around the world indicate that between 1 and 2.6 percent of all adults suffer from a bipolar disorder at any given time (Merikangas et al., 2007; Kessler et al., 2005). As many as 4 percent experience one of the bipolar disorders over the course of their lives. Bipolar I disorder seems to be a bit more common than bipolar II disorder (Rihmer & Angst, 2005; Kessler et al., 1994). The disorders appear to be equally common in women and men and among all socioeconomic classes and ethnic groups (Shastry, 2005; APA, 2000). However, women may experience more depressive episodes and more rapid cycling than men (Curtis, 2005; Papadimitiou et al., 2005). Onset usually occurs between the ages of 15 and 44 years. In most untreated cases of bipolar disorder, the manic and depressive episodes eventually subside, only to recur at a later time (APA, 2000). Generally, when episodes recur, the intervening periods of normality grow shorter and shorter (Goodwin & Jamison, 1984). It also appears that over time people with bipolar disorders develop more medical ailments than the rest of the population (Kupfer, 2005).

When a person experiences numerous periods of hypomanic symptoms and mild depressive symptoms, DSM-IV-TR assigns a diagnosis of **cyclothymic disorder.** The symptoms of this milder form of bipolar disorder continue for two or more years, interrupted occasionally by normal moods that may last for only days or weeks. This disorder, like bipolar I and bipolar II disorders, usually begins in adolescence or early adulthood and is equally common among women and men. At least 0.4 percent of the population develops cyclothymic disorder (APA, 2000). In some cases, the milder symptoms eventually blossom into a bipolar I or II disorder.

What Causes Bipolar Disorders?

Throughout the first half of the twentieth century, the search for the cause of bipolar disorders made little progress. Various explanations were proposed, but research did not support their validity. Psychodynamic theorists, for example, suggested that mania, like depression, emerges from the loss of a love object. Whereas some people introject the lost object and become depressed, others deny the loss and become manic. To avoid the terrifying conflicts generated by the loss, they escape into a dizzying round of activity (Lewin, 1950). Although case reports sometimes fit this explanation (Krishnan et al., 1984; Cohen et al., 1954), only a few controlled studies have found a relationship between loss early or later in life and the onset of manic episodes (Tsuchiya et al., 2005; Furukawa et al., 1999).

More recently, biological research has produced some promising clues. The biological insights have come from research into *neurotransmitter activity, ion activity, brain structure,* and *genetic factors.*

Neurotransmitters Remember from Chapter 3 that neurotransmitters released from neurons' axon endings carry messages to the dendrites of neighboring neurons by binding to receptor sites there. As you read, different psychological disorders have been linked to the abnormal functioning of various neurotransmitters, including norepinephrine. Could *overactivity* of norepinephrine be related to mania? This was the expectation of clinicians back in the 1960s after investigators first found a relationship between low norepinephrine activity and unipolar depression (Schildkraut, 1965). One study did indeed find the norepinephrine activity of persons with mania to be higher than that of depressed or control research participants (Post et al., 1980, 1978). In another study patients with a bipolar disorder were given *reserpine,* the blood pressure drug known to reduce norepinephrine activity in the brain, and the manic symptoms of some subsided (Telner et al., 1986).

Because serotonin activity often parallels norepinephrine activity in unipolar depression, theorists at first expected that mania would also be related to high serotonin

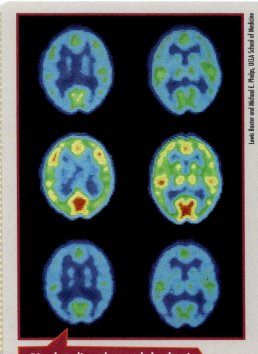

Lewis Baxter and Michael E. Phelps, UCLA School of Medicine

Bipolar disorder and the brain
These PET scans of the brain of a person with bipolar disorder were taken over the course of 10 days. The scans show the individual shifting from depression (top row) to mania (middle row) and back to depression (bottom row). As in all PET scans, red, orange, and yellow colors indicate higher levels of brain activity, while blue and green colors indicate lower levels.

•**cyclothymic disorder**•A disorder marked by numerous periods of hypomanic symptoms and mild depressive symptoms.

PSYCH WATCH · Abnormality and the Arts

Abnormality and Creativity: A Delicate Balance

Up to a point, states of depression, mania, anxiety, and even confusion can be useful. This may be particularly true in the arts. The ancient Greeks believed that various forms of "divine madness" inspired creative acts, from poetry to performance (Ludwig, 1995). In the eighteenth century, romantic notions of the "mad genius" led asylum superintendents to encourage their patients to write; the patients' creations were published in asylum literary journals (Gamwell & Tomes, 1995).

Even today many people expect "creative geniuses" to be psychologically disturbed. A popular image of the artist includes a glass of liquor, a cigarette, and a tormented expression. Classic examples include writer William Faulkner, who suffered from alcoholism and received electroconvulsive therapy for depression; poet Sylvia Plath, who experienced depression most of her life and eventually committed suicide at age 31; and dancer Vaslav Nijinsky, who suffered from schizophrenia and spent many years in institutions. In fact, a number of studies indicate that artists and writers are somewhat more likely than others to suffer from mental disorders, particularly mood disorders (Sample, 2005; Lauronen et al., 2004; Jamison, 1995; Ludwig, 1995, 1994).

Why might creative people be prone to psychological disorders? Some may be predisposed to such disorders long before they begin their artistic careers; the careers may simply bring attention to their emotional struggles (Ludwig, 1995). Indeed, creative people often have a family history of psychological problems. A number also have experienced intense psychological trauma during childhood. English novelist and essayist Virginia Woolf, for example, endured sexual abuse as a child.

Another reason for the creativity link may be that creative endeavors create emotional turmoil that is overwhelming. Truman Capote said that writing his famous book *In Cold Blood* "killed" him psychologically. Before writing this account of the brutal murders of a family, he considered himself "a stable person. . . . Afterward something happened to me" (Ludwig, 1995).

Yet a third explanation for the link between creativity and psychological disorders is that the creative professions offer a welcome climate for those with psychological disturbances. In the worlds of poetry, painting, and acting, for example, emotional expression, unusual thinking, and/or personal turmoil are valued as sources of inspiration and success (Sample, 2005; Ludwig, 1995).

Much remains to be learned about the relationship between emotional turmoil and creativity, but work in this area has already clarified two important points. First, psychological disturbance is hardly a requirement for creativity. Many "creative geniuses" are, in fact, psychologically stable and happy throughout their entire lives (Schlesinger & Ismail, 2004). Second, *mild* psychological disturbances relate to creative achievement much more strongly than severe disturbances do. For example, mild patterns of mania, or *hypomania,* often produce sharpened and creative thinking and greater productivity (Jamison, 1995). Extreme disturbance, however, such as severe mania, depression, or anxiety or a pattern of alcoholism, tends to reduce the quality and quantity of creative work and often ruins careers (Ludwig, 1995). Nineteenth-century composer Robert Schumann produced 27 works during one hypomanic year but next to nothing during years when he was severely depressed and suicidal (Jamison, 1995).

Some artists worry that their creativity would disappear if their psychological suffering were to stop. In fact, however, research suggests that successful treatment for severe psychological disorders more often than not improves the creative process (Jamison, 1995; Ludwig, 1995). Romantic notions aside, severe mental dysfunctioning has little redeeming value, in the arts or anywhere else.

Chris Pizzello/AP Photo

Metallica: Some Kind of Monster Recognizing the links between creativity, psychological dysfunction, and interpersonal distress, heavy metal band Metallica hired a therapist to work with them as they tried to record the album *St. Anger,* a therapy endeavor on display in the 2004 documentary film *Metallica: Some Kind of Monster.* The therapy sessions have been credited with preventing a meltdown and perhaps saving the band.

activity, but no such relationship has been found. Instead, research suggests that mania, like depression, may be linked to *low* serotonin activity (Shastry, 2005; Sobczak et al., 2002). Perhaps low activity of serotonin, acting again as a neuromodulator, opens the door to a mood disorder and *permits* the activity of norepinephrine (or perhaps other neurotransmitters) to define the particular form the disorder will take. That is, low serotonin activity accompanied by low norepinephrine activity may lead to depression; low serotonin activity accompanied by high norepinephrine activity may lead to mania.

Ion Activity While neurotransmitters play a significant role in the communication *between* neurons, ions seem to play a critical role in relaying messages *within* a neuron. That is, ions help transmit messages down the neuron's axon to the nerve endings. Positively charged *sodium ions* (*Na+*) sit on both sides of a neuron's cell membrane. When the neuron is at *rest,* more sodium ions sit outside the membrane. When the neuron receives an incoming message at its receptor sites, pores in the cell membrane open, allowing the sodium ions to flow to the inside of the membrane, thus increasing the positive charge inside the neuron. This starts a wave of electrical activity that travels down the length of the neuron and results in its "firing." After the neuron "fires," *potassium ions* (*K+*) flow from the inside of the neuron across the cell membrane to the outside, helping to return the neuron to its original resting state (see Figure 8-5).

If messages are to be relayed effectively down the axon, the ions must be able to travel easily between the outside and the inside of the neural membrane. Some theorists believe that irregularities in the transport of these ions may cause neurons to fire too easily (resulting in mania) or to stubbornly resist firing (resulting in depression) (Li & El-Mallakh, 2004; El-Mallakh & Huff, 2001). Not surprisingly, investigators have found

BETWEEN THE LINES

Cause for Admission

Up to 40 percent of all bipolar patients admitted to a psychiatric facility are in the midst of a *mixed* bipolar episode (Kruger et al., 2005).

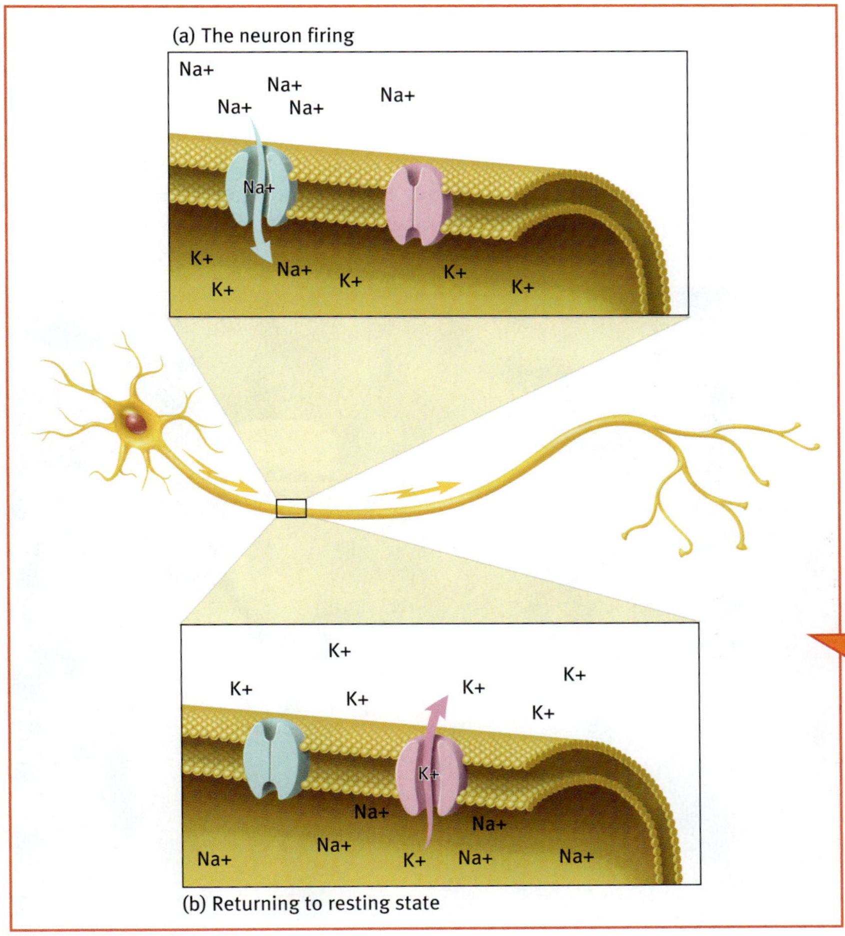

Figure 8-5
Ions and the firing of neurons Neurons relay messages in the form of electrical impulses that travel down the axon toward the nerve endings. As an impulse travels along the axon, sodium ions (Na^+), on the outside of the neuron's membrane, flow inside, causing the impulse to continue down the axon. Once sodium ions flow in, potassium ions (K^+) flow out, returning the membrane's electrical balance to its resting state, ready for the arrival of a new impulse

membrane defects in the neurons of people suffering from bipolar disorder and have observed abnormal functioning in the proteins that help transport ions across a neuron's membrane (Sassi & Soares, 2002; Wang et al., 1999).

Brain Structure Brain imaging and postmortem studies have identified a number of abnormal brain structures in people with bipolar disorders (Lambert & Kinsley, 2005; Shastry, 2005; Baumann & Bogerts, 2001; Stoll et al., 2000). In particular, the basal ganglia and cerebellum of these individuals tend to be smaller than those of other people. In addition, their dorsal raphe nucleus, striatum, amygdala, and prefontal cortex have some structural abnormalities. It is not clear what role such structural abnormalities play in bipolar disorders. It may be that they help produce the neurotransmitter and ion abnormalities that you read about earlier. The dorsal raphe nucleus, for example, is one of the brain sites where serotonin is produced. Alternatively, the structural problems may simply be the result of the neurotransmitter or ion abnormalities or of the medications that many patients with bipolar disorders now take.

Genetic Factors Many theorists believe that people inherit a biological predisposition to develop bipolar disorders. Family pedigree studies support this idea (Maier et al., 2005; Shastry, 2005; Gershon & Nurnberger, 1995). Identical twins of persons with a bipolar disorder have a 40 percent likelihood of developing the same disorder, and fraternal twins, siblings, and other close relatives of such persons have a 5 to 10 percent likelihood, compared to the 1 to 2.6 percent prevalence rate in the general population.

Researchers have also conducted *genetic linkage* studies to identify possible patterns in the inheritance of bipolar disorders. They select large families that have had high rates of a disorder over several generations, observe the pattern of distribution of the disorder among family members, and determine whether it closely follows the distribution pattern of a known genetically transmitted family trait (called a *genetic marker*), such as color blindness, red hair, or a particular medical syndrome.

After studying the records of Israeli, Belgian, and Italian families that had shown high rates of bipolar disorders across several generations, one team of researchers seemed to have linked bipolar disorders to genes on the X chromosome (Mendlewicz et al., 1987, 1980). Other research teams, however, later used techniques from *molecular biology* to examine genetic patterns in large families, and they linked bipolar disorders to genes on chromosomes 1, 4, 6, 10, 11, 12, 13, 15, 18, 21, and 22 (Maier et al., 2005; Baron, 2002).

Extended families and genetic research
Closely knit families in which there is little intermarriage across generations are attractive candidates for genetic linkage studies, which seek to identify possible patterns in the inheritance of disorders. The possible genetic patterns of bipolar disorders have, for example, been studied in some Amish families in Pennsylvania.

Jerry Irwin

Such wide-ranging findings suggest that a number of genetic abnormalities probably combine to help bring about bipolar disorders (Payne, Potash, & DePaulo, 2005).

PUTTING IT... together

Making Sense of All That Is Known

With mood disorders so prevalent in all societies, it is no wonder that they have been the focus of so much research. Great quantities of data about these disorders have been gathered. Still, clinicians have yet to understand fully all that they know.

Several factors have been tied closely to unipolar depression, including biological abnormalities, a reduction in positive reinforcements, negative ways of thinking, a perception of helplessness, and life stress and other sociocultural influences. Indeed, more contributing factors have been associated with unipolar depression than with most other psychological disorders. Precisely how all of these factors relate to unipolar depression, however, is unclear. Several relationships are possible:

1. *One of the factors* may be the key cause of unipolar depression. That is, one theory may be more useful than any of the others for predicting and explaining how unipolar depression occurs. If so, cognitive or biological factors are leading candidates, for these kinds of factors have each been found, at times, to precede and predict depression.

2. *Different factors* may be capable of initiating unipolar depression in different persons. Some people may, for example, begin with low serotonin activity, which predisposes them to react helplessly in stressful situations, interpret events negatively, and enjoy fewer pleasures in life. Others may first suffer a severe loss, which triggers helplessness reactions, low serotonin activity, and reductions in positive rewards. Regardless of the initial cause, these factors may merge into a "final common pathway" of unipolar depression.

3. An *interaction between two or more specific factors* may be necessary to produce unipolar depression (Klocek, Oliver, & Ross, 1997). Perhaps people will become depressed only if they have low levels of serotonin activity, feel helpless, *and* repeatedly blame themselves for negative events.

4. The *various factors may play different roles* in unipolar depression. Some may cause the disorder, some may result from it, and some may keep it going. Peter Lewinsohn and his colleagues (1988) assessed more than 500 nondepressed persons on the various factors linked to depression. They then assessed the study's participants again eight months later to see who had in fact become depressed and which of the factors had predicted depression. Negative thinking, self-dissatisfaction, and life stress were found to precede and predict depression; poor social relationships and reductions in positive rewards did not. The researchers concluded that the former factors help cause unipolar depression, while the latter simply accompany or result from depression and perhaps help maintain it.

As with unipolar depression, clinicians and researchers have learned much about bipolar disorders during the past 35 years. But bipolar disorders appear to be best explained by a focus on *one* kind of variable—biological factors. The evidence suggests that biological abnormalities, perhaps inherited and perhaps triggered by life stress, cause bipolar disorders. Whatever roles other factors may play, the primary one appears to lie in this realm.

Thus we see that one kind of mood disorder may result from multiple causes, while another may result largely from a single factor. Although today's theorists are increasingly looking for intersecting factors to explain various psychological disorders, this is not always the most enlightening course. It depends on the disorder. What is important is that the cause or causes of a disorder be recognized. Scientists can then invest their

Ognen Teofilovski/Reuters

Loneliness and depression: not for humans only
A chimpanzee named Koko looks out from his cage at the Skopje Zoo in Macedonia, a poor country in southeastern Europe. Authorities believe that Koko, the only chimp in the zoo, suffers from depression after having lived alone and in terrible conditions for many years.

BETWEEN THE LINES

Medical Problems and Depression

50% Stroke victims who experience clinical depression ‹‹

30% Cancer patients who experience depression ‹‹

20% Heart attack victims who become depressed ‹‹

18% People with diabetes who are depressed ‹‹

(NIMH, 2004; Simpson, 1996)

energies more efficiently and clinicians can better understand the persons with whom they work.

There is no question that investigations into the mood disorders have been fruitful, and valuable insights should continue to unfold in the years ahead. Now that clinical researchers have gathered so many important pieces of the puzzle, they must put the pieces together into a still more meaningful picture that will suggest even better ways to predict, prevent, and treat these disorders.

‹‹‹[SUMMING UP]›››

○ **Mood disorders** People with mood disorders have mood problems that tend to last for months or years, dominate their interactions with the world, and disrupt their normal functioning. *Depression* and *mania* are the key moods in these disorders. *p. 241*

○ **Unipolar depression** People with *unipolar depression,* the most common pattern of mood disorder, suffer exclusively from depression. The symptoms of depression span five areas of functioning: emotional, motivational, behavioral, cognitive, and physical. Depressed people are also at greater risk for suicidal thinking and behavior. Women are at least twice as likely as men to experience severe unipolar depression. *pp. 242–246*

○ **Explanations of unipolar disorder** Each of the leading models has offered explanations for unipolar depression. The biological, cognitive, and sociocultural views have received the greatest research support.

According to the *biological view,* low activity of two neurotransmitters, *norepinephrine* and *serotonin,* helps cause depression. *Hormonal factors* may also be at work. So too may deficiencies of key proteins and other chemicals *within* certain neurons. Brain imaging research has also tied depression to abnormalities in a circuit of brain areas, including the *prefrontal cortex, hippocampus, amygdala,* and *Brodmann Area 25.* All such biological problems may be linked to *genetic factors.*

According to the *psychodynamic view,* certain people who experience *real or imagined losses* may *regress* to an earlier stage of development, *introject* feelings for the lost object, and eventually become depressed.

The *behavioral view* says that when people experience a large reduction in their positive rewards in life, they may display fewer and fewer positive behaviors. This response leads to a still lower rate of positive rewards and eventually to depression.

The leading *cognitive explanations* of unipolar depression focus on *negative thinking* and *learned helplessness.* According to Beck's theory of negative thinking, *maladaptive attitudes,* the *cognitive triad, errors in thinking,* and *automatic thoughts* help produce unipolar depression. According to Seligman's learned helplessness theory, people become depressed when they believe that they have lost control over the reinforcements in their lives and when they attribute this loss to causes that are *internal, global,* and *stable.*

Sociocultural theories propose that unipolar depression is influenced by social and cultural factors. *Family-social* theorists point out that a low level of social support is often linked to unipolar depression. And *multicultural* theorists have noted that the character and prevalence of depression often varies by gender and sometimes by culture. *pp. 247–263*

○ **Bipolar disorders** In *bipolar disorders,* episodes of mania alternate or intermix with episodes of depression. These disorders are much less common than unipolar depression. They may take the form of *bipolar I, bipolar II,* or *cyclothymic disorder. pp. 263–267*

○ **Explanations of bipolar disorders**   Mania may be related to *high norepinephrine activity along with a low level of serotonin activity.* Some researchers have also linked bipolar disorders to *improper transport of ions* back and forth between the outside and the inside of a neuron's membrane; others have focused on deficiencies of key proteins and other chemicals within certain neurons; and still others have uncovered abnormalities in key brain structures. Genetic studies suggest that people may *inherit* a predisposition to these biological abnormalities. *pp. 267–271*

ᴡ CRITICAL THOUGHTS ᴡ

1. Almost every day we experience ups and downs in mood. How can we distinguish the everyday blues from clinical depression? *pp. 242–246*

2. In one study, students who listened to a sad song became more depressed than those who listened to a happy song (Stratton & Zalanow, 1999, 1994). Yet the sad-song students reported "enjoying" their musical experience more than the happy-song students. What might be going on here? *pp. 242–246*

3. Can you remember instances when a stressful event or period in your life triggered depressed feelings? Can you think of other times in your life when a similar event did not lead to depressed feelings? What was different about you or about this period of time that prevented a negative reaction? *pp. 247–263*

4. Many comedians report that they have grappled with depression. Is there something about performing that might improve their mood? Is there something about being depressed that might make them more skilled at thinking or acting funny? *pp. 247–263*

5. One-third of people who felt unhappy as children continue to feel unhappy as adults. In contrast, fewer than one-tenth of those who were happy as children become unhappy adults (Freeman et al., 1999). How might different theorists explain this correlation between childhood and adult happiness? *pp. 247–263*

6. Several different kinds of theories keep pointing to the social sphere as a key factor in depression—for example, social loss, social ties, social rewards, and social attitudes. Why might problems in the social arena be particularly tied to depression? *pp. 251–263*

⚹⚹ **cyberstudy** ⚹⚹   SEARCH

Search the *Abnormal Psychology* Video Tool Kit
www.worthpublishers.com/apvtk

▲ Chapter 8 Video Cases
   Depression: A Pervasive Disorder
   "Wire Mothers" and Attachment: Harlow's Monkeys
   Seeking Happiness: To Each His Own
▲ Video case discussions, study guides, and questions

Log on to the Comer Web Page
www.worthpublishers.com/comer

▲ Chapter 8 outline, learning objectives, research exercises, study tools, and practice test questions
▲ Additional Chapter 8 case studies, Web links, and FAQs

TREATMENTS FOR MOOD DISORDERS

I think depression has made me a stronger person somehow. I mean in learning to handle this kind of thing. I think that I've had to develop skills and abilities that I wouldn't otherwise. And sensitivities too. I think it's made me more compassionate. I think, because of it, I know what it's like to go through something like that and I'm more curious about other people and what they're going through. [I'm also] more intent in trying to make some meaning out of the whole thing [life]. . . .

Anonymous (in Karp, 1996, p. 130)

I will take Zoloft for the rest of my life. I'm quite content to do it.

Mike Wallace, television news journalist (in Biddle et al., 1996)

In my case, ECT [electroconvulsive therapy] was miraculous. My wife was dubious, but when she came into my room afterward, I sat up and said, "Look who's back among the living." It was like a magic wand.

Dick Cavett, talk show host (in People, 1992)

[T]he hospital was my salvation, and it is something of a paradox that in this austere place with its locked and wired doors and desolate green hallways . . . I found the repose, the assuagement of the tempest in my brain, that I was unable to find in my quiet farmhouse. . . . For me the real healers were seclusion and time.

William Styron, novelist (in Styron, 1990, pp. 68–69)

Because I thought I ought to be able to handle my increasingly violent mood swings by myself, for the first ten years I did not seek any kind of treatment. Even after my condition became a medical emergency, I still intermittently resisted the medications. . . . Having finally cottoned onto the disastrous consequences of starting and stopping lithium, I took it faithfully and found that life was a much stabler and more predictable place than I had ever reckoned. My moods were still intense and my temperament rather quick to the boil, but I could make plans with far more certainty and the periods of absolute blackness were fewer and less extreme. . . . I am [now] too frightened that I will again become morbidly depressed or virulently manic—either of which would, in turn, rip apart every aspect of my life, relationships, and work that I find most meaningful—to seriously consider any change in my medical treatment.

Kay Redfield Jamison, clinical researcher (in Jamison, 1995, pp. 5, 153, 212)

Each of these people suffered from and overcame a severe mood disorder. And, clearly, all believe that the treatment they received was the key to their improvement—the key that opened the door to a normal, stable, and productive life. Yet the treatments that seemed to help them differed greatly. Psychotherapy helped bring control, compassion, and meaning back to the life of the first individual. Electroconvulsive therapy, popularly known as shock treatment, lifted Dick Cavett from the black hole of severe unipolar depression. Hospitalization and its temporary retreat was the answer for William Styron, and antidepressant drugs were the key for Mike Wallace. Kay Jamison escaped the roller-coaster ride of bipolar disorders with the help of lithium, a common, inexpensive element found in mineral salts.

How could such diverse therapies be so helpful to people suffering from the same or similar disorders? As this chapter will show, mood disorders—as painful

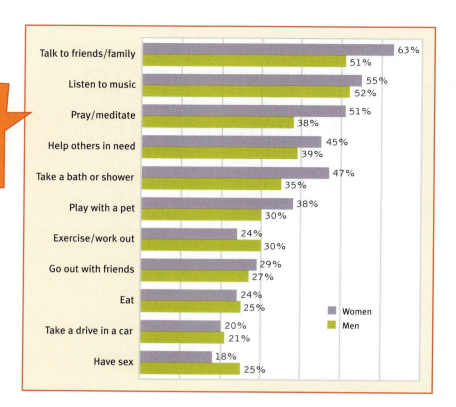

Figure 9-1

What do people do to improve their mood? Almost two-thirds of women talk to friends and family members, half listen to music, and half pray or meditate. Around half of men talk to friends and family members, half listen to music, one-third take a bath or shower, and one-quarter have sex (Wallis, 2005).

and disabling as they tend to be—respond more successfully to more kinds of treatment than do most other forms of psychological dysfunction (see Figure 9–1). This range of treatment options has been a source of reassurance and hope for the millions of people who desire desperately to regain some measure of control over their moods (Lewis & Hoofnagle, 2005).

✿ Treatments for Unipolar Depression

Around one-third of persons with unipolar depression (major depressive or dysthymic disorder) receive treatment from a mental health professional each year (Wang et al., 2005). In addition, many other people in therapy experience depressed feelings as part of another disorder, such as an eating disorder, or in association with changes or general problems that they are encountering in life (see *The Media Speaks* on the facing page). Thus much of the therapy being administered today is for unipolar depression.

A variety of treatment approaches are currently in widespread use for unipolar depression. This chapter will first look at the psychological approaches, focusing on the psychodynamic, behavioral, and cognitive therapies. You will then read about the sociocultural approaches, including a highly regarded intervention called interpersonal psychotherapy. Last, the chapter will look at effective biological approaches, including electroconvulsive therapy, antidepressant drugs, and new brain stimulation interventions. In the process, you will see that unipolar patterns of depression are indeed among the most successfully treated of all psychological disorders.

Psychological Approaches

The psychological treatments used most often to combat unipolar depression come from the psychodynamic, behavioral, and cognitive schools of thought. Psychodynamic therapy, the oldest of all modern psychotherapies, continues to be used widely for depression even though research has not offered strong evidence of its effectiveness. Behavioral therapy, effective primarily for mild or moderate depression, is practiced less

How Well Do Colleges Treat Depression?

BY DANIEL MCGINN AND RON DEPASQUALE, *NEWSWEEK*, AUGUST 23, 2004

On the long list of worries that Mom and Dad have when a child goes to college—grades, homesickness, partying— there's a new issue gaining prominence: the apparent rise in mental illness on campus. More than 1,100 college students commit suicide each year, according to estimates by mental-health groups. And even when students aren't in acute distress, they're suffering in surprisingly large numbers. In a 2003 survey by the American College Health Association, more than 40 percent of students reported feeling "so depressed it was difficult to function" at least once during the year. Thirty percent identified themselves as suffering from an anxiety disorder or depression. . . .

Nathan Lau/Design Pics/Corbis

Given that kind of assessment, it's inevitable that mental-health issues are starting to filter into admissions conversations. One counselor at an East Coast private high school says that during the 2003–04 admissions cycle, officials from two colleges confided they were particularly focused on admitting a class that was "rock solid" emotionally, both to help prevent suicides and to reduce the toll on overbooked school therapists. . . .

Since the admissions process requires students to appear flawless, many families avoid disclosing a child's history of emotional problems, especially before they get an acceptance letter. However, parents are starting to ask tough questions about just which kind of mental-health services they can expect from schools. . . . .

. . . While nearly every school has a counseling office, almost half lack a full-fledged staff psychiatrist, according to Robert Gallagher, a University of Pittsburgh professor who conducts an annual survey of college counseling offices. That means it may be difficult for a student to receive prescription drugs to treat depression or anxiety, and that students with serious problems may be referred off campus for treatment. "Not only are the [on-campus] services more accessible, but the people providing the services are more familiar with college pressures," says Gallagher. And while some schools offer unlimited therapy for students, others restrict them to eight or 10 appointments a year. That may be fine for the average student, who often sees a counselor just once or twice to discuss homesickness, a bad grade or a relationship breakup. For those with more serious problems, such limits may mean rushed care.

Experts cite a mix of reasons that campus therapists' offices are so crowded. Harvard provost Steven Hyman, former director of the National Institute of Mental Health, says that until a few years ago teenagers with mental illness weren't as likely to get good treatment, leading many to stay home after finishing high school. "These kids very likely underperformed [academically] and may not have been able to attend college at all, let alone

a challenging, selective institution," says Hyman. Today, with drugs and earlier intervention, many can. . . .

But the cries for help appear to have other causes, too. The quest to get into a top college has grown so cutthroat for many that more students are emerging from it emotionally damaged. "Kids are burning out sooner and sooner," says Leigh Martin Lowe, director of college counseling at Roland Park Country School in Baltimore. "They're not being allowed to enjoy their teenage years, and many of them end up in college and they don't have the energy or stamina to really turn it on." . . .

For students with [emotional problems], college counselors and therapists say that fact should play some role in their college search. . . . There may also be benefits in choosing smaller schools. . . . According to the University of Pittsburgh study, at colleges with 2,500 or fewer students, health centers had one counselor for every 818 students. At colleges with more than 15,000 students, the counselor-to-student ratio jumped to 1 to 2,426.

The trickiest task faces parents whose children seem 100 percent healthy when they leave for college. Donna Satow . . . and her husband run the Jed Foundation, which helps colleges develop strategies for dealing with student depression. She'd like all colleges to screen incoming students for depression, the same way they make sure they've had all their immunizations. Satow advises parents of every student to become informed about mental-health services at their child's school. "You don't ask, 'What kind of support do you have in case my youngster gets in trouble?'" But in a world where families agonize over finding the cushiest dorm room and the perfect meal plan, it's a question that deserves to be asked.

A place for laughter
Many comedians have histories of depression. Drew Carey, for example, suffered from severe depression for much of his life. The popular host of the TV game show *The Price Is Right* reports that he has been able to overcome this mood disorder successfully by developing a positive outlook—through reading psychology books, listening to tapes on positive thinking, and, of course, generating and communicating humorous thoughts.

Frederick M. Brown/Getty Images

often today than it was in past decades. Cognitive therapy and cognitive-behavioral therapies have performed so well in research that they have a large and growing following among clinicians.

Psychodynamic Therapy Believing that unipolar depression results from unconscious grief over real or imagined losses, compounded by excessive dependence on other people, psychodynamic therapists seek to help clients bring these underlying issues to consciousness and work them through. Using the arsenal of basic psychodynamic procedures, they encourage the depressed client to associate freely during therapy; suggest interpretations of the client's associations, dreams, and displays of resistance and transference; and help the person review past events and feelings (Busch et al., 2004). Free association, for example, helped one man recall the early experiences of loss that, according to his therapist, had set the stage for his depression:

Among his earliest memories, possibly the earliest of all, was the recollection of being wheeled in his baby cart under the elevated train structure and left there alone. Another memory that recurred vividly during the analysis was of an operation around the age of five. He was anesthetized and his mother left him with the doctor. He recalled how he had kicked and screamed, raging at her for leaving him.

(Lorand, 1968, pp. 325–326)

Psychodynamic therapists expect that in the course of treatment depressed clients will eventually gain awareness of the losses in their lives, become less dependent on others, cope with losses more effectively, and make corresponding changes in their functioning. The transition of a therapeutic insight into a real-life change is seen in the case of a middle-aged executive:

The patient's father was still living and in a nursing home, where the patient visited him regularly. On one occasion, he went to see his father full of high expectations, as he had concluded a very successful business transaction. As he began to describe his accomplishments to his father, however, the latter completely ignored his son's remarks and viciously berated him for wearing a pink shirt, which he considered unprofessional. Such a response from the father was not unusual, but this time, as a result of the work that had been accomplished in therapy, the patient could objectively analyze his initial sense of disappointment and deep feeling of failure for not pleasing the older man. Although this experience led to a transient state of depression, it also revealed to the patient his whole dependent lifestyle—his use of others to supply him with a feeling of worth. This experience added a dimension of immediate reality to the insights that had been achieved in therapy and gave the patient the motivation to change radically his childhood system of perceiving himself in relation to paternal transference figures.

(Bemporad, 1992, p. 291)

Despite successful case reports such as this, researchers have found that long-term psychodynamic therapy is only occasionally helpful in cases of unipolar depression (Prochaska & Norcross, 2007). Two features of the approach may help limit its effectiveness. First, depressed clients may be too passive and feel too weary to join fully into the subtle therapy discussions (Widloecher, 2001). And second, they may become discour-

BETWEEN THE LINES

Where Do Depressed Persons First Seek Treatment?

Initially, 41 percent of persons with depression go to a physician with complaints of feeling generally ill, including complaints of pain, general tiredness, and fatigue (Katon & Walker, 1998). ‹‹

aged and end treatment too early when this long-term approach is unable to provide the quick relief that they desperately seek. Generally, psychodynamic therapy seems to be of greatest help in cases of depression that clearly involve a history of childhood loss or trauma, a long-standing sense of emptiness, feelings of perfectionism, and extreme self-criticism (Blatt, 1999, 1995). Short-term psychodynamic therapies have performed better than the traditional approaches (Prochaska & Norcross, 2007; Leichsenring, 2001).

Behavioral Therapy Behaviorists, whose theories of depression tie mood to the rewards in a person's life, have developed corresponding treatments for unipolar depression. Most such treatments are modeled after the intervention proposed by Peter Lewinsohn, the behavioral theorist whose theory of depression was described in Chapter 8 (see page 255). In a typical behavioral approach, therapists (1) reintroduce depressed clients to pleasurable events and activities, (2) appropriately reinforce their depressive and non-depressive behaviors, and (3) help them improve their social skills (Farmer & Chapman, 2008, Addis & Martell, 2004; Lewinsohn et al., 1990, 1982).

First, the therapist selects activities that the client considers pleasurable, such as going shopping or taking photos, and encourages the person to set up a weekly schedule for engaging in them. Studies have shown that adding positive activities to a person's life—sometimes called behavioral activation—can indeed lead to a better mood (Farmer & Chapman, 2008; Leenstra, Ormel, & Giel, 1995). The following case description exemplifies this process:

This patient was a forty-nine-year-old [woman]. . . . Her major interest in life was painting, and indeed she was an accomplished artist. She developed a depression characterized by apathy, self-derogation, and anxiety while she was incapacitated with a severe respiratory infection. She was unable to paint during her illness and lost interest and confidence in her art work when she became depressed. Her therapist thought that she could reinstitute her sources of "reinforcement" if she could be motivated to return to the easel. After providing a supportive relationship for a month, the therapist scheduled a home visit to look at her paintings and to watch and talk with her while she picked up her brush and put paint to canvas. By the time he arrived, she had already begun to paint and within a few weeks experienced a gradual lessening of her depression.

(Liberman & Raskin, 1971, p. 521)

While reintroducing pleasurable events into a client's life, the therapist makes sure that the person's various behaviors are rewarded correctly. Behaviorists argue that when people become depressed, their negative behaviors—crying, ruminating, complaining, or self-depreciation—keep others at a distance, reducing chances for rewarding experiences and interactions. To change this pattern, therapists guide clients to monitor their negative behaviors and to try new, more positive ones (Farmer & Chapman, 2008; Addis & Martell, 2004). In addition, the therapist may use a *contingency management* approach, systematically ignoring a client's depressive behaviors while praising or otherwise rewarding constructive statements and behavior, such as going to work. Sometimes family members and friends are recruited to help with this feature of treatment (Liberman & Raskin, 1971).

Finally, behavioral therapists may train clients in effective social skills (Segrin, 2000; Hersen et al., 1984). In group therapy programs, for example, members may work together to improve eye contact, facial expression, posture, and other behaviors that send social messages.

These behavioral techniques seem to be of only limited help when just one of them is applied. In one study, for example, depressed people who were instructed to increase their pleasant activities showed no more improvement than those in a control group who were told simply to keep track of their activi-

Stretching one's emotions
Although formal treatment is typically needed for severe depression, personal efforts such as going on vacation or spending time with friends can often make a significant difference for people who are struggling with mild depression. Research shows, for example, that regular exercise can help prevent or reduce feelings of depression as well as other psychological symptoms (Dunn et al., 2005).

Pete Saloutos/Corbis

Figure 9-2

Increasing activity In the early stages of cognitive therapy for depression, the client and therapist prepare an activity schedule such as this. Activities as simple as watching television and calling a friend are specified. (Adapted from Beck et al., 1979, p. 122.)

	Monday	Tuesday	Wednesday	Thursday	Fr
9–10		Go to grocery store	Go to museum	Get ready to go out	
10–11		Go to grocery store	Go to museum	Drive to doctor's appointment	
11–12	Doctor's appointment	Call friend	Go to museum	Doctor's appointment	
12–1	Lunch	Lunch	Lunch at museum		
1–2	Drive home	Clean front room	Drive home		
2–3	Read novel	Clean front room	Washing		
3–4	Clean bedroom	Read novel	Washing		
4–5	Watch TV	Watch TV	Watch TV		
5–6	Fix dinner	Fix dinner	Fix dinner		
6–7	Eat with family	Eat with family	Eat with family		
7–8	Clean kitchen	Clean kitchen	Clean kitchen		
8–12	Watch TV, read novel, sleep	Call sister, watch TV, read novel, sleep	Work on rug, read novel, sleep		

cognitive therapy A therapy developed by Aaron Beck that helps people identify and change the maladaptive assumptions and ways of thinking that help cause their psychological disorders.

ties (Hammen & Glass, 1975). However, when two or more behavioral techniques are combined, behavioral treatment does appear to reduce depressive symptoms, particularly if the depression is mild (Farmer & Chapman, 2008; Jacobson et al., 2001, 1996; Teri & Lewinsohn, 1986). It is worth noting that Lewinsohn himself has combined behavioral techniques with cognitive strategies in recent years, in an approach similar to the cognitive-behavioral treatments discussed in the next section.

Cognitive Therapy In Chapter 8 you saw that Aaron Beck viewed unipolar depression as resulting from a pattern of negative thinking that may be triggered by current upsetting situations (see *A Closer Look* on page 282). *Maladaptive attitudes* lead people repeatedly to view themselves, their world, and their future in negative ways—the so-called *cognitive triad*. Such biased views combine with *illogical thinking* to produce *automatic thoughts,* unrelentingly negative thoughts that flood the mind and produce the symptoms of depression.

To help clients overcome this negative thinking, Beck has developed a treatment approach that he calls **cognitive therapy.** He uses this label because the approach is designed primarily to help clients recognize and change their negative cognitive processes and thus to improve their mood (Beck & Weishaar, 2005; Beck, 2002, 1985, 1967). However, as you will see, the approach also includes a number of *behavioral* techniques (Figure 9-2), particularly as therapists try to get clients moving again and encourage them to try out new behaviors. Thus, many theorists consider this approach a *cognitive-behavioral therapy* rather than the purely cognitive intervention implied by its name (Farmer & Chapman, 2008). Beck's approach is similar to Albert Ellis's *rational-emotive therapy* (discussed in Chapters 3 and 5), but it is tailored to the specific cognitive errors found in depression. The approach follows four phases and usually requires fewer than 20 sessions (see Table 9-1).

Phase 1: Increasing activities and elevating mood Using behavioral techniques to set the stage for cognitive treatment, therapists first encourage individuals to become more active and confident. Clients spend time during each session preparing a detailed schedule of hourly activities for the coming week. As they become more active from week to week, their mood is expected to improve.

Phase 2: Challenging automatic thoughts Once people are more active and feeling some emotional relief, cognitive therapists begin to educate them about their negative automatic thoughts. The individuals are instructed to recognize and record automatic thoughts as they occur and to bring their lists to each session. Therapist and client then test the reality behind the thoughts, often concluding that they are groundless. Beck offers the following exchange as an example of this sort of review:

Therapist: Why do you think you won't be able to get into the university of your choice?
Patient: Because my grades were really not so hot.
Therapist: Well, what was your grade average?
Patient: Well, pretty good up until the last semester in high school.
Therapist: What was your grade average in general?
Patient: A's and B's.
Therapist: Well, how many of each?
Patient: Well, I guess, almost all of my grades were A's but I got terrible grades my last semester.
Therapist: What were your grades then?
Patient: I got two A's and two B's.
Therapist: Since your grade average would seem to me to come out to almost all A's, why do you think you won't be able to get into the university?

Patient: *Because of competition being so tough.*
Therapist: *Have you found out what the average grades are for admission to the college?*
Patient: *Well, somebody told me that a B+ average would suffice.*
Therapist: *Isn't your average better than that?*
Patient: *I guess so.*

(Beck et al., 1979, p. 153)

BETWEEN THE LINES

In Their Words

"Start every day off with a smile; get it over with."

(W. C. Fields, 1879–1946)

Phase 3: Identifying negative thinking and biases As people begin to recognize the flaws in their automatic thoughts, cognitive therapists show them how illogical thinking processes are contributing to these thoughts. The depressed student, for example, was using dichotomous (all-or-nothing) thinking when she concluded that any grade lower than A was "terrible." The therapists also guide clients to recognize that almost all their interpretations of events have a negative bias and to change that style of interpretation.

Phase 4: Changing primary attitudes Therapists help clients change the maladaptive attitudes that set the stage for their depression in the first place. As part of the process, therapists often encourage clients to test their attitudes, as in the following therapy discussion:

Therapist: *On what do you base this belief that you can't be happy without a man?*
Patient: *I was really depressed for a year and a half when I didn't have a man.*
Therapist: *Is there another reason why you were depressed?*
Patient: *As we discussed, I was looking at everything in a distorted way. But I still don't know if I could be happy if no one was interested in me.*
Therapist: *I don't know either. Is there a way we could find out?*
Patient: *Well, as an experiment, I could not go out on dates for a while and see how I feel.*
Therapist: *I think that's a good idea. Although it has its flaws, the experimental method is still the best way currently available to discover the facts. You're fortunate in being able to run this type of experiment. Now, for the first time in your adult life you aren't attached to a man. If you find you can be happy without a man, this will greatly strengthen you and also make your future relationships all the better.*

(Beck et al., 1979, pp. 253–254)

table: 9-1

Mood Disorders and Treatment

Disorder	Most Effective Treatment	Average Length of Initial Treatment (Weeks)	Percent Improved by Treatment
Major depressive disorder	Cognitive, cognitive-behavioral, or interpersonal psychotherapy	20	60%
	Antidepressant drugs	20	60
	ECT	2	60
Dysthymic disorder	Cognitive, cognitive-behavioral, or interpersonal psychotherapy	20	60
	Antidepressant drugs	20	60
Bipolar I disorder	Antibipolar (mood-stabilizing) drugs	Indefinite	60
Bipolar II disorder	Antibipolar (mood-stabilizing) drugs	Indefinite	60
Cyclothymic disorder	Psychotherapy or antibipolar drugs	20 to indefinite	Unknown

The Grieving Process

Each year tens of millions of people experience the death of a close relative or friend. Reactions to such painful losses can be so similar to clinical depression that Freud and Abraham based the psychoanalytic explanation of depression on them. But mourning is a natural process that allows us eventually to come to grips with our loss and resume our lives.

Unfortunately, there are many common misconceptions about grieving. The most common is the belief that there is a set timetable for mourning (Oyebode, 2008; Hansson & Stroebe, 2007). Friends and acquaintances often allow the mourner only a few weeks to return to normal life. In fact, it is sometimes many months before a person is ready to do so. The amount of time needed depends on such factors as the relationship of the mourner to the deceased, the age of the mourner, and the mourner's gender or personality (Oyebode, 2008; Stroebe et al., 2007, 2005, 2000).

The bereavement process is also experienced differently in different cultural groups (Walker, 2008; Stroebe & Schut, 2005; Morgan & Laungani, 2002; Wikan, 1991). Japanese Buddhists believe in maintaining contact with dead ancestors,

and almost all homes have an altar dedicated to them. Offering food and speaking to the dead are common practices. The Hopi Indians, though, believe that contact with death brings pollution, so they quickly rid the home of all reminders of their deceased relatives. Muslims in Egypt believe that the bereaved should dwell on their loss and surround themselves with others who share their sorrow, but Muslims in Bali are taught to contain their grief, to laugh and be joyful.

Western society tends to view bereavement as an interference in the daily routine, a troublesome, debilitating emotional response that one must overcome as quickly and efficiently as possible (Oyebode, 2008). This view was not always the norm in the West. In the mid-nineteenth century, for example, communication with the dead through séances and mediums was popular. The amount of grief one felt after the death of a loved one was held to indicate the relationship's strength and significance, and the bereaved were expected to focus on a reunion with the deceased in heaven.

Despite individual variations, many mourners in Western society today go

through a predictable sequence of emotions (Thompson et al., 2007; Osterweis & Townsend, 1988). The bereavement process may begin with *shock:* the survivor has difficulty believing that the person has died. This is frequently followed by a sense of *loss and separation,* a feeling that sometimes leads to misperceptions and illusions—glimpses of the dead person in the street or dreams that the person is alive. Once the mourner fully accepts the fact that the deceased is not coming back, *despair* may set in. Depression, irritability, guilt, spiritual doubts, and anger are natural responses at this stage. Social relationships may deteriorate at this time, and some mourners may suffer from medical problems (Stroeb et al., 2007).

Once the mourning process is complete, it becomes possible to think of the deceased person without being overwhelmed by despair and a sense of loss. At this point, the bereaved is prepared to get on with his or her life, although anniversaries and other meaningful dates may rekindle mourning for many years to come.

Whatever a culture's or individual's reaction to grief may be, research suggests that social support plays an important role during the bereavement process (Sandler et al., 2008; Schneider, 2006; Hullett, 2005). Thus, it is not surprising that numerous self-help bereavement groups have emerged across the world, giving mourners opportunities to gather with others who have lost loved ones and discuss the emotional and practical problems they all face. These groups, which are apparently helpful for many mourners, allow a necessary process to proceed as it should—without pressure, misinterpretation, or judgment.

Mass grief When famous or important people die, it is common for hundreds, or even thousands, of people to come together to mourn the loss of life. In 2005, for example, millions of Catholics and non-Catholics worldwide flocked to Rome for the funeral of Pope John Paul II, whose body is carried here through a crowd of tens of thousands of mourners.

"You're sad about the wrong things, Albert."

Over the past three decades, hundreds of studies have shown that Beck's therapy and similar cognitive and cognitive-behavioral approaches help with unipolar depression. Depressed adults who receive these therapies improve much more than those who receive placebos or no treatment at all (Taube-Schiff & Lau, 2008; Hollon et al., 2006, 2005, 2002; DeRubeis et al., 2005). Around 50 to 60 percent show a near-total elimination of their symptoms. In view of this strong research support, many depression therapists have adopted cognitive and cognitive-behavioral approaches, some offering them in group therapy formats (Petrocelli, 2002).

It is worth noting that a growing number of today's cognitive-behavioral therapists do not agree with Beck's proposition that individuals must fully discard their negative cognitions in order to overcome depression. These therapists, the new wave cognitive-behavioral therapists about whom you read in Chapters 3 and 5, including those who practice *acceptance and commitment therapy* (ACT), guide depressed clients to recognize and accept their negative cognitions simply as streams of thinking that flow through their minds, rather than as valuable guides for behavior and decisions. As clients increasingly accept their negative thoughts for what they are, they can better work around the thoughts as they navigate their way through life (Zettle, 2007, Hayes et al., 2006).

Sociocultural Approaches

As you read in Chapter 8, sociocultural theorists trace the causes of unipolar depression to the broader social structure in which people live and the roles they are required to play. Two groups of sociocultural treatments are now widely applied in cases of unipolar depression—*multicultural approaches* and *family-social approaches.*

Multicultural Treatments
In Chapter 3, you read that *culture-sensitive therapies* seek to address the unique issues faced by members of cultural minority groups (Carten, 2006; Comas-Diaz, 2006). Such approaches typically include special cultural training of the therapists; heightened awareness by therapists of their clients' cultural values and the culture-related stressors, prejudices, and stereotypes faced by the clients; and efforts by therapists to help clients achieve a comfortable (for them) bicultural balance and recognize the impact of their own culture and the dominant culture on their self-views and behaviors (Prochaska & Norcross, 2007).

In the treatment of unipolar depression, culture-sensitive approaches increasingly are being combined with traditional forms of psychotherapy to help maximize the likelihood of minority clients overcoming their disorders. A number of today's therapists, for example, offer cognitive-behavioral therapy for depressed minority clients while also

•interpersonal psychotherapy (IPT)•
A treatment for unipolar depression that is based on the belief that clarifying and changing one's interpersonal problems will help lead to recovery.

•couple therapy•A therapy format in which the therapist works with two people who share a long-term relationship.

•electroconvulsive therapy (ECT)•A treatment for depression in which electrodes attached to a patient's head send an electrical current through the brain, causing a convulsion.

focusing on the clients' economic pressures, minority identity, and related cultural issues (Stacciarini et al., 2007; Satterfield, 2002). A range of studies indicate that Hispanic American, African American, Native American, and Asian American clients are more likely to overcome their depressive disorders when a culture-sensitive focus is added to the form of psychotherapy that they are otherwise receiving (Ward, 2007). Unfortunately, this kind of combination therapy for depression, while on the increase, is still unavailable to most minority clients (Dwight-Johnson & Lagomasino, 2007).

It also appears that the medication needs of many depressed minority clients, especially those who are poor, are inadequately addressed. As you will see later in this chapter, minority clients are less likely than European American clients to receive the most helpful antidepressant medications.

Family-Social Treatments Therapists who use family and social approaches to treat depression help clients change how they deal with the close relationships in their lives. The most effective family-social approaches are *interpersonal psychotherapy* and *couple therapy.*

INTERPERSONAL PSYCHOTHERAPY Developed by clinical researchers Gerald Klerman and Myrna Weissman, **interpersonal psychotherapy (IPT)** holds that any of four interpersonal problem areas may lead to depression and must be addressed: interpersonal loss, interpersonal role dispute, interpersonal role transition, and interpersonal deficits (Weissman & Markowitz, 2002; Klerman & Weissman, 1992). Over the course of around 16 sessions, IPT therapists address these areas.

First, depressed persons may, as psychodynamic theorists suggest, be experiencing a grief reaction over an important *interpersonal loss,* the loss of a loved one. In such cases, IPT therapists encourage clients to explore their relationship with the lost person and express any feelings of anger they may discover. Eventually clients develop new ways of remembering the lost person and also seek new relationships.

Second, depressed people may find themselves in the midst of an *interpersonal role dispute.* Role disputes occur when two people have different expectations of their relationship and of the role each should play. IPT therapists help clients examine whatever role disputes they may be involved in and then develop ways of resolving them.

Depressed people may also be experiencing an *interpersonal role transition,* brought about by major life changes such as divorce or the birth of a child. They may feel overwhelmed by the role changes that accompany the life change. In such cases IPT therapists help them develop the social supports and skills the new roles require.

Finally, some depressed people display *interpersonal deficits,* such as extreme shyness or social awkwardness, that prevent them from having intimate relationships. IPT therapists may help such individuals recognize their deficits and teach them social skills and assertiveness in order to improve their social effectiveness. In the following discussion, the therapist encourages a depressed man to recognize the effect his behavior has on others:

> Client: (After a long pause with eyes downcast, a sad facial expression, and slumped posture) People always make fun of me. I guess I'm just the type of guy who really was meant to be a loner, damn it. (Deep sigh)
> Therapist: Could you do that again for me?
> Client: What?
> Therapist: The sigh, only a bit deeper.
> Client: Why? (Pause) Okay, but I don't see what . . . okay. (Client sighs again and smiles)
> Therapist: Well, that time you smiled, but mostly when you sigh and look so sad I get the feeling that I better leave you alone in your misery, that I should walk on eggshells and not get too chummy or I might hurt you even more.
> Client: (A bit of anger in his voice) Well, excuse me! I was only trying to tell you how I felt.

Therapist: I know you felt miserable, but I also got the message that you wanted to keep me at a distance, that I had no way to reach you.
Client: (Slowly) I feel like a loner, I feel that even you don't care about me—making fun of me.
Therapist: I wonder if other folks need to pass this test, too?

(Beier & Young, 1984, p. 270)

Studies suggest that IPT and related interpersonal treatments for depression have a success rate similar to that of cognitive and cognitive-behavioral therapies (Markowitz, 2006; Weissman & Markowitz, 2002). That is, symptoms almost totally disappear in 50 to 60 percent of clients who receive treatment. After IPT, clients not only experience a reduction of depressive symptoms but also function more effectively in their social and family interactions. Not surprisingly, IPT is considered especially useful for depressed people who are struggling with social conflicts or undergoing changes in their careers or social roles (Weissman & Markowitz, 2002).

COUPLE THERAPY As you have read, depression can result from marital discord, and recovery from depression is often slower for people who do not receive support from their spouse (Franchi, 2004). In fact, as many as half of all depressed clients may be in a dysfunctional relationship. Thus it is not surprising that many cases of depression have been treated by **couple therapy,** the approach in which a therapist works with two people who share a long-term relationship.

Therapists who offer *behavioral marital therapy* help spouses change harmful marital behavior by teaching them specific communication and problem-solving skills (see Chapter 3). When the depressed person's marriage is filled with conflict, this approach and similar ones may be as effective as individual cognitive therapy, interpersonal psychotherapy, or drug therapy in helping to reduce depression (Snyder & Castellani, 2006; Franchi, 2004). In addition, depressed clients who receive couple therapy are more likely than those in individual therapy to be more satisfied with their marriage after treatment.

Biological Approaches

Like several of the psychological and sociocultural therapies, biological treatments can bring great relief to people with unipolar depression. Usually biological treatment means *antidepressant drugs* or popular herbal supplements (see *Psych Watch* on pages 286–287), but for severely depressed individuals who do not respond to other forms of treatment, it sometimes means *electroconvulsive therapy,* an approach that has been around for more than 70 years, or *brain stimulation,* a relatively new group of approaches.

Electroconvulsive Therapy
One of the most controversial forms of treatment for depression is **electroconvulsive therapy,** or **ECT.** One patient describes his experience:

Strapped to a stretcher, you are wheeled into the ECT room. The electroshock machine is in clear view. It is a solemn occasion; there is little talk. The nurse, the attendant, and the anesthetist go about their preparation methodically. Your psychiatrist enters. He seems quite matter-of-fact, businesslike—perhaps a bit rushed. "Everything is going to be just fine. I have given hundreds of these treatments. No one has ever died." You flinch inside. Why did he say that? But there is no time to dwell on it. They are ready. The electrodes are in place. The long clear plastic tube running from the bottle above ends with a needle

Role transition
Major life changes such as marriage, the birth of a child, or divorce can present difficulties in role transition, one of the interpersonal problem areas addressed by IPT therapists in their work with depressed clients.

Nature's Way

Today more than one-third of all Americans take "herbal" supplements and "natural" hormones to help combat ills ranging from depression to pain (Euler, 2008; Magee, 2007). Such supplements—collectively called *dietary supplements* or *nutraceuticals*—are experiencing a remarkable growth in popularity (Rossler et al., 2007), but they are hardly new. Chinese healers compiled the first of their 11,000 medicinal herb formulas as far back as 3000 B.C.

Dietary supplements are a $25 billion industry in the United States, with sales increasing by about $1 billion each year (Thurston, 2008). This sales explosion can be traced to the 1994 passage of the Dietary Supplement Health and Education Act, which provides that dietary supplements are not bound by the same legal requirements as medicinal drugs. To receive approval for a drug, its manufacturer must prove it safe and effective through a testing process that costs manufacturers hundreds of millions of dollars. Dietary supplements, in contrast, are assumed to be safe unless the U.S. Food and Drug Administration (FDA) can prove them harmful. In the wake of this law, 4,000 manufacturers have rushed dietary supplements into the marketplace, typically without research and often with a number of extraordinary claims about their healing powers.

Many other countries—including Canada, Germany, and China—regulate supplements more stringently than the United States, requiring prescriptions by physicians and encouraging ongoing research. In fact, most of the research on supplements has been conducted outside the United States (Linden et al., 2008). Over the past several years, however, the United States has begun to increase its research on supplements (Miller et al., 2004). In 1998, for example, Congress established the National Center for Complementary and Alternative Medicine to sponsor such research. The center has funded rigorous studies of supplements such as *Saint-John's-wort* and *gingko biloba* (NCCAM, 2008). Nevertheless, research on supplements remains modest in comparison with the extensive investigations conducted on medicinal drugs, and there remains a serious shortage of knowledge about the effectiveness of most supplements, as well as their safety, proper dosages, unintended effects, and interactions with other substances (McIntosk & Kleiman, 2007).

Reuters/Umit Bektas

Special mud? In Turkey, a popular alternative treatment for both psychological and physical problems is to visit the resort town of Dalyan and bathe in its special mud.

in your vein. An injection is given. Suddenly—terrifyingly—you can no longer breathe; and then . . . You awaken in your hospital bed. There is a soreness in your legs and a bruise on your arm you can't explain. You are confused to find it so difficult to recover memories. Finally, you stop struggling in the realization that you have no memory for what has transpired. You were scheduled to have ECT, but something must have happened. Perhaps it was postponed. But the nurse keeps coming over to you and asking, "How are you feeling?" You think to yourself: "It must have been given"; but you can't remember. Confused and uncomfortable, you begin to dread the return to the ECT room. You have forgotten, but something about it remains. You are frightened.

(Taylor, 1975)

Compounding these research problems is the reluctance of patients to discuss their use of supplements with their therapists or physicians. As many as three-quarters of those who use unconventional therapies fail to tell their health care provider about them (Sibinga et al., 2004; Kessler, 2002). Yet nutraceuticals can be potent and may interact dangerously with conventional medications (Magee, 2007; Zhou et al., 2004; Schwartz, 2000). In addition, patients often take nutraceuticals incorrectly, partly because they learn about them primarily from friends or from the Internet, where misinformation on this subject abounds (McIntosh & Kleiman, 2007; Walji et al., 2004). The supplement gingko biloba, for instance, does offer patients with Alzheimer's disease the possibility of some improved cognitive functioning (Sommer & Schatzberg, 2002), but it does not work immediately (Maher et al., 2002). People who expect instant results from the herb may be disappointed and discontinue its use before they have had time to receive its therapeutic benefits.

Despite such drawbacks, a number of nutraceuticals do appear to offer considerable promise as treatments for psychological disorders. Gingko biloba's potential benefits for patients with Alzheimer's disease have already been noted. Here are some others:

SAM-e In 1999, *s-adenosylmethionine,* or *SAM-e* (pronounced "Sammy"), entered the United States marketplace after more than 20 years of use in Italy and 13 other countries. A common molecule produced by all living cells, this compound is used in cases of depression. It has the advantages of taking effect in about a week and producing relatively few undesired effects. In contrast, pharmaceutical antidepressants take about a month to be of help and often produce at least inconvenient effects (Brown, Gerbarg, & Bottiglieri, 2002). At the same time, SAM-e itself has certain drawbacks, including its price—it costs several dollars a day for a therapeutic dose.

Saint-John's-wort Research suggests that this common flower can be quite helpful in cases of mild depression (McIntosh & Kleiman, 2007; Seelinger & Mannel, 2007; Linde et al., 2005). Moreover, it is relatively inexpensive and produces few undesired effects. However, it does not appear to benefit people with severe depression.

DHEA This compound seems to sometimes help improve cognitive functioning in cases of Alzheimer's disease and other forms of dementia (Krug et al., 2008). DHEA is not a recent discovery; published reports on its therapeutic potential first appeared in 1952 (Wolkowitz & Reus, 2002).

Black cohosh This herb shows some promise as a treatment for the symptoms of premenstrual syndrome and menopause (Briese et al., 2007; Spangler et al., 2007; Dentali, 2002). A host of other herbs have also been touted for these conditions, including *evening primrose oil, wild yam,* and *chaste berry* (Chavez & Spitzer, 2002).

Zinc People with the eating disorder anorexia nervosa sometimes benefit from dietary supplements of zinc. Studies show that this mineral helps produce weight gain in such individuals and may also help decrease their levels of anxiety and depression (Su & Birmingham, 2002).

Melatonin This hormone, which is secreted naturally by the brain's pineal gland, has been touted to do everything from alleviating depression to improving sexual performance and even increasing the life span. However, the hormone has not received clear research support in most of these realms. It has received modest research support as a treatment for certain sleep difficulties (Braam et al., 2008; Armour & Paton, 2004). It can also help reduce jet lag by resetting the body's internal clock, tricking the body into believing that it is still nighttime. And melatonin can be useful for night-shift workers and blind or elderly people (including Alzheimer's patients), whose circadian rhythms may be out of sync (Lewy et al., 2004; Mahlberg et al., 2004).

Clinicians and patients alike vary greatly in their opinions of ECT. Some consider it a safe biological procedure with minimal risks; others believe it to be an extreme measure that can cause troublesome memory loss and even neurological damage. Despite the heat of this controversy, ECT is used frequently, largely because it is an effective and fast-acting intervention for unipolar depression.

THE TREATMENT PROCEDURE In an ECT procedure, two electrodes are attached to the patient's head, and 65 to 140 volts of electricity are passed through the brain for a half second or less. This results in a *brain seizure* that lasts from 25 seconds to a few minutes. After 6 to 12 such treatments, spaced over two to four weeks, most patients feel less depressed (Garrett, 2008; Fink, 2007, 2001). In *bilateral ECT* one electrode is applied to each side of the forehead, and a current passes through both sides of the

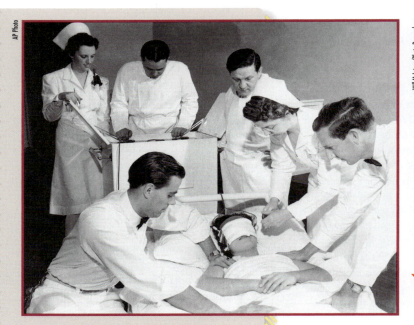

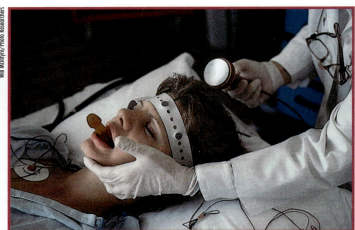

ECT: past and present
The techniques for administering ECT have changed significantly since the treatment's early days. In the 1930s and 1940s (left), patients were awake and held down by attendants throughout the procedure. Today (right), patients are given drugs to help them sleep, muscle relaxants to prevent severe jerks of the body and broken bones, and oxygen to guard against brain damage.

brain. In *unilateral ECT,* the electrodes are placed so that the current passes through only one side.

THE ORIGINS OF ECT The discovery that electric shock can be therapeutic was made by accident. In the 1930s, clinical researchers mistakenly came to believe that brain seizures, or the *convulsions* (severe body spasms) that accompany them, could cure schizophrenia and other psychotic disorders. They observed that people with psychosis rarely suffered from *epilepsy* (*brain seizure disorder*) and that people with epilepsy rarely were psychotic, and so concluded that brain seizures or convulsions somehow prevented psychosis. We now know that the observed correlation between seizures and lack of psychotic symptoms does not necessarily imply that one event caused the other. Nevertheless, swayed by faulty logic, clinicians in the 1930s searched for ways to induce seizures as a treatment for patients with psychosis.

A Hungarian physician named Joseph von Meduna gave the drug *metrazol* to patients suffering from psychosis, and a Viennese physician named Manfred Sakel gave them large doses of insulin (*insulin coma therapy*). These procedures produced the desired brain seizures, but each was quite dangerous and sometimes even caused death. Finally, an Italian psychiatrist named Ugo Cerletti discovered that he could produce seizures more safely by applying electric currents to patients' heads, and he and his colleague Lucio Bini soon developed electroconvulsive therapy as a treatment for psychosis (Cerletti & Bini, 1938). As you might expect, much uncertainty and confusion accompanied their first clinical application of ECT. Did experimenters have the right to impose such an untested treatment against a patient's will?

BETWEEN THE LINES

Why Was Insulin Initially Used to Induce Seizures?

When patients are given large doses of insulin, their blood sugar drops so dramatically that they may sink into a coma and experience brain seizures. ‹‹

The schizophrenic arrived by train from Milan without a ticket or any means of identification. Physically healthy, he was bedraggled and alternately was mute or expressed himself in incomprehensible gibberish made up of odd neologisms. The patient was brought in but despite their vast animal experience there was great apprehension and fear that the patient might be damaged, and so the shock was cautiously set at 70 volts for one-tenth of a second. The low dosage predictably produced only a minor spasm, after which the patient burst into song. Cerletti suggested another shock at a higher voltage, and an excited and voluble discussion broke out among the spectators. . . . All of the staff objected to a further shock, protesting that the patient would probably die. Cerletti was familiar with committees and knew that postponement would inevitably mean prolonged and possibly permanent procrastination, and so he decided to proceed at 110 volts for one-half second. However, before he could do so, the patient who had heard but so far not participated in the discussion sat up and pontifically proclaimed in clear Italian without hint of jargon, "Non una seconda! Mortifera!" (Not again! It will kill me!). Professor Bini hesitated but gave the order to proceed. After recovery, Bini asked the patient "What has been happening to you?" and the man replied "I don't know; perhaps I've been asleep." He remained jargon-free and gave a complete account of himself, and was discharged completely recovered after 11 complete and 3 incomplete treatments over a course of 2 months.

(Brandon, 1981, pp. 8–9)

ECT soon became popular and was tried out on a wide range of psychological problems, as new techniques so often are. Its effectiveness with severe depression in particular became apparent. Ironically, however, doubts were soon raised concerning its usefulness for psychosis, and many researchers have since judged it ineffective for psychotic disorders, except for cases that also include severe depressive symptoms (Taube-Schiff & Lau, 2008).

CHANGES IN ECT PROCEDURES Although Cerletti gained international fame for his procedure, eventually he abandoned ECT and spent his later years seeking other treatments for mental disorders (Karon, 1985). The reason: he abhorred the broken bones and dislocations of the jaw or shoulders that sometimes resulted from ECT's severe convulsions, as well as the memory loss, confusion, and brain damage that the seizures could cause. Other clinicians have stayed with the procedure, however, and have changed it over the years to reduce its undesirable consequences. Today's practitioners give patients strong *muscle relaxants* to minimize convulsions, thus eliminating the danger of fractures or dislocations. They also use *anesthetics (barbiturates)* to put patients to sleep during the procedure, reducing their terror. With these precautions, ECT is medically more complex than it used to be, but also less dangerous and somewhat less disturbing (Garrett, 2008; Gitlin, 2002).

Patients who receive ECT, particularly bilateral ECT, typically have difficulty remembering the events immediately before and after their treatments. In most cases, this memory loss clears up within a few months (Calev et al., 1995, 1991; Squire & Slater, 1983). Some patients, however, experience gaps in more distant memory, and this form of amnesia can be permanent (Wang, 2007; Squire, 1977). Understandably, these individuals may be left embittered by the procedure.

EFFECTIVENESS OF ECT ECT is clearly effective in treating unipolar depression. Studies find that between 60 and 80 percent of ECT patients improve (Richard & Lyness, 2006; Pagnin et al., 2004). The procedure seems to be particularly effective in severe cases of depression that include delusions. It has been difficult, however, to determine why ECT works so well (Garrett, 2008; Lambert & Kinsley, 2005). After all, this procedure delivers a broad insult to the brain that activates a number of brain areas, causes neurons all over the brain to fire, and leads to the release of all kinds of neurotransmitters, and it affects many other systems throughout the body as well.

Although ECT is effective and ECT techniques have improved, its use has generally declined since the 1950s. It is estimated that more than 100,000 patients a year underwent ECT in the United States during the 1940s and 1950s. Today as few as 50,000 per year are believed to receive it (Cauchon, 1999). Two of the reasons for this decline are the memory loss caused by ECT and the frightening nature of the procedure. Another is the emergence of effective *antidepressant drugs.*

Antidepressant Drugs Two kinds of drugs discovered in the 1950s reduce the symptoms of depression: *monoamine oxidase* (*MAO*) *inhibitors* and *tricyclics*. These drugs have been joined in recent years by a third group, the so-called *second-generation antidepressants* (see Table 9-2).

MAO INHIBITORS The effectiveness of **MAO inhibitors** as a treatment for unipolar depression was discovered accidentally. Physicians noted that *iproniazid,* a drug being tested on patients with tuberculosis, had an interesting effect: it seemed to make the patients happier (Sandler, 1990). It was found to have the same effect on depressed patients (Kline, 1958; Loomer, Saunders, & Kline, 1957). What this and several related drugs had in common biochemically was that they slowed the body's production of the enzyme *monoamine oxidase* (*MAO*). Thus they were called MAO inhibitors.

Normally, brain supplies of the enzyme MAO break down, or degrade, the neurotransmitter norepinephrine. MAO inhibitors block MAO from carrying out this activity and thereby stop the destruction of norepinephrine. The result is a rise in norepinephrine activity and, in turn, a reduction of depressive symptoms. Approximately half of depressed patients who take MAO inhibitors are helped by them (Thase, Trivedi, & Rush, 1995). There is, however, a potential danger with regard to these drugs. People who take them experience a dangerous rise in blood pressure if they eat foods containing the chemical *tyramine,* including such common foods as cheeses, bananas, and certain wines. Thus people on MAO inhibitors must stick to a rigid diet. In recent years, a new MAO inhibitor has become available in the form of a *skin patch* that allows for slow, continuous absorption of the drug into the client's body (Julien, 2008; Amsterdam, 2003). Because the doses absorbed across the skin are low, dangerous food interactions do not appear to be as common with this kind of MAO inhibitor.

TRICYCLICS The discovery of **tricyclics** in the 1950s was also accidental. Researchers who were looking for a new drug to combat schizophrenia ran some tests on a drug called *imipramine* (Kuhn, 1958). They discovered that imipramine was of no help in cases of schizophrenia, but it did relieve unipolar depression in many people. The new drug (trade name Tofranil) and related ones became known as tricyclic antidepressants because they all share a three-ring molecular structure.

•**MAO inhibitor**•An antidepressant drug that prevents the action of the enzyme monoamine oxidase.

•**tricyclic**•An antidepressant drug such as imipramine that has three rings in its molecular structure.

"Katia, I know that with the right combination of therapy and medication I could have a committed relationship with you."

In hundreds of studies, depressed patients taking tricyclics have improved much more than similar patients taking placebos, although the drugs must be taken for at least 10 days before such improvements take hold (Julien, 2008; APA, 1993). About 60 to 65 percent of patients who take tricyclics are helped by them (Gitlin, 2002; Hirschfeld, 1999). The case of Derek, whom you met in Chapter 8, is typical:

One winter Derek signed up for an evening course called "The Use and Abuse of Psychoactive Drugs" because he wanted to be able to provide accurate background information in future newspaper articles on drug use among high school and college students. The course covered psychiatric as well as recreational drugs. When the professor listed the symptoms of . . . mood disorders on the blackboard, Derek had a flash of recognition. Perhaps he suffered from depression. . . .

Derek then consulted with a psychiatrist, who confirmed his suspicion and prescribed [an antidepressant drug]. A week later, Derek was sleeping until his alarm went off. Two weeks later, at 9:00 A.M. he was writing his column and making difficult decisions about editorials on sensitive topics. He started writing some feature stories on drugs just because he was interested in the subject. Writing was more fun than it had been in years. His images of his own violent death disappeared. His wife found him more responsive. He conversed with her enthusiastically and answered her questions without . . . long delays.

(Lickey & Gordon, 1991, p. 185)

If depressed people stop taking tricyclics immediately after obtaining relief, they run a high risk of relapsing within a year. If, however, they continue taking the drugs for five months or more after being free of depressive symptoms—a practice called "continuation therapy"—their chances of relapse decrease considerably (Mauri et al., 2005; Kessler, 2002). Certain studies further suggest that patients who take these antidepressant drugs for three or more years after initial improvement—a practice called "maintenance therapy"—may reduce the risk of relapse even more. As a result, clinicians often keep patients on the antidepressant drugs indefinitely.

Most researchers have concluded that tricyclics reduce depression by acting on neurotransmitter "reuptake" mechanisms (Julien, 2008). Remember from Chapter 3 that messages are carried from the "sending" neuron across the synaptic space to a receiving neuron by a neurotransmitter, a chemical released from the axon ending of the sending neuron. However, there is a complication in this process. While the sending neuron releases the neurotransmitter, a pumplike mechanism in the neuron's ending immediately starts to reabsorb it in a process called *reuptake*. The purpose of this reuptake process is to control how long the neurotransmitter remains in the synaptic space and to prevent it from overstimulating the receiving neuron. Unfortunately, reuptake does not always progress properly. The reuptake mechanism may be too efficient in some people—cutting off norepinephrine or serotonin activity too soon, preventing messages from reaching the receiving neurons, and producing clinical depression. Tricyclics *block* this reuptake process, allowing neurotransmitters to remain in the synapse longer, and thus increasing their stimulation of the receiving neurons (see Figure 9-3 on the next page).

If tricyclics act immediately to increase norepinephrine and serotonin activity, why do the symptoms of depression continue for 10 or more days after drug therapy begins? Growing evidence suggests that when tricyclics are ingested, they initially slow down the activity of the neurons that use norepinephrine and serotonin (Lambert & Kinsley, 2005; Blier & de Montigny, 1994). Granted, the reuptake mechanisms of these cells are

table: 9-2

Drugs That Reduce Unipolar Depression

Class/Generic Name	Trade Name
Monoamine oxidase inhibitors	
Isocarboxazid	Marplan
Phenelzine	Nardil
Tranylcypromine	Parnate
Selegiline	Eldepril
Tricyclics	
Imipramine	Tofranil
Amitriptyline	Elavil
Doxepin	Adapin; Sinequan
Trimipramine	Surmontil
Desipramine	Norpramin; Pertofrane
Nortriptyline	Aventil; Pamelor
Protriptyline	Vivactil
Second-Generation Antidepressants	
Maprotiline	Ludiomil
Amoxapine	Asendin
Trazodone	Desyrel
Clomipramine	Anafranil
Fluoxetine	Prozac
Sertraline	Zoloft
Paroxetine	Paxil
Venlafaxine	Effexor
Fluvoxamine	Generic only
Nefazodone	Generic only
Bupropion	Wellbutrin
Mirtazapine	Remeron
Citalopram	Celexa
Escitalopram	Lexapro
Duloxetine	Cymbalta
Reboxetine	Edronax
Atomoxetine	Strattera

(Julien, 2008)

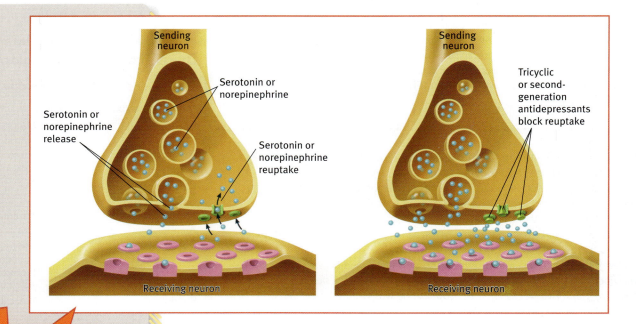

immediately corrected, thus allowing more efficient transmission of the neurotransmitters, but the neurons themselves respond to the change by releasing smaller amounts of the neurotransmitters. After a week or two, the neurons finally adapt to the tricyclic drugs and go back to releasing normal amounts of the neurotransmitters. Now the corrections in the reuptake mechanisms begin to have the desired effect: the neurotransmitters reach the receiving neurons in greater numbers, hence triggering more neural firing and producing a decrease in depression.

Soon after the discovery of tricyclics, this group of antidepressant drugs started being prescribed more often than MAO inhibitors. Tricyclics did not require dietary restrictions as MAO inhibitors did, and people taking them typically showed higher rates of improvement than those taking MAO inhibitors. On the other hand, some individuals respond better to MAO inhibitors than to either tricyclics or the new antidepressants described next, and such persons continue to be given MAO inhibitors (Julien, 2008; Thase, 2006).

SECOND-GENERATION ANTIDEPRESSANTS A third group of effective antidepressant drugs, structurally different from the MAO inhibitors and tricyclics, has been developed during the past few decades. Most of these second-generation antidepressants are labeled **selective serotonin reuptake inhibitors (SSRIs)** because they increase serotonin activity specifically, without affecting norepinephrine or other neurotransmitters. The SSRIs include *fluoxetine* (trade name Prozac), *sertraline* (Zoloft), and *escitalopram* (Lexapro). Newly developed *selective norepinephrine reuptake inhibitors,* such as *atomoxetine* (Strattera), which increase norepinephrine activity only, and *serotonin-norepinephrine reuptake inhibitors,* such as *venlafaxine* (Effexor), which increase both serotonin and norepinephrine activity, are also now available.

In effectiveness and speed of action the second-generation antidepressant drugs are about on a par with the tricyclics (Julien, 2008), yet their sales have skyrocketed. Clinicians often prefer the new antidepressants because it is harder to overdose on them than on the other kinds of antidepressants. In addition, they do not pose the dietary problems of the MAO inhibitors or produce some of the unpleasant effects of the tricyclics, such as dry mouth and constipation. At the same time, the new antidepressants can produce undesirable side effects of their own. Some people experience a reduction in their sex drive, for example (Julien, 2008; Taube-Schiff & Lau, 2008). Decisions about which kinds of antidepressants are prescribed for patients can also be influenced by other factors, such as insurance coverage or financial means (see *Eye on Culture* on the facing page).

First Dibs on Antidepressant Drugs?

In our society, the likelihood of being treated for depression and the types of treatment received by clients often differ greatly from ethnic group to ethnic group. In revealing studies, researchers have examined the antidepressant prescriptions written for depressed individuals, particularly Medicaid recipients with depression (Melfi et al., 2000; Strothers et al., 2005; Stagnitti, 2005; Schulte, 2003). The following patterns emerged:

▶ Almost 40 percent of depressed Medicaid recipients are seen by a mental health provider, irrespective of gender, race, or ethnic group.

▶ African Americans, Hispanic Americans, and Native Americans were half as likely as white Americans to be prescribed antidepressant medications on their initial therapy visits.

▶ Although African Americans are less likely to receive antidepressant drugs, some (but not all) clinical trials suggest that they may be more likely than white Americans to respond to proper antidepressant medications (Lesser et al., 2007; Lawson, 1996, 1986).

▶ African Americans also receive fewer prescriptions than white Americans for most nonpsychiatric disorders (HJK, 2008; Khandker & Simoni-Wastila, 1998).

▶ Among those individuals prescribed antidepressant drugs, African Americans are significantly more likely than white Americans to receive tricyclic and older second-generation antidepressant drugs, while white Americans were more likely than African Americans to receive newer second-generation antidepressant drugs. The older drugs tend to be less expensive for insurance providers.

▶ Although African Americans are more likely to be prescribed tricyclic antidepressants, clinical trials suggest that they may be more susceptible than white Americans to the undesired effects of those kinds of drugs (Sramek, 1996; Strickland et al., 1991).

▶ Elderly depressed individuals are more likely than other depressed persons to receive antidepressant medications.

Preferential treatment? A technician at the pharmaceutical company Eli Lilly examines a large sample of *duloxetine* (brand name Cymbalta), one of the company's second-generation antidepressants. Studies reveal that, on average, depressed African American and Hispanic American patients are less likely than White American patients to be prescribed antidepressant drugs, especially newer second-generation antidepressants.

AP Photo/Darron Cummings

Brain Stimulation Although often effective, the various therapies described so far in this chapter do not help everyone who is suffering from depression. In fact, a careful look at therapy outcome studies reveals that one-third or more of people with unipolar depression are not helped by those treatments. Thus, clinical investigators continue to search for alternative approaches to depression. In recent years, three promising biological approaches have been developed—*vagus nerve stimulation, transcranial magnetic stimulation,* and *deep brain stimulation.*

VAGUS NERVE STIMULATION We each have two *vagus nerves,* one on each side of our body. The vagus nerve, the longest nerve in the human body, runs from the brain stem through the neck down the chest and on to the abdomen, serving as a primary channel of communication between the brain and major organs such as the heart, lungs, and intestines.

A number of years ago, a group of depression researchers surmised that they might be able to stimulate the brain by electrically stimulating the vagus nerve. They were hoping to mimic the positive effects of ECT without, at the same time, producing the undesired effects or trauma associated with ECT. Their efforts gave birth to a new treatment for depression—**vagus nerve stimulation.**

In this procedure, a surgeon implants a small device called a *pulse generator* under the skin of the chest. The surgeon then guides a wire, which extends from the pulse generator, up to the neck and attaches it to the left vagus nerve (see Figure 9-4 on the next page).

•**selective serotonin reuptake inhibitors (SSRIs)**•A group of second-generation antidepressant drugs that increase serotonin activity specifically, without affecting other neurotransmitters.

•**vagus nerve stimulation**•A treatment procedure for depression in which an implanted pulse generator sends regular electrical signals to a person's vagus nerve; the nerve, in turn, stimulates the brain.

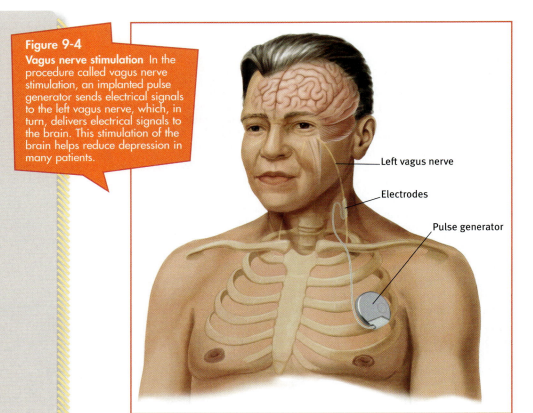

Figure 9-4
Vagus nerve stimulation In the procedure called vagus nerve stimulation, an implanted pulse generator sends electrical signals to the left vagus nerve, which, in turn, delivers electrical signals to the brain. This stimulation of the brain helps reduce depression in many patients.

Left vagus nerve

Electrodes

Pulse generator

Electrical signals travel from the pulse generator through the wire to the vagus nerve. In turn, the stimulated vagus nerve delivers electrical signals to the brain. Typically in this procedure, the pulse generator, which runs on battery power, is programmed to stimulate the vagus nerve (and, in turn, the brain) every five minutes for a period of 30 seconds.

In 2005, the U.S. Food and Drug Administration (FDA) approved this treatment procedure for long-term, recurrent, and/or severe depression and for cases of depression that have not improved even after the use of at least four other treatments. The reason for this approval? Ever since vagus nerve stimulation was first tried on depressed human beings in 1998, research has found that the procedure brings significant relief. Indeed, in studies of severely depressed people who have not responded to any other form of treatment, as many as 40 percent improve significantly when treated with vagus nerve stimulation (Graham, 2007; Nahas et al., 2005).

As with ECT, researchers do not yet know precisely why vagus nerve stimulation reduces depression. After all, like ECT, the procedure activates neurotransmitters and brain areas all over the brain. This includes, but is not limited to, serotonin and norepinephrine and the brain areas that have been implicated in depression (George et al., 2000; Jobe et al., 1999).

TRANSCRANIAL MAGNETIC STIMULATION Transcranial magnetic stimulation (TMS) is another technique that seeks to stimulate the brain without subjecting depressed individuals to the undesired effects or trauma of electroconvulsive therapy. In this procedure, first developed in 1985, the clinician places an electromagnetic coil on or above the patient's head. The coil sends a current into the prefrontal cortex. As you'll remember from the previous chapter, at least some parts of the prefrontal cortex of depressed people are underactive; TMS appears to increase neuron activity in those regions.

TMS has been tested by researchers on a range of disorders, including depression. A number of studies have found that the procedure reduces depression when it is administered daily for two to four weeks (Garrett, 2008; Triggs et al., 1999; George et al., 1995). Moreover, according to a few investigations, TMS may be just as helpful as

•**transcranial magnetic stimulation**• A treatment procedure for depression in which an electromagnetic coil, which is placed on or above a person's head, sends a current into the individual's brain.

•**deep brain stimulation**•A treatment procedure for depression in which a pacemaker powers electrodes that have been implanted in Brodmann Area 25, thus stimulating that brain area.

electroconvulsive therapy when it is administered to severely depressed people who have been unresponsive to other forms of treatment (Grunhaus et al., 2003; Janicak et al., 2002). It has, however, not yet been approved by the FDA as a treatment for depression, partly because the procedure can cause significant discomfort to the patient's scalp and can, in some cases, produce seizures (Carlson, 2008).

DEEP BRAIN STIMULATION As you read in the previous chapter, researchers have recently linked depression to high activity in *Brodmann Area 25,* a brain area located just below the cingulate cortex, and some suspect that this area may be a kind of "depression switch." This finding led neurologist Helen Mayberg and her colleagues (2005) to administer an experimental treatment called **deep brain stimulation (DBS)** to six severely depressed patients who had previously been unresponsive to all other forms of treatment, including electroconvulsive therapy.

Mayberg's approach was modeled after deep brain stimulation approaches that had been applied successfully in cases of brain seizure disorder and Parkinson's disease, both disorders that are related to overly active brain areas. For depression, the Mayberg team drilled two tiny holes into the patient's skull and implanted electrodes in Area 25. The electrodes were connected to a battery, or "pacemaker," that was implanted in the patient's chest (for men) or stomach (for women). The pacemaker powered the electrodes, sending a steady stream of low-voltage electricity to Area 25. Mayberg's expectation was that this repeated stimulation would reduce Area 25 activity to a normal level and "recalibrate" and regulate the depression brain circuit.

In the initial study of DBS, four of the six severely depressed patients became almost depression-free within a matter of months (Mayberg et al., 2005). Subsequent research with other severely depressed individuals has also yielded promising findings (Burkholder, 2008). In addition to significant mood improvements, patients undergoing the procedure have reported improvements in their short-term memory and quality of life.

Understandably, all of this has produced considerable enthusiasm in the clinical field (Dobbs, 2006). Nevertheless, it is important to recognize that research on DBS is in its earliest stages. Investigators have yet to run properly controlled studies of the procedure using larger numbers of research participants, to determine its long-term safety, or to fully clarify its undesired effects. We must remember that in the past, certain promising brain interventions for psychological disorders, such as the lobotomy, later proved problematic or even dangerous upon closer inspection.

How Do the Treatments for Unipolar Depression Compare?

For most kinds of psychological disorders, no more than one or two treatments or combinations of treatments, if any, emerge as highly successful. Unipolar depression seems to be an exception. One of the most treatable of all abnormal patterns, it may respond to any of several approaches. During the past 20 years researchers have conducted a number of treatment outcome studies, which have revealed some important trends:

1. Cognitive, cognitive-behavioral, interpersonal, and biological therapies are all highly effective treatments for unipolar depression, from mild to severe (DeRubeis et al., 2005; Hollon et al., 2005, 2002). In most head-to-head comparisons, they seem to be equally effective at reducing depressive symptoms; however, there are indications that some populations of depressed patients respond better to one therapy than to another (Weissman & Markowitz, 2002; Thase et al., 2000).

   A particularly ambitious study of depression therapy was a six-year investigation sponsored by the National Institute of Mental Health (Elkin, 1994; Elkin et al., 1989, 1985). Experimenters separated 239 moderately and severely depressed people into four treatment groups. One group was treated with 16 weeks of Beck's cognitive therapy, another with 16 weeks of interpersonal psychotherapy, and a third with the tricyclic drug *imipramine.* The

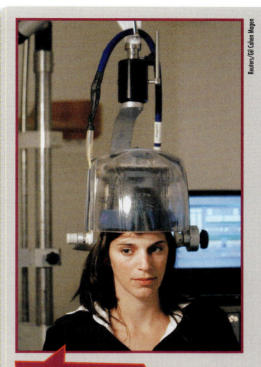

Reuters/Gil Cohen Magen

Stimulating the brain
In this version of transcranial magnetic stimulation, a woman sits under a helmet. The helmet contains an electromagnetic coil that sends currents into and stimulates her brain.

BETWEEN THE LINES

Drugs for Everyone?

Can antidepressant drugs also improve the spirits of nondepressed persons? Yes and no, it appears. When given to volunteers who had no clinical symptoms, antidepressants seemed to help reduce negative emotions such as hostility and fear, but they failed to increase positive feelings such as happiness and excitement (Knutson et al., 1998). ‹‹

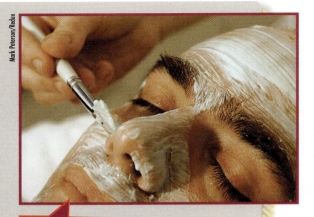

Makeover therapy?
Research suggests that minor improvements in appearance can produce positive cognitive changes such as rises in self-concept and self acceptance (Finzi & Wasserman, 2006). Thus, some cognitive-behavioral therapists encourage clients to purchase new clothes, style their hair differently, undergo facials, or take other such actions. This man is receiving a facial exfoliation, the removal of older surface skin so that fresher and smoother skin may come to the surface.

fourth group received a placebo. A total of 28 therapists conducted these treatments.

Using a depression assessment instrument called the *Hamilton Rating Scale for Depression,* the investigators found that each of the three therapies almost completely eliminated depressive symptoms in 50 to 60 percent of the subjects who completed treatment, whereas only 29 percent of those who received the placebo showed such improvement—a trend that also held, although somewhat less powerfully, when other assessment measures were used. These findings are consistent with those of most other comparative outcome studies (Hollon et al., 2006, 2005, 2002).

The study found that drug therapy reduced depressive symptoms more quickly than the cognitive and interpersonal therapies did, but these psychotherapies had matched the drugs in effectiveness by the final four weeks of treatment. In addition, some recent studies suggest that cognitive and cognitive-behavioral therapy may be more effective than drug therapy at preventing recurrences of depression except when drug therapy is continued for an extended period of time (Hollon et al., 2006, 2005, 2002). Despite the comparable or even superior showing of cognitive and cognitive-behavioral therapies, the past few decades have witnessed a significant increase in the number of physicians prescribing antidepressants. Indeed, the number of antidepressant prescriptions has grown from 2.5 million in 1980 to 4.7 million in 1990 to 203 million today (Horwitz & Wakefield, 2007; Koerner, 2007; Olfson & Klerman, 1993).

2. Although the cognitive, cognitive-behavioral, and interpersonal therapies may lower the likelihood of relapse, they are hardly relapse-proof. Some studies suggest that as many as 30 percent of the depressed patients who respond to these approaches may, in fact, relapse within a few years after the completion of treatment (Weissman & Markowitz, 2002; Cameron et al., 1999). In an effort to head off relapse, some of today's cognitive, cognitive-behavioral, and interpersonal therapists continue to offer treatment, perhaps on a less frequent basis and sometimes in group or classroom formats, after the depression lifts—an approach similar to the "continuation" or "maintenance" approaches used with antidepressant drugs. Early indications are that treatment extensions of this kind do in fact reduce the rate of relapse among successfully treated patients (Taube-Schiff & Lau, 2008; Hollon et al., 2005; Klein et al., 2004). In fact, some research suggests that people who have recovered from depression are less likely to relapse if they receive continuation or maintenance therapy in either drug or psychotherapy form, irrespective of which kind of therapy they originally received (Reynolds et al., 1999).

3. When people with unipolar depression experience significant discord in their marriages, couple therapy tends to be as helpful as cognitive, cognitive-behavioral, interpersonal, or drug therapy.

4. In head-to-head comparisons, depressed people who receive strictly behavioral therapy have shown less improvement than those who receive cognitive, cognitive-behavioral, interpersonal, or biological therapy. Behavioral therapy has, however, proved more effective than placebo treatments or no attention at all (Farmer & Chapman, 2008; Emmelkamp, 1994). Also, as you have seen, behavioral therapy is of less help to people who are severely depressed than to those with mild or moderate depression.

5. Most studies suggest that traditional psychodynamic therapies are less effective than these other therapies in treating all levels of unipolar depression (Svartberg & Stiles, 1991; McLean & Hakstian, 1979). Many psychodynamic clinicians argue, however, that this system of therapy simply does not lend itself to empirical research, and its effectiveness should be judged more by therapists' reports of individual recovery and progress (Busch et al., 2004).

6. Studies have found that a combination of psychotherapy (usually cognitive, cognitive-behavioral, or interpersonal) and drug therapy is modestly more helpful to depressed people than either treatment alone (Taube-Schiff & Lau, 2008; Hollon et al., 2006, 2002).

7. As you will see in Chapter 17, these various trends do not always carry over to the treatment of depressed children and adolescents. For example, a broad six-year project called the *Treatment for Adolescents with Depression Study (TADS)* indicates that a combination of cognitive and drug therapy may be *much* more helpful to depressed teenagers than either treatment alone (TADS, 2007).

8. Among biological treatments, ECT appears to be somewhat more effective than antidepressant drugs for reducing depression (Pagnin et al., 2004). ECT also acts more quickly. Half of patients treated by either intervention, however, relapse within a year unless the initial treatment is followed up by continuing drug treatment or by psychotherapy (Gitlin, 2002; Fink, 2007, 2001). In addition, the newly developed brain stimulation treatments seem helpful for some severely depressed individuals who have been repeatedly unresponsive to drug therapy, ECT, or psychotherapy.

When clinicians today choose a biological treatment for mild to severe unipolar depression, they generally prescribe one of the antidepressant drugs. In some cases, clients may actually request specific ones based on recommendations from friends or on ads they have seen (see *Psych Watch* on pages 298–299). Clinicians are not likely to refer patients for ECT unless the depression is severe and has been unresponsive to drug therapy and psychotherapy (Gitlin, 2002). ECT appears to be helpful for 50 to 80 percent of the severely depressed patients who do not respond to antidepressant drugs (APA, 1993; Avery & Lubrano, 1979). If depressed persons seem to be at high risk for suicide, clinicians sometimes refer them for ECT treatment more readily (Gitlin, 2002; Fink, 2007, 2001). Although ECT clearly has a beneficial effect on suicidal behavior in the short run, studies have not clearly indicated that it has a long-term effect on suicide rates (Prudic & Sackeim, 1999).

Flower power
Extracts from *Hypericum perforatum*, popularly known as Saint-John's-wort, are currently among the hottest-selling treatments for depression. Saint-John's-wort is a low, wild-growing shrub with yellow flowers that has been used for 2,400 years in folk and herbal remedies.

"Of course your daddy loves you. He's on Prozac—he loves everybody."

"Ask Your Doctor If This Medication Is Right for You"

Maybe you are suffering from depression" . . . "Ask your doctor about Zoloft" . . . "There is no need to suffer any longer." Anyone who watches television is familiar with phrases such as these. They are at the heart of *direct-to-consumer* (DTC) drug advertising—advertisements in which pharmaceutical companies appeal directly to consumers, coaxing them to ask their physicians to prescribe particular drugs for them. Research shows that consumers are, on average, familiar with 4 of every 10 drug ads (Wilkes et al., 2000). DTC drug ads on television are so commonplace that it is easy to forget they have been a major part of our viewing pleasure for only

a short while (Koerner, 2007). It was not until 1997, when the FDA relaxed the rules of pharmaceutical advertising, that these ads really took off.

Antidepressants are among the leading drugs to receive DTC television advertising, along with oral antihistamines, cholesterol reducers, and anti-ulcer drugs (Koerner, 2007; Rosenthal et al., 2002). Sales of antidepressants now total around $12 billion each year in the United States alone (Vedantam, 2007), and at least some of the success of these drugs is because of DTC ads.

Altogether, pharmaceutical companies now spend more than $4 billion a year on

American television advertising, around 12 times the amount spent in 1997 (Macias, Pashupati, & Lewis, 2007; Rosenthal et al., 2002; Kaiser Family Foundation, 2001). In fact, 30 percent of adults say they have asked their doctors about specific medications that they saw advertised, and half of these individuals report that their doctors gave them a prescription for the advertised drug (Hausman, 2008; Kaiser Family Foundation, 2001). With results like that, it is small wonder that the pharmaceutical companies are increasing their DTC expenditures by at least 33 percent each year (Fetto, 2002).

But how did we get here? Where did this tidal wave of advertising come from? And what's with those endless "side effects" that are recited so rapidly at the end of each and every commercial? It's a long and complex story, but here are some of the key plot twists that helped set the stage for the emergence of DTC television drug advertising.

1938: Food, Drug, and Cosmetic Act

Congress passed the *Food, Drug, and Cosmetic Act*, which gave the FDA jurisdiction over the labels on prescriptions and over-

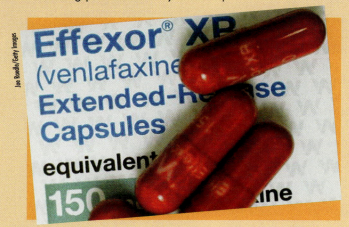

Jon Riscello/Getty Images

•lithium•A metallic element that occurs in nature as a mineral salt and is an effective treatment for bipolar disorders.

•mood stabilizing drugs•Psychotropic drugs that help stabilize the moods of people suffering from bipolar mood disorder. Also known as *antibipolar drugs*.

✿Treatments for Bipolar Disorders

Until the latter part of the twentieth century, people with bipolar disorders were destined to spend their lives on an emotional roller coaster. Psychotherapists reported almost no success, and antidepressant drugs were of limited help (Prien et al., 1974). In fact, the drugs sometimes triggered a manic episode (Post, 2005; Suppes et al., 2005). ECT, too, only occasionally relieved either the depressive or the manic episodes of bipolar disorders.

This gloomy picture changed dramatically in 1970 when the FDA approved the use of **lithium,** a silvery-white element found in various simple mineral salts throughout the natural world, as a treatment for bipolar disorder. Other **mood stabilizing,** or **antibipolar, drugs,** have since been developed, and several of them are now used more widely than lithium, either because they produce fewer undesired effects or because they are even more effective than lithium.

the-counter drugs and over most related forms of drug advertising (Kessler & Pines, 1990).

1962: Kefauver-Harris Drug Amendments

In the spirit of consumer protection, Congress passed a law requiring that all pharmaceutical drugs be proved safe and effective. The law also transferred still more authority for prescription drug ads from the Federal Trade Commission (which regulates most other kinds of advertising) to the FDA (Wilkes et al., 2000).

Finally, and perhaps most important, the law set up rules that companies were required to follow in their drug advertisements, including a detailed summary of the drug's contraindications, side effects, and effectiveness and a "fair balance" coverage of risks and benefits.

1962–1981: Drug Ads for Physicians

For the next two decades, pharmaceutical companies targeted their ads to the physicians who were writing the prescriptions. As more and more *psychotropic* drugs were developed, psychiatrists were included among those targeted.

1981: First Pitch

The pharmaceutical drug industry proposed shifting the advertising of drugs directly to consumers—an approach previously inconceivable because of the paternalized role of physicians (Curtiss, 2002; Wilkes et al., 2000). The argument was based on the notion that such advertising would protect consumers by directly educating them about those drugs that were available.

1983: First DTC Drug Ad

The first direct-to-consumer drug ad appeared. In turn, the FDA imposed a voluntary moratorium on such ads until it could develop a formal policy (Pines, 1999).

1985: Lifting the Ban

The FDA lifted the moratorium and allowed DTC drug ads as long as the ads adhered to the physician-directed promotion standards. That is, each consumer-oriented ad also had to include a summary of the drug's side effects, contraindications, and effectiveness; avoid false advertising; and offer a fair balance in its information about effectiveness and risks (Curtiss, 2002; Ostrove, 2001; Pines, 1999).

Because so much background information was required in each ad, the companies effectively were forced to limit their DTC ads primarily to magazines and ad brochures.

1997: FDA Makes Television-Friendly Changes

Recognizing that its previous guidelines could not readily be applied to brief TV ads, which may run for only 30 seconds, the FDA changed its guidelines for DTC television drug ads. It passed a *Draft Guidance*, which ruled that DTC television advertisements must simply mention a drug's important risks and must indicate where consumers can get further information about the drug. The company must also make such information available by providing a toll-free phone number and a Web site. In addition, it must refer consumers to a magazine ad or other printed material that contains more detailed information, and it must recommend that consumers speak with a doctor about the drug (Wilkes et al., 2000).

Nevertheless, it was lithium that first brought hope to those suffering from bipolar disorder. Anna, who began taking lithium in the 1960s when it was still considered an experimental drug, was one such individual.

Anna was a 21-year-old college student. Before she became ill, Anna was sedate and polite, perhaps even a bit prim. During the fall of her sophomore year at college, she had an episode of mild depression that began when she received a C on a history paper she had worked quite hard on. The same day she received a sanctimonious letter from her father reminding her of the financial hardships he was undergoing to send her to college. He warned her to stick to her books and not to play around with men. Anna became discouraged. She doubted that she deserved her parents' sacrifice. Anna's depression did not seem unusual to her roommate, to her other friends, or even to Anna herself. It seemed

Hopelessness before lithium
Influential English novelist and essayist Virginia Woolf (1882–1941) suffered major episodes of depression and mania at the ages of 13, 22, 28, and 30, and less severe mood swings throughout the rest of her life. Effective bipolar treatments did not exist in Woolf's lifetime, and at the age of 59 she took her own life by drowning, fearing that she was "going mad again."

a natural reaction to her father's unreasonable letter and her fear that she could not live up to the standards he set. In retrospect, this mild depression was the first episode of her bipolar illness.

Several months later, Anna became restless, angry, and obnoxious. She talked continuously and rapidly, jumping from one idea to another. Her speech was filled with rhymes, puns, and sexual innuendoes. During Christmas vacation, she made frequent and unwelcome sexual overtures to her brother's friend in the presence of her entire family. When Anna's mother asked her to behave more politely, Anna began to cry and then slapped her mother across the mouth. Anna did not sleep that night. She sobbed. Between sobs she screamed that no one understood her problems, and no one would even try. The next day, Anna's family took her to the hospital. . . . When she was discharged two weeks later, she was less angry and no longer assaultive. But she was not well and did not go back to school. Her thought and speech were still hypomanic. She had an exaggerated idea of her attractiveness and expected men to fall for her at the first smile. She was irritated when they ignored her attentions. Depressive symptoms were still mixed with the manic ones. She often cried when her bids for attention were not successful or when her parents criticized her dress or behavior.

Anna returned to school the following fall but suffered another depressive episode, followed by another attack of mania within seven months. She had to withdraw from school and enter the hospital. This time . . . the psychiatrists diagnosed her illness as bipolar disorder [and] began treatment with . . . lithium. . . . After seventeen days on lithium, Anna's behavior was quite normal. She was attractively and modestly dressed for her psychiatric interviews. Earlier, she had been sloppily seductive; hair in disarray, half-open blouse, smeared lipstick, bright pink rouge on her cheeks, and bright green make-up on her eyelids. With the help of lithium, she gained some ability to tolerate frustration. During the first week of her hospital stay, she had screamed at a nurse who would not permit her to read late into the night in violation of the ward's 11:00 P.M. "lights out" policy. On lithium, Anna was still annoyed by this "juvenile" rule, but she controlled her anger. She gained some insight into her illness, recognizing that her manic behavior was destructive to herself and others. She also recognized the depression that was often mixed with the mania. . . . She admitted, "Actually, when I'm high, I'm really feeling low. I need to exaggerate in order to feel more important."

Because Anna was on a research ward, the effectiveness of lithium had to be verified by removal of the drug. When she had been off lithium for four to five days, Anna began to show symptoms of both mania and depression. She threatened her psychiatrist, and as before, the threats were grandiose with sexual overtones. In a slinky voice, she warned, "I have ways to put the director of this hospital in my debt. He crawled for me before and he'll do it again. When I snap my fingers, he'll come down to this ward and squash you under his foot." Soon afterward, she threatened suicide. She later explained, "I felt so low last night that if someone had given me a knife or gun, POW." By the ninth day off lithium, Anna's speech was almost incomprehensible: "It's sad to be so putty, pretty, so much like water dripping from a faucet. . . ." Lithium therapy was reinstituted, and within about sixteen days, Anna again recovered and was discharged on lithium.

(Lickey & Gordon, 1991, pp. 236–239)

Lithium and Other Mood Stabilizers

The discovery that lithium effectively reduces bipolar symptoms was, like so many other medical discoveries, quite accidental. In 1949 an Australian psychiatrist, John Cade, hypothesized that manic behavior is caused by a toxic level of uric acid in the body. He set out to test this theory by injecting guinea pigs with uric acid, but first he combined it with lithium to increase its solubility.

To Cade's surprise, the guinea pigs became not manic but quite lethargic after their injections. Cade suspected that the lithium had produced this effect. When he later administered lithium to 10 human beings who had mania, he discovered that it calmed and normalized their mood. Many countries began using lithium for bipolar disorders soon after, but, as noted earlier, it was not until 1970 that the FDA approved it.

Determining the correct lithium dosage for a given patient is a delicate process requiring regular analyses of blood and urine samples and other laboratory tests. Too low a dose will have little or no effect on the bipolar mood swings, but too high a dose can result in lithium intoxication (literally, poisoning), which can cause nausea, vomiting, sluggishness, tremors, dizziness, slurred speech, seizures, kidney dysfunction, and even death. With the correct dose, however, lithium often produces a noticeable change. Some patients respond better to the other mood stabilizing drugs, such as the antiseizure drugs *carbamazepine* (Tegretol) or *valproate* (Depakote), or to a combination of such drugs (Bowden & Singh, 2005; Singh et al., 2005). And still others respond best to a combination of mood stabilizers and atypical antipsychotic drugs, medications that you will read about in Chapter 15 (Dunner, 2005; Kasper, 2005).

Given the effectiveness of lithium and other mood stabilizers, around one-third of all persons with a bipolar disorder now seek treatment from a mental health professional in any given year. Another 15 percent are treated or monitored by family physicians (Wang et al., 2005).

Effectiveness of Lithium and Other Mood Stabilizers

All manner of research has attested to the effectiveness of lithium and other mood stabilizers in treating *manic* episodes (Grof, 2005). More than 60 percent of patients with mania improve on these medications. In addition, most such individuals experience fewer new episodes as long as they continue taking the medications (Carney & Goodwin, 2005). One study found that the risk of relapse is 28 times greater if patients stop taking a mood stabilizer (Suppes et al., 1991). These findings suggest that the mood stabilizers are also prophylactic drugs, ones that actually help prevent symptoms from developing (Julien, 2008). Thus, today's clinicians usually continue patients on some level of a mood stabilizing drug even after their manic episodes subside (Swann, 2005; Cusack, 2002).

The mood stabilizers also help those with bipolar disorder overcome their *depressive* episodes, though to a lesser degree than they help with their manic episodes (Hlastala et al., 1997). Given the drugs' less powerful impact on depressive episodes, many clinicians use a combination of mood stabilizers and antidepressant drugs to treat bipolar depression (Swann, 2005; Grunze, 2005). In addition, continued doses of mood stabilizers (or mood stabilizers combined with antidepressant drugs) apparently reduce the risk of future depressive episodes and future suicide attempts, just as they seem to prevent the return of manic episodes (Carney & Goodwin, 2005).

These findings have led researchers to wonder whether mood stabilizing drugs might also be helpful in cases of unipolar depression. Here the results have been mixed. A few studies suggest that mood stabilizers do help some patients with unipolar depression (Lenox et al., 1998) and occasionally prevent recurrences of that pattern (Abou-Saleh, 1992). Of course, it is possible that the "unipolar" depressed patients helped by mood stabilizers actually have a bipolar disorder whose manic episode has yet to appear (Post, 2005; Sharma et al., 2005).

In the same vein, lithium and other mood stabilizers often seem to enhance the effectiveness of antidepressant drugs prescribed for unipolar depression (Fava, 2000). In one study, for example, up to two-thirds of "tricyclic nonrespondent" patients responded when lithium was added to their antidepressant drug therapy (Joffe et al., 1993).

Mode of Operation of Mood Stabilizers

Researchers do not fully understand how mood stabilizing drugs operate (Lambert & Kinsley, 2005). They suspect that the drugs change synaptic activity in neurons, but in a way different from that of antidepressant drugs. The firing of a

"Now that I've swung back to depression, I'm truly sorry for what I did when I was manic."

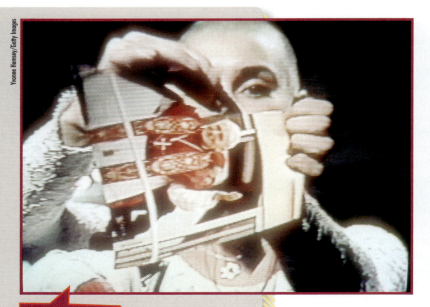

Yvonne Hemsey/Getty Images

AP Photo/Richard Drew

Bipolar struggle
Throughout the 1990s Grammy-winning Irish singer Sinead O'Connor was known for her shaved head, edgy songs, and notorious rebelliousness, including an appearance on the TV show *Saturday Night Live* in 2002 (left) in which she ripped up a picture of Pope John Paul II before the cameras. (Right) More recently, she has received a diagnosis of bipolar disorder and is being successfully treated for it. She now performs a more spiritual kind of music, on display in her CD album *Theology*.

•**second messengers**•Chemical changes within a neuron just after the neuron receives a neurotransmitter message and just before it responds.

neuron actually consists of several phases that ensue at lightning speed. When the neurotransmitter binds to a receptor on the receiving neuron, a series of changes occur *within* the receiving neuron to set the stage for firing. The substances in the neuron that carry out those changes are often called **second messengers** because they relay the original message from the receptor site to the firing mechanism of the neuron. (The neurotransmitter itself is considered the *first messenger*.) Whereas antidepressant drugs affect a neuron's initial reception of neurotransmitters, mood stabilizers appear to affect a neuron's second messengers (Julien, 2008).

Different second-messenger systems are at work in different neurons (Andreasen, 2001). In one of the most important systems, chemicals called *phosphoinositides* are produced once neurotransmitters are received. Research suggests that lithium, and perhaps the other mood stabilizers as well, affect this particular messenger system (Manji et al., 1999). It may be that these drugs affect the activity of any neuron that uses this second-messenger system and in so doing correct the biological abnormalities that lead to bipolar disorders.

In a similar vein, it has been found that lithium and other mood stabilizing drugs also increase the production of *neuroprotective proteins*—key proteins within certain neurons whose job is to prevent cell death. In so doing, the drugs may increase the health and functioning of those cells and, in turn, reduce bipolar symptoms (Gray et al., 2003; Ren et al., 2003).

Alternatively, it may be that the mood stabilizers correct bipolar functioning by directly changing sodium and potassium ion activity in neurons (Swonger & Constantine, 1983). In Chapter 8 you read that bipolar disorders may be triggered by unstable alignments of ions along the membranes of certain neurons in the brain. If this instability is the key to bipolar problems, mood stabilizers would be expected to have some kind of effect on the ion activity. Several studies in fact suggest that lithium ions often substitute, although imperfectly, for sodium ions (Lambert & Kinsley, 2005; Baer et al., 1971), and other research suggests that lithium changes the transport mechanisms that move ions back and forth across the neural membrane (Soares et al., 1999; Lenox et al., 1998).

Adjunctive Psychotherapy

Psychotherapy alone is rarely helpful for persons with bipolar disorders. At the same time, clinicians have learned that mood stabilizing drugs alone are not always sufficient either. Thirty percent or more of patients with these disorders may not respond to lithium or a related drug, may not receive the proper dose, or may relapse while taking it. In addition, a number of patients stop taking mood stabilizers on their own because they are bothered by the drugs' unwanted effects, feel too well to recognize the need for the drugs, miss the euphoria felt during manic episodes, or worry about becoming less productive when they take the drugs (Julien, 2008; Lewis, 2005).

In view of these problems, many clinicians now use individual, group, or family therapy as an *adjunct* to mood stabilizing drugs (Leahy, 2005; Vieta, 2005). Most often, therapists use these formats to emphasize the importance of continuing to take medications; to improve social skills and relationships that may be affected by bipolar episodes; to educate patients and families about bipolar disorders; to help patients solve the family, school, and occupational problems caused by their disorder; and to help prevent patients from attempting suicide. Few controlled studies have tested the effectiveness of such adjunctive therapy, but those that have been done, along with numerous clinical reports, suggest that it helps reduce hospitalization, improves social functioning, and increases patients' ability to obtain and hold a job (Scott & Colom, 2005; Vieta, 2005; Colom et al., 2003). Psychotherapy plays a more central role in the treatment of cyclothymic disorder, the mild bipolar pattern that you read about in Chapter 8. In fact, patients with this problem typically receive psychotherapy, alone or in combination with mood stabilizers (Klerman et al., 1994).

PUTTING IT... together

With Success Come New Questions

Mood disorders are among the most treatable of all psychological disorders. The choice of treatment for bipolar disorders is narrow and simple: drug therapy, perhaps accompanied by psychotherapy, is the single most successful approach. The picture for unipolar depression is more varied and complex, although no less promising. Cognitive, cognitive-behavioral, interpersonal, and antidepressant drug therapy are all helpful in cases of any severity; couple therapy is helpful in select cases; pure behavioral therapy helps in mild to moderate cases; and ECT is useful and effective in severe cases.

Why are several very different approaches highly effective in the treatment of unipolar depression? Two explanations have been proposed. First, if many factors contribute to unipolar depression, it is plausible that the removal of any one of them could improve all areas of functioning. In fact, studies have sometimes found that when one kind of therapy is effective, clients tend to function better in all spheres. When certain antidepressant drugs are effective, for instance, clients make the same improvements in their thinking and social functioning that cognitive and interpersonal therapy would bring about (Meyer et al., 2003; Weissman, 2000).

A second explanation suggests that there are various kinds of unipolar depression, each of which responds to a different kind of therapy. There is evidence that interpersonal psychotherapy is more helpful in depressions brought on by social problems than in depressions that seem to occur spontaneously (Weissman & Markowitz, 2002; Thase et al., 1997). Similarly, antidepressant medications seem more helpful than other treatments in cases marked by appetite and sleep problems, sudden onset, and a family history of depression (McNeal & Cimbolic, 1986).

Whatever the ultimate explanation, the treatment picture is very promising both for people with unipolar depression and for those with bipolar disorders. The odds are that one or a combination of the therapies now in use will relieve their symptoms. Yet the sobering fact remains that as many as 40 percent of people with a mood disorder do not improve under treatment and must suffer their mania or depression until it has run its course (Gitlin, 2002).

Reverse order
Now that antidepressants have proved helpful for so many humans, many veterinarians are administering the drugs to animals in distress. Here a dose of Prozac is given to Phoenix, an unhappy and stressed out cockatiel who has been plucking out his feathers.

Reuters/Mike Hutchings

‹‹‹[SUMMING UP]›››

○ **Treatments for mood disorders** More than 60 percent of people with mood disorders can be helped by treatment. *pp. 275–276*

○ **Treatments for unipolar depression** Various treatments have been used with unipolar depression. *Psychodynamic therapists* try to help depressed persons be-come aware of and work through their real or imagined losses and their excessive dependence on others. *Behavioral therapists* reintroduce clients to events and ac-tivities that they once found pleasurable, reinforce nondepressive behaviors, and teach interpersonal skills. *Cognitive therapists* help depressed persons identify and change their dysfunctional cognitions, and *cognitive-behavioral therapists* try to re-duce depression by combining cognitive and behavioral techniques. *pp. 276–283*

Sociocultural theorists trace unipolar depression to interpersonal, social, and cultural factors. One family-social approach, *interpersonal psychotherapy,* is based on the premise that depression stems from social problems, and so therapists try to help clients develop insight into their interpersonal problems, change them and the conditions that are causing them, and learn skills to protect themselves in the future. Another family-social approach, *couple therapy,* may be used when depressed people are in a dysfunctional relationship. *pp. 283–285*

Most *biological treatments* consist of antidepressant drugs, but electroconvulsive therapy is still used to treat some severe cases of depression, and several *brain stimu-lation* techniques recently have been developed to treat severely depressed patients who are unresponsive to all other forms of treatment. *Electroconvulsive therapy (ECT)* remains a controversial procedure, although it is a fast-acting interven-tion that is particularly effective when depression is severe, unresponsive to other kinds of treatment, or characterized by delusions. *Antidepressant drugs* include three classes: MAO inhibitors, tricyclics, and second-generation antidepressants. *MAO inhibitors* block the degradation of norepinephrine, allowing the levels of this neu-rotransmitter to build up and relieve depressive symptoms. People taking MAO inhibitors must be careful to avoid eating foods with tyramine. *Tricyclics* improve depression by blocking neurotransmitter *reuptake* mechanisms, thereby increasing the activity of norepinephrine and serotonin. The *second-generation antidepressants* include *selective serotonin reuptake inhibitors,* or *SSRIs,* drugs that selectively increase the activity of serotonin. These drugs are as effective as tricyclics and have fewer undesired effects. And, finally, the *brain stimulation* techniques include *vagus nerve stimulation* (which has been approved by the FDA for use in cases of depression), *transcranial magnetic stimulation,* and *deep brain stimulation. pp. 285–295*

○ **Comparing treatments for unipolar depression** The cognitive, interper-sonal, and biological therapies appear to be the most successful for mild to severe depression. Couple therapy is helpful when the individual's depression is ac-companied by significant marital discord. Behavioral therapy is helpful in mild to moderate cases. And ECT and brain stimulation treatments are effective in severe cases. Combinations of psychotherapy and drug therapy tend to be modestly more helpful than any one approach on its own. *pp. 295–298*

○ **Treatments for bipolar disorders** *Lithium* and other *mood stabilizing drugs,* such as *carbamazepine* or *valproate,* have proved to be very effective in alleviating and preventing both the manic and the depressive episodes of bipolar disorders. They are helpful in 60 percent or more of cases. These drugs may reduce bipolar symptoms by affecting the activity of *second-messenger* systems or key proteins or other chemicals in certain neurons throughout the brain. Alternatively, lithium and other mood stabilizers may directly change the activity of *sodium and other ions* in neurons, for example, by altering the transportation of the ions across neu-ral membranes.

In recent years clinicians have learned that patients may fare better when mood stabilizers are supplemented by adjunctive psychotherapy. The issues most often addressed by psychotherapists are medication management, social skills and relationships, education of patients, and solving the family, school, and occupational problems caused by bipolar episodes. *pp. 298–303*

⫸ CRITICAL THOUGHTS ⫷

1. What kinds of transference issues might psychodynamic therapists expect to arise in treatment with depressed persons? *pp. 278–279*

2. Friends and family members try, with limited success, to convince depressed people that their gloom-and-doom view of things is wrong. How does the successful cognitive approach to unipolar depression differ from such efforts at friendly persuasion? *pp. 280–283*

3. If antidepressant drugs are highly effective, why would people seek out herbal supplements, such as Saint-John's-wort or melatonin, for depression? *pp. 286–287, 297*

4. Some people argue that antidepressant drugs serve to curb useful behavior, destroy individuality, and blunt people's concerns about societal ills. Are such concerns justified? *pp. 290–292*

5. A growing number of troubled pets are now being treated with Prozac or other antidepressant drugs. Are such uses of psychotropic drugs appropriate? What other human treatments (psychological or medical) have been applied to pets? *pp. 290–292, 303*

6. Although *deep brain stimulation* has shown great promise as a treatment for severe depression, many clinicians express grave reservations about its use and point to the field's naive use of the lobotomy a half century ago as a cautionary tale. Are such clinicians misguided, or are their concerns valid? *p. 295*

SUICIDE

The war in Iraq never ended for Jonathan Michael Boucher. Not when he flew home from Baghdad, not when he moved to Saratoga Springs for a fresh start and, especially, not when nighttime arrived.

Tortured by what he saw as an 18-year-old Army private during the 2003 invasion and occupation, Boucher was diagnosed with post-traumatic stress disorder (PTSD) and honorably discharged from the military less than two years later.

On May 15, three days before his 24th birthday, the young veteran committed suicide in his apartment's bathroom, stunning friends and family. . . . There was no note. . . .

Boucher's short but intense life was marked by an adventurous spirit and a love for his family, his country and its military. He grew up with a zest for the outdoors and snowboarding and often visited family in the Saratoga area. He had an enormous work ethic and moral compass, family members said. . . .

Johnny Boucher joined the Army right after graduating from East Lyme High School in Connecticut in 2002 because he was emotionally moved by the Sept. 11, 2001, terrorist attacks. "He felt it was his duty to do what he could for America," his father, Steven Boucher, 50, said.

Shortly after enlisting, the 6-foot-2-inch soldier deployed with the "Wolf Pack"—1st Battalion, 41st Field Artillery—and fought his way north in Iraq. He landed with his unit at Baghdad International Airport and was responsible for helping guard it. The battalion earned a Presidential Unit Citation for "exceptional bravery and heroism in the liberation of Baghdad."

But it was during those early months of the war that Johnny Boucher had the evils of combat etched into his mind. The soldier was devastated by seeing a young Iraqi boy holding his dead father, who had been shot in the head. Later, near the airport, the soldier saw four good friends in his artillery battery killed in a vehicle accident minutes after one of them relieved him from duty, his father said.

Boucher tried to rescue the soldiers. Their deaths and other things his son saw deeply impacted his soul after he returned because he was sensitive about family and very patriotic, Steven Boucher said. . . .

But when the sun set, memories of combat and lost friends rose to the top, causing the former artilleryman severe nightmares. Sometimes he would curl up in a ball and weep, causing his parents to try to comfort him. . . . "At nighttime, he was just haunted," Steven Boucher said. . . . "Haunted, I think, by war." Bitterness about the war had crept in, and the troubled former soldier started drinking to calm himself. . . .

Supported by a huge family he adored . . . , Johnny Boucher recently got his own apartment on Franklin Street and appeared to be getting back on track. He seemed to be calm and enjoying life. But it was difficult to tell, and he was still fearful of sleep, his father said. They had plans for a hike, a birthday party and attending his brother Jeffrey's graduation. . . . Then, without warning, Johnny Boucher was gone. He hanged himself next to a Bible, his Army uniform and a garden statue of an angel, said his mother, who discovered him after he failed to show up to work for two days. . . .

Yusko, 2008

"Never was a story of more woe . . ." Two of the most famous suicides in English literature are those of Shakespeare's star-crossed lovers Romeo and Juliet. They each ended their own life when confronted by the perceived death of the other.

Salmon spawn and then die, after an exhausting upstream swim to their breeding ground. Lemmings rush to the sea and drown. But only humans knowingly take their own lives. The actions of salmon and lemmings are instinctual responses that may even help their species survive in the long run. Only in the human act of suicide do beings act for the specific purpose of putting an end to their lives.

Suicide has been recorded throughout history. The Old Testament described King Saul's suicide: "There Saul took a sword and fell on it." The ancient Chinese, Greeks, and Romans also provided examples. In more recent times, twentieth-century suicides by such celebrated individuals as writer Ernest Hemingway, actress Marilyn Monroe, and rock star Kurt Cobain both shocked and fascinated the public (*Psych Watch: Abnormality and the Arts* on the facing page). Even more disturbing are mass suicides such as those of the Heaven's Gate cult in 1997.

Before you finish reading this page, someone in the United States will try to kill himself. At least 60 Americans will have taken their own lives by this time tomorrow. . . . Many of those who attempted will try again, a number with lethal success.

(Shneidman & Mandelkorn, 1983)

Today suicide is one of the leading causes of death in the world. It has been estimated that 700,000 or more people may die by it each year, more than 31,000 in the United States alone (Sadock & Sadock, 2007; Stolberg et al., 2002) (see Table 10-1). Millions of other people throughout the world—600,000 in the United States—make unsuccessful attempts to kill themselves; such attempts are called **parasuicides.** Actually, it is difficult to obtain accurate figures on suicide, and many investigators believe that estimates are often low. For one thing, suicide can be difficult to distinguish from unintentional drug overdoses, automobile crashes, drownings, and other accidents (Wertheimer, 2001; Lester, 2000). Many apparent "accidents" were probably intentional. For another, since suicide is frowned on in our society, relatives and friends often refuse to acknowledge that loved ones have taken their own lives.

•parasuicide• A suicide attempt that does not result in death.

table: 10-1

Most Common Causes of Death in the United States

Rank	Cause	Deaths Per Year	Percentage of Total Deaths
1	Heart disease	696,947	28.5
2	Cancer	557,271	22.8
3	Stroke	162,672	6.7
4	Chronic respiratory diseases	124,816	5.1
5	Accidents	106,742	4.4
6	Diabetes	73,249	3.0
7	Pneumonia and influenza	65,681	2.7
8	Alzheimer's	58,866	2.4
9	Kidney disease	40,974	1.7
10	Septicemia	33,965	1.4
11	**Suicide**	**31,655**	**1.3**

Source: National Center for Health Statistics, *National Vital Health Statistics Report* (2005).

Abnormality and the Arts

Suicide in the Family

On July 1, 1996, model and actress Margaux Hemingway killed herself by taking an overdose of barbiturates. She was the fifth person in four generations of her family to commit suicide. Her death came almost 35 years to the day after the suicide of her famous grandfather, novelist Ernest Hemingway, by shotgun. Severely depressed about his progressive physical illnesses, he had failed to respond to two series of

Karsh/Woodfin Camp & Associates

electroconvulsive shock treatments. The novelist's father, brother, and sister also committed suicide.

Margaux Hemingway had suffered from severe depression, alcoholism, and bulimia nervosa. She had had a successful modeling and acting career in the 1970s, but in later years her work consisted primarily of infomercials and low-budget movies. According to friends, she had tried for years to handle her anguish and setbacks with grace. "I was taught it was Hemingwayesque to take your blows and walk stoically through them."

Famous cases such as this remind us that suicide sometimes runs in families. One study found that 11 percent of individuals who committed suicide had a close relative who had done the same, compared to none of the individuals in a control group, people who died of natural causes (Maris, 2001). But, as with other family-linked disorders, we cannot be certain whether genetic factors, environmental factors, or both produce family patterns of suicide.

Indeed, for members of celebrity families, the family name itself may add considerable stress to their lives. Just as Margaux Hemingway believed that she had to attempt to be "Hemingwayesque," members of celebrity families may feel trapped by the instant recognition, close scrutiny, and high expectations that go along with their family name.

Marc. C. Biggins/Gamma Liaison

Suicide is not classified as a mental disorder by DSM-IV-TR, but clinicians are aware of the high frequency with which psychological dysfunctioning—a breakdown of coping skills, emotional turmoil, a distorted view of life—plays a role in this act. Although suicide is frequently linked to depression, around half of all suicides result from other mental disorders, such as schizophrenia or alcohol dependence, or involve no clear psychological disorder at all (Maris, 2001). Jonathan Boucher, the young combat veteran about whom you read at the beginning of this chapter, had intense feelings of depression and developed a severe drinking problem, but these symptoms and his act of suicide seemed to derive from the posttraumatic stress disorder that engulfed his life and functioning.

People from all walks of life commit suicide, and they do so for a wide range of reasons. The public is often misinformed about the symptoms and causes of suicide. A generation ago, when researchers gave a suicide "fact test" to several hundred undergraduates, the average score was only 59 percent correct (McIntosh, Hubbard, & Santos, 1985). As suicide has become a major focus of the clinical field, however, people's insights are improving, and more recent scores on similar tests by students in both Canada and the United States have been higher (MacDonald, 2007).

BETWEEN THE LINES

Looking Back

In ancient Rome, if people wished to commit suicide, they applied to the Senate and, if their petitions were approved, were given free hemlock. ‹‹

BETWEEN THE LINES

Suicides by Musicians: Post–Kurt Cobain

Phyllis Hyman, jazz singer (1995) ‹‹

Jason Thirsk, punk band Pennywise (1996) ‹‹

Faron Young, country music (1996) ‹‹

Rob Pilatus, Milli Vanilli (1998) ‹‹

Wendy O. Williams, punk singer (1998) ‹‹

Screaming Lord Sutch, British rock singer (1999) ‹‹

Susannah McCorkle, jazz singer (2001) ‹‹

Herman Brood, Dutch rock singer (2001) ‹‹

Leslie Cheung, Chinese singer (2003) ‹‹

Elliott Smith, rock singer (2003) ‹‹

Gary Stuart, country singer (2003) ‹‹

Robert Quine, punk guitarist (2004) ‹‹

Dave Schulthise, bassist for Dead Milkman (2004) ‹‹

Derrick Plourde, rock drummer (2005) ‹‹

Jerry Hadley, opera tenor (2007) ‹‹

Brad Delp, lead singer for rock band Boston (2007) ‹‹

BETWEEN THE LINES

Left Behind

It is estimated that each suicide victim leaves behind an average of six close survivors who may be confused, guilt-ridden, and traumatized by the suicidal act (Hoyert et al., 2001). ‹‹

☼What Is Suicide?

Not every self-inflicted death is a suicide. A man who crashes his car into a tree after falling asleep at the steering wheel is not trying to kill himself. Thus Edwin Shneidman (2005, 1993, 1981, 1963), one of the most influential writers on this topic, defines **suicide** as an intentioned death—a self-inflicted death in which one makes an intentional, direct, and conscious effort to end one's life.

Intentioned deaths may take various forms. Consider the following examples. All three of these people intended to die, but their motives, concerns, and actions differed greatly.

Dave was a successful man. By the age of 50 he had risen to the vice presidency of a small but profitable investment firm. He had a caring wife and two teenage sons who respected him. They lived in an upper-middle-class neighborhood, had a spacious house, and enjoyed a life of comfort.

In August of his fiftieth year, everything changed. Dave was fired. Just like that. The economy had gone bad once again, the firm's profits were down and the president wanted to try new, fresher investment strategies and marketing approaches. He wanted to try a younger person in Dave's position.

The experience of failure, loss, and emptiness was overwhelming for Dave. He looked for another position, but found only low-paying jobs for which he was overqualified. Each day as he looked for work Dave became more depressed, anxious, and desperate. He thought of trying to start his own investment company or to be a consultant of some kind, but, in the cold of night, he knew he was just fooling himself with such notions. The economy was going to Hell—optimism, effort, and talent were not going to make a difference. Dave also became convinced that his wife and sons would not love him if he could not maintain their lifestyle. Even if they did, he could not love himself under such circumstances. He kept sinking, withdrew from others, and felt increasingly hopeless.

Six months after losing his job, Dave began to consider ending his life. The pain was too great, the humiliation unending. He hated the present and dreaded the future. Throughout February he went back and forth. On some days he was sure he wanted to die. On other days, an enjoyable evening or uplifting conversation might change his mind temporarily. On a Monday late in February he heard about a job possibility, and the anticipation of the next day's interview seemed to lift his spirits. But Tuesday's interview did not go well. It was clear to him that he would not be offered the job. He went home, took a recently purchased gun from his locked desk drawer, and shot himself.

Demaine never truly recovered from his mother's death. He was only 7 years old and unprepared for such a loss. His father sent him to live with his grandparents for a time, to a new school with new kids and a new way of life. In Demaine's mind, all these changes were for the worse. He missed the joy and laughter of the past. He missed his home, his father, and his friends. Most of all he missed his mother.

He did not really understand her death. His father said that she was in heaven now, at peace, happy; that she had not wanted to die or leave Demaine; that an accident had taken her life. Demaine's unhappiness and loneliness continued day after day and he began to put things together in his own way. He believed he would be happy again if he could join his mother. He felt she was waiting for him, waiting for him to come to her. These thoughts seemed so right to him; they brought him comfort and hope. One evening, shortly after saying good night to his grandparents, Demaine climbed out of bed, went up the stairs to the roof of their apartment house, and jumped to his death. In his mind he was joining his mother in heaven.

Tya and Noah had been going together for a year. It was Tya's first serious relationship; it was her whole life. Thus when Noah told her that he no longer loved her and was leaving her for someone else, she was shocked and shaken.

As the weeks went by, Tya was filled with two competing feelings—depression and anger. Several times she called Noah, begged him to reconsider, and pleaded for a chance to win him back. At the same time, she hated him for putting her through such misery.

Tya's friends became more and more worried about her. At first they sympathized with her pain, assuming it would soon lift. But as time went on, her depression and anger worsened, and Tya began to act strangely. Always a bit of a drinker, she started to drink heavily and to mix her drinks with various kinds of drugs.

One night Tya went into her bathroom, reached for a bottle of sleeping pills, and swallowed a handful of them. She wanted to make her pain go away, and she wanted Noah to know just how much pain he had caused her. She continued swallowing pill after pill, crying and swearing as she gulped them down. When she began to feel drowsy, she decided to call her close friend Dedra. She was not sure why she was calling, perhaps to say good-bye, to explain her actions, or to make sure that Noah was told; or perhaps to be talked out of it. Dedra pleaded and reasoned with her and tried to motivate her to live. Tya was trying to listen, but she became less and less coherent. Dedra hung up the phone and quickly called Tya's neighbor and the police. When reached by her neighbor, Tya was already in a coma. Seven hours later, while her friends and family waited for news in the hospital lounge, Tya died.

•**suicide**•A self-inflicted death in which the person acts intentionally, directly, and consciously.

•**death seeker**•A person who clearly intends to end his or her life at the time of a suicide attempt.

•**death initiator**•A person who attempts suicide believing that the process of death is already under way and that he or she is simply hastening the process.

•**death ignorer**•A person who attempts suicide without recognizing the finality of death.

•**death darer**•A person who is ambivalent about the wish to die even as he or she attempts suicide.

While Tya seemed to have mixed feelings about her death, Dave was clear in his wish to die. Whereas Demaine viewed death as a trip to heaven, Dave saw it as an end to his existence. Such differences can be important in efforts to understand and treat suicidal persons. Accordingly, Shneidman has distinguished four kinds of people who intentionally end their lives: the *death seeker, death initiator, death ignorer,* and *death darer.*

Death seekers clearly intend to end their lives at the time they attempt suicide. This singleness of purpose may last only a short time. It can change to confusion the very next hour or day, and then return again in short order. Dave, the middle-aged investment counselor, was a death seeker. He had many misgivings about suicide and was ambivalent about it for weeks, but on Tuesday night he was a death seeker—clear in his desire to die and acting in a manner that virtually guaranteed a fatal outcome.

Death initiators also clearly intend to end their lives, but they act out of a belief that the process of death is already under way and that they are simply hastening the process. Some expect that they will die in a matter of days or weeks. Many suicides among the elderly and very sick fall into this category. Robust novelist Ernest Hemingway was profoundly concerned about his failing body as he approached his sixty-second birthday (a lifetime of drinking had affected his health and he also suffered from cardiovascular problems)—a concern that some observers believe was at the center of his suicide.

Death ignorers do not believe that their self-inflicted death will mean the end of their existence. They believe they are trading their present lives for a better or happier existence. Many child suicides, like Demaine's, fall into this category, as do those of adult believers in a hereafter who commit suicide to reach another form of life. In 1997, for example, the world was shocked to learn that 39 members of an unusual cult named Heaven's Gate had committed suicide at an expensive house outside San Diego. It turned out that these members had acted out of the belief that their deaths would free their spirits and enable them to ascend to a "Higher Kingdom."

Death darers experience mixed feelings, or ambivalence, in their intent to die even at the moment of their attempt, and they show this ambivalence in the act itself. Although to some degree they wish to die, and they often do die, their risk-taking behavior does not guarantee death. The person who plays Russian roulette—that is, pulls the trigger of a revolver randomly loaded with one bullet—is a death darer. Many death darers are as interested in gaining attention, making someone feel

Death darers?
A sky surfer tries to ride the perfect cloud over Sweden. Are thrill-seekers daredevils searching for new highs, as many of them claim, or are some actually death darers?

Pressebild/Adventure

•**subintentional death**•A death in which the victim plays an indirect, hidden, partial, or unconscious role.

•**retrospective analysis**•A psychological autopsy in which clinicians and researchers piece together information about a person's suicide from the person's past.

guilty, or expressing anger as in dying per se (Brent et al., 1988). Tya might be considered a death darer. Although her unhappiness and anger were great, she was not sure that she wanted to die. Even while taking pills, she called her friend, reported her actions, and listened to her friend's pleas.

When individuals play *indirect, covert, partial,* or *unconscious* roles in their own deaths, Shneidman (2001, 1993, 1981) classifies them in a suicide-like category called **subintentional death.** Seriously ill people who consistently mismanage their medicines may belong in this category. In related work, influential clinical theorist Karl Menninger (1938) distinguished a category called *chronic suicide.* These people behave in life-endangering ways over an extended period of time, perhaps consuming excessive alcohol, abusing drugs, or indulging in risky activities or occupations. Although their deaths may represent a form of suicide, their true intent is unclear, and so these individuals are not included in the discussions of this chapter.

How Is Suicide Studied?

Suicide researchers face a major obstacle: the individuals they study are no longer alive. How can investigators draw accurate conclusions about the intentions, feelings, and circumstances of people who can no longer explain their actions? Two research methods attempt to deal with this problem, each with only partial success.

One strategy is **retrospective analysis,** a kind of psychological autopsy in which clinicians and researchers piece together data from the suicide victim's past (Wetzel & Murphy, 2005). Relatives, friends, therapists, or physicians may remember past statements, conversations, and behaviors that shed light on a suicide. Retrospective information may also be provided by the suicide notes that some victims leave behind (Handelman & Lester, 2007) (see *A Closer Look* on the facing page).

However, such sources of information are not always available. Around half of all suicide victims have never been in psychotherapy (Stolberg et al., 2002), and less than one-third leave notes (Maris, 2001). Nor is retrospective information necessarily valid. A grieving, perhaps guilt-ridden relative or a distraught therapist may be incapable of objective recollections or simply reluctant to discuss an act that is so stigmatizing in our society (Sudak et al., 2008; Lukas & Seiden, 2007).

Because of these limitations, many researchers also use a second strategy—*studying people who survive their suicide attempts.* It is estimated that there are 8 to 20 nonfatal suicide attempts for every fatal suicide (Maris, 2001). However, it may be that people who survive suicide differ in important ways from those who do not (Cutler et al., 2001; Diekstra et al., 1995). Many of them may not really have wanted to die, for example. Nevertheless, suicide researchers have found it useful to study survivors of suicide, and this chapter shall consider those who attempt suicide and those who commit suicide as more or less alike.

Patterns and Statistics

Suicide happens within a larger social setting, and researchers have gathered many statistics regarding the social contexts in which such deaths take place. They have found, for example, that suicide rates vary from country to country (Sadock & Sadock, 2007; Humphrey, 2006). Russia, Hungary, Germany, Austria, Finland, Denmark, China, and Japan have very high rates, more than 20 suicides annually per 100,000 persons; conversely, Egypt, Mexico, Greece, and Spain have relatively low rates, fewer than 5 per 100,000. The United States and Canada fall in between, each with a suicide rate of around 12 per 100,000 persons; England has a rate of 9 per 100,000.

Religious affiliation and beliefs may help account for these national differences (Sadock & Sadock, 2007; Brown, 2002). For example, countries that are largely Catholic, Jewish, or Muslim tend to have low suicide rates. It has been suggested that in these countries, strict prohibitions against suicide or a strong religious tradition deter many people from committing suicide (Matsumoto &

Retrospective analysis
The very public *retrospective analysis* of the 1994 suicide of rock star Kurt Cobain was given new impetus in 2002 with the publication of his personal diaries—800 pages that included Cobain's descriptions of his thoughts and concerns, bouts with depression, and drug addiction.

A CLOSER LOOK

Suicide Notes

Bill: I am sorry for causing you so much trouble. I really didn't want to and if you would have told me at the first time the truth probably both of us would be very happy now. Bill I am sorry but I can't take the life any more, I don't think there is any goodness in the world. I love you very very much and I want you to be as happy in your life as I wanted to make you. Tell your parents I am very sorry and please if you can do it don't ever let my parents know what happened.

Please, don't hate me Bill, I love you.
Mary////

(LEENAARS, 1991)

Many suicides go undetected or unconfirmed because the only people who could tell us the truth are gone from the world. Many other people who commit suicide, however—an estimated 12 to 33 percent—leave notes that reveal their intentions and psychological state only hours or minutes before they died (Girdhar et al., 2004; Maris, 2001; Lester, 2000).

Each suicide note is a personal document, unique to the writer and the circumstances (Leenaars, 2002, 1989). Some are barely a single sentence; others run several pages. People who leave notes clearly wish to send a powerful message to those they leave behind, whether it be "a cry for help, an epitaph, or a last will and testament" (Frederick, 1969, p. 17). Most suicide notes are addressed to specific individuals.

Survivors' reactions to suicide notes vary (Wertheimer, 2001; Leenaars, 1989). A note can clarify the cause of death, thus saving relatives the ordeal of a legal investigation. Friends and relatives may find that it eases their grief to know the person's reasons for committing suicide. Yet some suicide notes, especially ones that are passive-aggressive or outright hostile, add to the confusion, guilt, or horror that survivors experience, as in the following case:

Rather than permit his wife to leave him, twenty-year-old Mr. Jefferson hanged himself in the bathroom, leaving a note on the front door for his wife, saying, "Cathy I love you. You're right, I am crazy . . . and thank you for trying to love me. Phil." Mrs. Jefferson felt and frequently insisted that she "killed Phil." She attempted suicide herself a week after.////

(WALLACE, 1981, P. 79)

Clinical researchers have tried to improve their understanding of suicide by studying differences between the notes of suicide attempters and completers; genuine and fake suicide notes; the age, culture, and sex of note writers; the grammar of notes; the type and frequency of words used; conscious and unconscious contents; handwriting; and emotional, cognitive, and motivational themes (Handelman & Lester, 2007; Lester et al., 2004; O'Connor & Leenaars, 2004; Black & Lester, 2003). One important finding is that suicide notes vary significantly with age. Younger persons express more hostility toward themselves and cite more interpersonal problems and social isolation in their notes; those between 40 and 49 report being unable to cope with life; those between 50 and 59 tend not to cite a reason for their suicide; and those over 60 are motivated by such problems as illness, pain, disability, loneliness, and other deprivations (Zhang & Lester, 2008; Hokans & Lester, 2007; Lester et al., 2004).

A number of studies have also been conducted on writings that are similar to suicide notes. For example, one team of investigators compared poems by nine poets who committed suicide to those written by nine poets who did not commit suicide (Stirman & Pennebaker, 2001). The poets who committed suicide used more first-person self-references in their works, such as "I" and "me," as well as more words associated with death. In addition, the poets who committed suicide used fewer communication terms (such as "talk" and "listen") in the poems they had written close to the time of their suicides, while the nonsuicidal poets actually increased their use of such words during that same period of time. Thus, it may be that people who are contemplating suicide tend to

AP Photo/Omaha Police Handout

A confused good-bye On December 6, 2007, a depressed 19-year-old named Robert Hawkins shot eight Christmas shoppers and then himself at an Omaha shopping mall in the aftermath of a breakup with his long-term girlfriend and the loss of his job. In a suicide note left to his friends, Hawkins expressed a range of feelings, from love and appreciation to hostility and regret. In addition, he used his final words in life to declare once and for all that he did not commit certain acts of which he had been accused.

use language in distinct ways—ways that may eventually help clinicians identify a person's risk for suicide.

Of course, keep in mind that the writers of suicide notes themselves may not be fully aware of their motives; their desperate thinking may prevent them from being truly insightful. Thus, suicide notes are "not the royal road to an easy understanding of suicidal phenomena" (Shneidman, 1973, p. 380). Nevertheless, in combination with other sources they can point clinicians and researchers in the right direction.

Juang, 2008; Stack & Kposowa, 2008). Yet there are exceptions to this tentative rule. Austria, a predominantly Roman Catholic country, has one of the highest suicide rates in the world.

Research is beginning to suggest that religious doctrine may not help prevent suicide as much as the degree of an individual's *devoutness*. Regardless of their particular persuasion, very religious people seem less likely to commit suicide (Thio, 2006; Stack & Kposowa, 2008). Similarly, it seems that people who hold a greater reverence for life are less prone to consider or attempt self-destruction (Lee, 1985).

The suicide rates of men and women also differ (see Figure 10-1). Three times as many women attempt suicide as men, yet men succeed at more than three times the rate of women (Sadock & Sadock, 2007; Humphrey, 2006). Around the world 19 of every 100,000 men kill themselves each year; the suicide rate for women is 4 per 100,000 (Levi et al., 2003).

Figure 10-1

Current U.S. suicide rates (a) Elderly people are more likely to commit suicide than those in other age groups; (b) males commit suicide at higher rates than females of corresponding ages; (c) white Americans commit suicide at higher rates than African Americans of corresponding ages; (d) elderly white American men have the highest risk of suicide. (Adapted from CDC, 2008; U.S. Census Bureau, 2008, 1994, 1990.)

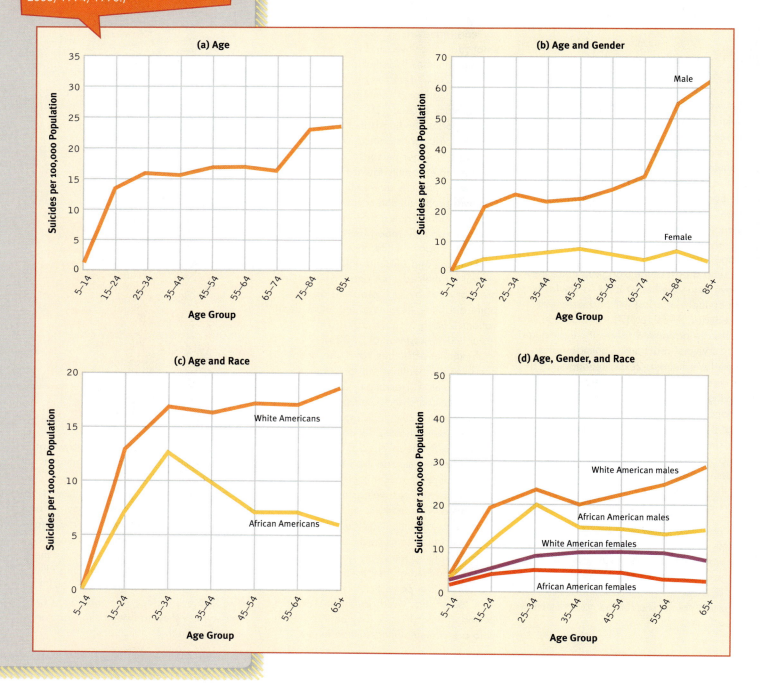

One reason for these differing rates appears to be the different methods used by men and women. Men tend to use more violent methods, such as shooting, stabbing, or hanging themselves, whereas women use less violent methods, such as drug overdose. Guns are used in nearly two-thirds of the male suicides in the United States, compared to 40 percent of the female suicides (Maris, 2001).

Suicide is also related to social environment and marital status (Cutright et al., 2007). In one study, around half of the individuals who had committed suicide were found to have no close friends (Maris, 2001). Fewer still had close relationships with parents and other family members. In a related vein, research has revealed that divorced persons have a higher suicide rate than married or cohabitating individuals (Stolberg et al., 2002).

Finally, in the United States at least, suicide rates seem to vary according to race. The overall suicide rate of white Americans, 12 per 100,000 persons, is almost twice as high as that of African Americans, Hispanic Americans, and Asian Americans (Walker et al., 2008; Oquendo et al., 2005; Stolberg et al., 2002). A major exception to this pattern is the very high suicide rate of Native Americans, which overall is one and a half times the national average (Alcantar & Gone, 2008; Humphrey, 2006). Although the extreme poverty of many Native Americans may partly explain this trend, studies show that factors such as alcohol use, modeling, and the availability of guns may also play a role (Goldston et al., 2008; Berman & Jobes, 1995, 1991). Studies of Native Americans in Canada yield similar results (Matsumoto & Juang, 2008).

Some of these statistics on suicide have been questioned (Leach & Leong, 2008). One analysis suggests that the actual rate of suicide may be 15 percent higher for African Americans and 6 percent higher for women than usually reported (Phillips & Ruth, 1993). People in these groups are more likely than others to use methods of suicide that can be mistaken for causes of accidental death, such as poisoning, drug overdose, single-car crashes, and pedestrian accidents.

✿What Triggers a Suicide?

Suicidal acts may be connected to recent events or current conditions in a person's life. Although such factors may not be the basic motivation for the suicide, they can precipitate it. Common triggering factors include *stressful events, mood and thought changes, alcohol and other drug use, mental disorders,* and *modeling.*

Stressful Events and Situations

Researchers have counted more stressful events in the recent lives of suicide attempters than in the lives of nonattempters (Kessler et al., 2008; Hendin et al., 2001). In one study, suicide attempters reported twice as many stressful events in the year before their attempts as nonsuicidal depressed patients or patients with other kinds of psychological problems (Cohen-Sandler et al., 1982). One stressor that has been consistently linked to suicide is combat stress. Research indicates that combat veterans across several wars are more than twice as likely to commit suicide as nonveterans (Kaplan et al., 2007). At the beginning of this chapter, for example, you read about a young man who committed suicide upon returning to civilian life, after experiencing the enormous stressors of combat in Iraq.

The stressors that help lead to suicide do not need to be as horrific as those tied to combat. Common forms of *immediate stress* seen in cases of suicide are the loss of a loved one through death, divorce, or rejection (Ajdacic-Gross et al., 2008); loss of a job (Yamasaki et al., 2005); and the stress associated with hurricanes or other natural disasters, even among very young children. A suicide attempt may also be precipitated

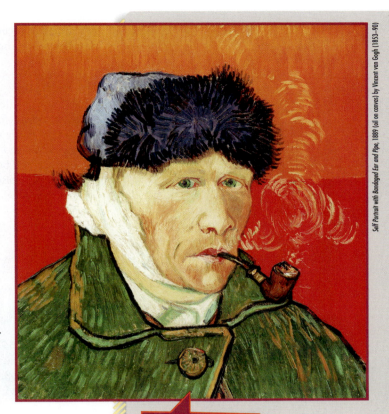

Self-Portrait with Bandaged Ear and Pipe, 1889 (oil on canvas) by Vincent van Gogh (1853–90)

Prelude to suicide?
Famed artist Vincent van Gogh, seen here in a self-portrait, lived a tortured and unhappy life and killed himself with a revolver in 1890. He had displayed acts of self-abuse and self-mutilation during his life, including a legendary incident on Christmas Eve in 1888, when he cut off part of his ear after a quarrel with his friend, artist Paul Gauguin.

BETWEEN THE LINES

"Birthday Blues" and Suicide
Despite a popular notion, individuals do not appear more likely to attempt suicide on or close to their birthdays (Reulbach et al., 2007). ‹‹

by a series of recent events that have a combined impact, rather than by a single event, as in the following case:

Sally's suicide attempt took place in the context of a very difficult year for the family. Sally's mother and stepfather separated after 9 years of marriage. After the father moved out, he visited the family erratically. Four months after he moved out of the house, the mother's boyfriend moved into the house. The mother planned to divorce her husband and marry her boyfriend, who had become the major disciplinarian for the children, a fact that Sally intensely resented. Sally also complained of being "left out" in relation to the closeness she had with her mother. Another problem for Sally had been two school changes in the last 2 years which left Sally feeling friendless. In addition, she failed all her subjects in the last marking period.

(Pfeffer, 1986, pp. 129–130)

People may also attempt suicide in response to long-term rather than recent stress. Three long-term stressors are particularly common—serious illness, an abusive environment, and occupational stress.

Serious Illness People whose illnesses cause them great pain or severe disability may try to commit suicide, believing that death is unavoidable and imminent (Schneider & Shenassa, 2008; Hendin, 2002, 1999). They may also believe that the suffering and problems caused by their illnesses are more than they can endure. Studies suggest that as many as one-third of individuals who die by suicide have been in poor physical health during the months prior to their suicidal acts (Sadock & Sadock, 2007; Conwell et al., 1990). Indeed, illness-linked suicides have become more common, and controversial, in recent years (Dickens et al., 2008). Although physicians can now keep seriously ill people alive much longer, they often fail to extend the quality and comfort of the patients' lives (Werth, 2001).

Abusive Environment Victims of an abusive or repressive environment from which they have little or no hope of escape sometimes commit suicide. For example, prisoners of war, inmates of concentration camps, abused spouses, abused children, and prison inmates have tried to end their lives (Konrad et al., 2007; Thio, 2006; Akyuz et al., 2005) (see Figure 10-2). Like those who have serious illnesses, these people may have felt that they could endure no more suffering and believed that there was no hope for improvement in their condition.

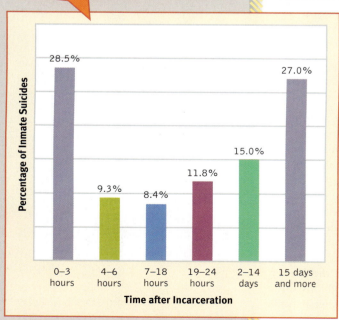

Figure 10-2

Suicide in prisons Approximately 107 of every 100,000 inmates in U.S. jails commit suicide each year, many times the national rate. Most such suicides occur during the first day of incarceration. (Adapted from Cerny & Noffsinger, 2006; Dahle et al., 2005; Bonner, 1992; Hayes & Rowan, 1988.)

Occupational Stress Some jobs create feelings of tension or dissatisfaction that may precipitate suicide attempts. Research has found particularly high suicide rates among psychiatrists and psychologists, physicians, nurses, dentists, lawyers, police officers, farmers, and unskilled laborers (Tanner, 2008; Sadock & Sadock, 2007; Stack, 2005). Such correlations do not necessarily mean that occupational pressures directly cause suicidal actions. Perhaps unskilled workers are responding to financial insecurity rather than job stress when they attempt suicide (Wasserman & Stack, 2000). Similarly, rather than reacting to the emotional strain of their work, suicidal psychiatrists and psychologists may have long-standing emotional problems that stimulated their career interest in the first place.

Clinicians once believed that married women who held jobs had higher suicide rates than other women, perhaps because of conflicts between the demands of their families and their jobs (Stack, 1987; Stillion, 1985). However, recent studies suggest that being employed is actually linked to lower suicide rates among married women, just as it is among men (Kalist et al., 2007; Stack, 1998).

Mood and Thought Changes

Many suicide attempts are preceded by a change in mood (see *Psych Watch: Abnormality and the Arts* on pages 318–319). The change may not be severe enough to warrant a diagnosis of a mental disorder, but it does represent a significant shift from the person's past mood. The most common change is an increase in sadness. Also common are increases in feelings of anxiety, tension, frustration, anger, or shame (Fawcett, 2007; Werth, 2004). In fact, Shneidman (2005, 2001) suggests that the key to suicide is "psychache," a feeling of psychological pain that seems intolerable to the person. A recent study of 88 patients found that those who scored higher on a measure called the Psychological Pain Assessment Scale were indeed more likely than others to commit suicide (Pompili et al., 2008). Said one man who survived his self-inflicted gunshot wound:

My mind became locked on my target. My thoughts were: Soon it will all be over. I would obtain the peace I had so long sought. The will to survive and succeed had been crushed and defeated. I was like a general on a battlefield being encroached on by my enemy and its hordes: fear, hate, self-depreciation, desolation . . .

(Shneidman, 1987, p. 56)

Suicide attempts may also be preceded by shifts in patterns of thinking. Individuals may become preoccupied with their problems, lose perspective, and see suicide as the only effective solution to their difficulties (Shneidman, 2005, 2001, 1987). They often develop a sense of **hopelessness**—a pessimistic belief that their present circumstances, problems, or mood will not change. In fact, one study found that individuals who generally expressed feelings of hopelessness were 11 times more likely to commit suicide over a 13-year follow-up period than people who did not feel hopeless (Kuo et al., 2004). Thus, some clinicians believe that a feeling of hopelessness is the single most likely indicator of suicidal intent, and they take special care to look for signs of hopelessness when they assess the risk of suicide (Van Orden et al., 2008; Sadock & Sadock, 2007).

Many people who attempt suicide fall victim to **dichotomous thinking,** viewing problems and solutions in rigid either/or terms (Shneidman, 2005, 2001, 1993). Indeed, Shneidman has said that the "four-letter word" in suicide is "only," as in "suicide was the *only* thing I could do" (Maris, 2001). In the following statement a woman who survived her leap from a building describes her dichotomous thinking at the time. She saw death as the only alternative to her pain:

I was so desperate. I felt, my God, I couldn't face this thing. Everything was like a terrible whirlpool of confusion. And I thought to myself: There's only one thing to do. I just have to lose consciousness. That's the only way to get away from it. The only way to lose consciousness, I thought, was to jump off something good and high. . . .

(Shneidman, 1987, p. 56)

Alcohol and Other Drug Use

Studies indicate that as many as 70 percent of the people who attempt suicide drink alcohol just before the act (Lejoyeux et al., 2008; McCloud et al., 2004). Autopsies reveal that about one-fourth of these people are legally intoxicated (Flavin et al., 1990). In fact, since coroners are more likely to classify deaths as accidental when they detect high alcohol levels (Crompton, 1985), the excessive use of alcohol just before suicide is

Multiple risks
People who experience multiple suicide factors are at particular risk for self-destruction (Wunderlich et al., 1998). In 2005, famous writer Hunter S. Thompson, pioneer of so-called gonzo journalism and author of the book *Fear and Loathing in Las Vegas,* shot himself to death. Thompson's suicide is thought to have been motivated by a combination of chronic pain (caused by medical problems) and depression.

•**hopelessness**•A pessimistic belief that one's present circumstances, problems, or mood will not change.

•**dichotomous thinking**•Viewing problems and solutions in rigid either/or terms.

Abnormality and the Arts

Can Music Inspire Suicide?

In 2008, a 13-year-old girl in Britain hanged herself (Woodward, 2008). The cause, according to a coroner, was in large part her obsession with emo music, music that mixes a guitar-based sound, punk rock, and strong doses of emotionality ("emo" is short for "emotional hardcore"). The coroner pointed in particular to the music of the popular emo band My Chemical Romance, her favorite group. Friends reported at the inquest into her death that the suicide victim had previously discussed the "glamour of suicide" that attracted her to emo music and had posted a picture of an emo girl with bloody wrists online. The British press, in turn, described My Chemical Romance as a "suicide cult band," prompting the band to defend itself and emo music in general as "antisuicide" and filled with positive messages in its lyrics (Woodward, 2008).

This tragedy is hardly the first time that music has been blamed by the public for suicidal acts. In fact, over the years, music genres as varied as country, opera, heavy metal, and pop rock have been pointed to as negative influences, particularly on teenagers, that can lead to suicide attempts (Copley, 2008; Snipes & Maguire, 1995;

Eye of the storm In a celebrated case, the British press have blamed the music of emo group My Chemical Romance for the recent suicide of a 13-year-old girl.

Reuters/Stringer Vietnam

probably much higher. It may be that the use of alcohol lowers the individuals' fears of committing suicide, releases underlying aggressive feelings, or impairs their judgment and problem-solving ability. Research shows that the use of other kinds of drugs may have a similar tie to suicide, particularly in teenagers and young adults (Darke et al., 2005; Lester, 2000). A high level of heroin, for example, was found in the blood of Kurt Cobain at the time of his suicide in 1994 (Colburn, 1996).

Mental Disorders

Although people who attempt suicide may be troubled or anxious, they do not necessarily have a psychological disorder as defined in DSM-IV-TR. Nevertheless, the majority of all suicide attempters do display such a disorder (Tatarelli et al., 2007; Carrier & Ennis, 2004). Research suggests that as many as half of all suicide victims had been experiencing severe *depression*, 20 percent *chronic alcoholism*, and 10 percent *schizophrenia* (see Table 10-2 on page 320). Correspondingly, as many as 15 percent of people with each of these disorders try to kill themselves. People who are both depressed and

Stack et al., 1994; Litman & Farberow, 1994; Stack & Gundlach, 1992; Wass et al, 1991). Little research has been conducted on this issue, and that which has been done fails to provide clear support for such claims. But the concerns go on. Indeed, such concerns helped lead to the current music rating system, which informs consumers (and their parents) about the kinds of language and themes that will appear on the CDs or music downloads they are about to buy.

Two famous cases in the 1980s first brought this concern into public awareness. One involved the music of Ozzy Osbourne, leader of the band Black Sabbath. In the early days of Black Sabbath, Osbourne and the band centered much of their music on psychological themes, and the band's music was even perceived by many as having a "satanic" bent. The band's 1970 album *Paranoid* became its biggest success.

Osbourne departed the band for a solo career between 1979 and the late 1990s. During this solo period, his music was blamed for three suicides. In 1984 a 19-year-old boy shot himself in the head while listening to Osbourne's song "Suicide Solution." A lawyer for the boy's family and lawyers for two other families whose children committed suicide claimed that the theme of the song encouraged suicide as an acceptable solution to one's problems. The lawyers also claimed that the song contained tones known as "hemisync" (a process that uses sound waves to influence an individual's mental state) and that these tones left the suicidal boys unable to resist what was being said in the song. Finally, the lawyers claimed that the song had *subliminal* lyrics—words sung much faster than the normal rate of speech and unrecognizable to first-time listeners. Supposedly, the subliminal lyrics in the song were "Why try, why try? Get the gun and try it! Shoot, Shoot, Shoot." Osbourne's lawyers claimed that all of this was nonsense and further argued that the musician had a First Amendment right to write about anything he wanted. The court agreed and dismissed all three cases by 1986.

A second famous case involved the music of the heavy metal band Judas Priest. In 1985 two boys shot themselves in the head with a shotgun; one of them died immediately and the other boy three years later. The boys had been drunk and on drugs and shot themselves in a "suicide pact" after listening to a Judas Priest album for hours. Lawyers for the boys' families claimed that Judas Priest's 1977 song "Better by You, Better Than Me" contained, when played backward, the subliminal message "Do it" as well as "Try suicide" and "Let's be dead." The band's lawyers countered that any song played backward might seem to have a hidden message. The trial judge agreed, and in 1990, after a month-long trial featuring various audio experts, he dismissed the $6.2 million lawsuit. He ruled that even if the lyrics conveyed subliminal messages, such messages had been unintentional.

If the music in these cases did not itself lead to suicide, what did? According to many experts, other nonmusical factors were probably to blame. A number of clinicians have argued that the individuals in these cases were probably suffering from several kinds of factors typically linked to suicide—depression, stress, and the like.

Of course, the dismissal of these suits did not put to rest the concerns of parents, and in fact such concerns grow still greater whenever parents read about a teenager—like the 13-year-old in Britain—who commits suicide while listening to death-themed music. While such events are not common in our society, they do, sadly, occur on occasion.

dependent on alcohol seem particularly prone to suicidal impulses (Sadock & Sadock, 2007; Sher et al., 2005). Certain anxiety disorders, including posttraumatic stress disorder and panic disorder, have also been linked to suicide, but in most cases of suicide these disorders occur in conjunction with major depressive disorder, a substance-related disorder, or schizophrenia (Inoue et al., 2007; Fawcett, 2007). It is also the case that many people with borderline personality disorder, a broad pattern that you will read about in Chapter 16, try to harm themselves or make suicidal gestures as part of their disorder (Weinberg & Maltzberger, 2007). The issues with which these individuals are grappling and the treatments to which they respond are often quite different from those of other suicidal persons. Thus, the suicidal features and treatments of borderline personality disorder will be examined in Chapter 16.

As you saw in Chapter 8, people with major depressive disorder often experience suicidal thoughts. Those whose depression includes a very strong sense of hopelessness seem particularly likely to attempt suicide. One program in Sweden was able to reduce the community suicide rate by teaching physicians how to recognize and treat depression at an early stage (Rihmer, Rutz, & Pihlgren, 1995). Even when depressed people

BETWEEN THE LINES

Still at Risk

Approximately 4 percent of all suicides are committed by people who are inpatients at mental hospitals or other psychiatric facilities. ‹‹

(Cassells et al., 2005)

table: **10-2**

Common Predictors of Suicide

1. Depressive disorder and certain other mental disorders
2. Alcoholism and other forms of substance abuse
3. Suicide ideation, talk, preparation; certain religious ideas
4. Prior suicide attempts
5. Lethal methods
6. Social withdrawal, isolation, living alone, loss of support
7. Hopelessness, feeling trapped, cognitive rigidity
8. Impulsivity and risk-taking behavior
9. Being an older white American male
10. Modeling, suicide in the family, genetics
11. Economic or work problems; certain occupations
12. Marital problems, family pathology
13. Dramatic changes in mood
14. Anxiety
15. Stress and stressful events
16. Anger, aggression, irritability
17. Psychosis
18. Physical illness

Source: Adapted from Van Orden et al., 2008;
Rudd et al., 2006; Papolos et al., 2005.

BETWEEN THE LINES

Media Impact

One study concludes that media reports on contemporary suicides have probably played a role in 10 percent of suicides by people under 25 years of age. They have either given youths the idea to commit suicide or provided them with information about specific methods (Bailey, 2003). ‹‹

---

are showing improvements in mood, however, they may remain high suicide risks. In fact, among those who are severely depressed, the risk of suicide may actually increase as their mood improves and they have more energy to act on their suicidal wishes (Sadock & Sadock, 2007). Recall, for example, Jonathan Boucher, the combat veteran whose case opened this chapter. Just prior to his suicide, he had seemed to be calm and enjoying life again, according to family members and friends.

Severe depression also may play a key role in suicide attempts by persons with serious physical illnesses (Werth, 2004). A study of 44 patients with terminal illnesses revealed that fewer than one-quarter of them had thoughts of suicide or wished for an early death and that those who did were all suffering from major depressive disorder (Brown et al., 1986).

A number of the people who drink alcohol or use drugs just before a suicide attempt actually have a long history of abusing such substances (Lejoyeux et al., 2008; Cottler et al., 2005). The basis for the link between substance-related disorders and suicide is not clear. Perhaps the tragic lifestyle of many persons with these disorders or their sense of being hopelessly trapped by a substance leads to suicidal thinking. Alternatively, a third factor—psychological pain, for instance, or desperation—may cause both substance abuse and suicidal thinking (Sher et al., 2005). Such people may be caught in a downward spiral: they are driven toward substance use by psychological pain or loss, only to find themselves caught in a pattern of substance abuse that aggravates rather than solves their problems (Maris, 2001).

People with schizophrenia, as you will see in Chapter 14, may hear voices that are not actually present (hallucinations) or hold beliefs that are clearly false and perhaps bizarre (delusions). The popular notion is that when such persons kill themselves, they must be responding to an imagined voice commanding them to do so or to a delusion that suicide is a grand and noble gesture. Research indicates, however, that suicides by people with schizophrenia more often reflect feelings of demoralization or fears of further mental deterioration (Heisel, 2008; Pompili & Lester, 2007). Many of the suicides in this population are committed by young and unemployed sufferers who have had relapses over several years and have come to believe that the disorder will forever disrupt their lives. Still others are committed by those who have been disheartened by their substandard living conditions. Suicide is the leading cause of premature death among people with schizophrenia (Pompili & Lester, 2007; Pompili et al., 2004).

Modeling: The Contagion of Suicide

It is not unusual for people, particularly teenagers, to try to commit suicide after observing or reading about someone else who has done so (Feigelman & Gorman, 2008; Stack, 2005, 2003). Perhaps these people have been struggling with major problems and the other person's suicide seems to reveal a possible solution, or perhaps they have been thinking about suicide and the other person's suicide seems to give them permission or finally persuades them to act. Either way, one suicidal act apparently serves as a *model* for another. Suicides by celebrities, other highly publicized suicides, and suicides by co-workers or colleagues are particularly common triggers.

Celebrities Research suggests that suicides by entertainers, political figures, and other well-known persons are regularly followed by unusual increases in the number of suicides across the nation (Cheng et al., 2007; Stack, 2005, 1987). During the week after the suicide of Marilyn Monroe in 1963, for example, the national suicide rate rose 12 percent (Phillips, 1974).

Other Highly Publicized Cases Suicides with bizarre or unusual aspects often receive intense coverage by the news media (Blood et al., 2007; Wertheimer, 2001). Such highly publicized accounts may lead to similar suicides (Gould et al., 2007). During the year after a widely publicized, politically motivated suicide by self-burning in England, for example, 82 other people set themselves on fire, with equally fatal results (Ashton & Donnan, 1981). Inquest reports revealed that most of those people had histories of emotional problems and that none of the suicides had the political motivation of the publicized suicide. The imitators seemed to be responding to their own problems in a manner triggered by the suicide they had observed or read about.

Even a media program that is clearly intended to educate and help viewers may have the paradoxical effect of spurring imitators. One study found a dramatic increase in the rate of suicide among West German teenagers after the airing of a television documentary showing the suicide of a teenager who jumped under a train (Schmidtke & Häfner, 1988). The number of railway suicides by male teenagers increased by 175 percent after the program was aired.

Some clinicians argue that more responsible reporting could reduce this frightening impact of highly publicized suicides (Blood et al., 2007; Cheng et al., 2007; Gould et al., 2007). A careful approach to reporting was seen in the media's coverage of the suicide of Kurt Cobain. MTV's repeated theme on the evening of the suicide was "Don't do it!" In fact, thousands of young people called MTV and other radio and television stations in the hours after Cobain's death, upset, frightened, and in some cases suicidal. Some of the stations responded by posting the phone numbers of suicide prevention centers, presenting interviews with suicide experts, and offering counseling services and advice directly to callers. Perhaps because of such efforts, the usual rate of suicide both in Seattle, Cobain's hometown, and elsewhere held steady during the weeks that followed (Colburn, 1996).

Co-workers and Colleagues The word-of-mouth publicity that attends suicides in a school, workplace, or small community may trigger suicide attempts. The suicide of a recruit at a U.S. Navy training school, for example, was followed within two weeks by another and also by an attempted suicide at the school. To head off what threatened to become a suicide epidemic, the school began a program of staff education on suicide and group therapy sessions for recruits who had been close to the suicide victims (Grigg, 1988). The kinds of postsuicide programs put into action by this school and by MTV in the aftermath of Kurt Cobain's death are often referred to by clinicians as *postvention*.

❋ What Are the Underlying Causes of Suicide?

Most people faced with difficult situations never try to kill themselves. In an effort to understand why some people are more prone to suicide than others, theorists have proposed more fundamental explanations for self-destructive actions than the immediate triggers considered in the previous section. The leading theories come from the psychodynamic, sociocultural, and biological perspectives. As a group, however, these hypotheses have received limited research support and fail to address the full range of suicidal acts. Thus the clinical field currently lacks a satisfactory understanding of suicide.

The Psychodynamic View

Many psychodynamic theorists believe that suicide results from depression and from anger at others that is redirected toward oneself. This theory was first stated by Wilhelm Stekel at a meeting in Vienna in 1910, when he proclaimed that "no one kills himself who has not wanted to kill another or at least wished the death of another" (Shneidman,

Reuters/Hugo Philpott MD

Suicidal thoughts
In a recent interview, J. K. Rowling, creator of the *Harry Potter* book series, revealed that she had "suicidal thoughts" while suffering from clinical depression in the mid-1990s. With this revelation, the author was hoping to counter the stigma associated with depression, but some also worry about the contagion effect that suicidal actions or admissions by famous people can have, particularly on teenagers.

BETWEEN THE LINES

Lingering Impact of Child Abuse

Adults who were sexually or physically abused in childhood harm themselves, think about suicide, and attempt suicide more than do adults without this history (Joiner et al., 2007; Read et al., 2001; Dinwiddie et al., 2000). ‹‹

New Line/Avery Pix/The Kobal Collection/Richard Cartright

Acting Happy
Some people are able to mask emotional pain and even suicidal thoughts as they carry out their professional work or social interactions. Thus, fans of actor Owen Wilson, known for his comic film portrayals, were shocked when they heard in 2007 that he had attempted suicide. Wilson (left) is seen here with actor Vince Vaughn in the movie *Wedding Crashers*, playing the happy-go-lucky character John Beckwith.

Gamma Liaison

Mass suicide
In 1997 the world learned of the bizarre beliefs held by the Heaven's Gate cult when 39 of its members committed suicide in a suburban San Diego house. Influenced by the cult's leader, Marshall Herff Applewhite (pictured here), the members believed that their bodies were "containers" for higher heavenly spirits and that their deaths would free them to fly to a higher kingdom on a UFO.

1979). Some years later Sigmund Freud (1920) wrote, "No neurotic harbors thoughts of suicide which he has not turned back upon himself from murderous impulses against others." Agreeing with this notion, Karl Menninger called suicide "murder in the 180th degree."

As you read in Chapter 8, Freud (1917) and Abraham (1916, 1911) proposed that when people experience the real or symbolic loss of a loved one, they come to "introject" the lost person; that is, they unconsciously incorporate the person into their own identity and feel toward themselves as they had felt toward the other. For a short while, negative feelings toward the lost loved one are experienced as self-hatred. Anger toward the loved one may turn into intense anger against oneself and finally into depression. Suicide is thought to be an extreme expression of this self-hatred. The following description of a suicidal patient demonstrates how such forces may operate:

A 27-year-old conscientious and responsible woman took a knife to her wrists to punish herself for being tyrannical, unreliable, self-centered, and abusive. She was perplexed and frightened by this uncharacteristic self-destructive episode and was enormously relieved when her therapist pointed out that her invective described her recently deceased father much better than it did herself.

(Gill, 1982, p. 15)

In support of Freud's view, researchers have often found a relationship between childhood losses—real or symbolic—and later suicidal behaviors (Ehnvall et al., 2008; Read et al., 2001). A classic study of 200 family histories, for example, found that early parental loss was much more common among suicide attempters (48 percent) than among nonsuicidal individuals (24 percent) (Adam, Bouckoms, & Streiner, 1982). Common forms of loss were death of the father and divorce or separation of the parents. Similarly, a recent study of 343 depressed individuals found that those who had felt rejected or neglected as children by their parents were more likely than other individuals to attempt suicide as adults (Ehnvall et al., 2008).

Late in his career, Freud proposed that human beings have a basic "death instinct." He called this instinct *Thanatos* and said that it opposes the "life instinct." According to Freud, while most people learn to redirect their death instinct by aiming it toward others, suicidal people, caught in a web of self-anger, direct it squarely toward themselves.

Sociological findings are consistent with this explanation of suicide. National suicide rates have been found to drop in times of war (Sadock & Sadock, 2007; Maris, 2001), when, one could argue, people are encouraged to direct their self-destructive energy against "the enemy." In addition, in many parts of the world, societies with high rates of homicide tend to have low rates of suicide, and vice versa (Bills & Gouhua, 2005). However, research has failed to establish that suicidal people are in fact dominated by intense feelings of anger. Although hostility is an important element in some suicides (Sher et al., 2005), several studies find that other emotional states are even more prevalent (Castrogiovanni et al., 1998).

By the end of his career, Freud himself expressed dissatisfaction with his theory of suicide. Other psychodynamic theorists have also challenged his ideas over the years, yet themes of loss and self-directed aggression generally remain at the center of most psychodynamic explanations (King, 2003).

Durkheim's Sociocultural View

Toward the end of the nineteenth century, Emile Durkheim (1897), a sociologist, developed a broad theory of suicidal behavior. Today this theory continues to be influential and is often supported by research (Fernquist, 2007). According to Durkheim, the probability of suicide is determined by how attached a person is to such social groups as the family, religious institutions, and community. The more thoroughly a person belongs, the lower the risk of suicide. Conversely, people who have poor relationships with their society are at greater risk of killing themselves. He defined several categories of suicide, including *egoistic, altruistic,* and *anomic* suicide.

Egoistic suicides are committed by people over whom society has little or no control. These people are not concerned with the norms or rules of society, nor are they integrated into the social fabric. According to Durkheim, this kind of suicide is more likely in people who are isolated, alienated, and nonreligious. The larger the number of such people living in a society, the higher that society's suicide rate.

Altruistic suicides, in contrast, are committed by people who are so well integrated into the social structure that they intentionally sacrifice their lives for its well-being. Soldiers who threw themselves on top of a live grenade to save others, Japanese kamikaze pilots who crashed their planes into enemy ships during World War II, and Buddhist monks and nuns who protested the Vietnam War by setting themselves on fire may have been committing altruistic suicide (Leenaars, 2004; Stack, 2004). According to Durkheim, societies that encourage altruistic deaths and deaths to preserve one's honor (as Far Eastern societies do) are likely to have higher suicide rates.

Anomic suicides, another category proposed by Durkheim, are those committed by people whose social environment fails to provide stable structures, such as family and religion, to support and give meaning to life. Such a societal condition, called *anomie* (literally, "without law"), leaves individuals without a sense of belonging. Unlike egoistic suicide, which is the act of a person who rejects the structures of a society, anomic suicide is the act of a person who has been let down by a disorganized, inadequate, often decaying society.

John Kaplan/Media Alliance

In the service of others
According to Durkheim, people who intentionally sacrifice their lives for others are committing altruistic suicide. Betsy Smith, a heart transplant recipient who was warned that she would probably die if she did not terminate her pregnancy, elected to have the baby and died giving birth.

Altruistic suicide?
A clay sculpture of a suicide bomber is displayed at a Baghdad art gallery. Some sociologists believe that the acts of such bombers fit Durkheim's definition of altruistic suicide, arguing that the bombers believe they are sacrificing their lives for the well-being of their society. Other theorists, however, point out that many such bombers seem indifferent to the innocent lives they are destroying and categorize the bombers instead as mass murderers motivated by hatred rather than feelings of altruism (Humphrey, 2006).

Durkheim argued that when societies go through periods of anomie, their suicide rates increase. Historical trends support this claim. Periods of economic depression may bring about some degree of anomie in a country, and national suicide rates tend to rise during such times (Maris, 2001). Periods of population change and increased immigration, too, tend to bring about a state of anomie, and again suicide rates rise (Kposowa et al., 2008; Ferrada et al., 1995).

A major change in an individual's immediate surroundings, rather than general societal problems, can also lead to anomic suicide. People who suddenly inherit a great deal of money, for example, may go through a period of anomie as their relationships with social, economic, and occupational structures are changed. Thus Durkheim predicted that societies with greater opportunities for change in individual wealth or status would have higher suicide rates, and this prediction, too, is supported by research (Cutright & Fernquist, 2001; Lester, 2000, 1985). Conversely, people who are removed from society and sent to a prison environment may experience anomie. As you read earlier, research confirms that such individuals have a heightened suicide rate (Konrad et al., 2007; Tartaro & Lester, 2005).

Although today's sociocultural theorists do not always embrace Durkheim's particular ideas, most agree that social structure and cultural stress often play major roles in suicide (see *Eye on Culture* on page 326). In fact, the sociocultural view pervades the study of suicide. Recall the earlier discussion of the many studies linking suicide to broad factors such as religious affiliation, marital status, gender, race, and societal stress. You will also see the impact of such factors when you read about the ties between suicide and age.

Despite the influence of sociocultural theories such as Durkheim's, these theories cannot by themselves explain why some people who experience particular societal pressures commit suicide while the majority do not. Durkheim himself concluded that the final explanation probably lies in the interaction between societal and individual factors.

The Biological View

For years biological researchers relied largely on family pedigree studies to support their position that biological factors contribute to suicidal behavior. They repeatedly have found higher rates of suicide among the parents and close relatives of suicidal people than among those of nonsuicidal people (Bronisch & Lieb, 2008; Mittendorfer-Rutz et al., 2008; Brent & Mann, 2003). Indeed, one study found that over one-third of its teenage participants who committed suicide had a relative who had attempted suicide (Gould et al., 2003, 1990). Such findings may suggest that genetic, and so biological, factors are at work.

Studies of twins also have supported this view of suicide. In a famous study, researchers who studied twins born in Denmark between 1870 and 1920 located 19 identical pairs and 58 fraternal pairs in which at least one twin had committed suicide (Juel-Nielsen & Videbech, 1970). In four of the identical pairs the other twin also committed suicide (21 percent), while none of the other twins among the fraternal pairs had done so.

As with all family pedigree and twin research, there are nonbiological interpretations for these findings as well. Psychodynamic clinicians might argue that children whose close relatives commit suicide are prone to depression and suicide because they have lost a loved one at a critical stage of development. Behavioral theorists might emphasize the modeling role played by parents or close relatives who attempt suicide.

In the past two decades, laboratory research has offered more direct support for a biological view of suicide. The activity level of the neurotransmitter serotonin has often been found to be low in people who commit suicide (Mann & Currier, 2007; Chen et al., 2005). An early hint of this relationship came from a study by psychiatric researcher Marie Asberg and her colleagues (1976). They studied 68 depressed patients and found that 20 of the patients had particularly low levels of serotonin activity. It turned out that 40 percent of the low-serotonin research participants attempted suicide, compared with 15 percent of the higher-serotonin participants. The researchers interpreted this to mean that low serotonin activity may be "a predictor of suicidal acts." Later studies found that suicide attempters with low serotonin activity are 10 times more likely to make a repeat attempt and succeed than are suicide attempters with higher serotonin activity (Roy, 1992).

Subsequent studies that examined the autopsied brains of suicide victims pointed in the same direction (Mann & Currier, 2007; Stanley et al., 2000, 1986, 1982). Some of these studies found, for example, that people who committed suicide tended to have fewer receptor sites on neurons that normally receive serotonin than did people who do not commit suicide. Similarly, recent PET scan studies have revealed that people who contemplate or attempt suicide display abnormal activity in areas of the brain that are comprised of many serotonin-using neurons—areas you read about in Chapters 5 and 8, such as the prefrontal cortex, orbitofrontal cortex, and cingulate cortex (Mann & Currier, 2007; Oquendo et al., 2003).

At first glance, these and related studies may appear to tell us only that depressed people often attempt suicide. After all, depression is itself related to low serotonin activity. On the other hand, there is evidence of low serotonin activity even among suicidal individuals who have no history of depression (Mann & Currier, 2007). That is, low serotonin activity also seems to play a role in suicide separate from depression.

How, then, might low serotonin activity increase the likelihood of suicidal behavior? One possibility is that it contributes to aggressive and impulsive behaviors. It has been found, for example, that serotonin activity is lower in aggressive men than in nonaggressive men and that serotonin activity is often low in those who commit such aggressive acts as arson and murder (Oquendo et al., 2006, 2004; Stanley et al., 2000). Moreover, PET scan studies of people who are aggressive and impulsive (but not necessarily depressed) reveal abnormal activity in the prefrontal cortex, orbitofrontal cortex, cingulate cortex, and other serotonin-rich areas of the brain (Mann & Currier, 2007; New et al., 2004, 2002). And, finally, studies have found that depressed patients with particularly low serotonin activity try to commit suicide more often, use more lethal methods, and score higher in hostility and impulsivity on personality inventories than do depressed patients with relatively higher serotonin activity (Oquendo et al., 2003; Malone et al., 1996; Van Praag, 1983). Such findings suggest that low serotonin activity helps produce aggressive feelings and impulsive behavior. In people who are clinically depressed, low serotonin activity may produce aggressive tendencies that cause them to be particularly vulnerable to suicidal thoughts and acts. Even in the absence of a depressive disorder, however, people with low serotonin activity may develop such aggressive feelings that they, too, are dangerous to themselves or to others.

Is aggression the key? Biological theorists believe that heightened feelings of aggression and impulsivity, produced by low serotonin activity, are key factors in suicide. In 2007, World Heavyweight Wrestling Champion Chris Benoit—here receiving a body kick during a match—killed his wife and son and then hanged himself, a tragedy that seemed to provide anecdotal support for this biological theory. In addition, toxicology reports found steroids in Benoit's body, drugs known by researchers to help cause aggression and impulsivity.

Is Suicide Linked to Age?

The likelihood of committing suicide generally increases with age, although people of all ages may try to kill themselves. Currently, 1 of every 100,000 children in the United States (age 10 to 14) kills himself or herself each year, compared to 7.3 of every 100,000 teenagers, 12.1 of every 100,000 young adults, 16.6 of every 100,000 middle-aged adults, and 19 of every 100,000 persons over age 65 (CDC, 2008; Cohen, 2008; NAHIC, 2006). It is worth noting that, these overall age trends not withstanding, the rate of teenage suicides fell sharply (by 30 percent) between 1993 and 2003, while that of middle-age suicides rose sharply (20 percent) during that same period of time, trends that are not fully understood. Similar rate changes in these particular age groups were observed in Britain and other countries (Biddle et al., 2008).

Clinicians have paid particular attention to self-destructive behavior in three age groups: *children*, *adolescents*, and the *elderly*. Although the features and theories of suicide discussed throughout this chapter apply to all age groups, each group faces unique problems that may play key roles in the suicidal acts of its members.

EYE ON CULTURE

Suicide among the Japanese

According to a comparison of American and Japanese medical students, Americans tend to regard suicide as an expression of anger or aggression, whereas the Japanese view it as normal, reasonable behavior (Domino & Takahashi, 1991). Sociologist Mamoru Iga (2001, 1993) holds that this difference reflects the cultures' religious and philosophical understandings of life and death.

The Shinto and Buddhist traditions stress eternal change and the transience of life. In the Buddhist view, life is sorrowful, and death is a way of freeing oneself from illusion and suffering. Furthermore, the highest aim of many Japanese is complete detachment from earthly concerns, total self-negation. Within this framework,

death can be seen as positive, as an expression of sincerity (*makoto*) or an appropriate reaction to shame. Thus, according to Iga, "In Japan, suicide has traditionally been an accepted, if not a welcomed, way of solving a serious problem. . . . Suicide is not a sin in Japan; it is not punishable by God. Suicide is not viewed as a social or national issue but a personal problem."

Many of the factors that trigger suicide in the West—physical illness, alcohol abuse, mental disorders—are also at work in Japanese suicides (Fushimi et al., 2005; Lester & Saito, 1999). However, the different attitudes of the two cultures toward death and suicide may help explain the sizable difference between the rates of

suicide in Japan (26 per 100,000 persons) and the United States (12 per 100,000).

Iga and other theorists also point to the absence of a humanistic tradition in Japan. Self-expression, self-enhancement, and self-love are prominent values in the West, and out of such a tradition comes the impulse to prevent suicide. Japanese society, however, values the subjugation of the individual to the social order (Young, 2002) and stresses harmony between humanity and nature: humans must bow to nature. Thus no deep-rooted principle in Japan requires that people be stopped from taking their own lives.

Finally, Iga points to several other sociocultural factors that may contribute to the high rate of suicide in Japan. One is the long-standing, pervasive sexism in Japanese culture. Others are increasing academic pressure on young people and increasing work pressure on middle-aged men. Nor should economic pressure in Japan be overlooked (Fushimi et al., 2005; Yamasaki et al., 2005, 2004). During the country's severe recession of the late 1990s, the number of suicides increased by more than one-third.

Of course, in today's world East and West meet regularly, and in fact interactions between the cultures have had an impact on Japanese attitudes in respect to one facet of suicide—*suicide prevention*. After visiting the Los Angeles Suicide Prevention Center, some Japanese psychologists and psychiatrists opened the first suicide prevention center in Japan in 1971. They worried at first that shame would deter the Japanese from seeking help (Matsumoto & Juang, 2008), but the center was so successful that by 1990 it was operating branches in 33 Japanese cities. Still other efforts at suicide prevention have followed (Shiho et al., 2005; Ueda & Matsumoto, 2003).

H. Yamaguchi/Gamma Liaison

Stress The students in this classroom are participating in summer *juku*, a Japanese camp where they receive remedial help, extra lessons, and exam practice 11 hours a day.

Children

> *Tommy [age 7] and his younger brother were playing together, and an altercation arose that was settled by the mother, who then left the room. The mother recalled nothing to distinguish this incident from innumerable similar ones. Several minutes after she left, she considered Tommy strangely quiet and returned to find him crimson-faced and struggling for air, having knotted a jumping rope around his neck and jerked it tight.*
>
> (French & Berlin, 1979, p. 144)

> *Dear Mom and Dad,*
> *I love you. Please tell my teacher that I cannot take it anymore. I quit. Please don't take me to school anymore. Please help me. I will run away so don't stop me. I will kill myself. So don't look for me because I will be dead. I love you. I will always love you. Remember me.*
> *Help me.*
> *Love Justin [age 10]*
>
> (Pfeffer, 1986, p. 273)

Although suicide is infrequent among children, it has been increasing over the past several decades (Dervic, Brent, & Oquendo, 2008). Indeed, more than 6 percent of all deaths among children between the ages of 10 and 14 years are caused by suicide (Arias et al., 2003). Boys outnumber girls by as much as 5 to 1. In addition, it has been estimated that 1 of every 100 children tries to harm himself or herself, and many thousands of children are hospitalized each year for deliberately self-destructive acts, such as stabbing, cutting, burning, overdosing, jumping from high places, or shooting themselves (Fortune & Hawton, 2007; Cytryn & McKnew, 1996).

Researchers have found that suicide attempts by the very young are commonly preceded by such behavioral patterns as running away from home; accident-proneness; aggressive acting out; temper tantrums; self-criticism; social withdrawal and loneliness; extreme sensitivity to criticism by others; low tolerance of frustration; dark fantasies, daydreams, or hallucinations; marked personality change; and overwhelming interest in death and suicide (Dervic et al., 2008; Cytryn & McKnew, 1996). Studies further have linked child suicides to the recent or anticipated loss of a loved one, family stress and a parent's unemployment, abuse by parents, and a clinical level of depression (Renaud et al., 2008; Van Orden et al., 2008).

Most people find it hard to believe that children fully comprehend the meaning of a suicidal act. They argue that because a child's thinking is so limited, children who attempt suicide fall into Shneidman's category of "death ignorers," like Demaine, who sought to join his mother in heaven. Many child suicides, however, appear to be based on a clear understanding of death and on a clear wish to die (Pfeffer, 2003). In addition, suicidal thinking among even normal children is apparently more common than most people once believed (Kovacs et al., 1993). Clinical interviews with schoolchildren have revealed that between 6 and 33 percent have thought about suicide (Riesch et al., 2008; Culp, Clyman, & Culp, 1995).

Adolescents

> *Dear Mom, Dad, and everyone else,*
> *I'm sorry for what I've done, but I loved you all and I always will, for eternity. Please, please, please don't blame it on yourselves. It was all my fault and not yours or anyone*

else's. *If I didn't do this now, I would have done it later anyway. We all die some day, I just died sooner.*

Love,
John

(Berman, 1986)

The suicide of John, age 17, was not an unusual occurrence. Suicidal actions become much more common after the age of 14 than at any earlier age. According to official records, overall 1,500 teenagers (age 15 to 19), or 7 of every 100,000, commit suicide in the United States each year (Van Orden et al., 2008). In addition, at least 1 in 12 teenagers make suicide attempts and 1 in 6 think about suicide each year (Goldston et al., 2008). Because fatal illnesses are uncommon among the young, suicide has become the third leading cause of death in this age group, after accidents and homicides (Shain, 2008). Around 11 percent of all adolescent deaths are the result of suicide (Arias et al., 2003).

About half of teenage suicides, like those of people in other age groups, have been tied to clinical depression (see *A Closer Look* on the facing page), low self-esteem, and feelings of hopelessness, but many teenagers who try to kill themselves also appear to struggle with anger and impulsiveness or to have serious alcohol or drug problems (Renaud et al., 2008; Witte et al., 2008). In addition, some have deficiencies in their ability to sort out and solve problems (Brent, 2001).

Teenagers who consider or attempt suicide are often under great stress. They may experience long-term pressures such as poor (or missing) relationships with parents, family conflict, inadequate peer relationships, and social isolation (Capuzzi & Gross, 2008; Apter & Wasserman, 2007; Stellrecht et al., 2006). Alternatively, their actions also may be triggered by more immediate stress, such as a parent's unemployment or medical illness, financial setbacks for the family, or a social loss such as a break-up with a boyfriend or girlfriend (Orbach & Iohan, 2007; Fergusson et al., 2000). Stress at school seems to be a particularly common problem for teenagers who attempt suicide. Some have trouble keeping up at school, while others may be high achievers who feel pressured to be perfect and to stay at the top of the class (Ho et al., 1995; Delisle, 1986; Leroux, 1986).

Some theorists believe that the period of adolescence itself produces a stressful climate in which suicidal actions are more likely (King & Apter, 2003). Adolescence is a period of rapid growth that is often marked by conflicts, depressed feelings, tensions, and difficulties at home and school. Adolescents tend to react to events more sensitively, angrily, dramatically, and impulsively than individuals in other age groups; thus the likelihood of suicidal acts during times of stress is increased (Greening et al., 2008). Finally, the suggestibility of adolescents and their eagerness to imitate others, including others who attempt suicide, may set the stage for suicidal action (Apter & Wasserman, 2007). One study found that 93 percent of adolescent suicide attempters had known someone who had attempted suicide (Conrad, 1992).

Teen Suicides: Attempts versus Completions Far more teenagers attempt suicide than actually kill themselves—the ratio may be as high as 200 to 1. The unusually large number of unsuccessful suicides may mean that teenagers are less certain than older persons who make such attempts. While some do indeed wish to die, many may simply want to make others understand how desperate they are, get help, or teach others a lesson (Apter & Wasserman, 2007; Leenaars et al., 2001). Up to half of teenage attempters make new suicide attempts in the future, and as many as 14 percent eventually die by suicide (Wong et al., 2008; Borowsky et al., 2001; Diekstra et al., 1995).

Why is the rate of suicide attempts so high among teenagers (as well as among young adults)? Several explanations, most pointing to societal factors, have been proposed. First, as the number and proportion of teenagers and young adults in the general population have risen, the competition for jobs, college positions, and academic and athletic honors has intensified for them, leading increasingly to shattered dreams and ambitions

The Black Box Controversy: Do Antidepressants Cause Suicide?

A major controversy in the clinical field is whether antidepressant drugs are highly dangerous for depressed children and teenagers. Throughout the 1990s, most psychiatrists believed that antidepressants—particularly the second-generation antidepressants—were safe and effective for children and adolescents, just as they seemed to be for adults, and they prescribed those medications readily (Kutcher & Gardner, 2008; Holden, 2004). However, after reviewing a large number of clinical reports and studying 3,300 patients on antidepressants, the United States Food and Drug Administration (FDA) concluded in 2004 that the drugs produce a real, though small, increase in the risk of suicidal behavior for certain children and adolescents, especially during the first few months of treatment, and it ordered that all antidepressant containers carry "black box" warnings stating that the drugs "increase the risk of suicidal thinking and behavior in children." In 2007 the FDA expanded this warning to include young adults (Howland, 2008).

Although many clinicians have been pleased by the FDA order, others worry that it may be ill-advised. They argue that while the drugs may indeed increase the risk of suicidal thoughts and attempts in as many as 2 to 3 percent of young patients, the risk of suicide is actually reduced in the vast majority of children and teenagers who take the drugs (Kutcher & Gardner, 2008; Henderson, 2005). To support this argument, they point out that the overall rate of teenage suicides decreased by 30 percent in the decade leading up to 2004, as the number of antidepressant prescriptions provided to children and teenagers were soaring.

The critics of the black box warnings also point to the initial effect that the warnings had on prescription patterns

Difficult years The angst, confusion, conflict, and impulsivity that typically characterize adolescence provide fertile ground for the growth of suicidal thoughts and attempts at suicide.

and teenage suicide rates in the United States and other countries. Some studies suggest that during the first two years following the institution of the black box warnings, the number of antidepressant prescriptions fell 22 percent in the United States and the Netherlands while the rate of teenage suicides rose 14 percent in the United States and 49 percent in the Netherlands, the largest suicide rate increases since 1979 (Fawcett, 2007). Although other studies challenge these numbers (Wheeler et al., 2008), it is certainly possible that black box warnings were indirectly depriving many young patients of a medication that they truly needed to help fight depression and head off suicide. Antidepressant prescriptions for depressed teenagers now seem to be rising again, and the effect of this trend reversal on teenage suicide rates certainly awaits careful scrutiny.

Notwithstanding the possible drawbacks of the FDA black box action, the field's growing recognition that antidepressants sometimes cause suicidal thinking is of obvious value to that small percentage of young patients who may be affected adversely by such drugs. The heightened vigilance of these individuals while they are on the drugs, as well as that of their parents and clinicians, may well save their lives.

Yet another benefit of the black box controversy is that the FDA recently has expanded its interest in suicidal side effects to drugs other than antidepressants. It now requires pharmaceutical companies to test proactively for suicidal side effects in newly developed drugs such as those for obesity and epilepsy (Carey, 2008; Harris, 2008). In the past, lethal effects of this kind never came to light until well after drugs had been approved and used by millions of patients.

(Holinger & Offer, 1993, 1991, 1982). Other explanations point to weakening ties in the family (which may produce feelings of alienation and rejection in many of today's young people) and to the easy availability of alcohol and other drugs and the pressure to use them among teenagers and young adults (Brent, 2001; Cutler et al., 2001).

The mass media coverage of suicides by teenagers and young adults may also contribute to the high rate of suicide attempts among the young (Apter & Wasserman, 2007; Gould et al., 2007). The detailed descriptions of teenage suicide that the media and the arts often offer may serve as models for young people who are contemplating suicide (Cheng et al., 2007; Wertheimer, 2001). In one of the most famous examples of this phenomenon, just days after the highly publicized suicides of four adolescents in a New Jersey town in 1987, dozens of teenagers across the United States took similar actions (at least 12 of them fatal)—two in the same garage just one week later. Similarly, one study found that the rate of adolescent suicide rose about 7 percent in New York City during the week following a television film on suicide, in contrast to a 0.5 percent increase in the adult suicide rate during the same week (Maris, 2001).

Teen Suicides: Multicultural Issues

Teenage suicide rates vary by ethnicity in the United States. Around 7.5 of every 100,000 white American teenagers commit suicide each year, compared to 5 of every 100,000 African American teens and 4.8 of every 100,000 Hispanic American teens (Goldston et al., 2008; NAHIC, 2006). Although these numbers certainly indicate that white American teens are more prone to suicide, the rates of the three groups are in fact becoming closer. The white American rate was 150 percent greater than the African American and Hispanic American rates in 1980; today it is only 50 percent greater. This closing trend may reflect increasingly similar pressures on young African, Hispanic, and white Americans—competition for grades and college opportunities, for example, is now intense for all three groups. The growing suicide rates for young African and Hispanic Americans may also be linked to rising unemployment among them, the many anxieties and economic pressures of inner city life, and the rage felt by many of them over racial inequities and discrimination in our society (Duarte-Velez & Bernal, 2008; Goldston et al., 2008; Kubrin et al., 2006). Recent studies further indicate that 4.5 of every 100,000 Asian American teens now commit suicide each year.

The highest teenage suicide rate of all is displayed by Native Americans. Currently, more than 15 of every 100,000 Native American teenagers commit suicide each year, double the rate of white American teenagers and triple that of other minority teenagers. Clinical theorists attribute this extraordinarily high rate to factors such as the extreme poverty faced by most Native American teens, their limited educational and employment opportunities, their particularly high rate of alcohol abuse, and the geographical isolation experienced by those who live on reservations (Alcantara & Gone, 2008; Goldston et al., 2008; Beals et al., 2005). In addition, it appears that certain Native American reservations have extreme suicide rates—called *cluster suicides*—and that teenagers who live in such communities are usually likely to be exposed to suicide, to have their lives disrupted, to observe suicidal models, and to be at risk for suicide contagion (Bender, 2006; Chekki, 2004).

The Elderly

Rose Ashby walks to the dry cleaner's to pick up her old but finest dinner dress. Although shaken at the cost of having it cleaned, Rose tells the sympathetic girl behind the counter, "Don't worry. It doesn't matter. I won't be needing the money any more."

Walking through the streets of St. Petersburg, Florida, she still wishes it had been Miami. The west coast of the fountain-of-youth peninsula is not as warm as the east. If only Chet had left more insurance money, Rose could have afforded Miami. In St. Petersburg, Rose failed to unearth de León's promised fount.

From the highest of highs
In 1994, when 12-year-old Vicki Van Meter became the youngest person ever to pilot a plane from the United States to Europe, the sky literally seemed to be the limit for her. However, in 2008, battling severe depression at the age of 26, Van Meter could see only one option for herself and shot herself to death.

BETWEEN THE LINES

In Their Words

"Old age, more to be feared than death." ‹‹

Juvenal, *Satires XI*

"My work is done, why wait?" ‹‹

George Eastman, founder of Kodak, suicide note, 1932

Last week, she told the doctor she felt lonely and depressed. He said she should perk up. She had everything to live for. What does he know? Has he lost a husband like Chet and his left breast to cancer all in one year? Has he suffered arthritis all his life? Were his ovaries so bad he had to undergo a hysterectomy? Did he have to suffer through menopause just to end up alone without family or friends? Does he have to live in a dungeon? Is his furniture worn, his carpet threadbare? What does he know? Might his every day be the last one for him?

As Rose turns into the walk to her white cinderblock apartment building, fat Mrs. Green asks if she is coming to the community center that evening. Who needs it? The social worker did say Rose should come. Since Rose was in such good health, she could help those not so well as she.

Help them do what? Finger-paint like little children? Make baskets like insane people? Sew? Who can see to sew? Besides, who would appreciate it? Who would thank her? Who could she tell about her troubles? Who cares?

When she told the doctor she couldn't sleep, he gave her the prescription but said that all elderly people have trouble sleeping. What does he know? Does he have a middle-aged daughter who can only think about her latest divorce, or grandchildren who only acknowledge her birthday check by the endorsement on the back? Are all his friends dead and gone? Is all the money from his dead husband's insurance used up? What does he know? Who could sleep in this dungeon?

Back in her apartment, Rose washes and sets her hair. It's good she has to do it herself. Look at this hair. So thin, so sparse, so frowsy. What would a hairdresser think?

Then make-up. Base. Rouge. Lipstick. Bright red. Perfume? No! No cheap perfume for Rose today. Remember the bottles of Joy Chet would buy for her? He always wanted her to have the best. He would boast that she had everything, and that she never had to work a day in her life for it.

"She doesn't have to lift her little finger," Chet would say, puffing on his cigar. Where is the Joy now? Dead and gone. With Chet. Rose manages a wry laugh at the play on words.

Slipping into her dinner dress, she looks into the dresser mirror. "It's good you can't see this face now, Chet. How old and ugly it looks."

Taking some lavender notepaper from the drawer, she stands at the dresser to write. Why didn't anyone warn her that growing old was like this? It is so unfair. But they don't care. People don't care about anyone except themselves.

Leaving the note on the dresser, she suddenly feels excited. Breathing hard now, she rushes to the sink—who could call a sink in the counter in the living room a kitchen?—and gets a glass of water.

Trying to relax, Rose arranges the folds in her skirt as she settles down on the chaise. Carefully sipping the water as she takes all the capsules so as to not smear her lipstick, Rose quietly begins to sob. After a lifetime of tears, these will be her last. Her note on the dresser is short, written to no one and to everyone.

You don't know what it is like to have to grow old and die.

(Gernsbacher, 1985, pp. 227–228)

In Western society the elderly are more likely to commit suicide than people in any other age group. About 19 of every 100,000 persons over the age of 65 in the United States commit suicide. Elderly persons commit over 19 percent of all suicides in the United States, yet they account for only 12 percent of the total population.

Many factors contribute to this high suicide rate (Vannoy et al., 2008; Oyama et al., 2005). As people grow older, all too often they become ill, lose close friends and relatives, lose control over their lives, and lose status in our society. Such experiences may result in feelings of hopelessness, loneliness, depression, or inevitability among aged persons and so increase the likelihood that they will attempt suicide. One study found that two-thirds of elderly individuals (above 80 years old) who committed suicide had experienced a medical hospitalization within two years preceding the suicide (Erlangsen

The power of respect
Elderly persons are held in high esteem in many traditional societies because of the store of knowledge they have accumulated. Perhaps not so coincidentally, suicides among the elderly seem to be less common in these cultures than in those of many modern industrialized nations.

et al., 2005). Other research reveals that the suicide rate of elderly people who have recently lost a spouse is particularly high (Ajdacic-Gross et al., 2008). The risk is greatest during the first weeks of bereavement, but it remains high in later months and years as well. And in one investigation, 44 percent of elderly people who committed suicide gave some indication that their act was prompted by the fear of being placed in a nursing home (Loebel et al., 1991).

Elderly persons are typically more determined than younger persons in their decision to die and they give fewer warnings, so their success rate is much higher (Woods, 2008; DeLeo et al., 2001). Apparently one of every four elderly persons who attempts suicide succeeds. Given the resolve of aged persons and their physical decline, some people argue that older persons who want to die are clear in their thinking and should be allowed to carry out their wishes (see *Psych Watch* on pages 334–335). However, clinical depression appears to play an important role in as many as 60 percent of suicides by the elderly, suggesting that more elderly persons who are suicidal should be receiving treatment for their depressive disorders (Awata et al., 2005; Peter et al., 2004).

The suicide rate among the elderly in the United States is lower in some minority groups (Alcantara & Gone, 2008; Leach & Leong, 2008; Utsey et al., 2008; McIntosh & Santos, 1982). Although Native Americans have the highest overall suicide rate, for example, the rate among elderly Native Americans is relatively low. The aged are held in high esteem by Native Americans and are looked to for the wisdom and experience they have acquired over the years, and this may help account for their low suicide rate. Such high regard is in sharp contrast to the loss of status often experienced by elderly white Americans.

Similarly, the suicide rate is only one-third as high among elderly African Americans as among elderly white Americans. One reason for this low suicide rate may be the pressures faced by African Americans: "only the strongest survive" (Seiden, 1981). Those who reach an advanced age have overcome great adversity and often feel proud of what they have accomplished. Because reaching old age is not in itself a form of success for white Americans, their attitude toward aging is more negative. Another possible explanation is that aged African Americans have successfully overcome the rage that prompts many suicides in younger African Americans.

✿Treatment and Suicide

Treatment of suicidal people falls into two major categories: *treatment after suicide has been attempted* and *suicide prevention*. While treatment may also be beneficial to relatives and friends, whose feelings of loss, guilt, and anger after a suicide fatality or attempt can be intense (Cerel et al., 2008; Wertheimer, 2001), the discussion here is limited to the treatment afforded suicidal people themselves.

What Treatments Are Used after Suicide Attempts?

After a suicide attempt, most victims need medical care. Some are left with severe injuries, brain damage, or other medical problems. Once the physical damage is treated, psychotherapy or drug therapy may begin, on either an inpatient or outpatient basis.

Unfortunately, even after trying to kill themselves, many suicidal people fail to receive systematic follow-up care (Goldney, 2003; Beautrais, Joyce, & Mulder, 2000). In a random survey of several hundred teenagers, 9 percent were found to have made at least one suicide attempt, and of those only half had received later psychological treatment (Harkavy & Asnis, 1985). Similarly, in another study, one-third of adolescent attempters reported that they had not received any help after trying to end their lives (Larsson &

Ivarsson, 1998). In some cases, health care professionals are at fault. In others, the person who has attempted suicide refuses follow-up therapy.

The goals of therapy are to keep people alive, help them achieve a nonsuicidal state of mind, and guide them to develop better ways of handling stress (Reinecke et al., 2008; Shneidman, 2001). Various therapies have been employed, including drug, psychodynamic, cognitive, cognitive-behavioral, group, and family therapies (Tarrier et al., 2008; Baldessarini & Tondo, 2007; Hawton, 2001). Treatment appears to help. Studies have found that 30 percent of suicide attempters who do not receive treatment try again, compared with 16 percent of patients in treatment (Nordstrom et al., 1995; Allard et al., 1992).

Research indicates that cognitive and cognitive-behavioral therapies may be particularly helpful for suicidal individuals (Ghahramanlou-Holloway et al., 2008; Tarrier et al., 2008). These approaches focus to a large degree on the painful thoughts, sense of hopelessness, dichotomous thinking, poor coping skills, and other cognitive and behavioral features that characterize the functioning of suicidal persons. Using elements of Beck's cognitive therapy (see pages 280–283), therapists may help their suicidal clients to assess, challenge, and change many of their negative attitudes and illogical thinking processes (Brown et al., 2005). Applying the principles of mindfulness-based cognitive therapy (see pages 69 and 283), therapists may also guide suicidal clients to become acutely aware of the painful thoughts and feelings that stream through their minds and to *accept* many such thoughts and feelings rather than try to eliminate them (Zettle, 2007). Acceptance of this kind is expected to increase the clients' tolerance of psychological distress. And finally, employing therapy exercises, homework assignments, and other cognitive-behavioral tools, therapists may try to teach clients better coping and problem-solving skills (Chiles & Strosahl, 2005).

Not just another bridge
The Golden Gate Bridge in San Francisco is believed to be the site of more jumping suicides than any other location in the world—with an estimated 1,400 suicides occurring there since the bridge opened in 1937. Falling 260 feet, jumpers hit the frigid water below at 80 miles per hour, an impact that is almost always fatal. Thousands of people have petitioned the city to construct suicide barriers on the bridge that would make it harder for people to jump from it.

What Is Suicide Prevention?

During the past 50 years, emphasis around the world has shifted from suicide treatment to suicide prevention (Kerkhof, 2005). In some respects this change is most appropriate: the last opportunity to keep many potential suicide victims alive comes before the first attempt.

The first **suicide prevention program** in the United States was founded in Los Angeles in 1955; the first in England, called the *Samaritans,* was started in 1953. There are now hundreds of suicide prevention centers in the United States and England. In addition, many of today's mental health centers, hospital emergency rooms, pastoral counseling centers, and poison control centers include suicide prevention programs among their services.

There are also hundreds of *suicide hotlines* in the United States, 24-hour-a-day telephone services. Callers reach a counselor, typically a *paraprofessional,* a person trained in counseling but without a formal degree, who provides services under the supervision of a mental health professional.

Suicide prevention programs and hotlines respond to suicidal people as individuals *in crisis*—that is, under great stress, unable to cope, feeling threatened or hurt, and interpreting their situations as unchangeable. Thus the programs offer **crisis intervention:** they try to help suicidal people see their situations more accurately, make better decisions, act more constructively, and overcome their crises (Van Orden et al., 2008; Frankish, 1994). Because crises can occur at any time, the centers advertise their hot lines and also welcome people who walk in without appointments.

Today suicide prevention takes place not only in special settings but also in therapists' offices. Suicide experts encourage all therapists to look for and address signs of suicidal thinking and behavior in their clients, regardless of the broad reasons that the clients are seeking treatment (McGlothlin, 2008; Lester et al., 2007). With this in mind, a number of guidelines have been developed to help therapists effectively uncover, assess, prevent, and treat suicidal thinking and behavior in their daily work with clients (Van Orden et al., 2008; Fawcett, 2004; Schneidman & Farberow, 1968).

•**suicide prevention program**•A program that tries to identify people who are at risk of killing themselves and to offer them crisis intervention.

•**crisis intervention**•A treatment approach that tries to help people in a psychological crisis to view their situation more accurately, make better decisions, act more constructively, and overcome the crisis.

PSYCH WATCH

The Right to Commit Suicide

In the fall of 1989, a Michigan doctor, Jack Kevorkian, built a "suicide device." A person using it could, at the touch of a button, change a saline solution being fed intravenously into the arm to one containing chemicals that would bring unconsciousness and a swift death. The following June, under the doctor's supervision, Mrs. J. Adkins took her life. She left a note explaining: "This is a decision taken in a normal state of mind and is fully considered. I have Alzheimer's disease and I do not want to let it progress any further. I do not want to put my family or myself through the agony of this terrible disease." Mrs. Adkins believed that she had a right to choose death. Michigan authorities promptly prohibited further use of Kevorkian's device, but the physician continued to assist in the suicides of medically ill persons throughout the 1990s.

(ADAPTED FROM BELKIN, 1990; MALCOLM, 1990)

In 1999 Dr. Kevorkian was convicted of second-degree murder and sentenced to prison for an assisted suicide that he had conducted, filmed, and aired on the television news show *60 Minutes*. He was released from prison on parole in 2007. However, his many court battles have helped bring an important question to the public's attention: Do individuals have a right to commit suicide, or does society have the right to stop them (Dickens et al., 2008; Strate et al., 2005)?

The ancient Greeks valued physical and mental well-being in life and dignity in death. Therefore, individuals with a grave illness or mental anguish were permitted to commit suicide. Citizens could obtain official permission from the Senate to take their own lives, and judges were allowed to give them hemlock (Humphry & Wickett, 1986).

Western traditions, in contrast, discourage suicide, on the basis of belief in the "sanctity of life" (Dickens et al., 2008; Eser, 1981). People in Western cultures speak of "committing" suicide, as though it were a criminal act (Wertheimer, 2001), and allow the state to use force, including involuntary commitment to a mental hospital, to prevent it. But times and attitudes are changing. Today the ideas of a "right to suicide" and "rational suicide" are receiving more support from the public and from many psychotherapists and physicians (Curlin et al., 2008; Leenaars et al., 2001).

Public support for a right to suicide seems strongest in connection with great pain and terminal illness (Werth, 2004, 2000, 1999, 1996). Surveys show that more than two-thirds of all Americans believe that terminally ill persons should be free to take their lives or to seek a physician's assistance to do so (Harris Poll, 2005). In line with this belief, the state of Oregon in 1997 passed the "Death with Dignity" Act, allowing a doctor to assist a suicide (by administering a lethal dose of drugs) if two physicians determine that the patient has less than six months to live and is not basing the decision to die on depression or another mental disorder. More than 350 people have used this law to end their lives since 1997, an average of 32 each year (Hoffman, 2007). Most of these individuals had cancer, and their median age was 74. In 2006, after an extended legal battle between the federal government and Oregon, the U.S. Supreme Court upheld the law by a 6-to-3 vote, ruling that individual states have the constitutional right to pass such legislation. Other states have considered similar laws, but none has yet passed such a statute, and, in fact, 35 states have laws explicitly criminalizing assisted suicide (Hoffman, 2007).

Although specific techniques vary from therapist to therapist or from prevention center to prevention center, the general approach used by the Los Angeles Suicide Prevention Center reflects the goals and techniques of many clinicians and organizations. During the initial contact at the center, the counselor has several tasks:

Establishing a positive relationship As callers must trust counselors in order to confide in them and follow their suggestions, counselors try to set a positive and comfortable tone for the discussion. They convey that they are listening, understanding, interested, nonjudgmental, and available.

Understanding and clarifying the problem Counselors first try to understand the full scope of the caller's crisis and then help the person see the crisis in clear and constructive terms. In particular, they try to help callers see the central issues and the transient nature of their crises and recognize the alternatives to suicide.

Assessing suicide potential Crisis workers at the Los Angeles Suicide Prevention Center fill out a questionnaire, often called a lethality scale, to estimate the caller's potential for suicide. It helps them determine the degree of stress the caller is under, relevant personality characteristics, how detailed the suicide plan is, the severity of symptoms, and the coping resources available to the caller.

Critics of the Oregon law and the right-to-suicide movement argue that the suicidal acts of patients with severe or fatal illnesses may often spring largely from psychological distress (Foley & Hendin, 2002; Akechi et al., 2001). Indeed, a number of studies suggest that half or more of severely ill patients who are suicidal may be clinically depressed (Werth, 2004; Chochinov & Schwartz, 2002). Thus, in some cases, it may be more beneficial to help individuals come to terms with a fatal illness than to offer them a license to end their lives. On the other hand, according to yet other research, decisions to seek physician-assisted suicide are often made in the absence of clinical depression (Rosenfeld, 2004).

Some clinicians also worry that the right to suicide could be experienced more as a "duty to die" than as the ultimate freedom (Foley & Hendin, 2003; Brock, 2001). Elderly people might feel selfish in expecting relatives to support and care for them when suicide is a socially approved alternative (Sherlock, 1983). Moreover, as care for the terminally ill grows ever more costly, might suicide be subtly encouraged among the poor and disadvantaged? Could assisted suicide become a form of medical cost control (Brock, 2001)? In the Netherlands, where physician-assisted suicide and euthanasia were approved by law in 2001 after years of informal acceptance, euthanasia is clearly on the increase (Rurup et al., 2005). Around 2.6 percent of all deaths in that country are now the result of physician-assisted suicide and voluntary euthanasia (Hendin, 2002). In fact, almost 1 percent of deaths are the result of *involuntary* euthanasia—the termination of life without an explicit request from the patient.

How are these issues to be resolved? Understanding and preventing suicide remain challenges for the future, as do questions about whether and when we should stand back and do nothing. Whatever one's position on this issue, it is a matter of life and death.

KEYT-TV/AP Photo

KEYT 3 Santa Barbara

A right to die? Multiple sclerosis patient Rebecca Badger conducts a TV interview from her bed in 1996, just two days before she committed suicide with the assistance of Dr. Jack Kevorkian. Badger stated that the constant pain and torment of immobility caused by her illness eventually made her long for death.

Assessing and mobilizing the caller's resources Although they may view themselves as ineffectual, helpless, and alone, people who are suicidal usually have many strengths and resources, including relatives and friends. It is the counselor's job to recognize, point out, and activate those resources.

Formulating a plan Together the crisis worker and caller develop a plan of action. In essence, they are agreeing on a way out of the crisis, an alternative to suicidal action. Most plans include a series of follow-up counseling sessions over the next few days or weeks, either in person at the center or by phone. Each plan also requires the caller to take certain actions and make certain changes in his or her personal life. Counselors usually negotiate a no-suicide contract with the caller—a promise not to attempt suicide, or at least a promise to reestablish contact if the caller again considers suicide. Although such contracts are popular, their usefulness has been called into question in recent years (Rudd et al., 2006). In addition, if callers are in the midst of a suicide attempt, counselors will try to find out their whereabouts and get medical help to them immediately.

Although crisis intervention may be sufficient treatment for some suicidal people, longer-term therapy is needed for most (Lester et al., 2007; Stolberg et al., 2002). If a crisis intervention center does not offer this kind of therapy, its counselors will refer the clients elsewhere.

BETWEEN THE LINES

Linguistic Roots

The word *euthanasia* comes from the Greek *eu* ("good" or "noble") and *thanatos* ("death") (Foley & Hendin, 2002). ‹‹

Working with suicide
An individual breaks free from police and falls from a bridge in New York City. The scene reminds us that many kinds of professionals face suicidal behavior. Police departments typically provide special crisis intervention training so that officers can develop the skills to address suicidal individuals.

As the suicide prevention movement spread during the 1960s, many clinicians came to believe that crisis intervention techniques should also be applied to problems other than suicide. Crisis intervention has emerged during the past three decades as a respected form of treatment for such wide-ranging problems as drug and alcohol abuse, rape victimization, and spouse abuse.

Yet another way to help prevent suicide may be to reduce the public's access to common means of suicide (Hawton, 2007; Nordentoft et al., 2007; Reisch et al, 2007). In 1960, for example, around 12 of every 100,000 persons in Britain killed themselves by inhaling coal gas (which contains carbon monoxide). In the 1960s Britain replaced coal gas with natural gas (which contains no carbon monoxide) as an energy source, and by the mid-1970s the rate of coal gas suicide fell to zero (Maris, 2001). In fact, England's overall rate of suicide, at least for older people, dropped as well. On the other hand, the Netherlands' drop in gas-induced suicides was compensated for by an increase in other methods, particularly drug overdoses.

Similarly, ever since Canada passed a law in the 1990s restricting the availability of and access to certain firearms, a decrease in firearm suicides has been observed across the country (Leenaars, 2007). Some studies suggest that this decrease has not been displaced by increases in other kinds of suicides; other studies, however, have found an increase in the use of other suicide methods (Caron, Julien, & Huang, 2008; Leenaars, 2007). Thus, although many clinicians hope that measures such as gun control, safer medications, better bridge barriers, and car emission controls will lower suicide rates, there is no guarantee that they will.

Do Suicide Prevention Programs Work?

It is difficult for researchers to measure the effectiveness of suicide prevention programs (De Leo & Evans, 2004). There are many kinds of programs, each with its own procedures and serving populations that vary in number, age, and the like. Communities with high suicide risk factors, such as a high elderly population or economic problems, may continue to have higher suicide rates than other communities regardless of the effectiveness of their local prevention centers.

Do suicide prevention centers reduce the number of suicides in a community? Clinical researchers do not know (Van Orden et al., 2008; De Leo & Evans, 2004). Studies comparing local suicide rates before and after the establishment of community prevention centers have yielded different findings. Some find a decline in a community's suicide rates, others no change, and still others an increase (De Leo & Evans, 2004; Leenaars & Lester, 2004). Of course, even an increase may represent a positive impact, if it is lower than the larger society's overall increase in suicidal behavior. One investigator found that although suicide rates did increase in certain cities with prevention programs, they increased even more in cities without such programs (Lester, 1991, 1974).

Do suicidal people contact prevention centers? Apparently only a small percentage do. Moreover, the typical caller to an urban prevention center appears to be young, African American, and female, whereas the greatest number of suicides are committed by older white men (Maris, 2001; Lester, 2000, 1989, 1972; Canetto, 1995). A key problem is that people who are suicidal do not necessarily admit or talk about their feelings in discussions with others, even with professionals (Stolberg et al., 2002). In fact, one study discovered that more than half of the depressed patients in a mental hospital who killed themselves had previously denied having suicidal thoughts or had, at most, admitted to vague thoughts about it (Fawcett, 1988).

Prevention programs do seem to reduce the number of suicides among those high-risk people who do call. One study identified 8,000 high-risk individuals who contacted the Los Angeles Suicide Prevention Center (Farberow & Litman, 1970). Approximately

BETWEEN THE LINES

Clinical Encounters

Suicide is the most common clinical emergency encountered in mental health practice (Stolberg et al., 2002; Beutler et al., 2000). ‹‹

Suicidal behavior or thinking is the most common reason for admission to a mental hospital. Around two-thirds of patients who are admitted have aroused concern that they will harm themselves (Jacobson, 1999). ‹‹

Robert Sollett/Staten Island Advance

2 percent of these callers later committed suicide, compared to the 6 percent suicide rate usually found in similar high-risk groups. Clearly, centers need to be more visible and available to people who are thinking of suicide. The growing number of advertisements and announcements in newspapers and on television, radio, and billboards indicate a movement in this direction (Oliver et al., 2008).

Partly because of the many suicide prevention programs and the data they have generated, today's clinicians have a better understanding of suicide and greater ability to assess its risk than those of the past. Studies reveal that the professionals who are most knowledgeable about suicide are psychologists, psychiatrists, and personnel who actually work in prevention programs (MacDonald, 2007; Domino & Swain, 1986). Other professionals whom suicidal persons might contact, such as members of the clergy, are sometimes less well informed (Leane & Shute, 1998; Domino & Swain, 1986).

Several theorists have called for more effective public education about suicide as the ultimate form of prevention, and at least some *suicide education* programs—most of them concentrating on teachers and students—have begun to emerge (Gibbons & Studer, 2008; Van Orden et al., 2008). The curriculum for such programs has been the subject of much debate, but clinicians typically agree with the goals behind them and, more generally, with Shneidman when he states:

> The primary prevention of suicide lies in education. The route is through teaching one another and . . . the public that suicide can happen to anyone, that there are verbal and behavioral clues that can be looked for . . . , and that help is available. . . .
>
> In the last analysis, the prevention of suicide is everybody's business.
>
> *(Shneidman, 1985, p. 238)*

Raising public awareness
In order to better educate the public about suicide's far reach, many states now hold special remembrances and offer informative programs about suicide. Here, during a gathering to commemorate Suicide Awareness Week in Montgomery, Alabama, a police officer looks at a large quilt dedicated to those who have committed suicide.

PUTTING IT... together

Psychological and Biological Insights Lag Behind

Once a mysterious and hidden problem, hardly acknowledged by the public and barely investigated by professionals, suicide today is the focus of much attention. During the past 35 years in particular, investigators have learned a great deal about this life-or-death problem.

In contrast to most other problems covered in this textbook, suicide has received much more examination from the sociocultural model than from any other. Sociocultural theorists have, for example, highlighted the importance of societal change and stress, national and religious affiliation, marital status, gender, race, and the mass media. The insights and information gathered by psychological and biological researchers have been more limited.

Although sociocultural factors certainly shed light on the general background and triggers of suicide, they typically leave us unable to predict that a given person will attempt suicide. When all is said and done, clinicians do not yet fully understand why some people kill themselves while others in similar circumstances manage to find better ways of addressing their problems. Psychological and biological insights must catch up to the sociocultural insights if clinicians are truly to explain and understand suicide.

Treatments for suicide also pose some difficult problems. Clinicians have yet to develop clearly successful therapies for suicidal persons. Although suicide prevention programs certainly show the clinical field's commitment to helping people who are suicidal, it is not yet clear how much such programs actually reduce the overall risk or rate of suicide.

At the same time, the growth in the amount of research on suicide offers great promise. And perhaps most promising of all, clinicians are now enlisting the public

BETWEEN THE LINES

Deal Breaker

If clients state an intention to commit suicide, therapists may break the doctor-patient confidentiality agreement that usually governs treatment discussions. ‹‹

Murder-suicide in the twenty-first century
An increasingly common form of murder-suicide involves individuals who massacre large numbers of people and then take their own lives. In November 2007, for example, 18-year-old Pekka-Eric Auvinen killed nine people and then himself at his high school in Finland, his actions coming one day after he had posted a video on YouTube announcing the massacre.

BETWEEN THE LINES

In Their Words

"I'll tell you what I can't get out of my head . . . it's watching my hands come off that railing and thinking to myself, My God, what have I just done? Because I know that almost everyone else who's gone off that bridge, they had that exact same thought at that moment. All of a sudden, they didn't want to die, but it was too late. Somehow I made it; they didn't." «

Survivor of a leap from the Golden Gate Bridge, 2008

in the fight against this problem. They are calling for broader public education about suicide—for programs aimed at both young and old. It is reasonable to expect that the current commitment will lead to a better understanding of suicide and to more successful interventions. Such goals are of importance to everyone. Although suicide itself is typically a lonely and desperate act, the impact of such acts is very broad indeed.

‹‹‹ SUMMING UP ›››

○ **What is suicide?** *Suicide* is a self-inflicted death in which one makes an intentional, direct, and conscious effort to end one's life. Four kinds of people who intentionally end their lives have been distinguished: the *death seeker*, the *death initiator*, the *death ignorer*, and the *death darer. pp. 310–312*

○ **Research strategies** Two major strategies are used in the study of suicide: *retrospective analysis* (a psychological autopsy) and the *study of people who survive suicide attempts*, on the assumption that they are similar to those who commit fatal suicides. Each strategy has limitations. *p. 312*

○ **Patterns and statistics** Suicide ranks among the top 10 causes of death in Western society. Rates vary from country to country. One reason seems to be cultural differences in *religious affiliation, beliefs*, or *degree of devoutness*. Suicide rates also vary according to *race, gender*, and *marital status. pp. 312–315*

○ **Factors that trigger suicide** Many suicidal acts are triggered by the current events or conditions in a person's life. The acts may be triggered by *recent stressors*, such as loss of a loved one and job loss, or *long-term stressors*, such as serious illness, an abusive environment, and job stress. They may also be preceded by *changes in mood or thought*, particularly increases in one's sense of *hopelessness*. In addition, the *use of alcohol or other kinds of substances, mental disorders*, or *news of another's suicide* may precede suicide attempts. *pp. 315–321*

○ **Explanations** The leading explanations for suicide come from the psychodynamic, sociocultural, and biological models. Each has received only limited support. *Psychodynamic* theorists believe that suicide usually results from depression and self-directed anger. Emile Durkheim's *sociocultural* theory defines three categories of suicide based on the person's relationship with society: *egoistic, altruistic*, and *anomic* suicides. And *biological* theorists suggest that the activity of the neurotransmitter serotonin is particularly low in individuals who commit suicide. *pp. 321–325*

○ **Suicide in different age groups** The likelihood of suicide varies with age. It is uncommon among *children*, although it has been increasing in that group during the past several decades.

Suicide by *adolescents* is a more common occurrence than suicide by children, but it has been decreasing over the past decade. Adolescent suicide has been linked to clinical depression, anger, impulsiveness, major stress, and adolescent life itself. *Suicide attempts* by this age group are numerous. The high attempt rate among adolescents and young adults may be related to the growing number and proportion of young people in the general population, the weakening of family ties, the increased availability and use of drugs among the young, and the broad media coverage of suicide attempts by the young. The rate of suicide among Native Americans teens is twice as high as that among white American teens and three times as high as the African, Hispanic, and Asian American teen suicide rates.

In Western society the *elderly* are more likely to commit suicide than people in any other age group. The loss of health, friends, control, and status may produce feelings of hopelessness, loneliness, depression, or inevitability in this age group. *pp. 325–332*

○ **Treatment and suicide** Treatment may *follow* a suicide attempt. In such cases, therapists seek to help the person achieve a nonsuicidal state of mind and develop better ways of handling stress and solving problems.

Over the past 30 years, emphasis has shifted to *suicide prevention*. Suicide prevention programs include 24-hour-a-day hotlines and walk-in centers staffed largely by *paraprofessionals*. During their initial contact with a suicidal person, counselors seek to establish a positive relationship, to understand and clarify the problem, to assess the potential for suicide, to assess and mobilize the caller's resources, and to formulate a plan for overcoming the crisis. Beyond such *crisis intervention*, most suicidal people also need *longer-term therapy*. In a still broader attempt at prevention, *suicide education programs* for the public are beginning to appear. *pp. 332–338*

⫸ CRITICAL THOUGHTS ⫷

1. As you read in the case of Margaux Hemingway and Ernest Hemingway, suicide sometimes runs in families. Why might this be the case? *p. 309*

2. A person's wish to die is often ambivalent. In addition, most people who think about suicide do not act. How, then, should clinicians decide whether to hospitalize a person who is considering suicide or even one who has made an attempt? *pp. 311–312, 328–330, 332–337*

3. Suicide rates vary widely from country to country. What factors besides religion might help account for the differences? *pp. 312, 314–315, 328*

4. Often people view the suicide of an elderly or chronically sick person as less tragic than that of a young or healthy person. Why might they think this way, and is their reasoning valid? *pp. 316, 330–332, 334–335*

5. Some schools are reluctant to offer suicide education programs, especially if they have never experienced a suicide attempt by one of their students. What might be their concerns? How valid is their position? *pp. 321, 337*

6. Why might people in past times have been inclined to punish those who committed suicide and their surviving relatives? Why do most people take a different view today? *p. 331*

🌌 cyberstudy 👀   SEARCH

Search the *Abnormal Psychology* Video Tool Kit
www.worthpublishers.com/apvtk

▲ Chapter 10 Video Cases
  Inside the Suicidal Mind
  Case of the "3-Star" Chef: Fame Is No Protection
  An Ethical Dilemma: Do People Have the Right to Take Their Own Lives?

▲ Video case discussions, study guides, and questions

Log on to the Comer Web Page
www.worthpublishers.com/comer

▲ Chapter 10 outline, learning objectives, research exercises, study tools, and practice test questions
▲ Additional Chapter 10 case studies, Web links, and FAQs

EATING DISORDERS

Janet Caldwell was . . . five feet, two inches tall and weighed 62 pounds. . . . Janet began dieting at the age of 12 when she weighed 115 pounds and was chided by her family and friends for being "pudgy." She continued to restrict her food intake over a two-year period, and as she grew thinner, her parents became increasingly more concerned about her eating behavior. . . .

Janet . . . felt that her weight problem began at the time of puberty. She said that her family and friends had supported her efforts to achieve a ten-pound weight loss when she first began dieting at age 12. Janet did not go on any special kind of diet. Instead, she restricted her food intake at meals, generally cut down on carbohydrates and protein intake, tended to eat a lot of salads, and completely stopped snacking between meals. At first, she was quite pleased with her progressive weight reduction, and she was able to ignore her feelings of hunger by remembering the weight loss goal she had set for herself. However, each time she lost the number of pounds she had set for her goal she decided to lose just a few more pounds. Therefore she continued to set new weight goals for herself. In this manner, her weight dropped from 115 pounds to 88 pounds during the first year of her weight loss regimen.

Janet felt that, in her second year of dieting, her weight loss had continued beyond her control. . . . She became convinced that there was something inside of her that would not let her gain weight. . . . Janet commented that although there had been occasions over the past few years when she had been fairly "down" or unhappy, she still felt driven to keep on dieting. As a result, she frequently went for walks, ran errands for her family, and spent a great deal of time cleaning her room and keeping it in a meticulously neat and unaltered arrangement.

When Janet's weight loss continued beyond the first year, her parents insisted that she see their family physician, and Mrs. Caldwell accompanied Janet to her appointment. Their family practitioner was quite alarmed at Janet's appearance and prescribed a high-calorie diet. Janet said that her mother spent a great deal of time pleading with her to eat, and Mrs. Caldwell planned various types of meals that she thought would be appealing to Janet. Mrs. Caldwell also talked a great deal to Janet about the importance of good nutrition. Mr. Caldwell, on the other hand, became quite impatient with these discussions and tended to order Janet to eat. Janet then would try to eat something, but often became tearful and ran out of the room because she could not swallow the food she had been ordered to eat. She said that she often responded to her parents' entreaties that she eat by telling them that she indeed had eaten but they had not seen her do so. She often listed foods that she said she had consumed which in fact she had flushed down the toilet. She estimated that she only was eating about 300 calories a day.

Leon, 1984, pp. 179–184

It has not always done so, but Western society today equates thinness with health and beauty (see Figure 11-1 on the next page). In fact, in the United States thinness has become a national obsession. Most of us are as preoccupied with how much we eat as with the taste and nutritional value of our food. Thus it is not surprising that during the past three decades we have also witnessed an increase in two eating disorders that have at their core a morbid fear of gaining weight. Sufferers of *anorexia nervosa*, like Janet Caldwell, are convinced that they need to be extremely thin, and they lose so much weight that they may starve themselves to death. People with *bulimia nervosa* go on frequent eating binges, during which

Percentage Dissatisfied with Their:

	1972		1997	
Overall body	Females 25% / Males 15%		Females 56% / Males 43%	
Weight	Females 48% / Males 35%		Females 66% / Males 52%	
Muscle tone	Females 30% / Males 25%		Females 57% / Males 45%	
Breasts/Chest	Females 26% / Males 18%		Females 34% / Males 38%	
Abdomen	Females 50% / Males 36%		Females 71% / Males 63%	
Hips and upper thighs	Females 49% / Males 12%		Females 61% / Males 29%	

Figure 11-1

Body dissatisfaction on the rise According to surveys, people in our society—both women and men—are much more dissatisfied with their bodies now than they were a generation ago. (Adams et al., 2005; Garner et al., 1997; Rodin, 1992)

table: 11-1

DSM Checklist

ANOREXIA NERVOSA

1. Refusal to maintain body weight above a minimally normal weight for age and height.

2. Intense fear of gaining weight, even though underweight.

3. Disturbed body perception, undue influence of weight or shape on self-evaluation, or denial of the seriousness of the current low weight.

4. In postmenarcheal females, amenorrhea.

Based on APA, 2000.

they uncontrollably consume large quantities of food, and then force themselves to vomit or take other extreme steps to keep from gaining weight.

The news media have published many reports about anorexic or bulimic behavior. One reason for the surge in public interest is the frightening medical consequences that can result (Kerr, Lindner, & Blaydon, 2007). The public first became aware of such consequences in 1983 when Karen Carpenter, a popular singer and entertainer, died from medical problems related to anorexia (see *Psych Watch: Abnormality and the Arts* on the facing page). Another reason for concern is the disproportionate prevalence of these disorders among adolescent girls and young women.

Clinicians now understand that the similarities between anorexia nervosa and bulimia nervosa can be as important as the differences between them. For example, many people with anorexia nervosa binge as they persist in losing dangerous amounts of weight; some later develop bulimia nervosa (Fairburn et al., 2008; Tozzi et al., 2005; APA, 2000). Conversely, people with bulimia nervosa sometimes develop anorexia nervosa as time goes on.

Anorexia Nervosa

Janet Caldwell, 14 years old and in the eighth grade, displays many symptoms of **anorexia nervosa:** she refuses to maintain more than 85 percent of her normal body weight, intensely fears becoming overweight, has a distorted view of her weight and shape, and has stopped menstruating (see Table 11-1).

Like Janet, at least half of the people with anorexia nervosa reduce their weight by restricting their intake of food, a pattern called *restricting-type anorexia nervosa*. First they tend to cut out sweets and fattening snacks; then, increasingly, they eliminate other foods (APA, 2000). Eventually people with this kind of anorexia nervosa show almost no variability in diet. Others, however, lose weight by forcing themselves to vomit after meals or by abusing laxatives or diuretics, and they may even engage in eating binges, a pattern called *binge-eating/purging-type anorexia nervosa,* which you will observe in more detail in the section on bulimia nervosa (APA, 2000).

Approximately 90 to 95 percent of all cases of anorexia nervosa occur in females (Zerbe, 2008; Freeman, 2005). Although the disorder can appear at any age, the peak

PSYCH WATCH Abnormality and the Arts

We've Only Just Begun

Given the hard-living, substance-abusing, risk-taking image cultivated by many pop, rock, and rap music artists, you are probably not shocked when you read about certain untimely deaths, from Elvis Presley, Jimi Hendrix, or Sid Vicious to Kurt Cobain, Tupac Shakur, Notorious B.I.G., or Russell Jones (Ol' Dirty Bastard). The 1983 death of Karen Carpenter, from the effects of anorexia nervosa, in contrast, stunned the country. Karen, the 32-year-old velvet-voiced lead singer of the soft-rock brother-and-sister duo The Carpenters, did not drink, take drugs, drive fast cars, or tear up the roadside on a motorcycle. She never appeared in the pages of the tabloids. Until her late twenties—well into her fame—she even continued to live at home with her parents and brother, Richard, in suburban Downey, California. Indeed, she and Richard were icons of unrebellious, quiet youthful virtue.

The pressure to maintain this wholesome image may have contributed to Karen's destruction. After reading an early concert review describing her as "chubby," Karen began a downward spiral into anorexia nervosa. Always a dutiful family member and content to let Richard make all the management and artistic decisions for their group, Karen seemed to have little control over her fame. One friend and fellow sufferer later said about Karen's eating disorder, "When you start denying yourself food, and begin feeling you have control over a life that has been pretty much controlled for you, it's exhilarating" (O'Neill, as cited in Levin, 1983).

For nine years Karen starved herself, abused laxatives and thyroid pills, and purged by repeatedly swallowing drugs that induce vomiting. Her weight dropped from a high of 140 pounds at the beginning of her singing career to a devastating low of 80 pounds. Ironically, in the last year of her life, it looked as though she had gotten a handle on her disorder. She had increased her weight to an almost-normal 108 pounds after a year of therapy. Yet on a visit home to her parents' house in California, on February 4, 1983, she collapsed. Paramedics could not revive her, and she died an hour later of cardiac arrest. Traces of a vomit-inducing drug were found in her bloodstream.

Until Karen's death, the public knew little about anorexia nervosa, and what it knew did not sound serious—it seemed more like the latest celebrity fad diet than a dangerous, potentially fatal condition. But that lighthearted view changed dramatically with her death, as scores of articles in newspapers and magazines detailed not only the tragically short life of Karen Carpenter but also the disorder that killed her. Anorexia nervosa was no longer something to be taken casually. Since then numerous other famous personalities in diverse fields have gone public about their own struggles with eating disorders.

B. Schiffman/Gamma Liaison

age of onset is between 14 and 18 years (APA, 2000). Between 0.5 and 2 percent of all females in Western countries develop the disorder in their lifetime, and many more display at least some of its symptoms (Culbert & Klump, 2008; Hudson et al., 2007). It seems to be on the increase in North America, Europe, and Japan.

Typically the disorder begins after a person who is slightly overweight or of normal weight has been on a diet (Couturier & Lock, 2006). The escalation toward anorexia nervosa may follow a stressful event such as separation of parents, a move away from home, or an experience of personal failure (Wilson et al., 2003). Although most victims recover, between 2 and 6 percent of them become so seriously ill that they die, usually from medical problems brought about by starvation or from suicide (Pompili et al., 2007; Millar et al., 2005).

•**anorexia nervosa**•A disorder marked by the pursuit of extreme thinness and by extreme loss of weight.

Wallace Kirkland, *Life* ©Time Warner, Inc.

Laboratory starvation
Thirty-six conscientious objectors who were put on a semistarvation diet for six months developed many of the symptoms seen in anorexia nervosa and bulimia nervosa (Keys et al., 1950).

•**amenorrhea**•The cessation of menstrual cycles.

•**bulimia nervosa**•A disorder marked by frequent eating binges that are followed by forced vomiting or other extreme compensatory behaviors to avoid gaining weight. Also known as *binge-purge syndrome.*

•**binge**•An episode of uncontrollable eating during which a person ingests a very large quantity of food.

The Clinical Picture

Becoming thin is the key goal for people with anorexia nervosa, but *fear* provides their motivation. People with this disorder are afraid of becoming obese, of giving in to their growing desire to eat, and more generally of losing control over the size and shape of their bodies. In addition, despite their focus on thinness and the severe restrictions they may place on their food intake, people with anorexia are *preoccupied with food.* They may spend considerable time thinking and even reading about food and planning their limited meals (Herzig, 2004; King et al., 1991). Many report that their dreams are filled with images of food and eating (Knudson, 2006; Levitan, 1981).

This preoccupation with food may in fact be a result of food deprivation rather than its cause. In a famous "starvation study" conducted in the late 1940s, 36 normal-weight conscientious objectors were put on a semi-starvation diet for six months (Keys et al., 1950). Like people with anorexia nervosa, the volunteers became preoccupied with food and eating. They spent hours each day planning their small meals, talked more about food than about any other topic, studied cookbooks and recipes, mixed food in odd combinations, and dawdled over their meals. Many also had vivid dreams about food.

Persons with anorexia nervosa also *think in distorted ways.* They usually have a low opinion of their body shape, for example, and consider themselves unattractive (Eifert et al., 2007; Kaye et al., 2002). In addition, they are likely to overestimate their actual proportions. While most women in Western society overestimate their body size, the estimates of those with anorexia nervosa are particularly high. A 23-year-old patient said:

I look in a full-length mirror at least four or five times daily and I really cannot see myself as too thin. Sometimes after several days of strict dieting, I feel that my shape is tolerable, but most of the time, odd as it may seem, I look in the mirror and believe that I am too fat.

(Bruch, 1973)

This tendency to overestimate body size has been tested in the laboratory (Farrell, Lee, & Shafran, 2005). In a popular assessment technique, research participants look at a photograph of themselves through an adjustable lens. They are asked to adjust the lens until the image that they see matches their actual body size. The image can be made to vary from 20 percent thinner to 20 percent larger than actual appearance. In one study, more than half of the individuals with anorexia nervosa were found to overestimate their body size, stopping the lens when the image was larger than they actually were.

The distorted thinking of anorexia nervosa also takes the form of certain maladaptive attitudes and misperceptions (Fairburn et al., 2008; Vartanian et al., 2004). Sufferers tend to hold such beliefs as "I must be perfect in every way"; "I will become a better person if I deprive myself"; and "I can avoid guilt by not eating." A woman who later recovered from anorexia nervosa recalled that at age 15 "my thought processes became very unrealistic. I felt I had to do something I didn't want to do for a higher purpose. That took over my life. It all went haywire" (Bruch, 1978, p. 17).

People with anorexia nervosa also display certain *psychological problems,* such as depression and anxiety and low self-esteem (Godart et al., 2005; O'Brien & Vincent, 2003). Some also experience insomnia or other sleep disturbances. A number grapple with substance abuse. And many display obsessive-compulsive patterns. They may set rigid rules for food preparation or even cut food into specific shapes. Broader obsessive-compulsive patterns are common as well (Culbert & Klump, 2008; Sansone et al., 2005). Many, for example, exercise compulsively, giving this activity higher priority than most other activities in their lives (Fairburn et al., 2008). In some research, people with anorexia nervosa and others with obsessive-compulsive disorder score equally high for obsessiveness and compulsiveness (Culbert & Klump, 2008; Bastiani et al., 1996). Finally, persons with anorexia nervosa tend to be perfectionistic, a characteristic that typically precedes the onset of the disorder (Pinto et al., 2008; Shafran, Cooper, & Fairburn, 2002).

Medical Problems

The starvation habits of anorexia nervosa cause medical problems (Zerbe, 2008; Tyre, 2005). Women develop **amenorrhea,** the absence of menstrual cycles. Other problems include lowered body temperature, low blood pressure, body swelling, reduced bone mineral density, and slow heart rate. Metabolic and electrolyte imbalances also may occur and can lead to death by heart failure or circulatory collapse. The poor nutrition of people with anorexia nervosa may also cause skin to become rough, dry, and cracked; nails to become brittle; and hands and feet to be cold and blue. Some people lose hair from the scalp, and some grow lanugo (the fine, silky hair that covers some newborns) on their trunk, extremities, and face.

   Clearly, people with this disorder are caught in a vicious cycle. Their fear of obesity and distorted body image lead them to starve themselves. Starvation in turn leads to a preoccupation with food, increased anxiety and depression, and medical problems, causing them to feel even more afraid that they will lose control over their weight, their eating, and themselves. They then try still harder to achieve thinness by not eating.

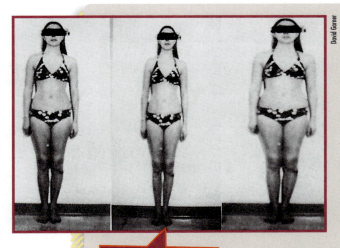

Seeing is deceiving
In one research technique, people look at photographs of themselves through a special lens and adjust the lens until they see what they believe is their actual image. A research participant may change her actual image (left) from 20 percent thinner (middle) to 20 percent larger (right).

✿Bulimia Nervosa

People with **bulimia nervosa**—a disorder also known as **binge-purge syndrome**—engage in repeated episodes of uncontrollable overeating, or **binges.** A binge occurs over a limited period of time, often an hour, during which the person eats much more food than most people would eat during a similar time span (Stewart & Williamson, 2008; APA, 2000). In addition, people with this disorder repeatedly perform inappropriate *compensatory behaviors,* such as forcing themselves to vomit; misusing laxatives, diuretics, or enemas; fasting; or exercising excessively (Kerr et al., 2007) (see Table 11-2 on the next page). If the compensatory behaviors regularly include forced vomiting or misuse of laxatives, diuretics, or enemas, the specific diagnosis is *purging-type bulimia nervosa.* If individuals instead compensate by fasting or exercising frantically, the specific diagnosis is *nonpurging-type bulimia nervosa.* A married woman with the former pattern, since recovered, describes a morning during her disorder:

Today I am going to be really good and that means eating certain predetermined portions of food and not taking one more bite than I think I am allowed. I am very careful to see that I don't take more than Doug does. I judge by his body. I can feel the tension building. I wish Doug would hurry up and leave so I can get going!

   As soon as he shuts the door, I try to get involved with one of the myriad of responsibilities on the list. I hate them all! I just want to crawl into a hole. I don't want to do anything. I'd rather eat. I am alone, I am nervous, I am no good, I always do everything wrong anyway, I am not in control, I can't make it through the day, I just know it. It has been the same for so long.

   I remember the starchy cereal I ate for breakfast. I am into the bathroom and onto the scale. It measures the same, BUT I DON'T WANT TO STAY THE SAME! I want to be thinner! I look in the mirror, I think my thighs are ugly and deformed looking. I see a lumpy, clumsy,

table: 11-2

DSM Checklist

BULIMIA NERVOSA

1. Recurrent episodes of binge eating.
2. Recurrent inappropriate compensatory behavior in order to prevent weight gain.
3. Symptoms continuing, on average, at least twice a week for three months.
4. Undue influence of weight or shape on self-evaluation.

Based on APA, 2000.

pear-shaped wimp. There is always something wrong with what I see. I feel frustrated trapped in this body and I don't know what to do about it.

I float to the refrigerator knowing exactly what is there. I begin with last night's brownies. I always begin with the sweets. At first I try to make it look like nothing is missing, but my appetite is huge and I resolve to make another batch of brownies. I know there is half of a bag of cookies in the bathroom, thrown out the night before, and I polish them off immediately. I take some milk so my vomiting will be smoother. I like the full feeling I get after downing a big glass. I get out six pieces of bread and toast one side in the broiler, turn them over and load them with patties of butter and put them under the broiler again till they are bubbling. I take all six pieces on a plate to the television and go back for a bowl of cereal and a banana to have along with them. Before the last toast is finished, I am already preparing the next batch of six more pieces. Maybe another brownie or five, and a couple of large bowlfuls of ice cream, yogurt or cottage cheese. My stomach is stretched into a huge ball below my ribcage. I know I'll have to go into the bathroom soon, but I want to postpone it. I am in never-never land. I am waiting, feeling the pressure, pacing the floor in and out of the rooms. Time is passing. Time is passing. It is getting to be time.

I wander aimlessly through each of the rooms again tidying, making the whole house neat and put back together. I finally make the turn into the bathroom. I brace my feet, pull my hair back and stick my finger down my throat, stroking twice, and get up a huge pile of food. Three times, four and another pile of food. I can see everything come back. I am glad to see those brownies because they are SO fattening. The rhythm of the emptying is broken and my head is beginning to hurt. I stand up feeling dizzy, empty and weak. The whole episode has taken about an hour.

(Hall, 1980, pp. 5–6)

Like anorexia nervosa, bulimia nervosa usually occurs in females, again in 90 to 95 percent of the cases (Stewart & Williamson, 2008). It begins in adolescence or young adulthood (most often between 15 and 21 years of age) and often lasts for several years, with periodic letup. The weight of people with bulimia nervosa usually stays within a normal range, although it may fluctuate markedly within that range (APA, 2000). Some people with this disorder, however, become seriously underweight and may eventually qualify for a diagnosis of anorexia nervosa instead (see Figure 11–2). Clinicians have also observed that certain people, a number of them overweight, display a pattern of binge eating without vomiting or other inappropriate compensatory behaviors. This pattern,

Figure 11-2

Overlapping patterns of anorexia nervosa, bulimia nervosa, and obesity Some people with anorexia nervosa binge and purge their way to weight loss, and some obese persons binge-eat. However, most people with bulimia nervosa are not obese, and most overweight people do not binge-eat. (Adapted from APA, 2000; Garner & Fairburn, 1988; Russell, 1979.)

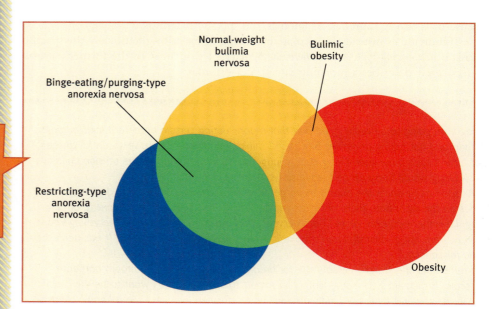

Scott Gries/Getty Images

often called *binge-eating disorder,* is not yet listed separately in the DSM, although it is likely to be in the next edition (Fairburn et al., 2008; Mitchell et al., 2008). Between 2 and 7 percent of the population and as many as one-quarter of severely overweight people are thought to have this disorder.

Many teenagers and young adults go on occasional eating binges or experiment with vomiting or laxatives after they hear about these behaviors from their friends or the media. Indeed, according to global studies, 25 to 50 percent of students report periodic binge-eating or self-induced vomiting (Zerbe, 2008; McDermott & Jaffa, 2005). Only some of these individuals, however, qualify for a diagnosis of bulimia nervosa. Surveys in several Western countries suggest that as many as 5 percent of women develop the full syndrome (Stewart & Williamson, 2008; Favaro et al., 2003). Among college students the rate may be much higher (Zerbe, 2008; Feldman & Meyer, 2007).

Binges

People with bulimia nervosa may have between 1 and 30 binge episodes per week (Fairburn et al., 2008). In most cases, the binges are carried out in secret. The person eats massive amounts of food very rapidly, with minimal chewing—usually sweet, high-calorie foods with a soft texture, such as ice cream, cookies, doughnuts, and sandwiches. The food is hardly tasted or thought about. Binge-eaters commonly consume more than 1,000 calories (often more than 3,000) during an episode.

Binges are usually preceded by feelings of great tension (Crowther et al., 2001). The person feels irritable, "unreal," and powerless to control an overwhelming need to eat "forbidden" foods. During the binge, the person feels unable to stop eating. Although the binge itself may be experienced as pleasurable in the sense that it relieves the unbearable tension, it is followed by feelings of extreme self-blame, shame, guilt, and depression, as well as fears of gaining weight and being discovered (Fairburn et al., 2008; Hayaki et al., 2002). Such feelings are on display in this description by a successful public relations executive:

Here I had everything society tells us should make us happy: success, money, access, but not one thing in my life gave me pleasure. In the middle of all of this action and all of these people, I felt like I was in solitary confinement. And I began to cope with these feelings of emptiness and dread by numbing the pain with food—the only thing I looked

Eating for sport
Many people go on occasional eating binges. In fact, sometimes binges are officially endorsed, as you see in this photo from the 2008 Nathan's Famous International Hot Dog eating contest at Brooklyn's Coney Island, New York. However, individuals are considered to have an eating disorder only when the binges recur, the pattern endures, and the issues of weight or shape dominate self-evaluation.

forward to after a sixteen-hour day. On the way home, I would pick up snack foods, ice cream, party mix, cheese . . . mix them with leftovers from restaurant dinners, and eat until I was beyond full. But my hunger increased week by week, until every half hour I would get out of bed and go to the refrigerator for a snack. I was gaining weight; the more weight I gained the more disgust I felt; the more self-disgust I felt the more I wanted to hide from the pain by eating and sleeping. Like every drug, the food gave me less relief each day, but I clung to it. It was the only thing in my life that could soothe me—the only crutch I had to help me limp around my intolerable feelings. But what started as a source of comfort became another prison.

The saddest thing about all this is that I was able to go so long without anyone really noticing or at least feeling like they could say something. Every shred of energy I could muster after a night of sleep interrupted by binge eating went into servicing my clients and doing my superwoman act: competent, together, single woman making it on willpower alone; I was the poster girl for ambition and achievement, the Strong Black Woman. Strangely, sadly, the façade held up. As far as my colleagues and clients were concerned, the work got done and got done well.

(Williams, 2008, p. xxiii)

Compensatory Behaviors

After a binge, people with bulimia nervosa try to compensate for and undo its effects. Many resort to vomiting. But vomiting actually fails to prevent the absorption of half of the calories consumed during a binge. Furthermore, repeated vomiting affects one's general ability to feel satiated; thus it leads to greater hunger and more frequent and intense binges. Similarly, the use of laxatives or diuretics largely fails to undo the caloric effects of bingeing (Fairburn et al., 2008).

Vomiting and other compensatory behaviors may temporarily relieve the uncomfortable physical feelings of fullness or reduce the feelings of anxiety and self-disgust attached to binge eating (Stewart & Williamson, 2008). Over time, however, a cycle develops in which purging allows more bingeing, and bingeing necessitates more purging. The cycle eventually causes people with this disorder to feel powerless and disgusted with themselves (Hayaki et al., 2002). Most recognize fully that they have an eating disorder. The married woman you met earlier recalls how the pattern of bingeing, purging, and self-disgust took hold while she was a teenager in boarding school:

BETWEEN THE LINES

Saintly Restraint

During the Middle Ages, restrained eating, prolonged fasting, or purging by a number of female saints was greatly admired and was even counted among their miracles. Catherine of Siena sometimes pushed twigs down her throat to bring up food; Mary of Oignes and Beatrice of Nazareth vomited from the mere smell of meat; and Columba of Rieti died of self-starvation (Brumberg, 1988). ‹‹

Every bite that went into my mouth was a naughty and selfish indulgence, and I became more and more disgusted with myself. . . .

The first time I stuck my fingers down my throat was during the last week of school. I saw a girl come out of the bathroom with her face all red and her eyes puffy. She had always talked about her weight and how she should be dieting even though her body was really shapely. I knew instantly what she had just done and I had to try it. . . .

I began with breakfasts which were served buffet-style on the main floor of the dorm. I learned which foods I could eat that would come back up easily. When I woke in the morning, I had to make the decision whether to stuff myself for half an hour and throw up before class, or whether to try and make it through the whole day without overeating. . . . I always thought people noticed when I took huge portions at mealtimes, but I figured they assumed that because I was an athlete, I burned it off. . . . Once a binge was under way, I did not stop until my stomach looked pregnant and I felt like I could not swallow one more time.

That year was the first of my nine years of obsessive eating and throwing up. . . . I didn't want to tell anyone what I was doing, and I didn't want to stop. . . . [Though] being in love or other distractions occasionally lessened the cravings, I always returned to the food.

(Hall, 1980, pp. 9–12)

As with anorexia nervosa, a bulimic pattern typically begins during or after a period of intense dieting, often one that has been successful and earned praise from family members and friends (Couturier & Lock, 2006; Helgeson, 2002). Studies have found that normal research participants placed on very strict diets also develop a tendency to binge (Eifert et al., 2007). Some of the participants in the conscientious objector "starvation study," for example, later binged when they were allowed to return to regular eating, and a number of them continued to be hungry even after large meals (Keys et al., 1950). A later study examined the binge-eating behavior of individuals at the end of a very low-calorie weight-loss program (Telch & Agras, 1993). Immediately after the program, 62 percent of the participants, who had not previously been binge eaters, reported binge-eating episodes, although the episodes did decrease during the three months after treatment stopped.

BETWEEN THE LINES

Royal Bulimia?

During her three years as queen of England, Anne Boleyn, King Henry VIII's second wife, displayed a habit, first observed during her coronation banquet, of vomiting during meals. In fact, she assigned a lady-in-waiting the task of holding up a sheet when the queen looked likely to vomit (Shaw, 2004). ‹‹

Schindler Family Photo/AP Photo

Was bulimia nervosa the cause?
One of the most publicized cases of 2005 was that of Terri Schiavo, shown in this photo shortly after she suffered an apparent heart attack in 1990. After experiencing cardiac arrest, she suffered extensive brain damage and was left in what was termed a "persistent vegetative state." Following a series of legal battles, a court ordered in 2005 that Schiavo's feeding tube be removed, and she died a week later. One question at the center of this case was whether Schiavo's heart dysfunction had been the result of bulimia nervosa. Blood tests revealed that she had a potassium deficiency (a dangerous medical complication of bulimia nervosa); her weight had fluctuated significantly during the years prior to her collapse; a number of friends reported observing bulimia-like patterns of behavior; and, in fact, a jury eventually awarded Schiavo more than $1 million in a malpractice suit against the obstetrician who had been treating her for infertility prior to her collapse, contending that he had failed to test her for or diagnose an eating disorder. On the other hand, Schiavo's autopsy offered no direct proof of an eating disorder, and alternative explanations for her collapse and cardiac arrest have been proposed.

Bulimia Nervosa vs. Anorexia Nervosa

Bulimia nervosa is similar to anorexia nervosa in many ways. Both disorders typically begin after a period of dieting by people who are fearful of becoming obese; driven to become thin; preoccupied with food, weight, and appearance; and struggling with depression, anxiety, obsessiveness, and the need to be perfect (Fairburn et al., 2008, 2003). Individuals with either of the disorders have a heightened risk of attempts at suicide (Pompili et al., 2007; Ruuska et al., 2005). Substance abuse may accompany either disorder, perhaps beginning with the excessive use of diet pills. People with either disorder believe that they weigh too much and look too heavy regardless of their actual weight or appearance (Stewart & Williamson, 2008; Kaye et al., 2002). And both disorders are marked by disturbed attitudes toward eating.

Yet the two disorders also differ in important ways (see Table 11–3). Although people with either disorder worry about the opinions of others, those with bulimia nervosa tend to be more concerned about pleasing others, being attractive to others, and having intimate relationships (Zerbe, 2008; Eddy et al., 2004; Striegel-Moore et al., 1993). They also tend to be more sexually experienced and active than people with anorexia nervosa. Particularly troublesome, they are more likely to have long histories of mood swings, become easily frustrated or bored, and have trouble coping effectively or controlling their impulses (Claes et al., 2002; APA, 2000). Individuals with bulimia nervosa also tend to be ruled by strong emotions and may change friends and relationships frequently. And more than one-third of them display the characteristics of a personality disorder, particularly borderline personality disorder, which you will be looking at more closely in Chapter 16 (Stewart & Williamson, 2008). This subgroup of people with bulimia nervosa may also display self-injurious behavior such as cutting their arms with razors, knives, or glass.

table: 11-3

Anorexia Nervosa versus Bulimia Nervosa

Restricting-type Anorexia Nervosa	Bulimia Nervosa
Refusal to maintain a minimum body weight for healthy functioning	Underweight, normal weight, near-normal weight, or overweight
Hunger and disorder denied; often proud of weight management and more satisfied with body	Intense hunger experienced; binge-purge experienced as abnormal; greater body dissatisfaction
Less antisocial behavior	Greater tendency to antisocial behavior and alcohol abuse
Amenorrhea of at least 3 months' duration common	Irregular menstrual periods common; amenorrhea uncommon unless body weight is low
Mistrust of others, particularly professionals	More trusting of people who wish to help
Tend to be obsessive	Tend to be dramatic
Greater self-control, but emotionally overcontrolled, with problems experiencing and expressing feelings	More impulsivity and emotional instability
More likely to be sexually immature and inexperienced	More sexually experienced and sexually active
Females more likely to reject traditional feminine role	Females more likely to embrace traditional feminine role
Age of onset often around 14–18	Age of onset around 15–21
Greater tendency for maximum pre-disorder weight to be near normal for age	Greater tendency for maximum pre-disorder weight to be slightly greater than normal
Lesser familial predisposition to obesity	Greater familial predisposition to obesity
Greater tendency toward pre-disorder compliance with parents	Greater tendency toward pre-disorder conflict with parents
Tendency to deny family conflict	Tendency to perceive intense family conflict

Source: Zerbe, 2008; APA, 2000, 1994; Levine, 1987; Andersen, 1985; Garner et al., 1985; Neuman & Halvorson, 1983.

Another difference is the nature of the medical complications that accompany the two disorders (Birmingham & Beumont, 2004). Only half of women with bulimia nervosa are amenorrheic or have very irregular menstrual periods, compared to almost all of those with anorexia nervosa (Zerbe, 2008; Crow et al., 2002). On the other hand, repeated vomiting bathes teeth and gums in hydrochloric acid, leading some women with bulimia nervosa to experience serious dental problems, such as breakdown of enamel and even loss of teeth (Stewart & Williamson, 2008; Helgeson, 2002). Moreover, frequent vomiting or chronic diarrhea (from the use of laxatives) can cause dangerous potassium deficiencies, which may lead to weakness, intestinal disorders, kidney disease, or heart damage (Zerbe, 2008; Turner et al., 2000).

✿What Causes Eating Disorders?

Most of today's theorists and researchers use a **multidimensional risk perspective** to explain eating disorders. That is, they identify several key factors that place individuals at risk for these disorders (Zerbe, 2008). The more of these factors that are present, the greater the likelihood that a person will develop an eating disorder. The factors cited most often include psychological problems (ego, cognitive, and mood disturbances), biological factors, and sociocultural conditions (societal, family, and multicultural pressures).

Psychodynamic Factors: Ego Deficiencies

Hilde Bruch, a pioneer in the study and treatment of eating disorders, developed a largely psychodynamic theory of the disorders. She argued that disturbed mother–child interactions lead to serious *ego deficiencies* in the child (including a poor sense of independence and control) and to severe *perceptual disturbances* that jointly help produce disordered eating patterns (Bruch, 2001, 1991, 1962).

According to Bruch, parents may respond to their children either effectively or ineffectively. *Effective parents* accurately attend to their children's biological and emotional needs, giving them food when they are crying from hunger and comfort when they are crying out of fear. *Ineffective parents,* by contrast, fail to attend to their children's needs, deciding that their children are hungry, cold, or tired without correctly interpreting the children's actual condition. They may feed the children at times of anxiety rather than hunger or comfort them at times of tiredness rather than anxiety. Children who receive such parenting may grow up confused and unaware of their own internal needs, not knowing for themselves when they are hungry or full and unable to identify their own emotions.

Unable to rely on internal signals, these children turn instead to external guides, such as their parents. They seem to be "model children," but they fail to develop genuine self-reliance and "experience themselves as not being in control of their behavior, needs, and impulses, as not owning their own bodies" (Bruch, 1973, p. 55). Adolescence increases their basic desire to establish independence, yet they feel unable to do so. To overcome their sense of helplessness, they seek excessive control over their body size and shape and over their eating habits. Helen, an 18-year-old, describes her experience:

There is a peculiar contradiction—everybody thinks you're doing so well and everybody thinks you're great, but your real problem is that you think that you are not good enough. You are afraid of not living up to what you think you are expected to do. You have one great fear, namely that of being ordinary, or average, or common—just not good enough. This peculiar dieting begins with such anxiety. You want to prove that you have control, that you can do it. The peculiar part of it is that it makes you feel good about yourself, makes you feel "I can accomplish something." It makes you feel "I can do something nobody else can do."

(Bruch, 1978, p. 128)

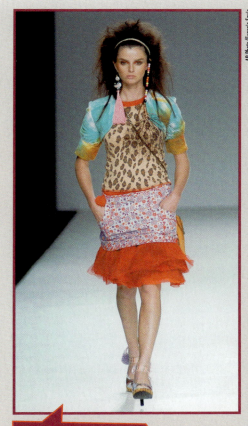

AP Photo/Eugenio Savio

Dangerous profession
Although a number of supermodels have publicly acknowledged disordered eating patterns in recent years, the fashion world was shocked when 21-year-old Brazilian model Ana Carolina Reston died in 2006 of complications from anorexia nervosa. Told during a 2004 casting call that she was "too fat," Reston began restricting her diet to only apples and tomatoes, culminating in a generalized infection and eventually death. The 5'8" model weighed 88 pounds at the time of her death.

•**multidimensional risk perspective**•
A theory that identifies several kinds of risk factors that are thought to combine to help cause a disorder. The more factors present, the greater the risk of developing the disorder.

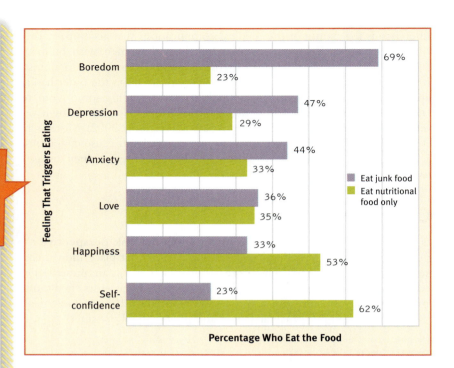

Figure 11-3

When do people seek junk food? Apparently, when they feel bad (Haberman, 2007; Hudd et al., 2000). People who eat junk food when they are feeling bad outnumber those who eat nutritional food under similar circumstances. In contrast, more people seek nutritional food when they are feeling good. (Rowan, 2005; Lyman, 1982).

Models and mannequins

Mannequins were once made extra-thin to show the lines of the clothing for sale to best advantage. Today the shape of the ideal woman is indistinguishable from that of a mannequin, and a growing number of young women try to achieve this ideal.

Clinical reports and research have provided some support for Bruch's theory (Eifert et al., 2007; Pearlman, 2005). Clinicians have observed that the parents of teenagers with eating disorders do tend to define their children's needs rather than allow the children to define their own needs (Ihle et al., 2005; Steiner et al., 1991). When Bruch interviewed the mothers of 51 children with anorexia nervosa, many proudly recalled that they had always "anticipated" their young child's needs, never permitting the child to "feel hungry" (Bruch, 1973).

Research has also supported Bruch's belief that people with eating disorders perceive internal cues, including emotional cues, inaccurately (Fairburn et al., 2008; Bydlowski et al., 2005). When research participants with an eating disorder are anxious or upset, for example, many of them mistakenly think they are also hungry (see Figure 11-3), and they respond as they might respond to hunger—by eating. In fact, people with eating disorders are often described by clinicians as *alexithymic,* meaning they have great difficulty putting descriptive labels on their feelings (Zerbe, 2008). And finally, studies support Bruch's argument that people with eating disorders rely excessively on the opinions, wishes, and views of others. They are more likely than other people to worry about how others view them, to seek approval, to be conforming, and to feel a lack of control over their lives (Travis & Meltzer, 2008; Button & Warren, 2001).

Cognitive Factors

If you look closely at Bruch's explanation of eating disorders, you'll see that it contains several *cognitive* features. She held, for example, that as a result of ineffective parenting, victims of eating disorders improperly label their internal sensations and needs, generally feel little control over their lives, and, in turn, desire excessive control over their body size, shape, and eating habits. According to cognitive theorists, these deficiencies contribute to a broad cognitive distortion that lies at the center of disordered eating, namely, people with anorexia nervosa and bulimia nervosa judge themselves—often exclusively—based on their shape and weight and their ability to control them (Fairburn et al., 2008; Eifert et al., 2007). This "core pathology," say cognitive theorists, gives rise to all other features of the disorders, including the individuals' repeated efforts to lose weight and their preoccupation with thoughts about shape, weight, and eating.

According to cognitive theorists, such distorted thinking is clearly on display in cases of restrictive-type anorexia nervosa, but it is just as influential in cases of bulimia nervosa (Fairburn et al., 2008). Given their disproportionate concerns about shape and weight, bulimic individuals try to stick to numerous extreme and specific dietary rules. When they inevitably break these rules—if they commit even a minor slip—the individuals interpret the slips as clear evidence of lack of self-control, feel like total failures, and temporarily abandon all efforts to restrict their eating. That is, they binge. In short order, the binge eating intensifies the core concerns about the control of eating, shape, and weight; triggers immediate efforts to correct the situation (purging); and leads to broad efforts to reestablish dietary restraint.

As you saw earlier in the chapter, research indicates that people with eating disorders do indeed display the various cognitive deficiencies pointed to in this explanation of eating disorders (Eifert et al., 2007; Vartanian et al., 2004). Although studies have not clarified that such deficiencies are the *cause* of eating disorders, many cognitive-behavioral therapists proceed from this assumption and center their treatment for the disorders on correcting the clients' cognitive distortions and their accompanying behaviors. As you'll soon see, cognitive-behavioral therapies of this kind are among the most widely used of all treatments for eating disorders (Fairburn et al., 2008).

Saying "no" to anorexia
In 2007 the manufacturer of the clothing brand Nolita launched a campaign against anorexia nervosa, displaying shocking billboards throughout Italy. Here two young women stop and stare in rapt attention at one such billboard—that of an emaciated naked woman appearing beneath the words "No Anorexia."

Mood Disorders

Many people with eating disorders, particularly those with bulimia nervosa, experience symptoms of depression (Stewart & Williamson, 2008; Speranza et al., 2005). This finding has led some theorists to suggest that mood disorders set the stage for eating disorders.

Their claim is supported by four kinds of evidence. First, many more people with an eating disorder qualify for a clinical diagnosis of major depressive disorder than do people in the general population (Stewart & Williamson, 2008; Duncan et al., 2005). Second, the close relatives of people with eating disorders seem to have a higher rate of mood disorders than do close relatives of people without such disorders (Moorhead et al., 2003; APA, 2000). Third, as you will soon see, many people with eating disorders, particularly bulimia nervosa, have low activity of the neurotransmitter serotonin, similar to the serotonin abnormalities found in depressed people. And finally, people with eating disorders are often helped by some of the same antidepressant drugs that reduce depression.

Although such findings suggest that depression may help cause eating disorders, other explanations are possible. For example, the pressure and pain of having an eating disorder may *cause* a mood disorder. Whatever the correct interpretation, many people struggling with eating disorders also suffer from depression, among other psychological problems.

Biological Factors

Biological theorists suspect that certain genes may leave some persons particularly susceptible to eating disorders (Kaplan, 2005). Consistent with this idea, relatives of people with eating disorders are up to six times more likely than other individuals to develop the disorders themselves (Stewart & Williamson, 2008; Strober et al., 2001, 2000). Moreover, if one identical twin has anorexia nervosa, the other twin also develops the disorder in as many as 70 percent of cases; in contrast, the rate for fraternal twins, who are genetically less similar, is 20 percent. In the case of bulimia nervosa, identical twins

BETWEEN THE LINES

Smoking, Eating, and Weight
- Smokers weigh less than nonsmokers.
- 75 percent of people who quit smoking gain weight.
- Nicotine, a stimulant substance, suppresses appetites and increases metabolic rate, perhaps because of its impact on the lateral hypothalamus. ‹‹

(Higgins & George, 2007)

Laboratory obesity
Biological theorists believe that certain genes leave some individuals particularly susceptible to eating disorders. To help support this view, researchers have created mutant ("knockout") mice—mice without certain genes. The mouse on the left is missing a gene that helps produce obesity, and it is thin. In contrast, the mouse on the right, which retains that gene, is indeed obese.

•**hypothalamus**•A part of the brain that helps regulate various bodily functions, including eating and hunger.

•**lateral hypothalamus (LH)**•A brain region that produces hunger when activated.

•**ventromedial hypothalamus (VMH)**• A brain region that depresses hunger when activated.

•**weight set point**•The weight level that a person is predisposed to maintain, controlled in part by the hypothalamus.

display a concordance rate of 23 percent, compared to a rate of 9 percent among fraternal twins (Zerbe, 2008; Kendler et al., 1995, 1991). Although such family and twin findings do not rule out environmental explanations, they have encouraged biological researchers to look further still for specific biological causes.

One factor that has interested investigators is the possible role of *serotonin*. Several research teams have found a link between eating disorders and the genes responsible for the production of this neurotransmitter, and still others have measured low serotonin activity in many people with eating disorders (Stewart & Williamson, 2008; Eifert et al., 2007). Given serotonin's role in depression and obsessive-compulsive disorder—problems that often accompany eating disorders—it is possible that low serotonin activity has more to do with those other disorders than with the eating disorders per se. On the other hand, perhaps low serotonin activity contributes directly to eating disorders—for example, by causing the body to crave and binge on high-carbohydrate foods (Kaye et al., 2005, 2002, 2000).

Other biological researchers explain eating disorders by pointing to the **hypothalamus,** a part of the brain that regulates many bodily functions (Zerbe, 2008; Higgins & George, 2007; Uher & Treasure, 2005). Researchers have located two separate areas in the hypothalamus that help control eating. One, the **lateral hypothalamus (LH),** consisting of the side areas of the hypothalamus, produces hunger when it is activated. When the LH of a laboratory animal is stimulated electrically, the animal eats, even if it has been fed recently. In contrast, another area, the **ventromedial hypothalamus (VMH),** consisting of the bottom and middle of the hypothalamus, reduces hunger when it is activated. When the VMH is electrically stimulated, laboratory animals stop eating (see *A Closer Look* on pages 356–357).

These areas of the hypothalamus and related brain structures are apparently activated by chemicals from the brain and body, depending on whether the person is eating or fasting (Zerbe, 2008). Two such brain chemicals are the natural appetite suppressants *cholecystokinin* (*CCK*) and *glucagon-like peptide-1* (*GLP-1*) (Higgins & George, 2007; Turton et al., 1996). When, for example, a team of researchers collected and injected GLP-1 into the brains of rats, the chemical traveled to receptors in the hypothalamus and caused the rats to reduce their food intake almost entirely even though they had not eaten for 24 hours. Conversely, when "full" rats were injected with a substance that blocked the reception of GLP-1 in the hypothalamus, they more than doubled their food intake.

Some researchers believe that the LH, VMH, related brain areas, and chemicals such as CCK and GLP-1, working together, comprise a "weight thermostat" of sorts in the body, which is responsible for keeping an individual at a particular weight level called the **weight set point** (Higgins & George, 2007; Keesey & Corbett, 1983). Genetic inheritance and early eating practices seem to determine each person's weight set point (Stewart & Williamson, 2008). When a person's weight falls below his or her particular set point, the LH and certain other brain areas are activated and seek to restore the lost weight by producing hunger and lowering the body's *metabolic rate,* the rate at which the body expends energy. When a person's weight rises above his or her set point, the VMH and certain other brain areas are activated, and they seek to remove the excess weight by reducing hunger and increasing the body's metabolic rate.

According to the weight set point theory, when people diet and fall to a weight below their weight set point, their brain starts trying to restore the lost weight. Hypothalamic and related brain activity produce a preoccupation with food and a desire to binge. It also triggers bodily changes that make it harder to lose weight and easier to gain weight, however little is eaten (Higgins & George, 2007; Spalter et al., 1993). Once the brain and body begin conspiring to raise weight in this way, dieters actually enter into a battle against themselves. Some people apparently manage to shut down the inner "thermostat" and control their eating almost completely. These people move toward restricting-type anorexia nervosa. For others, the battle spirals toward a binge-purge pattern. Although the weight set point explanation has received considerable debate in the clinical field, it remains widely accepted by theorists and practitioners (Higgins & George, 2007; Pinel et al., 2000).

Societal Pressures

Eating disorders are more common in Western countries than in other parts of the world (see *Eye on Culture* on page 359). Correspondingly, many theorists believe that Western standards of female attractiveness are partly responsible for the emergence of the disorders (Russo & Tartaro, 2008; Jambor, 2001). Western standards of female beauty have changed throughout history, with a noticeable shift toward preference for a thin female frame in recent decades (Gilbert et al., 2005). One study that tracked the height, weight, and age of contestants in the Miss America Pageant from 1959 through 1978 found an average decline of 0.28 pound per year among the contestants and 0.37 pound per year among winners (Garner et al., 1980). The researchers also examined data on all *Playboy* magazine centerfold models over the same time period and found that the average weight, bust, and hip measurements of these women had decreased steadily. More recent studies of Miss America contestants and *Playboy* centerfolds indicate that these trends have continued (Rubinstein & Caballero, 2000).

Because thinness is especially valued in the subcultures of fashion models, actors, dancers, and certain athletes, members of these groups are likely to be particularly concerned about their weight. Studies have indeed found that people in these professions are more prone than others to eating disorders (Kerr et al., 2007; Couturier & Lock, 2006). In fact, many famous young women from these fields have publicly acknowledged grossly disordered eating patterns in recent years. Surveys of athletes at colleges around the United States reveal that more than 9 percent of female college athletes suffer from an eating disorder and another 50 percent display eating behaviors that put them at risk for such disorders (Kerr et al., 2007; Johnson, 1995). A full 20 percent of surveyed gymnasts appear to have an eating disorder (see Figure 11-4).

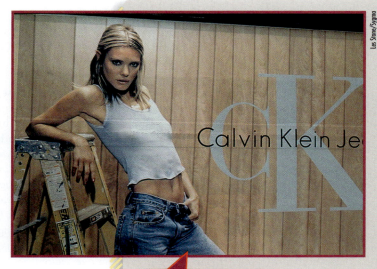

Harmful advertising
When Calvin Klein posed young teenagers in sexually suggestive clothing ads in 1995, the public protested and the ads were halted. However, what some researchers consider even more damaging—the use of very thin young models who influence the body ideals and dietary habits of millions of teenage girls—continues uninterrupted.

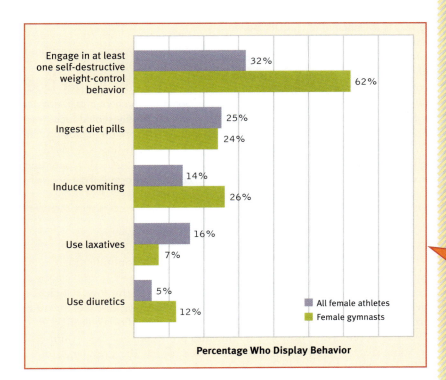

Percentage Who Display Behavior

Figure 11-4
Dangerous shortcuts According to surveys, in sports ranging from field hockey to gymnastics, many female athletes engage in one or more self-destructive behaviors to control their weight (Kerr et al., 2007; Taylor & Ste-Marie, 2001). One study found that close to two-thirds of female college gymnasts engage in at least one such behavior. (Adapted from Rosen & Hough, 1988; Rosen et al., 1986.)

Obesity: To Lose or Not to Lose

Body-mass index (*BMI*) is a formula used to indicate whether a person's weight is appropriate for his or her height. It is calculated as the person's weight (in kilograms) divided by the square of his or her height (in meters). According to the World Health Organization, people whose BMI is above 25 are overweight; those with a BMI above 30 are considered obese. By such standards, one-third of adults in the United States are overweight or obese (Freking, 2007; Hilbert et al., 2005). In fact, despite the public's focus on thinness, obesity has become increasingly common in many countries (Johnston, 2004).

Being overweight is not a mental disorder, nor in most cases is it the result of abnormal psychological processes (Mitchell et al., 2008). Nevertheless, it causes great anguish, and not just because of its physical effects (Norton, 2007). The media, people on the streets, and even many health professionals treat obesity as shameful (Goode & Vail, 2008). Obese people are often the unrecognized victims of discrimination in efforts to gain admission to college, obtain jobs, and receive promotions (Grilo, 2006).

Mounting evidence indicates that overweight persons are not to be derided as lacking in self-control and that obesity results from multiple factors (Hilbert et al., 2005). First, genetic and biological factors seem to play large roles. Researchers have found that children of obese biological parents are more likely to be obese than children whose biological parents are not obese, whether or not they are raised by obese parents (Higgins & George, 2007; Stunkard et al., 1986). Other researchers have identified several genes that seem to be linked to obesity. And still others have identified chemicals in the body, including the hormone *leptin* and the protein *glucagon-like peptide-1* (*GLP-1*), that apparently act as natural appetite suppressants (Costa et al., 2002). Suspicion is growing that the brain receptors for these chemicals may be defective in overweight persons.

Environment also plays a causal role in obesity. Studies have shown that people eat more when they are in the company of others, particularly if the other people are eating (Johnston & Tyler, 2008; Logue, 1991). In addition, research finds that people in low socioeconomic environments are more likely to be obese than those of high socioeconomic backgrounds (Benedict et al., 2007; Martin et al., 2008).

Health Risk?

Do mildly to moderately obese people have a greater risk of coronary disease, cancer, or other disease? Investigations into this question have produced conflicting results (Mitchell et al., 2008; Bender et al., 1999). One long-term study found that while moderately overweight participants had a 30 percent higher risk of early death, underweight participants had a low likelihood of dying at an early age as long as their thinness could not be attributed to smoking or illness (Manson et al., 2004, 1995). However, another study found that the mortality rate of underweight individuals was as high as that of overweight individuals regardless of smoking behavior or illness (Berrigan et al., 2006, 2003; Troiano et al., 1996). These conflicting findings suggest that the jury is still out on this issue.

Does Dieting Work?

There are scores of diets and diet pills. There is almost no evidence, however, that any diet yet devised can ensure long-term weight loss (Mann et al., 2007; Grilo, 2006). In fact, long-term studies reveal a *rebound effect*, a net gain in weight in obese people who have lost weight on very low-calorie diets. Research also suggests that the feelings of failure that accompany diet rebounds may lead to dysfunctional eating patterns, including binge eating (Eifert et al., 2007; Venditti et al., 1996).

Efforts are now underway to develop new kinds of drugs that will operate directly on the genes, hormones, proteins, and brain regions that have been linked to obesity (Marchione, 2005; Carek & Dickerson, 1999). Theoretically, these drugs will counteract the bodily reactions that undermine efforts at dieting. Whether such interventions can provide safe and permanent weight loss remains to be seen.

What Is the Proper Goal?

Some researchers argue that attempts to reduce obesity should focus less on weight loss and more on improving general health and attitudes (Travis & Meltzer, 2008; Painot et al., 2001). If poor eating habits can be corrected, if a poor self-concept and

Attitudes toward thinness may also help explain economic differences in the rates of eating disorders. In the past, women in the upper socioeconomic classes expressed more concern about thinness and dieting than women of the lower socioeconomic classes (Margo, 1985; Stunkard, 1975). Correspondingly, eating disorders were more common among women higher on the socioeconomic scale (Foreyt et al., 1996; Rosen et al., 1991). In recent years, however, dieting and preoccupation with thinness have increased to some degree in all socioeconomic classes, as has the prevalence of eating disorders (Germer, 2005; Striegel-Moore et al., 2005).

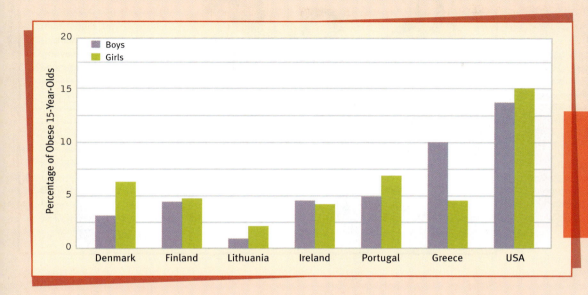

distorted body image can be improved, if proper exercise can be instituted, and if overweight people can be educated about the myths and truths regarding obesity, perhaps everyone will be better off.

Most experts agree that extreme obesity is indeed a clear health hazard and that weight loss is advisable in such cases. For these individuals, the most promising path to long-term weight loss may be to set realistic, attainable goals, behaviors, and exercise levels rather than unrealistic ideals (Travis & Meltzer, 2008; Brownell & O'Neil, 1993). As for people who are mildly and even moderately overweight, a growing number of experts now suggest that perhaps they should be left alone or, at the very least, encouraged to set more modest and realistic goals (Butryn & Wadden, 2005). In addition, it is critical that the public overcome its prejudice against people who are overweight and come to appreciate that obesity is, at worst, a problem that requires treatment and is perhaps simply another version of the normal human condition.

Obesity among Children and Adolescents

A matter of growing concern centers on recent increases in the rates of overweight children and adolescents, particularly in the United States (Johnston & Tyler, 2008). Indeed, since 1974, the obesity rate has quadrupled for children and doubled for adolescents in the United States (Ogden et al., 2002). Compared to most European countries, the United States has by far the highest percentage of obese young people (see the accompanying figure). Two key reasons for this difference are *diet* and *exercise*. American children and adolescents apparently drink more sugary soft drinks and eat more unhealthy food than young people in other countries (Malik et al., 2006), a trend that has been increasing for the past several decades. One study found, for example, that one-third of American teenagers eat at least one fast-food meal each day (Bowman et al., 2003). Moreover, on average, teenagers in the United States walk and bike less than their counterparts from other industrialized countries, and they are more likely to drive cars to get around (Matsumoto & Juang, 2008; Arnett & Balle-Jensen, 1993). Whatever the precise causes, the trends are alarming. Aside from the health hazards posed directly to the overweight children and adolescents, studies reveal that most overweight and obese children grow up to become overweight and obese adults (Matsumoto & Juang, 2008).

Western society not only glorifies thinness but also creates a climate of prejudice against overweight people (Russo & Tartaro, 2008; Goode & Vail, 2008). Whereas slurs based on ethnicity, race, and gender are considered unacceptable, cruel jokes about obesity are standard fare on television and in movies, books, and magazines (Gilbert et al., 2005). Research indicates that the prejudice against obese people is deep-rooted (Grilo et al., 2005). Prospective parents who were shown pictures of a chubby child and a medium-weight or thin child rated the former as less friendly, energetic, intelligent, and desirable than the latter. In another study, preschool children who were given a

The ad!

An advertising campaign that created a great stir in 2005 was the "Dove girls" ad. The manufacturer of Dove Firming products recruited six young women with no prior modeling experience, had them pose in their underwear, and displayed the ad in magazines and on billboards across the country. Many people praised Dove for "courageously" using less than perfectly shaped women in the ad, while others had a decidedly less positive reaction. The point that both sides overlooked is that the women were far from overweight, with dress sizes ranging from 6 to 12 (the average American woman is a size 14). Thus, the controversy reflected once again the predominant belief in Western society that extreme—typically unattainable—thinness is the aesthetic ideal for women.

choice between a chubby and a thin rag doll chose the thin one, although they could not say why. It is small wonder that as many as half of elementary school girls have tried to lose weight and 61 percent of middle school girls are currently dieting (Hill, 2006; Stewart, 2004).

Family Environment

Families may play an important role in the development of eating disorders (Stewart & Williamson, 2008; Eifert et al., 2007). Research suggests that as many as half of the families of people with eating disorders have a long history of emphasizing thinness, physical appearance, and dieting. In fact, the mothers in these families are more likely to diet themselves and to be generally perfectionistic than are the mothers in other families (Zerbe, 2008; Woodside et al., 2002). Tina, a 16-year-old, describes her view of the roots of her eating disorder:

When I was a kid, say 6 or 7, my Mom and I would go to the drugstore all the time. She was heavy and bought all kinds of books and magazines on how to lose weight. Whenever we talked, like after I got home from school, it was almost always about dieting and how to lose weight. . . . I [went] on diets with my Mom, to keep her company.

I just got better at it than she did. My eating disorder is my Mom's therapy. . . . It's also the way we have time together—working on the diets and exercise and all of that. We've stopped talking about diets since I got anorexia, and now I don't know what we can talk about.

(Zerbe, 2008, pp. 20–21)

Abnormal interactions and forms of communication within a family may also set the stage for an eating disorder (Reich, 2005; Vidovic et al., 2005). Family systems theorists argue that the families of people who develop eating disorders are often dysfunctional to begin with and that the eating disorder of one member is a reflection of the larger problem. Influential family theorist Salvador Minuchin, for example, believes that what

BETWEEN THE LINES

Teasing and Eating

In one study, researchers found that adolescents who were teased about their weight by family members were twice as likely as non-teased teens of similar weight to become overweight within 5 years and 1.5 times more likely to become binge-eaters and use extreme weight control measures (Neumark-Sztainer et al., 2007). ‹‹

Eating Disorders across the World

Up until the past decade, anorexia nervosa and bulimia nervosa were generally considered culture-bound abnormalities. Although prevalent in the United States and other Western countries, they were uncommon in non-Western cultures (Matsumoto & Juang, 2008). A study conducted during the mid-1990s, for example, compared students in the African nation of Ghana and those in the United States on issues such as eating disorders, weight, body perception, and attitudes toward thinness (Cogan et al., 1996). The Ghanaians were more likely to rate larger body sizes as ideal, while the Americans were more likely to diet and to display eating disorders. Similarly, in countries, such as Saudi Arabia, where attention was not drawn to the female figure and the female body was almost entirely covered, eating disorders were rarely mentioned in the clinical literature (Matsumoto & Juang, 2008; Al-Subaie & Alhamad, 2000).

However, studies conducted over the past decade reveal that disordered eating behaviors and attitudes are on the rise in non-Western countries, a trend that seems to correspond to those countries' increased exposure to Western culture. Researchers have found, for example, that eating disorders are increasing in Pakistan, particularly among women who have been more exposed to Western culture (Suhail & Nisa, 2002).

The spread of eating disorders to non-Western lands has been particularly apparent in a series of studies conducted on the Fiji Islands in the South Pacific (Becker et al., 2007, 2003, 2002, 1999). In 1995 satellite television began beaming Western shows and fashions to remote parts of the islands for the first time. Just a few years later, researchers found that Fijian teenage girls who watched television at least three nights per week were more likely than others to feel "too big or fat." In addition, almost two-thirds of them had dieted in the previous month, and 15 percent had vomited to control weight within the previous year (compared to 3 percent before television).

Chris Moore/Catwalking/Getty Images

Embracing diversity? The fashion industry prides itself on the range of nationalities now represented in its ranks. However, the Western ideal of extreme thinness remains the standard for all models, irrespective of their cultural background. Many psychologists worry that the success of supermodels such as Ethiopia's Liya Kebede (shown here) and Sudan's Alek Wek may contribute to thinner body ideals, greater body dissatisfaction, and more eating disorders in their African countries.

he calls an **enmeshed family pattern** often leads to eating disorders (Eifert et al., 2007; Minuchin, Rosman, & Baker, 1978).

In an enmeshed system, family members are overinvolved in each other's affairs and overconcerned with the details of each other's lives. On the positive side, enmeshed families can be affectionate and loyal. On the negative side, they can be clingy and foster dependency. Parents are too involved in the lives of their children, allowing little room for individuality and independence. Minuchin argues that adolescence poses a special problem for these families. The teenager's normal push for independence threatens the family's apparent harmony and closeness. In response, the family may subtly force the child to take on a "sick" role—to develop an eating disorder or some other illness. The child's disorder enables the family to maintain its appearance of harmony. A sick child needs her family, and family members can rally to protect her. Some case studies have supported such family systems explanations, but systematic research fails to show that particular family patterns consistently set the stage for the development of eating disorders (Wilson et al., 2003, 1996). In fact, the families of people with either anorexia nervosa or bulimia nervosa vary widely.

•**enmeshed family pattern**•A family system in which members are overinvolved with each other's affairs and overconcerned about each other's welfare.

Multicultural Factors: Racial and Ethnic Differences

In the popular 1995 movie *Clueless,* Cher and Dionne, wealthy teenage friends of different races, have similar tastes, beliefs, and values about everything from boys to schoolwork. In particular, they have the same kinds of eating habits and beauty ideals, and they are even similar in weight and physical form. But does the story of these young women reflect the realities of white American and African American females in our society?

In the early 1990s, the answer to this question appeared to be a resounding no. Most studies conducted up to the time of the movie's release indicated that the eating behaviors, values, and goals of young African American women were considerably healthier than those of young white American women (Lovejoy, 2001; Cash & Henry, 1995; Parker et al., 1995). A widely publicized 1995 study at the University of Arizona, for example, found that the eating behaviors and attitudes of young African American women were more positive than those of young white American women. It found, specifically, that nearly 90 percent of the white American respondents were dissatisfied with their weight and body shape, compared to around 70 percent of the African American teens.

The study also suggested that white American and African American adolescent girls had different ideals of beauty. The white American teens, asked to define the "perfect girl," described a girl of 5′7″ weighing between 100 and 110 pounds—proportions that mirror those of so-called supermodels. Attaining a perfect weight, many said, was the key to being "totally happy," and they indicated that thinness was a requirement for popularity. In contrast, the African American respondents emphasized personality traits over physical characteristics. They defined the "perfect" African American girl as smart, fun, easy to talk to, not conceited, and funny; she did not necessarily need to be "pretty," as long as she was well groomed. The body dimensions the African American teens described were more attainable for the typical girl; they favored fuller hips, for example. Moreover, the African American respondents were less likely than the white American respondents to diet for extended periods.

Unfortunately, research conducted over the past decade suggests that body image concerns, dysfunctional eating patterns, and eating disorders are on the rise among young African American women as well as among women of other minority groups (Stewart & Williamson, 2008). For example, a recent survey conducted by *Essence,* the largest-circulation African American magazine, and studies by several teams of researchers have found that the risk of today's African American women developing eating disorders is approaching that of white American women. Similarly, their attitudes regarding body image, weight, and eating are closing in on those of white American women (Annunziato et al., 2007; Walcott et al., 2003; Mulholland & Mintz, 2001; Pumariega et al., 1994). In the *Essence* survey, 65 percent of African American respondents reported

Multiple influences

An individual's weight is influenced by a range of factors, from genetic to sociocultural. Although the Pima Native Americans in Arizona (left) and their relatives in Mexico (right, during a Holy Week festival) share common genetics, the former weigh more on average. High-fat foods dominate the diets of Arizonan Pimas, while Mexican Pimas subsist on grains and vegetables.

dieting behavior, 39 percent said that food controlled their lives, 19 percent avoided eating when hungry, 17 percent used laxatives, and 4 percent vomited to lose weight. The racial gap may be closing all the more in young girls. In one study of more than 2,000 girls aged 9 to 10 years, 40 percent of the respondents—African American and white American participants in equal measure—reported wanting to lose weight (Schreiber et al., 1996).

The shift in the eating behaviors and eating problems of African American women appears to be partly related to their *acculturation* (Stewart & Williamson, 2008). One study compared African American women at a predominately white American university with those at a predominately African American university. Those at the former school had significantly higher depression scores, and those scores were positively correlated with eating problems (Ford, 2000).

Still other studies indicate that Hispanic American female adolescents and young adults engage in disordered eating behaviors and express body dissatisfaction at rates about equal to those of white American women (Stewart & Williamson, 2008; Erickson & Gerstle, 2007; Germer, 2005). Moreover, those who consider themselves more oriented to the white American culture appear to have a particularly high rate of eating disorders (Cachelin et al., 2006). One study even found that Hispanic American women who were dissatisfied with their weight displayed more severe binge-eating behavior than white American or African American women with similar concerns (Fitzgibbon et al., 1998).

Eating disorders also appear to be on the increase among young Asian American women and young women in several Asian countries (Stewart & Williamson, 2008; Pike & Borovoy, 2004). Indeed, a study in Taiwan surveyed 843 schoolgirls, aged 10 to 14 years, and found that 8 percent were severely underweight and 10 percent were somewhat underweight (Wong & Huang, 2000). Around 65 percent of the underweight girls nevertheless wished they were thinner.

Multicultural Factors: Gender Differences

Males account for only 5 to 10 percent of all cases of eating disorders (Kerr et al., 2007; Langley, 2006). The reasons for this striking gender difference are not entirely clear, but Western society's double standard for attractiveness is, at the very least, one reason. Our society's emphasis on a thin appearance is clearly aimed at women much more than men, and some theorists believe that this difference has made women much more inclined to diet and more prone to eating disorders (Cole & Daniel, 2005). Surveys of college men have, for example, found that the majority select "muscular, strong and broad shoulders" to describe the ideal male body and "thin, slim, slightly underweight" to describe the ideal female body (Toro et al., 2005; Kearney-Cooke & Steichen-Ash, 1990).

A second reason for the different rates of eating disorders between men and women may be the different methods of weight loss favored by the two genders. According to some clinical observations, men are more likely to use exercise to lose weight, whereas women more often diet (Toro et al., 2005; Braun, 1996). And, as you have read, dieting often precedes the onset of eating disorders.

Why do some men develop eating disorders? In a number of cases, the disorder is linked to the *requirements and pressures of a job or sport* (Kerr et al., 2007; Beals, 2004). According to one study, 37 percent of males with eating disorders had jobs or played sports for which weight control was important, compared to 13 percent of women with such disorders (Braun, 1996). The highest rates of male eating disorders have been found among jockeys, wrestlers, distance runners, body builders, and swimmers. Jockeys commonly spend hours before a race in a sauna, shedding up to seven pounds of weight, and may restrict their food intake, abuse laxatives and diuretics, and force vomiting (Kerr et al., 2007). Similarly, male wrestlers in high school and college commonly restrict their food for up to three days before a match in order to "make weight." Some lose up to five pounds of water weight by practicing or running in several layers of warm or rubber clothing before weighing in for a match.

Not for women only
A growing number of today's men are developing eating disorders. Some of them aspire to a very lean body shape, such as that displayed by a new breed of ultra-thin male models (left), and develop anorexia nervosa or bulimia nervosa. Others aspire to the ultra-muscular look displayed by bodybuilders (right) and develop a new kind of eating disorder called *muscle dysmorphobia*. The men in this latter category inaccurately consider themselves to be scrawny and small and keep striving for a perfect body through excessive weight lifting and abuse of steroids.

Herb McCauley, a top jockey who competed in more than 20,000 races and earned $70 million in winnings, suffered from an eating disorder for 20 years, until after his career ended. He describes his purge use of the laxative Ex-Lax and the diuretic Lasix:

"I tried everything. I took so many slabs of Ex-Lax that to this day I can't eat a Hershey bar." When commenting about Lasix, he said: "That takes five to six pounds off, but it also takes all the fluids, electrolytes and minerals out of your body. All of a sudden your body cramps up and you're not the jockey you're supposed to be. You come down the stretch and think a hot poker is going through your hips."

(Fountaine, 2000, p. 2)

BETWEEN THE LINES

GI Joe

Contemporary male action figures, such as GI Joe and Luke Skywalker, have acquired the physiques of body builders in recent years, with sharp muscle definition in the chest, shoulders, and abdominals (Pope et al., 1999). If GI Joe were a real man, he would have larger biceps than any body builder in history, with a 5'10" frame and 29-inch biceps, a 32-inch waist, and a 55-inch chest. ‹‹

For other men who develop eating disorders, *body image* appears to be a key factor, just as it is in women. Many of these individuals report that they want a "lean, toned, thin" shape similar to the ideal female body, rather than the muscular, broad-shouldered shape of the typical male ideal (Soban, 2006; Kearney-Cooke & Steichen-Ash, 1990). This is not to say that those who aspire to the typical male ideal are immune to eating disorders. A study of 548 males—both young and old—revealed that 43 percent of them were dissatisfied with their bodies to some degree, with many of them expressing a desire to increase their muscle mass, especially in their abdomen and chest (Garner & Kearney-Cooke, 1997). The most dissatisfied men were those in their 30s and 50s; the least dissatisfied were men in their 20s.

Given such concerns, it may not be surprising that a new kind of eating disorder has emerged, found almost exclusively among men, called *reverse anorexia nervosa* or *muscle dysmorphobia*. This disorder is displayed by men who are very muscular but still see themselves as scrawny and small and therefore continue to strive for a perfect body through extreme measures such as excessive weight lifting or the abuse of steroids (Stewart & Williamson, 2008; Goldfried et al., 2006). Individuals with muscle dysmorphobia typically experience shame about their body image, and many have a history of depression, anxiety, and self-destructive compulsive behavior. About one-third of them also display related dysfunctional behaviors such as bingeing.

✿How Are Eating Disorders Treated?

Today's treatments for eating disorders have two goals. The first is to correct the dangerous eating pattern as quickly as possible. The second is to address the broader psychological and situational factors that have led to and now maintain the eating problem. Family and friends can also play an important role in helping to overcome the disorder.

Treatments for Anorexia Nervosa

The immediate aims of treatment for anorexia nervosa are to help individuals regain their lost weight, recover from malnourishment, and eat normally again. Therapists must then help them to make psychological and perhaps family changes to lock in those gains.

How Are Proper Weight and Normal Eating Restored? A variety of treatment methods are used to help patients with anorexia nervosa gain weight quickly and return to health within weeks. In the past, treatment almost always took place in a hospital, but now it is often offered in outpatient settings (Vitousek & Gray, 2006; Gowers et al., 2000).

In life-threatening cases, clinicians may need to force *tube and intravenous feedings* on a patient who refuses to eat (Tyre, 2005). Unfortunately, this use of force may breed distrust in the patient (Robb et al., 2002). In contrast, behavioral weight-restoration approaches have clinicians use *rewards* whenever patients eat properly or gain weight and offer no rewards when they eat improperly or fail to gain weight (Tacon & Caldera, 2001).

Perhaps the most popular weight-restoration technique of recent years has been a combination of *supportive nursing care,* nutritional counseling, and a relatively high-calorie diet (Sorrentino et al., 2005; Roloff, 2001). Here nurses *gradually* increase a patient's diet over the course of several weeks to more than 3,000 calories a day (Zerbe, 2008; Herzog et al., 2004). The nurses educate patients about the program, track their

Taking the first bite
Two terrified teenagers hold hands and try to support one another while struggling to take small bites of their desserts. The girls, in treatment for eating disorders at the Renfrew Center in Florida, are required to eat the desserts as part of their inpatient program.

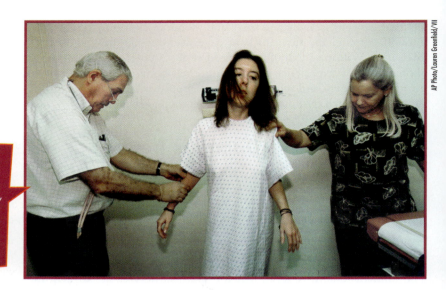

"Blind-weighed"
During inpatient treatment for anorexia nervosa, this 24-year-old woman, like many others in her program, cannot bear to see how much weight she may have gained. Thus she is "blind-weighed" by staff members: she mounts the scale backward so as not to view the weight gain. Clearly, gaining back her proper weight is a frightening and traumatic ordeal for her.

progress, provide encouragement, and help them recognize that their weight gain is under control and will not lead to obesity. Studies find that patients in nursing-care programs usually gain the necessary weight over 8 to 12 weeks.

How Are Lasting Changes Achieved? Clinical researchers have found that individuals with anorexia nervosa must overcome their underlying psychological problems in order to achieve lasting improvement. Therapists typically use a combination of education, psychotherapy, and family approaches to help achieve this broader goal (Zerbe, 2008; Hechler et al., 2005). Psychotropic drugs have also been helpful in some cases, but research has found that such medications are typically of limited benefit over the long-term course of anorexia nervosa (Zerbe, 2008).

COGNITIVE-BEHAVIORAL THERAPY In most treatment programs for anorexia nervosa a combination of behavioral and cognitive interventions are applied. Such techniques are designed to help clients appreciate and alter the behaviors and thought processes that help keep their restrictive eating going (Fairburn et al., 2008; Gleaves & Latner, 2008). On the behavioral side, clients are typically required to monitor (perhaps by keeping a diary) their feelings, hunger levels, and food intake and the ties between these variables. On the cognitive side, they are taught to identify their "core pathology"—the deep-seated belief that they should in fact be judged by their shape and weight and by their ability to control these physical characteristics. Inasmuch as restrictive eating represents a form of coping behavior, the clients may also be taught alternative, more appropriate ways of coping with stress and of solving problems. Such cognitive-behavioral approaches can take place in either individual therapy or group therapy formats.

The therapists who use these approaches are particularly careful to help patients with anorexia nervosa recognize their need for independence and teach them more appropriate ways to exercise control (Zerbe, 2008; Dare & Crowther, 1995). The therapists may also teach them to identify better and trust their internal sensations and feelings (Fairburn et al., 2008; Kaplan & Garfinkel, 1999). In the following session, a therapist tries to help a 15-year-old client recognize and share her feelings:

Patient: I don't talk about my feelings; I never did.
Therapist: Do you think I'll respond like others?
Patient: What do you mean?
Therapist: I think you may be afraid that I won't pay close attention to what you feel inside, or that I'll tell you not to feel the way you do—that it's foolish to feel frightened,

BETWEEN THE LINES

The Lure of "Ana"

Eating disorder specialists are concerned about a widespread underground movement that actively promotes self-starvation, often using the fictitious character "Ana" to give advice on the Web about what to eat and to mock people who do not lose weight. Many followers of Ana (short for anorexia) wear red Ana bracelets, follow the "Ana creed" of control and self-starvation, and offer each other words of "thinspiration" on Web pages and blogs. A Stanford University survey of teens with eating disorders found that 40 percent had visited Web sites that promote eating disorders (Irvine, 2005).

to feel fat, to doubt yourself, considering how well you do in school, how you're appreciated by teachers, how pretty you are.

Patient: (Looking somewhat tense and agitated) *Well, I was always told to be polite and respect other people, just like a stupid, faceless doll. (Affecting a vacant, doll-like pose)*

Therapist: *Do I give you the impression that it would be disrespectful for you to share your feelings, whatever they may be?*

Patient: *Not really; I don't know.*

Therapist: *I can't, and won't, tell you that this is easy for you to do. . . . But I can promise you that you are free to speak your mind, and that I won't turn away.*

(Strober & Yager, 1985, pp. 368–369)

Cognitive-behavioral therapists also take particular care to help clients with anorexia nervosa change their attitudes about eating and weight (Gleaves & Latner, 2008; McFarlane, Carter, & Olmsted, 2005) (see Table 11-4). The therapists may guide clients to identify, challenge, and change maladaptive assumptions, such as "I must always be perfect" or "My weight and shape determine my value" (Fairburn et al., 2008; Lask & Bryant-Waugh, 2000). They may also educate clients about the body distortions typical of anorexia nervosa and help them see that their own assessments of their size are incorrect. Even if a client never learns to judge her body shape accurately, she may at least reach a point where she says, "I know that a key feature of anorexia nervosa is a misperception of my own size, so I can expect to feel fat regardless of my actual size."

table: 11-4

Sample Items from the Eating Disorder Inventory

For each item, decide if the item is true about you ALWAYS (A), USUALLY (U), OFTEN (O), SOMETIMES (S), RARELY (R), or NEVER (N). Circle the letter that corresponds to your rating.

A	U	O	S	R	N	
A	U	O	S	R	N	I think that my stomach is too big.
A	U	O	S	R	N	I eat when I am upset.
A	U	O	S	R	N	I stuff myself with food.
A	U	O	S	R	N	I think about dieting.
A	U	O	S	R	N	I think that my thighs are too large.
A	U	O	S	R	N	I feel extremely guilty after overeating.
A	U	O	S	R	N	I am terrified of gaining weight.
A	U	O	S	R	N	I get confused about what emotion I am feeling.
A	U	O	S	R	N	I have gone on eating binges where I felt that I could not stop.
A	U	O	S	R	N	I get confused as to whether or not I am hungry.
A	U	O	S	R	N	I think my hips are too big.
A	U	O	S	R	N	If I gain a pound, I worry that I will keep gaining.
A	U	O	S	R	N	I have the thought of trying to vomit in order to lose weight.
A	U	O	S	R	N	I think my buttocks are too large.
A	U	O	S	R	N	I eat or drink in secrecy.
A	U	O	S	R	N	I would like to be in total control of my bodily urges.

Source: Garner, 2005; Garner, Olmsted, & Polivy, 1991, 1984.

Although cognitive-behavioral techniques are often of great help to clients with anorexia nervosa, research suggests that the techniques typically must be supplemented by other approaches to bring about better results (Zerbe, 2008). Family therapy, for example, is often included in treatment.

CHANGING FAMILY INTERACTIONS Family therapy can be an invaluable part of treatment for anorexia nervosa, particularly for children and adolescents with the disorder (Gleaves & Latner, 2008; Lock & le Grange, 2005; Reich, 2005). As in other family therapy situations, the therapist meets with the family as a whole, points out troublesome family patterns, and helps the members make appropriate changes. In particular, family therapists may try to help the person with anorexia nervosa separate her feelings and needs from those of other family members. Although the role of family in the development of anorexia nervosa is not yet clear, research strongly suggests that family therapy (or at least parent counseling) can be helpful in the treatment of this disorder (Gleaves & Latner, 2008; McDermott & Jaffa, 2005).

> **Mother:** I think I know what [Susan] is going through: all the doubt and insecurity of growing up and establishing her own identity. (Turning to the patient, with tears) If you just place trust in yourself, with the support of those around you who care, everything will turn out for the better.
>
> **Therapist:** Are you making yourself available to her? Should she turn to you, rely on you for guidance and emotional support?
>
> **Mother:** Well, that's what parents are for.
>
> **Therapist:** (Turning to patient) What do you think?
>
> **Susan:** (To mother) I can't keep depending on you, Mom, or everyone else. That's what I've been doing, and it gave me anorexia. . . .
>
> **Therapist:** Do you think your mom would prefer that there be no secrets between her and the kids—an open door, so to speak?
>
> **Older sister:** Sometimes I do.
>
> **Therapist:** (To patient and younger sister) How about you two?
>
> **Susan:** Yeah. Sometimes it's like whatever I feel, she has to feel.
>
> **Younger sister:** Yeah.
>
> *(Strober & Yager, 1985, pp. 381–382)*

What Is the Aftermath of Anorexia Nervosa?

The use of combined treatment approaches has greatly improved the outlook for people with anorexia nervosa, although the road to recovery can be difficult and research findings are sometimes mixed. The course and outcome of this disorder vary from person to person, but researchers have noted certain trends.

On the positive side, weight is often quickly restored once treatment for the disorder begins (McDermott & Jaffa, 2005), and treatment gains may continue for years (Haliburn, 2005; Ro et al., 2005). As many as 83 percent of patients continue to show improvement when they are interviewed several years or more after their initial recovery: around 25 percent are fully recovered and 58 percent partially improved (Zerbe, 2008; Herzog et al., 1999; Treasure et al., 1995).

Another positive note is that most females with anorexia nervosa menstruate again when they regain their weight, and other medical improvements follow (Zerbe, 2008; Fombonne, 1995). Also encouraging is that the death rate from anorexia nervosa seems to be falling. Earlier diagnosis and safer and faster weight-restoration techniques may account for this trend. Deaths that do occur are usually caused by suicide, starvation, infection, gastrointestinal problems, or electrolyte imbalance.

On the negative side, close to 20 percent of persons with anorexia nervosa remain seriously troubled for years (Haliburn, 2005; APA, 2000). Furthermore, recovery, when

Eric Young/Winona Daily News/AP Photo

New efforts at prevention
A number of innovative educational programs have been developed to help promote healthy body images and prevent eating disorders. Here, a Winona State University freshman swings a maul over her shoulder and into bathroom scales as part of Eating Disorders Awareness Week. The scale smashing is an annual event.

BETWEEN THE LINES

Poetic Concerns

Famed poet Lord Byron (1788–1824) wrote: "A woman should never be seen eating and drinking unless it be lobster salad and champagne." Friends noted that the poet himself had "a horror of fat." He regularly abstained from eating, believing that he would lose his creativity if he ate normally (Brumberg, 1988). ‹‹

it does occur, is not always permanent. Anorexic behavior recurs in at least one-third of recovered patients, usually triggered by new stresses, such as marriage, pregnancy, or a major relocation (Eifert et al., 2007; Fennig et al., 2002). Even years later, many recovered individuals continue to express concerns about their weight and appearance. Some continue to restrict their diets to a degree, experience anxiety when they eat with other people, or hold some distorted ideas about food, eating, and weight (Fairburn et al., 2008; Fichter & Pirke, 1995).

About half of those who have suffered from anorexia nervosa continue to experience certain emotional problems—particularly depression, obsessiveness, and social anxiety—years after treatment. Such problems are particularly common in those who have not succeeded in reaching a fully normal weight (Steinhausen, 2002; Halmi, 1995).

The more weight persons have lost and the more time that has passed before they entered treatment, the poorer the recovery rate (Fairburn et al., 2008). Individuals who had psychological or sexual problems before the onset of the disorder tend to have a poorer recovery rate than those without such a history (Finfgeld, 2002; Lewis & Chatoor, 1994). Teenagers seem to have a better recovery rate than older patients (Richard, 2005; Steinhausen et al., 2000). Females have a better recovery rate than males.

Treatments for Bulimia Nervosa

Treatment programs for bulimia nervosa are often offered in eating disorder clinics. Such programs share the immediate goal of helping clients to eliminate their binge-purge patterns and establish good eating habits and the more general goal of eliminating the underlying causes of bulimic patterns. The programs emphasize education as much as therapy (Fairburn et al., 2008; Zerbe, 2008). Cognitive-behavioral therapy is particularly helpful in cases of bulimia nervosa—even more helpful than in cases of anorexia nervosa (Gleaves & Latner, 2008). And antidepressant drug therapy, which is of limited help to people with anorexia nervosa, appears to be quite effective in many cases of bulimia nervosa (Zerbe, 2008; Steffen et al., 2006).

Cognitive-Behavioral Therapy
When treating clients with bulimia nervosa, cognitive-behavioral therapists employ many of the same techniques that they apply in cases of anorexia nervosa. Here, however, they tailor the techniques to the unique features of bulimia (for example, bingeing and purging behavior) and to the specific beliefs at work in bulimia nervosa.

BEHAVIORAL TECHNIQUES The therapists often instruct clients with bulimia nervosa to keep diaries of their eating behavior, changes in sensations of hunger and fullness, and the ebb and flow of other feelings (Stewart & Williamson, 2008; Latner & Wilson, 2002). This helps the clients to observe their eating patterns more objectively and recognize the emotions and situations that trigger their desire to binge.

The therapists may also use the behavioral technique of *exposure and response prevention* to help break the binge-purge cycle. As you read in Chapter 5, this approach consists of exposing people to situations that would ordinarily raise anxiety and then preventing them from performing their usual compulsive responses until they learn that the situations are actually harmless and their compulsive acts unnecessary. For bulimia nervosa, the therapists require clients to eat particular kinds and amounts of food and then prevent them from vomiting to show that eating can be a harmless and even constructive activity that needs no undoing (Williamson et al., 2004; Toro et al., 2003). Typically the therapist sits with the client during the eating of forbidden foods and stays until the urge to purge has passed. Studies find that this treatment often helps reduce eating-related anxieties, bingeing, and vomiting.

COGNITIVE TECHNIQUES Beyond such behavioral techniques, a primary focus of cognitive-behavioral therapists is to help clients with bulimia nervosa recognize and change their maladaptive attitudes toward food, eating, weight, and shape (Fairburn et al., 2008; Stewart & Williamson, 2008). The therapists typically teach the individuals to identify

BETWEEN THE LINES

Celebrities Who Acknowledge Having Had Eating Disorders

Alanis Morrissette, singer ‹‹

Kate Winslet, actress ‹‹

Mary-Kate Olsen, actress ‹‹

Jessica Alba, actress ‹‹

Elton John, singer ‹‹

Fiona Apple, singer ‹‹

Sally Field, actress ‹‹

Christina Ricci, actress ‹‹

Justine Bateman, actress ‹‹

Geri Halliwell ("Ginger Spice"), singer ‹‹

Daniel Johns, rock singer (Silverchair) ‹‹

Karen Elson, model ‹‹

Tracey Gold, actress ‹‹

Cynthia French, singer ‹‹

Jane Fonda, actress ‹‹

Jamie-Lynn Sigler, actress ‹‹

Paula Abdul, singer, dancer ‹‹

Victoria Beckham ("Posh Spice"), singer ‹‹

Princess Diana, British royalty ‹‹

Kate Beckinsale, actress ‹‹

Zina Garrison, tennis star ‹‹

Cathy Rigby, Olympic gymnast ‹‹

Kathy Johnson, Olympic gymnast ‹‹

Nadia Comaneci, Olympic gymnast ‹‹

Magali Amadei, supermodel ‹‹

Unfair game

As we are reminded by one of the leading characters in the highly successful film *Austin Powers 2: The Spy Who Shagged Me*, overweight people in Western society typically are treated with insensitivity. They are the targets of humor in magazines, books, television shows, and movies.

BETWEEN THE LINES

Fonda Women

In her 2005 book *My Life So Far*, Jane Fonda describes her five-decades-long battle with bulimia nervosa. She traces her disorder to her adolescence, when, after her mother's death, she longed to acquire love and recognition from her aloof father, actor Henry Fonda, who wanted "Fonda Women" to be trim. She recalls that by her teenage years, "the only time my father ever referred to how I looked was when he thought I was too fat" (p. 84). ‹‹

---

and challenge the negative thoughts that regularly precede their urge to binge—"I have no self-control," "I might as well give up," "I look fat" (Fairburn, 1985). They may also guide clients to recognize, question, and eventually change their perfectionistic standards, sense of helplessness, and low self-concept (see *Psych Watch* on the facing page). Cognitive-behavioral approaches seem to help as many as 65 percent of patients stop bingeing and purging (Eifert et al., 2007; Mitchell et al., 2002).

Other Forms of Psychotherapy Because of its effectiveness in the treatment of bulimia nervosa, cognitive-behavioral therapy is often tried first, before other therapies are considered. If clients do not respond to this approach, approaches with promising but less impressive track records may then be tried. A common alternative is *interpersonal psychotherapy,* the treatment that seeks to improve interpersonal functioning (Eifert et al., 2007; Phillips et al., 2003). *Psychodynamic therapy* has also been used in cases of bulimia nervosa, but only a few research studies have tested and supported its effectiveness (Zerbe, 2008, 2001; Valbak, 2001). The various forms of psychotherapy—cognitive-behavioral, interpersonal, and psychodynamic—are often supplemented by family therapy (le Grange et al., 2008, 2007)

Cognitive-behavioral, interpersonal, and psychodynamic therapy may each be offered in either individual or group therapy format. Group formats, including self-help groups, give clients with bulimia nervosa an opportunity to share their concerns and experiences with one another (Kalodner & Coughlin, 2004; Riess, 2002). Group members learn that their disorder is not unique or shameful, and they receive support from one another, along with honest feedback and insights. In the group they can also work directly on underlying fears of displeasing others or being criticized. Research suggests that group formats are at least somewhat helpful in as many as 75 percent of bulimia nervosa cases (Valbak, 2001; McKisack & Waller, 1997).

Antidepressant Medications During the past decade, antidepressant drugs—all groups of antidepressant drugs—have been used to help treat bulimia nervosa (Steffen et al., 2006; Sloan et al., 2004). In contrast to anorexia nervosa, people with bulimia nervosa are often helped considerably by these drugs (Zerbe, 2008). According to research, the drugs help as many as 40 percent of patients, reducing their binges by an average of 67 percent and vomiting by 56 percent. Once again, drug therapy seems to work best in combination with other forms of therapy, particularly cognitive-behavioral therapy (Stewart & Williamson, 2008). Alternatively, some therapists wait to see whether cognitive-behavioral therapy or another form of psychotherapy is effective before trying antidepressants (Wilson, 2005).

What Is the Aftermath of Bulimia Nervosa? Left untreated, bulimia nervosa can last for years, sometimes improving temporarily but then returning (APA, 2000). Treatment, however, produces immediate, significant improvement in approximately 40 percent of clients: they stop or greatly reduce their bingeing and purging, eat properly, and maintain a normal weight (Richard, 2005). Another 40 percent show a moderate response—at least some decrease in bingeing and purging. As many as 20 percent show little immediate improvement. Follow-up studies suggest that by 10 years after treatment, 89 percent of persons with bulimia nervosa have recovered either fully (70 percent) or partially (19 percent) (Zerbe, 2008; Herzog et al., 1999; Keel et al., 1999). Those with partial recoveries continue to have recurrent binges or purges. Research also indicates that treatment helps many, but not all, people with bulimia nervosa attain lasting improvements in their overall psychological and social functioning (Keel et al., 2002, 2000; Stein et al., 2002).

Relapse can be a problem even among people who respond successfully to treatment (Olmsted et al., 2005; Herzog et al., 1999). As with anorexia nervosa, relapses are usually triggered by a new life stress, such as an upcoming exam, job change, marriage, or divorce (Liu, 2007; Abraham & Llewellyn-Jones, 1984). One study found that close to one-third of persons who had recovered from bulimia nervosa relapsed within two years of treatment, usually within six months (Olmsted, Kaplan, & Rockert, 1994).

And She Lived Happily Ever After?

Back in 1996 Alicia Machado, a 19-year-old woman from Venezuela, was crowned Miss Universe. Then her problems began. During the first eight months of her reign, her weight rose from 118 to 160 pounds, angering pageant officials and sparking rumors that she was about to be relieved of her crown. The "problem" received broad newspaper and television coverage and much ridicule on talk radio programs around the world.

Ms. Machado explained, "I was a normal girl, but my life has had big changes. I travel to many countries, eat different foods." Nevertheless, in response to all the pressure, she undertook a special diet and an extensive exercise program to lose at

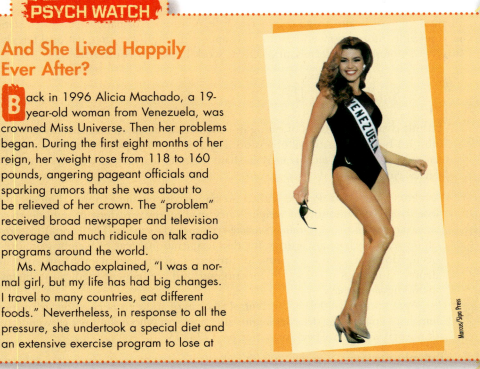

Marcus/Sipa Press

least some of the weight she had gained. Her trainer claimed that a weight of 118 pounds was too low for her frame and explained that she had originally attained it by taking diet pills.

In the meantime, the whole episode served to demonstrate once again the powerful role of society in defining female beauty, acceptable weight, and "proper" eating. Ironically, many of the individuals who harshly criticized Ms. Machado or made fun of her—that is, the female critics—were themselves victims of the demanding and unrealistic standards of Western cultures that drive so many individuals toward dysfunctional patterns of eating.

Relapse is more likely among persons who had longer histories of bulimia nervosa before treatment, had vomited more frequently during their disorder, had histories of substance abuse, made slower progress in the early stages of treatment, and continue to be lonely or to distrust others after treatment (Fairburn et al., 2004; Stewart, 2004; Keel et al., 2002, 1999).

PUTTING IT.....together

A Standard for Integrating Perspectives

You have observed throughout this book that it is often useful to consider sociocultural, psychological, and biological factors jointly when trying to explain or treat various forms of abnormal functioning. Nowhere is the argument for combining these perspectives more powerful than in the case of eating disorders. According to the multidimensional risk perspective embraced by many theorists, varied factors act together to spark the development of eating disorders. One case may result from societal pressures, autonomy issues, the physical and emotional changes of adolescence, and hypothalamic overactivity, while another case may result from family pressures, depression, and the effects of dieting. No wonder that the most helpful treatment programs for eating disorders combine sociocultural, psychological, and biological approaches. When the multidimensional risk perspective is applied to eating disorders, it demonstrates that scientists and practitioners who follow very different models can work together productively in an atmosphere of mutual respect.

Research on eating disorders keeps revealing new surprises that force clinicians to adjust their theories and treatment programs. For example, researchers have learned that people with bulimia nervosa sometimes feel strangely positive about their symptoms (Serpell & Treasure, 2002). A recovered patient, for example, said, "I still miss my bulimia as I would an old friend who has died" (Cauwels, 1983, p. 173). Given such feelings, many therapists now help clients work through grief reactions over their lost symptoms, reactions that may occur as the individuals begin to overcome their eating disorders (Zerbe, 2008).

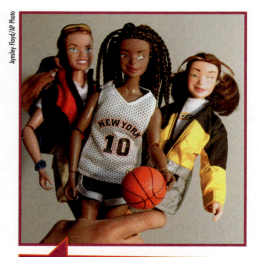

Ayrsley Floyd/AP Photo

New dolls for a new generation
After nearly 50 years of Barbie and her extremely thin waistline, some manufacturers are now introducing very different-looking dolls to the marketplace. The dolls, such as these Get Real Girls dolls, often emphasize fitness and health, multicultural appearance, and sports, business, and other professional roles for females. Observers hope that such products will have a positive effect on the body satisfaction and self-image of young girls and also help prevent eating disorders.

While clinicians and researchers seek more answers about eating disorders, clients themselves have begun to take an active role. A number of patient-run organizations now provide information, education, and support through Web sites, national telephone hot lines, professional referrals, newsletters, workshops, and conferences.

‹‹‹[SUMMING UP]›››

○ **Eating disorders** Rates of eating disorders have increased dramatically as thinness has become a national obsession. The two leading disorders in this category, *anorexia nervosa* and *bulimia nervosa,* share many similarities, as well as key differences. *pp. 341–342*

○ **Anorexia nervosa** People with anorexia nervosa pursue extreme thinness and lose dangerous amounts of weight. They may follow a pattern of *restricting-type anorexia nervosa* or *binge-eating/purging-type anorexia nervosa.* The central features of anorexia nervosa are a drive for thinness, irrational fear of weight gain, preoccupation with food, cognitive disturbances, psychological problems such as depressed feelings or obsessive functioning, and consequent medical problems, including *amenorrhea.*

Approximately 90 to 95 percent of all cases of anorexia nervosa occur among females. Typically the disorder begins after a person who is slightly overweight or of normal weight has been on a diet. *pp. 342–345*

○ **Bulimia nervosa** Individuals with bulimia nervosa go on frequent *eating binges* and then force themselves to vomit or perform other inappropriate *compensatory behaviors.* They may follow a pattern of *purging-type bulimia nervosa* or *nonpurging-type bulimia nervosa.* The binges often occur in response to increasing tension and are followed by feelings of guilt and self-blame.

Compensatory behavior is at first reinforced by the temporary relief from uncomfortable feelings of fullness or the reduction of feelings of anxiety, self-disgust, and loss of control attached to bingeing. Over time, however, sufferers feel generally disgusted with themselves, depressed, and guilty.

People with bulimia nervosa may experience mood swings or have difficulty controlling their impulses. Some display a personality disorder. Around half are amenorrheic, a number develop dental problems, and some develop a potassium deficiency.

Clinicians have also observed that certain people display a pattern of binge eating without vomiting or other inappropriate compensatory behaviors. This pattern, often called *binge-eating disorder,* is not yet listed in the DSM, although it is being considered for inclusion in the next edition. *pp. 345–351*

○ **Explanations** Most theorists now apply a *multidimensional risk perspective* to explain eating disorders and identify several key contributing factors. Principal among these are *ego deficiencies; cognitive factors; mood disorder; biological factors* such as activity of the *hypothalamus, biochemical activity,* and the body's *weight set point; society's emphasis on thinness and bias against obesity; family environment; racial and ethnic differences;* and *gender differences. pp. 351–363*

○ **Treatments** The first step in treating *anorexia nervosa* is to increase calorie intake and quickly restore the person's weight, using a strategy such as *supportive nursing care.* The second step is to deal with the underlying psychological and family problems, often using a combination of *education, cognitive-behavioral approaches,* and *family approaches.* As many as 83 percent of people who receive successful treatment for anorexia nervosa continue to show full or partial improvements years later. However, some of them relapse along the way, many continue to worry about their weight and appearance, and half continue to experience some emotional problems. Most menstruate again when they regain weight. *pp. 363–367*

Treatments for *bulimia nervosa* focus first on stopping the binge-purge pattern and then on addressing the underlying causes of the disorder. Often several treatment strategies are combined, including *education*, *psychotherapy* (particularly *cognitive-behavioral therapy*), and *antidepressant medications*. Approximately 89 percent of those who receive treatment eventually improve either fully or partially. While relapse can be a problem and may be precipitated by a new stress, treatment leads to lasting improvements in psychological and social functioning for many individuals. *pp. 367–369*

⋙ CRITICAL THOUGHTS ⋙

1. Many, perhaps most, women in Western society feel as if they are dieting or between diets their entire adult lives. Is it possible to be a woman in this society and not struggle with at least some issues of eating and appearance? Who is responsible for the standards and pressures that affect so many women? *pp. 341–342, 355–358*

2. The prevalence of eating disorders is particularly low in cultures that restrict female social roles and reduce a woman's freedom to make decisions about her life (Miller & Pumariega, 1999; Bemporad, 1997). How might you explain this relationship? *pp. 351–353*

3. The most successful of today's fashion models, often referred to as supermodels, have a celebrity status that was not conferred upon models in the past. Why do you think the fame and status of models have risen in this way? *pp. 351–353, 359*

4. The prevalence of eating disorders among men currently appears to be on the rise. What do you think is the reason for this trend? *pp. 361–363*

5. Relapse is a problem for some people who recover from anorexia nervosa and bulimia nervosa. Why might people remain vulnerable even after recovery? How might they and their therapists reduce the chances of relapse? *pp. 363–369*

6. What does the 1996 Miss Universe flap suggest about the role of societal factors in the development of eating problems? Why do you think so many people held such strong, often critical, opinions about Ms. Machado's weight? *p. 369*

⊞ cyberstudy ⊞   SEARCH

Search the *Abnormal Psychology* Video Tool Kit
www.worthpublishers.com/apvtk

▲ Chapter 11 Video Cases
 Imprisoned by an Eating Disorder
 Anorexia Nervosa: Not for Women Only
 Weight Gain: A Surprise Factor
▲ Video case discussions, study guides, and questions

Log on to the Comer Web Page
www.worthpublishers.com/comer

▲ Chapter 11 outline, learning objectives, research exercises, study tools, and practice test questions
▲ Additional Chapter 11 case studies, Web links, and FAQs

SUBSTANCE-RELATED DISORDERS

" "I am Duncan. I am an alcoholic." The audience settled deeper into their chairs at these familiar words. Another chronicle of death and rebirth would shortly begin [at] Alcoholics Anonymous. . . .

. . . "I must have been just past my 15th birthday when I had that first drink that everybody talks about. And like so many of them . . . it was like a miracle. With a little beer in my gut, the world was transformed. I wasn't a weakling anymore, I could lick almost anybody on the block. And girls? Well, you can imagine how a couple of beers made me feel like I could have any girl I wanted. . . .

"Though it's obvious to me now that my drinking even then, in high school, and after I got to college, was a problem, I didn't think so at the time. After all, everybody was drinking and getting drunk and acting stupid, and I didn't really think I was different. . . . I guess the fact that I hadn't really had any blackouts and that I could go for days without having to drink reassured me that things hadn't gotten out of control. And that's the way it went, until I found myself drinking even more—and more often—and suffering more from my drinking, along about my third year of college.

. . . "My roommate, a friend from high school, started bugging me about my drinking. It wasn't even that I'd have to sleep it off the whole next day and miss class, it was that he had begun to hear other friends talking about me, about the fool I'd made of myself at parties. He saw how shaky I was the morning after, and he saw how different I was when I'd been drinking a lot—almost out of my head was the way he put it. And he could count the bottles that I'd leave around the room, and he knew what the drinking and carousing was doing to my grades. . . . [P]artly because I really cared about my roommate and didn't want to lose him as a friend, I did cut down on my drinking by half or more. I only drank on weekends—and then only at night. . . . And that got me through the rest of college and, actually, through law school as well. . . .

"Shortly after getting my law degree, I married my first wife, and . . . for the first time since I started, my drinking was no problem at all. I would go for weeks at a time without touching a drop. . . .

"My marriage started to go bad after our second son, our third child, was born. I was very much career-and-success oriented, and I had little time to spend at home with my family. . . . My traveling had increased a lot, there were stimulating people on those trips, and, let's face it, there were some pretty exciting women available, too. So home got to be little else but a nagging, boring wife and children I wasn't very interested in. My drinking had gotten bad again, too, with being on the road so much, having to do a lot of entertaining at lunch when I wasn't away, and trying to soften the hassles at home. I guess I was putting down close to a gallon of very good scotch a week, with one thing or another.

"And as that went on, the drinking began to affect both my marriage and my career. With enough booze in me and under the pressures of guilt over my failure to carry out my responsibilities to my wife and children, I sometimes got kind of rough physically with them. I would break furniture, throw things around, then rush out and drive off in the car. I had a couple of wrecks, lost my license for two years because of one of them. Worst of all was when I tried to stop. By then I was totally hooked, so every time I tried to stop drinking, I'd experience withdrawal in all its horrors . . . with the vomiting and the 'shakes' and being unable to sit still or to lie down. And that would go on for days at a time. . . .

"Then, about four years ago, with my life in ruins, my wife given up on me and the kids with her, out of a job, and way down on my luck, [Alcoholics Anonymous] and I found each other. . . . I've been dry now for a little over two years, and with luck and support, I may stay sober. . . ."

Spitzer et al., 1983, pp. 87–89

Human beings enjoy a remarkable variety of foods and drinks. Every substance on earth probably has been tried by someone, somewhere, at some time. We also have discovered substances that have interesting nonnutritive effects—both medical and pleasurable—on our brains and the rest of our bodies. We may swallow an aspirin to quiet a headache, an antibiotic to fight an infection, or a tranquilizer to calm us down. We may drink coffee to get going in the morning or wine to relax with friends. We may smoke cigarettes to soothe our nerves. However, many of the substances we consume can harm us or disrupt our behavior or mood. The misuse of such substances has become one of society's biggest problems; it has been estimated that the cost of drug misuse is more than $200 billion each year in the United States alone (ONDCP, 2008).

A *drug* is defined as any substance other than food that affects our bodies or minds. It need not be a medicine or be illegal. The term "substance" is now frequently used in place of "drug," in part because many people fail to see that such substances as alcohol, tobacco, and caffeine are drugs, too. When a person ingests a substance—whether it be alcohol, cocaine, marijuana, or some form of medication—trillions of powerful molecules surge through the bloodstream and into the brain. Once there, the molecules set off a series of biochemical events that disturb the normal operation of the brain and body. Not surprisingly, then, substance misuse may lead to various kinds of abnormal functioning.

Drugs may cause *temporary* changes in behavior, emotion, or thought. As Duncan found out, for example, an excessive amount of alcohol may lead to *intoxication* (literally, "poisoning"), a temporary state of poor judgment, mood changes, irritability, slurred speech, and poor coordination. Drugs such as LSD may produce a particular form of intoxication, sometimes called *hallucinosis,* which consists of perceptual distortions and hallucinations.

Some substances can also lead to *long-term* problems. People who regularly ingest them may develop maladaptive patterns of behavior and changes in their body's physical responses (APA, 2000). In one such pattern, called **substance abuse,** they rely on the drug excessively and chronically and in so doing damage their family and social relationships, function poorly at work, or put themselves and others in danger. A more advanced pattern, **substance dependence,** is also known as **addiction.** In this pattern, people not only abuse the drug but also center their lives on it and perhaps acquire a physical dependence on it, marked by a *tolerance* for it, *withdrawal* symptoms, or both (see Table 12-1). When people develop **tolerance,** they need increasing doses of a drug in order to keep getting the desired effect. **Withdrawal** consists of unpleasant and even dangerous symptoms—cramps, anxiety attacks, sweating, nausea—that occur when individuals suddenly stop taking or cut back on the drug.

Duncan, who described his problems to fellow members at an Alcoholics Anonymous meeting, was caught in a pattern of alcohol dependence. When he was a college student and later a lawyer, alcohol damaged his family, social, academic, and work life. He also built up a tolerance for the substance over time and experienced withdrawal symptoms such as vomiting and shaking when he tried to stop using it. In any given year, 9.2 percent of all teens and adults in the United States, around 23 million people, display a pattern of substance abuse or dependence (NSDUH, 2008). The highest rate

table: 12-1

DSM Checklist

SUBSTANCE ABUSE

1. A maladaptive pattern of substance use leading to significant impairment or distress
2. At least one of the following features occurring within one year:
   (a) Recurrent substance use, resulting in failure to fulfill major role obligations at work, school, or home
   (b) Recurrent substance use in situations in which it is physically hazardous
   (c) Recurrent substance-related legal problems
   (d) Substance use that continues despite its causing or increasing persistent social or interpersonal problems

SUBSTANCE DEPENDENCE

1. A maladaptive pattern of substance use leading to significant impairment or distress
2. At least three of the following:
   (a) Tolerance
   (b) Withdrawal
   (c) Substance often taken in larger amounts over a longer period than was intended
   (d) Persistent desire for substance or unsuccessful efforts to control substance use
   (e) Considerable time spent trying to obtain, use, or recover from the substance
   (f) Substance use in place of important activities
   (g) Substance use that continues despite its causing or increasing persistent physical or psychological problems

Based on APA, 2000.

of substance abuse or dependence in the United States is found among Native Americans (19 percent), while the lowest is among Asian Americans (4.3 percent). White Americans, Hispanic Americans, and African Americans display rates between 9 and 10 percent (NSDUH, 2008) (see Figure 12-1). Only 26 percent of all people with a pattern of substance abuse or dependence receive treatment from a mental health professional (Wang et al., 2005).

Many drugs are available in our society, and new ones are introduced almost every day. Some are harvested from nature, others derived from natural substances, and still others produced in the laboratory. Some, such as antianxiety drugs and barbiturates, require a physician's prescription for legal use. Others, such as alcohol and nicotine, are legally available to adults. Still others, such as heroin, are illegal under all circumstances. In 1962 only 4 million people in the United States had ever used marijuana, cocaine, heroin, or another illegal substance; today the number has climbed to more than 94 million (NSDUH, 2008). In fact, 28 million people have used illegal substances within the past year, and 20.4 million are using one currently. Almost 22 percent of all high school seniors have used an illegal drug within the past month (Johnston et al., 2007).

The substances people misuse fall into several categories: *depressants,* such as alcohol and opioids, which slow the central nervous system; *stimulants* of the central nervous system, such as cocaine and amphetamines; *hallucinogens,* such as LSD, which cause delusions, hallucinations, and other powerful changes in sensory perception; and *cannabis* substances, such as marijuana, which cause a mixture of hallucinogenic, depressant, and stimulant effects. Many people take more than one of these substances at a time, a practice known as *polydrug use.* In this chapter you will read about some of the most problematic substances and the abnormal patterns they may produce. After first examining the substances separately, the chapter will consider the causes and treatments of substance-related disorders together as a group.

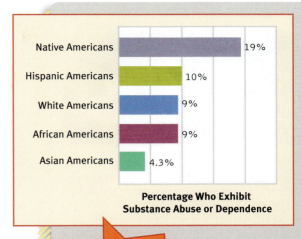

Figure 12-1

How do races differ in substance abuse and dependence? In the United States, Native Americans are much more likely than members of other ethnic or cultural groups to abuse or be dependent on substances. Conversely, Asian Americans are less likely to display substance abuse or dependence (NSDUH, 2008).

☼Depressants

Depressants slow the activity of the central nervous system. They reduce tension and inhibitions and may interfere with a person's judgment, motor activity, and concentration. The three most widely used groups of depressants are *alcohol, sedative-hypnotic drugs,* and *opioids.*

Alcohol

The World Health Organization estimates that 2 billion people worldwide consume **alcohol.** In the United States more than half of all residents at least from time to time drink beverages that contain alcohol (NSDUH, 2008). Purchases of beer, wine, and liquor amount to tens of billions of dollars each year in the United States alone.

When people consume five or more drinks on a single occasion, it is called a *binge-drinking* episode. Twenty-three percent of people in the United States over the age of 11 (57 million people) binge-drink each month (NSDUH, 2008). Over the past decade, the number of binge-drinking episodes per person has increased by 35 percent—by 25 percent among drinkers over 25 years of age and by 56 percent among underage drinkers (Naimi et al., 2003). Men account for 81 percent of binge-drinking episodes.

Nearly 7 percent of persons over 11 years of age, around 17 million people, are heavy drinkers, consuming at least five drinks on at least five occasions each month (NSDUH, 2008). Among heavy drinkers, males outnumber females by more than two to one, around 8 percent to 4 percent.

All alcoholic beverages contain *ethyl alcohol,* a chemical that is quickly absorbed into the blood through the lining of the stomach and the intestine. The ethyl alcohol immediately begins to take effect as it is carried in the bloodstream to the central nervous system (the brain and spinal cord), where it acts to depress, or slow, functioning by binding to various neurons. One important group of neurons to which ethyl alcohol binds

•**substance abuse**•A pattern of behavior in which people rely on a drug excessively and regularly, bringing damage to their relationships, functioning poorly at work, or putting themselves or others in danger.

•**substance dependence**•A pattern of behavior in which people organize their lives around a drug, possibly building a tolerance to it, experiencing withdrawal symptoms when they stop taking it, or both. Also called *addiction.*

•**tolerance**•The adjustment that the brain and the body make to the regular use of certain drugs so that ever larger doses are needed to achieve the earlier effects.

•**withdrawal**•Unpleasant, sometimes dangerous reactions that may occur when people who use a drug regularly stop taking or reduce their dosage of the drug.

•**alcohol**•Any beverage containing ethyl alcohol, including beer, wine, and liquor.

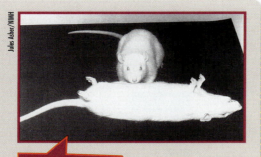

The GABA effect
After researchers blocked GABA receptors in the brain of the rat at the back of this photo, the rat showed no ill effects from ingesting alcohol. In contrast, the rat in front, whose unblocked GABA receptors remained open and available to alcohol, became obviously intoxicated when ingesting the same amount of alcohol.

are those that normally receive the neurotransmitter GABA. As you saw in Chapter 5, GABA carries an *inhibitory* message—a message to stop firing—when it is received at certain neurons. When alcohol binds to receptors on those neurons, it apparently helps GABA to shut down the neurons, thus helping to relax the drinker (Ksir et al., 2008; Staley et al., 2005).

At first ethyl alcohol depresses the areas of the brain that control judgment and inhibition; people become looser, more talkative, and often more friendly. As their inner control breaks down, they may feel relaxed, confident, and happy. When more alcohol is absorbed, it slows down additional areas in the central nervous system, leaving the drinkers less able to make sound judgments, their speech less careful and less coherent, and their memory weaker. Many people become highly emotional and perhaps loud and aggressive.

Motor difficulties increase as drinking continues, and reaction times slow. People may be unsteady when they stand or walk and clumsy in performing even simple activities. They may drop things, bump into doors and furniture, and misjudge distances. Their vision becomes blurred, particularly peripheral, or side, vision, and they have trouble hearing. As a result, people who have drunk too much alcohol may have great difficulty driving or solving simple problems.

The extent of the effect of ethyl alcohol is determined by its *concentration,* or proportion, in the blood. Thus a given amount of alcohol will have less effect on a large person than on a small one (see Table 12-2). Gender also affects the concentration of alcohol in the blood. Women have less of the stomach enzyme *alcohol dehydrogenase,* which breaks down alcohol in the stomach before it enters the blood. Thus, women become more intoxicated than men on equal doses of alcohol, and women may be at greater risk for physical and psychological damage from alcohol than men who drink similar quantities of alcohol (Brady & Back, 2008; Ksir et al., 2008).

table: 12-2

Relationships between Sex, Weight, Oral Alcohol Consumption, and Blood Alcohol Level

Absolute Alcohol (oz.)	Beverage Intake*	Blood Alcohol Level (percent)					
		Female (100 lb.)	Male (100 lb.)	Female (150 lb.)	Male (150 lb.)	Female (200 lb.)	Male (200 lb.)
½	1 oz. spirits[†] 1 glass wine 1 can beer	0.045	0.037	0.03	0.025	0.022	0.019
1	2 oz. spirits 2 glasses wine 2 cans beer	0.090	0.075	0.06	0.050	0.045	0.037
2	4 oz. spirits 4 glasses wine 4 cans beer	0.180	0.150	0.12	0.100	0.090	0.070
3	6 oz. spirits 6 glasses wine 6 cans beer	0.270	0.220	0.18	0.150	0.130	0.110
4	8 oz. spirits 8 glasses wine 8 cans beer	0.360	0.300	0.24	0.200	0.180	0.150
5	10 oz. spirits 10 glasses wine 10 cans beer	0.450	0.370	0.30	0.250	0.220	0.180

*In 1 hour.
†100-proof spirits.
Source: Ksir et al., 2008, p. 209.

Levels of impairment are closely related to the concentration of ethyl alcohol in the blood. When the alcohol concentration reaches 0.06 percent of the blood volume, a person usually feels relaxed and comfortable. By the time it reaches 0.09 percent, however, the drinker crosses the line into intoxication. If the level goes as high as 0.55 percent, death will probably result. Most people lose consciousness before they can drink enough to reach this level; nevertheless, more than 1,000 people in the United States die each year from too high a blood alcohol level (Ksir et al., 2008).

The effects of alcohol subside only when the alcohol concentration in the blood declines. Most of the alcohol is broken down, or *metabolized,* by the liver into carbon dioxide and water, which can be exhaled and excreted. The average rate of this metabolism is 25 percent of an ounce per hour, but different people's livers work at different speeds; thus rates of "sobering up" vary. Despite popular belief, only time and metabolism can make a person sober. Drinking black coffee, splashing cold water on one's face, or "pulling oneself together" cannot hurry the process.

Alcohol Abuse and Dependence Though legal, alcohol is actually one of the most dangerous of recreational drugs, and its reach extends across the life span. In fact, around 10 percent of elementary school students admit to some alcohol use, while nearly 45 percent of high school seniors drink alcohol each month (most to the point of intoxication) and 3 percent report drinking every day (Johnston et al., 2007). Similarly, alcohol misuse is a major problem on college campuses (see *Psych Watch* on the next page).

In any given year, 6.6 percent of the world's population fall into a long-term pattern of alcohol abuse or dependence, either of which is known in popular terms as *alcoholism,* and 13.2 percent experience one of the patterns sometime during their lifetime (Somers et al., 2004). Similarly, surveys indicate that over a one-year period, 7.6 percent of all adults in the United States, almost 19 million people, display an alcohol use disorder (NSDUH, 2008). Between 9 and 18 percent of the nation's adults display such a disorder at some time in their lives, with men outnumbering women by at least 2 to 1 (Kessler et al., 2005; NSDUH, 2005). Many teenagers also experience alcohol abuse or dependence (Johnston et al., 2007).

The prevalence of alcoholism in a given year is around the same (7 to 9 percent) for white Americans, African Americans, and Hispanic Americans (SAMHSA, 2008). The men in these groups, however, show strikingly different age patterns. For white American and Hispanic American men, the rate of alcoholism is highest—over 18 percent—during young adulthood, compared to 8 percent among African American men in that age group. For African American men, the rate is highest during late middle age, 15 percent compared to 8 percent among white American and Hispanic American men in that age group.

Native Americans, particularly men, tend to display a higher rate of alcohol abuse and dependence than any of these groups. Overall 15 percent of them abuse or depend on alcohol, although their specific prevalence rates differ across the various Native American reservation communities (SAMHSA, 2008; Beals et al., 2005). Generally, Asians in the United States and elsewhere have a lower rate of alcoholism (3 percent) than do people from other cultures. As many as one-half of these individuals have a deficiency of alcohol dehydrogenase, the chemical responsible for breaking down alcohol, so they react quite negatively to even a modest intake of alcohol. Such reactions in turn prevent extended use (Wall et al., 2001; APA, 2000).

ALCOHOL ABUSE Generally speaking, people who abuse alcohol drink large amounts regularly and rely on it to enable them to do things that would otherwise make them anxious. Eventually the drinking interferes with their social behavior and ability to think and work. They may have frequent arguments with family members or friends, miss work repeatedly, and even lose

Dealing with DUI
In an effort to better publicize, prevent, and punish intoxicated driving, Phoenix, Arizona, has recently created DUI chain gangs for all to see. Members of these chain gangs, men convicted of drunken driving, don bright pink shirts and perform tasks such as the burial of people who have died of alcohol abuse or dependence.

AP Photo/Matt York

College Binge Drinking: An Extracurricular Crisis

Drinking large amounts of alcohol in a short time, or *binge drinking*, is a serious problem on college campuses, as well as in many other settings (NSDUH, 2008). Studies show that 40 percent of college students binge-drink at least once each year, some of them six times or more per month (NCASA, 2007; Sharma, 2005; Wechsler et al., 2004). These are higher rates than those displayed by people of the same age who are not in college (Ksir et al., 2008). In many circles, alcohol use is an accepted part of college life. Are we as a society taking the issue too lightly? Consider some of the following statistics:

- Alcohol-related arrests account for 83 percent of all campus arrests (NCASA, 2007).
- Alcohol may be a factor in nearly 40 percent of academic problems and 28 percent of all college dropouts (Anderson, 1994).
- Alcohol affects not only those who drink but also those who do not; approximately 600,000 students each year are physically or emotionally traumatized or assaulted by a student drinker (NCASA, 2007; Hingson et al., 2002).
- Binge drinking has been linked to severe health problems and serious injury, auto crashes, unplanned and unprotected sex, aggressive behaviors, and various psychological problems. Binge drinking by college students has been associated with 1,700 deaths, 500,000 injuries, and tens of thousands of cases of sexual assault, including date rape, every year (NCASA, 2007; Wechsler & Wuethrich, 2002; Wechsler et al., 2000).
- Teenagers who begin binge drinking at age 13 and continue through

Andrew Lichtenstein/Corbis Sygma

Testing the limits Binge drinking, similar to this display at a college campus party, has led to a number of deaths in recent years.

adolescence are nearly four times more likely than non-binge-drinking peers to be overweight or have high blood pressure at age 24 (Oesterle et al., 2004).

- The number of female binge drinkers among college students has increased 31 percent over the past decade.

These findings have led some educators to describe binge drinking as "the No. 1 public health hazard" for full-time college students, and many researchers and clinicians have turned their attention to it. Researchers at the Harvard School of Public Health, for example, have surveyed more than 50,000 students at 120 college campuses around the United States (Wechsler & Nelson, 2008; Wechsler et al., 2004, 1995, 1994). According to their surveys, students most likely to binge-drink were those who lived in a fraternity or sorority house, pursued a party-centered lifestyle, and engaged in high-risk behaviors such as substance misuse or having multiple sex partners. The study also found that students

who were binge drinkers in high school were more likely to binge-drink in college.

Efforts to change such patterns have begun to make a difference. For example, some universities now provide substance-free dorms: 36 percent of the residents in such dorms were binge drinkers, according to one study, compared to 75 percent of those who lived in a fraternity or sorority house (Wechsler et al., 2002).

The results of such studies are based on self-administered questionnaires, and participants' responses may have been biased. Perhaps binge drinkers are more (or less) likely than nondrinkers to even respond to such questionnaires. Still, the implications are clear: college drinking, certainly binge drinking, may be more common and more harmful than was previously believed. At the very least, it is a problem whose research time has come.

their jobs. MRI scans of chronic heavy drinkers have revealed damage in various regions of their brains and, correspondingly, impairments in their short–term memory, speed of thinking, attention skills, and balance (Grilly, 2006; Meyerhoff et al., 2004).

Individually, people vary in their patterns of alcohol abuse. Some drink large amounts of alcohol every day and keep drinking until intoxicated. Others go on periodic binges of heavy drinking that can last weeks or months. They may remain intoxicated for days and later be unable to remember anything about the period. Still others may limit their excessive drinking to weekends, evenings, or both.

ALCOHOL DEPENDENCE For many people, the pattern of alcohol misuse includes dependence. Their bodies build up a tolerance for alcohol, and they need to drink ever greater amounts to feel its effects. They also experience withdrawal when they stop drinking. Within hours their hands, tongue, and eyelids begin to shake; they feel weak and nauseated; they sweat and vomit; their heart beats rapidly; and their blood pressure rises. They may also become anxious, depressed, unable to sleep, or irritable (APA, 2000).

A small percentage of people who are dependent on alcohol experience a particularly dramatic withdrawal reaction called **delirium tremens ("the DTs"),** or **alcohol withdrawal delirium.** It consists of terrifying visual hallucinations that begin within three days after they stop or reduce their drinking. Some people see small, frightening animals chasing or crawling on them or objects dancing about in front of their eyes. Mark Twain gave a classic picture of delirium tremens in Huckleberry Finn's description of his father:

Substance misuse and sports fans
A problem that has received growing attention in recent years is the excessive intake of alcohol by fans at sporting events. While two soccer players were jumping for a high ball at this 2002 play-off game in Athens, Greece, fans of the rival teams—many of them intoxicated—ripped out plastic seats, threw flares on the field, and hurled coins and rocks at the players.

> *I don't know how long I was asleep, but . . . there was an awful scream and I was up. There was Pap looking wild, and skipping around every which way and yelling about snakes. He said they was crawling up on his legs; and then he would give a jump and scream, and say one had bit him on the cheek—but I couldn't see no snakes. He started and run round . . . hollering "Take him off! he's biting me on the neck!" I never see a man look so wild in the eyes. Pretty soon he . . . fell down panting; then he rolled over . . . kicking things every which way, and striking and grabbing at the air with his hands, and screaming . . . there was devils a-hold of him. He wore out by and by. . . . He says . . .*
> *"Tramp-tramp-tramp: that's the dead; tramp-tramp-tramp; they're coming after me; but I won't go. Oh, they're here; don't touch me. . . . They're cold; let go. . . ."*
> *Then he went down on all fours and crawled off, begging them to let him alone. . . .*
>
> *(Twain, 1885)*

Like most other alcohol withdrawal symptoms, the DTs usually run their course in two to three days. However, people who experience severe withdrawal reactions such as this may also have seizures, lose consciousness, suffer a stroke, or even die. Today certain medical procedures can help prevent or reduce such extreme reactions (Doweiko, 2006).

What Is the Personal and Social Impact of Alcoholism?
Alcoholism destroys millions of families, social relationships, and careers (Murphy et al., 2005; Nace, 2005). Medical treatment, lost productivity, and losses due to deaths from alcoholism cost society many billions of dollars annually. The disorder also plays a role in more than one-third of all suicides, homicides, assaults, rapes, and accidental deaths, including 30 percent of all fatal automobile accidents in the United States (Ksir et al., 2008; Doweiko, 2006; Yi et al., 2005). Altogether, intoxicated drivers are responsible for 12,000 deaths each year. More than 30 million adults (12.4 percent) have driven while intoxicated at least once in the past year (NSDUH, 2008).

•**delirium tremens (DTs)**•A dramatic withdrawal reaction experienced by some people who are alcohol-dependent. It consists of confusion, clouded consciousness, and terrifying visual hallucinations. Also called *alcohol withdrawal delirium.*

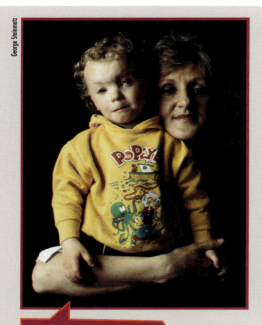

George Steinmetz

Fetal alcohol syndrome
Excessive alcohol use during pregnancy may cause a baby to be born with fetal alcohol syndrome. Individuals with this syndrome display a range of intellectual and physical problems, including the facial irregularities you see on this child.

•**Korsakoff's syndrome**•An alcohol-related disorder marked by extreme confusion, memory impairment, and other neurological symptoms.

•**fetal alcohol syndrome**•A cluster of problems in a child, including low birth weight, irregularities in the head and face, and intellectual deficits, caused by excessive alcohol intake by the mother during pregnancy.

•**sedative-hypnotic drug**•A drug used in low doses to reduce anxiety and in higher doses to help people sleep. Also called *anxiolytic drug.*

•**barbiturates**•Addictive sedative-hypnotic drugs that reduce anxiety and help produce sleep.

Alcoholism has serious effects on the 30 million children of persons with this disorder. Home life for these children is likely to include much conflict and perhaps sexual or other forms of abuse. In turn, the children themselves have higher rates of psychological problems such as anxiety, depression, phobias, conduct disorder, attention-deficit/hyperactivity disorder, and substance-related disorders during their lifetimes (Hall & Webster, 2002; Mylant et al., 2002). Many have low self-esteem, poor communication skills, poor sociability, and marital problems (Watt, 2002; Lewis-Harter, 2000).

Long-term excessive drinking can also seriously damage one's physical health (Myrick & Wright, 2008; Nace, 2005). It so overworks the liver that people may develop an irreversible condition called *cirrhosis,* in which the liver becomes scarred and dysfunctional. Cirrhosis accounts for more than 27,000 deaths each year (CDC, 2008). Alcohol abuse and dependence may also damage the heart and lower the immune system's ability to fight off cancer and bacterial infections and to resist the onset of AIDS after infection.

Long-term excessive drinking also causes major nutritional problems. Alcohol makes people feel full and lowers their desire for food, yet it has no nutritional value. As a result, chronic drinkers become malnourished, weak, and prone to disease. Their vitamin and mineral deficiencies may also cause problems. An alcohol-related deficiency of vitamin B (thiamine), for example, may lead to **Korsakoff's syndrome,** a disease marked by extreme confusion, memory loss, and other neurological symptoms (Doweiko, 2006). People with Korsakoff's syndrome cannot remember the past or learn new information and may make up for their memory losses by *confabulating*—reciting made-up events to fill in the gaps.

Finally, women who drink during pregnancy place their fetuses at risk (Finnegan & Kandall, 2008). Excessive alcohol use during pregnancy may cause a baby to be born with **fetal alcohol syndrome,** a pattern of abnormalities that can include mental retardation, hyperactivity, head and face deformities, heart defects, and slow growth (Grilly, 2006; Hankin, 2002). It has been estimated that in the overall population between 0.2 and 1.5 of every 1,000 babies is born with this syndrome (Ksir et al., 2008; Floyd & Sidhu, 2004). The rate may increase to as many as 29 of every 1,000 babies of women who are problem drinkers. If all alcohol-related birth defects are counted (known as *fetal alcohol effect*), the rate becomes 80 to 200 such births per 1,000 heavy-drinking women. In addition, heavy drinking early in pregnancy often leads to a miscarriage. According to surveys, 11.2 percent of pregnant American women have drunk alcohol during the past month and 4.5 percent of pregnant women had binge-drinking episodes (NSDUH, 2008).

Sedative-Hypnotic Drugs

Sedative-hypnotic drugs, also called **anxiolytic** (meaning "anxiety-reducing") **drugs,** produce feelings of relaxation and drowsiness. At low dosages, the drugs have a calming or sedative effect. At higher dosages, they are sleep inducers, or hypnotics. The sedative-hypnotic drugs include *barbiturates* and *benzodiazepines.*

Barbiturates
First discovered in Germany more than 100 years ago, **barbiturates** were widely prescribed in the first half of the twentieth century to fight anxiety and to help people sleep. Although still prescribed by some physicians, these drugs have been largely replaced by benzodiazepines, which are generally safer drugs. Barbiturates can cause many problems, not the least of which are abuse and dependence. Several thousand deaths a year are caused by accidental or suicidal overdoses.

Barbiturates are usually taken in pill or capsule form. In low doses they reduce a person's level of excitement in the same way that alcohol does, by attaching to receptors on the neurons that receive the inhibitory neurotransmitter GABA and by helping GABA operate at those neurons (Ksir et al., 2008; Grilly, 2006; Gao & Greenfield, 2005). People can get intoxicated from large doses of barbiturates, just as they do from alcohol. And, like alcohol, barbiturates are broken down in the liver. At high doses, barbiturates also depress the *reticular formation,* the part of the brain that normally keeps people awake, thus causing the person to get sleepy. At too high a level, the drugs can halt breathing, lower blood pressure, and lead to coma and death.

Repeated use of barbiturates can quickly result in a pattern of abuse (Dupont & Dupont, 2005). Users may spend much of the day intoxicated, irritable, and unable to do their work. Dependence can also result. The user organizes his or her life around the drug and needs increasing amounts of it to calm down or fall asleep. A great danger of barbiturate dependence is that the lethal dose of the drug remains the same even while the body is building up a tolerance for its sedating effects. Once the prescribed dose stops reducing anxiety or inducing sleep, the user is all too likely to increase it without medical supervision and eventually may ingest a dose that proves fatal. Those caught in a pattern of barbiturate dependence may also experience withdrawal symptoms such as nausea, anxiety, and sleep problems. Barbiturate withdrawal is particularly dangerous because it can cause convulsions.

Benzodiazepines Chapter 5 described **benzodiazepines,** the antianxiety drugs developed in the 1950s, as the most popular sedative-hypnotic drugs available. Xanax, Ativan, and Valium are just three of the dozens of these compounds in clinical use. Altogether, about 100 million prescriptions are written annually for this group of drugs (Bisaga, 2008). Like alcohol and barbiturates, they calm people by binding to receptors on the neurons that receive GABA and by increasing GABA's activity at those neurons (Ksir et al., 2008). These drugs, however, relieve anxiety without making people as drowsy as other kinds of sedative-hypnotics. They are also less likely to slow a person's breathing, so they are less likely to cause death in the event of an overdose (Nishino et al., 1995).

When benzodiazepines were first discovered, they seemed so safe and effective that physicians prescribed them generously, and their use spread. Eventually it became clear that in high enough doses the drugs can cause intoxication and lead to abuse or dependence (Bisaga, 2008; Dupont & Dupont, 2005). As many as 1 percent of the adults in North America abuse or become physically dependent on these antianxiety drugs at some point in their lives (Sareen et al., 2004; Goodwin et al, 2002; APA, 2000) and thus become subject to some of the same dangers that researchers have identified in barbiturate misuse.

Opioids

Opioids include opium—taken from the sap of the opium poppy—and the drugs derived from it, such as heroin, morphine, and codeine. **Opium** itself has been in use for thousands of years. In the past it was used widely in the treatment of medical disorders because of its ability to reduce both physical and emotional pain. Eventually, however, physicians discovered that the drug was physically addictive.

In 1804 a new substance, **morphine,** was derived from opium. Named after Morpheus, the Greek god of sleep, this drug relieved pain even better than opium did and initially was considered safe. However, wide use of the drug eventually revealed that it, too, could lead to addiction. So many wounded soldiers in the United States received morphine injections during the Civil War that morphine dependence became known as "soldiers' disease."

In 1898 morphine was converted into yet another new pain reliever, **heroin.** For several years heroin was viewed as a wonder drug and was used as a cough medicine and for other medical purposes. Eventually, however, physicians learned that heroin is even more addictive than the other opioids. By 1917 the U.S. Congress had concluded that all drugs derived from opium were addictive (see Table 12-3 on the next page), and it passed a law making opioids illegal except for medical purposes.

•**benzodiazepines**•The most common group of antianxiety drugs, which includes Valium and Xanax.

•**opioid**•Opium or any of the drugs derived from opium, including morphine, heroin, and codeine.

•**opium**•A highly addictive substance made from the sap of the opium poppy.

•**morphine**•A highly addictive substance derived from opium that is particularly effective in relieving pain.

•**heroin**•One of the most addictive substances derived from opium.

Purer blend
Heroin, derived from poppies such as these in Mexico, is purer and stronger today than it was in the 1980s (65 percent pure versus 5 percent pure).

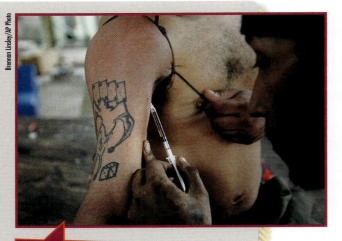

Injecting heroin
Opioids may be taken by mouth, inhaled, snorted, injected just beneath the surface of the skin, or injected intravenously. Here, one addict injects another with heroin inside one of the many so-called shooting galleries where addicts gather in downtown San Juan, Puerto Rico.

Still other drugs have been derived from opium, and *synthetic* (laboratory-blended) opioids such as *methadone* have also been developed. All these opioid drugs—natural and synthetic—are known collectively as *narcotics.* Each drug has a different strength, speed of action, and tolerance level. Morphine and *codeine* are medical narcotics usually prescribed to relieve pain. Heroin is illegal in the United States in all circumstances.

Narcotics are smoked, inhaled, snorted, injected by needle just beneath the skin ("skin popped"), or injected directly into the bloodstream ("mainlined"). Injection seems to be the most common method of narcotic use, although the other techniques have been used increasingly in recent years (NSDUH, 2008). An injection quickly brings on a *rush*—a spasm of warmth and ecstasy that is sometimes compared with orgasm. The brief spasm is followed by several hours of a pleasant feeling called a *high* or *nod.* During a high, the drug user feels relaxed, happy, and unconcerned about food, sex, or other bodily needs.

Opioids create these effects by depressing the central nervous system, particularly the centers that help control emotion. The drugs attach to brain receptor sites that ordinarily receive **endorphins**—neurotransmitters that help relieve pain and reduce emotional tension (Kreek, 2008; Ksir et al., 2008). When neurons at these receptor sites receive opioids, they produce pleasurable and calming feelings just as they would do if they were receiving endorphins. In addition to reducing pain and tension, opioids cause nausea, narrowing of the pupils ("pinpoint pupils"), and constipation—bodily reactions that can also be brought about by releases of endorphins in the brain.

Heroin Abuse and Dependence Heroin use exemplifies the kinds of problems posed by opioids. After taking heroin repeatedly for just a few weeks, users may become caught in a pattern of abuse: the drug interferes significantly with their social and occupational functioning. In most cases, heroin abuse leads to a pattern of dependence as well, and users soon center their lives on the substance, build a tolerance for it, and experience a withdrawal reaction when they stop taking it (Kreek, 2008; Ksir et al., 2008). At first the withdrawal symptoms are anxiety, restlessness, sweating, and rapid breathing; later they include severe twitching, aches, fever, vomiting, diarrhea, loss of appetite, high blood pressure, and weight loss of up to 15 pounds (due to loss of bodily fluids). These symptoms usually peak by the third day, gradually subside, and disappear by the eighth day. A person in withdrawal can either wait out the symptoms or end withdrawal by taking heroin again.

table: 12-3

Risks and Consequences of Drug Misuse

	Potential Intoxication	Dependency Potential	Risk of Organ Damage or Death	Risk of Severe Social or Economic Consequences	Risk of Severe or Long-Lasting Mental and Behavioral Change
Opioids	High	High	Low	High	Low to moderate
Sedative-hypnotics					
Barbiturates	Moderate	Moderate to high	Moderate to high	Moderate to high	Low
Benzodiazepines	Moderate	Moderate	Low	Low	Low
Stimulants (cocaine, amphetamines)	High	High	Moderate	Low to moderate	Moderate to high
Alcohol	High	Moderate	High	High	High
Cannabis	High	Low to moderate	Low	Low to moderate	Low
Mixed drugs	High	High	High	High	High

Source: Ksir et al., 2008; APA, 2000; Gold, 1986, p. 28.

People who are dependent on heroin soon need the drug just to avoid going into withdrawal, and they must continually increase their doses in order to achieve even that relief. The temporary high becomes less intense and less important. The individuals may spend much of their time planning their next dose, in many cases turning to criminal activities, such as theft and prostitution, to support the expensive "habit" (Allen, 2005).

Surveys suggest that close to 1 percent of adults in the United States become addicted to heroin or other opioids at some time in their lives (APA, 2000). The rate of such dependence dropped considerably during the 1980s, rose in the early 1990s, fell in the late 1990s, and now seems to be relatively high once again (NSDUH, 2008). The number of persons currently addicted to these drugs is estimated to be as much as 323,000. The actual number may be even higher, however, given the reluctance of many people to admit an illegal activity.

What Are the Dangers of Heroin Abuse? The most immediate danger of heroin use is an overdose, which closes down the respiratory center in the brain, almost paralyzing breathing and in many cases causing death. Death is particularly likely during sleep, when a person is unable to fight this effect by consciously working to breathe. People who resume heroin use after having avoided it for some time often make the fatal mistake of taking the same dose they had built up to before. Because their bodies have been without heroin for some time, however, they can no longer tolerate this high level. Each year approximately 2 percent of persons dependent on heroin and other opioids die under the drug's influence, usually from an overdose (Theodorou & Haber, 2005; APA, 2000).

Users run other risks as well. Often pushers mix heroin with a cheaper drug or even a deadly substance such as cyanide or battery acid. In addition, dirty needles and other unsterilized equipment spread infections such as AIDS, hepatitis C, and skin abscesses (Batki & Nathan, 2008; Kennedy et al., 2005). In some areas of the United States the HIV infection rate among persons dependent on heroin is reported to be as high as 60 percent (APA, 2000).

✿Stimulants

Stimulants are substances that increase the activity of the central nervous system, resulting in increased blood pressure and heart rate, greater alertness, and sped-up behavior and thinking. Among the most troublesome stimulants are *cocaine* and *amphetamines*, whose effects on people are very similar. When users report different effects, it is often because they have ingested different amounts of the drugs. Two other widely used and legal stimulants are *caffeine* and *nicotine* (see *A Closer Look* on the next page).

Cocaine

Cocaine—the central active ingredient of the coca plant, found in South America—is the most powerful natural stimulant now known. The drug was first separated from the plant in 1865. Native people of South America, however, have chewed the leaves of the plant since prehistoric times for the energy and alertness the drug offers. Processed cocaine (*hydrochloride powder*) is an odorless, white, fluffy powder. For recreational use, it is most often snorted so that it is absorbed through the mucous membrane of the nose. Some users prefer the more powerful effects of injecting cocaine intravenously or smoking it in a pipe or cigarette.

Sherlock Holmes took his bottle from the corner of the mantelpiece, and his hypodermic syringe from its neat morocco case. With his long white nervous fingers, he adjusted the delicate needle and rolled back his left shirtcuff. For some little time his eyes rested thoughtfully upon the sinewy forearm and wrist, all dotted and scarred with innumerable

•**endorphins**•Neurotransmitters that help relieve pain and reduce emotional tension. They are sometimes referred to as the body's own opioids.

•**cocaine**•An addictive stimulant obtained from the coca plant. It is the most powerful natural stimulant known.

▮▮▮ BETWEEN THE LINES ▮▮▮

Celebrities Who Have Acknowledged Past Substance Abuse or Dependence

Amy Winehouse, singer/songwriter ‹‹

Lindsay Lohan, actress ‹‹

Pete Doherty, rock musician ‹‹

David Crosby, musician ‹‹

Eminem, rapper ‹‹

Christian Slater, actor ‹‹

Drew Barrymore, actress ‹‹

Scott Weiland, rock singer ‹‹

Robert Downey Jr., actor ‹‹

Ron Wood, guitarist ‹‹

Melanie Griffith, actress ‹‹

Nick Cave, rock singer ‹‹

Juliette Lewis, actress ‹‹

Greg Allman, rock singer ‹‹

Dr. John, rock singer ‹‹

Charlie Sheen, actor ‹‹

Whitney Houston, singer ‹‹

James Hetfield, singer ‹‹

Matthew Perry, actor ‹‹

Pat O'Brien, interviewer ‹‹

Tobacco, Nicotine, and Addiction

Almost 30 percent of all Americans over the age of 11, around 73 million people, regularly smoke tobacco (NSDUH, 2008). Surveys also suggest that 22 percent of all high school seniors have smoked in the past month (Johnston et al., 2007). At the same time, 440,000 persons in the United States die each year as a result of smoking. Smoking is directly tied to high blood pressure, coronary heart disease, lung disease, cancer, strokes, and other deadly medical problems (George & Weinberger, 2008; Hymowitz, 2005; DeLaune & Schmitz, 2004). Nonsmokers who inhale cigarette smoke from their environment have a higher risk of lung cancer and other diseases. And the 16.4 percent of all pregnant women who smoke are more likely than nonsmokers to deliver premature and underweight babies (Ksir et al., 2008; NSDUH, 2008).

Research suggests that smoking may actually increase stress levels (Parrott, 2000, 1999), and most smokers know that smoking is unhealthy. Indeed, nearly 70 percent of all adolescents believe that it poses a great risk (NSDUH, 2008). So why do people continue to smoke? Because *nicotine,* the active substance in tobacco and a stimulant of the central nervous system, is as addictive as heroin, perhaps even more so (Ksir et al., 2008; Report of the Surgeon General, 1988). Indeed, the World Health

Organization estimates that 1.1 billion people worldwide are addicted to nicotine (Hasman & Holm, 2004). Regular smokers develop a tolerance for nicotine and must smoke more and more in order to achieve the same results (Hymowitz, 2005). When they try to stop smoking, they experience withdrawal symptoms—irritability, increased appetite, sleep disturbances, slower metabolism, cognitive difficulties, and cravings to smoke (Dodgen, 2005; APA, 2000). Nicotine acts on the same neurotransmitters and reward center in the brain as amphetamines and cocaine (George & Weinberger, 2008; Grilly, 2006). Inhaling a puff of cigarette smoke delivers a dose of nicotine to the brain faster than it could be delivered by injection into the bloodstream.

The declining acceptability of smoking in our society has created a market for products and techniques to help people kick the habit. Most of these methods do not work very well. Self-help kits, commercial programs, and support groups are of limited help. Smokers who do quit permanently tend to be successful only after several failed attempts.

One fairly successful behavioral treatment for nicotine addiction is *aversion therapy.* In one version of this approach, known as *rapid smoking,* the smoker sits in a closed room and puffs quickly on a

cigarette, as often as once every six seconds, until he or she begins to feel ill and cannot take another puff. The feelings of illness become associated with smoking, and the smoker develops an aversion to cigarettes (George & Weinberger, 2008; Spiegler & Guevremont, 2003).

Several biological treatments have also been developed. A common one is the use of *nicotine gum,* an over-the-counter product that contains a high level of nicotine that is released as the smoker chews. Theoretically, people who obtain nicotine by chewing will no longer feel a need to smoke. A similar approach is the *nicotine patch,* which is attached to the skin like a Band-Aid. Its nicotine is absorbed through the skin throughout the day, supposedly easing withdrawal and reducing the smoker's need for nicotine. Studies find that both nicotine gum and the nicotine patch help people to abstain from smoking (George & Weinberger, 2008; Grilly, 2006). Combining the two techniques, in proper quantities, has also shown promise.

Still another popular biological product is *nicotine lozenges.* In addition, *nicotine nasal spray,* a biological approach available by prescription, delivers nicotine to the brain much more rapidly than other methods. It can be used several times an hour, whenever the urge to smoke arises. Finally, the antidepressant drug *bupropion* (brand names Zyban and Wellbutrin) has demonstrated some success as a treatment for cigarette smoking (Buccafusco, 2004).

The more one smokes, the harder it is to quit. On the positive side, however, former smokers' risk of disease and death decreases steadily the longer they continue to avoid smoking. This assurance may be a powerful motivator for many smokers, and, in fact, around 46 percent of regular smokers want to stop and are eventually able to stop permanently (NSDUH, 2008). In the meantime, more than 1,000 people die of smoking-related diseases each day.

Genetics or modeling? A man smokes a cigarette while reading to his daughter under an overpass in Beijing, China. The tendency to smoke tobacco and become dependent on nicotine often runs in families. Researchers have found that both genetics and environment play key roles in such family trends (Rende et al., 2005).

Greg Baker/AP Photo

puncture-marks. Finally, he thrust the sharp point home, pressed down the tiny piston, and sank back into the velvet-lined armchair with a long sigh of satisfaction.

Three times a day for many months I had witnessed this performance, but custom had not reconciled my mind to it. . . .

"Which is it today," I asked, "morphine or cocaine?"

He raised his eyes languidly from the old black-letter volume which he had opened.

"It is cocaine," he said, "a seven-per-cent solution. Would you care to try it?"

"No, indeed," I answered brusquely. "My constitution has not got over the Afghan campaign yet. I cannot afford to throw any extra strain upon it."

He smiled at my vehemence. "Perhaps you are right, Watson," he said. "I suppose that its influence is physically a bad one. I find it, however, so transcendently stimulating and clarifying to the mind that its secondary action is a matter of small moment."

"But consider!" I said earnestly. "Count the cost! Your brain may, as you say, be roused and excited, but it is a pathological and morbid process which involves increased tissue-change and . . . a permanent weakness. You know, too, what a black reaction comes upon you. Surely, the game is hardly worth the candle."

(Doyle, 1938, pp. 91–92)

For years people believed that cocaine posed few problems aside from intoxication and, on occasion, temporary psychosis. Like Sherlock Holmes, many felt that the benefits outweighed the costs. Only later did researchers come to appreciate its many dangers. Their insights came after society witnessed a dramatic increase in the drug's popularity and in problems related to its use. In the early 1960s an estimated 10,000 persons in the United States had tried cocaine. Today 28 million people have tried it, and 2.4 million—most of them teenagers or young adults—are using it currently (NSDUH, 2008). In fact, 2 percent of all high school seniors have used cocaine within the past month and almost 6 percent have used it within the past year (Johnston et al., 2007).

Cocaine brings on a euphoric rush of well-being and confidence. Given a high enough dose, this rush can be almost orgasmic, like the one produced by heroin. At first cocaine stimulates the higher centers of the central nervous system, making users feel excited, energetic, talkative, and even euphoric. As more is taken, it stimulates other centers of the central nervous system, producing a faster pulse, higher blood pressure, faster and deeper breathing, and further arousal and wakefulness.

Cocaine apparently produces these effects largely by increasing supplies of the neurotransmitter *dopamine* at key neurons throughout the brain (Haney, 2008; Kosten et al., 2008; Messas et al., 2005) (see Figure 12-2). More precisely, cocaine prevents the neurons that release dopamine from reabsorbing it, as they normally would do. So excessive amounts of dopamine travel to receiving neurons throughout the central nervous system and over-stimulate them. In addition, cocaine appears to increase the activity of the neurotransmitters *norepinephrine* and *serotonin* in some areas of the brain (Haney, 2008; Ksir et al., 2008; Hall et al., 2004).

High doses of the drug produce *cocaine intoxication,* whose symptoms are poor muscle coordination, grandiosity, bad judgment, anger, aggression, compulsive behavior, anxiety, and confusion. Some people experience hallucinations, delusions, or both, a condition known as *cocaine-induced psychotic disorder* (APA, 2000).

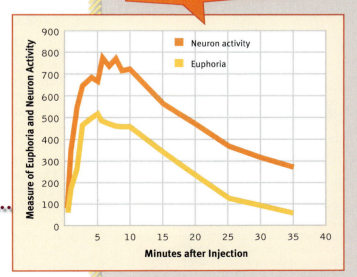

Figure 12-2

Biochemical euphoria The subjective experiences of euphoria after a cocaine injection closely parallel cocaine's action at dopamine-using neurons. The peak experience of euphoria seems to occur around the same time as the peak of neuron activity (Fowler, Volkow, & Wolf, 1995, p. 110; Cook, Jeffcoat, & Perez-Reyes, 1985).

A young man described how, after free-basing, he went to his closet to get his clothes, but his suit asked him, "What do you want?" Afraid, he walked toward the door, which told him, "Get back!" Retreating, he then heard the

Smoking crack
Crack, a powerful form of free-base cocaine, is produced by boiling cocaine down into crystalline balls and is smoked with a crack pipe.

sofa say, "If you sit on me, I'll kick your ass." With a sense of impending doom, intense anxiety, and momentary panic, the young man ran to the hospital where he received help.

(Allen, 1985, pp. 19–20)

As the stimulant effects of cocaine subside, the user experiences a depression-like letdown, popularly called crashing, a pattern that may also include headaches, dizziness, and fainting (Doweiko, 2002). For occasional users, the aftereffects usually disappear within 24 hours, but they may last longer for people who have taken a particularly high dose. These individuals may sink into a stupor, deep sleep, or, in some cases, coma.

Cocaine Abuse and Dependence Regular use of cocaine may lead to a pattern of abuse in which the person remains under its effects much of each day and functions poorly in social relationships and at work. Regular drug use may also cause problems in short-term memory or attention (Kubler et al., 2005). Dependence may also develop, so that cocaine dominates the person's life, higher doses are needed to gain the desired effects, and stopping it results in depression, fatigue, sleep problems, irritability, and anxiety (Ksir et al., 2008; Acosta et al., 2005). These withdrawal symptoms may last for weeks or even months after drug use has ended.

In the past, cocaine use and impact were limited by the drug's high cost. Moreover, cocaine was usually snorted, a form of ingestion that has less powerful effects than either smoking or injection. Since 1984, however, the availability of newer, more powerful, and sometimes cheaper forms of cocaine has produced an enormous increase in abuse and dependence. Currently, 0.7 percent of all people over the age of 11 in the United States, 1.7 million people, manifest cocaine abuse or dependence (NSDUH, 2008). Altogether one user in five falls into such a pattern. Many people now ingest cocaine by **free-basing,** a technique in which the pure cocaine basic alkaloid is chemically separated, or "freed," from processed cocaine, vaporized by heat from a flame, and inhaled through a pipe.

Millions more people use **crack,** a powerful form of free-base cocaine that has been boiled down into crystalline balls. It is smoked with a special pipe and makes a crackling sound as it is inhaled (hence the name). Crack is sold in small quantities at a fairly low cost, a practice that has resulted in crack epidemics among people who previously could not have afforded cocaine, primarily those in poor urban areas (Acosta et al., 2005). Almost 2 percent of high school seniors report having used crack within the past year, up from 1.5 percent in 1993, yet down from a peak of 2.7 percent in 1999 (Johnston et al., 2007).

What Are the Dangers of Cocaine? Aside from cocaine's harmful effects on behavior, the drug poses serious physical dangers (Kosten et al., 2008; Doweiko, 2006). Its growing use in powerful forms has caused the annual number of cocaine-related emergency room incidents in the United States to multiply 44 times since 1982, from around 4,000 cases to 450,000 (SAMHSA, 2007). In addition, cocaine use has been linked to as many as 20 percent of all suicides by men under 61 years of age (Garlow, 2002).

The greatest danger of cocaine use is an overdose. Excessive doses have a strong effect on the respiratory center of the brain, at first stimulating it and then depressing it, to the point where breathing may stop. Cocaine can also create major, even fatal, heart irregularities or brain seizures that bring breathing or heart functioning to a sudden stop (Ksir et al., 2008; Doweiko, 2006). In addition, pregnant women who use cocaine run the risk of having a miscarriage and of having children with abnormalities in immune functioning, attention and learning, thyroid size, and dopamine and serotonin activity in the brain (Kosten et al., 2008; Ksir et al., 2008; Delaney-Black et al., 2004).

•**free-base**•A technique for ingesting cocaine in which the pure cocaine basic alkaloid is chemically separated from processed cocaine, vaporized by heat from a flame, and inhaled with a pipe.

•**crack**•A powerful, ready-to-smoke free-base cocaine.

•**amphetamine**•A stimulant drug that is manufactured in the laboratory.

•**methamphetamine**•A powerful amphetamine drug that has experienced a surge in popularity in recent years, posing major health and law enforcement problems.

Amphetamines

The **amphetamines** are stimulant drugs that are manufactured in the laboratory. Some common examples are amphetamine (Benzedrine), dextroamphetamine (Dexedrine), and methamphetamine (Methedrine). First produced in the 1930s to help treat asthma, amphetamines soon became popular among people trying to lose weight; athletes seeking an extra burst of energy; soldiers, truck drivers, and pilots trying to stay awake; and students studying for exams through the night. Physicians now know the drugs are far too dangerous to be used so casually, and they prescribe them much less freely.

Amphetamines are most often taken in pill or capsule form, although some people inject the drugs intravenously or smoke them for a quicker, more powerful effect. Like cocaine, amphetamines increase energy and alertness and reduce appetite when taken in small doses; produce a rush, intoxication, and psychosis in high doses; and cause an emotional letdown as they leave the body. Also like cocaine, amphetamines stimulate the central nervous system by increasing the release of the neurotransmitters dopamine, norepinephrine, and serotonin throughout the brain, although the actions of amphetamines differ somewhat from those of cocaine (Haney, 2008; Ksir et al., 2008; Rawson & Ling, 2008).

Tolerance to amphetamines builds very quickly, so users are at great risk of becoming dependent (Acosta et al., 2005). People who start using the drug to reduce their appetite and weight, for example, may soon find they are as hungry as ever and increase their dose in response. Athletes who use amphetamines to increase their energy may also find before long that larger and larger amounts of the drug are needed. So-called speed freaks, who pop pills all day for days at a time, have built a tolerance so high that they now take as much as 200 times their initial amphetamine dose. When people who depend on the drug stop taking it, they plunge into a deep depression and extended sleep identical to the withdrawal from cocaine. Around 0.4 percent of adults—390,000 people—display amphetamine abuse or dependence each year (NSDUH, 2008). Approximately 1.5 to 2 percent become dependent on amphetamines at some point in their lives (APA, 2000; Anthony et al., 1995).

One kind of amphetamine, **methamphetamine** (nicknamed *crank*), has had a major surge in popularity in recent years and so warrants special focus. Almost 6 percent of all persons over the age of 11 in the United States have used this stimulant at least once. Around 0.3 percent, 731,000 individuals, use it currently (NSDUH, 2008). It is available in the form of crystals (also known by the street names *ice* and *crystal meth*), which are smoked by users.

Most of the nonmedical methamphetamine in the United States is made in small "stovetop laboratories," which typically operate for a few days in a remote area and then move on to a new—safer—location (Ksir et al., 2008). Such laboratories have been around since the 1960s, but they have increased eightfold—in number, production, and confiscations by authorities—over the past decade. A major health concern is that the secret laboratories expel dangerous fumes and residue (Burgess, 2001).

Since 1989, when the media first began reporting about the dangers of smoking methamphetamine crystals, the rise in usage has been dramatic. In 1994 fewer than 4 million Americans had tried this stimulant at least once. That number rose to more than 9 million in 1999 and is 15 million today (NSDUH, 2008). Until recently, use of this drug has been much more prevalent in western parts of the United States (NSDUH, 2007). Just a few years ago people in western states were more than twice as likely to use methamphetamine as those in midwestern and southern states and 12 times as likely as those in northeastern states. However, there is evidence that its use is now spreading east. For example, treatment admissions for methamphetamine abuse are on the increase in New York, Atlanta, Minneapolis/St. Paul, and St. Louis (Ksir et al., 2008; CEWG, 2004). Similarly, methamphetamine-linked emergency room visits are rising in hospitals throughout all parts of the country (DAWN, 2008).

National Pictures/Topham/The Image Works

DON'T LET DRUG DEALERS CHANGE THE FACE OF YOUR NEIGHBOURHOOD.
Call Crimestoppers anonymously on 0800 555 111.

Methamphetamine dependence: spreading the word
This powerful ad shows the degenerative effects of methamphetamine addiction on a woman over a four-year period—from age 36 in the top photo to age 40 in the bottom one.

Over-the-counter problems
Partly because many over-the-counter cold and allergy medicines contain *pseudoephedrine,* a key ingredient in the production of methamphetamine, a number of states have passed laws that restrict or limit the sale of such medicines.

Methamphetamine is about as likely to be used by women as men. Around 40 percent of current users are women (NSDUH, 2008). The drug is particularly popular today among biker gangs, rural Americans, and urban gay communities and has gained wide use as a "club drug," the term for those drugs that regularly find their way to all night dance parties, or "raves" (Ksir et al., 2008).

Like other kinds of amphetamines, methamphetamine increases activity of the neurotransmitters dopamine, serotonin, and norepinephrine, producing increased arousal, attention, and related effects (Rawson & Ling, 2008). It can have serious negative effects on a user's physical, mental, and social life (NSDUH, 2007). Of particular concern is that it damages nerve endings—a *neurotoxicity* that is accentuated by the fact that the drug stays in the brain and body for a relatively long time (more than 6 hours) (Rawson & Ling, 2008). But among users, such issues are overridden by methamphetamine's immediate positive impact, including perceptions by many that it makes them feel hypersexual and uninhibited (Jefferson, 2005)—all of which has contributed to several major societal problems. In the public health arena, for example, one-third of all men who tested positive for HIV in Los Angeles in 2004 reported having used this drug. In the area of law enforcement, one survey of police agencies had 58 percent of them reporting that methamphetamine is the leading drug they battle today. Similarly, surveys indicate that over the past few years, an increasing number of domestic violence incidents, assaults, and robberies have been tied to the use of methamphetamine.

Caffeine

Caffeine is the world's most widely used stimulant. Around 80 percent of the world's population consumes it daily (Rogers, 2005). Most of this caffeine is taken in the form of coffee (from the coffee bean); the rest is consumed in tea (from the tea leaf), cola (from the kola nut), so-called *energy drinks,* chocolate (from the cocoa bean), and numerous prescription and over-the-counter medications, such as Excedrin.

Around 99 percent of ingested caffeine is absorbed by the body and reaches its peak concentration within an hour. It acts as a stimulant of the central nervous system, again producing a release of the neurotransmitters dopamine, serotonin, and norepinephrine in the brain (Julien, 2008; Cauli & Morelli, 2005). Thus it increases arousal and motor activity and reduces fatigue. It can also disrupt mood, fine motor movement, and reaction time and may interfere with sleep (Judelson et al., 2005; Thompson & Keene, 2004). Finally, at high doses, it increases the rate of breathing and gastric acid secretions in the stomach (Ksir et al., 2008).

More than two to three cups of brewed coffee (250 milligrams of caffeine) can produce caffeine intoxication, which may include such symptoms as restlessness, nervousness, anxiety, stomach disturbances, twitching, and increased heart rate (Paton & Beer, 2001; APA, 2000). Grand mal seizures and fatal respiratory failure or circulatory failure can occur at doses greater than 10 grams of caffeine (about 100 cups of coffee).

Many people who suddenly stop or cut back on their usual intake of caffeine experience withdrawal symptoms—even some individuals whose regular consumption is low (two and a half cups of coffee daily or seven cans of cola). One study had adult participants consume their usual caffeine-filled drinks and foods for two days, then abstain from all caffeine-containing foods for two days while taking placebo pills that they thought contained caffeine, and then abstain from such foods for two days while taking actual caffeine pills (Silverman et al., 1992). More participants experienced headaches (52 percent), depression (11 percent), anxiety (8 percent), and fatigue (8 percent) during the two-day placebo period than during the caffeine periods. In addition, people reported using more unauthorized medications (13 percent) and performed experimental tasks more slowly during the placebo period than during the caffeine periods.

Investigators often assess caffeine's impact by measuring coffee consumption, yet coffee also contains other chemicals that may be dangerous to one's health. Although some early studies hinted at links between caffeine and cancer (particularly pancreatic cancer), the evidence is not conclusive (Ksir et al., 2008). On the other hand, studies do

BETWEEN THE LINES

Coffee Shops: A Growth Industry

200	The number of specialty coffee shops in the U.S. in 1989 ‹‹
15,000	The number of such shops today ‹‹

(Pressler, 2004)

"Say when."

suggest that there may be correlations between high doses of caffeine and heart rhythm irregularities (arrhythmias), high cholesterol levels, and risk of heart attacks (Ksir et al., 2008). And it appears that high doses of caffeine during pregnancy increase the risk of miscarriage (Weng, Odouli, & Li, 2008). As public awareness of these possible health risks has increased, caffeine consumption has declined and the consumption of decaffeinated drinks has increased over the past few decades. There are, however, indications that caffeine consumption may currently be on the rise once again (Ksir et al., 2008; Vega, 2008; Pressler, 2004).

☀Hallucinogens, Cannabis, and Combinations of Substances

Other kinds of substances may also cause problems for their users and for society. *Hallucinogens* produce delusions, hallucinations, and other sensory changes. *Cannabis substances* produce sensory changes, but they also have depressant and stimulant effects, and so they are considered apart from hallucinogens in DSM-IV-TR. And many individuals take *combinations of substances.*

Hallucinogens

Hallucinogens are substances that cause powerful changes in sensory perception, from strengthening a person's normal perceptions to inducing illusions and hallucinations. They produce sensations so out of the ordinary that they are sometimes called "trips." The trips may be exciting or frightening, depending on how a person's mind interacts with the drugs. Also called *psychedelic drugs,* the hallucinogens include LSD, mescaline, psilocybin, and MDMA (Ecstasy) (see *Psych Watch* on pages 392–393). Many of these substances come from plants or animals; others are laboratory-produced.

LSD (lysergic acid diethylamide), one of the most famous and most powerful hallucinogens, was derived by Swiss chemist Albert Hoffman in 1938 from a group of naturally occurring drugs called *ergot alkaloids.* During the 1960s, a decade of social rebellion and experimentation, millions of persons turned to the drug as a way of

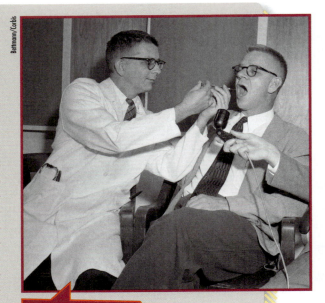

Early LSD research

In the 1950s, researchers came to believe that LSD produced a "model psychosis" and that studying its effects might offer insights into schizophrenia. Not yet recognizing how powerful and dangerous this drug can be, however, early investigators sometimes conducted LSD research in a naïve and casual manner. This 1955 photo shows one researcher administering LSD to another in Emory University's Pharmacological Department.

•**cannabis drugs**•Drugs produced from the varieties of the hemp plant *Cannabis sativa.* They cause a mixture of hallucinogenic, depressant, and stimulant effects.

•**marijuana**•One of the cannabis drugs, derived from buds, leaves, and flowering tops of the hemp plant *Cannabis sativa.*

•**tetrahydrocannabinol (THC)**•The main active ingredient of cannabis substances.

expanding their experience. Within two hours of being swallowed, LSD brings on a state of *hallucinogen intoxication,* sometimes called *hallucinosis,* marked by a general strengthening of perceptions, particularly visual perceptions, along with psychological changes and physical symptoms. People may focus on small details—the pores of the skin, for example, or individual blades of grass. Colors may seem enhanced or take on a shade of purple. Illusions may be experienced in which objects seem distorted and may appear to move, breathe, or change shape. A person under the influence of LSD may also hallucinate—seeing people, objects, or forms that are not actually present.

Hallucinosis may also cause one to hear sounds more clearly, feel tingling or numbness in the limbs, or confuse the sensations of hot and cold. Some people have been badly burned after touching flames that felt cool to them under the influence of LSD. The drug may also cause different senses to cross, an effect called *synesthesia.* Colors, for example, may be "heard" or "felt."

LSD can also induce strong emotions, from joy to anxiety or depression. The perception of time may slow dramatically. Long-forgotten thoughts and feelings may resurface. Physical symptoms can include sweating, palpitations, blurred vision, tremors, and poor coordination. All of these effects take place while the user is fully awake and alert, and they wear off in about six hours.

It seems that LSD produces these symptoms primarily by binding to some of the neurons that normally receive the neurotransmitter *serotonin,* changing the neurotransmitter's activity at those sites (Julien, 2008; Ksir et al., 2008; Appel, West, & Buggy, 2004). These neurons ordinarily help the brain send visual information and control emotions (as you saw in Chapter 8); thus LSD's activity there produces various visual and emotional symptoms.

More than 14 percent of all persons in the United States have used LSD or another hallucinogen at some point in their lives. Around 0.4 percent, or 1.6 million persons, are currently using them (NSDUH, 2008). Although people do not usually develop tolerance to LSD or have withdrawal symptoms when they stop taking it, the drug poses dangers for both one-time and long-term users. It is so powerful that any dose, no matter how small, is likely to produce enormous perceptual, emotional, and behavioral reactions. Sometimes the reactions are extremely unpleasant—an experience called a "bad trip." Reports of LSD users who injure themselves or others usually involve a reaction of this kind:

A 21-year-old woman was admitted to the hospital along with her lover. He had had a number of LSD experiences and had convinced her to take it to make her less constrained sexually. About half an hour after ingestion of approximately 200 microgm., she noticed that the bricks in the wall began to go in and out and that light affected her strangely. She became frightened when she realized that she was unable to distinguish her body from the chair she was sitting on or from her lover's body. Her fear became more marked after she thought that she would not get back into herself. At the time of admission she was hyperactive and laughed inappropriately. Her stream of talk was illogical and affect labile. Two days later, this reaction had ceased.

(Frosch, Robbins, & Stern, 1965)

Another danger is the long-term effect that LSD may have (Weaver & Schnoll, 2008). Some users eventually develop psychosis or a mood or anxiety disorder. And a number have *flashbacks*—a recurrence of the sensory and emotional changes after the LSD has left the body (Doweiko, 2006; Halpern et al., 2003). Flashbacks may occur days or even months after the last LSD experience. Although they typically become less severe and disappear within several months, some people report flashbacks a year or more after taking the drug.

Cannabis

Cannabis sativa, the hemp plant, grows in warm climates throughout the world. The drugs produced from varieties of hemp are, as a group, called **cannabis.** The most powerful of them is *hashish;* the weaker ones include the best-known form of cannabis, **marijuana,** a mixture derived from the buds, crushed leaves, and flowering tops of hemp plants. Each of these drugs is found in various strengths because the potency of a cannabis drug is greatly affected by the climate in which the plant is grown, the way it was prepared, and the manner and duration of its storage. Of the several hundred active chemicals in cannabis, **tetrahydrocannabinol (THC)** appears to be the one most responsible for its effects. The greater the THC content, the more powerful the cannabis: hashish contains a large portion, while marijuana's is small.

Vaughan Fleming/Science Photo Library/Photo Researchers

When smoked, cannabis produces a mixture of hallucinogenic, depressant, and stimulant effects. At low doses, the smoker typically has feelings of joy and relaxation and may become either quiet or talkative. Some smokers, however, become anxious, suspicious, or irritated, especially if they have been in a bad mood or are smoking in an upsetting environment. Many smokers report sharpened perceptions and fascination with the intensified sounds and sights around them. Time seems to slow down, and distances and sizes seem greater than they actually are. This overall "high" is technically called *cannabis intoxication.* Physical changes include reddening of the eyes, fast heartbeat, increases in blood pressure and appetite, dryness in the mouth, and dizziness. Some people become drowsy and may fall asleep.

In high doses, cannabis produces odd visual experiences, changes in body image, and hallucinations. Smokers may become confused or impulsive. Some worry that other people are trying to hurt them. Most of the effects of cannabis last two to six hours. The changes in mood, however, may continue longer.

Marijuana Abuse and Dependence Until the early 1970s, the use of marijuana, the weak form of cannabis, rarely led to a pattern of abuse or dependence. Today, however, many people, including large numbers of high school students, are caught in a pattern of marijuana abuse, getting high on marijuana regularly and finding their social and occupational or academic lives greatly affected (see Figure 12-3). Many regular users also become physically dependent on marijuana. They develop a tolerance for it and may experience flulike symptoms, restlessness, and irritability when they stop smoking (Chen et al., 2005; Smith, 2002; Kouri & Pope, 2000). Around 1.7 percent of all persons in the United States—4.2 million people—have displayed marijuana abuse or dependence in the past year; between 4 and 5 percent fall into one of these patterns at some point in their lives (NSDUH, 2008; APA, 2000).

Why have patterns of marijuana abuse and dependence increased in the last three decades? Mainly because the drug has changed (Doweiko, 2006). The marijuana widely available in the United States today is at least four times more powerful

Figure 12-3

How easy is it for teenagers to acquire substances? Most surveyed tenth graders say it is easy to get cigarettes, alcohol, and marijuana, and around one-third say it is easy to get Ecstasy, amphetamines, steroids, and barbiturates (Johnston et al., 2007).

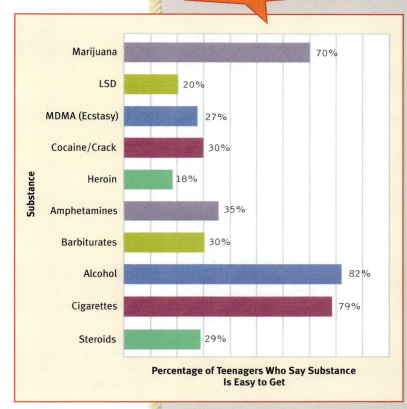

Percentage of Teenagers Who Say Substance Is Easy to Get

Substance	%
Marijuana	70%
LSD	20%
MDMA (Ecstasy)	27%
Cocaine/Crack	30%
Heroin	18%
Amphetamines	35%
Barbiturates	30%
Alcohol	82%
Cigarettes	79%
Steroids	29%

Club Drugs: X Marks the (Wrong) Spot

Club drugs, drugs that are extremely popular at those all-night techno-dance parties known as "raves," seem to follow a particular course. Typically, the drugs have been around for awhile prior to their emergence as the substance du jour, their "special" effects are at some point discovered by young partygoers, their popularity spreads far beyond the party scene, the drugs eventually receive serious research, they are found to produce some significant undesired effects, and their popularity as recreational drugs start to decline. This pattern was followed by past club drugs such as *GHB, Rohypnol,* and *LSD,* and it now seems to be under way for today's leading club drugs, *crystal meth* and *MDMA.* Let's take a closer look at MDMA to see how the pattern is playing out so far.

You probably know of the drug *MDMA (3,4-methylenedioxymethamphetamine)* by its common street name, *Ecstasy.* It is also known as X, Adam, hug, beans, and love drug. This laboratory-produced drug is technically a *stimulant,* similar to amphetamines, but it also produces hallucinogenic effects and so is often considered a *hallucinogenic* drug. MDMA was developed as far back as 1910, but only in the past two decades has it gained life as a club drug. Today, in the United States alone, consumers collectively take hundreds of thousands of doses of MDMA weekly (Weaver & Schnoll, 2008; McDowell, 2005).

What is Ecstasy's allure? As a stimulant and hallucinogen, it helps to raise the mood of many partygoers and provides them with an energy boost that enables them to keep dancing and partying. Suspecting that Ecstasy might have a number of hidden dangers, the federal government banned its use in 1985. However, this taboo status seemed only to make it more attractive to many consumers, and its popularity has continued to climb ever since. Altogether, 12 million Americans over the age of 11 have now tried MDMA at least once in their lifetimes, 2 million in the past year (NSDUH, 2008). Around 6.5 percent of all high school seniors have used it within the past year, and, indeed, more than 1.6 percent of seniors have used it within the past month (Johnston et al., 2007). Use of the drug is even more widespread among 18-to-25-year-olds (NSDUH, 2008).

Houston Scott/Corbis Sygma

Feeling the effects Shortly after taking MDMA, this couple manifests a shift in mood, energy, and behavior. Although this drug can feel pleasurable and energizing, often it produces undesired immediate effects, including confusion, depression, anxiety, sleep difficulties, and paranoid thinking.

than that used in the early 1970s. The THC content of today's marijuana is, on average, 8 percent, compared to 2 percent in the late 1960s (APA, 2000). Marijuana is now grown in places with a hot, dry climate, which increases the THC content.

Is Marijuana Dangerous? As the strength and use of marijuana have increased, researchers have discovered that smoking it may pose certain dangers. It occasionally causes panic reactions similar to the ones caused by hallucinogens, and some smokers may fear they are losing their minds (Doweiko, 2006; APA, 2000). Typically such reactions end in three to six hours, along with marijuana's other effects.

Because marijuana can interfere with the performance of complex sensorimotor tasks and with cognitive functioning, it has caused many automobile accidents (Kauert & Iwersen-Bergmann, 2004; Ramaekers et al., 2006). Furthermore, people on a marijuana high often fail to remember information, especially anything that has been recently

What Are the Dangers of Using Ecstasy?

As MDMA has gained wider and wider use, the drug has received increasing research scrutiny. As it turns out, the mood and energy lift produced by MDMA comes at a high price (Ksir et al., 2008; Weaver & Schnoll, 2008; Wiegand et al., 2008; Zakzanis et al., 2007; Braback & Humble, 2001). The problems that the drug may cause include the following:

- Immediate psychological problems such as confusion, depression, sleep difficulties, severe anxiety, and paranoid thinking. These symptoms may also continue for weeks after ingestion of MDMA.

- Significant impairment of memory and other cognitive skills.

- Physical symptoms such as muscle tension, nausea, blurred vision, faintness, and chills or sweating. MDMA also causes many people to clench and grind their teeth for hours at a time.

- Increases in heart rate and blood pressure, which place people with heart disease at special risk.

- Reduced sweat production. At a hot, crowded dance party, taking Ecstasy can even cause heat stroke, or *hyperthermia*. Users generally try to remedy this problem by drinking lots of water, but since the body cannot sweat under the drug's influence, the excess fluid intake can result in an equally perilous condition known as *hyponatremia*, or "water intoxication."

- Potential liver damage. This may happen when users take MDMA in combination with other drugs that are broken down by the same liver enzyme, such as the cheaper compound *DXM*, which is commonly mixed in with Ecstasy by dealers.

How Does MDMA Operate in the Brain?

MDMA works by causing the neurotransmitters *serotonin* and (to a lesser extent) *dopamine* to be released all at once throughout the brain, at first increasing and then depleting a person's overall supply of the neurotransmitters (Ksir et al., 2008; Malberg & Bonson, 2001). MDMA also interferes with the body's ability to produce new supplies of serotonin, reducing the availability of the neurotransmitter still further. With chronic use, the brain eventually produces less and less serotonin and shuts down the neuron receptors to which it normally binds (Baggot & Mendelson, 2001).

Ecstasy's impact on these neurotransmitters accounts for its various psychological effects—and associated problems. High levels of serotonin, such as those produced after one first ingests MDMA, produce feelings of well-being, sociability, and even euphoria. Remember, though, that MDMA also increases levels of dopamine. As you will see in Chapter 14, very high levels of that neurotransmitter can produce paranoid—even psychotic—thinking.

Conversely, abnormally low serotonin levels are associated with depression and anxiety. This is why "coming down" off a dose of Ecstasy often produces those psychological symptoms (Malberg & Bonson, 2001). Moreover, because repeated use of Ecstasy leads to long-term serotonin deficits, the depression and anxiety may be long-lasting. Finally, serotonin is linked to our ability to concentrate; thus the repeated use of Ecstasy may produce problems in memory and learning (Zakzanis et al., 2007; Heffernan et al., 2001; Rodgers, 2000).

End of the Honeymoon?

The dangers of MDMA do not yet seem to outweigh its pleasures in the minds of many individuals. In fact, use of the drug is still expanding to many social settings beyond raves, dance clubs, and college scenes (Weaver & Schnoll, 2008). Clearly, the honeymoon for this drug is not yet over. MDMA emergency room visits are on the rise, however, as is the number of deaths caused by the drug, for reasons ranging from kidney failure (the result of heat stroke) to liver failure to a heart attack. Like other club drugs over the years, it will probably lose its popularity eventually, but obviously not before it has taken a considerable toll.

---

learned, no matter how hard they try to concentrate; thus heavy marijuana smokers are at a serious disadvantage at school or work (Lundqvist, 2005; Ashton, 2001).

One study compared blood flow in the brain arteries of chronic marijuana users and nonusers (Herning et al., 2005). After one month of abstinence from smoking marijuana, chronic users continued to display higher blood flow than nonusers. Though still higher than normal, the blood flow of light marijuana users (fewer than 16 smokes per week) and of moderate users (fewer than 70 smokes per week) did improve somewhat over the course of the abstinence month. The blood flow of heavy users, however, showed no improvement. This lingering effect may help explain the memory and thinking problems of chronic heavy users of marijuana.

There are indications that regular marijuana smoking may also lead to long-term health problems (Deplanque, 2005). It may, for example, contribute to lung disease. Studies show that marijuana smoking reduces the ability to expel air from the lungs

(Tashkin, 2001) even more than tobacco smoking does (NIDA, 2002). In addition, marijuana smoke contains more tar and benzopyrene than tobacco smoke (Ksir et al., 2008). Both of these substances have been linked to cancer. Another concern is the effect of regular marijuana smoking on human reproduction. Studies since the late 1970s have discovered lower sperm counts in men who are chronic smokers of marijuana, and abnormal ovulation has been found in female smokers (Schuel et al., 2002).

Efforts to educate the public about the growing dangers of repeated marijuana use appeared to have paid off throughout the 1980s. The percentage of high school seniors who smoked the substance on a daily basis decreased from 11 percent in 1978 to 2 percent in 1992 (Johnston et al., 1993). Furthermore, in 1992 about 77 percent of high school seniors believed that regular marijuana smoking poses a serious health risk, a much higher percentage than that in earlier years. However, marijuana use among the young jumped up again during the 1990s. Today 5 percent of high school seniors smoke marijuana daily, and around 55 percent believe that regular use can be harmful (Johnston et al., 2007) (see Figure 12-4).

Cannabis and Society: A Rocky Relationship For centuries cannabis played a respected role in medicine. It was recommended as a surgical anesthetic by Chinese physicians 2,000 years ago and was used in other lands to treat cholera, malaria, coughs, insomnia, and rheumatism. When cannabis entered the United States in the early twentieth century, mainly in the form of marijuana, it was likewise used for various medical purposes. Soon, however, more effective medicines replaced it, and the favorable view of cannabis began to change. Marijuana began to be used as a recreational drug, and its illegal distribution became a law enforcement problem. Authorities assumed it was highly dangerous and outlawed the "killer weed."

But marijuana didn't go away. During the 1960s, a time of disillusionment, protest, and self-exploration, young people discovered the pleasures of getting high from smoking marijuana. By the end of the 1970s, 16 million people reported using it at least once, and 11 percent of the population were recent users.

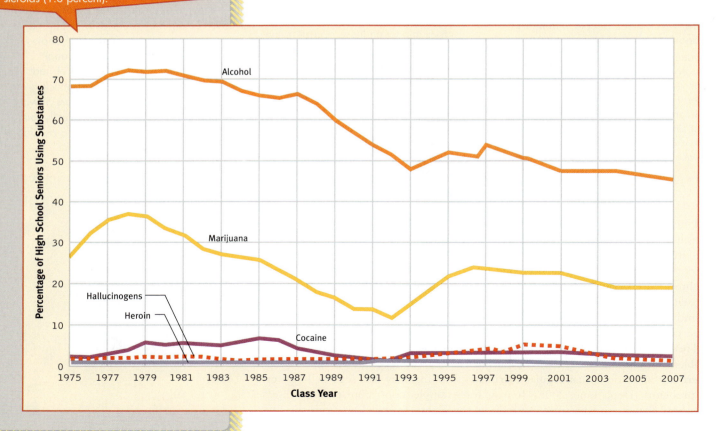

Figure 12-4

Teenagers and substance use The overall percentage of high school seniors who admitted to using substances illicitly at least once within the previous 30 days rose in the 1970s, declined in the 1980s, rose again in the early 1990s, and has been declining slightly since 1997 (Johnston et al., 2007). In addition to the drugs shown in this figure, other drugs used by high school seniors within the past month include MDMA, or Ecstasy (1.6 percent); inhalants (1.2 percent); methamphetamine (1.2 percent); and steroids (1.0 percent).

In the 1980s researchers developed precise techniques for measuring THC and for extracting pure THC from cannabis; they also developed laboratory forms of THC. These inventions opened the door to new medical applications for cannabis (Mack & Joy, 2001; Watson et al., 2000), such as its use in treating glaucoma, a severe eye disease. Cannabis was also found to help patients with chronic pain or asthma, to reduce the nausea and vomiting of cancer patients in chemotherapy, and to improve the appetites of AIDS patients and so combat weight loss in people with that disorder.

In light of these findings, several interest groups campaigned during the late 1980s for the *medical legalization* of marijuana, which operates on the brain and body more quickly than the THC capsules developed in the laboratory. In 1992, however, the Food and Drug Administration stopped reviewing requests for the "compassionate use" of marijuana. They held that prescriptions for pure THC served all needed medical functions. In turn, advocates of the medical use of marijuana stepped up their efforts, and indeed since 1996, 12 states have passed legislation giving physicians the right to prescribe marijuana for "seriously ill" or "terminally ill" patients, and the *New England Journal of Medicine,* one of the world's most prestigious medical publications, has even published an editorial favoring the medical use of marijuana.

Unfazed, the federal government has continued to fight and punish the production and distribution of marijuana for medical purposes. In 2005, the United States Supreme Court ruled 6 to 3 that medically ill marijuana smokers and those who help them grow or obtain marijuana can be prosecuted, even if their physicians prescribe it and even if they live in states where medical marijuana use is legal. Although this ruling was initially considered a blow to the medical marijuana cause, proponents have fought on; many are following the advice of Supreme Court Justice John Paul Stevens, who, writing for the majority in the ruling, suggested that users of medical marijuana look to Congress to overturn the laws against medical marijuana. And, indeed, Congress is currently considering several bills and amendments that would protect both medical marijuana patients and prescribing physicians.

In the meantime, the Canadian government has taken a different tack. Based on a series of studies and trial programs, Health Canada, the country's health care regulator, now permits the medical use of marijuana by individuals who are suffering from severe and debilitating illnesses, and it allows the sale of medical marijuana in select pharmacies, making Canada the second country in the world, after the Netherlands, to do so.

Dino Vournas/AP Photo

Medicinal use
Prior to the 2005 Supreme Court ruling that even medically ill marijuana smokers can be prosecuted for use of the substance, a number of medicinal cannabis shops opened throughout the United States. Here a medical marijuana patient (left), assisted by a volunteer, smells the different offerings at one such venue, the Love Shack medicinal cannabis shop in San Francisco.

Combinations of Substances

Because people often take more than one drug at a time, a pattern called *polysubstance use,* researchers have studied the ways in which drugs interact with one another. Two important discoveries have emerged from this work: the phenomena of *cross-tolerance* and *synergistic effects.*

Sometimes two or more drugs are so similar in their actions on the brain and the body that as people build a tolerance for one drug, they are simultaneously developing a tolerance for the other, even if they have never taken the latter. Correspondingly, users who display such **cross-tolerance** can reduce the symptoms of withdrawal from one drug by taking the other. Alcohol and antianxiety drugs are cross-tolerant, for example, so it is sometimes possible to reduce the alcohol withdrawal reaction of delirium tremens by administering benzodiazepines, along with vitamins and electrolytes (Ksir et al., 2008; Doweiko, 2006).

When different drugs are in the body at the same time, they may multiply, or potentiate, each other's effects. The combined impact, called a **synergistic effect,** is often greater than the sum of the effects of each drug taken alone: a small dose of one

•**cross-tolerance**•Tolerance for a substance one has not taken before as a result of using another substance similar to it.

•**synergistic effect**•In pharmacology, an increase of effects that occurs when more than one substance is acting on the body at the same time.

Frank Franklin II/AP Photo

Continuing problem
A number of popular performers have been victims of polysubstance misuse or abuse. The 2004 death of popular rap musician Russell Jones (left), known to fans as Ol' Dirty Bastard, was attributed to a lethal mixture of cocaine and pain medication. Similarly, the 2008 death of actor Heath Ledger (right), seen here as the Joker in the film *The Dark Knight*, was caused by a lethal combination of prescribed pain relievers, benzodiazepines, a sleep medication, and an antihistamine.

LILO/SIPA/Newscom

•**polysubstance-related disorder**•A long-term pattern of maladaptive behavior centered on abuse of or dependence on a combination of drugs.

drug mixed with a small dose of another can produce an enormous change in body chemistry.

One kind of synergistic effect occurs when two or more drugs have *similar actions.* For instance, alcohol, benzodiazepines, barbiturates, and opioids—all depressants—may severely depress the central nervous system when mixed (Ksir et al., 2008). Combining them, even in small doses, can lead to extreme intoxication, coma, and even death. A young man may have just a few alcoholic drinks at a party, for example, and shortly afterward take a moderate dose of barbiturates to help him fall asleep. He believes he has acted with restraint and good judgment—yet he may never wake up.

A different kind of synergistic effect results when drugs have *opposite,* or *antagonistic, actions.* Stimulant drugs, for example, interfere with the liver's usual disposal of barbiturates and alcohol. Thus people who combine barbiturates or alcohol with cocaine or amphetamines may build up toxic, even lethal, levels of the depressant drugs in their systems. Students who take amphetamines to help them study late into the night and then take barbiturates to help them fall asleep are unknowingly placing themselves in serious danger.

Each year tens of thousands of people are admitted to hospitals with a multiple-drug emergency, and several thousand of them die (SAMHSA, 2007). Sometimes the cause is carelessness or ignorance. Often, however, people use multiple drugs precisely because they enjoy the synergistic effects. In fact, **polysubstance-related disorders** are becoming as common as individual substance-related disorders in the United States, Canada, and Europe (Rosenthal & Levounis, 2005; Wu et al., 2005). As many as 90 percent of persons who use one illegal drug are also using another to some extent. A look-in on a group therapy session for users of crack reveals that several of the group members have used other substances in addition:

Therapist: Okay. Now, can you give me a list of all the drugs you've used? Gary?
   Gary: Pot. Coke. Crack. Mescaline. Acid. Speed. Crystal meth. Smack. Base dust. Sometimes alcohol.
  Dennis: Alcohol. Pot. Coke. Mescaline. LSD. Amyl nitrate. Speed and Valium.
    Davy: Coke. Crack. Reefer. Alcohol. Acid. Mescaline. Mushrooms. Ecstasy. Speed. Smack.
    Rich: Alcohol. Pot. Ludes [Quaaludes]. Valium. Speed. Ups [amphetamines]. Downs [barbiturates]. Acid. Mescaline. Crack. Base. Dust. That's about it.
   Carol: Alcohol. Pot. Cocaine. Mescaline. Valium. Crack.

(Chatlos, 1987, pp. 30–31)

Fans still mourn the deaths of many celebrities who have been the victims of poly-substance use. Elvis Presley's delicate balancing act of stimulants and depressants eventually killed him. Janis Joplin's mixtures of wine and heroin were ultimately fatal. And John Belushi's and Chris Farley's liking for the combined effect of cocaine and opioids ("speedballs") also ended in tragedy.

🌞What Causes Substance-Related Disorders?

Clinical theorists have developed sociocultural, psychological, and biological explanations for why people abuse or become dependent on various substances. No single explanation, however, has gained broad support. Like so many other disorders, excessive and chronic drug use is increasingly viewed as the result of a combination of these factors.

The Sociocultural View

A number of sociocultural theorists propose that people are most likely to develop patterns of substance abuse or dependence when they live under stressful socioeconomic conditions. In fact, studies have found that regions with higher levels of unemployment have higher rates of alcoholism. Similarly, lower socioeconomic classes have substance-abuse rates that are higher than those of the other classes (Franklin & Markarian, 2005; Khan, Murray, & Barnes, 2002). In a related vein, 18.5 percent of unemployed adults currently use an illegal drug, compared to 8.8 percent of full-time employed workers and 9.4 percent of part-time employees (NSDUH, 2008).

Other sociocultural theorists propose that substance abuse and dependence are more likely to appear in families and social environments where substance use is valued, or at least accepted. Researchers have, in fact, found that problem drinking is more common among teenagers whose parents and peers drink, as well as among teenagers whose family environments are stressful and unsupportive (Ksir et al., 2008; Lieb et al., 2002). Moreover, lower rates of alcohol abuse are found among Jews and Protestants, groups in which drinking is typically acceptable only as long as it remains within clear limits, whereas alcoholism rates are higher among the Irish and Eastern Europeans, who do not, on average, draw as clear a line (Ksir et al., 2008; Ledoux et al., 2002).

The Psychodynamic View

Psychodynamic theorists believe that people who abuse substances have powerful *dependency* needs that can be traced to their early years (Lightdale et al., 2008; Stetter, 2000). They claim that when parents fail to satisfy a young child's need for nurturance, the child is likely to grow up depending excessively on others for help and comfort, trying to find the nurturance that was lacking during the early years. If this search for outside support includes experimentation with a drug, the person may well develop a dependent relationship with the substance.

Some psychodynamic theorists also believe that certain people respond to their early deprivations by developing a *substance abuse personality* that leaves them particularly prone to drug abuse. Personality inventories and patient interviews have in fact indicated that people who abuse or depend on drugs tend to be more dependent, antisocial, impulsive, novelty-seeking, and depressive than other people (Ksir et al., 2008; Coffey et al., 2003). These findings are correlational, however, and do not clarify whether such personality traits lead to drug use or whether drug use causes people to be dependent, impulsive, and the like.

In an effort to establish clearer causation, one longitudinal study measured the personality traits of a large group of nonalcoholic young men and then kept track of each man's development (Jones, 1971, 1968). Years later, the traits of the men who developed alcohol problems in middle age were compared with the traits of those who did not. The men who developed alcohol problems had been more impulsive as teenagers and

Common substance, uncommon danger
A 13-year-old boy sniffs glue as he lies dazed near a garbage heap. In the United States, at least 6 percent of all people have tried to get high by inhaling the hydrocarbons found in common substances such as glue, gasoline, paint thinner, cleaners, and spray-can propellants (APA, 2000). Such behavior may lead to *inhalant abuse* or *dependence* and poses a number of serious medical dangers.

continued to be so in middle age, a finding suggesting that impulsive men are indeed more prone to develop alcohol problems. Similarly, in one laboratory investigation, "impulsive" rats—those that generally had trouble delaying their rewards—were found to drink more alcohol when offered it than other rats (Poulos, Le, & Parker, 1995).

A major weakness of this line of argument is the wide range of personality traits that have been tied to substance abuse and dependence. In fact, different studies point to different "key" traits. Inasmuch as some people with a drug addiction appear to be dependent, others impulsive, and still others antisocial, researchers cannot presently conclude that any one personality trait or group of traits stands out in substance-related disorders (Chassin et al., 2001).

The Cognitive-Behavioral Views

According to behaviorists, *operant conditioning* may play a key role in substance abuse (Ksir et al., 2008; Higgins et al., 2004). They argue that the temporary reduction of tension or raising of spirits produced by a drug has a rewarding effect, thus increasing the likelihood that the user will seek this reaction again. Similarly, the rewarding effects of a substance may eventually lead users to try higher dosages or more powerful methods of ingestion (see Table 12-4). Cognitive theorists further argue that such rewards eventually produce an *expectancy* that substances will be rewarding, and this expectation helps motivate individuals to increase drug use at times of tension (Chassin et al., 2001).

In support of these behavioral and cognitive views, studies have found that many people do in fact drink more alcohol or seek heroin when they feel tense (Ham et al., 2002; Cooper, 1994). In one study, as participants worked on a difficult anagram task, a confederate planted by the researchers unfairly criticized and belittled them (Marlatt, Kosturn, & Lang, 1975). The participants were then asked to participate in an "alcohol taste task," supposedly to compare and rate alcoholic beverages. The individuals who had been harassed drank more alcohol during the taste task than did the control participants who had not been criticized. A third group of participants was harassed while doing the anagrams but were given an opportunity to retaliate against their critics. These individuals drank relatively little during the tasting. Their retaliatory behavior had apparently reduced their tension and lessened their need for alcohol.

In a manner of speaking, the cognitive-behavioral theorists are arguing that many people take drugs to "medicate" themselves when they feel tense. If so, one would expect higher rates of drug abuse among people who suffer from anxiety, depression, and other such problems. And, in fact, more than 22 percent of all adults who suffer from psychological disorders have been dependent on or abused alcohol or other substances within the past year. Research indicates, for example, that around one-quarter of severely depressed people abuse or depend on drugs (NSDUH, 2008).

Of course, not all drug users find drugs pleasurable or reinforcing when they first take them. Many people report that they did not get high the first time they smoked marijuana, for example, and some opioid users were unaffected or sickened by their initial experiences with opioids. Moreover, even when drugs do initially produce pleasant feelings and rewards, a user's response to them tends to change over time. A number of people become anxious and depressed as they take more and more drugs (Ksir et al., 2008; Roggla & Uhl, 1995; Vaillant, 1993). Why, then, do users keep on taking drugs?

Some theorists use Richard Solomon's *opponent-process theory* to answer this question. Solomon (1980) held that the brain is structured in such a way that pleasurable emotions, such as drug-induced euphoria, inevitably lead to opponent processes—negative aftereffects—that leave the person feeling worse than usual. People who continue to use pleasure-giving drugs inevitably develop opponent aftereffects, such as cravings for more of the drug, an increasing need for the drug, and withdrawal responses. According to Solomon, the opponent processes eventually dominate, and avoidance of the negative aftereffects replaces pursuit of pleasure as the primary factor in drug taking. Although a highly regarded theory, the opponent-process explanation has not received systematic research support.

Still other behaviorists have proposed that *classical conditioning* may play a role in substance abuse and dependence (Haney, 2008; Drobes, Saladin, & Tiffany, 2001). As you'll remember from Chapters 3 and 5, classical conditioning occurs when two stimuli that appear close together in time become connected in a person's mind, so that eventually, the person responds similarly to each stimulus. Cues or objects present in the environment at the time drugs are taken may act as classically conditioned stimuli and come to produce some of the same pleasure brought on by the drugs themselves. Just the sight of a hypodermic needle, drug buddy, or regular supplier, for example, has been known to comfort people who abuse heroin or amphetamines and to relieve their withdrawal

table: 12-4

Methods of Taking Substances

Method	Route	Time to Reach Brain
Inhaling	Drug in vapor form is inhaled through mouth and lungs into circulatory system.	7 seconds
Snorting	Drug in powdered form is snorted into the nose. Some of the drug lands on the nasal mucous membranes, is absorbed by blood vessels, and enters the bloodstream.	4 minutes
Injection	Drug in liquid form directly enters the body through a needle. Injection may be intravenous or intramuscular (subcutaneous). intravenous intramuscular	 20 seconds 4 minutes
Oral ingestion	Drug in solid or liquid form passes through esophagus and stomach and finally to the small intestines. It is absorbed by blood vessels in the intestines.	30 minutes
Other routes	Drugs can be absorbed through areas that contain mucous membranes. Drugs can be placed under the tongue, inserted anally and vaginally, and administered as eyedrops.	Variable

Source: Ksir et al., 2008; Landry, 1994, p. 24.

•**reward center**•A dopamine-rich pathway in the brain that produces feelings of pleasure when activated.

•**reward-deficiency syndrome**•A condition, suspected to be present in some individuals, in which the brain's reward center is not readily activated by the usual events in their lives.

symptoms. In a similar manner, cues or objects that are present during withdrawal distress may produce withdrawal-like symptoms. One man who had formerly been dependent on heroin experienced nausea and other withdrawal symptoms when he returned to the neighborhood where he had gone through withdrawal in the past—a reaction that led him to start taking heroin again (O'Brien et al., 1975). Although classical conditioning certainly appears to be at work in particular cases or aspects of drug abuse and dependence, it has not received widespread research support as the *key* factor in such patterns (Drobes et al., 2001).

The Biological View

In recent years researchers have come to suspect that drug misuse may have biological causes. Studies on genetic predisposition and specific biochemical processes have provided some support for these suspicions.

Genetic Predisposition For years breeding experiments have been conducted to see whether certain animals are genetically predisposed to become dependent on drugs (Kreek, 2008; Li, 2000; Kurtz et al., 1996). In several studies, for example, investigators have first identified animals that prefer alcohol to other beverages and then mated them to one another. Generally, the offspring of these animals have been found also to display an unusual preference for alcohol (Melo et al., 1996).

Similarly, some research with human twins has suggested that people may inherit a predisposition to abuse substances. One classic study found an alcohol abuse *concordance* rate of 54 percent in a group of identical twins; that is, if one identical twin abused alcohol, the other twin also abused alcohol in 54 percent of the cases. In contrast, a group of fraternal twins had a concordance rate of only 28 percent (Kaij, 1960). Other studies have found similar twin patterns (Legrand et al., 2005; Tsuang et al., 2001; Kendler et al., 1994, 1992). As you have read, however, such findings do not rule out other interpretations. For one thing, the parenting received by two identical twins may be more similar than that received by two fraternal twins.

A stronger indication that genetics may play a role in substance abuse and dependence comes from studies of alcoholism rates in people adopted shortly after birth (Walters, 2002; Cadoret et al., 1995; Goldstein, 1994). These studies have compared adoptees whose biological parents are dependent on alcohol with adoptees whose biological parents are not. By adulthood, the individuals whose biological parents are dependent on alcohol typically show higher rates of alcohol abuse than those with nonalcoholic biological parents.

Genetic linkage strategies and *molecular biology* techniques provide more direct evidence in support of a genetic explanation (Gelernter & Kransler, 2008). One line of investigation has found an abnormal form of the so-called *dopamine-2 (D2) receptor gene* in a majority of research participants with alcohol, nicotine, or cocaine dependence but in less than 20 percent of nondependent participants (Preuss et al., 2007; Connor et al., 2002; Blum et al., 1996, 1990). Other studies have tied still other genes to substance-related disorders (Gelernter & Kransler, 2008; Kreek, 2008).

Biochemical Factors Over the past few decades, researchers have pieced together several biological explanations of drug tolerance and withdrawal symptoms (Kleber & Galanter, 2008; Koob, 2008; Kosten et al., 2005). According to one of the leading explanations, when a particular drug is ingested, it increases the activity of certain neurotransmitters whose normal purpose is to calm, reduce pain, lift mood, or increase alertness. When a person keeps on taking the drug, the brain apparently makes an adjustment and reduces its own production of the neurotransmitters. Because the drug is increasing neurotransmitter activity or efficiency, release of the neurotransmitter by the brain is less necessary. As drug intake increases, the body's production of the neurotransmitters continues to decrease, leaving the person in need of more and more of the drug to achieve its effects. In this way, drug takers build tolerance for a drug, becoming more and more reliant on it rather than on their own biological processes to feel comfortable, happy, or

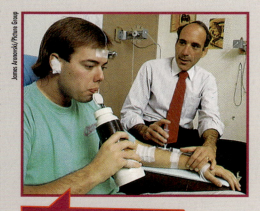

James Aronovski/Picture Group

Searching for genetic clues
A research participant drinks various substances to help determine whether the effects of alcohol and the causes of alcohol abuse are linked to genetic factors.

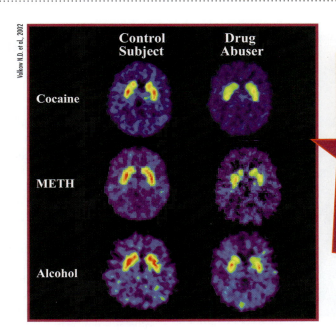

Volkow N.D. et al., 2002

	Control Subject	Drug Abuser
Cocaine		
METH		
Alcohol		

Victims of a reward deficiency syndrome? Theorists suspect that the brain reward centers of people who become dependent on substances are inadequately activated by events in life—a problem called the *reward deficiency syndrome*. With the colors red and orange indicating greater brain activity, these PET scans show that prior to their use of drugs, the reward centers of cocaine, methamphetamine, and alcohol abusers (right) are indeed generally less active than the reward centers of nonabusers (left) (Volkow et al., 2004, 2002).

alert. If they suddenly stop taking the drug, their natural supply of neurotransmitters will be low for a time, producing the symptoms of withdrawal. Withdrawal continues until the brain resumes its normal production of the neurotransmitters.

Which neurotransmitters are affected depends on the drug used. A chronic and excessive use of alcohol or benzodiazepines may lower the brain's production of the neurotransmitter GABA, regular use of opioids may reduce the brain's production of endorphins, and regular use of cocaine or amphetamines may lower the brain's production of dopamine (Haney, 2008; Volkow et al., 2004, 1999). In addition, researchers have identified a neurotransmitter called *anandamide* that operates much like THC; excessive use of marijuana may reduce the production of this neurotransmitter (Hitti, 2004; Johns, 2001).

This theory helps explain why people who regularly take substances experience tolerance and withdrawal reactions. But why are drugs so rewarding, and why do certain people turn to them in the first place? A number of brain-imaging studies suggest that many, perhaps all, drugs eventually activate a **reward center,** or "pleasure pathway," in the brain (Haney, 2008; Koob & LeMoal, 2008; Schultz, 2006). This reward center apparently extends from the brain area called the *ventral tegmental area* (in the midbrain) to an area known as the *nucleus accumbens* and on to the *frontal cortex* (see Figure 12-5). A key neurotransmitter in this pleasure pathway appears to be *dopamine* (Higgins & George, 2007; Volkow et al., 2004). When dopamine is activated along the pleasure pathway, a person experiences pleasure. Music may activate dopamine in the reward center. So may a hug or a word of praise. And so do drugs. Some researchers believe that other neurotransmitters may also play important roles in the reward center.

Certain drugs apparently stimulate the reward center directly. Remember that cocaine, amphetamines, and caffeine directly increase dopamine activity. Other drugs seem to stimulate it in roundabout ways. The biochemical reactions triggered by alcohol, opioids, and marijuana probably set in motion a series of chemical events that eventually lead to increased dopamine activity in the reward center.

A number of theorists suspect that people who abuse drugs suffer from a **reward–deficiency syndrome:** their reward center is not readily activated by the usual events in their lives (Blum et al., 2000; Nash, 1997) so they turn to drugs to stimulate this pleasure pathway, particularly in times of stress. Abnormal genes, such as the abnormal D2 receptor gene, have been cited as a possible cause of this syndrome (Finckh, 2001; Lawford et al., 1997).

Figure 12-5

Pleasure centers in the brain One of the reasons drugs produce feelings of pleasure is because they increase levels of the neurotransmitter dopamine along a "pleasure pathway" in the brain that extends from the ventral tegmental area to the nucleus accumbens and then to the frontal cortex. This activation of pleasure centers plays a role in addiction.

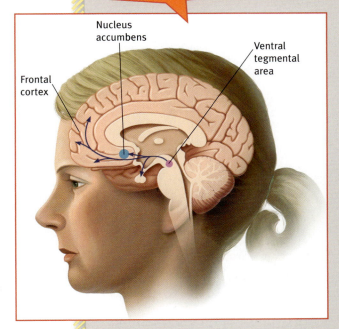

Nucleus accumbens

Ventral tegmental area

Frontal cortex

Sniffing for drugs
An increasingly common scene in schools, airports, storage facilities, and similar settings is that of trained dogs sniffing for marijuana, cocaine, opioids, and other substances. Here one such animal sniffs lockers at a school in Texas to see whether students have hidden any illegal substances among their books or other belongings.

✿How Are Substance-Related Disorders Treated?

Many approaches have been used to treat substance-related disorders, including psychodynamic, behavioral, cognitive-behavioral, and biological approaches, along with several sociocultural therapies. Although these treatments sometimes meet with great success, more often they are only moderately helpful (Myrick & Wright, 2008; Frances et al., 2005; Prendergast et al., 2002). Today the treatments are typically used on either an outpatient or inpatient basis or a combination of the two (Carroll, 2008, 2005; Weiss et al., 2008) (see Figure 12-6).

The value of a treatment for substance abuse or dependence can be difficult to determine. After all, different substance-related disorders pose different treatment problems. Moreover, some people recover without any intervention at all, while others recover and then relapse (Miller, 2000). Finally, different criteria are used by different clinical researchers. How long, for example, must a person refrain from substance use in order to be called a treatment success? And is total abstention the only criterion, or is a reduction of drug use acceptable?

Psychodynamic Therapies

Psychodynamic therapists first guide clients to uncover and work through the underlying needs and conflicts that they believe have led to the disorder. The therapists then try to help the individuals change their substance-related styles of living (Lightdale et al., 2008; Dodes & Khantzian, 2005). Although often applied, this approach has not been found to be particularly effective in cases of substance-related disorders (Cornish et al., 1995; Holder et al., 1991). It may be that drug abuse or dependence, regardless of its causes, eventually becomes a stubborn independent problem that must be the direct target of treatment if people are to become drug-free. Psychodynamic therapy tends to be of greater help when it is combined with other approaches in a multidimensional treatment program (Lightdale et al., 2008; Galanter & Brooks, 2001).

Behavioral Therapies

A widely used behavioral treatment for substance-related disorders is **aversion therapy,** an approach based on the principles of classical conditioning. Individuals are repeatedly presented with an unpleasant stimulus (for example, an electric shock) at the very moment that they are taking a drug. After repeated pairings, they are expected to react negatively to the substance itself and to lose their craving for it.

Aversion therapy has been applied to alcohol abuse and dependence more than to other substance-related disorders. In one version of this therapy, drinking behavior is paired with drug-induced nausea and vomiting (Owen-Howard, 2001; Welsh & Liberto, 2001). Another version, *covert sensitization,* requires people with alcoholism to imagine extremely upsetting, repulsive, or frightening scenes while they are drinking (Cautela, 2000; Kassel et al., 1999). The pairing of the imagined scenes with liquor is expected to produce negative responses to liquor itself. Here are the kinds of scenes therapists may guide a client to imagine:

•**aversion therapy**•A treatment in which clients are repeatedly presented with unpleasant stimuli while performing undesirable behaviors such as taking a drug.

I'd like you to vividly imagine that you are drinking and tasting (beer, whiskey, etc.). You are in a (restaurant, pub, etc.) where others are drinking. "See" yourself there, having a drink. Capture the exact taste of it, the color and the smell. Use all of your senses. Imagine that

Paul Howell/Liaison/Getty Images

you are actually drinking it, tasting it, swallowing it, feel the glass in your hand; and be aware of its temperature, taste and smell, but especially the taste.

As you swallow the drink, a man sitting not far from you gives a low groan, replaces his glass on the table and pushes it away. His head remains lowered as he grasps his stomach with both hands and continues moaning. His eyes are closed now as he grimaces and slowly shakes his head. His face has become a sickly pale color, and his hands are trembling as he starts to make quick swallowing motions. He opens his eyes and claps both hands over his mouth, but he cannot hold it in and the vomit bursts out. You can see it so clearly. Pieces of food run down his face, soaking his clothes and even reaching his glass. He continues to throw up and particles of his last meal stick to his chin and the hot sticky smell of alcohol reaches you. He really is a disgusting sight. He's got the dry heaves now, there's nothing left to bring up, but his face is still pale and he continues moaning.

I'd like you to vividly imagine that you are tasting the (beer, whiskey, etc.). See yourself tasting it, capture the exact taste, color and consistency. Use all of your senses. After you've tasted the drink you notice that there is something small and white floating in the glass—it stands out. You bend closer to examine it more carefully, your nose is right over the glass now and the smell fills your nostrils as you remember exactly what the drink tastes like. Now you can see what's in the glass. There are several maggots floating on the surface. As you watch, revolted, one manages to get a grip on the glass and, undulating, creeps up the glass. There are even more of the repulsive creatures in the glass than you first thought. You realise that you have swallowed some of them and you're very aware of the taste in your mouth. You feel very sick and wish you'd never reached for the glass and had the drink at all.

(Clarke & Saunders, 1988, pp. 143–144)

A behavioral approach that has been effective in the short-term treatment of people who abuse cocaine and some other drugs is *contingency management,* which makes incentives (such as cash, vouchers, prizes, or privileges) contingent on the submission of drug-free urine specimens (Higgins & Silverman, 2008; Kosten et al, 2008). In one pioneering study, 68 percent of cocaine abusers who completed a six-month contingency training program achieved at least eight weeks of continuous abstinence (Higgins et al., 1993).

Behavioral interventions for substance abuse and dependence have usually had only limited success when they are the sole form of treatment (Carroll, 2008). A major problem is that the approaches can be effective only when individuals are motivated to continue with them despite their unpleasantness or demands (DiClemente et al., 2008).

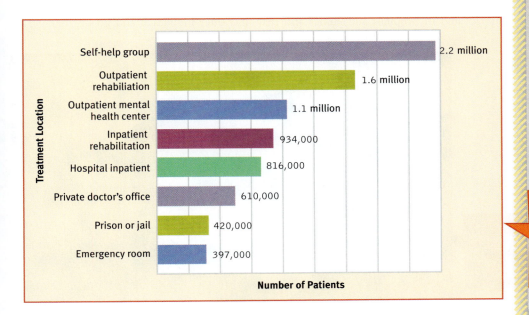

Figure 12-6
Where do people receive treatment? Most people receive treatment for substance abuse and dependence in a self-help group, an outpatient rehabilitation program, or a mental health center (NSDUH, 2008)

•**behavioral self-control training (BSCT)**•A cognitive-behavioral approach to treating alcohol abuse and dependence in which clients are taught to keep track of their drinking behavior and to apply coping strategies in situations that typically trigger excessive drinking.

•**relapse-prevention training**•An approach to treating alcohol abuse that is similar to BSCT and also has clients plan ahead for risky situations and reactions.

•**detoxification**•Systematic and medically supervised withdrawal from a drug.

•**antagonist drugs**•Drugs that block or change the effects of an addictive drug.

Generally, behavioral treatments work best in combination with either biological or cognitive approaches (Higgins & Silverman, 2008; Grilly, 2006).

Cognitive-Behavioral Therapies

Two popular approaches combine cognitive and behavioral techniques to help people gain *control* over their substance-related behaviors (Carroll, 2008). In one, **behavioral self-control training (BSCT),** applied to alcoholism in particular, therapists first have clients keep track of their own drinking behavior (Bishop, 2008; Adelson, 2005; Miller et al., 1992; Miller, 1983). Writing down the times, locations, emotions, bodily changes, and other circumstances of their drinking, they become more aware of the situations that place them at risk for excessive drinking. They are then taught coping strategies to use when such situations arise. They learn, for example, to set limits on their drinking (see *A Closer Look* on the facing page), to recognize when the limits are being approached, to control their rate of drinking (perhaps by spacing their drinks or by sipping them rather than gulping), and to practice relaxation techniques, assertiveness skills, and other coping behaviors in situations in which they would otherwise be drinking. Approximately 70 percent of the people who complete this training apparently show some improvement, particularly those who are young and not physically dependent on alcohol (Deas et al., 2008; Ksir et al., 2008; Walters, 2000).

In a related cognitive-behavioral approach, **relapse-prevention training,** heavy drinkers are assigned many of the same tasks as clients in BSCT (Witkiewitz & Marlatt, 2007, 2004). They are also taught to plan ahead of time how many drinks are appropriate, what to drink, and under what circumstances. The approach often lowers the frequency of intoxication, although the majority of clients achieve success only after repeated relapse prevention treatments (Witkiewitz & Marlatt, 2007, 2004). The approach has also been used, with some success, in the treatment of marijuana and cocaine abuse as well as with other kinds of disorders such as sexual paraphilias (see Chapter 13).

Biological Treatments

Biological approaches may be used to help people withdraw from substances, abstain from them, or simply maintain their level of use without further increases. As with the other forms of treatment, biological approaches alone rarely bring long-term improvement, but they can be helpful when combined with other approaches.

Detoxification **Detoxification** is systematic and medically supervised withdrawal from a drug. Some detoxification programs are offered on an outpatient basis. Others are located in hospitals and clinics and may also offer individual and group therapy, a

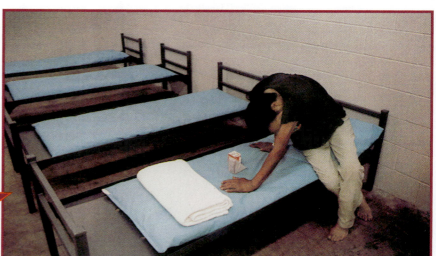

Patrick Davison/The Dallas Morning News

Forced detoxification Abstinence is not always medically supervised, nor is it necessarily planned or voluntary. This sufferer of alcoholism begins to experience symptoms of withdrawal soon after being imprisoned for public intoxication.

Controlled Drug Use versus Abstinence

I s total abstinence the only cure for drug abuse and dependence, or can people with substance-related disorders learn to keep drug use under control? This issue has been debated for years, especially when the drug in question is alcohol (Ksir et al., 2008; Adelson, 2005).

Some cognitive-behavioral theorists believe that people can continue to drink in moderation if they learn to set appropriate drinking limits. They argue that demanding strict abstinence of people may in fact cause them to lose self-control entirely if they have a single drink (Witkiewitz & Marlatt, 2007, 2004; Marlatt et al., 2001). In contrast, those who view alcoholism as a disease take the AA position of "Once an alcoholic, always an alcoholic" and argue that people with alcoholism are in fact more likely to relapse when they believe that they can safely take one drink (Pendery et al., 1982). This misguided belief, they hold, will sooner or later open the door to alcohol once again and lead back to uncontrollable drinking.

Feelings run so strongly that in the 1980s the people on one side challenged the motives and honesty of those on the other (Sobell & Sobell, 1984, 1973; Pendery et al., 1982). Research indicates, however, that both controlled drinking and abstinence may be useful treatment goals, depending on the individual's personality and on the nature of the particular

drinking problem. Studies suggest, for example, that abstinence is a more appropriate goal for people who have a long-standing dependence on alcohol, while controlled drinking can be helpful to younger drinkers whose pattern does not include physical dependence. The latter individuals may in fact need to be taught a nonabusive form of drinking (Deas et al., 2008; Ksir et al., 2008; Witkiewitz & Marlatt, 2007, 2004). Studies also suggest that abstinence is appropriate for people who believe that it is the only answer for them (Carbonari & Di Clemente, 2000; Rosenberg, 1993). These individuals are indeed more likely to relapse after having just one drink.

Generally speaking, both abstinence and controlled drinking are extremely difficult for persons with alcoholism to achieve. Although treatment may help them to improve for a while, many of them relapse (Myrick & Wright, 2008; Adelson, 2005; Allsop et al., 2000). Such statistics serve as a harsh reminder that substance abuse and dependence remain among society's most disabling problems.

Failure of forced abstinence Although individual efforts at voluntary abstinence from alcohol are often successful, broad social programs that try to force individuals to abstain from drinking usually meet with failure. During the period of "prohibition" in the United States (1920–1933), for example, the consumption of alcohol initially decreased but then soon increased, contributing to the repeal of "the noble experiment" in 1933. During this social ban on alcohol, people developed ingenious techniques for concealing and transporting this substance. Here, for example, a tube of liquor was hidden in the heel of a shoe available in shoe stores throughout the country.

AP Photo

"full-service" institutional approach that has become popular. One detoxification approach is to have clients withdraw gradually from the substance, taking smaller and smaller doses until they are off the drug completely (Wright & Thompson, 2002). A second—often medically preferred—detoxification strategy is to give clients other drugs that reduce the symptoms of withdrawal (Ksir et al., 2008; Oslin, 2006). Antianxiety drugs, for example, are sometimes used to reduce severe alcohol withdrawal reactions such as delirium tremens and seizures. Detoxification programs seem to help motivated people withdraw from drugs (Diclemente et al., 2008; Allan et al., 2000). However, relapse rates tend to be high for those who fail to receive a follow-up form of treatment—psychological, biological, or sociocultural—after successful detoxification (Polydorou & Kleber, 2008).

Antagonist Drugs After successfully stopping a drug, people must avoid falling back into a pattern of abuse or dependence. As an aid to resisting temptation, some people with substance-related disorders are given **antagonist drugs,** which block or change

Pros and cons of methadone treatment
Methadone is itself a narcotic that can
be as dangerous as other opioids when
not taken under safe medical supervision.
Here a couple protest against a proposed
methadone treatment facility in Maine.
Their 19-year-old daughter, who was not
an opioid addict, had died months earlier
after taking methadone to get high.

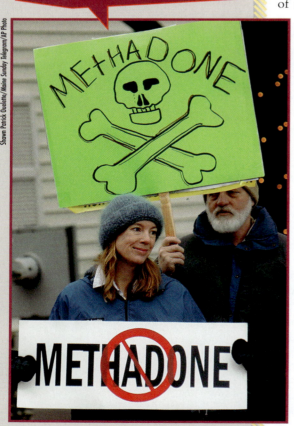

Shawn Patrick Ouellette/Maine Sunday Telegram/AP Photo

the effects of the addictive drug (O'Brien & Kampman, 2008; McCance-Katz & Kosten, 2005). *Disulfiram* (Antabuse), for example, is often given to people who are trying to stay away from alcohol. By itself a low dose of this drug seems to have few negative effects, but a person who drinks alcohol while taking disulfiram will experience intense nausea, vomiting, blushing, faster heart rate, dizziness, and perhaps fainting. People taking disulfiram are less likely to drink alcohol because they know the terrible reaction that awaits them should they have even one drink. Disulfiram has proved helpful, but again only with people who are motivated to take it as prescribed (Diclemente et al., 2008; Grilly, 2006).

Several other antagonist drugs are now being tested as possible treatments for people who abuse alcohol (Ehrenfeld, 2005). Unlike disulfiram, these drugs do not make the individuals ill when mixed with alcohol, but they do alter the brain's release of GABA, the neurotransmitter affected by alcohol use, and, in turn, seem to reduce the individuals' cravings for alcohol. One such drug under study is *topiramate* (Topamax), a medication that has been used for years to help treat people with brain seizure disorder (DeSousa et al., 2008).

In the realm of opioid dependence, several *narcotic antagonists,* such as *naloxone* and *naltrexone,* are used to treat people who are addicted to drugs of that kind (O'Brien & Kampman, 2008; Kirchmayer et al., 2002). These antagonists attach to *endorphin* receptor sites throughout the brain and make it impossible for the opioids to have their usual effect. Without the rush or high, continued drug use becomes pointless. Although narcotic antagonists have been helpful—particularly in emergencies, to rescue people from an overdose of opioids—some clinicians consider them too dangerous for regular treatment of opioid dependence. These antagonists must be given very carefully because of their ability to throw a person with an addiction into severe withdrawal. So-called *partial antagonists,* narcotic antagonists that produce less severe withdrawal symptoms, have also been developed (Ksir et al., 2008; O'Brien & Kampman, 2008).

Recent studies indicate that narcotic antagonists may also be useful in the treatment of alcohol and cocaine dependence (Bishop, 2008; Oslin, 2006; O'Brien & McKay, 2002). In some studies, for example, the narcotic antagonist naltrexone has helped reduce cravings for alcohol (O'Malley et al., 2000, 1996, 1992). Why should narcotic antagonists, which operate at the brain's endorphin receptors, help with alcoholism, which has been tied largely to activity at GABA sites? The answer may lie in the reward center of the brain (Gianoulakis, 2001). If various drugs eventually stimulate the same pleasure pathway, it seems reasonable that antagonists for one drug may, in a roundabout way, affect the impact of other drugs as well.

Drug Maintenance Therapy A drug-related lifestyle may be a greater problem than the drug's direct effects. Much of the damage caused by heroin addiction, for example, comes from overdoses, unsterilized needles, and an accompanying life of crime. Thus clinicians were very enthusiastic when **methadone maintenance programs** were developed in the 1960s to treat heroin addiction (Dole & Nyswander, 1967, 1965). In these programs, people with an addiction are given the laboratory opioid *methadone* as a substitute for heroin. Although they then become dependent on methadone, their new addiction is maintained under safe medical supervision. Unlike heroin, methadone can be taken by mouth, thus eliminating the dangers of needles, and needs to be taken only once a day.

At first, methadone programs seemed very effective, and many of them were set up throughout the United States, Canada, and England. These programs became less popular during the 1980s, however, because of the dangers of methadone itself. Many clinicians came to believe that substituting one addiction for another is not an acceptable "solution" for substance dependence, and many persons with an addiction complained that methadone addiction was creating an additional drug problem that simply complicated their original one (McCance-Katz & Kosten, 2005). In fact, methadone is sometimes harder to withdraw from than heroin because the withdrawal symptoms can last longer (Ksir et al., 2008; Backmund et al.,

2001). Moreover, pregnant women maintained on methadone have the added concern of the drug's effect on their fetus.

Despite such concerns, maintenance treatment with methadone—or with *buprenorphine,* another widely used substitute drug—has again sparked interest among clinicians in recent years, partly because of new research support (Strain & Lofwall, 2008) and partly because of the rapid spread of the HIV virus and the hepatitis C virus among intravenous drug abusers and their sex partners and children (Galanter & Kleber, 2008; Schottenfeld, 2008). More than one-quarter of AIDS cases reported in the early 1990s were directly tied to drug abuse, and intravenous drug abuse is the indirect cause in 60 percent of childhood AIDS cases. Not only is methadone treatment safer than street opioid use, but many methadone programs now include AIDS education and other health instructions in their services (Sorensen & Copeland, 2000). Research suggests that methadone maintenance programs are most effective when they are combined with education, psychotherapy, family therapy, and employment counseling (Schottenfeld, 2008; O'Brien & McKay, 2002). Today thousands of clinics provide methadone treatment across the United States (MTC, 2008; ONDCP, 2002, 2000).

Sociocultural Therapies

As you have read, sociocultural theorists—both *family-social* and *multicultural* theorists—believe that psychological problems emerge in a social setting and are best treated in a social context (see *The Media Speaks* on the next page). Three sociocultural approaches have been applied to substance-related disorders: (1) *self-help programs,* (2) *culture- and gender-sensitive programs,* and (3) *community prevention programs* (Ritvo & Causey, 2008).

Self-Help and Residential Treatment Programs
Many people who abuse drugs have organized among themselves to help one another recover without professional assistance. The drug self-help movement dates back to 1935, when two Ohio men suffering from alcoholism met and wound up discussing alternative treatment possibilities. The first discussion led to others and to the eventual formation of a self-help group whose members discussed alcohol-related problems, traded ideas, and provided support. The organization became known as **Alcoholics Anonymous (AA).**

Today AA has more than 2 million members in 113,000 groups across the United States and 180 other countries (AA World Services, 2008). It offers peer support along

Layne Kennedy, Minneapolis

Spreading the word
The AA message to accept one's powerlessness over alcohol and abstain from drinking "one day at a time" has been embraced by all kinds of people in all kinds of places. Here, for example, sober bikers get together at the Dry Gulch, a favorite spot in St. Paul, Minnesota.

HOME   SEND   EXPLORE

SEARCH

In Real Time, Amy Winehouse's Deeper Descent

BY JON PARELES, THE *NEW YORK TIMES*, JANUARY 24, 2008

AP Photo/Brian Kersey

It was witty, with a fillip of transgression, when Amy Winehouse sang, "They tried to make me go to rehab/I said no, no, no" on her album "Back to Black". . . . But there was nothing amusing, and barely any surprise, in Ms. Winehouse's recent, notorious and possibly inadvertent public appearance: on a video released by an English tabloid, *The Sun*.

The homemade clip . . . shows Ms. Winehouse, with her recent blond hairdo, in her London apartment, using a glass pipe to smoke what *The Sun* says is crack. And it was no surprise because she has been a very public wreck. Performers thrive on attention, and sometimes admit that it's an addiction; now, the Internet enables that addiction all too easily. The unintended consequence is that we can now watch stars self-destruct in real time.

Images of Ms. Winehouse looking intoxicated, disheveled, half-dressed and wild-eyed are all over the tabloids and the Internet. She has appeared to be drunk onstage, barely able to get through a song. . . . Ms. Winehouse, who writes her own lyrics, . . . has often sung about harmful appetites, not just in "Rehab" but in "Addicted" (about a freeloading pot smoker) and in "Back to Black," in which she sings, "You love blow and I love puff/And life is like a pipe." . . . What made "Rehab" amusing when it appeared was that Ms. Winehouse was mocking what had become such a standard celebrity way station.

Addiction might start with experiments by performers so young they feel invulnerable; it might seem to be, at first, a way to ease the stress of a peculiar job. It might be a way to act out the old Romantic image of the artist as daredevil. And there's no shortage of temptation in a musician's work environment of bars, clubs, late nights and party people. Rock stars weren't the first musicians to drink or drug themselves to death.

What's different, in the 21st century, is that we can watch the breakdowns almost as they happen. One day there's a grainy video of Ms. Winehouse spreading across the Internet. Now the video has been given to the British police for investigation while Ms. Winehouse, black-haired and neatly made up, is photographed professionally on the way to a doctor visit.

In the '60s and '70s there were occasional photos of Janis Joplin hoisting a bottle of Southern Comfort, and word-of-mouth about many bands' backstage excesses or drunken exploits, but those were occasional glimpses and dispatches. Rockers dosed themselves, mostly, behind closed doors.

Now digital video and photography, coupled with the Internet, can add up to near-constant surveillance. It's voluntary for people who post daily photos on their Facebook pages, perhaps less so for celebrities trailed by paparazzi. There's an entire industry in celebrity scandal, much of it remarkably callous.

In their times the deaths of Jim Morrison and Kurt Cobain were sudden and shocking, leaving them a legacy as handsome rock martyrs. . . . But they were pre-Internet stars. Now, there's a sleazy symbiosis that connects instantaneous worldwide visibility, publicity, marketing and narcissism. Attention addicts can get their fix with a few mouse clicks.

Why, for instance, was Ms. Winehouse letting someone shoot video, in a private setting, of her puffing that pipe in the first place? Maybe it's some version of "keepin' it real," the fallacy that insists art must be autobiographical to be worthwhile, as if art were documentation rather than storytelling. Maybe it's obliviousness, although, since the camera followed her around, she was likely to know it was there. Maybe she mistakenly trusted that whoever made the video would resist another temptation: the potential profit to be made providing it to a tabloid.

Perhaps Ms. Winehouse misunderstood what should be clear in the age of the Internet: Everything recorded can be duplicated and distributed. And possibly the video was, in its own bleary way, a kind of performance. She is keeping her audience informed if not exactly entertained.

Mostly, however, she's just supplying material for the sphere of celebrity interaction that only wants to see idols torn down. Her fans—those of us who believe she has more superb songs yet to write—would prefer she grow less visible and considerably more boring. . . . [S]he would do well to disappear for a while, into rehab or private recovery, and then to hole up in a recording studio and work up some new songs. (She definitely has enough ups and downs to write about, realistically or not.) In the era of total exposure Ms. Winehouse would serve herself and her listeners best by working behind closed doors.

[Note: Two weeks after this article was printed, Amy Winehouse won five Grammy Awards, including ones for best new artist, song of the year ("Rehab"), and best pop vocal album (Back to Black).]

with moral and spiritual guidelines to help people overcome alcoholism. Different members apparently find different aspects of AA helpful (Tonigan & Connors, 2008). For some it is the peer support; for others it is the spiritual dimension. Meetings take place regularly, and members are available to help each other 24 hours a day.

By offering guidelines for living, the organization helps members abstain "one day at a time," urging them to accept as "fact" the idea that they are powerless over alcohol and that they must stop drinking entirely and permanently if they are to live normal lives (Nace, 2008). Related self-help organizations, *Al-Anon* and *Alateen,* offer support for people who live with and care about persons with alcoholism (Galanter, 2008). Self-help programs such as *Narcotics Anonymous* and *Cocaine Anonymous* have been developed for other substance-related disorders.

Many self-help programs have expanded into **residential treatment centers,** or **therapeutic communities**—such as *Daytop Village* and *Phoenix House*—where people formerly dependent on drugs live, work, and socialize in a drug-free environment while undergoing individual, group, and family therapies and making a transition back to community life (Brook, 2008; De Leon, 2008).

The evidence that keeps self-help and residential treatment programs going comes largely in the form of individual testimonials. Many tens of thousands of persons have revealed that they are members of these programs and credit them with turning their lives around. Studies of the programs have also had favorable findings, but their numbers have been limited (De Leon, 2008; Moos & Timko, 2008; Tonigan & Connors, 2008).

Culture- and Gender-Sensitive Programs

Many persons who abuse substances live in a poor and perhaps violent setting. A growing number of today's treatment programs try to be sensitive to the special sociocultural pressures and problems faced by drug abusers who are poor, homeless, or members of minority groups (Cabaj, 2008; Westermeyer & Dickerson, 2008). Therapists who are sensitive to their clients' life challenges can do more to address the stresses that often lead to relapse.

Similarly, therapists have become more aware that women often require treatment methods different from those designed for men (Brady & Back, 2008; Blume & Zilberman, 2005). Women and men often have different physical and psychological reactions to drugs, for example. In addition, treatment of women who abuse substances may be complicated by the impact of sexual abuse, the possibility that they may be or may become pregnant while taking drugs, the stresses of raising children, and the fear of criminal prosecution for abusing drugs during pregnancy (Finnegan & Kandall, 2008). Thus many women with such disorders feel more comfortable seeking help at gender-sensitive clinics or residential programs; some such programs also allow children to live with their recovering mothers.

•**residential treatment center**•A place where people formerly dependent on drugs live, work, and socialize in a drug-free environment. Also called a *therapeutic community.*

Fighting drug abuse while in prison
Inmates at a county jail in Texas exercise and meditate as part of a drug and alcohol rehabilitation program. The program also includes psychoeducation and other interventions to help inmates address their substance abuse problems.

Joshua Lutz/Redux

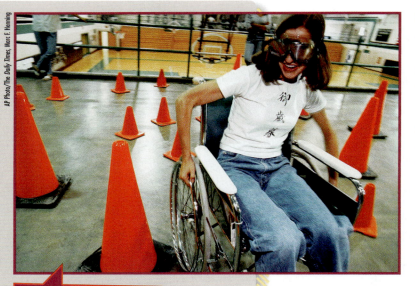

Simulation as prevention

A 16-year-old student weaves her way through an obstacle course while wearing a pair of alcohol-impaired goggles. The exercise is part of a DUI prevention program at her New Mexico high school, designed to give students hands-on experience regarding alcohol's effects on vision and balance.

Community Prevention Programs Perhaps the most effective approach to substance-related disorders is to prevent them (Clayton et al., 2008; Ksir et al., 2008). The first drug-prevention efforts were conducted in schools. Today prevention programs are also offered in workplaces, activity centers, and other community settings, and even through the media (NSDUH, 2008). Over 11 percent of adolescents report that they have participated in substance use prevention programs outside school within the past year. Around 80 percent have seen or heard a substance use prevention message. And almost 60 percent have talked to their parents in the past year about the dangers of alcohol and other drugs.

Some prevention programs argue for total abstinence from drugs, while others teach responsible use. Some seek to interrupt drug use; others try to delay the age at which people first experiment with drugs. Programs may also differ in whether they offer drug education, teach alternatives to drug use, try to change the psychological state of the potential user, seek to change relationships with peers, or combine these techniques.

Prevention programs may focus on the *individual* (for example, by providing education about unpleasant drug effects), the *family* (by teaching parenting skills), the *peer group* (by teaching resistance to peer pressure), the *school* (by setting up firm enforcement of drug policies), or the *community* at large (by public service announcements such as the "Just say no" campaign of the 1980s and 1990s). The most effective prevention efforts focus on several of these areas to provide a consistent message about drug abuse in all areas of individuals' lives (Clayton et al., 2008; Ksir et al., 2008). Some prevention programs have even been developed for preschool children.

PUTTING IT... together

New Wrinkles to a Familiar Story

In some respects the story of the misuse of drugs is the same today as in the past. Substance use is still rampant, often creating damaging psychological disorders. New drugs keep emerging, and the public goes through periods of believing, naively, that they are "safe." Only gradually do people learn that these drugs, too, pose dangers. And treatments for substance-related disorders continue to have only limited effect.

Yet there are important new wrinkles in this familiar story. Researchers have begun to develop a clearer understanding of how drugs act on the brain and body. In treatment, self-help groups and rehabilitation programs are flourishing. And preventive education to make people aware of the dangers of drug misuse is also expanding and seems to be having an effect. One reason for these improvements is that investigators and clinicians have stopped working in isolation and are instead looking for intersections between their own work and work from other models. The same kind of integrated efforts that have helped with other psychological disorders are bringing new promise and hope to the study and treatment of substance-related disorders.

Perhaps the most important insight to be gained from these integrated efforts is that several of the models were already on the right track. Social pressures, personality characteristics, rewards, and genetic predispositions all seem to play roles in substance-related disorders, and in fact to operate together. For example, some people may inherit a malfunction of the biological reward center and so may need special doses of external stimulation—say, intense relationships, an abundance of certain foods, or drugs—to stimulate their reward center. Their pursuit of external rewards may take on the character of an addictive personality (Ebstein & Kotler, 2002). Such individuals may be especially prone to experimenting with drugs, particularly when their social group makes the drugs available or when they are faced with intense social and personal stress.

Fred Squillante/The Columbus Dispatch

Listen to my story
A prisoner stands shackled before students at an Ohio high school and discusses his drunk-driving conviction (his intoxicated driving resulted in a fatal automobile crash). Such high school visits by inmates are part of the school's "Make the Right Choice" prevention program.

Just as each model has identified important factors in the development of substance-related disorders, each has made important contributions to treatment. As you have seen, the various forms of treatment seem to work best when they are combined with approaches from the other models, making integrated treatment the most productive approach.

These recent developments are encouraging. At the same time, however, enormous and increasing levels of drug use continue. New drugs and drug combinations are discovered almost daily, and with them come new problems, new questions, and the need for new research and new treatments. Perhaps the most valuable lesson is an old one: there is no free lunch. The pleasures derived from these substances come with high psychological and biological costs, some not yet even known.

‹‹‹[SUMMING UP]›››

○ **Substance misuse** The misuse of *substances* (or *drugs*) may lead to temporary changes in behavior, emotion, or thought, including *intoxication*. Chronic and excessive use can lead to *substance abuse* or *substance dependence*. People who become dependent on a drug may develop a *tolerance* for it, experience unpleasant *withdrawal symptoms* when they abstain from it, or both. *pp. 373–375*

○ **Depressants** *Depressants* are substances that slow the activity of the central nervous system. Each of the major depressants presents certain problems and dangers. Chronic and excessive use of these substances can lead to a pattern of abuse or dependence.

Alcoholic beverages contain *ethyl alcohol*, which is carried by the blood to the central nervous system, depressing its function. Intoxication occurs when the concentration of alcohol in the bloodstream reaches 0.09 percent. Among other actions, alcohol increases the activity of the neurotransmitter GABA at key sites in the brain. Excessive use has been tied to accidents, health problems, and certain psychological disorders. The *sedative-hypnotic drugs,* which produce feelings of relaxation and drowsiness, include *barbiturates* and *benzodiazepines*. These drugs also increase the activity of GABA.

continued

BETWEEN THE LINES

Drugs and the Law

There are more than 230,000 drug-law violators incarcerated in state prisons and local jails and 60,000 in federal prisons (Beck, 2004). ‹‹

Fifty-seven percent of state prisoners and 45 percent of federal prisoners in the United States report using illicit drugs in the month before committing their offense (Bureau of Justice Statistics, 1999). ‹‹

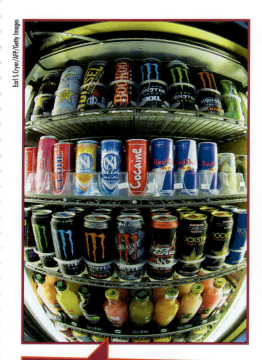

Earl S. Cryer/AFP/Getty Images

Energy drinks: a growing trend

Here a California store displays cans of *energy drinks*, popular high-stimulant soft drinks with edgy names such as *Rockstar, Full Throttle,* and *Cocaine.* Energy drinks, which typically contain very high levels of caffeine and other supplements, have become a major force in the soft drink industry, particularly among young consumers.

Opioids include *opium* and drugs derived from it, such as *morphine* and *heroin,* as well as laboratory-made opioids. They all reduce tension and pain and cause other reactions. Opioids operate by binding to neurons that ordinarily receive *endorphins. pp. 375–383*

○ **Stimulants** *Stimulants* are substances that increase the activity of the central nervous system. They may lead to intoxication, abuse, and dependence, including a withdrawal pattern marked by depression, fatigue, and irritability. *Cocaine, amphetamines,* and *caffeine* (less potent but more widely used) produce their effects by increasing the activity of dopamine, norepinephrine, and serotonin in the brain. *pp. 383–389*

○ **Hallucinogens** *Hallucinogens,* such as *LSD,* are substances that cause powerful changes primarily in sensory perception. Perceptions are intensified and illusions and hallucinations can occur. LSD apparently causes such effects by disturbing the release of the neurotransmitter serotonin. LSD is extremely potent, and it may lead to a "bad trip" or to *flashbacks. pp. 389–390*

○ **Cannabis** The main ingredient of *Cannabis sativa,* a hemp plant, is *tetrahydrocannabinol* (THC). *Marijuana,* the most popular form of cannabis, is more powerful today than it was in years past. It can cause intoxication, and regular use can lead to abuse and dependence. *pp. 391–395*

○ **Combinations of substances** Many people take more than one drug at a time, and the drugs interact. The use of two or more drugs at the same time— *polysubstance use*—has become increasingly common. Similarly, *polysubstance-related disorders* have also become a major problem. *pp. 395–397*

○ **Explanations for substance-related disorders** Several explanations for substance abuse and dependence have been put forward. No single one of them has gained unqualified research support, but together they are beginning to shed light on the disorders. According to the *sociocultural* view, the people most likely to abuse drugs are those living in socioeconomic conditions that generate stress or whose families value or tolerate drug use. In the *psychodynamic view,* people who turn to substance abuse have excessive *dependency* needs traceable to the early stages of life. Some psychodynamic theorists also believe that certain people have a *substance abuse personality* that makes them prone to drug use. The leading *behavioral* view proposes that drug use is reinforced initially because it reduces tensions and raises spirits. According to *cognitive* theorists, such reductions may also lead to an *expectancy* that drugs will be comforting and helpful.

The *biological* explanations are supported by twin, adoptee, genetic linkage, and molecular biology studies, suggesting that people may inherit a predisposition to substance dependence. Researchers have also learned that drug tolerance and withdrawal symptoms may be caused by cutbacks in the brain's production of particular neurotransmitters during excessive and chronic drug use. Finally, biological studies suggest that many, perhaps all, drugs may ultimately lead to increased *dopamine* activity in the brain's *reward center. pp. 397–401*

○ **Treatments for substance-related disorders** Treatments for substance abuse and dependence vary widely. Usually several approaches are combined. *Psychodynamic* therapies try to help clients become aware of and correct the underlying needs and conflicts that may have led to their use of drugs. A common *behavioral* technique is *aversion therapy,* in which an unpleasant stimulus is paired with the drug that the person is abusing. *Cognitive behavioral* techniques have been combined in such forms as *behavioral self-control training* (BSCT) and *relapse-prevention training. Biological* treatments include *detoxification, antagonist drugs,* and *drug maintenance* *therapy. Sociocultural* treatments approach substance-related disorders in a social context by means of *self-help groups* (for example, *Alcoholics Anonymous*), *culture-* and *gender-sensitive treatments,* and *community prevention programs. pp. 402–410*

≫CRITICAL THOUGHTS≫

1. Various kinds of *club drugs* (e.g., Ecstasy and crystal meth), drugs used at all-night dance parties called "raves," seem to fall in and out of favor rather quickly. Why might young people readily move from one such drug to another? *pp. 387–388, 392–393*

2. What effects might the use of drugs by some rock performers have on teenagers and young adults? Who has the greater impact on the drug behaviors of teenagers and young adults: rock performers who speak out against drugs or rock performers who praise the virtues of drugs? *pp. 395–397, 410*

3. What different kinds of issues might be confronted by drug abusers from different ethnic groups or genders, and how might such issues influence their efforts at recovery? *pp. 397, 409*

4. Different ethnic, religious, and national groups have different rates of alcohol abuse. What social factors might help explain this observation? Can we be certain that biological factors are not involved? *pp. 397–401*

5. Popular talk show host Oprah Winfrey has revealed, with great emotion, that she had been physically dependent on cocaine in the mid-1970s. What impact might admissions like Winfrey's have on people's willingness to seek treatment for substance abuse? *pp. 402–410*

6. Since the major dangers of heroin come from overdose, unsterilized needles, and a criminal lifestyle, society has periodically tried legal, medically supervised use of heroin (in Great Britain) or a heroin substitute (in the United States) to combat this drug problem. Generally, such approaches have had limited effectiveness. Why? *pp. 406–407*

◖◖ cyberstudy ◗◗

SEARCH

Search the *Abnormal Psychology* Video Tool Kit
www.worthpublishers.com/apvtk

▲ Chapter 12 Video Cases
  Craving for Cocaine
  Using Marijuana for Medicinal Purposes
  Hallucinogens and the Brain

▲ Video case discussions, study guides, and questions

Log on to the Comer Web Page
www.worthpublishers.com/comer

▲ Chapter 12 outline, learning objectives, research exercises, study tools, and practice test questions

▲ Additional Chapter 12 case studies, Web links, and FAQs

SEXUAL DISORDERS AND GENDER IDENTITY DISORDER

R *obert, a 57-year-old man, came to sex therapy with his wife because of his inability to get erections. He had not had a problem with erections until six months earlier, when they attempted to have sex after an evening out, during which he had had several drinks. They attributed his failure to get an erection to his being "a little drunk," but he found himself worrying over the next few days that he was perhaps becoming impotent. When they next attempted intercourse, he found himself unable to get involved in what they were doing because he was so intent on watching himself to see if he would get an erection. Once again he did not, and they were both very upset. His failure to get an erection continued over the next few months. Robert's wife was very upset and . . . frustrated, accusing him of having an affair, or of no longer finding her attractive. Robert wondered if he was getting too old, or if his medication for high blood pressure, which he had been taking for about a year, might be interfering with erection. . . . When they came for sex therapy, they had not attempted any sexual activity for over two months.*

LoPiccolo, 1992, p. 492

Sexual behavior is a major focus of both our private thoughts and public discussions. Sexual feelings are a crucial part of our development and daily functioning, sexual activity is tied to the satisfaction of our basic needs, and sexual performance is linked to our self-esteem. Most people are fascinated by the abnormal sexual behavior of others and worry about the normality of their own sexuality.

Experts recognize two general categories of sexual disorders: sexual dysfunctions and paraphilias. People with *sexual dysfunctions* experience problems with their sexual responses. Robert, for example, had a dysfunction known as erectile disorder, a repeated failure to attain or maintain an erection during sexual activity. People with *paraphilias* have repeated and intense sexual urges or fantasies in response to objects or situations that society deems inappropriate, and they may behave inappropriately as well. They may be aroused by the thought of sexual activity with a child, for example, or of exposing their genitals to strangers, and they may act on those urges. In addition to the sexual disorders, DSM includes a diagnosis called *gender identity disorder*, a sex-related pattern in which people persistently feel that they have been born to the wrong sex and in fact identify with the other gender.

As you will see throughout this chapter, except for gender differences, relatively little is known about racial and other cultural differences in sexuality. This is true for normal sexual patterns, sexual dysfunctions, and paraphilias alike. Although different cultural groups have for years been labeled hypersexual, "hot blooded," exotic, passionate, submissive, and the like, such incorrect stereotypes have grown strictly from ignorance or prejudice (McGoldrick et al., 2007; Lewis, 2006), not from objective observations or research. In fact, sex therapists and sex researchers have only recently begun to attend systematically to the importance of culture and race (McGoldrick et al., 2007).

✿ Sexual Dysfunctions

Sexual dysfunctions, disorders in which people cannot respond normally in key areas of sexual functioning, make it difficult or impossible to enjoy sexual intercourse. A large study suggests that as many as 31 percent of men and 43 percent of

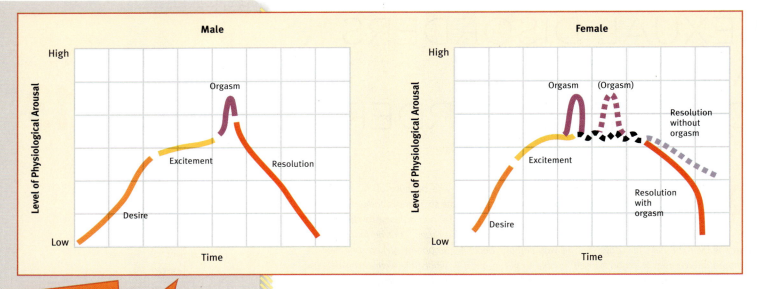

Figure 13-1
The normal sexual response cycle
Researchers have found a similar sequence of phases in both males and females. Sometimes, however, women do not experience orgasm; in that case, the resolution phase is less sudden. And sometimes women experience two or more orgasms in succession before the resolution phase. (Adapted from Kaplan, 1974; Masters & Johnson, 1970, 1966.)

•**sexual dysfunction**•A disorder marked by a persistent inability to function normally in some area of the human sexual response cycle.

•**desire phase**•The phase of the sexual response cycle consisting of an urge to have sex, sexual fantasies, and sexual attraction to others.

•**hypoactive sexual desire disorder**• A disorder marked by a lack of interest in sex and hence a low level of sexual activity.

women in the United States suffer from such a dysfunction during their lives (Laumann et al., 2005, 1999; Heiman, 2002). Sexual dysfunctions are typically very distressing, and they often lead to sexual frustration, guilt, loss of self-esteem, and interpersonal problems (Basson, 2007; Basson et al., 2001). Often these dysfunctions are interrelated; many patients with one dysfunction experience another as well. Sexual dysfunctioning will be described here for heterosexual couples, the majority of couples seen in therapy. Homosexual couples have the same dysfunctions, however, and therapists use the same basic techniques to treat them (LoPiccolo, 2004, 1995).

The human sexual response can be described as a *cycle* with four phases: *desire, excitement, orgasm,* and *resolution* (see Figure 13-1). Sexual dysfunctions affect one or more of the first three phases. Resolution consists simply of the relaxation and reduction in arousal that follow orgasm. Some people struggle with a sexual dysfunction their whole lives (labeled *lifelong type* in DSM-IV-TR); in other cases, normal sexual functioning preceded the dysfunction (*acquired type*). In some cases the dysfunction is present during all sexual situations (*generalized type*); in others it is tied to particular situations (situational type) (APA, 2000).

Disorders of Desire

The **desire phase** of the sexual response cycle consists of an urge to have sex, sexual fantasies, and sexual attraction to others (see Figure 13-2). Two dysfunctions—*hypoactive sexual desire disorder* and *sexual aversion disorder*—affect the desire phase. A client named Clara Bryarton experiences both of these disorders:

[Randall and Clara Bryarton] have been married for 14 years and have three children, ages 8 through 12. They [complain that Clara] has never enjoyed [sex] since they have been married.

Before their marriage, although they had intercourse only twice, [Clara] had been highly aroused by kissing and petting and felt she used her attractiveness to "seduce" her husband into marriage. She did, however, feel intense guilt about their two episodes of premarital intercourse; during their honeymoon, she began to think of sex as a chore that could not be pleasing. Although she periodically passively complied with intercourse, she had almost no spontaneous desire for sex. She never masturbated, had never reached orgasm, thought of all variations such as oral sex as completely repulsive, and was preoccupied with a fantasy of how disapproving her family would be if she ever engaged in any of these activities.

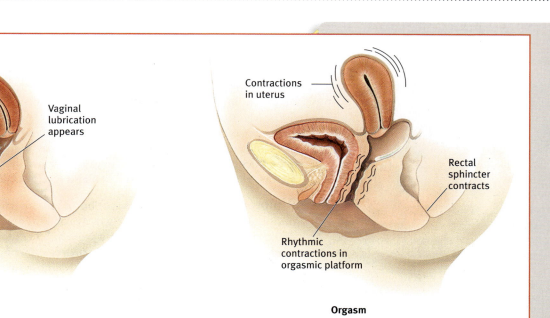

Figure 13-2
Normal female sexual anatomy
Changes in the female anatomy occur during the different phases of the sexual response cycle. (Adapted from Hyde, 1990, p. 200.)

[Clara feels] certain that no woman she respects in any older generation has [truly] enjoyed sex, and that despite the "new vogue" of sexuality, only sleazy, crude women let themselves act like "animals." These beliefs have led to a pattern of regular, but infrequent, sex that at best is accommodating and gives little or no pleasure to her or her husband. Whenever [Clara] comes close to having a feeling of sexual arousal, numerous negative thoughts come into her mind, such as "What am I, a tramp?" "If I like this, he'll just want it more often." Or "How could I look myself in the mirror after something like this?" These thoughts almost inevitably are accompanied by a cold feeling and an insensitivity to sensual pleasure. As a result, sex is invariably an unhappy experience. Almost any excuse, such as fatigue or being busy, is sufficient for her to rationalize avoiding intercourse.

Yet, intellectually [Clara] wonders, "Is something wrong with me?"

(Spitzer et al., 1994, p. 251)

People with **hypoactive sexual desire disorder** lack interest in sex and, in turn, display little sexual activity (see Table 13-1 on the next page). Nevertheless, when these individuals do have sex, their physical responses may be normal and they may enjoy the experience. While our culture portrays men as wanting all the sex they can get, hypoactive sexual desire may be found in as many as 16 percent of men, and the number seeking therapy has increased during the past decade (Maurice, 2007; Laumann et al., 2005, 1999). It may also be found in 33 percent of women. Surveys in the United Kingdom have yielded similar figures (Mercer et al., 2003). A number of people experience normal sexual interest and arousal but choose, as a matter of lifestyle, not to engage in sexual relations. These individuals are not diagnosed as having hypoactive sexual desire disorder.

DSM-IV-TR defines hypoactive sexual desire as "deficient or absent sexual fantasies and desire for sexual activity," but it does not specify what a "deficient" level is. In fact, this criterion is difficult to define (Basson, 2007; Maurice, 2007; LoPiccolo, 2004, 1995). Age, number of years married, education, social class, and other factors may all influence the frequency of sex (see *Psych Watch* on page 419). In one survey, 93 happily married couples were asked to report how often they desire sexual encounters. Almost all of them said that they desire sex at least once every two weeks, and around 85 percent reported a desire rate of several times a week or more. On the basis of this survey, sexual desire would be considered hypoactive only when a person desires sex less frequently than once every two weeks.

BETWEEN THE LINES

Eye of the Beholder

In the movie *Annie Hall,* Annie's psychotherapist asks her how often she and her boyfriend, Alvie Singer, sleep together. Simultaneously, across town, Alvie's therapist asks him the same question. Alvie answers, "Hardly ever, maybe three times a week," while Annie responds, "Constantly, I'd say three times a week." ‹‹

table: 13-1

DSM Checklist

HYPOACTIVE SEXUAL DESIRE DISORDER

1. Persistent or recurrent deficiency of sexual fantasies and desire for sexual activity.
2. Significant distress or interpersonal difficulty.

SEXUAL AVERSION DISORDER

1. Persistent or recurrent extreme aversion to, and avoidance of, almost all genital contact with a sexual partner.
2. Significant distress or interpersonal difficulty.

Based on APA, 2000.

•**sexual aversion disorder**•A disorder characterized by an aversion to and avoidance of genital sexual interplay.

People with **sexual aversion disorder** find sex distinctly unpleasant or repulsive. Sexual advances may sicken, disgust, or frighten them. Some people are repelled by a particular aspect of sex, such as penetration of the vagina; others experience a general aversion to all sexual stimuli, including kissing or touching. Aversion to sex seems to be quite rare in men and somewhat more common in women (Wincze, Bach, & Barlow, 2008; Maurice, 2007; Heiman, 2002).

A person's sex drive is determined by a combination of biological, psychological, and sociocultural factors, and any of them may reduce sexual desire. Most cases of low sexual desire or sexual aversion are caused primarily by sociocultural and psychological factors, but biological conditions can also lower sex drive significantly.

Biological Causes A number of hormones interact to produce sexual desire and behavior, and abnormalities in their activity can lower the sex drive (Ashton, 2007; Maurice, 2007; Hyde, 2005). In both men and women, a high level of the hormone *prolactin,* a low level of the male sex hormone *testosterone,* and either a high or low level of the female sex hormone *estrogen* can lead to low sex drive. Low sex drive has been linked to the high levels of estrogen contained in some birth control pills, for example. Conversely, it has also been tied to the low level of estrogen found in many postmenopausal women or women who have recently given birth. Long-term physical illness can also lower the sex drive (Basson, 2007; Stevenson & Elliott, 2007). The low drive may be a direct result of the illness or an indirect result because of stress, pain, or depression brought on by the illness.

Sex drive can be lowered by some pain medications, certain psychotropic drugs, and a number of illegal drugs such as cocaine, marijuana, amphetamines, and heroin (Stevenson & Elliott, 2007; Clayton et al., 2002). Low levels of alcohol may enhance the sex drive by lowering a person's inhibitions, yet high levels may reduce it (Ksir et al., 2008).

Psychological Causes A general increase in anxiety, depression, or anger may reduce sexual desire in both men and women (Basson, 2007; Hartmann et al., 2004). Frequently, as cognitive theorists have noted, people with hypoactive sexual desire and sexual aversion have particular attitudes, fears, or memories that contribute to their dysfunction, such as a belief that sex is immoral or dangerous (Wincze et al., 2008; LoPiccolo, 2004, 1995). Other people are so afraid of losing control over their sexual urges that they try to resist them completely. And still others fear pregnancy.

Certain psychological disorders may also contribute to hypoactive sexual desire and sexual aversion. Even a mild level of depression can interfere with sexual desire, and some people with obsessive-compulsive symptoms find contact with another person's body fluids and odors to be highly unpleasant (Basson, 2007; Maurice, 2007; LoPiccolo, 2004, 1995).

Sociocultural Causes The attitudes, fears, and psychological disorders that contribute to hypoactive sexual desire and sexual aversion occur within a social context, and thus certain sociocultural factors have also been linked to these dysfunctions. Many sufferers are feeling situational pressures—divorce, a death in the family, job stress, infertility difficulties, having a baby (Basson, 2007; Laumann et al., 2005). Others may be having problems in their relationships (Wincze et al., 2008). People who are in an unhappy relationship, have lost affection for their partner, or feel powerless and dominated by their partner can lose interest in sex (Maurice, 2007; Metz & Epstein, 2002). Even in basically happy relationships, if one partner is a very unskilled, unenthusiastic lover, the other can begin to lose interest in sex. And sometimes partners differ in their needs for closeness. The one who needs more personal space may develop hypoactive sexual desire as a way of keeping distance (LoPiccolo, 2004, 1997, 1995).

Cultural standards can also set the stage for hypoactive sexual desire and sexual aversion. Some men adopt our culture's double standard and thus cannot feel sexual desire for a woman they love and respect (Maurice, 2007). More generally, because our society equates sexual attractiveness with youthfulness, many middle-aged and older men and women lose interest in sex as their self-image or their attraction to their partner diminishes with age (LoPiccolo, 2004, 1995).

Lifetime Patterns of Sexual Behavior

Sexual dysfunctions are, by definition, different from the usual patterns of sexual functioning. But in the sexual realm, what is "the usual"? In the mid-1980s, clinicians found their efforts to prevent the spread of AIDS hindered by a lack of available data and began to conduct large surveys on sexual behavior. Collectively, studies conducted over the past two decades provide a wealth of useful, sometimes eye-opening information about sexual patterns in the "normal" populations of North America (CDC, 2007; Lindau et al., 2007; McAnulty & Burnette, 2006; Smith, 2006; Kelly, 2005; Laumann et al., 2005, 1999, 1994; Brown & Ceniceros, 2001; Seidman & Rieder, 1995; Janus & Janus, 1993).

Teenagers

More than 90 percent of boys masturbate by the end of adolescence, compared to 50 percent of girls. For the vast majority of them, masturbation began by age 14. Males report masturbating an average of one to two times a week, females once a month.

Around 20 percent of teenagers have heterosexual intercourse by the age of 15, and 80 percent by age 19. Today's teenagers are having intercourse younger than those of past generations. Most teens who are sexually experienced engage in only one sexual relationship at a time. Over the course of their teen years, however, most have at least two sex partners.

Extended periods without sex are still common, even for teenagers in a relationship. Half of sexually experienced adolescent girls have intercourse once a month or less. Sexually experienced teenage boys spend an average of six months of the year without intercourse.

Condom use by teenagers has increased somewhat during the past decade, partly because of warnings about AIDS. However, at most half of teenagers report having used a condom the last time they had sex. Less than a third of teenagers use condoms consistently and appropriately.

Early Adulthood (Ages 18–24)

More than 80 percent of unmarried young adults have intercourse in a given year. Of those who are sexually active, around a third have intercourse two or three times a month and another third engage in it two or three times a week. Masturbation remains common in young adulthood: close to 60 percent of men masturbate, a third of them at least once a week, and 36 percent of women masturbate, a tenth of them at least once a week.

Mid-Adulthood (Ages 25–59)

From the ages of 25 to 59, sexual relationships last longer and are more monogamous. More than 90 percent of people in this age range have sexual intercourse in a given year. Half of the unmarried men have two or more partners in a given year, compared to a quarter of the unmarried women.

Among sexually active adults, close to 60 percent of men have intercourse up to three times a week and around 60 percent of women once or twice a week. Middle-aged adults are still masturbating. Half of all middle-aged men masturbate at least monthly. Half of all women between 25 and 50 masturbate at least monthly, but only a third of those between 51 and 64 do so.

Old Age (Over Age 60)

More and more people stop having intercourse as the years go by—a total of 10 percent in their 40s, 15 percent in their 50s, 30 percent in their 60s, and 45 percent in their 70s. The decline in men's sexual activity usually comes gradually as they advance in age and their health fails. Sexual activity is more likely to drop off sharply for elderly women, commonly because of the death or illness of a partner. Elderly women also seem to lose interest in sex before elderly men do. Half of the women in their 60s report limited sexual interest, compared to fewer than 10 percent of the men.

Among elderly persons who remain sexually active, those in their 60s have intercourse an average of four times a month, those in their 70s two or three times a month. Around 70 percent of elderly men and 50 percent of elderly women continue to have sexual fantasies. Around half of men and a fourth of women continue to masturbate into their 90s.

Clearly sexual interests and behaviors remain an important part of life for large numbers of people, even as they grow older and as their sexual responses change to some degree.

"Lovapalooza" During early adulthood, more than 80 percent of individuals are sexually active. The feelings behind such activity are on display at the *Lovapalooza* kissing festival in Manila, Philippines, where more than 5,000 young couples lock lips for at least 10 seconds as part of the city's Valentine's Day celebration.

The trauma of sexual molestation or assault is especially likely to produce the fears, attitudes, and memories found in these sexual dysfunctions. Sexual aversion is very common in victims of sexual abuse and may persist for years, even decades (Hall, 2007; Heiman & Heard-Davison, 2004). In some cases, individuals may experience vivid flashbacks of the assault during adult sexual activity.

Disorders of Excitement

The **excitement phase** of the sexual response cycle is marked by changes in the pelvic region, general physical arousal, and increases in heart rate, muscle tension, blood pressure, and rate of breathing. In men, blood pools in the pelvis and leads to erection of the penis; in women, this phase produces swelling of the clitoris and labia, as well as lubrication of the vagina. Dysfunctions affecting the excitement phase are *female sexual arousal disorder* (once referred to as "frigidity") and *male erectile disorder* (once called "impotence").

Female Sexual Arousal Disorder
Women with a **female sexual arousal disorder** are persistently unable to attain or maintain proper lubrication or genital swelling during sexual activity (see Table 13-2). Understandably, many of them also experience an orgasmic disorder or other sexual dysfunction. In fact, this disorder is rarely diagnosed alone (Heiman, 2007; Heard-Davison et al., 2004). Studies vary widely in their estimates of its prevalence, but most agree that more than 10 percent of women experience it (Laumann et al., 2005, 1999, 1994; Bancroft et al., 2003). Because lack of sexual arousal in women is so often tied to an orgasmic disorder, researchers usually study and explain the two problems together. Correspondingly, this chapter will consider the causes of these problems together in the section on orgasmic disorder.

Male Erectile Disorder
Men with **male erectile disorder** persistently fail to attain or maintain an adequate erection during sexual activity. This problem occurs in about 10 percent of the general male population, including Robert, the man whose difficulties opened this chapter (Laumann et al., 2005, 1999; Heiman, 2002). Carlos Domera also has erectile disorder:

Carlos Domera is a 30-year-old dress manufacturer who came to the United States from Argentina at age 22. He is married to . . . Phyllis, also age 30. They have no children. Mr. Domera's problem was that he had been unable to have sexual intercourse for over a year due to his inability to achieve or maintain an erection. He had avoided all sexual contact with his wife for the prior five months, except for two brief attempts at lovemaking which ended when he failed to maintain his erection.

The couple separated a month ago by mutual agreement due to the tension that surrounded their sexual problem and their inability to feel comfortable with each other. Both professed love and concern for the other, but had serious doubts regarding their ability to resolve the sexual problem. . . .

[Carlos] conformed to the stereotype of the "macho Latin lover," believing that he "should always have erections easily and be able to make love at any time." Since he couldn't "perform" sexually, he felt humiliated and inadequate, and he dealt with this by avoiding not only sex, but any expression of affection for his wife.

[Phyllis] felt "he is not trying; perhaps he doesn't love me, and I can't live with no sex, no affection, and his bad moods." She had requested the separation temporarily, and he readily agreed. However, they had recently been seeing each other twice a week. . . .

During the evaluation he reported that the onset of his erectile difficulties was concurrent with a tense period in his business. After several "failures" to complete intercourse, he concluded he was "useless as a husband" and therefore a "total failure." The anxiety of attempting lovemaking was too much for him to deal with.

He reluctantly admitted that he was occasionally able to masturbate alone to a full, firm erection and reach a satisfying orgasm. However, he felt ashamed and guilty about

table: 13-2

DSM Checklist

FEMALE SEXUAL AROUSAL DISORDER

1. Persistent or recurrent inability to attain, or to maintain until completion of the sexual activity, adequate lubrication or swelling response of sexual excitement.
2. Significant distress or interpersonal difficulty.

MALE ERECTILE DISORDER

1. Persistent or recurrent inability to attain, or to maintain until completion of the sexual activity, an adequate erection.
2. Significant distress or interpersonal difficulty.

Based on APA, 2000.

this, from both childhood masturbatory guilt and a feeling that he was "cheating" his wife. It was also noted that he had occasional firm erections upon awakening in the morning. Other than the antidepressant, the patient was taking no drugs, and he was not using much alcohol. There was no evidence of physical illness.

(Spitzer et al., 1983, pp. 105–106)

Unlike Carlos, most men with an erectile disorder are over the age of 50, largely because so many cases are associated with ailments or diseases of older adults (Cameron et al., 2005). The disorder is experienced by 7 percent of men who are under 30 years old and increases to 50 percent of men over 60 (Rosen, 2007). Moreover, according to surveys, half of all adult men experience erectile difficulty during intercourse at least some of the time.

Most cases of erectile disorder result from an interaction of biological, psychological, and sociocultural processes (Rosen, 2007). One study found that only 10 of 63 cases of this disorder were caused by purely psychosocial factors, and only 5 were the result of physical impairment alone (LoPiccolo, 1991).

BIOLOGICAL CAUSES The same hormonal imbalances that can cause hypoactive sexual desire can also produce erectile disorder (Hyde, 2005). More commonly, however, vascular problems—problems with the body's blood vessels—are involved (Wincze et al., 2008; Rosen, 2007; Bach et al., 2001). An erection occurs when the chambers in the penis fill with blood, so any condition that reduces blood flow into the penis, such as heart disease or clogging of the arteries, may lead to the disorder. It can also be caused by damage to the nervous system as a result of diabetes, spinal cord injuries, multiple sclerosis, kidney failure, or treatment by dialysis (Wincze et al., 2008; Stevenson & Elliott, 2007). In addition, as is the case with hypoactive sexual desire, the use of certain medications and various forms of substance abuse, from alcohol abuse to cigarette smoking, may interfere with erections.

Medical procedures, including ultrasound recordings and blood tests, have been developed for diagnosing biological causes of erectile disorder. Measuring **nocturnal penile tumescence (NPT),** or erections during sleep, is particularly useful in assessing whether physical factors are responsible. Men typically have erections during *rapid eye movement (REM) sleep,* the phase of sleep in which dreaming takes place. A healthy man is likely to have two to five REM periods each night, and perhaps two to three hours of penile erections (see Figure 13-3 on the next page). Abnormal or absent nightly erections usually (but not always) indicate some physical basis for erectile failure. As a rough screening device, a patient may be instructed to fasten a simple "snap gauge" band around his penis before going to sleep and then check it the next morning. A broken band indicates that erection has occurred during the night. An unbroken band indicates a lack of nighttime erections and suggests that the person's general erectile problem may have a physical basis. A newer version of this device further attaches the band to a computer, which provides precise measurements of erections throughout the night (Wincze et al., 2008). Such devices are less likely to be in clinical practice today than in past years. As you'll see later in the chapter, Viagra and other drugs for erectile disorder are typically given to patients without much formal evaluation of their problem (Rosen, 2007).

PSYCHOLOGICAL CAUSES Any of the psychological causes of hypoactive sexual desire can also interfere with arousal and lead to erectile disorder (Rosen, 2007). As many as 90 percent of all men with severe depression, for example, experience some degree of erectile dysfunction (Stevenson & Elliott, 2007).

One well-supported psychological explanation for erectile disorder is the cognitive-behavioral theory developed by William Masters and Virginia Johnson (1970). The explanation emphasizes **performance anxiety** and the **spectator role.** Once a man begins to experience erectile problems, for

•nocturnal penile tumescence (NPT)• Erection during sleep.

•performance anxiety• The fear of performing inadequately and a related tension experienced during sex.

•spectator role• A state of mind that some people experience during sex, focusing on their sexual performance to such an extent that their performance and their enjoyment are reduced.

Psychological or organic? The *RigiScan* is a device that measures a male patient's erections during sleep. It consists of a computer and two bands that are worn around the penis. If the computer readout indicates that the bands have expanded throughout the night, it is concluded that the man has experienced normal erections during REM sleep and that his erectile failures during intercourse are probably caused by psychological factors.

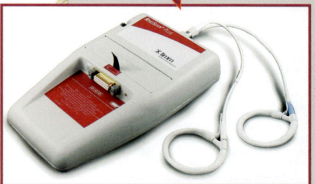

Courtesy Timm Medical Technologies, Eden Prairie, Minnesota

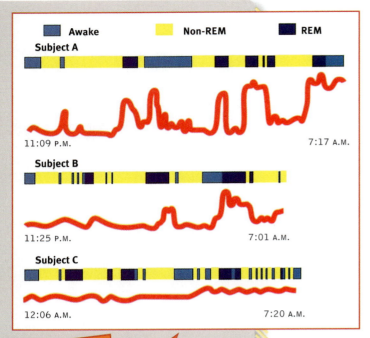

Figure 13-3

Measurements of erections during sleep
Research participant A, a man without
erectile problems, has normal erections
during REM sleep. Paricipant B has erectile
problems that seem to be at least partly
psychogenic—otherwise he would not
have any erections during REM sleep.
Participant C's erectile disorder is related
to organic problems, an interpretation supported by his lack of erections during REM
sleep. (Adapted from Bancroft, 1989.)

•**orgasm phase**•The phase of the
sexual response cycle during which an
individual's sexual pleasure peaks and
sexual tension is released as muscles in
the pelvic region contract rhythmically.

•**rapid ejaculation**•A dysfunction
in which a man reaches orgasm and
ejaculates before, on, or shortly after
penetration. and before he wishes to.
Also known as *premature ejaculation*.

whatever reason, he becomes fearful about failing to have an erection
and worries during each sexual encounter. Instead of relaxing and enjoying the sensations of sexual pleasure, he remains distanced from the
activity, watching himself and focusing on the goal of reaching erection. Instead of being an aroused participant, he becomes a judge and
spectator. Whatever the initial reason for the erectile dysfunction, the
resulting spectator role becomes the reason for the ongoing problem.
In this vicious cycle, the original cause of the erectile failure becomes
less important than fear of failure.

SOCIOCULTURAL CAUSES Each of the sociocultural factors that contribute
to hypoactive sexual desire has also been tied to erectile disorder. Men
who have lost their jobs and are under financial stress, for example, are
more likely to develop erectile difficulties than other men (Morokoff
& Gillilland, 1993). Marital stress, too, has been tied to this dysfunction (Wincze et al., 2008; Metz & Epstein, 2002). Two relationship
patterns in particular may contribute to it (Rosen, 2007; Perelman,
2005; LoPiccolo, 2004, 1991). In one, the wife provides too little
physical stimulation for her aging husband, who, because of normal
aging changes, now requires more intense, direct, and lengthy physical
stimulation of the penis for erection to occur. In the second relationship pattern, a couple believes that only intercourse can give the wife
an orgasm. This idea increases the pressure on the man to have an erection and makes
him more vulnerable to erectile dysfunction. If the wife reaches orgasm manually or
orally during their sexual encounter, his pressure to perform is reduced.

Disorders of Orgasm

During the **orgasm phase** of the sexual response cycle, an individual's sexual pleasure
peaks and sexual tension is released as the muscles in the pelvic region contract, or
draw together, rhythmically (see Figure 13-4). The man's semen is ejaculated, and the
outer third of the woman's vaginal wall contracts. Dysfunctions of this phase of the
sexual response cycle are *rapid*, or *premature, ejaculation; male orgasmic disorder;* and *female
orgasmic disorder.*

Rapid, or Premature, Ejaculation
Eddie is typical of many men in his experience of rapid ejaculation:

*Eddie, a 20-year-old student, sought treatment after his girlfriend ended their relation-
ship because his premature ejaculation left her sexually frustrated. Eddie had had only
one previous sexual relationship, during his senior year in high school. With two friends he
would drive to a neighboring town and find a certain prostitute. After picking her up, they
would drive to a deserted area and take turns having sex with her, while the others waited
outside the car. Both the prostitute and his friends urged him to hurry up because they
feared discovery by the police, and besides, in the winter it was cold. When Eddie began
his sexual relationship with his girlfriend, his entire sexual history consisted of this rapid
intercourse, with virtually no foreplay. He found caressing his girlfriend's breasts and genitals and her touching of his penis to be so arousing that he sometimes ejaculated before
complete entry of the penis, or after at most only a minute or so of intercourse.*

(LoPiccolo, 1995, p. 495)

A man suffering from **rapid, or premature, ejaculation** persistently reaches orgasm
and ejaculates with very little sexual stimulation before, on, or shortly after penetration,

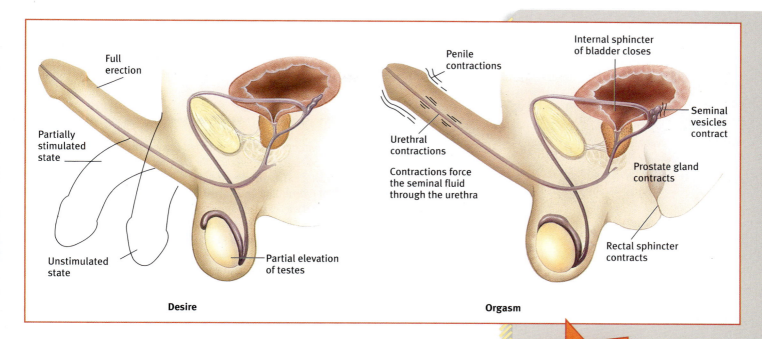

Figure 13-4
Normal male sexual anatomy Changes in the male anatomy occur during the different phases of the sexual response cycle. (Adapted from Hyde, 1990, p. 199.)

and before he wishes to (see Table 13–3 on the next page). As many as 30 percent of men in the United States experience rapid ejaculation at some time (Jannini & Lenzi, 2005; Laumann et al., 2005, 1999, 1994). The typical duration of intercourse in our society has increased over the past several decades, in turn increasing the distress of men who suffer from rapid ejaculation. Although the dysfunction is certainly experienced by many young men, it is not solely a young man's disorder. Research suggests that men of any age may suffer from rapid ejaculation (Althof, 2007; Laumann et al., 2005, 1999).

Psychological, particularly behavioral, explanations of rapid ejaculation have received more research support than other kinds of explanations. The dysfunction is common, for example, among young, sexually inexperienced men such as Eddie, who simply have not learned to slow down, control their arousal, and extend the pleasurable process of making love (Althof, 2007; Metz & Pryor, 2000). In fact, rapid ejaculation often occurs when a young man has his first sexual encounter. With continued sexual experience, most men acquire greater control over their sexual responses. Men of any age who have sex only occasionally are also prone to ejaculate rapidly (Althof, 2007; LoPiccolo, 2004, 1985).

Clinicians have also suggested that rapid ejaculation may be related to anxiety, hurried masturbation experiences during adolescence (in fear of being "caught" by parents), or poor recognition of one's own sexual arousal (Althof, 2007; Westheimer & Lopater, 2005). However, these theories have only sometimes received clear research support.

There is a growing belief among many clinical theorists that biological factors may also play a key role in many cases of rapid ejaculation. Research is at the earliest of stages, but three biological theories have emerged from the limited investigations done so far (Althof, 2007; Mirone et al., 2001; Waldinger et al., 1998). One theory states that some men are born with a genetic predisposition to develop this dysfunction. Indeed, one study found that 91 percent of a small sample of men suffering from rapid ejaculation had first-degree relatives who also displayed the dysfunction. A second theory argues that the brains of men with rapid ejaculation contain certain serotonin receptors that are overactive and others that are underactive. The theory is based on research with rodents. A third explanation holds that men with this dysfunction experience greater sensitivity or nerve conduction in the area of their penis, a notion that has received inconsistent research support thus far.

"Everybody's a critic."

•**male orgasmic disorder**•A male dysfunction characterized by repeated inability to reach orgasm or long delays in reaching orgasm after normal sexual excitement.

•**female orgasmic disorder**•A dysfunction in which a woman rarely has an orgasm or repeatedly experiences a very delayed one.

table: 13-3

DSM Checklist

PREMATURE EJACULATION

1. Persistent or recurrent ejaculation with minimal sexual stimulation before, on, or shortly after penetration and before the person wishes it.
2. Significant distress or interpersonal difficulty.

MALE ORGASMIC DISORDER

1. Persistent or recurrent delay in, or absence of, orgasm following a normal sexual excitement phase during sexual activity.
2. Significant distress or interpersonal difficulty.

FEMALE ORGASMIC DISORDER

1. Persistent or recurrent delay in, or absence of, orgasm following a normal sexual excitement phase during sexual activity.
2. Significant distress or interpersonal difficulty.

Based on APA, 2000.

Male Orgasmic Disorder A man with **male orgasmic disorder** is repeatedly unable to reach orgasm or is very delayed in reaching orgasm after normal sexual excitement. The disorder occurs in 8 percent of the male population (Hartmann & Waldinger, 2007; Laumann et al., 2005, 1999) and is typically a source of great frustration and upset, as in the case of John:

> John, a 38-year-old sales representative, had been married for 9 years. At the insistence of his 32-year-old wife, the couple sought counseling for their sexual problem—his inability to ejaculate during intercourse. During the early years of the marriage, his wife had experienced difficulty reaching orgasm until he learned to delay his ejaculation for a long period of time. To do this, he used mental distraction techniques and regularly smoked marijuana before making love. Initially, John felt very satisfied that he could make love for longer and longer periods of time without ejaculation and regarded his ability as a sign of masculinity.
>
> About 3 years prior to seeking counseling, after the birth of their only child, John found that he was losing his erection before he was able to ejaculate. His wife suggested different intercourse positions, but the harder he tried, the more difficulty he had in reaching orgasm. Because of his frustration, the couple began to avoid sex altogether. John experienced increasing performance anxiety with each successive failure, and an increasing sense of helplessness in the face of his problem.
>
> *(Rosen & Rosen, 1981, pp. 317–318)*

A low testosterone level, certain neurological diseases, and some head or spinal cord injuries can interfere with ejaculation (Stevenson & Elliott, 2007; McKenna, 2005). Drugs that slow down the sympathetic nervous system (such as alcohol, some medications for high blood pressure, and certain psychotropic medications) can also affect ejaculation. For example, the drug *fluoxetine,* or Prozac, and other serotonin-enhancing antidepressants appear to interfere with ejaculation in at least 30 percent of men who take them (Ashton, 2007; Clayton et al., 2002).

A leading psychological cause of male orgasmic disorder appears to be performance anxiety and the spectator role, the cognitive-behavioral factors also involved in male erectile disorder. Once a man begins to focus on reaching orgasm, he may stop being an aroused participant in his sexual activity and instead become an unaroused, self-critical, and fearful observer (Hartmann & Waldinger, 2007; Wiederman, 2001). Another psychological cause of male orgasmic disorder may be past masturbation habits. If, for example, a man has masturbated all his life by rubbing his penis against sheets, pillows, or other such objects, he may have difficulty reaching orgasm in the absence of the sensations and mechanics tied to those objects (Wincze et al., 2008). Finally, male orgasmic disorder may develop out of hypoactive sexual desire (Apfelbaum, 2000; Rosen & Leiblum, 1995). A man who engages in sex largely because of pressure from his partner, without any real desire for it, simply may not get aroused enough to reach orgasm.

Female Orgasmic Disorder Stephanie and Bill, married for three years, came for sex therapy because of her lack of orgasm.

> Stephanie had never had an orgasm in any way, but because of Bill's concern, she had been faking orgasm during intercourse until recently. Finally she told him the truth, and they sought therapy together. Stephanie had been raised by a strictly religious family. She could not recall ever seeing her parents kiss or show physical affection for each other. She was severely punished on one occasion when her mother found her looking at her own

genitals, at about age 7. Stephanie received no sex education from her parents, and when she began to menstruate, her mother told her only that this meant that she could become pregnant, so she mustn't ever kiss a boy or let a boy touch her. Her mother restricted her dating severely, with repeated warnings that "boys only want one thing." While her parents were rather critical and demanding of her (asking her why she got one B among otherwise straight A's on her report card, for example), they were loving parents and their approval was very important to her.

(LoPiccolo, 1995, p. 496)

Women with **female orgasmic disorder** rarely reach orgasm or generally experience a very delayed one. Around 24 percent of women apparently have this problem—including more than a third of postmenopausal women (Heiman, 2007, 2002; Laumann et al., 2005, 1999, 1994; Rosen & Leiblum, 1995). Studies indicate that 10 percent or more of women have never had an orgasm, either alone or during intercourse, and at least another 9 percent rarely have orgasms (Bancroft et al., 2003; LoPiccolo, 1995). At the same time, half of all women experience orgasm in intercourse at least fairly regularly (LoPiccolo & Stock, 1987). Women who are more sexually assertive (Hurlbert, 1991) and more comfortable with masturbation (Kelly, Stressberg, & Kircher, 1990) tend to have orgasms more regularly. Female orgasmic disorder appears to be more common among single women than among women who are married or living with someone (Laumann et al., 2005, 1999, 1994).

Most clinicians agree that orgasm during intercourse is not mandatory for normal sexual functioning (Wincze et al., 2008). Many women instead reach orgasm with their partners by direct stimulation of the clitoris (LoPiccolo, 2002, 1995). Although early psychoanalytic theory considered a lack of orgasm during intercourse to be pathological, evidence suggests that women who rely on stimulation of the clitoris for orgasm are entirely normal and healthy (Heiman, 2007).

As you saw earlier, female orgasmic disorder typically is linked to female sexual arousal disorder, and the two tend to be studied, explained, and treated together. Once again, biological, psychological, and sociocultural factors may combine to produce these disorders (Heiman, 2007).

BIOLOGICAL CAUSES A variety of physiological conditions can affect a woman's arousal and orgasm (Wincze et al., 2008; Heiman, 2007). Diabetes can damage the nervous system in ways that interfere with arousal, lubrication of the vagina, and orgasm. Lack of orgasm has sometimes been linked to multiple sclerosis and other neurological diseases, to the same drugs and medications that may interfere with ejaculation in men, and to changes, often postmenopausal, in skin sensitivity and structure of the clitoris, vaginal walls, or the labia—the folds of skin on each side of the vagina.

PSYCHOLOGICAL CAUSES The psychological causes of hypoactive sexual desire and sexual aversion, including depression, may also lead to the female arousal and orgasmic disorders (Heiman, 2007; Heard-Davison et al., 2004). In addition, as psychodynamic theorists might predict, memories of childhood traumas and relationships have sometimes been associated with these disorders. In one large study, memories of an unhappy childhood or loss of a parent during childhood were tied to lack of orgasm in adulthood (Raboch & Raboch, 1992). In other studies, childhood memories of a dependable father, a positive relationship with one's mother, affection between the parents, the mother's positive personality, and the mother's expression of positive emotions were all predictors of orgasm (Heiman, 2007; Heiman et al., 1986).

SOCIOCULTURAL CAUSES For years many clinicians have believed that female arousal and orgasmic disorders may result from society's recurrent message to women that they should repress and deny their sexuality, a message that has often led to "less permissive" sexual attitudes and behavior among women than

Grand Theft Auto: the sexual controversy
One of today's most popular video game series is *Grand Theft Auto*. The violence in these games has raised widespread concerns. Just as controversial is their sexually explicit content. Fearing that the sexual material in one of the games, *Grand Theft Auto: San Andreas*, was too graphic and suggestive for children, parents and politicians pressured the producer to stop manufacturing the initial version of that game and to develop enhanced security measures to prevent children's access to the game's sexual features.

Paul Sakuma/AP Photo

Figure 13-5

Is sex in a casual relationship acceptable? Men and women around the globe have different opinions on this issue. In one study, college women from the United States, Russia, and Japan rated casual sex as "unacceptable" on average, whereas the ratings by men in those countries ranged from "fairly acceptable" to "quite acceptable" (Sprecher & Hatfield, 1996). Both men and women from the various countries typically considered sex among engaged or pre-engaged couples to be "quite acceptable."

among men (see Figure 13-5). In fact, many women with female arousal and orgasmic disorders report that they had an overly strict religious upbringing, were punished for childhood masturbation, received no preparation for the onset of menstruation, were restricted in their dating as teenagers, and were told that "nice girls don't" (LoPiccolo & van Male, 2000; LoPiccolo, 1997) (see *A Closer Look* on the facing page).

A sexually restrictive history, however, is just as common among women who function well in sexual encounters (LoPiccolo, 2002, 1997; LoPiccolo & Stock, 1987). In addition, cultural messages about female sexuality have been more positive in recent years, while the rate of female arousal and orgasmic disorders remains the same. Why, then, do some women and not others develop sexual arousal and orgasmic dysfunctions? Researchers suggest that unusually stressful events, traumas, or relationships may help produce the fears, memories, and attitudes that often characterize these dysfunctions (Westheimer & Lopater, 2005; Heiman & Heard-Davison, 2004). For example, many women molested as children or raped as adults have arousal and orgasm dysfunctions (Hall, 2007; Heiman, 2007).

Research has also related orgasmic behavior to certain qualities in a woman's intimate relationships (Heiman, 2007; Metz & Epstein, 2002; Heiman et al., 1986). Studies have found, for example, that the likelihood of reaching orgasm may be tied to how much emotional involvement a woman had during her first experience of intercourse and how long that relationship lasted, the pleasure the woman obtained during the experience, her current attraction to her partner's body, and her marital happiness. Interestingly, the same studies have found that erotic fantasies during sex with their current partner are more common in orgasmic than in nonorgasmic women.

Disorders of Sexual Pain

Two sexual dysfunctions do not fit neatly into a specific phase of the sexual response cycle. These are the sexual pain disorders, *vaginismus* and *dyspareunia,* each marked by enormous physical discomfort when sexual activity is attempted.

Vaginismus In **vaginismus,** involuntary contractions of the muscles around the outer third of the vagina prevent entry of the penis (see Table 13-4). Severe cases can prevent a couple from ever having intercourse. This problem has received relatively little research, but estimates are that perhaps 20 percent of women occasionally experience pain during intercourse and that vaginismus occurs in less than 1 percent of all women (LoPiccolo & van Male, 2000; LoPiccolo, 1995).

Most clinicians agree with the cognitive-behavioral position that vaginismus is usually a learned fear response, set off by a woman's expectation that intercourse will be

table: 13-4

DSM Checklist

VAGINISMUS

1. Recurrent or persistent involuntary spasm of the muscles of the outer third of the vagina that interferes with sexual intercourse.
2. Significant distress or interpersonal difficulty.

DYSPAREUNIA

1. Recurrent or persistent genital pain associated with sexual intercourse in either a male or female.
2. Significant distress or interpersonal difficulty.

Based on APA, 2000.

A CLOSER LOOK

Common Sex-Role Myths

Myths of Male Sexuality

▶ A real man isn't into stuff like feelings and communicating.

▶ A man is always interested in and ready for sex.

▶ Sex is centered on a hard penis and what is done with it.

▶ A man should be able to make the earth move for his partner.

▶ Men don't have to listen to women in sex.

▶ Bigger is better.

▶ Men should be able to last all night during sex.

▶ Women typically dislike or disapprove of men who are unable to have an erection.

▶ If a man can't have an erection, he must not really love his partner.

▶ If a man knows that he might not be able to get an erection, it's unfair for him to start sexual activity with a partner.

▶ Focusing more intensely on one's erection—trying harder—is the best way to get an erection.

Myths of Female Sexuality

▶ Sex is only for women under 30.

▶ Normal women have an orgasm every time they have sex.

▶ All women can have multiple orgasms.

▶ Pregnancy and delivery reduce women's sexual responsiveness.

▶ A woman's sex life ends with menopause.

▶ A sexually responsive woman can always be aroused by her partner.

▶ Nice women aren't aroused by erotic books or films.

▶ Women are "frigid" if they don't like the more exotic forms of sex.

▶ If a woman can't have an orgasm quickly and easily, there's something wrong with her.

▶ Feminine women don't initiate sex or become unrestrained during sex.

▶ Contraception is a woman's responsibility, and she's just making up excuses if she says contraception issues are inhibiting her sexually.

Myths of Male and Female Sexuality

▶ All touching is sexual or should lead to sex.

▶ Sex equals intercourse.

▶ Good sex requires orgasm.

▶ It isn't romantic if a person asks the partner what he or she enjoys.

▶ Too much masturbation is bad.

▶ Someone with a sex partner does not masturbate.

▶ Fantasizing about someone else during sex means a person is not happy with the person he or she is in a relationship with.

(Wincze et al., 2008; Bach et al., 2001)

---

painful and damaging. A variety of factors apparently can set the stage for this fear, including anxiety and ignorance about intercourse, exaggerated stories about how painful and bloody the first occasion of intercourse is for women, trauma caused by an unskilled lover who forces his penis into the vagina before the woman is aroused and lubricated, and the trauma of childhood sexual abuse or adult rape (Binik et al., 2007; Hall, 2007; Heiman & Heard-Davison, 2004).

Some women experience painful intercourse because of an infection of the vagina or urinary tract, a gynecological disease such as herpes simplex, or the physical effects of menopause. In such cases vaginismus can be overcome only if the women receive medical treatment for these conditions (LoPiccolo, 2002, 1995). Many women who have vaginismus also have other sexual dysfunctions (Heard-Davison et al., 2004; Reissing et al., 2003). Some, however, enjoy sex greatly, have a strong sex drive, and reach orgasm with stimulation of the clitoris. They just fear penetration of the vagina.

Dyspareunia A person with **dyspareunia** (from Latin words meaning "painful mating") experiences severe pain in the genitals during sexual activity. Surveys suggest that as many as 14 percent of women and 3 percent of men suffer from this problem to some degree (Heiman, 2007, 2002; Laumann et al., 2005, 1999). As many as 8 percent of women experience painful intercourse on all or most occasions (Wincze et al., 2008). Sufferers typically enjoy sex and get aroused but find their sex lives very limited by the pain that accompanies what used to be a positive event.

Dyspareunia in women usually has a physical cause (Binik et al., 2007; Bergeron et al., 2002). Among the most common are injury to the vagina, cervix, uterus, or pelvic ligaments during childbirth. Similarly, the scar left by an episiotomy (a cut often made to

•**vaginismus**•A condition marked by involuntary contractions of the muscles around the outer third of the vagina, preventing entry of the penis.

•**dyspareunia**•A disorder in which a person experiences severe pain in the genitals during sexual activity.

enlarge the vaginal entrance and ease delivery) can cause pain. Dyspareunia has also been tied to collision of the penis with remaining parts of the hymen; yeast and other infections of the vagina; wiry pubic hair that rubs against the labia during intercourse; pelvic diseases; tumors; cysts; and allergic reactions to the chemicals in vaginal douches and contraceptive creams, the rubber in condoms or diaphragms, or the protein in semen.

Although psychological factors (for instance, heightened anxiety or overattentiveness to one's body) or relationship problems may contribute to this disorder, psychosocial factors alone are rarely responsible for it (Binik et al., 2007, 2002). In cases that are truly psychogenic, the woman is in fact likely to be suffering from hypoactive sexual desire (Steege & Ling, 1993). That is, penetration into an unaroused, unlubricated vagina is painful.

Treatments for Sexual Dysfunctions

The last 35 years have brought major changes in the treatment of sexual dysfunctions. For the first half of the twentieth century, the leading approach was long-term psychodynamic therapy. Clinicians assumed that sexual dysfunctioning was caused by failure to progress properly through the psychosexual stages of development, and they used techniques of free association and therapist interpretations to help clients gain insight about themselves and their problems. Although it was expected that broad personality changes would lead to improvement in sexual functioning, psychodynamic therapy was typically unsuccessful (Bergler, 1951).

In the 1950s and 1960s, behavioral therapists offered new treatments for sexual dysfunctions. Usually they tried to reduce the fears that they believed were causing the dysfunctions by applying such procedures as relaxation training and systematic desensitization (Lazarus, 1965; Wolpe, 1958). These approaches had some success, but they failed to work in cases where the key problems included misinformation, negative attitudes, and lack of effective sexual technique (LoPiccolo, 2002, 1995).

A revolution in the treatment of sexual dysfunctions occurred with the publication of William Masters and Virginia Johnson's landmark book *Human Sexual Inadequacy* in 1970. The *sex therapy* program they introduced has evolved into a complex approach, which now includes interventions from the various models, particularly cognitive-behavioral, couple, and family systems therapies, along with a number of sex-specific techniques (Leiblum, 2007; Bach et al., 2001). In recent years, biological interventions, particularly drug therapies, have been added to the treatment arsenal (Leiblum, 2007; Segraves & Althof, 2002).

What Are the General Features of Sex Therapy?

Modern sex therapy is short-term and instructive, typically lasting 15 to 20 sessions. It centers on specific sexual problems rather than on broad personality issues (Wincze et al., 2008; LoPiccolo, 2002, 1995). Carlos Domera, the Argentine man with an erectile disorder whom you met earlier, responded successfully to the multiple techniques of modern sex therapy:

At the end of the evaluation session the psychiatrist reassured the couple that Mr. Domera had a "reversible psychological" sexual problem that was due to several factors, including his depression, but also more currently his anxiety and embarrassment, his high standards, and some cultural and relationship difficulties that made communication awkward and relaxation nearly impossible. The couple was advised that a brief trial of therapy, focused directly on the sexual problem, would very likely produce significant improvement within ten to fourteen sessions. They were assured that the problem was almost certainly not physical in origin, but rather psychogenic, and that therefore the prognosis was excellent.

Mr. Domera was shocked and skeptical, but the couple agreed to commence the therapy on a weekly basis, and they were given a typical first "assignment" to do at home: a caressing massage exercise to try together with specific instructions not to attempt genital stimulation or intercourse at all, even if an erection might occur.

Not surprisingly, during the second session Mr. Domera reported with a cautious smile that they had "cheated" and had had intercourse "against the rules." This was their first successful intercourse in more than a year. Their success and happiness were acknowledged by the therapist, but they were cautioned strongly that rapid initial improvement often occurs, only to be followed by increased performance anxiety in subsequent weeks and a return of the initial problem. They were humorously chastised and encouraged to try again to have sexual contact involving caressing and non-demand light genital stimulation, without an expectation of erection or orgasm, and to avoid intercourse.

During the second and fourth weeks [Carlos] did not achieve erections during the love play, and the therapy sessions dealt with helping him to accept himself with or without erections and to learn to enjoy sensual contact without intercourse. His wife helped him to believe genuinely that he could please her with manual or oral stimulation and that, although she enjoyed intercourse, she enjoyed these other stimulations as much, as long as he was relaxed.

[Carlos] struggled with his cultural image of what a "man" does, but he had to admit that his wife seemed pleased and that he, too, was enjoying the nonintercourse caressing techniques. He was encouraged to view his new lovemaking skills as a "success" and to recognize that in many ways he was becoming a better lover than many husbands, because he was listening to his wife and responding to her requests.

By the fifth week the patient was attempting intercourse successfully with relaxed confidence, and by the ninth session he was responding regularly with erections. If they both agreed, they would either have intercourse or choose another sexual technique to achieve orgasm. Treatment was terminated after ten sessions.

(Spitzer et al., 1983, pp. 106–107)

"*When I touch him he rolls into a ball.*"

As Carlos Domera's treatment indicates, modern sex therapy includes a variety of principles and techniques. The following ones are applied in almost all cases, regardless of the dysfunction:

1. **Assessment and conceptualization of the problem.** Patients are initially given a medical examination and are interviewed concerning their "sex history" (see Figure 13-6 on the next page). The therapist's focus during the interview is on gathering information about past life events and, in particular, current factors that are contributing to the dysfunction (Heiman, 2007; Leiblum, 2007; Bach et al., 2001). Sometimes proper assessment requires a team of specialists, perhaps including a psychologist, urologist, and neurologist.

2. **Mutual responsibility.** Therapists stress the principle of *mutual responsibility*. Both partners in the relationship share the sexual problem, regardless of who has the actual dysfunction, and treatment will be more successful when both are in therapy (Hall, 2007; Bach et al., 2001).

3. **Education about sexuality.** Many patients who suffer from sexual dysfunctions know very little about the physiology and techniques of sexual activity (Wincze et al., 2008; Heiman, 2007; Rosen, 2007). Thus sex therapists may discuss these topics and offer educational materials, including instructional books, videos, and Internet sites.

4. **Attitude change.** Following a cardinal principle of cognitive therapy, sex therapists help patients examine and change any beliefs about sexuality that are

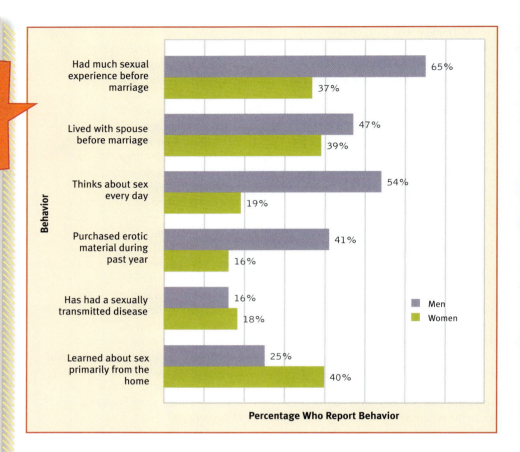

Figure 13-6

Sexual behavior and gender According to questionnaires, men are much more likely than women to think about sex on a daily basis and to have purchased sexual material, such as erotic magazines, within the past year. Women are more likely to have learned about sex from the home. (Adapted from Michael et al., 1994; Janus & Janus, 1993).

preventing sexual arousal and pleasure (Wincze et al., 2008; Heiman, 2007). Some of these mistaken beliefs are widely shared in our society and can result from past traumatic events, family attitudes, or cultural ideas.

5. **Elimination of performance anxiety and the spectator role.** Therapists often teach couples *sensate focus,* or *nondemand pleasuring,* a series of sensual tasks, sometimes called "petting" exercises, in which the partners focus on the sexual pleasure that can be achieved by exploring and caressing each other's body at home, without demands to have intercourse or reach orgasm—demands that may be interfering with arousal. Couples are told at first to refrain from intercourse at home and to restrict their sexual activity to kissing, hugging, and sensual massage of various parts of the body, but not of the breasts or genitals. Over time, they learn how to give and receive greater sexual pleasure and they build back up to the activity of sexual intercourse.

6. **Increasing sexual and general communication skills.** Couples are taught to use their sensate-focus skills and apply new sexual techniques and positions at home. They may, for example, try sexual positions in which the person being caressed can guide the other's hands and control the speed, pressure, and location of sexual contact (Heiman, 2007). Couples are also taught to give instructions to each other in a nonthreatening, informative manner ("It feels better over here, with a little less pressure"), rather than a threatening uninformative manner ("The way you're touching me doesn't turn me on"). Moreover, couples are often given broader training in how best to communicate with each other (Wincze et al., 2008; Basson, 2007; Bach et al., 2001).

7. **Changing destructive lifestyles and marital interactions.** A therapist may encourage a couple to change their lifestyle or take other steps to improve a situation that is having a destructive effect on their relationship—to distance themselves from interfering in-laws, for example, or to change a job that is

too demanding. Similarly, if the couple's general relationship is marked by conflict, the therapist will try to help them improve it, often before work on the sexual problems per se begins (Rosen, 2007; Metz & Epstein, 2002).

8. **Addressing physical and medical factors.** When sexual dysfunctions are caused by a medical problem, such as disease, injury, medication, or substance abuse, therapists try to address that problem (Ashton, 2007; Basson, 2007). If antidepressant medications are causing a man's erectile disorder, for example, the clinician may lower the dosage of the medication, change the time of day when the drug is taken, or consider prescribing a different antidepressant.

What Techniques Are Applied to Particular Dysfunctions?

In addition to the general components of sex therapy, specific techniques can help in each of the sexual dysfunctions.

Hypoactive Sexual Desire and Sexual Aversion
Hypoactive sexual desire and sexual aversion are among the most difficult dysfunctions to treat because of the many issues that may feed into them (Maurice, 2007; LoPiccolo, 2004, 2002). Thus therapists typically apply a combination of techniques. In a technique called *affectual awareness,* patients visualize sexual scenes in order to discover any feelings of anxiety, vulnerability, and other negative emotions they may have concerning sex. In another technique, patients receive cognitive *self-instruction training* to help them change their negative reactions to sex. That is, they learn to replace negative statements during sex with "coping statements," such as "I can allow myself to enjoy sex; it doesn't mean I'll lose control."

Therapists may also use behavioral approaches to help heighten a patient's sex drive. They may instruct clients to keep a "desire diary" in which they record sexual thoughts and feelings, to read books and view films with erotic content, and to fantasize about sex. Pleasurable shared activities such as dancing and walking together are also encouraged (LoPiccolo, 2002, 1997).

For sexual aversion that has resulted from sexual assault or childhood molestation, additional techniques may be needed (Hall, 2007). A patient may be encouraged to remember, talk about, and think about the assault until the memories no longer arouse fear or tension. Or the individual may be instructed to have a mock dialogue with the molester in order to express lingering feelings of rage and powerlessness (LoPiccolo, 2002, 1995).

These and related psychological approaches apparently help many women and men with hypoactive sexual desire and aversion disorders eventually to have intercourse more than once a week (Heard-Davison et al., 2004; Hurlbert, 1993). However, only a few controlled studies have been conducted.

Finally, biological interventions, such as hormone treatments, have been used, particularly for women whose problems arose after removal of their ovaries or later in life. The interventions have received some preliminary research support (Ashton, 2007; Davis, 2000, 1998). However, relatively few human studies have actually been conducted on such hormone treatments, and the field's understanding of the complex effects produced by hormone administration remains limited (Blaustein, 2008).

Erectile Disorder
Treatments for erectile disorder focus on reducing a man's performance anxiety, increasing his stimulation, or both, using a range of behavioral, cognitive, and relationship interventions (Rosen, 2007; Segraves & Althof, 2002). In one technique, the couple may be instructed to try the *tease technique* during sensate-focus exercises: the partner keeps caressing the man, but if the man gets an erection, the partner stops caressing him until he loses it. This exercise reduces pressure on the man to perform and at the same time teaches the couple that erections occur naturally in response to stimulation, as long as the partners do not keep focusing on performance. In another technique, the couple

Grooming is key
Humans are far from the only animals that follow a sexual response cycle or, for that matter, display sexual dysfunctions. Here a male Macaque monkey grooms a female monkey while they sit in a hot spring in the snow in central Japan. Research shows that such grooming triples the likelihood that the female will engage in sexual activity with the male.

AP Photo/Shuji Kajiyama

may be instructed to use manual or oral sex to try to achieve the woman's orgasm, again reducing pressure on the man to perform (LoPiccolo, 2004, 2002, 1995).

Biological approaches gained great momentum with the development in 1998 of *sildenafil* (trade name Viagra) (Rosen, 2007). This drug increases blood flow to the penis within one hour of ingestion; the increased blood flow enables the user to attain an erection during sexual activity (see *Eye on Culture* below). Sildenafil appears to be relatively safe except for men with certain coronary heart diseases and cardiovascular diseases, particularly those who are taking nitroglycerin and other heart medications (Stevenson & Elliott, 2007). Over the past decade, two other erectile dysfunction drugs have been approved—*tadalofil* (Cialis) and *vardenafil* (Levitra)—and are now actively competing with Viagra for a share of the lucrative marketplace. Collectively, the three drugs are the most common form of treatment for erectile disorder (Rosen, 2007). They effectively restore erections in 75 percent of men who use them.

EYE ON CULTURE

Sexism, Viagra, and the Pill

Many of us believe that we live in an enlightened world, where sexism is declining and where health care and benefits are available to men and women in equal measure. Periodically, however, such illusions are shattered. The responses of government agencies and insurance companies to the discovery and marketing of Viagra in 1998 may be a case in point.

Consider, first, the nation of Japan. In early 1999, just six months after Viagra's sensational introduction in the United States, the drug was approved for use among men in Japan (Martin, 2000). In contrast, low-dose contraceptives—"the pill"—were not approved for use among women in that country until June 1999—a full 40 years after their introduction

elsewhere! Many observers believe that birth control pills would still be unavailable to women in Japan had Viagra not received its quick approval.

Has the United States been able to avoid such an apparent double standard in its health care system? Not really. Before Viagra was introduced, insurance companies were not required to reimburse women for the cost of prescription contraceptives. As a result, women had to pay 68 percent more out-of-pocket expenses for health care than did men, largely because of uncovered reproductive health care costs (Hayden, 1998). Some legislators had sought to correct this problem by requiring contraceptive coverage in health insurance plans, but their efforts failed in state after state for more than a decade.

In contrast, when Viagra was introduced in 1998, many insurance companies readily agreed to cover the new drug, and many states included Viagra as part of Medicaid coverage. As the public outcry grew over the contrast between coverage of Viagra for men and lack of coverage of oral contraceptives for women, laws across the country finally began to change. In fact, by the end of 1998, nine

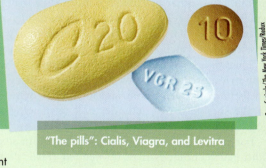
"The pills": Cialis, Viagra, and Levitra

Tony Cenicola/The New York Times/Redux

states required prescription contraceptive coverage (Hayden, 1998). Today 22 states require such coverage by private insurance companies and 35 states require it for state employees (CRR, 2005). Moreover, if the proposed Equity in Prescription Insurance and Contraceptive Coverage Act is passed by Congress, all insurers in the nation will be required to reimburse women for the cost of oral contraceptives.

In the meantime, wishful thinkers express hope that generous private donors will help foot the bill for oral contraceptives as some donors have done for Viagra. Immediately after Viagra's approval, one noted philanthropist donated $1 million to provide this drug to the needy. In explaining his action, he said, "I saw an article saying that at $10 apiece, a lot of impotent men wouldn't be able to afford it. So I said [to my wife], . . . 'let's help,' and by Tuesday we had it done" (Carlson, 1998).

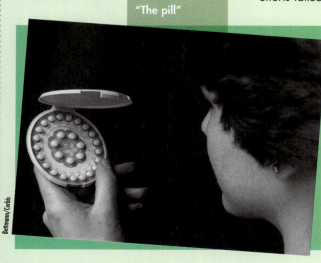
"The pill"

Bettmann/Corbis

Prior to the development of Viagra, Cialis, and Levitra, a range of other medical procedures were developed for erectile disorder. These procedures are now viewed as "second-line" treatments that are applied primarily when the medications are unsuccessful or too risky for individuals (Rosen, 2007; Frohman, 2002). Such procedures include gel suppositories, injections of drugs into the penis, and a *vacuum erection device* (*VED*), a hollow cylinder that is placed over the penis. Here a man uses a hand pump to pump air out of the cylinder, drawing blood into his penis and producing an erection. In another biological approach, now performed only rarely, surgeons implant a *penile prosthesis*—a semirigid rod made of rubber and wire—to produce an artificial erection (Rosen, 2007).

Male Orgasmic Disorder Like the treatments for male erectile disorder, therapies for male orgasmic disorder include techniques to reduce performance anxiety and increase stimulation (Hartmann & Waldinger, 2007; LoPiccolo, 2004). In one of many such techniques, a man may be instructed to masturbate to orgasm in the presence of his partner or to masturbate just short of orgasm before inserting his penis for intercourse (Marshall, 1997). This increases the likelihood that he will ejaculate during intercourse. He then is instructed to insert his penis at ever earlier stages of masturbation.

When male orgasmic disorder is caused by physical factors such as neurological damage or injury, treatment may include a drug to increase arousal of the sympathetic nervous system (Stevenson & Elliott, 2007). However, few studies have systematically tested the effectiveness of such treatments (Hartmann & Waldinger, 2007; Rosen & Leiblum, 1995).

Rapid Ejaculation Rapid, or premature, ejaculation has been treated successfully for years by behavioral procedures (Althof, 2007; Masters & Johnson, 1970). In the *stop-start,* or *pause,* procedure, the penis is manually stimulated until the man is highly aroused. The couple then pauses until his arousal subsides, after which the stimulation is resumed. This sequence is repeated several times before stimulation is carried through to ejaculation, so the man ultimately experiences much more total time of stimulation than he has ever experienced before (LoPiccolo, 2004, 1995). Eventually the couple progresses to putting the penis in the vagina, making sure to withdraw it and to pause whenever the man becomes too highly aroused. According to clinical reports, after two or three months many couples can enjoy prolonged intercourse without any need for pauses (Althof, 2007; LoPiccolo, 2004, 2002).

In a related procedure, the *squeeze technique,* a man with this dysfunction reaches near-ejaculation and then he or his partner applies a firm squeeze to the ridge of his penis below its head. If done correctly, the squeeze causes a partial or total loss of erection (Masters & Johnson, 1970). As in the stop-start procedure, this sequence is repeated several times. Again, research suggests that this technique often leads to significant improvements (Althof, 2007). Many men who respond to the squeeze, stop-start, or other behavioral techniques are, however, known to relapse, so relapse prevention strategies—periodic "booster" or maintenance sessions after therapy has been stopped—have been added to such programs of treatment.

Some clinicians treat rapid ejaculation with SSRIs, the serotonin-enhancing antidepressant drugs. Because these drugs often reduce sexual arousal or orgasm, the reasoning goes, they may be helpful to men who experience rapid ejaculation. Many studies report positive results with this approach (Althof, 2007, 1995; Ashton, 2007; Stevenson & Elliott, 2007). The effect of this approach is consistent with the biological theory, mentioned earlier, that serotonin receptors in the brains of men with rapid ejaculation may function abnormally.

Female Arousal and Orgasmic Disorders Specific treatments for female arousal and orgasmic dysfunctions include cognitive-behavioral techniques, self-exploration, enhancement of body awareness, and directed masturbation training (Heiman, 2007, 2002, 2000; Millner, 2005; LoPiccolo, 2002, 1997). These procedures are especially useful for women who have never had an orgasm under any circumstances. Biological treatments,

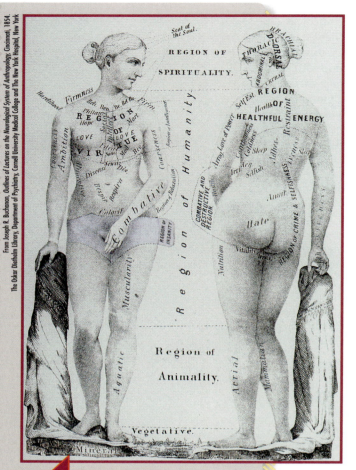

From Joseph R. Buchanan, *Outlines of Lectures on the Neurological System of Anthropology*, Cincinnati, 1854.
The Oskar Diethelm Library, Department of Psychiatry, Cornell University Medical College and The New York Hospital, New York

"The region of insanity"
Medical authorities described "excessive passion" in Victorian women as danger-ous and as a possible cause of insanity (Gamwell & Tomes, 1995). This illustration from a nineteenth-century medical text-book even labels a woman's reproductive organs as her "region of insanity."

including hormone therapy or the use of sildenafil (Viagra), have also been tried, but research has not found such interventions to be consistently help-ful (Heiman, 2007; Davis, 2000, 1998).

In **directed masturbation training,** a woman is taught step by step how to masturbate effectively and eventually to reach orgasm during sexual interactions. The training includes use of diagrams and reading material, private self-stimulation, erotic material and fantasies, "orgasm triggers" such as holding her breath or thrusting her pelvis, sensate focus with her partner, and sexual positioning that produces stimulation of the clitoris during intercourse. This training program appears to be highly effective: over 90 percent of women learn to have an orgasm during masturbation, about 80 percent during caressing by their partners, and about 30 percent during intercourse (Heiman, 2007; LoPiccolo, 2002, 1997).

As you read earlier, a lack of orgasm during intercourse is not neces-sarily a sexual dysfunction, provided the woman enjoys intercourse and can reach orgasm through caressing, either by her partner or by herself. For this reason some therapists believe that the wisest course is simply to educate women whose only concern is lack of orgasm during intercourse, informing them that they are quite normal.

Vaginismus Specific treatment for vaginismus, involuntary contractions of the muscles around the vagina, typically takes two approaches (Kabakci & Batur, 2003; Heiman, 2002). First, a woman may practice tightening and relaxing her vaginal muscles until she gains more voluntary control over them. Second, she may receive gradual behavioral exposure treatment to help her overcome her fear of penetration, beginning, for example, by in-serting increasingly large dilators in her vagina at home and at her own pace and eventually ending with the insertion of her partner's penis (Binik et al., 2007; Rosenbaum, 2007). Most women treated for vaginismus with such procedures eventually have pain-free intercourse (Heiman, 2002; Beck, 1993). In recent years, some medical interventions have also been applied. For example, several clinical investigators have injected the problematic vaginal muscles with Botox to help reduce spasms in those muscles (Ghazizadeh & Nikzad, 2004; Romito et al., 2004). However, studies of this approach have been unsystematic. Generally, many women with this problem report that they received ineffective or inaccurate forms of treatment when they first sought help from their physicians (Ogden & Ward, 1995).

Dyspareunia As you saw earlier, the most common cause of dyspareunia, genital pain during intercourse, is physical, such as pain-causing scars, lesions, or infection aftereffects. When the cause is known, pain management procedures (see pages 194–196, 198) and sex therapy techniques may be tried, including helping a couple to learn intercourse positions that avoid putting pressure on the injured area. Medical interventions—from topical creams to surgery—may also be tried, but they must still be combined with other sex therapy techniques to overcome the years of sexual anxiety and lack of arousal (Binik et al., 2007; Heard-Davison et al., 2004; Bergeron et al., 2002, 2001). Because many cases of dyspareunia are in fact caused by undiagnosed physical problems, it is very important that clients receive expert gynecological exams. Indeed, many experts believe that most cases of vaginismus and dyspareunia are best assessed and treated by a *team* of profession-als, including a gynecologist, physical therapist, and sex therapist or other mental health professional (Rosenbaum, 2007).

What Are the Current Trends in Sex Therapy?

Sex therapists have now moved well beyond the approach first developed by Masters and Johnson. For example, today's sex therapists regularly treat partners who are living together but not married. They also treat sexual dysfunctions that arise from psychological disorders such as depression, mania, schizophrenia, and certain personality disorders (Leiblum, 2007; Bach et al., 2001). In addition, sex therapists no longer screen out clients with severe marital discord, the elderly, the medically ill, the physically handicapped, gay clients, or individuals who have no long-term sex partner (Nichols & Shernoff, 2007; Stevenson & Elliott, 2007). Sex therapists are also paying more attention to excessive sexuality, sometimes called *hypersexuality* or *sexual addiction* (Kafka, 2007, 2000).

Many sex therapists have expressed concern about the sharp increase in the use of drugs and other medical interventions for sexual dysfunctions, particularly for hypoactive sexual desire and male erectile disorder. Their concern is that therapists will increasingly choose the biological interventions rather than integrating biological, psychological, and sociocultural interventions. In fact, a narrow approach of any kind probably cannot fully address the complex factors that cause most sexual problems (Leiblum, 2007; Rosen, 2007). It took sex therapists years to recognize the considerable advantages of an integrated approach to sexual dysfunctions. The development of new medical interventions should not lead to its abandonment.

Paraphilias

Paraphilias are disorders in which individuals repeatedly have intense sexual urges or fantasies or display sexual behaviors that involve nonhuman objects, children, nonconsenting adults, or the experience of suffering or humiliation. Many people with a paraphilia can become aroused only when a paraphilic stimulus is present, fantasized about, or acted out. Others need the stimulus only during times of stress or under other special circumstances.

According to DSM-IV-TR, a diagnosis of paraphilia should be applied only when the urges, fantasies, or behaviors last at least six months (see Table 13-5). For most paraphilias, the urges, fantasies, or behaviors must also cause great distress or interfere with one's social life or job performance in order for a diagnosis to be applied (APA, 2000). For certain paraphilias, however, DSM-IV-TR clarifies that performance of the sexual behavior indicates a disorder even if the individual experiences no distress or impairment (APA, 2000). People who initiate sexual contact with children, for example, warrant a diagnosis of pedophilia regardless of how troubled the individuals may or may not be over their behavior.

Some people with one kind of paraphilia display others as well (Marshall et al., 2008; Langstrom & Zucker, 2005). Relatively few people receive a formal diagnosis of paraphilia, but the large Internet and consumer market in paraphilic pornography leads clinicians to suspect that the patterns may be quite common (APA, 2000). People whose paraphilias involve children or nonconsenting adults often come to the attention of clinicians when they get into legal trouble (Maletzky & Steinhauser, 2004). Some experts argue that, with the exception of such nonconsensual paraphilias, paraphilic activities should be considered a disorder only when they are the exclusive or preferred means of achieving sexual excitement and orgasm (Marshall et al., 2008).

Although theorists have proposed various explanations for paraphilias, there is little formal evidence to support them (Abramowitz, 2008; McConaghy, 2005). Moreover, none of the many treatments applied to paraphilias have received much research or proved clearly effective (Roche & Quayle, 2007; McConaghy, 2005; Maletzky, 2002). Psychological and sociocultural treatments for paraphilias have been available the longest, but today's professionals are also using biological interventions. Some practitioners administer drugs called *antiandrogens* that lower the production of testosterone, the male sex hormone, and reduce the sex drive (Marshall et al., 2008; Hyde & DeLamater, 2006; Briken et al., 2003). Although antiandrogens do indeed reduce paraphilic patterns, several of them disrupt normal sexual feelings and behavior as well. Thus the drugs tend to be applied primarily when the paraphilias are of danger either to the individuals themselves or to other people. Clinicians are also increasingly administering SSRIs, the serotonin-enhancing antidepressant medications, to treat persons with paraphilias,

•**directed masturbation training**• A sex therapy approach that teaches women with female arousal or orgasmic disorders how to masturbate effectively and eventually to reach orgasm during sexual interactions.

•**paraphilias**•Disorders characterized by recurrent and intense sexual urges, fantasies, or behaviors involving nonhuman objects, children, nonconsenting adults, or experiences of suffering or humiliation.

table: 13-5

DSM Checklist

PARAPHILIA

1. Over a period of at least six months, recurrent, intense sexually arousing fantasies, sexual urges, or behaviors involving certain inappropriate stimuli or situations (nonhuman objects; the suffering or humiliation of oneself or one's partner; or children or other nonconsenting persons).

2. Significant distress or impairment over the fantasies, urges, or behaviors. (In some paraphilias—pedophilia, exhibitionism, voyeurism, frotteurism, and sexual sadism—the performance of paraphilic behaviors indicates a disorder, even in the absence of distress or impairment.)

Based on APA, 2000.

•**fetishism**•A paraphilia consisting of recurrent and intense sexual urges, fantasies, or behaviors that involve the use of a nonliving object, often to the exclusion of all other stimuli.

•**masturbatory satiation**•A behavioral treatment in which a client masturbates for a very long period of time while fantasizing in detail about a paraphilic object. The procedure is expected to produce a feeling of boredom that in turn becomes linked to the object.

•**orgasmic reorientation**•A procedure for treating certain paraphilias by teaching clients to respond to new, more appropriate sources of sexual stimulation.

•**transvestic fetishism**•A paraphilia consisting of repeated and intense sexual urges, fantasies, or behaviors that involve dressing in clothes of the opposite sex. Also known as *transvestism* or *cross-dressing*.

hoping that the drugs will reduce these compulsion-like sexual behaviors just as they help reduce other kinds of compulsions (Wright & Hatcher, 2006). In addition, of course, a common effect of the SSRIs is to lower sexual arousal.

Fetishism

Key features of **fetishism** are recurrent intense sexual urges, sexually arousing fantasies, or behaviors that involve the use of a nonliving object, often to the exclusion of all other stimuli. Usually the disorder, which is far more common in men than in women, begins in adolescence. Almost anything can be a fetish; women's underwear, shoes, and boots are particularly common (APA, 2000). Some people with fetishism commit thievery in order to collect as many of the desired objects as possible. The objects may be touched, smelled, worn, or used in some other way while the person masturbates, or the individual may ask a partner to wear the object when they have sex (Marshall et al., 2008). Several of these features are seen in the following case:

A 32-year-old, single male . . . related that although he was somewhat sexually attracted by women, he was far more attracted by "their panties."

To the best of the patient's memory, sexual excitement began at about age 7, when he came upon a pornographic magazine and felt stimulated by pictures of partially nude women wearing "panties." His first ejaculation occurred at 13 via masturbation to fantasies of women wearing panties. He masturbated into his older sister's panties, which he had stolen without her knowledge. Subsequently he stole panties from her friends and from other women he met socially. He found pretexts to "wander" into the bedrooms of women during social occasions, and would quickly rummage through their possessions until he found a pair of panties to his satisfaction. He later used these to masturbate into, and then "saved them" in a "private cache." The pattern of masturbating into women's underwear had been his preferred method of achieving sexual excitement and orgasm from adolescence until the present consultation.

(Spitzer et al., 1994, p. 247)

Researchers have not been able to pinpoint the causes of fetishism. Psychodynamic theorists view fetishes as defense mechanisms that help people avoid the anxiety

Mrs. Robinson's stockings
The 1967 film *The Graduate* helped define a generation by focusing on the personal confusion, apathy, and sexual adventures of a young man in search of meaning. Marketers decided to promote this film by using a fetishistic-like photo of Mrs. Robinson putting on her stockings under Benjamin's watchful eye, a scene forever identified with the movie.

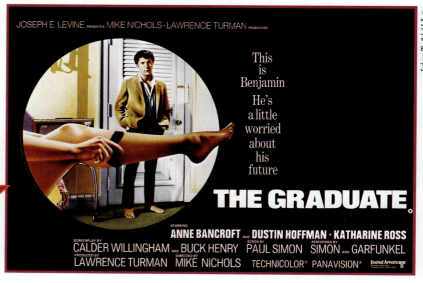

produced by normal sexual contact. Psychodynamic treatment for this problem, however, has met with little success (LoPiccolo, 1992).

Behaviorists propose that fetishes are acquired through classical conditioning (Roche & Quayle, 2007; Akins, 2004; Doctor & Neff, 2001). In a pioneering behavioral study, male participants were shown a series of slides of nude women along with slides of boots (Rachman, 1966). After many trials, the participants became aroused by the boot photos alone. If early sexual experiences similarly occur in the presence of particular objects, perhaps the stage is set for development of fetishes.

Behaviorists have sometimes treated fetishism with *aversion therapy* (Wright & Hatcher, 2006; Krueger & Kaplan, 2002). In one study, an electric shock was administered to the arms or legs of participants with fetishes while they imagined their objects of desire (Marks & Gelder, 1967). After two weeks of therapy all men in the study showed at least some improvement. In another aversion technique, *covert sensitization,* people with fetishism are guided to imagine the pleasurable object and repeatedly to pair this image with an *imagined* aversive stimulus until the object of sexual pleasure is no longer desired.

Another behavioral treatment for fetishism is **masturbatory satiation** (Wright & Hatcher, 2006; Krueger & Kaplan, 2002). In this method, the client masturbates to orgasm while fantasizing about a sexually appropriate object, then switches to fantasizing in detail about fetishistic objects while masturbating again and continues the fetishistic fantasy for an hour. The procedure is meant to produce a feeling of boredom, which in turn becomes linked to the fetishistic object.

Yet another behavioral approach to fetishism, also used for other paraphilias, is **orgasmic reorientation,** which teaches individuals to respond to more appropriate sources of sexual stimulation (Wright & Hatcher, 2006). People are shown conventional stimuli while they are responding to unconventional objects. A person with a shoe fetish, for example, may be instructed to obtain an erection from pictures of shoes and then to begin masturbating to a picture of a nude woman. If he starts to lose the erection, he must return to the pictures of shoes until he is masturbating effectively, then change back to the picture of the nude woman. When orgasm approaches, he must direct all attention to the conventional stimulus.

Transvestic Fetishism

Transvestic fetishism, also known as **transvestism** or **cross-dressing,** is a recurrent need or desire to dress in clothes of the opposite sex in order to achieve sexual arousal. In the following passage, a 42-year-old married father describes his pattern:

I have been told that when I dress in drag, at times I look like Whistler's Mother [laughs], especially when I haven't shaved closely. I usually am good at detail, and I make sure when I dress as a woman that I have my nails done just so, and that my colors match. Honestly, it's hard to pin a date on when I began cross dressing. . . . If pressed, I would have to say it began when I was about 10 years of age, fooling around with and putting on my mom's clothes. . . . I was always careful to put everything back in its exact place, and in 18 years of doing this in her home, my mother never, I mean never, suspected, or questioned me about putting on her clothes. I belong to a transvestite support group . . . , a group for men who cross dress. Some of the group are homosexuals, but most are not. A true transvestite—and I am one, so I know—is not homosexual. We don't discriminate against them in the group at all; hey, we have enough trouble getting acceptance as normal people and not just a bunch of weirdos ourselves. They are a bunch of nice guys . . . , really. Most of them are like me.

Most of [the men in the group] have told their families about their dressing inclinations, but those that are married are a mixed lot; some

A group approach
Crossroads is a self-help group for men with transvestic fetishism, a recurrent need to dress in women's clothing as a means to achieve sexual arousal.

wives know and some don't, they just suspect. I believe in honesty, and told my wife about this before we were married. We're separated now, but I don't think it's because of my cross dressing. . . . Some of my friends, when I was growing up, suggested psychotherapy, but I don't regard this as a problem. If it bothers someone else, then they have the problem. . . . I function perfectly well sexually with my wife, though it took her some time to be comfortable with me wearing feminine underwear; yes, sometimes I wear it while making love, it just makes it more exciting.

(Janus & Janus, 1993, p. 121)

Professional motives
Dressing in clothes of the opposite sex does not necessarily convey a paraphilia or gender identity disorder. Indeed, two of the most acclaimed movie performances of 2007 were Cate Blanchett's portrayal of musical legend Bob Dylan in *I'm Not There* and John Travolta's role as Edna Turnblad in *Hairspray*. On the other hand, the enormous attention that surrounded these performances probably does say something about the public's fascination with the issue of cross-dressing.

Like this man, the typical person with transvestism, almost always a heterosexual male (Marshall et al., 2008), begins cross-dressing in childhood or adolescence (Langstrom & Zucker, 2005; Doctor & Neff, 2001). He is the picture of characteristic masculinity in everyday life and is usually alone when he cross-dresses. A small percentage of such men cross-dress to visit bars or social clubs. Some wear a single item of women's clothing, such as underwear or hosiery, under their masculine clothes. Others wear makeup and dress fully as women. Some married men with transvestism involve their wives in their cross-dressing behavior (Kolodny, Masters, & Johnson, 1979). The disorder is often confused with gender identity disorder, but, as you will see, they are two separate patterns that overlap only in some individuals.

The development of transvestic fetishism sometimes seems to follow the behavioral principles of operant conditioning. In such cases, parents or other adults may openly encourage the individuals to cross-dress as children or even reward them for this behavior. In one case, a woman was delighted to discover that her young nephew enjoyed dressing in girls' clothes. She had always wanted a niece, and she proceeded to buy him dresses and jewelry and sometimes dressed him as a girl and took him out shopping.

Exhibitionism

A person with **exhibitionism** has recurrent urges to expose his genitals to another person, almost always a member of the opposite sex, or has sexually arousing fantasies of doing so. He may also carry out those urges but rarely attempts to initiate sexual activity with the person to whom he exposes himself (APA, 2000; Maletzky, 2000). More often, he wants to provoke shock or surprise. Sometimes an exhibitionist will expose himself in a particular neighborhood at particular hours. In a survey of 2,800 men, 4.3 percent of them reported that they perform exhibitionistic behavior (Langstrom & Seto, 2006). Yet between one-third and half of all women report having seen or had direct contact with an exhibitionist, or so-called flasher (Marshall et al., 2008). The urge to exhibit typically becomes stronger when the person has free time or is under significant stress.

Generally the disorder begins before age 18 and is most common in males (APA, 2000). Some studies suggest that persons with exhibitionism are typically immature in their dealings with the opposite sex and have difficulty in interpersonal relationships (Marshall et al., 2008; Murphy & Page, 2006). Around 30 percent of them are married and another 30 percent divorced or separated; their sexual relations with their wives are not usually satisfactory (Doctor & Neff, 2001). Many have doubts or fears about their masculinity, and some seem to have a strong bond to a possessive mother. As with other paraphilias, treatment generally includes aversion therapy and masturbatory satiation, possibly combined with orgasmic reorientation, social skills training, or cognitive-behavioral therapy (Marshall et al., 2008; Murphy & Page, 2006; Maletzky 2002, 2000).

Voyeurism

A person who engages in **voyeurism** has recurrent and intense urges to secretly observe unsuspecting people as they undress or to spy on couples having intercourse. The person may also masturbate during the act of observing or when thinking about it afterward but does not generally seek to have sex with the person being spied on. This disorder usually begins before the age of 15 and tends to persist (APA, 2000).

The vulnerability of the people being observed and the probability that they would feel humiliated if they knew they were under observation are often part of the individual's enjoyment. In addition, the risk of being discovered often adds to the excitement, as you can see in the following statement by a man with this disorder:

> *Looking at a nude girlfriend wouldn't be as exciting as seeing her the sneaky way. It's not just the nude body but the sneaking out and seeing what you're not supposed to see. The risk of getting caught makes it exciting. I don't want to get caught, but every time I go out I'm putting myself on the line.*
>
> (Yalom, 1960, p. 316)

Voyeurism, like exhibitionism, is often a source of sexual excitement in fantasy; it can also play a role in normal sexual interactions, but in such cases it is engaged in with the consent or understanding of the partner. The clinical disorder of voyeurism is marked by the repeated invasion of other people's privacy. Some people with voyeurism are unable to have normal sexual relations; others, however, have a normal sex life apart from their voyeurism.

Many psychodynamic clinicians propose that people with voyeurism are seeking by their actions to gain power over others, possibly because they feel inadequate or are sexually or socially shy (Metzl, 2004). Others have explained voyeurism as an attempt to reduce fears of castration, originally produced by the sight of an adult's genitals. Theoretically, people with voyeurism are repeating the behavior that produced the original fright to reassure themselves that there is nothing to fear (Fenichel, 1945). Behaviorists explain the disorder as a learned behavior that can be traced to a chance and secret observation of a sexually arousing scene. If such observations are repeated on several occasions while the onlooker masturbates, a voyeuristic pattern may develop.

Frotteurism

A person who develops **frotteurism** has repeated and intense sexual urges to touch and rub against a nonconsenting person or has sexually arousing fantasies of doing so. The person may also act on the urges. Frottage (from French *frotter*, "to rub") is usually committed in a crowded place, such as a subway or a busy sidewalk (Horley, 2001; Krueger & Kaplan, 2000). The person, almost always a male, may rub his genitals against the victim's thighs or buttocks or fondle her genital area or breasts with his hands. Typically he fantasizes during the act that he is having a caring relationship with the victim. This paraphilia usually begins in the teenage years or earlier, often after the person observes others committing an act of frottage. After the person reaches the age of about 25, the acts gradually decrease and often disappear (APA, 2000).

Pedophilia

A person with **pedophilia** gains sexual gratification by watching, touching, or engaging in sexual acts with prepubescent children, usually 13 years old or younger (see *Psych Watch* on the next page). Some people with this disorder are satisfied by child pornography (Linz & Imrich, 2001) or seemingly innocent material such as children's underwear ads; others are driven to actually watch, fondle, or engage in sexual intercourse with children (Durkin & Hundersmarck, 2008). Some people with pedophilia are attracted only to children; others are attracted to adults as well (Roche & Quayle, 2007; APA, 2000). Both boys and girls can be pedophilia victims, but there is evidence suggesting that two-thirds of them are girls (Doctor & Neff, 2001; Koss & Heslet, 1992).

•**exhibitionism**•A paraphilia in which persons have repeated sexually arousing urges or fantasies about exposing their genitals to another person, and may act upon those urges.

•**voyeurism**•A paraphilia in which a person has repeated and intense sexual desires to observe unsuspecting people in secret as they undress or to spy on couples having intercourse and may act upon these desires.

•**frotteurism**•A paraphilia consisting of repeated and intense sexual urges, fantasies, or behaviors that involve touching and rubbing against a nonconsenting person.

•**pedophilia**•A paraphilia in which a person has repeated and intense sexual urges or fantasies about watching, touching, or engaging in sexual acts with prepubescent children and may carry out these urges or fantasies.

Serving the Public Good

As clinical practitioners and researchers conduct their work, should they consider the potential impact of their decisions on society? Many people, including a large number of clinicians, believe that the answer to this question is a resounding yes. A decade ago two important clashes between the clinical field and the public interest—each centering on the disorder of *pedophilia*—brought this issue to life.

In 1994, the then-newly published DSM-IV ruled that people should receive a diagnosis of pedophilia only if their recurrent fantasies, urges, or behaviors involving sexual activity with children cause them significant distress or impairment in social, occupational, or other spheres of functioning. Critics worried that this criterion seemed to suggest that pedophilic behavior is acceptable, even normal, as long as it causes no distress or impairment. Even the U.S. Congress condemned the DSM-IV definition.

In response to these criticisms, the American Psychiatric Association clarified its position in 1997, stating, "An adult who engages in sexual activity with a child is performing a criminal and immoral act which never can be considered moral or socially acceptable behavior." In 2000 the Association went further still and changed the criteria for pedophilia in its newly published DSM-IV-TR; the disorder is now diagnosed if persons act on their sexual urges, regardless of whether they experience distress or impairment (APA, 2000). Similarly, acting on one's recurrent sexual urges or fantasies warrants a diagnosis in cases of exhibitionism, voyeurism, frotteurism, and sexual sadism.

Another clash between the clinical field and public sensibilities occurred in 1998 when a review article in the prestigious journal *Psychological Bulletin* concluded that the effects of child sexual abuse are not as long-lasting as usually believed. The study set off a firestorm, with critics arguing that the conclusion runs counter to evidence from a number of studies. Furthermore, many people worried that the article's conclusions could be used to legitimize pedophilia. After a groundswell of criticism, the American Psychological Association, publisher of the journal, acknowledged that it should have given more thought to how the study would be received and should have either presented the article with an introduction outlining the Association's stance against child abuse or paired it with articles offering different viewpoints. The Association also said that in the future it would more carefully weigh the potential consequences of research publications.

People with pedophilia usually develop their disorder during adolescence. Some were themselves sexually abused as children, and many were neglected, excessively punished, or deprived of genuinely close relationships during their childhood (McAnulty, 2006; Sawle & Kear, 2001; Berlin, 2000). It is not unusual for them to be married and to have sexual difficulties or other frustrations in life that lead them to seek an area in which they can be masters. Often these individuals are immature: their social and sexual skills may be underdeveloped, and thoughts of normal sexual relationships fill them with anxiety (McAnulty, 2006; Emmers-Sommer et al., 2004). Some people with pedophilia also exhibit distorted thinking, such as, "It's all right to have sex with children as long as they agree" (Roche & Quayle, 2007; Abel et al., 2001, 1994, 1984). Similarly, it is not uncommon for pedophiles to blame the children for adult–child sexual contacts or to assert that the children benefited from the experience (Durkin & Hundersmarck, 2008; Lanning, 2001).

While many people with pedophilia believe that their feelings are indeed wrong and abnormal, others consider adult sexual activity with children to be acceptable and normal. Some even have joined pedophile organizations that advocate abolishing the age of consent laws. The Internet has opened the channels of communication among such individuals. Indeed, there is

Pedophilia and the arts
The growing public awareness of pedophilia has led to an increase in the number of books, plays, movies, and television shows about the subject. Indeed, a recent production of the much-loved 1893 opera *Hansel and Gretel* was presented as an adults-only "study of pedophilia." In this scene from the opera, the witch gestures in front of a picture of one of the young victims.

Jens Meyer/AP Photo

now a wide range of Web sites, newsgroups, chat rooms, and discussion forums centered on pedophilia and adult-child sex (Durkin & Hundersmarck, 2008). Studies have found that most men with this disorder also display at least one additional psychological disorder, such as an anxiety or mood disorder, substance-related disorder, another paraphilia, or personality disorder (McAnulty, 2006; Cohen & Galynker, 2002). In recent years, some theorists have proposed that pedophilia may be related to a biochemical or brain structure abnormality (Cantor et al., 2004; Maes et al., 2001), but clear biological factors have yet to emerge in research.

Most pedophilic offenders are imprisoned or forced into treatment if they are caught (Stone et al., 2000). After all, they are committing child sexual abuse when they take any steps toward sexual contact with a child. Moreover, there are now numerous residential registration and community notification laws across the United States that help law enforcement agencies and the public account for and control where convicted child sex offenders live and work.

Treatments for pedophilia include those already mentioned for other paraphilias, such as aversion therapy, masturbatory satiation, orgasmic reorientation, cognitive-behavioral therapy, and antiandrogen drugs (Krueger & Kaplan, 2002; LoPiccolo, 1992). One widely applied cognitive-behavioral treatment for pedophilia, *relapse-prevention training,* is modeled after the relapse-prevention programs used in the treatment of substance dependence (Wright & Hatcher, 2006; Marques et al., 2005; Witkiewitz & Marlatt, 2004) (see page 404). In this approach, clients identify the kinds of situations that typically trigger their pedophilic fantasies and actions (such as depressed mood or distorted thinking). They then learn strategies for avoiding the situations or coping with them more effectively. Relapse-prevention training has sometimes, but not consistently, been of help in pedophilia and in certain other paraphilias (Marshall et al., 2008).

THERAPY: THE POSSIBILITY OF CHANGING BEHAVIOR

Civil commitment for sex offenders

A mural painted by patients at the Atascadero state mental hospital in California is meant to depict the pain of inmates at the forensic facility. By law, certain sex offenders may be committed to the hospital after they have completed a prison sentence if a court decides that they are not yet safe for release. At the hospital they undergo a five-phase relapse prevention treatment program, with the final phase being release into community outpatient treatment.

Sexual Masochism

A person with **sexual masochism** is intensely sexually aroused by the act or thought of being humiliated, beaten, bound, or otherwise made to suffer. Many people have fantasies of being forced into sexual acts against their will, but only those who are very distressed or impaired by the fantasies receive this diagnosis. Some people with the disorder act on the masochistic urges by themselves, perhaps tying, sticking pins into, or even cutting themselves. Others have their sexual partners restrain, tie up, blindfold, spank, paddle, whip, beat, electrically shock, "pin and pierce," or humiliate them (APA, 2000).

An industry of products and services has arisen to meet the desires of people with sexual masochism. Here a 34-year-old woman describes her work as the operator of a sadomasochism house:

> I get people here who have been all over looking for the right kind of pain they feel they deserve. Don't ask me why they want pain, I'm not a psychologist; but when they have found us, they usually don't go elsewhere. It may take some of the other girls an hour or even two hours to make these guys feel like they've had their treatment—I can achieve that in about 20 minutes. . . . Remember, these are businessmen, and they are not only buying my time, but they have to get back to work, so time is important.
>
> Among the things I do, that work really quickly and well, are: I put clothespins on their nipples, or pins in their [testicles]. Some of them need to see their own blood to be able to get off. . . .
>
> . . . All the time that a torture scene is going on, there is constant dialogue. . . . I scream at the guy, and tell him what a no-good rotten bastard he is, how this is even too good for him, that he knows he deserves worse, and I begin to list his sins. It works every time. Hey, I'm not nuts, I know what I'm doing. I act very tough and hard, but I'm really a

•sexual masochism• A paraphilia characterized by repeated and intense sexual urges, fantasies, or behaviors that involve being humiliated, beaten, bound, or otherwise made to suffer.

•**sexual sadism**•A paraphilia characterized by repeated and intense sexual urges, fantasies, or behaviors that involve inflicting suffering on others.

•**gender identity disorder**•A disorder in which a person persistently feels extremely uncomfortable about his or her assigned sex and strongly wishes to be a member of the opposite sex. Also known as *transsexualism*.

very sensitive woman. But you have to watch out for a guy's health . . . you must not kill him, or have him get a heart attack. . . . I know of other places that have had guys die there. I've never lost a customer to death, though they may have wished for it during my "treatment." Remember, these are repeat customers. I have a clientele and a reputation that I value.

(*Janus & Janus, 1993, p. 115*)

In one form of sexual masochism, *hypoxyphilia,* people strangle or smother themselves (or ask their partner to strangle them) in order to enhance their sexual pleasure. There have, in fact, been a disturbing number of clinical reports of *autoerotic asphyxia,* in which individuals, usually males and as young as 10 years old, may accidentally induce a fatal lack of oxygen by hanging, suffocating, or strangling themselves while masturbating. There is some debate as to whether the practice should be characterized as sexual masochism, but it is at least sometimes accompanied by other acts of bondage (Blanchard & Hucker, 1991).

Most masochistic sexual fantasies begin in childhood. However, the person does not act out the urges until later, usually by early adulthood. The disorder typically continues for many years. Some people practice more and more dangerous acts over time or during times of particular stress (Santtila et al., 2006, 2002; APA, 2000).

In many cases sexual masochism seems to have developed through the behavioral process of classical conditioning (Akins, 2004). A classic case study tells of a teenage boy with a broken arm who was caressed and held close by an attractive nurse as the physician set his fracture, a procedure done in the past without anesthesia (Gebhard, 1965). The powerful combination of pain and sexual arousal the boy felt then may have been the cause of his later masochistic urges and acts.

Sexual Sadism

A person with **sexual sadism,** usually male, is intensely sexually aroused by the thought or act of inflicting suffering on others by dominating, restraining, blindfolding, cutting, strangling, mutilating, or even killing the victim (Marshall & Kennedy, 2003). The label is derived from the name of the famous Marquis de Sade (1740–1814), who tortured others in order to satisfy his sexual desires. People who fantasize about sadism typically imagine that they have total control over a sexual victim who is terrified by the sadistic act. Many carry out sadistic acts with a consenting partner, often a person with sexual masochism. Some, however, act out their urges on nonconsenting victims (Marshall et al., 2008; Marshall & Hucker, 2006). A number of rapists and sexual murderers, for example, exhibit sexual sadism. In all cases, the real or fantasized victim's suffering is the key to arousal.

Fantasies of sexual sadism, like those of sexual masochism, may first appear in childhood (Johnson & Becker, 1997); the sadistic acts, when they occur, develop by early adulthood (APA, 2000). The pattern is long-term. Sadistic acts sometimes stay at the same level of cruelty, but often they become more and more severe over the years (Santtila et al., 2006, 2002). Obviously, people with severe forms of the disorder may be highly dangerous to others.

Some behaviorists believe that classical conditioning is at work in sexual sadism (Akins, 2004). While inflicting pain, perhaps unintentionally, on an animal or person, a teenager may feel intense emotions and sexual arousal. The association between inflicting pain and being aroused sexually sets the stage for a pattern of sexual sadism. Behaviorists also propose that the disorder may result from modeling, when adolescents observe others achieving sexual satisfaction by

Cinematic introduction
In one of filmdom's most famous scenes, Alex, the sexually sadistic character in *A Clockwork Orange,* is forced to observe violent images while he experiences painful stomach spasms. Public attitudes toward aversion therapy were greatly influenced by this 1971 portrayal of the treatment approach.

Courtesy of the Everett Collection

inflicting pain. The many Internet sex sites, sexual magazines, books, and videos in our society make such models readily available (Seto, Maric, & Barbaree, 2001).

Psychodynamic and cognitive theorists view people with sexual sadism as having underlying feelings of sexual inadequacy; they inflict pain in order to achieve a sense of power or control, which in turn increases their sexual arousal (Doctor, 2003; Rathbone, 2001). In contrast, certain biological studies have found signs of possible abnormalities in the endocrine systems of persons with sadism (Langevin et al., 1988). None of these explanations, however, has been thoroughly investigated.

Sexual sadism has been treated by aversion therapy. The public's view of and distaste for this procedure have been influenced by Anthony Burgess's novel (later a movie) *A Clockwork Orange,* which describes simultaneous presentations of sadistic images and drug-induced stomach spasms to a sadistic young man until he is conditioned to feel nausea at the sight of such images. It is not clear that aversion therapy is helpful in cases of sexual sadism. However, relapse-prevention training, used in some criminal cases, may be of value (Wright & Hatcher, 2006; Marques et al., 2005; Maletzky, 2003, 2002).

A Word of Caution

The definitions of the paraphilias, like those of sexual dysfunctions, are strongly influenced by the norms of the particular society in which they occur (McConaghy, 2005; APA, 2000). Some clinicians argue that except when people are hurt by them, many paraphilic behaviors should not be considered disorders at all. Especially in light of the stigma associated with sexual disorders and the self-revulsion that many people experience when they believe they have such a disorder, we need to be very careful about applying these labels to others or to ourselves. Keep in mind that for years clinicians considered homosexuality a paraphilia, and their judgment was used to justify laws and even police actions against gay individuals (Kirby, 2000) (see *Eye on Culture* on the next page). Only when the gay rights movement helped change society's understanding of and attitudes toward homosexuality did clinicians stop considering it a disorder. In the meantime, the clinical field had unintentionally contributed to the persecution, anxiety, and humiliation of millions of people because of personal sexual behavior that differed from the conventional norms.

✿Gender Identity Disorder

As children and adults, most people feel like and identify themselves as males or females —a feeling and identity that is consistent with the gender to which they are born. But society and the clinical field have come to appreciate that many people do not experience such gender clarity. Instead, they have *transgender experiences*—a sense that their actual gender identity is different from the gender category to which they were born physically or that it lies outside the usual male versus female categories (Carroll, 2007). Many people with such transgender experiences come to terms with their gender inconsistencies, blend gender in some way, and become comfortable with their atypical gender identify (Carroll, 2007). However, a number of others experience *gender dysphoria*—unhappiness with their given gender—and often seek treatment for their problem. DSM-IV-TR categorizes these individuals as having **gender identity disorder,** a disorder in which people persistently feel that a vast mistake has been made and they have been born to the wrong sex (see Table 13-6).

The DSM-IV-TR categorization of gender identity disorder has become controversial in recent years. Many people believe that transgender experiences reflect alternative—not pathological—ways of experiencing one's gender identity. Moreover, they argue, even transgender experiences that bring unhappiness, such as those called gender dysphoria, should not be considered a disorder. At the other end of the spectrum, many argue that gender identity disorder is in fact a medical problem that may produce personal unhappiness. According to this position, gender identity disorder should not be categorized as a psychological disorder, just as kidney disease and cancer, medical

BETWEEN THE LINES

Sex and the Law, Take 2

In 1996 the California state legislature passed the first law in the United States allowing state judges to order *antiandrogen* drug treatments, often referred to as "chemical castration," for repeat sex crime offenders, such as men who repeatedly commit pedophiliac acts or rape. ‹‹

table: 13-6

DSM Checklist

GENDER IDENTITY DISORDER

1. Strong and persistent cross-gender identification (for example, a stated desire to be the other sex, frequent passing as the other sex, desire to live or be treated as the other sex, or the conviction that one has the typical feelings and reactions of the other sex).

2. Persistent discomfort with one's sex or a sense of inappropriateness in the gender role of that sex (for example, preoccupation with getting rid of primary and secondary sex characteristics or belief that one was born the wrong sex).

3. Significant distress or impairment.

Based on APA, 2000.

EYE ON CULTURE

Homosexuality and Society

Homosexuality is not new; it has always existed in all cultures, as has the controversy that surrounds it. While most cultures do not openly advocate homosexuality, over the course of history few have condemned it as fiercely as Western culture does today (Kauth, 2006; Minton, 2002). Nevertheless, research shows that a society's acceptance or rejection of gay people does not affect the rate of homosexuality.

Before 1973, the DSM listed homosexuality as a sexual disorder. Protests by gay activist groups and many psychotherapists eventually led to its elimination from the diagnostic manual as a sexual disorder (Robertson, 2004). Most clinicians in the Western world now view homosexuality as a variant of normal sexual behavior, not a disorder (Crary, 2007).

Despite the growing acceptance of gay behavior by the clinical field, many people in Western society continue to hold anti-homosexual or homophobic attitudes and to spread myths about the lifestyles of gay persons (Kirby, 2000; Parker & Bhugra, 2000). Contrary to these myths, research has shown that gay people do not suffer from gender confusion, and there is not an identifiable "homosexual personality."

Psychologists do continue to debate one issue: whether homosexuality is the result of psychological factors (for example, cognitive-emotional or information-processing factors) or biological factors (for example, genetic predispositions or in utero events). The debate has been fueled by a range of findings that both support and contradict these various factors (Kauth, 2006; Hyde, 2005; Savic et al., 2005; Minton, 2002). Given such mixed results, several

interactionist theories have also been proposed, but these have yet to be tested systematically (Kauth, 2006, 2000; Diamond, 2003; Woodson & Gorski, 2000).

Gay people are found in every socio-economic group, every race, and every profession. It is impossible to identify a characteristic that consistently separates them from the rest of the population other than their sexual orientation. The gay community argues that since sexual orientation is the only variable that consistently separates homosexual from heterosexual couples, gay couples should have the same rights as heterosexual ones. Today, a number of marriages are performed for same-sex couples (Kauth, 2006; Leiblum, 2004). Furthermore, gay couples are increasingly asserting their rights in areas previously reserved for heterosexual couples only,

from spousal health insurance coverage and housing opportunities to fairer tax and inheritance laws and social security benefits; recent court decisions have endorsed a number of these rights.

A consistent 4 to 7 percent of all Americans continue to identify themselves as gay. Now that most psychologists agree that homosexuality is not a disorder, a key issue remains: How will society react to a significant proportion of its population that typically differs from the rest in but one way—their sexual orientation? So far, Western society cannot claim to have dealt very effectively or fairly with this question, but at least a trend toward understanding and equality seems to be unfolding. Research suggests that through continued education and exposure, people of different sexual orientations can often learn to accept and work with one another (Guth et al., 2004).

The great debate: gay marriage Del Martin and Phyllis Lyon, long-time gay activists who had been together for more than 50 years, cut their wedding cake after saying their vows in the San Francisco mayor's office on June 16, 2008. The joy on their faces belies the intense social controversy swirling around the issue of gay marriage in the United States. Martin died just a few months after fulfilling her dream.

conditions that may also produce unhappiness, are not categorized as psychological disorders. Although one of these views may indeed prove to be a more appropriate perspective, this chapter largely will follow DSM-IV-TR's current position that gender identity disorder is more than a variant lifestyle and far from a clearly defined medical problem, and it will examine what clinical theorists believe they know about the pattern and its treatment.

People with gender identity disorder would like to get rid of their primary and secondary sex characteristics—many of them find their own genitals repugnant—and acquire the characteristics of the other sex (APA, 2000). Men with gender identity disorder outnumber women by around 2 to 1. People with the problem often experience anxiety or depression and may have thoughts of suicide (Hepp et al., 2005; Bradley, 1995). Such reactions may be related to the confusion and pain brought on by the disorder itself, or they may also be tied to the prejudice typically experienced by individuals who display this pattern (Whittle, 2002; Lombardi et al., 2001). Studies also suggest that some people with gender identity disorder further manifest a personality disorder (Hepp et al., 2005). Among most of today's clinicians, the term "gender identity disorder" has replaced the old term *transsexualism,* although the label "transsexual" is still commonly applied to those individuals who desire and seek *full* gender change.

Sometimes gender identity disorder emerges in children (Carroll, 2007; Zucker, 2005). Like adults with this disorder, the children feel uncomfortable about their assigned sex and yearn to be members of the opposite sex. This childhood pattern usually disappears by adolescence or adulthood, but in some cases it develops into adult gender identity disorder (Cohen-Kettenis, 2001). Thus adults with this disorder may have had a childhood gender identity disorder, but most children with the disorder do not become adults with the disorder. Surveys of mothers indicate that about 1 to 2 percent of young boys wish to be a girl, and 3 to 4 percent of young girls wish to be a boy (Carroll, 2007; Zucker & Bradley, 1995). Yet, considerably less than 1 percent of adults manifest gender identity disorder. This age shift in the prevalence of gender identity disorder is, in part, why today's leading *standards of care manual for gender dysphoria* strongly recommends against any form of *physical* treatment for this pattern until individuals are at least 16 years of age (HBIGDA, 2001).

Explanations of Gender Identity Disorder

Various theories have been proposed to explain gender identity disorder (Carroll, 2007; Gehring & Knudson, 2005; Doctor & Neff, 2001), but research to test these views has been limited and generally weak. Many clinicians suspect that biological—perhaps genetic or prenatal—factors play a key role in the disorder (Henningsson et al., 2005; Bailey, 2003).

Jim Wilson/The New York Times/Redux

A delicate matter
A 5-year-old boy (left), who identifies and dresses as a girl and asks to be called "she," plays with a female friend. Sensitive to the gender identity rights movement and to the special needs of children with gender dysphoria, a growing number of parents, educators, and clinicians are now supportive of children like this boy.

Alessandro Bianchi/Reuters

Growing acceptance
An important milestone in the gender identity rights movement was the 2006 election of actress and television personality Vladimir Luxuria to the Italian Parliament, the first transgender individual ever to attain such legislative status. Luxuria, sitting here at the tribune of the parliament, has not undergone sex change surgery and currently remains physically male. She lost her Parliament seat in the 2008 general election.

Consistent with a genetic explanation is evidence that the disorder sometimes runs in families (Green, 2000). In addition, one biological study has received considerable attention (Zhou et al., 1997, 1995). Dutch investigators autopsied the brains of six people who had changed their sex from male to female. They found that a cluster of cells in the hypothalamus called the *bed nucleus of stria terminalis* (*BST*) was only half as large in these people as it was in a control group of "normal" men. Usually, a woman's BST is much smaller than a man's, so in effect the men with gender identity disorder were found to have a female-sized BST. Recent studies tell a similar story (Swaab, 2005). Scientists do not know for certain what the BST does in humans, but they know that it helps regulate sexual behavior in male rats. Although other interpretations are possible, it may be that men who develop gender identity disorder have a key biological difference that leaves them very uncomfortable with their assigned sex characteristics.

Treatments for Gender Identity Disorder

In order to more effectively assess and treat those with gender identity disorder, clinical theorists have tried to distinguish the most common patterns of gender dysphoria encountered in clinical practice.

Types of Gender Dysphoria Clients

Richard Carroll (2007), a Northwestern University professor and expert on gender dysphoria, has described the three patterns of gender identity disorder for which individuals most commonly seek treatment: (1) *female-to-male gender dysphoria,* (2) *male-to-female gender dysphoria: androphilic type,* and (3) *male-to-female gender dysphoria: autogynephilic type.*

FEMALE-TO-MALE GENDER DYSPHORIA People with a female-to-male gender dysphoria pattern are born female but appear or behave in a stereotypically masculine manner from early on—often as young as 3 years of age or younger. As children they always play rough games or sports, prefer the company of boys, hate "girlish" clothes, and state their wish to be male. As adolescents, they become disgusted by the physical changes of puberty and are sexually attracted to females. Although they may have lesbian relationships as teenagers and adults, this never feels like a satisfactory solution to their gender dysphoric feelings because they want other women to be attracted to them as males, not as females.

MALE-TO-FEMALE GENDER DYSPHORIA: ANDROPHILIC TYPE People with an androphilic type of male-to-female gender dysphoria are born male but appear or behave in a stereotypically female manner from birth. As children, they are viewed as effeminate, pretty, and gentle; avoid rough games; and hate to dress in boys' clothing. As adolescents, they become sexually attracted to males, and they often come out as gay and develop gay relationships (the term "androphilic" means *attracted to males*). But by adulthood, it becomes clear to them that such gay relationships do not truly address their gender dysphoric feelings because they want to be with heterosexual men who are attracted to them as women.

MALE-TO-FEMALE GENDER DYSPHORIA: AUTOGYNEPHILIC TYPE People with an autogynephilic type of male-to-female gender dysphoria are not sexually attracted to males within their pattern of gender dysphoria; rather, they are attracted to the fantasy of themselves being females (the term "autogynephilic" means *attracted to oneself as a female*). Like males with the paraphilia *transvestic fetishism* (see pages 437–438), persons with this form of gender dysphoria behave in a stereotypically masculine manner as children, start to enjoy dressing in female clothing during childhood, and, after puberty, become sexually aroused when they cross-dress. Also, like males with transvestic fetishism, they are attracted to females during and beyond adolescence but also become aware that their sexual arousal in these heterosexual relationships is greatest when they are able to dress in female clothing and to fantasize about having a female body. Unlike individuals with transvestic fetishism, however, the fantasies of becoming female become stronger and stronger during adulthood for those who develop this kind of male-to-female gender dysphoria. Eventually they are consumed with the need to be female.

•**sex-change surgery**•A surgical procedure that changes a person's sex organs, features, and, in turn, sexual identity. Also known as *sexual reassignment surgery.*

In short, cross-dressing is characteristic of both men with the paraphilia transvestic fetishism and men with this type of male-to-female gender dysphoria. But the former individuals cross-dress strictly to become sexually aroused, whereas the latter develop much deeper reasons for cross-dressing, reasons of gender identity.

Types of Treatment for Gender Identity Disorder Many people with gender identity disorder receive psychotherapy (Affatati et al., 2004); however, controlled studies indicate that most adults with the disorder do not come to accept completely their birth gender through psychological treatment (Carroll, 2007). Thus, a large number of individuals seek to address their concerns and conflicts through biological interventions (see *The Media Speaks* on the next page). For example, many adults with this disorder change their sexual characteristics by means of *hormone treatments* (Andreasen & Black, 2006; Hepp et al., 2002). Physicians prescribe the female sex hormone *estrogen* for male patients, causing breast development, loss of body and facial hair, and change in body fat distribution. Similar treatments with the male sex hormone *testosterone* are given to women with gender identity disorder.

Hormone therapy and psychotherapy enable many persons with this disorder to lead a satisfactory existence in the gender role that they believe represents their true identity. For others, however, this is not enough, and their dissatisfaction leads them to undergo one of the most controversial practices in medicine: **sex-change,** or **sexual reassignment, surgery** (Andreasen & Black, 2006; Hepp et al., 2002). This surgery is preceded by one to two years of hormone therapy. The operation itself involves, for men, amputation of the penis, creation of an artificial vagina, and face-changing plastic surgery. For women, surgery may include bilateral mastectomy and hysterectomy. The procedure for creating a functioning penis, called *phalloplasty,* is performed in some cases, but it is not yet perfected (Doctor & Neff, 2001). Doctors have, however, developed a silicone prosthesis that gives the patient the appearance of having male genitals. Studies in Europe suggest that 1 of every 30,000 men and 1 of every 100,000 women seek sex-change surgery (Carroll, 2007; Bakker et al., 1993). In the United States, more than 6,000 persons are estimated to have undergone this surgical procedure (Doctor & Neff, 2001).

Clinicians have debated heatedly whether sexual reassignment is an appropriate treatment for gender identity disorder. Some consider it a humane solution, perhaps the most satisfying one to people with the pattern. Others argue that sexual reassignment is a "drastic nonsolution" for a complex disorder. Either way, sexual reassignment surgery appears to be on the increase (Olsson & Moller, 2003).

Research into the outcomes of gender reassignment surgery points in favorable directions, although generally most such research has significant methodological flaws (Carroll, 2007). According to these investigations, the majority of patients—both female and male—state satisfaction with the outcome of the surgery and report subsequent improvements in the social, psychological, and occupational spheres of their lives, particularly improvements in self-satisfaction and interpersonal interactions (Michel et al., 2002). Improvements in sexual functioning after surgery, however, are often lacking (Schroder & Carroll, 1999).

The rate of "poor" sexual reassignment outcomes appears to be at least 8 percent (Carroll, 2007; Abramowitz, 1986). Female-to-male patients consistently show the most favorable psychosocial outcomes. Those who display the autogynephilic type of gender dysphoria (that is, those whose problems seem to evolve from transvestic fetishism) are more

BETWEEN THE LINES

Landmark Case

The first sex-change operation took place in 1931, but the procedure did not gain acceptance in the medical world until 1952, when an operation converted an ex-soldier named George Jorgensen into a woman, renamed Christine Jorgensen. This transformation made headlines around the world. ‹‹

James and Jan
Feeling like a woman trapped in a man's body, British writer James Morris (left) underwent sex-change surgery, described in his 1974 autobiography, *Conundrum.* Today Jan Morris (right) is a successful author and seems comfortable with her change of gender.

Bettmann Archives

David Levenson/Rex USA Ltd

HOME | SEND | EXPLORE

SEARCH

Battling a Culture of Shame

BY MARTIN ABBUGAO, AGENCE FRANCE-PRESSE, SEPTEMBER 10, 2007

She loves children and her lifelong dream is to be a wife and a mother, but the raspy voice and masculine frame betray the fact that Leona Lo was born a man.

Unlike many other transsexuals in Asia who prefer to live privately because of the social stigma of sex change, the British-educated, Singaporean transsexual woman has chosen to live a normal life, but in public. Smart, confident and articulate, the communications specialist who heads her own public relations company has embarked on a mission to help turn around the "culture of shame" surrounding transsexuals in Singapore and the region. "Somewhere out there, not just in Singapore but throughout Asia, there are lots of young people who are suffering the way I suffered years ago," Leona, 32, [says] in an interview.

In her former life as a man, she was called Leonard. These days, she draws on her experiences of gender identity crisis, rejection and discrimination to challenge social mores on behalf of the so-called silent community. "It's this entire culture of shame that gets under your skin. It's not something that you can isolate and demolish because it is so much a part of our culture," she says. While a few transsexuals are gaining prominence in Asia . . . most continue to live in silence. . . .

Slim and taller than the average local woman, Leona packs charm and gets animated when talking about children. But her lipsticked mouth creases into a pensive smile when she says: "I can't bear children. I have to be on hormones for life and I have this body structure of a guy." The hormone treatment has "feminised" the former man. While traces of masculinity are evident, Leona says she has already come to terms with being a woman—although a transsexual one. "I can't deny that biologically I'm different," says Leona, wearing a blue dress, the muscles on her shoulders and arms clearly visible.

Discrimination is the biggest challenge faced by transsexuals, she says, recalling repeated rejection by prospective employers in Singapore despite her academic credentials. "Singapore may be a cosmopolitan city but many things are still swept under the carpet," Leona says. . . . It's because a lot of transsexual women face discrimination at work and experience failure of relationships that a lot end up in suicide, depression. They end up on the streets as prostitutes," she says.

This is why she has taken time away from her thriving public relations consultancy promoting beauty products to wage her campaign. After much persuasion, one local university allowed her to speak to an audience of students but she is finding it hard to pry open a window to share her thoughts in the corporate world. . . . On September 14 she is to launch her autobiography, "From Leonard to Leona—A Singapore Transsexual's Journey to Womanhood." From Singapore, Leona plans to travel across Asia to bring her message for greater tolerance of gender diversity. . . .

As early as 10, Leonard had already started developing feelings for boys. But he was forced to remain silent because of a dearth of information about transsexualism and for fear his traditional Chinese family would be scandalized. "I did not think I was gay, I just felt that I was a woman trapped in a man's body," says Leona, who has a younger sister. At age 15, Leonard discovered a book about transsexualism, which sowed the seeds of his eventual decision to undergo a sex-change operation in 1997. "I discovered that book in the library and I said 'Oh my God! There are actually people like me!'" she reminisces. That changed my life and I discovered that I could go for the sex change operation." . . .

After military service, Leonard in 1996 went to study in Britain, where a more tolerant university environment allowed him to cross-dress for a year as part of his preparation for sex-change surgery. In 1997, Leonard flew with his tuition money from Britain to Bangkok, where he walked into a clinic for the life-altering operation. "I was afraid. I could go in and I could die. But I knew at that point that I was going to change my life forever," she recalls. "I had carried that burden within me for so long and I couldn't live anymore without doing it." Leona endured a lot of pain during the procedure . . . but the feeling of having a new identity was "wonderful, euphoric!" . . .

What is her dream now? "To be a wife and a mother," she says. "I look forward to a fulfilling relationship with a loving man, getting married and adopting three children. I've also reached a critical juncture where I'm more self-assured and finally able to lay to rest the painful aspects of my past and move confidently as a woman."

Fighting stigmatization Leona Lo describes her efforts to turn around the "culture of shame" currently surrounding her and other transsexuals throughout Asia.

Roslan Rahman/AFP/Getty Images

likely than those with the other types of gender dysphoria to regret sexual reassign-ment surgery and to have poor outcomes. Finally, patients with serious pretreatment psychological disturbances (for example, a personality disorder) are particularly likely to regret the surgery and are more likely than others to later attempt suicide. All of this argues for careful screening prior to proceeding on to this treatment approach and, of course, for continued research to better understand both the patterns themselves and the long-term impact of the surgical procedure.

Our gender is so basic to our sense of identity that it is hard for most of you to imagine wanting to change it, much less to imagine the feelings of conflict and stress experienced by those who question their assigned gender. Whether the underlying cause is biological, psychological, or sociocultural, gender identity disorder is a dramatic problem that often shakes the foundations of the sufferer's existence.

PUTTING IT... together

A Private Topic Draws Public Attention

For all the public interest in sexual disorders, clinical theorists and practitioners have only recently begun to understand their nature and how to treat them. As a result of research done over the past few decades, people with sexual dysfunctions are no longer doomed to a lifetime of sexual frustration. At the same time, however, insights into the causes and treatment of other kinds of sexual disorders—paraphilias and gender identity disorder—remain limited.

Studies of sexual dysfunctions have pointed to many psychological, sociocultural, and biological causes. Often, as you have seen with so many disorders, the various causes may *interact* to produce a particular dysfunction, as in erectile disorder and female orgasmic disorder. For some dysfunctions, however, one cause alone is dominant, and integrated explanations may be inaccurate and unproductive. Dyspareunia, for example, usually has a physical cause.

Recent work has also yielded important progress in the treatment of sexual dys-functions, and people with such problems are now often helped greatly by therapy. Sex therapy today is usually a complex program tailored to the particular problems of an individual or couple. Techniques from the various models may be combined, although in some instances the particular problem calls primarily for one approach (Bach et al., 2001).

One of the most important insights to emerge from all of this work is that *educa-tion* about sexual dysfunctions can be as important as therapy. Sexual myths are still taken so seriously that they often lead to feelings of shame, self-hatred, isolation, and hopelessness—feelings that themselves contribute to sexual difficulty. Even a modest amount of education can help persons who are in treatment.

In fact, most people can benefit from a more accurate understanding of sexual func-tioning. Public education about sexual functioning—through books, television and radio, school programs, group presentations, and the like—has become a major clinical focus. It is important that these efforts continue and even increase in the coming years.

«‹(SUMMING UP)›»

○ **Sexual dysfunctions** *Sexual dysfunctions* make it difficult or impossible for a person to have or enjoy sexual intercourse. *pp. 415–416*

○ **Disorders of desire** DSM-IV-TR lists two disorders of the *desire phase* of the *sexual response cycle: hypoactive sexual desire disorder,* marked by a lack of interest in sex, and *sexual aversion disorder,* marked by a persistent revulsion to sexual activity.

continued

BETWEEN THE LINES

Sexual Timeline

1905 Freud's "Three Essays on Sexuality" provides misinformation on the female orgasm. ‹‹

1953 Alfred Kinsey publishes the first major U.S. survey on women's sexual habits. ‹‹

1960 The U.S. Food and Drug Administration approves birth control pills. ‹‹

1965 The Supreme Court rules that the government cannot regulate the use of birth control in marriage. ‹‹

1966 Masters and Johnson find that half of U.S. marriages are marked by some kind of sexual inadequacy. ‹‹

1981 Massachusetts and New Jersey courts rule that husbands can be prosecuted for raping their wives. ‹‹

1998 Viagra is approved and marketed. ‹‹

2007 Between 25 and 30 million men worldwide take Viagra, Levitra, or Cialis. ‹‹

(Rosen, 2007; Deveny, 2003)

BETWEEN THE LINES

Sexual Census

The World Health Organization estimates that around 115 million acts of sexual intercourse occur each day. ‹‹

Eric Risberg/AP Photo

Do "date rape drugs" increase sexual arousal?
Many people mistakenly believe that so-called date rape drugs operate primarily by sexually arousing female victims. In fact, however, these tasteless, odorless, and colorless drugs (GHB, rohypnol, and ketamine) that sexual predators slip into the drinks or food of unsuspecting individuals, operate largely by producing a near-unconscious yet responsive state in victims, eliminating clear thinking, reducing inhibitions, and impairing memory. To help women detect such drugs, special "detection coasters," such as the ones in this photo, have been manufactured. Such coasters are supposed to turn dark blue within 30 seconds if splashes of alcohol from the drinks sitting on them contain a date rape drug.

Biological causes for these disorders include abnormal hormone levels, certain drugs, and some medical illnesses. Psychological and sociocultural causes include specific fears, situational pressures, relationship problems, and the trauma of having been sexually molested or assaulted. *pp. 416–420*

○ **Disorders of excitement** Disorders of the *excitement phase* are *female sexual arousal disorder,* marked by a persistent inability to attain or maintain adequate lubrication or genital swelling during sexual activity, and *male erectile disorder,* a repeated inability to attain or maintain an erection during sexual activity. Biological causes of male erectile disorder include abnormal hormone levels, vascular problems, medical conditions, and certain medications. Psychological and sociocultural causes include the combination of *performance anxiety* and the *spectator role,* situational pressures such as job loss, and relationship problems. *pp. 420–422*

○ **Disorders of orgasm** *Rapid,* or *premature, ejaculation,* a persistent tendency to reach orgasm and ejaculate before or shortly after penetration, has been attributed most often to behavioral causes, such as inappropriate early learning and inexperience. In recent years, possible biological factors have been proposed as well. *Male orgasmic disorder,* a repeated absence of or long delay in reaching orgasm, can have biological causes, such as low testosterone levels, neurological diseases, and certain drugs, and psychological causes, such as performance anxiety and the spectator role. The dysfunction may also develop from hypoactive sexual desire.

Female orgasmic disorder is a persistent absence of or long delay in orgasm in women. It, along with female sexual arousal disorder, has been tied to biological causes such as medical diseases and changes that occur after menopause, psychological causes such as memories of childhood traumas, and sociocultural causes such as relationship problems. Most clinicians agree that orgasm during intercourse is not critical to normal sexual functioning, provided a woman can reach orgasm with her partner during direct stimulation of the clitoris. *pp. 422–426*

○ **Sexual pain disorders** In *vaginismus,* involuntary contractions of the muscles around the outer third of the vagina prevent entry of the penis. In *dyspareunia,* the person experiences severe pain in the genitals during sexual activity. Dyspareunia usually occurs in women and typically has a physical cause, such as injury resulting from childbirth. *pp. 426–428*

○ **Treatments for sexual dysfunctions** In the 1970s the work of William Masters and Virginia Johnson led to the development of *sex therapy.* Today sex therapy combines a variety of cognitive, behavioral, couple, and family systems therapies. It generally includes features such as careful assessment, education, acceptance of mutual responsibility, attitude changes, *sensate-focus* exercises, improvements in communication, and couple therapy. In addition, specific techniques have been developed for each of the sexual dysfunctions. The use of biological treatments for sexual dysfunctions is also increasing. *pp. 428–435*

○ **Paraphilias** Paraphilias are disorders characterized by recurrent and intense sexual urges, fantasies, or behaviors involving either nonhuman objects, children, nonconsenting adults, or experiences of suffering or humiliation. The disorders are found primarily in men. The paraphilias include *fetishism, transvestic fetishism (transvestism), exhibitionism, voyeurism, frotteurism, pedophilia, sexual masochism,* and *sexual sadism.* Although various explanations have been proposed for these disorders, research has revealed little about their causes. A range of treatments have been tried, including *aversion therapy, masturbatory satiation, orgasmic reorientation,* and *relapse-prevention training. pp. 435–443*

○ **Gender identity disorder** People with *gender identity disorder* persistently feel that they have been assigned to the wrong sex. In recent years, a number of theorists have criticized the categorization of such gender identity patterns as clinical disorders. Men with gender identity disorder apparently outnumber females by around 2 to 1. Its causes are not well understood. *Hormone treatments* and *psychotherapy* have been used to help some people adopt the gender role they believe to be right for them. *Sex-change operations* have also been performed, but the appropriateness of surgery as a form of "treatment" has been debated heatedly. *pp. 443–449*

CRITICAL THOUGHTS

1. Prevalence rates for sexual behavior are typically based on surveys of the general population. How-ever, many people feel that sex is private and refuse to participate in such surveys, and those who do respond tend to be more liberal, sexually experienced, and unconventional than the norm. What problems might this cause for sex researchers? *pp. 415–428*

2. Why do you think the clinical field has been so slow to investigate possible cultural and racial differences in sexual behaviors, sexual dysfunctions, and paraphilias across the United States? *pp. 415–449*

3. Some theorists suggest that recent increases in the number of men receiving treatment for hypoactive sexual desire disorder may be linked to the impact of the women's movement. If this is the case, what factors might account for it? *pp. 416–420*

4. Some theorists cite performance anxiety and the spectator role as contributing factors in certain sexual dysfunctions. Are there other areas of dysfunction in life that might also be explained by performance anxiety and the spectator role? *pp. 421–422*

5. A key technique in sex therapy is to have a couple explore and caress each other's body (*sensate focus*) while resisting orgasm or intercourse. Why might people become more aroused during sexual caressing if they are prohibited from reaching orgasm or having intercourse? *p. 430*

6. Sex is one of the topics most commonly searched on the Internet. Why might it be such a popular search topic? Is the availability of sex chat groups and other sexual material on the Internet psychologically healthy or damaging? *pp. 430, 415–449*

cyberstudy

SEARCH

Search the *Abnormal Psychology* Video Tool Kit
www.worthpublishers.com/apvtk

▲ Chapter 13 Video Cases
  Viagra: Pathway to Sexual Happiness?
  Sex Offenders: Criminals or Patients?
  The Case of David Reimer: "The Boy Who Was Turned into a Girl"
▲ Video case discussions, study guides, and questions

Log on to the Comer Web Page
www.worthpublishers.com/comer

▲ Chapter 13 outline, learning objectives, research exercises, study tools, and practice test questions
▲ Additional Chapter 13 case studies, Web links, and FAQs

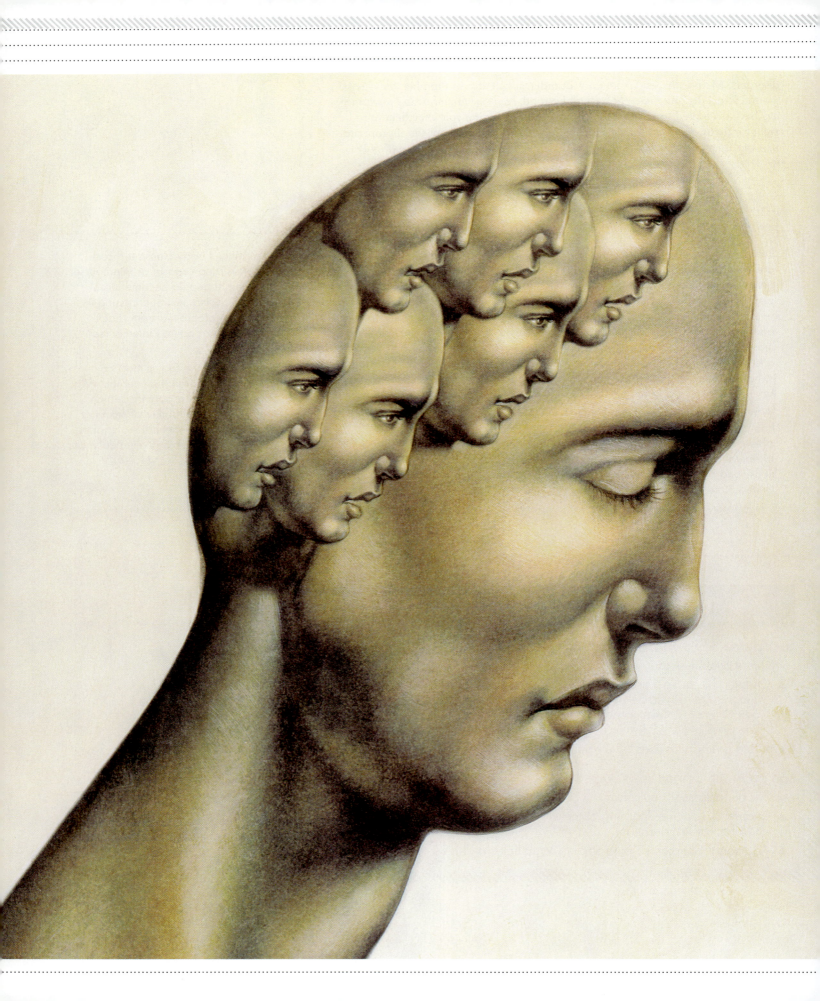

SCHIZOPHRENIA

W hat . . . does schizophrenia mean to me? It means fatigue and confusion, it means trying to separate every experience into the real and the unreal and sometimes not being aware of where the edges overlap. It means trying to think straight when there is a maze of experiences getting in the way, and when thoughts are continually being sucked out of your head so that you become embarrassed to speak at meetings. It means feeling sometimes that you are inside your head and visualizing yourself walking over your brain, or watching another girl wearing your clothes and carrying out actions as you think them. It means knowing that you are continually "watched," that you can never succeed in life because the laws are all against you and knowing that your ultimate destruction is never far away.

Rollin, 1980, p. 162

Does it surprise you to see such a coherent firsthand description of how it feels to suffer from **schizophrenia?** People who have this disorder, though they previously functioned well or at least acceptably, deteriorate into an isolated wilderness of unusual perceptions, odd thoughts, disturbed emotions, and motor abnormalities. In Chapter 15 you will see that schizophrenia is no longer the hopeless disorder of times past and that some sufferers, though certainly not all, now make remarkable recoveries. However, in this chapter let us first take a look at the symptoms of this disorder and at the theories that have been developed to explain them.

People with schizophrenia experience **psychosis,** a loss of contact with reality. Their ability to perceive and respond to the environment becomes so disturbed that they may not be able to function at home, with friends, in school, or at work. They may have hallucinations (false sensory perceptions) or delusions (false beliefs), or they may withdraw into a private world. As you saw in Chapter 12, taking LSD or abusing amphetamines or cocaine may produce psychosis. So may injuries or diseases of the brain. Most commonly, however, psychosis appears in the form of schizophrenia.

Schizophrenia appears to have been with us throughout history; it is one of the conditions commonly described as "madness" (Lavretsky, 2008; Cutting, 1985). The Bible, for example, speaks of King Saul's mad rages and terrors and of David feigning madness in order to escape his enemies. In 1865 a Belgian psychiatrist named Benedict Morel (1809–1873) applied the label *démence précoce* ("early dementia") to a 14-year-old boy who showed the symptoms of this disorder, and in 1899 Emil Kraepelin introduced the use of the Latin form of Morel's label, *dementia praecox*. In 1911, however, Swiss psychiatrist Eugen Bleuler (1857–1939) coined a new term, "schizophrenia," by combining Greek words that mean "split mind." Bleuler meant this name to imply (1) a fragmentation of thought processes, (2) a split between thoughts and emotions, and (3) a withdrawal from reality.

Approximately 1 of every 100 people in the world suffers from schizophrenia during his or her lifetime (APA, 2000). An estimated 24 million people worldwide are afflicted with this disorder, 2.5 million in the United States (Lambert & Kinsley, 2005; Bichsel, 2001). Its financial cost is enormous—according to some estimates, more than $63 billion each year in the United States, including the costs of hospitalization, lost wages, and disability benefits (Wu et al., 2005). The emotional cost is even greater. In addition, sufferers have an increased risk of suicide and of

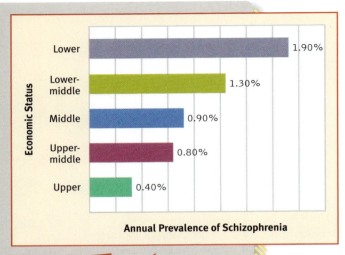

Figure 14-1
Socioeconomic class and schizophrenia
Poor people in the United States are more likely than wealthy people to experience schizophrenia. (Adapted from Keith et al., 1991.)

physical—often fatal—illness (Rystedt & Bartels, 2008; Kim et al., 2003). As you read in Chapter 10, it is estimated that at least 15 percent of people with the disorder attempt suicide (Heisel, 2008; Pompili & Lester, 2007).

Although schizophrenia appears in all socioeconomic groups, it is found more frequently in the lower levels (Lambert & Kinsley, 2005) (see Figure 14-1), leading some theorists to believe that the stress of poverty is itself a cause of the disorder. However, it could be that schizophrenia causes its victims to fall from a higher to a lower socioeconomic level or to remain poor because they are unable to function effectively (Priebe & Fakhoury, 2008; Ritsner & Gibel, 2007), they are depleted financially by health care costs (Samnaliev & Clark, 2008), or their stigmatizing labels severely limit workplace options (Corrigan & Larson, 2008). This is sometimes called the *downward drift* theory.

Equal numbers of men and women receive a diagnosis of schizophrenia (Seeman, 2008). In men, however, the disorder often begins earlier and may be more severe (Folsom et al., 2006). The average age of onset for men is 21 years, compared to 27 years for women. Almost 3 percent of all those who are divorced or separated suffer from schizophrenia sometime during their lives, compared to 1 percent of married people and 2 percent of people who remain single. Again, however, it is not clear whether marital problems are a cause or a result (Solter et al., 2004; Keith et al., 1991).

People today, like those of the past, show great interest in schizophrenia, flocking to plays and movies (including the remarkably popular horror movies) that explore or exploit our fascination with the disorder (see *PsychWatch: Abnormality and the Arts* on pages 456–457). Yet, as you will read, all too many people with schizophrenia are neglected in our country, their needs almost entirely ignored. Although effective interventions have been developed, most sufferers live without adequate treatment and without nearly fulfilling their potential as human beings (Ritsner & Gibel, 2007; Torrey, 2001).

✿The Clinical Picture of Schizophrenia

For years schizophrenia was a "wastebasket category" for diagnosticians, particularly for those in the United States, where the label might be assigned to anyone who acted unpredictably or strangely. Some clinicians were known to say that "even a trace of schizophrenia is schizophrenia" (Lewis & Piotrowski, 1954). The disorder is defined more precisely today, but still its symptoms vary greatly, and so do its triggers, course, and responsiveness to treatment (APA, 2000). In fact, a number of clinicians believe that schizophrenia is actually a group of distinct disorders that happen to have some features in common (Tamminga et al., 2008; Cohen & Docherty, 2005). To see the variety of forms schizophrenia may take, consider three people who were diagnosed as suffering from it. The cases are taken from the files of Silvano Arieti (1974), a famous theorist on the disorder.

Ann, 26 years old: *Ann graduated from high school and from a school for commercial art. . . . At the age of 18 she began going out with Henry. . . . They became engaged shortly thereafter and went out together frequently until their marriage . . . . Married life was considered a boring routine by both Ann and Henry. There was very little conversation between them. . . .*

Ann's disappointment in Henry increased. They had nothing in common; she was artistically inclined, whereas he had only an ordinary, conventional outlook toward life. It was at this time that she started to go dancing and then met Charles. Her interest in him increased, but . . . a divorce was not compatible with the precepts of the Catholic church. Her conflict grew and put her in a state of great agitation. . . .

. . . One evening she came home from dancing and told her mother that she was going to give up her husband Henry, marry Charles, go to Brazil with him, and have twenty

•schizophrenia•A psychotic disorder in which personal, social, and occupational functioning deteriorate as a result of strange perceptions, unusual emotions, and motor abnormalities.

•psychosis•A state in which a person loses contact with reality in key ways.

babies. She was talking very fast and saying many things, several of which were incomprehensible. At the same time she also told her mother that she was seeing the Virgin Mary in visions. She then went to her mother-in-law and told her to take back her son Henry, because he was too immature. The following day Ann went to work and tried to get the entire office down on their knees with her to recite the rosary. A few days later, her mother took her to a priest, whom she "told off" in no uncertain terms. She finally spit at him. A psychiatrist was consulted, and he recommended hospitalization.

(pp. 173–177)

Richard, 23 years old: *In high school, Richard was an average student. After graduation from high school, he [entered] the army. . . . Richard remembered [the] period . . . after his discharge from the army . . . as one of the worst in his life. . . . Any, even remote, anticipation of disappointment was able to provoke attacks of anxiety in him. . . .*

Approximately two years after his return to civilian life, Richard left his job because he became overwhelmed by these feelings of lack of confidence in himself, and he refused to go look for another one. He stayed home most of the day. His mother would nag him that he was too lazy and unwilling to do anything. He became slower and slower in dressing and undressing and taking care of himself. When he went out of the house, he felt compelled "to give interpretations" to everything he looked at. He did not know what to do outside the house, where to go, where to turn. If he saw a red light at a crossing, he would interpret it as a message that he should not go in that direction. If he saw an arrow, he would follow the arrow interpreting it as a sign sent by God that he should go in that direction. Feeling lost and horrified, he would go home and stay there, afraid to go out because going out meant making decisions or choices that he felt unable to make. He reached the point where he stayed home most of the time. But even at home, he was tortured by his symptoms. He could not act; any motion that he felt like making seemed to him an insurmountable obstacle, because he did not know whether he should make it or not. He was increasingly afraid of doing the wrong thing. Such fears prevented him from dressing, undressing, eating, and so forth. He felt paralyzed and lay motionless in bed. He gradually became worse, was completely motionless, and had to be hospitalized. . . .

Being undecided, he felt blocked, and often would remain mute and motionless, like a statue, even for days.

(pp. 153–155)

Laura, 40 years old: *Laura's desire was to become independent and leave home [in Austria] as soon as possible. . . . She became a professional dancer at the age of 20 . . . and was booked for . . . theaters in many European countries. . . .*

It was during one of her tours in Germany that Laura met her husband. . . . They were married and went to live in a small provincial town in France where the husband's business was. . . . She spent a year in that town and was very unhappy. . . . [Finally] Laura and her husband decided to emigrate to the United States. . . .

They had no children, and Laura . . . showed interest in pets. She had a dog to whom she was very devoted. The dog became sick and partially paralyzed, and veterinarians felt that there was no hope of recovery. . . . Finally [her husband] broached the problem to his wife, asking her "Should the dog be destroyed or not?" From that time on Laura became restless, agitated, and depressed. . . .

. . . Later Laura started to complain about the neighbors. A woman who lived on the floor beneath them was knocking on the wall to irritate her. According to the husband, this woman had really knocked on the wall a few times; he had heard the noises. However, Laura became more and more concerned about it. She would wake up in the middle of the night under the impression that she was hearing noises from the apartment downstairs. She would become upset and angry at the neighbors. . . . Later she became

Inner torment
Like this young woman, people with schizophrenia often appear to be trying to fight off the strange thoughts and perceptions that pervade their minds.

David Grossman/Photo Researchers

PSYCH WATCH Abnormality and the Arts

A Beautiful Mind: Movies versus Reality

Mental disorders and the people who experience them are popular subjects throughout the arts, including, of course, the cinema. One of the most successful such movies in recent years was *A Beautiful Mind,* based on the true story of John Forbes Nash. As the movie reveals, Nash is a brilliant mathematician who developed schizophrenia early in his academic and research career and struggled with the disorder for 35 years, unable to hold an academic position or function independently for most of those years. Nevertheless, in 1994 he was awarded the Nobel Prize in Economics for his earlier doctoral work on *game theory,* a mathematical model of conflict resolution. For his doctoral thesis in 1951, Nash had altered this theory in key ways, and while he was later struggling with schizophrenia, his revised theory went on to influence greatly the field of economics—thus his Nobel Prize in that field.

The movie is true to the spirit of Nash's battle against and ultimate triumph over schizophrenia. Similarly, it does capture the essence of Nash's relationship with his wife, Alicia, whose loving devotion, support, and patience have, by everyone's

The actor Portraying Nash in the movie *A Beautiful Mind,* Russell Crowe uses a window at Princeton University to work out a complex mathematical problem.

The mathematician John Forbes Nash gazes out the window of his house in Princeton, New Jersey, shortly after winning the Nobel Prize in Economics.

account, been key to his improvement and later accomplishments. At the same time, the movie takes certain liberties with the facts of Nash's life and struggle. Because this film has been so popular and influential—it

has provided millions of people with their primary education on schizophrenia—it may be useful to correct some of the movie's misrepresentations, each done in the spirit of artistic license.

more disturbed. She started to feel that the neighbors were now recording everything she said; maybe they had hidden wires in the apartment. She started to feel "funny" sensations. There were many strange things happening, which she did not know how to explain; people were looking at her in a funny way in the street; in the butcher shop, the butcher had purposely served her last, although she was in the middle of the line. During the next few days she felt that people were planning to harm either her or her husband. . . . In the evening when she looked at television, it became obvious to her that the programs referred to her life. Often the people on the programs were just repeating what she had thought. They were stealing her ideas. She wanted to go to the police and report them.

(pp. 165–168)

What Are the Symptoms of Schizophrenia?

Ann, Richard, and Laura all deteriorated from a normal level of functioning to become ineffective in dealing with the world. Each experienced some of the symptoms found in schizophrenia. The symptoms can be grouped into three categories: *positive symptoms*

Movie	Reality
Nash's hallucinations and delusions begin in 1948, when he is a 20-year-old graduate student at Princeton University.	His symptoms first appeared in 1958, when he was 30 years old, teaching and conducting research at MIT. In that same year, *Fortune* magazine had named him one of the country's leading mathematicians (Wallace, 2002).
Nash regularly interacts with a high-spirited roommate at Princeton and with a secretive federal agent at MIT, each of whom is but a visual hallucination.	In his battle with schizophrenia, Nash experienced only auditory hallucinations (voices), never visual ones.
Nash is hospitalized on one occasion for his psychotic symptoms.	He was committed to mental hospitals several times throughout the course of his disorder.
Nash meets his wife at MIT in 1952, when Alicia, a physics major, takes his calculus course. They marry in 1957 and remain married to the present day.	After Nash's disorder worsened and his accusations against her intensified, an exasperated and frightened Alicia divorced him in 1963. She remained devoted to him, however. After Nash's mother died in 1970, Alicia agreed to reunite with him, and they have continued to be together since then. They remarried in 2001 (Nasar, 2002).
Although Nash stops taking antipsychotic drugs for years, he returns to them by the movie's end, saying that he has been helped by new (atypical) antipsychotic drugs.	Nash refused to take any more medications in 1970, and he reports that he has not taken any such drugs since then (Duncan, 2002).
Nash has one child, a son named John Charles Nash, born to him and Alicia.	Nash also has an older son named John David Stier, born to him and a woman with whom Nash had a relationship before his marriage to Alicia. Nash currently has close relationships with both sons.
Nash's son, John Charles Nash, is depicted as a healthy child, free of psychological disorders.	Like his father, John Charles Nash went on to develop schizophrenia. Despite this disorder, the son, too, has earned a Ph.D. in mathematics.

(excesses of thought, emotion, and behavior), *negative symptoms* (deficits of thought, emotion, and behavior), and *psychomotor symptoms* (unusual movements or gestures). It appears that some people with schizophrenia are more dominated by positive symp–toms and others by negative symptoms, although both kinds of symptoms are typically displayed to some degree (Vahia & Cohen, 2008; Alves et al., 2005). On average, men with schizophrenia seem more likely to display negative symptoms than women, but both sexes display positive symptoms to the same degree (Usall et al., 2002). In addition, around half of people with schizophrenia display significant difficulties with memory and other kinds of cognitive functioning (Julien, 2008; Rogers et al., 2007).

Positive Symptoms

Positive symptoms are "pathological excesses," or bizarre additions, to a person's behavior. *Delusions, disorganized thinking and speech, heightened perceptions and hallucinations,* and *inappropriate affect* are the ones most often found in schizophrenia.

DELUSIONS Many people with schizophrenia develop **delusions,** ideas that they believe wholeheartedly but have no basis in fact. The deluded person may consider the ideas enlightening or may feel confused by them. Some people hold a single delusion that

•**positive symptoms**•Symptoms of schizophrenia that seem to be excesses of or bizarre additions to normal thoughts, emotions, or behaviors.

•**delusion**•A strange false belief firmly held despite evidence to the contrary.

Delusions of grandeur
In 1892, an artist who was a patient at a mental hospital claimed credit for this painting, *Self-Portrait as Christ.* Although few people with schizophrenia have his artistic skill, a number display similar delusions of grandeur.

•**formal thought disorder**•A disturbance in the production and organization of thought.

•**loose associations**•A common thinking disturbance in schizophrenia, characterized by rapid shifts from one topic of conversation to another. Also known as *derailment.*

dominates their lives and behavior, whereas others have many delusions. *Delusions of persecution* are the most common in schizophrenia (APA, 2000). People with such delusions believe they are being plotted or discriminated against, spied on, slandered, threatened, attacked, or deliberately victimized. Laura believed that her neighbors were trying to irritate her and that other people were trying to harm her and her husband. Another woman with schizophrenia vividly recalled her delusions of persecution:

> I felt as if I was being put on a heavenly trial for misdeeds that I had done and was being held accountable by God. Other times I felt as if I was being pursued by the government for acts of disloyalty. . . . I felt that the government agencies had planted transmitters and receivers in my apartment so that I could hear what they were saying and they could hear what I was saying. I also felt as if the government had bugged my clothing, so that whenever I went outside my apartment I felt like I was being pursued. I felt like I was being followed and watched 24 hours a day.
>
> I would like to point out that these were my feelings then, and in hindsight I hold nothing against these government agencies. I now know that this constant monitoring was either punishment at the hands of God's servants for deeds I committed earlier in my life (sort of like being punished in hell but while I was still alive) or alternatively, but less likely, that I just imagined these things.
>
> *(Anonymous, 1996, p. 183)*

People with schizophrenia may also experience *delusions of reference:* they attach special and personal meaning to the actions of others or to various objects or events. Richard, for example, interpreted arrows on street signs as indicators of the direction he should take. People who experience *delusions of grandeur* believe themselves to be great inventors, religious saviors, or other specially empowered persons. And those with *delusions of control* believe their feelings, thoughts, and actions are being controlled by other people. This man hospitalized for schizophrenia imagined he was being controlled by telepathy:

> The inmates, here, hate me extremely because I am sane. . . . They talk to me telepathically, continuously and daily almost without cessation, day and night. . . . By the power of their imagination and daily and continuously, they create extreme pain in my head, brain, eyes, heart, stomach and in every part of my body. Also by their imagination and daily and continuously, they lift my heart and stomach and they pull my heart, and they stop it, move it, twist it and shake it and pull its muscles and tissues. . . . By telepathy and imagination, they force me to say orally whatever they desire, whenever they desire and as long as they desire. I never said a word of my own. I never created a thought or image of my own.
>
> *(Arieti, 1974, pp. 404–405)*

DISORGANIZED THINKING AND SPEECH People with schizophrenia may not be able to think logically and may speak in peculiar ways. These **formal thought disorders** can cause the sufferer great confusion and make communication extremely difficult. Often they take the form of positive symptoms (pathological excesses), as in loose associations, neologisms, perseveration, and clang.

People who have **loose associations,** or **derailment,** the most common formal thought disorder, rapidly shift from one topic to another, believing that their incoherent statements make sense. A single, perhaps unimportant word in one sentence becomes the focus of the next. One man with schizophrenia, asked about his itchy arms, responded:

The problem is insects. My brother used to collect insects. He's now a man 5 foot 10 inches. You know, 10 is my favorite number. I also like to dance, draw, and watch television.

Some people with schizophrenia use *neologisms,* made-up words that typically have meaning only to the person using them. One individual stated, for example, "I am here from a foreign university . . . and you have to have a *'plausity'* of all acts of amendment to go through for the children's code . . . it is an *'amorition'* law . . . the children have to have this *'accentuative'* law so they don't go into the mortite law of the church" (Vetter, 1969, p. 189). Others may display the formal thought disorder of *perseveration,* in which they repeat their words and statements again and again. Finally, some use *clang,* or rhyme, to think or express themselves. When asked how he was feeling, one man replied, "Well, hell, it's well to tell." Another described the weather as "So hot, you know it runs on a cot."

Formal thought disorders are not unique to schizophrenia. Loose associations and perseverations are common in cases of severe mania, for example. Even people who function normally may organize statements loosely or may on occasion use words that others fail to understand, especially when they are fatigued or feeling ill; but the instances of formal thought disorder in schizophrenia are much more common and severe (Rogers et al., 2007; Holzman, 1986). Research suggests that some disorganized speech or thinking may appear long before a full pattern of schizophrenia unfolds (Covington et al., 2005; Metsanen et al., 2005).

HEIGHTENED PERCEPTIONS AND HALLUCINATIONS A deranged character in Edgar Allan Poe's "The Tell-Tale Heart" asks, "Have I not told you that what you mistake for madness is but the overacuteness of the senses?" Similarly, the perceptions and attention of some people with schizophrenia seem to intensify. The persons may feel that their senses are being flooded by all the sights and sounds that surround them. This makes it almost impossible for them to attend to anything important:

Everything seems to grip my attention. . . . I am speaking to you just now, but I can hear noises going on next door and in the corridor. I find it difficult to shut these out, and it makes it more difficult for me to concentrate on what I am saying to you.

(McGhie and Chapman, 1961)

Laboratory studies repeatedly have found problems of perception and attention among people with schizophrenia (Savla et al., 2008; Rogers et al., 2007). In one study, participants were instructed to listen for a particular syllable recorded against an ongoing background of speech (Harris et al., 1985). As long as the background speech was kept simple, participants with and without schizophrenia were equally successful at picking out the syllable in question; but when the background speech was made more distracting, the individuals with schizophrenia became less able to identify the syllable. In many studies, people with this disorder have also demonstrated deficiencies in *smooth pursuit eye movement,* weaknesses that may be related again to attention problems. When asked to keep their head still and track a moving object back and forth with their eyes, research participants with schizophrenia tend to perform more poorly than those without schizophrenia (Tamminga et al., 2008; Boudet et al., 2005).

The various perception and attention problems found in schizophrenia may develop years before the onset of the actual disorder (Cornblatt & Keilp, 1994). It is also possible that such problems further contribute to the memory impairments that are experienced by many individuals with the disorder (Savla et al., 2008; Hartman et al., 2003).

BETWEEN THE LINES

Neologisms No More

In *Alice in Wonderland,* Lewis Carroll often combined two legitimate words to form a nonsensical word. Some such words are now part of the English language (e.g., "chortle" and "galumph"). ‹‹

One of the 100 new words added to the Merriam-Webster college dictionary in 2008 was *ginormous* (a combination of "gigantic" and "enormous") ‹‹

Poor tracking
Clinical researcher Michael Obuchowski demonstrates a device that reveals how well a person's eyes track a moving laser dot. People with schizophrenia tend to perform poorly on this and other eye pursuit tasks.

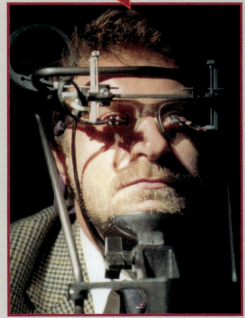

Ed Betz/AP Photo

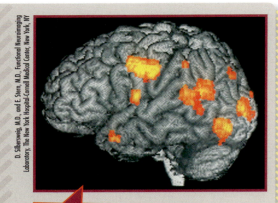

D. Silbersweig, M.D. and E. Stern, M.D., Functional Neuroimaging Laboratory, The New York Hospital-Cornell Medical Center, New York, NY

The human brain during hallucinations

This PET scan, taken at the moment a patient was experiencing auditory and visual hallucinations, shows heightened activity (yellow-orange) in *Broca's area,* a brain region that helps people produce speech, and the *auditory cortex,* the brain area that helps people hear sounds (Silbersweig et al., 1995). Conversely, the *prefrontal cortex,* an area at the front of the brain that is responsible for determining the source of sounds, was quiet during the hallucinations. Thus persons who are hallucinating seem to hear sounds produced by their own brains, but the brains cannot recognize that the sounds are actually coming from within.

•**hallucination**•The experiencing of sights, sounds, or other perceptions in the absence of external stimuli.

•**inappropriate affect**•Display of emotions that are unsuited to the situation; a symptom of schizophrenia.

•**negative symptoms**•Symptoms of schizophrenia that seem to be deficits in normal thought, emotions, or behaviors.

Another kind of perceptual problem in schizophrenia consists of **hallucinations,** perceptions that occur in the absence of external stimuli. People who have *auditory* hallucinations, by far the most common kind in schizophrenia, hear sounds and voices that seem to come from outside their heads (Waters, Badcock, & Maybery, 2007; Folsom et al., 2006). Auditory hallucinations are hardly unique to schizophrenia. Many normal people hear sounds or voices just as they are about to drift off to sleep. Moreover, auditory hallucinations may be experienced by people suffering from migraine headaches, hyperthyroidism, temporal lobe epilepsy, or dementia (Smith, 2007).

Among people with schizophrenia, the auditory hallucinations may talk directly to the hallucinator, perhaps giving commands or warning of dangers, or they may be experienced as overheard:

The voices . . . were mostly heard in my head, though I often heard them in the air, or in different parts of the room. Every voice was different, and each beautiful, and generally, speaking or singing in a different tone and measure, and resembling those of relations or friends. There appeared to be many in my head, I should say upwards of fourteen. I divide them, as they styled themselves, or one another, into voices of contrition and voices of joy and honour.

("Perceval's Narrative," in Bateson, 1974)

Research suggests that people with auditory hallucinations actually produce the nerve signals of sound in their brains, "hear" them, and then believe that external sources are responsible (Woodruff, 2004; Keefe et al., 2002). One line of research measured blood flow in Broca's area, the region of the brain that helps people produce speech (Waters et al., 2007; McGuire et al., 1996, 1995, 1993). The investigators found more blood flow in Broca's area while patients were experiencing auditory hallucinations. A related study instructed six men with schizophrenia to press a button whenever they experienced an auditory hallucination (Silbersweig et al., 1995). PET scans revealed increased activity near the surfaces of their brains, in the tissues of the brain's hearing center, when they pressed the button.

Hallucinations can also involve any of the other senses. *Tactile* hallucinations may take the form of tingling, burning, or electric-shock sensations. *Somatic* hallucinations feel as if something is happening inside the body, such as a snake crawling inside one's stomach. *Visual* hallucinations may produce vague perceptions of colors or clouds or distinct visions of people or objects. People with *gustatory* hallucinations regularly find that their food or drink tastes strange, and people with *olfactory* hallucinations smell odors that no one else does, such as the smell of poison or smoke.

Hallucinations and delusional ideas often occur together (Bach, 2007). A woman who hears voices issuing commands, for example, may have the delusion that the commands are being placed in her head by someone else. A man with delusions of persecution may hallucinate the smell of poison in his bedroom or the taste of poison in his coffee. Might one symptom cause the other? Whatever the cause and whichever comes first, the hallucination and delusion eventually feed into each other (see *Psych Watch* on the facing page):

I thought the voices I heard were being transmitted through the walls of my apartment and through the washer and dryer and that these machines were talking and telling me things. I felt that the government agencies had planted transmitters and receivers in my apartment so that I could hear what they were saying and they could hear what I was saying.

(Anonymous, 1996, p. 183)

Howling for Attention

It's when I was bitten by a rabid dog. . . . When I'm emotionally upset, I feel as if I am turning into something else: my fingers go numb, as if I had pins and needles right in the middle of my hand; I can no longer control myself. . . . I get the feeling I'm becoming a wolf. I look at myself in the mirror and I witness my transformation. It's no longer my face; it changes completely. I stare, my pupils dilate, and I feel as if hairs are growing all over my body, as if my teeth are getting longer. . . . I feel as if my skin is no longer mine.

(BENEZECH, DEWITTE, & BOURGEOIS, 1989)

Lycanthropy, the delusion of being an animal, is a rare psychological syndrome (Nejad, 2007). The word "lycanthropy" comes from the Greek *lykos*, "wolf," and *anthropos*, "man." Accounts have been found all over the world of people who take on the characteristics and behavior of wolves or other animals. Belief in these tales has persisted for centuries. In the Middle Ages, lycanthropy was thought to be the result of demonic possession (Kemp, 2000; Lehmann, 1985). In some societies it occurred after special ointments, probably hallucinogenic drugs, were applied, often for religious purposes (Rao, 2005; Lévi-Strauss, 1977). In other societies, cases seem to have been linked closely to mental disorders, including schizophrenia, severe mood disorders, and certain forms of brain damage.

Mention of lycanthropy continues to produce an image of a werewolf baring its fangs at a terrified villager on a fog-shrouded moor. The legend was that the former had been bitten by another werewolf in an unbroken chain that passes on the legacy. But there are now more reasonable explanations for this type of behavior. One explanation is that some people afflicted with lycanthropy actually suffer from *congenital generalized hypertrichosis*, an extremely rare disease marked by excessive amounts of hair on the face and upper body (Kemp, 2000; Maugh, 1995). Others may suffer from *porphyria*, an inherited blood disease whose victims sprout extra facial hair and are sensitive to sunlight (Osterweil, 2003). Still another current explanation ties lycanthropy to a disturbance in the activity of the *temporal lobe* of the brain, which is close to areas of the brain that may be responsible for visual hallucinations.

Despite these rational hypotheses, beliefs in werewolves as supernatural beings are likely to continue for the foreseeable future. Tales of demonic possession are more alluring than histories of congenital disease or temporal lobe abnormalities. Nor are publishers or movie producers likely to say good-bye to such good friends. Old explanations of lycanthropy may be flawed scientifically, but the profits they produce are far from a delusion.

Polygram/Universal/The Kobal Collection

Crying wolf In the film *An American Werewolf in London*, a possessed man cries out in terror as his body changes into that of a wolf.

INAPPROPRIATE AFFECT Many people with schizophrenia display **inappropriate affect**, emotions that are unsuited to the situation. They may smile when making a somber statement or upon being told terrible news, or they may become upset in situations that should make them happy. They may also undergo inappropriate shifts in mood. During a tender conversation with his wife, for example, a man with schizophrenia suddenly started yelling obscenities at her and complaining about her inadequacies.

In at least some cases, these emotions may be merely a response to other features of the disorder. Consider a woman with schizophrenia who smiles when told of her husband's serious illness. She may not actually be happy about the news; in fact, she may not be understanding or even hearing it. She could, for example, be responding instead to another of the many stimuli flooding her senses, perhaps a joke coming from an auditory hallucination.

Negative Symptoms
Negative symptoms are those that seem to be "pathological deficits," characteristics that are lacking in an individual. *Poverty of speech, blunted and flat affect, loss of volition,* and *social withdrawal* are commonly found in schizophrenia. Such deficits greatly affect one's life and activities.

•**alogia**•A decrease in speech or speech content; a symptom of schizophrenia. Also known as *poverty of speech.*

•**flat affect**•A marked lack of expressed emotions; a symptom of schizophrenia.

•**avolition**•A symptom of schizophrenia marked by apathy and an inability to start or complete a course of action.

•**catatonia**•A pattern of extreme psychomotor symptoms found in some forms of schizophrenia, which may include catatonic stupor, rigidity, or posturing.

POVERTY OF SPEECH People with schizophrenia often display **alogia,** or **poverty of speech,** a reduction in speech or speech content. Some people with this negative kind of formal thought disorder think and say very little. Others say quite a bit but still manage to convey little meaning. These speech problems do not necessarily carry over to the realm of writing (Salome et al., 2002). Nevertheless, they are revealed in the following diary entry written on February 27, 1919, by Vaslav Nijinsky, one of the twentieth century's great ballet dancers, as his schizophrenic disorder was unfolding:

I do not wish people to think that I am a great writer or that I am a great artist nor even that I am a great man. I am a simple man who has suffered a lot. I believe I suffered more than Christ. I love life and want to live, to cry but cannot—I feel such a pain in my soul—a pain which frightens me. My soul is ill. My soul, not my mind. The doctors do not understand my illness. I know what I need to get well. My illness is too great to be cured quickly. I am incurable. Everyone who reads these lines will suffer—they will understand my feelings. I know what I need. I am strong, not weak. My body is not ill—it is my soul that is ill. I suffer, I suffer. Everyone will feel and understand. I am a man, not a beast. I love everyone, I have faults, I am a man—not God. I want to be God and therefore I try to improve myself. I want to dance, to draw, to play the piano, to write verses, I want to love everybody. That is the object of my life.

(Nijinsky, 1936)

BLUNTED AND FLAT AFFECT Many people with schizophrenia have a *blunted affect*—they show less anger, sadness, joy, and other feelings than most people. And some show almost no emotions at all, a condition known as **flat affect.** Their faces are still, their eye contact is poor, and their voices are monotonous. In some cases, people with these problems may have *anhedonia,* a general lack of pleasure or enjoyment. In other cases, however, blunted or flat affect may reflect an inability to express emotions as others do. One study had participants view very emotional film clips. The participants with schizophrenia showed less facial expression than the others; however, they reported feeling just as much positive and negative emotion and in fact displayed greater skin arousal (Kring & Neale, 1996).

LOSS OF VOLITION Many people with schizophrenia experience **avolition,** or apathy, feeling drained of energy and of interest in normal goals and unable to start or follow through on a course of action (Lysaker & Bell, 1995). This problem is particularly common in people who have had schizophrenia for many years, as if they have been worn down by it. Similarly, individuals with the disorder may display *ambivalence,* or conflicting feelings, about most things. The avolition and ambivalence of Richard, the young man you read about earlier, made eating, dressing, and undressing impossible ordeals for him.

SOCIAL WITHDRAWAL People with schizophrenia may withdraw from their social environment and attend only to their own ideas and fantasies. Because their ideas are illogical and confused, the withdrawal has the effect of distancing them still further from reality. In fact, studies have found that participants with this disorder are typically less knowledgeable about everyday social issues than are other people (Venneri et al., 2002; Cutting & Murphy, 1990, 1988). The social withdrawal seems also to lead to a breakdown of social skills, including the ability to recognize other people's needs and emotions accurately (Tenhula & Bellack, 2008; Moore & Walkup, 2007).

Psychomotor Symptoms People with schizophrenia sometimes experience *psychomotor symptoms,* for example, awkward movements or repeated grimaces and odd gestures. These unusual gestures often seem to have a private purpose—perhaps ritualistic or magical.

The psychomotor symptoms of schizophrenia may take certain extreme forms, collectively called **catatonia** (Weder et al., 2008). People in a *catatonic stupor* stop responding to their environment, remaining motionless and silent for long stretches of time. Recall how Richard would lie motionless and mute in bed for days. People who display *catatonic rigidity* maintain a rigid, upright posture for hours and resist efforts to be moved. Others exhibit *catatonic posturing,* assuming awkward, bizarre positions for long periods of time. They may spend hours holding their arms out at a 90-degree angle or balancing in a squatting position. They may also display "waxy flexibility," indefinitely maintaining postures into which they have been placed by someone else. If a nurse raises a patient's arm or tilts the patient's head, for example, the individual will remain in that position until moved again. Finally, people who display *catatonic excitement,* a different form of catatonia, move excitedly, sometimes with wild waving of arms and legs.

The Oskar Diethelm Library, History of Psychiatry Section, Department of Psychiatry, Cornell University Medical College and The New York Hospital, New York, NY

A catatonic pose
These patients, photographed in the early 1900s, display features of catatonia, including catatonic posturing, in which they assume bizarre positions for long periods of time.

What Is the Course of Schizophrenia?

Schizophrenia usually first appears between the person's late teens and mid-30s (APA, 2000). Although its course varies widely from case to case, many sufferers seem to go through three phases—prodromal, active, and residual (Hafner & an der Heiden, 2008; Andreasen, 2001). During the *prodromal phase,* symptoms are not yet obvious, but the individuals are beginning to deteriorate. They may withdraw socially, speak in vague or odd ways, develop strange ideas, or express little emotion. During the *active phase,* symptoms become apparent. Sometimes this phase is triggered by stress in the person's life. For Laura, the middle-aged woman described earlier, the immediate trigger was the loss of her cherished dog. Finally, many people with schizophrenia eventually enter a *residual phase,* in which they return to a prodromal-like level of functioning. The striking symptoms of the active phase lessen, but some negative symptoms, such as blunted emotions, may remain. Although one-quarter or more of patients recover completely from schizophrenia, the majority continue to have at least some residual problems for the rest of their lives (Fischer & Carpenter, 2008; Roe & Davidson, 2008).

Each of these phases may last for days or for years. A fuller recovery from schizophrenia is more likely in persons who functioned quite well before the disorder (had good *premorbid functioning*) or whose disorder was initially triggered by stress, came on abruptly, or developed during middle age (Conus et al., 2007; Mamounas et al., 2001). Relapses are apparently more likely during times of life stress (Bebbington & Kuipers, 2008).

Diagnosing Schizophrenia

DSM-IV-TR calls for a diagnosis of schizophrenia only after symptoms of the disorder continue for six months or more. In addition, people suspected of having this disorder must show a deterioration in their work, social relations, and ability to care for themselves (see Table 14-1). Emil Kraepelin, writing in 1896, distinguished three patterns of schizophrenia: *hebephrenic* (now called "disorganized"), *catatonic,* and *paranoid*. To these categories DSM-IV-TR adds two other types of schizophrenia: *undifferentiated* and *residual*.

The central symptoms of *disorganized type of schizophrenia* are confusion, incoherence, and flat or inappropriate affect. Attention and perception problems, extreme social withdrawal, and odd mannerisms or grimaces are common. So is flat or inappropriate affect. Silliness, in particular, is common; some patients giggle constantly without apparent reason. This is why the pattern was first called "hebephrenic," after Hebe, the goddess who, according to Greek mythology, often acted like a clown to make the other gods laugh. Not surprisingly, people with disorganized schizophrenia are typically unable to take good care of themselves, maintain social relationships, or hold a job.

The central feature of *catatonic type of schizophrenia* is a psychomotor disturbance of some sort. Some of the people in this category spend their time in a catatonic stupor,

table: 14-1

DSM Checklist

SCHIZOPHRENIA

1. At least two of the following symptoms, each present for a significant portion of time during a one-month period:
   (a) Delusions.
   (b) Hallucinations.
   (c) Disorganized speech.
   (d) Grossly disorganized or catatonic behavior.
   (e) Negative symptoms.

2. Functioning markedly below the level achieved prior to onset.

3. Continuous signs of the disturbance for at least six months, at least one month of which includes symptoms in full and active form (as opposed to attenuated form).

Based on APA, 2000.

others in the throes of catatonic excitement. Richard, the unemployed young man who became mute and statuelike, might receive a diagnosis of this type of schizophrenia.

People with *paranoid type of schizophrenia* have an organized system of delusions and auditory hallucinations that may guide their lives. Laura would receive this diagnosis. She believed people were out to get her (delusions of persecution) and that people on television were stealing her ideas (delusions of reference). In addition, she heard noises from the apartment downstairs and felt "funny sensations" that confirmed her beliefs.

When people with this disorder do not fall neatly into one of the other categories, they are diagnosed with *undifferentiated type of schizophrenia*. Because this category is somewhat vague, it has been assigned to a wide assortment of unusual patterns over the years. Many clinicians believe that it is in fact overused.

When the symptoms of schizophrenia lessen in strength and number yet remain in a residual form, the patient's diagnosis is usually changed to *residual type of schizophrenia*. As you saw earlier, people with this pattern may continue to display blunted or inappropriate emotions, as well as social withdrawal, eccentric behavior, and some illogical thinking.

Apart from these DSM-IV categories, many researchers believe that a distinction between so-called Type I and Type II schizophrenia helps predict the course of the disorder. People with *Type I schizophrenia* are thought to be dominated by positive symptoms, such as delusions, hallucinations, and certain formal thought disorders (Crow, 2008, 1995, 1985, 1980). Those with *Type II schizophrenia* display negative symptoms, such as flat affect, poverty of speech, and loss of volition. Type I patients generally seem to have a better adjustment prior to the disorder, later onset of symptoms, and greater likelihood of improvement. In addition, as you will soon see, the positive symptoms of Type I schizophrenia may be linked more closely to *biochemical* abnormalities in the brain, while the negative symptoms of Type II schizophrenia may be tied largely to *structural* abnormalities in the brain.

✿How Do Theorists Explain Schizophrenia?

As with many other kinds of disorders, biological, psychological, and sociocultural theorists have each proposed explanations for schizophrenia. So far, the biological explanations have received by far the most research support. This is not to say that psychological and sociocultural factors play no role in the disorder. Rather, a *diathesis-stress relationship* may be at work: people with a biological predisposition will develop schizophrenia only if certain kinds of events or stressors are also present (Glatt, 2008; Tamminga et al., 2008). Similarly, a diathesis-stress relationship often seems to be operating in the development of other kinds of psychotic disorders (see *A Closer Look* on pages 468–469).

Biological Views

What is arguably the most enlightening research on schizophrenia during the past several decades has come from genetic and biological investigations (Downar & Kapur, 2008; Glatt, 2008). These studies have revealed the key roles of inheritance and brain activity in the development of this disorder and have opened the door to important changes in its treatment.

Genetic Factors Following the principles of the diathesis-stress perspective, genetic researchers believe that some people inherit a biological predisposition to schizophrenia and develop the disorder later when they face extreme stress, usually during late adolescence or early adulthood (Glatt, 2008). The genetic view has been supported by studies of (1) relatives of people with schizophrenia, (2) twins with this disorder, (3) people with schizophrenia who are adopted, and (4) genetic linkage and molecular biology.

ARE RELATIVES VULNERABLE? Family pedigree studies have found repeatedly that schizophrenia is more common among relatives of people with the disorder (Tamminga et al.,

Genetic diversity: laboratory style
These lab mice represent different breeds that are being crossbred into a new large rodent population. The larger population is intended to mimic the genetic diversity of human beings, enabling researchers to investigate better the causes and treatment of schizophrenia and other disorders.

AP Photo/Oak Ridge National Lab, Curtis Boles

2008; Higgins & George, 2007). And the more closely related the relatives are to the person with schizophrenia, the greater their likelihood of developing the disorder (see Figure 14-2).

As you saw earlier, 1 percent of the general population develops schizophrenia. The prevalence rises to 3 percent among second-degree relatives with this disorder—that is, half-siblings, uncles, aunts, nephews, nieces, and grandchildren (Gottesman & Reilly, 2003; Gottesman, 1991; Gottesman & Shields, 1983)—and it reaches an average of 10 percent among first-degree relatives (parents, siblings, and children). Of course, this trend by itself does not establish a genetic basis for the disorder. Neuroscientist Solomon Snyder (1980) points out, "Attendance at Harvard University also runs in families but would hardly be considered a genetic trait." Close family members are exposed to many of the same environmental influences as the person with schizophrenia, and it may be these influences that lead to the disorder.

IS AN IDENTICAL TWIN MORE VULNERABLE THAN A FRATERNAL TWIN?

Twins, who are among the closest of relatives, have received particular study by schizophrenia researchers. If both members of a pair of twins have a particular trait, they are said to be *concordant* for that trait. If genetic factors are at work in schizophrenia, identical twins (who share all their genes) should have a higher concordance rate for this disorder than fraternal twins (who share only some genes). This expectation has been supported consistently by research (Higgins & George, 2007; Folsom et al., 2006; Gottesman, 1991). Studies have found that if one identical twin develops schizophrenia, there is a 48 percent chance that the other twin will do so as well. If the twins are fraternal, on the other hand, the second twin has approximately a 17 percent chance of developing the disorder.

Once again, however, factors other than genetics may explain these concordance rates. For example, if one twin is exposed to a particular danger during the prenatal period, such as an injury or virus, the other twin is likely to be exposed to it as well (Davis & Phelps, 1995). This is especially true for identical twins, whose prenatal environment is particularly similar. Thus a predisposition to schizophrenia could be the result of a prenatal problem, and twins, particularly identical twins, would still be expected to have a higher concordance rate.

ARE THE BIOLOGICAL RELATIVES OF AN ADOPTEE VULNERABLE?

Adoption studies look at adults with schizophrenia who were adopted as infants and compare them with both their biological and their adoptive relatives. Because they were reared apart from their biological relatives, similar symptoms in those relatives would indicate genetic influences. Conversely, similarities to their adoptive relatives would suggest environmental influences.

Seymour Kety and his colleagues (1988, 1978, 1975, 1968) conducted a pioneering study in Copenhagen, Denmark, where detailed records of adoptions and mental disorders are available. In a sample of nearly 5,500 adults who had been adopted early in life, the researchers found 33 with schizophrenia. They then selected 33 matching control participants from the same large sample—normal adoptees similar in age, sex, and schooling to the individuals with schizophrenia. Next the investigators located 365 biological and adoptive relatives of these 66 adoptees, including both parents and siblings, and separated the relatives into four groups: (1) biological relatives of adoptees with schizophrenia; (2) adoptive relatives of adoptees with schizophrenia; (3) biological relatives of normal adoptees; and (4) adoptive relatives of normal adoptees. Thirty-seven of the relatives were found to qualify for a diagnosis of either schizophrenia or a schizophrenia-like disorder (see Table 14-2 on the next page). Most of them turned

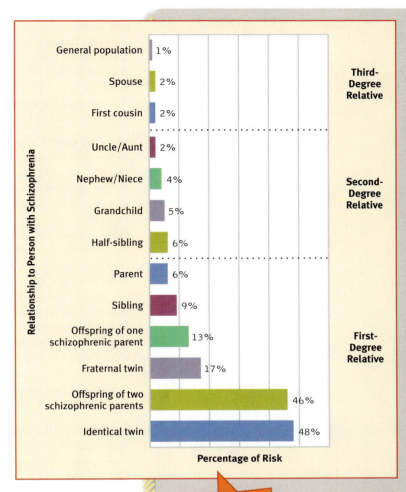

Figure 14-2
Family links People who are biologically related to individuals with schizophrenia have a heightened risk of developing the disorder during their lifetimes. The closer the biological relationship (that is, the more similar the genetic makeup), the greater the risk of developing the disorder. (Coon & Mitterer, 2007; Gottesman, 1991, p. 96.)

BETWEEN THE LINES

Specific Genes Linked to Schizophrenia

DTNBP1 (on chromosome 6) ‹‹

NRG1 (on chromosome 8) ‹‹

CHRNA7 (on chromosome 15) ‹‹

DAO, DAOA (on chromosome 13) ‹‹

RGS4 (on chromosome 1) ‹‹

DISC1 (on chromosome 1) ‹‹

(Deutsch et al., 2005; Kirov et al., 2005; DeLuca et al., 2004)

out to be biological relatives of the adoptees with schizophrenia, a result that strongly supports the genetic explanation. Altogether 14 percent of the biological relatives of the adoptees with the disorder were themselves classified as schizophrenic, whereas only 2.7 percent of their adoptive relatives received this classification. The biological and adoptive relatives of the normal adoptees had schizophrenia prevalence rates of 3.4 percent and 5.5 percent, respectively. More recent adoption studies in other countries have yielded similar findings (Janicak et al., 2001).

WHAT DO GENETIC LINKAGE AND MOLECULAR BIOLOGY STUDIES SUGGEST? As with bipolar disorders (see Chapter 8), researchers have run studies of *genetic linkage* and *molecular biology* to pinpoint the possible genetic factors in schizophrenia (Glatt, 2008; Walsh et al., 2008). In one approach, they select large families in which schizophrenia is very common, take blood and DNA samples from all members of the families, and then compare gene fragments from members with and without schizophrenia. Applying this procedure to families from around the world, various studies have identified possible gene defects on chromosomes 1, 6, 8, 10, 13, 15, 18, and 22 and on the X chromosome, each of which may help predispose individuals to develop schizophrenia (Folsom et al., 2006; Harrison & Weinberger, 2005).

These varied findings may indicate that some of the suspected gene sites are cases of mistaken identity and do not actually contribute to schizophrenia. Alternatively, it may be that different kinds of schizophrenia are linked to different genes. It is most likely, however, that schizophrenia, like a number of other disorders, is a *polygenic disorder,* caused by a combination of gene defects (Tamminga et al., 2008; Harrison & Weinberger, 2005).

How might genetic factors lead to the development of schizophrenia? Research has pointed to two kinds of biological abnormalities that could conceivably be inherited—*biochemical abnormalities* and *abnormal brain structure.*

Biochemical Abnormalities As you have read, the brain is made up of neurons whose electrical impulses (or "messages") are transmitted from one to another by neurotransmitters. After an impulse arrives at a receiving neuron, it travels down the axon of that neuron until it reaches the nerve ending. The nerve ending then releases neurotransmitters that travel across the synaptic space and bind to receptors on yet another neuron, thus relaying the message to the next "station." This neuron activity is known as "firing."

table: 14-2

An Array of Psychotic Disorders

Disorder	Key Features	Duration	Lifetime Prevalence
Schizophrenia	Various psychotic symptoms such as delusions, hallucinations, disorganized speech, flat or inappropriate affect, and catatonia	6 months or more	1.0%
Brief psychotic disorder	Various psychotic symptoms such as delusions, hallucinations, disorganized speech, flat or inappropriate affect, and catatonia	Less than 1 month	Unknown
Schizophreniform disorder	Various psychotic symptoms such as delusions, hallucinations, disorganized speech, flat or inappropriate affect, and catatonia	1 to 6 months	0.2%
Schizoaffective disorder	Marked symptoms of both schizophrenia and a mood disorder	6 months or more	Unknown
Delusional disorder	Persistent delusions that are not bizarre and not due to schizophrenia; persecutory, jealous, grandiose, and somatic delusions are common	1 month or more	0.1%
Shared psychotic disorder	Person adopts delusions that are held by another individual, such as a parent or sibling; Also known as *folie à deux*	No minimum length	Unknown
Psychotic disorder due to a general medical condition	Hallucinations or delusions caused by a medical illness or brain damage	No minimum length	Unknown
Substance-induced psychotic disorder	Hallucinations or delusions caused directly by a substance, such as an abused drug	No minimum length	Unknown

Over the past three decades, researchers have developed a **dopamine hypothesis** to explain their findings on schizophrenia: certain neurons that use the neurotransmitter dopamine fire too often and transmit too many messages, thus producing the symptoms of the disorder (McGowan et al., 2004). This hypothesis has undergone challenges and adjustments in recent years, but it is still the foundation for present biochemical explanations of schizophrenia. The chain of events leading to this hypothesis began with the accidental discovery of **antipsychotic drugs,** medications that help remove the symptoms of schizophrenia. As you will see in Chapter 15, the first group of antipsychotic medications, the **phenothiazines,** were discovered in the 1950s by researchers who were looking for better *antihistamine* drugs to combat allergies. Although phenothiazines failed as antihistamines, their effectiveness in reducing schizophrenic symptoms became obvious, and clinicians began to prescribe them widely.

Researchers soon learned that these early antipsychotic drugs often produce troublesome muscular tremors, symptoms that are identical to the central symptom of *Parkinson's disease,* a disabling neurological illness. This undesired reaction to antipsychotic drugs offered the first important clue to the biology of schizophrenia. Scientists already knew that people who suffer from Parkinson's disease have abnormally low levels of the neurotransmitter dopamine in some areas of the brain and that lack of dopamine is the reason for their uncontrollable shaking. If antipsychotic drugs produce Parkinsonian symptoms in persons with schizophrenia while removing their psychotic symptoms, perhaps the drugs reduce dopamine activity. And, scientists reasoned further, if lowering dopamine activity helps remove the symptoms of schizophrenia, perhaps schizophrenia is related to excessive dopamine activity in the first place.

HOW STRONG IS THE DOPAMINE-SCHIZOPHRENIA LINK? Since the 1960s, research has supported and helped clarify the dopamine hypothesis. It has been found, for example, that some people with Parkinson's disease develop schizophrenia-like symptoms if they take too much *L-dopa,* a medication that raises dopamine levels in patients with that disease (Grilly, 2002; Carey et al., 1995). The L-dopa apparently raises the dopamine activity so much that it produces psychosis.

Support for the dopamine hypothesis has also come from research on *amphetamines,* drugs that, as you saw in Chapter 12, stimulate the central nervous system. Investigators first noticed during the 1970s that people who take high doses of amphetamines may develop *amphetamine psychosis*—a syndrome very similar to schizophrenia. They also found that antipsychotic drugs can reduce the symptoms of amphetamine psychosis, just as they reduce the symptoms of schizophrenia (Janowsky et al., 1973). Eventually researchers learned that amphetamines increase dopamine activity in the brain, thus producing schizophrenia-like symptoms.

Investigators have located areas of the brain that are rich in dopamine receptors and have found that phenothiazines and other antipsychotic drugs bind to many of these receptors (Burt et al., 1977; Creese et al., 1977). Apparently the drugs are dopamine *antagonists*—drugs that bind to dopamine receptors, *prevent* dopamine from binding there, and so prevent the neurons from firing (Iversen, 1975). Researchers have identified five kinds of dopamine receptors in the brain—called the D-1, D-2, D-3, D-4, and D-5 receptors—and have found that phenothiazines bind most strongly to the *D-2 receptors* (Julien, 2008).

WHAT IS DOPAMINE'S PRECISE ROLE? These and related findings suggest that in schizophrenia, messages traveling from dopamine-sending neurons to dopamine receptors on other neurons, particularly to the D-2 receptors, may be transmitted too easily or too often. This theory is appealing because certain dopamine neurons are known to play a key role in guiding attention (Sikstrom & Soderlund, 2007). People whose attention is severely disturbed by excessive dopamine activity might well be expected to suffer from the problems of attention, perception, and thought found in schizophrenia.

Why might dopamine be overactive in people with schizophrenia? It may be that people with this disorder have a larger-than-usual number of dopamine receptors, particularly D-2 receptors, or their dopamine receptors may operate abnormally (Tamminga et

•**dopamine hypothesis**•The theory that schizophrenia results from excessive activity of the neurotransmitter dopamine.

•**antipsychotic drugs**•Drugs that help correct grossly confused or distorted thinking.

•**phenothiazines**•A group of antihistamine drugs that became the first group of effective antipsychotic medications.

BETWEEN THE LINES

Primary Causes of Premature Death among People with Schizophrenia

Suicide ‹‹

Accidents ‹‹

Inadequate medical care ‹‹

Infections, heart disease, diabetes ‹‹

Unhealthy lifestyles ‹‹

Homelessness ‹‹

(Torrey, 2001)

Postpartum Psychosis: The Case of Andrea Yates

On the morning of June 20, 2001, the nation's television viewers watched in horror as officials escorted 36-year-old Andrea Yates to a police car. Just minutes before, she had called police and explained that she had drowned her five children in the bathtub because "they weren't developing correctly" and because she "realized [she had not been] a good mother to them." Homicide sergeant Eric Mehl described how she looked him in the eye, nodded, answered with a polite "Yes, sir" to many of his questions, and twice recounted the order in which the children had died: first 3-year-old Paul, then 2-year-old Luke, followed by 5-year-old John and 6-month-old Mary. She then described how she had had to drag 7-year-old Noah to the bathroom and how he had come up twice as he fought for air. Signs of mental disturbance were present during this 17-minute conversation. Yates sat in silence if Mehl asked too many questions and could give only short answers to simple questions. Later she told doctors she wanted her hair shaved so she could see the number 666—the mark of the Antichrist—on her scalp (Roche, 2002).

In Chapter 9 you observed that as many as 80 percent of mothers experience "baby blues" soon after giving birth, while between 10 and 30 percent display the

Courtesy of Yates Family/Getty Images

Family tragedy In this undated photograph, Andrea Yates poses with her husband and four of the five children she later drowned.

clinical syndrome of *postpartum depression*. Yet another postpartum disorder that has become all too familiar to the public in recent times, by way of cases such as that of Andrea Yates, is *postpartum psychosis*.

Postpartum psychosis affects about 1 to 2 of every 1,000 mothers who have recently given birth. The symptoms apparently are triggered by the enormous shift in hormone levels that occur after delivery (Blackmore et al., 2008; Nonacs, 2007,

al., 2008; Sedvall, 1990; Seidman, 1990). Remember that when dopamine carries a message to a receiving neuron, it must bind to a receptor on the neuron. A greater number of receptors or abnormal operation by the receptors could result in more dopamine binding and thus more neuron firing. Autopsies have in fact found an unusually large number of dopamine receptors in people with schizophrenia (Owen et al., 1987, 1978; Lee & Seeman, 1980), and imaging studies have revealed particularly high occupancy levels of dopamine at D-2 receptors in patients with schizophrenia (Tamminga et al., 2008).

Though enlightening, the dopamine hypothesis has certain problems. The greatest challenge to it has come with the recent discovery of a new group of antipsychotic drugs, referred to as **atypical antipsychotic drugs,** which are often more effective than the traditional ones. The new drugs bind not only to D-2 dopamine receptors, like the traditional, or conventional, antipsychotic drugs, but also to many D-1 receptors and to receptors for other neurotransmitters such as *serotonin* (Goldman–Rakic et al., 2004; Roth et al., 2004). Thus, it may be that schizophrenia is related to abnormal activity or interactions of both dopamine and serotonin and perhaps other neurotransmitters (for

•**atypical antipsychotic drugs**•A relatively new group of antipsychotic drugs whose biological action is different from that of the traditional antipsychotic drugs.

2002; Sit et al., 2006). Within days or at most a few months of childbirth, the woman develops signs of losing touch with reality, such as delusions (for example, she may become convinced that her baby is the devil); hallucinations (perhaps hearing voices); extreme anxiety, confusion, and disorientation; disturbed sleep; and illogical or chaotic thoughts (for example, thoughts about killing herself or her child).

Women with a history of bipolar disorder, schizophrenia, or depression are particularly vulnerable to the disorder (Read & Purse, 2007; Nonacs, 2007, 2002; Sit et al., 2006). In addition, women who have previously experienced postpartum depression or postpartum psychosis have an increased likelihood of developing this disorder after subsequent births (Nonacs, 2007; Ruta & Cohen, 1998). Andrea Yates, for example, had developed signs of postpartum depression (and perhaps postpartum psychosis) and attempted suicide after the birth of her fourth child. At that time, however, she appeared to respond well to a combination of medications, including antipsychotic drugs, and so she and her husband later decided to conceive a fifth child. Although they were warned that she was at risk for serious postpartum symptoms once again, they believed that

the same combination of medications would help if the symptoms were to recur (King, 2002).

After the birth of her fifth child, the symptoms did in fact recur, along with features of psychosis. Yates again attempted suicide. Although she was hospitalized twice and treated with various medications, her condition failed to improve as various medications were added and withdrawn. Six months after giving birth to Mary, her fifth child, she drowned all five of her children.

Most clinicians who are knowledgeable about this rare disorder agree that Yates was indeed a victim of postpartum psychosis. Although only a fraction of women with the disorder actually harm their children (estimates run as high as 4 percent), the Yates case reminds us that such an outcome is indeed possible (Read & Purse, 2007; Dobson & Sales, 2000). The case also reminds us that early detection and intervention are critical.

Could more have been done for this woman as her disorder was progressing? In retrospect, obviously. And, in fact, fingers have been pointed at her husband, her doctors, her insurers, and others who failed to appreciate or respond properly to the severity of her disorder, failed to make

long-term hospitalization available to her, offered her relatively little in the way of treatment options, allowed her to be alone at home with her children while her stress built up and her symptoms continued, and failed to dissuade her from having a fifth child.

On March 13, 2002, a Texas jury found Andrea Yates guilty of murdering her children and she was sentenced to life in prison. She had pleaded *not guilty by reason of insanity* during her trial, but the jury concluded within hours that despite her profound disorder (which even the prosecutors had acknowledged), she did know right from wrong. The verdict itself stirred debate throughout the United States, but clinicians and the public alike were united in the belief that, at the very least, the mental health system had tragically failed this woman and her five children.

A Texas appeals court later reversed Yates's conviction, citing the inaccurate testimony of a prosecution witness, and on July 26, 2006, after a new trial, Yates was found *not guilty by reason of insanity* and was sent to a high-security mental health facility for treatment. In 2007, she was transferred to a low-security state mental hospital where she continues to receive treatment today.

example, *glutamate* and *GABA*) as well, rather than to abnormal dopamine activity alone (Bach, 2007; Folsom et al., 2006).

In yet another challenge to the dopamine hypothesis, some theorists claim that excessive dopamine activity contributes primarily to the positive symptoms of schizophrenia such as delusions and hallucinations. In support of that notion, it turns out that positive symptoms respond well to the conventional antipsychotic drugs, which bind so strongly to D-2 receptors, whereas some of the negative symptoms (such as flat affect and loss of volition) respond best to the atypical antipsychotic drugs, which bind less strongly to D-2 receptors (Julien, 2008; Arango et al., 2004). Still other studies suggest that negative symptoms may be related primarily to abnormal brain structure, rather than to dopamine overactivity (Maruff et al., 2005).

Abnormal Brain Structure During the past decade, researchers also have linked schizophrenia, particularly cases dominated by negative symptoms, to abnormalities in brain structure (Eyler, 2008; Weyandt, 2006). Using CAT and MRI scans, they have

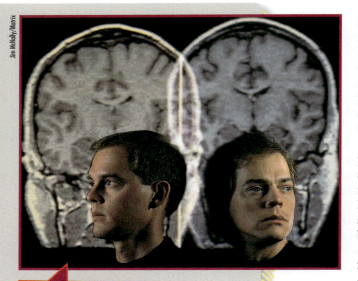

Not-so-identical twins
The man on the left is normal, while his identical twin, on the right, has schizophrenia. Magnetic resonance imaging (MRI), shown in the background, clarifies that the brain of the twin with schizophrenia is smaller overall than his brother's and has larger ventricles, indicated by the dark butterfly-shaped spaces.

found, for example, that many people with schizophrenia have *enlarged ventricles*—the brain cavities that contain cerebrospinal fluid (Cahn et al., 2002; Lieberman et al., 2001). On average the ventricles of these individuals are 15 percent larger than those of other persons (Torrey, 2002, 2001). In addition to displaying more negative symptoms and fewer positive ones, patients who have enlarged ventricles tend to experience a poorer social adjustment prior to the disorder, greater cognitive disturbances, and poorer responses to conventional antipsychotic drugs (Bornstein et al., 1992).

It may be that enlarged ventricles are actually a sign that nearby parts of the brain have not developed properly or have been damaged, and perhaps these problems are the ones that help produce schizophrenia. In fact, studies suggest that some patients with schizophrenia also have smaller temporal lobes and frontal lobes than other people, smaller amounts of cortical gray matter, and, perhaps most important, abnormal blood flow—either reduced or heightened—in certain areas of the brain (Tamminga et al., 2008; Higgins & George, 2007; Whitford et al., 2005). Still other studies have linked schizophrenia to size, structural, and cellular abnormalities of the hippocampus, amygdala, and thalamus, among other brain areas (Folsom et al., 2006; Spaniel et al., 2003) (see Figure 14-3).

Viral Problems What might cause the biochemical and structural abnormalities found in many cases of schizophrenia? Various studies have pointed to genetic factors, poor nutrition, fetal development, birth complications, immune reactions, and toxins (Ellman & Cannon, 2008; Bach, 2007). In addition, some investigators suggest that the brain abnormalities may result from exposure to *viruses* before birth. Perhaps the viruses enter the fetus's brain and interrupt proper brain development, or perhaps the viruses remain quiet until puberty or young adulthood, when, activated by changes in hormones or by another viral infection, they help to bring about schizophrenic symptoms (Lambert & Kinsley, 2005; Torrey, 2001, 1991).

Some of the evidence for the viral theory comes from animal model investigations, and some is circumstantial evidence, such as the finding that an unusually large number of people with schizophrenia are born during the winter (Meyer et al., 2005; Torrey, 2001, 1991). The winter birth rate among people with schizophrenia is 5 to 8 percent higher than among other persons (Tamminga et al., 2008). This finding could be because of an

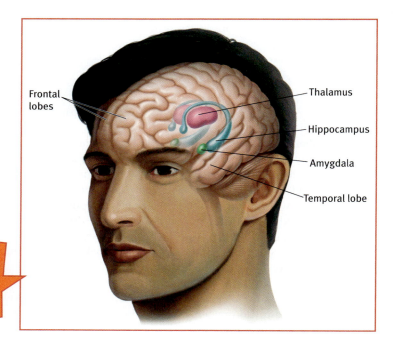

Figure 14-3
Biology of schizophrenia Some studies show that people with schizophrenia have relatively small temporal and frontal lobes, as well as abnormalities in structures such as the hippocampus, amygdala, and thalamus.

Frontal lobes

Thalamus

Hippocampus

Amygdala

Temporal lobe

increase in fetal or infant exposure to viruses at that time of year. The viral theory has also received support from investigations of *fingerprints.* Normally, identical twins have almost identical numbers of fingerprint ridges. People with schizophrenia, however, often have significantly more or fewer ridges than their nonschizophrenic identical twins (Van Os et al., 1997; Torrey et al., 1994). Fingerprints form in the fetus during the second trimester of pregnancy, just when the fetus is most vulnerable to certain viruses. Thus the fingerprint irregularities of some people with schizophrenia could reflect a viral infection contracted during the prenatal period, an infection that also predisposed the individuals to schizophrenia.

More direct evidence for the viral theory of schizophrenia comes from studies showing that mothers of individuals with schizophrenia were more likely to have been exposed to the influenza virus during pregnancy than were mothers of people without schizophrenia (Brown et al., 2004; Limosin et al., 2003). Other studies have found antibodies to particular viruses, including viruses usually found in animals, in the blood of 40 percent of research participants with schizophrenia (Leweke et al., 2004; Torrey et al., 1994). The presence of such antibodies suggests that these people had at some time been exposed to those particular viruses.

Together, the biochemical, brain structure, and viral findings are shedding much light on the mysteries of schizophrenia. At the same time, it is important to recognize that many people who display these biological abnormalities never develop schizophrenia. Why not? Possibly, as you read earlier, because biological factors merely set the stage for schizophrenia, while key psychological and sociocultural factors must be present for the disorder to appear.

Psychological Views

When schizophrenia investigators began to identify genetic and biological factors during the 1950s and 1960s, many clinicians abandoned the psychological theories of the disorder. During the past decade, however, the tables have been turned and psychological factors are once again being considered as important pieces of the schizophrenia puzzle. The leading psychological theories come from the psychodynamic, behavioral, and cognitive perspectives.

The Psychodynamic Explanation
Freud (1924, 1915, 1914) believed that schizophrenia develops from two psychological processes: (1) *regression* to a pre-ego stage and (2) efforts to *reestablish* ego control. He proposed that when their world is extremely harsh or withholding—for example, when parents are cold or unnurturing—people who develop schizophrenia regress to the earliest point in their development, to the pre-ego state of *primary narcissism,* in which they recognize and meet only their own needs. Their near-total regression leads to self-centered symptoms such as neologisms, loose associations, and delusions of grandeur. Once people regress to such an infantile state, Freud continued, they then try to reestablish ego control and contact with reality. Their efforts give rise to yet other schizophrenic symptoms. Auditory hallucinations, for example, may be an individual's attempt to substitute for a lost sense of reality.

Years later, noted psychodynamic clinician Frieda Fromm-Reichmann (1948) elaborated on Freud's notion that cold or unnurturing parents may set schizophrenia in motion. She described the mothers of people who develop this disorder as cold, domineering, and uninterested in their children's needs. According to Fromm-Reichmann, these mothers may appear to be self-sacrificing but are actually using their children to meet their own needs. At once overprotective and rejecting, they confuse their children and set the stage for schizophrenic functioning. She called them **schizophrenogenic** (schizophrenia-causing) **mothers.**

Fromm-Reichmann's theory, like Freud's, has received little research support (Willick, 2001). The majority of people with schizophrenia do not appear to have mothers who fit the schizophrenogenic description. In fact, some studies have suggested that quite a different personality style may prevail among their mothers. In one study the mothers

•**schizophrenogenic mother**•A type of mother—supposedly cold, domineering, and uninterested in the needs of others—who was once thought to cause schizophrenia in her child.

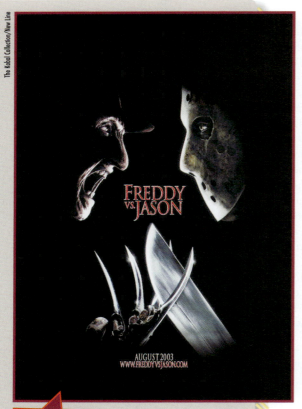

Movie myth
Movies, especially slasher films like *Freddie vs. Jason,* often depict people with psychosis as extremely violent, guided by their hallucinations and delusions to commit brutal assaults and murders. In fact, individuals with schizophrenia are much more likely to be victims than perpetrators of violence (Walsh et al., 2005).

of individuals with this disorder were found to be shy, withdrawn, and anxious, among other qualities, while the mothers of nonschizophrenic persons seemed more likely to display what Fromm-Reichmann would have called a schizophrenogenic maternal style (Waring & Ricks, 1965).

Most of today's psychodynamic theorists have, in fact, rejected the views of Freud and Fromm-Reichmann. Although these theorists may retain some of the early notions (Karon, 2008; Spielrein, 1995), more and more of them believe that biological abnormalities leave certain persons particularly prone to extreme regression or other unconscious acts that may contribute to schizophrenia (Berzoff, Flanagan, & Hertz, 2008; Willick, Milrod, & Karush, 1998). For example, self theorists, who believe that schizophrenia reflects a struggling fragmented self, suggest that biological deficiencies explain the failure of people with this disorder to develop an integrated self (Lysaker & Hermans, 2007; Kohut & Wolf, 1978).

The Behavioral View Behaviorists usually cite *operant conditioning* and principles of reinforcement as the cause of schizophrenia. They propose that most people become quite proficient at reading and responding to social cues—that is, other people's smiles, frowns, and comments. People who respond to such cues in a socially acceptable way are better able to satisfy their own emotional needs and achieve their goals (Bach, 2007; Liberman, 1982; Ullmann & Krasner, 1975). Some people, however, are not reinforced for their attention to social cues, either because of unusual circumstances or because important figures in their lives are socially inadequate. As a result, they stop attending to such cues and focus instead on irrelevant cues—the brightness of light in a room, a bird flying above, or the sound of a word rather than its meaning. As they attend more and more to irrelevant cues, their responses become increasingly bizarre. Because the bizarre responses are rewarded with attention or other types of reinforcement, they are likely to be repeated again and again.

Support for the behavioral position has been circumstantial. As you'll see in Chapter 15, researchers have found that patients with schizophrenia are capable of learning at least some appropriate verbal and social behaviors if hospital personnel consistently ignore their bizarre responses and reinforce normal responses with cigarettes, food, attention, or other rewards (Kopelowicz, Liberman, & Zarate, 2007). If bizarre verbal and social responses can be eliminated by appropriate reinforcements, perhaps they were acquired through improper learning in the first place. Of course, an effective treatment does not necessarily indicate the cause of a disorder. Today the behavioral view is usually considered at best a partial explanation for schizophrenia. Although it may help explain why a given person displays more schizophrenic behavior in some situations than in others, it is too limited, in the opinion of many, to account for schizophrenia's origins and its many symptoms.

The Cognitive View A leading cognitive explanation of schizophrenia agrees with the biological view that during hallucinations and related perceptual difficulties the brains of people with schizophrenia are actually producing strange and unreal sensations—sensations triggered by biological factors. According to the cognitive explanation, however, further features of the disorder emerge when the individuals attempt to understand their unusual experiences (Tarrier, 2008; Waters et al., 2007). When first confronted by voices or other troubling sensations, these people turn to friends and relatives. Naturally, the friends and relatives deny the reality of the sensations, and eventually the sufferers conclude that the others are trying to hide the truth. They begin to reject all feedback, and some develop beliefs (delusions) that they are being persecuted, especially if the voices are perceived as negative or malicious (Perez-Alvarez et al., 2008; Bach, 2007). In short, according to this theory, people with schizophrenia take a "rational path to madness" (Zimbardo, 1976).

Researchers have established that people with schizophrenia do indeed experience sensory and perceptual problems. As you saw earlier, many of them have hallucinations, for example, and most have trouble keeping their attention focused. But researchers have yet to provide clear, direct support for the cognitive notion that misinterpretations of such sensory problems actually produce a syndrome of schizophrenia.

Sociocultural Views

Sociocultural theorists, recognizing that people with mental disorders are subject to a wide range of social and cultural forces, claim that *multicultural factors, social labeling,* and *family dysfunctioning* all contribute to schizophrenia. At the same time, although these forces are each considered to play roles in the disorder, research has yet to clarify what the precise causal relationships might be.

Multicultural Factors Rates of schizophrenia appear to differ between racial and ethnic groups, particularly between African Americans and white Americans. As many as 2.1 percent of African Americans receive a diagnosis of schizophrenia, compared with 1.4 percent of white Americans (Lawson, 2008; Folsom et al., 2006). Similarly, studies find that African American patients are more likely than white American patients to be assessed as having symptoms of hallucinations, paranoia, and suspiciousness (Mark et al., 2003; Trierweiler et al., 2000). And still other studies suggest that African Americans with schizophrenia are overrepresented in state hospitals (Lawson, 2008; Barnes, 2004). For example, in Tennessee's state hospitals 48 percent of those with a diagnosis of schizophrenia are African American, although only 16 percent of the state population is African American (Lawson, 2008; Barnes, 2004).

It is not clear why African Americans have a higher likelihood than white Americans of receiving this diagnosis. One possibility is that African Americans are more prone to develop the disorder. Another possibility is that clinicians from majority groups are unintentionally biased in their diagnoses of African Americans or misread cultural differences as symptoms of schizophrenia (Lawson, 2008; Barnes, 2004).

Yet another explanation for the difference between African Americans and white Americans may lie in the economic sphere. On average, African Americans are more likely than white Americans to be poor, and, indeed, when economic differences are controlled for, the prevalence rates of schizophrenia become closer for the two racial groups. Consistent with the economic explanation is the finding that Hispanic Americans, who are, on average, also economically disadvantaged, appear to have a much higher likelihood of receiving a diagnosis of schizophrenia than white Americans, although their diagnostic rate is not as high as that of African Americans (Blow et al., 2004).

BETWEEN THE LINES

Multicultural Views

Research indicates that African Americans are *more likely* than white Americans to believe that people with schizophrenia or major depression may do something violent to people. ‹‹

On the other hand, African Americans are *less likely* than white Americans to believe that people with severe psychological disorders should be blamed and punished for violent behaviors. ‹‹

(Anglin, Link, & Phelan, 2006)

Silvia Izquierdo/AP Photo

Coming together
Different countries and cultures each have their own way of viewing and interacting with schizophrenic people and other disturbed individuals. Here members of the community and people with severe psychological disorders come together and dance during the annual Carnival parade in front of the Psychiatric Institute in Rio de Janeiro, Brazil.

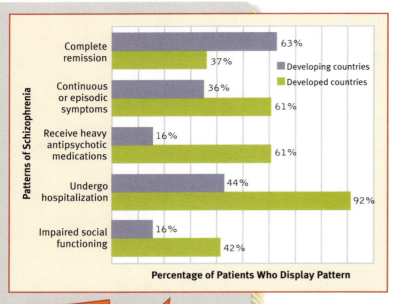

Patterns of Schizophrenia

- Complete remission: 63% (Developing countries), 37% (Developed countries)
- Continuous or episodic symptoms: 36% (Developing countries), 61% (Developed countries)
- Receive heavy antipsychotic medications: 16% (Developing countries), 61% (Developed countries)
- Undergo hospitalization: 44% (Developing countries), 92% (Developed countries)
- Impaired social functioning: 16% (Developing countries), 42% (Developed countries)

Legend:
- Developing countries
- Developed countries

Percentage of Patients Who Display Pattern

Figure 14-4

Do the course and outcome of schizophrenia differ from country to country? Yes, according to a World Health Organization study. In developing countries, patients with schizophrenia seem to recover more quickly, more often, and more completely than patients in developed countries. (Adapted from Jablensky, 2000.)

It also appears that schizophrenia differs from country to country in key ways. Although the overall prevalence of this disorder is stable—around 1 percent—in countries across the world, the *course* and *outcome* of the disorder may vary considerably. According to a 10-country study conducted by the World Health Organization (WHO), the 25 million schizophrenic patients who live in *developing* countries have better recovery rates than schizophrenic patients in Western and other *developed* countries (Vahia & Vahia, 2008; Jablensky, 2000). The WHO study followed the progress of 467 patients from developing countries (Colombia, India, and Nigeria) over a two-year period and compared it to that of 603 patients from developed countries (Czech Republic, Denmark, Ireland, Japan, Russia, the United Kingdom, and the United States). As you can see in Figure 14-4, during the course of a two-year observation period, the schizophrenic patients from the developing countries were more likely than those in the developed countries to recover from their disorder and less likely to experience continuous or episodic symptoms, display impaired social functioning, require heavy antipsychotic drugs, or require hospitalization.

Some clinical theorists believe that these differences partly reflect genetic differences from population to population. However, others argue that the psychosocial environments of developing countries tend to be more supportive and therapeutic than those of developed countries, leading to more favorable outcomes for people with schizophrenia (Vahia & Vahia, 2008; Jablensky, 2000). Developing countries, for example, seem to provide more family and social support to people with schizophrenia, make available more relatives and friends to help care for such individuals, and act less judgmental, critical, and hostile toward persons with schizophrenia. The Nigerian culture, for example, is generally more tolerant of the presence of voices than are Western cultures (Matsumoto & Juang, 2008).

Social Labeling Many sociocultural theorists believe that the features of schizophrenia are influenced by the diagnosis itself (Modrow, 1992). In their opinion, society assigns the label "schizophrenic" to people who fail to conform to certain norms of behavior. Once the label is assigned, justified or not, it becomes a self-fulfilling prophecy that promotes the development of many schizophrenic symptoms. Certainly sufferers of schizophrenia have attested to the power that labeling has had on their lives:

Like any worthwhile endeavor, becoming a schizophrenic requires a long period of rigorous training. My training for this unique calling began in earnest when I was six years old. At that time my somewhat befuddled mother took me to the University of Washington to be examined by psychiatrists in order to find out what was wrong with me. These psychiatrists told my mother: "We don't know exactly what is wrong with your son, but whatever it is, it is very serious. We recommend that you have him committed immediately or else he will be completely psychotic within less than a year." My mother did not have me committed since she realized that such a course of action would be extremely damaging to me. But after that ominous prophecy my parents began to view and treat me as if I were either insane or at least in the process of becoming that way. Once, when my mother caught me playing with some vile muck I had mixed up—I was seven at the time—she gravely told me, "They have people put away in mental institutions for doing things like that." Fear was written all over my mother's face as she told me this. . . . The slightest odd behavior on my part was enough to send my parents into paroxysms of apprehension. My parents' apprehensions in turn made me fear that I was going insane. . . . My fate had been sealed not by my genes, but by the attitudes, beliefs, and expectations of my parents. . . . I find it extremely difficult to condemn my parents for behaving as if I were going insane when the psychiatric authorities told them that this was an absolute certainty.

(Modrow, 1992, pp. 1–2)

Like this man, people who are called schizophrenic may be viewed and treated as "crazy." Perhaps the expectations of other people subtly encourage the individuals to display psychotic behaviors. In turn, they come to accept their assigned role and learn to play it convincingly.

We have already seen the very real dangers of diagnostic labeling. In the famous Rosenhan (1973) study, discussed in Chapter 3, eight normal people presented themselves at various mental hospitals, complaining that they had been hearing voices utter the words "empty," "hollow," and "thud." They were quickly diagnosed as schizophrenic, and all eight were hospitalized. Although the pseudopatients then dropped all symptoms and behaved normally, they had great difficulty getting rid of the label and gaining release from the hospital.

The pseudopatients reported that staff members were authoritarian in their behavior toward patients, spent limited time interacting with them, and responded curtly and uncaringly to questions. In fact, they generally treated patients as though they were invisible. "A nurse unbuttoned her uniform to adjust her brassiere in the presence of an entire ward of viewing men. One did not have the sense that she was being seductive. Rather, she didn't notice us." In addition, the pseudopatients described feeling powerless, bored, tired, and uninterested. The deceptive design and possible implications of this study have aroused the emotions of clinicians and researchers, pro and con. The investigation does demonstrate, however, that the label "schizophrenic" can itself have a negative effect not just on how people are viewed but on how they themselves feel and behave.

Family Dysfunctioning

Theorists have suggested for years that certain patterns of family interactions can promote—or at least sustain—schizophrenic symptoms. One leading theory has focused on *double-bind communications.*

DO DOUBLE-BIND COMMUNICATIONS CAUSE SCHIZOPHRENIA? One of the best-known family theories of schizophrenia is the **double-bind hypothesis** (Visser, 2003; Bateson, 1978; Bateson et al., 1956). It says that some parents repeatedly communicate pairs of mutually contradictory messages that place children in so-called double-bind situations: the children cannot avoid displeasing their parents because nothing they do is right. In theory, the symptoms of schizophrenia represent the child's attempt to deal with the double binds.

Double-bind messages typically consist of a verbal communication (the *primary communication*) and an accompanying—and contradictory—nonverbal communication (the *metacommunication*). If one person says to another, "I'm glad to see you," yet frowns and avoids eye contact, the two messages are incongruent. According to this theory, a child who is repeatedly exposed to double-bind communications will adopt a special life strategy for coping with them. One strategy, for example, is always to ignore primary communications and respond only to metacommunications: be suspicious of what anyone is saying, wonder about its true meaning, and focus on clues only in gestures or tones. People who increasingly respond to messages in this way may progress toward paranoid schizophrenia.

The double-bind hypothesis is closely related to the psychodynamic notion of a schizophrenogenic mother. When Fromm-Reichmann described schizophrenogenic mothers as overprotective and rejecting at the same time, she was in fact describing someone who is likely to send double-bind messages. Like the schizophrenogenic mother theory, the double-bind hypothesis has been popular in the clinical field over the years, but systematic investigations have not supported it (Chaika, 1990). In one study, clinicians analyzed letters written by parents to their children in the hospital

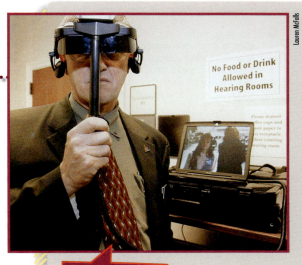

Lauren McFalls

No Food or Drink Allowed in Hearing Rooms

Virtual lobbying
This Washington state lawmaker wears the *Hallucinator Simulator*, a virtual-reality headset that produces disorienting sounds and visions similar to those experienced by people with psychosis. Mental health advocates convinced many of the state's legislators to wear the simulator prior to voting on a mental health funding bill, hoping that the experience would bring to life the needs of people with severe mental disorders.

•**double-bind hypothesis**•A theory that some parents repeatedly communicate pairs of messages that are mutually contradictory, helping to produce schizophrenia in their children.

©HessDesignWorks.com

TREATMENTS FOR SCHIZOPHRENIA AND OTHER SEVERE MENTAL DISORDERS

They call us insane—and in reality they are as inconsistent as we are, as flighty and change- able. This one in particular. One day he derides and ridicules me unmercifully; the next he talks to me sadly and this morning his eyes misted over with tears as he told me of the fate ahead. Damn him and all of his wisdom!

He has dinned into my ears a monotonous dirge—"Too Egotistical—too Egotistical—too Egotis- tical. Learn to think differently."—And how can I do it? How—how—can I do it? How the hell can I do it? I have tried to follow his suggestions but have not learned to think a bit differently. It was all wasted effort. Where has it got me?

Jefferson, 1948

With these words, Lara Jefferson, a young woman with schizophrenia, described her treatment experience in the 1940s. Her pain and frustration were typical of those experienced by hundreds of thousands of similar patients during that period of time. In fact, for much of human history, persons with schizophrenia were con- sidered beyond help. They and their therapists faced the daunting task of trying to communicate while speaking virtually different languages. The disorder is still ex- tremely difficult to treat, but clinicians are much more successful today than they were in the past (Roe & Davidson, 2008). Much of the credit goes to *antipsychotic drugs,* medications that help many people with schizophrenia think clearly and profit from therapies that previously would have had little effect on them.

As you will see, each of the models offers treatments for schizophrenia, and all have been influential at one time or another. However, a mere description of the different approaches cannot convey the unhappiness and pain suffered by the victims of this disorder as the various methods of treatment evolved over the years. People with schizophrenia have been subjected to more mistreatment and indifference than perhaps any other group of patients. Even today the majority of them do not receive adequate care, largely for reasons of economics and political priorities (Torrey, 2001).

To better convey the plight of people with schizophrenia, this chapter will depart from the usual format and discuss the treatments from a historical perspec- tive. Ultimately, a look at how treatment has changed over the years will help us understand the nature, problems, and promise of today's approaches. As you saw in Chapter 14, throughout much of the twentieth century the label "schizophrenia" was assigned to most people with psychosis—that is, a loss of contact with reality. However, clinical theorists now realize that many people with psychotic symp- toms are in fact manifesting a severe form of bipolar disorder or major depressive disorder and that many such individuals were in past times inaccurately given a diagnosis of schizophrenia. Thus, our discussions of past treatments for schizophre- nia, particularly the failures of institutional care, are as applicable to those other severe mental disorders as they are to schizophrenia.

<state hospitals>Public mental hospitals in the United States, run by the individual states.

Today, improvements in diagnostic procedures and in the DSM have helped disentangle schizophrenia from the other disorders. Nevertheless, any disorder that includes psychotic features presents formidable obstacles to treatment, and so even some of our discussions about current approaches to schizophrenia, such as the community mental health movement, apply to other severe mental disorders as well.

Institutional Care in the Past

For more than half of the twentieth century, most people diagnosed with schizophrenia were *institutionalized* in a public mental hospital. Because patients with this disorder failed to respond to traditional therapies, the primary goals of these establishments were to restrain them and give them food, shelter, and clothing. Patients rarely saw therapists and generally were neglected. Many were abused. Oddly enough, this state of affairs unfolded in an atmosphere of good intentions.

As you read in Chapter 1, the move toward institutionalization in hospitals began in 1793 when French physician Philippe Pinel "unchained the insane" at La Bicêtre asylum and began the practice of "moral treatment." For the first time in centuries, patients with severe disturbances were viewed as human beings who should be cared for with sympathy and kindness. As Pinel's ideas spread throughout Europe and the United States, they led to the creation of large mental hospitals rather than asylums to care for those with severe mental disorders (Goshen, 1967).

These new mental hospitals, typically located in isolated areas where land and labor were cheap, were meant to protect patients from the stresses of daily life and offer them a healthful psychological environment in which they could work closely with therapists (Grob, 1966). States throughout the United States were even required by law to establish public mental institutions, **state hospitals,** for patients who could not afford private ones.

Eventually, however, the state hospital system encountered serious problems. Between 1845 and 1955 nearly 300 state hospitals opened in the United States, and the number of hospitalized patients on any given day rose from 2,000 in 1845 to nearly 600,000 in 1955. During this expansion, wards became overcrowded, admissions kept rising, and state funding was unable to keep up. Too many aspects of treatment became the responsibility of nurses and attendants, whose knowledge and experience at that time were limited.

The priorities of the public mental hospitals, and the quality of care they provided, changed over those 110 years. In the face of overcrowding and understaffing, the emphasis shifted from giving humanitarian care to keeping order. In a throwback to the asylum period, difficult patients were restrained, isolated, and punished; individual attention disappeared. Patients were transferred to *back wards,* or chronic wards, if they failed to improve quickly (Bloom, 1984). Most of the patients on these wards suffered from schizophrenia (Hafner & an der Heiden, 1988). The back wards were in fact human warehouses filled with hopelessness. Staff members relied on straitjackets and handcuffs to deal with difficult patients. More "advanced" forms of treatment included medical approaches such as *lobotomy* (see *A Closer Look* on the facing page).

Many patients not only failed to improve under these conditions but also developed additional symptoms, apparently as a result of institutionalization itself. The most common pattern of decline was called the *social breakdown syndrome:* extreme withdrawal, anger, physical aggressiveness, and loss of interest in personal appearance and functioning (Oshima et al., 2005; Gruenberg, 1980). Often more troublesome than patients' original symptoms, this new syndrome made it impossible for them to return to society even if they somehow recovered from the symptoms that had first brought them to the hospital.

Overcrowded conditions
A night nurse sits in the ward of a public mental hospital in 1956 darning socks while the patients sleep. The beds in the ward are crammed close together, leaving no personal space of any kind for the patients.

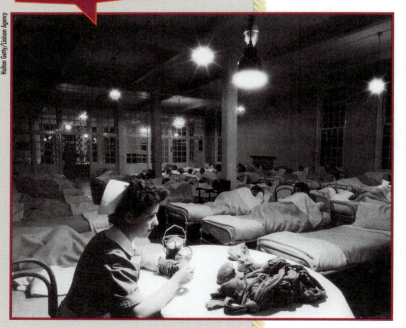

Hulton Getty/Liaison Agency

Lobotomy: How Could It Happen?

In 1949 a *New York Times* article reported on a medical procedure that appeared to offer hope to sufferers of severe mental disorders, people for whom no future had seemed possible outside of very overcrowded state mental institutions:

> Hypochondriacs no longer thought they were going to die, would-be suicides found life acceptable, sufferers from persecution complex forgot the machinations of imaginary conspirators. Prefrontal lobotomy, as the operation is called, was made possible by the localization of fears, hates, and instincts [in the prefrontal cortex of the brain]. It is fitting, then, that the Nobel Prize in medicine should be shared by Hess and Moniz. Surgeons now think no more of operations on the brain than they do of removing an appendix.

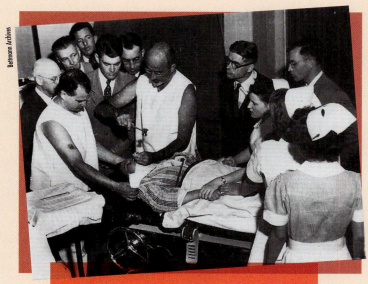

Lessons in psychosurgery Neuropsychiatrist Walter Freeman performs a lobotomy in 1949 before a group of interested onlookers by inserting a needle through a patient's eye socket into the brain.

We now know that the lobotomy was hardly a miracle treatment. Far from "curing" people with mental disorders, the procedure left thousands upon thousands extremely withdrawn, subdued, and even stuporous. The first lobotomy was performed by Portuguese neuropsychiatrist Egas Moniz in 1935 (Tierney, 2000). His particular procedure, called a prefrontal leukotomy, consisted of drilling two holes in either side of the skull and inserting an instrument resembling an icepick into the brain tissue to cut or destroy nerve fibers. Moniz believed that severe abnormal thinking could be changed by cutting the nerve pathways that carried such thoughts from one part of the brain to another. In the 1940s Walter Freeman and his surgical partner, James Watts, developed a second kind of psychosurgery called the transorbital lobotomy, in which the surgeon inserted a needle into the brain through the eye socket and rotated it in order to destroy the brain tissue.

Altogether, an estimated 50,000 people in the United States alone received lobotomies (Johnson, 2005). Why was the lobotomy so enthusiastically accepted by the medical community in the 1940s and 1950s? Neuroscientist Elliot Valenstein (1986) points first to the extreme overcrowding in mental hospitals at the time. This crowding was making it difficult to maintain decent standards in the hospitals. Valenstein also points to the personalities of the inventors of the procedure as important factors. Although these individuals were gifted and dedicated physicians, Valenstein also believes that their professional ambitions led them to move too quickly and boldly in applying the procedure. Indeed, in 1949 Moniz was awarded the Nobel Prize for his work.

The prestige and diplomatic skills of Moniz and Freeman were so great and the field of neurology was so small that their procedures drew little criticism. Physicians may also have been misled by the seemingly positive findings of early studies of the lobotomy, which, as it turned out, were not based on sound methodology (Swayze, 1995; Valenstein, 1986).

By the 1950s, better studies revealed that in addition to having a fatality rate of 1.5 to 6 percent, lobotomies could cause serious problems such as brain seizures, huge weight gain, loss of motor coordination, partial paralysis, incontinence, endocrine malfunctions, and very poor intellectual and emotional responsiveness. When the public became concerned that the procedure might be used to control violent criminals, the lobotomy became a civil rights issue as well. Finally, the discovery of effective antipsychotic drugs put an end to this inhumane treatment for mental disorders (Mashour et al., 2005; Tierney, 2000).

Today's psychosurgical procedures are greatly refined and hardly resemble the lobotomies of 50 years back. Moreover, such procedures are considered experimental and are used only as a last resort in the most severe cases of obsessive-compulsive disorder and depression (McNeely et al., 2008; Anderson & Booker, 2006). Even so, many professionals believe that any kind of surgery that destroys brain tissue is inappropriate and perhaps unethical and that it keeps alive one of the clinical field's most shameful and ill-advised efforts at cure.

✿Institutional Care Takes a Turn for the Better

In the 1950s, clinicians developed two institutional approaches that finally brought some hope to patients who had lived in institutions for years: *milieu therapy,* based on humanistic principles, and the *token economy program,* based on behavioral principles. These approaches particularly helped improve the personal care and self-image of patients, problem areas that had been worsened by institutionalization. The approaches were soon adapted by many institutions and are now standard features of institutional care.

Milieu Therapy

In the opinion of humanistic theorists, institutionalized patients deteriorate because they are deprived of opportunities to exercise independence, responsibility, and positive self-regard and to engage in meaningful activities. Thus the premise of **milieu therapy** is that institutions cannot be of help to patients unless they can somehow create a social climate, or milieu, that promotes productive activity, self-respect, and individual responsibility.

The pioneer of this approach was Maxwell Jones, a London psychiatrist who in 1953 converted a ward of patients with various psychological disorders into a therapeutic community. The patients were referred to as "residents" and were regarded as capable of running their own lives and making their own decisions. They participated in community government, working with staff members to establish rules and determine sanctions. In fact, patients and staff members alike were valued as important therapeutic agents. The atmosphere was one of mutual respect, support, and openness. Patients could also take on special projects, jobs, and recreational activities. In short, their daily schedule was designed to resemble life outside the hospital.

Milieu-style programs have since been set up in institutions throughout the Western world. The programs vary from setting to setting, but at a minimum staff members try to encourage interactions (especially group interactions) between patients and staff, to keep patients active, and to raise patients' expectations of what they can accomplish.

Research over the years has shown that patients with schizophrenia and other severe mental disorders in milieu hospital programs often improve and that they leave the hospital at higher rates than patients in programs offering primarily custodial care (Paul, 2000; Paul & Lentz, 1977; Cumming & Cumming, 1962). Many of these persons remain impaired, however, and must live in sheltered settings after their release. Despite its limitations, milieu therapy continues to be practiced in many institutions, often combined with other hospital approaches (Gunter, 2005; Dobson et al., 1995). Moreover, you will see later in this chapter that many of today's halfway houses and other community programs for individuals with severe mental disorders are run in accordance with the same principles of resident self-government and work schedules that have proved effective in hospital milieu programs.

A graphic reminder During the rise of the state hospital system, tens of thousands of patients with schizophrenia and other severe mental disorders were abandoned by their families and spent the rest of their lives in the back wards of the public mental institutions. We are reminded of their tragic plight by the numerous brass urns filled with unclaimed ashes currently stored in a building at Oregon State Hospital. Officials are working to find a proper burial place for the remains and to perhaps establish a memorial.

Greg Wahl-Stephens/AP Photo

The Token Economy

In the 1950s behaviorists had little status in mental institutions and were permitted to work only with patients whose problems seemed hopeless. Among the "hopeless" were patients diagnosed with schizophrenia. Through years of experimentation, behaviorists discovered that the systematic application of *operant conditioning* techniques on hospital wards could help change the behaviors of these individuals (Ayllon, 1963; Ayllon & Michael, 1959). Programs that apply these techniques are called **token economy programs.**

In token economies patients are rewarded when they behave acceptably and are not rewarded when they behave unacceptably. The immediate rewards for acceptable behavior are often tokens that can later be exchanged for food, cigarettes, hospital privileges, and other desirable items, thus creating a "token economy." Acceptable behaviors likely to be targeted include caring for oneself and for one's possessions (making the bed, getting dressed), going to a work program, speaking normally, following ward rules, and showing self-control.

How Effective Are Token Economy Programs?

Researchers have found that token economies do help reduce psychotic and related behaviors (Combs et al., 2008; Dickerson et al., 2005). In one very successful program, Gordon Paul and Robert Lentz (1977) set up a hospital token economy for 28 patients diagnosed with chronic schizophrenia, most of whom improved greatly. After four and a half years, 98 percent of the patients had been released, mostly to sheltered-care facilities, compared with 71 percent of patients treated in a milieu program and 45 percent of patients who received custodial care only.

What Are the Limitations of Token Economies?

Some clinicians have voiced reservations about the claims made for token economy programs. One problem is that many token economy studies, unlike Paul and Lentz's, are uncontrolled. When administrators set up a token economy, they usually bring all ward patients into the program rather than dividing the ward into a token economy group and a control group. As a result, patients' improvements can be compared only with their own past behaviors—a comparison that may be misleading. Changes in the physical setting, for example, or a general increase in staff attention could be causing patients' improvement, rather than the token economy.

Many clinicians have also raised ethical and legal concerns. If token economy programs are to be effective, administrators need to control the important rewards in a patient's life, perhaps including such basic ones as food and a comfortable bed. But aren't there some things in life to which all human beings are entitled? Court decisions have now ruled that patients do indeed have certain basic rights that clinicians cannot violate, regardless of the positive goals of a treatment program. They have a right to food, storage space, and furniture, as well as freedom of movement (Emmelkamp, 1994).

•**milieu therapy**•A humanistic approach to institutional treatment based on the belief that institutions can help patients recover by creating a climate that promotes self-respect, responsible behavior, and meaningful activity.

•**token economy program**•A behavioral program in which a person's desirable behaviors are reinforced systematically throughout the day by the awarding of tokens that can be exchanged for goods or privileges.

Jianan Yu/Reuters

Institutional life
In a scene reminiscent of ward life at most public mental hospitals in the United States throughout the 1960s and 1970s, these two recently photographed patients spend their day watching television at a psychiatric hospital in China. Because of a shortage of therapists, only a small fraction of the Chinese people who experience psychological disorders receive proper professional care today.

Still other clinicians have questioned the quality of the improvements made under token economy programs. Are behaviorists changing a patient's psychotic thoughts and perceptions or simply improving the patient's ability to imitate normal behavior? This issue is illustrated by the case of a middle-aged man named John, who had the delusion that he was the U.S. government (Comer, 1973). Whenever he spoke, he spoke as the government. "We are happy to see you. . . . We need people like you in our service. . . . We are carrying out our activities in John's body." When John's hospital ward was converted into a token economy, the staff members targeted his delusional statements and required him to identify himself properly to earn tokens. If he called himself John, he received tokens; if he insisted on describing himself as the government, he received nothing. After a few months on the token economy program, John stopped referring to himself as the government. When asked his name, he would say, "John." Although staff members were understandably pleased with his improvement, John himself had a different view of the situation. In a private discussion he said:

We're tired of it. Every damn time we want a cigarette, we have to go through their bullshit. "What's your name? . . . Who wants the cigarette? . . . Where is the government?" Today, we were desperate for a smoke and went to Simpson, the damn nurse, and she made us do her bidding. "Tell me your name if you want a cigarette. What's your name?" Of course, we said, "John." We needed the cigarettes. If we told her the truth, no cigarettes. But we don't have time for this nonsense. We've got business to do, international business, laws to change, people to recruit. And these people keep playing their games.

(Comer, 1973)

Critics of the behavioral approach would argue that John was still delusional and therefore as psychotic as before. Behaviorists, however, would argue that at the very least, John's judgment about the consequences of his behavior had improved. Learning to keep his delusion to himself might even be a step toward changing his private thinking.

Last, it has often been difficult for patients to make a satisfactory transition from hospital token economy programs to community living. In an environment where rewards are contingent on proper conduct, proper conduct becomes contingent on continued rewards. Some patients who find that the real world doesn't reward them so concretely abandon their newly acquired behaviors.

Nevertheless, token economies have had a most important effect on the treatment of people with schizophrenia and other severe mental disorders. They were among the first hospital treatments that actually changed psychotic symptoms and got chronic patients moving again. These programs are no longer as popular as they once were, but they are still used in many mental hospitals, usually along with medication, and in many community residences as well (Kopelowicz, Liberman, & Zarate, 2008). The approach has also been applied to other clinical problems, including mental retardation, delinquency, and hyperactivity, as well as in other fields, such as education and business (Spiegler & Guevremont, 2003).

✿Antipsychotic Drugs

Milieu therapy and token economy programs helped improve the gloomy outlook for patients diagnosed with schizophrenia, but it was the discovery of **antipsychotic drugs** in the 1950s that truly revolutionized treatment for this disorder. These drugs eliminate many of its symptoms and today are almost always a part of treatment (see Figure 15-1). What is more, as you saw in Chapter 14, they have influenced the way clinicians now view schizophrenia.

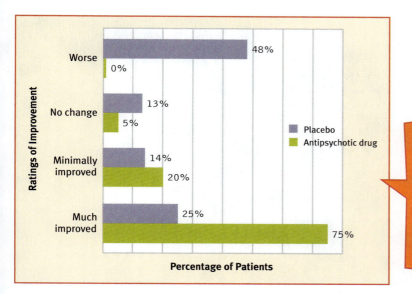

Figure 15-1

The effectiveness of antipsychotic drugs An early study found that after six weeks of treatment, 75 percent of patients with schizophrenia who had been given antipsychotic drugs were much improved, compared to only 25 percent of patients given placebos. In fact, close to half of those on the placebos worsened. The findings of this pioneering study have been confirmed in literally thousands of drug treatment outcome studies conducted over the past 45 years. (Adapted from Cole et al., 1964.)

The discovery of antipsychotic medications dates back to the 1940s, when researchers developed the first *antihistamine drugs* to combat allergies. Although antihistamines also produced considerable tiredness and drowsiness, they quickly became popular, and many such drugs were developed. The French surgeon Henri Laborit soon discovered that one group of antihistamines, *phenothiazines,* could also be used to help calm patients about to undergo surgery. After experimenting with several phenothiazine antihistamines and becoming most impressed with one called *chlorpromazine,* Laborit reported, "It provokes not any loss of consciousness, not any change in the patient's mentality but a slight tendency to sleep and above all 'disinterest' for all that goes on around him."

Laborit suspected that chlorpromazine might also have a calming effect on persons with severe psychological disorders. Psychiatrists Jean Delay and Pierre Deniker (1952) therefore tested the drug on six patients with psychotic symptoms and did indeed observe a sharp reduction in their symptoms. In 1954, chlorpromazine was approved for sale in the United States as an antipsychotic drug under the trade name Thorazine.

Since the discovery of the phenothiazines, other kinds of antipsychotic drugs have been developed. The ones developed throughout the 1960s, 1970s, and 1980s are now referred to as *"conventional" antipsychotic drugs* in order to distinguish them from the *"atypical" antipsychotics* (also called *"second generation" antipsychotic drugs*) that have been developed in recent years. The conventional drugs are also known as **neuroleptic drugs** because they often produce undesired movement effects similar to the symptoms of neurological diseases. Among the best known conventional drugs are *thioridazine* (Mellaril), *fluphenazine* (Prolixin), *trifluoperazine* (Stelazine), and *haloperidol* (Haldol). As you saw in Chapter 14, antipsychotic drugs reduce psychotic symptoms at least in part by blocking excessive activity of the neurotransmitter *dopamine,* particularly at the brain's dopamine D-2 receptors (Combs et al., 2008; Julien, 2008).

How Effective Are Antipsychotic Drugs?

Research repeatedly has shown that antipsychotic drugs reduce symptoms in at least 65 percent of patients diagnosed with schizophrenia (Julien, 2008; Sadock & Sadock, 2007). Moreover, in direct comparisons the drugs appear to be a more effective treatment for schizophrenia than any of the other approaches used alone, such as psychodynamic therapy, milieu therapy, or electroconvulsive therapy (May, Tuma, & Dixon, 1981; May & Tuma, 1964).

In most cases, the drugs produce the maximum level of improvement within the first six months of treatment (Kutscher, 2008; Szymanski et al., 1996); however, symptoms may return if patients stop taking the drugs too soon (Saba et al., 2007). In one study, when

•**antipsychotic drugs**•Drugs that help correct grossly confused or distorted thinking.

•**neuroleptic drugs**•Conventional antipsychotic drugs, so called because they often produce undesired effects similar to the symptoms of neurological disorders.

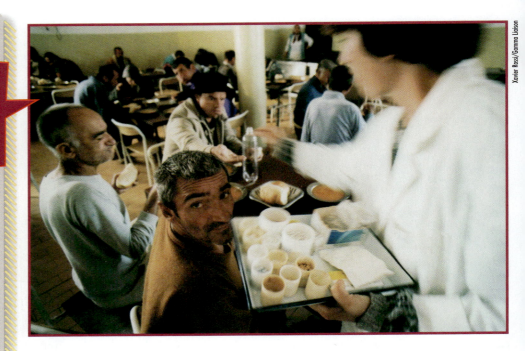

Xavier Rossi/Gamma Liaison

the antipsychotic medications of people with chronic schizophrenia were changed to a placebo after five years, 75 percent of the patients relapsed within a year, compared to 33 percent of similar patients who continued to receive medication (Sampath et al., 1992).

As you observed in Chapter 14, antipsychotic drugs, particularly the conventional ones, reduce the positive symptoms of schizophrenia, such as hallucinations and delusions, more completely, or at least more quickly, than the negative symptoms, such as flat affect, poverty of speech, and loss of volition (Combs et al., 2008; Julien, 2008). Correspondingly, people who display largely positive symptoms generally have better rates of recovery from schizophrenia than those with predominantly negative symptoms. Inasmuch as men with schizophrenia tend to have more negative symptoms than women, it is not surprising that they require higher doses and respond less readily to the antipsychotic drugs (Seeman, 2008; Szymanski et al., 1996, 1995).

Although antipsychotic drugs are now widely accepted, patients often dislike the powerful effects of the drugs—both intended and unintended—and some refuse to take them (Saba et al., 2007; Gilmer et al., 2004). But like Edward Snow, a writer who overcame schizophrenia, many are greatly helped by the medications.

In my case it was necessary to come to terms with a specified drug program. I am a legalized addict. My dose: 100 milligrams of Thorazine and 60 milligrams of Stelazine daily. I don't feel this dope at all, but I have been told it is strong enough to flatten a normal person. It keeps me—as the doctors agree—sane and in good spirits. Without the brain candy, as I call it, I would go—zoom—right back into the bin. I've made the institution scene enough already to be familiar with what it's like and to know I don't want to go back.

(Snow, 1976)

The Unwanted Effects of Conventional Antipsychotic Drugs

In addition to reducing psychotic symptoms, the conventional antipsychotic drugs sometimes produce disturbing movement problems (Julien, 2008). These effects are called **extrapyramidal effects** because they appear to be caused by the drugs' impact on the extrapyramidal areas of the brain, areas that help control motor activity. These undesired effects are so common that they are listed as a separate category of disorders—*medication-induced movement disorders*—in DSM-IV-TR (APA, 2000). They include *Parkinsonian and related symptoms, neuroleptic malignant syndrome,* and *tardive dyskinesia.*

Parkinsonian and Related Symptoms

The most common extra-pyramidal effects are *Parkinsonian symptoms,* reactions that closely resemble the features of the neurological disorder Parkinson's disease. At least half of patients on conventional antipsychotic drugs experience muscle tremors and muscle rigidity at some point in their treatment; they may shake, move slowly, shuffle their feet, and show little facial expression (Combs et al., 2008; Janno et al., 2004; APA, 2000). Some also display related symptoms such as *dystonia,* involuntary muscle contractions that produce bizarre and uncontrollable movements of the face, neck, tongue, and back, and *akathisia,* great restlessness, agitation, and discomfort in the limbs, which causes individuals to move their arms and legs continually in search of relief.

The Parkinsonian and related symptoms seem to be the result of medication-induced reductions of dopamine activity in the *basal ganglia* and the *substantia nigra,* parts of the brain that coordinate movement and posture (Combs et al., 2008; Julien, 2008). In most cases, the symptoms can be reversed if an anti-Parkinsonian drug is taken along with the antipsychotic drug. Alternatively, clinicians may have to reduce the dose of the antipsychotic drug or stop it altogether.

Neuroleptic Malignant Syndrome

In as many as 1 percent of patients, particularly elderly ones, conventional antipsychotic drugs produce *neuroleptic malignant syndrome,* a severe, potentially fatal reaction consisting of muscle rigidity, fever, altered consciousness, and improper functioning of the autonomic nervous system (Strawn et al., 2007; Keltner & Folks, 2001). As soon as the syndrome is recognized, drug use is discontinued and each neuroleptic symptom is treated medically. In addition, individuals may be given dopamine-enhancing drugs.

Tardive Dyskinesia

Whereas most undesired drug effects appear within days or weeks, a reaction called **tardive dyskinesia** (meaning "late-appearing movement disorder") does not usually unfold until after a person has taken conventional antipsychotic drugs for more than a year. Sometimes it does not even appear until after the medications are stopped (Julien, 2008; Wyatt, 1995). This syndrome may include involuntary writhing or ticlike movements of the tongue, mouth, face, or whole body; involuntary chewing, sucking, and lip smacking; and jerky movements of the arms, legs, or entire body. It is sometimes accompanied by memory difficulties (Sorokin et al., 1988).

Most cases of tardive dyskinesia are mild and involve a single symptom, such as tongue flicking; however, some are severe and include such features as continual rocking back and forth, irregular breathing, and grotesque twisting of the face and body. It is believed that more than 10 percent of the people who take conventional drugs for an extended time develop tardive dyskinesia to some degree, and the longer the drugs are taken, the greater the risk becomes (Julien, 2008; APA, 2000). Patients over 50 years of age seem to be at greater risk.

Tardive dyskinesia can be difficult, sometimes impossible, to eliminate (Combs et al., 2008). If it is discovered early and the conventional drugs are stopped immediately, it eventually disappears in most cases (Grilly, 2002; APA, 2000). Early detection, however, is elusive because some of the symptoms are similar to psychotic symptoms. Clinicians may easily overlook them, continue to administer the drugs, and unintentionally create a more serious case of tardive dyskinesia. The longer patients are on the conventional antipsychotic drugs, the less likely it is that their tardive dyskinesia will disappear, even when the drugs are stopped. Researchers do not fully understand why conventional antipsychotic drugs cause tardive dyskinesia; however, they suspect that, once again, the problem is related to the drugs' effect on dopamine receptors in the basal ganglia and substantia nigra (Julien, 2008).

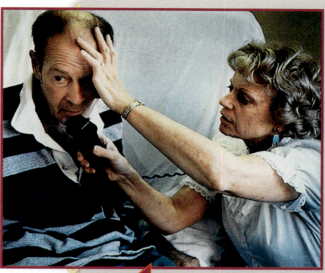

Unwanted effects This man has a severe case of Parkinson's disease, a disorder caused by low dopamine activity, and his muscle tremors prevent him from shaving himself. The conventional antipsychotic drugs often produce similar Parkinsonian symptoms.

•**extrapyramidal effects**•Unwanted movements, such as severe shaking, bizarre-looking grimaces, twisting of the body, and extreme restlessness, sometimes produced by conventional antipsychotic drugs.

•**tardive dyskinesia**•Extrapyramidal effects that appear in some patients after they have taken conventional antipsychotic drugs for an extended time.

table: 15-1

Antipsychotic Drugs

Class/Generic Name	Trade Name
Conventional antipsychotics	
Chlorpromazine	Thorazine
Triflupromazine	Vesprin
Thioridazine	Mellaril
Mesoridazine	Serentil
Trifluoperazine	Stelazine
Fluphenazine	Prolixin, Permitil
Perphenazine	Trilafon
Acetophenazine	Tindal
Chlorprothixene	Taractan
Thiothixene	Navane
Haloperidol	Haldol
Loxapine	Loxitane
Molindone hydrochloride	Moban, Lidone
Pimozide	Orap
Atypical antipsychotics	
Risperidone	Risperdal
Clozapine	Clozaril
Olanzapine	Zyprexa
Quetiapine	Seroquel
Ziprasidone	Geodon
Aripiprazole	Abilify

How Should Conventional Antipsychotic Drugs Be Prescribed?

Today clinicians are more knowledgeable and more cautious about prescribing conventional antipsychotic drugs than they have been in the past. Previously, when patients did not improve with such a drug, their clinicians would keep increasing the dose (Kane, 1992); today a clinician will typically stop the drug. Similarly, today's clinicians try to prescribe the lowest effective dose for each patient and to gradually reduce or even stop medication weeks or months after the patient begins functioning normally (Addington & Addington, 2008; Kutscher, 2008).

New Antipsychotic Drugs

Chapter 14 noted that "atypical" antipsychotic drugs have been developed in recent years (see Table 15-1). The most effective and widely used of these new drugs are *clozapine* (trade name Clozaril), *risperidone* (Risperdal), *olanzapine* (Zyprexa), *quetiapine* (Seroquel), *ziprasidone* (Geodon), and *aripiprazole* (Abilify). As you have read, the drugs are called *atypical* because their biological operation differs from that of the conventional antipsychotic medications: the atypicals are received at fewer dopamine D-2 receptors and more D-1, D-4, and serotonin receptors than the others (Julien, 2008).

In fact, atypical antipsychotic drugs appear to be more effective than the conventional drugs, helping as many as 85 percent of persons with schizophrenia, compared with the 65 percent helped by most of the conventional drugs (Julien, 2008). Unlike the conventional drugs, the new drugs reduce not only the positive symptoms of schizophrenia, but also the negative ones (Combs et al., 2008; deLima et al., 2005). Another major benefit of the atypical antipsychotic drugs is that they cause fewer extrapyramidal symptoms and do not seem to produce tardive dyskinesia (Dolder, 2008; Conley & Kelley, 2005) (see Figure 15-2). Given such advantages, it is not surprising that over half of all medicated patients with schizophrenia now take the atypical drugs and that these drugs are considered the first line of treatment for the disorder (Combs et al., 2008; Sajatovic et al., 2008) (see *Eye on Culture* on the facing page). Moreover, many patients with bipolar or other severe mental disorders also seem to be helped by several of the atypical antipsychotic drugs. Studies indicate, for example, that olanzapine, prescribed alone or in combination with mood-stabilizing drugs, is very effective in cases of acute mania (Julien, 2008; Dennehy et al., 2003).

Yet the atypical antipsychotic drugs have serious problems as well (Folsom et al., 2006). For example, people who use one of the atypical drugs, clozapine, have around a

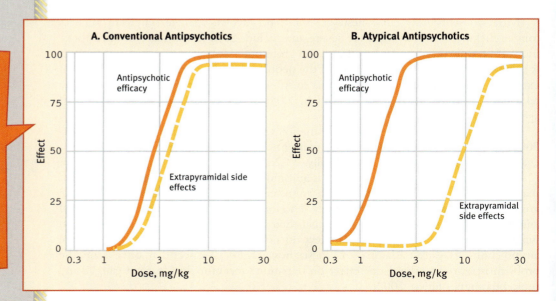

Figure 15-2

Conventional versus atypical antipsychotic drugs: the side effect advantage Conventional antipsychotic drugs are much more likely than atypical antipsychotic drugs to produce undesired extrapyramidal symptoms. (A) The dose-response curve for conventional drugs shows that, beginning with low doses of the drugs, extrapyramidal side effects emerge and keep intensifying right along with increases in the drug doses. (B) In contrast, the dose-response curve for atypical antipsychotic drugs indicates that extrapyramidal side effects typically do not even appear until a patient is taking relatively high doses of the drugs. (Adapted from Casey, 1995, p. 107.)

First Dibs on Atypical Antipsychotic Drugs?

As you saw in Chapter 9, depressed African Americans in the United States are less likely than depressed white Americans to be prescribed second-generation antidepressant drugs, the newer antidepressants that have fewer side effects than tricyclics and MAO inhibitors (see page 293). Thus many African Americans may be receiving less effective biological care than white Americans for their depressive disorders.

Unfortunately, a similar pattern appears to be at work in cases of schizophrenia when people are prescribed atypical antipsychotic medications, the second-generation antipsychotic medications that are often more effective and have fewer undesired effects than conventional antipsychotic medications. The following racial prescription patterns have emerged in several studies:

- African Americans and Hispanic Americans with schizophrenia and other psychotic disorders are significantly less likely than white Americans to be prescribed atypical antipsychotic drugs (Herbeck et al., 2004; Covell et al., 2002).

- African Americans and Hispanic Americans with schizophrenia are much more likely (as much as twice as likely) than white Americans to be prescribed conventional antipsychotic

drugs (Herbeck et al., 2004; Covell et al., 2002).

- In turn, African American and Hispanic American patients are less likely to be helped by their antipsychotic medications and more likely to experience tardive dyskinesia and extrapyramidal effects in response to their medications for schizophrenia.

- One reason for this racial disparity may be economic. On average, African American and Hispanic American patients are less likely than white Americans to have private health insurance or any health insurance at all (Ni & Cohen, 2004). Schizophrenic patients without private insurance are more likely to be prescribed

conventional antipsychotic medications, which are much cheaper, and are less likely to receive atypical antipsychotics, which are much more expensive (Herbeck et al., 2004).

- Another reason for this racial disparity may be the agents of treatment. In general, African American and Hispanic American patients are more likely to have a family physician rather than a psychiatrist prescribe their psychotropic drugs (Mark et al., 2002; Pingitore et al., 2001). It turns out that many family physicians are more inclined to prescribe conventional antipsychotic drugs than atypical antipsychotic drugs (Mark et al., 2003, 2002).

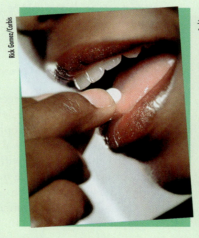

Rick Gomez/Corbis

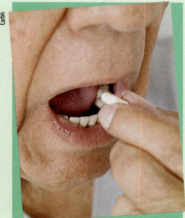

Corbis

1 percent risk of developing **agranulocytosis,** a life-threatening drop in white blood cells (other atypical antipsychotic drugs do not produce this undesired effect). Patients who take clozapine must therefore have frequent blood tests so that this effect can be spotted early and the drug stopped (Sajatovic et al., 2008). In addition, some of the atypical antipsychotic drugs may cause weight gain, particularly among women; dizziness; and significant elevations in blood sugar. They are also very expensive (Dolder, 2008; Seeman, 2008).

⚙Psychotherapy

Before the discovery of antipsychotic drugs, psychotherapy was not really an option for people diagnosed with schizophrenia. Most were too far removed from reality to profit from it. Only a handful of therapists, apparently blessed with extraordinary patience and skill, specialized in the psychotherapeutic treatment of this disorder and reported a

•**agranulocytosis**•A life-threatening reduction in white blood cells. This condition is sometimes produced by the atypical antipsychotic drug *clozapine.*

measure of success (Will, 1967, 1961; Sullivan, 1962, 1953; Fromm-Reichmann, 1950, 1948, 1943). These therapists believed that the first task of such therapy was to win the trust of patients with schizophrenia and build a close relationship with them.

Well-known clinical theorist and therapist Frieda Fromm-Reichmann, for example, would initially tell her patients that they could continue to exclude her from their private world and hold onto their disorder as long as they wished. She reported that eventually, after much testing and acting out, the patients would accept, trust, and grow attached to her and begin to talk to her about their problems. Case studies seemed to attest to the effectiveness of such approaches and to the importance of trust and emotional bonding in treatment. Here a recovered woman tells her therapist how she had felt during their early interactions:

At the start, I didn't listen to what you said most of the time but I watched like a hawk for your expression and the sound of your voice. After the interview, I would add all this up to see if it seemed to show love. The words were nothing compared to the feelings you showed. I sense that you felt confident I could be helped and that there was hope for the future. . . .

The problem with schizophrenics is that they can't trust anyone. They can't put their eggs in one basket. The doctor will usually have to fight to get in no matter how much the patient objects. . . .

Loving is impossible at first because it turns you into a helpless little baby. The patient can't feel safe to do this until he is absolutely sure the doctor understands what is needed and will provide it.

(Hayward & Taylor, 1965)

Today psychotherapy is successful in many more cases of schizophrenia (Kopelowicz et al., 2008). By helping to relieve thought and perceptual disturbances, antipsychotic drugs allow people with schizophrenia to learn about their disorder, participate actively in therapy, think more clearly about themselves and their relationships, make changes in their behavior, and cope with stressors in their lives (Rosenberg & Mueser, 2008; Awad & Voruganti, 2007). The most helpful forms of psychotherapy include cognitive-behavioral therapy and two broader sociocultural therapies—family therapy and social therapy. Often the various approaches are combined and tailored to a patient's particular needs (Kopelowicz et al., 2008).

Cognitive-Behavioral Therapy

As you read in the previous chapter, the cognitive explanation for schizophrenia starts with the premise that people with this disorder do indeed actually hear voices (or experience other kinds of hallucinations) as a result of biologically triggered sensations. According to this theory, the journey into schizophrenia takes shape when individuals try to make sense of these strange sensations and conclude incorrectly that the voices are coming from external sources, that they are being persecuted, that they are receiving divine guidance, or other such notions. These misinterpretations are essentially delusions, and they help set up the further symptoms—emotional, behavioral, and cognitive—of schizophrenia.

With this view of hallucinations and delusions in mind, an increasing number of clinicians now employ a cognitive-behavioral treatment for schizophrenia that seeks to change how individuals view and react to their hallucinatory experiences (Morrison, 2008; Tarrier, 2008). The therapists believe that if individuals can be guided to interpret such experiences in a more accurate way, they will not suffer the fear, confusion, and other symptoms generated by their delusional misinterpretations. To change clients' interpretations and reactions, these therapists use a combination of behavioral and cognitive techniques:

1. They provide clients with education and evidence about the biological causes of hallucinations.

2. They help clients learn more about the "comings and goings" of their own hallucinations and delusions. The individuals learn, for example, to monitor which kinds of events and situations trigger the voices in their heads. Similarly, the clients systematically observe the many "avoidance" and "safety" behaviors that they have come to adopt in response to their hallucinations and delusions.

3. The therapists challenge their clients' inaccurate ideas about the power of their hallucinations, such as their notions that the voices are all-powerful, uncontrollable, and must be obeyed. Correspondingly, the therapists have the clients conduct behavioral experiments to put such notions to the test. What happens, for example, if the clients occasionally resist following the orders from their hallucinatory voices?

4. The therapists teach clients to reattribute and more accurately interpret their hallucinations. Clients may, for example, increasingly adopt and apply alternative conclusions such as, "It's not a real voice, it's my illness."

5. While clients are developing more and more doubts about the merits of their hallucinations and delusions, they are also being taught techniques for coping with their unpleasant sensations (hallucinations). They may, for example, learn ways to reduce the physical arousal that accompanies hallucinations—applying special breathing and relaxation techniques, positive self-statements, and the like. Similarly, they may learn to switch their focus of attention or distract themselves whenever the hallucinations occur. In one reported case, a therapist repeatedly walked behind his schizophrenic client and made harsh and critical statements, seeking to simulate the clients' auditory hallucinations and then guiding him to focus his attention past the voices and on to the task at hand (Veiga-Marinez et al., 2008).

The systematic application of these behavioral and cognitive techniques helps schizophrenic individuals gain a greater sense of control over their hallucinations, develop more functional ways of reacting to their hallucinations, reduce their delusional ideas and other negative emotions and behaviors, and move forward in life with less confusion, greater happiness, and more purpose (Tarrier, 2008). At the same time, the techniques do not eliminate the hallucinations. They simply render the hallucinations less powerful and less destructive. Can anything be done further to lessen the hallucinations' unpleasant impact on the individual? Yes, say *new-wave cognitive-behavioral therapists.*

As you read in Chapter 3, a new wave of cognitive-behavioral therapists, including practitioners of *Acceptance and Commitment Therapy,* believe that the most useful goal of treatment is often to help clients *accept* their streams of problematic thoughts rather than to judge them, act on them, or try fruitlessly to change them (Hayes et al., 2004; Hayes, 2002). Such therapists, for example, help highly anxious individuals to become simply *mindful* of the worries that engulf their thinking and to *accept* such negative thoughts as but harmless events of the mind (see page 130). Similarly, in cases of schizophrenia, new-wave cognitive-behavioral therapists try to help clients become detached and comfortable observers of their hallucinations—merely mindful of the unusual sensations and accepting of them—while the individuals otherwise move forward with the tasks and events of their lives (Bach, 2007; Gaudiano, 2005; Bach & Hayes, 2002).

Studies indicate that these various cognitive-behavioral treatments for schizophrenia are often very helpful to clients with schizophrenia (Morrison, 2008; Tarrier, 2008; Saba et al., 2007; Gaudiano & Herbert, 2006). Many clients who receive such treatments report feeling less distressed by their hallucinations and display fewer delusions. Indeed,

BETWEEN THE LINES

In Their Words

"Last night I saw upon the stair
A little man who wasn't there.
He wasn't there again today.
Oh, how I wish he'd go away!"

Nursery rhyme

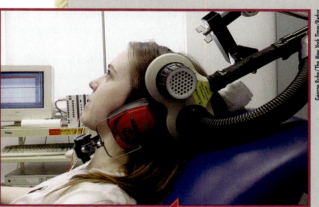

Reducing auditory sensations
While cognitive-behavioral therapists try to help schizophrenic people more accurately interpret their hallucinations as brain-produced sensations, biological researchers keep trying to rid sufferers of those sensations. Yale researcher Ralph Hoffman and his colleagues, for example, have used a *transcranial magnetic stimulation* procedure to stimulate the auditory brain centers of schizophrenic patients. The procedure, shown here, has indeed reduced the hallucinations of many patients, apparently by reducing neural excitability in their auditory brain areas (Hoffman et al., 2007, 2000).

the individuals are often able to shed the diagnosis of schizophrenia. Rehospitalizations decrease by 50 percent among clients treated with cognitive-behavioral therapy.

The cognitive-behavioral view that hallucinations should be accepted (rather than misinterpreted or overreacted to) is, in fact, compatible with a popular notion already

HOME   SEND   EXPLORE

Can You Live with the Voices in Your Head?

BY DANIEL B. SMITH, THE *NEW YORK TIMES*, MARCH 25, 2007

Angelo, a London-born scientist in his early 30s with sandy brown hair, round wire-frame glasses and a slight, unobtrusive stammer, vividly recalls the day he began to hear voices. It was Jan. 7, 2001, and he had recently passed his Ph.D. oral exams in chemistry at an American university. . . . Angelo was walking home from the laboratory when, all of a sudden, he heard two voices in his head. "It was like hearing thoughts in my mind that were not mine," he explained recently. "They identified themselves as Andrew and Oliver, two angels." . . . What the angels said, to Angelo's horror, was that in the coming days, he would die of a brain hemorrhage. Terrified, Angelo hurried home and locked himself into his apartment. For three long days he waited out his fate, at which time his supervisor drove him to a local hospital, where Angelo was admitted to the psychiatric ward. It was his first time under psychiatric care. He had never heard voices before. His diagnosis was schizophrenia with depressive overtones.

Angelo remembers his time at the hospital as the deepening of a nightmare. On top of his natural confusion and fear over the shattering of his psychological stability, Angelo did not react well to the antipsychotic he'd been prescribed. . . . His voices remained strong and disturbing. . . . Several days into his stay, Angelo's parents flew to the United States from London and took him back home.

More than six years later, Angelo still lives at his parents' house. He currently takes a cocktail of antidepressants and antipsychotics, with tolerable side effects. . . . The pills help Angelo to manage his voices, but they have not been able to eradicate them. . . . Despite these setbacks, Angelo has maintained his optimism. He is eager to discover new ways to combat his voices. Not long ago, he found one. In November, his psychologist informed him of a local support group for people who hear voices, from which he thought Angelo might benefit. Angelo began to attend the group late last year.

I first met Angelo at a meeting of the group in mid-January. (I was given permission to sit in on the condition that I not divulge the participants' last names.) The meeting took place in the bright, cheerfully decorated back room of a community mental-health center in North Finchley. . . . The gathering was small but eclectic. In addition to the group's facilitators—Jo Kutchinsky, an occupational therapist, and Liana Kaiser, a social-work student—five men and women assembled in a circle of bulky wool-knit chairs around a worn coffee table. Besides Angelo, there was Stewart, . . . Jenny, . . . Michelle, . . . and David. . . .

. . . When Kutchinsky opened the meeting by asking each member to discuss the previous week's experience hearing voices, . . . most of the members spoke of their voices in the way that comedians speak of mothers-in-law: burdensome and irritating, but an inescapable part of life that you might as well learn to deal with. When David's name was called, he lifted his head and discussed his struggle to accept his voices as part of his consciousness. "I've learned over time that my voices can't be rejected," he said. "No matter what I do, they won't go away. I have to find a way to live with them." Jenny discussed how keeping busy quieted her voices; she seemed to have taken a remarkable number of adult-education courses. Michelle expressed her belief that her voices were nothing more exotic than powerfully negative thoughts. "Negative thoughts are universal," she said. "Everyone has them. Everyone. What matters is how you cope with them: that's what counts."

I had trouble gauging Angelo's reaction throughout these testimonies, so afterward I pulled him aside and asked him what he thought. "It's interesting to hear people's stories," he said. "Before I started coming, I hadn't realized just how long some people have suffered. I've heard voices for six years. Some people have heard them for 15 or 20. . . . Still, he appeared to appreciate the camaraderie. For years, he had been socially isolated. . . . It was comforting, he said, to speak at last with people who understood.

The meeting that I attended in London is one of dozens like it affiliated with a small but influential grass-roots organization known as Hearing Voices Network. . . . H.V.N. groups must accept all interpretations of auditory hallucinations as equally valid. If an individual comes to a group claiming that he is hearing the voice of the queen of England, and he finds this belief useful, no attempt is made to divest him of it, but rather to figure out what it means to him. . . .

. . . H.V.N.'s brief . . . can be boiled down to two core positions. The first is that many more people hear voices, and hear many more kinds of voices, than is usually assumed. The second is that auditory hallucination—or "voice-hearing," H.V.N.'s more neutral preference—should be thought of not as a

held by many people who hallucinate. There are now many self-help groups comprised of people with auditory hallucinations whose guiding principles are that hallucinations themselves are harmless and valid experiences and that sufferers often do best if they simply can accept and learn to live with these experiences (see *The Media Speaks* below).

"And only you can hear this whistle?"

pathological phenomenon in need of eradication but as a meaningful, interpretable experience, intimately linked to a hearer's life story. . . .

The concept of "coping" is central to H.V.N., based on its belief that people feel better not when their voices are extinguished but when the person hearing voices learns to listen to his hallucinations without anguish. Jacqui Dillon, the national chairwoman of H.V.N., embraces this credo based on personal experience. Dillon, a mother of two, has heard voices for more than 30 years and has never taken medication for them. Mostly, she says, her voices are supportive and even witty, though occasionally they are cruel—they swear and tell her to harm herself. But she no longer heeds their commands or allows them to bother her. . . .

It was just before noon on a mild Friday in January when the North Finchley hearing-voices group reconvened after a 15-minute coffee break. . . . Earlier in the day, Kutchinsky and Kaiser printed out a list of coping strategies that another group's members had found useful [to deal with the voices in their heads], cutting each description into thin rectangles, which they now spread across the table, facedown. The participants were asked to choose one and discuss. Angelo picked first: "Hobbies." He cleared his throat, and in a gentle, measured voice, began: "Collecting, day or evening classes, visiting a library, computer skills, reading and sport. All these activities are not only fun and relaxing; they can fill voids in our lives and help

to occupy us during the day or evening. They can improve concentration and reduce isolation. They can also boost our morale and confidence and give us a feel-good factor." Finished, Angelo lifted his head from the paper and looked around.

"Well, do you have any hobbies, Angelo?" Kutchinsky asked.

"I like to play chess," he said. "And, as I've said, I like to read. But it's difficult. I can really only handle something light or humorous. Like Dave Barry."

"I see. Does reading help to block the voices at all?"

Angelo's eyes seemed to darken. "No. I'm afraid nothing at all blocks the voices. Even if I play music really loud, it doesn't help at all."

The coping strategies that followed were within the same vein as the first—commonsensical lifestyle suggestions geared toward improving one's frame of mind, or sanding down the edges of the experience's effects. Liana chose "Exercise"; Jenny chose "Religious Activities"; David chose "Pamper Yourself." . . . The most novel strategy, and the only one that seemed to cause the group's members to perk up, came under the heading of "Mobile Phones." If you have the temptation to yell at your voices in public, one suggestion went, you should do so with a phone to your ear. That way you can feel free to let loose, and no one who sees you will think you're crazy. Chris in particular seemed to cozy to the suggestion. "I sometimes talk to my voices in public," he said matter-of-factly. "It's very upsetting. I have to bite my knuckles to suppress the urge."

Participants in H.V.N.'s self-help groups take comfort from strategies like these not least because they approach voices as you would approach any other painful but normal experience, like anxiety or stress. . . .

As for Angelo, his concern is not to choose one option over another—but only to recover. "I have found the group interesting," Angelo wrote via e-mail three weeks after we met. "It has made me realize that many voice-hearers have had the problem for many years, and that many never stop hearing the voices, though some are successful in that regard. One lady has recently quit the group as she no longer hears voices. I also see that some hearers are quite high-functioning and are able to hold down a job despite the voices. I hope to do this myself. Perhaps the right combination of drugs will make this possible."

Family Therapy

Over 50 percent of persons who are recovering from schizophrenia and other severe mental disorders live with their families: parents, siblings, spouses, or children (Barrowclough & Lobban, 2008). Such situations create special pressures; even if family stress was not a factor in the onset of the disorder, a patient's recovery may be influenced greatly by the behavior and reactions of his or her relatives at home.

Generally speaking, persons with schizophrenia who feel positively toward their relatives do better in treatment (Camacho et al., 2005; Lebell et al., 1993). As you observed in Chapter 14, recovered patients living with relatives who display high levels of *expressed emotion*—that is, relatives who are very critical, emotionally overinvolved, and hostile—often have a much higher relapse rate than those living with more positive and supportive relatives (Ritsner & Gibel, 2007; Janicak et al., 2001).

For their part, family members may be affected greatly by the social withdrawal and unusual behaviors of a relative with schizophrenia (Barrowclough & Lobban, 2008; Magaña et al., 2007; Creer & Wing, 1974). One individual complained, "In the evening you go into the sitting room and it's in darkness. You turn on the light and there he is just sitting there, staring in front of him."

To address such issues, clinicians now commonly include family therapy in their treatment of schizophrenia, providing family members with guidance, training, practical advice, psychoeducation about the disorder, and emotional support and empathy (Kopelowicz et al., 2008). In family therapy, relatives develop more realistic expectations and become more tolerant, less guilt-ridden, and more willing to try new patterns of communication. Family therapy also helps the person with schizophrenia cope with the pressures of family life, make better use of family members, and avoid troublesome interactions.

Research has found that family therapy—particularly when it is combined with drug therapy—helps reduce tensions within the family and so helps relapse rates go down (Barrowclough & Lobban, 2008; Falloon, 2002). The principles of this approach are evident in the following description:

Mark was a 32-year-old single man living with his parents. He had a long and stormy history of schizophrenia with many episodes of psychosis, interspersed with occasional brief periods of good functioning. Mark's father was a bright but neurotically tormented man gripped by obsessions and inhibitions. Mark's mother appeared weary, detached, and embittered. Both parents felt hopeless about Mark's chances of recovery and resentful that needing to care for him would always plague their lives. They acted as if they were being intentionally punished. It gradually emerged that the father, in fact, was riddled with guilt and self-doubt; he suspected that his wife had been cold and rejecting toward Mark as an infant and that he had failed to intervene, due to his unwillingness to confront his wife and the demands of graduate school that distanced him from home life. He entertained the fantasy that Mark's illness was a punishment for this. Every time Mark did begin to show improvement—both in reduced symptoms and in increased functioning—his parents responded as if it were just a cruel torment designed to raise their hopes and then to plunge them into deeper despair when Mark's condition deteriorated. This pattern was especially apparent when Mark got a job. As a result, at such times, the parents actually became more critical and hostile toward Mark. He would become increasingly defensive and insecure, finally developing paranoid delusions, and usually would be hospitalized in a panicky and agitated state.

All of this became apparent during the psychoeducational sessions. When the pattern was pointed out to the family, they were able to recognize their self-fulfilling prophecy and were motivated to deal with it. As a result, the therapist decided to see the family together. Concrete instances of the pattern and its consequences were explored, and alternative responses by the parents were developed. The therapist encouraged both the parents and Mark to discuss their anxieties and doubts about Mark's progress, rather than to stir up one another's expectations of failure. The therapist had regular individual sessions with Mark as well as the family sessions. As a result, Mark has successfully held a job for an unprecedented 12 months.

(Heinrichs & Carpenter, 1983, pp. 284–285)

The families of persons with schizophrenia may also turn to family support groups and family psychoeducational programs for assistance, encouragement, and advice (Chien et al., 2004; Powder, 2004). In such programs, family members meet with others in the same situation to share their thoughts and emotions, provide mutual support, and learn about schizophrenia. Although research has yet to determine the usefulness of these groups, the approach has become popular.

Social Therapy

Many clinicians believe that the treatment of people with schizophrenia should include techniques that address social and personal difficulties in the clients' lives. These clinicians offer practical advice; work with clients on problem solving, decision making, and social skills; make sure that the clients are taking their medications properly; and may even help them find work, financial assistance, appropriate health care, and proper housing (Ridgeway, 2008; Sherrer & O'Hare, 2008; Kersting, 2005).

Research finds that this practical, active, and broad approach, called *social therapy* or *personal therapy,* does indeed help keep people out of the hospital (Hogarty, 2002). One study compared the progress of four groups of patients with chronic schizophrenia after their discharge from a state hospital (Hogarty et al., 1986, 1974). One group received both antipsychotic medications and social therapy in the community, while the other groups received medication only, social therapy only, or no treatment of any kind. The researchers' first finding was that chronic patients need to continue taking medication after being released in order to avoid rehospitalization. Over a two-year period, 80 percent of those who did not continue medication needed to be hospitalized again, compared to 48 percent of those who received medication. They also found that among the patients on medication, those who also received social therapy adjusted to the community and avoided rehospitalization most successfully. Clearly, social therapy played an important role in their recovery.

✿The Community Approach

The broadest approach for the treatment of schizophrenia and other severe mental disorders is the *community approach.* In 1963, partly in response to the terrible conditions in public mental institutions and partly because of the emergence of antipsychotic drugs, the U.S. government ordered that patients be released and treated in the community. Congress passed the *Community Mental Health Act,* which stipulated that patients with psychological disorders were to receive a range of mental health services—outpatient therapy, inpatient treatment, emergency care, preventive care, and aftercare—in their communities rather than being transported to institutions far from home. The act was aimed at a variety of psychological disorders, but patients diagnosed with schizophrenia, especially those who had been institutionalized for years, were affected most. Other countries around the world put similar sociocultural treatment programs into action shortly thereafter (Wiley-Exley, 2007; Hafner & an der Heiden, 1988).

Thus began four decades of **deinstitutionalization,** an exodus of hundreds of thousands of patients with schizophrenia and other long-term mental disorders from state institutions into the community. On a given day in 1955 close to 600,000 patients were living in state institutions; today only around 60,000 patients reside in those

•**deinstitutionalization**•The discharge of large numbers of patients from long-term institutional care so that they might be treated in community programs.

AP Photo/M. Spencer Green

A place to call home
One of the most important features of community mental health is to live in a proper and appealing residence. This man, recovering from schizophrenia and bipolar disorder, joyfully assumes a yoga pose in the living room of his new Chicago apartment. He found the residence with the help of a program called Direct Connect, which has helped many such individuals move into their own apartments.

•**community mental health center**• A treatment facility that provides medication, psychotherapy, and emergency care for psychological problems and coordinates treatment in the community.

•**aftercare**•A program of posthospitalization care and treatment in the community.

•**day center**•A program that offers hospital-like treatment during the day only. Also known as a *day hospital*.

•**halfway house**•A residence for people with schizophrenia or other severe problems, often staffed by paraprofessionals. Also known as a *group home* or *crisis house*.

settings (Salzer et al., 2006; Torrey, 2001). Clinicians have learned that patients recovering from schizophrenia and other severe disorders can profit greatly from community programs. As you will see, however, the actual quality of community care for these people has often been inadequate throughout the United States. The result is a "revolving door" syndrome for many patients: they are released to the community, readmitted to an institution within months, released a second time, admitted yet again, and so on, over and over (Sadock & Sadock, 2007; Torrey, 2001).

What Are the Features of Effective Community Care?

People recovering from schizophrenia and other severe disorders need medication, psychotherapy, help in handling daily pressures and responsibilities, guidance in making decisions, training in social skills, residential supervision, and vocational counseling—a combination of services sometimes called *assertive community treatment* (DeLuca, Moser, & Bond, 2008; Coldwell & Bender, 2007). Those whose communities help them meet these needs make greater progress than those living in other communities. Some of the key features of effective community care programs are (1) coordination of patient services, (2) short-term hospitalization, (3) partial hospitalization, (4) supervised residencies, and (5) occupational training.

Coordinated Services When the Community Mental Health Act was first passed, it was expected that community care would be provided by a **community mental health center,** a treatment facility that would supply medication, psychotherapy, and inpatient emergency care to people with severe disturbances, as well as coordinate the services offered by other community agencies. Each center was expected to serve a geographic area with a population of 50,000 to 200,000 people.

When community mental health centers are available and do provide these services, patients with schizophrenia and other severe disorders often make significant progress

Art that heals
Art and other creative activities can be therapeutic for people with schizophrenia and other severe mental disorders. More than 250,000 pieces of patient-produced art are on display at the Museum of the Unconscious in Rio de Janeiro, Brazil, where supervisors work closely with patients every day. One of the museum's most famous and talented patients, Fernando Diniz, poses with some of his extraordinary artwork.

From *The Power to Heal: Ancient Arts & Modern Medicine*, RX Media Group © Claus Meyer/Black Star

(Rapp & Goscha, 2008; Fenton et al., 2002). They are better integrated into the community and function more effectively than patients who receive only standard outpatient care (Madianos & Madianou, 1992). Coordination of services is particularly important for the so-called *mentally ill chemical abusers* (*MICAs*), patients with psychotic disorders as well as substance-related disorders (see *Psych Watch* on pages 500–501).

Short-Term Hospitalization

When people develop severe psychotic symptoms, today's clinicians first try to treat them on an outpatient basis, usually with a combination of antipsychotic medication and psychotherapy (Addington & Addington, 2008). If this approach fails, *short-term hospitalization*—in a mental hospital or a general hospital's psychiatric unit—that lasts a few weeks (rather than months or years) may be tried (Soliman, Santos, & Lohr, 2008; Sadock & Sadock, 2007). Soon after the patients improve, they are released for **aftercare,** a general term for follow-up care and treatment in the community. Short-term hospitalization usually leads to greater improvement and a lower rehospitalization rate than extended institutionalization (Soliman et al., 2008; Caton, 1982). Countries throughout the world now favor this policy (Wiley-Exley, 2007).

Partial Hospitalization

People's needs may fall between full hospitalization and outpatient therapy, and so some communities offer **day centers** or **day hospitals,** all-day programs in which patients return to their homes for the night. Such programs actually originated in Moscow in 1933, when a shortage of hospital beds necessitated the premature release of many patients. Today's day centers provide patients with daily supervised activities, therapy, and programs to improve social skills. People recovering from schizophrenia and other severe disorders in day centers often do better than those who spend extended periods in a hospital or in traditional outpatient therapy (Mayahara & Ito, 2002; Yoshimasu et al., 2002).

Another kind of institution that has become a popular setting for the treatment of people with schizophrenia and other severe disorders is the *semihospital,* or *residential crisis center.* Semihospitals are houses or other structures in the community that provide 24-hour nursing care for people with severe mental disorders (Soliman et al., 2008; Torrey, 2001). Many individuals who would otherwise be cared for in state hospitals are now being transferred to these semihospitals.

Supervised Residences

Many people do not require hospitalization but, at the same time, are unable to live alone or with their families. **Halfway houses,** also known as *crisis houses* or *group homes,* often serve individuals well (Levy et al., 2005). Such residences may shelter between one and two dozen people. The live-in staff usually are *paraprofessionals*—lay people who receive training and ongoing supervision from outside mental health professionals. The houses are usually run with a *milieu therapy* philosophy that emphasizes mutual support, resident responsibility, and self-government. Research indicates that halfway houses help many people recovering from schizophrenia and other severe disorders adjust to community life and avoid rehospitalization (Hansson et al., 2002; McGuire, 2000). Here is how one woman described living in a halfway house after 10 hospitalizations in 12 years:

Christopher Morris/Black Star

Community care in action
Clinicians have learned that people with schizophrenia and other severe disorders often make great progress in well-coordinated community treatment programs. Here patients begin their day with breakfast at New York City's Fountain House, a day center that provides daily activities and therapy as well as extensive occupational training.

The halfway house changed my life. First of all, I discovered that some of the staff members had once been clients in the program! That one single fact offered me hope. For the first time, I saw proof that a program could help someone, that it was possible to regain control over one's life and become independent. The house was democratically run; all residents had one vote and the staff members, outnumbered 5 to 22, could not make

PSYCH WATCH

Mentally Ill Chemical Abusers: A Challenge for Treatment

A state appeals court yesterday ordered Larry Hogue, who has for years frightened residents of Manhattan's Upper West Side with his bizarre behavior, to remain in a state mental hospital until a hearing next week. . . . Before he was arrested, Mr. Hogue had attacked passers-by and cars in the area around West 96th Street and Amsterdam Avenue. . . .

. . . Mr. Hogue has been arrested 30 times and served at least six terms in prison, ranging from five days to a year, according to law-enforcement records. He now faces charges of criminal mischief for scraping the paint off a car last August.

(NEW YORK TIMES, FEBRUARY 9, 1993)

During the 1990s, Larry Hogue, nicknamed the "Wild Man of West 96th Street" by neighbors, became the best-known *mentally ill chemical abuser* (MICA) in the United States. MICAs, also known as *dual diagnosis* patients, are individuals who suffer from both a mental disorder (in Hogue's case schizophrenia) *and* a substance-related disorder. Today the MICA problem in the United States appears to be bigger than ever. Between 20 and 50 percent of all people with chronic mental disorders may be MICAs (Kavanagh, 2008; Torrey, 2001).

MICAs tend to be young and male. They often rate below average in social functioning and school achievement and above average in poverty, acting-out behavior, emergency room visits, and encounters with the criminal justice system (McKendrick et al., 2007; Sullivan et al., 2007). MICAs commonly report greater distress and have poorer treatment outcomes than people with mental disorders who do not abuse substances (Potvin et al., 2008).

The relationship between substance abuse and mental dysfunctioning is complex. A mental disorder may precede substance abuse, and the drug may be taken as a form of self-medication or as a result of impaired judgment (Potvin et al., 2008; Ziedonis et al., 2000). Conversely, substance abuse may cause or exacerbate psychopathology. Cocaine and amphetamines, for example, exacerbate the symptoms of psychosis and can quickly intensify the symptoms of schizophrenia. Whichever begins first, substance abuse and mental disorders interact to create a complex and distinct problem that is greater than the sum of its parts (Kavanagh, 2008; Meydan et al., 2005). The course and outcome of each disorder can be significantly influenced by the other.

Andrew Savulich/New York Times Pictures

Wild Man of West 96th Street The case of Larry Hogue, the so-called Wild Man of West 96th Street, helped bring the plight of MICAs to public attention. Here Hogue roams the streets while displaying the combined effects of schizophrenia and substance abuse.

rules or even discharge a client from the program without majority sentiment. There was a house bill of rights that was strictly observed by all. We helped one another and gave support. When residents were in a crisis, no staff member hustled them off or increased their medication to calm them down. Residents could cry, be comforted and hugged until a solution could be found, or until they accepted that it was okay to feel bad. Even anger was an acceptable feeling that did not have to be feared, but could be expressed and turned into constructive energy. If you disliked some aspect of the program or the behavior of a staff member, you could change things rather than passively accept what was happening. Choices were real, and failure and success were accepted equally. . . . Bit by bit, my distrust faltered and the fears lessened. I slept better and made friends. . . . Other residents and staff members who had hallucinated for years and now were able to control their hallucinations shared with me some of the techniques that had worked for them. Things like diet . . . and interpersonal relationships became a few of my tools.

(Lovejoy, 1982, pp. 605–609)

Treatment of MICAs has been undermined by the tendency of patients to hide their drug abuse problems and for clinicians to underdiagnose them (Wohlheiter & Dixon, 2008; Lehman et al., 1996). Unrecognized substance abuse may lead to misdiagnosis and misunderstanding of the disorders. The treatment of MICAs is further complicated by the fact that many treatment facilities are designed and funded to treat *either* mental disorders *or* substance abuse; only some are equipped or willing to treat both. As a result, it is not uncommon for MICA patients to be rejected as inappropriate for treatment in both substance abuse and mental health programs (NSDUH, 2008, 2005; Torrey, 2001). Many such individuals fall through the cracks in this way and find themselves in jail, like Larry Hogue, or in homeless shelters for want of the treatment they sought in vain (Egelko et al., 2002; Blanchard et al., 2000).

Experts describe the ideal MICA treatment program as a safe and supportive therapeutic environment that offers techniques for treating both mental disorders and substance abuse and takes into account the unique effects of both problems (Kavanagh, 2008; Akerele & Levin, 2002). One particularly inspiring development is

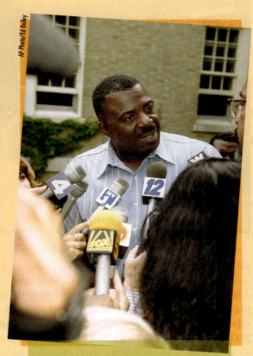

Not-So-Wild Man of West 96th Street Here Larry Hogue speaks to reporters immediately following one of his stays at a psychiatric hospital. Now on antipsychotic medication and off of alcohol and other substances, he expresses his desire to be a good neighbor and to become an advocate for the homeless.

the establishment of self-help groups for MICAs living in the community.

The problem of falling through the cracks is perhaps most poignantly seen in the case of *homeless* MICAs (Felix et al., 2008; Blanchard et al., 2000). Researchers estimate that 10 to 20 percent of the homeless population may be MICAs (NCH, 2007). MICAs typically remain homeless longer than other homeless people and are more likely to experience extremely harsh conditions, such as living on the winter streets rather than in a homeless shelter. They are also more likely to be jailed, to trade sexual favors for food or money, to share needles, to engage in unprotected sex, and to be victimized in other ways (Felix et al., 2008; Susser et al., 1996). Homeless MICAs need programs committed to building trust and providing intensive case management and long-term practical assistance (Coldwell & Bender, 2007; Egelko et al., 2002). In short, therapists must tailor treatment programs to MICAs' unique combination of problems rather than expecting the MICAs to adapt to traditional forms of care.

Occupational Training Paid employment provides income, independence, self-respect, and the stimulation of working with others. It also brings companionship and order to one's daily life. For these reasons, occupational training and placement are important services for people with schizophrenia and other severe mental disorders (Becker, 2008; DeLuca et al., 2008).

Many people recovering from such disorders receive occupational training in a **sheltered workshop**—a supervised workplace for employees who are not ready for competitive or complicated jobs. The workshop replicates a typical work environment: products such as toys or simple appliances are manufactured and sold, workers are paid according to performance, and all are expected to be at work regularly and on time. For some, the sheltered workshop becomes a permanent workplace. For others, it is an important step toward better-paying and more demanding employment or a return to a previous job (Becker, 2008; Chalamat et al., 2005). In the United States, occupational training is not consistently available to people with severe mental disorders (Torrey, 2001). Some studies find that fewer than 15 percent of such people are competitively employed (Honberg, 2005; Blyler, 2003).

•**sheltered workshop**•A supervised workplace for people who are not yet ready for competitive jobs.

Many of the people with schizophrenia and other severe disorders return to their families and receive medication and perhaps emotional and financial support, but little else in the way of treatment (Barrowclough & Lobban, 2008). Around 8 percent enter an alternative institution such as a nursing home or rest home, where they receive only custodial care and medication (Torrey, 2001). As many as 18 percent are placed in privately run residences where supervision is provided by untrained individuals—foster homes (small or large), boardinghouses, congregate care homes, and similar facilities. These residences vary greatly in quality. Some of them are legitimate "bed and care" facilities, providing three meals a day, medication reminders, and at least a small degree of staff supervision. However, many fail to offer even these minimal services.

Another 31 percent of people with schizophrenia and other severe disorders live in totally unsupervised settings. Some of these individuals are equal to the challenge of living alone, support themselves effectively, and maintain nicely furnished apartments. But many cannot really function independently and wind up in rundown single-room-occupancy hotels (SROs) or rooming houses, often located in inner-city neighborhoods (Torrey, 2001). They may live in conditions that are substandard and unsafe.

Most of the residents in poorly supervised or unsupervised settings survive on government disability payments (Torrey, 2001; Barker et al., 1992), and many spend their days wandering through neighborhood streets. Thus it is sometimes said that people with severe mental disorders are now "dumped" in the community, just as they were once "warehoused" in institutions.

Finally, a great number of people with schizophrenia and other severe disorders have become homeless (Felix, Herman, & Susser, 2008; Folsom et al., 2006). There are between 400,000 and 800,000 homeless people in the United States, and approximately one-third have a severe mental disorder, commonly schizophrenia (Coldwell & Bender, 2007; NCH, 2007; Sadock & Sadock, 2007). Many such persons have been released from hospitals. Others are young adults who were never hospitalized in the first place. Another 135,000 or more people with severe mental disorders end up in prisons because their disorders have led them to break the law (Morrissey & Cuddeback, 2008; Peters et al., 2008; Perez et al., 2003). Certainly deinstitutionalization and the community mental health movement have failed these individuals, and many report actually feeling relieved if they are able to return to hospital life.

The Promise of Community Treatment

Despite these very serious problems, proper community care has shown great potential for assisting in the recovery from schizophrenia and other severe disorders, and clinicians and many government officials continue to press to make it more available. In addition, a number of *national interest groups* have formed in countries around the world that push for better community treatment (Frese, 2008; Archibald, 2007; Torrey, 2001). In the United States, for example, the *National Alliance on Mental Illness* began in 1979 with 300 members and has expanded to around 220,000 members in more than 1,100 chapters (NAMI, 2008, 2002). Made up largely of relatives of people with severe mental disorders (particularly schizophrenia, bipolar disorders, and major depressive disorder), this group has become not only a source of information and support for its members but also a powerful lobbying force in state legislatures; additionally, it has pressured community mental health centers to treat more persons with schizophrenia and other severe disorders.

Today community care is a major feature of treatment for people recovering from severe mental disorders in countries around the world (Wiley-Exley, 2007). Some countries, learning from the mistakes of deinstitutionalization in the United States, have organized their own community programs better and as a result have had more success with them (Honkonen et al., 2003; Fakhoury & Priebe, 2002). Both in the United States and abroad, varied and well-coordinated community treatment is seen as an important part of the solution to the problem of schizophrenia and other severe disorders (DeLuca et al., 2008; Rapp & Goscha, 2008).

Incarceration posing as treatment
A man with a severe mental disorder sits alone in the dayroom of a maximum security prison in Idaho. Too dysfunctional to be treated as an outpatient and too dangerous for treatment at a low security hospital, he is one of many such individuals sent to this prison for "treatment."

AP Photo/Troy Maben

AP Photo/Javier Galeano

Healthy competition
As part of the community mental health philosophy, individuals with schizophrenia and other severe mental disorders are also encouraged to participate in normal activities, athletic endeavors, and artistic undertakings. Here mental health patients compete in the men's 100-meter event during an annual sports festival held in Havana Cuba for psychiatric patients.

PUTTING IT... together

An Important Lesson

After years of frustration and failure, clinicians now have an arsenal of weapons to use against schizophrenia and other disorders marked by psychosis—medication, institutional programs, psychotherapy, and community programs. It has become very clear that antipsychotic medications open the door for recovery from these disorders, but in most cases other kinds of treatment are also needed to help the recovery process along. The various approaches must be combined in a way that meets each individual's specific needs.

Working with schizophrenia and other severe disorders has taught therapists an important lesson: no matter how compelling the evidence for biological causation may be, a strictly biological approach to the treatment of psychological disorders is a mistake more often than not. Largely on the basis of biological discoveries and pharmacological advances, hundreds of thousands of patients with schizophrenia and other severe mental disorders were released to their communities in the 1960s. Little attention was paid to the psychological and sociocultural needs of these individuals, and many of them have been trapped in their pathology ever since. Clinicians must remember this lesson, especially in today's climate, when managed care and government priorities often promote medication as the sole treatment for psychological problems.

When Kraepelin described schizophrenia at the turn of the twentieth century, he estimated that only 13 percent of its victims ever improved. Today, even with shortages in community care, many more such individuals show improvement (Roe & Davidson, 2008; McGuire, 2000). Twenty-five percent or more are believed to recover from schizophrenia completely, and another 35 percent return to relatively independent lives, although their occupational and social functioning may continue to fall short of earlier levels (Combs et al., 2008; Harrow et al., 2005; Jobe & Harrow, 2005). These improvements notwithstanding, the clinical field still has far to go (Conley et al., 2005). Studies suggest that the recovery rates could be considerably higher (McGuire, 2000). It is unacceptable that so many people with this and other severe mental disorders receive few or none of the effective community interventions that have been developed, worse still that tens of thousands have become homeless. Although many factors have contributed to this state of affairs, neglect by clinical practitioners has certainly played a big role in it. It is now up to these professionals, along with public officials, to address the needs of all people with schizophrenia and other severe disorders.

BETWEEN THE LINES

Schizophrenia and Jail

There are more people with schizophrenia and other severe mental disorders in jails and prisons than there are in all hospitals and other treatment facilities. ‹‹

Persons with severe mental disorders account for 10 to 16 percent of the jail populations in the United States. ‹‹

Inmates in jails and prisons have rates of schizophrenia that are four times higher than that of the general public. ‹‹

The Los Angeles County Jail, where 3,300 of the 21,000 inmates require daily mental health services, is now de facto the largest mental institution in the United States. ‹‹

(Morrissey & Cuddeback, 2008; Peters et al., 2008; Skelton, 2004; Torrey, 2001, 1999; Grinfield, 1993)

‹‹‹[SUMMING UP]›››

○ **Overview of treatment** For years all efforts to treat schizophrenia brought only frustration. The disorder is still difficult to treat, but today's therapies are more successful than those of the past. *pp. 481–482*

○ **Past institutional care** For more than half of the twentieth century, the main treatment for schizophrenia and other severe mental disorders was *institutionalization* and *custodial care*. Because patients failed to respond to traditional therapies, they were usually placed in overcrowded public institutions (*state hospitals* in the United States), typically in *back wards* where the primary goal was to maintain and restrain them. Between 1845 and 1955 the number of state hospitals and mental patients rose steadily, while the quality of care declined. *pp. 482–483*

○ **Improved institutional care** In the 1950s two in-hospital approaches were developed, *milieu therapy* and *token economy programs*. They often brought improvement and particularly helped patients to care for themselves and feel better about themselves. *pp. 484–486*

○ **Antipsychotic drugs** The discovery of *antipsychotic drugs* in the 1950s revolutionized the treatment of schizophrenia and other disorders marked by psychosis. Today they are almost always a part of treatment. Theorists believe that the first generation of antipsychotic drugs operate by reducing excessive dopamine activity in the brain. These "conventional" antipsychotic drugs reduce the positive symptoms of schizophrenia more completely, or more quickly, than the negative symptoms.

The conventional antipsychotic drugs can also produce dramatic unwanted effects, particularly movement abnormalities called extrapyramidal effects, which include Parkinsonian and related symptoms, neuroleptic malignant syndrome, and tardive dyskinesia. Tardive dyskinesia apparently occurs in more than 10 percent of the people who take conventional antipsychotic drugs for an extended time and can be difficult or impossible to eliminate, even when the drugs are stopped. Recently atypical antipsychotic drugs (such as clozapine, risperidone, and olanzapine) have been developed, which seem to be more effective than the conventional drugs and to cause fewer or no extrapyramidal effects. *pp. 486–491*

○ **Psychotherapy** Today *psychotherapy* is often employed successfully in combination with antipsychotic drugs. Helpful forms include *cognitive-behavioral therapy, family therapy,* and *social therapy. Family support groups* and *family psychoeducational programs* are also growing in number. *pp. 491–497*

○ **The community approach** A *community approach* to the treatment of schizophrenia and other severe mental disorders began in the 1960s, when a policy of *deinstitutionalization* in the United States brought about a mass exodus of hundreds of thousands of patients from state institutions into the community. Among the key elements of effective community care programs are coordination of patient services by a *community mental health center, short-term hospitalization* (followed by *aftercare*), *day centers, halfway houses,* and *occupational training.*

Unfortunately, the quality and funding of community care for people with schizophrenia and other severe disorders have been inadequate throughout the United States, often resulting in a "revolving door" syndrome. One consequence is that many people with such disorders are now homeless or in jail. Still others live in *nursing homes* or *rest homes* where they do not receive effective treatment, and many live in *boardinghouses* or *single-room-occupancy hotels. pp. 497–504*

○ **The promise of community treatment** The potential of proper community care to help people recovering from schizophrenia and other severe disorders continues to capture the interest of clinicians and policy makers. One major development has been the formation of *national interest groups* that are successfully promoting community treatment for people with these disorders. *pp. 504–505*

⫸ CRITICAL THOUGHTS ⫷

1. Why have more people with schizophrenia than people with other disorders been the victims of mistreatment (lobotomy or deinstitutionalization, for example)? *pp. 481–505*

2. In the early years of antipsychotic drug use, patients who failed to respond to these drugs were likely to receive higher and higher dosages until many of them seemed to be walking zombies. Why might clinicians have used this medication strategy, even when the drugs failed to reduce symptoms? *pp. 486–490*

3. Although both cognitive-behavioral therapists and self-help programs such as *Hearing Voices Network* believe that people who hallucinate should "accept" the voices that spring forth from their brains, there are differences between the status and meaning that they each assign to hallucinations. What are these differences, and why are they important? *pp. 492–495*

4. The public often perceives people with schizophrenia as dangerous and violent even though most persons with this disorder are far from dangerous. Why does the public hold such a perception, and how can it be changed? *pp. 502–506*

5. As a result of deinstitutionalization, some of today's homeless shelters use buildings that were once state hospitals, and, in fact, some of the homeless mentally ill now find themselves back in the same place where they were confined years earlier, only under totally different circumstances. How might individuals react when they return to their former hospital residences under such circumstances? *pp. 503–504*

⫸⫷ cyberstudy ⫸⫷   SEARCH

Search the *Abnormal Psychology* Video Tool Kit
www.worthpublishers.com/apvtk

▲ Chapter 15 Video Cases
   Antipsychotic Drugs: Before and After
   Treating MICAs: "Wild Man of West 96th Street"
   John Nash's Beautiful Mind

▲ Video case discussions, study guides, and questions

Log on to the Comer Web Page
www.worthpublishers.com/comer

▲ Chapter 15 outline, learning objectives, research exercises, study tools, and practice test questions

▲ Additional Chapter 15 case studies, Web links, and FAQs

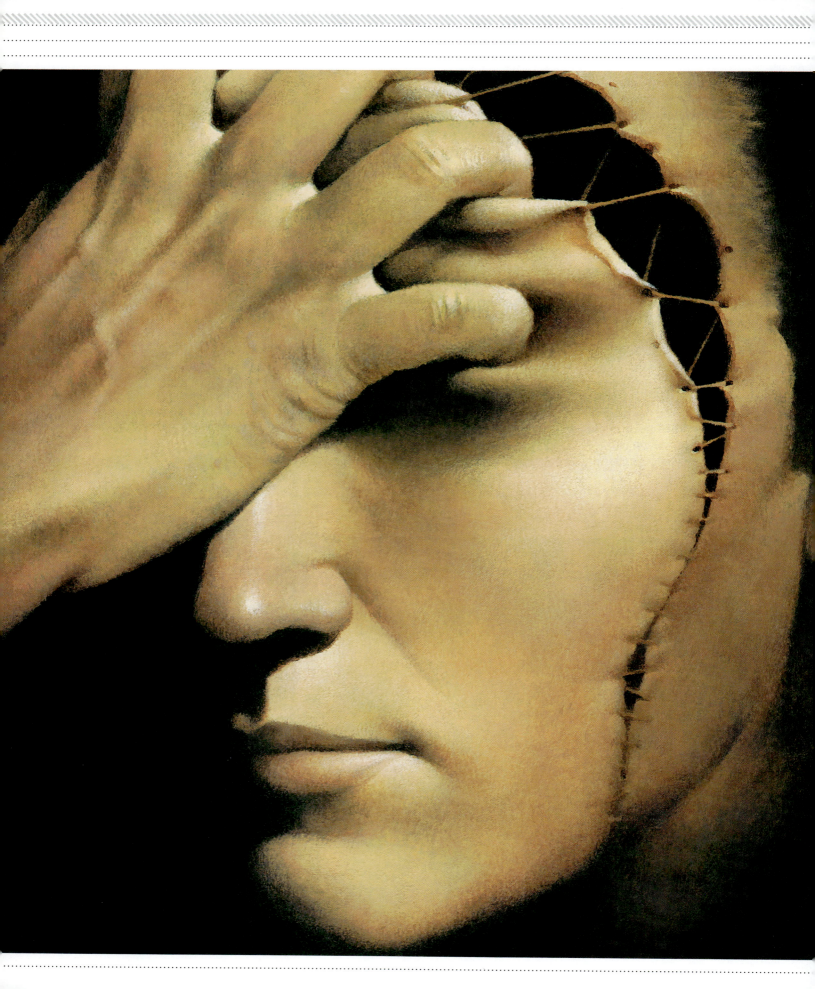

PERSONALITY DISORDERS

W hile interviewing for the job of editor, Frederick said, "This may sound self-serving, but I am extraordinarily gifted. I am certain that I will do great things in this position, that I and the newspaper will soon set the standard for journalism in this city." The committee was impressed. Certainly, Frederick's credentials were strong, but even more important, his self-confidence and boldness had wowed them.

A year later, many of the same individuals were describing Frederick differently—arrogant, self-serving, cold, ego-maniacal, draining. He had performed well as editor (though not as spectacularly as he seemed to think), but that performance could not outweigh his impossible personality. Colleagues below and above him had grown weary of his manipulations, his emotional outbursts, his refusal ever to take the blame, his nonstop boasting, and his grandiose plans. Once again Frederick had outworn his welcome.

To be sure, Frederick had great charm, and he knew how to make others feel important, when it served his purpose. Thus he always had his share of friends and admirers. But in reality they were just passing through, until Frederick would tire of them or feel betrayed by their lack of enthusiasm for one of his self-serving interpretations or grand plans. Or until they simply could take Frederick no longer.

Bright and successful though he was, Frederick always felt entitled to more than he was receiving—to higher grades at school, greater compensation at work, more attention from girlfriends. If criticized even slightly, he reacted with fury, and was certain that the critic was jealous of his superior intelligence, skill, or looks. At first glance, Frederick seemed to have a lot going for him socially. Typically, he could be found in the midst of a deep, meaningful romantic relationship—one in which he might be tender, attentive, and seemingly devoted to his partner. But Frederick would always tire of his partner within a few weeks or months and would turn cold or even mean. Often he started affairs with other women while still involved with the current partner. The breakups—usually unpleasant and sometimes ugly—rarely brought sadness or remorse to him, and he would almost never think about his former partner again. He always had himself.

Each of us has a *personality*—a unique and enduring pattern of inner experience and outward behavior. We tend to react in our own predictable and consistent ways. These consistencies, often called *personality traits,* may be the result of inherited characteristics, learned responses, or a combination of the two. Yet our personalities are also flexible. We learn from experience. As we interact with our surroundings, we try out various responses to see which are more effective. This is a flexibility that people who suffer from a personality disorder usually do not have.

A **personality disorder** is an inflexible pattern of inner experience and outward behavior. The pattern is seen in most of the person's interactions, continues for years, and differs markedly from the experiences and behaviors usually expected of people (see Table 16–1 on the next page). Frederick seems to display such a disorder. For most of his life, his narcissism, grandiosity, outbursts, and insensitivity to others have been excessive and have dominated his functioning. The rigid traits of people with personality disorders often lead to psychological pain for the individual and social or occupational difficulties (see *A Closer Look* on

table: 16-1

DSM Checklist

PERSONALITY DISORDER

1. An enduring pattern of inner experience and behavior that deviates markedly from the expectations of the individual's culture, with at least two of the following areas affected: • cognition • affectivity • interpersonal functioning • impulse control.

2. Pattern is inflexible and pervasive across a broad range of personal and social situations.

3. Pattern is stable and long-lasting, and its onset can be traced back at least to adolescence or early adulthood.

4. Significant distress or impairment.

Based on APA, 2000.

page 512). The disorders may also bring pain to others. Witness the upset and turmoil experienced by Frederick's co-workers and girlfriends.

Personality disorders typically become recognizable in adolescence or early adulthood, although some start during childhood (Kernberg & Wiener, 2004; APA, 2000). These are among the most difficult psychological disorders to treat. Many sufferers are not even aware of their personality problems and fail to trace their difficulties to their inflexible style of thinking and behaving. It has been estimated that between 9 and 13 percent of all adults may have a personality disorder (O'Connor, 2008; Lenzenweger et al., 2007).

As you saw in Chapter 4, DSM-IV-TR distinguishes Axis II disorders, disorders of long standing that usually begin well before adulthood and continue into adult life, from Axis I disorders, more acute disorders that often begin as a noticeable change in a person's usual behavior and are, in many cases, of limited duration. The personality disorders are Axis II disorders; these patterns are not typically marked by changes in intensity or periods of clear improvement.

It is common for a person with a personality disorder also to suffer from an acute (Axis I) disorder, a relationship called *comorbidity* (Fowler, O'Donohue, & Lilienfeld, 2007). Perhaps personality disorders predispose people to develop certain Axis I disorders. For example, people with avoidant personality disorder, who fearfully shy away from all relationships, may be prone to develop a social phobia. Or certain Axis I disorders may set the stage for a personality disorder. Or perhaps some biological factor creates a predisposition to both (Patrick, 2007). Whatever the reason for the relationship, research indicates that the presence of a personality disorder complicates a person's chances for a successful recovery from psychological problems (Skodol et al., 2005; Tyrer & Simmonds, 2003).

DSM-IV-TR identifies 10 personality disorders and separates them into three groups, called *clusters* (APA, 2000). One cluster, marked by odd or eccentric behavior, consists of the *paranoid, schizoid,* and *schizotypal* personality disorders. A second group features dramatic behavior and consists of the *antisocial, borderline, histrionic,* and *narcissistic* personality disorders. The final cluster features a high degree of anxiety and includes the *avoidant, dependent,* and *obsessive-compulsive* personality disorders.

The personality disorders listed in DSM IV-TR overlap so much that it can be difficult to distinguish one from the other (see Figure 16-1). In fact, diagnosticians sometimes determine that particular individuals have more than one such personality disorder (O'Connor, 2008). In addition, clinicians often disagree as to the correct diagnosis for people with a DSM-IV-TR personality disorder. This lack of agreement has raised serious questions about the *validity* (accuracy) and *reliability* (consistency) of the present DSM categories (Fowler et al., 2007). In fact, as you will see later in the chapter, there is a growing movement in the clinical field to eliminate the current categories and adopt instead an alternative—"dimensional"—way of thinking about and classifying disorders of personality. Before considering this alternative approach, however, let us examine DSM-IV-TR's 10 current categories. Two of these categories—*antisocial* and *borderline* personality disorders—will receive particular attention, as they have received much more attention than the other personality disorders by clinicians, research, and the public.

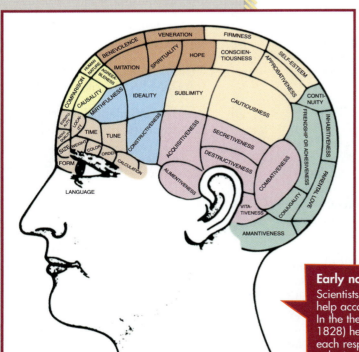

Early notions of personality

Scientists have long suspected that biological factors help account for personality and personality disorders. In the theory of phrenology, Franz Joseph Gall (1758–1828) held that the brain consists of distinct portions, each responsible for some aspect of personality. Phrenologists tried to assess personality by feeling bumps and indentations on a person's head.

As you start to read about the DSM-IV-TR personality disorders, you should be clear that diagnoses of such disorders can easily be overdone. We may catch glimpses of ourselves or of people we know in the descriptions of these disorders, and we may be tempted to conclude that we or they have a personality disorder. In the vast majority of instances, such interpretations are incorrect. We all display personality traits. Only occasionally are they so inflexible, maladaptive, and distressful that they can be considered disorders.

•**personality disorder**•A very rigid pattern of inner experience and outward behavior that differs from the expectations of one's culture and leads to dysfunctioning.

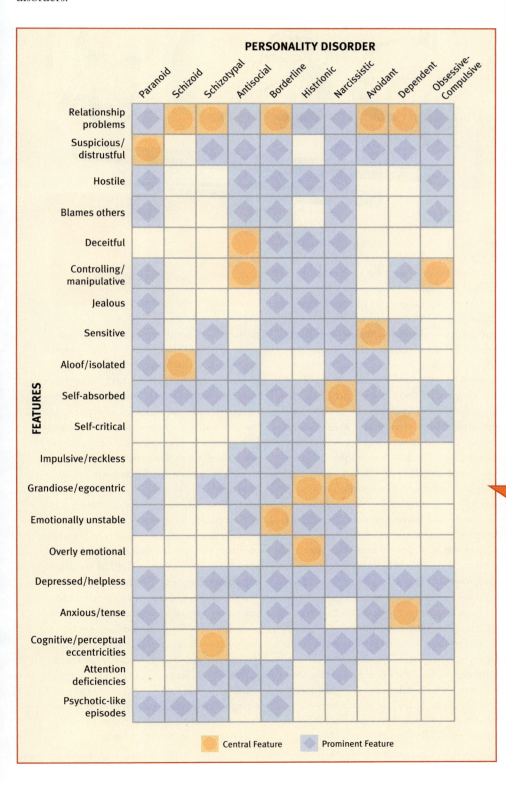

Figure 16-1

Prominent and central features of DSM-IV-TR's 10 personality disorders The symptoms of the various disorders often overlap greatly, leading to frequent misdiagnosis or to multiple diagnoses for a given client.

Personality and the Brain: The Case of Phineas Gage

Most of us are aware that damage to particular regions in the brain can cause motor dysfunction, memory or language problems, or even the loss of particular senses such as vision or hearing. However, clinical scientists have come to appreciate that damage to the brain from strokes, injury, or tumors can also bring about major changes in personality. The tragic story of Phineas Gage provided science with history's most memorable evidence of this fact.

In 1848, 25-year-old Gage was laying tracks for a railroad, a hazardous but common occupation in those years. The smart, careful, and friendly Gage was admired and liked by the men he supervised, and the company that wrote the paychecks called him "the most efficient and capable" employee they had. But that was all to change in a few seconds' time, when a rock-blasting mishap hurled a three-foot-long tamping iron under Gage's left cheek and straight through the top of his skull, piercing a one-and-a-half-inch hole through his brain's frontal lobes (Damasio, 1994).

Miraculously, Gage's body survived. But you could say that Gage himself, at least as others had known him, did not. From an even-tempered, responsible, and likable young man, Gage turned into a disrespectful, profane, impulsive, stubborn, and indecisive individual who had trouble planning for the future and sometimes had fits of temper. Beyond losing his sight in one eye, Gage suffered no lasting physical defects. He remained nimble, alert, and able to speak and think. The wound in his head laid waste to his personality alone.

After the accident, Gage could not keep his job, as he no longer had the motivation to perform up to expectations. His newly unpleasant behavior drove friends away and destroyed the possibility of finding a romantic partner with whom to share his life. Gage moved from job to job, including a stint in a circus sideshow in New York. This once-promising and ambitious young man eventually ended up a penniless ward of his mother and sister.

AP Photo/Courtesy of Harvard Medical School

Irreparable harm An 1850s artist offered these drawings of the injury suffered by Phineas Gage when a three-foot tamping iron penetrated his brain. Although the holes in Gage's head eventually healed, his previous personality did not survive.

He died of a brain seizure at the age of 38 (Damasio, 1994).

What, exactly, was the critical injury suffered by Gage? *Why* did his personality change so profoundly? In his book *Descartes' Error* (1994), neuroscientist Antonio Damasio speculates that the destruction of Gage's frontal lobe resulted in his inability to experience appropriate emotion. Imagine being unable to experience shame at saying rude things to your host at a dinner, anger at being duped by a con man who invests your money in a speculative venture, or fear at walking through a dangerous area of town at midnight. Imagine being unable to feel affection for a spouse or child or pleasure at engaging in one activity versus another. All of these failures of emotion would leave you socially helpless, indecisive, and unable to behave consistently in ways designed to further your own interests. You would be, in any sense of the word, perfectly unreasonable. In short, you might be much like Phineas Gage.

Gage is not the only person to have lost this critical faculty. Damasio (1994) documents a number of such patients who display startling results in tests of their emotional capacities. When shown emotion-arousing pictures that raise the galvanic skin responses (GSRs) of most people, patients with damage to their frontal lobes register no GSR reaction at all. When

performing "gambling" tasks in certain studies, normal individuals adopt low-risk strategies, while frontally damaged patients engage in high-risk and bankrupting tactics. Most telling, when the individuals in such studies are hooked to a polygraph, the GSRs of the normal gamblers increase (signaling increasing dread and nervousness) throughout the task, while those of the frontally damaged gamblers remain constant.

If the ability to *feel* appropriately has such a profound impact on a person's personality and successes, then you shouldn't be surprised to hear that scientists in the sometimes controversial field of *evolutionary psychology* have argued persuasively that emotions are adaptive, indeed critical, to an organism's survival. This goes even for those darker emotions we normally view as counterproductive, such as jealousy (Buss, 2000) and vengefulness (Cosmides & Tooby, 2000). Such emotions, although unpleasant, may help us to navigate dangers and respond to social threats that a completely dispassionate, cool-headed person might miss.

⚙ "Odd" Personality Disorders

The cluster of *"odd" personality disorders* consists of the *paranoid, schizoid,* and *schizotypal* personality disorders. People with these disorders typically display odd or eccentric behaviors that are similar to but not as extensive as those seen in schizophrenia, including extreme suspiciousness, social withdrawal, and peculiar ways of thinking and perceiving things. Such behaviors often leave the person isolated. Some clinicians believe that these personality disorders are actually related to schizophrenia, and they call them *schizophrenia-spectrum disorders.* In support of this idea, people with these personality disorders often qualify for an additional diagnosis of schizophrenia or have close relatives with schizophrenia (Bollini & Walker, 2007; APA, 2000).

Clinicians have learned much about the symptoms of the odd personality disorders but have not been so successful in determining their causes or how to treat them. In fact, people with these disorders rarely seek treatment (Mittal et al., 2007).

Paranoid Personality Disorder

People with **paranoid personality disorder** deeply distrust other people and are suspicious of their motives (APA, 2000). Because they believe that everyone intends them harm, they shun close relationships. Their trust in their own ideas and abilities can be excessive, though, as you can see in the case of Amaya:

She believed, without cause, that her neighbors were harassing her by allowing their young children to make loud noise outside her apartment door. Rather than asking the neighbors to be more considerate, she stopped speaking to them and began a campaign of unceasingly antagonistic behavior: giving them "dirty looks," pushing past them aggressively in the hallway, slamming doors, and behaving rudely toward their visitors. After over a year had passed, when the neighbors finally confronted her about her obnoxious behavior, she accused them of purposely harassing her. "Everyone knows that these doors are paper thin," she said, "and that I can hear everything that goes on in the hallway. You are doing it deliberately." Nothing that the neighbors said could convince her otherwise. Despite their attempts to be more considerate about the noise outside her apartment, she continued to behave in a rude and aggressive manner toward them.

Neighbors and visitors commented that [Amaya] appeared tense and angry. Her face looked like a hard mask. She was rarely seen smiling. She walked around the neighborhood wearing dark sunglasses, even on cloudy days. She was often seen yelling at her children, behavior that had earned her the nickname "the screamer" among the parents at her children's school. She had forced her children to change schools several times within the same district because she was dissatisfied with the education they were receiving. An unstated reason, perhaps, was that she had alienated so many other parents. [Amaya] worked at home during the day at a job that required her to have little contact with other people. She had few social contacts, and in conversation was often perceived to be sarcastic and hypercritical.

(Bernstein & Useda, 2007, p. 42)

Ever on guard and cautious and seeing threats everywhere, people like Amaya continually expect to be the targets of some trickery (see Figure 16-2). They find "hidden" meanings, which are usually belittling or threatening, in everything. In a study that required individuals to role-play, participants with paranoia were more likely than control participants to read hostile intentions into the actions of others. In addition, they more often chose anger as the appropriate role-play response (Turkat et al., 1990).

•**paranoid personality disorder**•A personality disorder marked by a pattern of distrust and suspiciousness of others.

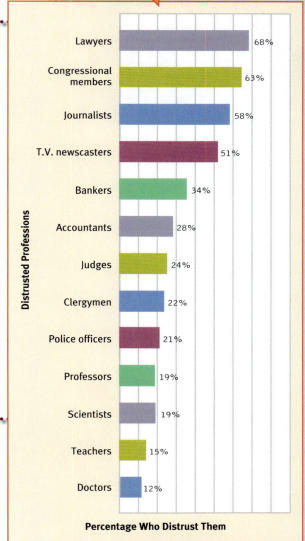

Figure 16-2

Whom do you distrust? Although distrust and suspiciousness are the hallmarks of paranoid personality disorder, even persons without this disorder are surprisingly untrusting. In a broad survey, the majority of respondents said they distrust lawyers, congressional members, journalists, and television newscasters (Harris Poll, 2006).

Distrusted Professions	Percentage Who Distrust Them
Lawyers	68%
Congressional members	63%
Journalists	58%
T.V. newscasters	51%
Bankers	34%
Accountants	28%
Judges	24%
Clergymen	22%
Police officers	21%
Professors	19%
Scientists	19%
Teachers	15%
Doctors	12%

Is hatred a disorder?
With the term "skinhead" tattooed on the back of his head, this man awaits trial in Germany for committing neo-Nazi crimes against foreigners and liberals. Clinicians regularly confront extreme racism, homophobia, and other forms of prejudice in their practices, particularly among clients with paranoid, antisocial, and certain other personality disorders. There is a small, but growing, movement in the clinical field to classify extreme hatred and prejudice as a psychological disorder (Vedantam, 2005).

BETWEEN THE LINES

Distrusting Souls

According to surveys, the people who tend to be the most distrustful in the United States are those who were warned repeatedly by their parents against trusting strangers. Other characteristics: they are socially isolated and report having no religious affiliation (Pew Research Center, 1997). «

Quick to challenge the loyalty or trustworthiness of acquaintances, people with paranoid personality disorder remain cold and distant. A woman might avoid confiding in anyone, for example, for fear of being hurt, or a husband might, without any justification, persist in questioning his wife's faithfulness. Although inaccurate and inappropriate, their suspicions are not usually *delusional;* the ideas are not so bizarre or so firmly held as to clearly remove the individuals from reality (Bernstein & Useda, 2007).

People with this disorder are critical of weakness and fault in others, particularly at work. They are unable to recognize their own mistakes, however, and are extremely sensitive to criticism. They often blame others for the things that go wrong in their lives, and they repeatedly bear grudges. Between 0.5 and 3 percent of adults are believed to experience this disorder, apparently more men than women (O'Connor, 2008; Mattia & Zimmerman, 2001).

How Do Theorists Explain Paranoid Personality Disorder?

The proposed explanations of paranoid personality disorder, like those of most other personality disorders, have received little systematic research (Bernstein & Useda, 2007). Psychodynamic theories, the oldest of the explanations for this disorder, trace the pattern to early interactions with demanding parents, particularly distant, rigid fathers and overcontrolling, rejecting mothers (Kernberg & Caligor, 2005; Sperry, 2003). (You will see that psychodynamic explanations for almost all the personality disorders begin the same way—with repeated mistreatment during childhood and lack of love.) According to one psychodynamic view, some individuals come to view their environment as hostile as a result of their parents' persistently unreasonable demands. They must always be on the alert because they cannot trust others, and they are likely to develop feelings of extreme anger. They also project these feelings onto others and, as a result, feel increasingly persecuted (Koenigsberg et al., 2001). Similarly, some cognitive theorists suggest that people with paranoid personality disorder generally hold broad maladaptive assumptions such as "People are evil" and "People will attack you if given the chance" (Beck et al., 2004, 2001).

Biological theorists propose that paranoid personality disorder has genetic causes (Bernstein & Useda, 2007; Jang & Vernon, 2001). One study that looked at self-reports of suspiciousness in 3,810 Australian twin pairs found that if one twin was excessively suspicious, the other had an increased likelihood of also being suspicious (Kendler et al., 1987). Once again, however, it is important to note that such similarities between twins might also be the result of common environmental experiences.

Treatments for Paranoid Personality Disorder People with paranoid personality disorder do not typically see themselves as needing help, and few come to treatment willingly (O'Connor, 2008). Furthermore, many who are in treatment view the role of patient as inferior and distrust and rebel against their therapists (Bender, 2005). Thus it is not surprising that therapy for this disorder, as for most other personality disorders, has limited effect and moves very slowly (Piper & Joyce, 2001).

Object relations therapists—the psychodynamic therapists who give center stage to relationships—try to see past the patient's anger and work on what they view as his or her deep wish for a satisfying relationship (Salvatore et al., 2005). Self-therapists—the psychodynamic clinicians who focus on the need for a healthy and unified self—try to help clients reestablish self-cohesion (a unified personality), which they believe has been lost in the person's continuing negative focus on others (Silverstein, 2007). Cognitive and behavioral techniques have also been applied in cases of paranoid personality disorder, often combined into an integrated cognitive-behavioral approach. On the behavioral side, therapists help the individuals to master anxiety-reduction techniques and to improve their skills at solving interpersonal problems. On the cognitive side, therapists guide the clients to develop more realistic interpretations of other people's words and actions and to become more aware of other people's points of view (Farmer & Nelson-Gray, 2005; Leahy, Beck, & Beck, 2005). Drug therapy seems to be of limited help (Agronin, 2006).

Schizoid Personality Disorder

People with **schizoid personality disorder** persistently avoid and are removed from social relationships and demonstrate little in the way of emotion (APA, 2000). Like people with paranoid personality disorder, these individuals do not have close ties with other people. The reason they avoid social contact, however, has nothing to do with paranoid feelings of distrust or suspicion; it is because they genuinely prefer to be alone. Take Roy:

> Roy was a successful sanitation engineer involved in the planning and maintenance of water resources for a large city; his job called for considerable foresight and independent judgment but little supervisory responsibility. In general, he was appraised as an undistinguished but competent and reliable employee. There were few demands of an interpersonal nature made of him, and he was viewed by most of his colleagues as reticent and shy and by others as cold and aloof.
>
> Difficulties centered about his relationship with his wife. At her urging they sought marital counseling for, as she put it, "he is unwilling to join in family activities, he fails to take an interest in the children, he lacks affection and is disinterested in sex."
>
> The pattern of social indifference, flatness of affect and personal isolation which characterized much of Roy's behavior was of little consequence to those with whom a deeper or more intimate relationship was not called for; with his immediate family, however, these traits took their toll.
>
> (Millon, 1969, p. 224)

People like Roy, often described as "loners," make no effort to start or keep friendships, take little interest in having sexual relationships, and even seem indifferent to their families. They seek out jobs that require little or no contact with others. When necessary, they can form work relations to a degree, but they prefer to keep to themselves. Many live by themselves as well. Not surprisingly, their social skills tend to be weak. If they marry, their lack of interest in intimacy may create marital or family problems, as it did for Roy.

People with schizoid personality disorder focus mainly on themselves and are generally unaffected by praise or criticism. They rarely show any feelings, expressing neither joy nor anger. They seem to have no need for attention or acceptance; are typically viewed as cold, humorless, or dull; and generally succeed in being ignored. This disorder is estimated to be present in fewer than 1 percent of the population (Mittal et al., 2007; Samuels et al., 2002). It is slightly more likely to occur in men than in women, and men may also be more impaired by it (APA, 2000).

How Do Theorists Explain Schizoid Personality Disorder?

Many psychodynamic theorists, particularly object relations theorists, propose that schizoid personality disorder has its roots in an unsatisfied need for human contact (Kernberg, 2005; Kernberg & Caligor, 2005). The parents of people with this disorder, like those of people with paranoid personality disorder, are believed to have been unaccepting or even abusive of their children. Whereas individuals with paranoid symptoms react to such parenting chiefly with distrust, those with schizoid personality disorder are left unable to give or receive love. They cope by avoiding all relationships (Sperry, 2003).

Cognitive theorists propose, not surprisingly, that people with schizoid personality disorder suffer from deficiencies in their thinking. Their thoughts tend to be vague and empty, and they have trouble scanning the environment to arrive at accurate perceptions.

•**schizoid personality disorder**•
A personality disorder characterized by persistent avoidance of social relationships and little expression of emotion.

MCT/Newscom

A darker knight
In this scene from the hugely popular 2008 movie *The Dark Knight*, Bruce Wayne confronts Batman, Wayne's alter-ego and only real friend. During the 1980s, writer-artist Frank Miller revolutionized the personality of the crime-fighter, presenting Batman as a singularly driven loner incapable of forming or sustaining relationships. Indeed, some clinical observers have argued that in key ways the current *Dark Knight* version of Batman displays the features of schizoid personality disorder.

•**schizotypal personality disorder**•
A personality disorder characterized by extreme discomfort in close relationships, odd forms of thinking and perceiving, and behavioral eccentricities.

Unable to pick up emotional cues from others, they simply cannot respond to emotions (Smith, 2006; Beck & Freeman, 1990). As this theory might predict, children with schizoid personality disorder develop language and motor skills very slowly, whatever their level of intelligence (Wolff, 2000, 1991).

Treatments for Schizoid Personality Disorder Their social withdrawal prevents most people with schizoid personality disorder from entering therapy unless some other disorder, such as alcoholism, makes treatment necessary (Mittal et al., 2007). These clients are likely to remain emotionally distant from the therapist, seem not to care about their treatment, and make limited progress at best (Millon, 1999).

Cognitive-behavioral therapists have sometimes been able to help people with this disorder experience more positive emotions and more satisfying social interactions (Farmer & Nelson-Gray, 2005; Beck et al., 2004). On the cognitive end, their techniques include presenting clients with lists of emotions to think about or having them write down and remember pleasurable experiences. On the behavioral end, therapists have sometimes had success teaching social skills to such clients, using role-playing, exposure techniques, and homework assignments as tools. Group therapy is apparently useful when it offers a safe setting for social contact, although people with this disorder may resist pressure to take part (Piper & Joyce, 2001). As with paranoid personality disorder, drug therapy seems to offer limited help (Koenigsberg et al., 2002).

Schizotypal Personality Disorder

People with **schizotypal personality disorder** display a range of interpersonal problems marked by extreme discomfort in close relationships, very odd patterns of thinking and perceiving, and behavioral eccentricities (APA, 2000). Anxious around others, they seek isolation and have few close friends. Many feel intensely lonely. The disorder is more severe than the paranoid and schizoid personality disorders, as we see in the case of Harold:

Harold was the fourth of seven children. . . . "Duckie," as Harold was known, had always been a withdrawn, frightened and "stupid" youngster. The nickname "Duckie" represented a peculiar waddle in his walk; it was used by others as a term of derogation and ridicule. Harold rarely played with his sibs or neighborhood children; he was teased unmercifully because of his "walk" and his fear of pranksters. Harold was a favorite neighborhood scapegoat; he was intimidated even by the most innocuous glance in his direction. . . .

Harold's family was surprised when he performed well in the first few years of schooling. He began to falter, however, upon entrance to junior high school. At about the age of 14, his schoolwork became extremely poor, he refused to go to classes and he complained of a variety of vague, physical pains. By age 15 he had totally withdrawn from school, remaining home in the basement room that he shared with two younger brothers. Everyone in his family began to speak of him as "being touched." He thought about "funny religious things that didn't make sense"; he also began to draw "strange things" and talk to himself. When he was 16, he once ran out of the house screaming "I'm gone, I'm gone, I'm gone . . . ," saying that his "body went to heaven" and that he had to run outside to recover it; rather interestingly, this event occurred shortly after his father had been committed by the courts to a state mental hospital. By age 17, Harold was ruminating all day, often talking aloud in a meaningless jargon; he refused to come to the family table for meals.

(Millon, 1969, pp. 347–348)

As with Harold, the thoughts and behaviors of people with schizotypal personality disorder can be noticeably disturbed. These symptoms may include *ideas of reference*—beliefs that unrelated events pertain to them in some important way—and *bodily illusions*, such as sensing an external "force" or presence. A number of people with this disorder see themselves as having special extrasensory abilities, and some believe that they have magical control over others. Examples of schizotypal eccentricities include repeatedly arranging cans to align their labels, organizing closets extensively, or wearing an odd assortment of clothing. The emotions of these individuals may be inappropriate, flat, or humorless.

People with schizotypal personality disorder often have great difficulty keeping their attention focused. Correspondingly, their conversation is typically digressive and vague, even sprinkled with loose associations (O'Connor, 2008). They tend to drift aimlessly and lead an idle, unproductive life (Skodol et al., 2002). They are likely to choose undemanding jobs in which they can work below their capacity and are not required to interact with other people. It has been estimated that 2 to 4 percent of all people—slightly more males than females—may have a schizotypal personality disorder (Bollini & Walker, 2007; Mattia & Zimmerman, 2001).

How Do Theorists Explain Schizotypal Personality Disorder?
Because the symptoms of schizotypal personality disorder so often resemble those of schizophrenia, researchers have hypothesized that similar factors are at work in both disorders (Koenigsberg et al., 2005). They have in fact found that schizotypal symptoms, like schizophrenic patterns, are often linked to family conflicts and to psychological disorders in parents (Millon & Grossman, 2007; Carlson & Fish, 2005; Asarnow et al., 1991). They have also learned that defects in attention and short-term memory may contribute to schizotypal personality disorder, just as they apparently do to schizophrenia (Bollini & Walker, 2007). For example, research participants with either disorder perform poorly on *backward masking,* a laboratory test of attention that requires individuals to identify a visual stimulus immediately after a previous stimulus has flashed on and off the screen. People with these disorders have a hard time shutting out the first stimulus in order to focus on the second. Finally, researchers have begun to link schizotypal personality disorder to some of the same biological factors found in schizophrenia, such as high activity of the neurotransmitter dopamine, enlarged brain ventricles, smaller temporal lobes, and loss of gray matter (Bollini & Walker, 2007; Coccaro, 2001; Downhill et al., 2001). As you read in Chapter 14, there are indications that these biological factors may have a genetic base.

Although these findings do suggest a close relationship between schizotypal personality disorder and schizophrenia, the personality disorder also has been linked to mood disorders. Over half of people with the personality disorder also suffer from major depressive disorder at some point in their lives (APA, 2000). Moreover, relatives of people with depression have a higher than usual rate of schizotypal personality disorder, and vice versa. Thus, at the very least, this personality disorder is not tied exclusively to schizophrenia.

Treatments for Schizotypal Personality Disorder
Therapy is as difficult in cases of schizotypal personality disorder as it is in cases of paranoid and schizoid personality disorders. Most therapists agree on the need to help these clients "reconnect" with the world and recognize the limits of their thinking and their powers. The therapists may thus try to set clear limits—for example, by requiring punctuality—and work on helping the clients recognize where their views end and those of the therapist begin (Stone, 1989). Other therapy goals are to increase positive social contacts, ease loneliness, reduce overstimulation, and help the individuals become more aware of their personal feelings (Sperry, 2003; Piper & Joyce, 2001).

Cognitive-behavioral therapists further combine cognitive and behavioral techniques to help people with schizotypal personality disorder function more effectively. Using cognitive interventions, they try to teach clients to evaluate their unusual thoughts or perceptions objectively and to ignore the inappropriate ones (Leahy et al., 2005; Beck et al., 2004). Therapists may keep track of clients' odd or magical predictions, for example, and later point out their inaccuracy. When clients are speaking and begin to digress, the therapists might ask them to sum up what they are trying to say. In addition, specific behavioral methods, such as speech lessons, social skills training, and

When personality disorders explode
In a rambling video, Seung-Hui Cho, a student at Virginia Tech, describes the slights he experienced throughout his life and his desire for violent revenge. After making this DVD and mailing it to NBC News, he proceeded, on April 16, 2007, to kill 32 people, including himself, and to wound 25 others in a campus shooting rampage. His disorder? Most clinical observers agree that he displayed a combination of features from the antisocial, borderline, paranoid, schizoid, schizotypal, and narcissistic personality disorders, including boundless fury and hatred, extreme social withdrawal, persistent distrust, strange thinking, intimidating behavior and arrogance, disregard for others, and violation of social boundaries.

Sipa Press/Newscom

tips on appropriate dress and manners, have sometimes helped clients learn to blend in better with and be more comfortable around others (Farmer & Nelson-Gray, 2005).

Antipsychotic drugs have been given to people with schizotypal personality disorder, again because of the disorder's similarity to schizophrenia (Bollini & Walker, 2007). In low doses the drugs appear to have helped some people, usually by reducing certain of their thought problems (Markovitz, 2004, 2001; Koenigsberg et al., 2003, 2002).

✿"Dramatic" Personality Disorders

The cluster of *"dramatic" personality disorders* includes the *antisocial, borderline, histrionic,* and *narcissistic* personality disorders. The behaviors of people with these problems are so dramatic, emotional, or erratic that it is almost impossible for them to have relationships that are truly giving and satisfying.

These personality disorders are more commonly diagnosed than the others. However, only the antisocial and borderline personality disorders have received much study, partly because they create so many problems for other people. The causes of the disorders, like those of the odd personality disorders, are not well understood. Treatments range from ineffective to moderately effective.

Antisocial Personality Disorder

Sometimes described as "psychopaths" or "sociopaths," people with **antisocial personality disorder** persistently disregard and violate others' rights (APA, 2000). Aside from substance-related disorders, this is the disorder most closely linked to adult criminal behavior. DSM-IV-TR stipulates that a person must be at least 18 years of age to receive this diagnosis; however, most people with antisocial personality disorder displayed some patterns of misbehavior before they were 15, including truancy, running away, cruelty to animals or people, and destroying property.

Robert Hare (1993), a leading researcher of antisocial personality disorder, recalls an early professional encounter with a prison inmate named Ray:

In the early 1960s, I found myself employed as the sole psychologist at the British Columbia Penitentiary. . . . I wasn't in my office for more than an hour when my first "client" arrived. He was a tall, slim, dark-haired man in his thirties. The air around him seemed to buzz, and the eye contact he made with me was so direct and intense that I wondered if I had ever really looked anybody in the eye before. That stare was unrelenting—he didn't indulge in the brief glances away that most people use to soften the force of their gaze.

Without waiting for an introduction, the inmate—I'll call him Ray—opened the conversation: "Hey, Doc, how's it going? Look, I've got a problem. I need your help. I'd really like to talk to you about this."

Eager to begin work as a genuine psychotherapist, I asked him to tell me about it. In response, he pulled out a knife and waved it in front of my nose, all the while smiling and maintaining that intense eye contact.

Once he determined that I wasn't going to push the button, he explained that he intended to use the knife not on me but on another inmate who had been making overtures to his "protégé," a prison term for the more passive member of a homosexual pairing. Just why he was telling me this was not immediately clear, but I soon suspected that he was checking me out, trying to determine what sort of a prison employee I was. Following our session, in which he described his "problem" not once or twice but many times, I kept quiet about the knife. To my relief, he didn't stab the other inmate, but it soon became evident that Ray had caught me in his trap: I had shown myself to be a soft touch who would overlook clear violations of fundamental prison rules in order to develop "professional" rapport with the inmates.

•antisocial personality disorder•
A personality disorder marked by a general pattern of disregard for and violation of other people's rights.

From that first meeting on, Ray managed to make my eight-month stint at the prison miserable. His constant demands on my time and his attempts to manipulate me into doing things for him were unending. On one occasion, he convinced me that he would make a good cook . . . and I supported his request for a transfer from the machine shop (where he had apparently made the knife). What I didn't consider was that the kitchen was a source of sugar, potatoes, fruit, and other ingredients that could be turned into alcohol. Several months after I had recommended the transfer, there was a mighty eruption below the floorboards directly under the warden's table. When the commotion died down, we found an elaborate system for distilling alcohol below the floor. Something had gone wrong and one of the pots had exploded. There was nothing unusual about the presence of a still in a maximum-security prison, but the audacity of placing one under the warden's seat shook up a lot of people. When it was discovered that Ray was the brains behind the bootleg operation, he spent some time in solitary confinement.

Once out of "the hole," Ray appeared in my office as if nothing had happened and asked for a transfer from the kitchen to the auto shop—he really felt he had a knack, he saw the need to prepare himself for the outside world, if he only had the time to practice he could have his own body shop on the outside. . . . I was still feeling the sting of having arranged the first transfer, but eventually he wore me down.

Soon afterward I decided to leave the prison to pursue a Ph.D. in psychology, and about a month before I left Ray almost persuaded me to ask my father, a roofing contractor, to offer him a job as part of an application for parole.

Ray had an incredible ability to con not just me but everybody. He could talk, and lie, with a smoothness and a directness that sometimes momentarily disarmed even the most experienced and cynical of the prison staff. When I met him he had a long criminal record behind him (and, as it turned out, ahead of him); about half his adult life had been spent in prison, and many of his crimes had been violent. . . . He lied endlessly, lazily, about everything, and it disturbed him not a whit whenever I pointed out something in his file that contradicted one of his lies. He would simply change the subject and spin off in a different direction. Finally convinced that he might not make the perfect job candidate in my father's firm, I turned down Ray's request—and was shaken by his nastiness at my refusal.

Before I left the prison for the university, I took advantage of the prison policy of letting staff have their cars repaired in the institution's auto shop—where Ray still worked, thanks (he would have said no thanks) to me. The car received a beautiful paint job and the motor and drivetrain were reconditioned.

With all our possessions on top of the car and our baby in a plywood bed in the backseat, my wife and I headed for Ontario. The first problems appeared soon after we left Vancouver, when the motor seemed a bit rough. Later, when we encountered some moderate inclines, the radiator boiled over. A garage mechanic discovered ball bearings in the carburetor's float chamber; he also pointed out where one of the hoses to the radiator had clearly been tampered with. These problems were repaired easily enough, but the next one, which arose while we were going down a long hill, was more serious. The brake pedal became very spongy and then simply dropped to the floor—no brakes, and it was a long hill. Fortunately, we made it to a service station, where we found that the brake line had been cut so that a slow leak would occur. Perhaps it was a coincidence that Ray was working in the auto shop when the car was being tuned up, but I had no doubt that the prison "telegraph" had informed him of the owner of the car.

(Hare, 1993)

Like Ray, people with antisocial personality disorder lie repeatedly (Patrick, 2007). Many cannot work consistently at a job; they are absent frequently and are likely to quit their jobs altogether. Usually they are also careless with money and frequently fail to pay their debts. They are often impulsive, taking action without thinking of the consequences (Blair, Mitchell, & Blair, 2005) (see *A Closer Look* on the next page). Correspondingly, they may be irritable, aggressive, and quick to start fights. Many travel from place to place.

Gambling and Other Impulse Problems

Impulsivity is a symptom of many psychological disorders, including the antisocial and borderline personality disorders. DSM-IV-TR also lists several disorders of which impulsivity, rather than personality, is the *main* feature. People with these *impulse-control disorders* fail to resist an impulse, drive, or temptation to perform acts that are harmful to themselves or others (APA, 2000). Usually they experience growing tension before the act and relief when they give in to the impulse. Some, but not all, feel regret or guilt afterward. Around 9 percent of adults display an impulse-control disorder in a given year (Kessler et al., 2006, 2005). The impulse-control disorders include pyromania, kleptomania, intermittent explosive disorder, trichotillomania, and pathological gambling.

- *Pyromania* is the deliberate and repeated setting of fires to achieve intense pleasure or relief from tension. It is different from *arson,* the setting of fires for revenge or financial gain.
- *Kleptomania* is a recurrent failure to resist the impulse to steal. People with this disorder often have more than enough money to pay for the things they steal.
- Individuals with *intermittent explosive disorder* have periodic aggressive outbursts in which they may seriously attack people and destroy property. Their explosiveness far exceeds any provocation.
- People with *trichotillomania* repeatedly pluck hair from various parts of their bodies, particularly the scalp, eyebrows, and eyelashes.

- The most common of the impulse-control disorders is *pathological gambling,* persistent and repeated gambling behavior that disrupts one's life at home or at work (APA, 2000).

It is estimated that as many as 2.3 percent of adults and 3 to 8 percent of teenagers and college students suffer from pathological gambling (Griffiths, 2006; APA, 2000). Clinicians are careful, however, to distinguish between pathological and social gambling (Kaminer et al., 2002). Pathological gambling is defined less by the amount of time or money spent in gambling than by the addictive and impulsive nature of the behavior (Petry, 2005, 2001). People with this disorder cannot walk away from a bet and are restless and irritable if gambling is denied them. Repeated losses of money lead to more gambling in an effort to win the money back, and the gambling continues even in the face of financial, social, and health problems (Griffiths, 2006).

A great deal of attention has been directed in recent years toward the treatment of pathological gambling. Treatments that combine cognitive, behavioral, biological, and yet other approaches and that help build coping skills tend to be the most effective (Black et al., 2008, 2007; Weinstein, 2007). People who join self-help support groups, such as *Gamblers Anonymous,* a network patterned after Alcoholics

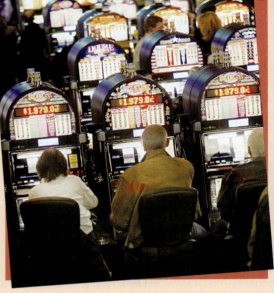

Anonymous, seem to have a higher recovery rate, perhaps in part because they have admitted that they have a problem and are seeking to conquer it.

Journalists and others have sometimes asked whether the "medicalization" of gambling has the effect of somehow excusing a pattern of irresponsible, sometimes illegal, behavior (Castellani, 2000). However, several studies suggest that pathological gambling and other impulse-control disorders are complex problems that often involve a variety of causes, including biochemical ones (Petry, 2005; Szegedy-Maszak, 2005).

Recklessness is another common trait: people with antisocial personality disorder have little regard for their own safety or for that of others, even their children. They are self-centered as well, and are likely to have trouble maintaining close relationships. Usually they develop a knack for gaining personal profit at the expense of other people. Because the pain or damage they cause seldom concerns them, clinicians commonly say that they lack a moral conscience (Kantor, 2006). They think of their victims as weak and deserving of being conned, robbed, or even physically harmed (see Table 16–2).

Surveys indicate that 2 to 3.5 percent of people in the United States meet the criteria for antisocial personality disorder (O'Connor, 2008; Mattia & Zimmerman, 2001). The disorder is as much as four times more common among men than women (Patrick, 2007).

Because people with this disorder are often arrested, researchers frequently look for people with antisocial patterns in prison populations (Hare, 2003; Blair et al., 2005). In fact, it is estimated that around 30 percent of people in prison meet the diagnostic criteria for this disorder (O'Connor, 2008). Among men in urban jails, the antisocial personality pattern has been linked strongly to past arrests for crimes of violence (De Matteo et al., 2005; Abram & Teplin, 1990). For many people with this disorder, criminal behavior declines after the age of 40; some, however, continue their criminal activities throughout their lives (Hurt & Oltmanns, 2002).

Studies and clinical observations also indicate higher rates of alcoholism and other substance-related disorders among people with antisocial personality disorder than in the rest of the population (Patrick, 2007; Westermeyer & Thuras, 2005). Perhaps intoxication and substance abuse help trigger the development of antisocial personality disorder by loosening a person's inhibitions. Perhaps this personality disorder somehow makes a person more prone to abuse substances. Or perhaps antisocial personality disorder and substance abuse both have the same cause, such as a deep-seated need to take risks. Interestingly, drug users with the personality disorder often cite the recreational aspects of drug use as their reason for starting and continuing it (Mirin & Weiss, 1991).

Finally, children with conduct disorder and an accompanying attention-deficit/hyperactivity disorder may have a heightened risk of developing antisocial personality disorder (Lahey et al., 2005; APA, 2000). These two childhood disorders, which you will read about in Chapter 17, often bear similarities to antisocial personality disorder. Like adults with antisocial personality disorder, children with a conduct disorder persistently lie and violate rules and other people's rights, and children with attention-deficit/hyperactivity disorder lack foresight and judgment and fail to learn from experience. Intriguing as these observations may be, however, the precise connection between the childhood disorders and the personality disorder has been difficult to pinpoint.

How Do Theorists Explain Antisocial Personality Disorder?

Explanations of antisocial personality disorder come from the psychodynamic, behavioral, cognitive, and biological models. As with many other personality disorders, psychodynamic theorists propose that this one, too, begins with an absence of parental love during infancy, leading to a lack of basic trust (Sperry, 2003). In this view, some children—the ones who develop antisocial personality disorder—respond to the early inadequacies by becoming emotionally distant, and they bond with others through the use of power and destructiveness. In support of the psychodynamic explanation, researchers have found that people with this disorder are more likely than others to have had significant stress in their childhoods, particularly in such forms as family poverty, family violence, and parental conflict or divorce (Martens, 2005; Paris, 2001).

Many behavioral theorists have suggested that antisocial symptoms may be learned through *modeling,* or imitation (Gaynor & Baird, 2007). As evidence, they point to the higher rate of antisocial personality disorder found among the parents of people with this disorder (Paris, 2001). Other behaviorists have suggested that some parents unintentionally teach antisocial behavior by regularly rewarding a child's aggressive behavior (Kazdin, 2005). When the child misbehaves or becomes violent in reaction to the parents' requests or orders, for example, the parents may give in to restore peace. Without meaning to, they may be teaching the child to be stubborn and perhaps even violent.

table: 16-2

Hate Crimes in the United States, 2006

Group Attacked	Number of Reported Incidents
Racial/ethnic group	
• Anti-White	890
• Anti-African American	2,640
• Anti-Native American	60
• Anti-Hispanic American	576
• Anti-Asian American	181
• Anti-Other racial/ethnic group	637
All racial/ethnic groups	**4,984**
Religious group	
• Anti-Jewish	967
• Anti-Catholic	76
• Anti-Protestant	59
• Anti-Islamic	156
• Anti-Other religious group	204
All religious groups	**1,462**
Sexual orientation group	
• Anti-Homosexual	1,148
• Anti-Heterosexual	26
• Anti-Bisexual	21
All sexual orientation groups	**1,195**
Group with disability	
• Anti-Physically disabled	17
• Anti-Mentally disabled	62
All groups with disability	**79**

Source: Infoplease, 2006; FBI, Uniform Crime Reports, 2004.

Negative models Behavioral theorists claim that aggressive and other antisocial behaviors may be learned through modeling, or imitation—a learning process that can begin very early in life. The heightened rate of such behaviors found among the parents of people with antisocial personality disorder is consistent with this claim.

The cognitive view says that people with antisocial personality disorder hold attitudes that trivialize the importance of other people's needs (Elwood et al., 2004; Levenson, 1992). Such a philosophy of life, some theorists suggest, may be far more common in our society than people recognize (see Figure 16-3). Cognitive theorists further propose that people with this disorder have genuine difficulty recognizing a point of view other than their own.

Finally, studies suggest that biological factors may play an important role in antisocial personality disorder. Researchers have found that antisocial people, particularly those who are highly impulsive and aggressive, display lower serotonin activity than other individuals (Patrick, 2007). As you'll recall (see page 325), both impulsivity and aggression also have been linked to low serotonin activity in other kinds of studies, so the presence of this biological factor in people with antisocial personality disorder is not surprising.

Other studies further indicate that individuals with this disorder display deficient functioning in their frontal lobes (Morgan & Lilienfeld, 2000). Among other duties, the frontal lobes help individuals to plan and execute realistic strategies and to experience personal characteristics such as sympathy, judgment, and empathy (Lambert & Kinsley, 2005). These are, of course, all qualities found wanting in people with antisocial personality disorder.

In yet another line of research, investigators have found that individuals with this disorder often experience less anxiety than other people, and so lack a key ingredient for learning (Blair et al., 2005). This would help explain why they have so much trouble learning from negative life experiences or tuning in to the emotional cues of others. Why should individuals with antisocial personality disorder experience less anxiety than other people? The answer may lie once again in the biological realm (Kumari et al., 2005; Retz et al., 2004). Research participants with the disorder often respond to warnings or expectations of stress with low brain and bodily arousal, such as slow autonomic arousal and slow EEG waves (Gaynor & Baird, 2007; Lindberg et al., 2005). Perhaps because of the low arousal, the individuals easily tune out threatening or emotional situations, and so are unaffected by them.

It could also be argued that because of their physical underarousal, people with antisocial personality disorder would be more likely than other people to take risks and seek thrills. That is, they may be drawn to antisocial activity precisely because it meets an underlying biological need for more excitement and arousal. In support of this idea, as you read earlier, antisocial personality disorder often goes hand in hand with sensation-seeking behavior (Patrick, 2007).

Mixed verdict Crime boss Tony Soprano of *The Sopranos* displays many symptoms of antisocial personality disorder, including his persistent disregard for and violation of others' rights, incessant lying, self-centeredness, and lack of conscience after cheating, robbing, or even killing other people. Nevertheless, clinicians point out that this character also possesses several qualities uncharacteristic of the disorder, such as genuine love and concern for his children and friends, bouts of overwhelming anxiety, and a capacity to persevere in and profit from long-term therapy.

Treatments for Antisocial Personality Disorder Treatments for people with antisocial personality disorder are typically ineffective (Hilarski, 2007; Reid & Gacono, 2000). A major obstacle to treatment is the individuals' lack of conscience or desire to change (Kantor, 2006). Most of those in therapy have been forced to participate by an employer, their school, or the law, or they come to the attention of therapists when they also develop another psychological disorder (Agronin, 2006).

Some cognitive therapists try to guide clients with antisocial personality disorder to think about moral issues and about the needs of other people (Leahy et al., 2005; Beck et al., 2004). In a similar vein, a number of hospitals and prisons have tried to create a therapeutic community for people with this disorder, a structured environment that teaches responsibility toward others (Harris & Rice, 2006; Piper & Joyce, 2001). Some patients seem to profit from such approaches, but it appears that most do not. In recent years, clinicians have also used psychotropic medications, particularly atypical antipsychotic drugs, to treat people with antisocial personality disorder. Some report that these drugs help reduce certain features of the disorder, but systematic studies of this claim are still needed (Markovitz, 2004).

Borderline Personality Disorder

People with **borderline personality disorder** display great instability, including major shifts in mood, an unstable self-image, and impulsivity. These characteristics combine to make their relationships very unstable as well (Paris, 2005; APA, 2000). Some of Ellen Farber's difficulties are typical:

Ellen Farber, a 35-year-old, single insurance company executive, came to a psychiatric emergency room of a university hospital with complaints of depression and the thought of driving her car off a cliff. An articulate, moderately overweight, sophisticated woman, Ms. Farber appeared to be in considerable distress. She reported a 6-month period of increasingly persistent dysphoria and lack of energy and pleasure. Feeling as if she were "made of lead," Ms. Farber had recently been spending 15–20 hours a day in her bed. She also reported daily episodes of binge eating, when she would consume "anything I can find," including entire chocolate cakes or boxes of cookies. She reported problems with intermittent binge eating since adolescence, but these had recently increased in frequency, resulting in a 20-pound weight gain over the last few months. In the past her weight had often varied greatly as she had gone on and off a variety of diets. . . .

She attributed her increasing symptoms to financial difficulties. Ms. Farber had been fired from her job two weeks before coming to the emergency room. She claimed it was because she "owed a small amount of money." When asked to be more specific, she reported owing $150,000 to her former employers and another $100,000 to various local banks. Further questions revealed that she had always had difficulty managing her money and had been forced to declare bankruptcy at age 27. From age 30 to age 33, she had used her employer's credit cards to finance weekly "buying binges," accumulating the $150,000 debt. She . . . reported that spending money alleviated her chronic feelings of loneliness, isolation, and sadness. Experiencing only temporary relief, every few days she would impulsively buy expensive jewelry, watches, or multiple pairs of the same shoes. . . .

In addition to lifelong feelings of emptiness, Ms. Farber described chronic uncertainty about what she wanted to do in life and with whom she wanted to be friends. She had many brief, intense relationships with both men and women, but her quick temper led

Figure 16-3
Are some cultures more antisocial than others? In a cross-cultural study, teenagers were asked to write stories describing how imaginary characters would respond to various conflicts. About one-third of the respondents from New Zealand, Australia, Northern Ireland, and the United States described violent responses, compared to less than one-fifth of the subjects from Korea, Sweden, and Mexico. (Adapted from Archer & McDaniel, 1995.)

•**borderline personality disorder**•
A personality disorder characterized by repeated instability in interpersonal relationships, self-image, and mood and by impulsive behavior.

to frequent arguments and even physical fights. Although she had always thought of her childhood as happy and carefree, when she became depressed, she began to recall [being abused verbally and physically by her mother].

(Spitzer et al., 1994, pp. 395–397)

Like Ellen Farber, people with borderline personality disorder swing in and out of very depressive, anxious, and irritable states that last anywhere from a few hours to a few days or more (see Table 16-3). Their emotions seem to be always in conflict with the world around them. They are prone to bouts of anger, which sometimes result in physical aggression and violence. Just as often, however, they direct their impulsive anger inward and inflict bodily harm on themselves. Many seem troubled by deep feelings of emptiness.

Borderline personality disorder is a complex disorder, and it is fast becoming one of the more common conditions seen in clinical practice. Many of the patients who come to mental health emergency rooms are individuals with this disorder who have intentionally hurt themselves. Their impulsive, self-destructive activities may range from alcohol and substance abuse to delinquency, unsafe sex, and reckless driving (Sherry & Whilde, 2008; Trull et al., 2003, 2000). Many engage in so-called self-injurious or self-mutilation behaviors, such as cutting or burning themselves or banging their heads (Conklin & Westen, 2005). Although these behaviors typically cause immense physical suffering, those with borderline personality disorder often feel as if the physical discomfort offers relief from their emotional suffering. It may serve as a distraction from their emotional or interpersonal upsets, "snapping" them out of an "emotional overload" (Stanley & Brodsky, 2005). Scars and bruises may also provide the individuals with a kind of documentation or concrete evidence of their emotional distress (Plante, 2006;

table: 16-3

Comparison of Personality Disorders

	DSM-IV Cluster	Similar Disorders on Axis I	Responsiveness to Treatment
Paranoid	Odd	Schizophrenia; delusional disorder	Modest
Schizoid	Odd	Schizophrenia; delusional disorder	Modest
Schizotypal	Odd	Schizophrenia; delusional disorder	Modest
Antisocial	Dramatic	Conduct disorder	Poor
Borderline	Dramatic	Mood disorders	Moderate
Histrionic	Dramatic	Somatoform disorders; mood disorders	Modest
Narcissistic	Dramatic	Cyclothymic disorder (mild bipolar disorder)	Poor
Avoidant	Anxious	Social phobia	Moderate
Dependent	Anxious	Separation anxiety disorder; dysthymic disorder (mild depressive disorder)	Moderate
Obsessive-compulsive	Anxious	Obsessive-compulsive anxiety disorder	Moderate

Paris, 2005). Finally, like Ellen Farber, many people with borderline personality disorder try to hurt themselves as a way of dealing with their chronic feelings of emptiness, boredom, and identity confusion (see *The Media Speaks* on pages 526–527).

Suicidal threats and actions are also common. Studies suggest that around 75 percent of people with borderline personality disorder attempt suicide at least once in their lives; as many as 10 percent actually commit suicide (Sherry & Whilde, 2008; Soloff et al., 2005). The rate of suicide among individuals with the disorder may be as much as 50 times higher than the rate found in the general population. Not surprisingly, it is also common for people with this disorder to enter clinical treatment by way of the emergency room after a suicide attempt (Lambert, 2003).

People with borderline personality disorder frequently form intense, conflict-ridden relationships in which their feelings are not necessarily shared by the other person. They may come to idealize another person's qualities and abilities after just a brief first encounter. They also may violate the boundaries of relationships (Skodol et al., 2002). Thinking in dichotomous (black-and-white) terms, they quickly become furious when their expectations are not met; yet they remain very attached to the relationships (Bender et al., 2001). In fact, people with this disorder have recurrent fears of impending abandonment and frequently engage in frantic efforts to avoid real or imagined separations from important people in their lives (Sherry & Whilde, 2008). Sometimes they cut themselves or carry out other self-destructive acts to prevent partners from leaving.

Sufferers of borderline personality disorder typically experience dramatic shifts in their identity. An unstable sense of self may produce rapid shifts in goals, aspirations, friends, and even sexual orientation (Skodol, 2005). The individuals may also experience an occasional sense of dissociation, or detachment, from their own thoughts or bodies. Indeed, at times they may experience no sense of themselves at all, leading to the feelings of emptiness described earlier (Linehan, Cochran, & Kehrer, 2001).

Between 1 and 2.5 percent of the general population are thought to suffer from borderline personality disorder (Sherry & Whilde, 2008; Arntz, 2005). Close to 75 percent of the patients who receive the diagnosis are women. The course of the disorder varies from person to person. In the most common pattern, the individual's instability and risk of suicide peak during young adulthood and then gradually wane with advancing age (Hurt & Oltmanns, 2002; APA, 2000). Males with borderline personality disorder may display more aggressive, disruptive, and antisocial behaviors than females (Bradley et al., 2005). Given the chaotic and unstable relationships characteristic of borderline personality disorder, it is not surprising that this disorder tends to interfere with job performance more than most other personality disorders do (Zanarini et al., 2005).

How Do Theorists Explain Borderline Personality Disorder?
Because a fear of abandonment tortures so many people with borderline personality disorder, psychodynamic theorists have looked once again to early parental relationships to explain the disorder (Gunderson, 2001, 1996). Object relations theorists, for example, propose that an early lack of acceptance by parents may lead to a loss of self-esteem, increased dependence, and an inability to cope with separation (Sherry & Whilde, 2008; Kernberg & Caligor, 2005).

Research has found that the early childhoods of people with the disorder are often consistent with this view. In many cases, the parents of such individuals neglected or rejected them, verbally abused them, or otherwise behaved inappropriately (Bradley et al., 2005; Guttman, 2002). Similarly, their childhoods were often marked by multiple parent substitutes, divorce, death, or traumas such as physical or sexual abuse (Sansone et al., 2005; Yen et al., 2002). Indeed, research suggests that early sexual abuse is a common contributor to the development of borderline personality disorder (Bradley et al., 2005); children who experience such abuse are four times more likely to develop the

Suzanne Tenner/Columbia Tristar/The Kobal Collection

Personality disorders— at the movies
In this scene from the 1999 film *Girl, Interrupted*, based on a best-selling memoir, Susanna Kaysen (left, played by actress Winona Ryder) is befriended by Lisa Rowe (played by Angelina Jolie) at a psychiatric hospital. Kaysen, who had recently made a suicide attempt, received a diagnosis of borderline personality disorder at the hospital, while Rowe's diagnosis was antisocial personality disorder. However, Rowe's rages, dramatic mood shifts, impulsivity, and other symptoms were actually more characteristic of a borderline picture than were Kaysen's.

BETWEEN THE LINES

In Their Words

"Anger is a brief lunacy." ‹‹
Horace, Roman poet

Finally, some sociocultural theorists suggest that cases of borderline personality disorder are particularly likely to emerge in cultures that change rapidly. As a culture loses its stability, they argue, it inevitably leaves many of its members with problems of identity, a sense of emptiness, high anxiety, and fears of abandonment (Paris, 1991). Family units may come apart, leaving people with little sense of belonging. Changes of this kind in society today may explain growing reports of the disorder.

Treatments for Borderline Personality Disorder It appears that psychotherapy can eventually lead to some degree of improvement for people with borderline personality disorder (Sperry, 2003; Gunderson, 2001). It is, however, extraordinarily difficult for a therapist to strike a balance between empathizing with the borderline client's dependency and anger and challenging his or her way of thinking (Sherry & Whilde, 2008; Goin, 2001). Given the emotionally draining demands of clients with borderline personality disorder, some therapists refuse to treat such individuals. The wildly fluctuating interpersonal attitudes of clients with the disorder can also make it difficult for therapists to establish collaborative and productive working relationships with them (Bender & Oldham, 2005). Moreover, such clients may violate the boundaries of the client–therapist relationship (for example, calling the therapist's emergency contact number to discuss matters of a less urgent nature) (Gutheil, 2005).

Traditional psychoanalysis has not been effective with these individuals (Bender & Oldham, 2005). The clients often experience the psychoanalytic therapist's reserved style and encouragement of free association as suggesting disinterest and abandonment. The clients may also have difficulties tolerating interpretations made by psychoanalytic therapists, experiencing them as attacks.

Contemporary psychodynamic approaches, such as *relational psychoanalytic therapy* (see page 62), in which therapists take a more supportive and egalitarian posture, have proved to be more effective than traditional psychoanalytic approaches (Bender & Oldham, 2005). In such contemporary approaches, therapists work to provide an empathic setting within which borderline clients can explore their unconscious conflicts and pay particular attention to their central relationship disturbance, poor sense of self, and pervasive loneliness and emptiness (Gabbard, 2001; Piper & Joyce, 2001). Research has found that contemporary psychodynamic approaches sometimes help reduce suicide attempts, self-harm behaviors, and the number of hospitalizations and bring at least some improvement to individuals with the disorder (Bradley et al., 2007; Roth & Fonagy, 2005; Clarkin et al., 2001).

Over the past two decades, an integrative treatment for borderline personality disorder, called *dialectical behavior therapy* (*DBT*), has received growing research support and is now considered the treatment of choice in many clinical circles (Linehan & Dexter-Mazza, 2008; Linehan et al., 2006, 2002, 2001; Linehan, 1993, 1992). DBT grows largely from the cognitive-behavioral treatment model and, as such, includes a number of the same cognitive and behavioral techniques that are applied to other disorders: homework assignments, psychoeducation, the teaching of social and other skills, therapist modeling, clear goal setting, ongoing assessment of the client's behaviors and treatment progress, and collaborative examinations by client and therapist of the client's ways of thinking (Sherry & Whilde, 2008). In addition, DBT borrows heavily from humanistic and contemporary psychodynamic approaches, placing the client–therapist relationship itself at the center of treatment interactions, making sure that appropriate treatment boundaries are adhered to, and, at the same time, providing acceptance and validation of the client. Indeed, DBT therapists regularly empathize with their borderline clients and with the emotional turmoil they are experiencing, locate kernels of truth in the clients' complaints or demands, and examine alternative ways for them to address valid needs. Frequently, DBT is supplemented by the clients' participation in social skill-building groups where they can practice new ways of relating to other persons in a safe environment and at the same time receive validation and support from other group members.

DBT has received more research support than any other treatment for borderline personality disorder (Linehan & Dexter-Mazza, 2008; Linehan et al., 2006, 2002, 2001;

Lieb et al., 2004). Many clients who receive this treatment come to display an increased ability to tolerate stress; develop new, more appropriate, social skills; and respond more effectively to life situations. Such individuals also display significantly fewer suicidal behaviors and require fewer hospitalizations than those who receive other forms of treatment. Finally, DBT clients are more likely to remain in this form of treatment and to report less anger, greater social gratification, improved work performance, and reductions in substance abuse.

Finally, antidepressant, antibipolar, antianxiety, and antipsychotic drugs have helped calm the emotional and aggressive storms of some people with borderline personality disorder (Agronin, 2006; Gruettert & Friege, 2005). However, given the numerous suicide attempts by individuals with this disorder, the use of drugs on an outpatient basis is controversial. Additionally, clients with the disorder have been known to adjust or discontinue their medication dosages without consulting their clinicians. Today, many professionals believe that psychotropic drug treatment for borderline personality disorder should be used largely as an adjunct to psychotherapy approaches, and indeed many clients seem to benefit from a combination of psychotherapy and drug therapy (Soloff, 2005; Livesley, 2000).

Histrionic Personality Disorder

People with **histrionic personality disorder,** once called **hysterical personality disorder,** are extremely emotional—they are typically described as "emotionally charged"—and continually seek to be the center of attention (APA, 2000). Their exaggerated moods can complicate life considerably, as we see in the case of Hilde:

Hilde is a 42-year-old homemaker who [had] . . . a combination of complaints, including headaches, mild depression, and marital difficulties. . . . Hilde, still quite attractive, obviously spent a great deal of time on her personal appearance. She was cooperative in the initial interview with the psychiatrist, though at times rambled so much that he had to bring her back to the subject at hand. As she talked, it became apparent that she had not really reflected in any depth on the issues that she discussed and was only pumping out information, much as a computer would. She showed a significant amount of [emotion] during the interview, but it was often exaggerated in response to the content she was discussing at the time. She delighted in giving extensive historical descriptions of her past life. . . .

In fact, many of the descriptions she gave appeared to be more for the purpose of impressing the therapist than in order to come to grips with her problems. When confronted with any irrelevancies in her stories, she first adopted a cute and charming manner, and if this proved ineffective in persuading the psychiatrist to change topics, she then became petulant and irritated.

When she described her present difficulties, she was always inclined to ascribe the responsibility to some person or situation other than herself. She stated that her husband was indifferent to her. . . . This situation, along with a "lot of stress in my life" were given as the reason for [her] headaches and depression. When pressed for more details, she found it hard to describe interactions with her husband in any meaningful detail.

A parallel interview with her husband revealed that he felt he "had simply become tired of dealing with her." He admitted that his original attraction to Hilde was for her social status, her "liveliness," and her physical attractiveness. Over the years, it became clear that her liveliness was not the exuberance and love of life of an integrated personality, but simply a chronic flamboyance and intensity that was often misplaced. Her physical attractiveness was naturally declining, and she was spending inordinate amounts of time and money attempting to keep it up. . . . [He] had . . . grown tired of her childish and superficial manner. . . .

Hilde was raised as a prized child of a moderately wealthy family. Her father owned a successful [business]. Her mother was active socially, joining virtually every socially

•**histrionic personality disorder**•
A personality disorder characterized by a pattern of excessive emotionality and attention seeking. Once called *hysterical personality disorder.*

Lying: "Oh What a Tangled Web . . . "

A college student fakes her own kidnapping, triggering a massive manhunt to locate her.

A 59-year-old great-grandmother falsely claims to the national news media that she is pregnant with twins.

A woman disappears shortly before her wedding, setting off a three-day nationwide search, then calls home from across the country with the false claim that she had been kidnapped and sexually assaulted.

In a critically acclaimed memoir, an author writes about growing up as a half-white, half-Native American foster child in South Central Los Angeles, running drugs for gang members. It was later discovered that she had been born to and raised by an all-white family in a wealthy area of Los Angeles.

After emerging from a very troubled adolescence as a transgendered, abused, homeless drug addict and male prostitute, a young male writer achieves enormous literary success and a cult-like following. However, the writer turns out to be a 40-year-old woman who had made up this entire persona.

A 71-year-old woman reveals as false a best-selling memoir that describes her early years as a Jewish child wandering through Europe during the Holocaust in search of her deported parents.

These are among the more famous examples of lying that have surfaced almost daily on the Internet and in the media. As each such fabrication has been revealed, people scratch their heads and ask, "What was he thinking?" or "What's wrong with her?" The answers to those questions remain elusive.

Psychologists have offered various theories about why people lie, but research has produced limited insight into this subject (Dike et al., 2005; Grubin, 2005). In fact, lying—even *extreme* or *compulsive lying*—is not, by itself, considered a psychological disorder, although it is sometimes characteristic of people with antisocial, borderline, histrionic, or narcissistic personality disorders.

Let's take a brief look at what the field of psychology knows about lying. First, researchers have determined that most people lie some of the time. Almost everyone has been in a situation when lying seems preferable to telling the truth (Ennis et al., 2008). Sometimes these lies are told to protect another person from being hurt by the truth (such as when you tell a friend his or her new haircut looks great even if it doesn't). This is often referred to as an "altruistic" or "white" lie since it is not told for self-serving reasons (Whitty & Carville, 2008).

Altruistic lies can be distinguished from "defensive" lies, self-serving lies that people offer to save face or avoid getting into trouble (such as telling your professor that the computer wouldn't print your paper when in fact you hadn't finished writing it). It is worth noting that people are more likely to tell defensive lies in some situations than in others. E-mail lying is, for example, more likely than phone call lying, and both are more likely than face-to-face lying (Whitty & Carville, 2008).

Although most people have told white or defensive lies when confronted with an uncomfortable situation, few can be classified as "pathological" liars. Pathological liars do not lie to protect themselves or others; rather, their lies have no situational gain. Pathological lies tend to be compulsive or fantastic in nature and can often be refuted easily by others (Dike et al., 2006, 2005; Ford et al., 1988; Selling, 1942).

Various explanations have been offered for why people lie. Psychodynamic theorists view lying as an important and normal mechanism by which young children and adolescents can separate themselves from their parents and become autonomous beings (Tosone, 2006; Kohut, 1966).

Behaviorists claim that people learn to lie by being exposed to others (for example, parents) who lie. The more often people hear those around them lie, the more likely they are to tell their own lies. Parental reactions to a child's lies can also influence his or her future propensity to lie (Crossman & Lewis, 2006).

Sociocultural theorists suggest that one's culture can also have a large effect on one's attitudes toward lying. According to this theory, lying is more acceptable in some cultures than in others. One study of college students, for example, found that white American students rated lies as more acceptable than Ecuadorian students (Mealy et al., 2007). In fact, in some

---

Steven came to the attention of a therapist when his wife insisted that they seek marital counseling. According to her, Steve was "selfish, ungiving and preoccupied with his work." Everything at home had to "revolve about him, his comfort, moods and desires, no one else's." She claimed that he contributed nothing to the marriage, except a rather meager income. He shirked all "normal" responsibilities and kept "throwing chores in her lap," and she was "getting fed up with being the chief cook and bottlewasher, tired of being his mother and sleep-in maid."

On the positive side, Steven's wife felt that he was basically a "gentle and good-natured guy with talent and intelligence." But this wasn't enough. She wanted a husband, someone with whom she could share things. In contrast, he wanted, according to her, "a mother, not a wife"; he didn't want "to grow up, he didn't know how to give affection, only to take it when he felt like it, nothing more, nothing less."

"I would've told you all this yesterday, but I just made it up today."

Across the world, around 53 percent of people believe that they can consistently detect lies (Bond, 2004). Although most of us are less good at this task than we suspect, some cultures are more confident than others about their lie-detector abilities. Americans believe, for example, that they can detect lies less than half the time, while Norwegians and Swedes rate themselves lower. At the other end of the spectrum, Turks and Armenians believe they can spot liars 70 percent of the time (Bond, 2004; Mann, 2004; Warner, 2004).

How can we protect ourselves from being deceived? How can we tell when someone is lying to us? A variety of informal clues to detect lies have been cited by researchers (Geary & DePaulo, 2007; Bond, 2004; Ekman, et al, 1999). An observer may, for example, be able to spot deception from behavioral cues such as the deceiver's slowness to respond, frequent pauses, inappropriate message duration, or unusual physical gestures such as arm raising and staring (Porter & ten Brinke, 2008; Bond, 2004). When persons ask someone to "Look me in the eye when you say that," they are often trying to pick up on subtle cues to determine whether the speaker is uttering a falsehood or telling the truth. We should beware, however, that such "telltale" signs are far from foolproof (Vrij, 2008; Geary & DePaulo, 2007).

cultures, the clever deceit of others may be highly regarded.

Finally, some biological researchers report that pathological lying may be tied to brain structure and brain chemistry. In one study, for example, researchers found more white matter in the prefrontal cortex of pathological liars than of other people (Yang et al., 2007; Spence, 2005).

Researchers are often less interested in why people lie and instead focus on ways to detect when people lie (Bond, 2004). The ability to detect a lie can be of obvious value in both our personal and professional lives and in court trials. (Weiss & Feldman, 2006). In Chapter 4 you read about formal efforts to detect deceit such as lie detector, voice stress, and integrity tests (Vrij, 2008), but as you saw, these methods have serious pitfalls and researchers have been trying to develop more reliable and valid ways of assessing honesty and integrity.

Steve presented a picture of an affable, self-satisfied and somewhat disdainful young man. He was employed as a commercial artist, but looked forward to his evenings and weekends when he could turn his attention to serious painting. He claimed that he had to devote all of his spare time and energies to "fulfill himself," to achieve expression in his creative work. . . .

His relationships with his present co-workers and social acquaintances were pleasant and satisfying, but he did admit that most people viewed him as a "bit self-centered, cold and snobbish." He recognized that he did not know how to share his thoughts and feelings with others, that he was much more interested in himself than in them and that perhaps he always had "preferred the pleasure" of his own company to that of others.

(Millon, 1969, pp. 261–262)

Peter Turnley/Corbis

A lonely life

This woman paints a sad and lonely figure as she sits by the Paris grave of the late Jim Morrison, lead singer of the rock group The Doors. Legions of Morrison fans have visited the grave for a variety of reasons—from curiosity to admiration—since his 1971 death. Clinicians believe, however, that in some cases the overly devoted fans of Morrison and other long-gone celebrities—particularly fans who build their lives around the celebrities—manifest *avoidant personality disorder.* Uncomfortable and inhibited in real social situations, some people with this personality disorder develop an inner world of fantasy and imagined relationships.

People like James actively avoid occasions for social contact. At the center of this withdrawal lies not so much poor social skills as a dread of criticism, disapproval, or rejection. They are timid and hesitant in social situations, afraid of saying something foolish or of embarrassing themselves by blushing or acting nervous. Even in intimate relationships they express themselves very carefully, afraid of being shamed or ridiculed.

People with this disorder believe themselves to be unappealing or inferior to others. They exaggerate the potential difficulties of new situations, so they seldom take risks or try out new activities. They usually have few or no close friends, though they actually yearn for intimate relationships, and frequently feel depressed and lonely. As a substitute, some develop an inner world of fantasy and imagination (Millon, 1990).

Avoidant personality disorder is similar to *social phobia* (see Chapter 5), and many people with one of these disorders also experience the other (Ralevski et al., 2005). The similarities include a fear of humiliation and low confidence. Some theorists believe that there is a key difference between the two disorders—namely, that people with a social phobia primarily fear social *circumstances,* while people with the personality disorder tend to fear close social *relationships.* Other theorists, however, believe that the two disorders reflect the same core of psychopathology and should be combined in future revisions of the DSM (Herbert, 2007).

Between 1 and 2 percent of adults have avoidant personality disorder, men as frequently as women (O'Connor, 2008; Mattia & Zimmerman, 2001). Many children and teenagers are also painfully shy and avoid other people, but this is usually just a normal part of their development.

How Do Theorists Explain Avoidant Personality Disorder? Theorists often assume that avoidant personality disorder has the same causes as anxiety disorders—such as early traumas, conditioned fears, upsetting beliefs, or biochemical abnormalities. However, with the exception of social phobia, research has not yet tied the personality disorder directly to the anxiety disorders (Herbert, 2007). In the meantime, psychodynamic, cognitive, and behavioral explanations of avoidant personality disorder are the most popular among clinicians.

Psychodynamic theorists focus mainly on the general sense of shame felt by people with avoidant personality disorder (Newman & Fingerhut, 2005; Gabbard, 1990). Some trace the shame to childhood experiences such as early bowel and bladder accidents. If parents repeatedly punish or ridicule a child for having such accidents, the child may develop a negative self-image. This may lead to the individual's feeling unlovable throughout life and distrusting the love of others.

Similarly, cognitive theorists believe that harsh criticism and rejection in early childhood may lead certain people to assume that others in their environment will always judge them negatively. These individuals come to expect rejection, misinterpret the reactions of others to fit that expectation, discount positive feedback, and generally fear social involvements—setting the stage for avoidant personality disorder (Beck et al., 2004, 2001). In several studies, participants with this disorder were asked to recall their childhood, and their descriptions supported both the psychodynamic and the cognitive theories (Herbert, 2007; Grilo & Masheb, 2002). They remembered, for example, feeling criticized, rejected, and isolated; receiving little encouragement from their parents; and experiencing few displays of parental love or pride.

Finally, behavioral theorists suggest that people with avoidant personality disorder typically fail to develop normal social skills, a failure that helps maintain the disorder. In support of this position, several studies have indeed found social skills deficits among individuals with avoidant personality disorder (Herbert, 2007). Most behaviorists agree, however, that the deficits first develop as a result of the individuals avoiding so many social situations.

Treatments for Avoidant Personality Disorder
People with avoidant personality disorder come to therapy in the hope of finding acceptance and affection. Keeping them in treatment can be a challenge, however, for many of them soon begin to avoid the sessions. Often they distrust the therapist's sincerity and start to fear his or her rejection. Thus, as with several of the other personality disorders, a key task of the therapist is to gain the individual's trust (Sadock & Sadock, 2007; Millon, 1999).

Beyond building trust, therapists tend to treat people with avoidant personality disorder much as they treat people with social phobias and other anxiety disorders (Svartberg, Stiles, & Seltzer, 2004; Markovitz, 2001). Such approaches have had at least modest success (Porcerelli et al., 2007; Crits-Christoph & Barber, 2002). Psychodynamic therapists try to help clients recognize and resolve the unconscious conflicts that may be operating (Sperry, 2003). Cognitive therapists help them change their distressing beliefs and thoughts, carry on in the face of painful emotions, and improve their self-image (Leahy et al., 2005; Beck et al., 2004). Behavioral therapists provide social skills training as well as exposure treatments that require people gradually to increase their social contacts (Herbert, 2007; Farmer & Nelson-Gray, 2005). Group therapy formats, especially groups that follow cognitive and behavioral principles, have the added advantage of providing clients with practice in social interactions (Herbert et al., 2005; Piper & Joyce, 2001). Antianxiety and antidepressant drugs are sometimes useful in reducing the social anxiety of people with the disorder, although the symptoms may return when medication is stopped (Herbert, 2007; Fava et al., 2002).

Dependent Personality Disorder

People with **dependent personality disorder** have a pervasive, excessive need to be taken care of (APA, 2000). As a result, they are clinging and obedient, fearing separation from their parent, spouse, or other person with whom they are in a close relationship. They rely on others so much that they cannot make the smallest decision for themselves. Matthew is a case in point.

Matthew is a 34-year-old single man who lives with his mother and works as an accountant. He is seeking treatment because he is very unhappy after having just broken up with his girlfriend. His mother had disapproved of his marriage plans, ostensibly because the woman was of a different religion. Matthew felt trapped and forced to choose between his mother and his girlfriend, and because "blood is thicker than water," he had decided not to go against his mother's wishes. Nonetheless, he is angry at himself and at her and believes that she will never let him marry and is possessively hanging on to him. His mother "wears the pants" in the family and is a very domineering woman who is used to getting her way. Matthew is afraid of disagreeing with his mother for fear that she will not be supportive of him and he will then have to fend for himself. He criticizes himself for being weak, but also admires his mother and respects her judgment—"Maybe Carol wasn't right for me after all." He alternates between resentment and a "Mother knows best" attitude. He feels that his own judgment is poor.

Matthew works at a job several grades below what his education and talent would permit. On several occasions he has turned down promotions because he didn't want the responsibility of having to supervise other people or make independent decisions. He has worked for the same boss for 10 years, gets on well with him, and is, in turn, highly regarded as a dependable and unobtrusive worker. He has two very close friends whom he has had since early childhood. He has lunch with one of them every single workday and feels lost if his friend is sick and misses a day.

BETWEEN THE LINES

Feelings of Shyness

48% Percentage of people in the United States who consider themselves to be shy to some degree ‹‹

62% Percentage of shy people who experience their feelings of shyness daily ‹‹

64% Percentage of shy people who believe that their shyness is the result of external factors beyond their control, such as early family experience ‹‹

(Carducci, 2000)

•**dependent personality disorder**•
A personality disorder characterized by a pattern of clinging and obedience, fear of separation, and an ongoing need to be taken care of.

Matthew is the youngest of four children and the only boy. He was "babied and spoiled" by his mother and elder sisters. He had considerable separation anxiety as a child—he had difficulty falling asleep unless his mother stayed in the room, mild school refusal, and unbearable homesickness when he occasionally tried "sleepovers." As a child he was teased by other boys because of his lack of assertiveness and was often called a baby. He has lived at home his whole life except for 1 year of college, from which he returned because of homesickness. . . .

(Spitzer et al., 1994, pp. 179–180)

It is normal and healthy to depend on others, but those with dependent personality disorder constantly need assistance with even the simplest matters and demonstrate extreme feelings of inadequacy and helplessness. Afraid that they cannot care for themselves, they cling desperately to friends or relatives.

As you just observed, people with avoidant personality disorder have difficulty *initiating* relationships. In contrast, people with dependent personality disorder have difficulty with *separation*. The individuals feel completely helpless and devastated when a close relationship ends, and they quickly seek out another relationship to fill the void. Many cling persistently to relationships with partners who physically or psychologically abuse them.

Lacking confidence in their own ability and judgment, people with this disorder seldom disagree with others and allow even important decisions to be made for them (Bornstein, 2007; APA, 2000). They may depend on a parent or spouse to decide where to live, what job to have, and which neighbors to befriend. Because they so fear rejection, they are overly sensitive to disapproval and keep trying to meet other people's wishes and expectations, even if it means volunteering for unpleasant or demeaning tasks.

Many people with dependent personality disorder feel distressed, lonely, and sad; often they dislike themselves. Thus they are at risk for depressive, anxiety, and eating disorders (Bornstein, 2007). Their fear of separation and their feelings of helplessness may leave them particularly prone to suicidal thoughts, especially when they believe that a relationship is about to end (Kiev, 1989).

Studies suggest that over 2 percent of the population experience dependent personality disorder (Mattia & Zimmerman, 2001). For years clinicians have believed that more women than men display this pattern (Anderson et al., 2001), but some research suggests that the disorder is just as common in men (APA, 2000).

How Do Theorists Explain Dependent Personality Disorder?

Psychodynamic explanations for this personality disorder are very similar to those for depression. Freudian theorists argue, for example, that unresolved conflicts during the oral stage of development can give rise to a lifelong need for nurturance, thus heightening the likelihood of a dependent personality disorder (Bornstein, 2007, 2005). Similarly, object relations theorists say that early parental loss or rejection may prevent normal experiences of *attachment* and *separation*, leaving some children with fears of abandonment that persist throughout their lives. Still other psychodynamic theorists suggest that, to the contrary, many parents of people with this disorder were overinvolved and overprotective, thus increasing their children's dependency, insecurity, and separation anxiety (Sperry, 2003).

Behaviorists propose that parents of people with dependent personality disorder unintentionally rewarded their children's clinging and "loyal" behavior, while at the same time punishing acts of independence, perhaps through the withdrawal of love. Alternatively, some parents' own dependent behaviors may have served as models for their children (Bornstein, 2007).

Finally, cognitive theorists identify two maladaptive attitudes as helping to produce and maintain this disorder: (1) "I am inadequate and helpless to deal with the world," and

Cell phone dependence Many clinicians believe that the proliferation of cell phones has created a widespread psychological dependence on these electronic devices. They note that, like the woman in this photo, many users are more focused on cellular connections than direct people connections. Studies reveal that some cell phone users react with intense anxiety and worry, physical discomfort, feelings of separation, and a loss of self-esteem when forced to shut off their portable phones for more than a few minutes (Chaparro, 2004).

Hans Neleman/zefa/Corbis

(2) "I must find a person to provide protection so I can cope" (Beck et al., 2004, 2001). Dichotomous (black-and-white) thinking may also play a key role: "If I am to be dependent, I must be completely helpless," or "If I am to be independent, I must be alone." Such thinking prevents sufferers from making efforts to be autonomous.

Treatments for Dependent Personality Disorder

In therapy, people with this personality disorder usually place all responsibility for their treatment and well-being on the clinician (Gutheil, 2005). Thus a key task of therapy is to help patients accept responsibility for themselves. Because the domineering behaviors of a spouse or parent may help foster a patient's symptoms, some clinicians propose couple or family therapy as well, or even separate therapy for the partner or parent (Nichols, 2004; Links et al., 2004).

Treatment for dependent personality disorder can be at least modestly helpful. Psychodynamic therapy for this pattern focuses on many of the same issues as therapy for depressed people, including the *transference* of dependency needs onto the therapist (Sperry, 2003; Gabbard, 2001). Cognitive-behavioral therapy combines behavioral and cognitive interventions to help the clients take control of their lives. On the behavioral end, the therapists often provide assertiveness training to help the individuals better express their own wishes in relationships (Farmer & Nelson-Gray, 2005). On the cognitive end, the therapists also try to help the clients challenge and change their assumptions of incompetence and helplessness (Beck et al., 2004; Freeman, 2002). Antidepressant drug therapy has been helpful for persons whose personality disorder is accompanied by depression (Fava et al., 2002).

Finally, as with avoidant personality disorder, a group therapy format can be helpful because it provides opportunities for the client to receive support from a number of peers rather than from a single dominant person (Perry, 2004; Sperry, 2003). In addition, group members may serve as models for one another as they practice better ways to express feelings and solve problems.

Obsessive-Compulsive Personality Disorder

People with **obsessive-compulsive personality disorder** are so preoccupied with order, perfection, and control that they lose all flexibility, openness, and efficiency. Their concern for doing everything "right" impairs their productivity, as in the case of Wayne:

Wayne was advised to seek assistance from a therapist following several months of relatively sleepless nights and a growing immobility and indecisiveness at his job. When first seen, he reported feelings of extreme self-doubt and guilt and prolonged periods of tension and diffuse anxiety. It was established early in therapy that he always had experienced these symptoms. They were now merely more pronounced than before.

The precipitant for this sudden increase in discomfort was a forthcoming change in his academic post. New administrative officers had assumed authority at the college, and he was asked to resign his deanship to return to regular departmental instruction. In the early sessions, Wayne spoke largely of his fear of facing classroom students again, wondered if he could organize his material well, and doubted that he could keep classes disciplined and interested in his lectures. It was his preoccupation with these matters that he believed was preventing him from concentrating and completing his present responsibilities.

At no time did Wayne express anger toward the new college officials for the "demotion" he was asked to accept. He repeatedly voiced his "complete confidence" in the "rationality of their decision." Yet, when face-to-face with them, he observed that he stuttered and was extremely tremulous.

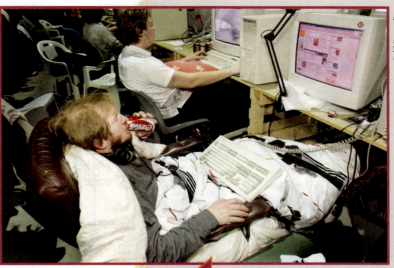

Fredrik Naumann/Panos

Internet dependence
The new term "Internet addiction" has entered the clinical vernacular to describe people whose excessive computer use and dependence interfere markedly with their daily lives. This pattern, which has been linked to dependent personality disorder, substance addiction, obsessive-compulsive disorder, and impulse-control disorders, includes excessive Internet browsing, social networking, e-mail and text messaging, blogging, shopping, gambling, or pornographic use. Research indicates that at least 1 percent of all people display this pattern, leading some theorists to argue that "Internet dependence" should be listed as a new category in the next DSM (Block, 2008; Young, 2007, 2005).

•**obsessive-compulsive personality disorder**•A personality disorder marked by such an intense focus on orderliness, perfectionism, and control that the individual loses flexibility, openness, and efficiency.

disorder (Sherry & Whilde, 2008; Hodges, 2003). In the absence of systematic research, however, alternative explanations like this remain untested and corresponding treatments undeveloped.

In a related vein, given the childhood experiences that typically precede borderline personality disorder, some multicultural theorists believe that the disorder may actually be a reaction to persistent feelings of marginality, powerlessness, and social failure (Sherry & Whilde, 2008; Miller, 1999, 1994). That is, the disorder may be attributable more to social inequalities (including sexism, racism, or homophobia) than to psychological factors.

Given such possibilities, it is most welcome that a few multicultural studies of borderline personality disorder have been conducted recently. In one, researchers assessed the prevalence of the personality disorder in racially diverse clinical populations from across the United States (Chavira et al., 2003). The study found that disproportionately more Hispanic American clients qualified for a diagnosis of borderline personality disorder than did white or African American clients. Could it be that Hispanic Americans generally are more likely than other cultural groups to display this disorder, and—if so—why?

Finally, some multicultural theorists have argued that the features of borderline personality disorder listed in DSM-IV-TR may be perfectly acceptable traits and behaviors in certain cultures. In Puerto Rican culture, for example, men are *expected* to display very strong emotions like anger, aggression, and sexual attraction (Sherry & Whilde, 2008; Casimir & Morrison, 1993). Could such culture-based characteristics help account for the higher rates of borderline personality disorder found among Hispanic American clients? And could these culturally based characteristics also help explain the fact that Hispanic men and women demonstrate similar rates of this disorder, in contrast to the usual 3 to 1 female-to-male ratio found in other cultural groups (Chavira et al., 2003; Akhtar et al., 1986)? Questions of this kind underline once again the need for more multicultural research into personality disorders.

❂What Problems Are Posed by the DSM-IV-TR Categories?

Most of today's clinicians believe that personality disorders are important and troubling patterns. Yet these disorders are particularly hard to diagnose and easy to misdiagnose, difficulties that indicate serious problems with the *validity* (accuracy) and *reliability* (consistency) of the DSM-IV-TR categories (Fowler et al., 2007).

One problem is that some of the criteria used to diagnose personality disorders cannot be observed directly. To distinguish paranoid from schizoid personality disorder, for example, clinicians must ask not only whether people avoid forming close relationships, but also *why*. In other words, the diagnoses often rely heavily on the impressions of the individual clinician. A related problem is that clinicians differ widely in their judgments about when a normal personality style crosses the line and deserves to be called a disorder (Widiger, 2007). Some even believe that it is wrong ever to think of personality styles as mental disorders, however troublesome they may be.

The similarity of personality disorders within a cluster, or even between clusters, poses yet another problem (Widiger, 2007). Within DSM-IV-TR's "anxious" cluster, for example, there is considerable overlap between the symptoms of avoidant personality disorder and those of dependent personality disorder. When clinicians see similar feelings of inadequacy, fear of disapproval, and the like, is it reasonable to consider them separate disorders? Also, the many borderline traits ("dramatic" cluster) found among some people with dependent personality disorder ("anxious" cluster) may indicate that these two disorders are but different versions of one basic pattern.

In fact, some research suggests that people with disorders of personality *typically* meet diagnostic criteria for several personality disorders (O'Connor, 2008; Langenbucher & Nathan, 2006). Once again, when two or more personality disorders occur in the same person, it is not clear whether the various disorders actually represent multiple pathologies or a single underlying pathology.

Yet another problem with the DSM-IV-TR categories is that people with quite different personalities may qualify for the same personality disorder diagnosis (Fowler et al., 2007; Widiger, 2007). Individuals must meet a certain number of criteria from DSM-IV-TR to receive a given diagnosis, but no single feature is necessary for that diagnosis. A diagnosis of borderline personality disorder, for example, requires that 5 of 9 possible symptoms be present. This means that 126 distinct symptom combinations can characterize people with the disorder (Skodol, 2005).

Partly because of these problems, diagnosticians keep changing the criteria used to assess each of the personality disorders. In fact, the diagnostic categories themselves have changed more than once, and they will no doubt change again. For example, DSM-IV-TR dropped a past category, **passive-aggressive personality disorder,** a pattern of negative attitudes and passive resistance to the demands of others, because research failed to show that this was more than a single trait. The pattern is now being studied more carefully and may be included once again in future editions of the DSM.

✿Are There Better Ways to Classify Personality Disorders?

In light of these concerns, it is not surprising that today's leading criticism of DSM-IV-TR's approach to personality disorders is that the classification system defines such disorders by using *categories*—rather than *dimensions*—of personality (Widiger, 2007). Like a light switch that is either on or off, DSM-IV-TR's categorical approach assumes that (1) problematic personality traits are either present or absent in people, (2) a personality disorder is either displayed or not displayed by an individual, and (3) a person who suffers from a personality disorder is not markedly troubled by personality traits outside of that disorder.

Many theorists disagree with these assumptions and believe instead that personality disorders differ more in *degree* than in type of dysfunction. Therefore, they propose that the disorders should be classified by the severity of key personality traits (or dimensions) rather than by the presence or absence of specific traits (Widiger, 2007, 2006). In such an approach, each key trait (for example, agreeableness or honesty or self-absorption) would be seen as varying along a continuum in which there is no clear boundary between normal and abnormal. People with a personality disorder would be those who display extreme degrees of several of these key traits—degrees not commonly found in the general population.

We can all probably generate an extensive list of traits, or dimensions, on which our friends vary. For example, they might differ in the extent to which they dwell on their problems, socialize with others, spend frivolously, and enjoy soft music. Clearly, some

•**passive-aggressive personality disorder**•A category of personality disorder listed in past versions of the DSM, marked by a pattern of negative attitudes and resistance to the demands of others.

Dysfunctional toons

As the messages and technology found in film animation have become more complex over time, so have the personality problems of animated characters. (Left) Troubled characters of the past were usually defined by a single undesirable personality trait, as demonstrated by Snow White's friend Grumpy, second from left. (Right) Today's characters have "clusters" of problematic traits. For example, some critics suggest that the *South Park* kids (especially Cartman, second from left) display enduring grumpiness; disrespect for authority, irreverence, and self-absorption; disregard for the feelings of others; general lack of conscience; and a tendency to get into trouble.

of these dimensions are more important than others to one's functioning. What key personality dimensions should clinicians use to help identify people with personality problems? Some theorists believe that they should rely upon the dimensions identified in the "Big Five" theory of personality—the dimensional theory that has been studied the most by personality theorists.

The "Big Five" Theory of Personality and Personality Disorders

A large body of research conducted with diverse populations consistently suggests that the basic structure of personality may consist of five "supertraits," or factors—*neuroticism, extroversion, openness to experiences, agreeableness,* and *conscientiousness* (Costa & McCrae, 2005). Each of these factors, which are frequently referred to as the "Big Five," consists of a number of subfactors. Anxiety and hostility, for example, are subfactors of the neuroticism factor, while optimism and friendliness are subfactors of the extroversion factor. Theoretically, everyone's personality can be summarized by a combination of these supertraits. One person may display high levels of neuroticism and agreeableness, medium extroversion, and low conscientiousness and openness to experiences. In contrast, another person may display high levels of agreeableness and conscientiousness, medium neuroticism and extroversion, and low openness to experiences. And so on.

Many proponents of the five-factor model further argue that it would be best to describe all people with personality disorders as being high, low, or in between on the five supertraits, and to drop the DSM's current use of personality disorder categories altogether (Clark, 2005; Costa & McCrae, 2005). Thus, a particular individual who currently qualifies for a diagnosis of avoidant personality disorder might instead be described as displaying a high degree of neuroticism, medium degrees of agreeableness and conscientiousness, and very low degrees of extroversion and openness to new experiences. Similarly, an individual currently diagnosed with narcissistic personality disorder might be described in the five-factor dimensional approach as displaying very high degrees of neuroticism and extroversion, medium degrees of conscientiousness and openness to new experiences, and a very low degree of agreeableness.

Alternative Dimensional Approaches

Although many of today's clinical theorists agree that a dimensional approach would reflect personality pathology more accurately than the categorical DSM-IV-TR approach, not all of them believe that the "Big Five" model is the most useful dimensional approach (Fowler et al., 2007). Some worry that too few trait adjectives are included in the five-factor model, and others suggest that ratings of simple adjective lists cannot capture the complex problems of people with personality disorders. Thus, alternative dimensional models have also been proposed (Bagby et al., 2005; Widiger & Simonsen, 2005). One such model, developed by researchers Jonathan Shedler and Drew Westen (2004), identifies 12 broad factors rather than 5 factors—broad factors that are collectively made up of 200 descriptive *statements* such as "The individual tends to elicit liking in others," "The individual tends to get into power struggles," and "The individual's emotions tend to change rapidly and exaggeratedly." Clinicians describe a person with a personality disorder by rating each of these 200 statements on a scale from 0 to 7. Research suggests that the resulting descriptions effectively capture the complexity of personality dysfunctioning and, at the same time, provide numerical scores that can be used in systematic studies of personality disorders (Westen & Muderrisoglo, 2006; Shedler & Westen, 2004).

It is not yet certain where these proposed dimensional models of personality pathology will lead, although many influential theorists predict that the next edition of the DSM (DSM-V) will use some such model rather than the current categorical model (Widiger, 2007). At the very least, the present debate indicates once again that most of today's clinicians believe personality dysfunctions to be important forms of abnormality that must be better understood and treated.

Personality au naturel
As suggested by the varied reactions of these polar bears to events at Canada's Hudson Bay, human beings are not the only creatures who demonstrate differences in personality, mood, and lifestyle. Natural data of this kind have led many theorists to suspect that inborn, biological factors contribute, at least in part, to personality differences and personality disorders.

PUTTING IT... together

Disorders of Personality Are Rediscovered

During the first half of the twentieth century, clinicians believed deeply in the unique, enduring patterns we call personality, and they tried to define important personality traits. They then discovered how readily people can be shaped by the situations in which they find themselves, and a backlash developed. The concept of personality seemed to lose legitimacy, and for a while it became almost an obscene word in some circles. The clinical category of personality disorders experienced a similar rejection. When psycho-dynamic and humanistic theorists dominated the clinical field, *neurotic character disorders,* a set of diagnoses similar to today's personality disorders, were considered useful clinical categories (Millon et al., 2000). But their popularity declined as other models grew in influence.

During the past two decades, serious interest in personality and personality disorders has rebounded (Lenzenweger & Clarkin, 2005). In case after case, clinicians have concluded that rigid personality traits do seem to pose special problems, and they have developed new objective tests and interview guides to assess these disorders, setting in motion a wave of systematic research (O'Connor, 2008; Weiner & Greene, 2008). So far, only the antisocial and borderline personality disorders have received much study. As other patterns of personality pathology attract their fair share of research attention, clinicians should be better able to answer some pressing questions: How common are the various personality disorders? How useful are the present categories? And what treatments are most effective?

One of the most important questions is "Why do people develop troubled patterns of personality?" As you have read, psychological, as opposed to biological and sociocultural, theories have offered the most suggestions so far, but these proposed explanations are not very precise, and they do not have strong research support. Given the current enthusiasm for biological explanations, genetic and biological factors are beginning to receive considerable study, a shift in the waters that should soon enable researchers to determine possible interactions between biological and psychological causes (Herbert, 2007). And one would hope that sociocultural factors will be studied as well. As you have seen, sociocultural theorists have only occasionally offered explanations for person-ality disorders, and multicultural factors have received little research. However, sociocul-tural factors may well play an important role in these disorders and should be examined more carefully, especially since, by definition, patterns diagnosed as a personality disorder differ markedly from the expectations of a person's culture.

BETWEEN THE LINES

Violent Models

By the age of 18, the average child in the United States has viewed 200,000 acts of violence on television alone (American Academy of Pediatrics, 1999; Prothrow-Stith & Spivak, 1999). ‹‹

The future is likely to bring major changes to the explanations and treatments for personality disorders, and the classification of personality disorders will probably undergo change as well. Such changes, however, are now more likely to be based on research than on clinical intuitions. For the many people caught in the web of rigid and maladaptive personality traits, these changes should make an important difference, and one long overdue.

‹‹‹[SUMMING UP]›››

○ **Personality disorders** A *personality disorder* is an inflexible pattern of inner experience and outward behavior. Such patterns are wide-ranging and enduring, differ markedly from social norms, and lead to distress or impairment. Explanations for most of the personality disorders have received only limited research support. DSM-IV-TR distinguishes 10 personality disorders and separates them into three *clusters*. *pp. 509–512*

○ **"Odd" personality disorders** Three of the personality disorders are marked by the kinds of odd or eccentric behavior often seen in the Axis I disorder of schizophrenia. People with *paranoid personality disorder* display a broad pattern of distrust and suspiciousness. Those with *schizoid personality disorder* persistently avoid social relationships, have little or no social interests, and show little emotional expression. Individuals with *schizotypal personality disorder* display a range of interpersonal problems marked by extreme discomfort in close relationships, very odd forms of thinking and behavior, and behavioral eccentricities. People with these three kinds of disorders usually are resistant to treatment, and treatment gains tend to be modest at best. *pp. 513–518*

○ **"Dramatic" personality disorders** Four of the personality disorders are marked by highly dramatic, emotional, or erratic symptoms. People with *antisocial personality disorder* display a pattern of disregard for and violation of the rights of others. No known treatment is notably effective. People with *borderline personality disorder* display a pattern of instability in interpersonal relationships, self-image, and mood, along with extreme impulsivity. Treatment apparently can be helpful and lead to some improvement. People with *histrionic personality disorder* (once called *hysterical personality disorder*) display a pattern of extreme emotionality and attention seeking. Clinical case reports suggest that treatment is helpful on occasion. Finally, people with *narcissistic personality disorder* display a pattern of grandiosity, need for admiration, and lack of empathy. It is one of the most difficult disorders to treat. *pp. 518–535*

○ **"Anxious" personality disorders** Three of the personality disorders are marked by the kinds of symptoms found in the Axis I anxiety and depressive disorders. People with *avoidant personality disorder* are consistently uncomfortable and inhibited in social situations, overwhelmed by feelings of inadequacy, and extremely sensitive to negative evaluation. People with *dependent personality disorder* have a persistent need to be taken care of, are submissive and clinging, and fear separation. Individuals with *obsessive-compulsive personality disorder* are so preoccupied with order, perfection, and control that they lose their flexibility, openness, and efficiency. A variety of treatment strategies have been used for people with these disorders and apparently have been modestly to moderately helpful. *pp. 535–541*

○ **Multicultural factors** Despite DSM-IV-TR's emphasis on cultural factors when defining personality disorders, relatively little research has been done on gender and other multicultural influences. Nevertheless, many clinicians believe that multicultural factors play key roles in the diagnosis and treatment of personality disorders, and researchers have recently begun to study this possibility. *pp. 541–542*

○ **Problems posed by the DSM-IV-TR Categories** It appears that the DSM-IV-TR personality disorders are commonly misdiagnosed, an indication of serious problems in the *validity* and *reliability* of the categories. Given the significant problems posed by DSM-IV-TR's *categorical* approach, a number of today's theorists believe that personality disorders should instead be described and classified by a *dimensional* approach, such as the *five-factor model*. *pp. 542–543*

⫸CRITICAL THOUGHTS⫷

1. It is common for people outside the clinical field to mistakenly diagnose mental disorders in themselves, relatives, or acquaintances, and the personality disorders are among the most favored of their diagnoses. Why do you think these disorders are particularly subject to such efforts at amateur psychology? *pp. 509–546*

2. Some observers suggest that personality disorders are little more than descriptions of undesirable personal styles, and they argue that such styles should not be considered psychological disorders, no matter how many problems they may create for the individuals themselves or for society. Take a try at arguing both for and against this position. *pp. 509–546*

3. How do various institutions in our society—business, government, academia, science, religion—view lying, and how might these views affect the prevalence and nature of individual lies? *pp. 532–533*

4. Why do people often admire someone who deceives—a flatterer, an art forger, a jewel thief? *pp. 532–533*

5. Some people believe that the past 15 years have witnessed an increase in narcissistic behavior and thinking in Western society. What features of Western society during this span of time (for example, child-rearing philosophies, advertising campaigns, sports heroes, book topics, television programming, and movies) may be contributing to a rise in narcissistic behavior? *p. 534*

6. Invent a way of organizing and defining personality disorders that improves upon the present diagnostic system. How would the DSM-IV-TR categories fit into your new scheme? *pp. 542–545*

⫸ cyberstudy ⫷

SEARCH

Search the *Abnormal Psychology* Video Tool Kit

www.worthpublishers.com/apvtk

▲ Chapter 16 Video Cases
Video Games: Do They Make People Violent?
Antisocial Personality Disorder: A Treatable Pattern?
Compulsive Gambling, the Brain, and Poor Impulse Control

▲ Video case discussions, study guides, and questions

Log on to the Comer Web Page

www.worthpublishers.com/comer

▲ Chapter 16 outline, learning objectives, research exercises, study tools, and practice test questions

▲ Additional Chapter 16 case studies, Web links, and FAQs

DISORDERS OF CHILDHOOD AND ADOLESCENCE

B illy, a 7-year-old . . . child, was brought to a mental health clinic by his mother because "he is unhappy and always complaining about feeling sick." . . . His mother describes Billy as a child who has never been very happy and never wanted to play with other children. From the time he started nursery school, he has complained about stomachaches, headaches, and various other physical problems. . . .

Billy did well in first grade, but in second grade he is now having difficulty completing his work. He takes a lot of time to do his assignments and frequently feels he has to do them over again so that they will be "perfect." Because of Billy's frequent somatic complaints, it is hard to get him off to school in the morning. If he is allowed to stay home, he worries that he is falling behind in his schoolwork. When he does go to school, he often is unable to do the work, which makes him feel hopeless about his situation. . . .

His worries have expanded beyond school, and frequently he is clinging and demanding of his parents. He is fearful that if his parents come home late or leave and go somewhere without him that something may happen to them. . . .

Although Billy's mother acknowledges that he has never been really happy, in the last 6 months, she feels, he has become much more depressed. He frequently lies around the house, saying that he is too tired to do anything. He has no interest or enjoyment in playing. His appetite has diminished. He has trouble falling asleep at night and often wakes up in the middle of the night or early in the morning. Three weeks ago, he talked, for the first time, about wanting to die. . . .

(Spitzer et al., 1994)

In the past year, Eddie [age 9] had been suspended twice for hyperactive and impulsive behavior. Most recently, he had climbed onto the overhead lights of the classroom and caused an uproar when he could not get himself down. His teachers complain that other children cannot concentrate when Eddie is in the room because he walks around constantly. Even when he is seated, his rapid foot and hand movements are disruptive to the other children. Eddie has almost no friends and does not play games with his classmates due to his impulsivity and overly active behavior. After school, he likes to play with his dog or ride his bike alone.

Eddie's mother reports that he has been excessively active since he was a toddler. At the age of three, Eddie would awaken at 4:30 AM each day and go downstairs without any supervision. Sometimes he would "demolish" the kitchen or living room, and at other times he would leave the house by himself. Once when he was four years old, he was found walking alone on a busy street in the early morning. Luckily, a passerby rescued him before he got into traffic.

After being rejected by a preschool because of his hyperactivity and impulsivity, Eddie attended a kindergarten and had a very difficult year. For first and second grade, he attended a special behavioral program. For third grade, he was allowed to attend a regular education class, with pull-out services for help with his behavior.

(Spitzer et al., 1994)

Billy and Eddie are both displaying psychological disorders. Their disorders are disrupting the boys' family ties, school performances, and social relationships, but each disorder does so in a particular way and for particular reasons. Billy, who may qualify for a diagnosis of *major depressive disorder*, struggles constantly with sadness, worry, and perfectionism, along with stomachaches and other physical ailments. Eddie, on the other hand, cannot concentrate and is overly active and impulsive—difficulties that comprise attention-deficit/hyperactivity disorder (ADHD). Like Billy, Eddie and others with ADHD may experience bouts of unhappiness, but for them such feelings are brought about by the repeated criticisms and social rebukes that they receive; in contrast, Billy's unhappiness is at the center of his disorder—it is the primary cause of his suffering and impaired functioning.

Abnormal functioning can occur at any time in life. Some patterns of abnormality, however, are more likely to emerge during particular periods—during childhood, for example, or, at the other end of the spectrum, during old age. In this chapter you will read about disorders that have their onset during childhood or early adolescence. In the next chapter you'll observe problems that are more common among the elderly.

✿Childhood and Adolescence

Theorists often view life as a series of stages on the road from birth to death. Most people pass through these stages in the same order, though at their own rates and in their own ways. As you saw in Chapter 3, Freud proposed that each child passes through the same five stages—the *oral, anal, phallic, latency,* and *genital stages.* The influential psycho-dynamic theorist Erik Erikson (1963) added old age as one of life's most meaningful stages. Although theorists may disagree with the details of these schemes, most agree that we confront key pressures during each stage in life and either grow or decline depending on how we meet those pressures. Each stage offers many opportunities for dysfunction, whether because of biological limitations, psychological struggles, or extraordinary environmental stress.

People often think of childhood as a carefree and happy time—yet it can also be frightening and upsetting. In fact, children of all cultures typically experience at least some emotional and behavioral problems as they encounter new people and situations. Surveys reveal that *worry* is a common experience: close to half of all children in the United States have multiple fears, particularly concerning school, health, and personal safety (Beidel & Turner, 2005; Szabo & Lovibond, 2004). Bed-wetting, nightmares, temper tantrums, and restlessness are other problems experienced by many children.

Adolescence can also be a difficult period. Physical and sexual changes, social and academic pressures, personal doubts, and temptations cause many teenagers to feel anxious, confused, and depressed (Weisz et al., 2006; King et al., 2005). Today's teens, although generally happy and optimistic and often spiritual, tend to feel less trusting, more sensitive, and more isolated from their families than adolescents of decades past (Begley, 2000).

Along with these common psychological difficulties, at least one-fifth of all children and adolescents in North America also experience a diagnosable psychological disorder (Steele, Roberts, & Elkin, 2008). Boys with disorders outnumber girls, even though most of the adult psychological disorders are more common among women. Some disorders of children—childhood anxiety disorders, childhood depression, and disruptive disorders—have adult counterparts, although they are also distinct in certain ways. Other childhood disorders—elimination disorders, for example—usually disappear or radically change form by adulthood. There are also disorders that begin at birth or in childhood and persist in stable forms into adult life. These include mental retardation and autism, the former an extensive disturbance in intellect, the latter marked by a lack of responsiveness to the environment.

"I wish I'd started therapy at your age."

✿Childhood Anxiety Problems

Anxiety is, to a degree, a normal and common part of childhood. Since children have had fewer experiences than adults, their world is often new and scary. They may be frightened by common events, such as the beginning of school, or by special upsets, such as moving to a new house or becoming seriously ill. In addition, each generation of children is confronted by new sources of anxiety. Today's children, for example, are repeatedly warned, both at home and at school, about the dangers of Internet surfing and networking, child abduction, drugs, and terrorism. They are bombarded by violent images on the Web, on television, or in movies. Even fairy tales and nursery rhymes contain frightening images that upset many children.

Because they are highly dependent on their parents for emotional support and guidance, children may also be affected greatly by parental problems or inadequacies (Baldwin & Dadds, 2008; Barrett & Shortt, 2003). If, for example, parents typically react to events with high levels of anxiety or overprotect their children, the children may be more likely to respond to the world with anxiety. Similarly, if parents repeatedly reject, disappoint, or avoid their children, the world may seem an unpleasant and anxious place for them. And if parents are divorced, become seriously ill, or must be separated from their children for a long period, childhood anxiety may result.

Nor are these the only factors that may contribute to childhood and adolescent anxiety (Baldwin & Dadds, 2008). There is genetic evidence that some children are prone to an anxious temperament. In addition, concerns about peers can upset many children. And childhood medical problems may produce considerable anxiety.

Steve Stoner/Fort Morgan Times/AP Photo

Oh, that first day!
The first day of kindergarten is overwhelming for this child and perhaps also for his mother, who tries her best to comfort him. Such anxiety reactions to the beginning of school and to being temporarily separated from one's parents are common among young children. However, 4 percent of children have broader fears and display separation anxiety disorder.

Childhood Anxiety Disorders

For some children, such anxieties become chronic and debilitating, interfering with their daily lives and their ability to function appropriately. These children may be suffering from an anxiety disorder. Surveys indicate that between 10 and 21 percent of all children and adolescents display an anxiety disorder (Baldwin & Dadds, 2008; Costello et al., 2003). Some of the childhood anxiety disorders are similar to their adult counterparts. When specific phobias are experienced by children, for example, they usually look and operate just like the phobias of adulthood. Indeed, a number of untreated childhood phobias grow into adult ones.

More often, however, the anxiety disorders of childhood take on a somewhat different character from that of adult anxiety disorders. Consider *generalized anxiety disorder,* marked by constant worrying, and *social phobia,* marked by fears of embarrassing oneself in front of others. In order to have such disorders, individuals must be able to anticipate future negative events (losing one's job, having a car accident, fainting in front of others), to take on the perspective of other people, and/or to recognize that the thoughts and beliefs of others differ from their own. These cognitive skills are simply beyond the capacity of very young children, and so the symptoms of generalized anxiety disorder and social phobia do not appear in earnest until children are 7 years old or older. In short, odd as it may sound, some patterns of anxiety cannot fully unfold until children are afforded the "benefits" of cognitive, physical, and emotional growth (Bengtsson, 2005; Selman, 1980).

What, then, do the anxiety disorders of young children look like? Typically they are dominated by behavioral and somatic symptoms rather than cognitive ones—symptoms such as clinging, sleep difficulties, and stomach pains (Kendall & Pimentel, 2003). They tend to center on specific, sometimes imaginary, objects and events, such as monsters, ghosts, or thunderstorms, rather than broad concerns about the future or one's place in the world. And they are more often than not triggered by current events and situations.

separation anxiety disorder• A childhood disorder marked by excessive anxiety, even panic, whenever the child is separated from home or parent.

play therapy• An approach to treating childhood disorders that helps children express their conflicts and feelings indirectly by drawing, playing with toys, and making up stories.

Separation anxiety disorder, one of the most common childhood anxiety disorders, follows this profile. This disorder is unique to childhood, begins as early as the preschool years, and is displayed by 4 percent of all children (Shear et al., 2006; Beidel & Turner, 2005). Sufferers feel extreme anxiety, often panic, whenever they are separated from home or a parent. Carrie, a 9-year-old girl, was referred to a local mental health center by her school counselor when she seemed to become extremely anxious at school for no apparent reason.

She initially reported feeling sick to her stomach and later became quite concerned over being unable to get her breath. She stated that she was too nervous to stay at school and that she wanted her mother to come get her and take her home. . . . The counselor indicated that a similar incident occurred the next day with Carrie ending up going home again. She had not returned to school since. . . .

At the time of the intake evaluation the mother indicated that she felt Carrie was just too nervous to go to school. She stated that she had encouraged her daughter to go to school on numerous occasions but that she seemed afraid to go and appeared to feel bad, so she had not forced her. . . . When asked if Carrie went places by herself, the mother stated that Carrie didn't like to do that and that the two of them typically did most everything together. The mother went on to note that Carrie really seemed to want to have her (the mother) around all the time and tended to become upset whenever the two of them were separated.

(Schwartz & Johnson, 1985, p. 188)

Children like Carrie have great trouble traveling away from their family, and they often refuse to visit friends' houses, go on errands, or attend camp or school. Many cannot even stay alone in a room and cling to their parent around the house. Some also have temper tantrums, cry, or plead to keep their parents from leaving them. The children may fear that they will get lost when separated from their parents or that the parents will meet with an accident or illness. As long as the children are near their parents and not threatened by separation, they may function quite normally. At the first hint of separation, however, the dramatic pattern of symptoms may be set in motion.

As in Carrie's case, a separation anxiety disorder may further take the form of a *school phobia,* or *school refusal,* a common problem in which children fear going to school and often stay home for a long period (Heyne et al., 2002). Many cases of school phobia, however, have causes other than separation fears, such as social or academic fears, depression, and fears of specific objects or persons at school.

Treatments for Childhood Anxiety Disorders

Despite the high prevalence of childhood and adolescent anxiety disorders, many anxious children go untreated (Baldwin & Dadds, 2008). Among the children who do receive treatment, psychodynamic, behavioral, cognitive, cognitive-behavioral, family, and group therapies, separately or in combination, have been applied most often—each with some degree of success (Baldwin & Dadds, 2008; Rapee, 2003). Such treatments parallel the adult anxiety approaches that you read about in Chapter 5, but they are, of course, tailored to the child's cognitive capacity, unique life situation, and limited control over his or her life. In addition, clinicians may offer psychoeducation and arrange school interventions to treat anxious children. Clinicians have also used drug therapy in a number of cases, particularly antianxiety and antidepressant medications, often in combination with psychotherapy. Drug

Drawing on one's experiences
Art therapy is often used to help young children express and work through anxiety and other upsetting emotions. This child, displaced from her home by Hurricane Katrina in 2005, was, at first, able to draw, rather than describe, her thoughts about losing her home and her fears about safety. These drawings then led to more direct discussions of her traumatic experiences.

Lori Waselchuk/The New York Times/Redux

therapy for childhood anxiety appears to be helpful, but it has begun only recently to receive much research attention (Walkup et al., 2008).

Because children typically have difficulty recognizing and understanding their feelings and motives, many therapists, particularly psychodynamic therapists, use **play therapy** as part of treatment (Hall et al., 2002). In this approach, the children play with toys, draw, and make up stories; in doing so they reveal the conflicts in their lives and their related feelings. The therapists then introduce more play and fantasy to help the children work through their conflicts and change their emotions and behavior. In addition, because children are often excellent hypnotic subjects, some therapists use *hypnotherapy* to help them overcome intense fears.

✿Childhood Mood Problems

Children may experience depression, as did Billy, the boy you observed at the beginning of this chapter. Bobby has similar symptoms:

In observing Bobby in the playroom it was obvious that his activity level was well below that expected for a child of 10. He showed a lack of interest in the toys that were available to him, and the interviewer was unable to get him interested in any play activity for more than a few minutes. In questioning him about home and school, Bobby indicated that he didn't like school because he didn't have any friends, and he wasn't good at playing games like baseball and soccer like the other kids were, stating "I'm not really very good at anything." . . . When asked what he would wish for if he could have any three wishes granted he indicated, "I would wish that I was the type of boy my mother and father want, I would wish that I could have friends, and I would wish that I wouldn't feel sad so much."

In speaking with the parents, the mother reported that she and her husband had become increasingly concerned about their son during the past year. She indicated that he always seemed to look sad and cried a lot for no apparent reason and that he appeared to have lost interest in most of the things that he used to enjoy doing. The mother confirmed Bobby's statements that he had no friends, indicating that he had become more and more of a loner during the past 6 to 9 months. She stated that his schoolwork had also suffered in that he is unable to concentrate on school assignments and seems to have "just lost interest." The mother notes, however, that her greatest concern is that he has recently spoken more and more frequently about "killing himself," saying that the parents would be better off if he wasn't around.

(Schwartz & Johnson, 1985, p. 214)

Major Depressive Disorder

Like Bobby, around 2 percent of children and 9 percent of adolescents currently experience major depressive disorder. Indeed, as many as 15 percent of adolescents experience at least one depressive episode (Avenevoli et al., 2008; Curry & Becker, 2008).

As with anxiety disorders, very young children lack some of the cognitive skills that help produce clinical depression, thus accounting for the low rate of depression among the very young (Hankin et al., 2008; Weiss & Garber, 2003). For example, in order to experience the sense of hopelessness typically found in depressed adults, children must demonstrate an ability to hold expectations about the future, a skill rarely in full bloom before the age of 7.

Nevertheless, if life situations or biological predispositions are significant enough, even very young children sometimes experience severe and enduring downward turns of mood (Cummings & Fristad, 2008; Nantel-Vivier & Pihl, 2008). Depression in the young may be triggered by negative life events (particularly losses), major changes,

Grief camp
Research indicates that people who lose parents or close relatives early in life have an increased likelihood of experiencing depression, either immediately or later as adults. With this in mind, a number of "grief camps" have been developed around the country for children, usually between the ages of 6 and 16, who have lost a loved one. At one such program, this young girl, whose uncle was killed while fighting in Iraq, puts a clipping representing what she feels about his death in a bag.

rejection, or ongoing abuse (Abela & Hankin, 2008; Molnar et al., 2001). Some of the features of childhood depression differ from those that characterize adult depression. For example, a depressed child's inability to experience pleasure (*anhedonia*) is typically expressed as a disinterest in toys and games, as opposed to a reduced desire for sex in depressed adults (Weiss & Garber, 2003). In addition, childhood depression is more commonly characterized by such symptoms as headaches, stomach pain, and irritability (Hankin et al., 2008).

Clinical depression is much more common among teenagers than among young children. Adolescence is, under the best of circumstances, a difficult and confusing time, marked by angst, hormonal and bodily changes, mood changes, complex relationships, and new explorations (see *The Media Speaks* on the facing page). For some teens these "normal" upsets of adolescence cross the line into clinical depression. In fact, as you read in Chapter 10, suicidal thoughts and attempts are particularly common among adolescents—one in six teens think about suicide each year—and depression is the leading cause of such thoughts and attempts (Spirito & Esposito-Smythers, 2008).

Interestingly, while there is no difference between the rates of depression in boys and girls before the age of 13, girls are twice as likely as boys to be depressed by the age of 16. Why this gender shift? Several factors have been suggested, including hormonal changes, the fact that females increasingly experience more stressors than males, and the tendency of girls to become more emotionally invested than boys in social and intimate relationships as they mature (Hankin et al., 2008). One explanation also focuses on teenage girls' growing dissatisfaction with their bodies. Whereas boys tend to like the increase in muscle mass and other body changes that accompany puberty, girls often detest the increases in body fat and weight gain that they experience during puberty and beyond. Raised in a society that values and demands extreme thinness as the aesthetic female ideal, many adolescent girls feel imprisoned by their own bodies, experience low self-esteem, and become depressed (Stice et al., 2000; Allgood-Merten et al., 1990). Many also develop eating disorders, as you saw in Chapter 11.

Throughout the 1990s it was generally believed that childhood and teenage depression would respond well to the same treatments that have been of help to depressed adults—cognitive-behavioral therapy, interpersonal approaches, and antidepressant drugs—and, in fact, many studies have indicated the effectiveness of such approaches (Curry & Becker, 2008; Fombonne & Zinck, 2008; Reinecke & Ginsburg, 2008). Some recent studies and events, however, have raised questions about these approaches and findings.

First, the National Institute of Mental Health recently sponsored a six-year, 13-site study called the *Treatments for Adolescents with Depression Study (TADS),* which compared the effectiveness of cognitive-behavioral therapy alone, antidepressant therapy alone, cognitive-behavioral and antidepressant therapy combined, and placebo therapy for teenage depression (Curry & Becker, 2008; TADS, 2007, 2004). Three major surprises emerged from this highly regarded study. First, neither antidepressants alone nor cognitive-behavioral therapy alone was as effective for teenage depression as was a combination of antidepressants and cognitive-behavioral therapy. Second, antidepressants alone tended to be significantly more helpful to depressed teens than cognitive-behavioral therapy alone. And third, cognitive-behavioral therapy alone was barely more helpful than placebo therapy.

Given cognitive-behavioral therapy's strong performance in other adolescent depression studies, many researchers believe that certain peculiarities in the subject population of the TADS study may have been responsible for its unexpected findings. However, other clinical theorists believe that the TADS study is indeed the definitive research undertaking that it was designed to be and that many depressed teens may in fact respond less well to cognitive-behavioral therapy than adults do. The clinical community is currently trying to sort out this important issue.

A second development in recent years has been the discovery that antidepressant drugs may be highly dangerous for some depressed children and teenagers. Throughout

HOME   SEND   EXPLORE

SEARCH

Alone in a Parallel Life

BY BERNADINE HEALY, M.D., *U.S. NEWS & WORLD REPORT*, MAY 21, 2007

The world wide web began as a platform for information, communication, and entertainment. It's now emerging as a powerful social medium, in which people build communities of newfound friends with whom they form personal and emotional bonds. One has to be concerned about this seemingly innocuous exercise in networking, however, if these bonds with people known only to the imagination—typically anonymous, sometimes misrepresented, and never accountable—interfere with or replace real intimacies, particularly in those who are in a formative stage of social development. Researchers at the Annenberg School Center for the Digital Future at the University of Southern California, which has been tracking Internet behavior for six years, were taken by surprise when their latest survey found that more than 40 percent of users feel that their online friends are every bit as important to them as their real-life ones.

Beyond communities of presumably real people is the Internet game world, in which emotional contacts are made in three-dimensional virtual reality with fantasy people in fantasy places. . . .

Little is known about what might be [the] safety concerns related to games in which young people create avatars [virtual representations of themselves] and interact freely in vivid imaginary worlds, largely unsupervised. Sometimes the play involves any number of supercharged violent or objectionable actions against other imaginary humans—taken without remorse or empathy or personal consequence. To be sure, there is disagreement on the impact of such experiences. Some psychologists argue that they might encourage the behavior in the real world; others that it has no effect and may even be a way to drain off aggressive feelings. Or, as in one study, a 15-year-old girl, whose avatar was a cyberprostitute, believed that her online behavior wasn't bad since it wasn't real. In essence, this girl is saying, just chill.

The unknown. Should we chill? As Harvard cyberresearcher and psychiatrist Steven Locke acknowledges, we've only scratched the surface when it comes to understanding how imaginary experiences that are so vividly realistic might affect

brain development in children. We know that real ones do. We also have to consider a broader but more subtle risk: that for some kids, a dependence on virtual human interactions, be they with real or with fantasy people, might influence their evolving social intelligence, affecting whom they trust and how they set expectations, how they deal with both affirmation and rejection, and how they give and receive emotional support. Remember, the virtual world can be just what you want it to be and can become an escape from reality.

In this regard, psychologists are concerned about one form of virtual escape—Internet addiction disorder, which can be a big relationship buster. Those with IAD become so immersed online that they neglect studies, work, friends, and family and when deprived of Internet access grow anxious or depressed. IAD has been reported worldwide in at least 2 percent of Internet users, and the young are most susceptible. Concerned, China last month mandated antiaddiction software to limit young people's Internet access to three hours per day.

But it's cybersmart parents who are best suited to influence their children's time online and also the places they go. Maybe the first question at the next PTA meeting should be, "Where was your 13-year-old's avatar last night?"

Oleg Nikishin/Getty Images

the 1990s, most psychiatrists believed that second-generation antidepressants were safe and effective for children and adolescents, and they prescribed them readily (Kutcher & Gardner, 2008; Holden, 2004). However, as you read in Chapter 10, the United States Food and Drug Administration (FDA) concluded in 2004, based on a number of clinical reports, that the drugs may produce a real, though small, increase in the risk of suicidal behavior for certain children and adolescents, especially during the first few months of treatment, and it ordered that all antidepressant containers carry "black box" warnings stating that the drugs "increase the risk of suicidal thinking and behavior in children."

Separation and depression
This 3-year-old boy hugs his father as the soldier departs for three months of special training and then deployment to Iraq. Given a growing body of research evidence that extended family separations often produce depression in children, clinical theorists are particularly worried about the emotional welfare of the thousands of children from military families who have been left behind during the wars in Iraq and Afghanistan.

•**oppositional defiant disorder**•
A childhood disorder in which children argue repeatedly with adults, lose their temper, and swear, feeling intense anger and resentment.

•**conduct disorder**•A childhood disorder in which the child repeatedly violates the basic rights of others, displaying aggression and sometimes destroying others' property, stealing, or running away from home.

Arguments about the wisdom of this FDA order have since followed. Although most clinicians agree that the drugs may indeed increase the risk of suicidal thoughts and attempts in as many as 2 to 4 percent of young patients, a number of observers have noted that the overall risk of suicide may actually be reduced for the vast majority of children who take the drugs (Kutcher & Gardner, 2008; Henderson, 2005). They point out, for example, that suicides among children and teenagers decreased by 30 percent in the decade leading up to 2004, as the number of antidepressant prescriptions provided to children and teenagers were soaring.

While the findings of the TADS study and questions about antidepressant drug safety continue to be sorted out, these two recent developments do serve to highlight once again the importance of research, particularly in the treatment realm. We are reminded that treatments that work for individuals of a certain age, gender, race, or ethnic background may be ineffective or even dangerous for other groups of individuals.

Bipolar Disorder

For decades, conventional clinical wisdom held that bipolar disorder is exclusively an *adult* mood disorder, whose earliest age of onset is the late teens. However, since the mid-1990s, clinical theorists have done an about-face, and a rapidly growing number of them now believe that many children display bipolar disorder. Indeed, in a review of national diagnostic trends from 1994 through 2003, it was found that the number of children—often very young children—and adolescents diagnosed and treated for bipolar disorder in U. S. mental health settings increased 40-fold, from 25 such diagnoses per 100,000 individuals in 1994 to 1,000 per 100,000 individuals in 2003 (Moreno et al., 2007). Correspondingly, the number of private office visits for children with bipolar disorders increased from 20,000 in 1994 to 800,000 in 2003. Furthermore, most clinical observers agree that the number of children and adolescents diagnosed with bipolar disorder has continued to rise sharply since 2003 (Carey, 2007).

Most theorists believe that these numbers reflect not an increase in the prevalence of bipolar disorders among children but, rather, a new diagnostic trend. The question is whether this trend is accurate. In a national survey of adults with bipolar disorders, 33 percent of the respondents recalled that their symptoms actually began before they reached 15 years of age, and another 27 percent said their symptoms first appeared between the ages of 15 and 19 (Hirschfield et al., 2003). Such responses indicate that bipolar disorders among children and teenagers have indeed been around for years but were overlooked by diagnosticians and therapists.

Some clinical theorists, however, distrust the accuracy of such retrospective reports and believe that the diagnosis of bipolar disorder is currently being overapplied to children and adolescents (Carey, 2007; Moreno et al., 2007). Indeed, they suggest that the label has become a clinical "catchall" that is being applied to almost every explosive, aggressive child. In fact, symptoms of rage and aggression, along with depression, dominate the clinical picture of most children who receive a bipolar diagnosis. The children typically do not manifest the symptoms of mania or the mood swings that characterize cases of adult bipolar disorder. Moreover, two-thirds of the children and adolescents who receive a bipolar diagnosis are boys, while adult men and women have bipolar disorder in equal numbers. Could it be, critics ask, that the bipolar label is being applied conveniently to childhood patterns for which there is currently no clear DSM category?

The outcome of this debate is important, particularly because the current shift in diagnoses has been accompanied by an increase in the number of children who receive adult medications for bipolar disorder (Moreno et al., 2007; Olfman, 2007). Around one-half of children in treatment for bipolar disorder receive an antipsychotic drug; one-third receive an antibipolar, or mood stabilizing, drug; and many others receive antidepressant or stimulant drugs. The majority, in fact, receive a combination of two or more such drugs, yet relatively few of these drugs have been tested on and approved specifically for use with children. Around 40 percent of children in treatment for bipolar disorder receive psychotherapy, particularly family therapy and cognitive-behavioral therapy (Cummings & Fristad, 2008; Carey, 2007). Clearly this is an issue that requires careful study.

✿Oppositional Defiant Disorder and Conduct Disorder

Most children break rules or misbehave on occasion (see Figure 17-1 and *Psych Watch* on page 559). If they consistently display extreme hostility and defiance, however, they may qualify for a diagnosis of oppositional defiant disorder or conduct disorder. Those with **oppositional defiant disorder** are often hostile (they argue repeatedly with adults, lose their temper, feel great anger and resentment) and disobedient (they ignore adult rules and requests) and display negative behaviors (they may try to annoy other people and blame others for their own mistakes and problems). As many as 10 percent of children qualify for this diagnosis (McMahon & Kotler, 2008; Nock et al., 2007). The disorder is more common in boys than in girls before puberty but equal in both sexes after puberty.

Children with **conduct disorder,** a more severe problem, repeatedly violate the basic rights of others. They are often aggressive and may be physically cruel to people or animals, deliberately destroy other people's property, skip school, or run away from home (see Table 17-1 on the next page). Many steal from, threaten, or harm their victims, committing such crimes as shoplifting, forgery, breaking into buildings or cars, mugging, and armed robbery. As they get older, their acts of physical violence may include rape or, in rare cases, homicide (APA, 2000). The symptoms of conduct disorder are apparent in this summary of a clinical interview with a 15-year-old boy named Derek:

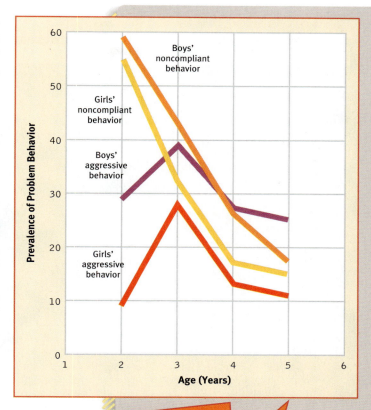

Figure 17-1
Early misbehavior Teachers' evaluations of more than 700 preschoolers indicated that the rates of both noncompliant and aggressive behavior dropped as the children grew older. (Adapted from Crowther et al., 1981.)

Questioning revealed that Derek was getting into . . . serious trouble of late, having been arrested for shoplifting 4 weeks before. Derek was caught with one other youth when he and a dozen friends swarmed a convenience store and took everything they could before leaving in cars. This event followed similar others at a compact disc store and a retail clothing store. Derek blamed his friends for getting caught because they apparently left him behind as he straggled out of the store. He was charged only with shoplifting, however, after police found him holding just three candy bars and a bag of potato chips. Derek expressed no remorse for the theft or any care for the store clerk who was injured when one of the teens pushed her into a glass case. When informed of the clerk's injury, for example, Derek replied, "I didn't do it, so what do I care?"

The psychologist decided to question Derek further about other legal violations in the past. He discovered a rather extended history of trouble. Ten months earlier, Derek had been arrested for vandalism—breaking windows and damaging cars—on school property. He was placed on probation for 6 months because this was his first offense. In addition, Derek boasted of other exploits for which he was not caught, including several shoplifting attempts, heavy marijuana use on the weekends, joyriding, and missing school. . . . Derek had missed 23 days (50 percent) of school since the beginning of the academic year. . . . In addition, Derek described break-in attempts of his neighbors' apartments and his precocious sexual activity. . . . Only rarely during the interview did Derek stray from his bravado.

(Kearney, 1999, pp. 104–105)

BETWEEN THE LINES

Narrowing the Gender Gap

The number of teenage girls arrested for aggravated assault has doubled over the past 20 years, compared to a rise of 13 percent among boys. ‹‹

Today, one of every three teens arrested for violent crimes is female. ‹‹

(Scelfo, 2005)

table: **17-1**

DSM Checklist

CONDUCT DISORDER

1. A repetitive and persistent pattern of behavior in which the basic rights of others or major age-appropriate societal norms or rules are violated, with at least three of the following present in the past twelve months (and at least one in the past six months):
    a. Frequent bullying or threatening of others.
    b. Frequent provoking of physical fights.
    c. Using dangerous weapons.
    d. Physical cruelty to people.
    e. Physical cruelty to animals.
    f. Stealing while confronting a victim.
    g. Forcing someone into sexual activity.
    h. Fire-setting.
    i. Deliberately destroying others' property.
    j. Breaking into a house, building, or car.
    k. Frequent manipulation of others.
    l. Stealing items of nontrivial value without confronting a victim.
    m. Frequent staying out beyond curfews, beginning before the age of 13.
    n. Running away from home overnight at least twice.
    o. Frequent truancy from school, beginning before the age of 13.

2. Significant impairment.

Based on APA, 2000.

Conduct disorder usually begins between 7 and 15 years of age (APA, 2000). As many as 10 percent of children, three-quarters of them boys, qualify for this diagnosis (Nock et al., 2006; Hibbs & Jensen, 2005). Children with a mild conduct disorder often improve over time, but severe cases may continue into adulthood and develop into antisocial personality disorder or other psychological problems (Phares, 2008). Usually, the earlier the onset of the conduct disorder, the poorer the eventual outcome. Research indicates that more than 80 percent of individuals who develop conduct disorder first display a pattern of oppositional defiant disorder (Lahey, 2008; Lahey & Loeber, 1994).

Many clinical theorists believe that there are actually several kinds of conduct disorder. One team of researchers, for example, distinguishes four patterns: (1) the *overt-destructive* pattern, in which individuals display openly aggressive and confrontational behaviors; (2) the *overt-nondestructive* pattern, dominated by openly offensive but nonconfrontational behaviors such as lying; (3) the *covert-destructive* pattern, characterized by secretive destructive behaviors such as violating other people's property, breaking and entering, and setting fires; and (4) the *covert-nondestructive* pattern, in which individuals secretly commit nonaggressive behaviors, such as being truant from school (McMahon & Frick, 2005). Some individuals with conduct disorder display only one of these patterns, while others display a combination of them. It may be that the different patterns have different causes.

Other researchers distinguish yet another pattern of aggression found in certain cases of conduct disorder, *relational aggression,* in which the individuals are socially isolated and primarily display social misdeeds such as slandering others, spreading rumors, and manipulating friendships (Underwood, 2003). Relational aggression is more common among girls than boys.

Unthinkable
A surveillance camera shows the 1993 abduction of 2-year-old James Bulger from a shopping mall in England. The child holds the hand of one of his abductors—two 10-year-old boys who were later convicted of his torture and murder. The legal case stirred the emotions of people around the world and clarified once again that some children are indeed capable of extreme anti-social behavior.

Photo by BWP Media via Getty Images

Bullying: A Growing Crisis?

Does bullying qualify as a national crisis? Even to pose the question sounds a bit silly, conjuring up images of the schoolyard thug from the *Calvin and Hobbes* comic strip or Bart's nemesis on *The Simpsons*. But many sober voices say that bullying is no laughing matter and warn that if society continues to overlook this problem, it will place its citizens, particularly its children, at considerable risk (Jacobs, 2008; Rigby, 2002).

A report examining the many school shootings that have taken place across the United States since 1997 found that bullying was a factor in two-thirds of them (Crisp, 2001). In some cases, the shooters had been bullies; much more often, they had been the *victims* of bullying. A survey released by the Kaiser Family Foundation and Nickelodeon asked a national sample of children aged 8 to 15 what issues in school concerned them most, and all age groups pointed to teasing and bullying as "big problems" that ranked higher than racism, AIDS, and peer pressure to try sex or alcohol (Cukan, 2001). More generally, over one-quarter of students report being bullied frequently and more than 70 percent report having been a victim at least once, with victims typically reacting with feelings of humiliation, anxiety, or dislike for school (Jacobs, 2008; Nishina et al., 2005). Just as troubling, the technological advances of our plugged-in world have broadened the ways in which children and adolescents can be bullied, and today bullying by e-mail, text-messaging, and the like is on the rise (Jacobs, 2008). Issues such as these have elevated bullying from a narrow concern that is best dealt with by students themselves (or perhaps by the teachers and parents of those directly involved) to a

Cyberbullying Tina Meier holds two pictures of her daughter Megan, a 13-year-old who hanged herself after receiving cruel messages on her MySpace page. Believing that she had struck up a warm online relationship with a 16-year-old boy, the girl became despondent when he began sending a barrage of hateful insults and mean messages to her. As it turned out, the boy did not exist and the messages had all been sent through a false-identity account by several persons who were trying to upset Megan.

widespread problem that requires the attention of school-level programs and statewide policies.

Thus, a growing number of schools—from elementary through high school—have implemented programs with features such as teaching students how to deal more

effectively with tormentors, working systematically to change the mind-set of bullies, teacher training, parent discussion groups, school prevention measures, and implementation of classroom rules and interventions (Jacobs, 2008; Frey et al., 2005; Twemlow et al., 2003; Rahey & Craig, 2002; Cunningham & Henggeler, 2001). In addition, public health campaigns have been developed to spread the word about antibullying programs, including the "Stop Bullying Now" campaign by the U.S. Department of Health and Human Services.

While acknowledging the important impact of bullying in school shootings, e-mail and text-messaging harassment, and the like, some experts worry that the public, school officials, and policy makers are focusing on this issue so intensely that more subtle and perhaps more significant factors are being ignored by clinicians and researchers. Why has the public concentrated so much attention on bullying as it tries to sort out school shootings and other unthinkable acts by children and teenagers? Perhaps, some experts argue, because bullying offers a quick explanation and a ready focus for intervention and change.

At the same time, some worry that the commonplace nature of bullying may in fact render it an elusive problem to address. How easy can it be for clinicians to identify which children will turn dangerously violent if indeed 70 percent of all children have experienced bullying? How can we rid ourselves of a problem as pervasive as this? As one commentator said, "Short of raising kids in isolation chambers . . . bullying behaviors can never be eliminated entirely from the sustained hazing ritual known as growing up" (Angier, 2001).

More than one-third of boys and one-half of girls with conduct disorder also display attention-deficit/hyperactivity disorder (ADHD), a disorder that you will read about shortly (Waschbusch, 2002). In most such cases, ADHD is believed to precede and help cause the conduct disorder. Individuals with both of these disorders typically have more severe symptoms, commit a higher number of aggressive acts, and display more violence when they become adults (McMahon & Frick, 2005).

Many children with conduct disorder also experience depression. In such cases, the conduct disorder typically precedes the onset of depressive symptoms. This combination of symptoms places the individuals at higher risk for suicide (Loeber & Keenan, 1994). Anxiety may also accompany conduct problems, especially among girls.

Many children with conduct disorder are suspended from school, placed in foster homes, or incarcerated. When children between the ages of 8 and 18 break the law, the legal system often labels them *juvenile delinquents* (Lahey, 2008; Heilbrun et al., 2005). More than half of the juveniles who are arrested each year are *recidivists,* meaning they have records of previous arrests. Boys are much more involved in juvenile crime than girls, although rates for girls are on the increase. Girls are most likely to be arrested for drug use, sexual offenses, and running away, boys for drug use and crimes against prop–erty. Arrests of teenagers for serious crimes have at least tripled during the past 20 years (U.S. Department of Justice, 2006, 2000, 1994).

A CLOSER LOOK

Child Abuse

What I remember most about my mother was that she was always beating me. She'd beat me with her high-heeled shoes, with my father's belt, with a potato masher. When I was eight, she black and blued my legs so badly, I told her I'd go to the police. She said, "Go, they'll just put you into the darkest prison." So I stayed. When my breasts started growing at 13, she beat me across the chest until I fainted. Then she'd hug me and ask forgiveness. . . . Most kids have nightmares about being taken away from their parents. I would sit on our front porch crooning softly of going far, far away to find another mother.

(*TIME*, SEPTEMBER 5, 1983, P. 20)

A problem that affects all too many children and has an enormous im-pact on their psychological development is *child abuse,* the nonaccidental use of excessive physical or psychological force by an adult on a child, often with the in-tention of hurting or destroying the child. At least 5 percent, and perhaps as many as 26 percent, of children in the United States are physically abused each year (Phares, 2008). Surveys suggest that 1 of every 10 children is the victim of severe violence, such as being kicked, bitten, hit, beaten, or threatened with a knife or a gun. In fact, some observers believe that physical abuse and neglect are the leading causes of death among young children.

Overall, girls and boys are physically abused at approximately the same rate (Humphrey, 2006). However, boys are at greatest risk when they are under the age of 12, while the risk for girls is high-est when they are older than 12 (Azar et al., 1998). Although child abuse occurs in all socioeconomic groups, it is apparently more common among the poor (Mammen et al., 2002).

Abusers are usually the child's parents (Faust et al., 2008; Humphrey, 2006). Clinical investigators have learned that abusive parents often have poor impulse control, low self-esteem, and weak parent-ing skills (Tolan et al., 2006; Mammen et al., 2002). Many have been abused them-selves as children and have had poor role models (McCaghy et al., 2006). In some cases, they are experiencing the stress of marital discord or family unemployment (Faust et al., 2008).

Studies suggest that the victims of child abuse may suffer both immediate and long-term psychological effects. Research has revealed, for example, that abused chil-dren have more performance and behavior problems in school. Long-term negative effects include lack of social acceptance, a higher number of medical and psychologi-cal disorders (including posttraumatic stress disorder and depression), more abuse of

alcohol and other substances, more ar-rests during adolescence and adulthood, a greater risk of becoming criminally violent, a higher unemployment rate, and a higher suicide rate (Faust et al., 2008; Harkness & Lumley, 2008; Safren et al., 2002; Mol-nar et al., 2001; Widom, 2001). Finally, as many as one-third of abuse victims grow up to be abusive, neglectful, or inadequate parents themselves (Heyman & Slep, 2002; Clarke et al., 1999).

Two forms of child abuse have re-ceived special attention: psychological and sexual abuse. *Psychological abuse* may include severe rejection, excessive discipline, scapegoating and ridicule, isolation, and refusal to provide help for a child with psychological problems (Faust et al., 2008). It probably accompanies all forms of physical abuse and neglect and often occurs by itself. *Child sexual abuse,* the use of a child for gratification of adult sexual desires, may occur outside of or within the home (Faust et al., 2008; Mc-Caghy et al., 2006). Surveys suggest that at least 13 percent of women were forced into sexual contact with an adult male during their childhood, many of them with their father or stepfather (Phares, 2008, 2003; Hill, 2003). At least 4 percent of men were also sexually abused during childhood (Romano & DeLuca, 2001).

What Are the Causes of Conduct Disorder?

Many cases of conduct disorder have been linked to genetic and biological factors, particularly cases marked by destructive behaviors (Blair et al., 2006; Simonoff, 2001). In addition, a number of cases have been linked to drug abuse, poverty, traumatic events, and exposure to violent peers or community violence (Hibbs & Jensen, 2005; Hill & Maughan, 2001). Most often, however, conduct disorder has been tied to troubled parent-child relationships, inadequate parenting, family conflict, marital conflict, and family hostility (Phares, 2003; Biederman et al., 2001). Children whose parents reject, leave, coerce, or abuse them or fail to provide appropriate and consistent supervision are apparently more likely to develop conduct problems. Similarly, children seem more prone to this disorder when their parents are antisocial, display excessive anger, or have substance–related, mood, or schizophrenic disorders (Julien, 2008) (see *A Closer Look* below).

Direct intervention Montana's Family Support Network tries to address reported cases of child abuse by directly teaching parents better ways of coping and interacting with their children. Here a clinician first uses a monitoring system to observe parents interacting with their children and then uses an earpiece and microphone to provide on-the-spot guidance and suggestions.

Child sexual abuse appears to be equally common across all socioeconomic classes, races, and ethnic groups (McCaghy et al., 2006).

A variety of therapies have been used in cases of child abuse, including groups sponsored by *Parents Anonymous,* which helps parents to develop insight into their behavior, provide training on alternatives to abuse, and teach parenting skills (Tolan et al., 2006; Wolfe et al., 1988). Still other treatments help parents deal more effectively with the stresses that often trigger the abuse, such as unemployment, marital conflict, and feelings of depression. In addition, prevention programs, often in the form of home visitations and parent training, have proved promising (Wekerle et al., 2007).

Finally, research suggests that the psychological needs of the child victims should be addressed as early as possible (Gray et al., 2000; Roesler & McKenzie, 1994). Clinicians and educators have launched *early detection programs* that aim to (1) educate all children about child abuse, (2) teach them skills for avoiding or escaping from abusive situations, (3) encourage children to tell another adult if they are abused, and (4) assure them that abuse is never their own fault (Godenzi & DePuy, 2001; Finkelhor et al., 1995). These programs seem to increase the likelihood that children will report abuse, reduce their tendency to blame themselves for it, and increase their feelings of efficacy (Goodman-Brown et al., 2003; MacIntyre & Carr, 1999).

Reuters/Courtesy of Waycross, Georgia, Police Dept./Handout

No age minimum
The numerous school shootings that have occurred over the past decade clarify that even very young children are sometimes capable of extreme violence. This photo, released by police in Georgia, shows the various weapons that a group of 9-year-olds recently brought to school in a plot to injure their teacher.

How Do Clinicians Treat Conduct Disorder?

Because aggressive behaviors become more locked in with age, treatments for conduct disorder are generally most effective with children younger than 13 (Hibbs & Jensen, 2005). A number of interventions, from sociocultural to child-focused, have been developed in recent years to treat children with the disorder. As you will see, several of these have had modest (and at times moderate) success, but clearly no one of them alone is the answer for this difficult problem. In fact, given that conduct disorder affects all spheres of the child's life—family, school, social, and community—today's clinicians are increasingly combining several approaches into a wide-ranging treatment program (Boxer & Frick, 2008).

Sociocultural Treatments Given the importance of family factors in conduct disorder, therapists often use family interventions. One such approach, used with preschoolers, is called *parent-child interaction therapy* (Querido & Eyberg, 2005). Here therapists teach parents to work with their child positively, to set appropriate limits, to act consistently, to be fair in their discipline decisions, and to establish more appropriate expectations regarding the child. The therapists also try to teach the child better social skills. Ideally, these efforts strengthen the relationship between the parents and child, improve the parents' attitudes, lead to greater parent control, and help bring about improvements in the child's behavior. A related family intervention for very young children, *video tape modeling,* works toward the same goals with the help of video tools (Webster-Stratton, 2005).

When children reach school age, therapists often use a family intervention called *parent management training.* In this approach (1) parents are again taught more effective ways to deal with their children and (2) parents and children meet together in behavior-oriented family therapy (McMahon & Kotler, 2008; Kazdin, 2007, 2003, 2002). Typically, the family and therapist target particular behaviors for change; then, with the help of written manuals, therapy rehearsals and practice, and homework, the parents are taught how to better identify problem behaviors, stop rewarding unwanted behaviors, and reward proper behaviors with consistency (Kendall, 2000). Like the preschool family interventions, parent management training has often achieved a measure of success (McMahon & Kotler, 2008).

Other sociocultural approaches, such as residential treatment in the community and programs at school, have also helped some children improve (Boxer & Frick, 2008; Henggeler & Lee, 2003). In one such approach, *treatment foster care,* delinquent boys and girls with conduct disorder are assigned to a foster home in the community by the juvenile justice system. While there, the children, foster parents, and biological parents all

Breeding ground for antisocial behavior?
Conduct disorders are more common among children who have been exposed regularly to community violence. Thus clinicians worry that life in war-torn areas may foster antisocial behaviors among the young residents who are raised there. Here an Iraqi girl "plays" with a plastic handgun, pointing it at the head of a young playmate, while a soldier looks on.

Cris Bouroncle/AFP/Getty Images

receive training and treatment interventions, including family therapy with both sets of parents, individual treatment for the child, and meetings with school, parole, and probation officers. In addition, the children and their parents continue to receive treatment and support after they leave foster care. This program is apparently most beneficial when all the intervention components are applied simultaneously.

In contrast to these sociocultural interventions, institutionalization in so-called *juvenile training centers* has not met with much success (Heilbrun et al., 2005; Tate et al., 1995). In fact, such institutions frequently serve to strengthen delinquent behavior rather than resocialize young offenders (see Figure 17-2).

Child-Focused Treatments

Treatments that focus primarily on the child with conduct disorder, particularly cognitive-behavioral interventions, have achieved some success in recent years (Kazdin, 2007, 2003, 2002; Lochman, Barry, & Pardini, 2003). In an approach called *problem-solving skills training,* therapists combine modeling, practice, role-playing, and systematic rewards to help teach children constructive thinking and positive social behaviors. During therapy sessions, the therapists may play games and solve tasks with the children and later help the children apply the lessons and skills derived from the games and tasks to real-life situations.

In another child-focused approach, the *Anger Coping and Coping Power Program,* children with conduct problems participate in group sessions that teach them to manage their anger more effectively, view situations in perspective, solve problems, become aware of their emotions, build social skills, set goals, and handle peer pressure. (While the children receive this group training, their parents participate in group sessions of their own.) Studies indicate that child-focused approaches such as these do indeed help reduce aggressive behaviors and prevent substance use in adolescence (Boxer & Frick, 2008; Lochman et al., 2003).

Recently, drug therapy has also been used on children with conduct disorder. Studies suggest that *stimulant drugs* may be particularly helpful in reducing their aggressive behaviors at home and at school (Connor et al., 2002; Gerardin et al., 2002).

Prevention

It may be that the greatest hope for dealing with the problem of conduct disorder lies in *prevention* programs that begin in the earliest stages of childhood (Boxer & Frick, 2008; Hill & Maughan, 2001). These programs try to change unfavorable social conditions before a conduct disorder is able to develop. The programs may offer training opportunities for young people, recreational facilities, and health care and may try to ease the stresses of poverty and improve parents' child-rearing skills. All such approaches work best when they educate and involve the family.

Figure 17-2
Teenage crime Although teenagers make up only 14 percent of the total population, they commit around 30 percent of all violent crimes and 34 percent of all murders. They are also the victims of 33 percent of all violent crimes. (Adapted from National Crime Victimization Survey, 2006, 1997, 1996, 1993; Levesque, 2002.)

Prevention: Scared Straight
Rather than waiting for children or adolescents to develop antisocial patterns, many clinicians call for better *prevention* programs. In one such program, "at-risk" children visit nearby prisons where inmates describe how drugs, gang life, and other antisocial behaviors led to their imprisonment. Here an inmate at a Wisconsin prison, serving life without parole for the killing of a friend, "explains" in no uncertain terms how his lifestyle led to his present predicament.

✿Attention-Deficit/Hyperactivity Disorder

Children who display **attention-deficit/hyperactivity disorder (ADHD)** have great difficulty attending to tasks, or behave overactively and impulsively, or both (see Table 17–2). The disorder often appears before the child starts school, as with Eddie, one of the boys we met at the beginning of this chapter. Steven is another child whose symptoms began very early in life:

Steven's mother cannot remember a time when her son was not into something or in trouble. As a baby he was incredibly active, so active in fact that he nearly rocked his crib apart. All the bolts and screws became loose and had to be tightened periodically. Steven was also always into forbidden places, going through the medicine cabinet or under the kitchen sink. He once swallowed some washing detergent and had to be taken to the emergency room. As a matter of fact, Steven had many more accidents and was more clumsy than his older brother and younger sister. . . . He always seemed to be moving fast. His mother recalls that Steven progressed from the crawling stage to a running stage with very little walking in between.

Trouble really started to develop for Steven when he entered kindergarten. Since his entry into school, his life has been miserable and so has the teacher's. Steven does not seem capable of attending to assigned tasks and following instructions. He would rather be talking to a neighbor or wandering around the room without the teacher's permission. When he is seated and the teacher is keeping an eye on him to make sure that he works, Steven's body still seems to be in motion. He is either tapping his pencil, fidgeting, or staring out the window and daydreaming. Steven hates kindergarten and has few long-term friends; indeed, school rules and demands appear to be impossible challenges for him. The effects of this mismatch are now showing in Steven's schoolwork and attitude. He has fallen behind academically and has real difficulty mastering new concepts; he no longer follows directions from the teacher and has started to talk back.

(Gelfand, Jenson, & Drew, 1982, p. 256)

The symptoms of ADHD often feed into one another (Stevens & Ward–Estes, 2006). Children who have trouble focusing attention may keep turning from task to task until they end up trying to run in several directions at once. Similarly, constantly moving children may find it hard to attend to tasks or show good judgment. In many cases one of these symptoms stands out much more than the other. About half of the children

"Playing" attention A range of techniques have been used to help understand and treat children with ADHD, including a computer program called Play Attention. Here, under the watchful eye of a behavior specialist, a girl with ADHD wears a bike helmet that measures brain waves while she performs tasks that challenge her to pay attention.

table: 17-2

DSM Checklist

ATTENTION-DEFICIT/HYPERACTIVITY DISORDER

1. Either of the following groups:
   A. At least six of the following symptoms of *inattention*, persisting for at least six months to a degree that is maladaptive and inconsistent with development level:
      a. Frequent failure to give close attention to details, or making careless mistakes.
      b. Frequent difficulty in sustaining attention.
      c. Frequent failure to listen when spoken to directly.
      d. Frequent failure to follow through on instructions and failure to finish work.
      e. Difficulty organizing tasks and activities.
      f. Avoidance of, dislike of, and reluctance to engage in tasks that require sustained mental effort.
      g. Frequent loss of items necessary for tasks or activities.
      h. Easy distraction by irrelevant stimuli.
      i. Forgetfulness in daily activities.

   B. At least six of the following symptoms of *hyperactivity-impulsivity,* persisting for at least six months to a degree that is maladaptive and inconsistent with developmental level:
      a. Fidgeting with hands or feet, or squirming in seat.
      b. Frequent wandering from seat in classroom or similar situation.
      c. Frequent running about or climbing excessively in situations in which it is inappropriate.
      d. Frequent difficulty playing or engaging in leisure activities quietly.
      e. Frequent "on the go" activity or acting as if "driven by a motor."
      f. Frequent excessive talking.
      g. Frequent blurting out of answers before questions have been completed.
      h. Frequent difficulty awaiting turn.
      i. Frequent interrupting of or intruding on others.

2. The presence of some symptoms before the age of 7.
3. Impairment from the symptoms in at least two settings.
4. Significant impairment.

Based on APA, 2000.

•**attention-deficit/hyperactivity disorder (ADHD)**•A disorder marked by inability to focus attention, or overactive and impulsive behavior, or both.

with ADHD also have learning or communication problems, many perform poorly in school, a number have difficulty interacting with other children, and about 80 percent misbehave, often quite seriously (Phares, 2008; Watson et al., 2008). It is also common for these children to have anxiety or mood problems (Julien, 2008).

Around 5 percent of schoolchildren display ADHD, as many as 90 percent of them boys (Hoza, Kaisar, & Hurt, 2008; Rapport et al., 2008). Those whose parents have had ADHD are more likely than others to develop it (APA, 2000). The disorder usually persists throughout childhood. Many children show a marked lessening of symptoms as they move into mid-adolescence, but between 35 and 60 percent of affected children continue to have ADHD as adults (Julien, 2008; Kessler et al., 2006, 2005). The symptoms of restlessness and overactivity are not usually as pronounced in adult cases.

What Are the Causes of ADHD?

Today's clinicians generally consider ADHD to have several interacting causes. Biological factors have been identified in many cases, particularly abnormal activity of the neurotransmitter *dopamine* and abnormalities in the *frontal-striatal* regions of the brain

BETWEEN THE LINES

ADHD in the Workplace

Young adults with ADHD are more likely than other young adults to be fired from their jobs, change jobs more frequently, and earn low work performance appraisals (Rapport et al., 2008). «

(Julien, 2008; Teicher et al., 2008). The disorder has also been linked to high levels of stress and to family dysfunctioning (Rapport et al., 2008; Barkley, 2006, 2004, 2002). In addition, sociocultural theorists have noted that ADHD symptoms and a diagnosis of ADHD may themselves create interpersonal problems and produce additional symptoms in the child. That is, children who are hyperactive tend to be viewed particularly negatively by their peers and by their parents, and they often view themselves negatively as well (Rapport et al., 2008; McCormick, 2000).

Three other explanations for attention-deficit/hyperactivity disorder have received considerable press coverage: (1) ADHD is caused by sugar or food additives, (2) ADHD results from environmental toxins such as lead, and (3) excessive exposure of children to television can contribute to ADHD. Only the third of these explanations has found any degree of research support. One study indicated, for example, a link between excessive TV watching during the first three years of life and weak attention at age 7 (Christakis et al., 2004).

How Do Clinicians Assess ADHD?

ADHD is a difficult disorder to assess (Rapport et al., 2008; Nichols & Waschbusch, 2004). Ideally, the child's behavior should be observed in several environmental settings (school, home, with friends) because the symptoms of hyperactivity and inattentiveness must be present across multiple settings in order to fit DSM-IV-TR's criteria. Because children with this disorder often give poor descriptions of their symptoms and tend to underreport the severity and impairment of their behaviors, it is important to obtain reports of the child's symptoms from his or her parents and teachers. In addition to these reports and to clinical observations, clinicians commonly employ diagnostic interviews, ratings scales, and psychological tests to assess ADHD. Intelligence tests and neuropsychological tests may also be used. Unfortunately, although ADHD can be diagnosed reliably only after a battery of observations, interviews, psychological tests, and physical exams, studies suggest that many children receive their diagnosis from pediatricians or family physicians and that only one-third to one-half of such diagnoses are based on psychological or educational testing (Hoagwood et al., 2000).

How Is ADHD Treated?

There is heated disagreement about the most effective treatment for ADHD (DuPaul & Barkley, 2008; Hoza et al., 2008). The most commonly applied approaches are drug therapy, behavioral therapy, or a combination of the two.

Drug Therapy Like Tom, millions of children and adults with ADHD are currently treated with **methylphenidate,** a stimulant drug that actually has been available for decades, or with certain other stimulants.

- -

When Tom was born, he acted like a "crack baby," his mother, Ann, says. "He responded violently to even the slightest touch, and he never slept." Shortly after Tom turned two, the local day care center asked Ann to withdraw him. They deemed his behavior "just too aberrant," she remembers. Tom's doctors ran a battery of tests to screen for brain damage, but they found no physical explanation for his lack of self-control. In fact, his IQ was high—even though he performed poorly in school. Eventually, Tom was diagnosed with attention-deficit/hyperactivity disorder (ADHD). . . . The psychiatrist told Ann that in terms of severity, Tom was 15 on a scale of one to 10. As therapy, this doctor prescribed methylphenidate, a drug better known by its brand name, Ritalin.

(Leutwyler, 1996, p. 13)

•**methylphenidate**•A stimulant drug, known better by the trade name Ritalin, commonly used to treat ADHD.

Although a variety of manufacturers now produce methylphenidate, the drug continues to be known to the public by its most famous trade name, **Ritalin.** As researchers have confirmed Ritalin's quieting effect on children with ADHD and its ability to help them focus, solve complex tasks, perform better at school, and control aggression, use of the drug has increased enormously—according to some estimates, at least a threefold increase since 1990 alone (Anderson, 2007; Barkley, 2006, 2004, 2002) (see Figure 17-3). This increase in use also extends to preschoolers (Zito et al., 2000).

As many as 10 to 12 percent of all American boys may take Ritalin for ADHD, and the number of girls taking it is growing. Around 8.5 tons of Ritalin are produced each year; 90 percent of it is used in the United States (DEA, 2000). In recent years, certain other stimulant drugs also have been found to be helpful in cases of ADHD, leading to corresponding increases in their use (Biederman, Spencer & Wilens, 2005). Collectively, the stimulant drugs are now the most common treatment for ADHD (Hoza et al., 2008). Many clinicians, however, worry about the possible long-term effects of the drugs, and others question whether the favorable findings of the drug studies (most of which have been done on white American children) are applicable to children from minority groups (Biederman et al., 2005, 2004).

Extensive investigations indicate that ADHD is overdiagnosed in the United States, so many children who are receiving Ritalin may, in fact, have been inaccurately diagnosed (Rapport et al., 2008; DEA, 2000; UNINCB, 1996). In addition, a number of clinicians and parents have questioned the safety of Ritalin. During the late 1980s, several lawsuits were filed against physicians, schools, and even the American Psychiatric Association, claiming misuse of Ritalin (Safer, 1994). Most of the suits were dismissed, yet the media blitz they engendered has affected public perceptions. At the same time, Ritalin has become a popular recreational drug among teenagers; some snort it to get high, and a number become dependent on it, further raising public concerns about the drug (Biederman et al., 2005).

On the positive side, Ritalin is apparently very helpful to children and adults who do suffer from ADHD. As you will see, behavioral programs are also effective in many cases, but not in all. Moreover, the behavioral programs tend to be most effective when they are combined with Ritalin or similar drugs (MTA Cooperative Group, 2004, 1999). When children with ADHD are taken off the drugs—frequently because of the drugs' negative publicity—many fare badly (Safer & Krager, 1992).

Most studies to date have indicated that Ritalin is safe for the majority of people with ADHD (Rapport et al., 2008; Biederman et al., 2005; Pennington, 2002). Its undesired effects are usually no worse than insomnia, stomachaches, headaches, or loss of appetite. However, a recent wave of research and case reports suggests that, in a small number of cases, Ritalin and related drugs may increase the risk of having a heart attack (particularly in adults with high blood pressure) and produce psychotic symptoms or facial tics (Carey, 2006). They also apparently can affect the growth of some children, thus requiring "drug holidays" to prevent such an effect. Clearly, more studies are needed to ascertain the full impact and long-term effects of Ritalin and other ADHD drugs (Biederman et al., 2005).

Behavior Therapy and Combination Therapies

Behavioral therapy has been applied in many cases of ADHD. Here parents and teachers learn how to reward attentiveness or self-control in the children, often placing them on a token economy program. Such operant conditioning treatments have been helpful for a number of

Figure 17-3

The rise of Ritalin The use of Ritalin has been increasing since the early 1980s, when researchers discovered that it helped people with ADHD. (Adapted from Drug Enforcement Administration, 2002, 2000, 1996.)

BETWEEN THE LINES

Divorce and Ritalin

A Canadian study found that children of divorced parents are almost twice as likely as other children to be prescribed Ritalin (6 percent versus 3.3 percent) (Anderson, 2007). ‹‹

Jose Azel/Aurora

Behavioral intervention
Educational and treatment programs for children with ADHD use behavioral principles that clearly spell out target behaviors and program rewards and systematically reinforce appropriate behaviors by the children.

children, especially when combined with stimulant drug therapy (Rapport et al., 2008; Barkley, 2006, 2004, 2002). Combining behavioral and drug therapies is also desirable because, according to research, children who receive both treatments require lower levels of medication, meaning, of course, that they are less subject to the medication's undesired effects (Hoza et al., 2008).

Because children with ADHD often display other (comorbid) psychological disorders as well, researchers have further tried to determine which treatments work best for different combinations of disorders. It appears that for children with ADHD alone, either medication or medication combined with behavioral therapy is more effective than behavioral therapy alone (MTA Cooperative Group, 2004, 1999). For children who display both ADHD and conduct disorder, medication appears to be the most effective approach. Children with ADHD and anxiety disorders seem to benefit from either medication or behavioral therapy, or both. Those with a combination of ADHD, conduct disorder, and anxiety symptoms respond best when treated with both medication and behavioral therapy (Stevens & Ward-Estes, 2006; Jensen et al., 2001). The treatments that are of help to children and adolescents also tend to be effective for adults with ADHD (Biederman et al., 2005; Faraone et al., 2004).

Multicultural Factors and ADHD

Throughout this book, you have seen that race often affects how persons are diagnosed and treated for various psychological disorders. Thus, you should not be totally surprised that race also seems to come into play with regard to ADHD.

A number of studies indicate that African American and Hispanic American children with significant attention and activity problems are less likely than white American children with similar symptoms to be assessed for ADHD, receive an ADHD diagnosis, or undergo treatment for this disorder (Bussing et al., 2005, 2003, 1998; Stevens et al., 2005). Moreover, among those who do receive an ADHD diagnosis and treatment, children from racial minorities are less likely than white American children to be treated with stimulant drugs or a combination of stimulants and behavioral therapy—the interventions that seem to be of most help to those with ADHD (Stevens et al., 2005; Cooper, 2004; Hoagwood et al., 2000). And, finally, among children who do receive stimulant drug treatment for ADHD, children from racial minorities are less likely than white American children to receive the promising (but more expensive) *long-acting* stimulant drugs that have been developed in recent years (Cooper, 2004). It is important to note that these patterns are not the result of racial differences in drug tolerance: research clarifies that children of all races respond similarly to the various stimulant drugs.

In part, these racial differences in diagnosis and treatment are tied to economic factors. Studies consistently reveal that poorer children are less likely than wealthier ones to be identified as having ADHD and are less likely to receive effective treatment, and racial minority families have, on average, lower incomes and weaker insurance coverage than white American families. Consistent with this point, one study found that privately insured African American children with ADHD do in fact receive higher, more effective doses of stimulant drugs than do Medicaid-insured African American children with ADHD (Lipkin et al., 2005).

A growing number of clinical theorists further believe that social bias and stereotyping may contribute to the racial differences in diagnosis and treatment that have been observed. The theorists argue that our society often views the learning and behavioral symptoms of ADHD as medical problems when exhibited by white American children but as indicators of poor parenting, lower IQ, substance use, or violence when displayed by African American and Hispanic American children (Kendall & Hatton, 2002). This notion has been supported by the finding that white American parents of ADHD children are more likely than African American parents to believe that ADHD is caused by genetic and biological problems and less likely than African American parents to cite parenting issues or life stressors as causes of ADHD (Stief, 2004). Small wonder that, according to several studies, African American and Hispanic American parents are less inclined than white American parents to believe that their children may have ADHD or to seek ADHD evaluations and treatments for their children (Stevens et al., 2005; Kendall & Hatton, 2002). In a similar vein, some studies have found that, all symptoms being equal, teachers are more likely to conclude that overactive white American children have ADHD but that overactive African American or Hispanic American children have other kinds of difficulties (Raymond, 1997; Samuel et al., 1997).

Whatever the reason—economic disadvantage, social bias, racial stereotyping, or other factors—it appears that children from racial minority groups are less likely to receive a proper ADHD diagnosis and treatment. While many of today's clinical theorists correctly alert us to the possibility that ADHD may be generally overdiagnosed and overtreated, it is important to also recognize that children from certain segments of society may, in fact, be underdiagnosed and undertreated.

⚙Elimination Disorders

Children with elimination disorders repeatedly urinate or pass feces in their clothes, in bed, or on the floor. They already have reached an age at which they are expected to control these bodily functions, and their symptoms are not caused by physical illness.

Enuresis

Enuresis is repeated involuntary (or in some cases intentional) bed-wetting or wetting of one's clothes. It typically occurs at night during sleep but may also occur during the day. Children must be at least 5 years of age to receive this diagnosis. The problem may be triggered by stressful events, such as a hospitalization, entrance into school, or family problems, as we see in the case of Amber:

Amber . . . was a 7-year-old . . . referred to an outpatient mental health clinic for children and families. At the time of her initial assessment, Amber was in second grade. She was referred to the clinic by her father, Mr. Dillon, who was quite upset about his daughter's problems. During the telephone screening interview, he reported that Amber was wetting her bed more at night and often needed to urinate during school. She was also experiencing minor academic problems. . . .

•**enuresis**•A childhood disorder marked by repeated bed-wetting or wetting of one's clothes.

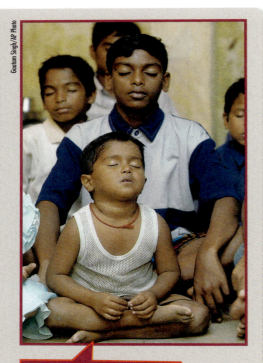

Meditation at an early age
To help survivors of the 2004 tsunami overcome their traumatic ordeal, the Art and Living Foundation organized meditation sessions throughout Asia. In this session a 4-year-old Indian child, along with several older survivors, learns how to meditate, with the hope that this technique, among others, will help prevent the onset of psychological disorders.

During [her] assessment session [with a psychologist] Amber said that she was getting into a lot of trouble at home and that her parents were mad at her. When asked why they were mad, Amber said she wasn't doing well in school and that she felt "nervous." . . . She said her grades had been getting worse over the course of the school year and that she was having trouble concentrating on her assigned work. She had apparently been a very good student the year before, especially in reading, but was now struggling with different subjects. . . .

[Amber acknowledged that] she wet her bed at night about once or twice a week. In addition, she often had to use the bathroom at school, going about three or four times a day. This was apparently a source of annoyance for her team teacher. . . . On one occasion, Amber said that she didn't make it to the bathroom in time and slightly wet her pants. Fortunately, this was not noticeable, but Amber was quite embarrassed about the incident. In fact, she now placed a wad of toilet tissue in her underwear to diminish the results of any possible mishaps in the future. . . .

[In a separate assessment interview, the psychologist asked Amber's parents] if any significant changes were going on at home. The question seemed to strike a nerve, as both parents paused and looked at each other nervously before answering. Finally, Mr. Dillon said that he and his wife had been having marital problems within the past year and that they were fighting more than usual. In fact, the possibility of divorce had been raised and both were now considering separation.

(Kearney, 1999, pp. 60–62)

The prevalence of enuresis decreases with age. As many as 10 percent of children who are 5 years old suffer from this disorder, compared to 3 to 5 percent of 10-year-olds and 1 percent of 15-year-olds. Those with enuresis typically have a close relative (parent, sibling) who has had or will have the same disorder (Friman, 2008; APA, 2000).

Research has not favored one explanation for enuresis over the others. Psychodynamic theorists explain it as a symptom of broader anxiety and underlying conflicts (Friman, 2008; Olmos de Paz, 1990). Family theorists point to disturbed family interactions (Fletcher, 2000). Behaviorists view the problem as the result of improper, unrealistic, or coercive toilet training (Christophersen & Purvis, 2001). And biological theorists suspect that children with this disorder often have a small bladder capacity or an inadequacy of the muscles that inhibit urination (Friman, 2008; Nield & Kamat, 2004).

Most cases of enuresis correct themselves even without treatment. However, therapy, particularly behavioral therapy, can speed up the process (Butler, 2004; Nield & Kamat,

SIPRESS

"We've been thinking a lot about what we want to do with your life."

2004). In a widely used classical conditioning approach, the *bell-and-battery technique,* a bell and a battery are wired to a pad consisting of two metallic foil sheets, and the entire apparatus is placed under the child at bedtime (Houts, 2003; Mowrer & Mowrer, 1938). A single drop of urine sets off the bell, awakening the child as soon as he or she starts to wet. Thus the bell (unconditioned stimulus) paired with the sensation of a full bladder (conditioned stimulus) produces the response of waking. Eventually, a full bladder alone awakens the child.

Another effective behavioral treatment method is *dry-bed training,* in which children receive training in cleanliness and retention control, are awakened periodically during the night, practice going to the bathroom, and are appropriately rewarded (Friman, 2008; Christophersen & Purvis, 2001). Like the bell-and-battery technique, this behavioral approach is often effective, according to research.

Encopresis

Encopresis, repeatedly defecating into one's clothing, is less common than enuresis, and it is also less well researched. This problem seldom occurs at night during sleep (Walker, 2003). It is usually involuntary, starts after the age of 4, and affects about 1 percent of 5-year-olds (see Table 17-3). The disorder is more common in boys than in girls (Friman, 2008; APA, 2000).

Encopresis causes intense social problems, shame, and embarrassment (Cox et al., 2002). Children who suffer from it usually try to hide their condition and to avoid situations, such as camp or school, in which they might embarrass themselves (APA, 2000). Cases may stem from stress, constipation, improper toilet training, or a combination of these factors. In fact, most children with encopresis have a history of repeated constipation, a history that may contribute to improper intestinal functioning (Friman, 2008; Partin et al., 1992). Because physical problems are so often linked to this disorder, a medical examination is typically conducted first, followed by a psychological evaluation.

The most common and successful treatments for encopresis are behavioral and medical approaches or a combination of the two (Friman, 2008; Christophersen & Purvis, 2001; McGrath et al., 2000). Among other features of treatment, practitioners may use biofeedback training (see pages 133 and 195) to help the children better detect when their bowels are full, try to eliminate the children's constipation, and stimulate regular bowel functioning with high-fiber diets, mineral oil, laxatives, and lubricants (Friman, 2008; McClung et al., 1993). Family therapy has also proved helpful (Murphy & Carr, 2000).

•**encopresis**•A childhood disorder characterized by repeated defecating in inappropriate places, such as one's clothing.

table: 17-3

Comparison of Childhood Disorders

Disorder	Usual Age of Identification	Prevalence Among All Children	Gender with Greater Prevalence	Elevated Family History	Recovery by Adulthood
Separation anxiety disorder	Before 12 years	4%	Females	Yes	Usually
Conduct disorder	7–15 years	1–10%	Males	Yes	Often
ADHD	Before 12 years	5%	Males	Yes	Often
Enuresis	5–8 years	5%	Males	Yes	Usually
Encopresis	After 4 years	1%	Males	Unclear	Usually
Learning disorders	6–9 years	5%	Males	Yes	Often
Autism	0–3 years	0.17%–0.63%	Males	Yes	Sometimes
Mental retardation	Before 10 years	1–3%	Males	Unclear	Sometimes

☀ Long-Term Disorders That Begin in Childhood

As you read at the beginning of this chapter, many childhood disorders change or subside as the person ages. Two groups of disorders that emerge during childhood, however, are likely to continue unchanged throughout life: the *pervasive developmental disorders* and *mental retardation*. Researchers have investigated both of these categories extensively. In addition, although it was not always so, clinicians have developed a range of treatment approaches that can make a major difference in the lives of people with these problems.

Pervasive Developmental Disorders

Pervasive developmental disorders are a group of disorders marked by impaired social interactions, unusual communications, and inappropriate responses to stimuli in the environment. The group includes *autistic disorder, Asperger's disorder, Rett's disorder,* and *childhood disintegrative disorder.* Because autistic disorder initially received more attention than the others, these disorders are often referred to as *autistic-spectrum disorders.* Although the patterns are similar in many ways, they do differ significantly in the degree of social impairment sufferers experience and in the time of onset. Given the low prevalence of Rett's disorder and childhood disintegrative disorder, we will examine only autistic disorder and Asperger's disorder in this chapter.

Autistic Disorder A child named Mark presents a typical picture of autism:

In retrospect [Susan, Mark's mother] can recall some things that appeared odd to her. For example, she remembers that . . . Mark never seemed to anticipate being picked up when she approached. In addition, despite Mark's attachment to a pacifier (he would complain if it were mislaid), he showed little interest in toys. In fact, Mark seemed to lack interest in anything. He rarely pointed to things and seemed oblivious to sounds. . . . Mark spent much of his time repetitively tapping on tables, seeming to be lost in his own world.

After his second birthday, Mark's behavior began to trouble his parents. . . . Mark, they said, would "look through" people or past them, but rarely at them. He could say a few words but didn't seem to understand speech. In fact, he did not even respond to his own name. Mark's time was occupied examining familiar objects, which he would hold in front of his eyes while he twisted and turned them. Particularly troublesome were Mark's odd movements—he would jump, flap his arms, twist his hands and fingers, and perform all sorts of facial grimaces, particularly when he was excited—and what Robert [Mark's father] described as Mark's rigidity. Mark would line things up in rows and scream if they were disturbed. He insisted on keeping objects in their place and would become upset whenever Susan attempted to rearrange the living room furniture. . . .

Slowly, beginning at age five, Mark began to improve. . . . The pronoun in the sentence was inappropriate and the sentence took the form of a question he had been asked previously, but the meaning was clear.

(Wing, 1976)

Mark was displaying **autistic disorder,** or **autism,** a pattern first identified by the American psychiatrist Leo Kanner in 1943. Children with this disorder are extremely unresponsive to others, uncommunicative, repetitive, and rigid (see Table 17-4). Their symptoms appear early in life, typically before 3 years of age. Just a decade ago, autism seemed to affect around 1 out of every 2,000 children (APA, 2000). However, in recent years there has been a steady increase in the number of children diagnosed with autism, and it now appears that at least 1 in 600 and perhaps as many as 1 in 160 children display the disorder (Teicher et al., 2008; Fombonne, 2003; Wing & Potter, 2002).

•**autistic disorder**•A pervasive developmental disorder marked by extreme unresponsiveness to others, poor communication skills, and highly repetitive and rigid behavior. Also known as *autism.*

Around 80 percent of all cases of autism occur in boys. As many as 90 percent of children with the disorder remain severely disabled into adulthood. They have enormous difficulty maintaining employment, performing household tasks, and leading independent lives (Siegel & Ficcaglia, 2006). Moreover, even the highest-functioning adults with autism typically have problems displaying closeness, empathy, and support in their social interactions and communications and have restricted interests and activities (Baron-Cohen & Wheelwright, 2003).

The individual's *lack of responsiveness*—including extreme aloofness, lack of interest in other people, low empathy, and inability to share attention with others—has long been considered the central feature of autism (Siegel & Ficcaglia, 2006). Like Mark, children with this disorder typically do not reach for their parents during infancy. Instead they may arch their backs when they are held and appear not to recognize or care about those around them.

Language and communication problems take various forms in autism. Approximately half of all sufferers fail to speak or develop language skills (Gillis & Romanczyk, 2007). Those who do talk may show peculiarities in their speech. One of the most common speech problems is *echolalia*, the exact echoing of phrases spoken by others. The individuals repeat the words with the same accent or inflection, but with no sign of understanding or intent of communicating. Some even repeat a sentence days after they have heard it (*delayed echolalia*).

Autistic acts
This autistic child is comforted by standing on her chair and watching television close up, and she often repeats this behavior. People with autism often interact with objects and people in unusual ways that seem to fascinate, stimulate, comfort, or reassure them.

table: 17-4

DSM Checklist

AUTISTIC DISORDER

1. A total of at least six items from the following groups of symptoms:

   A. Impairment in social interaction, as manifested by at least two of the following:
      a. Marked impairment in the use of multiple nonverbal behaviors such as eye-to-eye gaze, facial expression, body postures, and gestures to regulate social interaction.
      b. Failure to develop peer relationships appropriately.
      c. Lack of spontaneous seeking to share enjoyment, interests, or achievements with other people.
      d. Lack of social or emotional reciprocity.

   B. Impairment in communication, as manifested by at least one of the following:
      a. Delay in, or total lack of, the development of spoken language.
      b. In individuals with adequate speech, marked impairment in the ability to start or sustain a conversation with others.
      c. Stereotyped and repetitive use of language, or idiosyncratic language.
      d. Lack of varied, spontaneous make-believe play or social imitative play.

   C. Restricted repetitive and stereotyped patterns of behavior, interests, and activities, as manifested by at least one of the following:
      a. Abnormal preoccupation with one or more stereotyped and restricted patterns of interest.
      b. Inflexible adherence to specific nonfunctional routines or rituals.
      c. Stereotyped and repetitive motor mannerisms (e.g., hand or finger flapping or twisting).
      d. Persistent preoccupation with parts of objects.

2. Prior to 3 years of age, delay or abnormal functioning in either social interaction, language, or symbolic or imaginative play.

Based on APA, 2000.

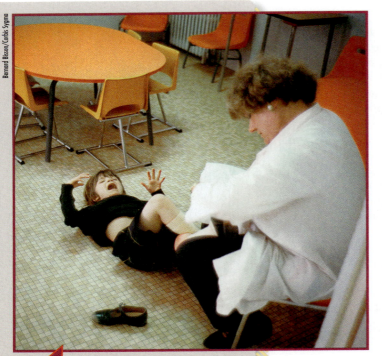

Autistic acts, take II
When upset, some children with autism, particularly those who cannot express themselves verbally, display physical outbursts. This 6-year-old child throws a tantrum and exhibits self-stimulatory hand shaking while under the care of a doctor at Bretonneau Hospital in Tours, France.

•**Asperger's disorder**•A pervasive developmental disorder in which individuals display profound social impairment yet maintain a relatively high level of cognitive functioning and language skills. Also known as *Asperger's syndrome.*

Because they have difficulty empathizing and sharing a frame of reference with others, individuals with autism may also display other speech oddities, such as *pronominal reversal,* or confusion of pronouns—for example, the use of "you" instead of "I." When Mark was hungry, he would say, "Do you want dinner?" In addition, individuals may have problems naming objects, using abstract language, employing a proper tone when talking, speaking spontaneously, using language for conversational purposes, or understanding speech.

Autism is also marked by *limited imaginative or abstract play* and by *very repetitive and rigid behavior.* Children with the disorder may be unable to play in a varied, spontaneous way. Unlike other individuals of the same age, the children may fail to include others in their play or to represent social experiences when they are playing; in fact, they often fail to see themselves as others see them and have no desire to imitate or be like others (Kasari et al., 2006; Siegel & Ficcaglia, 2006). Typically they become very upset at minor changes of objects, persons, or routines and resist any efforts to change their own repetitive behaviors. Mark, for example, lined things up and screamed if they were disturbed. Similarly, children with autism may react with tantrums if a parent wears an unfamiliar pair of glasses, a chair is moved to a different part of the room, or a word in a song is changed. Kanner (1943) labeled such reactions a *perseveration of sameness.* Furthermore, many sufferers become strongly attached to particular objects—plastic lids, rubber bands, buttons, water. They may collect these objects, carry them, or play with them constantly. Some are fascinated by movement and may watch spinning objects, such as fans, for hours.

The *motor movements* of people with autism may also be unusual. Mark would jump, flap his arms, twist his hands and fingers, rock, walk on his toes, spin, and make faces. These acts are called *self-stimulatory behaviors.* Some individuals also perform *self-injurious behaviors,* such as repeatedly lunging into or banging their head against a wall, pulling their hair, or biting themselves.

The symptoms of this disorder suggest a very disturbed and contradictory pattern of reactions to stimuli (see *Psych Watch* on page 576). Sometimes individuals with autism seem *overstimulated* by sights and sounds and appear to be trying to block them out, while at other times they seem *understimulated* and appear to be performing self-stimulatory actions. They may, for example, fail to react to loud noises yet turn around when they hear soda being poured. Similarly, they may fail to recognize that they have reached the edge of a dangerous high place yet immediately spot a small object that is out of position in their room.

Asperger's Disorder Around the time that Kanner first identified autism, a Viennese physician named Hans Asperger began to note a syndrome in which children display significant social impairments yet manage to maintain relatively high levels of cognitive function and language. Those with **Asperger's disorder,** or **Asperger's syndrome,** experience the kinds of social deficits, impairments in expressiveness, idiosyncratic interests, and restricted and repetitive behaviors that characterize individuals with autism, but at the same time they often have normal (or near normal) intellectual, adaptive, and language skills (Siegel & Ficcaglia, 2006; Ozonoff et al., 2002). Many individuals with this disorder want to fit in and interact with others, but their impaired social functioning makes it hard for them to do so. They wind up appearing awkward and unaware of conventional social rules (ASA, 2006).

Clinical research suggests that there may be several subtypes of Asperger's disorder, each having a particular set of symptoms. One team of researchers has distinguished three subtypes: rule boys, logic boys, and emotion boys (Sohn & Grayson, 2005). *Rule boys* are Asperger sufferers who need to have a set of rules that govern their lives. They are extremely stubborn about following these rules, and may become aggressive when the rules are not clearly laid out. At the same time, they are typically able to respect authority figures and structure. *Logic boys* are primarily interested in the *reasons* behind rules; rules alone are not sufficient. They want to know how the world works, often question the logic of others' reasoning, and may have their own reasons for why things are happening. In turn, they are typically unwilling to accept illogical events and often become overly analytical. *Emotion boys* tend to be run by their feelings. They have more tantrums than others with Asperger's disorder and seem less available to others. It is hard to sway them with rules or reason, and they often act out.

Asperger's disorder appears to be more prevalent than autism. Approximately 1 in 250 individuals displays this pattern, again 80 percent of them boys (CADDRE, 2004). It is important to diagnose and treat Asperger's disorder early in life so that the individual has a better chance of being successful at school and living independently. Although Asperger individuals must contend with deficits throughout their lives, many are able to complete a high level of education, such as college or trade school. Similarly, they may successfully hold jobs, particularly ones that require a focus on details and limited social interactions (ASA, 2005). Despite their social deficits, some people with Asperger's disorder further manage to have romantic—even marital—relationships, particularly with others who display the same disorder.

Asperger's disorder and personal achievement
Although significantly impaired by many autistic-like deficits and limitations, individuals with Asperger's disorder maintain relatively high language, intellectual, and adaptive skills; indeed, some reach impressive heights. A butterfly perches on the nose of this 14-year-old boy with Asperger's disorder, winner of a national achievement award for activities such as playing the piano at nursing homes and raising chickens, peacocks, strawberries, and more on his family's farm in Ohio.

What Are the Causes of Pervasive Developmental Disorders?
Much more research has been conducted on autism than on Asperger's disorder or other pervasive developmental disorders. Currently, many clinicians and researchers believe that the other pervasive developmental disorders are caused by factors similar to those responsible for autism and that people with the other disorders can often be helped by interventions similar to ones that bring positive change in cases of autism. It is quite possible, however, that in the coming years, as Asperger's disorder and other pervasive developmental disorders receive more and more study, clear differences in the causes and treatments of the various disorders will emerge.

A variety of explanations have been offered for autism. This is one disorder for which sociocultural explanations have probably been overemphasized. In fact, such explanations initially led investigators in the wrong direction. More recent work in the psychological and biological spheres has persuaded clinical theorists that cognitive limitations and brain abnormalities are the primary causes of autism.

SOCIOCULTURAL CAUSES At first, theorists thought that family dysfunction and social stress were the primary causes of autism. When he first identified autism, for example, Kanner (1954, 1943) argued that particular *personality characteristics of the parents* created an unfavorable climate for development and contributed to the child's disorder. He saw these parents as very intelligent yet cold—"refrigerator parents." These claims had enormous influence on the public and on the self-image of the parents themselves, but research has totally failed to support a picture of rigid, cold, rejecting, or disturbed parents (Jones & Jordan, 2008; Roazen, 1992).

Similarly, some clinical theorists have proposed that a high degree of *social and environmental stress* is a factor in autism. Once again, however, research has not supported this notion. Investigators who have compared children with autism to children without the disorder have found no differences in the rate of parental death, divorce, separation, financial problems, or environmental stimulation (Cox et al., 1975).

PSYCHOLOGICAL CAUSES According to certain theorists, people with autism have a central perceptual or cognitive disturbance that makes normal communication and interactions impossible. One influential explanation holds that individuals with the disorder fail to develop a **theory of mind**—an awareness that other people base their behaviors on their own beliefs, intentions, and other mental states, not on information that they have no way of knowing (Hale & Tager-Flusberg, 2005; Frith, 2000).

•theory of mind• Awareness that other people base their behaviors on their own beliefs, intentions, and other mental states, not on information they have no way of knowing.

A Special Kind of Talent

Most people are familiar with the savant syndrome, thanks to Dustin Hoffman's portrayal of a man with autism in the movie *Rain Man*. The savant skills that Hoffman portrayed—counting 246 toothpicks in the instant after they fall to the floor, memorizing the phone book through the Gs, and doing numerical calculations at lightning speed—were based on the astounding talents of certain real-life people who are otherwise limited by autism or mental retardation.

A *savant* (French for "learned" or "clever") is a person with a major mental disorder or intellectual handicap who has some spectacular ability, some area of exceptional brilliance. Often these abilities are remarkable only in light of the handicap, but sometimes they are remarkable by any standard (Yewchuk, 1999).

A common savant skill is calendar calculating, the ability to calculate what day of the week a date will fall on, such as New Year's Day in 2050 (Kennedy & Squire, 2007; Heavey et al., 1999). A common musical skill such individuals may possess is the ability to play a piece of classical music flawlessly from memory after hearing it only once. Other individuals can paint exact replicas of scenes they saw years ago (Hou et al., 2000).

Special insights One of the world's highest achieving autistic individuals is Dr. Temple Grandin, a professor at Colorado State University and leader in both the animal welfare movement and the autism advocacy movement. Applying her personal perspective and unique visualization skills, she has developed insight into the minds and sensitivities of cattle and has designed more humane animal-handling equipment and facilities. Indeed she argues that autistic savants and animals share cognitive similarities.

Some theorists believe that savant skills do indeed represent special forms of cognitive functioning; others propose that the skills are merely a positive side to certain cognitive deficits (Scheuffgen et al., 2000; Miller, 1999). Special memorization skills, for example, may be facilitated by the very narrow and intense focus often found in cases of autism.

By 3 to 5 years of age, most children can take the perspective of another person into account and use it to anticipate what the person will do. In a way, they learn to read others' minds. Let us say, for example, that we watch Jessica place a marble in a container and then we observe Frank move the marble to a nearby room while Jessica is taking a nap. We know that later Jessica will search first in the container for the marble because she is not aware that Frank moved it. We know that because we take Jessica's perspective into account. A normal child would also anticipate Jessica's search correctly. A person with autism would not. He or she would expect Jessica to look in the nearby room because that is where the marble actually is. Jessica's own mental processes would be unimportant to the person.

Studies show that people with autism do have this kind of "mindblindness," although they are not the only kinds of individuals with this limitation (Jones & Jordan, 2008; Dahlgren et al., 2003). They thus have great difficulty taking part in make-believe play, using language in ways that include the perspectives of others, developing relationships, or participating in human interactions. Why do people with autism have this and other cognitive limitations? Some theorists believe that they suffered early biological problems that prevented proper cognitive development.

BIOLOGICAL CAUSES For years researchers have tried to determine what biological abnormalities might cause theory-of-mind deficits and the other features of autism. They have not yet developed a detailed biological explanation, but they have uncovered some promising leads (Teicher et al., 2008; Rodier, 2000). First, examinations of the relatives of people with autism keep suggesting a *genetic factor* in this disorder. The prevalence of autism among their siblings, for example, is as high as 6 to 8 per 100 (Teicher et al., 2008; Gillis & Romanczyk, 2007), a rate much higher than the general population's. Moreover, the prevalence of autism among the identical twins of people with autism is 60 percent. In addition, chromosomal abnormalities have been discovered in 10 to 12 percent of people with the disorder (Sudhalter et al., 1990).

Some studies have also linked autism to *prenatal difficulties* or *birth complications* (Teicher et al., 2008; Rodier, 2000; Simon, 2000). The chances of developing the disorder are higher when the mother had rubella (German measles) during pregnancy, was exposed to toxic chemicals before or during pregnancy, or had complications during labor or delivery. In 1998 one team of investigators proposed that a *postnatal event*—the vaccine for measles, mumps, and rubella—might produce autism in some children, alarming many parents of toddlers. However, research has not confirmed a link between the vaccine and the disorder (Institute of Medicine, 2004).

Finally, researchers have identified specific *biological abnormalities* that may contribute to autism. One line of research has pointed to the **cerebellum,** for example (Teicher et al., 2008; DeLong, 2005; Pierce & Courchesne, 2002, 2001). Brain scans and autopsies reveal abnormal development in this brain area occurring early in the life of people with autism. Scientists have long known that the cerebellum coordinates movement in the body, but they now suspect that it also helps control a person's ability to shift attention rapidly. It may be that people whose cerebellum develops abnormally will have great difficulty adjusting their level of attention, following verbal and facial cues, and making sense of social information—all key features of autism.

In a similar vein, neuroimaging studies indicate that many children with autism have increased brain volume and white matter (Wicker, 2008) and structural abnormalities in the brain's limbic system, brain stem nuclei, and amygdala (Gillis & Romanczyk, 2007). Many individuals with the disorder also experience reduced activity in the brain's temporal and frontal lobes when they perform language and motor initiation tasks—tasks that normally require activity by the brain's left hemisphere (Escalante, Minshew, & Sweeney, 2003).

Many researchers believe that autism may in fact have multiple biological causes (Mueller & Courchesne, 2000). Perhaps all relevant biological factors (genetic, prenatal, birth, and postnatal) eventually lead to a common problem in the brain—a "final common pathway," such as neurotransmitter abnormalities, that produces the cognitive problems and other features of the disorder.

How Do Clinicians and Educators Treat Pervasive Developmental Disorders?
Treatment can help people with autism adapt better to their environment, although no treatment yet known totally reverses the autistic pattern. Treatments of particular help are *behavioral therapy, communication training, parent training,* and *community integration.* In addition, psychotropic drugs and certain vitamins have sometimes helped when combined with other approaches (Teicher et al., 2008; Volkmar, 2001).

BEHAVIORAL THERAPY Behavioral approaches have been used in cases of autism for more than 30 years to teach new, appropriate behaviors, including speech, social skills, classroom skills, and self-help skills, while reducing negative, dysfunctional ones. Most often, the therapists use modeling and operant conditioning. In modeling, they demonstrate a desired behavior and guide people with the disorder to imitate it. In operant conditioning, they reinforce such behaviors, first by shaping them—breaking them down so they can be learned step by step—and then rewarding each step clearly and consistently (Campbell et al., 2008; Lovaas, 2003, 1987). With careful planning and execution, these procedures often produce new, more functional behaviors.

•**cerebellum**•An area of the brain that coordinates movement in the body and perhaps helps control a person's ability to shift attention rapidly.

Creative interventions
The severe sensory, perceptual, cognitive, and social problems of individuals with autism often require teachers and therapists to develop innovative approaches. This teacher, for example, escorts an autistic child down the school hallway while the boy wears a full-body sack that helps minimize intolerable stimuli and increases his sense of security.

•**augmentative communication system**•A method for enhancing the communication skills of individuals with autism, mental retardation, or cerebral palsy by teaching them to point to pictures, symbols, letters, or words on a communication board or computer.

A long-term study compared the progress of two groups of children with autism (Campbell et al., 2008; McEachin et al., 1993; Lovaas, 1987). Nineteen received intensive behavioral treatments, and 19 served as a control group. The treatment began when the children were 3 years old and continued until they were 7. By the age of 7, the behavioral group was doing better in school and scoring higher on intelligence tests than the control group. Many were able to go to school in regular classrooms. The gains continued into the research participants' teenage years. In light of such findings, many clinicians now consider early behavioral programs to be the preferred treatment for autism.

A recent behavioral program that has achieved considerable success is the *Learning Experiences . . . An Alternative Program (LEAP)* for preschoolers with autism (Kohler, Strain, & Goldstein, 2005). In this program, four autistic children are integrated with 10 normal children in a classroom. The normal children learn how to use modeling and operant conditioning in order to help teach social, communication, play, and other skills to the autistic children. The program has been found to improve significantly the cognitive functioning of autistic children, as well as their social engagements, peer interactions, play behaviors, and other behaviors. Moreover, the normal children in the classroom experience no negative effects as a result of serving as intervention agents.

As such programs suggest, therapies for people with autism, particularly behavioral ones, tend to provide the most benefit when they are started early in the children's lives (Campbell et al., 2008; Palmer, 2003). Very young autistic children often begin with services at home, but ideally, by the age of 3 they attend special programs outside the home. The Individuals with Disabilities Education Act, a federal law, lists autism as 1 of 10 disorders for which school districts must provide a free education from birth to age 22, in the least restrictive or most appropriate setting possible. Typically, services are provided by education, health, or social service agencies until the children reach 3 years of age; then the department of education for each state determines what services will be offered (NRC, 2001).

Given the recent increases in the prevalence of autism, many school districts are now trying to provide education and training for autistic children in special classes that operate at the district's own facilities. However, most school districts remain ill equipped to meet the profound needs of students with autism. The most fortunate students are sent by their school districts to attend special schools, where education and therapy are combined. At such schools, specially trained teachers help the children improve their skills, behaviors, and interactions with the world. The higher-functioning students with autism may eventually spend at least part of their school day returning to normal classrooms in their own school district, where they can develop social and academic skills in the company of nonautistic students (Smith et al., 2002).

Although significantly impaired, children with Asperger's disorder have less profound educational and treatment needs than do those with autism. Once diagnosed, many such children are assigned to special programs (either within their own school system or at special schools) in which they receive a combination of education and cognitive-behavioral therapy tailored to their particular impairments. In one such program, *cognitive social integration therapy,* the children are taught to be more flexible with regard to social rules, problem solving, and behavioral choices (Sohn & Grayson, 2005). The teacher works with the Asperger students in groups, acknowledging their thoughts and feelings, teaching them how to prevent anxiety in the face of change, and helping them to develop new social skills and other kinds of abilities. The teacher also helps ensure that the newly learned skills generalize to the individual's life by using techniques such as rehearsal, role-playing, and visual imaging throughout the group sessions.

COMMUNICATION TRAINING Even when given intensive behavioral treatment, half of the people with autism remain speechless. As a result, they are often taught other forms of communication, including *sign language* and *simultaneous communication,* a method combining sign language and speech. They may also learn to use **augmentative communication systems,** such as "communication boards" or computers that use pictures, symbols, or written words to represent objects or needs (Gillis & Romanczyk, 2007). A child may point to a picture of a fork to give the message "I am hungry," for example, or point to a radio for "I want music."

Some programs now use *child-initiated interactions* to help improve the communication skills of autistic children (Koegel, Koegel, & Brookman, 2005). In such programs, teachers try to identify *intrinsic* reinforcers rather than trivial ones like food or candy. The children are first encouraged to choose items that they are interested in, and they then learn to initiate questions ("What's that?" "Where is it?" "Whose is it?") in order to obtain the items. Studies find that child-directed interventions of this kind often increase self-initiated communications, improve language development, and heighten participation in interactions (Koegel et al., 2005).

PARENT TRAINING Today's treatment programs involve parents in a variety of ways. Behavioral programs, for example, often train parents so that they can apply behavioral techniques at home (Schreibman & Koegel, 2005; Erba, 2000). Instruction manuals for parents and home visits by teachers and other professionals are often included in such programs. Research consistently has demonstrated that the behavioral gains produced by trained parents are typically equal to or greater than those generated by teachers. Moreover, parent-run interventions tend to produce greater generalization of skills.

In addition to parent-training programs, individual therapy and support groups are becoming more available to help the parents of autistic children deal with their own emotions and needs (Hastings, 2008). A number of parent associations and lobbies also offer emotional support and practical help.

COMMUNITY INTEGRATION Many of today's school-based and home-based programs for autism teach self-help, self-management, and living, social, and work skills as early as possible to help the children function better in their communities. In addition, greater numbers of carefully run *group homes* and *sheltered workshops* are now available for teenagers and young adults with autism. These and related programs help the individuals become a part of their community; they also reduce the concerns of aging parents whose children will always need supervision.

Learning to communicate
Behaviorists have had success teaching many children with autism to communicate. Here a speech language specialist combines behavioral techniques with the use of a communication board to teach a 3-year-old autistic child how to express herself better and understand others.

Mental Retardation

Ed Murphy, aged 26, can tell us what it's like to be diagnosed as retarded:

What is retardation? It's hard to say. I guess it's having problems thinking. Some people think that you can tell if a person is retarded by looking at them. If you think that way you don't give people the benefit of the doubt. You judge a person by how they look or how they talk or what the tests show, but you can never really tell what is inside the person.

(Bogdan & Taylor, 1976, p. 51)

For much of his life Ed was labeled mentally retarded and was educated and cared for in special institutions. During his adult years, clinicians discovered that Ed's intellectual ability was in fact higher than had been assumed. In the meantime, however, he

table: 17-5

DSM Checklist

MENTAL RETARDATION

1. Significantly subaverage intellectual functioning: an IQ of approximately 70 or below on an individually administered IQ test.

2. Concurrent deficits or impairments in present adaptive functioning in at least two of the following areas:
   a. Communication.
   b. Self-care.
   c. Home living.
   d. Social/interpersonal skills.
   e. Use of community resources.
   f. Self-direction.
   g. Functional academic skills.
   h. Work.
   i. Leisure.
   j. Health.
   k. Safety.

3. Onset before the age of 18.

Based on APA, 2000.

had lived the childhood and adolescence of a person labeled retarded, and his statement reveals the kinds of difficulties often faced by people with this disorder.

The term "mental retardation" has been applied to a varied population, including children in institutional wards who rock back and forth, young people who work in special job programs, and men and women who raise and support their families by working at undemanding jobs. In recent years, the less stigmatizing term *intellectual disability* has become synonymous with mental retardation in many clinical settings. As many as 3 of every 100 persons meet the criteria for this diagnosis (Leonard & Wen, 2002; APA, 2000). Around three-fifths of them are male, and the vast majority are considered *mildly* retarded.

According to DSM-IV-TR, people should receive a diagnosis of **mental retardation** when they display general *intellectual functioning* that is well below average, in combination with poor *adaptive behavior* (APA, 2000). That is, in addition to having a low IQ (a score of 70 or below), a person with mental retardation must have great difficulty in areas such as communication, home living, self-direction, work, or safety (APA, 2000). The symptoms must also appear before the age of 18 (see Table 17–5). Although these DSM-IV-TR criteria may seem straightforward, they are in fact hard to apply.

Assessing Intelligence Educators and clinicians administer intelligence tests to measure intellectual functioning (see Chapter 4). These tests consist of a variety of questions and tasks that rely on different aspects of intelligence, such as knowledge, reasoning, and judgment. Having difficulty in one or two of these subtests or areas of functioning does not necessarily reflect low intelligence (see *A Closer Look* on page 582). It is an individual's overall test score, or **intelligence quotient (IQ),** that is thought to indicate general intellectual ability.

Many theorists have questioned whether IQ tests are indeed valid. Do they actually measure what they are supposed to measure? The correlation between IQ and school performance is rather high—around .50—indicating that many children with lower IQs do, as one might expect, perform poorly in school, while many of those with higher IQs perform better (Sternberg et al., 2001). At the same time, the correlation also suggests that the relationship is far from perfect. That is, a particular child's school performance is often higher or lower than his or her IQ might predict. Moreover, the accuracy of IQ tests at measuring extremely low intelligence has not been evaluated adequately, so it is difficult to assess people with severe mental retardation properly (Bebko & Weiss, 2006).

Getting a head start Studies suggest that IQ scores and school performances of children from poor neighborhoods can be improved by enriching their daily environments at a young age through programs such as Head Start, thus revealing the powerful effect of the environment on IQ scores and intellectual performance. The teachers in this classroom try to stimulate further and enrich the lives of preschool children in a Head Start program in Oregon.

Don Ryan/AP Photo

Intelligence tests also appear to be socioculturally biased, as you read in Chapter 4 (Gopaul-McNicol & Armour-Thomas, 2002). Children reared in households at the middle and upper socioeconomic levels tend to have an advantage on the tests because they are regularly exposed to the kinds of language and thinking that the tests evaluate. The tests rarely measure the "street sense" needed for survival by people who live in poor, crime-ridden areas—a kind of know-how that certainly requires intellectual skills. Similarly, members of cultural minorities and people for whom English is a second language often appear to be at a disadvantage in taking these tests.

If IQ tests do not always measure intelligence accurately and objectively, then the diagnosis of mental retardation also may be biased. That is, some people may receive the diagnosis partly because of test inadequacies, cultural differences, discomfort with the testing situation, or the bias of a tester.

Assessing Adaptive Functioning Diagnosticians cannot rely solely on a cutoff IQ score of 70 to determine whether a person suffers from mental retardation. Some people with a low IQ are quite capable of managing their lives and functioning independently, while others are not. The cases of Brian and Jeffrey show the range of adaptive abilities.

Brian comes from a lower-income family. He always has functioned adequately at home and in his community. He dresses and feeds himself and even takes care of himself each day until his mother returns home from work. He also plays well with his friends. At school, however, Brian refuses to participate or do his homework. He seems ineffective, at times lost, in the classroom. Referred to a school psychologist by his teacher, he received an IQ score of 60.

Jeffrey comes from an upper-middle-class home. He was always slow to develop, and sat up, stood, and talked late. During his infancy and toddler years, he was put in a special stimulation program and given special help and attention at home. Still Jeffrey has trouble dressing himself today and cannot be left alone in the backyard lest he hurt himself or wander off into the street. Schoolwork is very difficult for him. The teacher must work slowly and provide individual instruction for him. Tested at age 6, Jeffrey received an IQ score of 60.

Brian seems well adapted to his environment outside of school. However, Jeffrey's limitations are pervasive. In addition to his low IQ score, Jeffrey has difficulty meeting challenges at home and elsewhere. Thus a diagnosis of mental retardation may be more appropriate for Jeffrey than for Brian.

Several scales, such as the *Vineland* and *AAMR Adaptive Behavior Scales* and the *Scales of Independent Behavior Revised,* have been developed to assess adaptive behavior. Here again, however, some people function better in their lives than the scales predict, while others fall short. Moreover, several clinicians and educators argue that the adaptive scales do not include a sufficient number of indicators of social, communicative, academic, physical, and community competence (Jacobson & Mulick, 1996).

Thus to properly diagnose mental retardation, clinicians should probably observe the functioning of each individual in his or her everyday environment, taking both the person's background and the community's standards into account. Even then, however, such judgments may be subjective, as clinicians may not be familiar with the standards of a particular culture or community.

What Are the Features of Mental Retardation? The most consistent feature of mental retardation is that the person learns very slowly (Sturmey, 2008; Hodapp & Dykens, 2003). Other areas of difficulty are attention, short-term memory, planning, and language. Those who are institutionalized with mental retardation are particularly likely

•**mental retardation**•A disorder marked by intellectual functioning and adaptive behavior that are well below average.

•**intelligence quotient (IQ)**•A score derived from intelligence tests that theoretically represents a person's overall intellectual capacity.

BETWEEN THE LINES

In Their Words

"The IQ test was invented to predict academic performance, nothing else. If we wanted something that would predict life success, we'd have to invent another test completely."

Robert Zajonc, psychologist, 1984

Reading and 'Riting and 'Rithmetic

Between 15 and 20 percent of children, boys more often than girls, develop slowly and function poorly compared to their peers in an area such as learning, communication, or coordination (Watson, Watson, & Ret, 2008; APA, 2000). The children do not suffer from mental retardation, and in fact they are often very bright, yet their problems may interfere with school performance, daily living, and in some cases social interactions. Similar difficulties may be seen in the children's close biological relatives (Watson et al., 2008). According to DSM-IV-TR, these children may be suffering from a *learning disorder*, a *communication disorder*, or a *developmental coordination disorder*.

The skill in arithmetic, written expression, or reading exhibited by children with *learning disorders* is well below their intellectual capacity and causes academic and personal dysfunctioning (APA, 2000). Across the United States, children with learning disorders comprise the largest subgroup of individuals placed in special education classes (Watson et al., 2008). One learning disorder is called *mathematics disorder* and is diagnosed in children who have markedly impaired mathematical skills. Children with *disorder of written expression* make extreme and persistent errors in spelling, grammar, punctuation, and paragraph organization. And children with *reading disorder*, also known as *dyslexia*, have great difficulty recognizing words and comprehending as they read. They typically read slowly and haltingly and may omit, distort, or substitute words as they go.

The *communication disorders* take various forms as well (APA, 2000). Children with *phonological disorder* consistently fail to make correct speech sounds at an appropriate age, so that many of them seem to be talking baby talk. Those with *expressive language disorder* have trouble using language to express themselves. They may struggle at learning new words, confine their speech to short simple sentences, or show a general lag in language development. Children with *mixed receptive/expressive language disorder* have difficulty comprehending and expressing language. And those who suffer from *stuttering* display a disturbance in the fluency and timing of their speech. They may repeat, prolong, or interject sounds, pause before finishing a word, or experience excessive tension in the muscles used for speech.

Finally, children with *developmental coordination disorder* perform coordinated motor activities at a level well below that of others their age (APA, 2000). Younger children with this disorder are clumsy and are slow to master skills such as tying shoelaces, buttoning shirts, and zipping pants. Older children with the disorder may have great difficulty assembling puzzles, building models, playing ball, and printing or writing.

Studies have linked these various developmental disorders to genetic defects, birth injuries, lead poisoning, inappropriate diet, sensory or perceptual dysfunction, and poor teaching (Golden, 2008; Teicher et al., 2008; Watson et al., 2008). Research implicating each of these factors has been limited, however, and the precise causes of the disorders remain unclear.

Some of the disorders respond to special treatment approaches (Watson et al., 2008; Pless & Carlsson, 2000; Merzenich et al., 1996). Reading therapy, for example, is very helpful in mild cases of reading disorder, and speech therapy brings about complete recovery in most cases of phonological disorder. Furthermore, learning, communication, and developmental coordination disorders often disappear before adulthood, even without any treatment (APA, 2000).

The inclusion of learning, communication, and coordination problems in the DSM is controversial. Many clinicians view them as strictly educational or social problems, best addressed at school or at home. The framers of DSM-IV-TR have reasoned, however, that the additional problems created by these disorders and their frequent links to other psychological and social problems justify their clinical classifications. Of special concern are studies that have found an increased risk of depression and even suicide in adolescents with certain of these problems (Piek et al., 2007; Alexander-Passe, 2006; Daniel et al. 2006).

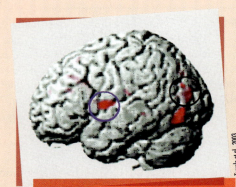

Temple et al., 2003

Dyslexia and the brain This fMRI brain scan reveals that, after successful reading and phonological training, not only could a child with dyslexia read better, but key areas (encircled) of his brain also were changed. Prior to the special training program, those brain areas had shown abnormally low activity when the child was confronted by challenging reading tasks; after training, those areas demonstrated higher levels of activity during such tasks.

to have these limitations. It may be that the unstimulating environment and minimal interactions with staff in many institutions contribute to such difficulties.

DSM-IV-TR describes four levels of mental retardation: *mild* (IQ 50–70), *moderate* (IQ 35–49), *severe* (IQ 20–34), and *profound* (IQ below 20). In contrast, the American

Association of Mental Retardation (1992) prefers to distinguish different kinds of mental retardation according to the level of support the person needs in various aspects of his or her life—*intermittent, limited, extensive,* or *pervasive.*

Mild Retardation

Some 80–85 percent of all people with mental retardation fall into the category of **mild retardation** (IQ 50–70) (Leonard & Wen, 2002; APA, 2000). They are sometimes called "educably retarded" because they can benefit from schooling and can support themselves as adults. Mild mental retardation is not usually recognized until children enter school and are assessed there. The individuals demonstrate rather typical language, social, and play skills, but they need assistance when under stress—a limitation that becomes increasingly apparent as academic and social demands increase. Interestingly, the intellectual performance of individuals with mild mental retardation often seems to improve with age; some even seem to leave the label behind when they leave school, and they go on to function well in the community (Sturmey, 2008). Their jobs tend to be unskilled or semiskilled.

Research has linked mild mental retardation mainly to sociocultural and psychological causes, particularly poor and unstimulating environments, inadequate parent-child interactions, and insufficient learning experiences during a child's early years (Sturmey, 2008; Stromme & Magnus, 2000). These relationships have been observed in studies comparing deprived and enriched environments (see Figure 17-4). In fact, some community programs have sent workers into the homes of young children with low IQ scores to help enrich the environment there, and their interventions have often improved the children's functioning. When continued, programs of this kind also help improve the individual's later performance in school and adulthood (Sparling et al., 2005; Ramey & Ramey, 2004, 1998, 1992).

Although sociocultural and psychological factors seem to be the leading causes of mild mental retardation, at least some biological factors also may be operating. Studies suggest, for example, that a mother's moderate drinking, drug use, or malnutrition during pregnancy may lower her child's intellectual potential (Ksir et al., 2008; Neisser et al., 1996; Stein et al., 1972). Similarly, malnourishment during a child's early years may hurt his or her intellectual development, although this effect can usually be reversed at least partly if a child's diet is improved before too much time goes by.

Moderate, Severe, and Profound Retardation

Approximately 10 percent of persons with mental retardation function at a level of **moderate retardation** (IQ 35–49). They typically receive their diagnosis earlier in life than do individuals with mild retardation, as they demonstrate clear deficits in language development and play during their preschool years. By middle school they further display significant delays in their acquisition of reading and number skills and adaptive skills. By adulthood, however, many individuals with moderate mental retardation manage to acquire a fair degree of communication skill, learn to care for themselves, benefit from vocational training, and can work in unskilled or semiskilled jobs, usually under supervision. Most such persons also function well in the community if they have supervision (Bebko & Weiss, 2006; APA, 2000).

Approximately 3 to 4 percent of people with mental retardation display **severe retardation** (IQ 20–34). They typically demonstrate basic motor and communication deficits during infancy. Many also show signs of neurological dysfunction and have an increased risk for brain seizure disorder, or epilepsy. In school, they may be able to string together only two or three words when speaking. Individuals in this category usually require careful supervision, profit somewhat from vocational training, and can perform only basic work tasks in structured and sheltered settings. Their understanding

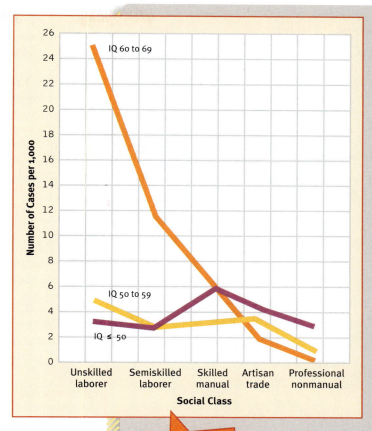

Figure 17-4

Mental retardation and socioeconomic class The prevalence of mild mental retardation is much higher in the lower socioeconomic classes than in the upper classes. In contrast, the forms of mental retardation that result in greater impairment are evenly distributed. (Adapted from Popper, 1988; Birch et al., 1970.)

•**mild retardation**•A level of mental retardation (IQ between 50 and 70) at which people can benefit from education and can support themselves as adults.

•**moderate retardation**•A level of mental retardation (IQ between 35 and 49) at which people can learn to care for themselves and can benefit from vocational training.

•**severe retardation**•A level of mental retardation (IQ between 20 and 34) at which individuals require careful supervision and can learn to perform basic work in structured and sheltered settings.

- **profound retardation**•A level of mental retardation (IQ below 20) at which individuals need a very structured environment with close supervision.

- **Down syndrome**•A form of mental retardation caused by an abnormality in the twenty-first chromosome.

- **fetal alcohol syndrome**•A group of problems in a child, including lower intellectual functioning, low birth weight, and irregularities in the hands and face, that result from excessive alcohol intake by the mother during pregnancy.

Reaching higher
Until the 1970s, clinicians were pessimistic about the potential of people with Down syndrome. Today these people are viewed as individuals who can learn and accomplish many things in their lives. Derek Finstad, a 16-year-old with this disorder, celebrates with his football teammates after the team's 56–0 season-opening victory.

Brian Davies/The Appeal-Democrat

of communication is usually better than their speech. Most are able to function well in the community if they live in group homes, in community nursing homes, or with their families (Bebko & Weiss, 2006; APA, 2000). They are rarely able to live independently.

Around 1 to 2 percent of all people with mental retardation fall into the category of **profound retardation** (IQ below 20). This level of retardation is very noticeable at birth or early infancy. With training, people with profound mental retardation may learn or improve basic skills such as walking, some talking, and feeding themselves. They need a very structured environment, with close supervision and considerable help, including a one-to-one relationship with a caregiver, in order to develop to the fullest (Sturmey, 2008; APA, 2000).

Severe and profound levels of mental retardation often appear as part of larger syndromes that include severe physical handicaps. The physical problems are often even more limiting than the individual's low intellectual functioning and in some cases can be fatal.

What Are the Causes of Mental Retardation?
The primary causes of moderate, severe, and profound retardation are biological, although people who function at these levels also are affected greatly by their family and social environment (Sturmey, 2008; Hodapp & Dykens, 2003). Sometimes genetic factors are at the root of these biological problems, in the form of chromosomal or metabolic disorders. In fact, researchers have identified 1,000 genetic causes of mental retardation, although few of them have undergone much study (Dykens & Hodapp, 2001; Azar, 1995). Other biological causes of these kinds of mental retardation come from unfavorable conditions that occur before, during, or after birth, such as birth injuries.

CHROMOSOMAL CAUSES The most common of the chromosomal disorders leading to mental retardation is **Down syndrome,** named after Langdon Down, the British physician who first identified it. Fewer than 1 of every 1,000 live births result in Down syndrome, but this rate increases greatly when the mother's age is over 35. Many older expectant mothers are now encouraged to undergo *amniocentesis* (testing of the amniotic fluid that surrounds the fetus) during the fourth month of pregnancy to identify Down syndrome and other chromosomal abnormalities.

Individuals with Down syndrome may have a small head, flat face, slanted eyes, high cheekbones, and, in some cases, protruding tongue. The latter may affect their ability to pronounce words clearly. They are often very affectionate with family members but in general display the same range of personality characteristics as people in the general population (Carr, 1994).

Several types of chromosomal abnormalities may cause Down syndrome (Teicher et al., 2008). The most common type (94 percent of cases) is *trisomy 21,* in which the individual has three free-floating twenty-first chromosomes instead of two. In a second type, *translocation,* the person has two normal twenty-first chromosomes and a third twenty-first chromosome fused with another chromosome (the fifteenth or thirteenth). And in a third extremely rare type, *mosaicism,* cells with two and cells with three twenty-first chromosomes are found in the same person. Most people with Down syndrome range in IQ from 35 to 55 (AAMR, 2005). The individuals appear to age early, and many even show signs of dementia as they approach 40 (Bebko & Weiss, 2006; Lawlor et al., 2001). Studies suggest that Down syndrome and early dementia often occur together because the genes that produce them are located close to each other on chromosome 21 (Selkoe, 1991).

Fragile X syndrome is the second most common chromosomal cause of mental retardation. Children born with a fragile X chromosome (that is, an X chromosome with a genetic abnormality that leaves it prone to breakage and loss) generally

Animal connection
At the National Aquarium in Havana, Cuba, regular sessions of stroking and touching dolphins, sea tortoises, and sea lions have helped many children with autism and others with mental retardation to behave more spontaneously and increase their independence and sociability.

display mild to moderate degrees of intellectual dysfunctioning, language impairments, and, in some cases, behavioral problems—difficulties that become particularly apparent as adolescence approaches (Teicher et al., 2008; Eliez & Feinstein, 2001). Typically, these individuals are shy and anxious, and males often display theory-of-mind deficits (AAMR, 2005).

METABOLIC CAUSES In metabolic disorders, the body's breakdown or production of chemicals is disturbed. The metabolic disorders that affect intelligence and development are typically caused by the pairing of two defective *recessive* genes, one from each parent. Although one such gene would have no influence if it were paired with a normal gene, its pairing with another defective gene leads to major problems for the child.

The most common metabolic disorder to cause mental retardation is *phenylketonuria* (*PKU*), which strikes 1 of every 14,000 children. Babies with PKU appear normal at birth but cannot break down the amino acid *phenylalanine*. The chemical builds up and is converted into substances that poison the system, causing severe retardation and several other symptoms. Today infants can be screened for PKU, and if started on a special diet before 3 months of age, they may develop normal intelligence.

Children with *Tay-Sachs disease,* another metabolic disorder resulting from a pairing of recessive genes, progressively lose their mental functioning, vision, and motor ability over the course of two to four years, and eventually die. One of every 30 persons of Eastern European Jewish ancestry carries the recessive gene responsible for this disorder, so that 1 of every 900 Jewish couples is at risk for having a child with Tay-Sachs disease.

PRENATAL AND BIRTH-RELATED CAUSES As a fetus develops, major physical problems in the pregnant mother can threaten the child's prospects for a normal life (Bebko & Weiss, 2006; Neisser et al., 1996). When a pregnant woman has too little iodine in her diet, for example, her child may develop *cretinism,* marked by an abnormal thyroid gland, slow development, mental retardation, and a dwarflike appearance. The disorder is rare today because the salt in most diets now contains extra iodine. Also, any infant born with this disorder may quickly be given thyroid extract to bring about a normal development.

Other prenatal problems may also cause mental retardation. As you saw in Chapter 12, children whose mothers drink too much alcohol during pregnancy may be born with **fetal alcohol syndrome,** a group of very serious problems that includes lower intellectual functioning. In fact, a generally safe level of alcohol consumption during pregnancy has not been established by research. In addition, certain maternal infections during pregnancy—*rubella* (German measles) and *syphilis,* for example—may cause childhood problems that include mental retardation.

BETWEEN THE LINES

About the Sex Chromosome

The 23rd chromosome, whose abnormality causes the Fragile X syndrome, is the smallest human chromosome.

The 23rd chromosome determines a person's sex and so it is also referred to as the sex chromosome.

In males, the 23rd chromosome pair consists of an X chromosome and a Y chromosome.

In females, the 23rd chromosome pair consists of two X chromosomes.

Birth complications can also lead to mental retardation. A prolonged period without oxygen (*anoxia*) during or after delivery can cause brain damage and retardation in a baby. Similarly, although premature birth does not necessarily lead to long-term problems for children, researchers have found that a birth weight of less than 3.5 pounds may sometimes result in retardation (Neisser et al., 1996).

CHILDHOOD PROBLEMS After birth, particularly up to age 6, certain injuries and accidents can affect intellectual functioning and in some cases lead to mental retardation. Poisonings, serious head injuries caused by accident or abuse, excessive exposure to X-rays, and excessive use of certain drugs pose special dangers (Evans, 2006). For example, a serious case of *lead poisoning,* from eating lead-based paints or inhaling high levels of automobile fumes, can cause retardation in children. Mercury, radiation, nitrite, and pesticide poisoning may do the same. In addition, certain infections, such as *meningitis* and *encephalitis,* can lead to mental retardation if they are not diagnosed and treated in time (MFA, 2008; Baroff & Olley, 1999).

Interventions for People with Mental Retardation The quality of life attained by people with mental retardation depends largely on sociocultural factors: where they live and with whom, how they are educated, and the growth opportunities available at home and in the community. Thus intervention programs for these individuals try to provide comfortable and stimulating residences, a proper education, and social and economic opportunities. At the same time, the programs seek to improve the self-image and increase the self-esteem of individuals with mental retardation. Once these needs are met, formal psychological or biological treatments are also of help in some cases.

WHAT IS THE PROPER RESIDENCE? Until recent decades, parents of children with mental retardation would send them to live in public institutions—**state schools**—as early as possible. These overcrowded institutions provided basic care, but residents were neglected, often abused, and isolated from society. Ed Murphy, the misdiagnosed man whom you met earlier, recalls his first day at a state school:

They had me scheduled to go to P-8—a back ward—when just one man looked at me. I was a wreck. I had a beard and baggy State clothes on. I had just arrived at the place. I was trying to understand what was happening. I was confused. What I looked like was P-8 material. There was this supervisor, a woman. She came on the ward and looked right at me and said: "I have him scheduled for P-8." An older attendant was there. He looked over at me and said, "He's too bright for that ward. I think we'll keep him." . . .

Of course I didn't know what P-8 was then, but I found out. I visited up there a few times on work detail. That man saved my life. Here was a woman that I had never known who they said was the building supervisor looking over me. At that point I'm pretty positive that if I went there I would have fitted in and I would still be there.

(Bogdan & Taylor, 1976, p. 49)

During the 1960s and 1970s, the public became more aware of these sorry conditions and, as part of the broader deinstitutionalization movement (see Chapter 15), demanded that many people with mental retardation be released from the state schools (Beyer, 1991). In many cases, the releases occurred without adequate preparation or supervision. Like deinstitutionalized people suffering from schizophrenia, the individuals were virtually dumped into the community. Often they failed to adjust and had to be institutionalized once again.

Since that time, reforms have led to the creation of *small institutions* and other *community residences* (group homes, halfway houses, local branches of larger institutions, and independent residences) that teach self-sufficiency, devote more staff time to patient care, and offer educational and medical services. Many of these settings follow the principles of **normalization** first started in Denmark and Sweden—they attempt to provide living conditions similar to those enjoyed by the rest of society, flexible routines, and normal developmental experiences, including opportunities for self-determination, sexual fulfillment, and economic freedom (Hodapp & Dykens, 2003).

Today the vast majority of children with mental retardation live at home rather than in an institution. During adulthood and as their parents age, however, some individuals with mental retardation require levels of assistance and opportunities that their families are unable to provide. A community residence becomes an appropriate alternative for these persons. Most people with mental retardation, including almost all with mild mental retardation, now spend their adult lives either in the family home or in a community residence (Sturmey, 2008).

WHICH EDUCATIONAL PROGRAMS WORK BEST? Because early intervention seems to offer such great promise, educational programs for individuals with mental retardation may begin during the earliest years. The appropriate education depends on the individual's degree of retardation (Bebko & Weiss, 2006; Patton et al., 2000). Educators hotly debate whether special classes or mainstreaming is most effective once the children enter school (Hardman, Drew, & Egan, 2002). In **special education,** children with mental retardation are grouped together in a separate, specially designed educational program. In contrast, **mainstreaming,** or **inclusion,** places them in regular classes with nonretarded students. Neither approach seems consistently superior (Bebko & Weiss, 2006). It may well be that mainstreaming is better for some areas of learning and for some children, special classes for others (Cummins & Lau, 2003).

Teacher preparedness is another factor that may play into decisions about mainstreaming and special education classes. Many teachers report feeling inadequately prepared to provide training and support for children with mental retardation, especially children who have additional disabilities or problems (Scheuermann et al., 2003). Brief training courses for teachers appear to address such concerns, build teacher confidence, and provide valuable information regarding children with special needs (Campbell, Gilmore, & Cuskelly, 2003).

Teachers who work with individuals with mental retardation often use operant conditioning principles to improve the self-help, communication, social, and academic skills of the individuals (Sturmey, 2008; Ardoin et al., 2004). They break learning tasks down into small steps, giving positive reinforcement as each increment is accomplished.

Early intervention
One of the most important research insights to emerge regarding treatments for autism and mental retardation is the value of early intervention—both psychological and physical. In this spirit, a 2-year-old boy is administered a session of aquatherapy, a program to help build both muscle strength and a sense of self-efficacy, as part of Missouri's First Steps program.

Life lessons
The normalization movement calls for people with mental retardation to be taught whatever skills are needed for normal and independent living. Here a psychologist (left) gives cooking lessons to young adults with mental retardation as part of a national program called You and I, which services more than 20,000 people. The program also provides lessons in dating, self-esteem, social skills, and sex education.

Working for money, independence, and self-respect
Individuals with mental retardation need the personal and financial rewards that come with work. Here a 28-year-old waiter serves beverages in a café in Slovakia. He is one of five waiters with mental retardation who work at the café.

In addition, many institutions, schools, and private homes have set up *token economy programs*—the operant conditioning programs that have also been used to treat institutionalized patients suffering from schizophrenia.

WHEN IS THERAPY NEEDED? Like anyone else, people with mental retardation sometimes experience emotional and behavioral problems. As many as 25 percent of them have a psychological disorder other than mental retardation (McBrien, 2003; Dykens & Hodapp, 2001). Furthermore, some suffer from low self-esteem, interpersonal problems, and difficulties adjusting to community life. These problems are helped to some degree by either individual or group therapy (Rush & Frances, 2000). In addition, large numbers of people with mental retardation are given psychotropic medications (Sturmey, 2008). Many clinicians argue, however, that too often the medications are used simply for the purpose of making the individuals easier to manage.

HOW CAN OPPORTUNITIES FOR PERSONAL, SOCIAL, AND OCCUPATIONAL GROWTH BE INCREASED?
People need to feel effective and competent in order to move forward in life. Those with mental retardation are most likely to achieve these feelings if their communities allow them to grow and to make many of their own choices. Denmark and Sweden, where the normalization movement began, have again been leaders in this area, developing youth clubs that encourage those with mental retardation to take risks and function independently (Flynn & Lemay, 1999; Perske, 1972). The Special Olympics program has also encouraged those with mental retardation to be active in setting goals, participate in their environment, and interact socially with others (Weiss et al., 2003).

Socializing, sex, and marriage are difficult issues for people with mental retardation and their families, but with proper training and practice, the individuals usually can learn to use contraceptives and carry out responsible family planning (Lumley & Scotti, 2001; Bennett-Gates & Zigler, 1999). The National Association for Retarded Citizens offers guidance in these matters, and some clinicians have developed *dating skills programs* (Segal, 2008; Valenti-Hein et al., 1994).

Some states restrict marriage for people with mental retardation (Levesque, 1996). These laws are rarely enforced, however, and in fact between one-quarter and one-half of all people with mild mental retardation eventually marry (Grinspoon et al., 1986). Contrary to popular myths, the marriages can be very successful. Moreover, although some individuals may be

Normal needs
The interpersonal and sexual needs of people with mental retardation are normal, and many, such as this engaged couple, demonstrate considerable ability to express intimacy.

incapable of raising children, many are quite able to do so, either on their own or with special help and community services (Sturmey, 2008).

Finally, adults with mental retardation—whatever the severity—need the personal and financial rewards that come with holding a job (Kiernan, 2000). Many work in **sheltered workshops,** protected and supervised workplaces that train them at a pace and level tailored to their abilities. After training in the workshops, many with mild or moderate retardation move on to hold regular jobs (Moore, Flowers, & Taylor, 2000).

Although training programs for people with mental retardation have improved greatly in quality over the past 30 years, there are too few of them. Consequently, most of these individuals fail to receive a complete range of educational and occupational training services. Additional programs are required so that more people with mental retardation may achieve their full potential, as workers and as human beings.

PUTTING IT... together

Clinicians Discover Childhood and Adolescence

Early in the twentieth century, mental health professionals virtually ignored children (Phares, 2008). At best, they viewed them as small adults and treated their psychological disorders as they would adult problems (Peterson & Roberts, 1991). Today the problems and special needs of young people have caught the attention of researchers and clinicians. Although all of the leading models have been used to help explain and treat these problems, the sociocultural perspective—especially the family perspective—is considered to play a special role.

Because children and adolescents have limited control over their lives, they are particularly affected by the attitudes and reactions of family members. Clinicians must therefore deal with those attitudes and reactions as they try to address the problems of the young. Treatments for conduct disorder, ADHD, mental retardation, and other problems of childhood and adolescence typically fall short unless clinicians educate and work with the family as well.

At the same time, clinicians who work with children and adolescents have learned that a narrow focus on any one model can lead to problems. For years autism was explained exclusively by family factors, misleading theorists and therapists alike and adding to the pain of parents already devastated by their child's disorder. Similarly, in the past, the sociocultural model often led professionals wrongly to accept anxiety among young children and depression among teenagers as inevitable, given the many new experiences confronted by the former and the latter group's preoccupation with peer approval.

The increased clinical focus on the young has also been accompanied by increased attention to their human and legal rights. More and more, clinicians have called on government agencies to protect the rights and safety of this often powerless group. In doing so, they hope to fuel the fights for greater educational resources and against child abuse and neglect, sexual abuse, malnourishment, and fetal alcohol syndrome.

As the problems and, at times, mistreatment of young people receive greater attention, the special needs of these individuals are becoming more visible. Thus the study and treatment of psychological disorders among children and adolescents are likely to continue at a rapid pace. Now that clinicians and public officials have "discovered" this population, they are not likely to underestimate their needs and importance again.

‹‹‹[SUMMING UP]›››

○ **Disorders of childhood and adolescence** Emotional and behavioral problems are common in childhood and adolescence, but in addition, at least one-fifth of all children and adolescents in the United States experience a diagnosable psychological disorder. *pp. 549–550*

continued

•**sheltered workshop**•A protected and supervised workplace that offers job opportunities and training at a pace and level tailored to people with various psychological disabilities.

BETWEEN THE LINES

Children, Teens, and Online Networking

One of seven individuals between 10 and 17 years of age acknowledges receiving at least one online sexual solicitation each year. ‹‹

4 percent of 10- to 17-year-olds acknowledge receiving "aggressive" online solicitations (a push for off-line contact). ‹‹

MySpace deletes 25,000 profiles weekly of users who do not meet the site's 14-year-old minimum age requirement. ‹‹

Two-thirds of parents have never talked with their teen child about his or her MySpace use. ‹‹

38 percent of parents have never seen their child's MySpace profile. ‹‹

(Andrews, 2006)

Anxiety disorders are particularly common among children and adolescents. This group of problems includes adult-like disorders, such as social phobia and generalized anxiety disorder, and the unique childhood pattern of *separation anxiety disorder,* which is characterized by excessive anxiety, often panic, whenever a child is separated from a parent. *Depression* is found in 2 percent of children and 9 percent of adolescents. The past 15 years have also witnessed an enormous increase in the number of children and adolescents who receive diagnoses of *bipolar disorder. pp. 551–557*

Children with *oppositional defiant disorder* and *conduct disorder* exceed the normal breaking of rules and act very aggressively. Children with oppositional defiant disorder argue repeatedly with adults, lose their temper, and feel intense anger and resentment. Those with conduct disorder, a more severe pattern, repeatedly violate the basic rights of others. Children with this disorder often are violent and cruel and may deliberately destroy property, steal, and run away. *pp. 557–563*

Children who display *attention-deficit/hyperactivity disorder (ADHD)* attend poorly to tasks, or behave overactively and impulsively, or both. *Ritalin* and other *stimulant drugs* and *behavioral programs* are often effective treatments. Children with an *elimination disorder*—*enuresis* or *encopresis*—repeatedly urinate or pass feces in inappropriate places. Behavioral approaches, such as the *bell-and-battery technique,* are effective treatments for enuresis. *pp. 564–571*

○ **Long-term disorders that begin in childhood** *Pervasive developmental disorders* and *mental retardation* are problems that emerge early and typically continue throughout a person's life. People with *autism,* the most heavily researched pervasive developmental disorder, are extremely unresponsive to others, have poor communication skills (including *echolalia* and *pronominal reversal*), and behave in a very rigid and repetitive manner (displaying *perseveration of sameness, strong attachments to objects, self-stimulatory behaviors,* and *self-injurious behaviors*). Individuals with *Asperger's disorder,* another kind of pervasive developmental disorder, display profound social impairment yet maintain relatively high levels of cognitive functioning and language skills.

The leading explanations of autism point to cognitive deficits, such as failure to develop a *theory of mind,* and biological abnormalities, such as abnormal development of the *cerebellum,* as causal factors. Although no treatment totally reverses the autistic pattern, significant help is available in the form of *behavioral treatments, communication training, treatment and training for parents,* and *community integration. pp. 572–579*

People with *mental retardation* are significantly below average in *intelligence* and *adaptive ability.* Approximately 3 of every 100 people qualify for this diagnosis. *Mild retardation,* by far the most common level of mental retardation, has been linked primarily to *environmental factors* such as understimulation, inadequate parent–child interactions, and insufficient early learning experiences. *Moderate, severe,* and *profound mental retardation* are caused primarily by *biological factors,* although individuals who function at these levels also are affected enormously by their family and social environment. The leading biological causes are *chromosomal abnormalities* (as in *Down syndrome*); *metabolic disorders* that typically are caused by the pairing of two defective *recessive genes* (for example, *phenylketonuria,* or *PKU,* and *Tay-Sachs disease*); disorders resulting from *prenatal problems* (cretinism and *fetal alcohol syndrome*); disorders resulting from *birth complications,* such as *anoxia* or *extreme prematurity;* and *childhood diseases* and *injuries.*

Today intervention programs for people with mental retardation emphasize the importance of a *comfortable and stimulating residence,* either the family home or a small institution or group home that follows the principles of *normalization.* Other important interventions include *proper education, therapy* for psychological problems, and programs offering *training in socializing, sex, marriage, parenting,* and *occupational skills.* One of the most intense debates in the field of education centers on whether individuals with mental retardation profit more from *special classes* or from *mainstreaming*. Research has not consistently favored one approach over the other. *pp. 579–589*

⫸ CRITICAL THOUGHTS ⫷

1. Although boys with psychological disorders outnumber girls, adult women with such disorders outnumber adult men. How might you explain this age-related shift? *pp. 549–571*

2. Do video games that feature violence help produce oppositional defiant disorder, conduct disorder, or other childhood problems? *pp. 557–563*

3. What psychological effects might bullying have on its victims? Why do many individuals seem able to overcome the trauma of being bullied, while others do not? *p. 559*

4. The overall rate of repeated arrests of adolescents sent to juvenile detention, or juvenile training, centers has been estimated to be as high as 80 percent. How might such centers themselves be contributing to this recidivism rate? *p. 560*

5. In past times, a child with a learning, communication, or coordination disorder might simply be called a "weak" reader, "clumsy," or the like. What are the advantages and disadvantages to the child of affixing clinical names to the patterns? *p. 582*

6. What might be the merits and flaws of *special classes* versus *mainstreaming* for people with mental retardation? *p. 587*

⫸ cyberstudy ⫷   SEARCH

Search the *Abnormal Psychology* Video Tool Kit
www.worthpublishers.com/apvtk

▲ Chapter 17 Video Cases
   The 9/11 Attacks: Effects on Children
   ADHD: A Family Problem
   Faces of Autism
▲ Video case discussions, study guides, and questions

Log on to the Comer Web Page
www.worthpublishers.com/comer

▲ Chapter 17 outline, learning objectives, research exercises, study tools, and practice test questions
▲ Additional Chapter 17 case studies, Web links, and FAQs

DISORDERS OF AGING AND COGNITION

Harry appeared to be in perfect health at age 58. . . . He worked in the municipal water treatment plant of a small city, and it was at work that the first overt signs of Harry's mental illness appeared. While responding to a minor emergency, he became confused about the correct order in which to pull the levers that controlled the flow of fluids. As a result, several thousand gallons of raw sewage were discharged into a river. Harry had been an efficient and diligent worker, so after puzzled questioning, his error was attributed to the flu and overlooked.

Several weeks later, Harry came home with a baking dish his wife had asked him to buy, having forgotten that he had brought home the identical dish two nights before. Later that week, on two successive nights, he went to pick up his daughter at her job in a restaurant, apparently forgetting that she had changed shifts and was now working days. A month after that, he quite uncharacteristically argued with a clerk at the phone company; he was trying to pay a bill that he had already paid three days before. . . .

Months passed and Harry's wife was beside herself. She could see that his problem was worsening. Not only had she been unable to get effective help, but Harry himself was becoming resentful and sometimes suspicious of her attempts. He now insisted there was nothing wrong with him, and she would catch him narrowly watching her every movement. . . . Sometimes he became angry—sudden little storms without apparent cause. . . . More difficult for his wife was Harry's repetitiveness in conversation: He often repeated stories from the past and sometimes repeated isolated phrases and sentences from more recent exchanges. There was no context and little continuity to his choice of subjects. . . .

Two years after Harry had first allowed the sewage to escape, he was clearly a changed man. Most of the time he seemed preoccupied; he usually had a vacant smile on his face, and what little he said was so vague that it lacked meaning. . . . Gradually his wife took over getting him up, toileted, and dressed each morning. . . .

Harry's condition continued to worsen slowly. When his wife's school was in session, his daughter would stay with him some days, and neighbors were able to offer some help. But occasionally he would still manage to wander away. On those occasions he greeted everyone he met—old friends and strangers alike—with "Hi, it's so nice." That was the extent of his conversation, although he might repeat "nice, nice, nice" over and over again. . . . When Harry left a coffee pot on a unit of the electric stove until it melted, his wife, desperate for help, took him to see another doctor. Again Harry was found to be in good health. [However] the doctor ordered a CAT scan [and eventually concluded] that Harry had "Pick-Alzheimer disease" and that there was no known cause and no effective treatment. . . .

Because Harry was a veteran . . . [he qualified for] hospitalization in a regional veterans' hospital about 400 miles away from his home. . . . Desperate, five years after the accident at work, [his wife] accepted with gratitude [this] hospitalization. . . .

At the hospital the nursing staff sat Harry up in a chair each day and, aided by volunteers, made sure he ate enough. Still, he lost weight and became weaker. He would weep when his wife came to see him, but he did not talk, and he gave no other sign that he recognized her. After a year, even the weeping stopped. Harry's wife could no longer bear to visit. Harry lived on until just after his sixty-fifth birthday, when he choked on a piece of bread, developed pneumonia as a consequence, and soon died.

(Heston, 1992, pp. 87–90)

Harry suffered from a form of *Alzheimer's disease.* This term is familiar to almost everyone in our society. It seems as if each decade is marked by a disease that everyone dreads—a diagnosis no one wants to hear because it feels like a death sentence. Cancer used to be such a diagnosis, then AIDS. But medical science has made remarkable strides with those diseases, and patients who now develop them have reason for hope and expectations of improvement. Alzheimer's disease, on the other hand, remains incurable and almost untreatable, although, as you will see later, researchers are currently making enormous progress toward understanding it and reversing, or at least slowing, its march.

What makes Alzheimer's disease particularly frightening is that it means not only eventual physical death but also, as in Harry's case, a slow psychological death—a progressive *dementia,* or deterioration of one's memory and related cognitive faculties. There are dozens of causes of dementia; however, Alzheimer's disease is the most common one.

Although dementia is currently the most publicized and feared psychological problem among the elderly, it is hardly the only one. Indeed, a variety of psychological disorders are tied closely to later life. As with childhood disorders, some of the disorders of old age are caused primarily by pressures that are particularly likely to appear at that time of life, others by unique traumatic experiences, and still others—like dementia—by biological abnormalities.

Old Age and Stress

Old age is usually defined in our society as the years past age 65. By this account, around 36 million people in the United States are "old," representing 12 percent of the total population; this is an 11-fold increase since 1900 (Edelstein, Stoner, & Woodhead, 2008) (see Figure 18-1). Moreover, it has been estimated that the U.S. population will consist of 65 million elderly people by the year 2030—20 percent of the population (Cherry, Galea, & Silva, 2007). Not only is the overall population of the elderly on the rise, but, furthermore, the number of people over 85 will double in the next 10 years. Indeed, people over 85 represent the fastest-growing segment of the population in the United States and in most countries around the world (Cherry et al., 2007). Older women outnumber older men by 3 to 2 (Etaugh, 2008).

Like childhood, old age brings special pressures, unique upsets, and profound biological changes (Edelstein et al., 2008). People become more prone to illness and injury as they age, and they are likely to experience the stress of loss—the loss of spouses, friends, and adult children and the loss of former activities and roles (Etaugh, 2008; Inselmann, 2004). Many lose their sense of purpose after they retire. Even favored pets and possessions are sometimes lost.

The stresses of elderly people need not necessarily result in psychological problems (Edelstein et al., 2008; Cherry et al., 2007). In fact, some older persons use the changes that come with aging as opportunities for learning and growth. For example, the number of elderly—often physically limited—people who use the Internet to connect with people of similar ages and interests doubled between 2000 and 2004, and then doubled again between 2004 and 2007 (APA, 2007). For other elderly people, however, the stresses of old age do lead to psychological difficulties (Aldwin, Spiro, & Park, 2006). Studies indicate that as many as 50 percent of elderly people would benefit from mental health services, yet fewer than 20 percent actually receive them. **Geropsychology,** the field of psychology dedicated to the mental health of elderly people, has developed almost entirely within the last 30 years, and at present fewer than 4 percent of all clinicians work primarily with elderly persons (Meyers, 2006; Dittman, 2005).

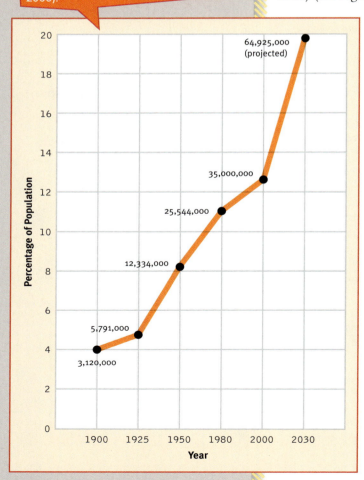

Figure 18-1

On the rise The population of people aged 65 and older in the United States increased 11-fold during the twentieth century. The percentage of elderly people in the population increased from 4 percent in 1900 to 12 percent in 2000 and is expected to be 20 percent in 2030 (Edelstein et al., 2008; U.S. Census, 2000).

The psychological problems of elderly persons may be divided into two groups. One group consists of disorders that may be common among people in all age groups but are often connected to the process of aging when they occur in an elderly person. These include *depressive, anxiety,* and *substance-related disorders.* The other group consists of disorders of cognition, such as *delirium* and *dementia,* that result from brain abnormalities. As in Harry's case, these brain abnormalities are most often tied to aging, but they also can sometimes occur in younger individuals. Elderly persons with one of these psychological problems often display other such problems. For example, many who suffer from dementia also experience depression and anxiety (Apostolova & Cummings, 2008). And those who are depressed have an increased likelihood of displaying a pattern of alcohol abuse (Devanand, 2002).

Owen Franken/Corbis

Making a difference
Many people come to feel unimportant and lonely and develop low self-esteem as they become older—ingredients that may contribute to depression. To help prevent these feelings, some older individuals now offer their expertise and wisdom to young people who are trying to master new skills, undertake business projects, and the like. This elderly man, who volunteers regularly at an elementary school, is teaching math to a first grader.

❋Depression in Later Life

Depression is one of the most common mental health problems of older adults. The features of depression are the same for elderly people as for younger people, including feelings of profound sadness and emptiness; low self-esteem, guilt, and pessimism; and loss of appetite and sleep disturbances (see *A Closer Look* on pages 596–597). Depression is particularly common among those who have recently experienced a trauma, such as the loss of a spouse or close friend or the development of a serious physical illness (Edelstein et al., 2008; Etaugh, 2008).

[Oscar] was an 83-year-old married man with an episode of major depressive disorder. . . . He said that about one and one-half years prior to beginning treatment, his brother had died. In the following months, two friends whom he had known since childhood died. Following these losses, he became increasingly anxious [and] grew more and more pessimistic. Reluctantly, he acknowledged, "I even thought about ending my life." Review of his symptoms indicated that while . . . anxiety was a prominent part of his clinical picture, so was depression. . . .

During . . . treatment, [Oscar] discussed his relationship with his brother. He discussed how distraught he was to watch his brother's physical deterioration from an extended illness. He described the scene at his brother's deathbed and the moment "when he took his final breath." He experienced guilt over the failure to carry out his brother's funeral services in a manner he felt his brother would have wanted. While initially characterizing his relationship with his brother as loving and amiable, he later acknowledged that he disapproved of many ways in which his brother acted. Later in therapy, he also reviewed different facets of his past relationships with his two deceased friends. He expressed sadness that the long years had ended. . . . [Oscar's] life had been organized around visits to his brother's home and outings with his friends. . . . [While] his wife had encouraged him to visit with other friends and family, it became harder and harder to do so as he became more depressed.

(Hinrichsen, 1999, p. 433)

Overall, as many as 20 percent of people experience depression at some point during old age (Knight et al., 2006; Blazer, 2002). The rate is highest in older women. This rate among the elderly is about the same as that among younger adults—even lower,

BETWEEN THE LINES

In Their Words

"What an amount of good nature and humor it takes to endure the gruesome business of growing old." ‹‹
Sigmund Freud, 1937

Sleep and Sleep Disorders among the Old and Not So Old

Sleep is affected by both physical and psychosocial factors. Sleep deprivation for 100 hours or more leads to hallucinations, paranoia, and bizarre behavior. When people remain awake for over 200 hours, they frequently experience periods of "microsleep," naps lasting two to three seconds. The body simply refuses to be entirely deprived of sleep for long.

To learn more about sleep, researchers bring people into the laboratory and record their activities as they sleep, using various types of recording devices. One important discovery has been that eyes move rapidly about 25 percent of the time a person is asleep, a phenomenon known as *rapid eye movement,* or *REM.* REM sleep is often called "paradoxical sleep" because it resembles both deep sleep and wakefulness (Wickwire et al., 2008). Despite small movements and muscle twitches, the body is immobilized, almost paralyzed. At the same time, the eyes are darting back and forth, blood flow to the brain increases, and brain-wave activity is almost identical to that of an awake and alert person. Eighty percent of subjects who are awakened from REM sleep report that they were dreaming.

DSM-IV-TR identifies a number of sleep disorders. The *dyssomnias* (insomnia, hypersomnia, breathing-related sleep disorder, narcolepsy, and circadian rhythm sleep disorder) involve disturbances in the amount, quality, or timing of sleep. The *parasomnias* (nightmare disorder, sleep terror disorder, and sleepwalking disorder) involve abnormal events that occur during sleep.

The most common of these disorders is *insomnia,* a dyssomnia in which people repeatedly have great difficulty falling asleep or maintaining sleep (Taylor et al., 2008). More than 20 percent of the entire population experience this pattern each year (APA, 2000). People with insomnia feel as though they are almost constantly awake. Often they are very sleepy during the day and have difficulty functioning effectively. The problem may be caused by factors such as anxiety or depression, medical ailments, pain, or medication effects (Andreasen & Black, 2006).

Sleep Disorders among the Elderly

Insomnia is more common among older persons than younger ones (Knight et al., 2006). At least 50 percent of the population over 65 years of age experience some measure of insomnia (Edelstein et al., 2008). Elderly people may be particularly prone to this problem because so many of them have medical ailments, experience pain, take medications, or grapple with depression and anxiety—each a known contributor to insomnia (Taylor et al., 2008; Asplund, 2005). In addition, some of the normal physical changes that occur as people age may heighten the chances of insomnia. As we age, for example, our body rhythms change, we naturally spend less time in deep sleep, our sleep is more readily interrupted, and we take longer to get back to sleep (Edelstein et al., 2008).

Another sleep disorder commonly found among the elderly is *breathing-related sleep disorder,* a respiratory problem in which persons are periodically deprived of oxygen to the brain while they sleep, so that they frequently wake up. *Sleep apnea,* the most common form of this disorder, may occur in more than 10 percent of the elderly population; it is less common in younger age groups (Wickwire et al, 2008; APA, 2000). Its victims, typically overweight persons who are heavy snorers, actually stop breathing for up to 30 seconds or more as they sleep. Hundreds of episodes may occur nightly, without the victim's awareness.

Sleep Disorders throughout the Life Span

As you have read, insomnia and breathing-related sleep disorder are particularly common among older persons, although they are found in younger persons as well. Other sleep disorders are just as common—in a few cases more common—among the other age groups.

according to some studies. However, it climbs much higher among aged persons who live in nursing homes, as opposed to those in the community (Carlson & Snowden, 2007; Fisher et al., 2001).

Several studies suggest that depression raises an elderly person's chances of developing significant medical problems (Edelstein et al., 2008; Alexopoulos, 2005). For example, older depressed people with high blood pressure are almost three times as likely to suffer a stroke as older nondepressed people with the same condition. Similarly, elderly people who are depressed recover more slowly and less completely from heart attacks, hip fractures, pneumonia, and other infections and illnesses. Small wonder that among the elderly, increases in clinical depression are tied to increases in the mortality rate (Holwerda et al., 2007).

As you read in Chapter 10, elderly persons are also more likely to commit suicide than younger ones, and often their suicides are related to depression (Vannoy et al., 2008). The overall rate of suicide in the United States is 12 per 100,000 persons; among

In contrast to insomnia, *hypersomnia* is a sleep disorder marked by a heightened need for sleep and excessive sleepiness. Sufferers may need extra hours of sleep each night and may need to sleep during the daytime as well (APA, 2000).

Narcolepsy, a disorder marked by repeated sudden bouts of REM sleep during waking hours, afflicts more than 135,000 people in the United States (NINDS, 2006). Although narcolepsy is a biological disorder, the bouts of REM sleep are often triggered by strong emotions. Sufferers may suddenly fall into REM sleep in the midst of an argument or during an exciting part of a football game.

People with *circadian rhythm sleep disorder* experience excessive sleepiness or insomnia as a result of a mismatch between their own sleep-wake pattern and the sleep-wake schedule of most other people in their environment. Often the disorder takes the form of falling asleep late and awakening late. This dyssomnia can result from night-shift work, frequent changes in work shifts, or repeated episodes of jet lag (Ohayon et al., 2002).

Nightmare disorder is the most common of the parasomnias. Although most people experience nightmares from time to time, in this disorder nightmares become frequent and cause such great distress that the individual must receive treatment. Such nightmares often increase under stress.

Persons with *sleep terror disorder* awaken suddenly during the first third of their evening sleep, screaming in extreme fear and agitation. They are in a state of panic, are often incoherent, and have a heart rate to match. Sleep terrors most often appear in children and disappear during adolescence. Up to 6 percent of children experience them at some time (APA, 2000).

People with a *sleepwalking disorder*—usually children—repeatedly leave their beds and walk around, without being conscious of the episode or remembering it later. The episodes occur in the first third of the individuals' nightly sleep. Those who are awakened while sleepwalking are confused for several moments. If allowed to continue sleepwalking, they eventually return to bed. Sleepwalkers usually manage to avoid obstacles, climb stairs, and perform complex activities, in a seemingly emotionless state. Accidents do happen, however: tripping, bumping into furniture, and even falling out of windows have all been reported. Up to 5 percent of children experience this disorder for an extended period of time, and as many as 40 percent have occasional episodes (Wickwire et al., 2008; APA, 2000). Sleepwalking usually disappears by age 15.

the elderly it is 19 per 100,000. Among 80- to 85-year-olds in particular, it is 27 per 100,000; among white American men over the age of 85, it is 65 per 100,000 (NCHS, 2006; CDC, 2001; Fisher et al., 2001).

Like younger adults, older individuals who are depressed may be helped by cognitive-behavioral therapy, interpersonal therapy, antidepressant medications, or a combination of these approaches (Knight et al., 2006; Alexopoulos, 2005). Both individual and group therapy formats have been used. More than half of elderly patients with depression improve with these various treatments. At the same time, it is sometimes difficult to use antidepressant drugs effectively and safely with older persons because the body breaks the drugs down differently in later life (Rubin, 2005; Sadavoy, 2004). Moreover, among elderly people, antidepressant drugs have a higher risk of causing some cognitive impairment (Edelstein et al., 2008). Electroconvulsive therapy, applied with certain modifications, also has been used for elderly people who are severely depressed and unhelped by other approaches (Wang, 2007; Blazer, 2002).

Rick Rickman/Matrix

© Mitch Wojnarowicz/The Image Works

Racing to mental health
Gerontologists propose that elderly people need to pursue pleasurable and personally meaningful activities in order to thrive psychologically. With this in mind, the elderly men on the left compete in a race in the Senior Olympics. On the other hand, the elderly gentleman on the right, also interested in racing, watches a competition at the Saratoga Springs horse racing track with the daily post parade statistics program resting on his head. Which of these two activities might clinical theorists have more confidence in as a key to successful psychological functioning during old age?

BETWEEN THE LINES

Bereavement and Gender

11.1 million Number of widows in the United States ‹‹

2.6 million Number of widowers in the United States ‹‹

(Etaugh, 2008; U.S. Census Bureau, 2005)

✿Anxiety Disorders in Later Life

Anxiety is also common among elderly people (Schuurmans et al., 2005). At any given time, around 6 percent of elderly men and 11 percent of elderly women in the United States experience at least one of the anxiety disorders (Fisher et al., 2001). Surveys indicate that generalized anxiety disorder is particularly common, experienced by up to 7 percent of all elderly persons (Holwerda et al., 2007; Flint, 1994). The prevalence of anxiety also increases throughout old age. For example, individuals over 85 years of age report higher rates of anxiety than those between 65 and 84 years. In fact, all of these numbers may be low, as anxiety in the elderly tends to be underreported (Jeste, Blazer, & First, 2005). Both the elderly individual and the clinician may interpret physical symptoms of anxiety, such as heart palpitations and sweating, as symptoms of a medical condition.

There are many things about aging that may heighten the anxiety levels of certain individuals. Declining health, for example, has often been pointed to, and in fact, older persons who experience significant medical illnesses or injuries report more anxiety than those who are healthy or injury-free (Nordhus & Nielsen, 2005). Researchers have not, however, been able to determine why certain individuals who experience such problems in old age become anxious while others who face similar circumstances remain relatively calm (see *Psych Watch* on page 600).

Older adults with anxiety disorders have been treated with psychotherapy of various kinds, particularly cognitive therapy (Knight et al., 2006; Mohlman et al., 2003). Many also receive benzodiazepines or other antianxiety medications; those with obsessive-compulsive disorder or panic disorder may be treated with serotonin-enhancing antidepressant drugs such as fluoxetine (Prozac), just as younger sufferers are. Again, however, all such drugs must be used cautiously with older people (Tamblyn et al., 2005).

✿Substance Abuse in Later Life

Although alcohol abuse and other forms of substance abuse are significant problems for many older persons, the prevalence of such patterns actually appears to decline after age 60, perhaps because of declining health or reduced financial status (Aldwin et al., 2006; Oslin & Holden, 2002). The majority of older adults do not misuse alcohol or other substances despite the fact that aging can sometimes be a time of considerable stress and that in our society alcohol and drugs are widely turned to in times of stress. At the same time, accurate data about the rate of substance abuse among older adults are difficult to gather because many elderly persons do not suspect or admit that they have such a problem (Jeste et al., 2005).

Surveys find that 4 to 7 percent of older people, particularly men, have alcohol-related disorders in a given year (Knight et al., 2006; Adams & Cox, 1997). Men under 30 are four times as likely as men over 60 to exhibit a behavioral problem associated with alcohol abuse, such as repeated falling, spells of dizziness or blacking out, secretive drinking, or social withdrawal. Older patients who are institutionalized, however, do display high rates of problem drinking. For example, alcohol problems among older persons admitted to general and mental hospitals range from 15 percent to 49 percent, and estimates of alcohol-related problems among patients in nursing homes range from 26 percent to 60 percent (Klein & Jess, 2002; Gallagher-Thompson & Thompson, 1995).

Researchers often distinguish between older problem drinkers who have had alcohol-related problems for many years, perhaps since their 20s, and those who do not start the pattern until their 50s or 60s. The latter group typically begins abusive drinking as a reaction to the negative events and pressures of growing older, such as the death of a spouse, living alone, or unwanted retirement (Onen et al., 2005). Alcohol abuse and dependence in elderly people are treated much as in younger adults (see Chapter 12), with such approaches as detoxification, Antabuse, Alcoholics Anonymous (AA), and cognitive-behavioral therapy (Knight et al., 2006; Gurnack et al., 2002).

A leading kind of substance problem in the elderly is the *misuse of prescription drugs* (Beckman, Parker, & Thorslund, 2005). Most often it is unintentional. Elderly people buy 30 percent of all prescription drugs and 40 percent of all over-the-counter drugs. In fact, older people receive twice as many prescriptions as younger persons; the average elderly individual takes four prescription drugs and two over-the-counter drugs (Edelstein et al., 2008; Wilder-Smith, 2005). Thus their risk of confusing medications or skipping doses is high. Research shows that across the world, more than 12 percent of elderly people do not take their medications properly (Cooper et al., 2005). To help address this problem, physicians and pharmacists often try to simplify medications, educate older patients about their prescriptions, clarify directions, and teach them to watch for undesired effects (Rubin, 2005).

On the other hand, physicians themselves are sometimes to blame in cases of prescription drug misuse, perhaps overprescribing medications for elderly patients or unwisely mixing certain medicines (Spinewine et al., 2005; Wilder-Smith, 2005). In a poignant letter published in the magazine *Aging,* a 72-year-old woman revealed that because of problems earlier in her life, her physician prescribed first tranquilizers, then a stimulant, and then medication for severe headaches. Eventually she increased the dosage of these various

BETWEEN THE LINES

Losing a Spouse

Widowed men suffer more depression, other psychological disorders, and physical illnesses than widowed women. ‹‹

In the United States, by two years after the death of their spouse, 19 percent of women are in a new romantic relationship and 5 percent are remarried. ‹‹

In the United States, by two years after the death of their spouse, 61 percent of men are in a new romantic relationship and 25 percent are remarried. ‹‹

(Etaugh, 2008; Fields, 2004; Wortman et al., 2004; Canetto, 2003)

"Am I the smart one and you're the pretty one or is it the other way around?"

The Oldest Old

Clinicians suggest that aging need not inevitably lead to psychological problems. Nor apparently does it always lead to physical problems.

When researchers have studied people over 95 years of age—often called the "oldest old"—they have been surprised to learn that these individuals are on average more healthy, clear-headed, and agile than those in their 80s and early 90s (Corliss & Lemonick, 2004; Duenwald, 2003; Perls, 1995). Although some certainly experience cognitive declines, more than half remain perfectly alert (Boeve et al., 2003). Many of the oldest old are, in fact, still employed, sexually active, and able to enjoy the outdoors and the arts. What is the greatest fear of these individuals? The fear

of significant cognitive decline. According to one study, many people in their 90s and above fear the prospect of mental deterioration more than they fear death (Boeve et al., 2003).

Some scientists believe that individuals who live this long carry "longevity" genes that make them resistant to disabling or terminal infections (Corliss & Lemonick, 2004; Perls, 1995). The individuals themselves often credit a good frame of mind or regular behaviors that they have maintained for many years—for example, eating healthful food, pursuing regular exercise, and not smoking. Said one 96-year-old retired math and science teacher, "You can't sit. . . . You have to keep moving" (Duenwald, 2003).

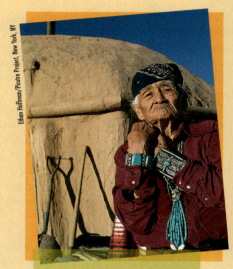

Ethan Hoffman/Picture Project, New York, NY

John Parrish, a 104-year-old medicine man living in Monument Valley, Arizona

Ageism in the United States

80% Percentage of elderly people who report experiencing ageism, such as people assuming they have memory or physical impairments due to their age ‹‹

58% Elderly people who report being told jokes that poke fun at older persons ‹‹

31% Elderly people who report being ignored or not taken seriously because of their age ‹‹

(Palmore, 2005, 2004, 2001)

medications, noting that the drugs no longer had the same effect and that she did not feel well. She said she felt no guilt about what had happened because "after all I was only following the doctor's orders at all times" (Reynolds, 1990, p. 27). Her functioning became so impaired, however, that she needed hospitalization and therapy to end her addiction.

Yet another drug-related problem, apparently on the increase, is the misuse of powerful medications at nursing homes. Research suggests that antipsychotic drugs are currently being given to almost 30 percent of the total nursing home population in the United States, despite the fact that many such individuals do not display psychotic functioning (Lagnado, 2007). Apparently, these powerful and (for some elderly patients) dangerous drugs are often given to sedate and manage the patients.

✿Psychotic Disorders in Later Life

Elderly people have a higher rate of psychotic symptoms than younger persons (Broadway & Mintzer, 2007; Hassett et al., 2005). Among aged people, these symptoms are usually due to underlying medical conditions such as delirium and dementia, the disorders of cognition that you will read about in the next section. However, some elderly persons suffer from *schizophrenia* or *delusional disorder*.

Actually, schizophrenia is less common in older persons than in younger ones. In fact, many persons with schizophrenia find that their symptoms lessen in later life (Meeks & Jeste, 2008; Fisher et al., 2001). Improvement can occur in people who have displayed schizophrenia for 30 or more years, particularly in such areas as social skills and work capacity, as we are reminded by the remarkable late-life improvement of the Nobel Prize recipient John Nash (see pages 456–457).

It is uncommon for *new* cases of schizophrenia to emerge in late life. Thus some of the elderly people with schizophrenia have been receiving antipsychotic drugs and psychotherapeutic interventions for many years and are continuing to do so in old age (Meeks & Jeste, 2008; Sadavoy, 2004). In contrast, others have been untreated for years and continue to be untreated as elderly persons, winding up in nursing homes, in run-down apartments, homeless, or in jail.

Another kind of psychotic disorder found among the elderly is *delusional disorder,* in which individuals develop beliefs that are false but not bizarre. This disorder is rare in most age groups—around 3 of every 10,000 persons—but its prevalence appears to increase in the elderly population (Chae & Kang, 2006; Fisher et al., 2001; APA, 2000). Older persons with a delusional disorder may develop deeply held suspicions of persecution; they believe that other persons—often family members, doctors, or friends—are conspiring against, cheating, spying on, or maligning them. They may become irritable, angry, or depressed or pursue legal action because of such ideas. It is not clear why this disorder increases among elderly people, but some clinicians suggest that the rise is related to the deficiencies in hearing, social isolation, greater stress, or heightened poverty experienced by many elderly persons.

Disorders of Cognition

Most of us worry from time to time that we are losing our memory and other mental abilities. You rush out the door without your keys, you meet a familiar person and cannot remember her name, or your mind goes blank in the middle of an important test. Actually such mishaps are a common and quite normal feature of stress or of aging (Edelstein et al., 2008; Hoyer & Verhaeghen, 2006). As people move through middle age, these memory difficulties and lapses of attention increase, and they may occur regularly by the age of 60 or 70. Sometimes, however, people experience memory and other cognitive changes that are far more extensive and problematic.

In Chapter 7 you saw that problems in memory and related cognitive processes can occur without biological causes, in the form of *dissociative disorders.* More often, however, cognitive problems do have organic roots, particularly when they appear late in life. The leading cognitive disorders among elderly persons are *delirium* and *dementia.*

Delirium

Delirium is a clouding of consciousness. As the person's awareness of the environment becomes less clear, he or she has great difficulty concentrating, focusing attention, and thinking sequentially, which leads to misinterpretations, illusions, and, on occasion, hallucinations (Trzepacz & Meagher, 2008; APA, 2000). Sufferers may believe that it is morning in the middle of the night or that they are home when actually they are in a hospital room.

This state of massive confusion typically develops over a short period of time, usually hours or days. Delirium apparently affects more than 2 million people in the United States each year (Clary & Krishnan, 2001). It may occur in any age group, including children, but is most common in elderly persons. In fact, when elderly people enter a hospital to be treated for a general medical condition, 1 in 10 of them shows the symptoms of delirium (Trzepacz & Meagher, 2008; APA, 2000). At least another 10 percent develop delirium during their stay in the hospital (Inouye et al., 2003, 2001, 1999).

Fever, certain diseases and infections, poor nutrition, head injuries, strokes, and stress (including the trauma of surgery) may all cause delirium (Wetterling, 2005; Schneider et al., 2002). So may intoxication by certain substances, such as prescription drugs. Partly because older people face so many of these problems, they are more likely than younger ones to experience delirium. If a clinician accurately identifies delirium, it can often be easy to correct—by treating the underlying infection, for example, or changing the patient's drug prescription (Sadavoy, 2004). However, the syndrome typically fails to be recognized for what it is (Hustey et al., 2003; Monette et al., 2001). One landmark study on a medical ward, for example, found that admission doctors detected only 1 of 15 consecutive cases of delirium (Cameron et al., 1987). Incorrect

•**delirium**•A rapidly developing clouding of consciousness; the person has great difficulty concentrating, focusing attention, and following an orderly sequence of thought.

Environmental comfort In addition to providing support, psychotropic medications, and other such measures to help calm and lift the spirits of elderly residents, some long-term care facilities have redesigned their buildings so that the settings themselves have soothing effects. At this facility in Baltimore, an elderly resident feels one of the fiber-optic light curtains that decorate the rooms. The rooms are also made more peaceful by the use of soft changing colors and sounds of the ocean, woods, and streams.

Ted Mathias/AP Photo

diagnoses of this kind may contribute to a high death rate for older people with delirium (Trzepacz & Meagher, 2008; Gonzalez et al., 2005).

Dementia

People with **dementia** experience significant memory losses along with losses in other cognitive functions such as abstract thinking or language (APA, 2000). Those with certain forms of dementia may also undergo personality changes—they may begin to behave inappropriately, for example—and their symptoms may worsen steadily.

At any given time, around 3 to 9 percent of the world's adult population are suffering from dementia (Berr et al., 2005). Its occurrence is closely related to age (see Figure 18-2). Among people 65 years of age, the prevalence is around 1 to 2 percent, increasing to as much as 50 percent among those over the age of 85 (Apostolova & Cummings, 2008; Knight et al., 2006).

Altogether, 5 million persons in the United States experience some form of dementia (Soukup, 2006; Reuters, 2004). More than 70 forms have been identified. Like delirium, dementia is sometimes the result of nutritional or other problems that can be corrected. Most forms of dementia, however, are caused by brain diseases or injuries, such as Alzheimer's disease or stroke, which are currently difficult or impossible to correct.

Alzheimer's Disease **Alzheimer's disease** is named after Alois Alzheimer, the German physician who formally identified it in 1907. Alzheimer first became aware of the syndrome in 1901 when a new patient, Auguste D., was placed under his care:

On November 25, 1901, a . . . woman with no personal or family history of mental illness was admitted to a psychiatric hospital in Frankfurt, Germany, by her husband, who could no longer ignore or hide quirks and lapses that had overtaken her in recent months. First, there were unexplainable bursts of anger, and then a strange series of memory problems. She became increasingly unable to locate things in her own home and began to make surprising mistakes in the kitchen. By the time she arrived at Städtische Irrenanstalt, the Frankfurt Hospital for the Mentally Ill and Epileptics, her condition was as severe as it was curious. The attending doctor, senior physician Alois Alzheimer, began the new file with these notes. . . .

She sits on the bed with a helpless expression.
"What is your name?"
Auguste.
"Last name?"
Auguste.
"What is your husband's name?"
Auguste, I think.
"How long have you been here?"
(She seems to be trying to remember.)
Three weeks.

It was her second day in the hospital. Dr. Alzheimer, a thirty-seven-year-old neuropathologist and clinician, . . . observed in his new patient a remarkable cluster of symptoms: severe disorientation, reduced comprehension, aphasia (language impairment), paranoia, hallucinations, and a short-term memory so incapacitated that when he spoke her full-name, ***Frau Auguste D_____,*** *and asked her to write it down, the patient got only as far as "Frau" before needing the doctor to repeat the rest.*

He spoke her name again. She wrote "Augu" and again stopped.

When Alzheimer prompted her a third time, she was able to write her entire first name and the initial "D" before finally giving up, telling the doctor, "I have lost myself."

Her condition did not improve. It became apparent that there was nothing that anyone at this or any other hospital could do for Frau D. except to insure her safety and try to

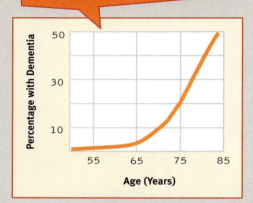

Figure 18-2

Dementia and age The occurrence of dementia is closely related to age. Fewer than 1 percent of all 60-year-olds have dementia, compared to as many as 50 percent of those who are 85. After 60, the prevalence of dementia doubles every six years up to age 85 or so, after which the increase tapers off. (Adapted from Julien, 2008; Nussbaum & Ellis, 2003; Alzheimer's Association, 1997).

•**dementia**•A syndrome marked by severe problems in memory and in at least one other cognitive function.

•**Alzheimer's disease**•The most common form of dementia, usually occurring after the age of 65.

keep her as clean and comfortable as possible for the rest of her days. Over the next four and a half years, she became increasingly disoriented, delusional, and incoherent. She was often hostile.

"Her gestures showed a complete helplessness," Alzheimer later noted in a published report. "She was disoriented as to time and place. From time to time she would state that she did not understand anything, that she felt confused and totally lost. . . . Often she would scream for hours and hours in a horrible voice."

By November 1904, three and a half years into her illness, Auguste D. was bedridden, incontinent, and largely immobile. . . . Notes from October 1905 indicate that she had become permanently curled up in a fetal position with her knees drawn up to her chest, muttering but unable to speak, and requiring assistance to be fed.

(Shenk, 2001, pp. 12–14)

Alzheimer's disease is the most common form of dementia, accounting for as many as two-thirds of all cases. Around 5 million people in the United States currently have this gradually progressive disease (Julien, 2008; Hebert et al., 2003). It sometimes appears in middle age (early onset), but in the vast majority of cases it occurs after the age of 65 (late onset), and its prevalence increases markedly among people in their late 70s and early 80s (see Table 18-1).

Although some people with Alzheimer's disease may survive for as many as 20 years, the time between onset and death is typically 8 to 10 years (Julien, 2008; Soukup, 2006). It usually begins with mild memory problems, lapses of attention, and difficulties in language and communication (Apostolova & Cummings, 2008; Lyketsos et al., 2002, 2000). As symptoms worsen, the person has trouble completing complicated tasks or remembering important appointments. Eventually sufferers also have difficulty with simple tasks, distant memories are forgotten, and changes in personality often become very noticeable. For example, a man may become uncharacteristically aggressive.

People with Alzheimer's disease may at first deny that they have a problem, but they soon become anxious or depressed about their state of mind; many also become agitated. A woman from Virginia describes her memory loss as the disease progresses:

Very often I wander around looking for something which I know is very pertinent, but then after a while I forget about what it is I was looking for. . . . Once the idea is lost, everything is lost and I have nothing to do but wander around trying to figure out what it was that was so important earlier.

(Shenk, 2001, p. 43)

As the symptoms of dementia intensify, people with Alzheimer's disease show less and less awareness of their limitations. They may withdraw from others during the late stages of the disorder, become more confused about time and place, wander, and show very poor judgment. Eventually they become fully dependent on other people. They may lose almost all knowledge of the past and fail to recognize the faces of even close relatives. They also become increasingly uncomfortable at night and take frequent naps during the day (Edelstein et al., 2008; Tractenberg, Singer, & Kaye, 2005). During the late phases of the disorder, the individuals require constant care.

Alzheimer's victims usually remain in fairly good health until the later stages of the disease. As their mental functioning declines, however, they become less active and spend much of their time just sitting or lying in bed (Apostolova & Cummings, 2008). As a result, they are prone to develop illnesses such as pneumonia, which can result in death. Alzheimer's disease is responsible for 71,000 deaths each year in the United States, which makes it the seventh leading cause of death in the country (CDC, 2008).

table: 18-1

DSM Checklist

DEMENTIA OF THE ALZHEIMER'S TYPE
1. The development of multiple cognitive deficits manifested by both memory impairment and at least one of the following cognitive disturbances:
   (a) Aphasia.
   (b) Apraxia.
   (c) Agnosia.
   (d) Disturbance in executive functioning.
2. Significant impairment in social or occupational functioning, along with significant decline from a previous level of functioning.
3. Gradual onset and continuing cognitive decline.

Based on APA, 2000.

BETWEEN THE LINES

Senior Moments . . . Not

When a 20-year-old forgets someone's name or misplaces a checkbook, we do not consider it a *20-something moment*. Accordingly, it has been argued, clinicians should not automatically assume that an instance of forgetting by an elderly person represents a *senior moment*.
(Cherry et al., 2007; Cruikshank, 2003)

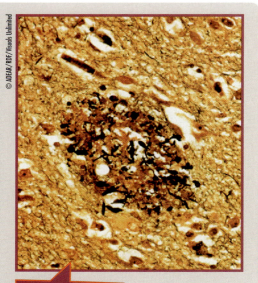

Biological culprits
Tissue from the brain of a man with Alzheimer's disease shows excessive amounts of plaque (white spheres), the clusters of beta-amyloid protein that form outside cells, and of neurofibrillary tangles (dark blobs), the twisted fibers within cells.

•**neurofibrillary tangles**•Twisted protein fibers that form within certain brain cells as people age. People with Alzheimer's disease have an excessive number of such tangles.

•**senile plaques**•Sphere-shaped deposits of beta-amyloid protein that form in the spaces between certain brain cells and in certain blood vessels as people age. People with Alzheimer's disease have an excessive number of such plaques.

•**short-term memory**•The memory system that collects new information. Also known as *working memory*.

•**long-term memory**•The memory system that contains all the information that we have stored over the years.

In most cases, Alzheimer's disease can be diagnosed with certainty only after death (Julien, 2008; APA, 2000), when structural changes in the person's brain, such as excessive *neurofibrillary tangles* and *senile plaques,* can be fully examined. **Neurofibrillary tangles,** twisted protein fibers found *within* the cells of the hippocampus and certain other brain areas, occur in all people as they age, but people with Alzheimer's disease form an extraordinary number of them.

Senile plaques are sphere-shaped deposits of a small molecule known as the *beta-amyloid protein* that form in the spaces *between* cells in the hippocampus, cerebral cortex, and certain other brain regions, as well as in some nearby blood vessels. The formation of plaques is also a normal part of aging, but again it is exceptionally high in people with Alzheimer's disease (Selkoe, 2002, 2000, 1992). For most people, the majority of their beta-amyloid proteins are composed of 40 amino acids (*AB40*), while a small percentage of their beta-amyloid proteins have 42 amino acids (*AB42*). Research suggests that people with Alzheimer's disease have a relatively high number of the AB42 kind of beta amyloids and that these are the kind that form plaques (Graff-Radford, 2005). Plaques may interfere with communications between cells and so cause cell breakdown or cell death.

Scientists do not fully understand why some people develop these problems and Alzheimer's disease. Research has suggested several possible causes, however, including genetic factors and abnormalities in brain structure and brain chemistry.

WHAT ARE THE GENETIC CAUSES OF ALZHEIMER'S DISEASE? It appears that Alzheimer's disease often has a genetic basis. Because many cases seem to run in families, clinicians distinguish between *familial* Alzheimer's disease and *sporadic* Alzheimer's disease, which is not associated with a family history of the brain disease. Studies have found that particular genes are responsible for the production of proteins called *beta-amyloid precursor protein* (*beta-APP*), *presenilin,* and *interleukin-1.* Many theorists now believe that some families transmit *mutations,* or abnormal forms, of these genes, increasing the likelihood of plaque and tangle formations and, in turn, of Alzheimer's disease (Jia et al., 2005; Doran & Larner, 2004; Farlow et al., 2001). Genetic studies have also linked certain kinds of Alzheimer's disease to defects on chromosomes 1, 14, 19, and 21 (Apostolova & Cummings, 2008). All of these discoveries are promising, but since many people with Alzheimer's disease do not have a clear family history of the disorder, scientists cannot be certain about the influence of genetic mutations on the disease's development in the population as a whole.

WHAT ARE THE STRUCTURAL AND BIOCHEMICAL CAUSES OF ALZHEIMER'S DISEASE? Whether it is genetic factors or other kinds of factors that predispose individuals to Alzheimer's disease, we still need to know what brain abnormalities they set in motion. That is, what abnormalities in brain structure or brain chemistry lead to Alzheimer's disease and to the excessive numbers of tangles and plaques that are its hallmark? Researchers have identified a number of possibilities. To understand these possible explanations, we need first to understand some basic information about the operation and biology of memory.

The human brain has two memory systems that work together to help us learn and recall. **Short-term memory,** or **working memory,** gathers new information. **Long-term memory** is the accumulation of information that we have stored over the years, information that first made its way through the short-term memory system. The information held in short-term memory must be transformed, or *consolidated,* into long-term memory if we are to hold on to it. Remembering information that has been stored in long-term memory is called *retrieval* and is described as going into one's long-term memory to bring it out for use again in short-term, or working, memory. Information in long-term memory can be classified as either procedural or declarative. *Procedural memories* are learned skills we perform without needing to think about them, such as walking, cutting with scissors, or writing. *Declarative memory* consists of names, dates, and other facts that have been learned. Declarative memory is usually affected more profoundly than procedural memory in cases of dementia.

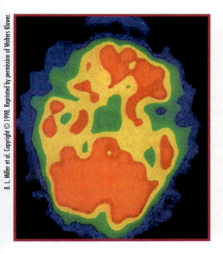

Artistic gain
The brain changes that cause dementia sometimes also produce temporary new skills. Here, the scan of a 64-year-old woman with dementia shows less activity in her left frontal lobe than her right one. Apparently, this brain change also helped cultivate her artistic ability, enabling her to do remarkable paintings such as the one shown here.

Certain *brain structures* seem to be especially important in memory. Among the most important structures in short-term memory are the *prefrontal lobes,* located just behind the forehead. When animals or humans acquire new information, their prefrontal lobes become more active (Jiang et al., 2000; Haxby et al., 1996). Apparently this activity enables them to hold information temporarily and to continue working with the information as long as it is needed. Among the brain areas most important to long-term memory are the *temporal lobes* (including the *hippocampus* and *amygdala,* key structures under the temporal lobes) and the *diencephalon* (including the *mammillary bodies, thalamus,* and *hypothalamus*), which seem to help transform short-term into long-term memory. Cases of dementia involve damage to one or more of these areas (van der Flier et al., 2005; Caine et al., 2001) (see *A Closer Look* on pages 606–607 and Figure 18-3).

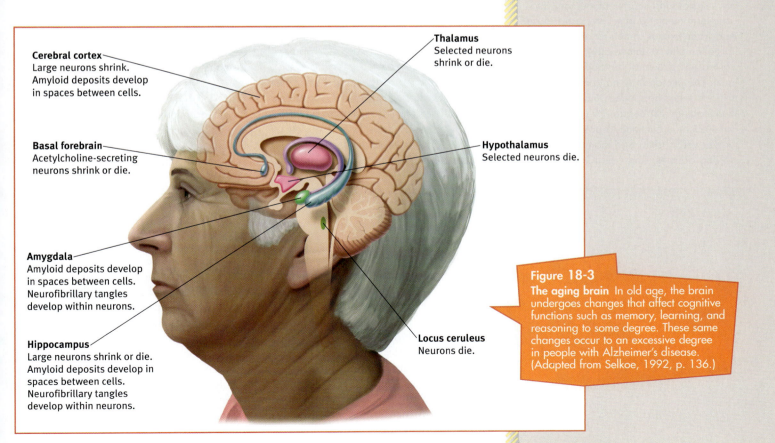

Cerebral cortex
Large neurons shrink. Amyloid deposits develop in spaces between cells.

Basal forebrain
Acetylcholine-secreting neurons shrink or die.

Amygdala
Amyloid deposits develop in spaces between cells. Neurofibrillary tangles develop within neurons.

Hippocampus
Large neurons shrink or die. Amyloid deposits develop in spaces between cells. Neurofibrillary tangles develop within neurons.

Thalamus
Selected neurons shrink or die.

Hypothalamus
Selected neurons die.

Locus ceruleus
Neurons die.

Figure 18-3

The aging brain In old age, the brain undergoes changes that affect cognitive functions such as memory, learning, and reasoning to some degree. These same changes occur to an excessive degree in people with Alzheimer's disease. (Adapted from Selkoe, 1992, p. 136.)

Amnestic Disorders: Forgetting to Remember

People who suffer from dementia experience both severe memory problems and other cognitive impairments. In contrast, those with *amnestic disorders*, another group of disorders caused by brain diseases or injuries, have memory problems only. Amnestic disorders are just as likely to occur in younger people as among the elderly.

Retrograde amnesia is an inability to remember events from the past. *Anterograde amnesia* is an ongoing inability to form new memories. People with amnestic disorders sometimes suffer from retrograde amnesia, depending on the particular disorder, but they almost always experience anterograde amnesia.

In anterograde amnesia, it is as though information from short-term memory can no longer cross over into long-term memory. Not surprisingly, it is often the result of damage to the brain's *temporal lobes* or *diencephalon*, the areas largely responsible for transforming short-term memory into long-term memory. In severe forms of anterograde amnesia, new acquaintances are forgotten almost immediately, and problems solved one day must be tackled again the next. The person may not remember anything that has happened since his or her problem first began. Nevertheless, sufferers may continue to possess all of their earlier verbal skills and many problem-solving abilities, and their IQ is not changed. The best known of the amnestic disorders are *Korsakoff's syndrome* and disorders resulting from *head injuries* or *brain surgery*.

Korsakoff's Syndrome

Fred, a 69-year-old man, was admitted to a mental hospital in a state of confusion, the result of *Korsakoff's syndrome*, an amnestic disorder that causes its victims to keep forgetting newly learned information (anterograde amnesia):

Fred . . . had a history of many years of heavy drinking, although he denied drinking during the past several years. When seen in the admitting ward, the patient was neatly dressed, but there was some deterioration of his personal habits. Although pleasant and sociable with the interviewer and ward personnel, he was definitely confused. He wandered about the ward, investigating objects and trying on other people's clothing. He talked freely, though his speech tended to be rambling and at times incoherent. Most of his spontaneous conversation centered on himself, and there were a number of hypochondriacal complaints. Fred was disoriented for time and place, although he was able to give his name. He could not give his correct address, said his age was 91, and was unable to name the day, the month, or the year. He did not know where he was, although he said he was sent here by his landlord because he had been drinking. He admitted that he had been arrested for fighting and drinking, but he said that he had never had an attack of delirium tremens. [Fred] showed the characteristic symptom picture of Korsakoff's syndrome, with disorientation, confusion, and a strong tendency toward confabulation. When asked where he was, he said he was in a brewery. He gave the name of the brewery, but when asked the same question a few minutes later, he named another brewery. Similarly, he said that he knew the examiner, called him by an incorrect name, and a little later changed the name again. When leaving the examining room, he used still another name when he said politely, "Goodbye, Mr. Wolf!"

(KISKER, 1977, P. 308)

As you'll recall from Chapter 12, approximately 5 percent of people with chronic alcoholism develop Korsakoff's syndrome. A combination of excessive drinking and improper diet produce a deficiency of *vitamin B* (*thiamine*), which leads to damage in portions of the *diencephalon* (Sadock & Sadock, 2007; Harding et al., 2000). Sufferers of this disorder primarily lose memories of factual knowledge but still maintain their intellectual and language skills. This may explain why Korsakoff's patients tend to *confabulate*. Like Fred, they use their general intellect to make up elaborate stories and lies in an effort to replace the memories they keep losing.

Head Injuries and Brain Surgery

Both head injuries and brain surgery can cause amnestic disorders (Sadock & Sadock, 2007; Richardson, 2002; Zec et al., 2002, 2001). Either may destroy

---

Memory researchers have also identified *biochemical changes* that occur in cells as memories form. For example, when new information is acquired and stored, *proteins* are produced in key brain cells. Several chemicals are responsible for the production of proteins, including *acetylcholine, glutamate, RNA* (*ribonucleic acid*), and *calcium*. If the activity of any of these chemicals is disturbed, the proper production of proteins may be prevented and the formation of memories interrupted (Wu et al., 2008; Steward & Worley, 2002; Rosenzweig, 1996). For example, by blocking the activity of glutamate, animal researchers have prevented short-term memory. Similarly, by blocking the cellular production of RNA or of calcium, they have interrupted the formation of long-term memories.

With this background information in mind, let us return to the biological causes of Alzheimer's disease. One line of research suggests that some of the *proteins* involved in memory formation may take an abnormal form and essentially run amok in people with Alzheimer's disease (Apostolova & Cummings, 2008; Graff-Radford, 2005). Studies

Part of the game? Hard hits to the head are common in contact sports such as football, hockey, and boxing and often result in head injuries. One expert estimates that 350,000 athletes endure head injuries each year that cause them to lose consciousness (Gioia, 2007). Repeated hits may, in fact, lead to repeated concussions, further affecting memory and other cognitive functions and, in some cases, endangering the athlete's physical integrity or life.

memory-related brain structures. Television shows and movies often portray bumps on the head as a quick and easy way to lose one's memory. In fact, *mild* head injuries, such as a concussion that does not result in coma or a period of unconsciousness, rarely cause much memory loss, and what loss there is usually disappears within days or months. In contrast, almost half of all *severe* head injuries do cause some permanent learning and memory problems, both anterograde and retrograde. In everyday life, the leading causes of traumatic brain injuries are car accidents and falls.

Given the significant impact of head injuries, the public has become very concerned by the recent release of information that tens of thousands of U.S. soldiers in Iraq and Afghanistan have suffered head injuries from exposure to blasts during combat. Estimates on the low end are that at least 20,000 combat veterans have sustained such injuries, whereas high-end estimates suggest numbers as large as 320,000 (RAND, 2008; Department of Veterans Affairs, 2007; Marchione, 2007). While it may be that most such brain injuries were mild and will have only a temporary impact on the individuals, clinical practitioners and researchers caution that they do not yet know how severe or long lasting these injuries will turn out to be.

Brain surgery may create more specific memory problems. The most famous case of memory loss as a result of brain surgery was that of H.M., a man whose identity was protected for decades (Kensinger, Ullman, & Corkin, 2001; Corkin, 1984, 1968; Milner, 1971). H.M. suffered from severe *brain seizure disorder,* or *epilepsy,* a disorder that produced seizures in his temporal lobes. To reduce his symptoms, doctors removed parts of both of his temporal lobes in 1953, along with the amygdala and hippocampus. At that time, the involvement of these brain areas in the formation of memories was not known. (Today temporal lobe surgery is usually limited to either the right or left side of the brain). H.M. experienced severe anterograde amnesia from the time of his surgery more than a half-century ago until his death in 2008. He was unable to recognize or recall anyone he met after his operation.

suggest, for example, that two key proteins—*beta-amyloid protein* and *tau protein*—operate abnormally in such individuals. As you read earlier, abnormal structure and activity by the beta-amyloid protein seem to be involved in the formation of plaques in the hippocampus and certain other brain areas. Similarly, abnormal activity of the tau protein apparently leads to the formation of tangles in those brain areas.

Another line of research points to abnormal activity by the neurotransmitters and related chemicals involved in the production of the memory proteins. Many studies have found that *acetylcholine* and *glutamate* are in low supply, or at least function differently, in the brains of Alzheimer's victims (Chin et al., 2007; Akaike, 2006; Bissette et al., 1996). Still other studies suggest that victims may display an imbalance in the metabolism of *calcium.*

A third explanation for Alzheimer's disease holds that certain substances found in nature may act as toxins and damage the brain. For example, researchers have detected

Finding the right activity This patient picks tomatoes from a garden at Les Aurelias Home for Alzheimer's Victims in France. Recognizing the horticultural interests of this Alzheimer's patient, the staff created a therapeutic garden where she could be active and experience pleasure and satisfaction.

high levels of *zinc* in the brains of some Alzheimer's victims (Shcherbatykh & Carpenter, 2007). This finding has gained particular attention because in some animal studies zinc has been observed to trigger a clumping of the beta-amyloid protein, similar to the plaques found in the brains of Alzheimer's patients (Turkington & Harris, 2001).

Yet another explanation suggests that certain environmental toxins, such as *lead,* may contribute to the development of Alzheimer's disease (Ritter, 2008). Lead was phased out of gasoline products between 1976 and 1991, leading to an 80 percent drop of lead levels in people's blood. However, many of today's elderly population were exposed to high levels of lead in the 1960s and 1970s, regularly inhaling air pollution from vehicle exhausts—an exposure that might have damaged or destroyed many of their neurons. Could it be that this previous absorption of lead and other pollutants is now having a negative effect on their cognitive functioning? Some circumstantial evidence supports this notion. One study, for example, examined elderly people and scanned their shinbones for lead (Schwartz & Stewart, 2007). Interpreting shinbone levels of lead as indicators of the individuals' lifetime exposures to this toxin, the researchers found that the higher a person's lifetime lead exposure, the more poorly he or she performed on memory and language tests. Several other studies have also pointed to early lead exposure as a possible culprit in the development of Alzheimer's disease (Ritter, 2008; Hu et al., 2005). An important question here is: Why would cognitive dysfunction first appear decades after exposure to the toxin? Medical researcher Philip Landrigan (2007) suggests, "If a substance destroys brain cells in early life, the brain may cope by drawing on its reserve capacity until [eventually] it loses more cells with aging. . . . Only then would symptoms like forgetfulness or tremors begin."

Finally, two other explanations for Alzheimer's disease have been offered. One is the *autoimmune theory.* On the basis of certain irregularities found in the immune systems of people with Alzheimer's disease, several researchers have speculated that changes in aging brain cells may trigger an *autoimmune response* (that is, a mistaken attack by the immune system against itself) that leads to this disease (Zip & Aktas, 2006; McGeer & McGeer, 1996). The other explanation is a *viral theory.* Because Alzheimer's disease resembles *Creutzfeldt-Jakob disease,* another form of dementia that is known to be caused by a slow-acting virus, some researchers propose that a similar virus may cause Alzheimer's disease (Doty, 2008; Prusiner, 1991). However, no such virus has been detected in the brains of Alzheimer's victims.

Other Forms of Dementia A number of other disorders may also lead to dementia (Apostolova & Cummings, 2008). **Vascular dementia,** also known as **multi-infarct dementia,** may follow a cerebrovascular accident, or *stroke,* during which blood flow to specific areas of the brain was cut off, thus damaging the areas (Ghika & Bogousslavsky, 2002). In many cases, the patient may not even be aware of the stroke. Like Alzheimer's disease, vascular dementia is progressive, but its symptoms begin suddenly rather than gradually. Moreover, cognitive functioning may continue to be normal in areas of the brain that have not been affected by the stroke, in contrast to the broad cognitive deficiencies usually displayed by Alzheimer's patients. Vascular dementia accounts for 10 to 30 percent of all cases of dementia (Sadock & Sadock, 2007; Corey-Bloom, 2004). Some people have both Alzheimer's disease and vascular dementia.

Pick's disease, a rare disorder that affects the frontal and temporal lobes, offers a clinical picture similar to Alzheimer's disease, but the two diseases can be distinguished at autopsy. *Creutzfeldt-Jakob disease,* another source of dementia, has symptoms that often include spasms of the body. As you read earlier, this disease is caused by a slow-acting virus that may live in the body for years before the disease develops. Once launched, however, the disease has a rapid course. *Huntington's disease* is an inherited progressive

•**vascular dementia**•Dementia caused by a cerebrovascular accident, or stroke, which restricts blood flow to certain areas of the brain. Also known as *multi-infarct dementia.*

disease in which memory problems worsen over time, along with personality changes and mood difficulties. Huntington's victims have movement problems, too, such as severe twitching and spasms. Children of people with Huntington's disease have a 50 percent chance of developing it. *Parkinson's disease,* the slowly progressive neurological disorder marked by tremors, rigidity, and unsteadiness, can cause dementia, particularly in older people or individuals whose cases are advanced. And, finally, cases of dementia may also be caused by viral and bacterial *infectious disorders* such as HIV and AIDS, meningitis, and advanced syphilis; by *brain seizure disorder;* by *drug abuse;* or by *toxins* such as mercury, lead, or carbon monoxide.

The Assessment and Treatment of Dementia

As you saw earlier, most cases of Alzheimer's disease can be *diagnosed* with absolute certainty only after death, when an autopsy is performed. However, CAT and MRI scans, which reveal structural abnormalities in the brain, now are used commonly as assessment tools and often provide clinicians with considerable confidence in their diagnoses of Alzheimer's disease (Apostolova & Cummings, 2008; Julien, 2008). The *treatment* of this disease has been at best modestly helpful. However, growing research has raised hopes that Alzheimer's disease and other forms of dementia may be assessed and treated more effectively or even prevented in the near future.

CAN DEMENTIA BE PREDICTED? Several research teams currently are trying to develop tools that can identify persons likely to develop dementia. One of the most promising lines of work comes from the laboratory of brain researcher Lisa Mosconi and her colleagues (Mosconi et al., 2008; deLeon et al., 2007). Using a special kind of PET scan (*PET with fluoro-deoxyglucose*), this research team examined activity in certain parts of the *hippocampus* in dozens of older research participants and then conducted follow-up studies of these individuals for up to 24 years. (Recall that the hippocampus plays a major role in long-term memory.) Eventually, 43 percent of the study's participants developed either *mild cognitive impairment* (mild dementia) or Alzheimer's disease itself. The researchers found that those who developed these cognitive impairments had indeed displayed lower hippocampus activity on their initial PET scans than the participants who remained healthy. Overall, the special PET scans, administered years before the onset of symptoms, predicted mild cognitive impairment with an accuracy rate of 71 percent and Alzheimer's disease with an accuracy rate of 83 percent.

In another line of work researcher Neill Graff-Radford (2005) and his colleagues took repeated samples of blood from hundreds of normal elderly research participants over a period of years and measured levels of the beta-amyloid protein in the blood samples. (Recall that clusters of the beta-amyloid protein, particularly the AB42 kind, form senile plaques.) The research team found that participants whose blood contained an unusually high proportion of AB42 beta-amyloid proteins were three times more likely to develop mild dementia or Alzheimer's disease.

As you will see shortly, the most effective interventions for Alzheimer's disease and other kinds of dementia are those that help *prevent* these problems, or at least ones that are applied early. Clearly, then, it is essential to have tools that identify the disorders as early as possible, preferably years before the onset of symptoms. That is what makes the research advances in assessment and diagnosis so exciting.

Victims of Parkinson's disease
Two of today's most famous victims of Parkinson's disease, boxing legend Muhammad Ali (left) and actor Michael J. Fox (right), chat playfully prior to testifying before a Senate funding subcommittee about the devastating effects the disease has had on their lives and those of other persons.

Day treatment
Two women go their separate ways in a New Jersey day-care facility for patients with Alzheimer's disease. The individuals return to their families each night.

Cognitive fitness center
A number of senior living community programs now include cognitive fitness centers where elderly persons sit at computers and work on memory and cognitive software programs. Research on brain plasticity suggests that "cognitive calisthenics" of this kind may provide challenging workouts for the brain and help prevent or reverse certain symptoms of aging, including memory loss, declining vision and hearing, and reduced motor control.

BETWEEN THE LINES

Busy Mind, Healthier Brain

Researchers have found fewer plaques and tangles in the brains of lab mice that live in intellectually stimulating environments—chew toys, running wheels, and tunnels—than in those of mice that live in less stimulating settings (Lazarov et al., 2005). ‹‹

WHAT TREATMENTS ARE CURRENTLY AVAILABLE FOR DEMENTIA? Treatments for the cognitive features of Alzheimer's disease and most other forms of dementia have been at best modestly helpful. One common approach is the use of drugs that affect the neurotransmitters known to play important roles in memory (see *The Media Speaks* on the facing page). Four such drugs— *tacrine* (trade name Cognex), *donepezil* (Aricept), *rivastigmine* (Exelon), and *galantamine* (Reminyl)—prevent the breakdown of acetylcholine, one of the neurotransmitters in low supply among people with Alzheimer's disease (Julien, 2008). Some Alzheimer's patients who take these drugs improve slightly in short-term memory and reasoning ability, as well as in their use of language and their ability to cope under pressure (Apostolova & Cummings, 2008; Olsen et al., 2005). Although the benefits of the drugs are limited and the risk of harmful effects (particularly for tacrine) is sometimes high, these drugs have been approved by the Food and Drug Administration (FDA). Indeed, a skin patch for one of the drugs, *rivastigmine,* was sanctioned by the FDA in 2007 (Hitti, 2007). Clinicians believe that these drugs may be of greatest use to persons in the early stages of Alzheimer's disease or to those with mild cognitive impairment. Yet another approach, taking *vitamin E,* either alone or in combination with one of these drugs, also seems to help prevent further cognitive decline among people with mild dementia (Sano, 2003).

An alternative drug, *memantine* (Namenda), affects glutamate, another neurotransmitter linked to memory. This drug often improves cognition, even in severely impaired patients, although once again the improvement is modest (Julien, 2008; Soukup, 2006). In addition to these various drugs, a number of other possible drug treatments currently are being investigated.

The drugs discussed here are each prescribed *after* a person has developed mild cognitive improvement or Alzheimer's disease. In contrast, several research teams are currently trying to develop an *immunization* for the disease, although, so far, such efforts remain largely at the animal research stage (Bussiere et al., 2004; Bard et al., 2003, 2000; Cribbs et al., 2003). In a similar vein, a number of studies suggest that certain substances may help prevent or delay the onset of the disease. For example, one team of researchers concluded that women who took *estrogen,* the female sex hormone, for years after menopause cut their risk of developing Alzheimer's disease in half (Kawas et al., 1997). Also, long-term use of *nonsteroid anti-inflammatory drugs* such as *ibuprofen* and *naprosyn* (drugs found in Advil, Motrin, Nuprin, and other pain relievers) seems to reduce the risk of Alzheimer's disease (Julien, 2008), although recent research on this possibility has not always been supportive (Apostolova & Cummings, 2008; Weggen et al., 2003).

Cognitive treatments have been applied in cases of Alzheimer's disease, with some temporary success (Sadock & Sadock, 2007; Knight et al., 2006; Fabre, 2004). In Japan, for example, a number of persons with the disease meet regularly in classes, performing simple calculations and reading aloud essays and novels. Proponents of this approach claim that it serves as a mental exercise that helps rehabilitate those parts of the brain linked to memory, reasoning, and judgment. In a similar vein, research suggests that cognitive activities may actually help *prevent* or *delay* the onset of mild cognitive impairment or Alzheimer's disease (Meyers, 2008; Willis et al., 2006). One study of 700 80-year-old individuals found that those research participants who had pursued cognitive activities over a five-year period (for example, visiting libraries, reading newspapers or books, attending concerts or plays, and writing letters) were less than half as likely to develop Alzheimer's disease as mentally inactive participants (Wilson et al., 2007).

Behavioral interventions have also been applied to Alzheimer's patients, with modest success. The approaches typically focus on changing everyday patient behaviors that are stressful for the family, such as wandering at night, loss of bladder control, demands

The Media SPEAKS   HOME   SEND   EXPLORE

SEARCH

Doctor, Do No Harm

BY LAURIE TARKAN, THE *NEW YORK TIMES*, JUNE 24, 2008

Ramona Lamascola thought she was losing her 88-year-old mother to dementia. Instead, she was losing her to overmedication.

Last fall her mother, Theresa Lamascola, of the Bronx, suffering from anxiety and confusion, was put on the antipsychotic drug Risperdal. When she had trouble walking, her daughter took her to another doctor—the younger Ms. Lamascola's own physician—who found that she had unrecognized hypothyroidism, a disorder that can contribute to dementia.

Theresa Lamascola was moved to a nursing home to get these problems under control. But things only got worse. "My mother was screaming and out of it, drooling on herself and twitching," said Ms. Lamascola, a pediatric nurse. The psychiatrist in the nursing home stopped the Risperdal, which can cause twitching and vocal tics, and prescribed a sedative and two other antipsychotics. "I knew the drugs were doing this to her," her daughter said. "I told him to stop the medications and stay away from Mom." Not until yet another doctor took Mrs. Lamascola off the drugs did she begin to improve.

The use of antipsychotic drugs to tamp down the agitation, combative behavior and outbursts of dementia patients has soared, especially in the elderly. Sales of newer antipsychotics like Risperdal, Seroquel and Zyprexa totaled $13.1 billion in 2007, up from $4 billion in 2000. . . . Part of this increase can be traced to prescriptions in nursing homes. Researchers estimate that about a third of all nursing home patients have been given antipsychotic drugs.

The increases continue despite a drumbeat of bad publicity. A 2006 study of Alzheimer's patients found that for most patients, antipsychotics provided no significant improvement over placebos in treating aggression and delusions. . . . [The] Food and Drug Administration . . . has not approved marketing of these drugs for older people with dementia, but they are commonly prescribed to these patients "off label." . . .

[M]any doctors say misuse of the drugs is widespread. "These antipsychotics can be overused and abused," said Dr. Johnny Matson, a professor of psychology at Louisiana State University. "And there's a lot of abuse going on in a lot of these places.". . .

Nursing homes are short staffed, and insurers do not generally pay for the attentive medical care and hands-on psychosocial therapy that advocates recommend. It is much easier to use sedatives and antipsychotics, despite their side effects. . . .

Used correctly, the drugs do have a role in treating some seriously demented patients, who may be incapacitated by paranoia or are self-destructive or violent. Taking the edge off the behavior can keep them safe and living at home, rather than in a nursing home.

Roy McMahon/Corbis

If patients are prescribed an antipsychotic, it should be a very low dose for the shortest period necessary, said Dr. Dillip V. Jeste, a professor of psychiatry and neuroscience at the University of California, San Diego. It may take a few weeks or months to control behavior. In many cases, the patient can then be weaned off of the drugs or kept at a very low dose. . . .

Some doctors point out that simply paying attention to a nursing home patient can ease dementia symptoms. They note that in randomized trials of antipsychotic drugs for dementia, 30 to 60 percent of patients in the placebo groups improved.

"That's mind boggling," Dr. Jeste said. "These severely demented patients are not responding to the power of suggestion. They're responding to the attention they get when they participate in a clinical trial.

"They receive both T.L.C. and good general medical and humane care, which they did not receive until now. That's a sad commentary on the way we treat dementia patients.". . .

[Fortunately,] the physician [Ramona Lamascola] consulted [did] stop . . . her mother's antipsychotics and sedatives and prescribed Aricept. "It's not clear whether it was getting her . . . medical issues finally under control or getting rid of the offending medications," [the physician] said. "But she had a miraculous turnaround."

Theresa Lamascola still has dementia, but . . . as her daughter put it, "I got my mother back."

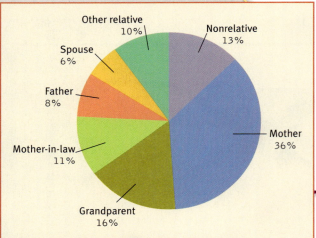

Figure 18-4

Whom do caregivers take care of? Caregivers provide care for their mother in 36 percent of Alzheimer's cases, their mother-in-law in 11 percent of cases, and their grandparent in 16 percent of cases. (Adapted from Kantrowitz & Springen, 2007; Alzheimer's Association, 2007.)

for attention, and inadequate personal care (Knight et al., 2006; Fisher & Carstensen, 1990). The behavioral therapists use a combination of role-playing exercises, modeling, and practice to teach family members how and when to apply reinforcement in order to shape more positive behaviors.

Caregiving can take a heavy toll on the close relatives of people with dementia (Sadock & Sadock, 2007; Cummings, 2005). Almost 90 percent of all people with dementia are cared for by their relatives (Alzheimer's Association, 2007; Kantrowitz & Springen, 2007) (see Figure 18-4). It is hard, however, to take care of someone who is becoming increasingly lost, helpless, and medically ill. And it is very painful to witness mental and physical decline in someone you love:

I have really struggled with the honesty issue. What do you say to someone who sits on her bed and says that she has never stayed out overnight without letting her parents know where she is? What do you say to someone who thinks she is a teacher and if she doesn't get home and into her classroom there will be a whole class of children left unattended? What do you say to someone who thinks she has no money to pay bills and will lose everything she owns if she doesn't get home to a job that you know she has been retired from for years? I couldn't find any reason for telling her over and over that she has a horrible terrible degenerating disease that was making her feel the way she does.

I found that she became less anxious if I just listened to what she was saying and feeling. Sometimes saying nothing was better than anything I could say. Telling her that I would take care of some of these things put her a bit more at ease. It may feel better for me to verbalize the facts, but what she needs is comfort and security—not the truth. The truth won't change anything.

(Shenk, 2001, p. 147)

One of the most frequent reasons for the institutionalization of Alzheimer's victims is that overwhelmed caregivers can no longer cope with the difficulties of keeping them at home (Apostolova & Cummings, 2008; Cummings, 2005). Many caregivers experience anger and depression, and their own physical and mental health often declines (Kantrowitz & Springen, 2007; Sherwood et al., 2005). Clinicians now recognize that one of the most important aspects of treating Alzheimer's disease and other forms of dementia is to focus on the emotional needs of the caregivers: their need for regular time out, for education about the disease, and for psychotherapy when stress begins to build (Knight et al., 2006; Gaugler et al., 2003). Some clinicians also provide caregiver support groups (Pillemer & Suitor, 2002; Gallagher-Thompson et al., 2000).

In recent years, sociocultural approaches have begun to play an important role in treatment (Brooks, 2005; Hirshom, 2004; Kalb, 2000) (see *Psych Watch: Abnormality and the Arts* on the facing page). A number of *day-care facilities* for patients with dementia have been developed, providing treatment programs and activities for outpatients during the day and returning them to their homes and families at night. In addition, many *assisted-living facilities* have been built, in which individuals suffering from dementia live in cheerful apartments, receive needed supervision, and take part in various activities that bring more joy and stimulation

Devoted and devastated

In a tender moment, this Alzheimer's patient holds the hand of her caregiving husband.

Abnormality and the Arts

"You Are the Music, while the Music Lasts"

BY CLAYTON S. COLLINS

Oliver Sacks [a well-known neurologist and writer] danced to the Dead. For three solid hours. At 60. And with "two broken knees." . . .

The power of music—. . . to "bring back" individuals rendered motionless and mute by neurological damage and disorders—is what's driving Sacks these days. The . . . author (*Migraine, A Leg to Stand On, The Man Who Mistook His Wife for a Hat, Seeing Voices* and *Awakenings*) . . . is working on another case-study book, one that deals in part with the role of music as a stimulus to minds that have thrown up stiff sensory barriers. . . . [Note: This book, *Musicophilia: Tales of Music and the Brain,* is now published.]

"One sees how robust music is neurologically," Sacks says. "You can lose all sorts of particular powers but you don't tend to lose music and identity." . . .

Much of what he has encountered, particularly in working with patients at Beth Abraham Hospital, Bronx, N.Y., . . . relates to music. . . .

"Deeply demented people respond to music, babies respond to music, fetuses probably respond to music. Various animals respond to music," Sacks says. "There is something about the animal nervous system . . . which seems to respond to music all the way down . . . ," Sacks says, citing the case of a patient with damage to the frontal lobes of his brain.

"When he sings, one almost has the strange feeling that [music] has given him his frontal lobes back, given him back, temporally, some function that has been lost on an organic basis," Sacks says, adding a quote from T. S. Eliot: "You are the music, while the music lasts."

The effects of music therapy may not always last. Sacks will take what he can get. "To organize a disorganized person for a minute is miraculous. And for half an hour, more so." . . .

The key, says Sacks, is for patients to "learn to be well" again. Music can restore to them, he says, the identity that predates the illness. "There's a health to music, a life to music." . . .

"Greg" was an amnesiac with a brain tumor and no coherent memories of life since about 1969—but an encyclopedic memory of the years that came before, and a real love of Grateful Dead tunes.

Sacks took Greg to that night's [Grateful Dead] performance. "In the first half of the concert they were doing early music, and Greg was enchanted by everything," Sacks recalls. "I mean, he was not an amnesiac. He was completely oriented and organized and with it." Between sets Sacks went backstage and introduced Greg to band member Micky Hart, who was impressed with Greg's knowledge of the group but quite surprised when Greg asked after Pigpen. When told the former band member had died 20 years before, "Greg was very upset," Sacks recalls. "And then 30 seconds later he asked 'How's Pigpen?'"

During the second half, the band played its newer songs. And Greg's world began to fall apart. "He was bewildered and enthralled and frightened. Because the music for him—and this is an extremely musical man, who understands the idiom of the Grateful Dead—was both familiar and unfamiliar. . . . He said, 'This is like the music of the future.'"

Sacks tried to keep the new memories fresh. But the next day, Greg had no

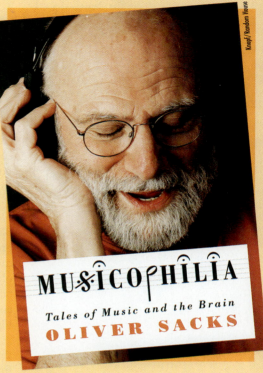

memory of the concert. It seemed as if all had been lost. "But—and this is strange—when one played some of the new music, which he had heard for the first time at the concert, he could sing along with it and remember it."

It is an encouraging development. . . . Children have been found to learn quickly lessons that are embedded in song. Sacks, the one-time quiet researcher, is invigorated by the possibilities. He wonders whether music could carry such information, to give his patient back a missing part of his life. To give Greg "some sense of what's been happening in the last 20 years, where he has no autobiography of his own."

That would have Sacks dancing in the aisles.

Excerpted by permission from *Profiles,* the magazine of Continental Airlines, February 1994.

to their lives. These apartments are typically designed to meet the special needs of the residents—providing more light, for example, or enclosing gardens with circular paths so the individuals can go for strolls alone without getting lost. Studies suggest that such facilities often help slow the cognitive decline of residents and enhance their enjoyment

Staying in touch
This Alzheimer's sufferer wears a tracking bracelet that enables his family members to locate him quickly if he wanders from home. This wrist device is a much less controversial solution for the problem of wandering than microchip implants or other invasive tracking techniques that have been proposed.

of life. In addition, a growing number of practical devices, such as tracking beacons worn on the wrists of Alzheimer's patients, have been developed to help locate patients who may wander off (Neergaard, 2007).

Given the progress now unfolding in the understanding and treatment of Alzheimer's disease and other forms of dementia, researchers are looking forward to advances in the coming years. The brain changes responsible for dementia are tremendously complex, but given the amount of research under way, most investigators believe that exciting breakthroughs are just over the horizon.

⚙Issues Affecting the Mental Health of the Elderly

As the study and treatment of elderly people have progressed, three issues have raised concern among clinicians: the problems faced by elderly members of racial and ethnic minority groups, the inadequacies of long-term care, and the need for a health-maintenance approach to medical care in an aging world (Gallagher-Thompson & Thompson, 1995).

First, *discrimination because of race and ethnicity has long been a problem in the United States* (see Chapter 3), and many people suffer as a result, particularly those who are old (Utsey et al., 2002; Cavanaugh, 1990). To be both old and a member of a minority group is considered a kind of "double jeopardy" by many observers. For older women in minority groups, the difficulties are sometimes termed "triple jeopardy," as many more older women than older men live alone, are widowed, and are poor. Clinicians must take into account their older patients' race, ethnicity, and gender as they try to diagnose and treat their mental health problems (Knight et al., 2006; Sadavoy et al., 2004) (see Figure 18-5).

Some elderly people in minority groups face language barriers that interfere with their medical and mental health care. Others may hold cultural beliefs that prevent them from seeking services. Moreover, many members of minority groups do not trust the majority establishment or do not know about medical and mental health services that are sensitive to their culture and their particular needs (Ayalon & Huyck, 2001; Ralston, 1991). As a result, it is common for elderly members of racial and ethnic minority groups to rely largely on family members or friends for remedies and health care.

Today, 10 to 20 percent of elderly people live with their children or other relatives, usually because of increasing health problems (Etaugh, 2008). In the United States, this

Social connections
Recognizing that elderly people continue to need social companionship and stimulation, many retirement homes now offer student visitation programs. The elderly residents benefit emotionally and cognitively from such visits, while the students learn much about aging and about life. The engaged looks on the faces of these residents during their interactions with several students are a far cry from the lost and lonely faces often found in less stimulating nursing and retirement homes.

living arrangement is more common for elderly people from ethnic minority groups than for elderly white Americans. Elderly Asian Americans are most likely to live with their children, African Americans and Hispanic Americans are less likely to do so, and white Americans are least likely (Etaugh, 2008; Armstrong, 2001).

Second, *many older people require care outside the family called long-term care,* a term that may refer variously to the services offered in a partially supervised apartment, in a senior housing complex for mildly impaired elderly persons, or in a nursing home where skilled medical and nursing care are available around the clock. The quality of care in such residences varies widely.

At any given time in the United States, only about 5 percent of the elderly population actually live in nursing homes, but 25 to 30 percent eventually wind up being placed in such facilities (Edelstein et al., 2008). Thus many older adults live in fear of being "put away." They fear having to move, losing independence, and living in a medical environment. Many elderly people know someone who died shortly after being admitted to a long-term care facility, and this increases their fears about the quality of life in such settings.

Many also worry about the cost of long-term care facilities (Papastavrou et al., 2007). Families today are trying to keep elderly relatives at home longer, and so most older people enter nursing homes only in the last stages of a disease and in need of almost total care. Around-the-clock nursing care is expensive, and nursing home costs continue to rise. The health insurance plans available today do not adequately cover the costs of long-term or permanent placement (Newcomer et al., 2001). Worry over these issues can greatly harm the mental health of older adults, perhaps leading to depression and anxiety as well as family conflict.

Finally, medical scientists suggest that *the current generation of young adults should take a health-maintenance,* or *wellness promotion, approach to their own aging process* (Meyers, 2008; Aldwin et al., 2006). In other words, they should do things that promote physical and mental health—avoid smoking, eat well-balanced and healthful meals, exercise regularly, engage in positive social relationships, and take advantage of psychoeducational, stress management, and other mental health programs (Cherry et al., 2007; Peterson, 2006). There is a growing belief that older adults will adapt more readily to changes and negative events if their physical and psychological health is good.

Working the mind
A staff member at New York's Museum of Modern Art leads a discussion about Henri Rousseau's *Sleeping Gypsy* during a guided tour for a group of Alzheimer's patients and their caregivers.

Figure 18-5

Ethnicity and old age The elderly population is becoming racially and ethnically more diverse. In the United States today, 82 percent of all people over the age of 65 are white Americans. By 2050, only 67 percent of the elderly will be in this group. (Adapted from Edelstein et al., 2008; Cavanaugh & Blanchard-Fields, 2006; U.S. Census, 2004, 2000; Hobbs, 1997.)

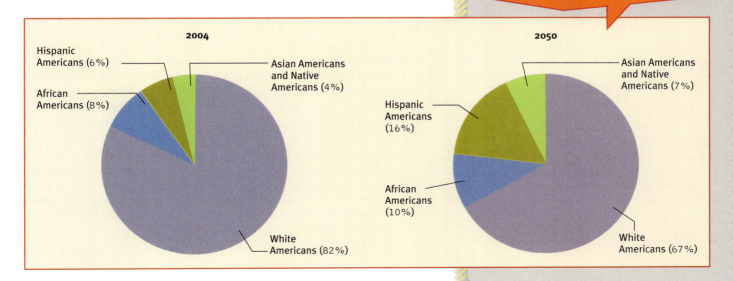

2004
Hispanic Americans (6%)
African Americans (8%)
Asian Americans and Native Americans (4%)
White Americans (82%)

2050
Hispanic Americans (16%)
African Americans (10%)
Asian Americans and Native Americans (7%)
White Americans (67%)

PUTTING IT . . . . together

Clinicians Discover the Elderly

Early in the twentieth century, mental health professionals focused little on the elderly. But like the problems of children, those of aging persons have now caught the attention of researchers and clinicians. Current work is bringing important changes in how we understand and treat the psychological problems of the elderly. No longer do clinicians simply accept depression or anxiety in elderly people as inevitable. No longer do they overlook the dangers of prescription drug misuse by the elderly. And no longer do they underestimate the dangers of delirium or the prevalence of dementia. Similarly, gero-psychologists have become more aware of the importance of addressing the health care and financial needs of the elderly as keys to their psychological well-being.

As the elderly population grows ever larger, the special needs of people in this age group are becoming more visible. Thus the study and treatment of their psychological problems, like those of children, will probably continue at a rapid pace. Clinicians and public officials are not likely to underestimate their needs and importance again.

Particularly urgent is dementia and its devastating impact on the elderly and their families. The complexity of the brain makes dementia difficult to understand, diagnose, and treat. However, researchers announce exciting new discoveries almost daily. To date, this research has been largely biological, but dementia has such a powerful impact on patients and their families that psychological and sociocultural investigations will not lag behind for long. In fact, society's special interest in and focus on Alzheimer's disease have reminded everyone about the importance of memory and related cognitive faculties. Memory is so central to our lives and to our self-concept that psychological and sociocultural research in this area is of potential value to every person's well-being. Thus, we can expect such work to grow and expand in the years to come.

‹‹‹[SUMMING UP]›››

○ **Disorders of later life** The problems of elderly people are often linked to the losses and other stresses and changes that accompany advancing age. As many as 50 percent of the elderly would benefit from mental health services, yet fewer than 20 percent receive them. *Depression* is a common mental health problem among this age group. Older people may also suffer from *anxiety disorders.* Between 4 and 6 percent exhibit *alcohol-related problems* in any given year, and many others *misuse prescription drugs.* In addition, some elderly persons display psychotic disorders such as *schizophrenia* or *delusional disorder. pp. 593–601*

○ **Disorders of cognition** Older people are more likely than people of other age groups to experience *delirium,* a clouding of consciousness in which a person has great difficulty concentrating, focusing attention, and following an orderly sequence of thought.

Dementia, a syndrome characterized by severe memory loss and other cognitive disturbances, becomes increasingly common in older age groups. It can result from dozens of brain illnesses or injuries, most commonly *Alzheimer's disease* or *vascular dementia.* Alzheimer's disease has been linked to an unusually high number of *neurofibrillary tangles* and *senile plaques* in the brain. A number of causes have been proposed for this disease, including *genetic factors; abnormal protein and neurotransmitter activity; high levels of zinc, lead, or other toxins; immune system problems;* and *slow-acting infections.*

Researchers are making significant strides at better assessing dementia and even at identifying persons who will eventually develop this problem. Drug, cognitive, and behavioral therapies have been applied to dementia, with limited success. Addressing the needs of *caregivers* is now also recognized as a key part of treatment. In addition, sociocultural approaches such as *day-care facilities* are on the rise. The coming years are expected to see major treatment breakthroughs. *pp. 601–614*

○ **Key issues** In studying and treating the problems of old age, clinicians have become concerned about three issues: *the problems of elderly members of racial and ethnic minority groups, inadequacies of long-term care,* and *the need for health maintenance by young adults. pp. 614–615*

⋙ CRITICAL THOUGHTS ⋘

1. Need aging lead to depression and other psychological problems? What kinds of attitudes, preparations, and activities might help an individual enter old age with peace of mind and even positive anticipation? *pp. 594–600*

2. What changes in medical practice, patient education, or family interactions might address the growing problem of misuse of prescription drugs among the elderly? *pp. 599–600*

3. The "oldest old" often seem particularly well adjusted. Does their positive frame of mind lead to longevity, or does outstanding health produce greater happiness? Why do many in this age group attribute their longevity to psychological factors, while scientists seem to prefer biological explanations? *p. 600*

4. Current research developments suggest that diagnosticians eventually may be able to identify victims of Alzheimer's disease years before

their memory begins to fail noticeably. Would people be better off knowing or not knowing that they will eventually develop a devastating disease that currently has no known cure? *p. 609*

5. If caregivers for elderly relatives often feel anxious, depressed, and overwhelmed, might those feelings be sensed by the elderly individuals, even those with dementia? How might this occur, and what impact might it have? *pp. 610–614*

⬙ cyberstudy ⬙   SEARCH

Search the *Abnormal Psychology* Video Tool Kit

www.worthpublishers.com/apvtk

▲ Chapter 18 Video Cases
Pets and the Elderly: The Impact of Companionship
Living without Memory
Suffering from Alzheimer's Disease

▲ Video case discussions, study guides, and questions

Log on to the Comer Web Page

www.worthpublishers.com/comer

▲ Chapter 18 outline, learning objectives, research exercises, study tools, and practice test questions

▲ Additional Chapter 18 case studies, Web links, and FAQs

LAW, SOCIETY, AND THE MENTAL HEALTH PROFESSION

Dear Jodie:

There is a definite possibility that I will be killed in my attempt to get Reagan. It is for this very reason that I am writing you this letter now. As you well know by now, I love you very much. The past seven months I have left you dozens of poems, letters and messages in the faint hope you would develop an interest in me. . . . Jodie, I would abandon this idea of getting Reagan in a second if I could only win your heart and live out the rest of my life with you, whether it be in total obscurity or whatever. I will admit to you that the reason I'm going ahead with this attempt now is because I just cannot wait any longer to impress you. I've got to do something now to make you understand in no uncertain terms that I am doing all of this for your sake. By sacrificing my freedom and possibly my life I hope to change your mind about me. This letter is being written an hour before I leave for the Hilton Hotel. Jodie, I'm asking you please to look into your heart and at least give me the chance with this historical deed to gain your respect and love. I love you forever.

JOHN HINCKLEY

John W. Hinckley Jr. wrote this letter to actress Jodie Foster in March 1981. Soon after writing it, he stood waiting, pistol ready, outside the Washington Hilton Hotel. Moments later, President Ronald Reagan came out of the hotel, and the popping of pistol fire was heard. As Secret Service men pushed Reagan into the limousine, a policeman and the president's press secretary fell to the pavement. The president had been shot, and by nightfall most of America had seen the face and heard the name of the disturbed young man from Colorado.

As you have seen throughout this book, the psychological dysfunctioning of an individual does not occur in isolation. It is influenced—sometimes caused—by societal and social pressures, and it affects the lives of relatives, friends, and acquaintances. The case of John Hinckley demonstrates in powerful terms that individual dysfunction may, in some cases, also affect the well-being and rights of people the person does not know.

By the same token, clinical scientists and practitioners do not conduct their work in isolation. As they study and treat people with psychological problems, they are affecting and being affected by other institutions of society. We have seen, for example, how the government regulates the use of psychotropic medications, how clinicians helped carry out the government's policy of deinstitutionalization, and how clinicians have called the psychological ordeal of Iraq combat veterans and, before them, Vietnam veterans, to the attention of society.

In short, like their clients, clinical professionals operate within a complex social system, and in fact, it is the system that defines and regulates their professional responsibilities. Just as we must understand the social context in which abnormal behavior occurs in order to understand the behavior, so must we understand the context in which this behavior is studied and treated.

Two social institutions have a particularly strong impact on the mental health profession—the legislative and judicial systems. These institutions—collectively, the *legal field*—have long been responsible for protecting both the public good

•**forensic psychology**•The branch of psychology concerned with intersections between psychological practice and research and the judicial system. Also related to the field of *forensic psychiatry.*

•**criminal commitment**•A legal process by which people accused of a crime are instead judged mentally unstable and sent to a mental health facility for treatment.

•**not guilty by reason of insanity (NGRI)**•A verdict stating that defendants are not guilty of committing a crime because they were insane at the time of the crime.

Would-be assassin
Few courtroom decisions have spurred as much debate or legislative action as the jury's verdict that John Hinckley, having been captured in the act of shooting President Ronald Reagan, was not guilty by reason of insanity.

AP/Wide World Photos

and the rights of individuals. Sometimes the relationship between the legal field and the mental health field has been friendly, and they have worked together to protect the rights and meet the needs of troubled individuals and of society at large. At other times they have clashed, and one field has imposed its will on the other.

This relationship has two distinct aspects. On the one hand, mental health professionals often play a role in the criminal justice system, as when they are called upon to help the courts assess the mental stability of people accused of crimes. They responded to this call in the Hinckley case, as you will see, and in thousands of other cases. This aspect of the relationship is sometimes termed *psychology in law;* that is, clinical practitioners and researchers operate within the legal system. On the other hand, there is another aspect to the relationship, called *law in psychology.* The legislative and judicial systems act upon the clinical field, regulating certain aspects of mental health care. The courts may, for example, force some individuals to enter treatment, even against their will. In addition, the law protects the rights of patients.

The intersections between the mental health field and the legal and judicial systems are collectively referred to as **forensic psychology** (McGrath & Torres, 2008; Packer, 2008). Forensic psychologists or psychiatrists (or related mental health professionals) may perform such varied activities as testifying in trials, researching the reliability of eyewitness testimony, or helping police profile the personality of a serial killer on the loose.

⚙Psychology in Law: How Do Clinicians Influence the Criminal Justice System?

To arrive at just and appropriate punishments, the courts need to know whether defendants are *responsible* for the crimes they commit and *capable* of defending themselves in court. If not, it would be inappropriate to find individuals guilty or punish them in the usual manner. The courts have decided that in some instances people who suffer from severe *mental instability* may not be responsible for their actions or may not be able to defend themselves in court, and so should not be punished in the usual way. Although the courts make the final judgment as to mental instability, their decisions are guided to a large degree by the opinions of mental health professionals.

When people accused of crimes are judged to be mentally unstable, they are usually sent to a mental institution for treatment, a process called **criminal commitment.** Actually there are several forms of criminal commitment. In one, individuals are judged mentally unstable *at the time of their crimes* and so innocent of wrongdoing. They may plead **not guilty by reason of insanity (NGRI)** and bring mental health professionals into court to support their claim. When people are found not guilty on this basis, they are committed for treatment until they improve enough to be released.

In a second form of criminal commitment, individuals are judged mentally unstable *at the time of their trial* and so are considered unable to understand the trial procedures and defend themselves in court. They are committed for treatment until they are competent to stand trial. Once again, the testimony of mental health professionals helps determine the defendant's psychological functioning.

These judgments of mental instability have stirred many arguments. Some people consider the judgments to be loopholes in the legal system that allow criminals to escape proper punishment for wrongdoing. Others argue that a legal system simply cannot be just unless it allows for extenuating circumstances, such as mental instability. The practice of criminal commitment differs from country to country. In this chapter you will see primarily how it operates in the United States. Although the specific principles and procedures of each country may differ, most countries grapple with the same issues, concerns, and decisions that you will be reading about here.

Criminal Commitment and Insanity during Commission of a Crime

Consider once again the case of John Hinckley. Was he insane at the time he shot the president? If insane, should he be held responsible for his actions? On June 21, 1982, 15 months after he shot four men in the nation's capital, a jury pronounced Hinckley not guilty by reason of insanity. Hinckley thus joined Richard Lawrence, a house painter who shot at Andrew Jackson in 1835, and John Schrank, a saloonkeeper who shot former president Teddy Roosevelt in 1912, as a would-be assassin who was found not guilty by reason of insanity.

Although most Americans were shocked by the Hinckley verdict, those familiar with the insanity defense were not so surprised. In this case, as in other federal court cases at that time, the prosecution had the burden of proving that the defendant was sane beyond a reasonable doubt. Many state courts placed a similar responsibility on the prosecution. To present a clear-cut demonstration of sanity can be difficult, especially when the defendant has exhibited bizarre behavior in other areas of life. In fact, a few years later, Congress passed a law making it the defense's burden in federal cases to prove that defendants are insane, rather than the prosecution's burden to prove them sane. Around 70 percent of state legislatures have since followed suit.

It is important to recognize that "insanity" is a *legal* term (Hartocollis, 2008). That is, the definition of "insanity" used in criminal cases was written by legislators, not by clinicians. Defendants may have mental disorders but not necessarily qualify for a legal definition of insanity. Modern Western definitions of insanity can be traced to the murder case of Daniel M'Naghten in England in 1843. M'Naghten shot and killed Edward Drummond, the secretary to British Prime Minister Robert Peel, while trying to shoot Peel. Because of M'Naghten's apparent delusions of persecution, the jury found him to be not guilty by reason of insanity. The public was outraged by this decision, and their angry outcry forced the British law lords to define the insanity defense more clearly. This legal definition, known as the **M'Naghten test,** or **M'Naghten rule,** stated that experiencing a mental disorder at the time of a crime does not by itself mean that the person was insane; the defendant also had to be *unable to know right from wrong.* The state and federal courts in the United States adopted this test as well.

In the late nineteenth century some state and federal courts in the United States, dissatisfied with the M'Naghten rule, adopted a different test—the **irresistible impulse test.** This test, which had first been used in Ohio in 1834, emphasized the inability to control one's actions. A person who committed a crime during an uncontrollable "fit of passion" was considered insane and not guilty under this test.

For years state and federal courts chose between the M'Naghten test and the irresistible impulse test to determine the sanity of criminal defendants. For a while a third test, called the **Durham test,** also became popular, but it was soon replaced in most courts. This test, based on a decision handed down by the Supreme Court in 1954 in the case of *Durham v. United States,* stated simply that people are not criminally responsible if their "unlawful act was the product of mental disease or mental defect." This test was meant to offer more flexibility in court decisions, but it proved too flexible. Insanity defenses could point to such problems as alcoholism or other forms of substance dependence and conceivably even headaches or ulcers, which were listed as psychophysiological disorders in DSM-I.

In 1955 the American Law Institute (ALI) formulated a test that combined aspects of the M'Naghten, irresistible impulse, and Durham tests. The **American Law Institute test** held that people are not criminally responsible if at the time of a crime they had a mental disorder or defect that prevented them from knowing right from wrong *or* from being able to control themselves and to follow the law. For a time the new test became the most widely accepted legal test of insanity. After the Hinckley verdict, however, there was a public uproar over the "liberal" ALI guidelines, and people called for tougher standards.

Partly in response to this uproar, the American Psychiatric Association recommended in 1983 that people should be found not guilty by reason of insanity *only if*

•**M'Naghten test**•A widely used legal test for insanity that holds people to be insane at the time they committed a crime if, because of a mental disorder, they did not know the nature of the act or did not know right from wrong. Also known as *M'Naghten rule.*

•**irresistible impulse test**•A legal test for insanity that holds people to be insane at the time they committed a crime if they were driven to do so by an uncontrollable "fit of passion."

•**Durham test**•A legal test for insanity that holds people to be insane at the time they committed a crime if their act was the result of a mental disorder or defect.

•**American Law Institute test**•A legal test for insanity that holds people to be insane at the time they committed a crime if, because of a mental disorder, they did not know right from wrong or could not resist an uncontrollable impulse to act.

BETWEEN THE LINES

In Their Words

"John Hinckley suffers [from] schizophrenia." ‹‹
    Expert defense witness, June 7, 1982

"Hinckley does not suffer from schizophrenia." ‹‹
    Expert prosecution witness, June 7, 1982

"[Hinckley had] a very severe depressive disorder." ‹‹
    Expert defense witness, May 20, 1982

"There is little to suggest he was seriously depressed [the day of the shootings]." ‹‹
    Expert prosecution witness, June 4, 1982

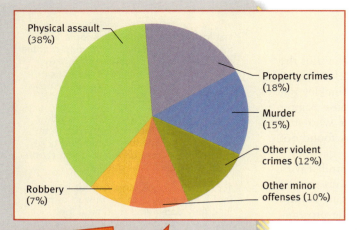

Figure 19-1
Crimes for which persons are found not guilty by reason of insanity (NGRI) A review of NGRI verdicts in eight states revealed that most people who were acquitted on this basis had been charged with a crime of violence. (Based on APA, 2003; Steadman et al., 1993; Callahan et al., 1991.)

Physical assault (38%)
Property crimes (18%)
Murder (15%)
Other violent crimes (12%)
Other minor offenses (10%)
Robbery (7%)

they did not know right from wrong at the time of the crime; an inability to control themselves and to follow the law should no longer be sufficient grounds for a judgment of insanity. In short, the association was calling for a return to the M'Naghten test. This test now is used in all cases tried in federal courts and in about half of the state courts (Doherty, 2007). The more liberal ALI standard is still used in the remaining state courts, except in Idaho, Kansas, Montana, Nevada, and Utah, which have, more or less, done away with the insanity plea altogether (Greenberg & Felthous, 2007; Lohr, 2007). Research has not found, however, that the stricter M'Naghten definition actually reduces the likelihood of verdicts of not guilty by reason of insanity (Ogloff et al., 1992).

People suffering from severe mental disorders in which confusion is a major feature may not be able to tell right from wrong or to control their behavior. It is therefore not surprising that approximately two-thirds of defendants who are acquitted of a crime by reason of insanity qualify for a diagnosis of schizophrenia (Novak et al., 2007; Steadman et al., 1993). The vast majority of these acquitted defendants have a history of past hospitalization, arrest, or both. About half who successfully plead insanity are white, and 86 percent are male. Their mean age is 32 years. The crimes for which defendants are found not guilty by reason of insanity vary greatly. However, approximately 65 percent are violent crimes of some sort (APA, 2003; Steadman et al., 1993). Close to 15 percent of those acquitted are accused specifically of murder (see Figure 19-1 and *A Closer Look* on pages 624–625).

What Concerns Are Raised by the Insanity Defense?
Despite the changes in the insanity tests, criticism of the insanity defense continues (Sales & Shuman, 2005; Slovenko, 2004, 2002). One concern is the fundamental difference between the law and the science of human behavior (Dennison, 2007). The law assumes that individuals have free will and are generally responsible for their actions. Several models of human behavior, in contrast, assume that physical or psychological forces act to determine the individual's behavior. Inevitably, then, legal definitions of insanity and responsibility will differ from those suggested by clinical research.

A second criticism points to the uncertainty of scientific knowledge about abnormal behavior. During a typical insanity defense trial, the testimony of defense clinicians conflicts with that of clinicians hired by the prosecution, and so the jury must weigh the claims of "experts" who disagree in their assessments (Koocher & Keith-Spiegel, 2008). Some people see this lack of professional agreement as evidence that clinical knowledge in some areas may be too incomplete to be allowed to influence important legal decisions. Others counter that the field has made great strides—for example, developing several psychological scales to help clinicians discriminate more consistently between the sane and insane as defined by the M'Naghten standard (Rogers, 2008).

Even with helpful scales in hand, however, clinicians making judgments of legal insanity face a problem that is difficult to overcome: they must evaluate a defendant's state of mind during an event that occurred weeks, months, or years earlier. Because mental states can and do change over time and across situations, clinicians can never be entirely certain that their assessments of mental instability at the time of the crime are accurate.

Perhaps the most often heard criticism of the insanity defense is that it allows dangerous criminals to escape punishment. Granted, some people who successfully plead insanity are released from treatment facilities just months after their acquittal. Yet the number of such cases is quite small (MHA, 2007, 2004; Steadman et al., 1993). According to surveys, the public dramatically overestimates the percentage of defendants who plead insanity, guessing it to be 30 to 40 percent, when in fact it is less than 1 percent. Moreover, only a minority of these persons fake or exaggerate their psychological symptoms (Resnick & Harris, 2002; Perlin, 2000), and only one-quarter of defendants who plead insanity are actually found not guilty on this basis (APA, 2003; Callahan et al., 1991). In the end, less than 1 of every 400 defendants in the United States is found not guilty by reason of insanity. It is also worth noting that in 80 percent of those cases in which defendants are acquitted by reason of insanity, the prosecution has agreed to the appropriateness of the plea.

During most of U.S. history, a successful insanity plea amounted to the equivalent of a long-term prison sentence. In fact, treatment in a mental hospital often resulted in a longer period of confinement than a verdict of guilty would have brought (Nwokike, 2005; Perlin, 2000). Because hospitalization resulted in little, if any, improvement, clinicians were reluctant to predict that the offenders would not repeat their crimes. Moreover, tragic cases would occasionally call into question clinicians' ability to make such judgments and to predict dangerousness (Hooper et al., 2005). In Idaho, for example, a young man raped two women and was found not guilty by reason of insanity. He was released after less than a year of treatment, shot a nurse, and this time was convicted of assault with intent to kill. The uproar over this 1981 case led the Idaho state legislature to abolish the insanity plea.

Today, however, offenders are being released from mental hospitals earlier and earlier. This trend is the result of the increasing effectiveness of drug therapy and other treatments in institutions, the growing reaction against extended institutionalization, and a greater emphasis on patients' rights (Slovenko, 2004; Salekin & Rogers, 2001). In 1992, in the case of *Foucha v. Louisiana,* the U.S. Supreme Court clarified that the *only* acceptable basis for determining the release of hospitalized offenders is whether or not they are still "insane"; they cannot be kept indefinitely in mental hospitals solely because they are dangerous. Some states are able to maintain control over offenders even after their release from hospitals (Swartz et al., 2002). The states may insist on community treatment, monitor the patients closely, and rehospitalize them if necessary.

What Other Verdicts Are Available?
Over the past few decades, 14 states have added another verdict option—**guilty but mentally ill.** Defendants who receive this verdict are found to have had a mental illness at the time of their crime, but the illness was not fully related to or responsible for the crime. The guilty-but-mentally-ill option enables jurors to convict a person they view as dangerous while also suggesting that the individual receive needed treatment. Defendants found to be guilty but mentally ill are given a prison term with the added recommendation that they also undergo treatment if necessary.

After initial enthusiasm for this verdict option, legal and clinical theorists have increasingly found it unsatisfactory (Melville & Naimark, 2002). According to research, it has not reduced the number of not-guilty-by-reason-of-insanity verdicts. Moreover, it often confuses jurors in both real and mock trials. And, perhaps most important, critics point out that appropriate mental health care is supposed to be available to all prisoners anyway, regardless of the verdict. They argue that the guilty-but-mentally-ill option differs from a guilty verdict in name only (Sadock & Sadock, 2007; Slovenko, 2004, 2002).

Some states allow still another kind of defense, *guilty with diminished capacity.* Here a defendant's mental dysfunctioning is viewed as an extenuating circumstance that the court should take into consideration in determining the precise crime of which he or she is guilty (Benitez & Chamberlain, 2008; Leong, 2000). The defense lawyer argues that because of mental dysfunctioning, the defendant could not have *intended* to commit a particular crime. The person can then be found guilty of a lesser crime—of manslaughter (unlawful killing without intent), say, instead of murder in the first degree (planned murder). The famous case of Dan White, who shot and killed Mayor George Moscone and City Supervisor Harvey Milk of San Francisco in 1978, illustrates the use of this verdict.

On the morning of November 27, 1978, Dan White loaded his .38 caliber revolver. White had recently resigned his position as a San Francisco supervisor because of family and financial pressures. Now, after a change of heart, he wanted his job back. When he

•**guilty but mentally ill**•A verdict stating that defendants are guilty of committing a crime but are also suffering from a mental illness that should be treated during their imprisonment.

A CLOSER LOOK

Famous Insanity Defense Cases

1977 In Michigan, Francine Hughes poured gasoline around the bed where her husband, Mickey, lay in a drunken stupor. Then she lit a match and set him on fire. At her trial she explained that he had beaten her repeatedly for 14 years and had threatened to kill her if she tried to leave him. The jury found her not guilty by reason of temporary insanity, making her into a symbol for many abused women across the nation. Some people saw the decision as confirmation of a woman's right to self-defense in her own home.

1978 David "Son of Sam" Berkowitz, a serial killer in New York City, explained that a barking dog had sent him demonic messages to kill. Although two psychiatrists assessed him as psychotic, he was found guilty of his crimes. Long after his trial, he said that he had actually made up the delusions.

1979 Kenneth Bianchi, one of the pair known as the Hillside Strangler, entered a plea of not guilty by reason of insanity but was found guilty along with his cousin of sexually assaulting and murdering women in the Los Angeles area in late 1977 and early 1978. He claimed that he had multiple personality disorder.

1980 In December, Mark David Chapman murdered John Lennon. Chapman later explained that he had killed the rock music legend because he believed Lennon to be a "sell-out." He also described hearing the voice of God, considered himself his generation's "catcher in the rye" (from the J. D. Salinger novel), and compared himself to Moses. Despite clinical testimony that supported Chapman's plea of not guilty by reason of insanity, he was ultimately convicted of murder.

1981 In an attempt to prove his love for actress Jodie Foster, John Hinckley Jr. tried to assassinate President Ronald Reagan. Hinckley was found not guilty by reason of insanity and was committed to St. Elizabeths Hospital for the criminally insane in Washington, D.C., where he remains today.

1992 Jeffrey Dahmer, a 31-year-old mass murderer in Milwaukee, was tried for the killings of 15 young men. Dahmer apparently drugged some of his victims and performed crude lobotomies on them in an attempt to create zombie-like companions for himself. He also dismembered his victims' bodies and stored their parts to be eaten. Although his defense attorney argued that Dahmer was not guilty by reason of insanity, the jury found him guilty as charged. He was beaten to death by another inmate in 1995.

1994 On June 23, 1993, 24-year-old Lorena Bobbitt cut off her husband's penis with a 12-inch kitchen knife while he slept. During her trial, defense attorneys argued that after years of abuse by John Bobbitt, his wife suffered a brief psychotic episode and was seized by an "irresistible impulse" to cut off his penis after he came home drunk and raped her. In 1994, the jury acquitted her of the charge of malicious wounding by reason of temporary insanity. She was committed to a state mental hospital for further assessment and treatment and released a few months later.

1997 John E. Du Pont, 57-year-old heir to his family's chemical fortune, shot and killed the Olympic wrestling champion

asked Mayor George Moscone to reappoint him, however, the mayor refused. Supervisor Harvey Milk was among those who had urged Moscone to keep White out, for Milk was America's first openly gay politician, and Dan White had been an outspoken opponent of measures supporting gay rights.

White avoided the metal detector at City Hall's main entrance by climbing through a basement window after telling construction workers who recognized him that he had forgotten his keys. After they unlocked the window for him, he went straight to the mayor's office. . . . White pulled out his gun and shot the mayor once in the arm and once in the chest. As Moscone lay bleeding on the floor, White walked over to him and, from only inches away, fired twice into Moscone's head.

White then reloaded his gun, ran down the hall, and spotted Harvey Milk. White asked to talk with him. Right after the two men went into White's former office, three more shots rang out. Milk crumpled to the floor. Once again White from point-blank range fired two more bullets into his victim's head. Shortly afterward he turned himself in to the police. Several months later the jury rendered its verdict: Dan White was not guilty of murder, only voluntary manslaughter.

Murder is the illegal killing of a human being with malice aforethought, that is, with the intent to kill. Manslaughter is the illegal killing of a human being without malice

Dave Schultz in January 1995. The murder took place on Du Pont's 800-acre estate, where he had built a sports center for amateur athletes. Schultz, his close friend, had coached wrestlers at the center. In 1997 Du Pont was found guilty of third-degree murder, but mentally ill. He was sentenced to prison for 13 to 30 years and assigned to receive treatment at the prison's mental health unit.

2003 For three weeks in October 2002, John Allen Muhammad and Lee Boyd Malvo went on a sniping spree in the Washington, D.C., area, shooting 10 people dead and wounding 3 others. Attorneys for Malvo, a teenager, argued that he had acted under the influence of the middle-aged Muhammad and that he should be found not guilty of the crimes by reason of insanity. The jury, however, found Malvo guilty of capital murder and sentenced him to life in prison.

2006 On June 20, 2001, Andrea Yates, a 36-year-old woman, drowned each of her five children in the bathtub. Yates had a history of *postpartum depression* and *postpartum psychosis:* she believed that she was the devil, that she had failed to be a good mother, and that her children were not developing correctly. She had in fact been hospitalized twice for her disorder and was in treatment just prior to the killings. Given such problems and history, she pleaded not guilty by reason of insanity during her trial in 2002. The jury agreed that she had a profound disorder, but it concluded that she did know right from wrong at the time of the murders, found her guilty, and sentenced her to life in prison in Texas. This verdict was later overturned when a Texas appeals court decided that a prosecution witness at the trial had provided misinformation in his testimony. On July 26, 2006, after a new trial, Yates was found not guilty by reason of insanity and was sent to a mental health facility for treatment.

Pool photo by Getty Images

Two verdicts Andrea Yates is led into a district court in Texas for arraignment on multiple counts of murder in the drowning of her five children. In a 2002 trial Yates was found guilty of murder and sentenced to life in prison. In a 2006 retrial, however, she was judged not guilty by reason of insanity and sent to a mental institution for treatment.

---

aforethought. The attacker may intend to harm the victim, but not to kill. If the victim nonetheless dies, the crime is voluntary manslaughter. Involuntary manslaughter is an illegal killing from negligence rather than intentional harm. . . .

. . . Defense attorney Douglas Schmidt argued that a patriotic, civic-minded man like Dan White—high school athlete, decorated war veteran, former fireman, policeman, and city supervisor—could not possibly have committed such an act unless something had snapped inside him. The brutal nature of the two final shots to each man's head only proved that White had lost his wits. White was not fully responsible for his actions because he suffered from "diminished capacity." Although White killed Mayor George Moscone and Supervisor Harvey Milk, he had not planned his actions. On the day of the shootings, White was mentally incapable of planning to kill, or even of wanting to do such a thing.

Well known in forensic psychiatry circles, Martin Blinder, professor of law and psychiatry at the University of California's Hastings Law School in San Francisco, brought a good measure of academic prestige to White's defense. White had been, Blinder explained to the jury, "gorging himself on junk food: Twinkies, Coca-Cola. . . . The more he consumed, the worse he'd feel and he'd respond to his ever-growing depression by consuming ever more junk food." Schmidt later asked Blinder if he could elaborate on this. "Perhaps if

Justice served?
Mass protests took place in San Francisco after Dan White was convicted of voluntary manslaughter rather than premeditated murder in the killings of Mayor George Moscone and Supervisor Harvey Milk, one of the nation's leading gay activists. For many, the 1979 verdict highlighted the serious pitfalls of the "diminished capacity" defense.

it were not for the ingestion of this junk food," Blinder responded, "I would suspect that these homicides would not have taken place." From that moment on, Blinder became known as the author of the Twinkie defense. . . .

Dan White was convicted only of voluntary manslaughter, and was sentenced to seven years, eight months. (He was released on parole January 6, 1984.) Psychiatric testimony convinced the jury that White did not wish to kill George Moscone or Harvey Milk.

The angry crowd that responded to the verdict by marching, shouting, trashing City Hall, and burning police cars was in good part homosexual. Gay supervisor Harvey Milk had worked well for their cause, and his loss was a serious setback for human rights in San Francisco. Yet it was not only members of the gay community who were appalled at the outcome. Most San Franciscans shared their feelings of outrage.

(Coleman, 1984, pp. 65–70)

Because of possible miscarriages of justice, many legal experts have argued against the "diminished capacity" defense, and a number of states have eliminated it, including California shortly after the Dan White verdict (Gado, 2008; Slovenko, 2002, 1992). Some studies find, however, that jurors are often capable of using the option in careful and appropriate ways (Finkel & Duff, 1989).

What Are Sex-Offender Statutes? Since 1937, when Michigan passed the first "sexual psychopath" law, a number of states have placed sex offenders in a special legal category (Strutin, 2007; Zonana et al., 2004). These states believe that some of the individuals who are repeatedly found guilty of sex crimes have a mental disorder, and so the states categorize them as *mentally disordered sex offenders.*

People classified in this way are convicted of a criminal offense and are thus judged to be responsible for their actions. Nevertheless, like people found not guilty by reason of insanity, mentally disordered sex offenders are instead committed to a mental health facility. In part, such laws reflect a belief held by many legislators that such sex offenders are psychologically disturbed. On a practical level, the laws help protect sex offenders from the physical abuse that they often receive in prison society.

Over the past two decades, however, most states have been changing or abolishing their mentally disordered sex offender laws, and at this point only a handful still have them (Sreenivasan et al., 2003). There are several reasons for this trend. First, states typi-

BETWEEN THE LINES

The Aftermath

Dan White Convicted of voluntary manslaughter in 1979, Dan White was released from prison in 1984. He committed suicide in 1985. ‹‹

Daniel M'Naghten Judged not guilty by reason of insanity, Daniel M'Naghten lived in a mental hospital until his death 22 years later (Slovenko, 2002, 1995). ‹‹

John Hinckley In 2008, officials at St. Elizabeths Hospital in Washington, D.C. asked a federal judge to grant John Hinckley more privileges, including 10-day visits to his mother's home rather than 6-day visits (Wilber, 2008). ‹‹

cally have found the laws difficult to apply. Some of the laws, for example, require that the offender be found "sexually dangerous beyond a reasonable doubt"—a judgment that is often beyond the reach of the clinical field's expertise. Similarly, the state laws may require that in order to be classified as mentally disordered sex offenders, individuals must be good candidates for treatment, another judgment that is difficult for clinicians to make, especially for this population. Third, evidence exists that racial bias often affects the use of the mentally disordered sex offender classification (Sturgeon & Taylor, 1980). From a defendant's perspective, this classification is considered an attractive alternative to imprisonment—an alternative available to white Americans much more often than to members of racial minority groups. Indeed, white Americans are twice as likely to be granted mentally disordered sex offender status as African Americans or Hispanic Americans who have been convicted of similar crimes.

But perhaps the primary reason that mentally disordered sex offender laws have lost favor is that state legislatures and courts are now less concerned than they used to be about the rights and needs of sex offenders, given the growing number of sex crimes taking place across the country, particularly those in which children are victims. In fact, in response to public outrage over the high number of sex crimes, 17 states have instead passed *sexually violent predator* laws (or *sexually dangerous persons* laws). These new laws call for certain sex offenders who have been convicted of sex crimes and have served their sentence in prison to be removed from prison before their release and committed involuntarily to a mental hospital for treatment if a court judges them likely to engage in further "predatory acts of sexual violence" as a result of "mental abnormality" or "personality disorder" (Jackson & Richards, 2008; Sreenivasan et al., 2003). That is, in contrast to the mentally disordered sex offender laws, which call for sex offenders to receive treatment *instead* of imprisonment, the sexually violent predator laws require certain sex offenders to receive imprisonment and then, *in addition*, be committed for a period of involuntary treatment. The constitutionality of the sexually violent predator laws was upheld by the Supreme Court in the 1997 case of *Kansas v. Hendricks* by a 5 to 4 margin. In California, one of the states with such a law, around 1 to 2 percent of convicted sex offenders have been committed to mental health treatment programs after serving their prison sentences (Sreenivasan et al., 2003).

Criminal Commitment and Incompetence to Stand Trial

Regardless of their state of mind at the time of a crime, defendants may be judged to be **mentally incompetent** to stand trial. The competence requirement is meant to ensure that defendants understand the charges they are facing and can work with their lawyers to prepare and conduct an adequate defense (Fitch, 2007). This minimum standard of competence was specified by the Supreme Court in the case of *Dusky v. United States* (1960).

The issue of competence is most often raised by the defendant's attorney, although prosecutors, arresting police officers, and even the judge may raise it as well. They prefer to err on the side of caution because some convictions have been reversed on appeal when a defendant's competence was not established at the beginning. When the issue of competence is raised, the judge orders a psychological evaluation, usually on an inpatient basis (see Table 19-1 on the next page). As many as 40,000 competency evaluations are conducted in the United States each year (Zapf & Roesch, 2006; Roesch et al., 1999). Approximately 20 percent of defendants who receive such an evaluation are in fact found to be incompetent to stand trial. If the court decides that the defendant is incompetent, the individual is typically assigned to a mental health facility until competent to stand trial (Fitch, 2007; Perlin, 2003).

One famous case of incompetence to stand trial is that of Russell Weston, a man who entered the United States Capitol building in

•**mental incompetence**•A state of mental instability that leaves defendants unable to understand the legal charges and proceedings they are facing and unable to prepare an adequate defense with their attorney.

Executing the mentally ill
One of the most controversial executions in the United States was that of Charles Singleton, a man who killed a store clerk in Arkansas, was sentenced to death in 1979, and then developed schizophrenia at some point after the trial. Inasmuch as the United States does not allow executions if persons cannot understand why they are being executed, state officials wanted Singleton to take medications to clear up his psychosis. After years of legal appeals, the U.S. Supreme Court ruled in 2003 that Singleton was, by then, taking medications voluntarily, and Singleton was executed by lethal injection in 2004.

Neemah Aaron/AP Photo

table: **19-1**

Multicultural Issues: Race and Forensic Psychology

- Psychologically disturbed people from racial minority groups are more likely than disturbed white Americans to be sent to prison, as opposed to mental health facilities.

- Among defendants evaluated for competence to stand trial, those from racial minority groups are more likely than white American defendants to be referred for *inpatient* evaluations.

- Among defendants evaluated for competence to stand trial, those from racial minority groups are more likely than white Americans to have the evaluation occur in a *strict-security inpatient* setting, rather than in the noncorrectional mental health system.

- When nonwhite and white defendants are evaluated for competence to stand trial, the defendants from racial minority groups are more likely to be found incompetent to stand trial.

- In New York State, 42 percent of all individuals ordered into *involuntary outpatient commitment* are African American, 34 percent are white American, and 21 percent are Hispanic American. In contrast, these three groups comprise, respectively, 17 percent, 61 percent, and 16 percent of New York's general population.

Source: Haroules, 2007; Pinals et al., 2004; Grekin et al., 1994; Arvanites, 1989.

Figure 19-2

Prison and mental health According to studies conducted in several Western countries, psychological disorders are much more prevalent in prison populations than in the general population. For example, schizophrenia is 4 times more common and personality disorders 5 times more common among prisoners than among nonprisoners. In fact, antisocial personality disorder is 10 times more common. (Based on Butler et al., 2006; Fazel & Danesh, 2002.)

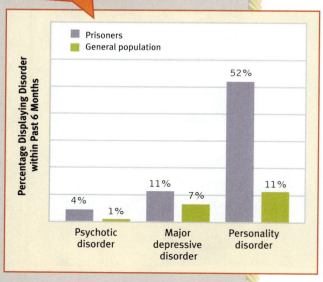

1998 apparently seeking out then–House Majority Whip Tom DeLay, among others. Weston proceeded to shoot two police officers to death before being apprehended. In 1999, the defendant, who had stopped taking medications for his severe psychosis, was found incompetent to stand trial and sent to a psychiatric institution. In 2001, a judge ruled that he should be forced to take medications again, but even with such drugs Weston continued to have severe symptoms and to this day remains incompetent to stand trial for the 1998 shootings.

Many more cases of criminal commitment result from decisions of mental incompetence than from verdicts of not guilty by reason of insanity (Zapf & Roesch, 2006; Roesch et al., 1999). However, the majority of criminals currently institutionalized for psychological treatment in the United States are not from either of these two groups. Rather, they are convicted inmates whose psychological problems have led prison officials to decide they need treatment—either in mental health units within the prison or in mental hospitals (Senior et al., 2007; Way et al., 2005) (see Figure 19-2).

It is possible that an innocent defendant, ruled incompetent to stand trial, could spend years in a mental health facility with no opportunity to disprove the criminal accusations. Some defendants have, in fact, served longer "sentences" in mental health facilities awaiting a ruling of competence than they would have served in prison had they been convicted. Such a possibility was reduced when the Supreme Court ruled, in the case of *Jackson v. Indiana* (1972), that an incompetent defendant cannot be indefinitely committed. After a reasonable amount of time, he or she should either be found competent and tried, set free, or transferred to a mental health facility under *civil* commitment procedures.

Until the early 1970s, most states required the commitment of mentally incompetent defendants to maximum-security institutions for the "criminally insane." Under current law, the courts have greater flexibility. In some cases, particularly when the charge is a minor one, the defendant may even be treated on an outpatient basis, an arrangement often called *jail diversion* because the disturbed individual is "diverted" from jail to the community for mental health care (Morrissey & Cuddeback, 2008).

✸Law in Psychology: How Do the Legislative and Judicial Systems Influence Mental Health Care?

Just as clinical science and practice have influenced the legal system, so the legal system has had a major impact on clinical practice. First, courts and legislatures have developed the process of **civil commitment,** which allows certain people to be forced into mental health treatment. Although many people who show signs of mental disturbance seek treatment voluntarily, a large number are not aware of their problems or are simply not interested in undergoing therapy. What are clinicians to do for these people? Should they force treatment upon them? Or do people have the right to feel miserable and function poorly? The law has answered this question by developing civil commitment guidelines under which certain people can be forced into treatment.

Second, the legal system, on behalf of the state, has taken on the responsibility for protecting patients' rights during treatment. This protection extends not only to patients who have been involuntarily committed but also to those who seek treatment voluntarily, even on an outpatient basis.

Civil Commitment

Every year in the United States large numbers of people with mental disorders are involuntarily committed to treatment. Typically they are committed to *mental institutions,* but 27 states also have *outpatient* civil commitment laws that allow patients to be forced into community treatment programs (Haroules, 2007; Monahan et al., 2005). Civil commitments have long caused controversy and debate. In some ways the law provides greater protection for people suspected of being criminals than for people suspected of being psychotic (Strachan, 2008; Burton, 1990).

Why Commit? Generally our legal system permits involuntary commitment of individuals when they are considered to be *in need of treatment* and *dangerous to themselves or others.* People may be dangerous to themselves if they are suicidal or if they act recklessly (for example, drinking a drain cleaner to prove that they are immune to its chemicals). They may be dangerous to others if they seek to harm them (see *Psych Watch* on the next page) or if they unintentionally place others at risk. The state's authority to commit disturbed individuals rests on its duties to protect the interests of the individual and of society: the principles of *parens patriae* and *police power* (Swallow et al., 2005). Under *parens patriae* ("parent of the country"), the state can make decisions that promote the patient's best interests and provide protection from self-harm, including a decision of involuntary hospitalization. Conversely, *police power* allows the state to take steps to protect society from a person who is violent or otherwise dangerous.

What Are the Procedures for Civil Commitment? Civil commitment laws vary from state to state (Bindman & Thornicroft, 2008). Some basic procedures, however, are common to most of these laws. Often family members begin commitment proceedings. In response to a son's psychotic behavior and repeated assaults on other people, for example, his parents may try to persuade him to seek admission to a mental institution. If the son refuses, the parents may go to court and seek an involuntary commitment order. If the son is a minor, the process is simple. The Supreme Court, in the case of *Parham v. J. R.* (1979), has ruled that a hearing is not necessary in such cases, as long as a qualified mental health professional considers commitment necessary. If the son is

•civil commitment• A legal process by which an individual can be forced to undergo mental health treatment.

Stalking: crime or disorder?

Jack Jordan, accused stalker of actress Uma Thurman, calmly eats a sandwich during a break in his 2008 trial, oblivious to the media circus that surrounded his case. Accused of harassing Thurman and her family members and friends with upsetting notes and letters, Jordan was found guilty of a criminal offense and placed on probation for three years. The clinical and legal fields have struggled with how best to deal with stalking—as a criminal offense or a psychological disorder. The pattern has a range of causes, may produce enormous stress for victims, and sometimes results in tragedy (Petherick, 2008; Martin, 2007).

John Marshall Mantel/The New York Times/Redux

Violence against Therapists

On a winter night in 2008, a 39-year-old man named David Tarloff went to the New York City office of psychiatrist Kent Shinbach. Tarloff had a long history of severe mental disorders, and apparently Dr. Shinbach had played a role in one of the diagnoses and institutionalizations of this individual back in 1991. Tarloff later explained to police that he went to the office to rob Dr. Shinbach, hoping to gain enough money to remove his mother from a nursing home and take her to Hawaii. Upon his arrival, however, Tarloff first came upon psychologist Dr. Kathryn Faughey, whose office was near Dr. Shinbach's. In the course of events, Tarloff slashed Dr. Faughey to death with a meat cleaver and seriously wounded Dr. Shinbach, who tried to come to the psychologist's aid.

As you have read, the vast majority of people with severe mental disorders are not violent and in fact are much more likely to be victims of violence than perpetrators. Nevertheless, periodic cases, like the tragic murder of Dr. Faughey, do occur,

reminding psychotherapists that there is indeed some degree of danger attached to their profession—a profession in which clients are invited to expose and address their innermost feelings and concerns. Such danger is particularly a possibility in cases in which clients generally have displayed a history of violence.

According to surveys, more than 80 percent of therapists have on at least one occasion feared that a client might physically attack them (Pope et al., 2006; Pope & Tabachnick, 1993). Are such concerns exaggerated? Not always (Lion, 2008;

Freed & Geller, 2005; Fry et al., 2002). It is estimated that as many as 13 percent of therapists have been attacked in some form by a patient at least once in private therapy, and an even larger percentage have been assaulted in mental hospitals (Barron, 2008; Tryon, 1987; Bernstein, 1981). Similarly, a number of therapists have been stalked or harassed by patients (Hudson-Allez, 2006).

Patients have used a variety of weapons in their attacks, including such common objects as shoes, lamps, fire extinguishers, and canes. Some have used guns or knives and have severely wounded or even killed a therapist, as we saw in the case of Dr. Faughey.

As you can imagine, many therapists who have been attacked continue to feel anxious and insecure in their work for a long time afterward. Some try to be more selective in accepting patients and to look for cues that signal impending violence. It is possible that such concerns represent a significant distraction from the task at hand when they are in session with clients.

an adult, however, the process is more involved. The court usually will order a mental examination and allow the person to contest the commitment in court, often represented by a lawyer.

Although the Supreme Court has offered few guidelines concerning specific procedures of civil commitment, one important decision, in the case of *Addington v. Texas* (1979), outlined the *minimum standard of proof* needed for commitment. Here the Court ruled that before an individual can be committed, there must be "clear and convincing" proof that he or she is mentally ill and has met the state's criteria for involuntary commitment. The ruling does not suggest what criteria should be used. That matter is still left to each state. But, whatever the state's criteria, clinicians must offer clear and convincing proof that the individual meets those criteria. When is proof clear and convincing, according to the Court? When it provides 75 percent certainty that the criteria of commitment have been met. This is far less than the near-total certainty ("beyond a reasonable doubt") required to convict people of committing a crime.

Emergency Commitment Many situations require immediate action; no one can wait for commitment proceedings when a life is at stake. Consider, for example, an emergency room patient who is suicidal or hearing voices demanding hostile actions against others. He or she may need immediate treatment and round-the-clock supervision. If treatment could not be given in such situations without the patient's full consent, the consequences could be tragic.

Therefore, many states give clinicians the right to certify that certain patients need temporary commitment and medication. In past years, these states required certification by two *physicians* (not necessarily psychiatrists in some of the states). Today states may allow certification by other mental health professionals as well. The clinicians must declare that the state of mind of the patients makes them dangerous to themselves or others. By tradition, the certifications are often referred to as *two-physician certificates,* or *2 PCs.* The length of such emergency commitments varies from state to state, but three days is often the limit (Strachan, 2008). Should clinicians come to believe that a longer stay is necessary, formal commitment proceedings may be initiated during the period of emergency commitment.

Who Is Dangerous? In the past, people with mental disorders were actually less likely than others to commit violent or dangerous acts. This low rate of violence was apparently related to the fact that so many such individuals lived in institutions. As a result of deinstitutionalization, however, hundreds of thousands of people with severe disturbances now live in the community, and many of them receive little, if any, treatment. Some of these individuals are indeed dangerous to themselves or others.

Although approximately 90 percent of people with mental disorders are in no way violent or dangerous (Pilgrim, 2003; Swanson et al., 1990), studies now suggest at least a small relationship between severe mental disorders and violent behavior (Norko & Baranoski, 2008; Cole & Glass, 2005). After reviewing a number of studies, John Monahan (2008, 2001, 1993, 1992), a law and psychology professor, concluded that the rate of violent behavior among persons with severe mental disorders is at least somewhat higher than that of people without such disorders:

- Approximately 15 percent of patients in mental hospitals have assaulted another person prior to admission.
- Around 25 percent of patients in mental hospitals assault another person during hospitalization.
- Approximately 12 percent of all people with schizophrenia, major depression, or bipolar disorder have assaulted other people, compared with 2 percent of persons without a mental disorder.
- Approximately 4 percent of people who report having been violent during the past year suffer from schizophrenia, whereas 1 percent of nonviolent persons suffer from schizophrenia.

Failure to predict
A relatively new form of dangerousness—children and adolescents who shoot family members, schoolmates, and teachers—began in earnest with a killing rampage at Columbine High School in Littleton, Colorado, on April 20, 1999, captured here on a school-cafeteria surveillance camera. Earlier videos made by Dylan Klebold and Eric Harris, the students who committed the mass murder, suggest that they had planned their attack for more than a year. Despite building a violent Web site, threatening other students, having problems with the law, and, in the case of one boy, receiving treatment for mental health problems, professionals were not able to predict or prevent their violent behavior.

Monahan cautions that the findings do not suggest that people with mental disorders are generally dangerous. Nor do they justify the "caricature of the mentally disordered" that is often portrayed by the media or the "lock 'em up" laws proposed by some politicians. But they do indicate that a severe mental disorder may be more of a risk factor for violence than mental health experts used to believe.

A judgment of *dangerousness* is often required for involuntary civil commitment. But can mental health professionals accurately predict who will commit violent acts? Research suggests that psychiatrists and psychologists are wrong more often than right when they make *long-term* predictions of violence (Litwack et al, 2006; Eccleston & Ward, 2004). Most often they overestimate the likelihood that a patient will eventually be violent. On the other hand, studies suggest that *short-term* predictions—that is, predictions of imminent violence—can be more accurate (Litwack et al, 2006). Researchers are now working, with some success, to develop new assessment techniques that use statistical approaches and are more objective in their predictions of dangerousness than the subjective judgments of clinicians (Norko & Baranoski, 2008; Heilbrun & Erickson, 2007).

What Are the Problems with Civil Commitment?

Civil commitment has been criticized on several grounds (Winick, 2008; Morse, 1982; Ennis & Emery, 1978). First is the difficulty of assessing a person's dangerousness. If judgments of dangerousness are often inaccurate, how can one justify using them to deprive people of liberty? Second, the legal definitions of "mental illness" and "dangerousness" are vague. The terms may be defined so broadly that they could be applied to almost anyone an evaluator views as undesirable (see *Eye on Culture* below). Indeed, many civil libertarians worry about the use of involuntary commitment to control people, as occurred in the former Soviet Union and now seems to be taking place in China, where mental hospitals house people with unpopular political views (Charatan, 2001). A third problem is the sometimes questionable therapeutic value of civil commitment. Research suggests that many people committed involuntarily do not typically respond well to therapy (Winick, 2008).

On the basis of these and other arguments, some clinicians suggest that involuntary commitment should be abolished (Haroules, 2007; Szasz, 2007, 1977, 1963). Others, however, advocate finding a more systematic way to evaluate dangerousness when decisions are to be made about commitment. They suggest instituting a process of *risk*

The Separation of Mind and State

During the presidential campaigns of 1992 and 1996, independent candidate Ross Perot was branded "emotionally unbalanced" by some of his detractors. Perot reacted with good humor and even adopted Willie Nelson's "Crazy" as his theme song. The strategy of questioning the psychological stability of political opponents was taken to the extreme in the former Soviet Union, particularly under the rule of Joseph Stalin, when many political dissidents were placed in mental hospitals to get them out of the way. Similarly, there is growing concern in Western countries that the government of China is now following a similar practice (Charatan, 2001).

Politically motivated labeling was at work during the mid-nineteenth-century debate over slavery in the United States, when those who favored slavery attacked Abraham Lincoln in the press as "insane" for his antislavery stance (Gamwell & Tomes, 1995). Many people, even among those who were against slavery, feared radical abolitionists and called them mentally unbalanced, blaming them for the nation's turmoil.

The trial of abolitionist John Brown brought the issue out front for all to see. Brown, a white opponent of slavery, organized a small force of African Americans and white Americans to attack the federal armory at Harpers Ferry in Virginia. He was captured after two days and tried for murder and treason. Many of Brown's supporters, including his own defense attorneys, urged him to plead not guilty by reason of insanity to avoid the death penalty (Gamwell & Tomes, 1995). Some fellow abolitionists, however, were offended by the suggestion that Brown's actions represented insanity, and Brown himself proudly maintained that he was mentally stable. In the end, Brown was convicted and executed.

As historians Lynn Gamwell and Nancy Tomes (1995) point out, it was in the interests of both sides of the case to have Brown declared legally insane. Many people who opposed slavery believed that an insanity verdict would distance Brown's radical behavior from their own efforts in the public's mind and would calm public fears of violence by abolitionists. Many of those who defended slavery believed that a judgment of insanity would hurt Brown's reputation and prevent him from becoming a martyr for the abolitionist cause—as in fact he did become. Obviously, the verdict pleased neither side.

Clinical labels have been used for political gain throughout the ages. We may not

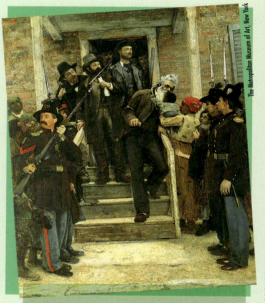

The Last Moments of John Brown Abolitionist John Brown's journey to execution is portrayed in Thomas Hovenden's painting *The Last Moments of John Brown*, 1884.

always be able to stop the practice, but we should at least be aware of it. As we read about historical events, we must be careful to weigh the available evidence and separate mental health labels that are used correctly from those that seek merely to further a political cause.

The Metropolitan Museum of Art, New York

To help protect the rights of patients, Congress passed the Protection and Advocacy for Mentally Ill Individuals Act in 1986. This law set up *protection and advocacy systems* in all states and U.S. territories and gave public advocates who worked for patients the power to investigate possible abuse and neglect and to correct those problems legally.

In recent years public advocates have argued that the right to treatment also should be extended to the tens of thousands of people with severe mental disorders who are repeatedly released from hospitals into ill-equipped communities. Many such people have no place to go and are unable to care for themselves, often winding up homeless or in prisons (Felix et al., 2008; Torrey, 2001). A number of advocates are now suing federal and state agencies throughout the country, demanding that they fulfill the promises of the community mental health movement (see Chapter 15).

How Is the Right to Refuse Treatment Protected?
During the past two decades the courts have also decided that patients, particularly those in institutions, have the **right to refuse treatment** (Rolon & Jones, 2008; Perlin, 2004, 2000). The courts have been reluctant to make a single general ruling on this right because there are so many different kinds of treatment, and a general ruling based on one of them might have unintended effects. Therefore, rulings usually target one specific treatment at a time.

Most of the right-to-refuse-treatment rulings center on *biological treatments* (Rolon & Jones, 2008). These treatments are easier to impose on patients without their cooperation than psychotherapy, and they often seem more hazardous. For example, state rulings have consistently granted patients the right to refuse *psychosurgery,* the most irreversible form of physical treatment—and therefore the most dangerous.

Some states have also acknowledged a patient's right to refuse *electroconvulsive therapy* (*ECT*), the treatment used in many cases of severe depression (see Chapter 9). However, the right-to-refuse issue is more complex with regard to ECT than to psychosurgery. ECT is very effective for many people with severe depression; yet it can cause great upset and can also be misused. Today many states grant patients—particularly voluntary patients—the right to refuse ECT. Usually a patient must be informed fully about the nature of the treatment and must give written consent to it. A number of states continue to permit ECT to be forced on committed patients (Baldwin & Oxlad, 2000), whereas others require the consent of a close relative or other third party in such cases.

In the past, patients did not have the right to refuse *psychotropic medications.* As you have read, however, many psychotropic drugs are very powerful, and some produce effects that are unwanted and dangerous. As these harmful effects have become more apparent, some states have granted patients the right to refuse medication. Typically, these states require physicians to explain the purpose of the medication to patients and obtain their written consent. If a patient's refusal is considered incompetent, dangerous, or irrational, the state may allow it to be overturned by an independent psychiatrist, medical committee, or local court (Rolon & Jones, 2008). However, the refusing patient is supported in this process by a lawyer or other patient advocate.

What Other Rights Do Patients Have?
Court decisions have protected still other patient rights over the past several decades. Patients who perform work in mental institutions, particularly private institutions, are now guaranteed at least a *minimum wage.* In addition, a district court ruled in 1974 that patients released from state mental hospitals have a right to *aftercare* and to an *appropriate community residence,* such as a group home, a right later confirmed by the Supreme Court in the 1999 case of *Olmstead v. L.C. et al.* And in the 1975 case of *Dixon v. Weinberger,* another district court ruled that people with psychological disorders should receive treatment in the *least restrictive facility* available. If an inpatient program at a community mental health center is available, for example, then that is the facility to which they should be assigned, not a mental hospital (Bindman & Thornicroft, 2008).

The "Rights" Debate
Certainly, people with psychological disorders have civil rights that must be protected at all times. However, many clinicians express concern that the patients' rights rulings and laws may unintentionally deprive these patients of

•**right to treatment**•The legal right of patients, particularly those who are involuntarily committed, to receive adequate treatment.

•**right to refuse treatment**•The legal right of patients to refuse certain forms of treatment.

BETWEEN THE LINES

At Special Risk

People with severe mental disorders are more likely to be victims than perpetrators of violence. In any given year at least 16 percent of those with severe disorders report being violently victimized (Walsh et al., 2003). Those who are homeless are at particular risk. ‹‹

"The Taser solution"
Advocates for the mentally ill are currently protesting the ever-increasing police use of stun guns, or Tasers, to subdue people with mental disorders. Tasers, weapons that immediately affect neuromuscular control and temporarily incapacitate people, are viewed by the advocates as a violation of the rights of mental patients—a quick but inhumane intervention that is a poor substitute for patience and support when dealing with extremely confused or frightened people.

opportunities for recovery. Consider the right to refuse medication. If medications can help a patient with schizophrenia to recover, doesn't the patient have the right to that recovery? If confusion causes the patient to refuse medication, can clinicians in good conscience delay medication while legal channels are cleared? Psychologist Marilyn Whiteside raised similar concerns in her description of a 25-year-old patient with mental retardation:

He was 25 and severely retarded. And after his favorite attendant left, he became self-abusive. He beat his fists against the side of his head until a football helmet had to be ordered for his protection. Then he clawed at his face and gouged out one of his eyes.

The institution psychologists began a behavior program that had mildly aversive consequences: they squirted warm water in his face each time he engaged in self-abuse. When that didn't work, they requested permission to use an electric prod. The Human Rights Committee vetoed this "excessive and inhumane form of correction" because, after all, the young man was retarded, not criminal.

Since nothing effective could be done that abridged the rights and negated the dignity of the developmentally disabled patient, he was verbally reprimanded for his behavior—and allowed to push his thumb through his remaining eye. He is now blind, of course, but he has his rights and presumably his dignity.

(Whiteside, 1983, p. 13)

Despite such legitimate concerns, keep in mind that the clinical field has not always done an effective job of protecting patients' rights. Over the years, many patients have been overmedicated and received improper treatments. Furthermore, one must ask whether the field's present state of knowledge justifies clinicians' overriding of patients' rights. Can clinicians confidently say that a given treatment will help a patient? Can they predict when a treatment will have harmful effects? Since clinicians themselves often disagree, it seems appropriate for patients, their advocates, and outside evaluators to play key roles in decision making.

BETWEEN THE LINES

No Right to Vote
Forty-four states deny voting privileges to subgroups of people with mental disorders. The wording in some of the state laws refers to the ineligible individuals as "incompetent," "insane," "incapacitated," "idiot," "lunatic," and of "unsound mind" (Tucker, 2007; Appelbaum, 2000; Moore, 1997). ‹‹

✿In What Other Ways Do the Clinical and Legal Fields Interact?

Mental health and legal professionals may influence each other's work in other ways as well. During the past two decades, their paths have crossed in four key areas: *malpractice suits, professional boundaries, jury selection,* and *psychological research of legal topics.*

Law in Psychology: Malpractice Suits

The number of **malpractice suits** against therapists has risen so sharply in recent years that clinicians have coined terms for the fear of being sued—"litigaphobia" and "litigastress." Claims have been made against clinicians in response to a patient's attempted suicide, sexual activity with a patient, failure to obtain informed consent for a treatment, negligent drug therapy, omission of drug therapy that would speed improvement, improper termination of treatment, and wrongful commitment (Koocher & Keith-Spiegel, 2008; Feldman, Moritz, & Benjamin, 2005).

Improper termination of treatment was at issue in one highly publicized case in 1985. A man being treated for alcohol-related depression was released from a state hospital in Alabama. Two and a half months later, he shot and killed a new acquaintance in a motel lounge. He was convicted of murder and sentenced to life in prison. The victim's father, claiming negligence, filed a civil suit against a psychologist, physician, and social worker at the state hospital, and after two years of legal action a jury awarded him a total of almost $7 million. The state supreme court later overturned the verdict, saying that a state hospital is entitled to a certain degree of immunity in such cases.

Two investigators who studied the effects of this case found that the hospital had released 11 percent of its patients during the six months before the lawsuit was filed, 10 percent during the two years it was being litigated, but only 7 percent during the six months after the verdict (Brodsky & Poythress, 1990). Although judgments about a patient's improvement are supposed to be made on their own merits, they were apparently being affected by a heightened fear of litigation at this hospital.

Similarly, a more recent study of 98 psychiatrists in northern England found that most of them were practicing "defensive medicine" at least some of the time—selecting certain treatments, tests, and procedures to protect themselves from criticism, rather than because such approaches were clearly best for their clients (Beezhold, 2002). Seventy-one of the psychiatrists reported that during the month preceding the study, they had indeed taken some defensive action in their work, including admitting patients to hospitals overcautiously (21 percent) and placing hospitalized patients on higher levels of staff observation (29 percent). Clearly, malpractice suits, or the fear of them, can have significant effects on clinical decisions and practice, for better or for worse (Feldman et al., 2005).

Law in Psychology: Professional Boundaries

During the past several years the legislative and judicial systems have helped to change the *boundaries* that distinguish one clinical profession from another. In particular, they have given more authority to psychologists and blurred the lines that once separated psychiatry from psychology. A growing number of states, for example, are ruling that psychologists can admit patients to the state's hospitals, a power previously held only by psychiatrists (Halloway, 2004).

In 1991, with the blessings of Congress, the Department of Defense (DOD) started to reconsider the biggest difference of all between the practices of psychiatrists and psychologists—the authority to prescribe drugs, a role heretofore denied to psychologists. The DOD set up a trial training program for Army psychologists. Given the apparent success of this trial program, the American Psychological Association later recommended that all psychologists be allowed to attend a special educational program in prescription services and receive certification to prescribe medications if they pass

•**malpractice suit**•A lawsuit charging a therapist with improper conduct in the course of treatment.

Eyewitness error
Psychological research has indicated that eyewitness testimony is often invalid. Here a woman talks to the man whom she had identified as her rapist back in 1984. DNA testing eventually proved that a different person had, in fact, raped her, and the incorrectly identified man was released. In the meantime, however, he had served 11 years of a life sentence in prison.

Chuck Burton/AP Photo

(Poling et al., 2008, 2007). New Mexico and Louisiana and the U.S. territory of Guam now do in fact grant prescription privileges to psychologists who receive special pharmacological training.

As the action by the American Psychological Association in the prescription matter suggests, the legislative and judicial systems do not simply take it upon themselves to interfere in the affairs of clinical professionals. In fact, professional associations of psychologists, psychiatrists, and social workers lobby in state legislatures across the country for laws and decisions that may increase the authority of their members. In each instance, clinicians seek the involvement of other institutions as well, a further demonstration of the way the mental health system interacts with other sectors of our society.

Psychology in Law: Jury Selection

During the past 25 years, more and more lawyers have turned to clinicians for psychological advice in conducting trials (Lieberman & Sales, 2007). A new breed of clinical specialists, known as "jury specialists," has evolved. They advise lawyers about which jury candidates are likely to favor their side and which strategies are likely to win jurors' support during trials. The jury specialists make their suggestions on the basis of surveys, interviews, analyses of jurors' backgrounds and attitudes, and laboratory simulations of upcoming trials. However, it is not clear that a clinician's advice is more valid than a lawyer's instincts or that the judgments of either are particularly accurate.

Psychology in Law: Psychological Research of Legal Topics

Psychologists have sometimes conducted studies and developed expertise on topics of great importance to the criminal justice system. In turn, these studies influence how the system carries out its work. Psychological investigations of two topics, *eyewitness testimony* and *patterns of criminality*, have gained particular attention.

Eyewitness Testimony
In criminal cases testimony by eyewitnesses is extremely influential. It often determines whether a defendant will be found guilty or not guilty. But how accurate is eyewitness testimony? This question has become urgent, as a troubling number of prisoners (many on death row) have recently had their convictions overturned after DNA evidence revealed that they could not have committed the crimes of which they had been convicted. It turns out that 90 percent of such wrongful convictions were based in large part on mistaken eyewitness testimony (Fisher & Reardon, 2007; Wells et al., 1998).

While some witnesses may have reason to lie (for example, prosecutors may reduce an eyewitness's own punishment in exchange for testimony), most eyewitnesses undoubtedly try to tell the truth about what or who they saw. Yet research indicates that eyewitness testimony can be highly unreliable, partly because most crimes are unexpected and fleeting and therefore not the sort of events remembered well (Lindsay et al., 2007; Wells & Loftus, 2006). During the crime, for example, lighting may be poor or other distractions may be present. Witnesses may have had other things on their minds, such as concern for their own safety or that of bystanders. Such concerns may greatly impair later memory.

Moreover, in laboratory studies researchers have found it easy to fool research participants who are trying to recall the details of an observed event simply by introducing misinformation. After a suggestive description by the researcher, stop signs can be transformed into yield signs, white cars into blue ones, and Mickey Mouse into Minnie Mouse (Pickel, 2004; Loftus, 2003). In addition, laboratory studies indicate that persons who are highly suggestible have the poorest recall of observed events (Liebman et al., 2002).

As for identifying actual perpetrators, research has found that accuracy is greatly influenced by the method used in identification (Fisher & Reardon, 2007; Wells & Olsen, 2003). The traditional police lineup, for example, is not always a highly reliable technique, and witnesses' errors committed during lineups tend to stick (Wells, 2008; Haw & Fisher, 2004). Researchers have also learned that witnesses' confidence is not necessarily related to accuracy (Ghetti et al., 2004). Witnesses who are "absolutely certain" may be no more correct in their recollections than those who are only "fairly sure." Yet the degree of a witness's confidence often influences whether jurors believe his or her testimony. In fact, judges often instruct jurors that they can use witness confidence as an indicator of accuracy (Greene & Ellis, 2007; Golding et al., 2003).

Psychological investigations into eyewitnesses' memory have not yet undone the judicial system's reliance on or respect for those witnesses' testimony. Nor should it. The distance between laboratory studies and real-life events is often great, and the implications of such research must be applied carefully (Wagstaff et al., 2003). Still, eyewitness research has begun to make an impact. Studies of hypnosis and of its ability to create false memories, for example, have led most states to prohibit eyewitnesses from testifying about events or details if their recall of the events was initially helped by hypnosis (Knight, Meyer, & Goldstein, 2007).

Patterns of Criminality

A growing number of television shows, movies, and books suggest that clinicians often play a major role in criminal investigations by providing police with *psychological profiles* of perpetrators—"He's probably white, in his 30s, has a history of animal torture, has few friends, and is subject to emotional outbursts." The study of criminal behavior patterns and the practice of profiling has increased in recent years; however, it is not nearly as revealing or influential as the media and the arts would have us believe (Turvey, 2008; Alison & Ogan, 2006).

On the positive side, researchers have gathered information about the psychological features of various criminals, and they have indeed found that perpetrators of particular kinds of crimes—serial murder or serial sexual assault, for example—frequently share a number of traits and background features (see *Psych Watch* on pages 640–641). But while such traits are *often* present, they are not *always* present, and so applying profile information to a particular crime can be wrong and misleading. Increasingly police are consulting psychological profilers, and this practice appears to be helpful as long as the limitations of profiling are recognized and the contributions of profilers are combined with other, often more compelling clues to help the police pursue leads and narrow their investigations (Turvey, 2008; Wright, Hatcher & Willerick, 2006; Palermo et al., 2005).

A reminder of the limitations of profiling information comes from the case of the snipers who terrorized the Washington, D.C., area for three weeks in October 2002, shooting 10 people dead and seriously wounding 3 others (Turvey & McGrath, 2006). Most of the profiling done by FBI psychologists had suggested that the sniper was acting alone; it turned out that the attacks were conducted by a pair: a middle-age man, John Allen Muhammad, and a teenage boy, Lee Boyd Malvo. Although profiles had suggested a young thrill-seeker, Muhammad was 41. Profilers had believed the attacker to be white, but neither Muhammad nor Malvo is white. The prediction of a *male* attacker was correct, but then again female serial killers are relatively rare (Scott, 2008). Given such limitations, it is not surprising that the factors most often leading to the capture of serial murderers are not psychological profiles but, rather, an eyewitness report, a past institutionalization of the murderer, the murderer's *modus operandi,* or *MO* (he or she had committed other crimes in a similar way), or apprehension of the criminal for another, often less serious, crime (Alison & Ogan, 2006).

Misleading profile
Massive numbers of police search for clues outside a Home Depot in Virginia in 2002, hoping to identify and capture the serial sniper who killed 10 people and terrorized residents throughout Washington, D.C., Maryland, and Virginia. As it turned out, psychological profiling in this case offered limited help and, in fact, misled the police in certain respects.

AP Photo/Ron Edmonds

PSYCH WATCH

Serial Murderers: Madness or Badness?

In late 2001, a number of anthrax-tainted letters were mailed to people throughout eastern parts of the United States, leading to 5 deaths and severe illness in 13 other people. The FBI immediately mounted a massive investigation to find the person behind these killings, but the individual eluded them for almost 7 years. Finally, in 2008 their investigation targeted a biodefense researcher named Bruce Ivins. With a murder indictment imminent, Ivins committed suicide by taking an overdose of medications on July 29, 2008. It appeared that the FBI had finally found the perpetrator of these terrible deeds. Media reports offered the following profile of this individual:

> Ivins, 62, worked as a civilian at the U.S. Army Medical Research Institute of Infectious Diseases (USAMRIID)

laboratories at Fort Detrick, MD, for 18 years. . . . A well-respected and award-winning scientist, [he] co-wrote a slew of anthrax studies, including a recent work on the treatment for inhalation anthrax. . . . The son of a pharmacist, Ivins graduated from the University of Cincinnati with a degree in microbiology. He received advanced degrees from there as well. . . .

> As a leading anthrax expert at Fort Detrick, Ivins [had] reportedly helped the FBI analyze the anthrax-containing powder involved in the 2001 incidents. . . . Once the government shifted its investigation [toward him] Ivins' demeanor changed. He seemed stressed out and, in the words of one colleague, was under treatment for depression. The colleague said that Ivins' access to his lab was decreased.

(WEEKS & KNOX, 2008)

Fearing for her safety and that of others, Jean Duley, a psychotherapist with whom

Ivins had been working, filed for a restraining order in a Maryland court just days before his self-inflicted death:

> In the taped testimony, Duley told the court that she had known Ivins for six months and had been meeting with him for group sessions weekly and for individual counseling every other week.

> She said that on July 9, Ivins showed up for a group session "extremely agitated, out of control." She said that when she asked him what was wrong, he said he had obtained a gun and described to the group "a very long and detailed homicidal plan" to kill his co-workers.

> Duley said she then called Ivins' two lawyers and the city police, who went to Ivins' workplace and had him committed to Frederick Memorial Hospital for a psychiatric evaluation. . . .

> [In her testimony, Duley said further,] "As far back as the year 2000, [Ivins] actually attempted to murder

Murder by mail A hazardous-material worker sprays his colleagues as they depart the Senate Office Building after searching the building for traces of anthrax, an acute infectious disease caused by a spore-forming bacterium. In late 2001, a number of anthrax-tainted letters were mailed to people throughout eastern parts of the United States, leading to 5 deaths and severe illness in 13 other people—serial murders that were not solved until 2008.

Photo by Alex Wong/Getty Images

✿What Ethical Principles Guide Mental Health Professionals?

Discussions of the legal and mental health systems may sometimes give the impression that clinicians as a group are uncaring and are considerate of patients' rights and needs only when they are forced to be. This, of course, is not true. Most clinicians care greatly about their clients and strive to help them while at the same time respecting their rights and dignity. In fact, clinicians do not rely exclusively on the legislative and court systems

several other people, [sometimes] through poisoning. He is a revenge killer. When he feels that he's been slighted . . . he plots and actually tries to carry out revenge killings.". . .

She added that Ivins "has been forensically diagnosed by several top psychiatrists as a sociopathic, homicidal killer. I have that in evidence. And through my working with him, I also believe that to be very true."

(DISHNEAU & JORDAN, 2008)

Given Ivins's suicide, some questions remain about his crimes and even about his guilt or innocence. However, the FBI has concluded that this troubled man was indeed the Anthrax killer. As such, he appears to have been one of a growing list of serial killers who have fascinated and horrified Americans over the years: Theodore Kaczynski ("Unabomber"), Ted Bundy, David Berkowitz ("Son of Sam"), Albert DeSalvo, John Wayne Gacy, Jeffrey Dahmer, John Allen Muhammad, John Lee Malvo, Dennis Rader ("BTK killer"), and more. The FBI estimates that there are between 35 and 100 serial killers at large in the United States at any given time (Hickey, 2002). Serial murderers often seem to kill for the sheer thrill of the experience. Clinical theorists do not yet understand these individuals, but they are beginning to use the information that has been gathered about them to speculate on the psychology behind their violence.

Each serial killer follows his or her own pattern (Kocsis, 2008; Homant & Kennedy, 2006), but many of them appear to have certain characteristics in common. Most—but certainly not all—are white males

between 25 and 34 years old, of average to high intelligence, generally clean-cut, smooth-talking, attractive, and skillful manipulators (Kocsis, 2008; Fox & Levin, 2005). Many have no permanent ties to any community and move from place to place in pursuit of the kill. Others, however, maintain a job and social life, and in fact between killings may go to work and spend time with friends. Serial killers typically select their victims carefully. Only 10 to 15 percent of the killers are women (Scott, 2008).

Many serial killers have mental disorders, but they do not typically fit the legal criteria of insanity (Kelleher & Van Nuys, 2002; Ferreira, 2000). Park Dietz, a psychiatrist and highly regarded expert on the subject, offers this explanation:

None of the serial killers I've had the occasion to study or examine has been legally insane, but none has been normal, either. They've all been people who've got mental disorders. But despite their mental disorders, which have to do with their sexual interests and their character, they've been people who knew what they were doing, knew what they were doing was wrong, but chose to do it anyway.

(DOUGLAS, 1996, PP. 344–345)

As a result, the plea of not guilty by reason of insanity is generally unsuccessful for serial killers. This outcome may also be influenced by the concern of communities that a defendant found not guilty by reason of insanity may be released too quickly.

A number of serial killers seem to display severe personality disorders

(Homant & Kennedy, 2006; Whitman & Akutagawa, 2004). Lack of conscience and an utter disregard for people and the rules of society—key features of antisocial personality disorder—are typical. Narcissistic thinking is quite common as well. The feeling of being special may even give the killer an unrealistic belief that he will not get caught (Kocsis, 2008; Wright et al., 2006). Often it is this sense of invincibility that leads to his capture.

Sexual dysfunction and fantasy also seem to play a part (Wright et al., 2006; Arndt et al., 2004). Studies have found that vivid fantasies, often sexual and sadistic, may help drive the killer's behavior (Kocsis, 2008; Homant & Kennedy, 2006). Some clinicians also believe that the killers may be trying to overcome general feelings of powerlessness by controlling, hurting, or eliminating those who are momentarily weaker (Fox & Levin, 2005, 1999). Studies show that many serial killers experienced traumas during their childhood, including having alcoholic, incarcerated, or psychologically unstable parents and experiencing extended separations from their parents; a number of them were abused as children—physically, sexually, and emotionally (Wright et al., 2006; Beasley, 2004; Hickey, 2002).

Despite such profiles and suspicions, clinical theorists do not yet understand why serial killers behave as they do. Thus most agree with Dietz when he asserts, "It's hard to imagine any circumstance under which they should be released to the public again" (Douglas, 1996, p. 349).

to ensure proper and effective clinical practice. They also regulate themselves by continually developing and revising ethical guidelines for members of the clinical field. Many legal decisions do nothing more than place the power of the law behind these already existing professional guidelines.

Each profession within the mental health field has its own **code of ethics** (Koocher & Keith-Spiegel, 2008). The code of the American Psychological Association (2002, 1992) is typical. This code, highly respected by other mental health professionals and public officials, includes specific guidelines:

•**code of ethics**•A body of principles and rules for ethical behavior, designed to guide decisions and actions by members of a profession.

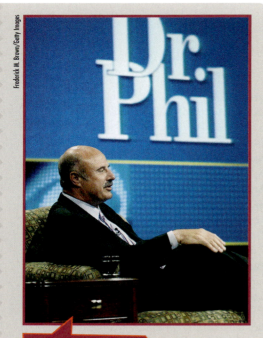

The ethics of giving professional advice
Like enormously popular psychologist Phil McGraw ("Dr. Phil"), many of today's clinicians offer advice to millions of people in books, at workshops, on television and radio, on DVDs, and on the Web. Their presentations often affect people greatly, and so they, too, are bound by the field's ethics code to act responsibly and to base their advice on appropriate psychological theories and findings.

•**confidentiality**•The principle that certain professionals will not divulge the information they obtain from a client.

•**duty to protect**•The principle that therapists must break confidentiality in order to protect a person who may be the intended victim of a client.

1. **Psychologists are permitted to offer advice** in self-help books, on DVDs, on television and radio programs, in newspaper and magazine articles, through mailed material, and in other places, provided they do so responsibly and professionally and base their advice on appropriate psychological literature and practices. Psychologists are bound by these same ethical requirements when they offer advice and ideas on-line, whether on individual Web pages, blogs, electronic groups and bulletin boards, or chat rooms (Koocher & Keith-Spiegel, 2008). Internet-based professional advice has proved difficult to regulate, however, because the number of such offerings keeps getting larger and larger and so many advice-givers (at least one-third of them) do not appear to have any professional training or credentials (Heinlen et al., 2003).

2. **Psychologists may not conduct fraudulent research, plagiarize the work of others, or publish false data.** During the past 25 years cases of scientific fraud or misconduct have been discovered in all of the sciences, including psychology. These acts have led to misunderstandings of important issues, taken scientific research in the wrong direction, and damaged public trust. Unfortunately, the impressions created by false findings may continue to influence the thinking of both the public and other scientists for years.

3. **Psychologists must acknowledge their limitations** with regard to patients who are disabled or whose gender, ethnicity, language, socioeconomic status, or sexual orientation differs from that of the therapist (Philogene, 2004). This guideline often requires psychotherapists to obtain additional training or supervision, consult with more knowledgeable colleagues, or refer clients to more appropriate professionals.

4. **Psychologists who make evaluations and testify in legal cases must base their assessments on sufficient information and substantiate their findings appropriately** (Koocher & Keith-Spiegel, 2008; Costanzo et al., 2007). If an adequate examination of the individual in question is not possible, psychologists must make clear the limited nature of their testimony.

5. **Psychologists may not take advantage of clients and students, sexually or otherwise.** This guideline relates to the widespread social problem of sexual harassment, as well as the problem of therapists who take sexual advantage of clients in therapy. The code specifically forbids a sexual relationship with a present or former therapy client for at least two years after the end of treatment; and even then such a relationship is permitted only in "the most unusual circumstances." Furthermore, psychologists may not accept as clients people with whom they have previously had a sexual relationship.

   Clients may suffer great emotional damage from sexual involvement with their therapists (Koocher & Keith-Spiegel, 2008; Pope & Wedding, 2008). A number of therapists report treating clients whose primary problem is that they previously experienced some form of sexual misconduct by a therapist. Many such clients experience the symptoms of posttraumatic stress disorder or major depressive disorder.

   How many therapists actually have a sexual relationship with a client? On the basis of various surveys, reviewers have estimated that some form of sexual misconduct with patients may be engaged in by around 5 to 6 percent of today's therapists, down from 10 percent more than a decade ago (Koocher & Keith-Spiegel, 2008; Pope & Wedding, 2008). Although the vast majority of therapists do not engage in sexual behavior of any kind with clients, their ability to control private feelings is apparently another matter. In surveys, close to 90 percent of therapists reported having been sexually attracted to a client, at least on occasion (Koocher & Keith-Spiegel, 2008; Pope & Vasquez, 2007; Pope et al., 2006). Although few of these therapists acted on their feelings, most of them felt guilty, anxious, or concerned about the attraction. Given such sexual issues, it is not surprising that sexual ethics training is given high priority in many of today's clinical training programs (Lamb et al., 2003).

6. **Psychologists must adhere to the principle of confidentiality.** All of the state and federal courts have upheld laws protecting therapist **confidentiality.** For peace of mind and to ensure effective therapy, clients must be able to trust that their private exchanges with a therapist will not be repeated to others (Green & Bloch, 2006). There are times, however, when the principle of confidentiality must be compromised (Koocher & Keith-Spiegel, 2008). A therapist in training, for example, must discuss cases on a regular basis with a supervisor. Clients, in turn, must be informed when such discussions are occurring.

A second exception arises in cases of outpatients who are clearly dangerous. The 1976 case of *Tarasoff v. Regents of the University of California,* one of the most important cases to affect client–therapist relationships, concerned an outpatient at a University of California hospital. He had confided to his therapist that he wanted to harm his former girlfriend, Tanya Tarasoff. Several days after ending therapy, the former patient fulfilled his promise. He stabbed Tanya Tarasoff to death.

Should confidentiality have been broken in this case? The therapist, in fact, felt that it should. Campus police were notified, but the patient was released after some questioning. In their suit against the hospital and therapist, the victim's parents argued that the therapist should have also warned them and their daughter that the patient intended to harm Ms. Tarasoff. The California Supreme Court agreed: "The protective privilege ends where the public peril begins."

The current code of ethics for psychologists thus declares that therapists have a **duty to protect**—a responsibility to break confidentiality, even without the client's consent, when it is necessary "to protect the client or others from harm." Since the *Tarasoff* ruling, California's courts further have held that therapists must also protect people who are close to a client's intended victim and thus in danger. A child, for example, is likely to be at risk when a client plans to assault the child's mother. In addition, the California courts have ruled that therapists must act to protect people even when information about the dangerousness of a client is received from the client's family, rather than from the client (Thomas, 2005). Many, but not all, states have adopted the California court rulings or similar ones, and a number have passed "duty to protect" bills that clarify the rules of confidentiality for therapists and protect them from certain civil suits (Koocher & Keith-Spiegel, 2008).

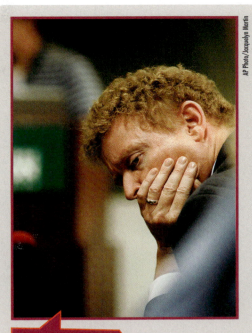

Failure to protect
The father of one of the 32 students and teachers slain in the 2007 massacre at Virginia Tech listens to a review panel investigating the shootings. The panel blamed mental health professionals and school administrators for failing to notice clear warning signs of psychological deterioration displayed by killer Seung-Hui Cho for two years prior to the shooting and for failing to force him into proper treatment.

✿Mental Health, Business, and Economics

The legislative and judicial systems are not the only social institutions with which mental health professionals interact. The *business* and *economic* fields are two other sectors that influence and are influenced by clinical practice and study. To be sure, health care in all its varieties is itself a business, and many decisions in the clinical field are based on economic considerations, but the mental health field in turn influences the conduct of business and economic programs.

Bringing Mental Health Services to the Workplace

It has been estimated that untreated psychological disorders cost the United States $105 billion in lost productivity each year (Armour, 2006). Collectively, such disorders are among the 10 leading categories of work-related disorders and injuries (Kessler & Stang, 2006; Kemp, 1994). In fact, almost 12 percent of all employees are said to experience psychological problems that are serious enough to affect their work. Psychological problems contribute to 60 percent of all absenteeism from work, up to 90 percent of industrial accidents, and to 65 percent of work terminations. Alcohol abuse and other substance-related disorders are particularly damaging, increasing absences by as much as six times, accidents by four times, and workers' compensation claims by five times (Martin, Kraft, & Roman, 1994; Wright, 1984). The business world has often turned to clinical professionals to help prevent and correct such problems (Wang, 2007). Two

BETWEEN THE LINES

Business and Mental Health

The American Psychiatric Association receives $13 million annually from advertising by pharmaceutical companies ‹‹

The American Medical Association receives $20 million annually from selling its membership list to pharmaceutical companies ‹‹

(Thomas, 2004)

common means of providing mental health care in the workplace are *employee assistance programs* and *problem-solving seminars*.

Employee assistance programs, mental health services made available by a place of business, are run either by mental health professionals who work directly for a company or by outside mental health agencies (Armour, 2006; Jacobson, 2005). Companies publicize such programs at the work site, educate workers about psychological dysfunctioning, and teach supervisors how to identify workers who are having psychological problems. Businesses believe that employee assistance programs save them money in the long run by preventing psychological problems from interfering with work performance and by reducing employee insurance claims, although these beliefs have not undergone extensive testing (Wang, 2007; Kessler & Stang, 2006).

Stress-reduction and problem-solving seminars are workshops or group sessions in which mental health professionals teach employees techniques for coping, solving problems, and handling and reducing stress (Russell, 2007; Daw, 2001). Programs of this kind are just as likely to be aimed at high-level executives as at assembly-line workers. Often employees are required to attend such workshops, which may run for several days, and are given time off from their jobs to do so.

David Butow/Redux

The drum circle
At Toyota's headquarters, a drum "facilitator" leads a group of executives as they generate various rhythms on hand drums. As the individuals produce and listen to such rhythms, they are expected to experience reductions in stress, learn to operate in sync with one another, and become better at resolving problems. This nontraditional version of stress-reduction and problem-solving seminars has been adopted by numerous corporations around the world.

The Economics of Mental Health

We have already seen how economic decisions by the government may influence the clinical field's treatment of people with severe mental disorders. For example, the desire of the state and federal governments to reduce costs was an important consideration in the country's deinstitutionalization movement, which contributed to the premature release of hospital patients into the community. Economic decisions by government agencies may affect other kinds of clients and treatment programs as well.

As you read in Chapter 15, government funding for services to people with psychological disorders has risen sharply over the past four decades, from $1 billion in 1963 to around $104 billion today (Mark et al., 2008, 2005; Redick et al., 1992). On the other hand, much of that money is spent on income support, housing subsidies, and other such expenses rather than directly on mental health medications and services (Sperling, 2005). Government funding currently covers around two-thirds of all mental health services, leaving a mental health expense of tens of billions of dollars for individual patients and their private insurance companies (Mark et al, 2008, 2005).

This large economic role of private insurance companies has had a significant effect on the way clinicians go about their work. As you'll remember from Chapter 1, to reduce their expenses and keep track of their payments, most of these companies have developed **managed care programs,** in which the insurance company decides such questions as which therapists clients may choose, the cost of sessions, and the number of sessions for which a client may be reimbursed (Koocher & Keith-Spiegel, 2008). These and other insurance plans may also control expenses through the use of **peer review systems,** in which clinicians who work for the insurance company periodically review a client's treatment program and recommend that insurance benefits be either continued or stopped. Typically, insurers require reports or session notes from the therapist, often including intimate personal information about the patient.

Many therapists and clients dislike managed care programs and peer reviews (Koocher & Keith-Spiegel, 2008; Mechanic, 2004). They believe that the reports required of therapists breach confidentiality, even when efforts are made to protect anonymity, and that the value of therapy in a given case is sometimes difficult to convey in a brief report. They also argue that the priorities of managed care programs inevitably shorten therapy, even if longer-term treatment would be advisable in particular cases. The priorities may also favor treatments that offer short-term results (for example, drug therapy) over more costly approaches that might achieve a more promising long-term improvement. As in the medical field, disturbing stories are often heard about patients who are prematurely cut off from mental health services by their managed care programs. In short, many clinicians fear that the current system amounts to regulation of therapy by insurance companies rather than by therapists.

The Person within the Profession

The actions of clinical researchers and practitioners not only influence and are influenced by other institutions but also are closely tied to their personal needs and goals. You have seen that the human strengths, imperfections, wisdom, and clumsiness of clinical professionals may affect their theoretical orientations, their interactions with clients, and the kinds of clients with whom they choose to work. You have also seen how personal leanings may sometimes override professional standards and scruples and, in extreme cases, lead clinical scientists to commit research fraud and clinical practitioners to engage in sexual misconduct with clients.

"Look, you're not the only one with problems."

Surveys of the mental health of therapists have found that as many as 84 percent report having been in therapy at least once (Klitzman, 2008; Pope et al., 2006; Pope & Brown, 1996; Pope & Tabachnick, 1994). Their reasons are largely the same as those of other clients, with emotional problems, depression, and anxiety topping the list. And, like other people, therapists often are reluctant to acknowledge their psychological problems, partly because of the stigma that still exists with regard to having certain psychological disorders (see *The Media Speaks* on pages 646–647). It is not clear why so many therapists seem to experience psychological problems. Perhaps their jobs are highly stressful; indeed, research suggests that therapists often experience some degree of job burnout (Rosenberg & Pace, 2006). Or perhaps therapists are simply more aware of their own negative feelings or are more likely to pursue treatment for their problems. Alternatively, individuals with personal concerns may be more inclined to choose clinical work as a profession. Whatever the reason, clinicians bring to their work a set of psychological issues that may, along with other important factors, affect how they listen and respond to clients (Friedman, 2008).

The science and profession of abnormal psychology seek to understand, predict, and change abnormal functioning. But we must not lose sight of the broader context in which its activities are conducted. Mental health researchers and clinicians are human beings, living within a society of human beings, working to serve human beings. The mixture of discovery, misdirection, promise, and frustration that you have encountered throughout this book is thus to be expected. When you think about it, could the study and treatment of human behavior really proceed in any other way?

PUTTING IT..... together

Operating within a Larger System

At one time clinical researchers and professionals conducted their work largely in isolation. Today, however, their activities have numerous ties to the legislative, judicial, economic, and other established systems. One reason for this growing interconnectedness is that the clinical field has achieved a high level of respect and acceptance in our society. Clinicians now serve millions of people in many ways. They have much to say about almost every aspect of society, from education to ecology, and are widely looked to as sources of expertise. When a field achieves such prominence, it inevitably affects how other institutions are run. It also attracts public scrutiny, and various institutions begin to keep an eye on its activities.

•**employee assistance program**•A mental health program offered by a business to its employees.

•**stress-reduction and problem-solving seminar**•A workshop or series of group sessions offered by a business in which mental health professionals teach employees how to cope with and solve problems and reduce stress.

•**managed care program**•An insurance program in which the insurance company decides the cost, method, provider, and length of treatment.

•**peer review system**•A system by which clinicians paid by an insurance company may periodically review a patient's progress and recommend the continuation or termination of insurance benefits.

The Media SPEAKS

HOME · SEND · EXPLORE

"Mad Pride" Fights a Stigma

BY GABRIELLE GLASER, THE *NEW YORK TIMES*, MAY 11, 2008

In the YouTube video, Liz Spikol is smiling and animated, the light glinting off her large hoop earrings. Deadpan, she holds up a diaper. It is not, she explains, a hygienic item for a giantess, but rather a prop to illustrate how much control people lose when they undergo electroconvulsive therapy, or ECT, as she did 12 years ago.

In other videos and blog postings, Ms. Spikol, a 39-year-old writer in Philadelphia who has bipolar disorder, describes a period of psychosis so severe she jumped out of her mother's car and ran away like a scared dog.

In lectures across the country, Elyn Saks, a law professor and associate dean at the University of Southern California, recounts the florid visions she has experienced during her lifelong battle with schizophrenia—dancing ashtrays, houses that spoke to her—and hospitalizations where she was strapped down with leather restraints and force-fed medications.

Like many Americans who have severe forms of mental illness such as schizophrenia and bipolar disorder, Ms. Saks and Ms. Spikol are speaking candidly and publicly about their demons. Their frank talk is part of a conversation about mental illness (or as some prefer to put it, "extreme mental states") that stretches from college campuses to community health centers, from YouTube to online forums.

"Until now, the acceptance of mental illness has pretty much stopped at depression," said Charles Barber, a lecturer in psychiatry at the Yale School of Medicine. "But a newer generation, fueled by the Internet and other sophisticated delivery systems, is saying, 'We deserve to be heard, too.'"

Just as gay-rights activists reclaimed the word queer as a badge of honor rather than a slur, these advocates proudly call themselves mad; they say their conditions do not preclude them from productive lives. Mad pride events, organized by loosely connected groups in at least seven countries including Australia, South Africa and the United States, draw thousands of participants. . . . Recent mad pride activities include a Mad Pride Cabaret in Vancouver, British Columbia; a Mad Pride March in Accra, Ghana; and a Bonkersfest in London that drew 3,000 participants. . . .

"It used to be you were labeled with your diagnosis and that was it; you were marginalized," said Molly Sprengelmeyer, an organizer for . . . a mad pride group in North Carolina. "If people found out, it was a death sentence, professionally and socially." She added, "We are hoping to change all that by talking."

The confessional mood encouraged by memoirs and blogs, as well as the self-help advocacy movement in mental health, have deepened the understanding of bipolar disorder and schizophrenia.. . . . and related illnesses. In recent years, groups have started antistigma campaigns, and even the federal government embraces the message, with an ad campaign aimed at young adults to encourage them to support friends with mental illness. . . .

Many [clinicians] now recognize that patients' candid discussions of their experiences can help their recoveries. "Problems are created when people don't talk to each other," said Dr. Robert W. Buchanan, the chief of the Outpatient Research Program at the Maryland Psychiatric Research Center. "It's critical to have an open conversation."

Ms. Spikol writes about her experiences with bipolar disorder in The Philadelphia Weekly, and posts videos on her blog, the Trouble With Spikol. . . . Thousands have watched her joke about her weight gain and loss of libido, and her giggle-

---

Today, when people with psychological problems seek help from a therapist, they are entering a complex system consisting of many interconnected parts. Just as their personal problems have grown within a social structure, so will their treatment be affected by the various parts of a larger system—the therapist's values and needs, legal and economic forces, societal attitudes, and yet other forces. These many forces influence clinical research as well.

The effects of this larger system on an individual's psychological needs can be positive or negative, like a family's impact on each of its members. When the system protects a client's rights and confidentiality, for example, it is serving the client well. When economic, legal, or other societal forces limit treatment options, cut off treatment prematurely, or stigmatize a person, the system is adding to the person's problems.

Because of the enormous growth and impact of the mental health profession in our society, it is important that we understand its strengths and weaknesses. As you have seen throughout this book, the field has gathered much knowledge, especially during the past several decades. What mental health professionals do not know and cannot do, how-

SEARCH

"Mad pride" Writer and blogger Liz Spikol sits in front of a laptop that displays her Web site. With a combination of wit and self-revelation, Spikol, who suffers from bipolar disorder, speaks out on her trials and tribulations—seeking to increase awareness and remove the stigma of mental disorders.

punctuated portrayal of ECT. But another video shows her face pale and her eyes red-rimmed as she reflects on the dark period in which she couldn't care for herself, or even shower. "I knew I was crazy but also sane enough to know that I couldn't make myself sane," she says in the video.

In a telephone interview, she described one medication that made her salivate so profusely she needed towels to mop it up. "Of course it's heartbreaking if you let it be," she said. "But it's also inherently funny. I'd sit there watching TV and drool so much, it would drip on the couch." Ms. Spikol said she has a kind doctor who treats her with respect, and she takes her pharmaceutical drugs to stabilize her mood. . . .

Ms. Saks, the U.S.C. professor, who recently published a memoir, "The Center Cannot Hold: My Journey Through Madness," has come to accept her illness. She manages her symptoms with a regimen that includes psychoanalysis and medication. But stigma, she said, is never far away. She said she waited until she had tenure at U.S.C. before going public with her experience. When she was hospitalized for cancer some years ago, she was lavished with flowers. During periods of mental illness, though, only good friends have reached out to her.

Ms. Saks said she hopes to help others in her position, find tolerance, especially those with fewer resources. "I have the kind of life that anybody, mentally ill or not, would want: a good place to live, nice friends, loved ones," she said. "For an unlucky person," Ms. Saks said, "I'm very lucky."

ever, still outweigh what they do know and can do. Everyone who turns to the clinical field—directly or indirectly—must recognize that it is young and imperfect. Society is vastly curious about behavior and often in need of information and help. What we as a society must remember, however, is that the field is still *putting it all together.*

⟨⟨⟨(SUMMING UP)⟩⟩⟩

○ **The legal system and the mental health field** The mental health profession interacts with the *legislative and judicial systems* in two key ways. First, clinicians help assess the mental stability of people accused of crimes. Second, the legislative and judicial systems help regulate mental health care. *pp. 619–620*

continued

○ **Criminal commitment** The punishment of persons convicted of crimes depends on the assumption that individuals are *responsible for their acts* and are *capable of defending themselves in court*. Evaluations by clinicians may help judges and juries decide the culpability of defendants and sometimes result in criminal commitment.

If defendants are judged to have been *mentally unstable at the time they committed a crime,* they may be found *not guilty by reason of insanity* and placed in a treatment facility rather than a prison. "Insanity" is a legal term, one defined by legislators, not by clinicians. In federal courts and about half the state courts, insanity is judged in accordance with the *M'Naghten test,* which holds that defendants were insane at the time of a criminal act if they did not know the nature or quality of the act or did not know right from wrong at the time they committed it. Other states use the broader *American Law Institute test.*

The insanity defense has been criticized on several grounds, and some states have added an additional option, *guilty but mentally ill.* Defendants who receive this verdict are sentenced to prison with the proviso that they will also receive psychological treatment. Still another verdict option is *guilty with diminished capacity.* A related category consists of convicted *sex offenders,* who are considered in some states to have a mental disorder and are therefore assigned to treatment in a mental health facility.

Regardless of their state of mind at the time of the crime, defendants may be found *mentally incompetent to stand trial,* that is, incapable of fully understanding the charges or legal proceedings that confront them. If so, they are typically sent to a mental hospital until they are competent to stand trial. *pp. 621–629*

○ **Civil commitment** The legal system also influences the clinical profession. First, courts may be called upon to commit noncriminals to mental hospitals for treatment, a process called *civil commitment.* Society allows involuntary commitment of people considered to be *in need of treatment* and *dangerous to themselves or others.* Laws governing civil commitment procedures vary from state to state, but a *minimum standard of proof*—clear and convincing evidence of the necessity of commitment—has been defined by the Supreme Court. *pp. 629–634*

○ **Protecting patients' rights** The courts and legislatures significantly affect the mental health profession by specifying legal rights to which patients are entitled. The rights that have received the most attention are the *right to treatment* and the *right to refuse treatment. pp. 634–636*

○ **Other clinical-legal interactions** Mental health and legal professionals also cross paths in four other areas. First, *malpractice suits* against therapists have increased in recent years. Second, the legislative and judicial systems help define *professional boundaries.* Third, lawyers may solicit the advice of mental health professionals regarding the *selection of jurors* and case strategies. Fourth, psychologists may *investigate legal phenomena* such as *eyewitness testimony* and *patterns of criminality. pp. 637–640*

○ **Ethical principles** Each clinical profession has a *code of ethics.* The psychologists' code includes prohibitions against *engaging in fraudulent research* and against *taking advantage of clients and students, sexually or otherwise.* It also establishes guidelines for respecting patient *confidentiality.* The case of *Tarasoff v. Regents of the University of California* helped to determine the circumstances in which therapists have a *duty to protect* the client or others from harm and must break confidentiality. *pp. 640–643*

○ **Mental health, business, and economics** Clinical practice and study also intersect with the business and economic worlds. Clinicians often help to address psychological problems in the workplace, for example, through *employee assistance programs* and *stress-reduction and problem-solving seminars.*

Reductions in government funding of clinical services have left much of the expense for these services to be paid by insurance companies. Private insurance companies are setting up *managed care programs* whose structure and reimbursement procedures influence and often reduce the duration and focus of therapy. Their procedures, which include *peer review systems,* may also compromise patient confidentiality and the quality of therapy services. *pp. 643–645*

○ **The person within the profession** Mental health activities are affected by the personal needs, values, and goals of the human beings who provide the clinical services. These factors inevitably affect the choice, direction, and even quality of their work. *p. 645*

⟫ CRITICAL THOUGHTS ⟫

1. In some states, the defense must prove that a defendant was not guilty by reason of insanity, while in other states the prosecution must prove that a defendant making this plea was not insane. Which burden of proof is more appropriate? *pp. 620–622*

2. After a patient has been criminally committed to an institution, why might a clinician be reluctant to declare that the person is mentally stable and unlikely to commit the same crime again, even if the patient shows significant improvement? *pp. 622–623*

3. How are people who have been institutionalized viewed and treated by others today? Is the stigma of hospitalization a legitimate argument against civil commitment? *pp. 629–634*

4. How might lingering anxiety affect the behavior and effectiveness of clinicians who have been attacked? *p. 630*

5. Most psychiatrists do not want psychologists to be granted the authority to prescribe psychotropic medications. Surprisingly, many psychologists oppose the idea as well (Poling et al., 2008, 2007). Why might they take this position? *pp. 637–638*

6. Although more than two-thirds of therapists have felt sexually attracted to a client on at least one occasion, only around one-third of clients have ever felt sexually attracted to their therapist (Pope & Brown, 1996). How might these different reactions be explained? *p. 642*

❧ cyberstudy ❧   SEARCH

Search the *Abnormal Psychology* Video Tool Kit
www.worthpublishers.com/apvtk

▲ Chapter 19 Video Cases
 Jeffrey Dahmer: Not Guilty by Reason of Insanity?
 Forcing People into Mental Health Treatment
 When Treatment Leads to Execution
▲ Video case discussions, study guides, and questions

Log on to the Comer Web Page
www.worthpublishers.com/comer

▲ Chapter 19 outline, learning objectives, research exercises, study tools, and practice test questions
▲ Additional Chapter 19 case studies, Web links, and FAQs

glossary

ABAB design A single-subject experimental design in which behavior is measured during a baseline period, after a treatment has been applied, after baseline conditions have been reintroduced, and after the treatment has been reintroduced. Also called a *reversal design*.

Abnormal psychology The scientific study of abnormal behavior in order to describe, predict, explain, and change abnormal patterns of functioning.

Acetylcholine A neurotransmitter that has been linked to depression and dementia.

Acute stress disorder An anxiety disorder in which fear and related symptoms are experienced soon after a traumatic event and last less than a month.

Addiction Physical dependence on a substance, marked by such features as tolerance, withdrawal symptoms during abstinence, or both.

Affect An experience of emotion or mood.

Aftercare A program of posthospitalization care and treatment in the community.

Agoraphobia An anxiety disorder in which a person is afraid to be in places or situations from which escape might be difficult (or embarrassing) or help unavailable if panic-like symptoms were to occur.

Agranulocytosis A life-threatening reduction in white blood cells. This condition is sometimes produced by clozapine, one of the atypical antipsychotic drugs.

Alcohol Any beverage containing ethyl alcohol, including beer, wine, and liquor.

Alcohol dehydrogenase An enzyme that breaks down alcohol in the stomach before it enters the blood.

Alcoholics Anonymous (AA) A self-help organization that provides support and guidance for persons with patterns of alcohol abuse or dependence.

Alcoholism A pattern of behavior in which a person repeatedly abuses or develops a dependence on alcohol.

Alogia A decrease in speech or speech content; a symptom of schizophrenia. Also known as *poverty of speech*.

Alprazolam A benzodiazepine drug shown to be effective in the treatment of anxiety disorders. Marketed as *Xanax*.

Altruistic suicide Suicide committed by people who intentionally sacrifice their lives for the well-being of society.

Alzheimer's disease The most common form of dementia, usually occurring after the age of 65.

Amenorrhea The absence of menstrual cycles.

American Law Institute (ALI) test A legal test for insanity that holds people to be insane at the time of committing a crime if, because of a mental disorder, they did not know right from wrong or could not resist an uncontrollable impulse to act.

Amnesia Loss of memory.

Amnestic disorders Organic disorders in which the primary symptom is memory loss.

Amniocentesis A prenatal procedure used to test the amniotic fluid that surrounds the fetus for the possibility of birth defects.

Amphetamine A stimulant drug that is manufactured in the laboratory.

Amygdala A structure in the brain that plays a key role in emotion and memory.

Anaclitic depression A pattern of depressed behavior found among very young children that is caused by separation from the mother.

Analog observation A method for observing behavior in which people are observed in artificial settings such as clinicians' offices or laboratories.

Analogue experiment A research method in which the experimenter produces abnormal-like behavior in laboratory subjects and then conducts experiments on the subjects.

Anal stage In psychoanalytic theory, the second 18 months of life, during which the child's focus of pleasure shifts to the anus.

Anesthesia A lessening or loss of sensation of touch or for pain.

Anomic suicide Suicide committed by individuals whose social environment fails to provide stability, thus leaving them without a sense of belonging.

Anorexia nervosa A disorder marked by the pursuit of extreme thinness and by an extreme loss of weight.

Anoxia A complication of birth in which the baby is deprived of oxygen.

Antabuse (disulfiram) A drug that causes intense nausea, vomiting, increased heart rate, and dizziness when taken with alcohol. It is often taken by people who are trying to refrain from drinking alcohol.

Antagonist drugs Drugs that block or change the effects of an addictive drug.

Anterograde amnesia The inability to remember new information acquired after the event that triggered amnesia.

Antianxiety drugs Psychotropic drugs that help reduce tension and anxiety. Also called *minor tranquilizers* or *anxiolytics*.

Antibipolar drugs Psychotropic drugs that help stabilize the moods of people suffering from a bipolar mood disorder. Also known as *mood stabilizing drugs*.

Antibodies Bodily chemicals that seek out and destroy foreign invaders such as bacteria or viruses.

Antidepressant drugs Psychotropic drugs that improve the mood of people with depression.

Antigen A foreign invader of the body, such as a bacterium or virus.

Antipsychotic drugs Drugs that help correct grossly confused or distorted thinking, such as that found in psychotic disorders.

Antisocial personality disorder A personality disorder marked by a general pattern of disregard for and violation of other people's rights.

Anxiety The central nervous system's physiological and emotional response to a vague sense of threat or danger.

Anxiety disorder A disorder in which anxiety is a central symptom.

Anxiety sensitivity A tendency of certain persons to focus on their bodily sensations, assess them illogically, and interpret them as harmful.

Anxiolytics Drugs that reduce anxiety.

Arbitrary inference An error in logic in which a person draws negative conclusions on the basis of little or even contrary evidence.

Asperger's disorder A pervasive developmental disorder in which individuals display profound social impairment yet maintain a relatively high level of cognitive functioning and language skills. Also known as *Asperger's syndrome*.

Assertiveness training A cognitive-behavioral approach to increasing assertive behavior that is socially desirable.

Assessment The process of collecting and interpreting relevant information about a client or subject.

Asthma A medical problem marked by narrowing of the trachea and bronchi, which results in shortness of breath, wheezing, coughing, and a choking sensation.

Asylum A type of institution first established in the sixteenth century to provide care for persons with mental disorders. Most became virtual prisons.

Attention-deficit/hyperactivity disorder (ADHD) A disorder in which persons are unable to focus their attention, behave overactively and impulsively, or both.

Attribution An explanation of things we see going on around us that points to particular causes.

Atypical antipsychotic drugs A new group of antipsychotic drugs that operate in a biological manner that is different from the way traditional antipsychotic drugs operate.

Auditory hallucination A hallucination in which a person hears sounds or voices that are not actually present.

Augmentative communication system A method for teaching communication skills to individuals with autism, mental retardation, or cerebral palsy by pointing to pictures, symbols, letters, or words on a communication board or computer.

Aura A warning sensation that may precede a migraine headache.

Autistic disorder A pervasive developmental disorder marked by extreme unresponsiveness to others, poor communication skills, and highly repetitive and rigid behavior. Also known as *autism*.

Autoerotic asphyxia A fatal lack of oxygen that persons may unintentionally produce while hanging, suffocating, or strangling themselves during masturbation.

Automatic thoughts Numerous unpleasant thoughts that come into the mind, helping to cause or maintain depression, anxiety, or other forms of psychological dysfunction.

Autonomic nervous system (ANS) The network of nerve fibers that connect the central nervous system to all the other organs of the body.

Aversion therapy A treatment based on the principles of classical conditioning in which people are repeatedly presented with shocks or another unpleasant stimulus while they are performing undesirable behaviors such as taking a drug.

Avoidant personality disorder A personality disorder in which an individual is consistently uncomfortable and restrained in social situations, overwhelmed by feelings of inadequacy, and extremely sensitive to negative evaluation.

Avolition A symptom of schizophrenia marked by apathy and an inability to start or complete a course of action.

Axon A long fiber extending from the body of a neuron.

Baroreceptors Sensitive nerves in the blood vessels that are responsible for signaling the brain that blood pressure is becoming too high.

Baseline data An individual's initial response level on a test or scale.

Basic irrational assumptions According to Albert Ellis, the inaccurate and inappropriate beliefs held by people with various psychological problems.

Battery A series of tests, each of which measures a specific skill area.

B-cell A lymphocyte that produces antibodies.

Behavioral medicine A field of treatment that combines psychological and physical interventions to treat or prevent medical problems.

Behavioral model A theoretical perspective that emphasizes behavior and the ways in which it is learned.

Behavioral self-control training (BSCT) A cognitive-behavioral approach to treating alcohol abuse and dependence in which people are taught to keep track of their drinking behavior and to apply coping strategies in situations that typically trigger excessive drinking.

Behavioral therapy A therapeutic approach that seeks to identify problem-causing behaviors and change them. Also known as *behavior modification*.

Behaviors The responses an organism makes to its environment.

Bender Visual-Motor Gestalt Test A neuropsychological test in which a subject is asked to copy a set of nine simple designs and later reproduce the designs from memory.

Benzodiazepines The most common group of antianxiety drugs, including Valium and Xanax.

Bereavement The process of working through the grief that one feels when a loved one dies.

Beta-amyloid protein A small molecule that forms sphere-shaped deposits called senile plaques, linked to aging and to Alzheimer's disease.

Bilateral electroconvulsive therapy (ECT) A form of electroconvulsive therapy in which one electrode is applied to each side of the forehead and electrical current is passed through the brain.

Binge An episode of uncontrollable eating during which a person eats a very large quantity of food.

Binge-eating disorder A type of eating disorder in which a person displays a pattern of binge eating without accompanying compensatory behaviors.

Binge-eating/purging-type anorexia nervosa A type of anorexia nervosa in which people have eating binges but still lose excessive weight by forcing themselves to vomit after meals or by abusing laxatives or diuretics.

Biofeedback training A treatment technique in which a person is given information about physiological reactions as they occur and learns to control the responses voluntarily.

Biological challenge test A procedure used to produce panic in subjects or clients by having them exercise vigorously or perform other tasks in the presence of a researcher or therapist.

Biological model The theoretical perspective that points to biological processes as the key to human behavior.

Biological therapy The use of physical and chemical procedures to help people overcome psychological problems.

Biopsychosocial theories Explanations that attribute the cause of abnormality to an interaction of genetic, biological, developmental, emotional, behavioral, cognitive, social, and societal influences.

Bipolar disorder A disorder marked by alternating or intermixed periods of mania and depression.

Bipolar I disorder A type of bipolar disorder in which a person experiences full manic and major depressive episodes.

Bipolar II disorder A type of bipolar disorder in which a person experiences mildly manic (hypomanic) episodes and major depressive episodes.

Birth complications Problematic biological conditions during birth that can affect the physical and psychological well-being of the child.

Blind design An experiment in which subjects do not know whether they are in the experimental or the control condition.

Blunted affect A symptom of schizophrenia in which a person shows less emotion than most people.

Body dysmorphic disorder A somatoform disorder marked by excessive worry that some aspect of one's physical appearance is defective. Also known as *dysmorphophobia*.

Borderline personality disorder A personality disorder in which an individual displays repeated instability in interpersonal relationships, self-image, and mood, as well as extremely impulsive behavior.

Brain region A distinct area of the brain formed by a large group of neurons.

Brain wave The fluctuations of electrical potential that are produced by neurons in the brain.

Breathing-related sleep disorder A sleep disorder in which sleep is frequently disrupted by a breathing problem, causing excessive sleepiness or insomnia.

Brief psychotic disorder Psychotic symptoms that appear suddenly after a very stressful event or a period of emotional turmoil and last anywhere from a few hours to a month.

Bulimia nervosa A disorder marked by frequent eating binges that are followed by forced vomiting or other extreme compensatory behaviors. Also known as *binge-purge syndrome*.

Cannabis drugs Drugs produced from the different varieties of the hemp plant, *Cannabis sativa*. They cause a mixture of hallucinogenic, depressant, and stimulant effects.

Case manager A community therapist who offers a full range of services for persons with schizophrenia or other severe disorders, including therapy, advice, medication, guidance, and protection of patients' rights.

Case study A detailed account of a person's life and psychological problems.

Catatonia A pattern of extreme psychomotor symptoms, found in some forms of schizophrenia, that may include catatonic stupor, rigidity, or posturing.

Catatonic excitement A form of catatonia in which a person moves excitedly, sometimes with wild waving of the arms and legs.

Catatonic stupor A symptom associated with schizophrenia in which a person becomes almost totally unresponsive to the environment, remaining motionless and silent for long stretches of time.

Catatonic type of schizophrenia A type of schizophrenia dominated by severe psychomotor disturbances.

Catharsis The reliving of past repressed feelings in order to settle internal conflicts and overcome problems.

Caudate nuclei Structures in the brain, within the region known as the basal ganglia, that help convert sensory information into thoughts and actions.

Central nervous system The brain and spinal cord.

Cerebellum An area of the brain that coordinates movement in the body and perhaps helps control a person's rapid attention to things.

Checking compulsion A compulsion in which people feel compelled to check the same things over and over.

Child abuse The nonaccidental use of excessive physical or psychological force by an adult on a child, often aimed at hurting or destroying the child.

Chlorpromazine A phenothiazine drug commonly used for treating schizophrenia. Marketed as *Thorazine*.

Chromosomes The structures located within a cell that contain genes.

Chronic headaches Frequent intense aches in the head or neck that are not caused by another medical disorder.

Circadian rhythms Internal "clocks" consisting of repeated biological fluctuations.

Circadian rhythm sleep disorder A sleep disorder caused by a mismatch between the sleep-wake cycle in a person's environment and the person's own circadian sleep-wake cycle.

Cirrhosis An irreversible condition, often caused by excessive drinking, in which the liver becomes scarred and begins to change in anatomy and functioning.

Civil commitment A legal process by which certain individuals can be forced to undergo mental health treatment.

Clang A rhyme used by some persons with schizophrenia as a guide to forming thoughts and statements.

Classical conditioning A process of learning by temporal association in which two events that repeatedly occur close together in time become fused in a person's mind and so produce the same response.

Classification system A list of disorders, along with descriptions of symptoms and guidelines for making appropriate diagnoses.

Cleaning compulsion A common compulsion in which people feel compelled to keep cleaning themselves, their clothing, and their homes.

Client-centered therapy The humanistic therapy developed by Carl Rogers in which clinicians try to help clients by being accepting, empathizing accurately, and conveying genuineness.

Clinical interview A face-to-face encounter in which clinicians ask questions of clients, weigh their responses and reactions, and learn about them and their psychological problems.

Clinical psychologist A mental health professional who has earned a doctorate in clinical psychology.

Clinical psychology The study, assessment, treatment, and prevention of abnormal behavior.

Clitoris The female sex organ located in front of the urinary and vaginal openings. It becomes enlarged during sexual arousal.

Clozapine A commonly prescribed atypical antipsychotic drug.

Cocaine An addictive stimulant taken from the coca plant; the most powerful natural stimulant known.

Code of ethics A body of principles and rules for ethical behavior, designed to guide decisions and actions by members of a profession.

Cognition The capacity to think, remember, and anticipate.

Cognitive behavior Thoughts and beliefs, many of which remain private.

Cognitive-behavioral model A theoretical perspective that views cognitions as learned behaviors.

Cognitive model A theoretical perspective that emphasizes the process and content of thinking as causes of psychological problems.

Cognitive therapy A therapy developed by Aaron Beck that helps people identify and change the maladaptive assumptions and ways of thinking that help cause their psychological disorders.

Cognitive triad The three forms of negative thinking that theorist Aaron Beck says lead people to feel depressed. The triad consists of a negative view of one's experiences, oneself, and the future.

Coitus Sexual intercourse.

Community mental health center A community treatment facility that provides medication, psychotherapy, and, ideally, emergency care to patients and coordinates their treatment in the community.

Community mental health treatment A treatment approach that emphasizes community care.

Comorbidity The occurrence of two or more disorders in the same person.

Compulsion A repetitive and rigid behavior or mental act that persons feel they must perform in order to prevent or reduce anxiety.

Compulsive ritual A detailed, often elaborate, set of actions that a person often feels compelled to perform, always in an identical manner.

Computerized axial tomography (CAT scan) A composite image of the brain created by compiling X-ray images taken from many angles.

Concordance A statistical measure of the frequency with which family members (often both members of a pair of twins) have the same particular characteristic.

Conditioned response (CR) A response previously associated with an unconditioned stimulus that comes to be produced by a conditioned stimulus.

Conditioned stimulus (CS) A previously neutral stimulus that comes to be associated with a nonneutral stimulus, and can then produce responses similar to those produced by the nonneutral stimulus.

Conditioning A simple form of learning in which a given stimulus comes to produce a given response.

Conditions of worth According to client-centered theorists, the internal standards by which a person judges his or her own lovability and acceptability, determined by the standards to which the person was held as a child.

Conduct disorder A childhood disorder in which the child repeatedly violates the basic rights of others, displaying aggression and sometimes destroying others' property, lying, or running away from home.

Confabulation A made-up description of one's experience to fill in a gap in one's memory.

Confederate An experimenter's accomplice, who helps create a particular impression in a study while pretending to be just another subject.

Confidentiality The principle that certain professionals will not divulge the information they obtain from a client.

Confound In an experiment, a variable other than the independent variable that may also be acting on the dependent variable.

Continuous amnesia An inability to recall newly occurring events as well as certain past events.

Control group In an experiment, a group of subjects who are not exposed to the independent variable.

Conversion disorder A somatoform disorder in which a psychosocial need or conflict is converted into dramatic physical symptoms that affect voluntary motor or sensory function.

Convulsion A brain seizure.

Coronary arteries Blood vessels that surround the heart and are responsible for carrying oxygen to the heart muscle.

Coronary heart disease Illness of the heart caused by a blockage of the coronary arteries.

Correlation The degree to which events or characteristics vary along with each other.

Correlational method A research procedure used to determine how much events or characteristics vary along with each other.

Correlation coefficient (r) A statistical term that indicates the direction and the magnitude of a correlation, ranging from −1.00 to +1.00.

Corticosteroids A group of hormones released by the adrenal glands at times of stress.

Cortisol A hormone released by the adrenal glands when a person is under stress.

Counseling psychology A mental health specialty similar to clinical psychology that requires completion of its own graduate training program.

Countertransference A phenomenon of psychotherapy in which therapists' own feelings, history, and values subtly influence the way they interpret a patient's problems.

Couple therapy A therapy format in which the therapist works with two people who share a long-term relationship. Also called *marital therapy*.

Covert desensitization Desensitization that focuses on imagining confrontations with the frightening objects or situations while in a state of relaxation.

Covert sensitization A behavioral treatment for eliminating unwanted behavior by pairing the behavior with unpleasant mental images.

Crack A powerful, ready-to-smoke freebase cocaine.

Cretinism A disorder marked by mental retardation and physical abnormalities; caused by low levels of iodine in the mother's diet during pregnancy.

Creutzfeldt-Jakob disease A form of dementia caused by a slow-acting virus that may live in the body for years before the disease unfolds.

Criminal commitment A legal process by which persons accused of a crime are instead judged mentally unstable and sent to a mental health facility for treatment.

Crisis intervention A treatment approach that tries to help people in a psychological crisis view their situation more accurately, make better decisions, act more constructively, and overcome the crisis.

Critical incident stress debriefing Training in how to help victims of disasters or other horrifying events talk about their feelings and reactions to the traumatic incidents.

Cross-tolerance Tolerance that a person develops for a substance as a result of regularly using another substance similar to it.

Culture A people's common history, values, institutions, habits, skills, technology, and arts.

Culture-sensitive therapies Treatment approaches that seek to address the unique issues faced by members of various cultural and ethnic groups.

Cyclothymic disorder A disorder marked by numerous periods of hypomanic symptoms and mild depressive symptoms.

Day center A program that offers hospital-like treatment during the day only. Also called *day hospital*.

Death darer A person who is ambivalent about the wish to die even as he or she attempts suicide.

Death ignorer A person who attempts suicide without recognizing the finality of death.

Death initiator A person who attempts suicide believing that the process of death is already under way and that he or she is simply quickening the process.

Death seeker A person who clearly intends to end his or her life at the time of a suicide attempt.

Declarative memory Memory of learned information such as names, dates, and other facts.

Deep brain stimulation A treatment procedure for depression in which a pacemaker powers electrodes that have been implanted in Brodmann Area 25, thus stimulating that brain area.

Deinstitutionalization The discharge of large numbers of patients from long-term institutional care so that they might be treated in community programs.

Déjà vu The haunting sense of having previously seen or experienced a new scene or situation.

Delirium A rapidly developing clouded state of consciousness in which a person has great difficulty concentrating, focusing attention, and keeping a straightforward stream of thought.

Delirium tremens (DTs) A dramatic withdrawal reaction experienced by some people who are alcohol-dependent; consists of mental confusion, clouded consciousness, and terrifying visual hallucinations. Also called *alcohol withdrawal delirium*.

Delusion A strange false belief firmly held despite evidence to the contrary.

Delusional disorder A disorder consisting of persistent, nonbizarre delusions that are not part of a schizophrenic disorder.

Delusion of control The belief that one's impulses, feelings, thoughts, or actions are being controlled by other people.

Delusion of grandeur The belief that one is a great inventor, historical figure, or other specially empowered person.

Delusion of persecution The belief that one is being plotted or discriminated against, spied on, slandered, threatened, attacked, or deliberately victimized.

Delusion of reference A belief that attaches special and personal meaning to the actions of others or to various objects or events.

Dementia A syndrome marked by severe problems in memory and at least one other cognitive function.

Demonology The belief that abnormal behavior results from supernatural causes such as evil spirits.

Dendrite An extension located at one end of a neuron that receives impulses from other neurons.

Denial An ego defense mechanism in which a person fails to acknowledge unacceptable thoughts, feelings, or actions.

Dependent personality disorder A personality disorder characterized by a pattern of clinging and obedience, fear of separation, and a persistent, excessive need to be taken care of.

Dependent variable The variable in an experiment that is expected to change as the independent variable is manipulated.

Depersonalization disorder A disorder marked by a persistent and recurrent feeling of being detached from one's own mental processes or body; that is, one feels unreal and alien.

Depressant A substance that slows the activity of the central nervous system and in sufficient dosages causes a reduction of tension and inhibitions.

Depression A low state marked by significant levels of sadness, lack of energy, low self-worth, guilt, or related symptoms.

Derailment A common thinking disturbance in schizophrenia, involving rapid shifts from one topic of conversation to another. Also called *loose associations*.

Desensitization *See* Systematic desensitization.

Desire phase The phase of the sexual response cycle consisting of an urge to have sex, sexual fantasies, and sexual attraction to others.

Detoxification Systematic and medically supervised withdrawal from a drug.

Deviance Variance from common patterns of behavior.

Diagnosis A determination that a person's problems reflect a particular disorder.

***Diagnostic and Statistical Manual of Mental Disorders* (DSM)** The classification system for mental disorders developed by the American Psychiatric Association.

Diathesis-stress view The view that a person must first have a predisposition to a disorder and then be subjected to immediate psychosocial stress in order to develop the disorder.

Diazepam A benzodiazepine drug, marketed as *Valium*.

Dichotomous thinking Viewing problems and solutions in rigid "either/or" terms.

Diencephalon A brain area (consisting of the mammillary bodies, thalamus, and hypothalamus) that plays a key role in transforming short-term to long-term memory, among other functions.

Directed masturbation training A sex therapy approach that teaches women with female arousal or orgasmic disorders how to masturbate effectively and eventually reach orgasm during sexual interactions.

Disaster Response Network (DRN) A network of thousands of volunteer mental health professionals who mobilize to provide free emergency psychological services at disaster sites throughout North America.

Disorganized type of schizophrenia A type of schizophrenia marked primarily by confusion, incoherence, and flat or inappropriate affect.

Displacement An ego defense mechanism that channels unacceptable id impulses toward another, safer substitute.

Dissociative amnesia A dissociative disorder marked by an inability to recall important personal events and information.

Dissociative disorders Disorders marked by major changes in memory that are not due to clear physical causes.

Dissociative fugue A dissociative disorder in which a person travels to a new location and may assume a new identity, simultaneously forgetting his or her past.

Dissociative identity disorder A disorder in which a person develops two or more distinct personalities. Also called *multiple personality disorder.*

Disulfiram (Antabuse) An antagonist drug used in treating alcohol abuse or dependence.

Dopamine The neurotransmitter whose high activity has been shown to be related to schizophrenia.

Dopamine hypothesis The theory that schizophrenia results from excessive activity of the neurotransmitter dopamine.

Double-bind hypothesis A theory that some parents repeatedly communicate pairs of messages that are mutually contradictory, helping to produce schizophrenia in their children.

Double-blind design Experimental procedure in which neither the subject nor the experimenter knows whether the subject has received the experimental treatment or a placebo.

Double depression A sequence in which dysthymic disorder leads to a major depressive disorder.

Down syndrome A form of mental retardation related to an abnormality in the twenty-first chromosome.

Drapetomania According to a nineteenth-century diagnostic category, an obsessive desire for freedom that drove some slaves to try to flee from captivity.

Dream A series of ideas and images that form during sleep and are interpreted by psychodynamic theorists as clues to the unconscious.

Drug Any substance other than food that affects the body or mind.

Drug maintenance therapy An approach to treating substance dependence in which clients are given legally and medically supervised doses of the drug on which they are dependent or a substitute drug.

Drug therapy The use of psychotropic drugs to reduce the symptoms of psychological disorders.

DSM-IV-TR The text revision of DSM-IV, the current edition of the *Diagnostic and Statistical Manual of Mental Disorders.*

Durham test A legal test for insanity that holds people to be insane at the time of committing a crime if the act was the result of a mental disorder or defect.

Duty to protect The principle that therapists must break confidentiality in order to protect a person who may be the intended victim of a client.

Dyslexia A disorder in which persons show a marked impairment in the ability to recognize words and to comprehend what they read. Also known as *reading disorder.*

Dyspareunia A disorder in which a person experiences severe pain in the genitals during sexual activity.

Dyssomnias Sleep disorders in which the amount, quality, or timing of sleep is disturbed.

Dysthymic disorder A mood disorder that is similar to but longer-lasting and less disabling than a major depressive disorder.

Echolalia A symptom of autism or schizophrenia in which a person responds to statements by repeating the other person's words.

Ego According to Freud, the psychological force that employs reason and operates in accordance with the reality principle.

Ego defense mechanisms According to psychoanalytic theory, strategies developed by the ego to control unacceptable id impulses and to avoid or reduce the anxiety they arouse.

Egoistic suicide Suicide committed by people over whom society has little or no control, people who are not concerned with the norms or rules of society.

Ego theory The psychodynamic theory that emphasizes the ego and considers it an independent force.

Eidetic imagery A strong visual image of an object or scene that persists in some persons long after the object or scene is removed.

Ejaculation Contractions of the muscles at the base of the penis that cause sperm to be ejected.

Electra complex According to Freud, the pattern of desires all girls experience during the phallic stage, in which they develop a sexual attraction to their father.

Electroconvulsive therapy (ECT) A form of treatment, used primarily in cases of unipolar depression, in which electrodes attached to a person's head send an electric current through the brain, causing a brain seizure.

Electroencephalograph (EEG) A device that records electrical impulses in the brain.

Electromyograph (EMG) A device that provides feedback about the level of muscular tension in the body.

Electrooculograph A device that records the movement of the eyes.

Emergency commitment Temporary commitment to a mental hospital of a patient who is behaving in a bizarre or violent way.

Employee assistance program A mental health program that some businesses offer to their employees.

Encopresis A childhood disorder characterized by repeated defecation in inappropriate places, such as into one's clothing.

Endocrine system The system of glands located throughout the body that helps control important activities such as growth and sexual activity.

Endogenous depression A depression that appears to develop without external reasons and is assumed to be caused by internal factors.

Endorphins Neurotransmitters that help relieve pain and reduce emotional tension; sometimes referred to as the body's own opioids.

Enmeshed family pattern A family system in which members are overinvolved with each other's affairs and overconcerned about each other's welfare.

Enuresis A childhood disorder marked by repeated bed-wetting or wetting of one's clothes.

Epidemiological study A study that measures the incidence and prevalence of a disorder in a given population.

Ergot alkaloid A naturally occurring compound from which LSD is derived.

Essential hypertension High blood pressure caused by a combination of psychosocial and physiological factors.

Estrogen The primary female sex hormone.

Ethyl alcohol The chemical compound in all alcoholic beverages that is rapidly absorbed into the blood and immediately begins to affect the person's functioning.

Evoked potentials The brain response patterns recorded on an electroencephalograph while a person performs a task such as observing a flashing light.

Excitement phase The phase of the sexual response cycle marked by changes in the pelvic region, general physical arousal, and increases in heart rate, muscle tension, blood pressure, and rate of breathing.

Exhibitionism A paraphilia in which persons have repeated sexually arousing urges or fantasies about exposing their genitals to another person and may act upon those urges.

Existential anxiety According to existential theorists, a universal fear of the limits and responsibilities of one's existence.

Existential model The theoretical perspective that human beings are born with the total freedom either to face up to one's existence and give meaning to one's life or to shrink from that responsibility.

Existential therapy A therapy that encourages people to accept responsibility for their lives and to live with greater meaning and values.

Exorcism The practice in early societies of treating abnormality by coaxing evil spirits to leave the person's body.

Experiment A research procedure in which a variable is manipulated and the effect of the manipulation is observed.

Experimental group In an experiment, the subjects who are exposed to the independent variable under investigation.

Exposure and response prevention A behavioral treatment for obsessive-compulsive disorder that exposes a client to anxiety-arousing thoughts or situations and then prevents the client from performing his or her compulsive acts. Also called *exposure and ritual prevention.*

Exposure treatments Behavioral treatments in which persons with fears are exposed to their dreaded objects or situations.

Expressed emotion The general level of criticism, disapproval, hostility, and intrusiveness expressed in a family.

External validity The degree to which the results of a study may be generalized beyond that study.

Extrapyramidal effects Unwanted movements, such as severe shaking, bizarre-looking twisting of the face and body, and extreme restlessness, sometimes produced by traditional antipsychotic drugs.

Eye movement desensitization and reprocessing A behavioral exposure treatment in which clients move their eyes in a saccadic (rhythmic) manner from side to side while flooding their minds with images of objects and situations they ordinarily avoid.

Factitious disorder An illness with no identifiable physical cause in which the patient is believed to be producing or faking symptoms intentionally in order to assume a sick role.

Family pedigree study A research design in which investigators determine how

many and which relatives of a person with a disorder have the same disorder.

Family systems theory A theory that views the family as a system of interacting parts and proposes that members interact in consistent ways and operate by unstated rules.

Family therapy A therapy format in which the therapist meets with all members of a family and helps them change in therapeutic ways.

Fantasy An ego defense mechanism in which a person uses imaginary events to satisfy unacceptable impulses.

Fear The central nervous system's physiological and emotional response to a serious threat to one's well-being.

Fear hierarchy A list of objects or situations that frighten a person, starting with those that are slightly feared and ending with those that are feared greatly; used in systematic desensitization.

Female orgasmic disorder A dysfunction in which a woman rarely has an orgasm or repeatedly experiences a very delayed one following a normal sexual excitement phase.

Female sexual arousal disorder A female dysfunction marked by a persistent inability to attain or maintain adequate lubrication or genital swelling during sexual activity.

Fetal alcohol syndrome A group of problems in a child, including lower intellectual functioning, low birth weight, and irregularities in the hands and face, that result from excessive alcohol intake by the mother during pregnancy.

Fetishism A paraphilia consisting of recurrent and intense sexual urges, fantasies, or behaviors that involve the use of a nonliving object, often to the exclusion of all other stimuli.

Fixation According to Freud, a condition in which the id, ego, and superego do not mature properly, causing the person to become entrapped at an early stage of development.

Flashback The recurrence of LSD-induced sensory and emotional changes long after the drug has left the body. Or, in posttraumatic stress disorder, the reexperiencing of past traumatic events.

Flat affect A symptom of schizophrenia in which the person shows almost no emotion at all.

Flooding A treatment for phobias in which a person is exposed repeatedly and intensively to a feared object and made to see that it is actually harmless.

Forensic psychology The branch of psychology concerned with intersections between psychological practice and research and the judicial system. Also related to the field of *forensic psychiatry.*

Formal thought disorder A disturbance in the production and organization of thought.

Free association A psychodynamic technique in which a person describes any thought, feeling, or image that comes to mind, even if it seems unimportant.

Free-base A technique for ingesting cocaine in which the pure-cocaine basic alkaloid is chemically separated from processed cocaine, vaporized by heat from a flame, and inhaled through a pipe.

Free-floating anxiety Chronic and persistent feelings of anxiety that are not clearly attached to a specific, identifiable threat.

Frotteurism A paraphilia consisting of repeated and intense sexual urges, fantasies, or behaviors that involve touching and rubbing against a nonconsenting person.

Fusion The final merging of two or more subpersonalities in multiple personality disorder.

Gamma aminobutyric acid (GABA) A neurotransmitter whose low activity has been linked to generalized anxiety disorder.

Gender dysphoria Unhappiness with one's given gender.

Gender identity disorder A disorder in which a person persistently feels extremely uncomfortable about his or her assigned sex and strongly wishes to be a member of the opposite sex.

Gender-sensitive therapies Treatment approaches geared to the special pressures of being a woman in Western society. Also called *feminist therapies.*

Generalized amnesia A loss of memory for events that occurred over a limited period of time as well as for certain events that occurred prior to that period.

Generalized anxiety disorder A disorder marked by persistent and excessive feelings of anxiety and worry about numerous events and activities.

General paresis An irreversible medical disorder whose symptoms include psychological abnormalities, such as delusions of grandeur; caused by syphilis.

Genes Chromosome segments that control the characteristics and traits we inherit.

Genetic linkage study A research approach in which extended families with high rates of a disorder over several generations are observed in order to determine whether the disorder closely follows the distribution pattern of other family traits.

Genital stage In Freud's theory, the stage beginning at approximately 12 years old, when the child begins to find sexual pleasure in heterosexual relationships.

Geropsychology The field of psychology concerned with the mental health of elderly people.

Gestalt therapy The humanistic therapy developed by Fritz Perls in which clinicians actively move individuals toward self-recognition and self-acceptance by using techniques such as role-playing and skillful frustration.

Glia Brain cells that support the neurons.

Glutamate A common neurotransmitter that has been linked to memory and to dementia.

Grief The reaction one experiences when a loved one is lost.

Group home A special home where people with disorders or disabilities live and are taught self-help, living, and working skills.

Group therapy A therapy format in which a group of people with similar problems meet together with a therapist to work on their problems.

Guided participation A modeling technique in which a client systematically observes and imitates the therapist while the therapist confronts feared items.

Guilty but mentally ill A verdict stating that defendants are guilty of committing a crime but are also suffering from a mental illness that should be treated during their imprisonment.

Halfway house A residence for people with severe psychological problems who cannot yet live alone or with their families; often staffed by paraprofessionals. Also known as *group home*.

Hallucination The experiencing of imagined sights, sounds, or other sensory experiences as if they were real.

Hallucinogens Substances that primarily cause powerful changes in sensory perception, including strengthening a person's perceptions and producing illusions and hallucinations. Also called *psychedelic drugs*.

Hallucinosis A form of intoxication caused by hallucinogens, consisting of perceptual distortions and hallucinations.

Hardiness A set of positive attitudes and reactions in response to stress.

Health maintenance The principle that young adults should act to promote their physical and mental health to best prepare for the aging process. Also called *wellness*.

Helper T-cell A lymphocyte that identifies foreign invaders and then both multiplies and triggers the production of other kinds of immune cells.

Heroin A highly addictive substance derived from morphine; illegal in the United States under all circumstances.

High The pleasant feeling of relaxation and euphoria that follows the rush from certain recreational drugs.

Hippocampus A brain area located below the cerebral cortex that is involved in memory.

Histrionic personality disorder A personality disorder in which an individual displays a pattern of excessive emotionality and attention seeking. Once called *hysterical personality disorder.*

Homosexuality Sexual preference for a person of one's own gender.

Hopelessness A pessimistic belief that one's present circumstances, problems, or mood will not change.

Hormones The chemicals released by glands into the bloodstream.

Humanistic model The theoretical perspective that human beings are born with a natural inclination to be friendly, cooperative, and constructive and are driven to self-actualize.

Humanistic therapy A system of therapy that tries to help clients look at themselves accurately and acceptingly so that they can fulfill their positive inborn potential.

Humors According to Greek and Roman physicians, bodily chemicals that influence mental and physical functioning.

Huntington's disease An inherited disease, characterized by progressive problems in cognition, emotion, and movement, which results in dementia.

Hypertension Chronic high blood pressure.

Hypnosis A sleeplike suggestible state during which a person can be directed to act in unusual ways, to experience unusual sensations, to remember seemingly forgotten events, or to forget remembered events.

Hypnotic amnesia Loss of memory produced by hypnotic suggestion.

Hypnotic therapy A treatment in which a person undergoes hypnosis and is then guided to recall forgotten events or perform other therapeutic activities. Also called *hypnotherapy*.

Hypnotism A procedure that places persons in a trancelike mental state during which they become extremely suggestible.

Hypoactive sexual desire disorder A disorder marked by a lack of interest in sex.

Hypochondriasis A somatoform disorder in which people mistakenly fear that minor changes in their physical functioning indicate a serious disease.

Hypomanic pattern A pattern in which a person displays symptoms of mania, but the symptoms are less severe and cause less impairment than a manic episode.

Hypothalamic-pituitary-adrenal (HPA) pathway One route by which the brain and body produce arousal and fear. At times of stress, the hypothalamus signals the pituitary gland, which in turn signals the adrenal glands. Stress hormones are then released to various body organs.

Hypothalamus A part of the brain that helps maintain various bodily functions, including eating and hunger.

Hypothesis A hunch or prediction that certain variables are related in certain ways.

Hypoxyphilia A pattern in which people strangle or smother themselves, or ask their partners to strangle or smother them, to increase their sexual pleasure.

Hysteria A term once used to describe what are now known as conversion disorder, somatization disorder, and pain disorder associated with psychological factors.

Hysterical disorder A disorder in which physical functioning is changed or lost, without an apparent physical cause.

Hysterical somatoform disorders Somatoform disorders in which people experience actual changes in their physical functioning.

Id According to Freud, the psychological force that produces instinctual needs, drives, and impulses.

Ideas of reference Beliefs that unrelated events pertain to oneself in some important way.

Identification Unconsciously incorporating the values and feelings of one's parents and fusing them with one's identity. Also, an ego defense mechanism in which persons take on the values and feelings of a person who is causing them anxiety.

Idiographic understanding An understanding of the behavior of a particular individual.

Illogical thinking According to cognitive theories, illogical ways of thinking that may lead to self-defeating conclusions and psychological problems.

Immune system The body's network of activities and cells that identify and destroy antigens and cancer cells.

Impulse-control disorders Disorders in which people repeatedly fail to resist an impulse, drive, or temptation to perform an act that is harmful to themselves or to others.

Inappropriate affect A symptom of schizophrenia in which a person displays emotions that are unsuited to the situation.

Incest Sexual relations between close relatives.

Incidence The number of new cases of a disorder occurring in a population over a specific period of time.

Independent variable The variable in an experiment that is manipulated to determine whether it has an effect on another variable.

Individual therapy A therapeutic approach in which a therapist sees a client alone for sessions that may last from 15 minutes to two hours.

Insanity defense A legal defense in which persons charged with a criminal offense claim to be not guilty by reason of insanity at the time of the crime.

Insomnia The most common dyssomnia, characterized by difficulties initiating and maintaining sleep.

Integrity test A test that seeks to measure whether the test taker is generally honest or dishonest.

Intellectual disability A disorder in which people display general intellectual functioning and adaptive behavior that are well below average. Also known as *mental retardation*.

Intelligence quotient (IQ) A general score derived from an intelligence test that theoretically represents a person's overall intellectual capacity.

Intelligence test A test designed to measure a person's intellectual ability.

Intermittent explosive disorder An impulse-control disorder in which people periodically fail to resist aggressive impulses and commit serious assaults on other people or destroy property.

Internal validity The accuracy with which a study can pinpoint one of various possible factors as the cause of a phenomenon.

International Classification of Diseases (ICD) The classification system for medical and mental disorders that is used by the World Health Organization.

Interpersonal psychotherapy (IPT) A treatment for unipolar depression that is based on the belief that clarifying and changing one's interpersonal problems will help lead to recovery.

Intoxication A temporary drug-induced state in which people display symptoms such as impaired judgment, mood changes, irritability, slurred speech, and loss of coordination.

In vivo desensitization Desensitization that makes use of actual objects or situations, as opposed to imagined ones.

Irresistible impulse test A legal test for insanity that holds people to be insane at the time of committing a crime if they were driven to do so by an uncontrollable "fit of passion."

Isolation An ego defense mechanism in which people unconsciously isolate and disown undesirable and unwanted thoughts, experiencing them as foreign intrusions.

Kleptomania An impulse-control disorder characterized by the recurrent failure to resist impulses to steal objects not needed for personal use or monetary value.

Korsakoff's syndrome An amnestic disorder marked by extreme confusion, memory impairment, and other neurological symptoms; caused by long-term alcoholism, an accompanying poor diet, and, in turn, a deficiency of vitamin B (thiamine).

Latent content The symbolic meaning behind a dream's content.

Lateral hypothalamus (LH) The region of the hypothalamus that, when activated, produces hunger.

L-dopa A drug used in the treatment of Parkinson's disease, a disease in which dopamine is low.

Learned helplessness The perception, based on past experiences, that one has no control over one's reinforcements.

Learning disorder A developmental disorder marked by impairments in cognitive skills such as reading, mathematics, or language.

Libido The sexual energy that fuels the id.

Life change units (LCUs) A system for measuring the stress associated with various life events.

Light therapy A treatment for seasonal affective disorder in which patients are exposed to extra light for several hours. Also called *phototherapy*.

Lithium A metallic element that occurs in nature as a mineral salt and is a highly effective treatment for bipolar disorders.

Lobotomy Psychosurgery in which a surgeon cuts the connections between the brain's frontal lobes and the lower centers of the brain.

Localized amnesia An inability to recall any of the events that occurred over a limited period of time.

Locus ceruleus A small area of the brain that seems to be active in the regulation of emotions. Many of its neurons use norepinephrine.

Longitudinal study A study that observes the same subjects on many occasions over a long period of time.

Long-term care Extended personal and medical support provided to elderly and other persons who may be impaired. It may range from partial support in a supervised apartment to intensive care at a nursing home.

Long-term memory The memory system that contains all the information that a person has stored over the years.

Loose associations A common thinking disturbance in schizophrenia, involving rapid shifts from one topic of conversation to another. Also known as *derailment*.

Lycanthropy A condition in which persons believe themselves to be possessed by wolves or other animals.

Lymphocytes White blood cells that circulate through the lymph system and bloodstream, helping the body identify and destroy antigens and cancer cells.

Lysergic acid diethylamide (LSD) A hallucinogenic drug derived from ergot alkaloids.

Mainstreaming An approach to educating children with mental retardation in which they are placed in regular classes with children who are not mentally retarded. Also called *inclusion*.

Major depressive disorder A severe pattern of depression that is disabling and is not caused by such factors as drugs or a general medical condition.

Male erectile disorder A dysfunction in which a man persistently fails to attain or maintain an erection during sexual activity.

Male orgasmic disorder A male dysfunction characterized by a repeated inability to reach orgasm or by long delays in reaching orgasm after normal sexual excitement.

Malingering Intentionally faking illness to achieve some external gains, such as financial compensation or military deferment.

Malpractice suit A lawsuit charging a therapist with improper conduct or decision-making in the course of treatment.

Managed care program A system of health care coverage in which the insurance company largely controls the cost, method, provider, and length of treatment.

Mania A state or episode of euphoria or frenzied activity in which people may have an exaggerated belief that the world is theirs for the taking.

Manifest content The consciously remembered content of a dream.

Mantra A sound, uttered or thought, used to focus one's attention and to turn away from ordinary thoughts and concerns during meditation.

MAO inhibitor An antidepressant drug that prevents the action of the enzyme monoamine oxidase.

Marijuana One of the cannabis drugs, derived from the leaves and flowering tops of the hemp plant, *Cannabis sativa*.

Marital therapy A therapy approach in which the therapist works with two people who share a long-term relationship. Also known as *couple therapy*.

Masturbation Self-stimulation of the genitals to achieve sexual arousal.

Masturbatory satiation A behavioral treatment in which a client masturbates for a very long period of time while fantasizing in detail about a paraphilic object. The procedure is expected to produce a feeling of boredom that in turn becomes linked to the object.

Mean The average of a group of scores.

Meditation A technique of turning one's concentration inward and achieving a slightly changed state of consciousness.

Melancholia A condition described by early Greek and Roman philosophers and physicians as consisting of unshakable sadness. Today it is known as *depression*.

Melatonin A hormone released by the pineal gland when a person's surroundings are dark.

Memory The faculty for recalling past events and past learning.

Mental incompetence A state of mental instability that leaves defendants unable to understand the legal charges and proceedings they are facing and unable to adequately prepare a defense with their attorneys.

Mentally ill chemical abusers (MICAs) Persons suffering from both schizophrenia (or another severe psychological disorder) and a substance-related disorder.

Mental retardation A disorder in which people display general intellectual functioning and adaptive behavior that are well below average. Also known as *intellectual disability.*

Mental status exam A set of interview questions and observations designed to reveal the degree and nature of a person's abnormal functioning.

Mesmerism The method employed by Austrian physician F. A. Mesmer to treat hysterical disorders; a precursor of *hypnotism.*

Metabolism An organism's chemical and physical breakdown of food and the process of converting it into energy. Also, an organism's biochemical transformation of various substances, as when the liver breaks down alcohol into acetylaldehyde.

Methadone A laboratory-made opioid-like drug.

Methadone maintenance program An approach to treating heroin dependence in which people are given legally and medically supervised doses of methadone, a laboratory-produced opioid, as a substitute for heroin.

Methylphenidate A stimulant drug, known better by the trade name Ritalin, commonly used to treat ADHD.

Migraine headache An extremely severe headache that occurs on one side of the head, often preceded by a warning sensation and sometimes accompanied by dizziness, nausea, or vomiting.

Mild retardation A level of mental retardation (IQ between 50 and 70) at which persons can benefit from education and support themselves as adults.

Milieu therapy Humanistic approach to institutional treatment based on the belief that institutions can help patients recover by creating a climate that builds self-respect, individual responsibility, and meaningful activity.

Mind-body dualism René Descartes's position that the mind is separate from the body.

Minnesota Multiphasic Personality Inventory (MMPI) A widely used personality inventory consisting of a large number of statements that subjects mark as being true or false for them.

Mixed design A research design in which a correlational method is mixed with an experimental method. Also known as *quasi-experiment.*

M'Naghten test A widely used legal test for insanity that holds people to be insane at the time of committing a crime if, because of a mental disorder, they did not know the nature of the act or did not know right from wrong.

Model A set of assumptions and concepts that helps scientists explain and interpret observations. Also called *paradigm.*

Modeling A process of learning in which an individual acquires responses by observing and imitating others. Also, a therapy approach based on the same principle.

Moderate retardation A level of mental retardation (IQ between 35 and 49) in which persons can learn to care for themselves and benefit from vocational training.

Monoamine oxidase (MAO) A body chemical that destroys the neurotransmitter norepinephrine.

Monoamine oxidase (MAO) inhibitors Antidepressant drugs that lower MAO activity and thus increase the level of norepinephrine activity in the brain.

Mood disorder A disorder affecting one's emotional state, including major depressive disorder and bipolar disorders.

Mood stabilizing drugs Psychotropic drugs that help stabilize the moods of people suffering from a bipolar mood disorder. Also known as *antibipolar drugs.*

Moral treatment A nineteenth-century approach to treating people with mental dysfunction that emphasized moral guidance and humane and respectful treatment.

Morphine A highly addictive substance derived from opium that is particularly effective in relieving pain.

Multiaxial system A classification system in which different "axes," or branches of information, are required from the diagnostician. DSM-IV-TR is a multiaxial system.

Multicultural perspective The view that each culture within a larger society has a particular set of values and beliefs, as well as special external factors, that help account for the behavior and functioning of its members. Also called *culturally diverse perspective.*

Multicultural psychology The field of psychology that examines the impact of culture, race, ethnicity, gender, and similar factors on our behaviors and thoughts and also focuses on how such factors may influence the origin, nature, and treatment of abnormal behavior.

Multidimensional risk perspective A theory that identifies several different kinds of risk factors that may combine to help cause a disorder. The more such factors present, the greater the risk of developing the disorder.

Multiple personality disorder A dissociative disorder in which a person develops two or more distinct personalities. Also called *dissociative identity disorder.*

Munchausen syndrome An extreme and long-term form of factitious disorder in which a person produces symptoms, gains admission to a hospital, and receives treatment.

Munchausen syndrome by proxy A factitious disorder in which parents make up or produce physical illnesses in their children.

Muscle contraction headache A headache caused by the narrowing of muscles surrounding the skull. Also called *tension headache.*

Narcolepsy A dyssomnia characterized by sudden onsets of REM sleep during waking hours, generally brought on by strong emotion.

Narcotic Any natural or synthetic opioid-like drug.

Narcotic antagonist A substance that attaches to opioid receptors in the brain and, in turn, blocks the effects of opioids.

Natural experiment An experiment in which nature, rather than an experimenter, manipulates an independent variable.

Naturalistic observation A method of observing behavior in which clinicians or researchers observe people in their everyday environments.

Negative correlation A statistical relationship in which the value of one variable increases while the other variable decreases.

Negative symptoms Symptoms of schizophrenia that seem to be deficits of normal thought, emotion, or behavior.

Neologism A made-up word that has meaning only to the person using it.

Nerve ending The region at the end of a neuron from which an impulse is sent to a neighboring neuron.

Neurofibrillary tangles Twisted protein fibers that form within certain brain cells as people age.

Neuroimaging techniques Neurological tests that provide images of brain structure or brain activity, including CT, PET, MRI, and fMRI scans.

Neuroleptic drugs A term used for the traditional antipsychotic drugs because they often produce undesired effects similar to the symptoms of neurological disorders.

Neuroleptic malignant syndrome A severe, potentially fatal reaction to antipsychotic drugs, marked by muscle rigidity, fever, altered consciousness, and autonomic dysfunction.

Neurological Relating to the structure or activity of the brain.

Neurological test A test that directly measures brain structure or activity.

Neuromodulator A neurotransmitter that helps modify or regulate the effect of other neurotransmitters.

Neuron A nerve cell. The brain contains billions of neurons.

Neuropsychological test A test that detects brain impairment by measuring a person's cognitive, perceptual, and motor performances.

Neurosis Freud's term for disorders characterized by intense anxiety, attributed to failure of a person's ego defense mechanisms to cope with unconscious conflicts.

Neurotransmitter A chemical that, released by one neuron, crosses the synaptic space to be received at receptors on the dendrites of neighboring neurons.

Neutralizing Attempting to eliminate thoughts that one finds unacceptable by thinking or behaving in ways that make up for those thoughts and so put matters right internally.

Nicotine patch A patch attached to the skin like a Band-Aid, with nicotine content that is absorbed through the skin, that supposedly eases the withdrawal reaction brought on by quitting cigarette smoking.

Nightmare disorder A parasomnia characterized by chronic distressful, frightening dreams.

Nocturnal penile tumescence (NPT) The occurrence of erections during sleep.

Nomothetic understanding A general understanding of the nature, causes, and treatments of abnormal psychological functioning in the form of laws or principles.

Norepinephrine A neurotransmitter whose abnormal activity is linked to depression and panic disorder.

Normalization The principle that institutions and community residences should expose persons with mental retardation to living conditions and opportunities similar to those found in the rest of society.

Norms A society's stated and unstated rules for proper conduct.

Not guilty by reason of insanity (NGRI) A verdict stating that defendants are not guilty of committing a crime because they were insane at the time of the crime.

Observer drift The tendency of an observer who is rating subjects in an experiment to change criteria gradually and involuntarily, thus making the data unreliable.

Obsession A persistent thought, idea, impulse, or image that is experienced repeatedly, feels intrusive, and causes anxiety.

Obsessive-compulsive disorder A disorder characterized by recurrent and unwanted thoughts and/or a need to perform rigidly repetitive physical or mental actions.

Obsessive-compulsive personality disorder A personality disorder in which an individual is so focused on orderliness, perfectionism, and control that he or she loses flexibility, openness, and efficiency.

Oedipus complex In Freudian theory, the pattern of desires emerging during the phallic stage in which boys become attracted to their mother as a sexual object and see their father as a rival they would like to push aside.

Operant conditioning A process of learning in which behavior that leads to satisfying consequences, or rewards, is likely to be repeated.

Opioid Opium or any of the drugs derived from opium, including morphine, heroin, and codeine.

Opium A highly addictive substance made from the sap of the opium poppy seed.

Oppositional defiant disorder A childhood disorder in which children argue repeatedly with adults, lose their temper, and feel great anger and resentment.

Oral stage The earliest developmental stage in Freud's conceptualization of psychosexual development during which the infant's main gratification comes from feeding and from the body parts involved in it.

Orbitofrontal cortex A region of the brain in which impulses involving excretion, sexuality, violence, and other primitive activities normally arise.

Orgasm A peaking of sexual pleasure, consisting of rhythmic muscular contractions in the pelvic region, during which a man's semen is ejaculated and the outer third of a woman's vaginal wall contracts.

Orgasmic reorientation A procedure for treating certain paraphilias by teaching clients to respond to new, more appropriate sources of sexual stimulation.

Orgasm phase The phase of the sexual response cycle during which an individual's sexual pleasure peaks and sexual tension is released as muscles in the pelvic region contract rhythmically.

Outpatient A person who receives diagnosis or treatment in a clinic, hospital, or therapist's office but is not hospitalized overnight.

Panic attack A short bout of panic that occurs suddenly, reaches a peak within minutes, and gradually passes.

Panic disorder An anxiety disorder marked by recurrent and unpredictable panic attacks.

Panic disorder with agoraphobia A panic disorder in which panic attacks lead to agoraphobic patterns of behavior.

Paranoid personality disorder A personality disorder marked by a pattern of extreme distrust and suspiciousness of others.

Paranoid type of schizophrenia A type of schizophrenia in which the person has an organized system of delusions and hallucinations.

Paraphilias Disorders characterized by recurrent and intense sexual urges, fantasies, or behaviors involving nonhuman objects, children, nonconsenting adults, or experiences of suffering or humiliation.

Paraprofessional A person without previous professional training who provides services under the supervision of a mental health professional.

Parasomnias Sleep disorders characterized by the occurrence of abnormal events during sleep.

Parasuicide A suicide attempt that does not result in death.

Parasympathetic nervous system The group of nerve fibers of the autonomic nervous system that help maintain normal organ functioning. They slow organ functioning after stimulation and help return other bodily processes to normal.

Parens patriae The principle by which the state can make decisions to promote the individual's best interests and protect him or her from self-harm or neglect.

Parkinsonian symptoms Symptoms similar to those found in Parkinson's disease. Patients with schizophrenia who take conventional antipsychotic medications may display one or more of these symptoms.

Parkinson's disease A slowly progressive neurological disease, marked by tremors and rigidity, that may also cause dementia.

Participant modeling A behavioral treatment in which people with fears observe a therapist (model) interacting with a feared object and then interact with the object themselves.

Passive-aggressive personality disorder A category of personality disorder, listed in past versions of DSM, marked by a pattern of negative attitudes and resistance to the demands of others.

Pathological gambling An impulse-control disorder characterized by recurrent and persistent maladaptive gambling behavior that disrupts personal, family, or vocational pursuits.

Pedophilia A paraphilia in which a person has repeated and intense sexual urges or fantasies about watching, touching, or engaging in sexual acts with prepubescent children and may carry out these urges or fantasies.

Peer review system A system by which clinicians paid by an insurance company may periodically review a patient's progress and recommend the continuation or termination of insurance benefits.

Penile prosthesis A surgical implant consisting of a semirigid rod made of rubber and wire that produces an artificial erection.

Performance anxiety The fear of performing inadequately and a related tension experienced during sex.

Perseveration The persistent repetition of words and statements.

Personality A unique and long-term pattern of inner experience and outward behavior that leads to consistent reactions across various situations.

Personality disorder A very rigid pattern of inner experience and outward behavior that differs from the expectations of one's culture and leads to dysfunctioning.

Personality inventory A test designed to measure broad personality characteristics that consists of statements about behaviors, beliefs, and feelings. People evaluate the statements as either characteristic or uncharacteristic of themselves.

Pervasive developmental disorders A broad category of disorders beginning in early childhood, characterized by severe and pervasive impairments in social interaction and communication or the presence of rigid and repetitive behaviors, interests, and activities.

Phallic stage In psychoanalytic theory, the period between the third and fourth years when the focus of sexual pleasure shifts to the genitals.

Phalloplasty A surgical procedure designed to create a functional penis.

Phenothiazines A group of antihistamine drugs that became the first group of effective antipsychotic medications.

Phenylketonuria (PKU) A metabolic disorder caused by the body's inability to break down the amino acid phenylalanine, resulting in mental retardation and other symptoms.

Phobia A persistent and unreasonable fear of a particular object, activity, or situation.

Pick's disease A neurological disease that affects the frontal and temporal lobes, causing dementia.

Placebo A sham treatment that a subject believes to be genuine.

Placebo therapy A sham treatment that the subject in an experiment believes to be genuine.

Play therapy An approach to treating childhood disorders that helps children express their conflicts and feelings indirectly by drawing, playing with toys, and making up stories.

Pleasure principle The pursuit of gratification that characterizes id functioning.

Plethysmograph A device used to measure sexual arousal.

Polygraph A test that seeks to determine whether or not the test taker is telling the truth by measuring physiological responses such as respiration level, perspiration level, and heart rate. Also known as a *lie-detector test*.

Polysubstance use The use of two or more substances at the same time.

Polysubstance-related disorder A long-term pattern of maladaptive behavior centered on the abuse of or dependence on a combination of drugs.

Positive correlation A statistical relationship in which the values of two variables increase together or decrease together.

Positive psychology The study and enhancement of positive feelings, traits, and abilities.

Positive symptoms Symptoms of schizophrenia that seem to be excesses, that is, bizarre additions to normal thoughts, emotions, or behaviors.

Positron emission tomography (PET scan) A computer-produced motion picture showing rates of metabolism throughout the brain.

Postpartum depression An episode of depression experienced by some new mothers that begins within four weeks after giving birth.

Postpartum psychosis An episode of psychosis experienced by a small percentage of new mothers that begins within days or weeks after giving birth.

Posttraumatic stress disorder An anxiety disorder in which fear and related symptoms continue to be experienced long after a traumatic event.

Poverty of content A lack of meaning in spite of high emotion that is found in the speech of some people with schizophrenia.

Predisposition An inborn or acquired vulnerability for developing certain symptoms or disorders.

Prefrontal lobes Regions of the brain that play a key role in short-term memory, among other functions.

Premature ejaculation A dysfunction in which a man reaches orgasm and ejaculates before, on, or shortly after penetration and before he wishes it. Also known as *rapid ejaculation*.

Premorbid The period prior to the onset of a disorder.

Preoccupation somatoform disorders Somatoform disorders in which people misinterpret and overreact to minor, even normal, bodily symptoms or features.

Preparedness A predisposition to develop certain fears.

Prevalence The total number of cases of a disorder occurring in a population over a specific period of time.

Prevention A key feature of community mental health programs that seek to prevent or minimize psychological disorders.

Primary gain In psychodynamic theory, the gain achieved when hysterical symptoms keep internal conflicts out of awareness.

Primary hypersomnia A sleep disorder in which the main problem is excessive sleepiness for at least a month.

Primary insomnia A sleep disorder in which the main problem is an inability to initiate or maintain sleep.

Primary personality The subpersonality that appears more often than the others in individuals with multiple personality disorder.

Private psychotherapy An arrangement in which a person directly pays a therapist for counseling services.

Proband The person who is the focus of a genetic study.

Procedural memory Memory of learned skills that a person performs without needing to think about them.

Prodromal phase The period during which the symptoms of schizophrenia are not yet prominent, but the person has begun to deteriorate from previous levels of functioning.

Profound retardation A level of mental retardation (IQ below 20) at which individuals need a very structured environment with constant aid and supervision.

Projection An ego defense mechanism whereby individuals attribute to other people characteristics or impulses they do not wish to acknowledge in themselves.

Projective test A test that consists of vague material that people interpret or respond to.

Protection and advocacy system The system by which lawyers and advocates who work for patients may investigate the patients' treatment and protect their rights.

Prozac Trade name for fluoxetine, a second-generation antidepressant.

Psychedelic drugs Substances such as LSD that cause profound perceptual changes. Also called *hallucinogenic drugs*.

Psychiatric social worker A mental health specialist who is qualified to conduct psychotherapy upon earning a master's degree or doctorate in social work.

Psychiatrist A physician who in addition to medical school has completed three to four years of residency training in the treatment of abnormal mental functioning.

Psychoanalysis Either the theory or the treatment of abnormal psychological functioning that emphasizes unconscious psychological forces as the cause of psychopathology.

Psychodynamic model The theoretical perspective that sees all human functioning as being shaped by dynamic (interacting) psychological forces and explains people's behavior by reference to unconscious internal conflicts.

Psychodynamic therapy A system of therapy whose goals are to help clients uncover past traumatic events and the inner conflicts that have resulted from them, settle those conflicts, and resume personal development.

Psychogenic perspective The view that the chief causes of abnormal functioning are psychological.

Psychological autopsy A procedure used to analyze information about a deceased person, for example, in order to determine whether the person's death was a suicide.

Psychological debriefing A form of crisis intervention in which victims of traumatic incidents are helped to talk about their feelings and reactions to the incidents. Also called *critical incident stress debriefing*.

Psychomotor symptoms Disturbances in movement sometimes found in certain disorders such as schizophrenia.

Psychoneuroimmunology The study of the connections among stress, the body's immune system, and illness.

Psychopathology An abnormal pattern of functioning that may be described as deviant, distressful, dysfunctional, and/or dangerous.

Psychopathy *See* Antisocial personality disorder.

Psychopharmacologist A psychiatrist who primarily prescribes medications. Also called *pharmacotherapist*.

Psychophysiological disorders Illnesses that result from an interaction of both psychosocial and physical factors. DSM-IV-TR labels these illnesses *psychological factors affecting medical condition*. Also called *psychosomatic disorders*.

Psychophysiological test A test that measures physical responses (such as heart rate and muscle tension) as possible indicators of psychological problems.

Psychosexual stages The developmental stages defined by Freud in which the id, ego, and superego interact.

Psychosis A state in which a person loses contact with reality in key ways.

Psychosomatic illnesses Illnesses that result from an interaction of both physical and psychosocial causes. DSM-IV-TR labels these illnesses *psychological factors affecting medical condition*. Also called *psychophysiological illnesses*.

Psychosurgery Brain surgery for mental disorders.

Psychotherapy A treatment system in which words and acts are used by a client (patient) and therapist in order to help the client overcome psychological difficulties.

Psychotropic medications Drugs that primarily affect the brain and reduce various symptoms of mental dysfunctioning.

Pyromania An impulse-control disorder characterized by a pattern of fire setting for pleasure, gratification, or relief from tension.

Rape Forced sexual intercourse or another sexual act upon a nonconsenting person or intercourse with an underage person.

Rap group A group that meets to help members talk about and explore problems in an atmosphere of mutual support.

Rapid eye movement (REM) sleep The period of the sleep cycle during which the eyes move quickly back and forth, indicating that the person is dreaming.

Rapprochement movement An effort to identify a set of common strategies that characterize the work of all effective therapists.

Rational-emotive therapy A cognitive therapy developed by Albert Ellis that helps people identify and change the irrational assumptions and thinking that help cause their psychological disorders.

Rationalization An ego defense mechanism in which one creates acceptable reasons for unwanted or undesirable behavior.

Reaction formation An ego defense mechanism whereby one counters an unacceptable desire by taking on a lifestyle that directly opposes the unwanted impulse.

Reactive depression A depression that appears to be triggered by clear events. Also known as *exogenous depression*.

Reactivity The extent to which the very presence of an observer affects a person's behavior.

Reality principle The recognition, characterizing ego functioning, that we cannot always express or satisfy our id impulses.

Receptor A site on a neuron that receives a neurotransmitter.

Regression An ego defense mechanism in which a person returns to a more primitive mode of interacting with the world.

Reinforcement The desirable or undesirable stimuli that result from an organism's behavior.

Relapse-prevention training An approach to treating alcohol abuse that is similar to behavioral self-control training but also has people plan ahead for risky situations and reactions.

Relational psychoanalytic therapy A form of psychodynamic therapy that considers therapists to be active participants in the formation of patients' feelings and reactions and therefore calls for therapists to disclose their own experiences and feelings in discussions with patients.

Relaxation training A treatment procedure that teaches people to relax at will.

Reliability A measure of the consistency of test or research results.

Repression A defense mechanism whereby the ego prevents unacceptable impulses from reaching consciousness.

Residential treatment center A place where people formerly dependent on

drugs live, work, and socialize in a drug-free environment. Also called a *therapeutic community*.

Residual type of schizophrenia A type of schizophrenia in which the acute symptoms of the disorder have lessened in strength and number yet remain in residual form.

Resistance A defense mechanism that blocks a person's free associations or causes the person to change the subject to avoid a painful discussion.

Resolution phase The fourth phase in the sexual response cycle, characterized by relaxation and a decline in arousal following orgasm.

Response inventories Tests designed to measure a person's responses in one specific area of functioning, such as affect, social skills, or cognitive processes.

Response prevention *See* Exposure and response prevention.

Response set A particular way of responding to questions or statements on a test, such as always selecting "true," regardless of the actual questions.

Restricting-type anorexia nervosa A type of anorexia nervosa in which people reduce their weight by severely restricting their food intake.

Reticular formation The brain's arousal center, which helps people to be awake, alert, and attentive.

Retrograde amnesia A lack of memory about events that occurred before the event that triggered amnesia.

Retrospective analysis A psychological autopsy in which clinicians and researchers piece together information about a person's suicide from the person's past.

Reversal design A single-subject experimental design in which behavior is measured to provide a baseline (A), then again after the treatment has been applied (B), then again after the conditions during baseline have been reintroduced (A), and then once again after the treatment is reintroduced (B). Also known as *ABAB design*.

Reward A pleasurable stimulus given to an organism that encourages a specific behavior.

Reward center A dopamine-rich pathway in the brain that produces feelings of pleasure when activated.

Reward-deficiency syndrome A condition, suspected to be present in some individuals, in which the brain's reward center is not readily activated by the usual events in their lives.

Right to refuse treatment The legal right of patients to refuse certain forms of treatment.

Right to treatment The legal right of patients, particularly those who are involuntarily committed, to receive adequate treatment.

Risperidone A commonly prescribed atypical antipsychotic drug.

Ritalin Trade name of methylphenidate, a stimulant drug that is helpful in many cases of attention-deficit/hyperactivity disorder (ADHD).

Role play A therapy technique in which clients are instructed to act out roles assigned to them by the therapist.

Rorschach test A projective test, in which a person reacts to inkblots, designed to help reveal psychological features of the person.

Rosenthal effect The general finding that the results of any experiment often conform to the expectations of the experimenter.

Rush A spasm of warmth and ecstasy that occurs when certain drugs, such as heroin, are ingested.

Savant A person with a mental disorder or significant intellectual deficits who has some extraordinary ability despite the disorder or deficits.

Schizoaffective disorder A disorder in which symptoms of both schizophrenia and a mood disorder are prominent.

Schizoid personality disorder A personality disorder in which a person persistently avoids social relationships and shows little emotional expression.

Schizophrenia A psychotic disorder in which personal, social, and occupational functioning deteriorate as a result of strange perceptions, disturbed thought processes, unusual emotions, and motor abnormalities.

Schizophreniform disorder A disorder in which all of the key features of schizophrenia are present but last only between one and six months.

Schizophrenogenic mother A type of mother—supposedly cold, domineering, and uninterested in the needs of others—who was once thought to cause schizophrenia in the child.

Schizotypal personality disorder A personality disorder in which a person displays a pattern of interpersonal problems marked by extreme discomfort in close relationships, odd forms of thinking and perceiving, and behavioral eccentricities.

School phobia A childhood pattern in which children fear going to school and often stay home for a long period of time. Also called *school refusal.*

Scientific method The process of systematically gathering and evaluating information through careful observations to gain an understanding of a phenomenon.

Seasonal affective disorder (SAD) A mood disorder in which mood episodes are related to changes in season.

Secondary gain In psychodynamic theory, the gain achieved when hysterical symptoms elicit kindness from others or provide an excuse for avoiding unpleasant activities.

Second-generation antidepressants New antidepressant drugs that differ structurally from tricyclics and MAO inhibitors.

Second messengers Chemical changes within a neuron just after the neuron receives a neurotransmitter message and just before it responds.

Sedative-hypnotic drug A drug used in low doses to reduce anxiety and in higher doses to help people sleep. Also called *anxiolytic drug.*

Selective amnesia An inability to recall some of the events that occurred over a limited period of time.

Selective serotonin reuptake inhibitors (SSRIs) A group of second-generation antidepressant drugs that increase serotonin activity specifically without affecting other neurotransmitters.

Self-actualization The humanistic process by which people fulfill their potential for goodness and growth.

Self-efficacy The judgment that one can master and perform needed behaviors whenever necessary.

Self-help group A group made up of people with similar problems who help and support one another without the direct leadership of a clinician. Also called *mutual help group.*

Self-hypnosis The process of hypnotizing oneself—for example, to forget unpleasant events.

Self-instruction training A cognitive treatment developed by Donald Meichenbaum that teaches people to use coping self-statements at times of stress or discomfort. Also called *stress inoculation training.*

Self-monitoring Clients' observation of their own behavior.

Self-statements According to some cognitive theorists, statements about oneself, sometimes counterproductive, that come to mind during stressful situations.

Self theory The psychodynamic theory that emphasizes the role of the self—a person's unified personality.

Senile Characteristic of or associated with old age.

Senile plaques Sphere-shaped deposits of beta-amyloid protein that form in the spaces between certain brain cells and in certain blood vessels as people age.

Sensate focus A treatment for sexual disorders that instructs couples to take the focus away from orgasm or intercourse and instead spend time concentrating on the pleasure achieved by such acts as kissing, hugging, and mutual massage. Also known as *nondemand pleasuring.*

Separation anxiety disorder A childhood disorder marked by excessive anxiety, even panic, whenever the child is separated from home or a parent.

Serotonin A neurotransmitter whose abnormal activity is linked to depression, obsessive-compulsive disorder, and eating disorders.

Severe retardation A level of mental retardation (IQ between 20 and 34) in which individuals require careful supervision and can learn to perform basic work in structured and sheltered settings.

Sex-change surgery A surgical procedure that changes a person's sex organs and features and thus sexual identity.

Sex offender statute The presumption by some state legislatures that people who are repeatedly found guilty of certain sex crimes have a mental disorder and should be categorized as "mentally disordered sex offenders."

Sexual aversion disorder A disorder characterized by an aversion to and avoidance of genital sexual interplay.

Sexual dysfunction A disorder marked by a persistent inability to function normally in some area of the human sexual response cycle.

Sexual masochism A paraphilia characterized by repeated and intense sexual urges, fantasies, or behaviors that involve being humiliated, beaten, bound, or otherwise made to suffer.

Sexual pain disorder A dysfunction in which a person experiences pain during sexual arousal or intercourse. *See also* Dyspareunia *and* Vaginismus.

Sexual response cycle The general sequence of behavior and feelings that occurs during sexual activity, consisting of desire, excitement, orgasm, and resolution.

Sexual sadism A paraphilia characterized by repeated and intense sexual urges, fantasies, or behaviors that involve inflicting suffering on others.

Shaping A learning procedure in which successive approximations of the desired behavior are rewarded until finally the exact and complete behavior is learned.

Shared psychotic disorder A disorder in which a person embraces delusions held by another individual. Also known as *folie à deux.*

Sheltered workshop A protected and supervised workplace that offers job opportunities and training at a pace and level tailored to people with various disabilities.

Short-term memory The memory system that collects new information. Also known as *working memory.*

Shuttle box A box separated in the middle by a barrier that an animal can jump over in order to escape or avoid shock.

Sildenafil A drug used to treat erectile disorder that helps increase blood flow to the penis during sexual activity. Marketed as *Viagra*.

Single-subject experimental design A research method in which a single subject is observed and measured both before and after the manipulation of an independent variable.

Situation anxiety The various levels of anxiety produced in a person by different situations. Also called *state anxiety*.

Sleep apnea A disorder in which a person frequently stops breathing for up to 30 or more seconds while asleep.

Sleep terror disorder A parasomnia in which persons awaken suddenly during the first third of sleep, screaming out in extreme fear and agitation.

Sleepwalking disorder A parasomnia in which people repeatedly leave their beds and walk around without being conscious of the episode or remembering it later.

Social phobia A severe and persistent fear of social or performance situations in which embarrassment may occur.

Social skills training A therapy approach that helps people learn or improve social skills and assertiveness through the use of role-playing and rehearsing of desirable behaviors.

Social therapy An approach to therapy in which the therapist makes practical advice and life adjustment a central focus of treatment for schizophrenia. Therapy also focuses on problem solving, decision making, development of social skills, and management of medications. Also known as *personal therapy*.

Sociocultural model The theoretical perspective that emphasizes the effect of society, culture, and social and family groups on individual behavior.

Sociopathy *See* Antisocial personality disorder.

Sodium amobarbital (Amytal) A drug used to put people into a near-sleep state during which some can better recall forgotten events.

Sodium pentobarbital (Pentothal) *See* Sodium amobarbital.

Somatization disorder A somatoform disorder marked by numerous recurring physical ailments without an organic basis. Also called *Briquet's syndrome*.

Somatoform disorder A physical illness or ailment that is largely explained by psychosocial causes, in which the patient experiences no sense of wanting or guiding his or her symptoms.

Somatogenic perspective The view that abnormal psychological functioning has physical causes.

Special education An approach to educating children with mental retardation in which they are grouped together and given a separate, specially designed education.

Specific phobia A severe and persistent fear of a specific object or situation (other than agoraphobia and social phobia).

Spectator role A state of mind that some people experience during sex in which they focus on their sexual performance to such an extent that their performance and their enjoyment are reduced.

Standardization The process of administering a test to a large group of persons whose performance then serves as a common standard or norm against which any individual's score can be measured.

State-dependent learning Learning that becomes associated with the conditions under which it occurred so that what is learned is best remembered under the same conditions.

State hospitals State-run public mental institutions in the United States.

State school A state-supported institution for individuals with mental retardation.

Statistical analysis The application of principles of probability to the findings of a study in order to learn how likely it is that the findings have occurred by chance.

Statistical significance A measure of the probability that a study's findings occurred by chance rather than because of the experimental manipulation.

Stimulant drug A substance that increases the activity of the central nervous system.

Stimulus generalization A phenomenon in which responses to one stimulus are also produced by similar stimuli.

Stress management program An approach to treating generalized and other anxiety disorders that teaches people techniques for reducing and controlling stress.

Stressor An event that creates a sense of threat by confronting a person with a demand or opportunity for change of some kind.

Stress-reduction seminar A workshop or series of group sessions offered by a business in which mental health professionals teach employees how to cope with and solve problems and reduce stress. Also known as *problem-solving seminar*.

Stress response A person's particular reactions to stress.

Structured interview An interview format in which the clinician asks prepared questions.

Stutter A disturbance in the normal fluency and timing of speech.

Subintentional death A death in which the victim plays an indirect, hidden, partial, or unconscious role.

Subject An individual chosen to participate in a study. Also called a *participant*.

Sublimation In psychoanalytic theory, the rechanneling of id impulses into endeavors that are both socially acceptable and personally gratifying. It can also be used as an ego defense mechanism.

Subpersonalities The distinct personalities found in individuals suffering from multiple personality disorder. Also known as *alternate personalities*.

Substance abuse Such excessive and repeated reliance on a drug that the behavior disrupts the person's life.

Substance dependence Such excessive reliance on a drug that one makes it the center of one's life and perhaps builds a tolerance to it, experiences withdrawal symptoms when one stops taking it, or both. Also known as *addiction*.

Substance-related disorder A pattern of maladaptive behavior centered on the use of, abuse of, or dependence on certain substances.

Suicide A self-inflicted death in which the person acts intentionally, directly, and consciously.

Suicide prevention program A program that tries to identify people who are at risk of killing themselves and to offer them crisis intervention.

Superego According to Freud, the psychological force that emphasizes one's conscience, values, and ideals.

Supportive nursing care A treatment, applied to anorexia nervosa in particular, in which trained nurses conduct a day-to-day hospital program.

Symbolic loss According to Freudian theory, the loss of a valued object (for example, a loss of employment) which is unconsciously interpreted as the loss of a loved one. Also called *imagined loss*.

Sympathetic nervous system The nerve fibers of the autonomic nervous system that quicken the heartbeat and produce other changes experienced as fear or anxiety.

Symptom A physical or psychological sign of a disorder.

Synapse The tiny space between the nerve ending of one neuron and the dendrite of another.

Syndrome A cluster of symptoms that usually occur together.

Synergistic effect In pharmacology, an increase of effects that occurs when more than one drug is acting on the body at the same time.

Synesthesia A crossing over of sensory perceptions caused by LSD and other hallucinogenic drugs. For example, a loud sound may be seen or a color may be felt.

Systematic desensitization A behavioral treatment that uses relaxation training and a fear hierarchy to help people with phobias react calmly to the objects or situations they dread.

Tarantism A disorder occurring throughout Europe between 900 and 1800 A.D. in which people would suddenly start to jump around, dance, and go into convulsions. Also known as *St. Vitus's dance.*

Tardive dyskinesia A condition characterized by extrapyramidal effects that appear in some patients after they have taken traditional antipsychotic drugs for an extended time.

Tay-Sachs disease A metabolic disorder that causes progressive loss of intellectual functioning, vision, and motor functioning, resulting in death.

Temporal lobes Regions of the brain that play a key role in transforming short-term memory to long-term memory, among other functions.

Tension headache *See* Muscle contraction headache.

Test A device for gathering information about a few aspects of a person's psychological functioning from which broader information about the person can be inferred.

Testosterone The principal male sex hormone.

Tetrahydrocannabinol (THC) The main active ingredient of cannabis substances.

Thanatos According to the Freudian view, the basic death instinct that functions in opposition to the life instinct.

Thematic Apperception Test (TAT) A projective test consisting of pictures that show people in ambiguous situations that the client is asked to interpret.

Theory of mind Awareness that other people base their behaviors on their own beliefs, intentions, and mental states, not on information they have no way of knowing.

Therapist A professional clinician who applies a system of therapy to help a person overcome psychological difficulties.

Therapy A systematic process for helping persons overcome their psychological problems. It consists of a patient, a trained therapist, and a series of contacts between them.

Token economy program A behavioral program in which a person's desirable behaviors are reinforced systematically throughout the day by the awarding of tokens that can be exchanged for goods or privileges.

Tolerance Upon regular use of a drug, the need of the brain and the body for ever-larger doses in order to achieve the drug's earlier effects.

Trait anxiety The general level of anxiety that a person brings to the various events in his or her life.

Tranquilizer A drug that reduces anxiety.

Transcranial magnetic stimulation A treatment procedure for depression in which an electromagnetic coil, which is placed on or above a person's head, sends a current into the individual's brain.

Transference According to psychodynamic theorists, a process in which a therapist's patients respond to the therapist as they did or do to important figures in their lives.

Transgender experience A sense that one's actual gender identity is different from the gender category to which one was born physically or that it lies outside the usual male versus female categories.

Transsexualism A term that now tends to be used to describe those people with gender identity disorder who desire and actually seek full gender change.

Transvestic fetishism A paraphilia consisting of repeated and intense sexual urges, fantasies, or behaviors that involve dressing in clothes of the opposite sex. Also known as *transvestism* or *cross-dressing.*

Treatment A procedure designed to help change abnormal behavior into more normal behavior. Also called *therapy.*

Trephination An ancient operation in which a stone instrument was used to cut away a circular section of the skull, perhaps to treat abnormal behavior.

Trichotillomania An impulse-control disorder (or compulsion) in which people repeatedly pull at and even yank out their hair, eyelashes, and eyebrows.

Tricyclic An antidepressant drug, such as imipramine, that has three rings in its molecular structure.

Trisomy A chromosomal abnormality in which an individual has three chromosomes of one kind rather than the usual two.

Tube and intravenous feeding Forced nourishment sometimes provided to sufferers of anorexia nervosa when their condition becomes life-threatening.

Type A personality style A personality pattern characterized by hostility, cynicism, drivenness, impatience, competitiveness, and ambition.

Type B personality style A personality pattern in which persons are more relaxed, less aggressive, and less concerned about time.

Type I schizophrenia According to some theorists, a type of schizophrenia dominated by positive symptoms, such as delusions, hallucinations, and certain formal thought disorders.

Type II schizophrenia According to some theorists, a type of schizophrenia dominated by negative symptoms, such as flat affect, poverty of speech, and loss of volition.

Tyramine A chemical that, if allowed to accumulate, can raise blood pressure dangerously. It is found in many common foods and is broken down by MAO.

Unconditional positive regard Full, warm acceptance of a person regardless of what he or she says, thinks, or feels; a critical component of client-centered therapy.

Unconditioned response (UCR) The natural, automatic response produced by an unconditioned stimulus.

Unconditioned stimulus (UCS) A stimulus that produces an automatic, natural response.

Unconscious The deeply hidden mass of memories, experiences, and impulses that is viewed in Freudian theory as the source of much behavior.

Undifferentiated type of schizophrenia A type of schizophrenia in which no single set of psychotic symptoms (incoherence, psychomotor disturbances, delusions, or hallucinations) dominates.

Undoing An ego defense mechanism in which a person unconsciously cancels out an unacceptable desire or act by performing another act.

Unilateral electroconvulsive therapy (ECT) A form of electroconvulsive therapy in which electrodes are attached to the head so that electrical current passes through only one side of the brain.

Unipolar depression Depression without a history of mania.

Unstructured interview An interview format in which the clinician asks spontaneous questions that are based on issues that arise during the interview.

Vaginismus A condition marked by involuntary contractions of the muscles around the outer third of the vagina during sexual activity, preventing entry of the penis.

Vagus nerve stimulation A treatment procedure for depression in which an implanted pulse generator sends regular electrical signals to a person's vagus nerve; the nerve, in turn, stimulates the brain.

Validity The accuracy of a test's or study's results; that is, the extent to which the test or study actually measures or shows what it claims to.

Valium The trade name of diazepam, an antianxiety drug.

Variable Any characteristic or event that can vary across time, locations, or persons.

Vascular dementia Dementia caused by a cerebrovascular accident, or stroke, that restricts blood flow to certain areas of the brain. Also called *multi-infarct dementia*.

Ventromedial hypothalamus (VMH) The region of the hypothalamus that, when activated, depresses hunger.

Visual hallucinations Hallucinations in which a person may either experience vague visual perceptions, perhaps of colors or clouds, or have distinct visions of people, objects, or scenes that are not there.

Voyeurism A paraphilia in which a person has repeated and intense sexual desires or urges to observe unsuspecting people secretly as they undress or have intercourse. The person may also act on these desires.

Weight set point The weight level that a person is predisposed to maintain, controlled, in part, by the hypothalamus.

Windigo An intense fear of being turned into a cannibal by a flesh-eating monster. The disorder was once found among Algonquin Indian hunters.

Withdrawal Unpleasant, sometimes dangerous reactions that may occur when people who use a drug regularly stop taking or reduce their dosage of the drug.

Working through The psychodynamic treatment process of repeatedly facing conflicts, reinterpreting feelings, and overcoming one's problems.

references

AA World Services (2008). AA fact file. New York: AA World Services.

AAAAI (American Academy of Allergy Asthma & Immunology). (2005, June). Topic of the Month: Enjoy summer vacation with allergies and asthma. Milwaukee, WI: Author.

AAMR (American Association on Mental Retardation). (2005). *AAMR fact sheets.* From AAMR.

AAP (American Academy of Pediatrics). (1999). Media education, policy statement. *Pediatrics, 104*(2), 341–343.

Abbey, S. E. (2005). Somatization and somatoform disorders. In J. L. Levenson (Ed.), *The American Psychiatric Publishing textbook of psychosomatic medicine* (pp. 271–296). Washington, DC: American Psychiatric Publishing.

Abdulhamid, I. (2002). Munchausen by proxy. *eMed. J., 3*(1).

Abel, G. G., Becker, J. V., & Cunningham-Rathner, J. (1984). Complications, consent, and cognitions in sex between children and adults. *Inter. J. Law Psychiat., 7,* 89–103.

Abel, G. G., Jordan, A., Hand, C. G., Holland, L. A., & Phipps, A. (2001). Classification models of child molesters utilizing the Abel Assessment for child sexual abuse interest. *Child Abuse Negl., 25*(5), 703–718.

Abel, G. G., Lawry, S. S., Karlstrom, E., Osborn, C. A., et al. (1994). Screening tests for pedophilia. *Criminal Justice and Behavior. 2*(1), 115–131.

Abela, J. R. Z., Brozina, K., & Seligman, M. E. P. (2004). A test of integration of the activation hypothesis and the diathesis-stress component of the hopelessness theory of depression. *Brit. J. Clin. Psychol., 32*(2), 111–128.

Abela, J. R. Z., & Hankin, B. L. (2008). Depression in children and adolescents: Causes, treatment, and prevention. In J. R. Z. Abela & B. L. Hankin (Eds.), *Handbook of depression in children and adolescents.* New York: Guilford Press.

Abercrombie, H. C., Schaefer, S. M., Larson, C. L., Oakes, T. R., Lindgren, K. A., Holden, J. E., et al. (1998). Metabolic rate in the right amygdala predicts negative affect in depressed patients. *Neuroreport, 9,* 3301–3307.

Abou-Saleh, M. T. (1992). Lithium. In E. S. Paykel (Ed.), Handbook of affective disorders. New York: Guilford Press.

Abou-Saleh, M. T., Ghubash, R., Karim, L., Krymski, M., & Anderson, D. N. (1999). The role of pterins and related factors in the biology of early postpartum depression. *Eur. Neuropsychopharmacology, 9*(4), 295–300.

Abraham, K. (1911). Notes on the psychoanalytic investigation and treatment of manic-depressive insanity and allied conditions. In *Selected papers on psychoanalysis* (pp. 137–156). New York: Basic Books. (Work republished 1960)

Abraham, K. (1916). The first pregenital stage of the libido. In *Selected papers on psychoanalysis* (pp. 248–279). New York: Basic Books. (Work republished 1960)

Abraham, S., & Llewellyn-Jones, D. (1984). *Eating disorders: The facts.* New York: Oxford University Press.

Abram, K. M., & Teplin, L. A. (1990). Drug disorder, mental illness, and violence. *Nat. Inst. Drug Abuse Res. Monogr. Ser., 103,* 222–238.

Abramowitz, J. S. (2008). Is nonparaphilic compulsive sexual behavior a variant of OCD? In J. S. Abramowitz, D. McKay, & S. Taylor (Eds.), *Obsessive-compulsive disorder: Subtypes and spectrum conditions.* Oxford, England: Elsevier.

Abramowitz, J. S., McKay, D., & Taylor, S. (Eds.). (2008). *Obsessive-compulsive disorder: Subtypes and spectrum conditions.* Oxford, England: Elsevier.

Abramowitz, S. I. (1986). Psychosocial outcomes of sex reassignment surgery. *J. Cons. Clin. Psychol., 54*(2), 183–189.

Abramson, L. Y., Alloy, L. B., Hankin, B. L., Haeffel, G. J., MacCoon, D. G., & Gibb, B. E. (2002). Cognitive vulnerability—Stress models of depression in a self-regulatory and psychobiological context. In I. H. Gotlib & C. L. Hammen (Eds.), *Handbook of depression* (pp. 268–294). New York: Guilford Press.

Abramson, L. Y., Metalsky, G. I., & Alloy, L. B. (1989). Hopelessness depression: A theory-based subtype of depression. *Psychol. Rev., 96*(2), 358–372.

Abramson, L. Y., Seligman, M. E., & Teasdale, J. D. (1978). Learned helplessness in humans: Critique and reformulation. *J. Abnorm. Psychol., 87*(1), 49–74.

Achenbach, T. M., Krukowski, R. A., Dumenci, L., & Ivanova, M. Y. (2005). Assessment of adult psychopathology: Meta-analyses and implications of cross-informant correlations. *Psychol. Bull., 131*(3), 361–382.

Acocella, J. (1999). *Creating hysteria: Women and multiple personality disorder.* San Francisco: Jossey-Bass.

Acosta, M. C., Haller, D. L., & Schnoll, S. H. (2005). Cocaine and stimulants. In R. J. Frances, A. H. Mack, & S. I. Miller (Eds.), *Clinical textbook of addictive disorders* (3rd ed., pp. 184–218). New York: Guilford Press.

Adam, K. S., Bouckoms, A., & Streiner, D. (1982). Parental loss and family stability in attempted suicide. *Arch. Gen. Psychiat., 39* (9), 1081–1085.

Adams, G., Turner, H., & Bucks, R. (2005). The experience of body dissatisfaction in men. *Body Image, 2*(3), 271–283.

Adams, R. E., & Boscarino, J. A. (2005). Stress and well-being in the aftermath of the World Trade Center attack: The continuing effects of a communitywide disaster. *J. Comm. Psychol., 33*(2), 175–190.

Adams, W. L. (2004). No frowny faces here. *Newsweek, 144*(6), 11.

Adams, W. L., & Cox, N. S. (1997). Epidemiology of problem drinking among elderly people. In A. Gurnack (Ed.), *Older adults' misuse of alcohol, medicines, and other drugs.* New York: Springer.

Addington, D., & Addington, J. (2008). First-episode psychosis. In K. T. Mueser & D. V. Jeste (Eds.), *Clinical handbook of schizophrenia* (pp. 367–379). New York: Guilford Press.

Addis, M. E., & Martell, C. R. (2004). *Overcoming depression one step at a time: The new behavioral activation approach to getting your life back.* Oakland, CA: New Harbinger.

Adelson, R. (2005). Limit violations just spur more drinking. *Monitor Psychol., 36*(9), 20–21.

Ader, R., Felten, D. L., & Cohen, N. (Eds.). (2001). *Psychoneuroimmunology* (3rd ed., Vols. 1 & 2). San Diego, CA: Academic Press.

Adler, G. (2000). The alliance and the more disturbed patient. In S. T. Levy (Ed.), *The therapeutic alliance. Workshop series of the American Psychoanalytic Association, Monograph 9.* Madison, CT: International Universities Press.

Adler, N. E., Boyce, T., Chesney, M. A., Cohen, S., Folkman, S., Kahn, R. L., et al. (1994). Socioeconomic status and health: The challenge of the gradient. *Amer. Psychologist, 49*(1), 15–24.

Affatati, V., Di Nicola, V., Santoro, M., Bellomo, A., Todarello, G., & Todarello, O. (2004). Psychotherapy of gender identity disorder: Problems and perspectives. *Medica Psicosomatica, 49*(1–2), 57–64.

Agras, W. S., Sylvester, D., & Oliveau, D. (1969). The epidemiology of common fears and phobias. *Comprehen. Psychiat., 10*(2), 151–156.

Agronin, M. E. (2006). Personality disorders. In D. V. Jeste & J. H. Friedman (Eds.), *Psychiatry for neurologists.* Totowa, NJ: Humana Press.

AHA (American Heart Association). (2005). Coronary heart disease and angina pectoris. Dallas, TX: Author.

Ahrens, C. E., Dean, K., Rozee, P. D., & McKenzie, M. (2008). Understanding and preventing rape. In F. L. Denmark & M. A. Paludi (Eds.), *Psychology of women: A handbook of issues and theories* (2nd ed.). Westport, CT: Praeger Publishers.

Aiken, L. R. (1985). *Psychological testing and assessment* (5th ed.). Boston: Allyn & Bacon.

Aiken, L. R., & Groth-Marnat, G. (2006). *Psychological testing and assessment* (12th ed.). New York: Pearson/Allyn & Bacon.

Airan, R. D., Meltzer, L. A., Madhuri, R., Gong, Y., Chen, H., & Deisseroth, K. (2007). High-speed imaging reveals neurophysiological links to behavior in an animal model of depression. *Science, 317,* 819–823.

Ajdacic-Gross, V., Ring, M., Gadola, E., Lauber, C., Bopp, M., Gutzwiller, F., et al. (2008). Suicide after bereavement: An overlooked problem. *Psychol. Med., 38*(5), 673–676.

Akaike, A. (2006). Preclinical evidence of neuroprotection by cholinesterase inhibitors. *Alz. Disease Assoc. Disord., 20*(2, Suppl. 1), S8–S11.

Akashi, Y. J., Nakazawa, K., Sakakibara, M., Miyaake, F., Musha, H., & Sasaka, K. (2004). ^{123}I-MIBG myocardial scintigraphy in patients with "takotsubo" cardiomyopathy. *J. Nuclear Med., 45*(July), 1121–1127.

Akechi, T., Okamura, H., Yamawaki, S., & Uchitomi, Y. (2001). Why do some cancer patients with depression desire an early death and others do not? *Psychosomatics, 42*(2), 141–145.

Akerele, E. O., & Levin, F. R. (2002). Substance abuse among patients with schizophrenia. *J. Psychiat. Prac., 8*(2), 70–80.

Akhtar, S., Byrne, J. P., & Doghramji, K. (1986). The demographic profile of borderline personality disorder. *J. Clin. Psychiat., 47,* 196–198.

Akhtar, S., Wig, N. H., Verma, V. K., Pershod, D., & Verma, S. K. (1975). A phenomenological analysis of symptoms in obsessive-compulsive neuroses. *Brit. J. Psychiat., 127,* 342–348.

Akins, C. K. (2004). The role of Pavlovian conditioning in sexual behavior: A comparative analysis of human and nonhuman animals. *Inter. J. Compat. Psychol., 17*(2–3), 241–262.

Akins, C. K., Panicker, S., & Cunningham, C. L. (Eds.). (2005). *Laboratory animals in research and teaching: Ethics, care, and methods.* Washington, DC: American Psychological Association.

Akiskal, H. S. (2005). Searching for behavioral indicators of bipolar II in patients presenting with major depressive episodes: The "red sign," the "rule of three" and other biographic signs of temperamental extravagance, activation and hypomania. *J. Affect. Disorders, 84*(2–3), 279–290.

Akiskal, H. S. (2005). The dark side of bipolarity: Detecting bipolar depression in its pleomorphic expressions. *J. Affect. Disorders, 84*(2–3), 107–115.

Akiskal, H. S., & Benazzi, F. (2008). Continuous distribution of atypical depressive symptoms between major depressive and bipolar II disorders: Dose-response relationship with bipolar family history. *Psychopathology, 41*(1), 39–42.

Akyuz, G., Sar, V., Kugu, N., & Dogan, O. (2005). Reported childhood trauma, attempted suicide and self-mutilative behavior among women in the general population. *Eur. Psychiat., 20*(3), 268–273.

Albert, U., Maina, G., Forner, F., & Bogetto, F. (2004). DSM-IV obsessive-compulsive personality disorder: Prevalence in patients with anxiety disorders and in healthy comparison subjects. *Comprehen. Psychiat., 45*(5), 325–332.

Alcántara, C., & Gone, J. P. (2008). Suicide in Native American communities: A transactional-ecological formulation of the problem. In M. M. Leach & F. T. L. Leong (Eds.), *Suicide among racial and ethnic minority groups: Theory, research, and practice* (pp. 173–199). New York: Routledge/Taylor & Francis Group.

Aldwin, C. M., Spiro, A., III, & Park, C. L. (2006). Health, behavior, and optimal aging: A life span developmental perspective. In J. E. Birren & K. W. Schaie (Eds.), *Handbook of the psychology of aging* (6th ed., pp. 85–104). San Diego, CA: Elsevier.

Alegria, M., Kessler, R. C., Bijl, R., Lin, E., Heeringa, S. G., Takeuchi, D. T., et al. (2000). Comparing data on mental health service use between countries. In G. Andrews & S. Henderson (Eds.), *Unmet need in psychiatry: Problems, resources, responses* (pp. 97–118). New York: Cambridge University Press.

Alegria, M., Mulvaney-Day, N., Torres, M., Polo, A., Cao, Z., & Canino, G. (2007). Prevalence of psychiatric disorders across Latino subgroups in the United States. *Amer. J. Publ. Hlth., 97*(1), 68–75.

Alegria, M., Takeuchi, D., Canino, G., Duan, N., Shrout, P., Meng, X. L., et al. (2004). Considering context, place and culture: The National Latino and Asian American Study. *Inter. J. Methods Psychiatr. Res., 13*(4), 208–220.

Alexander, J. F., Sexton, T. L., & Robbins, M. S. (2002). The developmental status of family therapy in family psychology intervention science. In H. A. Liddle, D. A. Santisteban, R. F. Levant, & J. H. Bray (Eds.), *Family psychology:*

Science-based interventions (pp. 17–40) Washington, DC: American Psychological Association.

Alexander-Passe, N. (2006). How dyslexic teenagers cope: An investigation of self-esteem, coping and depression. *Dyslexia: Inter. J. Res. Pract., 12*(4), 256–275.

Alexopoulos, G. S. (2005). Depression in the elderly. *Lancet, 365*(9475), 1961–1970.

Alison, L. J., & Ogan, J. S. (2006). Offender profiling. In R. D. McAnulty & M. M. Burnette (Eds.), *Sex and sexuality—Volume 3: Sexual deviation and sexual offenses.* Westport, CT: Praeger Publishers.

Allan, C. A., Smith, I., & Mellin, M. (2000). Detoxification from alcohol: A comparison of home detoxification and hospital-based day patient care. *Alcohol Alcoholism, 35*(1), 66–69.

Allard, R., Marshall, M., & Plante, M. C. (1992). Intensive follow-up does not decrease the risk of repeat suicide attempts. *Suic. Life-Threat. Behav., 22,* 303–314.

Allderidge, P. (1979). Hospitals, madhouses and asylums: Cycles in the care of the insane. *Brit. J. Psychiat., 134,* 321–334.

Allen, C. (2005). The links between heroin, crack cocaine and crime: Where does street crime fit in? *Brit. J. Criminol., 45*(3), 355–372.

Allen, D. F. (Ed.). (1985). *The cocaine crisis.* Plenum Press: New York.

Allen, J. G. (1993). Dissociative processes: Theoretical underpinnings of a working model for clinician and patient. *Bull. Menninger Clin., 57*(3), 287–308.

Allen, N. B., Gilbert, P., & Semedar, A. (2004). Depressed mood as an interpersonal strategy: The importance of relational models. In N. Haslem (Ed.), *Relational models theory: A contemporary overview* (pp. 309–334). Mahwah, NJ: Lawrence Erlbaum.

Allen, P., Larol, F., McGuire, P. K., & Aleman, A. (2008). The hallucinating brain: A review of structural and functional neuroimaging studies of hallucinations. *Neurosci. Biobehav. Rev., 32*(1), 175–191.

Allgood-Merten, B., Lewinsohn, P. M., & Hops, H. (1990). Sex differences and adolescent depression. *J. Abnorm. Psychol., 99*(1), 55–63.

Allison, C., Williams, J., Scott, F., Stott, C., Bolton, P., Baron-Cohen, S., & Brayne, C. (2007). The Childhood Asperger Syndrome Test (CAST): Test-retest reliability in a high scoring sample. *Autism, 11*(2), 173–185.

Allison, K. C., & Friedman, L. S. (2004, September 27). Soothing a sensitive gut. *Newsweek, 144*(13), 71.

Allsop, S., Saunders, B., & Phillips, M. (2000). The process of relapse in severely dependent male problem drinkers. *Addiction, 95*(1), 95–106.

Al-Subaie, A., & Alhamad, A. (2000). Psychiatry in Saudi Arabia. In I. Al-Jun[[uoverbar]] n (Eds.), *Mental illness in the Islamic world* (pp. 205–233). Madison, CT: International Universities Press.

Althof, S. E. (1995). Pharmacologic treatment of rapid ejaculation. Special issue: Clinical sexuality. *Psychiatr. Clin. N. Amer., 18*(1), 85–94.

Althof, S. E. (2007). Treatment of rapid ejaculation: Psychotherapy, pharmacotherapy, and combined therapy. In S. R. Leiblum, *Principles and practice of sex therapy* (4th ed., pp. 212–240). New York: Guilford Press.

Alves, T. M., Pereira, J. C. R., & Elkis, H. (2005). The psychopathological factors of

refractory schizophrenia. *Revista Brasileira de Psiquiatria, 27*(2), 108–112.

Alzheimer's Association. (2007). Care in the U.S. Graph cited in *Newsweek, CXLIX*(25), 56.

American Association on Mental Retardation. (1992). *Mental retardation: Definition, classification, and systems of supports* (9th ed.). Washington, DC: Author.

American Society for Aesthetic Plastic Surgery. (2004). 11.9 million cosmetic procedures in 2004: American society for aesthetic plastic surgery reports 44 percent increase. Press release from ASAPS.

Amsterdam, J. D. (2003). A double-blind, placebo-controlled trial of the safety and efficacy of Selegiline Transdermal System without dietary restrictions in patients with major depressive disorder. *J. Clin. Psychiat., 64,* 208–214.

Andersen, A. E. (1985). *Practical comprehensive treatment of anorexia nervosa and bulimia.* Baltimore: Johns Hopkins University Press.

Anderson, D. (1994). *Breaking the tradition on college campuses: Reducing drug and alcohol misuse.* Fairfax, VA: George Mason University Press.

Anderson, K. G., Sankis, L. M., & Widiger, T. A. (2001). Pathology versus statistical infrequency: Potential sources of gender bias in personality disorder criteria. *J. Nerv. Ment. Dis., 189*(10), 661–668.

Anderson, S. (2007, June 4). Ritalin use doubles after divorce, study finds. *Yahoo! News.* Retrieved June 5, 2007, from http://news.yahoo.com

Anderson-Fye, E. P. (2004). A "Coca-Cola" shape: Cultural change, body image, and eating disorders in San Andres, Belize. *Cult. Med. Psychiat., 28*(4), 561–595.

Andrasik, F., & Walch, S. E. (2003). Headaches. In A. M. Nezu, C. J. Nezu, P. A. Geller, & I. B. Weiner (Eds.), *Handbook of psychology: Health psychology* (Vol. 9, pp. 245–266). New York: Wiley.

Andreasen, N. C. (2001). *Brave new brain: Conquering mental illness in the era of the genome.* New York: Oxford University Press.

Andreasen, N. C. (Ed.). (2005). *Research advances in genetics and genomics: Implications for psychiatry.* Washington, DC: American Psychiatric Publishing.

Andreasen, N. C., & Black, D. W. (2006). *Introductory textbook of psychiatry* (4th ed.). Washington, DC: American Psychiatric Publishing.

Andresen, J. (2000). Meditation meets behavioral medicine: The story of experimental research on meditation. *J. Consciousness. Stud., 7*(11–12), 17–73.

Andrews, B., & Wilding, J. M. (2004). The relation of depression and anxiety to life-stress and achievement in students. *Brit. J. Psychol., 95*(4), 509–521.

Andrews, M. (2006, September 18). Decoding Myspace. *U.S. News & World Report, 141*(10), 46–60

Andrews, V. (1998, December 14). Abducted by aliens? Or just a little schizoid? *HealthScout.*

Angier, N. (2001, May 20). Bully for you: Why push comes to shove. *New York Times,* Sect. 4, p. 1.

Anglin, D. M., Link, B. G., & Phelan, J. C. (2006). Racial differences in stigmatizing attitudes toward people with mental illness. *Psychiatr. Serv., 57*(6), 857–862.

Angst, J., Gamma, A., Endrass, J., Goodwin, R., Ajdacic, V., Eich, D., et al. (2004).

Obsessive-compulsive severity spectrum in the community: Prevalence, comorbidity, and course. *Eur. Arch. Psychiat. Clin. Neurosci., 254*(3), 156–164.

Angst, J., Gamma, A., Endrass, J., Hantouche, E., Goodwin, R., Ajdacic, V., et al. (2005). Obsessive-compulsive syndromes and disorders: Significance of comorbidity with bipolar and anxiety syndromes. *Eur. Arch. Psychiat. Clin. Neurosci., 255*(1), 65–71.

Angst, J., Sellaro, R., Stassen, H. H., & Gamma, A. (2005). Diagnostic conversion from depression to bipolar disorders: Results of a long-term prospective study of hospital admissions. *J. Affect. Disorders, 84*(2–3), 149–157.

Annunziato, R. A., Lee, J. N., & Lowe, M. R. (2007). A comparison of weight-control behaviors in African American and Caucasian women. *Ethnicity Dis., 17,* 262–267.

Anonymous. (1996). First person account: Social, economic, and medical effects of schizophrenia. *Schizo. Bull., 22*(1), 183.

Anooshian, J., Streltzer, J., & Goebert, D. (1999). Effectiveness of a psychiatric pain clinic. *Psychosomatics, 40*(3), 226–232.

Anthony, J. C., Arria, A. M., & Johnson, E. O. (1995). Epidemiological and public health issues for tobacco, alcohol, and other drugs. In J. M. Oldham & M. B. Riba (Eds.), *American Psychiatric Press review of psychiatry* (Vol. 14). Washington, DC: American Psychiatric Press.

Antoni, M. H. (2005). Behavioural interventions and psychoneuroimmunology. In K. Vedhara & M. Irwin (Eds.), *Human psychoneuroimmunology.* Oxford, England: Oxford University Press.

Antony, M. M., & Barlow, D. H. (2002). Specific phobias. In D. H. Barlow (Ed.), Anxiety and its disorders: The nature and treatment of anxiety and panic (2nd ed., pp. 380–417). New York: Guilford Press.

Antony, M. M., & Swinson, R. P. (2000). *Phobic disorders and panic in adults: A guide to assessment and treatment.* Washington, DC: American Psychological Association.

Aouizerate, B., Rotge, J. Y., Martin-Guehl, C., Cuny, E., Rougier, A., Guehl, D., et al. (2006). A systematic review of psychosurgical treatments for obsessive-compulsive disorder: Does deep brain stimulation represent the future trend in psychosurgery? *Clin. Neuropsychiat.: J. Treat. Eval., 3*(6), 391–403.

APA (American Psychiatric Association). (1993). *Practice guideline for major depressive disorder in adults.* Washington, DC: Author.

APA (American Psychiatric Association). (1994). *Diagnostic and statistical manual of mental disorders* (4th ed.). Washington, DC: Author.

APA (American Psychiatric Association). (2000). *DSM-IV text revision.* Washington, DC: Author.

APA (American Psychiatric Association). (2003). Questions and answers on using "insanity" as a legal defense. *HealthyMinds.org.* Arlington, VA: American Psychiatric Association.

APA (American Psychological Association). (1992). Ethical principles of psychologists and code of conduct. Washington: DC: Author.

APA (American Psychological Association). (2002). Ethical principles of psychologists and code of conduct. Washington: DC: Author.

APA (American Psychological Association). (2005). Executive summary: Risk factors for

meeting the public's need for health service psychologists. Washington, DC: Author.

APA (American Psychological Association). (2005, March 3). American Psychological Association announces plans for next phase of tsunami relief efforts. Press release.

APA (American Psychological Association). (2008). The American Psychological Association's disaster response network. *APA Online.* Retrieved August 7, 2008, from http://www.apa.org/practice/drnindex.html

Apostolova, L. G., & Cummings, J. L. (2008). Neuropsychiatric aspects of Alzheimer's disease and other dementing illnesses. In S. C. Yudofsky & R. E. Hales (Eds.), *The American psychiatric publishing textbook of neuropsychiatry and behavioral neurosciences* (5th ed.). Washington, DC: American Psychiatric Publishing.

Appel, J. B., West, W. B., and Buggy, J. (2004). LSD, Serotonin (5 HT) and the evolution of a behavioral assay. *Neurosci. Biobehav. Rev., 27* 693–701.

Appelbaum, P. S. (2000). "I vote. I count": Mental disability and the right to vote. *Psychiatr. Serv., 51*(7), 849–850, 863.

Apter, A., & Wasserman, D. (2007). Suicide in psychiatric disorders during adolescence. In R. Tatarelli, M. Pompili, & P. Girardi (Eds.), *Suicide in psychiatric disorders.* New York: Nova Science Publishers.

ARA (American Retirement Association). (2007). Combating loneliness. *NJJN-Princeton Mercer Bucks,* November 13, 2007, 26.

Araf, J. (2008, January 6). The wounded chaplain. National Public Radio.

Arango, C., Buchanan, R. W., Kirkpatrick, B., et al. (2004). The deficit syndrome in schizophrenia: Implications for the treatment of negative symptoms. *Eur. Psychiat., 19,* 21–26.

Archer, D., & McDaniel, P. (1995). Violence and gender: Differences and similarities across societies. In R. B. Ruback & N. A. Weiner (Eds.), *Interpersonal violent behaviors: Social and cultural aspects.* New York: Springer.

Archibald, M. E. (2007). *The evolution of self-help: How a health movement became an institution.* New York: Palgrave Macmillan.

Ardoin, S. P., Martens, B. K., Wolfe, L. A., Hilt, A. M., & Rosenthal, B. D. (2004). A method for conditioning reinforcer preferences in students with moderate mental retardation. *J. Dev. Phys. Disabil., 16*(1), 33–51.

Arias, E., Anderson, R. N., Kung, H. C., Murphy, S. L., & Kochanek, K. D. (2003). Deaths: Final data for 2001. *National Vital Statistics Reports, 52.* Hyattsville, MD: National Center for Health Statistics.

Arieti, S. (1974). *Interpretation of schizophrenia.* New York: Basic Books.

Arieti, S., & Bemporad, J. (1978). *Severe and mild depression: The psychotherapeutic approach.* New York: Basic Books.

Arikha, N. (2007). *Passions and tempers: A history of the humours.* New York: Ecco/HarperCollins.

Aring, C. D. (1974). The Gheel experience: Eternal spirit of the chainless mind! *JAMA, 230*(7), 998–1001.

Aring, C. D. (1975). Gheel: The town that cares. *Fam. Hlth., 7*(4), 54–55, 58, 60.

Arliss, J. M., Kaplan, E. N., Galvin, S. L. Lynn, S. J., & Kirsch, I. (2005). The effect of the lunar cycle on frequency of births and birth

complications. *Amer. J. Obstet. Gynecol., 192*(5), 1462–1464.

Armour, D., & Paton, C. (2004). Melatonin in the treatment of insomnia in children and adolescents. *Psychiatr. Bull., 28*(6), 222–224.

Armour, S. (2006, August 22). Workplaces quit quietly ignoring mental illness. *USAtoday.com.* Retrieved July 6, 2007, from http://usatoday.com/money/workplace/2006-08-21-depressed-usat_x.htm?csp=N009

Armstrong, M. J. (2001). Ethnic minority women as they age. In J. D. Garner & S. O. Mercer (Eds.), *Women as they age* (2nd ed., pp. 97–114). New York: Haworth.

Arndt, W. B., Hietpas, T., & Kim, J. (2004). Critical characteristics of male serial murderers. *Amer. J. Criminal Justice, 29*(1), 117–131.

Arnett, J. J., & Balle-Jensen, L. (1993). Cultural bases of risk behavior: Danish adolescents. *Child Dev., 64*(6), 1842–1855.

Arntz, A. (2005). Introduction to special issue: Cognition and emotion in borderline personality disorder. *J. Behav. Ther. Exp. Psychiat., 36*(3), 167–172.

Arvanites, T. M. (1989). The differential impact of deinstitutionalization on white and nonwhite defendants found incompetent to stand trial. *Bull. Amer. Acad. Psychiat. Law, 17,* 311–320.

ASA (Autism Society of America). (2005). Asperger's syndrome. Retrieved from www.autism-society.org

ASA (Autism Society of America). (2006). Asperger's syndrome. Retrieved from www.autism-society.org

Asarnow, J. R., Asarnow, R. F., Hornstein, N., & Russell, A. (1991). Childhood-onset schizophrenia: Developmental perspectives on schizophrenic disorders. In E. F. Walker (Ed.), *Schizophrenia: A life-course developmental perspective.* San Diego: Academic Press.

Asberg, M., Traskman, L., & Thoren, P. (1976). 5 HIAA in the cerebrospinal fluid: A biochemical suicide predictor? *Arch. Gen. Psychiat., 33*(10), 1193–1197.

Ash, R. (1998). *The top 10 of everything 1999.* New York: DK Publishing.

Ash, R. (1999). *Fantastic book of 1001 facts.* New York: DK Publishing.

Ash, R. (2001). *The top 10 of everything 2002* (American ed.). New York: DK Publishing.

Ashton, A. K. (2007). The new sexual pharmacology: A guide for the clinician. In S. R. Leiblum (Ed.), *Principles and practice of sex therapy* (4th ed., pp. 509–540). New York: Guilford Press.

Ashton, C. H. (2001). Pharmacology and effects of cannabis: A brief review. *Brit. J. Psychiat., 178,* 101–106.

Ashton, J. R., & Donnan, S. (1981). Suicide by burning as an epidemic phenomenon: An analysis of 82 deaths and inquests in England and Wales in 1978–9. *Psychol. Med., 11*(4), 735–739.

Asimov, I. (1997). *Isaac Asimov's book of facts.* New York: Random House (Wings Books).

Asmundson, G. J. G., Stapleton, J. A., & Taylor, S. (2004). Are avoidance and numbing distinct PTSD symptom clusters? *J. Traum. Stress, 17*(6), 467–475.

Asmundson, G. J. G., & Taylor, S. (2005). *It's not all in your head. How worrying about your health could be making you sick — and what you can do about it.* New York: Guilford Press.

Asmundson, G. J. G., & Taylor, S. (2008). Health anxiety and its disorders. In M. Hersen

& J. Rosqvist (Eds.), *Handbook of psychological assessment, case conceptualization, and treatment, Vol. 1: Adults* (pp. 701–727). Hoboken, NJ: John Wiley & Sons.

Asnis, G. M., Kohn, S. R., Henderson, M., & Brown, N. L. (2004). SSRIs versus non-SSRIs in posttraumatic stress disorder: An update with recommendations. *Drugs, 64*(4), 383–404.

Asplund, R. (2005). Sleep and sensory organ functions in the elderly. *Sleep Hyp., 7*(2), 68–76.

Astin, J. A. (2004). Mind-body therapies for the management of pain. *Clin. J. Pain, 20*(1), 27–32.

Ator, N. A. (2005). Contributions of GABA-sub(A) receptor subtype selectivity to abuse liability and dependence potential of pharmacological treatments for anxiety and sleep disorders. *CNS Spectrums, 10*(1), 31–39.

Avenevoli, S., Knight, E., Kessler, R. C., & Merikangas, K. R. (2008). Epidemiology of depression in children and adolescents. In J. R. Z. Abela & B. L. Hankin (Eds.), *Handbook of depression in children and adolescents.* New York: Guilford Press.

Avery, D., & Lubrano, A. (1979). Depression treated with imipramine and ECT: The DeCarolis study reconsidered. *Amer. J. Psychiat., 136,* 559–569.

Awad, A. G., & Voruganti, L. N. P. (2007). Antipsychotic medications, schizophrenia and the issue of quality of life. In A. G. Awad & M. S. Ritsner (Eds.), *Quality of life impairment in schizophrenia, mood and anxiety disorders: New perspectives on research and treatment* (pp. 307–319). New York: Springer Science + Business Media.

Awata, S., Seki, T., Koizumi, Y., Sato, S., Hozawa, A., Omori, K., et al. (2005). Factors associated with suicidal ideation in an elderly urban Japanese population: A community-based, cross-sectional study. *Psychiat. Clin. Neurosci., 59*(3), 327–336.

Axelrod, B. N., & Wall, J. R. (2007). Expectancy of impaired neuropsychological test scores in a non-clinical sample. *Internat. J. Neurosci., 117*(11), 1591–1602.

Ayalon, L., & Huyck, M. H. (2001). Latino caregivers of relatives with Alzheimer's disease. *Clin. Geront., 24*(3–4), 93–106.

Ayalon, L., & Young, M. A. (2003). A comparison of depressive symptoms in African Americans and Caucasian Americans. *J. Cross-Cult. Psychol. 34*(1), 111–124.

Ayd, F. J., Jr. (1956). A clinical evaluation of Frenquel. *J. Nerv. Ment. Dis., 124,* 507–509.

Ayllon, T. (1963). Intensive treatment of psychotic behavior by stimulus satiation and

Ayllon, T., & Michael, J. (1959). The psychiatric nurse as a behavioural engineer. *J. Exp. Anal. Behav., 2,* 323–334.

Ayoub, C. C. (2006). Munchausen by proxy. In T. G. Plante (Ed.), *Mental disorders of the new millenium: Biology and function* (Vol. 3, pp. 173–193). Westport, CT: Praeger Publishers/Greenwood Publishing.

Ayoub, C. C., Deutsch, R. M., & Kinscherff, R. (2000). Munchausen by proxy: Definitions, identification, and evaluation. In R. M. Reece (Ed.), *Treatment of child abuse: Common ground for mental health, medical, and legal practitioners* (pp. 213–226). Baltimore: Johns Hopkins University Press.

Ayoub, C. C., Deutsch, R. M., & Kinscherff, R. (2000). Psychosocial management issues

in Munchausen by proxy. In R. M. Reese (Ed.), *Treatment of child abuse: Common ground for mental health, medical, and legal practitioners* (pp. 226–235). Baltimore: Johns Hopkins University Press.

Azar, B. (1995). Mental disabilities and the brain-gene link. *APA Monitor, 26*(12), 18.

Azar, S. T., Ferraro, M. H., & Breton, S. J. (1998). Intrafamilial child maltreatment. In T. H. Ollendick & M. Hersen (Eds.), *Handbook of child psychopathology* (3rd ed.). New York: Plenum.

Bach, A. K., Wincze, J. P., & Barlow, D. H. (2001). Sexual dysfunction. In D. H. Barlow (Ed.), *Clinical handbook of psychological disorders: A step-by-step treatment manual* (3rd ed., pp. 562–608). New York: Guilford Press.

Bach, P. A. (2007). Psychotic disorders. In D. W. Woods & J. W. Kanter (Eds.), *Understanding behavior disorders: A contemporary behavioral perspective.* Reno, NV: Context Press.

Bachmann, A. W., Sedgley, T. L., Jackson, R. V., Gibson, J. N., Young, R. McD., & Torpy, D. J. (2005). Glucocorticoid receptor polymorphisms and post-traumatic stress disorder. *Psychoneuroendocrinology, 30*(3), 297–306.

Backmund, M., Meyer, K., Eichenlaub, D., & Schuetz, C. G. (2001). Predictors for completing an inpatient detoxification program among intravenous heroin users, methadone substituted and codeine substituted patients. *Drug Alc. Dep., 64*(2), 173–180.

Baer, L. (2001). *The imp of the mind: Exploring the silent epidemic of obsessive bad thoughts.* New York: Dutton/Penguin Books.

Baer, L., Platman, S. R., Kassir, S., & Fieve, R. R. (1971). Mechanisms of renal lithium handling and their relationship to mineral corticoids: A dissociation between sodium and lithium ions. *J. Psychiatr. Res., 8*(2), 91–105.

Bagby, E. (1922). The etiology of phobias. *J. Abnorm. Psychol., 17,* 16–18.

Bagby, R. M., Costa, P. T., Jr., Widiger, T. A., Ryder, A. G., & Marshall, M. (2005). DSM-IV personality disorders and the five-factor model of personality: A multi-method examination of domain—and facet-level predictions. *Eur. J. Pers., 19*(4), 307–324.

Baggot, M., & Mendelson, J. (2001). Does MDMA cause brain damage? In J. Holland (Ed.), *Ecstasy: The complete guide: A comprehensive look at the risks and benefits of MDMA* (pp. 110–145). Rochester, VT: Park Street Press.

Bahrick, H. (1996, January). Cited in G. Neimeyer, Anecdotes for education. *Newsletter for Abnormal Psychology.*

Bailey, D. S. (2003). Compulsive cybersex can jeopardize marriage, rest of life. *Monitor Psychol., 34*(9), 20.

Bailey, D. S. (2003). Help the media prevent copycat suicides. *Monitor Psychol., 34*(9), 14.

Bailey, J. E., Argyropoulos, S. V., Lightman, S. L., & Nutt, D. J. (2003). Does the brain noradrenaline network mediate the effects of the CO-sub-2 challenge? *J. Psychopharmacol., 17*(3), 252–259.

Bailey, J. M. (2003). *The man who would be queen: The science of gender-bending and transsexualism.* Washington, DC: National Academy Press

Baker, R. (1992). Psychosocial consequences for tortured refugees seeking asylum and refugee status in Europe. In M. Basoglu (Ed.), *Torture*

and its consequences: Current treatment approaches (pp. 83–106). Cambridge, England: Cambridge University Press.

Bakker, A., van Kesteren, P. J., Gooren, L. J. G., & Bezemer, P. D. (1993). The prevalence of transsexualism in the Netherlands. *Acta Psychiatrica Scandinavica, 87,* 237–238.

Baldessarini, R. J., & Tondo, L. (2007). Psychopharmacology for suicide prevention. In R. atarelli, M. Pompili, & P. Girardi (Eds.), *Suicide in psychiatric disorders.* New York: Nova Science Publishers.

Baldwin, J. S., & Dadds, M. R. (2008). Anxiety disorders. In D. Reitman (Ed.), *Handbook of psychological assessment, case conceptualization, and treatment, Vol. 2: Children and adolescents.* Hoboken, NJ: John Wiley & Sons.

Baldwin, S., & Oxlad, M. (2000). *Electroshock and minors: A fifty-year review.* Westport, CT: Greenwood.

Bancroft, J. (1989). *Human sexuality and its problems.* New York: Churchill-Livingstone.

Bancroft, J., Loftus, J., & Long, J. S. (2003). Distress about sex: A national survey of women in heterosexual relationships. *Arch. Sex. Behav., 32*(3), 193–208.

Bandura, A. (1971). Psychotherapy based upon modeling principles. In A. E. Bergin & S. L. Garfield (Eds.), *Handbook of psychotherapy and behavior change.* New York: Wiley.

Bandura, A. (1977). Self-efficacy: Toward a unifying theory of behavioral change. *Psychol. Rev., 84*(2), 191–215.

Bandura, A. (2004). Swimming against the mainstream: The early years from chilly tributary to transformative mainstream. *Behav. Res. Ther., 42*(6), 613–630.

Bandura, A., Adams, N. E., & Beyer, J. (1977). Cognitive processes mediating behavioral change. *J. Pers. Soc. Psychol., 35*(3), 125–139.

Bandura, A., & Rosenthal, T. (1966). Vicarious classical conditioning as a function of arousal level. *J. Pers. Soc. Psychol., 3,* 54–62.

Bandura, A., Roth, D., & Ross, S. (1963). Imitation of film-mediated aggressive models. *J. Abnorm. Soc. Psychol., 66,* 3–11.

Bankert, E. A., & Madur, R. J. (2006). *Institutional review board: Management and function* (2nd ed.). Boston: Jones and Bartlett Publishers.

Bard, F., Barbour, R., Cannon, C., Carretto, R., Fox, M., Games, D., et al. (2003). Epitope and isotype specificities of antibodies to beta-amyloid peptide for protection against Alzheimer's disease-like neuropathology. *Proc. Natl. Acad. Sci. USA, 100,* 2023–2028.

Bard, F., Cannon, C., Barbour, R., Burke, R. L., Games, D., Grajeda, H., et al. (2000). Peripherally administered antibodies against amyloid beta-peptide enter the central nervous system and reduce pathology in a mouse model of Alzheimer disease. *Nat. Med., 6,* 916–919.

Bareggi, S. R., Bianchi, L., Cavallaro, R., Gervasoni, M., Siliprandi, F., & Bellodi, L. (2004). Citalopram concentrations and response in obsessive-compulsive disorder: Preliminary results. *CNS Drugs, 18*(5), 329–335.

Barker, P. R., Manderscheid, R. W., Hendershot, G. E., Jack, S. S., Schoenborn, C. A., & Goldstrom, I. (1992). Serious mental illness and disability as a function of the adult household population: United States, 1989. In R. W. Manderscheid & M. A. Sonnenschein (Eds.),

Mental health, United States, 1992. Washington, DC: U.S. Department of Health and Human Services.

Barkley, R. A. (Ed.). (2002). Taking charge of ADHD: The complete authoritative guide for parents, revised edition. *J. Amer. Acad. Child Adol. Psychiat., 41*(1), 101–102.

Barkley, R. A. (2004). Adolescents with attention-deficit/hyperactivity disorder: An overview of empirically based treatments. *J. Psychiatr. Pract., 10*(1), 39–56.

Barkley, R. A. (2006). *Attention deficit hyperactivity disorder* (3rd ed.). New York: Guilford Press.

Barnard, C. (2007). Ethical regulation and animal science: Why animal behaviour is special. *Animal Behav., 74*(1), 5–13.

Barnes, A. (2004). Race, schizophrenia, and admission to state psychiatric hospitals. *Admin. Policy Ment. Hlth, 31*(3), 241–252.

Barnes, G. E., & Prosen, H. (1985). Parental death and depression. *J. Abnorm. Psychol., 94*(1), 64–69.

Baroff, G. S., & Olley, J. G. (1999). *Mental retardation: Nature, cause, and management* (3rd ed.). Philadelphia: Brunner/Mazel.

Baron, M. (2002). Manic-depression genes and the new millennium: Poised for discovery. *Mol. Psychiat., 7*(4), 342–358.

Baron-Cohen, S., & Wheelwright, S. (2003). The Friendship Questionnaire: An investigation of adults with Asperger syndrome or high-functioning autism, and normal sex differences. *J. Autism Dev. Disorders, 33,* 509–517.

Barrett, N. (2000). Wasting away on the web: Shocking internet sites are encouraging anorexia as a "lifestyle". *Planetgrrl.* Retrieved from http:///btinternet.com/~virtuous/planetgrrlbabe/babearticles

Barrett, P. M., & Shortt, A. L. (2003). Parental involvement in the treatment of anxious children. In A. E. Kazdin & J. R. Weisz (Eds.), *Evidence-based psychotherapies for children and adolescents.* New York: Guilford Press.

Barron, J. (2008). Working in mental health, the prospect of violence is a part of the job. *New York Times,* February 14, 2008.

Barrowclough, C., & Lobban, F. (2008). Family intervention. In K. T. Mueser & D. V. Jeste (Eds.), *Clinical handbook of schizophrenia* (pp. 214–225). New York: Guilford Press.

Barsky, A. J., & Ahern, D. K. (2004). Cognitive behavior therapy for hypochondriasis: A randomized controlled trial. *JAMA, 291*(12), 1464–1470.

Bartholomew, K. (2000). Clinical protocol. *Psychoanal. Inq., 20*(2), 227–248.

Bartrop, R. W., Lockhurst, E., Lazarus, L., Kiloh, L. G., & Penny, R. (1977). Depressed lymphocyte function after bereavement. *Lancet, 1,* 834–836.

Bartz, J., Kaplan, A., & Hollander, E. (2007). Obsessive-compulsive personality disorder. In W. O'Donohue, K. A. Fowler, S. O. Lilienfeld (Eds.), *Personality disorders: Toward the DSM-V.* Los Angeles: Sage Publications.

Baskin, K. (2007). Not just any old butterflies. *The Washington Post.* January 9, 2007, HE01.

Basoglu, M., Jaranson, J. M., Mollica, R., & Kastrup, M. (2001). Torture and mental health: A research overview. In E. Gerrity, T. M. Keane, & F. Tuma (Eds.), *The mental health consequences of torture* (pp. 35–62). New York: Kluwer Academic/Plenum Publishers.

Basson, R. (2007). Sexual desire/arousal disorders in women. In S. R. Leiblum (Ed.), *Principles and practice of sex therapy* (4th ed., pp. 25–53). New York: Guilford Press.

Basson, R., Berman, J., Burnett, A., Derogatis, L., Ferguson, D., Fourcroy, J., et al. (2001). Report of the International Consensus Development Conference on Female Dysfunction: Definitions and classifications. *J. Sex Marital Ther., 27*(2), 83–94.

Bastiani, A. M., Altemus, M., Pigott, T. A., Rubenstein, C., et al. (1996). Comparison of obsessions and compulsions in patients with anorexia nervosa and obsessive-compulsive disorder. *Biol. Psychiat., 39,* 966–969.

Bates, G. W., Thompson, J. C., & Flanagan, C. (1999). The effectiveness of individual versus group induction of depressed mood. *J. Psychol., 133*(3), 245–252.

Bateson, G. (1974) *Perceval's narrative: A patient's account of his psychosis.* New York: William Morrow.

Bateson, G. (1978, April 21). The double-bind theory—Misunderstood? *Psychiatr. News,* p. 40.

Bateson, G., Jackson, D., Haley, J., & Weakland, J. (1956). Toward a theory of schizophrenia. *Behav. Sci., 1,* 251–264.

Batki, S. L., & Nathan, K. I. (2008). HIV/AIDS and hepatitis C. In H. D. Kleber & M. Galanter (Eds.), *The American Psychiatric Publishing textbook of substance abuse treatment* (4th ed., pp. 581–593). Arlington, VA: American Psychiatric Publishing.

Batres, A. R. (2003). Lessons from combat veterans. In J. K. Doka & M. Lattanzi-Licht (Eds.), *Living with grief: Coping with public tragedy.* New York: Brunner-Routledge.

Baucom, D. H., Epstein, N. B., & Gordon, K. C. (2000). Marital therapy: Theory, practice, and empirical status. In C. R. Snyder & R. E. Ingram (Eds.), *Handbook of psychological change: Psychotherapy processes & practices for the 21st century* (pp. 280–308). New York: Wiley.

Baucom, D. H., Epstein, N. B., & Stanton, S. (2006). The treatment of relationship distress: Theoretical perspectives and empirical findings. In A. L. Vangelisti & D. Perlman (Eds.), *The Cambridge handbook of personal relationships* (pp. 745–765). New York: Cambridge University Press.

Baucom, D. H., Gordon, K. C., & Snyder, D. K. (2005). Treating affair couples: An integrative approach. In J. Lebow (Ed.), *Handbook of clinical family therapy* (pp. 431–463). New York: Wiley.

Bauer, M. E. (2005). Stress, glucocorticoids and ageing of the immune system. *Stress: Inter. J. Biol. Stress, 8*(1), 69–83.

Baum, A., Gatchel, R. J., & Schaeffer, M. (1983). Emotional, behavioural and physiological effects of chronic stress at Three Mile Island. *J. Cons. Clin. Psychol., 51,* 565–572.

Baum, A., Wallander, J. L., Boll, T. J., & Frank, R. G. (Eds.). (2004). *Handbook of clinical health psychology, Vol. 3: Models and perspectives in health psychology.* Washington, DC: American Psychological Association.

Baumann, B., & Bogerts, B. (2001). Neuroanatomical studies on bipolar disorder. *Brit. J. Psychiat., 178,* 142–147.

Baxter, L. R., Jr., Ackermann, R. F., Swerdlow, N. R., Brody, A., Saxena, S., Schwartz, J. M., et al. (2000). Specific brain system mediation of obsessive-compulsive disorder responsive to either medication or behavior therapy. In W. K. Goodman, M. V. Rudorfer, & J. D. Maser (Eds.), *Obsessive-compulsive disorder: Contemporary issues in treatment* (pp. 573–609). Mahwah, NJ: Lawrence Erlbaum.

Baxter, L. R., Jr., Clark, E. C., Iqbal, M., & Ackermann, R. F. (2001). Cortical-subcortical systems in the mediation of obsessive-compulsive disorder: Modeling the brain's mediation of a classic "neurosis." In D. G. Lichter & J. L. Cummings (Eds.), *Frontal-subcortical circuits in psychiatric and neurological disorders* (pp. 207–230). New York: Guilford Press.

Baxter, L. R., Phelps, M. E., Mazziotta, J. C., Guze, B. H., et al. (1987). Local cerebral glucose metabolic rates in obsessive-compulsive disorder: A comparison with rates in unipolar depression and in normal controls. *Arch. Gen. Psychiat., 44*(3), 211–218.

Baxter, L. R., Schwartz, J. M., Bergman, K. S., Szuba, M. P., Guze, B. H., Mazziotta, J. C., et al. (1992). Caudate glucose metabolic rate changes with both drug and behavior therapy for obsessive-compulsive disorder. *Arch. Gen. Psychiat., 49,* 681–689.

Baxter, L. R., Schwartz, J. M., Guze, B. H., Bergman, K., et al. (1990). PET imaging in obsessive compulsive disorder with and without depression. Symposium: Serotonin and its effects on human behavior (1989, Atlanta, GA). *J. Clin. Psychiat., 51*(Suppl.), 61–69.

Bazargan, M., Bazargan-Hejazi, S., & Baker, R. S. (2005). Treatment of self-reported depression among Hispanics and African Americans. *J. Hlth Care Poor Underserved, 16,* 328–344.

Beals, J., Manson, S. M., Whitesell, N. R., Spicer, P., Novins, D. K., & Mitchell, C. M. (2005). Prevalence of DSM-IV disorders and attendant help-seeking in 2 American Indian reservation populations. *Arch. Gen. Psychiat., 62*(1), 99–108.

Beals, K. A. (2004). *Disordered eating among athletes.* Champaign, IL: Human Kinetics.

Beasley, J. O., II. (2004). Serial murder in America: Case studies of seven offenders. *Behav. Sci. Law, 22*(3), 395–414.

Beautrais, A., Joyce, P., & Mulder, R. (2000). Unmet need following serious suicide attempt: Follow-up of 302 individuals for 30 months. In G. Andrews & S. Henderson (Eds.), *Unmet need in psychiatry: Problems, resources, responses.* New York: Cambridge University Press.

Bebbington, P., & Kuipers, E. (2008). Psychosocial factors. In K. T. Mueser & D. V. Jeste (Eds.), *Clinical handbook of schizophrenia* (pp. 74–81). New York: Guilford Press.

Bebko, J. M., & Weiss, J. A. (2006). Mental retardation. In M. Hersen & J. C. Thomas (Series Eds.) & R. T. Ammerman (Vol. Ed.), *Comprehensive handbook of personality and psychopathology, Vol. 3: Child psychopathology* (pp. 233–253). Hoboken, NJ: Wiley.

Becchetti, L., & Santoro, M. (2007). The income-unhappiness paradox: A relational goods/Baumol disease explanation. In P. L. Porta & L. Bruni (Eds.), *Handbook on the economics of happiness* (pp. 239–262). Northampton, MA: Edward Elgar Publishing.

Beck, A. T. (1967). *Depression: Clinical, experimental and theoretical aspects.* New York: Harper & Row.

Beck, A. T. (1985). Theoretical perspectives on clinical anxiety. In A. H. Tuma & J. D. Maser

(Eds.), *Anxiety and the anxiety disorders.* Hillsdale, NJ: Lawrence Erlbaum.

Beck, A. T. (1991). Cognitive therapy: A 30-year retrospective. *Amer. Psychologist, 46*(4), 368–375.

Beck, A. T. (2002). Cognitive models of depression. In R. L. Leahy & E. T. Dowd (Eds.), *Clinical advances in cognitive psychotherapy: Theory and application* (pp. 29–61). New York: Springer.

Beck, A. T. (2004). A cognitive model of schizophrenia. *J. Cog. Psychother., 18*(3), 281–288.

Beck, A. T. (2004). Cognitive therapy, behavior therapy, psychoanalysis, and pharmacotherapy: A cognitive continuum. In M. J. Mahoney, P. DeVito, D. Martin, & A. Freeman (Eds.), *Cognition and psychotherapy* (2nd ed., pp. 197–220). New York: Springer Publishing.

Beck, A. T., Butler, A. C., Brown, G. K., Dahlsgaard, K. K., Newman, C. F., & Beck, J. S. (2001). Dysfunctional beliefs discriminate personality disorders. *Behav. Res. Ther., 39*(10), 1213–1225.

Beck, A. T., & Emery, G., with Greenberg, R. L. (1985). Differentiating anxiety and depression: A test of the cognitive content-specificity hypothesis. *J. Abnorm. Psychol., 96,* 179–183.

Beck, A. T., & Freeman, A. (1990). *Cognitive therapy of personality disorders.* New York: Guilford Press.

Beck, A. T., Freeman, A., Davis, D. D., et al. (2004). *Cognitive therapy of personality disorders* (2nd ed.). New York: Guilford Press.

Beck, A. T., Rush, A. J., Shaw, B. F., & Emery, G. (1979). *Cognitive therapy of depression.* New York: Guilford Press.

Beck, A. T., Ward, C. H., Mendelson, M., Mock, J. E., & Erbaugh, J. (1962). Reliability of psychiatric diagnosis: 2. A study of consistency of clinical judgments and ratings. *Amer. J. Psychiat., 119,* 351–357.

Beck, A. T., & Weishaar, M. E. (2008). Cognitive therapy. In R. J. Corsini & D. Wedding (Eds.), *Current psychotherapies* (8th ed). Belmont, CA: Brooks Cole.

Beck, J. G. (1993). Vaginismus. In W. O'Donohue & J. H. Geer (Eds.), *Handbook of sexual dysfunctions: Assessment and treatment* (pp. 381–397). Needham Heights, MA: Allyn & Bacon.

Beck, M. (2008). When fretting is in your DNA: Overcoming the worry gene. *The Wall Street Journal.* January 15, 2008, D1.

Becker, A. E., Burwell, R. A., Gilman, S. E., Herzog, D. B., & Hamburg, P. (2002). Eating behaviors and attitudes following prolonged exposure to television among ethnic Fijian adolescent girls. *Brit. J. Psychiat., 180,* 509–514.

Becker, A. E., Burwell, R. A., Narvara, K., & Gilman, S. E. (2003). Binge eating and binge eating disorder in a small scale indigenous society: The view from Fiji. *Inter. J. Eat. Disorders, 34,* 423–431.

Becker, A. E., Fay, A., Gilman, S. E., & Stiegel-Moore, R. (2007). Facets of acculturation and their diverse relations to body shape concerns in Fiji. *Inter. J. Eat. Disorders, 40*(1), 42–50.

Becker, A. E., Grinspoon, S. K., Klibanski, A., & Herzog, D. B . (1999). Eating disorders. *New England Journal of Medicine, 340,* 1092–1098.

Becker, D. R. (2008). Vocational rehabilitation. In K. T. Mueser & D. V. Jeste (Eds.), *Clinical hand-book of schizophrenia* (pp. 261–267). New York: Guilford Press.

Becker, K., & Schmidt, M. H. (2004). Internet chat rooms and suicide. *J. Amer. Acad. Child Adol. Psychat., 43*(3), 246.

Beckman, A. G. K., Parker, M. G., & Thorslund, M. (2005). Can elderly people take their medicine? *Patient Educ. Couns., 59*(2), 186–191.

Beebe, D. K. (1991). Emergency management of the adult female rape victim. *Amer. Fam. Physician, 43,* 2041–2046.

Beezhold, J. (2002). Cited in Psychiatrists "driven by fear." *BBC News: Health,* December 17, 2002.

Begley, S. (2000, May 8). A world of their own. *Newsweek,* pp. 52–63.

Begley, S. (2008, February 11). Happiness: Enough already. *Newsweek,* 50–52.

Beidel, D. C., & Turner, S. M. (2005). *Childhood anxiety disorders: A guide to research and treatment.* New York: Routledge/Taylor & Francis.

Beier, E. G., & Young, D. M. (1984). The silent language of psychotherapy: Social reinforcement of the unconscious processes (2nd ed.). Hawthorne, New York: Aldine.

Belkin, L. (1990, June 6). Doctor tells of first death using his suicide device. *New York Times,* A1, p. 3.

Bell, J. (2008, February 6). When anxiety is at the table. *New York Times.*

Bellinger, D. L., Madden, K. S., Felten, S. Y., & Felten, D. L. (1994). Neural and endocrine links between the brain and the immune system. In C. S. Lewis, C. O'Sullivan, & J. Barraclough (Eds.), *The psychoimmunology of cancer: Mind and body in the fight for survival.* Oxford, England: Oxford University Press.

Bellodi, L., Caldirola, D., & Bertani, A. (2003). Does the brain noradrenaline network mediate the effects of the CO-sub-2 challenge? *J. Psychopharmacol., 17*(3), 263–264.

Bemporad, J. R. (1992). Psychoanalytically orientated psychotherapy. In E. S. Paykel (Ed.), *Handbook of affective disorders.* New York: Guilford Press.

Bemporad, J. R. (1997). Cultural and historical aspects of eating disorders. *Theor. Med., 18*(4), 401–420.

Bender, D. S. (2005). The therapeutic alliance in the treatment of personality disorders. *J. Psychiat. Pract., 11*(2), 73–87.

Bender, D. S., Farber, B. A., & Geller, J. D. (2001). Cluster B personality traits and attachment. *J. Amer. Acad. Psychoanal., 29*(4), 551–563.

Bender, D. S., & Oldham, J. M. (2005). Psychotherapies for borderline personality disorder. In J. G. Gunderson & P. D. Hoffman (Eds.), *Understanding and treating borderline personality disorder* (pp. 21–41). Washington, DC: American Psychiatric Publishing.

Bender, D. S., Skodol, A. E., Dyck, I. R., Markowitz, J. C., Shea, M. T., Yen, S., et al. (2007). Ethnicity and mental health treatment utilization by patients with personality disorders. *J. Cons. Clin. Psychol., 75*(6), 992–999.

Bender, E. (2006, June 16). APA, AACAP suggest ways to reduce high suicide rates in Native Americans. *Psychiat. News, 41*(12), 6.

Bender, L. (1938). *A visual motor gestalt test and its clinical use.* New York: American Orthopsychiatric Assoc.

Bender, R., Jockel, K. H., Trautner, C., Spraul, M., & Berger, M. (1999). Effect of age on excess mortality in obesity. *JAMA, 281*(16), 1498–1504.

Benedict, S., Campbell, M., Doolen, A., Rivera, I., Negussi, T., & Turner-McGrievy, G. (2007). Seeds of HOPE: A model for addressing social and economic determinants of health in a women's obesity prevention project in two rural communities. *J. Women's Hlth., 16*(8), 1117–1124.

Benezech, M., DeWitte, J. J. E., & Bourgeois, M. (1989). A lycanthropic murderer [Letter to the editor]. *Amer. J. Psychiat., 146*(7), 942.

Bengtsson, H. (2005). Children's cognitive appraisal of others' distressful and positive experiences. *Inter. J. Behav. Dev., 29,* 457–466.

Benight, C. C., Harper, M. L., Zimmer, D. L., Lowery, M., Sanger, J., & Laudenslager, M. L. (2004). Repression following a series of natural disasters: Immune and neuroendocrine correlates. *Psychol. Hlth., 19*(3), 337–352.

Benitez, C. T., & Chamberlain, J. (2008). Methamphetamine-induced psychosis and diminished capacity to form intent to kill: Ultimate issue in expert testimony. *J. Amer. Acad. Psychiat. Law, 36*(2), 258–260.

Bennett, M. P. (1998). The effect of mirthful laughter on stress and natural killer cell cytotoxicity. *Diss. Abstr. Inter.: Sect. B: Sci. Eng., 58*(7–B), 3553.

Bennett-Gates, D., & Zigler, E. (1999). Effectance motivation and the performance of individuals with mental retardation. In E. Zigler & D. Bennett-Gates (Eds.), *Personality development in individuals with mental retardation* (pp. 145–164). New York: Cambridge University Press.

Berg, W. K., Wacker, D. P., Cigrand, K., Merkle, S., Wade, J., & Henry, K. (2007). Comparing functional analysis and paired-choice assessment results in classroom settings. *J. Appl. Behav. Anal., 40*(3), 545–552.

Bergeron, S., Binik, Y. M., Khalife, S., Pagidas, K., Glazer, H. I., Meana, M., et al. (2001). A randomized comparison of group cognitive-behavioral therapy, surface electromyographic biofeedback, and vestibulectomy in the treatment of dyspareunia resulting from vulvar vestibulitis. *Pain, 91,* 297–306.

Bergeron, S., Brown, C., Lord, M., Oala, M., Binik, Y. M., & Khalife, S. (2002). Physical therapy for vulvar vestibulitis syndrome: A retrospective study. *J. Sex Marital Ther., 28,* 183–192.

Bergin, A. E., & Richards, P. S. (2001). Religious values and mental health. In A. E. Kazdin (Ed.), *Encyclopedia of psychology.* New York: American Psychological Association & Oxford University Press.

Bergler, E. (1951). *Neurotic counterfeit sex.* New York: Grune & Stratton.

Bergquist, K. (2002). "War on crime adversely affects war on terrorism, professor says." http://www.ur.umich.edu/0203/Oct14_02/g_simon.shtml

Berk, S. N., & Efran, J. S. (1983). Some recent developments in the treatment of neurosis. In C. E. Walker (Ed.), *The handbook of clinical psychology: Theory, research, and practice* (Vol. 2). Homewood, IL: Dow Jones-Irwin.

Berlin, F. S. (2000). The etiology and treatment of sexual offending. In D. H. Fishbein (Ed.),

The science, treatment, and prevention of antisocial behaviors: Application to the criminal justice system (pp. 21-1–21-15). Kingston, NJ: Civic Research Institute.

Berman, A. L. (1986). Helping suicidal adolescents: Needs and responses. In C. A. Corr & J. N. McNeil (Eds.), *Adolescence and death.* New York: Springer.

Berman, A. L., & Jobes, D. A. (1991). *Adolescent suicide: Assessment and intervention.* Washington, DC: American Psychological Association.

Berman, A. L., & Jobes, D. A. (1995). Suicide prevention in adolescents (age 12–18). [Special issue: Suicide prevention: Toward the year 2000.] *Suic. Life-Threat. Behav., 25*(1), 143–154.

Bernert, R. A., Merrill, K. A., Braithwaite, S. R., Van Orden, K. A., & Joiner, T. E., Jr. (2007). Family life stress and insomnia symptoms in a prospective evaluation of young adults. *J. Fam. Psychol., 21*(1), 58–66.

Bernstein, D. P., & Useda, J. D (2007). Paranoid personality disorder. In W. O'Donohue, K. A. Fowler, & S. O. Lilienfeld (Eds.), *Personality disorders: Toward the DSM-V.* Los Angeles: Sage Publications.

Bernstein, H. A. (1981). Survey of threats and assaults directed toward psychotherapists. *Amer. J. Psychother., 35,* 542–549.

Berr, C., Wancata, J., & Ritchie, K. (2005). Prevalence of dementia in the elderly in Europe. *Eur. Neuropsychopharmacology, 15*(4), 463–471.

Berrettini, W. (2006). Genetics of bipolar and unipolar disorders. In D. J. Stein, D. J. Kupfer, & A. F. Schatzberg (Eds.), *The American Psychiatric Publishing textbook of mood disorders.* Washington, DC: American Psychiatric Publishing.

Berrigan, D., Dodd, K., Triano, R. P., Krebs-Smith, S. M., & Barbash, R. B. (2003). Patterns of health behavior in U.S. adults. *Prev. Med.: Inter. J. Devvoted to Pract. Theory, 36*(5), 615–623.

Berrigan, D., Troiano, R. P., McNeel, T., DiSogra, C., & Ballard-Barbash, R. (2006). Active transportation increases adherence to activity recommendations. *Amer. J. Prev. Med., 31*(3), 210–216.

Berthier, M. L., Kulisevsky, J., Gironell, A., & Lopez, O. L. (2001). Obsessive-compulsive disorder and traumatic brain injury: Behavioral, cognitive, and neuroimaging findings. *Neuropsychiat., Neuropsychol., Behav. Neurol., 14*(1), 23–31.

Berzoff, J., Flanagan, L. M., & Hertz, P. (Eds.). (2008). *Inside out and outside in: Psychodynamic clinical theory and psychopathology in contemporary multicultural contexts* (2nd ed.). Lanham, MD: Jason Aronson.

Beutler, L. E. (1991). Have all won and must all have prizes? Revisiting Luborsky et al.'s verdict. *J. Cons. Clin. Psychol., 59,* 226–232.

Beutler, L. E. (2000). David and Goliath: When empirical and clinical standards of practice meet. *Amer. Psychologist, 55*(9), 997–1007.

Beutler, L. E. (2002). The dodo bird is extinct. *Clin. Psychol.: Sci. Prac., 9*(1), 30–34.

Beutler, L. E., Clarkin, J. F., & Bongar, B. (2000). *Guidelines for the systematic treatment of the depressed patient.* New York: Oxford University Press.

Beutler, L. E., & Malik, M. L. (Eds.). (2002). *Rethinking the DSM: A psychological perspective. Decade of behavior.* Washington, DC: American Psychological Association.

Beutler, L. E., Williams, R. E., Wakefield, P. J., & Entwistle, S. R. (1995). Bridging scientist and practitioner perspectives in clinical psychology. *Amer. Psychologist, 50*(12), 984–994.

Beyer, H. A. (1991). Litigation involving people with mental retardation. In J. L. Matson & J. A. Mulick (Eds.), *Handbook of mental retardation* (2nd ed.). New York: Pergamon Press.

Bhushan, B., & Kumar, J. S. (2007). Emotional distress and posttraumatic stress in children surviving the 2004 tsunami. *J. Loss Trauma, 12*(3), 245–257.

Bichsel, S. (2001). Schizophrenia and severe mental illness: Guidelines for assessment, treatment, and referral. In E. R. Welfel & R. E. Ingersoll (Eds.), *The mental health desk reference* (pp. 142–154). New York: Wiley.

Bickman, L. (2005). A common factors approach to improving mental health services. *Ment. Hlth Serv. Res., 7*(1), 1–4.

Biddle, L., Brock, A., Brookes, S. T., & Gunnell, D. (2008). Suicide rates in young men in England and Wales in the 21st century: Time trend study. *Brit. Med. J., 336*(7643), 539.

Biddle, S., Akande, D., Armstrong, N., Ashcroft, M., Brooke, R., & Goudes, M. (1996). The self-motivation inventory modified for children: Evidenced on psychometric properties and its use in physical exercise. *International Journal of Sport Psychology, 27*(3), 237–250.

Biederman, J., Mick, E., Faraone, S. V., & Burback, M. (2001). Patterns of remission and symptom decline in conduct disorder: A four-year prospective study of an ADHD sample. *J. Amer. Acad. Child Adol. Psychiat., 40*(3), 290–298.

Biederman, J., Spencer, T., & Wilens, T. (2004). Evidence-based pharmacotherapy for attention-deficit hyperactivity disorder. *Inter. J. Neuropsychopharmacol., 7,* 77–97.

Biederman, J., Spencer, T., & Wilens, T. (2005). Evidence-based pharmacotherapy of attention-deficit hyperactivity disorder. In D. J. Stein, B. Lerer, & S. Stahl, *Evidence-based psychopharmacology* (pp. 255–289). New York: Cambridge University Press.

Bills, C. B., & Li, G. (2005). Correlating homicide and suicide. *Inter. J. Epidemiol., 34*(4), 837–845.

Bindman, J., & Thornicroft, G. (2008). In K. T. Mueser & D. V. Jeste (Eds.), *Clinical handbook of schizophrenia* (pp. 516–523). New York: Guilford Press.

Binet, A., & Simon, T. (1916). *The development of intelligence in children (The Binet-Simon Scale).* Baltimore: Williams & Wilkins.

Binik, Y. M., Bergeron, S., & Khalifé, S. (2007). Dyspareunia and vaginismus: So-called sexual pain. In S. R. Leiblum (Ed.), *Principles and practice of sex therapy* (4th ed., pp. 157–179). New York: Guilford Press.

Binik, Y. M., Reissing, E., Pukall, C., Flory, N., Payne, K. A., & Khalife, S. (2002). The female sexual pain disorders: Genital pain or sexual dysfunction? *Arch. Sex. Behav., 31*(5), 425–429.

Binik, Y. M., Servan-Schreiber, D., Freiwald, S., & Hall, K. S. (1988). Intelligent computer-based assessment and psychotherapy: An expert system for sexual dysfunction. *J. Nerv. Ment. Dis., 176*(7), 387–400.

Biondi, M., & Picardi, A. (2003). Increased probability of remaining in remission from panic disorder with agoraphobia after drug treatment in patients who received concurrent cognitive-behavioural therapy: A follow-up study. *Psychother. Psychosom., 72*(1), 34–42.

Birch, H. G., Richardson, S. A., Baird, D., et al. (1970). *Mental subnormality in the community—A clinical and epidemiological study.* Baltimore: Williams & Wilkins.

Birmingham, C. L., & Beumont, P. (2004). *Medical management of eating disorders: A practical handbook for health care professionals.* New York: Cambridge University Press.

Bisaga, A. (2008). Benzodiazepines and other sedatives and hypnotics. In H. D. Kleber & M. Galanter (Eds.), *The American Psychiatric Publishing textbook of substance abuse treatment* (4th ed., pp. 215–235). Arlington, VA: American Psychiatric Publishing.

Bishop, F. M. (2008). Alcohol abuse. In M. Hersen & J. Rosqvist (Eds.), *Handbook of psychological assessment, case conceptualization and treatment, Vol. 1: Adults.* Hoboken, NJ: John Wiley & Sons.

Bissette, G., Seidler, F. J., Nemeroff, C. B., & Slotkin, T. A. (1996). High affinity choline transporter status in Alzheimer's disease tissue from rapid autopsy. In R. J. Wurtman, S. Corkin, J. H. Growdon, & R. M. Nitsch (Eds.), *The neurobiology of Alzheimer's disease.* New York: New York Academy of Sciences.

Bisson, J. I., & Deahl, M. P. (1994). Psychological debriefing and prevention of post-traumatic stress: More research is needed. *Brit. J. Psychiat., 165*(6), 717–720.

Bisson, J. I., Jenkins, P. L., Alexander, J., & Bannister, C. (1997). Randomised controlled trial of psychological debriefing for victims of acute burn trauma. *Brit. J. Psychiat., 171,* 78–81.

Björgvinsson, T., & Hart, J. (2008). Obsessive-compulsive disorder. In M. Hersen & J. Rosqvist (Eds.), *Handbook of psychological assessment, case conceptualization, and treatment, Vol. 1: Adults* (pp. 237–262). Hoboken, NJ: John Wiley & Sons.

Black, D. W., Shaw, M. C., & Allen, J. (2008). Extended release carbamazepine in the treatment of pathological gambling: An open-label study. *Progress in Neuro-Psychpharmacology & Biological Psychiatry, 32*(5), 1191–1194.

Black, D. W., Shaw, M., Forbush, K. T., & Allen, J. (2007). An open-label trial of escitalopram in the treatment of pathological gambling. *Clin. Neuropharmacol., 30*(4), 206–212.

Black, D. W., Stephan, A., Coryell, W. H., Argo, T., Forbush, K. T., Shaw, M. C., Perry, P., & Allen, J. (2007). Buproprion in the treatment of pathological gambling: A randomized, double-blind, placebo-controlled, flexible-dose study. *J. Clin. Psychopharmacol. 27*(2), 143–150.

Black, K. J. (2005). Diagnosis. In E. H. Rubin & C. F. Zorumski (Eds.), *Adult psychiatry* (2nd ed.). Oxford, England: Blackwell Publishing.

Black, S. T., & Lester, D. (2003). The content of suicide notes: Does it vary by method of suicide, sex, or age? *Omega: J. Death Dying, 46*(3), 241–249.

Blackmore, E. R., Craddock, N., Walters, J., & Jones, I. (2008). Is the perimenopause a time of increased risk of recurrence in women with a history of bipolar affective postpartum psychosis? A case series. *Arch. Women's Ment. Hlth., 11*(1), 75–78.

Blagov, P. S., Fowler K. A., & Lilienfeld, S. O. (2007). Histrionic personality disorder. In W. O'Donohue, K. A. Fowler, & S. O. Lilienfeld (Eds.). *Personality disorders: Toward the DSM-V.* Los Angeles: Sage Publications.

Blair, J., Mitchell, D., & Blair, K. (2005). *The psychopath: Emotion and the brain.* Malden, MA: Blackwell Publishing.

Blair, R. J. R., Peschardt, K. S., Budhani, S., & Pine, D. S. (2006). Neurobiology of aggression in children. In R. J. Nelson (Ed.), *Biology of aggression* (pp. 351–370). New York: Oxford University Press.

Blanch, A. (2007). Integrating religion and spirituality in mental health: The promise and the challenge. *Psychosoc. Rehab. J., 30*(4), 251–260.

Blanchard, E. B., & Hickling, E. J. (2004). Psychophysiological assessment with MVA survivors. In E. J. Hickling & E. B. Blanchard, *After the crash: Psychological assessment and treatment of survivors of motor vehicle accidents* (2nd ed., pp. 213–229). Washington, DC: American Psychological Association.

Blanchard, E. B., Rowell, D., Kuhn, E., Rogers, R., & Wittrock, D. (2005). Posttraumatic stress and depression symptoms in a college population one year after the September 11 attacks: The effect of proximity. *Behav. Res. Ther., 43*(1), 143–150.

Blanchard, J. J., Brown, S. A., Horan, W. P., & Sherwood, A. R. (2000). Substance use disorders in schizophrenia: Review, integration, and a proposed model. *Clin. Psychol. Rev., 20*(2), 207–234.

Blanchard, R., & Hucker, S. J. (1991). Age, transvestism, bondage, and concurrent paraphilic activities in 117 fatal cases of autoerotic asphyxia. *Brit. J. Psychiat., 159,* 371–377.

Blanchflower, D. G., & Oswald, A. (2007, February). *Is well-being U-shaped over the life cycle?* (NBER Working Paper No. 12935). Cambridge, MA: National Bureau of Economic Research.

Blatt, S. J. (1995). The destructiveness of perfectionism. Implications for the treatment of depression. *Amer. Psychologist., 50*(12), 1003–1020.

Blatt, S. J. (1999). Personality factors in brief treatment of depression: Further analyses of the NIMH-sponsored Treatment for Depression Collaborative Research Program. In D. S. Janowsky (Ed.), *Psychotherapy indications and outcomes.* Washington, DC: American Psychiatric Press.

Blatt, S. J. (2004). Developmental origins (distal antecedents). In S. J. Blatt, *Experiences of depression: Theoretical, clinical, and research perspectives* (pp. 187–229). Washington, DC: American Psychological Association.

Blaustein, J. D. (2008). Neuroendocrine regulation of feminine sexual behavior: Lessons from rodent models and thoughts about humans. In S. Fiske, D. L. Schacter, & R. Sternberg (Eds.), *Annual review of psychology* (Vol. 59). Palo Alto, CA: Annual reviews.

Blazer, D. (2002). *Depression in late life* (3rd ed.). New York: Springer.

Blazer, D. G., Hughes, D., George, L. K., Swartz, M., & Boyer, R. (1991). Generalized anxiety disorder. In L. N. Robins & D. A. Regier (Eds.), *Psychiatric disorders in America: The Epidemiologic Catchment Area Study.* New York: Maxwell Macmillan International.

Blier, P., & de Montigny, C. (1994, July). Current advances and trends in the treatment of depression. *TIPS, 15,* 220–226.

Bliss, E. L. (1980). Multiple personalities: A report of 14 cases with implications for schizophrenia and hysteria. *Arch. Gen. Psychiat., 37*(12), 1388–1397.

Bliss, E. L. (1980). *Multiple personality, allied disorders and hypnosis.* New York: Oxford University Press.

Bliss, E. L. (1985). "How prevalent is multiple personality?": Dr. Bliss replies. *Amer. J. Psychiat., 142*(12), 1527.

Block, J. J. (2008). Issues for DSM-V: Internet addiction. *Amer. J. Psychiat., 165*(3), 306–307.

Blood, R. W., Pirkis, J., & Holland, K. (2007). Media reporting of suicide methods: An Australian perspective. *Crisis: J. Crisis Intervent. Suic. Prev., 28*(Suppl. 1), 64–69.

Bloom, B. L. (1984). *Community mental health: A general introduction* (2nd ed.). Monterey, CA: Brooks/Cole.

Bloom, J. D. (2004). Thirty-five years of working with civil commitment statutes. *J. Amer. Acad. Psychiat. Law, 32*(4), 430–439.

Bloom, M. (2008). Principles and approaches to primary prevention. In T. P. Gullotta & G. M. Blau (Eds.), *Handbook of childhood behavioral issues: Evidence-based approaches to prevention and treatment* (pp. 107–122). New York: Routledge/Taylor & Francis Group.

Blow, F. C., Zeber, J. E., McCarthy, J. F., Valenstein, M., Gillon, L., & Bingham, C. R. (2004). Ethnicity and diagnostic patterns in veterans with psychoses. *Soc. Psychiat. Psychiatr. Epidemiol., 39*(10), 841–851.

Bluglass, K. (2001). Treatment of perpetrators. In G. Adshead & D. Brooke (Eds.), *Munchausen's syndrome by proxy: Current issues in assessment, treatment and research* (pp. 175–184). London: Imperial College Press.

Blum, K., Braverman, E. R., Holder, J. M., Lubar, J. F., Monastra, V. J., Miller, D., et al. (2000). Reward deficiency syndrome: A biogenetic model for the diagnosis and treatment of impulsive, addictive, and compulsive behaviors. *J. Psychoact. Drugs, 32*(Suppl.), 1–68.

Blum, K., Cull, J. G., Braverman, E. R., & Comings, D. E. (1996). Reward deficiency syndrome. *Amer. Sci., 84*(2), 132–144.

Blum, K., Noble, E. P., Sheridan, P. J., Montgomery, A., Ritchie, T., Jagadeeswaran, P., et al. (1990). Allelic association of human dopamine D2 receptor gene in alcoholism. *JAMA, 263*(15), 2055–2060.

Blume, S. B., & Zilberman, M. L. (2005). Addictive disorders in women. In R. J. Frances, A. H. Mack, & S. I. Miller (Eds.), *Clinical textbook of addictive disorders* (3rd ed., pp. 437–453). New York: Guilford Press.

Blyler, C. R. (2003). Understanding the employment rate of people with schizophrenia: Different approaches lead to different implications for policy. In M. F. Lenzenweger & J. M. Hooley (Eds.), *Principles of experimental psychopathology: Essays in honor of Brendan A. Maher* (pp. 107–115). Washington, DC: American Psychological Association.

Boardman, S., & Makari, G. J. (2007). The lunatic asylum on Blackwell's Island and the New York press. *Amer. J. Psychiat., 164*(4), 581.

Bock, M. A. (2007). A social-behavioral learning strategy intervention for a child with Asperger syndrome: Brief report. *Remed. Spec. Educ. 28*(5), 258–265.

Bockoven, J. S. (1963). *Moral treatment in American psychiatry.* New York: Springer.

Boeve, B., McCormick, J., Smith, G., Ferman, T., Rummans, T., Carpenter, T., et al. (2003). Mild cognitive impairment in the oldest old. *Neurology, 60*(3), 477–480.

Bogart, L. M., Benotsch, E. G., & Pavlovic, J. D. (2004). Feeling superior but threatened: The relation of narcissism to social comparison. *Basic Appl. Soc. Psychol., 26*(1), 35–44.

Bogdan, R., & Taylor, S. (1976, January). The judged, not the judges: An insider's view of mental retardation. *Amer. Psychologist., 31*(1), 47–52.

Bolgar, H. (1965). The case study method. In B. B. Wolman (Ed.), *Handbook of clinical psychology.* New York: McGraw-Hill.

Bollini, A. M., & Walker, E. F. (2007). Schizotypal personality disorder. In W. O'Donohue, K. A. Fowler, S. O. Lilienfeld (Eds.). *Personality disorders: Toward the DSM-V.* Los Angeles: Sage Publications.

Bonanno, G. A. (2004). Loss, trauma, and human resilience. *Amer. Psychologist, 59*(1), 20–28.

Bond, C. (2004). International deception. Presentation at congressional briefing "Detecting deception: Research to secure the Homeland." Washington, DC. March 19, 2004.

Bond, L. A., & Hauf, A. M.-C. (2007). Community-based collaboration: An overarching best practice in prevention. *Couns. Psychologist, 35*(4), 567–575.

Bonner, R. L. (1992). Isolation, seclusion, and psychosocial vulnerability as risk factors for suicide behind bars. In R. W. Maris, A. L. Berman, J. T. Maltsberger, & R. I. Yufit (Eds.), *Assessment and prediction of suicide.* New York: Guilford Press.

Boodman, S. G. (2006, April 4). Treat mom, help child. *Washingtonpost.com.* Retrieved July 6, 2007, from http://www.washingtonpost.com

Bornstein, R. A., Schwarzkopf, S. B., Olson, S. C., & Nasrallah, H. A. (1992). Third-ventricle enlargement and neuropsychological deficit in schizophrenia. *Biol. Psychiat., 31*(9), 954–961.

Bornstein, R. F. (2005). Psychodynamic theory and personality disorders. In S. Strack (Ed.), *Handbook of personality and psychopathology* (pp. 164–180). Hoboken, NJ: Wiley.

Bornstein, R. F. (2007). Dependent personality disorder. In W. O'Donohue, K. A. Fowler, S. O. Lilienfeld (Eds.). *Personality disorders: Toward the DSM-V.* Los Angeles: Sage Publications.

Bornstein, R. F. (2007). Might the Rorschach be a projective test after all: Social projection of an undesired trait alters Rorschach oral dependency scores. *J. Pers. Assess., 88*(3), 354–367.

Bornstein, R. F. (2007). Nomothetic psychoanalysis. *Psychoanal. Psychol., 24*(4), 590–602.

Borowsky, I. L., Ireland, M., & Resnick M. D. (2001). Adolescent suicide attempts: Risks and protectors. *Pediatrics, 107,* 485–493.

Borthwick, A., Holman, C., Kennard, D., McFetridge, M., Messruther, K., & Wilkes, J. (2001). The relevance of moral treatment to contemporary mental health care. *J. Ment. Hlth UK., 10*(4), 427–439.

Boscarino, J. A., Adams, R. E., & Figley, C. R. (2004). Mental health service use 1 year after the World Trade Center disaster: Implications for mental health care. *Gen. Hosp. Psychiat., 26*(5), 346–358.

Bossolo, L., & Lichtenstein, B. (2002). Many Americans still feeling effects of September 11th; Are reexamining their priorities in life. *APA Online.*

Bott, E. (1928). Teaching of psychology in the medical course. *Bull. Assoc. Amer. Med. Colleges, 3,* 289–304.

Boudet, C., Bocca, M. L., Chabot, B., Dela-millieure, P., Brazo, P., Denise, P., & Doll-fus, S. (2005). Are eye movement abnormalities indicators of genetic vulnerability to schizo-phrenia? *Eur. Psychiat., 20*(4), 339–345.

Bouman, T. K. (2008). Hypochondriasis. In J. S. Abramowitz, D. McKay, & S. Taylor (Eds.), *Obsessive-compulsive disorder: Subtypes and spectrum conditions.* Oxford, England: Elsevier.

Bourin, M., Malinge, M., & Guitton, B. (1995). [Provocative agents in panic disorder.] *Therapie 50*(4), 301–306. [French]

Bourne, E. J., Brownstein, A., & Garano, L. (2004). *Natural relief for anxiety: Complementary strategies for easing fear, panic & worry.* Oakland, CA: New Harbinger Publications.

Bowden, C. L. (2005). A different depression: Clinical distinctions between bipolar and uni-polar depression. *J. Affect. Disorders, 84*(2–3), 117–125.

Bowden, C. L. (2005). Atypical antipsychotic augmentation of mood stabilizer therapy in bipolar disorder. *J. Clin. Psychiat., 66*(Suppl. 3), 12–19.

Bowden, C. L., & Singh, V. (2005). Valproate in bipolar disorder: 2000 onwards. *Acta Psychiatr. Scandin., 111*(Suppl. 426), 13–20.

Bowen, M. A. (1960). A family concept of schizophrenia. In D. D. Jackson (Ed.), *The etiol-ogy of schizophrenia.* New York: Basic Books.

Bower, G. H. (1981). Mood and memory. *Amer. Psychologist, 36*(2), 129–148.

Bowman, S. A., Gortmaker, S. L., Ebbel-ing, C. B., Pereira, M. A., & Ludwig, D. S. (2003). Effects of fast-food consumption on energy intake and diet quality among children in a national household survey. *Pediatrics, 113,* 112–118.

Boxer, P., & Frick, P. J. (2008). Treating conduct problems, aggression, and antisocial behavior in children and adolescents: An integrated view. In R. G. Steele, T. D. Elkin, & M. C. Roberts (Eds.), *Handbook of evidence-based therapies for children and adolescents: Bridging science and practice.* New York: Springer.

Boyce, W. T., Chesney, M., Alkon, A., Tschann, J. M., et al. (1995). Psychobiologic reactivity to stress and childhood respiratory illnesses: Results of two prospective studies. *Psy-chosom. Med., 57,* 411–422.

Boye, B., Bentsen, H., & Malt, U. F. (2002). Does guilt proneness predict acute and long-term distress in relatives of patients with schizophrenia? *Acta Pyschiatr. Scandin., 106*(5), 351–357.

Boyle, S. H., Williams, R. B., Mark, D. B., Brummett, B. H., Siegler, I. C., Helms, M. J., et al. (2004). Hostility as a predictor of survival in patients with coronary artery disease. *Psychosom. Med., 66*(5), 629–632.

Boyles, S. (2002, January 8). More people seek-ing treatment for depression. *WebMDHealth.* Retrieved January 9, 2002, from www.webcenter .health.web

Boysen, G. A. (2007). An evaluation of the DSM concept of mental disorder. *J. Mind Behav., 28*(2), 157–173.

Braam, W., Didden, R., Smits, M., & Curfs, L. (2008). Melatonin treatment in individuals with intellectual disability and chronic insom-nia: A randomized placebo-controlled study. *J. Intell. Disab. Res., 52*(3), 256–264.

Braback, L., & Humble, M. (2001). Young woman dies of water intoxication after taking one tablet of ecstasy. Today's drug panorama calls for increased vigilance in health care. *Lakartidningen, 98*(9), 817–819.

Bradley, B. P., Mogg, K., Falla, S. J., & Ham-ilton, L. R. (1998). Attentional bias for threat-ening facial expressions in anxiety: Manipula-tion of stimulus duration. *Cog. Emot., 12*(6), 737–753.

Bradley, R., Conklin, C. Z., & Westen, D. (2005). The borderline personality diagnosis in adolescents: Gender differences and subtypes. *J. Child Psychol. Psychiat., 46,* 1006–1019.

Bradley, R., Conklin, C. Z., & Westen, D. (2007). Borderline personality disorder. In W. O'Donohue, K. A. Fowler, S. O. Lilienfeld (Eds.). *Personality disorders: Toward the DSM-V.* Los Angeles: Sage Publications.

Bradley, R., Greene, J., Russ, E., Dutra, L., & Westen, D. (2005). A multidimensional meta-analysis of psychotherapy for PTSD. *Amer. J. Psychiat., 162*(2), 214–227.

Bradley, R., Jenei, J., & Westen, D. (2005). Etiology of borderline personality disorder: Dis-entangling the contributions of intercorrelated antecedents. *J. Nerv. Ment. Dis., 193,* 24–31.

Bradley, S. J. (1995). Psychosexual disorders in adolescence. In J. M. Oldham & M. B. Riba (Eds.), *American Psychiatric Press review of psy-chiatry* (Vol. 14). Washington, DC: American Psychiatric Press.

Brady, K. T., & Back, S. E. (2008). Women and addiction. In H. D. Kleber & M. Galanter (Eds.), *The American Psychiatric Publishing textbook of substance abuse treatment* (4th ed. pp. 555–564). Arlington, VA: American Psychiatric Publishing.

Brainerd, C. J., Reyna, V. F., & Ceci, S. J. (2008). Developmental reversals in false mem-ory: A review of data and theory. *Psychol. Bull., 134*(3), 343–382.

Bram, T., & Björgvinsson, T. (2004). A psy-chodynamic clinician's foray into cognitive-behavioral therapy utilizing exposure-response prevention for obsessive-compulsive disorder. *Am. J. Psychother., 58,* 304–320.

Brambrink, D. K. (2004). A comparative study for the treatment of anxiety in women using electromyographic biofeedback and progres-sive relaxation and coping with stress: A manual for women. *Diss. Abstr. Inter.: Sect. B: Sci. Eng., 65*(6-B), 3146.

Brandon, S. (1981). *The history of shock treatment. In Electroconvulsive therapy: An appraisal.* Oxford, England: Oxford University Press.

Braun, D. L. (1996, July 28). Interview. In S. Gil-bert, More men may seek eating-disorder help. *New York Times.*

Braxton, L. E., Calhoun, P. S., Williams, J. E., & Boggs, C. D. (2007). Validity rates of the Per-sonality Assessment Inventory and the Minnesota Multiphasic Personality Inventory-2 in a VA medical center setting. *J. Pers. Assess., 88*(1), 5–15.

Breedlove, L., Decker, C., Lakin, K. C., Prouty, R., & Coucouvanis, K. (2005).

Placement of children and youth in state insti-tutions: Forty years after the high point, it is time to just stop. *Ment. Retard., 43*(3), 235–238.

Bremer, H.-H. (2001). *Trafficking in women reaches new heights in Europe.* Retrieved April 3, 2007, from http://www.freerepublic.com/forum/a3ad2b4951392.htm

Bremner, J. D. (2002). *Does stress damage the brain? Understanding trauma-related disorders from a mind-body perspective.* New York: Norton.

Bremner, J. D. (2007). Does stress damage the brain? In M. Barad, L. Kirmayer, & R. Lemelson (Eds.), *Understanding trauma: Integrating biologi-cal, clinical, and cultural perspectives* (pp. 118–141). New York: Cambridge University Press.

Bremner, J. D., Vythilingam, M., Vermetten, E., Vaccarino, V., & Charney, D. S. (2004). Deficits in hippocampal and anterior cingulate functioning during verbal declarative memory encoding in midlife major depression. *Amer. J. Psychiat., 161*(4), 637–645.

Brende, J. O., & Parson, E. R. (1985). *Vietnam veterans.* New York: Plenum.

Brenner, I. (1999). Deconstructing DID. *Amer. J. Psychother., 53*(3), 344–360.

Brent, D. A. (2001). Assessment and treatment of the youthful suicidal patient. In H. Hendin & J. J. Mann (Eds.), *The clinical science of suicide prevention* (Vol. 932, pp. 106–131). New York: Annals of the New York Academy of Sciences.

Brent, D. A., & Mann, J. J. (2003). Familial factors in adolescent suicidal behavior. In A. Apter & R. A King (Eds.), *Suicide in children and adolescents* (pp. 86–117). New York: Cambridge University Press.

Brent, D. A., Kupfer, D. J., Bromet, E. J., & Dew, M. A. (1988). The assessment and treat-ment of patients at risk for suicide. In A. J. Fran-ces & R. E. Hales (Eds.), *American Psychiatric Press review of psychiatry* (Vol. 7). Washington, DC: American Psychiatric Press.

Breslau, J., Aguilar-Gaxiola, S., Borges, G., Kendler, K. S., Su, M., & Kessler, R. C. (2007). Risk for psychiatric disorder among immigrants and their US-born descendants: Evidence from the National Comorbidity Survey Replication. *J. Nerv. Ment. Dis., 195*(3), 189–195.

Breslau, J., Aguilar-Gaxiola, S., Kendler, K. S., Su, M., Williams, D., & Kessler, R. C. (2006). Specifying race-ethnic differences in risk for psychiatric disorder in a USA national sample. *Psychol. Med., 36,* 57–68.

Breslau, N., Roth, T., Burduvali, E., Kapke, A., Schults, L., & Roehrs, T. (2005). Sleep in lifetime posttraumatic stress disorder: A community-based polysomnographic study: Correction. *Arch. Gen. Psychiat., 62*(2), 172.

Brewin, D. R., Andrews, B., & Rose, S. (2003). Diagnostic overlap between acute stress disorder and PTSD in victims of violent crime. *Amer. J. Psychiat., 160,* 783–785.

Briese, V., Stammwitz, U., Friede, M., & Henneicke von Zepelin, H. H. (2007). Black cohosh with or without St. John's wort for symptom-specific climacteric treatment: Results of a large-scale, controlled, observational study. *Maturitas, 57*(4), 405–414.

Briken, P., Hill, A., & Berner, W. (2003). Phar-macotherapy of paraphilias with long-acting ago-nists of luteinizing hormone-releasing hormone: A systematic review. *J. Clin. Psychiat., 64*(8), 890–897.

Britt, R. R. (2005). The odds of dying. *LiveScience.com.* Rape and sexual assault: Reporting to police and medical attention, 1992–2000. Retrieved January 12, 2005, from www.ojp.usdoj.gov/bjs/abstract/rsarp00.htm

Broadway, J., & Mintzer, J. (2007). The many faces of psychosis in the elderly. *Curr. Opin. Psychiat., 20*(6), 551–558.

Brock, D. W. (2001). Physician-assisted suicide—The worry about abuse. In L. M. Kopelman & K. A. De Ville (Eds.), *Physician-assisted suicide: What are the issues?* (pp. 59–74). Dordrecht, Netherlands: Kluwer Academic.

Brodsky, S., & Poythress, N. (1990). Presentation. American Psychological Association Convention, Boston.

Brody, C. L., Hamer, D. H., & Haaga, D. A. F. (2005). Depression vulnerability, cigarette smoking, and the serotonin transporter gene. *Addict. Behav., 30*(3), 557–566.

Brody, H. (2000). Better health from your inner pharmacy. *Psychol. Today, 32*(4), 60–67.

Brommelhoff, J. A., Conway, K., Merikangas, K., & Levy, B. R. (2004). Higher rates of depression in women: Role of gender bias within the family. *J. Women's Hlth., 13*(1), 69–76.

Brondolo, E., Rieppi, R., Kelly, K. P., & Gerin, W. (2003). Perceived racism and blood pressure: A review of the literature and conceptual and methodological critique. *Ann. Behav. Med., 25*(1), 55–65.

Bronisch, T., & Lieb, R. (2008). Maternal suicidality and suicide risk in offspring. *Psychiatr. Clin. N. Amer., 31*(2), 213–221.

Brook, D. W. (2008). Group therapy. In H. D. Kleber & M. Galanter (Eds.), *The American Psychiatric Publishing textbook of substance abuse treatment* (4th ed., pp. 413–427). Arlington, VA: American Psychiatric Publishing.

Brooks, G. R., & Richardson, F. C. (1980). Emotional skills training: A treatment program for duodenal ulcer. *Behav. Ther., 11*(2), 198–207.

Brooks, M. K. (2005). Dementia and wandering behavior: Concern for the lost elder. *Soc. Work Hlth. Care, 41*(2), 95–97.

Brown, A. S. (2003). A review of the déjà vu experience. *Psychol. Bull., 129*(3), 394–413.

Brown, A. S. (2004). The déjà vu illusion. *Curr. Dir. Psychol. Sci., 13*(6), 256–259.

Brown, A. S., Begg, M. D., Gravenstein, S., Schaefer, C. A., Wyatt, R. J., Bresnahan, M., Babulas, V. P., & Susser, E. S. (2004). Serologic evidence of prenatal influenza in the etiology of schizophrenia. *Arch. Gen. Psychiat., 61*(8), 774–780.

Brown, G. P., & Beck, A. T. (2002). Dysfunctional attitudes, perfectionism, and models of vulnerability to depression. In G. L. Flett & P. L. Hewitt (Eds.), *Perfectionism: Theory, research, and treatment* (pp. 231–251). Washington, DC: American Psychological Association.

Brown, G. R., & Ceniceros, S. (2001). Human sexuality in health and disease. In D. Wedding (Ed.), *Behavior and medicine* (3rd ed., pp. 171–184). Seattle: Hogrefe & Huber.

Brown, G. W., & Harris, T. O. (1978). *Social origins of depression: A study of psychiatric disorder in women.* London: Tavistock.

Brown, G. W., Harris, T. O., & Hepworth, C. (1995). Loss, humiliation and entrapment among women developing depression: A patient and non-patient comparison. *Psychol. Med., 25,* 7–21.

Brown, J. H., Henteleff, P., Barakat, S., & Rowe, C. J. (1986). Is it normal for terminally ill patients to desire death? *Amer. J. Psychiat., 143*(2), 208–211.

Brown, R. J. (2002). The cognitive psychology of dissociative states. *Cog. Neuropsychiat., 7*(3), 221–235.

Brown, R. J., Cardena, E., Nijenhuis, E., Sar, V., & van der Hart, O. (2007). Should conversion disorder be reclassified as a dissociative disorder in DSM-V? *Psychosom.: J. Cons. Liaison Psychiat., 48*(5), 369–378.

Brown, R. J., Schrag, A., & Trimble, M. R. (2005). Dissociation, childhood interpersonal trauma, and family functioning in patients with somatization disorder. *Amer. J. Psychiat., 162*(5), 899–905.

Brown, R. P., Gerbarg, P., & Bottiglieri, T. (2002). S-adenosylmethionine (SAMe) for depression. *Psychiatr. Ann., 32*(1), 29–44.

Brown, T. A., Hertz, R. M., & Barlow, D. H. (1992). New developments in cognitive-behavioral treatment of anxiety disorders. In A. Tasman & M. B. Riba (Eds.), *Review of psychiatry* (Vol. 11). Washington, DC: American Psychiatric Press.

Brown, T. A., O'Leary, T. A., & Barlow, D. A. (2001). Generalized anxiety disorder. In D. H. Barlow (Ed.), *Clinical handbook of psychological disorders: A step-by-step treatment manual* (3rd ed. pp. 154–208). New York: Guilford Press.

Brownell, K. D., & Napolitano, M. A. (1995). Distorting reality for children: Body size proportions of Barbie and Ken dolls. *Inter. J. Eat. Disorders, 18*(3), 295–298.

Brownell, K. D., & O'Neil, P. M. (1993). Obesity. In D. H. Barlow (Ed.), *Clinical handbook of psychological disorders: A step-by-step treatment manual* (2nd ed.). New York: Guilford Press.

Bruch, H. (1962). Perceptual and conceptual disturbances in anorexia nervosa. *Psychosom. Med., 24,* 187–194.

Bruch, H. (1973). *Eating disorders: Obesity, anorexia nervosa and the person within.* New York: Basic Books.

Bruch, H. (1978). *The golden cage: The enigma of anorexia nervosa.* Cambridge, MA: Harvard University Press.

Bruch, H. (1991). The sleeping beauty: Escape from change. In S. I. Greenspan & G. H. Pollock (Eds.), *The course of life, Vol. 4: Adolescence.* Madison, CT: International Universities Press.

Bruch, H. (2001). *The golden cage: The enigma of anorexia nervosa.* Cambridge, MA: Harvard University Press.

Brumberg, J. J. (1988). *Fasting girls: The history of anorexia nervosa.* New York: Penguin Books.

Bryant, R. A., Guthrie, R. M., & Moulds, M. L. (2001). Hypnotizability in acute stress disorder. *Amer. J. Psychiat., 158*(4), 600–604.

Bryant, R. A., Moulds, M. L., Guthrie, R. M., & Nixon, R. D. V. (2005). The additive benefit of hypnosis and cognitive-behavioral therapy in treating acute stress disorder. *J. Cons. Clin. Psychol., 73*(2), 334–340.

Buccafusco, J. J. (2004). Neuronal nicotinic receptor subtypes: Defining therapeutic targets. *Molecular Interventions, 4,* 285–295.

Buchanan, J. A., & Houlihan, D. (2008). The use of in vivo desensitization for the treatment of a specific phobia of earthworms. *Clin. Case Stud., 7*(1), 12–24.

Bunney, W. E., & Bunney, B. G. (2000). Molecular clock genes in man and lower animals: Possible implications for circadian abnormalities in depression. *Neuropsychopharmacology, 22*(4), 335–345.

Bureau of Justice Statistics. (1999). *Report on U.S. prison population.* Washington, DC.

Bureau of Labor Statistics, U.S. Department of Labor. (2002). Counselors. In Bureau of Labor Statistics, *Occupational outlook handbook* (2004–05 ed.). Washington, DC: Author.

Bureau of Labor Statistics, U.S. Department of Labor. (2002). Social workers. In Bureau of Labor Statistics, *Occupational outlook handbook* (2004–05 ed.). Washington, DC: Author.

Bureau of Labor Statistics, U.S. Department of Labor. (2008). *Occupational Outlook Handbook, 2008–09 Edition,* Psychologists. Retrieved January 1, 2008, from http://www.bls.gov/oco/ocos056.htm

Burgess, J. L. (2001). Phosphine exposure from a methamphetamine laboratory investigation. *J. Toxicol. Clin. Toxicol. 39,* 165.

Burijon, B. N. (2007). *Biological bases of clinical anxiety.* New York: W. W. Norton & Company.

Burke, R. D. (1996). *When the music's over: My journey into schizophrenia.* New York: Plume.

Burkholder, A. (2008). Jolting the brain fights deep depression. *CNN.com/health,* May 2, 2008.

Burston, D. (2000). *The crucible of experience: R. D. Laing and the crisis of psychotherapy.* Cambridge, MA: Harvard University Press.

Burt, D. R., Creese, I., & Snyder, S. H. (1977). Anti-schizophrenic drugs: Chronic treatment elevates dopamine receptor binding in brain. *Science, 196*(4287), 326–328.

Burton, V. S. (1990). The consequences of official labels: A research note on rights lost by the mentally ill, mentally incompetent, and convicted felons. *Comm. Ment. Hlth. J., 26*(3), 267–276.

Busch, A. B., Huskamp, H. A., Normand, S. L. T., Young, A. S., Goldman, H., & Frank, R. G. (2006). The impact of parity on major depression treatment quality in the Federal Employees' Health Benefits Program after parity implementation. *Med. Care, 44*(6), 506–512.

Busch, F. N., Rudden, M. G., & Shapiro, T. (2004). *Psychodynamic treatment of depression.* Washington, DC: American Psychiatric Publishing.

Bushman, B. J., Baumeister, R. F., & Stack, A. D. (1999). Catharsis, aggression, and persuasive influence: Self-fulfilling or self-defeating prophecies? *J. Pers. Soc. Psychol., 76*(3), 367–376.

Buss, D. M. (2000). *The dangerous passion: Why jealousy is as necessary as love and sex.* New York: Free Press.

Bussiere, T., Bard, F., Barbour, R., Grajeda, H., Guido, T., Kahn, K. et al. (2004). Morphological characterization of Thioflavin-S-positive amyloid plaques in transgenic Alzheimer mice and effect of passive Abeta immunotherapy on their clearance. *Am. J. Pathol., 165,* 987–995.

Bussing, R., Koro-Ljungberg, M. E., Gary, F., Mason, D. M., & Garvan, C. W. (2005). Exploring help-seeking for ADHD symptoms: A mixed-methods approach. *Harvard Rev. Psychiat., 13*(2), 85–101.

Bussing, R., Zima, B. T., & Belin, T. R. (1998). Differential access to care for children with ADHD in special education programs. *Psychiatr. Serv., 49*(9), 1226–1229.

Bussing, R., Zima, B. T., Gary, F. A., & Garvan, C. W. (2003). Barriers to detection, help-seeking, and service use for children with

ADHD symptoms. *J. Behav. Hlth. Serv. Res., 30*(2), 176–189.

Butcher, J. N., Cabiya, J., Lucio, E., & Garrido, M. (2007). *Assessing Hispanic clients using the MMPI-2 and MMPI-A.* Washington, DC: American Psychological Association.

Butler, G., Fennel, M., Robson, P., & Gelder, M. (1991). A comparison of behavior therapy and cognitive behavior therapy in the treatment of generalized anxiety disorder. *J. Cons. Clin. Psychol., 59*(1), 167–175.

Butler, R. J. (2004). Childhood nocturnal enuresis: Developing a conceptual framework. *Clin. Psychol. Rev., 24,* 909–931.

Butler, T., Andrews, G., Allnutt, S., Sakashita, C., Smith, N. E., & Basson, J. (2006). "Mental disorders in Australian prisoners: A comparison with a community sample": Corrigendum. *Austral. New Zeal. J. Psychiat., 40*(8).

Butryn, M. L., & Wadden, T. A. (2005). Treatment of overweight in children and adolescents: Does dieting increase the risk of eating disorders? *Inter. J. Eat. Disorders, 37*(4), 285–293.

Button, E. J., & Warren, R. L. (2001). Living with anorexia nervosa: The experience of a cohort of sufferers from anorexia nervosa 7.5 years after initial presentation to a specialized eating disorders service. *Eur. Eating Disord. Rev., 9*(2), 74–96.

Bydlowski, S., Corcos, M., Jeammet, P., Paterniti, S., Berthoz, S., Laurier, C., et al. (2005). Emotion-processing deficits in eating disorders. *Inter. J. Eat. Disorders, 37*(4), 321–329.

Byrne, M., Carr, A., & Clark, M. (2004). The efficacy of behavioral couples therapy and emotionally focused therapy for couple distress. *Contemp. Fam. Ther.: Inter. J., 26*(4), 361–387.

Cabaj, R. P. (2008). Gay men and lesbians. In H. D. Kleber & M. Galanter (Eds.), *The American Psychiatric Publishing textbook of substance abuse treatment* (4th ed., pp. 623–638). Arlington, VA: American Psychiatric Publishing.

Cachelin, F. M., Phinney, J. S., Schug, R. A., & Striegel-Moore, R. M. (2006). Acculturation and eating disorders in a Mexican American community sample. *Psychol. Women Quart., 30*(4), 340–347.

CADDRE (Center for Autism and Developmental Disabilities Research and Epidemiology). (2004). *The epidemiology and etiology of autistic spectrum disorder: A prospective study.* Children's Hospital of Pennsylvania. Retrieved October 7, 2005, from www.aboard.org/aboard/presentations/Levy/CADDRE_files/Default.htm

Cadoret, R. J., Yates, W. R., Troughton, E., Woodworth, G., & Stewart, M. A. (1995). Adoption study demonstrating two genetic pathways to drug abuse. *Arch. Gen. Psychiatry, 52,* 42–52.

Caetano, R., & Babor, T. F. (2007). Diagnosis of alcohol dependence in epidemiological surveys: An epidemic of youthful alcohol dependence or a case of measurement error? In P. J. Sirovatka, D. A. Regier, J. B. Saunders, & M. A. Schuckit (Eds.), *Diagnostic issues in substance use disorders: Refining the research agenda for DSM-V* (pp. 195–201). Washington, DC: American Psychiatric Association.

Cahn, W., Pol, H. E. H., Bongers, M., Schnack, H. G., Mandi, R. C. W., Van

Haren, N. E. M., et al. (2002). Brain morphology in antipsychotic-naïve schizophrenia: A study of multiple brain structures. *Brit. J. Psychiat., 181*(Suppl 43), s66–s72.

Cain, D. J. (2007). What every therapist should know, be and do: Contributions from humanistic psychotherapies. *J. Contemp. Psychother., 37*(1), 3–10.

Caine, D., Patterson, K., Hodges, J. R., Heard, R., & Haliday, G. (2001). Severe anterograde amnesia with extensive hippocampal degeneration in a case of rapidly progressive frontotemporal dementia. *Neurocase, 7*(1), 57–64.

Calev, A., Gaudino, E. A., Squires, N. K., Zervas, I. M., & Fink, M. (1995). ECT and non-memory cognition: A review. *Br. J. Clin. Psychol., 34,* 505–515.

Calev, A., Nigal, D., Shapira, B., Tubi, N., Chazan, M. A., Ben-Yehuda, B. A., et al. (1991). Early and long-term effects of electroconvulsive therapy and depression on memory and other cognitive functions. *J. Nerv. Ment. Dis., 179*(9), 526–533.

Callahan, C. M., Wolinsky, F. D., Stump, T. E., Nienaber, N. A., Hui, S. L., & Tierney, W. M. (1998). Mortality, symptoms, and functional impairment in late-life depression. *J. Gen. Intern. Med., 13*(11), 746–752.

Callahan, L. A., Steadman, H. J., McGreevy, M. A., & Robbins, P. C. (1991). The volume and characteristics of insanity defense pleas: An eight-state study. *Bull. Amer. Acad. Psychiat. Law, 19*(4), 331–338.

Camacho, E. B., Leon, E. C., & Uribe, M. P. O. (2005). Nature and schizophrenia. *Salud Mental., 28*(2), 59–72.

Cameron, A., Rosen, R. C., & Swindle, R. W. (2005). Sexual and relationship characaristics among an internet-based sample of U.S. men with and without erectile dysfunction. *J. Sex Marital Ther., 31*(3), 229–242.

Cameron, D. J., Thomas, R. I., Mulvhill, M., & Bronheim, H. (1987). Delirium: A test of the Diagnostic and Statistical Manual III criteria on medical inpatients. *J. Amer. Ger. Soc., 35,* 1007–1010.

Cameron, P. M., Leszcz, M., Bebchuk, W., Swinson, R. P., Antony, M. M., Azim, H. F., et al. (1999). The practice and roles of the psychotherapies: A discussion paper. *Canad. J. Psychiat., 44*(Suppl 1), 18S-31S.

Campbell, J., Gilmore, L., & Cuskelly, M. (2003). Changing student teachers' attitudes towards disability and inclusion. *J. Intell. Dev. Disab., 28,* 369–379.

Campbell, J. M., Herzinger, C. V., & James, C. L. (2008). Evidence-based therapies for autistic disorder and pervasive developmental disorders. In R. G. Steele, T. D. Elkin, & M. C. Roberts (Eds.), *Handbook of evidence-based therapies for children and adolescents: Bridging science and practice.* New York: Springer.

Canetto, S. S. (1995). Elderly women and suicidal behavior. In S. S. Canetto & D. Lester (Eds.), *Women and suicidal behavior.* New York: Springer.

Canetto, S. S. (1995). Suicidal women: Prevention and intervention strategies. In S. S. Canetto & D. Lester (Eds.), *Women and suicidal behavior.* New York: Springer.

Canetto, S. S. (2003). Older adulthood. In L. Slater, J. H. Daniel, & A. Banks (Eds.) *The complete guide to women and mental health* (pp. 56–64). Boston: Beacon Press.

Cantor, J. M., Blanchard, R., Christensen, B. K., Dickey, R., Klassen, P. E., Beckstead, A. L., et al. (2004). Intelligence, memory, and handedness in pedophilia. *Neuropsychol., 18*(1), 3–14.

Caplan, P. J., & Cosgrove, L. (Eds.). (2004). *Bias in psychiatric diagnosis.* Northvale, NJ: Jason Aronson.

Capuzzi, D., & Gross, D. R. (Eds.). (2008). *Youth at risk: A prevention resource for counselors, teachers, and parents.* Alexandria, VA: American Counseling Association.

Carbonari, J. P., & DiClemente, C. C. (2000). Using transtheoretical model profiles to differentiate levels of alcohol abstinence success. *J. Cons. Clin. Psychol., 68*(5), 810–817.

Cardena, E. (2008). Dissociative disorders measures. In A. J. Rush, Jr., M. B. First, & D. Blacker (Eds.), *Handbook of psychiatric measures* (2nd ed., pp. 587–599). Arlington, VA: American Psychiatric Publishing.

Cardena, E., & Gleaves, D. H. (2007). Dissociative disorders. In M. Hersen, S. M. Turner, & D. C. Beidel (Eds.), *Adult psychopathology and diagnosis* (5th ed., pp. 473–503). Hoboken, NJ: Wiley.

Carducci, B. (2000). Shyness: The new solution. *Psychol. Today, 33*(1), 38–45.

Carek, P. J., & Dickerson, L. M. (1999). Current concepts in the pharmacological management of obesity. *Drugs, 57*(6), 883–904.

Carey, B. (2006). Heart risks with stimulant use? Maybe. Worry? For some. *New York Times,* Feb. 21, section F., p. 1.

Carey, B. (2007, September 4). Bipolar illness soars as a diagnosis for the young. *New York Times Online.* Retrieved September 17, 2007, from http://www.nytimes.com

Carey, B. (2008, February 10). Making sense of the great suicide debate. *New York Times.* Retrieved February 23, 2008, from www.nytimes.com

Carey, B. (2008, May 27). Lotus therapy. *New York Times Online.* Retrieved August 2, 2008, from http://www.nytimes.com/2008/05/27/health/research/27budd.html

Carey, R. J., Pinheiro-Carrerra, M., Dai, H., Tomaz, C., et al. (1995). L-DOPA and psychosis: Evidence for L-DOPA-induced increases in prefrontal cortex dopamine and in serium corticosterone. *Biol. Psychiat., 38*(10), 669–676.

Carll, E. K. (Ed.). (2007). *Trauma psychology: Issues in violence, disaster, health, and illness* (Vol. 1). Westport, CT: Praeger Publishers.

Carlson, G. A., & Fish, B. (2005). Longitudinal course of schizophrenia spectrum symptoms in offspring of psychiatrically hospitalized mothers. *J. Child Adol. Psychopharmacol., 15*(3), 362–383.

Carlson, M. (1998, June 22). The best things in life aren't free. *Time, 151,* p. 21.

Carlson, N. R. (2008). *Foundations of physiological psychology* (7th ed.). Boston: Pearson.

Carlson, W. L., & Snowden, M. (2007). Improving treatment for depression in the nursing home population: Integrating the model of depression care manager. *Harvard Rev. Psychiat., 15*(3), 128–132.

Carmichael, M. (2004, September 27). Cut stress–cut sugar. *Newsweek, 144*(13), p. 56.

Carney, S. M., & Goodwin, G. M. (2005). Lithium—A continuing story in the treatment of bipolar disorder. *Acta Psychiatr. Scandin., 111*(Suppl. 426), 7–12.

Caron, J., Julien, M., & Huang, J. H. (2008). Changes in suicide methods in Quebec between 1987 and 2000: The possible impact of Bill C-17 requiring safe storage of firearms. *Suic. Life-Threat. Behav., 38*(2), 195–208.

Carr, J. E. (1994). Annotation: Long term outcome for people with Down syndrome. *J. Child Psychol. Psychiat. Allied Disc, 35*(3), 425–439.

Carr, J. E. (2001). Stress and illness. In D. Wedding (Ed.), *Behavior and medicine* (3rd ed., pp. 231–246). Seattle: Hogrefe & Huber.

Carrier, J. W., & Ennis, K. (2004). Depression and suicide. In D. Capuzzi (Ed.), *Suicide across the life span: Implications for counselors* (pp. 39–62). Alexandria, VA: American Counseling Association.

Carroll, K. M. (2005). Matching and differential therapies: Providing substance abusers with appropriate treatment. In R. J. Frances, A. H. Mack, & S. I. Miller (Eds.), *Clinical textbook of addictive disorders* (3rd ed., pp. 637–662). New York: Guilford Press.

Carroll, K. M. (2008). Cognitive-behavioral therapies. In H. D. Kleber & M. Galanter (Eds.), *The American Psychiatric Publishing textbook of substance abuse treatment* (4th ed., pp. 349–360). Arlington, VA: American Psychiatric Publishing.

Garroll, R. A. (2007). Gender dysphoria and transgender experiences. In S. R. Leiblum (Ed.), *Principles and practice of sex therapy* (4th ed., pp. 477–508). New York: Guilford Press.

Carten, A. J. (2006). African Americans and mental health. In S. Rosenberg & J. Rosenberg (Eds.), *Community mental health: Challenges for the 21st century* (pp. 125–139). New York: Routledge.

Casey, D. E. (1995). Motor and mental aspects of EPS. *Inter. J. Psychopharmacology, 10*, [np].

Casey, L. M., Oei, T. P. S., & Newcombe, P. A. (2004). An integrated cognitive model of panic disorder: The role of positive and negative cognitions. *Clin. Psychol. Rev., 24*(5), 529–555.

Casey, P. (2001). Multiple personality disorder. *Prim. Care Psychiat., 7*(1), 7–11.

Cash, T. F., & Henry, P. E. (1995). Women's body images: The results of a national survey in the U. S. A. *Sex Roles, 33*(1/2), 19–28.

Casimir, G. J., & Morrison, B. J. (1993). Rethinking work with "multicultural populations." *Comm. Ment. Hlth. J., 29,* 547–559.

Cassells, C., Paterson, B., Dowding, D., & Morrison, R. (2005). Long- and short-term risk factors in the prediction of inpatient suicide: A review of the literature. *Crisis, 26*(2), 53–63.

Castellani, B. (2000). *Pathological gambling: The making of a medical problem.* Albany: State University of New York Press.

Castonguay, L. G., & Beutler, L. E. (2006). *Principles of psychotherapeutic change that work.* New York: Oxford University Press.

Castro, Y., Holm-Denoma, J. M., & Buckner, J. D. (2007). Introduction to empirically informed mental health services for diverse populations. In J. D. Buckner, Y. Castro, & J. M. Holm-Denoma (Eds.), *Mental health care for people of diverse backgrounds* (pp. 1–8). Abingdon, England: Radcliffe Publishing.

Castrogiovanni, P., Pieraccini, F., & Di Muro, A. (1998). Suicidality and aggressive behavior. *Acta Psychiatr. Scandin., 97*(2), 144–148.

Catan, T. (2007). Online anorexia sites shut down amid claims they glorify starvation. *TimesOnline* November 22, 2007. Retrieved from http://www.timesonline.uk/tol/life_and_style/health

Caton, C. L. (1982). Effect of length of inpatient treatment for chronic schizophrenia. *Amer. J. Psychiat., 139*(7), 856–861.

Cauchon, D. (1999, February). Patients often aren't informed of danger. *USA Today.*

Cauchon, D. (2004, November 16). Pennies pay off when Ohio collector cashes in. *USA Today,* p. 3A.

Cauli, O., & Morelli, M. (2005). Caffeine and the dopaminergic system. *Behav. Pharmacol., 16*(2), 63–77.

Cautela, J. R. (2000). Rationale and procedures for covert conditioning. *Psicoterapia Cognitiva e Comportamentale, 6*(2), 194–205.

Cauwels, J. M. (1983). *Bulimia: The binge-purge compulsion.* New York: Doubleday.

Cavanaugh, J. C. (1990). *Adult development and aging.* Belmont, CA: Wadsworth.

Cavanaugh, J. C., & Blanchard-Fields, F. (2006). *Adult development and aging* (5th ed.). Belmont, CA: Wadsworth/Thomson Learning.

Cavett, R. (1992, August 3). Goodbye, darkness. *Time, 38*(5), 88.

CBC. (2008, May 13). The world's worst natural disasters: Calamities of the 20th and 21st centuries. *CBC News.*

CDC (Centers for Disease Control and Prevention). (2001). Report. Atlanta, Georgia: Author.

CDC (Centers for Disease Control and Prevention). (2007). Four percent of American adults never had sex. Report cited in *YAHOO! News,* June 22, 2007.

CDC (Centers for Disease Control and Prevention). (2008). *Chronic liver disease/cirrhosis.* Hyattsville, MD: NCHS.

CDC (Centers for Disease Control and Prevention). (2008). U.S. life expectancy hits new high of nearly 78 years. *News Release.* Hyattsville, MD: U.S. Department of Health and Human Services, Centers for Disease Control and Prevention.

Cerel, J., Jordan, J. R., & Duberstein, P. R. (2008). The impact of suicide on the family. *Crisis: J. Crisis Intervent. Suic. Prev., 29*(1), 38–44.

Cerletti, U., & Bini, L. (1938). L'elettroshock. *Arch. Gen. Neurol. Psychiat. & Psychoanal., 19,* 266–268.

Cerny, C. A., & Noffsinger, S. (2006). Prisoner rights and suicide. *J. Amer. Acad. Psychiat. Law, 34*(4), 549–551.

CEWG (Community Epidemiology Work Group). (2004). *Trends in drug abuse, Vol. 1: Proceedings of the community epidemiology work group. NIH Pub. No 04-5364.* Washington, DC: U.S. Government Printing Office.

Chacón, F., & Vecina, M. L. (2007). The 2004 Madrid terrorist attack: Organizing a large-scale psychological response. In E. K. Carll (Ed.), *Trauma psychology: Issues in violence, disaster, health, and illness* (Vol. 1). Westport, CT: Praeger Publishers.

Chae, B. J., & Kang, B. J. (2006). Quetiapine for delusional jealousy in a deaf elderly patient. *Inter. Psychoger., 18*(1), 187–188.

Chaika, E. O. (1990). *Understanding psychotic speech: Beyond Freud and Chomsky.* Springfield, IL: Thomas.

Chalamat, M., Mihalopoulos, C., Carter, R., & Vos, T. (2005). Assessing cost-effectiveness in mental health: Vocational rehabilitation for schizophrenia and related conditions. *Austral. New Zeal. J. Psychiat., 39*(8), 693–700.

Chamberlain, S. R., Blackwell, A. D., Fineberg, N. A., Robbins, T. W., & Sahakian, B. J. (2005). The neuropsychology of obsessive compulsive disorder: The importance of failures in cognitive and behavioural inhibition as candidate endopyhenotypic markers. *Neurosci. Biobehav. Rev., 29*(3), 399–419.

Chambless, D. L. (2002). Identification of empirically supported counseling psychology interventions: Commentary. *Counseling Psychologist, 30*(2), 302–308.

Chaparro, S. (2004). Cited in T. Sauthoff, Professor assigns 48 hours without using cell phone. *The Daily Targum,* April 5, 2004, p. 1.

Charatan, F. (2001). World psychiatric association asked to take up case of Chinese dissidents. *British Medical Journal, 322*:7290, p. 817.

Charland, L. C. (2007). Benevolent theory: Moral treatment at the York Retreat. *Hist. Psychiat., 18*(1), 61–80.

Charman, D. P. (Ed.). (2004). *Core processes in brief psychodynamic psychotherapy: Advancing effective practice.* Mahwah, NJ: Lawrence Erlbaum.

Charney, D. S., Woods, S. W., Goodman, W. K., & Heninger, G. R. (1987). Neurobiological mechanisms of panic anxiety: Biochemical and behavioral correlates of yohimbine-induced anxiety. *Amer. J. Psychiat., 144*(8), 1030–1036.

Charney, D. S., Woods, S. W., Price, L. H., Goodman, W. K., Glazer, W. M., & Heninger, G. R. (1990). Noradrenergic dysregulation in panic disorder. In J. C. Ballenger (Ed.), *Neurobiology of panic disorder.* New York: Wiley-Liss.

Charuvastra, A., & Cloitre, M. (2008). Social bonds and posttraumatic stress disorder. In S. Fiske, D. L. Schacter, & R. Sternberg (Eds.), *Annual review of psychology* (Vol. 59). Palo Alto, CA: Annual reviews.

Chassin, L., Collins, R. L., Ritter, J., & Shirley, M. C. (2001). Vulnerability to substance use disorders across the life span. In R. E. Ingram & J. M. Price (Eds.), *Vulnerability to psychopathology: Risk across the lifespan* (pp. 165–172). New York: Guilford Press.

Chatlos, C. (1987). *Crack: What you should know about the cocaine epidemic.* New York: Perigee Books.

Chavez, M. L., & Spitzer, M. F. (2002). Herbals and other dietary supplements for premenstrual syndrome and menopause. *Psychiatr. Ann., 32*(1), 61–71.

Chavira, D. A., Grilo, C. M., Shea, M. T., Yen, S., Gunderson, J. G., Morey, L. C., et al. (2003). Ethnicity and four personality disorders. *Comprehen. Psychiat., 44*(6), 483–491.

Chekki, C. (2004, November 10). Treaty 3 cries for help. *The Chronicle Journal* (Thunder Bay, Ontario, Canada), p. A3.

Chen, T.-J., Yu, Y. W.-Y., Chen, M.-C., Wang, S.-Y., Tsai, S.-J., & Lee, T.-W. (2005). Serotonin dysfunction and suicide attempts in major depressives: An auditory event-related potential study. *Neuropsychobiology, 52*(1), 287–36.

Chen, Y. R., Swann, A. C., & Burt, D. B. (1996). Stability of diagnosis in schizophrenia. *Amer. J. Psychiat., 153*(5), 682–686.

Cheney, T. (2008, January 13). Take me as I am, whoever I am. *New York Times.* Retrieved from http://www.nytimes.com

Cheng, A. T. A., Hawton, K., Lee, C. T. C., & Chen, T. H. H. (2007). The influence of media reporting of the suicide of a celebrity on suicide rates: A population-based study. *Inter. J. Epidemiol., 36*(6), 1229–1234.

Cherry, K. E., Galea, S., & Silva, J. L. (2007). Successful aging in very old adults: Resiliency in the face of natural disaster. In M. Hersen & A. M. Gross (Eds.), *Handbook of clinical psychology, Vol. 1: Adults.* Hoboken, NJ: Wiley.

Chester, A., & Glass, C. A. (2006). Online counselling: A descriptive analysis of therapy services on the internet. *Brit. J. Guid. Couns., 34*(2), 145–160.

Chien, W. T., Norman, I., & Thompson, D. R. (2004). A randomized controlled trial of a mutual support group for family caregivers of patients with schizophrenia. *Inter. J. Nurs. Stud., 41*(6), 637–649.

Chiles, J. A., & Strosahl, K. D. (2005). *Clinical manual for assessment and treatment of suicidal patients.* Washington, DC: American Psychiatric Publishing.

Chin, J. H., Ma, L., MacTavish, D., & Jhamandas, J. H. (2007). Amyloid beta protein modulates glutamate-mediated neurotransmission in the rat basal forebrain: Involvement of presynaptic neuronal nicotinic acetylcholine and metabotropic glutamate receptors. *J. Neurosci., 27*(35), 9262–9269.

Chiu, L. H. (1971). Manifested anxiety in Chinese and American children. *J. Psychol., 79,* 273–284.

Cho, H. (2007). Influences of self-monitoring and goal-setting on drinking refusal self-efficacy and drinking behavior. *Alcoholism Treat. Quart., 25*(3), 53–65.

Cho, M. J., Moscicki, E. K., Narrow, W. E., Rae, D. S., Locke, B. Z., & Regier, D. A. (1993). Concordance between two measures of depression in the Hispanic Health and Nutrition Examination Survey. *Soc. Psychiat. Psychiatr. Epidemiol., 28*(4), 156–163.

Choca, J. P. (2004). Case reports. In J. P. Choca, *Interpretive guide to the Millon Clinical Multiaxial Inventory* (3rd ed., pp. 289–326). Washington, DC: American Psychological Association.

Chochinov, H. M., & Schwartz, L. (2002). Depression and the will to live in the psychological landscape of terminally ill patients. In K. Foley & H. Hendin (Eds.), *The case against assisted suicide: For the right to end-of-life care* (pp. 261–278). Baltimore, MD: The John Hopkins University Press.

Christakis, D. A., Zimmerman, F. J., DiGiuseppe, D. L., & McCarty, C. A. (2004). Early television exposure and subsequent attentional problems in children. *Pediatrics, 113,* 708–713.

Christensen, A., Atkins, D. C., Yi, J., Baucom, D. H., & George, W. H. (2006). Couple and individual adjustment for 2 years following a randomized clinical trial comparing traditional versus integrative behavioral couple therapy. *J. Cons. Clin. Psychol., 74*(6), 1180–1191.

Christensen, A., Sevier, M., Simpson, L. E., & Gattis, K. S. (2004). Acceptance, mindfulness, and change in couple therapy. In V. M. Follette, M. M. Linehan, & S. C. Hayes (Eds.), *Mindfulness and acceptance: Expanding the cognitive-behavioral tradition* (pp. 288–309). New York: Guilford Press.

Christensen, A. J., Dornick, R., Ehlers, S. L., & Schultz, S. K. (1999). Social environment and longevity in schizophrenia. *Psychosom. Med., 61*(2), 141–145.

Christopher, P. P., Foti, M. E., Roy-Bujnowski, K., & Appelbaum, P. S. (2007). Consent form readability and educational levels of potential participants in mental health research. *Psychiatr. Serv., 58*(2), 227–232.

Christophersen, E. R., & Purvis, P. C. (2001). Toileting problems in children. In C. E. Walker & M. C. Roberts (Eds.), *Handbook of clinical child psychopathology* (3rd ed., pp. 453–469). New York: Wiley.

Chung, M. C., Dennis, I., Easthope, Y., Werrett, J., & Farmer, S. (2005). A multiple-indicator multiple-case model for posttraumatic stress reactions: Personality, coping, and maladjustment. *Psychosom. Med., 67*(2), 251–259.

Chylinski, J., & Wright, M. W. (1967). Testing in Canada with the Minnesota Multiphasic Personality Inventory (MMPI) and the Edwards Personal Preference Schedule (EPPS). *Canad. Psychol., 8a*(3), 202–206.

Ciano-Federoff, L. M., & Sperry, J. A. (2005). On "converting" hand pain into psychological pain: Treating hand pain vicariously through exposure-based therapy for PTSD. *Clin. Case Stud., 4*(1), 57–71.

Cicero-Dominguez, S. A. (2005). Assessing the U.S.–Mexico fight against human trafficking and smuggling: Unintended results of U. S. immigration policy. *Northwestern Journal of International Human Rights, 4,* 303–330.

Cima, M., Nijman, H. L. I., Merckelbach, H., et al. (2004). Claims of crime-related amnesia in forensic patients. *Inter. J. Law Psychiat., 27,* 215–221.

Claes, L., Vandereycken, W., & Vertommen, H. (2002). Impulsive and compulsive traits in eating disordered patients compared with controls. *Pers. Individ. Diff., 32*(4), 707–714.

Clark, D. A. (2004). Cognitive-behavioral theory and treatment of obsessive-compulsive disorder: Past contributions and current developments. In R. L. Leahy (Ed.), *Contemporary cognitive therapy: Theory, research, and practice* (pp. 161–183). New York: Guilford Press.

Clark, D. A. (2004). *Cognitive-behavioral therapy for OCD.* New York: Guilford Press.

Clark, D. A., & Guyitt, B. D. (2008). Pure obsessions: Conceptual misnomer or clinical anomaly? In J. S. Abramowitz, D. McKay, & S. Taylor (Eds.), *Obsessive-compulsive disorder: Subtypes and spectrum conditions.* Oxford, England: Elsevier.

Clark, L. A. (2005, November). Dimensional bases of diagnosis. *Clinician's Res. Digest, Suppl. Bull. 33,* 1–2.

Clarke, G. N., Rohde, P., Lewinsohn, P. M., Hops, H., & Seeley, J. R. (1999). Cognitive-behavioral treatment of adolescent depression: Efficacy of acute group treatment and booster sessions. *J. Amer. Acad. Child Adol. Psychiat., 38*(3), 272–279.

Clarke, J. C., & Saunders, J. B. (1988). *Alcoholism and problem drinking: Theories and treatment.* Sydney: Pergamon Press.

Clarkin, J. F., Foelsch, P. A., Levy, K. N., Hull, J. W., Delaney, J. C., & Kernberg, O. F. (2001). The development of a psychodynamic treatment for patients with borderline personality disorder: A preliminary study of behavioral change. *J. Per. Disorders, 15,* 487–495.

Clary, G. L., & Krishnan, K. R. (2001). Delirium: Diagnosis, neuropathogenesis and treatment. *J. Psychiatr. Prac., 7*(5), 310–323.

Clayton, A. H., Pradko, J. F., Croft, H. A., Montano, C. B., Leadbetter, R. A., Bolden-Watson, C., et al. (2002). Prevalence of sexual dysfunction among newer antidepressants. *J. Clin. Psychiat., 63*(4), 357–366.

Clayton, R. R., Segress, M. J. H., & Caudill, C. A. (2008). Prevention of substance abuse. In H. D. Kleber & M. Galanter (Eds.), *The American Psychiatric Publishing textbook of substance abuse treatment* (4th ed.). (pp. 681–688). Arlington, VA: American Psychiatric Publishing.

Clay-Warner, J., & Burt, C. H. (2005). Rape reporting after reforms: Have times really changed? *Violence Against Women, 11*(2), 150–176.

Clifford, J. S., Norcross, J. C., & Sommer, R. (1998). *Autobiographies of mental patients: Psychologists' uses and recommendations.* Paper presented at the 69th annual meeting of the Eastern Psychological Association, Boston.

Clinton, D., Gierlach, E., Zack, S. E., Beutler, L. E., & Castonguay, L. G. (2007). Toward the integration of technical interventions, relationship factors, and participants variables. In J. Weinberger & S. G. Hofmann (Eds.), *The art and science of psychotherapy* (pp. 131–153). New York: Routledge/Taylor and Francis Group.

Cloitre, M., Yonkers, K. A., Pearlstein, T., Altemus, M., Davidson, K. W., Pigott, T. A., et al. (2004). Women and anxiety disorders: Implications for diagnosis and treatment. *CNS Spectrums, 9*(9 Suppl 8), 1–16.

Cloninger, C. F., & Svrakic, D. M. (2005). Personality disorders. In E. H. Rubin & C. F. Zorumski (Eds.), *Adult psychiatry* (2nd ed., pp. 290–306). Oxford, England: Blackwell Publishing.

Clum, G. A., & Febbraro, G. A. R. (2001). Phobias. In H. S. Friedman (Ed.), *Specialty articles from the encyclopedia of mental health.* San Diego: Academic Press.

CNN. (2004, June 4). Porn 3X more popular than searches. *CNNmoney.*

CNN. (2008). Girl's suicide leaves dozens ill from fumes. Retrieved on April 24, 2008, at www.CNN.com.

Coccaro, E. F. (2001). Biological and treatment correlates. In W. J. Livesley (Ed.), *Handbook of personality disorders: Theory, research, and treatment* (pp. 124–135). New York: Guilford Press.

Coetzer, B. R. (2004). Obsessive-compulsive disorder following brain injury: A review. *Inter. J. Psychiat. Med., 34*(4), 363–377.

Coffey, C., Carlin, J. B., Lynskey, M., Li, N., & Patton, G. C. (2003). Adolescent precursors of cannabis dependence: Findings from the Victorian Adolescent Health Cohort Study. *Brit. J. Psychiat., 182*(4), 330–336.

Coffey, S. F., Gudleski, G. D., Saladin, M. E., & Brady, K. T. (2003). Impulsivity and rapid discounting of delayed hypothetical rewards in cocaine-dependent individuals. *Exp. Clin. Psychopharmacol., 11*(1), 18–25.

Cogan, J. C., Bhalla, S. K., Sefa-Dedeh, A., & Rothblum, E. D. (1996). A comparison study of United States and African students on perceptions of obesity and thinness. *J. Cross-Cult. Psychol., 27,* 98–113.

Cohen, A. S., & Docherty, N. M. (2005). Symptom-oriented versus syndrome approaches to resolving heterogeneity of neuropsychological functioning in schizophrenia. *J. Neuropsychiat. Clin. Neurosci., 17*(3), 384–390.

Cohen, E. (2007). CDC: Antidepressants most prescribed drugs in U.S. *CNN.* Retrieved July 10, 2007, from http://www.cnn/2007/health/07/09/antidepressants/index.html#cnnSTCTest

Cohen, J., Goodman, R. F., Brown, E. J., & Mannarino, A. (2004). *Harvard Rev. Psychiatry, 12*(4), 213–216.

Cohen, L., Ardjoen, R. C., & Sewpersad, K. S. M. (1997). Type A behaviour pattern as a risk factor after myocardial infarction: A review. *Psychology and Health, 12,* 619–632.

Cohen, L. J., & Galynker, I. I. (2002). Clinical features of pedophilia and implications for treatment. *J. Psychiatr. Prac., 8*(5), 276–289.

Cohen, M. B., Baker, G., Cohen, R. A., Fromm-Reichmann, F., & Weigert, E. V. (1954). An intensive study of twelve cases of manic-depressive psychosis. *Psychiatry, 17,* 103–137.

Cohen, P. (2008). Midlife suicide rises, puzzling researchers. *New York Times, 157*(54), 225.

Cohen, S. (2002). Psychosocial stress, social networks, and susceptibility to infection. In H. G. Koenig & H. J. Cohen (Eds.), *The link between religion and health: Psychoneuroimmunology and the faith factor* (pp. 101–123). New York: Oxford University Press.

Cohen, S. (2005). Psychological stress, immunity and upper respiratory infections. In G. Miller & E. Chen (Eds.), *Current directions in health psychology.* Upper Saddle River, NJ: Pearson.

Cohen, S., Tyrrell, A. D., & Smith, A. P. (1991). Psychological stress and susceptibility to the common cold. *N. Engl. J. Med., 325,* 606–612.

Cohen-Kettenis, P. T. (2001). Gender identity disorder in DSM? *J. Amer. Acad. Child Adol. Psychiat., 40*(4), 391.

Cohen-Sandler, R., Berman, A. L., & King, R. A. (1982). A follow-up study of hospitalized suicidal children. *J. Amer. Acad. Child Psychiat., 214,* 398–403.

Colburn, D. (1996, November 19). Singer's suicide doesn't lead to "copycat" deaths. *Washington Post Health,* p. 5.

Coldwell, C. M., & Bender, W. S. (2007). The effectiveness of assertive community treatment for homeless populations with severe mental illness: A meta-analysis. *Amer. J. Psychiat., 164*(3), 393–399.

Coldwell, S. E., Wilhelm, F. H., Milgrom, P., Prall, C. W., Getz, T., Spadafora, A., et al. (2007). Combining alprazolam with systematic desensitization therapy for dental injection phobia. *J. Anx. Disorders, 21*(7), 871–887.

Cole, D. A., & Turner, J. E., Jr. (1993). Models of cognitive mediation and moderation in child depression. *J. Abnorm. Psychol., 102*(2), 271–281.

Cole, E., & Daniel, J. H. (Eds.). (2005). *Featuring females: Feminist analyses of media.* Washington, DC: American Psychological Association.

Cole, J. O., Klerman, G. L., Goldberg, S. C., et al. (1964). Phenothiazine treatment in acute schizophrenia. *Arch. Gen. Psychiatry, 10,* 246–261.

Cole, T. B., & Glass, R. M. (Eds.). (2005). Mental illness and violent death: Major issues for public health. *JAMA, 294*(5), 623–624.

Coleman, L. (1984). *The reign of error: Psychiatry, authority, and law.* Boston: Beacon.

Coles, M. E., Heimberg, R. G., Frost, R. O., & Steketee, G. (2005). Not just right experiences and obsessive-compulsive features: experimental and self-monitoring perspectives. *Behav. Res. Ther., 43,* 153–167.

Coles, M. E., & Pietrefesa, A. S. (2008). Symmetry, ordering, and arranging. In J. S. Abramowitz, D. McKay, & S. Taylor (Eds.), *Obsessive-compulsive disorder: Subtypes and spectrum conditions.* Oxford, England: Elsevier.

Colom, F., Vieta, E., Martinez, A. A., Reinares, M., Goikolea, J. M., Benabarre, A., et al. (2003). A randomized trial on the efficacy of group psychoeducation in the prophylaxis of recurrences in bipolar patients whose disease is in remission. *Arch. Gen. Psychiat., 60*(4), 402–407.

Colom, F., Vieta, E., Reinares, M., Martinez, A. A., Torrent, C., Goikolea, J. M., et al. (2003). Psychoeducation efficacy in bipolar disorders: Beyond compliance enhancement. *J. Clin. Psychiat., 64*(9), 1101–1105.

Comas-Diaz, L. (2006). Cultural variation in the therapeutic relationship. In C. D. Goodheart, A. E. Kazdin, & R. J. Sternberg (Eds.), *Evidence-based psychotherapy: Where practice and research meet* (pp. 81–105). Washington, DC: American Psychological Association.

Combs, D. R., Basso, M. R., Wanner, J. L., & Ledet, S. N. (2008). Schizophrenia. In M. Hersen & J. Rosqvist (Eds.), *Handbook of psychological assessment, case conceptualization and treatment, Vol. 1: Adults* (pp. 352–402). Hoboken, NJ: John Wiley & Sons.

Comer, J. S., & Kendall, P. C. (2007). Terrorism: The psychological impact on youth. *Clin. Psychol.: Sci. Pract., 14*(3), 178–212.

Comer, R. (1973). *Therapy interviews with a schizophrenic patient.* Unpublished manuscript.

Compas, B. E., & Gotlib, I. H. (2002). *Introduction to clinical psychology: Science and practice.* Boston: McGraw-Hill.

Conklin, C. Z., & Westen, D. (2005). Borderline personality disorder in clinical practice. *Amer. J. Psychiat., 162,* 867–875.

Conley, R. R., & Kelly D. L. (2005). Schizophrenia. In R. Rakel & E. Bopp (Eds.) *Conn's current therapy,* 2005 (pp. 1280–1284). Philadelphia: Saunders, Philadelphia.

Conley, R. R., Kelly, D. L., Nelson, M. W., Richardson, C. M., Feldman, S., Benham, R., et al. (2005). Risperidone, quetiapine, and fluphenazine in the treatment of patients with therapy-refractory schizophrenia. *Clin. Neuropharmacol., 28*(4), 163–168.

Connelly, M., & Dutton, S. (2002). Bearing the brunt: New Yorkers react to 9/11. *The Roper Center for Public Opinion Research, 13*(5), 25.

Connor, J. P., Young, R. McD., Lawford, B. R., Ritchie, T. L., & Noble, E. P. (2002). D_2 dopamine receptor (DRD2) polymorphism is associated with severity of alcohol dependence. *Eur. Psychiat., 17*(1), 17–23.

Connor-Greene, P. A. (2007). Observation or interpretation: Demonstrating unintentional subjectivity and interpretive variance. *Teach. Psychol., 34*(3), 167–171.

Conrad, N. (1992). Stress and knowledge of suicidal others as factors in suicidal behavior of high school adolescents. *Issues Ment. Hlth. Nurs., 13*(2), 95–104.

Conus, P., Cotton, S., Schimmelmann, B. G., McGorry, P. D., & Lambert, M. (2007). The first-episode psychosis outcome study: Premorbid and baseline characteristics of an epidemiological cohort of 661 first-episode psychosis patients. *Early Intervent. Psychiat., 1*(2), 191–200.

Conwell, Y., Caine, E. D., & Olsen, K. (1990). Suicide and cancer in late life. *Hosp. Comm. Psychiat., 43,* 1334–1338.

Cook, C. E., Jeffcoat, A. R., & Perez-Reyes, M. (1985). Pharmacokinetic studies of cocaine and phencyclidine in man. In G. Barnett & C. N. Chiang (Eds.), *Pharmacokinetics and pharmacodynamics of psychoactive drugs.* Foster City, CA: Biomedical Publications.

Cook, I. A., & Leuchter, A. F. (2001). Prefrontal changes and treatment response prediction in depression. *Seminars Clin. Neuropsychiat., 6,* 113–120.

Coon, D., & Mitterer, J. O. (2007). *Introduction to psychology: Gateways to mind and behavior* (11th ed.). Belmont, CA: Wadsworth.

Coons, P. M., & Bowman, E. S. (2001). Ten-year follow-up study of patients with dissociative identity disorder. *J. Trauma Dissoc., 2*(1), 73–89.

Coons, P. M., Bowman, E. S., & Milstein, V. (1988). Multiple personality disorder: A clinical investigation of 50 cases. *J. Nerv. Ment. Dis., 176*(9), 519–527.

Cooper, A. M., Scherer, C. R., Boies, S. C., & Gordon, B. L. (1999). Sexuality on the Internet: From sexual exploration to pathological expression. *Profess. Psychol.: Res. Pract., 30*(2), 154–164.

Cooper, J., Carty, J., & Creamer, M. (2005). Pharmacotherapy for posttraumatic stress disorder: Empirical review and clinical recommendations. *Austral. New Zeal. J. Psychiat., 39*(8), 674–682.

Cooper, J. L. (2004). Treatment for children with attention-deficit/hyperactivity disorder. *Diss. Abstr. Inter.: Sect. B: Sci. Eng., 65*(5-B), 2338.

Cooper, M. (2001). Eating disorders, culture, and cognition. In J. F. Schumaker & T. Ward (Eds.), *Cultural cognition and psychopathology.* Westport, CT: Praeger.

Cooper, M. L. (1994). Motivations for alcohol use among adolescents: Development and validation of a four-factor model. *Psychol. Assess., 6*(2), 117–128.

Copley, J. (2008, May 8). Psychology of heavy metal music. *Suite101.com.* Retrieved June 14, 2008, from www.suite101.com

Corcoran, K., Gorin, S., & Moniz, C. (2005). Managed care and mental health. In S. A. Kirk (Ed.), *Mental disorders in the social environment: Critical perspectives* (pp. 430–442). New York: Columbia University Press.

Corey, G. (2001). *Theory and practice of counseling and psychotherapy* (6th ed.). Belmont, CA: Brooks/Cole.

Corey, G. (2008). *Theory and practice of counseling and psychotherapy* (8th ed.). Belmont, CA: Brooks/Cole.

Corey-Bloom, J. (2004). Alzheimer's disease. *Continuum Lifelong Learn. Neurol., 10,* 29–57.

Corkin, S. (1968). Acquisition of motor skill after bilateral medial temporal-lobe excision. *Neuropsychologia, 6,* 255–264.

Corkin, S. (1984). Lasting consequences of bilateral medial temporal lobectomy: Clinical course and experimental findings in H. M. *Sem. in Neuro., 4,* 249–259.

Corliss, R., & Lemonick, M. D. (2004, August 30). How to live to be 100. *Time, 164*(9), 40–46.

Cornblatt, B. A., & Keilp, J. G. (1994). Impaired attention, genetics, and the pathophysiology of schizophrenia. *Schizo. Bull., 20*(1), 31–46.

Cornish, J. W., McNicholas, L. F., & O'Brien, C. P. (1995). Treatment of substance-related disorders. In A. F. Schatzberg & C. B. Nemeroff (Eds.), *The American Psychiatric Press textbook of psychopharmacology.* Washington, DC: American Psychiatric Press.

Corrie, S., & Callanan, M. M. (2001). Therapists' beliefs about research and the scientist-practitioner model in an evidence-based health care climate? A qualitative study. *Brit. J. Med. Psychol., 74*(2), 135–149.

Corrigan, P. W. (2007). How clinical diagnosis might exacerbate the stigma of mental illness. *Soc. Work, 52*(1), 31–39.

Corrigan, P. W., & Larson, J. E. (2008). Stigma. In K. T. Mueser & D. V. Jeste (Eds.), *Clinical handbook of schizophrenia* (pp. 533–540). New York: Guilford Press.

Corrigan, P. W., Larson, J. E., & Kuwabara, S. A. (2007a). Mental illness stigma and the fundamental components of supported employment. *Rehab. Psychol., 52*(4), 451–457.

Corrigan, P. W., Watson, A. C., Otey, E., Westbrook, A. L., Gardner, A. L., Lamb, T. A., & Fenton, W. S. (2007b). How do children stigmatize people with mental illness? *J. Appl. Soc. Psychol., 37*(7), 1405–1417.

Corsini, R. J. (2008). Introduction. In R. J. Corsini & D. Wedding (Eds.), *Current psychotherapies* (8th ed.). Belmont, CA: Thomson Brooks/Cole.

Cosgrove, L., & Riddle, B. (2004). Gender bias and sex distribution of mental disorders in the DSM-IV-TR. In L. Cosgrove & P. J. Caplan (Eds.), *Bias in psychiatric diagnosis* (pp. 127–140). Northvale, NJ: Jason Aronson.

Cosmides, L., & Tooby, J. (2000). Evolutionary psychology and the emotions. In M. Lewis & J. M. Haviland (Eds.), *Handbook of emotions* (2nd ed., pp. 91–115). New York: Guilford Press.

Costa, E. (1983). Are benzodiazepine recognition sites functional entities for the action of endogenous effectors or merely drug receptors? *Adv. in Biochem. & Psychopharm., 38,* 249–259.

Costa, E. (1985). Benzodiazepine-GABA interactions: A model to investigate the neurobiology of anxiety. In A. H. Tuma & J. Maser (Eds.), *Anxiety and the anxiety disorders.* Hillsdale, NJ: Lawrence Erlbaum.

Costa, J. L., Brennen, M. B., & Hochgeschwender, U. (2002). The human genetics of eating disorders: Lessons from the leptin/melanocortin system. *Child Adol. Psychiat. Clin. N. Amer., 11*(2), 387–397.

Costa, P. T., Jr., & McCrae, R. R. (2005). A five-factor model perspective on personality disorders. In S. Strack (Ed.), *Handbook of personality and psychopathology* (pp. 442–461). Hoboken, NJ: Wiley.

Costantino, G., Dana, R. H., & Malgady, R. G. (2007). *TEMAS (Tell-Me-A-Story) assessment in multicultural societies.* Mahwah, NJ: Lawrence Erlbaum.

Costanzo, M., Krauss, D., & Pezdek, K. (2007). *Expert psychological testimony for the courts.* Mahwah, NJ: Lawrence Erlbaum.

Costello, E. J., Mustillo, S., Erkanli, A., Keeler, G., & Angold, A. (2003). Prevalence and development of psychiatric disorders in childhood and adolescence. *Arch. Gen. Psychiat., 60,* 837–844.

Cottler, L. B., Campbell, W., Krishna, V. A. S., Cunningham-Williams, R. M., & Abdullah, A.-B. (2005). Predictors of high rates of suicidal ideation among drug users. *J. Nerv. Ment. Dis., 193*(7), 431–437.

Couturier, J., & Lock, J. (2006). Eating disorders: Anorexia nervosa, bulimia nervosa, and binge eating disorder. In T. G. Plante (Ed.), *Mental disorders of the new millennium, Vol. 3: Biology and function.* Westport, CT: Praeger Publishers.

Covell, N. H., Jackson, C. T., Evans, A. C., & Essock, M. S. (2002). Antipsychotic prescribing practices in Connecticut's public mental health system: Rates of changing medications and prescribing styles. *Schizo. Bull., 28*(1), 17–29.

Cowan, S. (2002). Public arguments for and against the establishment of community mental health facilities: Implications for mental health practice. *J. Ment. Hlth. UK, 11*(1), 5–15.

Cox, A., Rutter, M., Newman, S., & Bartak, L. (1975). A comparative study of infantile autism and specific developmental receptive language disorder: II. Parental characteristics. *Brit. J. Psychiat., 126,* 146–159.

Cox, D. J., Morris, J. B., Jr., Borowitz, S. M., & Sutphen, J. L. (2002). Psychological differences between children with and without chronic encopresis. *J. Pediatr. Psychol., 27*(7), 585–591.

Coy, T. V. (1998). The effect of repressive coping style on cardiovascular reactivity and speech disturbances during stress. *Diss. Abstr. Inter.: Sect. B: Sci. Eng., 58*(8–B), 4512.

Coyne, J. C. (2001). Depression and the response of others. In W. G. Parrott (Ed.), *Emotions in social psychology: Essential readings* (pp. 231–238). Philadelphia: Psychology Press/Taylor & Francis.

Coyne, J. C., & Calarco, M. M. (1995). Effects of the experience of depression: Application of focus group and survey methodologies. *Psychiat.: Interpers. Biol. Proc., 58*(2), 149–163.

Coyne, J. C., Schwenk, T. L., & Fechner-Bates, S. (1995). Nondetection of depression by primary care physicians reconsidered. *Gen. Hosp. Psychiat., 17*(1), 3–12.

Cozier-D'Amico, Y. C. (2004). Social factors, genetics, and hypertension in United States Black women. *Diss. Abstr. Inter.: Sect. B: Sci. Eng., 65*(3-B), 1275.

Crandall, C. S., Preisler, J. J., & Aussprung, J. (1992). Measuring life events stress in the lives of college students: The Undergraduate Stress Questionnaire (USQ). *Journal of Behavioral Medicine, 15*(6), 627–662.

Crary, D. (2007). Psychologists to review stance on gays. *Yahoo! News.* Retrieved July 10, 2007, from http://news.yahoo.com

Creamer, T. L., & Liddle, B. J. (2005). Secondary traumatic stress among disaster mental health workers responding to the September 11 attacks. *J. Traum. Stress, 18*(1), 89–96.

Creese, I., Burt, D. R., & Snyder, S. H. (1977). Dopamine receptor binding enhancement accompanies lesion-induced behavioral supersensitivity. *Science, 197,* 596–598.

Cribbs, D. H., Ghochikyan, A., Vasilevko, T., et al. (2003). Adjuvant-dependent modulation of Th1 and Th2 responses to immunization with beta-amyloid. *Inter. Immunol., 15,* 505–514.

Crisp, M. (2001, April 8). Sticks & stones: 'New Kid' puts comic spin on a serious situation. *Sunday News* (Lancaster, PA), p. H–1.

Crits-Christoph, P., & Barber, J. P. (2002). Psychological treatments for personality disorders. In P. E. Nathan & J. M. Gorman (Eds.), *A guide to treatments that work* (2nd ed., pp. 611–623). London: Oxford University Press.

Crits-Christoph, P., Gibbons, M. B. C., Losardo, D., Narducci, J., Schamberger, M., & Gallop, R. (2004). Who benefits from brief psychodynamic therapy for generalized anxiety disorder? *Canad. J. Psychoanal., 12*(2), 301–324.

Crits-Christoph, P., Wilson, G. T., & Hollon, S. D. (2005). Empirically supported psychotherapies: Comment on Westen, Novotny, and Thompson-Brenner (2004). *Psychol. Bull., 131*(3), 412–417.

Crompton, M. R. (1985). Alcohol and violent accidental and suicidal death. *Med. Sci. Law, 25,* 59–62.

Crossman, A. M., & Lewis, M. (2006). Adults' ability to detect children's lying. *Behav. Sci. Law, 24*(5), 703–715.

Crow, S. J., Thuras, P., Keel, P. K., & Mitchell, J. E. (2002). Long-term menstrual and reproductive function in patients with bulimia nervosa. *Amer. J. Psychiat., 159*(6), 1048–1050.

Crow, T. J. (1980). Positive and negative schizophrenic symptoms and the role of dopamine: II. *Brit. J. Psychiat., 137,* 383–386.

Crow, T. J. (1985). The two-syndrome concept: Origins and current status. *Schizo. Bull., 11*(3), 471–486.

Crow, T. J. (1995). Brain changes and negative symptoms in schizophrenia. *Psychopathology, 28*(1), 18–21.

Crow, T. J. (2008). The "big bang" theory of the origin of psychosis and the faculty of language. *Schizo. Res., 102*(1–3), 31–52.

Crowther, J. H., Bond, L. A., & Rolf, J. E. (1981). The incidence, prevalence, and severity of behavior disorder among preschool-age children in day care. *J. Abnorm. Child Psychol., 9,* 23–42.

Crowther, J. H., Snaftner, J., Bonifazi, D. Z., & Shepherd, K. L. (2001). The role of daily hassles in binge eating. *Inter. J. Eat. Disorders, 29*(4), 449–454.

CRR (Center for Reproductive Rights). (2005, August 1). Contraceptive coverage for all: EPICC Act is prescription for women's equality. (Item: F013). Retrieved October 16, 2005, from www.crlp.org/pub_fac_epicc.html

Cruikshank, M. (2003). *Learning to be old: Gender, culture, and aging.* Lanham, MD: Rowman & Littlefield.

Cukan, A. (2001, March 8). Confronting a culture of cruelty. General feature release. *United Press International.*

Culbert, K. M., & Klump, K. L. (2008). Should eating disorders be included in the obsessive-compulsive spectrum? In J. S. Abramowitz, D. McKay, & S. Taylor (Eds.), *Obsessive-compulsive disorder: Subtypes and spectrum conditions.* Oxford, England: Elsevier.

Culp, A. M., Clyman, M. M., & Culp, R. E. (1995). Adolescent depressed mood, reports of suicide attempts, and asking for help. *Adolescence, 30*(120), 827–837.

Cumming, J., & Cumming, E. (1962). *Ego and milieu: Theory and practice of environmental therapy.* New York: Atherton.

Cummings, C. J., & Fristad, M. A. (2008). Mood disorders in childhood. In R. G. Steele, T. D. Elkin, & M. C. Roberts (Eds.), *Handbook of evidence-based therapies for children and adolescents: Bridging science and practice.* New York: Springer.

Cummings, J. L. (2005). The neuropsychiatric burden of neurological diseases in the elderly. *Inter. Psychogeriatrics, 17*(3), 341–351.

Cummins, R. A., & Lau, A. L. (2003). Community integration or community exposure? A review and discussion in relation to people with an intellectual disability. *Journal of Applied Research in Intellectual Disabilities, 16,* 145–157.

Cunningham, P. B., & Henggeler, S. W. (2001). Implementation of an empirically based drug and violence prevention and intervention program in public school settings. *J. Clin. Child Psychol., 30,* 221–232.

Curlin, F. A., Nwodim, C., Vance, J. L., Chin, M. H., & Lantos, J. D. (2008). To die, to sleep: US physicians' religious and other objections to physician-assisted suicide, terminal sedation, and withdrawal of life support. *Amer. J. Hospice Pall. Med., 25*(2), 112–120.

Curry, J. F., & Becker, S. J. (2008). Empirically supported psychotherapies for adolescent depression and mood disorders. In R. G. Steele, T. D. Elkin, & M. C. Roberts (Eds.), *Handbook of evidence-based therapies for children and adolescents: Bridging science and practice.* New York: Springer.

Curtis, R., Groarke, A. M., Coughlan, R., & Gsel, A. (2004). The influence of disease severity, perceived stress, social support and coping in patients with chronic ilness: A 1-year follow-up. *Psychol. Hlth. Med., 9*(4), 456–475.

Curtis, V. (2005). Women are not the same as men: Specific clinical issues for female patients with bipolar disorder. *Bipolar Disord., 7*(Suppl. 1), 16–24.

Curtiss, L. M. (April, 2002). *The marketing of psychotropic drugs: Mind games with mind drugs or meeting the demand for information?* Unpublished thesis, Princeton University.

Cusack, J. R. (2002). Challenges in the diagnosis and treatment of bipolar disorder. *Drug Benef. Trends, 14*(10), 34–38.

Cutler, C. M. (2007). The changing relationship between health plans and their members. In D. A. Shore (Ed.), *The trust crisis in healthcare: Causes, consequences, and cures* (pp. 160–171). New York: Oxford University Press.

Cutler, D. L., Bigelow, D., Collins, V., Jackson, C., & Field, G. (2002). Why are severely mentally ill persons in jail and prison? In P. Backlar & D. L. Cutler (Eds.), *Ethics in community mental health care: Commonplace concerns* (pp. 137–154). New York: Kluwer Academic/Plenum Publishers.

Cutler, D. M., Glaeser, E. L., & Norberg, K. E. (2001). Explaining the rise in youth suicide. In J. Gruber (Ed.), *Risky behavior among youths: An economic analysis* (pp. 219–269). Chicago: University of Chicago Press.

Cutright, P., & Fernquist, R. M. (2001). The relative gender gap in suicide: Societal integration, the culture of suicide and period effects in 20 developed countries, 1955–1994. *Soc. Sci. Res., 30*(1), 76–99.

Cutright, P., Stack, S., & Fernquist, R. (2007). Marital status integration, suicide disapproval, and societal integration as explanations of marital status differences in female age-specific suicide rates. *Suic., Life-Threat. Behav., 37*(6), 715–724.

Cutting, J. (1985). *The psychology of schizophrenia.* Edinburgh, Scotland: Churchill-Livingstone.

Cutting, J., & Murphy, D. (1988). Schizophrenic thought disorder: A psychological and organic interpretation. *Brit. J. Psychiat., 152,* 310–319.

Cuvelier, M. (2002). Victim, not villain. The mentally ill are six to seven times more likely to be murdered. *Psychol. Today, 35*(3), 23.

Cytryn, L., & McKnew, D. H., Jr. (1996). *Growing up sad: Childhood depression and its treatment.* New York: Norton.

Dahle, K. P., Lohner, J. C., & Konrad, N. (2005). Suicide prevention in penal institutions: Validation and optimization of a screening tool for early identification of high-risk inmates in pretrial detention. *Inter. J. Forens. Ment. Hlth., 4*(1), 53–62.

Dahlgren, S., Sandberg, A. D., & Hjelmquist, E. (2003). The non-specificity of theory of mind deficits: Evidence from children with communicative disabilities. *Eur. J. Cog. Psychol., 15*(1), 129–155.

Dalby, J. T. (1997). Elizabethan madness: On London's stage. *Psychol Rep., 81,* 1331–1343.

Dale, R. C., Heyman, I., Surtees, R. A., Church, A. J., Giovannoni, G., Goodman, R., et al. (2004). Dyskinesias and associated psychiatric disorders following streptococcal infections. *Arch. Dis. Child., 89*(7), 604–610.

Damasio, A. R. (1994). *Descartes' error: Emotion, reason, and the human brain.* New York: Avon Books.

Dana, R. H. (2000). Culture and methodology in personality assessment. In I. Cuellar & F. A. Paniagua (Eds.), *Handbook of multicultural mental health* (pp. 97–120). San Diego, CA: Academic.

Dana, R. H. (2005). *Multicultural assessment: Principles, applications, and examples.* Mahwah, NJ: Lawrence Erlbaum.

Daniel, S. S., Walsh, A. K., Goldston, D. B., Arnold, E. M., Reboussin, B. A., & Wood, F. B. (2006). Suicidality, school dropout, and reading problems among adolescents. *J. Learn. Disabil., 39*(6), 507–514.

Daniels, C. W. (2002). Legal aspects of polygraph admissibility in the United States. In M. Klener (Ed.), *The handbook of polygraph testing.* San Diego, CA: Academic.

Danilenko, K. V., & Putilov, A. A. (2005). Melatonin treatment of winter depression following total sleep deprivation: Waking EEC and mood correlates. *Neuropsychopharmacology, 30*(7), 1345–1352.

Danner, M. (2004). *Torture and truth: America, Abu Ghraib, and the war on terror.* New York: New York Review of Books.

Dare, C., & Crowther, C. (1995). Psychodynamic models of eating disorders. In G. Szmukler, C. Dare, & J. Treasure (Eds.), *Handbook of eating disorders: Theory, treatment and research.* Chichester, England: Wiley.

Darke, S., Williamson, A., Ross, J., & Teesson, M. (2005). Attempted suicide among heroin users: 12-month outcomes from the Australian Treatment Outcome Study (ATOS). *Drug Alc. Depend., 78*(2), 177–186.

Darvres-Bornoz, J., Lemperiere, T., Degiovanni, A., & Gaillard, P. (1995). Sexual victimization in women with schizophrenia and bipolar disorder. *Soc. Psychiat. Psychiatr. Epidemiol., 30*(2), 78–84.

Darwin, C. A. (1872). *The expression of the emotions in man and animals.* London: John Murray, Albemarle Street.

Dass, R., & Levine, S. (2002). Guided meditation. In A. A. Sheikh (Ed.), *Handbook of therapeutic imagery techniques. Imagery and human development series* (pp. 351–353). Amityville, NY: Baywood Publishing Co.

Dattilio, F. M. (2001). Variations in cognitive responses to fear in anxiety disorder subtypes. *Arch. Psychiat. Psychother., 3*(1), 17–30.

Davidson, J. R. T. (2004). Use of benzodiazepines in social anxiety disorder, generalized anxiety disorder, and posttraumatic stress disorder. *J. Clin. Psychiat., 65*(Suppl. 5), 29–33.

Davidson, J. R. T., Connor, K. M., Hertzberg, M. A., Weisler, R. H., Wilson, W. H., & Payne, V. M. (2005). Maintenance therapy with fluoxetine in posttraumatic stress disorder: A placebo-controlled discontinuation study. *J. Clin. Psychopharmacol., 25*(2), 166–169.

Davis, J. O., & Phelps, J. A. (1995). Twins with schizophrenia: Genes or germs? *Schizo. Bull., 21*(1), 13–18.

Davis, M. (1992). Analysis of aversive memories using the fear potentiated startle paradigm. In N. Butters & L. R. Squire (Eds.), *The neuropsychology of memory* (2nd ed.). New York: Guilford Press.

Davis, R. C., Brickman, E., & Baker, T. (1991). Supportive and unsupportive responses of others to rape victims: Effects on concurrent victim adjustment. *Amer. J. Comm. Psychol., 19,* 443–451.

Davis, S. (2000). Testosterone and sexual desire in women. *J. Sex Educ. Ther., 25*(1), 25–32.

Davis, S. R. (1998). The clinical use of androgens in female sexual disorders. *J. Sex Marital Ther., 24*(3), 153–163.

Daw, J. (2001). APA's disaster response network: Help on the scene. *Monit. Psychol., 32*(10), 14–15.

Dawes, R. M., Faust, D., & Meehl, P. E. (2002). Clinical versus actuarial judgment. In D. Kahneman, T. Gilovich, & D. Griffin (Eds.), *Heuristics and biases: The psychology of intuitive judgment* (pp. 716–729). New York: Cambridge University Press.

DAWN (Drug Abuse Warning Network). (2008). Publications and tables from DAWN Emergency Department Data. Retrieved November 24, 2008, from www.dawninfo.net

Dawson, G. R., Collinson, N., & Atack, J. R. (2005). Development of subtype selective GABA-sub(A) modulators. *CNS Spectrums, 10*(1), 21–27.

de l'Etoile, S. K. (2002). The effect of musical mood induction procedure on mood state-dependent word retrieval. *J. Music Ther., 39*(2), 145–160.

De Leo, D., & Evans, R. (2004). *International suicide rates and prevention strategies.* Cambridge, MA: Hogrefe & Huber.

De Leo, D., Padoani, W., Scocco, P., Lie, D., Bille-Brahe, U., Arensman, E., et al. (2001). Attempted and completed suicide in older subjects: Results from the WHO/EURO Multicentre Study of Suicidal Behavior. *Inter. J. Ger. Psychiat., 16*(3), 300–310.

De Leon, G. (2008). Therapeutic communities. In H. D. Kleber & M. Galanter (Eds.), *The American Psychiatric Publishing textbook of substance abuse treatment* (4th ed., pp. 459–475). Arlington, VA: American Psychiatric Publishing.

de Leon, M. J., Mosconi, L., Blennow, K., De Santi, S., Zinkowski, R., Mehta, P. D., et al. (2007). Imaging and CSF studies in the preclinical diagnosis of Alzheimer's disease. In H. Federoff, M. J. de Leon, & D. A. Snider (Eds.), *Imaging and the aging brain* (pp. 114–145). Malden, MA: Blackwell.

de Maat, S. M., Dekker, J., Schoevers, R. A., & de Jonghe, F. (2007). Relative efficacy of psychotherapy and combined therapy in the treatment of depression: A meta-analysis. *Eur. Psychiat.,* 22(1), 1–8.

De Matteo, D., Heilbrun, K., & Marczyk, G. (2005). Psychopathy, risk of violence, and protective factors in a noninstitutionalized and noncriminal sample. *Inter. J. Forens. Ment. Hlth.,* 4(2), 147–157.

De Sousa, A. A., De Sousa, J. A., & Kapoor, H. (2008). An open randomized trial comparing disulfiram and topiramate in the treatment of alcohol dependence. *J. Substance Abuse Treat.,* 34(4), 460–463.

De Vries, R., DeBruin, D. A., & Goodgame, A. (2004). Ethics review of social, behavioral, and economic research: Where should we go from here? *Ethics Behav.,* 14(4), 351–368.

de Waal, M. W. M., Arnold, I. A., Eekhof, J. A. H., & van Hemert, A. M. (2004). Somatoform disorders in general practice: Prevalence, functional impairment and comorbidity with anxiety and depressive disorders. *Brit. J. Psychiat.,* 184(6), 470–476.

DEA (Drug Enforcement Administration). (1996). *Consumption of ritalin.* Washington, DC: Author.

DEA (Drug Enforcement Administration). (2000, May 16). DEA congressional testimony before the committee on education and the workforce: Subcommittee on early childhood and families.

DEA (Drug Enforcement Administration). (2002). Cited in R. Holland, The reaction against Ritalin. *Lexington Institute Issue Brief,* February, 2002.

DeAngelis, T. (2008). Helping families cope with PTSD. *Monitor on Psychology,* 39(1), 44–45.

DeAngelis, T. (2008). PTSD treatments grow in evidence, effectiveness. *Monitor on Psychology,* 39(1), 40–43.

Deas, D., Gray, K., & Upadhyaya, H. (2008). Evidence-based treatments for adolescent substance use disorders. In R. G. Steele, T. D. Elkin, M. C. Roberts (Eds.), *Handbook of evidence-based therapies for children and adolescents,* (pp. 429–444). New York: Springer.

Deb, P., Li, C., Trivedi, P. K., & Zimmer, D. M. (2006). The effect of managed care on use of health care services: Results from two contemporaneous household surveys. *Hlth. Econ.,* 15(7), 743–760.

Decker, H. S. (2004). The psychiatric works of Emil Kraepelin: A many-faceted story of modern medicine. *J. Hist. Neurosci.,* 13(3), 248–276.

Degun-Mather, M. (2002). Hypnosis in the treatment of a case of dissociative amnesia for a 12-year period. *Contemp. Hyp.,* 19(1), 34–31.

Deitz, S. M. (1977). An analysis of programming DRL schedules in educational settings. *Behav. Res. Ther.,* 15(1), 103–111.

Delahanty, D. L., Nugent, N. R., Christopher, N. C., & Walsh, M. (2005). Initial urinary epinephrine and cortisol levels predict acute PTSD symptoms in child trauma victims. *Psychoneuroendocrinology,* 30(2), 121–128.

Delaney-Black, V., Covington, C., Nordstrom, B., Ager, J., Janisse, J., Hannigan, J. H., et al. (2004). Prenatal cocaine: Quantity of exposure and gender moderation. *J. Dev. Behav. Pediatr.,* 25(4), 254–263.

DeLaune, K. A., & Schmitz, J. M. (2004). Treatment of nicotine addiction: A current perspective. *Addic. Disord. Treat.,* 3(3), 97–109.

Delay, J., & Deniker, P. (1952). Le traitment des psychoses par une méthode neurolytique derivée d'hibernothérapie: Le 4560 RP utilisé seul en cure prolongée et continuée. *Congrès des médicins aliénistes et neurologistes de France et des pays du langue francaise,* 50, 503–513.

DeLisi, L. E., & Fleischhaker, W. (2007). Schizophrenia research in the era of the genome, 2007. *Curr. Opin. Psychiat.,* 20(2), 109–110.

Delisle, J. R. (1986). Death with honors: Suicide among gifted adolescents [Special issue]. *J. Couns. Dev.,* 64(9), 558–560.

DeLong, G. R. (2005). The cerebellum in autism. In M. Coleman (Ed.), *The neurology of autism* (pp. 75–90). New York: Oxford University Press.

Delorme, R., Krebs, M. O., Chabane, N., Roy, I., Millet, B., Mouren-Simeoni, M. C., et al. (2004). Frequency and transmission of glutamate receptors GRIK2 and GRIK3 polymorphisms in patients with obsessive compulsive disorder. *Neurorep. Rapid Commun. Neurosci. Res.,* 15(4), 699–702.

DeLuca, N. L., Moser, L. L., & Bond, G. R. (2008). Assertive community treatment. In K. T. Mueser & D. V. Jeste (Eds.), *Clinical handbook of schizophrenia* (pp. 329–338). New York: Guilford Press.

Deniz, M. E., Hamarta, E., & Ari, R. (2005). An investigation of social skills and loneliness levels of university students with respect to their attachment styles in a sample of Turkish students. *Soc. Behav. Pers.,* 33(1), 19–32.

Dennehy, E. B., Doyle, K., & Suppes, T. (2003). The efficacy of olanzapine monotherapy for acute hypomania or mania in an outpatient setting. *Inter. Clin. Psychopharmacology,* 18, 143–145.

Dennison, S. (2007). Criminal responsibility. In D. Carson, R. Milne, F. Pakes, K. Shalev, & A. Shawyer (Eds.), *Applying psychology to criminal justice.* Hoboken, NJ: John Wiley & Sons.

Dentali, S. (2002). The uses of black cohosh in menopause and chaste tree fruit in premenstrual syndrome. In J. F. Rosenbaum & D. Mischoulon (Eds.), *Natural medications for psychiatric disorders: Considering the alternatives* (pp. 175–184). Philadelphia: Lippincott Williams & Wilkins.

Department of Veterans Affairs. (2007). Cited in G. Zoroya, Combat brain injuries multiply. *USA Today,* November 23, 2007, 1A.

Deplanque, D. (2005). Recreational cannabis use: not so harmless! *J Neurol Neurosurg Psychiat.,* 76(3), 306.

DeRubeis, R. J., Hollon, S. D., Amsterdam, J. D., Shelton, R. C., Young, P. R., Salomon, R. M., et al. (2005). Cognitive therapy vs. medications in the treatment of moderate to severe depression. *Arch. Gen. Psychiat.,* 62, 409–416.

Dervic, K., Brent, D. A., & Oquendo, M. A. (2008). Completed suicide in childhood. *Psychiatr. Clin. N. Amer.,* 31(2), 271–291.

Devanand, D. P. (2002). Comorbid psychiatric disorders in late life depression. *Biol. Psychiat.,* 52(3), 236–242.

DeVeaugh-Geiss, J., Moroz, G., Biederman, J., Cantwell, D. P., et al. (1992). Clomipramine hydrochloride in childhood and adolescent obsessive compulsive disorder. A multicenter trial. *J. Amer. Acad. Child Adol. Psychiat.,* 31(1), 45–49.

Deveny, K. (2003, June 30). We're not in the mood. *Newsweek,* 141(26), pp. 40–46.

Devineni, T., & Blanchard, E. B. (2005). A randomized controlled trial of an internet-based treatment for chronic headache. *Behav. Res. Ther.,* 43, 277–292.

Dhossche, D., van-der-Steen, F., Ferdinand, R. (2002). Somatoform disorders in children and adolescents: A comparison with other internalizing disorders. *Ann. Clin. Psychiat.,* 14(1), 23–31.

Diamond, G. S., & Diamond, G. M. (2002). Studying a matrix of change mechanisms: An agenda for family-based process research. In H. A. Liddle, D. A. Santisteban, R. F. Levant, & J. H. Bray (Eds.), *Family psychology: Science-based interventions* (pp. 41–66). Washington, DC: American Psychological Association.

Diamond, L. M. (2003). What does sexual orientation orient? A biobehavioral model distinguishing romantic love and sexual desire. *Psychol. Rev.,* 110(1), 173–192.

Dickens, B. M., Boyle, J. M., Jr., & Ganzini, L. (2008). Euthanasia and assisted suicide. In A. M. Viens & P. A. Singer (Eds.), *The Cambridge textbook of bioethics* (pp. 72–77). New York: Cambridge University Press.

Dickerson, F. B., Tenhula, W. N., & Green-Paden, L. D. (2005). The token economy for schizophrenia: Review of the literature and recommendations for future research. *Schizo. Res.,* 75(2–3), 405–416.

DiClemente, C. C., Garay, M., & Gemmell, L. (2008). Motivational enhancement. In H. D. Kleber & M. Galanter (Eds.), *The American Psychiatric Publishing textbook of substance abuse treatment* (4th ed., pp. 361–371). Arlington, VA: American Psychiatric Publishing.

Didion, J. (1970). *Play it as it lays.* New York: Farrar, Straus and Giroux.

Diekstra, R. F. W., Kienhorst, C. W. M., & de Wilde, E. J. (1995). Suicide and suicidal behaviour among adolescents. In M. Rutter & D. J. Smith, *Psychosocial disorders in young people.* Chichester, England: Wiley.

Diener, E. (2000, January). Subjective well-being: The science of happiness and a proposal for a national index. *Amer. Psychologist,* 55(1), 34–43.

Diener, E., & Diener, C. (1996). Most people are happy. *Psychol. Sci.,* 7(3), 181–185.

Diener, E., Lucas, R. E., & Scollon, C. N. (2006). Beyond the hedonic treadmill: Revising the adaptation theory of well-being. *Amer. Psychologist,* 61(4), 305–314.

Diener, E., Sandvik, E., Pavot, W., & Fujita, F. (1992). Extraversion and subjective well-being in a U.S. national probability sample. *J. Res. Pers.,* 26(3), 205–215.

Diener, E., Sandvik, E., Seidlitz, L., & Diener, M. (1993). The relationship between income and subjective well-being: Relative or absolute? *Soc. Indicators Res., 28*(3), 195–223.

Diener, E., & Seligman, M. E. P. (2002). Very happy people. *Psychol. Sci., 13*(1), 81–84.

Diener, E., & Seligman, M. E. P. (2004). Beyond money: Toward an economy of well-being. *Psychol. Sci. Publ. Interest, 5*(1), 1–31.

Dietrich, A. M. (2007). Traumatic impact of violence against women. In E. K. Carll (Ed.), *Trauma psychology: Issues in violence, disaster, health, and illness* (Vol. 2). Westport, CT: Praeger Publishers.

Dike, C. C., Baranoski, M., & Griffith, E. E. H. (2005). Pathological lying revisited. *J. Amer. Acad. Psychiat. Law, 33*(3), 342–349.

Dike, C. C., Baranoski, M., & Griffith, E. E. H. (2006). What is pathological lying? *Brit. J. Psychiat., 189*(1), 86.

Dikel, T. N., Engdahl, B., & Eberly, R. (2005). PTSD in former prisoners of war: Prewar, wartime, and postwar factors. *J. Traum. Stress, 18*(1), 69–77.

Dinwiddie, S. H., Heath, A. C., Dunne, M. P., Bucholz, K. K., Madden, P. A. F., Slutske, W. F., et al. (2000). Early sexual abuse and lifetime psychopathology: A co-twin-control study. *Psychol. Med., 30*(1), 41–52.

Dirkzwager, A. J. E., Bramsen, I., & van der Ploeg, H. M. (2005). Factors associated with posttraumatic stress among peacekeeping soldiers. *Anx., Stress, Coping: Inter. J., 18*(1), 37–51.

Dishneau, D., & Jordan, L. J. (2008, August 3). Report: Therapist feared scientist poisoned people. *Yahoo! News.* Retrieved August 3, 2008, from http://news.yahoo.com

Dittman, M. (2005). Postgrad growth areas: Geopsychology. *gradPSYCH, 3*(3), September.

DMR (Dream Mill Research). (2006). Debt and exams among top 10 teenage worries Samaritans research reveals. *Creativematch.* November 10, 2006.

Dobbs, D. (2006, April 2). A depression switch? *New York Times.* Retrieved May 25, 2008, from http://www.nytimes.com/2006/04/02/magazine/02depression.html

Dobson, D. J. G., McDougall, G., Busheikin, J., & Aldous, J. (1995). Effects of social skills training and social milieu treatment on symptoms of schizophrenia. *Psychiatr. Serv., 46*(4), 376–380.

Dobson, V., & Sales, B. (2000). The science of infanticide and mental illness. *Psychol. Pub. Pol. Law, 6*(4), 19–25.

Doctor, R. (2003). The role of violence in perverse psychopathology. In R. Doctor (Ed.), *Dangerous patients: A psychodynamic approach to risk assessment and management* (pp. 107–114). London: Karnac Books.

Doctor, R. M., & Neff, B. (2001). Sexual disorders. In H. S. Friedman (Ed.), *Specialty articles from the encyclopedia of mental health.* San Diego: Academic Press.

Dodes, L. M., & Khantzian, E. J. (2005). Individual psychodynamic psychotherapy. In R. J. Frances, A. H. Mack, & S. I. Miller (Eds.), *Clinical textbook of addictive disorders* (3rd ed., pp. 457–473). New York: Guilford Press.

Dodgen, C. E. (2005). Cravings and relapse prevention. In C. E. Dodgen (Ed.), *Nicotine dependence: Understanding and applying the most effective treatment interventions* (pp. 175–195). Washington, DC: American Psychological Association.

Doherty, B. (2007, July). "You can't see why on an fMRI": What science can, and can't, tell us about the insanity defense. *Reasononline.* Retrieved August 17, 2008, from http://www.reason.com/news/show/120266.html

Dohrmann, R. J., & Laskin, D. M. (1978). An evaluation of electromyographic feedback in the treatment of myofascial pain-dysfunction syndrome. *JAMA, 96,* 656–662.

Dolder, C. R. (2008). Side effects of antipsychotics. In K. T. Mueser & D. V. Jeste (Eds.), *Clinical handbook of schizophrenia* (pp. 168–177). New York: Guilford Press.

Dole, V. P., & Nyswander, M. (1965). A medical treatment for heroin addiction. *JAMA, 193,* 646–650.

Dole, V. P., & Nyswander, M. (1967). Heroin addiction, a metabolic disease. *Arch. Internal Med., 120,* 19–24.

Dolezal, D. N., Weber, K. P., Evavold, J. J., Wylie, J., & McLaughlin, T. F. (2007). The effects of a reinforcement package for on-task and reading behavior with at-risk and middle school students with disabilities. *Child Fam. Behav. Ther., 29*(2), 9–25.

Domino, G., & Swain, B. J. (1986). Recognition of suicide lethality and attitudes toward suicide in mental health professions. *Omega: J. Death Dying, 16*(4), 301–308.

Domino, G., & Takahashi, Y. (1991). Attitudes toward suicide in Japanese and American medical students. *Suic. Life-Threat. Behav., 21*(4), 345–359.

Donnellan, M. B., & Conger, R. D. (2007). Designing and implementing longitudinal studies. In R. F. Krueger, R. W. Robins, & R. C. Fraley (Eds.), *Handbook of research methods in personality psychology* (pp. 21–36). New York: Guilford Press.

Dorahy, M. J., & Huntjens, R. J. C. (2007). Memory and attentional processes in dissociative identity disorder: A review of the empirical literature. In D. Spiegel, E. Vermetten, & M. Dorahy (Eds.), *Traumatic dissociation: Neurobiology and treatment* (pp. 55–75). Washington, DC: American Psychiatric Publishing.

Doran, M., & Larner, A. J. (2004). Prominent behavioural and psychiatric symptoms in early-onset Alzheimer's disease in a sib pair with the presenilin-1 gene R269G mutation. *Eur. Arch. Psychiat. Clin. Neurosci., 254*(3), 187–189.

Doss, B. D., Mitchell, A. E., & De la Garza-Mercer, F. (2008). Marital distress. In M. Hersen, & J. Rosqvist (Eds.), *Handbook of psychological assessment, case conceptualization, and treatment, Vol. 1: Adults* (pp. 563–589). Hoboken, NJ: John Wiley & Sons.

Doty, R. L. (2008). The olfactory vector hypothesis of neurodegenerative disease: Is it viable? *Ann. Neurol., 63*(1), 7–15.

Doughty, C. J., Wells, J. E., Joyce, P. R., & Walsh, A. E. (2004). Bipolar-panic disorder comorbidity within bipolar disorder families: A study of siblings. *Bipolar Disord., 6,* 245–252.

Douglas, J. (1996). *Mind hunter: Inside the FBI's elite serial crime unit.* New York: Pocket Star.

Doweiko, H. E. (2002). *Concepts of chemical dependency.* Australia: Brooks/Cole.

Doweiko, H. E. (2006). *Concepts of chemical dependency* (6th ed.). Belmont, CA: Thomson Brooks/Cole.

Downar, J., & Kapur, S. (2008). Biological theories. In K. T. Mueser & D. V. Jeste (Eds.), *Clinical handbook of schizophrenia* (pp. 25–34). New York: Guilford Press.

Downey, R. G., Sinnett, E. R., & Seeberger, W. (1998). The changing face of MMPI practice. *Psychol. Rep., 83*(3, Pt. 2), 1267–1272.

Downhill, J. E., Jr., Buchsbaum, M. S., Hazlett, E. A., Barth, S., Roitman, S. L., Nunn, M., et al. (2001). Temporal lobe volume determined by magnetic resonance imaging in schizotypal personality disorder and schizophrenia. *Schizo. Res., 48*(2–3), 187–199.

Doyle, A. C. (1914). The valley of fear. In *The complete Sherlock Holmes.* Garden City, NY: Doubleday.

Doyle, A. C. (1938). The sign of the four. In *The complete Sherlock Holmes.* Garden City, NY: Doubleday.

Dozois, D. J. A., & Westra, H. A. (2004). The nature of anxiety and depression: Implications for prevention. In K. S. Dobson & D. J. A. Dozois (Eds.), *The prevention of anxiety and depression: Theory, research, and practice* (pp. 9–41). Washington, DC: American Psychological Association.

Draguns, J. G. (2006). Culture in psychopathology—psychopathology in culture: Taking a new look at an old problem. In T. G. Plante (Ed.), *Mental disorders of the new millennium, Vol. 2: Public and social problems.* Westport, CT: Praeger Publishers.

Draine, J., Salzer, M. S., Culhane, D. P., & Hadley, T. R. (2002). Role of social disadvantage in crime, joblessness, and homelessness among persons with serious mental illness. *Psychiatr. Serv., 53*(5), 565–573.

Dratcu, L. (2000). Panic, hyperventilation and perpetuation of anxiety. *Prog. Neuropsychopharmacol. Biol. Psychiat., 24*(7), 1069–1089.

Drevets, W. C. (2000). Functional anatomical abnormalities in limbic and prefrontal cortical structures in major depression. *Prog. Brain Res., 126,* 413–431.

Drevets, W. C. (2001). Neuroimaging and neuropathological studies of depression: Implications for the cognitive-emotional features of mood disorders. *Curr. Opin. Neurobiol. 11,* 240–249.

Drevets, W. C., Price, J. L., Simpson, J. R., Todd, R. D., Reich, T., Vannier, M., Raichle, M. E., et al. (1997). Subgenual prefrontal cortex abnormalities in mood disorders. *Nature, 386,* 824–827.

Drevets, W. C., & Todd, R. D. (2005). Depression, mania, and related disorders. In E. H. Rubin & C. F. Zorumski (Eds.), *Adult psychiatry* (2nd ed., pp. 91–129). Oxford, England: Blackwell Publishing.

Drevets, W. C., Videen, T. O., Price, J. L., Preskorn, S. H., Carmichael, S. T., & Raichle, M. E. (1992). A functional anatomical study of unipolar depression. *J. Neurosci., 12,* 3628–3641.

Drobes, D. J., Saladin, M. E., & Tiffany, S. T. (2001). Classical conditioning mechanisms in alcohol dependence. In N. Heather, T. J. Peters, & T. Stockwell (Eds.), *International handbook of alcohol dependence and problems* (pp. 281–297). New York: Wiley.

Druss, B. G., Wang, P. S., Sampson, N. A., Olfson, M., Pincus, H. A., Wells, K. B., & Kessler, R. C. (2007). Understanding mental health treatment in persons without mental diagnoses: Results from the National Comorbidity Survey Replication. *Arch. Gen. Psychiat.*, 64 (10), 1196–1203.

Duarte-Velez, Y. M., & Bernal, G. (2008). Suicide risk in Latino and Latina adolescents. In M. M. Leach & F. T. L. Leong (Eds.), *Suicide among racial and ethnic minority groups: Theory, research, and practice* (pp. 281–115). New York: Routledge/Taylor & Francis Group.

Duenwald, M. (2003, March 18). "Oldest old" still show alertness. *New York Times.* Retrieved August 2, 2008, from www.nytimes.com

Dugas, M. J., Buhr, K., & Ladouceur, R. (2002). The role of intolerance of uncertainty in the etiology and maintenance of generalized anxiety disorder. In R. G. Heimberg, C. L. Turk, & D. S. Mennin (Eds.), *Generalized anxiety disorder: Advances in research and practice.* New York: Guilford Press.

Dugas, M. J., Buhr, K., & Ladouceur, R. (2004). The role of intolerance of uncertainty in etiology and maintenance. In R. G. Heimberg, C. L. Turk, & D. S. Mennin (Eds.)., *Generalized anxiety disorder: Advances in research and practice* (pp. 143–163). New York: Guilford Press.

Dugas, M. J., Gagnon, F., Ladouceur, R., & Freeston, M. H. (1998). Generalized anxiety disorder: A preliminary test of a conceptual model. *Behav. Res. Ther.*, 36(2), 215–226.

Dugas, M. J., Gosselin, P., & Ladouceur, R. (2001). Intolerance of uncertainty and worry: Investigating specificity in a nonclinical sample. *Cog. Ther. Res.*, 25(5), 551–558.

Dugas, M. J., Marchand, A., & Ladouceur, R. (2005). Further validation of a cognitive-behavioral model of generalized anxiety disorder: Diagnostic and symptom specificity. *J. Anx. Disorders*, 19(3), 329–343.

Dunbar, F. (1948). *Synopsis of psychosomatic diagnosis and treatment.* St. Louis: Mosby.

Duncan, A. E., Neuman, R. J., Kramer, J., Kuperman, S., Hesselbrock, V., Reich, T., et al. (2005). Are there subgroups of bulimia nervosa based on comorbid psychiatric disorders? *Inter. J. Eat. Disord.*, 37(1), 19–25.

Duncan, B. L. (2002). Does drug company marketing now include product placement in the movies? *Ethical Human Sciences and Services,* 4(2), 147–150.

Dunn, A. L., Trivedi, M. H., Kampert, J. B., Clark, C. G., & Chambliss, H. O. (2005). Exercise treatment for depression: Efficacy and dose response. *Amer. J. Prev. Med.*, 28(1), 1–8.

Dunn, E. F., & Steiner, M. (2000). The functional neurochemistry of mood disorders in women. In M. Steiner, K. A. Yonkers, & E. Erikson (Eds.), *Mood disorders in women* (pp. 71–82). London: Martin Dunitz.

Dunner, D. L. (2005). Atypical antipsychotics: Efficacy across bipolar disorder subpopulations. *J. Clin. Psychiat.*, 66(Suppl. 3), 20–27.

DuPaul, G. J., & Barkley, R. A. (2008). Attention deficit hyperactivity disorder. In R. J. Morris & T. R. Kratochwill (Eds.), *The practice of child therapy* (4th ed., pp. 143–186). Mahwah, NJ: Lawrence Erlbaum.

Dupont, R. L., & Dupont, C. M. (2005). Sedatives/hypnotics and benzodiazepines. In R. J. Frances, A. H. Mack, & S. I. Miller (Eds.), *Clini-cal textbook of addictive disorders* (3rd ed., pp. 219–242). New York: Guilford Press.

Durkheim, E. (1897). *Suicide.* New York: Free Press. (Work republished 1951)

Durkin, K. F., & Hundersmarck, S. (2008). Pedophiles and child molesters. In E. Goode & D. A. Vail (Eds.), *Extreme deviance.* Los Angeles: Pine Forge Press.

Dwight-Johnson, M., & Lagomasino, I. T. (2007). Addressing depression treatment preferences of ethnic minority patients. *Gen. Hosp. Psychiat.*, 29(3), 179–181.

Dykens, E. M., & Hodapp, R. M. (2001). Research in mental retardation: Toward an etiologic approach. *J. Child Psychol. Psychiat. Allied Discl.*, 42(1), 49–71.

Easterbrook, G. (2005). The real truth about money. *Time,* 165(3), January 17, 2005, A32–A34.

Eaton, W. W., Kalaydjian, A., Scharfstein, D. O., Mezuk, B., & Ding, Y. (2007). Prevalence and incidence of depressive disorder: The Baltimore ECA follow-up, 1981–2004. *Acta Psychiatr. Scand.*, 116(3), 182–188.

Ebstein, R. P., & Kotler, M. (2002). Personality, substance abuse, and genes. In J. Benjamin, R. P. Ebstein, & R. H. Belmaker (Eds.), *Molecular genetics and the human personality* (pp. 151–163). Washington, DC: American Psychological Association.

Eccleston, L., & Ward, T. (2004). Assessment of dangerous and criminal responsibility. In W. T. O'Donohue & E. R. Levensky (Eds.), *Handbook of forensic psychology: Resource for mental health and legal professionals* (pp. 85–101). New York: Elsevier.

Eddy, K. T., Dutra, L., Bradley, R., & Westen, D. (2004). A multidimensional meta-analysis of psychotherapy and pharmacotherapy for obsessive-compulsive disorder. *Clin. Psychol. Rev.*, 24, 1011–1030.

Edelstein, B. A., Stoner, S. A., & Woodhead, E. (2008). Older adults. In M. Hersen & J. Rosqvist (Eds.), *Handbook of psychological assessment, case conceptualization and treatment, Vol. 1): Adults.* Hoboken, NJ: Wiley.

Edwards, O. W., & Oakland, T. D. (2006). Factorial invariance of Woodcock-Johnson III Scores for African Americans and Caucasian Americans. *J. Psychoeduc. Assess.*, 24(4), 358–366.

Egelko, S., Galanter, M., Dermatis, H., Jurewicz, E., Jamison, A., Dingle, S., et al. (2002). Improved psychological status in a modified therapeutic community for homeless MICA men. *J. Addic. Diseases,* 21(1), 75–92.

Ehlers, A., Clark, D. M., Hackman, A., McManus, F., & Fennell, M. (2005). Cognitive therapy for post-traumatic stress disorder: Development and evaluation. *Behav. Res. Ther.*, 43(4), 413–431.

Ehnvall, A., Parker, G., Hadzi, P. D., & Malhi, G. (2008). Perception of rejecting and neglectful parenting in childhood relates to lifetime suicide attempts for females—but not for males. *Acta Psychiatr. Scandin.*, 117(1), 50–56.

Ehrenfeld, T. (2005, June 13). An epilepsy drug may help alcoholics stop drinking. *Newsweek, 145,* 68.

Eifert, G. H., Greco, L. A., Heffner, M., & Louis, A. (2007). Eating disorders: A new behavioral perspective and acceptance-based treatment approach. In D. W. Woods & J. W. Kanter (Eds.), *Understanding behavior disorders: A contemporary behavioral perspective.* Reno, NV: Context Press.

Eifert, G. H., & Zvolensky, M. J. (2005). Somatoform disorders. In J. E. Maddux & B. A. Winstead (Eds.), *Psychopathology: Foundations for a contemporary understanding* (pp. 281–300). Mahwah, NJ: Lawrence Erlbaum.

Eifert, G. H., Zvolensky, M. J., & Louis, A. (2008). Somatoform disorders: Nature, psychological processes, and treatment strategies. In J. E. Maddux & B. A. Winstead (Eds.), *Psychopathology: Foundations for a contemporary understanding* (2nd ed., pp. 307–325). New York: Routledge/Taylor & Francis Group.

Eisner, A. (2005). Odd U.S. state laws ban owning skunks, swearing. *Reuters,* May 25, 2005.

Ekman, P., O'Sullivan, M., & Frank, M. G. (1999). A few can catch a liar. *Psychol. Sci., 10*(3), 263–266.

Elias, M. (1995, April 18). Therapist's program to go on-line. *USA Today,* p. 1D.

Eliez, S., & Feinstein, C. (2001). The fragile X syndrome: Bridging the gap from gene to behavior. *Curr. Opin. Psychiat.*, 14(5), 443–449.

Elkin, I. (1994). The NIMH Treatment of Depression Collaborative Research Program: Where we began and where we are. In A. E. Bergin & S. L. Garfield (Eds.), *Handbook of psychotherapy and behavior change* (4th ed.). New York: Wiley.

Elkin, I., Parloff, M. B., Hadley, S. W., & Autry, J. H. (1985). National Institute of Mental Health Treatment of Depression Collaborative Research Program: Background and research plan. *Arch. Gen. Psychiat.*, 42, 305–316.

Elkin, I., Shea, M. T., Watkins, J. T., Imber, S. D., et al. (1989). National Institute of Mental Health Treatment of Depression Collaborative Research Program: General effectiveness of treatments. *Arch. Gen. Psychiat.*, 46(11), 971–982.

Elkins, G., & Perfect, M. M. (2007). Hypnotherapy for the treatment of childhood somatoform disorders. In L. Sugarman & W. C. Wester, III (Eds.), *Therapeutic hypnosis with children and adolescents* (pp. 217–239). Norwalk, CT: Crown House Publishing Limited.

Ellenberger, H. F. (1970). *The discovery of the unconscious.* New York: Basic Books.

Ellenberger, H. F. (1972). The story of "Anna O.": A critical review with new data. *J. History Behav. Sci., 8,* 267–279.

Elliott, R. (2002). The effectiveness of humanistic therapies. In D. J. Cain & J. Seeman (Eds.), *Humanistic psychotherapies: Handbook of research and practice* (pp. 57–82). Washington, DC: American Psychological Association.

Ellis, A. (1962). *Reason and emotion in psychotherapy.* Secaucus, NJ: Lyle Stuart.

Ellis, A. (2001). *Overcoming destructive beliefs, feelings, and behaviors: New directions for rational emotive behavior therapy.* Amherst, NY: Prometheus.

Ellis, A. (2002). The role of irrational beliefs in perfectionism. In G. L. Flett & P. L. Hewitt (Eds.) *Perfectionism: Theory, research, and treatment* (pp. 217–229). Washington, DC: American Psychological Association.

Ellis, A. (2005). Rational-emotive therapy. In R. Corsini & D. Wedding (Eds.), *Current psychotherapies* (7th ed., pp. 166–201). Boston: Thomson/Brooks-Cole.

Ellis, A. (2008). Rational emotive behavior therapy. In R. J. Corsini & D. Wedding (Eds.), *Current psychotherapies* (8th ed.). Belmont, CA: Thomson Brooks/Cole.

Ellman, L. M., & Cannon, T. D. (2008). Environmental pre- and perinatal influences in etiology. In K. T. Mueser & D. V. Jeste (Eds.), *Clinical handbook of schizophrenia* (pp. 65–73). New York: Guilford Press.

El-Mallakh, R. S., & Huff, M. O. (2001). Mood stabilizers and ion regulation. *Harvard Rev. Psychiat., 9*(1), 23–32.

Elms, A. C. (2007). Psychobiography and case study methods. In R. F. Krueger, R. W. Robins, & R. C. Fraley (Eds.), *Handbook of research methods in personality psychology* (pp. 97–113). New York: Guilford Press.

Elwood, C. E., Poythress, N. G., & Douglas, K. S. (2004). Evaluation of the Hare P-SCAN in a non-clinical population. *Pers. Individ. Diff., 36*(4), 833–843.

Emanuel, E. J., Crouch, R. A., Arras, J. D., Moreno, J. D., & Grady, C. (Eds.). (2003). *Ethical and regulatory aspects of clinical research: Readings and commentary.* Baltimore: Johns Hopkins University Press.

Emmelkamp, P. M. (1982). Exposure in vivo treatments. In A. Goldstein & D. Chambless (Eds.), *Agoraphobia: Multiple perspectives on theory and treatment.* New York: Wiley.

Emmelkamp, P. M. (1994). Behavior therapy with adults. In A. E. Bergin & S. L. Garfield (Eds.), *Handbook of psychotherapy and behavior change* (4th ed.). New York: Wiley.

Emmers-Sommer, T. M., Allen, M., Bourhis, J., Sahlstein, E., Laskowski, K., Falato, W., et al. (2004). A meta-analysis of the relationship between social skills and sexual offenders. *Communic. Rep., 17*, 1–10.

Engel, G. L. (1968). A life setting conducive to illness: The giving-up-given-up complex. *Ann. Internal Med., 69*, 293.

Engel, J. M., Jensen, M. P., & Schwartz, L. (2004). Outcome of biofeedback-assisted relaxation for pain in adults with cerebral palsy: Preliminary findings. *Appl. Psychophysiol. Biofeedback, 29*(2), 135–140.

Engstrom, E. J., Weber, M. M., & Burgmair, W. (2006). Emil Wilhelm Magnus Georg Kraepelin (1856–1926). *Amer. J. Psychiat., 163*(10), 1710.

Ennis, B. J., & Emery, R. D. (1978). *The rights of mental patients* (ACLU Handbook Series). New York: Avon.

Ennis, E., Vrij, A., & Chance, C. (2008). Individual differences and lying in everyday life. *J. Soc. Pers. Relationships, 25*(1), 105–118.

Epstein, R. (2001). In her own words. *Psychol. Today, 34*(6), 36–37, 87.

Erba, H. W. (2000). Early intervention programs for children with autism: Conceptual frameworks for implementation. *Amer. J. Orthopsychiat., 70*(1), 82–94.

Erickson, S. J., & Gerstle, M. (2007). Investigation of ethnic differences in body image between Hispanic/biethnic-Hispanic and non-Hispanic white preadolescent girls. *Body Image, 4*(1), 69–78.

Erikson, E. (1963). *Childhood and society.* New York: Norton.

Erlangsen, A., Vach, W., & Jeune, B. (2005). The effect of hospitalization with medical illnesses on the suicide risk in the oldest old: A population-based register study. *J. Amer. Ger. Soc., 53*(5), 771–776.

Ervin, R. A., Schaughency, E., Matthews, A., Goodman, S. D., & McGlinchey, M. T. (2007). Primary and secondary prevention of behavior difficulties: Developing a data-informed problem-solving model to guide decision making at a school-wide level. *Psychol. Schools, 44*(1), 7–18.

Escalante, P. R., Minshew, N. J., & Sweeney, J. A. (2003). Abnormal brain lateralization in high-functioning autism. *J. Autism Dev. Disorders, 33*, 539–543.

Eschweiler, G. W., Vonthein, R., Bode, R., Huell, M., Conca, A., Peters, O., et al. (2007). Clinical efficacy and cognitive side effects of bifrontal versus right unilateral electroconvulsive therapy (ECT): A short-term randomised controlled trial in pharmaco-resistant major depression. *J. Affect. Disorders, 101*(1–3), 149–157.

Escobar, J. I. (1995). Transcultural aspects of dissociative and somatoform disorders. *Psychiatr. Clin. N. Amer., 18*(3), 555–569.

Escobar, J. I. (1998). Immigration and mental health: Why are immigrants better off? *Arch. Gen. Psychiat., 55*(9), 781–782.

Escobar, J. I. (2004, April 15). Transcultural aspects of dissociative and somatoform disorders. *Psychiatr. Times, XXI*(5), p. 10.

Escobar, J. I., Canino, G., Rubio-Stipec, M., & Bravo, M. (1992). Somatic symptoms after a natural disaster: A prospective study. *Amer. J. Psychiat., 149*(7), 965–967.

Escobar, J. I., Gara, M., Silver, R. C., Waitzkin, H., Holman, A., & Compton, W. (1998). Somatisation disorder in primary care. *Brit. J Psychiat., 173*, 262–266.

Escobar, J. I., Randolph, E. T., Puente, G., Spiwak, F., Asamen, J. K., Hill, M., et al. (1983). Posttraumatic stress disorder in Hispanic Vietnam veterans clinical phenomenology and sociocultural characteristics. *J. Nerv. Ment. Dis., 171*, 585–596.

Eser, A. (1981). "Sanctity" and "quality" of life in a historical comparative view. In S. E. Wallace & A. Eser (Eds.), *Suicide and euthanasia: The rights of personhood.* Knoxville: University of Tennessee Press.

Etaugh, C. (2008). Women in the middle and later years. In F. L. Denmark & M. A. Paludi (Eds.), *Psychology of women: A handbook of issues and theories* (2nd ed.). Westport, CT: Praeger Publishers.

Euler, D. (2008). Chinese herbal medicine for pain. In J. F. Audette & A. Bailey (Eds.), *Integrative pain medicine: The science and practice of complementary and alternative medicine in pain management* (pp. 471–493). Totowa, NJ: Humana Press.

Evans, G. W. (2006). Child development and the physical environment. *Annu. Rev. Psychol., 57*, 423–451.

Evans, J., Heron, J., Lewis, G., Araya, R., & Wolke, D. (2005). Negative self-schemas and the onset of depression in women: Longitudinal study. *Brit. J. Psychiat., 186*(4), 302–307.

Everson, S. A., Goldberg, D. E., Kaplan, G. A., Cohen, R. D., et al. (1996). Hopelessness and risk of mortality and incidence of myocardial infarction and cancer. *Psychosom. Med., 58*, 113–121.

Exner, J. E., Jr. (2003). *The Rorschach: A comprehensive system* (4th ed.). New York: Wiley.

Exner, J. E., Jr. (2007). A new U.S. adult non-patient sample. *J. Pers. Assess., 89*(Suppl.1), S154–S158.

Eyler, L. T. (2008). Brain imaging. In K. T. Mueser & D. V. Jeste (Eds.), *Clinical handbook of schizophrenia* (pp. 35–43). New York: Guilford Press.

Fabre, O. (2004). Therapy offers Alzheimer's hope to Japan's elderly. *Reuters (Sendai, Japan).*

Fábrega, H., Jr. (1990). The concept of somatization as a cultural and historical product of Western medicine. *Psychosom. Med., 52*(6), 653–672.

Fábrega, H., Jr. (2002). *Origins of psychopathology: The phylogenetic and cultural basis of mental illness.* New Brunswick, NJ: Rutgers University Press.

Fábrega, H., Jr. (2004). Psychiatric conditions in an evolutionary context. *Psychopath., 37*(6), 290–298.

Fábrega, H., Jr. (2006). Why psychiatric conditions are special: An evolutionary and cross-cultural perspective. *Perspect. Biol. Med., 49*(4), 586–601.

Fábrega, H., Jr. (2007, Summer). How psychiatric conditions were made. *Psychiat.: Interpers. Biol. Process., 130*–153.

Faedda, G. L., Tondo, L., Teichner, M. H., Baldessarini, R. J., Gelbard, H. A., & Floris, G. F. (1993). Seasonal mood disorders: Patterns of seasonal recurrence in mania and depression. *Arch. Gen. Psychiat., 50*(1), 17–23.

Fahrenberg, J., Foerster, F., & Wilmers, F. (1995). Is elevated blood pressure level associated with higher cardiovascular responsiveness in laboratory tasks and with response specificity? *Psychophysiology, 32*(1), 81–91.

Fairbank, J. A., & Keane, T. M. (1982). Flooding for combat-related stress disorders: Assessment of anxiety reduction across traumatic memories. *Behav. Ther., 13*, 499–510.

Fairburn, C. G. (1985). Cognitive-behavioural treatment for bulimia. In D. M. Garner & P. E. Garfinkel (Eds.), *Handbook of psychotherapy for anorexia nervosa and bulimia.* New York: Guilford Press.

Fairburn, C. G., Agras, W. S., Walsh, B. T., Wilson, G. T., & Stice, E. (2004). Prediction of outcome in bulimia nervosa by early change in treatment. *Amer. J. Psychiat., 161*(12), 2322–2324.

Fairburn, C. G., Cooper, Z., & Shafran, R. (2003). Cognitive behaviour therapy for eating disorders: A "transdiagnostic" theory and treatment. *Behav. Res. Ther., 41*(5), 509–528.

Fairburn, C. G., Cooper, Z., Shafran, R., & Wilson, G. T. (2008). Eating disorders: A transdiagnostic protocol. In D. H. Barlow (Ed.), *Clinical handbook of psychological disorders: A step-by-step treatment manual* (4th ed.). New York: Guilford Press.

Fakhoury, W., & Priebe, S. (2002). The process of deinstitutionalization: An international overview. *Curr. Opin. Psychiat., 15*(2), 187–192.

Faraone, S. V., Spencer, T., Aleardi, M., Pagano, C., & Biederman, J. (2004). Meta-analysis of the efficacy of methylphenidate for treating adult attention-deficit/hyperactivity disorder. *J. Clin. Psychopharmacol., 24*, 24–29.

Farberow, N. L., & Litman, R. E. (1970). *A comprehensive suicide prevention program.* Unpublished final report, Suicide Prevention Center of Los Angeles, Los Angeles.

Farlow, M. R., Murrell, J. R., Unverzagt F. W., Phillips, M., Takao, M., Hulette, C., et al. (2001). Familial Alzheimer's disease with spastic paraparesis associated with a mutation at codon 261 of the presenilin 1 gene. In I. Khalid, S. S. Sisodia, & B. Winblad (Eds.), *Alzheimer's disease: Advances in etiology, pathogenesis and therapeutics.* Chichester, England: Wiley.

Farmer, R. F., & Chapman, A. L. (2008). *Behavioral interventions in cognitive behavior therapy: Practical guidance for putting theory into action.* Washington, DC: American Psychological Association.

Farmer, R. F., & Nelson-Gray, R. O. (2005). Behavioral treatment of personality disorders. In R. F. Farmer & R. O. Nelson-Gray (Eds.), *Personality-guided behavior therapy* (pp. 203–243). Washington, DC: American Psychological Association.

Farrell, C., Lee, M., & Shafran, R. (2005). Assessment of body size estimation: A Review. *Eur. Eat. Disord. Rev., 13*(2), 75–88.

Fatality Facts. (2004). *Alcohol.* Washington, DC: Insurance Institute for Highway Safety.

Faust, J., Chapman, S., & Stewart, L. M. (2008). Neglected, physically abused, and sexually abused children. In D. Reitman (Ed.), *Handbook of psychological assessment, case conceptualization, and treatment, Vol. 2: Children and adolescents.* Hoboken, NJ: John Wiley & Sons.

Fava, M. (2000). New approaches to the treatment of refractory depression. *J. Clin. Psychiat., 61*(Suppl.), 26–32.

Fava, M., Farabaugh, A. H., Sickinger, A. H., Wright, E., Alpert, J. E., Sonawalla, S., et al. (2002). Personality disorders and depression. *Psychol. Med., 32*(6), 1049–1057.

Favaro, A., Ferrara, S., & Santonastaso, P. (2003). The spectrum of eating disorders in young women: A prevalence study in a general population sample. *Psychosom. Med., 65*(4), 701–708.

Fawcett, J. (1988). Predictors of early suicide: Identification and appropriate intervention. *J. Clin. Psychiat., 49*(Suppl.), 7–8.

Fawcett, J. (2004). Is suicide preventable? There is no room for complacency in patient treatment or clinician attitude when recognizing suicidal risk. *Psychiatr. Ann., 34*(5), 338–339.

Fawcett, J. (2007). Comorbid anxiety and suicide in mood disorders. *Psychiatr. Ann., 37*(10), 667–671.

Fawcett, J. (2007). What has the "black box" done to reduce suicide? *Psychiatr. Ann., 37*(10), 657, 662.

Fay, B. P. (1995). The individual versus society: The cultural dynamics of criminalizing suicide. *Hastings International and Comparative Law Review, 18,* 591–615.

Fayek, A. (2002). Analysis of a case of psychogenic amnesia: The issue of termination. *J. Clin. Psychoanal., 11*(4), 586–612.

Fazel, S., & Danesh, J. (2002). Serious mental disorder in 23,000 prisoners: A systematic review of 62 surveys. *Lancet, 359*(9306), 545–550.

Fazel, S., & Grann, M. (2006). The population impact of severe mental illness on violent crime. *Amer. J. Psychiat., 163*(8), 1397–1403.

Feigelman, W., & Gorman, B. S. (2008). Assessing the effects of peer suicide on youth suicide. *Suic. Life-Threat. Behav., 38*(2), 181–194.

Feldman, M. B., & Meyer, I. H. (2007). Childhood abuse and eating disorders in gay and bisexual men. *Inter. J. Eat. Disorders, 40*(5), 418–423.

Feldman, M. D. (2004). *Playing sick? Untangling the web of Munchausen syndrome, Munchausen by proxy, malingering and factitious disorder.* New York: Routledge.

Feldman, M. D., Ford, C. V., & Reinhold, T. (1994). *Patient or pretender: Inside the strange world of factitious disorders.* New York: Wiley.

Feldman, S. R., Moritz, S. H., & Benjamin, G. A. H. (2005). Suicide and the law: A practical overview for mental health professionals. *Women Ther., 28*(1), 95–103.

Felix, A., Herman, D., & Susser, E. (2008). Housing instability and homelessness. In K. T. Mueser & D. V. Jeste (Eds.), *Clinical handbook of schizophrenia* (pp. 411–423). New York: Guilford Press.

Fellenz, M. R. (2007). *The moral menagerie: Philosophy and animal rights.* Champaign, IL: University of Illinois Press.

Fenichel, O. (1945). *The psychoanalytic theory of neurosis.* New York: Norton.

Fennig, S., Fennig, S., & Roe, D. (2002). Cognitive-behavioral therapy for bulimia nervosa: Time course and mechanisms of change. *Gen. Hosp. Psychiat., 24*(2), 87–92.

Fenton, W. S., Hoch, J. S., Herrell, J. M., Mosher, L., & Dixon, L. (2002). Cost and cost-effectiveness of hospital vs. residential crisis care for patients who have serious mental illness. *Arch. Gen. Psychiat., 59*(4), 357–364.

Fergusson, D. M., Woodward, L. J., & Horwood, L. J. (2000). Risk factors and life processes associated with the onset of suicidal behavior during adolescence and early adulthood. *Psychol. Med., 30*(1), 23–39.

Fernquist, R. M. (2007). How do Durkheimian variables impact variation in national suicide rates when proxies for depression and alcoholism are controlled? *Arch. Suic. Res., 11*(4), 361–374.

Ferrada, N. M., Asberg, M., Ormstad, K., & Nordstrom, P. (1995). Definite and undetermined forensic diagnoses of suicide among immigrants in Sweden. *Acta Psychiatr. Scandin., 91*(2), 130–135.

Ferrari, R. (2006). *The whiplash encyclopedia: The facts and myths of whiplash.* Boston: Jones and Bartlett.

Ferreira, C. (2000). Serial killers—Victims of compulsion or masters of control? In D. H. Fishbein (Ed.), *The science, treatment, and prevention of antisocial behaviors: Application to the criminal justice system* (pp. 15-1–15-8). Kingston, NJ: Civic Research Institute.

Fetto, J. (2002, April 1). What seems to be the problem? *Amer. Demog.*

Fetto, J. (2002, May 1). Drugged out. *Amer. Demog.*

Fetto, J. (2002, May 1). You never call. *Amer. Demog. 4*(1), 8–9.

Feuer, C. A., Nishith, P., & Resick, P. (2005). Prediction of numbing and effortful avoidance in female rape surviv with chronic PTSD. *J. Traum. Stress, 18*(2), 165–170.

Fichter, M. M., & Pirke, K. M. (1995). Starvation models and eating disorders. In G. Szmukler, C. Dare, & J. Treasure (Eds.), *Handbook of eating disorders: Theory, treatment and research.* Chichester, England: Wiley.

Fichtner, C. G., Kuhlman, D. T., Gruenfeld, M. J., & Hughes, J. R. (1990). Decreased episodic violence and increased control of dissociation in a carbamazepine-treated case of multiple personality. *Biol. Psychiat., 27*(9), 1045–1052.

Field, A., & Davey, G. (2005). Experimental methods in clinical and health research. In J. Miles & P. Gilbert (Eds.), *A handbook of research methods for clinical and health psychology* (pp. 175–184). New York: Oxford University Press.

Fields, J. (2004). *America's families and living arrangements, 2003.* Current Population Reports, P20-553. Washington, DC: U.S. Census Bureau.

Fieve, R. R. (1975). *Moodswing.* New York: Morrow.

Figley, C. R. (1978). Symptoms of delayed combat stress among a college sample of Vietnam veterans. *Military Med., 143*(2), 107–110.

Finckh, U. (2001). The dopamine D2 receptor gene and alcoholism: Association studies. In D. P. Agarwal & H. K. Seitz (Eds.), *Alcohol in health and disease* (pp. 151–176). New York: Marcel Dekker.

Fine, C. G., & Madden, N. E. (2000). Group psychotherapy in the treatment of dissociative identity disorder and allied dissociative disorders. In R. H. Klein & V. L. Schermer (Eds.), *Group psychotherapy for psychological trauma* (pp. 298–325). New York: Guilford Press.

Finfgeld, D. L. (2002). Anorexia nervosa: Analysis of long-term outcomes and clinical implications. *Arch. Psychiatr. Nursing, 16*(4), 176–186.

Fink, M. (2001). Convulsive therapy: A review of the first 55 years. *J. Affect. Disorders, 63*(1–3), 1–15.

Fink, M. (2007). What we learn about continuation treatments from the collaborative electroconvulsive therapy studies. *J. ECT, 23*(4), 215–218.

Fink, P., Hansen, M. S., & Oxhoj, M. L. (2004). The prevalence of somatoform disorders among internal medical inpatients. *J. Psychosom. Res., 56*(4), 413–418.

Fink, P., Ørnbøl, E., Toft, T. T., Sparle, K. C., Frostholm, L., & Olesen, F. (2004). A new, empirically established hypochondriasis diagnosis. *Amer. J. Psychiat., 161*(9), 1680–1691.

Finkelhor, D., Asdigian, N., & Dziuba-Leatherman, J. (1995). Victimization prevention programs for children: A follow-up. *Amer. J. Pub. Hlth., 85*(12), 1684–1689.

Finnegan, L. P., & Kandall, S. R. (2008). Perinatal substance abuse. In H. D. Kleber & M. Galanter (Eds.), *The American Psychiatric Publishing textbook of substance abuse treatment* (4th ed., pp. 565–580). Arlington, VA: American Psychiatric Publishing.

Finzi, E., & Wasserman, E. (2006). Treatment of depression with botulism toxin A: A case series. *Dermatol. Surg., 32*(5), 645–650(6).

Fischer, B. A., IV, & Carpenter, W. T., Jr. (2008). Remission. In K. T. Mueser & D.V. Jeste (Eds.), *Clinical handbook of schizophrenia* (pp. 559–565). New York: Guilford Press.

Fishbain, D. A. (2000). Re: The meeting of pain and depression. Comorbidity in women. *Canad. J. Psychiat., 45*(1), 88.

Fisher, A. V., & Sloutsky, V. M. (2005). When induction meets memory: Evidence for gradual transition from similarity-based to category-based induction. *Child Dev., 76*(3), 583–597.

Fisher, J. E., & Carstensen, L. L. (1990). Behavior management of the dementias. *Clin. Psychol. Rev., 10,* 611–629.

Fisher, J. E., Zeiss, A. M., & Carstensen, L. L. (2001). Psychopathology in the aged. In P. B. Sutker & H. E. Adams (Eds.), *Comprehensive handbook of psychopathology* (3rd ed., pp. 921–952). New York: Kluwer Academic/Plenum.

Fisher, P. H., Masia-Warner, C., & Klein, R. G. (2004). Skills for social and academic success: A school-based intervention for social anxiety disorder in adolescents. *Clin. Child Fam. Psychol. Rev., 7*(4), 241–249.

Fisher, R. P., & Reardon, M. C. (2007). Eyewitness identification. In D. Carson, R. Milne, F. Pakes, K. Shalev, & A. Shawyer (Eds.), *Applying psychology to criminal justice.* Hoboken, NJ: John Wiley & Sons.

Fitch, W. L. (2007). AAPL practice guideline for the forensic psychiatric evaluation of competence to stand trial: An American legal perspective. *J. Amer. Acad. Psychiat. Law, 35*(4), 509–513.

Fitz, A. (1990). Religious and familial factors in the etiology of obsessive-compulsive disorder: A review. *J. Psychol. Theol., 18*(2), 141–147.

Fitzgibbon, M. L., Spring, B., Avellone, M. E., Blackman, L. R., Pingitore, R., & Stolley, M. R. (1998). Correlates of binge eating among Hispanic, Black and White women. *Inter. J. Eat. Disorders, 24,* 43–52.

Flahive, E. (2008). Are you tanorexic? *WebMD.* Retrieved May 4, 2008, from http://www.webmd.com/skin-beauty/features/you-tanorexic

Flavin, D. K., Franklin, J. E., & Frances, R. J. (1990). Substance abuse and suicidal behavior. In S. J. Blumenthal & D. J. Kupfer (Eds.), *Suicide over the life cycle: Risk factors, assessment, and treatment of suicidal patients.* Washington, DC: American Psychiatry Press.

Fleck, D. E., Keck, P. E., Corey, K. B., & Strakowski, S. M. (2005). Factors associated with medication adherence in African American and white patients with bipolar disorder. *J. Clin. Psychiat., 66*(5), 646–652.

Fletcher, T. B. (2000). Primary nocturnal enuresis: A structural and strategic family systems approach. *J. Ment. Hlth Couns., 22*(1), 32–44.

Flint, A. J. (1994). Epidemiology and comorbidity of anxiety disorders in the elderly. *Amer. J. Psychiat., 151*(5), 640–649.

Floyd, F. J., & Sidhu, J. S. (2004). Monitoring prenatal alcohol exposure. *Amer. J. Med. Genet (Seminars in Medical Genetics) 127C,* 3–9.

Flynn, R. J., & Lemay, R. A. (Eds.). (1999). *A quarter-century of normalization and social role valorization: Evolution and impact.* Ottawa, ON: University of Ottawa Press.

Foa, E. B., & Franklin, M. E. (2001). Obsessive-compulsive disorder. In D. H. Barlow (Ed.), *Clinical handbook of psychological disorders: A step-by-step treatment manual* (3rd ed.). New York: Guilford Press.

Foa, E. B., & Franklin, M. E. (2004). Psychotherapies for obsessive-compulsive disorder: A review. In M. Maj, N. Sartorius, A. Okasha, & J. Zohar (Eds.), *Obsessive-compulsive disorder* (pp. 93–115). New York: Wiley.

Foa, E. B., Hearst-Ikeda, D., & Perry, K. L. (1995). Evaluation of a brief cognitive-behavioral program for the prevention of chronic PTSD in recent assault victims. *J. Cons. Clin. Psychol., 63,* 948–955.

Foa, E. B., Liebowitz, M. R., Kozak, M. J., Davies, S., Campeas, R., Franklin, M. E., et al. (2005). Randomized placebo-controlled trial of exposure and ritual prevention, Clomip-ramine, and their combination in the treatment of obsessive-compulsive disorder. *Amer. J. Psychiat., 162*(1), 151–161.

Foa, E. B., Rothbaum, B. O., & Furr, J. M. (2003). Augmenting exposure therapy with other CBT procedures. *Psychiatr. Ann., 33*(1), 47–53.

Foley, K., & Hendin, H. (2002). Introduction: A medical, ethical, legal, and psychosocial perspective. In K. Foley & H. Hendin (Eds.), *The case against assisted suicide: For the right to end-of-life care* (pp. 1–16). Baltimore, MD: The John Hopkins University Press.

Foley, K., & Hendin, H. (Eds.). (2003). The case against assisted suicide: For the right to-end-life care. *J. Nerv. Ment. Dis., 191*(1), 62–64.

Folkman, S., & Moskowitz, J. T. (2004). Coping: Pitfalls and promise. *Annu. Rev. Psychol., 55,* 745–774.

Folsom, D. P., Fleisher, A. S., & Depp, C. A. (2006). Schizophrenia. In D.V. Jeste & J. H. Friedman (Eds.), *Psychiatry for neurologists* (pp. 59–66). Totowa, NJ: Humana Press.

Fombonne, E. (1995). Eating disorders: Time trends and possible explanatory mehanisms. In M. Rutter & D. J. Smith, *Psychosocial disorders in young people.* Chichester, England: Wiley.

Fombonne, E. (2003). Epidemiological surveys of autism and other pervasive developmental disorders: An update. *J. Autism Dev. Disorders, 33,* 365–382.

Fombonne, E., & Zinck, S. (2008). Psycho-pharmacological treatment of depression in children and adolescents. In J. R. Z. Abela & B. L. Hankin (Eds.), *Handbook of depression in children and adolescents* (pp. 207–223). New York: Guilford Press.

Fonagy, P., Gergely, G., Jurist, E. L., & Target, M. (2002). *Affect regulation, mentalization and the development of the self.* New York: Other Press.

Fonda, J. (2005). My life so far. New York: Random House:

Ford, C. V. (2005). Deception syndromes: Factitious disorders and malingering. In J. L. Levenson (Ed.), *The American Psychiatric Publishing textbook of psychosomatic medicine* (pp. 297–309). Washington, DC: American Psychiatric Publishing.

Ford, C. V., King, B. H., & Hollender, M. H. (1988). Lies and liars: Psychiatric aspects of prevarication. *Amer. J. Psychiat., 145*(5), 554–562.

Ford, J. D., & Stewart, J. (1999). Group psychotherapy for war-related PTSD with military veterans. In B. H. Young & D. D. Blake (Eds.), *Group treatments for post-traumatic stress disorder.* Philadelphia: Brunner/Mazel.

Ford, M. R., & Widiger, T. A. (1989). Sex bias in the diagnosis of histrionic and antisocial personality disorders. *J. Cons. Clin. Psychol., 57*(2), 301–305.

Ford, T. (2000). The influence of womanist identity on the development of eating disorders and depression in African American female college students. *Diss. Abstr. Inter., Sect. A: Human. Soc. Sci., 61,* 2194.

Foreman, W. (2005, June 26). Ghost fears keep visitors from Thailand. *Boston.com News.*

Foreyt, J. P., Poston, W. S. C., & Goodrick, G. K. (1996). Future directions in obesity and eating disorders. *Addic. Behav., 21*(6), 767–778.

Fortune, S. A., & Hawton, K. (2007). Suicide and deliberate self-harm in children and adolescents. *Paediatrics Child Hlth., 17*(11), 443–447.

Foster, J. D., Campbell, W. K., & Twenge, J. M. (2003). Individual differences in narcissicm: Inflated self-views across the lifespan and around the world. *Journal of Research in Personality, 37,* 469–486.

Fountaine, E. (2000). Stakes are high for overweight jockeys. *New York Thoroughbred Horsemen's Association Newsletter,* June. Online, available at www.nytha.com

Fowler, J. S., Volkow, N. D., & Wolf, A. P. (1995). PET studies of cocaine in human brain. In A. Biegon & N. D.Volkow (Eds.), *Sites of drug action in the human brain.* Boca Raton, FL: CRC Press.

Fowler, K. A., O'Donohue, W., Lilienfeld, S. O. (2007). Introduction: Personality disorders in perspective. In W. O'Donohue, K. A. Fowler, S. O. Lilienfeld (Eds.), *Personality disorders: Toward the DSM-V.* Los Angeles: Sage Publications.

Fox, J. A., & Levin, J. (2005). *Extreme killing: Understanding serial and mass murder.* Thousand Oaks, CA: Sage.

Frances, R. J., Mack, A., & Miller, S. I. (Eds.). (2005). *Clinical textbook of addictive disorders* (3rd ed.). New York: Guilford Press.

Franchi, S. (2004). Depression and marital discord. *Revista Argentina de Clinica Psicologica, 13*(3), 197–203.

Frank, J. D. (1973). *Persuasion and healing* (Rev. ed.). Baltimore: Johns Hopkins University Press.

Frankel, F. H. (1993). Adult reconstruction of childhood events in the multiple personality literature. *Amer. J. Psychiat., 150*(6), 954–958.

Frankish, C. J. (1994). Crisis centers and their role in treatment: Suicide prevention versus health promotion. In A. A. Leenaars, J. T. Maltsberger, & R. A. Neimeyer (Eds.), *Treatment of suicidal people.* Washington, DC: Taylor & Francis.

Franklin, J., & Markarian, M. (2005). Substance abuse in minority populations. In R. J. Frances, A. H. Mack, & S. I. Miller (Eds.), *Clinical textbook of addictive disorders* (3rd ed., pp. 321–339). New York: Guilford Press.

Franklin, M. E., Abramowitz, J. S., Bux, D. A., Jr., Zoellner, L. A., & Feeny, N. C. (2002). Cognitive-behavioral therapy with and without medication in the treatment of obsessive-compulsive disorder. *Profess. Psychol.: Res. Pract., 33*(2), 162–168.

Franklin, M. E., Riggs, D. S., & Pai, A. (2005). Obsessive-compulsive disorder. In M. M. Antony, D. R. Ledley, & R. G. Heimberg (Eds.), *Improving outcomes and preventing relapse in cognitive-behavioral therapy* (pp. 128–173). New York: Guilford Press.

Frare, F., Perugi, G., Ruffolo, G., & Toni, C. (2004). Obsessive-compulsive disorder and body dysmorphic disorder: A comparison of clinical features. *Eur. Psychiat., 19*(5), 292–298.

Fraser, G. A. (1993). Special treatment techniques to access the inner personality system of multiple personality disorder patients. *Dissociat.: Prog. Dissociat. Disorders, 6*(2–3), 193–198.

Fraser, J. S., & Solovey, A. D. (2007). Couples therapy. In J. S. Scott & A. D. Solovey (Eds.), *Second-order change in psychotherapy: The golden thread that unifies effective treatments* (pp. 191–221). Washington, DC: American Psychological Association.

Frederick, C. J. (1969). Suicide notes: A survey and evaluation. *Bull. Suicidol., 8,* 17–26.

Fredericks, L. E. (2001). *The use of hypnosis in surgery and anesthesiology: Psychological preparation of the surgical patient.* Springfield, IL: Thomas.

Fredrickson, B. L., Tugade, M. M., Waugh, C. E., & Larkin, G. R. (2003). What good are positive emotions in crisis? A prospective study of resilience and emotion following the terrorist attacks on the United States on September 11th, 2001. *J. Pers. Soc. Psychol., 84,* 365–376.

Freed, A. O., & Geller, J. L. (2005). Client violence in social work practice: Prevention, intervention, and research. *Psychiat. Serv., 56*(3), 366.

Freedman, R., Ross, R., Michels, R., Appelbaum, P., Siever, L., Binder, R., et al. (2007). Psychiatrists, mental illness, and violence. *Amer. J. Psychiat., 165*(9), 1315–1317.

Freeman, A. (2002). Cognitive-behavioral therapy for severe personality disorders. In S. G. Hofmann & M. C. Tompson (Eds.), *Treating chronic and severe mental disorders: A handbook of empirically supported interventions* (pp. 382–402). New York: Guilford Press.

Freeman, A. C. (2005). Eating disorders in males: A review. *S. Afr. Psychiat. Rev., 8*(2), 58–64.

Freking, K. (2007, August 27). Obesity rates show no decline in US. *Yahoo! News.* Retrieved August 27, 2007, from http://news.yahoo.com

Freking, K. (2007, October 14). Report ranks jobs by rates of depression. *Yahoo! News.* Retrieved October 14, 2007, from http://www.physorg.com/news111566913.html

French, A. P., & Berlin, I. N. (1979). Depression in children and adolescents. New York: Human Sciences Press.

Frese, F. J., III. (2008). Self-help activities. In D.V. Jeste, & K. T. Mueser (Eds.) *Clinical handbook of schizophrenia* (pp. 298–305). New York: Guilford Press.

Freud, S. (1885). On the general effects of cocaine. *Med. Chir. Centralb., 20,* 373–375.

Freud, S. (1894). The neuropsychoses of defense. In J. Strachey (Ed.), *The standard edition of the complete psychological works of Sigmund Freud* (Vol. 3). London: Hogarth Press. (Work republished 1962)

Freud, S. (1909). Analysis of a phobia in a five-year-old boy. In *Sigmund Freud: Collected papers* (Vol. 3). New York: Basic Books.

Freud, S. (1914). On narcissism. In *Complete psychological works* (Vol. 14). London: Hogarth Press. (Work republished 1957)

Freud, S. (1915). A case of paranoia counter to psychoanalytic theory. In *Complete psychological works* (Vol. 14). London: Hogarth Press. (Work republished 1957)

Freud, S. (1917). *A general introduction to psychoanalysis* (J. Riviere, Trans.). New York: Liveright. (Work republished 1963)

Freud, S. (1917). Mourning and melancholia. In *Collected papers* (Vol. 4, pp. 152–172). London: Hogarth Press and the Institute of Psychoanalysis. (Work republished 1950)

Freud, S. (1920). Beyond the pleasure principle. *S.E., 18,* 7–64.

Freud, S. (1924). The loss of reality in neurosis and psychosis. In *Sigmund Freud's collected papers* (Vol. 2, pp. 272–282). London: Hogarth Press.

Freud, S. (1933). *New introductory lectures on psychoanalysis.* New York: Norton.

Freud, S. (1961). *The future of an illusion.* New York: W. W. Norton.

Frey, K. S., & Hirschstein, M. K., Snell, J. L., Edstrom, L. V., MacKenzie, E. P., & Brod-

erick, C. J. (2005). Reducing playground bullying and supporting beliefs: An experimental trial of the Steps to Respect program. *Dev. Psychol., 41,* 479–491.

Friedman, M., & Rosenman, R. (1959). Association of specific overt behavior pattern with blood and cardiovascular findings. *JAMA, 169,* 1286.

Friedman, M., & Rosenman, R. (1974). *Type A behavior and your heart.* New York: Knopf.

Friedman, M., Thoresen, C., Gill, J., et al. (1984). Alteration of type A behavior and reduction in cardiac recurrences in postmyocardial infarction patients. *Am. Heart J., 108*(2), 653–665.

Friedman, R. A. (2007, December 18). Brought on by darkness, disorder needs light. *New York Times.* Retrieved December 20, 2007, from http://www.nytimes.com/2007/12/18/health/18mind.html

Friedman, R. A. (2008, February 19). "Have you ever been in psychotherapy, doctor?" *New York Times.* Retrieved February 25, 2008, from http://www.nytimes.com/2008/02/19/health/19mind.html

Friman, P. C. (2008). Evidence-based therapies for enuresis and encopresis. In R. G. Steele, T. D. Elkin, & M. C. Roberts (Eds.), *Handbook of evidence-based therapies for children and adolescents: Bridging science and practice.* New York: Springer.

Frith, U. (2000). Cognitive explanations of autism. In K. Lee (Ed.), *Childhood cognitive development: The essential readings. Essential readings in development psychology.* Malden, MA: Blackwell.

Fritsche, I., & Linneweber, V. (2005). Nonreactive methods in psychological research. In E. Diener & M. Eid (Eds.)., *Handbook of multimethod measurement in psychology* (pp. 189–203). Washington, DC: American Psychological Association.

Frodl, T., Meisenzahl, E. M., Zetzsche, R., Hohne, T., Banac, S., Schorr, C., et al. (2004). Hippocampal and amygdale changes in patients with major depressive disorder and healthy controls during a 1-year follow-up. *J. Clin. Psychiat., 65*(4), 492–499.

Frohman, E. M. (2002). Sexual dysfunction in neurological disease. *Clin. Neuropharmacol., 25*(3), 126–132.

Fromm-Reichmann, F. (1943). Psychotherapy of schizophrenia. *Amer. J. Psychiat., 111,* 410–419.

Fromm-Reichmann, F. (1948). Notes on the development of treatment of schizophrenia by psychoanalytic psychotherapy. *Psychiatry, 11,* 263–273.

Fromm-Reichmann, F. (1950). *Principles of intensive psychotherapy.* Chicago: University of Chicago.

Frosch, W. A., Robbins, E. S., & Stern, M. (1965). Untoward reactions to lysergic acid diethylamide (LSD) resulting in hospitalization. *N. Engl. J. Med., 273,* 1235–1239.

Frost, R. O., & Steketee, G. (2001). Obsessive-compulsive disorder. In H. S. Friedman (Ed.), *Specialty articles from the encyclopedia of mental health.* San Diego: Academic Press.

Frost, R. O., & Steketee, G. (Eds.). (2002). *Cognitive approaches to obsessions and compulsions: Theory, assessment, and treatment.* Amsterdam: Pergamon/Elsevier Science.

Fry, A. J., O'Riordan, D., Turner, M., & Mills, K. L. (2002). Survey of aggressive incidents

experienced by community mental health staff. *Inter. J. Ment. Hlth. Nurs., 11*(2), 112–120.

Furedi, F. (2007). "The only thing we have to fear is the 'culture of fear' itself". *Spiked.* Based on a talk at the NY Salon debate, 20 March 2007.

Furukawa, T. A., Ogura, A., Hirai, T., Fujihara, S., Kitamura, T., & Takahashi, K. (1999). Early parental separation experiences among patients with bipolar disorder and major depression: A case-control study. *J. Affect. Disorders, 52*(1–3), 85–91.

Fushimi, M., Sugawara, J., & Shimizu, T. (2005). Suicide patterns and characteristics in Akita, Japan. *Psychiat. Clin. Neurosci., 59*(3), 296–302.

Gabbard, G. O. (1990). *Psychodynamic psychiatry in clinical practice.* Washington, DC: American Psychiatric Press.

Gabbard, G. O. (2001). Psychoanalysis and psychoanalytic psychotherapy. In W. J. Livesley (Ed.), *Handbook of personality disorders: Theory, research, and treatment* (pp. 359–376). New York: Guilford Press.

Gado, M. (2008). The insanity defense: Twinkies as a defense. *trutv.com.* Retrieved August 17, 2008, from http://www.trutv.com/library/crime/criminal_mind/psychology/insanity

Galanter, M. (2008). Network therapy. In H. D. Kleber & M. Galanter (Eds.), *The American Psychiatric Publishing textbook of substance abuse treatment* (4th ed., pp. 401–412). Arlington, VA: American Psychiatric Publishing.

Galanter, M., & Brooks, D. (2001). Network therapy for addiction: Bringing family and peer support into office practice. *Inter. J. Group Psychother., 51*(1), 101–122.

Galanter, M., & Kleber, H. D. (Eds.). (2008). *The American Psychiatric Publishing textbook of substance abuse treatment* (4th ed.). Arlington, VA: American Psychiatric Publishing.

Galea, S., Ahern, J., Resnick, H., Kilpatrick, D., Bucuvalas, M., Gold, J., & Vlahov, D. (2002). Psychological sequelae of the September 11 terrorist attacks in New York City. *New Engl. J. Med., 13,* 982–987.

Galea, S., Ahern, J., Resnick, H., Kilpatrick, D., Bucuvalas, M., Gold, J., & Vlahov, D. (2007). Psychological sequelae of the September 11 terrorist attacks in New York City. In B. Trappler (Ed.), *Modern terrorism and psychological trauma* (pp. 14–24). New York: Gordian Knot Books/Richard Altschuler & Associates.

Galea, S., Ahern, J., Resnick, H., & Vlahov, D. (2006). Post-traumatic stress symptoms in the general population after a disaster: Implications for public health. In Y. Neria, R. Gross, R. D. Marshall, & E. S. Susser (Eds.), *9/11: Mental health in the wake of terrorist attacks* (pp. 19–44). New York: Cambridge University Press.

Gallagher, R. (1998, December 17). Interviewed in R. Vigoda, More college students showing signs of stress. *The Seattle Times.*

Gallagher-Thompson, D., Lovett, S., Rose, J., McKibbin, C., Coon, D., Futterman, A., & Thompson, L. W. (2000). Impact of psychoeducational interventions on distressed family caregivers. *J. Clin. Geropsychol., 6*(2), 91–110.

Gallagher-Thompson, D., & Thompson, L. W. (1995). Problems of aging. In R. J. Comer (Ed.), *Abnormal psychology.* New York: W. H. Freeman.

Gamwell, L., & Tomes, N. (1995). *Madness in America: Cultural and medical perceptions of mental illness before 1914*. Ithaca, NY: Cornell University Press.

Gao, L., & Greenfield, L. J. (2005). Activation of protein kinase C reduces benzodiazepine potency at GABA-sub(A) receptors in NT2-N neurons. *Neuropharmacology, 48*(3), 333–342.

Garb, H. N. (2006). The conjunction effect and clinical judgment. *J. Soc. Clin. Psychol., 25*(9), 1048–1056.

Garber, K. (2008). Who's behind the bible of mental illness. *U.S. News & World Report*, December 31, 2007/ January 7, 2008, 25.

Gardner, R. A. (2004). The psychodynamics of patients with False Memory Syndrome (FMS). *J. Amer. Acad. Psychoanal. Dynamic Psychiat., 32*(1), 77–90.

Gardyn, R. (2002). Family matters. *Am. Demogr., 24*(8), 34.

Garlow, S. J. (2002). Age, gender, and ethnicity differences in patterns of cocaine and ethanol use preceding suicide. *Amer. J. Psychiat., 159*(4), 615–619.

Garner, D. M. (1991). *Eating disorder inventory—2: Professional manual*. Odessa, FL: Psychological Assessment Resources.

Garner, D. M., & Fairburn, C. G. (1988). Relationship between anorexia nervosa and bulimia nervosa: Diagnostic implications. In D. M. Garner & P. E. Garfinkel (Eds.), *Diagnostic issues in anorexia nervosa and bulimia nervosa*. Brunner/Mazel eating disorders monograph series, No. 2. New York: Brunner/Mazel.

Garner, D. M., Garfinkel, P. E., & O'Shaughnessy, M. (1985). The validity of the distinction between bulimia with and without anorexia nervosa. *Amer. J. Psychiat., 142*, 581–587.

Garner, D. M., Garfinkel, P. E., Schwartz, D., & Thompson, M. (1980). Cultural expectations of thinness in women. *Psychol. Rep., 47*, 483–491.

Garner, D. M., Kearney, C. A., & Marano, H. E. (1997). The 1997 body image survey results. *Psychol. Today*, 30–44.

Garner, D. M., Olmsted, M. P., & Polivy, J. (1984). *The EDI*. Odessa, FL: Psychological Assessment Resources.

Garralda, M. E. (1996). Somatisation in children. *J. Child Psychol. Psychiat., 37*(1), 13–33.

Garrett, B. (2008). *Brain and behavior: An introduction to biological psychology* (2nd ed.). Los Angeles: Sage.

Garssen, B., & Goodkin, K. (1999). On the role of immunological factors as mediators between psychosocial factors and cancer progression. *Psychiat. Res., 85*(1), 51–61.

Gatchel, R. J. (2001). Biofeedback and self-regulation of physiological activity: A major adjunctive treatment modality in health psychology. In A. Baum, T. A. Revenson, & J. E. Singer (Eds.), *Handbook of health psychology* (pp. 95–104). Mahwah, NJ: Lawrence Erlbaum.

Gatchel, R. J. (2005). The biopsychosocial approach to pain assessment and management. In R. J. Gatchel (Ed.), *Clinical essentials of pain management* (pp. 23–46). Washington, DC: American Psychological Association.

Gatchel, R. J., & Maddrey, A. M. (2004). The biopsychosocial perspective of pain. In L. C. Leviton & J. M. Raczynski (Eds.), *Handbook of clinical health psychology, Vol. 2: Disorders of behavior and health* (pp. 357–378). Washington, DC: American Psychological Association.

Gatchel, R. J., Peng, Y. B., Peters, M. L., Fuchs, P. N., & Turk, D. C. (2007). The biopsychosocial approach to chronic pain: Scientific advances and future directions. *Psychol. Bull., 133*(4), 581–624.

Gaudiano, B. A. (2005). Cognitive behavior therapies for psychotic disorders: Current empirical status and future directions. *Clin. Psychol.: Sci. Prac., 12*, 33–49.

Gaugler, J. E., Jarrott, S. E., Zarit, S. H., Stephens, M. A. P., Townsend, A., & Greene, R. (2003). Adult day service use and reductions in caregiving hours: Effects on stress and psychological well-being for dementia caregivers. *Inter. J. Ger. Psychiat., 18*(1), 55–62.

Gay, P. (1999, March 29). Psychoanalyst Sigmund Freud. *Time*, pp. 66–69.

Gay, P. (2006). *Freud: A life for our time*. New York: W. W. Norton & Co.

Gaynor, S. T., & Baird, S. C. (2007). Personality disorders. In D. W. Woods & J. W. Kanter (Eds.), *Understanding behavior disorders: A contemporary behavioral perspective*. Reno, NV: Context Press.

Geary, J., & DePaulo, B. M. (2007). Issue 7: Can people accurately detect lies? In J. A. Nier, *Taking sides: Clashing views in social psychology* (2nd ed., pp. 138–151). New York: McGraw-Hill.

Gebhard, P. H. (1965). Situational factors affecting human sexual behavior. In F. Beach (Ed.), *Sex and behavior*. New York: Wiley.

Gehring, D., & Knudson, G. (2005). Prevalence of childhood trauma in a clinical population of transsexual people. *Inter. J. Transgenderism, 8*(1), 23–30.

Gelernter, J., & Kranzler, H. R. (2008). Genetics of addiction. In H. D. Kleber & M. Galanter (Eds.), *The American Psychiatric Publishing textbook of substance abuse treatment* (4th ed., pp. 17–27). Arlington, VA: American Psychiatric Publishing.

Gelfand, D. M., Jenson, W. R., & Drew, C. J. (1982). *Understanding child behavior disorders*. New York: Holt, Rinehart & Winston.

Genchi, A. J., Alvarado, R. I. N., & Portocarrero, A. N. (2004). Sleep characteristics in subjects with major depression. *Psiquiatria, 20*(3), 1–3.

General Social Survey, University of Chicago (GSS). (1998, February). Cited in *J. Student*, Am. Demogr.

George, M. S., Sackeim, H. A., Rush, A. J., Marangell, L. B., Nahas, Z., Husain, M. M., et al. (2000). Vagus nerve stimulation: A new tool for brain research and therapy. *Biol. Psychiat., 47*, 287–295.

George, M. S., Wassermann, E. M., Williams, W. A., Callahan, A., Ketter, T. A., Basser, P., et al. (1995). Daily repetitive transcranial magnetic stimulation (rTMS) improves mood in depression. *Neuroreport, 6*, 1853–1856.

George, T. P., & Weinberger, A. H. (2008). Nicotine and tobacco. In H. D. Kleber & M. Galanter (Eds.), *The American Psychiatric Publishing textbook of substance abuse treatment* (4th ed., pp. 201–213). Arlington, VA: American Psychiatric Publishing.

Gerardin, P., Cohen, D., Mazet, P., & Flament, M. F. (2002). Drug treatment of conduct disorder in young people. *Eur. Neuropsychopharmacology, 12*(5), 361–370.

Gerbasi, J. B., & Simon, R. I. (2003). Patients' rights and psychiatrists' duties: Discharging patients against medicine advice. *Harvard Rev. Psychiat., 11*(6), 333–343.

Geremia, G. M., & Neziroglu, F. (2001). Cognitive therapy in the treatment of body dysmorphic disorder. *Clin. Psychol. Psychother., 8*, 243–251.

Germer, J. (2005). The relationship between acculturation and eating disorders among Mexican American college females: An investigation. *Diss. Abstr. Inter.: Sect. B: Sci. Eng., 65*(7-B), 3706.

Gernsbacher, L. M. (1985). *The suicide syndrome*. New York: Human Sciences Press.

Gerrity, E., Keane, T. M., & Tuma, F. (2001). Introduction. In E. Gerrity, T. M. Keane, & F. Tuma (Eds.), *The mental health consequences of torture* (pp. 3–12). New York: Kluwer Academic/Plenum Publishers.

Gershon, E. S., & Nurnberger, J. I. (1995). Bipolar illness. In J. M. Oldham & M. B. Riba (Eds.), *American Psychiatric Press review of psychiatry* (Vol. 14). Washington, DC: American Psychiatric Press.

Gever, J. (2008, May 7). APA: PTSD may be major combat scar of Iraq vets. Retrieved May 19, 2008, from http://www.medpagetoday.com/MeetingCoverage/APA/9368

Ghahramanlou-Holloway, M., Brown, G. K., & Beck, A. T. (2008). Suicide. In M. A. Whisman (Ed.), *Adapting cognitive therapy for depression: Managing complexity and comorbidity* (pp. 159–184). New York: Guilford Press.

Ghazizadeh, S., & Nikzad, M. (2004). Botulinum toxin in the treatment of refractory vaginismus. *Obs. Gyn., 104*(5, Pt. 1), 922–925.

Gheorghiu, V. A., & Orleanu, P. (1982). Dental implant under hypnosis. *Amer. J. Clin. Hyp., 25*(1), 68–70.

Ghetti, S., Schaaf, J. M., Qin, J., & Goodman, G. S. (2004). Issues in eyewitness testimony. In W. T. O'Donohue & E. R. Levensky (Eds.), *Handbook of forensic psychology: Resource for mental health and legal professionals* (pp. 513–554). New York: Elsevier Science.

Ghika, J., & Bogousslavsky, J. (2002). Vascular dementia after stroke. In J. Bogousslavsky (Ed.), *Long-term effects of stroke* (pp. 235–262). New York: Marcel Dekker.

Ghosh, A., & Greist, J. H. (1988). Computer treatment in psychiatry. *Psychiatr. Ann., 18*(4), 246–250.

Gianaros, P. J., May, J. C., Siegle, G. J., & Jennings, J. R. (2005). Is there a functional neural correlate of individual differences in cardiovascular reactivity? *Psychosom. Med., 67*(1), 31–39.

Gianoulakis, C. (2001). Influence of the endogenous opioid system on high alcohol consumption and genetic predisposition to alcoholism. *J. Psychiat. Neurosci., 26*(4), 304–318.

Gibbons, M. M., & Studer, J. R. (2008). Suicide awareness training for faculty and staff: A training model for school counselors. *Profess. School Couns., 11*(4), 272–276.

Gibbs, M. S. (1989). Factors in the victim that mediate between disaster and psychopathology: A review. *J. Traum. Stress, 2*(4), 489–514.

Gilbert, S. C., Keery, H., & Thompson, J. K. (2005). The media's role in body image and eating disorders. In J. H. Daniel & E. Cole (Eds.), *Featuring females: Feminist analyses of media* (pp. 41–56). Washington, DC: American Psychological Association.

Gill, A. D. (1982). Vulnerability to suicide. In E. L. Bassuk, S. C. Schoonover, & A. D. Gill (Eds.), *Lifelines: Clinical perspectives on suicide.* New York: Plenum Press.

Gill, R. E. (2008). Historic parity bill expected to pass. *Natl. Psychologist, 17*(4), 1.

Gillham, J. E., Reivich, K. J., Jaycox, L. H., & Seligman, M. E. (1995). Prevention of depressive symptoms in schoolchildren: Two-year follow-up. *Psychol. Sci., 6*(6), 343–351.

Gillham, J. E., Shatte, A. J., & Freres, D. R. (2000). Preventing depression: A review of cognitive-behavioral and family interventions. *Appl. Prev. Psychol., 9,* 63–88.

Gillis, J. M., & Romanczyk, R. G. (2007). Autism spectrum disorders and related developmental disabilities. In M. Hersen & A. M. Gross (Eds.), *Handbook of clinical psychology* (Vol. 2). Hoboken, NJ: John Wiley & Sons.

Gioia, G. (2007). Expert: Millions get concussions. *Philly.com.* Retrieved April 23, 2007, from http://www.philly.com/dailynews/sports/20070421_Expert_Millions_get_concussions.html

Girdhar, S., Leenaars, A. A., Dogra, T. D., Leenaars, L., & Kumar, G. (2004). Suicide notes in India: What do they tell us? *Arch. Suic. Res., 8*(2), 179–185.

Gitlin, M. J. (2002). Pharmacological treatment of depression. In I. H. Gotlib & C. L. Hammen (Eds.), *Handbook of depression* (pp. 360–382). New York: Guilford Press.

Gjerdingen, D. K., & Center, B. A. (2005). First-time parents' postpartum changes in employment, childcare, and housework responsibilities. *Soc. Sci. Res., 34*(1), 103–116.

Glaser, G. (2008). Anxious about Earth's troubles? There's treatment. *New York Times,* Feb. 16, 2008.

Glass, C. R., & Merluzzi, T. V. (2000). Cognitive and behavioral assessment. In C. E. Watkins, Jr., & V. L. Campbell (Eds.), *Testing and assessment in counseling practice* (2nd ed.). Mahwah, NJ: Lawrence Erlbaum.

Glatt, S. J. (2008). Genetics. In K. T. Mueser & D. V. Jeste (Eds.), *Clinical handbook of schizophrenia* (pp. 55–64). New York: Guilford Press.

Glazer, M., Baer, R. D., Weller, S. C., de-Alba, J. E. G., & Liebowitz, S. W. (2004). Susto and soul loss in Mexicans and Mexican Americans. *J. Comp. Soc. Sci., 38*(3), 270–288.

Gleaves, D. H., & Latner, J. D. (2008). Evidence-based therapies for children and adolescents with eating disorders. In R. G. Steele, T. D. Elkin, & M. C. Roberts (Eds.), *Handbook of evidence-based therapies for children and adolescents: Bridging science and practice.* New York: Springer.

Glisky, E. L., Ryan, L., Reminger, S., Hardt, O., Hayes, S. M., & Hupbach, A. (2004). A case of psychogenic fugue: I understand, aber ich verstehe nichts. *Neuropsychologia, 42*(8), 1132–1147.

Gluck, J. P., & Bell, J. (2003). Ethical issues in the use of animals in biomedical and psychopharmacological research. *Psychopharmacology, 171*(1), 6–12.

Godart, N. T., Curt, F., Perdereau, F., Lang, F., Venisse, J. L., Halfon, O., et al. (2005). La frequence des troubles anxio-depressifs differe-t-elle entre les types diagnostiques d'anorexia mentale et de boulimie?/Are anxiety or depressive disorders more frequent among one of the anorexia or bulimia nervosa subtype? *L'Encephale, 31*(3), 279–288.

Goddard, J. (2003, February 22). Tragedy strikes United States once more. *The Scotsman.*

Godenzi, A., & DePuy, J. (2001). Overcoming boundaries: A cross-cultural inventory of primary prevention programs against wife abuse and child abuse. *J. Primary Prev., 21*(4), 455–475.

Goin, M. K. (2001). Borderline personality disorder: The importance of establishing a treatment framework. *Psychiatr. Serv., 52*(2), 167–168.

Goisman, R. M., Warshaw, M. G., & Keller, M. B. (1999). Psychosocial treatment prescriptions for generalized anxiety disorder, panic disorder, and social phobia, 1991–1996. *Amer. J. Psychiat., 156*(11), 1819–1821.

Gold, E. R. (1986). Long-term effects of sexual victimization in childhood: An attributional approach. *J. Cons. Clin. Psychol., 54,* 471–475.

Goldapple, K., Segal, Z., Garson, C., Lau, M., Bieling, P., Kennedy, S., & Mayberg, H. (2004). Modulation of cortical-limbic pathways in major depression. *Arch. Gen. Psychiat., 61*(1), 34–41.

Golden, C. J. (2008). Neurologically impaired children. In D. Reitman (Ed.), *Handbook of psychological assessment, case conceptualization, and treatment, Vol. 2: Children and adolescents.* Hoboken, NJ: John Wiley & Sons.

Golden, R. N., Gaynes, B. N., Ekstrom, R. D., Damer, R. M., Jacobsen, F. M., Suppes, T., et al. (2005). The efficacy of light therapy in the treatment of mood disorders: A review and meta-analysis of the evidence. *Amer. J. Psychiat., 162*(4), 656–662.

Goldenberg, I., & Goldenberg, H. (2008). Family therapy. In R. J. Corsini & D. Wedding (Eds.), *Current psychotherapies* (8th ed.). Belmont, CA: Thomson Brooks/Cole.

Goldfield, G. S., Blouin, A. G., & Woodside, D. B. (2006). Body image, binge eating, and bulimia nervosa in male bodybuilders. *Canadian Journal of Psychiatry, 51*(3), 160–168.

Goldfried, M. R., & Wolfe, B. E. (1996). Psychotherapy practice and research. Repairing a strained alliance. *Amer. Psychologist, 51*(10), 1007–1016.

Goldiamond, I. (1965). Self-control procedures in personal behavior problems. *Psychol. Rep., 17,* 851–868.

Golding, J., Fryman, H., Marsil, D., & Yozwiak, J. (2003). Big girls don't cry: The effect of child witness demeanor on juror decisions in a child sexual abuse trial. *Child Abuse Negl., 27,* 1311–1321.

Goldman, J. G. (1995). A mutual story-telling technique as an aid to integration after abreaction in the treatment of MPD. *Dissociat. Prog. Dissociat. Disorders 8*(1), 53–60.

Goldman-Rakic, P. S., Castner, S. A., Svensson, T. H., et al. (2004). Targeting the dopamine D1 receptor in schizophrenia: Insights for cognitive dysfunction. *Psychopharmacology, 174,* 3–16.

Goldney, R. D. (2003). Deinstitutionalization and suicide. *Crisis, 24*(1), 39–40.

Goldstein, A. (1994). *Addiction: From biology to drug policy.* New York: W. H. Freeman.

Goldston, D. B., Molock, S. D., Whitbeck, L. B., Murakami, J. L., Zayas, L. H., & Hall, G. C. N. (2008). Cultural considerations in adolescent suicide prevention and psychosocial treatment. *Amer. Psychologist, 63*(1), 14–31.

Gollan J. K., & Jacobson N. S. (2002). Developments in couple therapy research. In H. A. Liddle, D. A. Santiseban, R. F. Levant, & J. H. Bray (Eds.), *Family psychology: Science-based interventions.* Washington, DC: American Psychological Association.

Golub, D. (1995). Cultural variations in multiple personality disorder, In L. M. Cohen, J. N. Berzoff, M. R. Elin (Eds.), *Dissociative identity disorder.* Northvale, NJ: Jason Aronson.

Gonzalez, M., de Pablo, J., Valdes, M., Matrai, S., Peri, J. M., & Fuente, E. (2005). Delirium: A predictor of mortality in the elderly. *Eur. J. Psychiat., 19*(3), 165–171.

Gonzalez, M.-J., & Acevedo, G. (2006). Psychological intervention with Hispanic patients: A review of selected culturally syntonic treatment approaches. In S. Rosenberg & J. Rosenberg (Eds.), *Community mental health: Challenges for the 21st century* (pp. 153–165). New York: Routledge.

Gonzalez-Brignardello, M. P., & Vazquez, A. M. M. (2004). Intervention in a case of post-traumatic stress disorder with EMDR within a cognitive behavioral setting. *Clinica y Salud, 15*(3), 337–354.

Good, G. E., & Brooks, G. R. (Eds.). (2005). *The new handbook of psychotherapy and counseling with men: A comprehensive guide to settings, problems, and treatment approaches* (Rev. & abridged ed.). San Francisco, CA: Jossey-Bass.

Goode, E., & Vail, D. A. (Eds.). (2008). *Extreme deviance.* Los Angeles: Pine Forge Press.

Goodman, S. H. (2002). Depression and early adverse experiences. In I. H. Gotlib & C. L. Hammen (Eds.), *Handbook of depression* (pp. 245–267). New York: Guilford Press.

Goodman-Brown, T. B., Edelstein, R. S., Goodman, G. S., Jones, D. P. H., & Gordon, D. S. (2003). Why children tell: A model of children's disclosure of sexual abuse. *Child Abuse and Neglect, 27,* 525–540.

Goodwin, C. J. (2008). *Research in psychology: Methods and design* (5th ed.) Hoboken, NJ: John Wiley & Sons.

Goodwin, F. K., & Jamison, K. R. (1984). The natural course of manic-depressive illness. In R. M. Post & J. C. Ballenger (Eds.), *Neurobiology of mood disorders.* Baltimore: Williams & Wilkins.

Gopaul-McNicol, S., & Armour-Thomas, E. (2002). *Assessment and culture: Psychological tests with minority populations.* San Diego, CA: Academic.

Gordon, J. (2005). Diversity in health care. In N. Borkowski (Ed.), *Organizational behavior in health care* (pp. 15–41). Boston, MA: Jones & Bartlett Publishers.

Gordon, K. H., Perez, M., & Joiner, T. E., Jr. (2002). The impact of racial stereotypes on eating disorder recognition. *Int. J. Eat. Dis., 32,* 219–224.

Gorman, J. M. (2003). Does the brain noradrenaline network mediate the effects of the CO-sub-2 challenge? *J. Psychopharmacol., 17*(3), 265–266.

Gormley, M. (The Associated Press). (2008). MySpace agrees to new safety measures. Cited in *YAHOO! News,* January 14, 2008.

Goshen, C. E. (1967). Documentary history of psychiatry: A source book on historical principles. New York: Philosophy Library.

Gottesman, I. I. (1991). *Schizophrenia genesis.* New York: Freeman.

Gottesman, I. I., & Reilly, J. L. (2003). Strengthening the evidence for genetic factors in schizophrenia (without abetting genetic discrimination). In M. F. Lenzenweger & J. M. Hooley (Eds.), *Principles of experimental psychopathology: Essays in honor of Brendan A. Maher* (pp. 31–44). Washington, DC: American Psychological Association.

Gottesman, I. I., & Shields, J. (1983). Genetic theorizing and schizophrenia. In T. Millon (Ed.), *Theories of personality and psychopathology* (3rd ed.). New York: Holt, Rinehart and Winston.

Gottfredson, L. S. (2005). Suppressing intelligence research: Hurting those we intend to help. In N. A. Cummings, & R. H. Wright (Eds.), *Destructive trends in mental health: The well-intentioned path to harm* (pp. 155–186). New York: Routledge.

Gould, M. S., Midle, J. B., Insel, B., & Kleinman, M. (2007). Suicide reporting content analysis: Abstract development and reliability. *Crisis: J. Crisis Intervent. Suic. Prev., 28*(4), 165–174.

Gould, M. S., Shaffer, D., & Davies, M. (1990). Truncated pathways from childhood to adulthood: Attrition in follow-up studies due to death. In L. Robins & M. Rutter (Eds.), *Straight and devious pathways from childhood to adulthood.* Cambridge, England: Cambridge University Press.

Gould, M. S., Shaffer, D., & Greenberg, T. (2003). The epidemiology of youth suicide. In R. A. King & A. Apter (Eds.), *Suicide in children and adolescents* (pp. 1–40). Cambridge, England: Cambridge University Press.

Gowers, S. G., Weetman, J., Shore, A., Hossairn, F., & Elvins, R. (2000). Impact of hospitalization on the outcome of anorexia nervosa. *Br. J. Psychiat., 176*(2), 138–141.

Grace, S. L., Evindar, A., & Stewart, D. E. (2003). The effect of postpartum depression on child cognitive development and behavior: A review and critical analysis of the literature. *Arch. Women's Ment. Hlth., 6*(4), 263–274.

Grady, D. (2008, January 8). Empathy goes a long way. *New York Times.*

Graff-Radford, N. (2005). Plasma Aβ Levels as a premorbid biomarker for cognitive decline, mild cognitive impairment (MCI) and Alzheimer disease (AD). *Alzheimer's Association International Conference on Prevention of Dementia,* June 18, 2005, Washington, DC.

Graham, J. R. (2006). *MMPI-2: Assessing personality and psychopathology* (4th ed.). New York: Oxford University Press.

Graham, M. (2007). Brain "pacemaker" tickles your happy nerve. *Wired.* Retrieved May 26, 2008, from http://www.wired.com/science/discoveries/news/2007/05/nerve

Gray, H. (1959). *Anatomy of the human body* (27th ed.). Philadelphia: Lea & Febiger.

Gray, J. A., & McNaughton, N. (1996). The neuropsychology of anxiety: Reprise. In D. A. Hope (Ed.), *The Nebraska symposium on motivation* (Vol. 43). Lincoln: University of Nebraska Press.

Gray, J., Nielsen, D. R., Wood, L. E., Andresen, M., & Dolce, K. (2000). Academic progress of children who attended a preschool for abused children: A follow-up of the Keepsafe Project. *Child Abuse Negl., 24*(1), 25–32.

Gray, N. A., Zhou, R., Du, J., Moore, G. J., & Manji, H. K. (2003). The use of mood stabilizers as plasticity enhancers in the treatment of neuropsychiatric disorders. *J. Clin. Psychiat., 64*(Suppl. 5), 3–17.

Green, R. (2000). Family cooccurrence of "gender dysphoria": Ten siblings or parent-child pairs. *Arch. Sex. Behav., 29*(5), 499–507.

Green, S., & Bloch, S. (2006). *An anthology of psychiatric ethics.* New York: Oxford University Press.

Green, S. A. (1985). *Mind and body: The psychology of physical illness.* Washington, DC: American Psychiatric Press.

Greenberg, D., & Felthous, A. R. (2007). The insanity defense and psychopathic disorders in the United States and Australia. In A. Felthous & H. Sass, *International handbook of psychopathic disorders and the law* (Vol. 2). Hoboken, NJ: Wiley.

Greenberg, L. S., Elliott, R., & Lietaer, G. (1994). Research on experiential psychotherapies. In A. E. Bergin & S. L. Garfield (Eds.), *Handbook of psychotherapy and behavior change.* New York: Wiley.

Greenberg, L. S., Watson, J. C., & Lietaer, G. (Eds.). (1998). *Handbook of experiential psychotherapy.* New York: Guilford Press.

Greenberg, P. E., Kessler, R. C., Birnbaum, H. G., Leong, S. A., Lowe, S. W., Berglund, P. A., et al. (2003). The economic burden of depression in the United States: How did it change between 1990 and 2000? *J. Clin. Psychiat., 64*(12), 1465–1475.

Greene, E., & Ellis, L. (2007). Decision making in criminal justice. In D. Carson, R. Milne, F. Pakes, K. Shalev, & A. Shawyer (Eds.), *Applying psychology to criminal justice.* Hoboken, NJ: John Wiley & Sons.

Greene, R. L. (2006). Forensic applications of the Minnesota Multiphasic Personality Inventory-2. In A. M. Goldstein (Ed.), *Forensic psychology: Emerging topics and expanding roles* (pp. 73–96). Hoboken, NJ: Wiley.

Greening, L., Stoppelbein, L., Fite, P., Dhossche, D., Erath, S., Brown, J., et al. (2008). Pathways to suicidal behaviors in childhood. *Suic., Life-Threat. Behav., 38*(1), 35–45.

Greer, S. (1999). Mind-body research in psychooncology. *Adv. Mind-Body Med., 15*(4), 236–244.

Greeven, A., van Balkom, A. J. L. M., Visser, S., Merkelbach, J. W., van Rood, Y. R., van Dyck, R., et al. (2007). Cognitive behavior therapy and paroxetine in the treatment of hypochondriasis: A randomized controlled trial. *Amer. J. Psychiat., 164,* 91–99.

Gregory, R. J. (2004). *Psychological testing: History, principles, and applications.* Needham Heights, MA: Allyn and Bacon.

Grekin, P. M., Jemelka, R., & Trupin, E. W. (1994). Racial differences in the criminalization of the mentally ill. *Bull. Amer. Acad. Psychiat. Law, 22,* 411–420.

Griffiths, K. M., & Christensen, H. (2006). Review of randomised controlled trials of Internet interventions for mental disorders and related conditions. *Austral. Psychol. Soc., 10*(1), 16–29.

Grigg, J. R. (1988). Imitative suicides in an active duty military population. *Military Med., 153*(2), 79–81.

Grilly, D. M. (2002). *Drugs and human behavior* (4th ed.). Boston: Allyn and Bacon.

Grilly, D. M. (2006). *Drugs and human behavior* (5th ed.). Boston: Pearson.

Grilo, C. M. (2006). *Eating and weight disorders.* New York: Psychology Press.

Grilo, C. M., & Masheb, R. M. (2002). Childhood maltreatment and personality disorders in adult patients with binge eating disorder. *Acta Psychiat. Scandin., 106*(3), 183–188.

Grilo, C. M., Masheb, R. M., Brody, M., Toth, C., Burke-Martindale, C. H., & Rothschild, B. S. (2005). Childhood maltreatment in extremely obese male and female bariatric surgery candidates. *Obesity Res., 13,* 123–130.

Grinfield, M. J. (1993, July). Report focuses on jailed mentally ill. *Psychiat. Times,* pp. 1–3.

Grinspoon, L., et al. (Eds.). (1986). Paraphilias. *Harvard Med. Sch. Ment. Health Newsl., 3*(6), 1–5.

Grob, G. N. (1966). *State and the mentally ill: A history of Worcester State Hospital in Massachusetts, 1830–1920.* Chapel Hill: University of North Carolina Press.

Grof, P. (2005). Lithium in bipolar disorder. In S. Kasper & R. M. A. Hirschfeld (Eds.), *Handbook of bipolar disorder: Diagnosis and therapeutic approaches* (pp. 267–284). New York: Taylor & Francis.

Gross, D. (2005, June 21). Marijuana-flavored candy blasted. *Associated Press (Atlanta)/Netscape News.*

Grossman, R. (2004). Pharmacotherapy of personality disorders. In J. J. Magnavita (Ed.), *Handbook of personality disorders: Theory and practice.* Hoboken, NJ: Wiley.

Grove, W. M., Zald, D. H., Lebow, B. S., Snitz, B. E., & Nelson, C. (2000). Clinical versus mechanical prediction: A meta-analysis. *Psychol. Assess., 12,* 19–30.

Grubin, D. (2005). Commentary: Getting at the truth about pathological lying. *J. Amer. Acad. Psychiat. Law, 33*(3), 350–353.

Gruenberg, E. M. (1980). Mental disorders. In J. M. Last (Ed.), *Maxcy-Rosenau public health and preventive medicine* (11th ed.). New York: Appleton-Century-Crofts.

Gruettert, T., & Friege, L. (2005). Quetiapine in patients with borderline personality disorder and psychosis: A case series. *Inter. J. Psychiat. Clin. Pract., 9*(3), 180–186.

Grunhaus, L., Schreiber, S., Dolberg, O. T., Polak, D., & Dannon, P. N. (2003). A randomized controlled comparison of electroconvulsive therapy and repetitive transcranial magnetic stimulation in severe and resistant nonpsychotic major depression. *Biol. Psychiat., 53,* 324–331.

Grunze, H. (2005). Reevaluating therapies for bipolar depression. *J. Clin Psychiat., 66*(Suppl. 5), 17–25.

Gruttadaro, D. (2005). Federal leaders call on schools to help. *NAMI Advocate, 3*(1), 7.

Guimón, J. (2004). Evidence-based research studies on the results of group therapy: A critical review. *Eur. J. Psychiat., 18*(Suppl), 49–60.

Gunderson, J. G. (1988). Personality disorders. In A. M. Nicholi, Jr. (Ed.), *The new Harvard guide to psychiatry.* Cambridge, MA: Belknap Press.

Gunderson, J. G. (1996). The borderline patient's intolerance of aloneness: Insecure attachments and therapist availability. *Amer. J. Psychiat., 153*(6), 752–758.

Gunderson, J. G. (2001). *Borderline personality disorder: A clinical guide.* Washington, DC: American Psychiatric Publishing.

Gunter, M. (2005). Individual psychotherapy versus milieu therapy in childhood and adolescence. *Ther. Comm., 26*(2), 163–173.

Gurman, A. S. (2003). Marital therapies. In A. S. Gurman & S. B. Messer (Eds.), *Essential psychotherapies: Theory and practice* (2nd ed.). New York: Guilford Press.

Gurnack, A. M., Atkinson, R., & Osgood, N. J. (Eds.). (2002). *Treating alcohol and drug abuse in the elderly.* New York: Springer.

Guth, L. J., Lopez, D. F., Rojas, J., Clements, K. D., & Tyler, J. M. (2004). Experiential versus rational training: A comparison of student attitudes toward homosexuality. *J. Homosexuality, 48*(2), 83–102.

Gutheil, T. G. (2005). Boundary issues and personality disorders. *J. Psychiat. Pract., 11*(2), 88–96.

Guttman, H. A. (2002). The epigenesis of the family system as a context for individual development. *Fam. Process, 41*(3), 533–545.

Haberman, C. (2007). It's not the stress, it's how you deal with it. *New York Times, 156*(54), 109).

Hadley, S. W., & Strupp, H. H. (1976). Contemporary views of negative effects in psychotherapy: An integrated account. *Arch. Gen. Psychiat., 33*(1), 1291–1302.

Hafner, H., & an der Heiden, W. (1988). The mental health care system in transition: A study in organization, effectiveness, and costs of complementary care for schizophrenic patients. In C. N. Stefanis & A. D. Rabavilis (Eds.), *Schizophrenia: Recent biosocial developments.* New York: Human Sciences Press.

Hafner, H., & an der Heiden, W. (2008). Course and outcome. In K. T. Mueser & D. V. Jeste (Eds.), *Clinical handbook of schizophrenia* (pp. 100–113). New York: Guilford Press.

Hage, S. M., Romano, J. L., Conyne, R. K., Kenny, M., Matthews, C., Schwartz, J. P., et al. (2007). Best practice guidelines on prevention practice, research, training, and social advocacy for psychologists. *Counsel. Psychologist, 35*(4), 493–566.

Hakuhodo Institute of Life and Living. (2001). What price beauty? *From the HILL, 7*(4).

Hale, C. M., & Tager-Flusberg, H. (2005). Social communication in children with autism: The relationship between theory of mind and discourse development. *Autism, 9*(2), 157–178.

Hale, E. (1983, April 17). Inside the divided mind. *New York Times Magazine,* pp. 100–106.

Haliburn, J. (2005). Australian and New Zealand clinical practice guidelines for the treatment of anorexia nervosa. *Austral. New Zeal. J. Psychiat., 39*(7), 639–640.

Hall, C. W., & Webster, R. E. (2002). Traumatic symptomatology characteristics of adult children of alcoholics. *J. Drug Educ., 32*(3), 195–211.

Hall, F. S., Sora, I., Drgonova, J., Li, X. F., Goeb, M., & Uhl, G. R. (2004). Molecular mechanisms underlying the rewarding effects of cocaine. In T. Nabeshima, T. Yanagita, & S. Ali (Eds.), *Current status of drug dependence/abuse studies: Cellular and molecular mechanisms of drugs of abuse and neurotoxicity* (pp. 47–66). New York: New York Academy of Sciences.

Hall, K. (2007). Sexual dysfunction and childhood sexual abuse: Gender differences and treatment implications. In S. R. Leiblum (Ed.), *Principles and practice of sex therapy* (4th ed., pp. 350–370). New York: Guilford Press.

Hall, L., with Cohn, L. (1980). *Eat without fear.* Santa Barbara, CA: Gurze.

Hall, T. M., Kaduson, H. G., & Schaefer, C. E. (2002). Fifteen effective play therapy techniques. *Profess. Psychol.: Res. Pract., 33*(6), 515–522.

Halloway, J. D. (2004). California psychologists prepare for hospital privileges battle. *APA Monitor on Psychology, 35*(1), 28–29.

Halls, S. B., & Hanson, J. (2003). Women's average weight chart and percent distribution. Retrieved January 2006 from www.halls.md/chart/height-weight.htm

Halmi, K. A. (1995). Current concepts and definitions. In G. Szmukler, C. Dare, & J. Treasure (Eds.), *Handbook of eating disorders: Theory, treatment and research.* Chichester, England: Wiley.

Ham, L. S., Hope, D. A., White, C. S., & Rivers, P. C. (2002). Alcohol expectancies and drinking behavior in adults with social anxiety disorder and dysthymia. *Cog. Ther. Res., 26*(2), 275–288.

Hammen, C. L., & Glass, D. R. (1975). Expression, activity, and evaluation of reinforcement. *J. Abnorm. Psychol., 84*(6), 718–721.

Hammen, C. L., & Krantz, S. (1976). Effect of success and failure on depressive cognitions. *J. Abnorm. Psychol., 85*(8), 577–588.

Han, C., Pae, C. U., Lee, B. H., Ko, Y. H., Masand, P. S., Patkar, A. A., et al. (2008). Fluoxetine versus sertraline in the treatment of patients with undifferentiated somatoform disorder: A randomized, open-label, 12-week, parallel-group trial. *Prog. Neuropsychopharmacol. Biol. Psychiat., 32*(2), 437–444.

Handelman, L. D., & Lester, D. (2007). The content of suicide notes from attempters and completers. *Crisis, 28,* 102–104.

Haney, M. (2008). Neurobiology of stimulants. In H. D. Kleber & M. Galanter (Eds.), *The American Psychiatric Publishing textbook of substance abuse treatment* (4th ed., pp. 143–155). Arlington, VA: American Psychiatric Publishing.

Hankin, B. L., & Abramson, L. Y. (2001). Development of gender differences in depression: An elaborated cognitive vulnerability-transactional stress theory. *Psychol. Bull., 127,* 773–796.

Hankin, B. L., Grant, K. E., Cheeley, C., Wetter, E., Farahmand, F. K., & Westerholm, R. I. (2008). Depressive disorders. In D. Reitman (Ed.), *Handbook of psychological assessment, case conceptualization, and treatment, Vol. 2: Children and adolescents.* Hoboken, NJ: John Wiley & Sons.

Hankin, J. R. (2002). Fetal alcohol syndrome prevention research. *Alc. Res. Hlth., 26*(1), 58–65.

Hansson, L., Middelboe, T., Sorgaard, K. W., Bengtsson, T. A., Bjarnason, O., Merinder, L., et al. (2002). Living situation, subjective quality of life and social network among individuals with schizophrenia living in community settings. *Acta Pyschiatr. Scandin., 106*(5), 343–350.

Hansson, R. O., & Stroebe, M. S. (2007). *Bereavement in late life: Coping, adaptation, and developmental influences.* Washington, DC: American Psychological Association.

Hardin, S. B., Weinrich, S., Weinrich, M., Garrison, C., Addy, C., & Hardin, T. L. (2002). Effects of a long-term psychosocial nursing intervention on adolescents exposed to catastrophic stress. *Issues Ment. Hlth. Nurs., 23*(6), 537–551.

Harding, A., Halliday, G., Caine, D., & Kril, J. (2000). Degeneration of anterior thalamic nuclei differentiates alcoholics with amnesia. *Brain, 123*(1), 141–154.

Hardman, M. L., Drew, C. J., & Egan, M. W. (2002). *Human exceptionality: Society, school and family.* Boston: Allyn & Bacon.

Hare, R. D. (1993). *Without conscience: The disturbing world of the psychopaths among us.* New York: Pocket Books.

Harkavy, J. M., & Asnis, G. (1985). Suicide attempts in adolescence: Prevalence and implications. *N. Engl. J. Med., 313,* 1290–1291.

Harkness, K. L., & Lumley, M. N. (2008). Child abuse and neglect and the development of depression in children and adolescents. In J. R. Z. Abela & B. L. Hankin (Eds.), *Handbook of depression in children and adolescents.* New York: Guilford Press.

Harlow, H. F., & Harlow, M. K. (1965). The affectional systems. In A. Schrier, H. Harlow, & F. Stollnitz (Eds.), *Behavior of nonhuman primates* (Vol. 2). New York: Academic Press.

Harlow, H. F., & Zimmermann, R. R. (1996). Affectional responses in the infant monkey. In L. C. Drickamer & L. D. Houck (Eds.), *Foundations of animal behavior: Classic papers with commentaries* (pp. 376–387). Chicago, IL: University of Chicago Press.

Haroules, B. (2007). Involuntary commitment is unconstitutional. In A. Quigley (Ed.), *Current controversies: Mental health.* Detroit: Greenhaven Press/Thomson Gale.

Harper, P. B., & Dwivedi, K. N. (Eds.). (2004). *Promoting the emotional well-being of children and adolescents and preventing their mental ill health: A handbook.* Philadelphia: Jessica Kingsley.

Harris Poll. (2005, April 27). *Majorities of U.S. adults favor euthanasia and physician-assisted suicide by more than two-to-one* (Harris Poll, No. 32). Retrieved June 9, 2008, from www. harrisinteractive.com.harris_poll

Harris Poll. (2006, August 8). *Doctors and teachers most trusted among 22 occupations and professions: Fewer adults trust the president to tell the truth* (Harris Poll, No. 61). Retrieved June 9, 2008, from http://www.harrisinteractive.com/harris_poll

Harris Poll. (2007, July 31). *Harris Poll shows number of "cyberchondriacs"—adults who have ever gone online for health information—increases to an estimated 160 million nationwide* (Harris Poll, No. 76). New York: Harris Interactive.

Harris Poll. (2008, April 4). *Cell phone usage continues to increase* (Harris Poll, No. 36). Retrieved June 9, 2008, from http://www.harrisinteractive.com/harris_poll

Harris Poll. (2008, April 22). *Americans who are religious and older people are happier. Harris Poll Interactive, #46.*

Harris, A., Ayers, T., & Leek, M. R. (1985). Auditory span of apprehension deficits in schizophrenia. *J. Nerv. Ment. Dis., 173*(11), 650–657.

Harris, E. C., & Barraclough, B. (1998). Excess mortality of mental disorder. *Brit. J. Psychiat., 173,* 11–53.

Harris, G. (2008, January 24). F.D.A. requiring suicide studies in drug trials. *New York Times.* Retrieved January 24, 2008, from www.nytimes.com

Harris, G. T., & Rice, M.,E. (2006). Treatment of psychopathy: A review of empirical findings. In C. J. Patrick (Ed.), *Handbook of psychopathy.* New York: Guilford Press.

Harris, K. M., Carpenter, C., & Bao, Y. (2006). The effects of state parity laws on the use of mental health care. *Med. Care., 44*(6), 499–505.

Harris, R. J. (2003). Traditional nomothetic approaches. In S. F. Davis (Ed.), *Handbook of research methods in experimental psychology* (pp. 42–65). Malden, MA: Blackwell Publishers.

Harrison, P. J., & Weinberger, D. R. (2005). Schizophrenia genes, gene expression, and neuropathology: On the matter of their convergence. *Mol. Psychiat., 10*(8), 804.

Harrow, M., Grossman, L. S., Jobe, T. H., & Herbener, E. S. (2005). Do patients with schizophrenia ever show periods of recovery? A 15-year multi-site follow-up study. *Schizo. Bull., 31,* 723–734.

Hartley, T. A., Violanti, J. M., Fekedulegn, D., Andrew, M. E., & Burchfield, C. M. (2007). Associations between major life events, traumatic incidents, and depression among Buffalo police officers. *Inter. J. Emerg. Ment. Hlth., 9*(1), 25–35.

Hartman, M., Steketee, M. C., Silva, S., Lanning, K., & McCann, H. (2003). Working memory and schizophrenia: Evidence for slowed encoding. *Schizo. Res., 59*(2–3), 99–113.

Hartmann, U., Philippsohn, S., Heiser, K., & Rüffer-Hesse, C. (2004). Low desire in midlife and older women: Personality factors, psychosocial development, present sexuality. *Menopause, 11*(6), 726–740.

Hartmann, U., & Waldinger, M. D. (2007). Treatment of delayed ejaculation. In S. R. Leiblum (Ed.), *Principles and practice of sex therapy* (4th ed., pp.241–276). New York: Guilford Press.

Hartocollis, A. (2008, February 20). Actions considered insane often don't meet the standards of New York's legal system. *New York Times.* Retrieved February 25, 2008, from http:/// www.nytimes.com

Harway, M. (Ed.). (2005). *Handbook of couples therapy.* New York: Wiley.

Hasman, A., & Holm, S. (2004). Nicotine conjugate vaccine: Is there a right to a smoking future? *J. Med. Ethics, 30*(4), 344–345.

Hassett, A., Ames, D., & Chiu, E. (Eds.). (2005). *Psychosis in the elderly.* New York: Taylor & Francis.

Hastings, R. P. (2008). Stress in parents of children with autism. In E. McGregor, M. Núñez, K. Cebula, & J. C. Gómez (Eds.), *Autism: An integrated view from neurocognitive, clinical, and intervention research.* Malden, MA: Blackwell Publishing.

Hätönen, T., Alila, A., & Laakso, M. L. (1996). Exogenous melatonin fails to counteract the light-induced phase delay of human melatonin rhythm. *Brain Res., 710*(1–2), 125–130.

Hausman, A. (2008). Direct-to-consumer advertising and its effect on prescription requests. *J. Advert. Res., 48*(1), 42–56.

Haw, R. M., & Fisher, R. P. (2004). Effects of administrator-witness contact on identification accuracy. *J. Appl. Psychol., 89,* 1106–1112.

Hawkins, J. R. (2004). The role of emotional repression in chronic back pain: A study of chronic back pain patients undergoing psychodynamically oriented group psychotherapy as treatment for their pain. *Diss. Abstr. Inter.: Sect. B: Sci. Eng., 64*(8-B), 4038.

Hawkrigg, J. J. (1975). Agoraphobia. *Nursing Times, 71,* 1280–1282.

Hawton, K. (2001). The treatment of suicidal behavior in the context of the suicidal process. In K. van Heeringen (Ed.), *Understanding suicidal behavior: The suicidal process approach to research, treatment and prevention* (pp. 212–229). Chichester, England: Wiley.

Hawton, K. (2007). Restricting access to methods of suicide: Rationale and evaluation of this approach to suicide prevention. *Crisis: J. Crisis Intervent. Suic. Prev., 28*(Suppl. 1), 4–9.

Haxby, J. V., Ungerleider, L. G., Horwitz, B., Maisog, J. M., Rapoport, S. I., & Grady, C. L. (1996). Face encoding and recognition in the human brain. *Proc. Nat. Acad. Sci. USA, 93*(2), 922–927.

Hayaki, J., Friedman, M. A., & Brownell, K. D. (2002). Shame and severity of bulimic symptoms. *Eat. Behav., 3*(1), 73–83.

Hayden, L. A. (1998). Gender discrimination within the reproductive health care system: Viagra v. birth control. *J. Law Health, 13,* 171–198.

Hayes, L. M., & Rowan, J. R. (1988). *National study of jail suicides: Seven years later.* Alexandria, VA: National Center for Institutions and Alternatives.

Hayes, S. C. (2002). Acceptance, mindfulness, and science. *Clin. Psychol.: Sci. Prac., 9,* 101–106.

Hayes, S. C. (2004). Acceptance and commitment therapy and the new behavior therapies. In S. C. Hayes, V. M. Follette, & M. M. Linehan (Eds.), *Mindfulness and acceptance: Expanding the cognitive-behavioral tradition* (pp. 1–29). New York: Guilford Press.

Hayes, S. C., Follette, V. M., & Linehan, M. M. (Eds.). (2004). *Mindfulness and acceptance: Expanding the cognitive-behavioral tradition.* New York: Guilford Press.

Hayes, S. C., Luoma, J. B., Bond, F. W., Masuda, A., & Lillis, J. (2006). Acceptance and commitment therapy: Model, processes and outcomes. *Behav. Res. Ther., 44,* 1–25.

Haynes, S. G., Feinleib, M., & Kannel, W. B. (1980). The relationship of psychosocial factors to coronary heart disease in the Framingham study: III. Eight-year incidence of coronary heart disease. *Amer. J. Epidemiol., 111,* 37–58.

Haynes, S. N. (2001). Clinical applications of analog behavioral observations: Dimensions of psychometric evaluations. *Psychol. Assess., 13*(1), 73–85.

Haynes, S. N. (2001). Introduction to the special section on clinical applications of analogue behavioral observation. *Psychol. Assess., 13*(1), 3–4.

Hayward, M. D., & Taylor, J. E. (1965). A schizophrenic patient describes the action of intensive psychotherapy. *Psychiat. Quart., 30.*

HBIGDA (Harry Benjamin International Gender Dysphoria Association). (2001). The standards of care for gender identity disorders (6th version). *International Journal of Transgenderism, 5*(1).

Heard-Davison, A., Heiman, J. R., & Briggs, B. (2004). Sexual disorders affecting women. In L. J. Haas (Ed.), *Handbook of primary care psychology* (pp. 495–509). New York: Oxford University Press.

Heavey, L., Pring, L., & Hermelin, B. (1999). A date to remember: The nature of memory in savant calendrical calculators. *Psychol. Med., 29*(1), 145–160.

Hebert, L. E., Scherr, P. A., Bienias, J. L., Bennett, D. A., & Evans, D. A. (2003). Alzheimer disease in the US population. *Archives of Neurology, 60*(8), 1119–1122.

Hechler, T., Beumont, P., Marks, P., & Touyz, S. (2005). How do clinical specialists understand the role of physical activity in eating disorders? *Eur. Eat. Disord. Rev., 13*(2), 125–132.

Hecimovic, H., & Gilliam, F. G. (2006). Neurobiology of depression and new opportunities for treatment. In F. G. Gilliam, A. M. Kanner, & Y. I. Sheline (Eds.), *Depression and brain dysfunction* (pp. 51–84). New York: Taylor & Francis.

Heffernan, T. M., Jarvis, H., Rodgers, J., Scholey, A. B., & Ling, J. (2001). Prospective memory, everyday cognitive failure and central executive function in recreational users of Ecstasy. *Human Psychopharmacol. Clin. Exp., 16*(8), 607–612.

Heilbrun, K., & Erickson, J. (2007). A behavioural science perspective on identifying and managing hindsight bias and unstructured judgement: Implications for legal decision making. In D. Carson, R. Milne, F. Pakes, K. Shalev, & A. Shawyer (Eds.), *Applying psychology to criminal justice.* Hoboken, NJ: John Wiley & Sons.

Heilbrun, K., Goldstein, N. E. S, & Redding, R. E. (Eds.). (2005). *Juvenile delinquency: Prevention, assessment, and intervention* (pp. 85–110). New York: Oxford University Press.

Heiman, J. R. (2000). Organic disorders in women. In S. R. Leiblum & R. C. Rosen (Eds.), *Principles and practice of sex therapy* (3rd ed., pp. 118–153). New York: Guilford Press.

Heiman, J. R. (2002). Psychologic treatments for female sexual dysfunction: Are they effective and do we need them? *Arch. Sex. Behav., 31,* 445–450.

Heiman, J. R. (2002). Sexual dysfunction: Overview of prevalence, etiological factors, and treatments. *J. Sex Res., 39*(1), 73–78.

Heiman, J. R. (2007). Orgasmic disorders in women. In S. R. Leiblum (Ed.), *Principles and practice of sex therapy* (4th ed., pp. 84–123). New York: Guilford Press.

Heiman, J. R., Gladue, B. A., Roberts, C. W., & LoPiccolo, J. (1986). Historical and current factors discriminating sexually functional from sexually dysfunctional married couples. *J. Marital Fam. Ther., 12*(2), 163–174.

Heiman, J. R., & Heard-Davison, A. R. (2004). Child sexual abuse and adult sexual relationships: Review and perspective. In L. K. Koenig, L. Doll, A. O'Leary, & W. Pequegnat (Eds.), *From child sexual abuse to adult sexual risk: Trauma, revictimization, and intervention* (pp. 13–47). Washington, DC: American Psychological Association.

Heinlen, K. T., Welfel, E. R., Richmond, E. N., & O'Donnell, M. S. (2003). The nature, scope, and ethics of psychologist's E-therapy Web sites: What consumers find when surfing the Web. *Psychotherapy, 40,* 112–124.

Heinrichs, D. W., & Carpenter, W. T., Jr. (1983). The coordination of family therapy with other treatment modalities for schizophrenia. In

W. McFarlane (Ed.), *Family therapy in schizophrenia.* New York: Guilford Press.

Heisel, M. J. (2008). Suicide. In K. T. Mueser & D. V. Jeste (Eds.), *Clinical handbook of schizophrenia* (pp. 491–504). New York: Guilford Press.

Helgeson, V. S. (2002). *The psychology of gender.* Upper Saddle River, NJ: Prentice Hall.

Helmeke, K. B., & Sori, C. F. (Eds.). *The therapist's notebook for integrating spirituality in counseling II: Homework, handouts and activities for use in psychotherapy.* New York: Haworth Press.

Helzer, J. E., Burnam, A., & McEvoy, L. T. (1991). Alcohol abuse and dependence. In L. N. Robins & D. S. Regier (Eds.), *Psychiatric disorders in America: The Epidemiological Catchment Area Study.* New York: Free Press.

Henderson, S. (2005, June 7). Court loss for medical marijuana. *Philadelphia Inquirer.*

Hendin, H. (1999). Suicide, assisted suicide, and medical illness. *J. Clin. Psychiat., 60*(Suppl. 2), 46–50.

Hendin, H. (2002). The Dutch experience. In K. Foley & H. Hendin (Eds.), *The case against assisted suicide: For the right to end-of-life care* (pp. 97–121). Baltimore, MD: The John Hopkins University Press.

Hendin, H., Maltsberger, J. T., Lipschitz, A., Haas, A. P., & Kyle, J. (2001). Recognizing and responding to a suicide crisis. In H. Hendin & J. J. Mann (Eds.), *The clinical science of suicide prevention* (Vol. 932, pp. 169–187). New York: Annals of the New York Academy of Sciences.

Henggeler, S. W., & Lee, T. (2003). Multisystemic treatment of serious clinical problems. In A. E. Kazdin & J. R. Weisz (Eds.), *Evidence-based psychotherapies for children and adolescents.* New York: Guilford Press.

Henley, T. C., & Thorne, B. M. (2005). The lost millennium: Psychology during the Middle Ages. *Psychol. Rec., 55*(1), 103–113.

Henn, F. A., & Vollmayr, B. (2005). Stress models of depression: Forming genetically vulnerable strains. *Neurosci. Biobehav. Rev., 29*(4–5), 799–804.

Hennig, C. W., Crabtree, C. R., & Baum, D. (1998). Mental health CPR: Peer contracting as a response to potential suicide in adolescents. *Arch. Suic. Res., 4*(2), 169–187.

Henningsson, S., Westberg, L., Nilsson, S., Lundstrom, B., Ekselius, L., Bodlund, O., et al. (2005). Sex steroid-related genes and male-to-female transsexualism. *Psychoneuroendocrinology, 30*(7), 657–664.

Hepp, U., Klaghofer, R., Burkhard, K., & Buddeberg, C. (2002). Treatment history of transsexual patients: A retrospective follow-up study. *Nervenarzt, 73*(3), 283–288.

Hepp, U., Kraemer, B., Schnyder, U., Miller, N., & Delsignore, A. (2005). Psychiatric comorbidity in gender identity disorder. *J. Psychosom. Res., 58*(3), 259–261.

Herba, C. M., Ferdinand, R. F., van der Ende, J., & Verhulst, F. C. (2007). Long-term associations of childhood suicide ideation. *J. Amer. Acad. Child Adol. Psychiat., 46*(11), 1473–1481.

Herbeck, D. M., West, J. C., Ruditis, I., Duffy, F. F., Fitek, D. J., Bell, C. C., et al. (2004). Variations in use of second-generation antipsychotic medication by race among adult psychiatric patients. *Psychiatr. Serv., 55*(6), 677–684.

Herbert, J. D. (2007). Avoidant personality disorder. In W. O'Donohue, K. A. Fowler, S. O.

Lilienfeld (Eds.). *Personality disorders: Toward the DSM-V.* Los Angeles: Sage Publications.

Herbert, J. D., Gaudiano, B. A., Rheingold, A., Harwell, V., Dalrymple, K., & Nolan, E. M. (2005). Social skills training augments the effectiveness of cognitive behavior group therapy for social anxiety disorder. *Behavior Therapy, 36,* 125–138.

Herman, N. J. (1999). Road rage: An exploratory analysis. *Michigan Sociol. Rev., 13,* 65–79.

Herning, R. I., Better, W. E., Tate, K., & Cadet, J. L. (2005). Cerebrovascular perfusion in marijuana users during a month of monitored abstinence. *Neurology, 64,* 488–493.

Hersen, M. (Ed.). (2004). *Psychological assessment in clinical practice: A pragmatic guide.* New York: Brunner-Routledge.

Hersen, M., Bellack, A. S., Himmelhoch, J. M., & Thase, M. E. (1984). Effects of social skill training, amitriptyline, and psychotherapy in unipolar depressed women. *Behav. Ther., 15,* 21–40.

Hersen, M., & Thomas, J. C. (Eds.). (2007). *Handbook of clinical interviewing with adults.* Thousand Oaks, CA: Sage Publishing.

Herzig, H. (2004). *Medical information.* Somerset, England: Somerset and Wessex Eating Disorders Association.

Herzog, D. B., Dorer, D. J., Keel, P. K., Selwin, S. E., Ekeblad, E. R., Flores, A. T., et al. (1999). Recovery and relapse in anorexia and bulimia nervosa: A 7.5–year follow-up study. *J. Amer. Acad. Child Adol. Psychiat., 38*(7), 829–837.

Herzog, T., Zeeck, A., Hartmann, A., & Nickel, T. (2004). Lower targets for weekly weight gain lead to better results in inpatient treatment of anorexia nervosa: A pilot study. *Eur. Eat. Disord. Rev., 12*(3), 164–168.

Hess, N. (1995). Cancer as a defence against depressive pain. University College Hospital/Middlesex Hospital Psychotherapy Department. *Psychoanalytic Psychother., 9*(2), 175–184.

Heston, L. L. (1992). *Mending minds: A guide to the new psychiatry of depression, anxiety, and other serious mental disorders.* New York: W. H. Freeman.

Hettema, J. M., Annas, P., Neale, M. C., Kendler, K. S., & Fredrikson, M. (2003). A twin study of the genetics of fear conditioning. *Arch. Gen. Psychiat., 60*(7), 702–708.

Hettema, J. M., Neale, M. C., & Kendler, K. S. (2001). A review and meta-analysis of genetic epidemiology off anxiety disorders. *Amer. J. Psychiat., 158*(10), 1568–1578.

Hettema, J. M., Prescott, C. A., & Kendler, K. S. (2001). A population-based twin study of generalized anxiety disorder in men and women. *J. Nerv. Ment. Dis., 189*(7), 413–420.

Hettema, J. M., Prescott, C. A., Myers, J. M., Heale, M. C., & Kendler, K. S. (2005). The structure of genetic and environmental risk factors for anxiety disorders in men and women. *Arch. Gen. Psychiat., 62*(2), 182–189.

Heydebrand, G., & Wetzel, R. D. (2005). Psychological testing. In E. H. Rubin & C. F. Zorumski (Eds.), *Adult psychiatry* (2nd ed.). Oxford, England: Blackwell Publishing.

Heyman, R. E., & Slep, A. M. S. (2002). Do child abuse and interparental violence lead to adulthood family violence? *J. Marr. Fam., 64*(4), 864–870.

Heyne, D., King, N. J., Tonge, B. J., Rollings, S., Young, D., Pritchard, M., & Ollendick, T. H. (2002). Evaluation of child therapy and

caregiver training in the treatment of school refusal. *J. Amer. Acad. Child Adoles. Psychiat., 41*(6), 687–695.

Hibbs, E. D., & Jensen, P. S. (2005). Analyzing the research. In E. D. Hibbs & P. S. Jensen (Eds.), *Psychosocial treatments for child and adolescent disorders: Empirically based strategies for clinical practice* (2nd ed., pp. 3–8). Washington, DC: American Psychological Association.

Hickey, E. (2002). *Serial murderers and their victims* (3rd ed.). Belmont: Wadsworth.

Hickling, E. J., & Blanchard, E. B. (2007). Motor vehicle accidents and psychological trauma. In E. K. Carll (Ed.), *Trauma psychology: Issues in violence, disaster, health, and illness* (Vol. 2). Westport, CT: Praeger Publishers.

Hiday, V. A. (2006). Putting community risk in perspective: A look at correlations, causes and controls. *Inter. J. Law Psychiat., 29*(4), 316–331.

Hiday, V. A., & Wales, H. W. (2003). Civil commitment and arrests. *Curr. Opin. Psychiat., 16*(5), 575–580.

Higgins, E. S., & George, M. S. (2007). *The neuroscience of clinical psychiatry: The pathophysiology of behavior and mental illness.* Philadelphia: Wolters Kluwer/Lippincott Williams & Wilkins.

Higgins, S. T., Budney, A. J., Bickel, W. K., Hughes, J., Foerg, F., & Badger, G. (1993). Achieving cocaine abstinence with a behavioral approach. *Amer. J. Psychiat., 150*(5), 763–769.

Higgins, S. T., Heil, S. H., & Lussier, J. P. (2004). Clinical implications of reinforcement as a determinant of substance use disorders. *Annu. Rev. Psychol., 55,* 401–430.

Higgins, S. T., & Silverman, K. (2008). Contingency management. In H. D. Kleber & M. Galanter (Eds.), *The American Psychiatric Publishing textbook of substance abuse treatment* (4th ed., pp. 387–399). Arlington, VA: American Psychiatric Publishing.

Highet, N., Thompson, M., & McNair, B. (2005). Identifying depression in a family member: The carers' experience. *J. Affect. Disorders, 87*(1), 25–33.

Hilarski, C. (2007). Antisocial personality disorder. In J. S. Wodarski & B. A. Thyer (Eds.), *Social work in mental health: An evidence-based approach.* Hoboken, NJ: Wiley.

Hilbert, A., Schnur, A. B., & Wilfley, D. E. (2005). Obesity and binge eating disorder. In E. H. Rubin & C. F. Zorumski (Eds.), *Adult psychiatry* (2nd ed., pp. 247–260). Oxford, England: Blackwell Publishing.

Hildebrand, K. M., Johnson, D. J., Dewayne, J., & Bogle, K. (2001). Comparison of patterns of alcohol use between high school and college athletes and non-athletes. *Coll. Student J., 35,* 358–365.

Hilgard, E. R. (1977). Controversies over consciousness and the rise of cognitive psychology. *Austral. Psychologist, 12*(1), 7–26.

Hilgard, E. R. (1987). Research advances in hypnosis: Issues and methods. *Inter. J. Clin. Exp. Hyp., 35,* 248–264.

Hilgard, E. R. (1992). Dissociation and theories of hypnosis. In E. Fromm & M. R. Nash (Eds.), *Contemporary hypnosis research.* New York: Guilford Press.

Hill, A. J. (2006). Body dissatisfaction and dieting in children. In P. J. Cooper & A. Stein (Eds.), *Childhood feeding problems and adolescent eating disorders.* London: Routledge (Taylor & Francis Group).

Hill, J. (2003). Childhood trauma and depression. *Curr. Opin. Psychiat., 16*(1), 3–6.

Hill, J., & Maughan, B. (Eds.). (2001). *Conduct disorders in childhood and adolescence.* New York: Cambridge University Press.

Hingson, R., Heeren, T., Zakocs, R., Kopstein, A., & Wechsler, H. (2002). Magnitude of alcohol-related morbidity, mortality, and alcohol dependence among U.S. college students age 18–24. *J. Stud. Alc., 63*(2), 136–144.

Hinrichsen, G. A. (1999). Interpersonal psychotherapy for late-life depression In M. Duffy (Ed.), *Handbook of counseling and psychotherapy with older adults.* New York: Wiley.

Hinton, D., Um, K., & Ba, P. (2001). Kyol goeu ("wind overload") Part I: A cultural syndrome of orthostatic panic among Khmer refugees. *Transcultur. Psychiat., 38*(4), 403–432.

Hinton, D., Um, K., & Ba, P. (2001). Kyol goeu ("wind overload") Part II: Prevalence, characteristics, and mechanisms of kyol goeu and near-kyol goeu episodes of Khmer patients attending a psychiatric clinic. *Transcultur. Psychiat., 38*(4), 433–460.

Hiroeh, U., Appleby, L., Mortensen, P.-B., & Dunn, G. (2001). Death by homicide, suicide, and other unnatural causes in people with mental illness: A population-based study. *Lancet, 358*(9299), 2110–2112.

Hirschfeld, R. M. (1999). Efficacy of SSRIs and newer antidepressants in severe depression: Comparison with TCAs. *J. Clin. Psychiat., 60*(5), 326–335.

Hirschfeld, R. M., Lewis, L., & Vornik, L. A. (2003). Perceptions and impact of bipolar disorder: How far have we really come? Results of the National Depressive and Manic-Depressive Associations 2000 Survey of Individuals with Bipolar Disorder. *J. Clin. Psychiat., 64*(2), 161–174.

Hirshom, E. (2004). Review of design for assisted living: Guidelines for housing the physically and mentally frail. *Amer. J. Alz. Disease Other Dement., 19*(2), 136.

Hitti, M. (2004). Brain chemicals suggest marijuana's effects. *WebMD.* Retrieved September 24, 2004, from my.webmd.com/content/Article/94/102660.htm

Hitti, M. (2007, July 9). FDA OKs 1st Alzheimer's skin patch: Once-daily exelon patch also approved to treat mild to moderate Parkinson's disease dementia. *WebMD.com.* Retrieved August 13, 2008, from http://www.webmd.com/alzheimers/news/20070709/fda-oks-1st-alzheimer-skin-patch

Hjerl, K., Andersen, E. W., Keiding, N., Mouridsen, H. T., Mortensen, P. B., & Jorgensen, T. (2003). Depression as a prognostic for breast cancer mortality. *Psychosom. J. Cons. Liaison Psychiat., 44*(1), 24–30.

HJK (The Henry J. Kaiser Family Foundation). (2008). *Kaiser Health Tracking Poll: Election 2008, Issue 9,* August.

Hlastala, S. A., Frank, E., Mallinger, A. G., Thase, M. E., Ritenour, A. M., & Kupfer, D. J. (1997). Bipolar depression: An underestimated treatment challenge. *Depress. Anx., 5,* 73–83.

Ho, T. P., Hung, S. F., Lee, C. C., & Chung, K. F. (1995). Characteristics of youth suicide in Hong Kong. *Soc. Psychiat. Psychiatr. Epidemiol., 30*(3), 107–112.

Hoagwood, K., Kelleher, K. J., Feil, M., & Comer, D. M. (2000). Treatment services for children with ADHD: A national perspective. *J. Amer. Acad. Child Adol. Psychiat., 39*(2), 198–206.

Hobbs, F. B. (1997). The elderly population. *U.S. Census Bureau: The official statistics.* Washington, DC: U.S. Census Bureau.

Hobson, C. J., Kamen, J., Szostek, J., Nethercut, C. M., Tiedmann, J. W., & Wojnarowicz, S. (1998). Stressful life events: A revision and update of the Social Readjustment Rating Scale. *Inter. J. Stress Manag., 5*(1), 1–23.

Hodapp, R. M., & Dykens, E. M. (2003). Mental retardation (intellectual disabilities). In E. J. Mash & R. A. Barkley (Eds.), *Child psychopathology* (2nd ed.). New York: Guilford Press.

Hodges, S. (2003). Borderline personality disorder and posttraumatic stress disorder: Time for integration? *J. Couns. Dev., 81*(4), 409–417.

Hodgson, R. J., & Rachman, S. (1972). The effects of contamination and washing in obsessional patients. *Behav. Res. Ther., 10,* 111–117.

Hoffman, K. B. (2007, May 26). Kevorkian's cause founders as he's freed. *Yahoo! News.* Retrieved May 26, 2007, from http://news.yahoo.com

Hoffman, R. E., Boutros, N. N., Hu, S., et al. (2000). Transcranial magnetic stimulation and auditory hallucinations in schizophrenia [Letter]. *Lancet, 355*(9209), 1073–1075.

Hoffman, R. E., Hampson, M., Wu, K., Anderson, A. W., Gore, J. C., Buchanan, R. J., et al. (2007, February 13). Probing the pathophysiology of auditory/verbal hallucinations by combining functional magnetic resonance imaging and transcranial magnetic stimulation. *Cerebral Cortex.* Retrieved August 5, 2008, from http://cercor.oxfordjournals.org/cgi/content/abstractbhl183

Hofmann, S. G., & Weinberger, J. (Eds.). (2007). *The art and science of psychotherapy.* New York: Routledge/Taylor & Francis Group.

Hogan, R. A. (1968). The implosive technique. *Behav. Res. Ther., 6,* 423–431.

Hogarty, G. E. (2002). Personal therapy for schizophrenia and related disorders: A guide to individualized treatment. New York: Guilford Press.

Hogarty, G. E., Anderson, C. M., Reiss, D. J., Kornblith, S. J., Greenwald, D. P., Javna, C. D., et al. (1986). Family psychoeducation, social skills training, and maintenance chemotherapy in the aftercare treatment of schizophrenia: I. One-year effects of a controlled study on relapse and expressed emotion. *Arch. Gen. Psychiat., 43*(7), 633–642.

Hoge, C. W., Castro, C. A., Messer, S. C., McGurk, D., Cotting, D. I., & Koffman, R. L. (2004). Combat duty in Iraq and Afghanistan, mental health problems, and barriers to care. *N. Engl. J. Med., 351,* 13–22.

Hohagen, F., Winkelmann, G., Rasche-Raeuchle, H., Hand, I., Koenig, A., Muenchau, N., et al. (1998). Combination of behaviour therapy with fluvoxamine in comparison with behaviour therapy and placebo: Results of a multicentre study. *Brit. J. Psychiat., 173*(Suppl. 35), 71–78.

Hojnoski, R. L., Morrison, R., Brown, M., & Matthews, W. J. (2006). Projective test use among school psychologists: A survey and critique. *J. Psychoeduc. Assess., 24*(2), 145–159.

Hokans, K. D., & Lester, D. (2007). Motives for suicide in adolescents: A preliminary study. *Psychol. Rep., 101*(3), 778.

Holaway, R. M., Rodebaugh, T. L., & Heimberg, R. G. (2006). The epidemiology of worry and generalized anxiety disorder. In G. C. L. Davey & A. Wells (Eds.), *Worry and psychological disorders: Theory, assessment and treatment.* Chichester, England: Wiley.

Holden, C. (2004, February 6). FDA weighs suicide risk in children on antidepressants. *Science, 303,* p. 745.

Holder, H., Longabaugh, R., Miller, W., et al. (1991). The cost effectiveness of treatment for alcoholism: A first approximation. *J. Stud. Alc., 52,* 517–540.

Holinger, P. C., & Offer, D. (1982). Prediction of adolescent suicide: A population model. *Amer. J. Psychiat., 139,* 302–307.

Holinger, P. C., & Offer, D. (1991). Sociodemographic, epidemiologic, and individual attributes. In L. Davidson & M. Linnoila (Eds.), *Risk factors for youth suicide.* New York: Hemisphere.

Holinger, P. C., & Offer, D. (1993). *Adolescent suicide.* New York: Guilford Press.

Hollon, S. D., DeRubeis, R. J., Shelton, R. C., Amsterdam, J. D., Salomon, R. M., O'Reardon, J. P., et al. (2005). Prevention of relapse following cognitive therapy v. medications in moderate to severe depression. *Arch. Gen. Psychiat., 62,* 417–422.

Hollon, S. D., Haman, K. L., & Brown, L. L. (2002). Cognitive behavioral treatment of depression. In I. H. Gotlib & C. L. Hammen (Eds.), *Handbook of depression* (pp. 383–403). New York: Guilford Press.

Hollon, S. D., Stewart, M. O., & Strunk D. (2006). Enduring effects for cognitive behavior therapy in the treatment of depression and anxiety. *Annu. Rev. Psychol., 57,* 285–315.

Holmans, P., Weissman, M. M., Zubenko, G. S., Scheftner, W. A., Crowe, R. R., DePaulo, J. R., Jr., et al. (2007). Genetics of recurrent early-onset major depression (GenRED): Final genome scan report. *Amer. J. Psychiat., 164*(2), 248–258.

Holmes, T. H., & Rahe, R. H. (1967). The Social Readjustment Rating Scale. *J. Psychosom. Res., 11,* 213–218.

Holmes, T. H., & Rahe, R. H. (1989). The Social Readjustment Rating Scale. In T. H. Holmes & E. M. David (Eds.), *Life change, life events, and illness: Selected papers.* New York: Praeger.

Holstein, J. A. (1993). *Court-ordered insanity: Interpretive practice and involuntary commitment.* New York: Aldine de Gruyter.

Holwerda, T. J., Schoevers, R. A., Dekker, J., Deeg, D. J. H., Jonker, C., & Beekman, A. T. F. (2007). The relationship between generalized anxiety disorder, depression and mortality in old age. *Inter. J. Ger. Psychiat., 22*(3), 241–249.

Holzman, P. S. (1986). Quality of thought disorder in differential diagnosis. *Schizo. Bull., 12,* 360–372.

Homant, R. J., & Kennedy, D. B. (2006). Serial murder: A biopsychosocial approach. In W. Petherick (Ed.), *Serial crime: Theoretical and practical issues in behavioral profiling* (pp. 189–228). San Diego, CA: Elsevier.

Honberg, R. (2005). Decriminalizing mental illness. *NAMI Advocate, 3*(1), 4–5.

Hong, J. P., Samuels, J., Bienvenu, O. J., III, Cannistraro, P., Grados, M., Riddle, M. A.,

et al. (2004). Clinical correlates of recurrent major depression in obsessive-compulsive disorder. *Depress. Anx., 20*(2), 86–91.

Honikman, J. I. (1999). Role of self-help techniques for postpartum mood disorders. In L. J. Miller (Ed.), *Postpartum mood disorders.* Washington, DC: American Psychiatric Press.

Honkonen, T., Karlsson, H., Koivisto, A. M., Stengard, E., & Salokangas, R. K. R. (2003). Schizophrenic patients in different treatment settings during the era of deinstitutionalization: Three-year follow-up of three discharge cohorts in Finland. *Austral. New Zeal. J. Psychiat., 37*(2), 160–168.

Hooper, J. F., McLearen, A. M., & Barnett, M. E. (2005). The Alabama structured assessment of treatment completion for insanity acquittees (The AlaSATcom). *Inter. J. Law Psychiat., 28*(6), 604–612.

Hopko, D. R., Robertson, S. M. C., Widman, L., & Lejuez, C. W. (2008). Specific phobias. In M. Hersen & J. Rosqvist (Eds.), *Handbook of psychological assessment, case conceptualization, and treatment, Vol. 1: Adults* (pp. 139–170). Hoboken, NJ: John Wiley & Sons.

Horley, J. (2001). Frotteurism: A term in search of an underlying disorder? *J. Sex. Aggress., 7*(1), 51–55.

Horney, K. (1937). *The neurotic personality of our time.* New York: Norton.

Hornyak, L. M., & Green, J. P. (Eds.). (2000). *Healing from within: The use of hypnosis in women's health care.* Washington, DC: American Psychological Association.

Horowitz, J. A., Damato, E. G., Duffy, M. E., & Solon, L. (2005). The relationship of maternal attributes, resources, and perceptions of postpartum experiences to depression. *Res. Nursing Hlth., 28*(2), 159–171.

Horowitz, J. A., Damato, E., Solon, L., Metzsch, G., & Gill, V. (1995). Postpartum depression: Issues in clinical assessment. *J. Perinat. Med., 15*(4), 268–278.

Horwitz, A. V., & Wakefield, J. C. (2007, December 9). Sadness is not a disorder. *The Philadelphia Inquirer,* pp. C1, C5.

Hou, C., Miller, B. L., Cummings, J. L., Goldberg, M., Mychack, P., Bottino, V., et al. (2000). Artistic savants. *Neuropsychiat., Neuropsychol., Behav. Neurol., 13*(1), 29–38.

Houts, A. C. (2003). Behavioral treatment for enuresis. In A. E. Kazdin & J. R. Weisz (Eds.), *Evidence-based psychotherapies for children and adolescents.* New York: Guilford Press.

Hoven, C. W., Duarte, C. S., Lucas, C. P., Wu, P., Mandell, D. J., Goodwin, R. D., et al. (2005). Psychopathology among New York City public school children 6 months after September 11. *Arch. Gen. Psychiat., 62*(5), 545–551.

Howe, R., & Nugent, T. (1996, April 22). The gory details. *People,* pp. 91–92.

Howells, J. G., & Guirguis, W. R. (1985). *The family and schizophrenia.* New York: International Universities Press.

Howland, R. H. (2008). Antidepressants and suicide: Putting the risk in perspective. *Psychiatr. Ann., 38*(3), 198–201.

Hoyer, W. J., & Verhaeghen, P. (2006). Memory aging. In J. E. Birren & K. W. Schaie (Eds.), *Handbook of the psychology of aging* (6th ed., pp. 209–232). San Diego, CA: Elsevier.

Hoyert, D. L., Kung, H. C., & Smith, B. L. (2005). *Deaths: Preliminary data for 2003.*

National Vital Statistics Reports 53, no. 15. Hyattsville, MD: National Center for Health Statistics.

Hoza, B., Kaiser, N., & Hurt, E. (2008). Evidence-based treatments for attention-deficit/hyperactivity disorder (ADHD). In R. G. Steele, T. D. Elkin, & M. C. Roberts (Eds.), *Handbook of evidence-based therapies for children and adolescents: Bridging science and practice.* New York: Springer.

Hrobjartsson, A., & Gotzsche, P. C. (2001). Is the placebo powerless? An analysis of clinical trials comparing placebo with no treatment. *N. Engl. J. Med., 344*(21), 1594–1602.

Hrobjartsson, A., & Gøtzsche, P. C. (2004). Is the placebo effect powerless? Update of a systematic review with 52 new randomized trials comparing placebo with no treatment. *J. Inter. Med., 256,* 91–100.

Hrobjartsson, A., & Gotzsche, P. C. (2006). Unsubstantiated claims of large effects of placebo on pain: Serious errors in meta-analysis of placebo analgesia mechanism studies. *J. Clin. Epidemiol., 59,* 336–338.

Hu, W., Ranaivo, H. R., Craft, J. M., Van Eldik, L. J., & Watterson, D. M. (2005). Validation of the neuroinflammation cycle as a drug discovery target using integrative chemical biology and lead compound development with an Alzheimer's disease-related mouse model. *Curr. Alz. Res., 2*(2), 197–205.

Huda, S. (2006). Sex trafficking in South Asia. *Inter. J. Gynecol. Obstet., 94,* 374–381.

Hudd, S., Dumlao, J., Erdmann-Sager, D., Murray, D., Phan, E., Soukas, N., et al. (2000). Stress at college: Effects on health habits, health status and self-esteem. *Coll. Student J., 34*(2), 217–227.

Hudson, J. I., Hiripi, E., Pope, H. G., Jr., & Kessler, R. C. (2007). The prevalence and correlates of eating disorders in the National Comorbidity Survey Replication. *Biol. Psychiat., 61*(3), 348–358.

Hudson, J. L., & Rapee, R. M. (2004). From anxious temperament to disorder: An etiological model of generalized anxiety disorder. In R. G. Heimberg, C. L. Turk, & D. S. Mennin (Eds.), *Generalized anxiety disorder: Advances in research and practice* (pp. 51–74). New York: Guilford Press.

Hudson-Allez, G. (2006). The stalking of psychotherapists by current or former clients: Beware of the insecurely attached! *Psychodyn. Pract.: Indiv. Groups Org., 12*(3), 249–260.

Hugdahl, K. (1995). *Psychophysiology: The mind-body perspective.* Cambridge, MA: Harvard University Press.

Hullett, C. R. (2005). Grieving families: Social support after the death of a loved one. In E. B. Ray (Ed.), *Health communication in practice: A case study approach* (pp. 211–221). Mahwah, NJ: Lawrence Erlbaum.

Humphrey, J. A. (2006). *Deviant behavior.* Upper Saddle River, NJ: Pearson/Prentice Hall.

Humphreys, K. (1996). Clinical psychologists as psychotherapists. History, future, and alternatives. *Amer. Psychologist, 51*(3), 190–197.

Humphreys, K., & Rappaport, J. (1993). From the community mental health movement to the war on drugs: A study in the definition of social problems. *Amer. Psychologist, 48*(8), 892–901.

Humphry, D., & Wickett, A. (1986). *The right to die: Understanding euthanasia.* New York: Harper & Row.

Hunt, C., & Andrews, G. (1995). Comorbidity in the anxiety disorders: The use of a life-chart approach. *J. Psychiatr. Res., 29*(6), 467–480.

Huntjens, R. J. C., Peters, M. L., Postma, A., Woertman, L., Effting, M., & van der Hart, O. (2005). Transfer of newly acquired stimulus valence between identities in dissociative identity disorder (DID). *Behav. Res. Ther., 43*(2), 243–255.

Huprich, S. K. (Ed.). (2006). *Rorschach assessment to the personality disorders.* Mahwah, NJ: Lawrence Erlbaum.

Hurlbert, D. F. (1991). The role of assertiveness in female sexuality: A comparative study between sexually assertive and sexually non-assertive women. *J. Sex Marital Ther., 17*(3), 183–190.

Hurlbert, D. F. (1993). A comparative study using orgasm consistency training in the treatment of women reporting hypoactive sexual desire. *J. Sex Marital Ther., 19,* 41–55.

Hurlbert, D. F., Apt, C., & Rabehl, S. M. (1993). Key variables to understanding female sexual satisfaction: An examination of women in non-distressed marriages. J. *Sex Marital Ther., 19,* 154–165.

Hurlburt, R. T., & Knapp, T. J. (2006). Munsterberg in 1898, not Allport in 1937, introduced the terms "idiographic" and "nomothetic" to American psychology. *Theory Psychol., 16*(2), 287–293.

Hurt, S., & Oltmanns, T. F. (2002). Personality traits and pathology in older and younger incarcerated women. *J. Clin. Psychol., 58*(4), 457–464.

Hustey, F. M., Meldon, S. W., Smith, M. D., et al. (2003). The effect of mental status screening on the care of elderly emergency department patients. *Ann. Emerg. Med., 41,* 678–684.

Hyde, J. S. (1990). *Understanding human sexuality* (4th ed.). New York: McGraw-Hill.

Hyde, J. S. (2005). The genetics of sexual orientation. In J. S. Hyde (Ed.), *Biological substrates of human sexuality.* Washington, DC: American Psychological Association.

Hyde, J. S., & DeLamater, J. D. (2006). *Understanding human sexuality* (9th ed.). Boston: McGraw-Hill.

Hyman, I. E., Jr., & Loftus, E. F. (2002). False childhood memories and eyewitness memory errors. In M. L. Eisen (Ed.), *Memory and suggestibility in the forensic interview. Personality and clinical psychology series* (pp. 63–84). Mahwah, NJ: Lawrence Erlbaum.

Hymowitz, N. (2005). Tobacco. In R. J. Frances, A. H. Mack, & S. I. Miller (Eds.), *Clinical textbook of addictive disorders* (3rd ed., pp. 105–137). New York: Guilford Press.

Ibanez, G. E., Buck, C. A., Khatchikian, N., & Norris, F. H. (2004). Qualitative analysis of coping strategies among Mexican disaster survivors. *Anx., Stress, Coping: Inter. J., 17*(1), 69–85.

Iga, M. (1993). Japanese suicide. In A. A. Leenaars (Ed.), *Suicidology.* Northvale, NJ: Jason Aronson.

Iga, M. (2001). The thorn in the chrysanthemum: Suicide and economic success in modern Japan. In E. S. Shneidman (Ed.), *Comprehending suicide: Landmarks in 20th-century suicidology* (pp. 59–68). Washington, DC: American Psychological Association.

Ihle, W., Jahnke, D., Heerwagen, A., & Neuperdt, C. (2005). Depression, anxiety, and eating disorders and recalled parental rearing behavior. *Kindheit Entwicklung, 14*(1), 30–38.

Imbesi, L. (2000). On the etiology of narcissistic personality disorder. *Issues Psychoanal. Psychol., 22*(2), 43–58.

Ingram, R. E., Nelson, T., Steidtmann, D. K., & Bistricky, S. L. (2007). Comparative data on child and adolescent cognitive measures associated with depression. *J. Cons. Clin. Psychol., 75*(3), 390–403.

Innes, M. (2002). Satir's therapeutically oriented educational process: A critical appreciation. *Contemp. Fam. Therap: Internat. J., 24*(1), 35–56.

Inoue, K., Tanii, H., Nishimura, Y., Masaki, M., Yokoyama, C., Kajiki, N., et al. (2007). Suicide in panic disorder. *Inter. Med. J., 14*(3), 199–202.

Inouye, S. K. (1999). Predisposing and precipitating factors for delirium in hospitalized older patients. *Dement. Ger. Cogn. Disord., 10*(5), 393–400.

Inouye, S. K., Bogardus, S. T., Jr., Williams, C. S., et al. (2003). The role of adherence on the effectiveness of nonpharmacologic interventions: Evidence from the delirium prevention trial. *Arch. Internal Med., 163,* 958–964.

Inouye, S. K., Foreman, M. D., Mion, L. C., et al. (2001). Nurses' recognition of delirium and its symptoms: Comparison of nurse and researcher ratings. *Arch. Internal Med., 161,* 2467–2473.

Insel, T. R. (2007). Shining light on depression. *Science, 317*(5839), 757–758.

Inselmann, U. (2004). Bio-psycho-social burdens at old age: Theoretical and psychotherapeutic implications of the experience of loss. *Psychother. Forum, 12*(3), 140–146.

Institute of Medicine (of the National Academies). (2004). *Immunization safety review: Autism and vaccines.* Washington, DC: National Academies Press.

Irvine, M. (2005, May 30). Cult-like lure of "Ana" attracts anorexics. *Associated Press (Chicago)/Netscape News with CNN.*

Irwin, M. R., & Cole, J. C. (2005). Depression and psychonueroimmunology. In K. Vedhara & M. Irwin (Eds.), *Human psychoneuroimmunology.* Oxford, England: Oxford University Press.

Isenberg, D. H., Loomis, C., Humphreys, K., & Maton, K. I. (2004). Self-help research: Issues of power sharing. In L. A. Jason, C. B. Keys, Y. Suarez-Balcazar, R. R. Taylor, & M. L. Davis (Eds.), *Participatory community research: Theories and methods in action.* Washington, DC: American Psychological Association.

Ito, A., Ichihara, M., Hisanaga, N., Ono, Y., et al. (1992). Prevalence of seasonal mood changes in low latitude area: Seasonal Pattern Assessment Questionnaire score of Quezon City workers. *Jpn. J. Psychiatry, 46,* 249.

Iversen, L. L. (1975). Dopamine receptors in the brain. *Science, 188,* 1084–1089.

Iverson, G. L., Williamson, D. J., Ropacki, M., & Reilly, K. J. (2007) Frequency of abnormal scores on the Neuropsychological Assessment Battery Screening Module (S-NAM) in a mixed neurological sample. *Appl. Neuropsychol., 14*(3), 178–182.

Jablensky, A. (2000). Epidemiology of schizophrenia: The global burden of disease and disability. *Eur. Arch. Psychiat. Clin. Neurosci., 250,* 274–285.

Jackson, J. S., Torres, M., Caldwell, C. H., Neighbors, H. W., Nesse, R. M., Taylor, R. J., et al. (2004). The National Survey of American Life: A study of racial, ethnic and cultural influences on mental disorders and mental health. *Inter. J. Methods Psychiatr. Res., 13*(4), 196–207.

Jackson, R. L., & Richards, H. J. (2008). Evaluations for the civil commitment of sexual offenders. In R. Jackson (Ed.), *Learning forensic assessment* (pp. 183–209). New York: Routledge/Taylor & Francis Group.

Jackson, Y. (Ed.). (2006) *Encyclopedia of multicultural psychology.* Thousand Oaks, CA: Sage Publications.

Jacobs, A. K. (2008). Components of evidence-based interventions for bullying and peer victimization. In R. G. Steele, T. D. Elkin, & M. C. Roberts (Eds.), *Handbook of evidence-based therapies for children and adolescents: Bridging science and practice.* New York: Springer.

Jacobs, M. (2003). *Sigmund Freud.* London: Sage.

Jacobs, M. K., Christensen, A., Snibbe, J. R., Dolezal-Wood, S., Huber, A., & Polterok, A. (2001). A comparison of computer-based versus traditional individual psychotherapy. *Profess. Psychol.: Res. Pract., 32*(1), 92–96.

Jacobson, G. (1999). The inpatient management of suicidality. In D. G. Jacobs (Ed.), *The Harvard Medical School guide to suicide assessment and intervention.* San Francisco: Jossey-Bass.

Jacobson, J. M. (2005). Guest editorial: Workplace crisis intervention and employee assistance programs (EAPs). *Inter. J. Emerg. Ment. Hlth., 7*(3), 155–156.

Jacobson, J. W., & Mulick, J. A. (1996). Definition of mental retardation. In J. W. Jacobson & J. A. Mulick (Eds.), *Manual of diagnosis and professional practice in mental retardation* (pp. 13–53). Washington, DC: American Psychological Association.

Jacobson, N. S., Dobson, K. S., Truax, P. A., Addis, M. E., et al. (1996). A component analysis of cognitive-behavioral treatment for depression. *J. Consult. Clin. Psychol., 64*(2), 295–304.

Jacobson, N. S., Martell, C. R., & Dimidjian, S. (2001). Behavioral activation treatment for depression: Returning to contextual roots. *Clin. Psychol.: Sci. Prac., 8,* 255–270.

Jambor, E. (2001). Media involvement and the idea of beauty. In R. McComb & J. Jacalyn (Eds.), *Eating disorders in women and children: Prevention, stress management, and treatment* (pp. 179–183). Boca Raton, FL: CRC Press.

James, W. (1890). *Principles of psychology* (Vol. 1). New York: Holt, Rinehart & Winston.

Jamison, K. R. (1995). *An unquiet mind.* New York: Vintage Books.

Jamison, K. R. (1995, February). Manic-depressive illness and creativity. *Scientif. Amer.,* pp. 63–67.

Jang, K. L., & Vernon, P. A. (2001). Genetics. In W. J. Livesley (Ed.), *Handbook of personality disorders: Theory, research, and treatment* (pp. 177–195). New York: Guilford Press.

Janicak, P. G., Davis, J. M., Preskorn, S. H., & Ayd, F. J. (2001). *Principles and practice of psychopharmacotherapy* (3rd ed.). Philadelphia: Lippincott Williams & Wilkin.

Janicak, P. G., Dowd, S. M., Martis, B., Alam, D., Beedle, D., Krasuski, J., et al. (2002). Repetitive transcranial magnetic stimulation versus electroconvulsive therapy for major depression: Preliminary results of a randomized trial. *Biol. Psychiat., 51,* 659–667.

Jannini, E., & Lenzi, A. (2005). Ejaculatory disorders: Epidemiology and current approaches to definition, classification and subtyping. *World Journal of Urology, 23,* 68–75.

Janowsky, D. S., El-Yousef, M. K., Davis, J. M., & Sekerke, H. J. (1973). Provocation of schizophrenic symptoms by intravenous administration of methylphenidate. *Arch. Gen. Psychiat., 28,* 185–191.

Janus, S. S., & Janus, C. L. (1993). *The Janus report on sexual behavior.* New York: Wiley.

Jefferson, D. J. (2005, August 8). America's most dangerous drug. *Newsweek, 146*(6), 40–48.

Jenike, M. A. (1992). New developments in treatment of obsessive-compulsive disorder. In A. Tasman & M. B. Riba (Eds.), *Review of psychiatry* (Vol. 11). Washington, DC: American Psychiatric Press.

Jenkins, R. L. (1968). The varieties of children's behavioral problems and family dynamics. *Amer. J. Psychiat., 124*(10), 1440–1445.

Jensen, G. M. (1998). The experience of injustice: Health consequences of the Japanese American internment. *Diss. Abstr. Inter.: Sect. A: Human Soc. Sci., 58*(7–A), 2718.

Jensen, P. S., Hinshaw, S. P., Kraemer, H. C., Lenora, N., Newcorn, J. H., Abikoff, H. B., et al. (2001). ADHD comorbidity findings from the MTA study: Comparing comorbid subgroups. *J. Amer. Acad. Child Adol. Psychiat., 40*(2), 147–158.

Jeste, D. V., Blazer, D. G., & First, M. (2005). Aging-related diagnostic variations: Need for diagnostic criteria appropriate for elderly psychiatric patients. *Biol. Psychiat., 58*(4), 265–271.

Jia, J., Xu, E., Shao, Y., Jia, J., Sun, Y., & Li, D. (2005). One novel presenilin-1 gene mutation in a Chinese predigree of familial Alzheimer's disease. *J. Alzheimer Dis., 7*(2), 119–124.

Jiang, Y., Haxby J. V., Martin, A., Ungerleider, L. G., & Parasuraman R. (2000). Complementary neural mechanisms for tracking items in human working memory. *Science, 287*(5453), 643–646.

Jobe, P. C., Dailey, J. W., & Wernicke, J. F. (1999). A noradrenergic and serotonergic hypothesis of the linkage between epilepsy and affective disorders. *Crit. Rev. Neurobiol., 13*(4), 317–356.

Jobe, T. H., & Harrow, M. (2005). Long-term outcome of patients with schizophrenia: A review. *Canad. J. Psychiat., 50,* 892–900.

Joffe, C., Brodaty, H., Luscombe, G., & Ehrlich, F. (2003). The Sydney Holocaust study: Posttraumatic stress disorder and other psychosocial morbidity in an aged community sample. *J. Traum. Stress., 16*(1), 39–47.

Joffe, R. T., Singer, W., Levitt, A. J., & MacDonald, C. (1993). A placebo-controlled comparison of lithium and triiodothyronine augmentation of tricyclic antidepressants in unipolar refractory depression. *Arch. Gen. Psychiat., 50,* 387–393.

Johns, A. (2001). Psychiatric effects of cannabis. *Brit. J. Psychiat., 178,* 116–122.

Johnson, B. R., & Becker, J. V. (1997). Natural born killers?: The development of the sexually sadistic serial killer. *J. Amer. Acad. Psychiat. Law., 25*(3), 335–348.

Johnson, C. (1995, February 8). National Collegiate Athletic Association study. In *The Hartford Courant.*

Johnson, L. A. (2005, July 21). Lobotomy back in spotlight after 30 years. *Netscape News.*

Johnson, M. E., Jones, G., & Brems, C. (1996). Concurrent validity of the MMPI-2 feminine gender role (GF) and masculine gender role (GM) scales. *J. Pers. Assess., 66*(1), 153–168.

Johnson, C. A., & Tyler, C. (2008). Evidence-based therapies for pediatric overweight. In R. G. Steele, T. D. Elkin, & M. C. Roberts (Eds.), *Handbook of evidence-based therapies for children and adolescents: Bridging science and practice.* New York: Springer.

Johnston, J. M. (2004). Eating disorders and childhood obesity: Who are the real gluttons? *Canad. Med. Assoc. J., 171*(12), 1459–1460.

Johnston, L. D., O'Malley, P. M., & Bachman, J. G. (1993). *National survey results on drug use from the Monitoring the Future Study, 1975–1992.* Rockville, MD: National Institute on Drug Abuse.

Johnston, L. D., O'Malley, P. M., Bachman, J. G., & Schulenberg, J. E. (2007). *Monitoring the future national results on adolescent drug use: Overview of key findings, 2006* (NIH Publication No. 07-6202). Bethesda, MD: National Institute on Drug Abuse.

Joiner, T. E., Jr. (2002). Depression in its interpersonal context. In I. H. Gotlib & C. L. Hammen (Eds.), *Handbook of depression* (pp. 295–313). New York: Guilford Press.

Joiner, T. E., Jr., & Metalsky, G. I. (1995). A prospective test of an integrative interpersonal theory of depression: A naturalistic study of college roommates. *J. Pers. Soc. Psychol., 69,* 778–788.

Joiner, T. E., Jr., & Metalsky, G. I. (2001). Excessive reassurance seeking: Delineating a risk factor involved in the development of depressive symptoms. *Psychol. Sci., 12*(5), 371–378.

Joiner, T. E., Sachs-Ericsson, N. J., Wingate, L. R., & Brown, J. S. (2007). Childhood physical and sexual abuse and lifetime number of suicide attempts: A resilient and theoretically important relationship. *Behav. Res. Ther., 45,* 539–547.

Jones, G., & Jordan, R. (2008). Research base for intervention in autism spectrum disorders. In E. McGregor, M. Núñez, K. Cebula, & J. C. Gómez (Eds.), *Autism: An integrated view from neurocognitive, clinical, and intervention research.* Malden, MA: Blackwell Publishing.

Jones, M. C. (1968). Personality correlates and antecedents of drinking patterns in males. *J. Cons. Clin. Psychol., 32,* 2–12.

Jones, M. C. (1971). Personality antecedents and correlates of drinking patterns in women. *J. Cons. Clin. Psychol., 36,* 61–69.

Joseph, J. (2006). *The missing gene: Psychiatry, heredity, and the fruitless search for genes.* New York: Algora Publishing.

Joy, M. (2005). Humanistic psychology and animal rights: Reconsidering the boundaries of the humanistic ethic. *J. Human. Psychol., 45*(1), 106–130.

Judd, L. L., Akiskal, H. S., & Paulus, M. P. (1997). The role and clinical significance of subsyndromal depressive symptoms (SSD) in unipolar major depressive disorder. *J. Affect. Disorders, 45*(1–2), 5–17.

Judd, L. L., Rapaport, M. H., Yonkers, K. A., Rush, A. J., Frank, E., Thase, M. E., et al.

(2004). Randomized, placebo-controlled trial of fluoxetine for acute treatment of minor depressive disorder. *Amer. J. Psychiat., 161*(10), 1864–1871.

Judd, L. L., Schettler, P. J., & Akiskal, H. S. (2002). The prevalence, clinical relevance, and public health significance of subthreshold depressions. *Psychiatr. Clin. N. Amer., 25*(4), 685–698.

Judelson, D. A., Armstrong, L. E., Sokmen, B., Roti, M. W., Casa, D. J., & Kellogg, M. D. (2005). Effect of chronic caffeine intake on choice reaction time, mood, and visual vigilance. *Physiol. Behav., 85*(5), 629–634.

Juel-Nielsen, N., & Videbech, T. (1970). A twin study of suicide. *Acta Genet. Med. Gemellol., 19,* 307–310.

Julien, R. M. (2005). *A primer of drug action* (10th ed.). New York: Worth Publishers.

Julien, R. M. (2008). *A primer of drug action* (11th ed.). New York: Worth Publishers.

Jung, C. J. (1971). *Psychological types: The relations between the ego and the unconscious.* From *The collected works* (Vol. 6). Princeton, NJ: Princeton University Press. (Original work published 1921)

Kabakci, E., & Batur, S. (2003). Who benefits from cognitive behavioral therapy for vaginismus? *J. Sex Marital Ther., 29,* 277–288.

Kabat-Zinn, J. (2005). *Wherever you go, there you are: Mindfulness meditation in everyday life.* New York: Hyperion.

Kabat-Zinn, J., Massion, A. O., Kristeller, J., Peterson, L. G., et al. (1992). Effectiveness of a meditation-based stress reduction program in the treatment of anxiety disorders. *Amer. J. Psychiat., 149*(7), 936–943.

Kafka, M. P. (2000). The paraphilia-related disorders: Nonparaphilic hypersexuality and sexual compulsivity/addiction. In S. R. Leiblum & R. C. Raymond (Eds.), *Principles and practice of sex therapy* (3rd ed., pp. 471–503). New York: Guilford Press.

Kafka, M. P. (2007). Paraphilia-related disorders: The evaluation and treatment of nonparaphilic hypersexuality. In S. R. Leiblum (Ed.), *Principles and practice of sex therapy* (4th ed., pp. 442–476). New York: Guilford Press.

Kagan, J. (2003). Biology, context and developmental inquiry. *Ann. Rev. Psychol., 54,* 1–23.

Kagan, J. (2007). The limitations of concepts in developmental psychology. In G. W. Ladd (Ed.), *Appraising the human developmental sciences: Essays in honor of Merrill-Palmer Quarterly* (pp. 30–37). Detroit, MI: Wayne State University Press.

Kagan, J., & Snidman, N. (1991). Infant predictors of inhibited and uninhibited profiles. *Psychol. Sci., 2,* 40–44.

Kagan, J., & Snidman, N. (1999). Early childhood predictors of adult anxiety disorders. *Biol. Psychiat., 46*(11), 1536–1541.

Kahn, A. P., & Fawcett, J. (1993). *The encyclopedia of mental health.* New York: Facts on File.

Kaij, L. (1960). *Alcoholism in twins: Studies on the etiology and sequels of abuse of alcohol.* Stockholm: Almquist & Wiksell.

Kaiser Family Foundation. (2001, November). *Understanding the effects of direct-to-consumer prescription drug advertising.* The Health Care Marketplace Project Publications: Menlo Park, CA.

Kalb, C. (2000, January 31). Coping with the darkness: Revolutionary new approaches in pro-

viding care for helping people with Alzheimer's stay active and feel productive. *Newsweek,* pp. 52–54.

Kalb, C. (2004, September 6). Know the numbers. *Newsweek, 144*(10), 72–73.

Kalidindi, S., & McGuffin, P. (2003). The genetics of affective disorders: Present and future. In R. Plomin, J. C. DeFries, I. W. Craig, & P. McGuffin (Eds.), *Behavioral genetics in the postgenomic era* (pp. 481–501). Washington, DC: American Psychological Association.

Kalin, N. H. (1993, May). The neurobiology of fear. *Scientif. Amer.,* pp. 94–101.

Kalist, D. E., Molinari, N. A. M., & Siahaan, F. (2007). Income, employment and suicidal behavior. *J. Ment. Hlth. Policy Econ., 10*(4), 177–187.

Kalodner, C. R., & Coughlin, J. W. (2004). Psychoeducational and counseling groups to prevent and treat eating disorders and disturbances. In J. L. DeLucia-Waack, D. A. Gerrity, C. R. Kalodner, & M. T. Riva (Eds.), *Handbook of group counseling and psychotherapy* (pp. 481–496). Thousand Oaks, CA: Sage.

Kaminer, Y., Burleson, J. A., & Jadamec, A. (2002). Gambling behavior in adolescent substance abuse. *Subs. Abuse, 23*(3), 191–198.

Kamphaus, R. W., & Frick, P. J. (2002). *Clinical assessment of child and adolescent personality and behavior* (2nd ed.). Boston: Allyn and Bacon.

Kane, J. M. (1992). Clinical efficacy of clozapine in treatment-refractory schizophrenia: An overview. *Brit. J. Psychiat., 160*(Suppl. 17), 41–45.

Kanner, B. (1995). *Are you normal?: Do you behave like everyone else?* New York: St. Martin's Press.

Kanner, B. (1998, February). Are you normal? Turning the other cheek. *American Demog.*

Kanner, B. (1998, May). Are you normal? Creatures of habit. *Am. Demogr.*

Kanner, B. (1999, January). Hungry, or just bored? *Am. Demogr.*

Kanner, B. (2005). *Are you normal about sex, love, and relationships?* New York: St. Martin's Press.

Kanner, L. (1943). Autistic disturbances of affective contact. *Nerv. Child. 2,* 217.

Kanner, L. (1954). To what extent is early infantile autism determined by constitutional inadequacies? *Proceedings of the Assoc. Res. Nerv. Ment. Dis., 33,* 378–385.

Kantor, M. (2006). The psychopathy of everyday life. In T. G. Plante (Ed.), *Mental disorders of the new millennium, Vol. 1: Behavioral issues.* Westport, CT: Praeger Publishers.

Kantrowitz, B., & Springen, K. (2004, August 9). What dreams are made of. *Newsweek, 144*(6), 40–47.

Kantrowitz, B., & Springen, K. (2007). Confronting Alzheimer's. *Newsweek, CXLIX*(25), 54–61.

Kaplan, A. S. (2005). From genes to treatment response: New research into the psychobiology of anorexia nervosa. *Inter. J. Eat. Disord., 37*(Suppl.), S87–S89.

Kaplan, A. S., & Garfinkel, P. E. (1999). Difficulties in treating patients with eating disorders: A review of patient and clinician variables. *Canad. J. Psychiat., 44*(7), 665–670.

Kaplan, H. S. (1974). *The new sex therapy: Active treatment of sexual dysfunction.* New York: Brunner/Mazel.

Kaplan, M. S., Huguet, N., McFarland, H., & Newsom, J. T. (2007). Suicide among male veterans: A prospective population-based study. *J. Epidemiol. Comm. Hlth., 61,* 619–624.

Kaplan, R. M. (2000). Two pathways to prevention. *Amer. Psychologist, 55*(4), 382–396.

Kardiner, A. (1977). *My analysis with Freud: Reminiscences.* New York: Norton.

Karon, B. P. (1985). Omission in review of treatment interactions. *Schizo. Bull., 11*(1), 16–17.

Karon, B. P. (2008). An "incurable" schizophrenic: The case of Mr. X. *Pragmat. Case Stud. Psychother., 4*(1), 1–24.

Karp, D. A. (1996). *Speaking of sadness: Depression, disconnection, and the meanings of illness.* New York: Oxford University Press.

Kasari, C., Freeman, S., & Paparella, T. (2006). Joint attention and symbolic play in young children with autism: A randomized controlled intervention study. *J. Child Psychol. Psychiat., 47,* 611–620.

Kasper, S. (2005). Atypical antipsychotics in bipolar disorder. In S. Kasper & R. M. A. Hirschfeld (Eds.), *Handbook of bipolar disorder: Diagnosis and therapeutic approaches* (pp. 315–330). New York: Taylor & Francis.

Kassel, J. D., Wagner, E. F., & Unrod, M. (1999). Alcoholism-behavior therapy. In M. Hersen & A. S. Bellack (Eds.), *Handbook of comparative interventions for adult disorders* (2nd ed.). New York: Wiley.

Katel, P., & Beck, M. (1996, March 29). Sick kid or sick Mom? *Newsweek,* p. 73.

Katon, W. J., & Walker, E. A. (1998). Medically unexplained symptoms in primary care. *J. Clin. Psychiat., 59*(Suppl. 20), 15–21.

Kauert, G., & Iwersen-Bergmann, S. (2004). Illicit drugs as cause of traffic crashes, focus on cannabis. *Sucht (German Journal of Addiction Research and Practice), 50*(5), 327–333.

Kaufman, J., & Charney, D. (2000). Comorbidity of mood and anxiety disorders. *Depress. Anx., 12*(suppl. 1), 69–76.

Kauth, M. R. (2000). *True nature: A theory of sexual attraction.* New York: Kluwer Academic/Plenum.

Kauth, M. R. (2006). Sexual orientation and identity. In R. D. McAnulty & M. M. Burnette (Eds.), *Sex and sexuality, Vol. 1: Sexuality today: Trends and controversies.* Westport, CT: Praeger Publishers.

Kavanagh, D. J. (2008). Management of co-occurring substance use disorders. In K. T. Mueser & D. V. Jeste (Eds.), *Clinical handbook of schizophrenia* (pp. 459–470). New York: Guilford Press.

Kawas, C., Resnick, S., Morrison, A., Brookmeyer, R., Corrada, M., Zonderman, A., et al. (1997). A prospective study of estrogen replacement therapy and the risk of developing Alzheimer's disease: The Baltimore Longtitudinal Study of Aging. *Neurology, 48*(6), 1517–1521.

Kaye, W. H., Frank, G. K., Bailer, U. F., Henry, S. E., Meltzer, C. C., Price, J. C., et al. (2005). Serotonin alterations in anorexia and bulimia nervosa: New insights from imaging studies. *Physiolog. Behav., 85*(1), 73–81.

Kaye, W. H., Gendall, K. A., Fernstrom, M. H., Fernstrom, J. D., McConaha, C. W., & Weltzin, T. E. (2000). Effects of acute tryptophan depletion on mood in bulimia nervosa. *Biol. Psychiat., 47*(2), 151–157.

Kaye, W. H., Strober, M., & Rhodes, L. (2002). Body image disturbance and other core symptoms in anorexia and bulimia nervosa. In D. J. Castle & K. A. Phillips (Eds.), *Disorders of body image* (pp. 67–82). Petersfield, England: Wrightson Biomedical.

Kazdin, A. E. (1994). Methodology, design, and evaluation in psychotherapy research. In A. E. Bergin & S. L. Garfield (Eds.), *Handbook of psychotherapy and behavior change* (4th ed.). New York: Wiley.

Kazdin, A. E. (2000). *Psychotherapy for children and adolescents: Directions for research and practice.* New York: Oxford University Press.

Kazdin, A. E. (2002). Psychosocial treatments for conduct disorder in children and adolescents. In P. E. Nathan & J. M. Gorman (Eds.), *A guide to treatments that work* (2nd ed., pp. 57–85). London: Oxford University Press.

Kazdin, A. E. (Ed.). (2003). *Methodological issues & strategies in clinical research* (3rd ed.). Washington, DC: American Psychological Association.

Kazdin, A. E. (2003). Problem-solving skills training and parent management training for conduct disorder. In A. E. Kazdin & J. R. Weisz (Eds.), *Evidence-based psychotherapies for children and adolescents.* New York: Guilford Press.

Kazdin, A. E. (2004). Evidence-based treatments: Challenges and priorities for practice and research. *Child Adol. Psychiat. Clinics N. Amer., 13*(4), 923–940.

Kazdin, A. E. (2005). *Parent management training: Treatment for oppositional, aggressive, and antisocial behavior in children and adolescents.* New York: Oxford University Press.

Kazdin, A. E. (2006). Assessment and evaluation in clinical practice. In R. J. Sternberg, C. D. Goodheart, & A. E. Kazdin (Eds.), *Evidence-based psychotherapy: Where practice and research meet* (pp. 153–177). Washington, DC: American Psychological Association.

Kazdin, A. E. (2006). Mechanisms of change in psychotherapy: Advances, breakthroughs, and cutting-edge research (do not yet exist). In P. E. McKnight & R. R. Bootzin (Eds.), *Strengthening research methodology: Psychological measurement and evaluation* (pp. 77–101). Washington, DC: American Psychological Association.

Kazdin, A. E. (2007). Psychosocial treatments for conduct disorder in children and adolescents. In P. E. Nathan & J. M. Gorman (Eds.), *A guide to treatments that work* (3rd ed., pp. 71–104). New York: Oxford University Press.

Kearney, C. A. (1999). *Casebook in child behavior disorders.* Belmont, CA: Wadsworth.

Kearney, C. A. (2005). *Social anxiety and social phobia in youth: Characteristics, assessment, and psychological treatment.* New York: Springer Publishing.

Kearney, C. A., & Steichen-Asch, P. (1990). Men, body image, and eating disorders. In A. E. Andersen (Ed.), *Males with eating disorders.* New York: Brunner/Mazel.

Keefe, R. S. E., Arnold, M. C., Bayen, U. J., McEvoy, J. P., & Wilson, W. H. (2002). Source-monitoring deficits for self-generated stimuli in schizophrenia: Multinomial modeling of data from three sources. *Schizo. Res., 57*(1), 51–68.

Keel, P. K., Mitchell, J. E., Davis, T. L., & Crow, S. J. (2002). Long-term impact of treatment in women diagnosed with bulimia nervosa. *Inter. J. Eat. Disorders, 31*(2), 151–158.

Keel, P. K., Mitchell, J. E., Miller, K. B., Davis, T. L., & Crow, S. J. (1999). Long-term outcome of bulimia nervosa. *Arch. Gen. Psychiat., 56*(1), 63–69.

Keel, P. K., Mitchell, J. E., Miller, K. B., Davis, T. L., & Crow, S. J. (2000). Social adjustment over 10 years following diagnosis with bulimia nervosa. *Inter. J. Eat. Disorders, 27*(1), 21–28.

Keen, E. (1970). *Three faces of being: Toward an existential clinical psychology.* By the Meredith Corp. Reprinted by permission of Irvington Publishers.

Keenan, K., Wakschlag, L., Danis, B., Hill, C., Humphries, J., Duax, J., et al. (2007). Further evidence of the reliability and validity of DSM-IV ODD and CD in preschool children. *J. Amer. Acad. Child Adol. Psychat., 46,* 457–468.

Keesey, R. E., & Corbett, S. W. (1983). Metabolic defense of the body weight set-point. In A. J. Stunkard & E. Stellar (Eds.), *Eating and its disorders.* New York: Raven Press.

Keith, S. J., Regier, D. A., & Rae, D. S. (1991). Schizophrenic disorders. In L. N. Robins & D. S. Regier (Eds.), *Psychiatric disorders in America: The Epidemiological Catchment Area Study.* New York: Free Press.

Kelleher, M. D., & Van Nuys, D. (2002). *This is the Zodiac speaking: Into the mind of a serial killer.* Westport, CT: Praeger/Greenwood.

Kellerman, H., & Burry, A. (2007). *Handbook of psychodiagnostic testing: Analysis of personality in the psychological report.* New York: Springer Publishing.

Kelly, K. (2005). Just don't do it! *U. S. News & World Report, 139*(14), 44–49.

Kelly, K. A. (1993). Multiple personality disorders: Treatment coordination in a partial hospital setting. *Bull. Menninger Clin., 57*(3), 390–398.

Kelly, M. P., Strassberg, D. S., & Kircher, J. R. (1990). Attitudinal and experiental correlates of anorgasmia. *Arch. Sex. Behav., 19,* 165–172.

Kemp, C. (2000, June 15–21). The curse of the werewolf. *Citybeat.com.* Retrieved July 30, 2008, from http://citybeat.com/2005-06-15/scitech.shtml

Kemp, D. R. (1994). *Mental health in the workplace: An employer's and manager's guide.* Westport, CT: Quorum Books.

Kendall, J., & Hatton, D. (2002). Racism as a source of health disparity in families with children with attention deficit hyperactivity disorder. *Adv. Nurs. Sci., 25*(2), 22–39.

Kendall, P. C. (2000). *Childhood disorders.* Hove, England: Psychology Press/Taylor & Francis.

Kendall, P. C., & Pimentel, S. S. (2003). On the physiological constellation in youth with generalized anxiety disorder (GAD). *J. Anx. Disorders, 17,* 211–221.

Kendler, K. S., Heath, A., & Martin, N. G. (1987). A genetic epidemiologic study of self-report suspiciousness. *Comprehen. Psychiat., 28*(3), 187–196.

Kendler, K. S., Heath, A., Neale, M., Kessler, R., & Eaves, L. (1992). A population-based twin study of alcoholism in women. *JAMA, 268*(14), 1877–1882.

Kendler, K. S., Karkowski, L. M., & Prescott, C. A. (1999). Causal relationship between stressful life events and the onset of major depression. *Amer. J. Psychiat., 156*(6), 837–848.

Kendler, K. S., Kuhn, J. W., & Prescott, C. A. (2004). Childhood sexual abuse, stressful life events and risk for major depression in women. *Psychol. Med., 34*(8), 1475–1482.

Kendler, K. S., Myers, J., & Prescott, C. A. (2005). Sex differences in the relationship between social support and risk for major depression: A longitudinal study of opposite-sex twin pairs. *Amer. J. Psychiat., 162*(2), 250–256.

Kendler, K. S., Neale, M. C., Heath, A. C., Kessler, R. C., & Eaves, L. J. (1994). A twin-family study of alcoholism in women. *Amer. J. Psychiat., 151*(5), 707–715.

Kendler, K. S., Neale, M. C., Kessler, R. C., Heath, A. C., & Eaves, L. J. (1993). Panic disorder in women: A population-based twin study. *Psychol. Med., 23*, 397–406.

Kendler, K. S., Ochs, A. L., Gorman, A. M., Hewitt, J. K., Ross, D. E., & Mirsky, A. F. (1991). The structure of schizotypy: A pilot multitrait twin study. *Psychiat. Res., 36*(1), 19–36.

Kendler, K. S., Walters, E. E., & Kessler, R. C. (1997). The prediction of length of major depressive episodes: Results from an epidemiological sample of female twins. *Psychol. Med., 27*(1), 107–117.

Kendler, K. S., Walters, E. E., Neale, M. C., Kessler, R. C., et al. (1995). The structure of the genetic and environmental risk factors for six major psychiatric disorders in women: Phobia, generalized anxiety disorder, panic disorder, bulimia, major depression, and alcoholism. *Arch. Gen. Psychiat., 52*(5), 374–383.

Kennedy, C. A., Hill, J. M., & Schleifer, S. J. (2005). HIV/AIDS and substance use disorders. In R. J. Frances, A. H. Mack, & S. I. Miller (Eds.), *Clinical textbook of addictive disorders* (3rd ed., pp. 411–436). New York: Guilford Press.

Kennedy, D. P., & Squire, L. R. (2007). An analysis of calendar performance in two autistic calendar savants. *Learning & Memory, 14*(8), 533–538.

Kennedy, P. (2004, June 13). One room, 3,000 brains. *The Boston Globe*, 3rd ed..

Kenny, M. C., Alvarez, K., Donohue, B. C., & Winick, C. B. (2008). Overview of behavioral assessment with adults. In M. Hersen & J. Rosqvist (Eds.), *Handbook of psychological assessment, case conceptualization and treatment, Vol. 1: Adults.* Hoboken, NJ: John Wiley & Sons.

Kensinger, E. A., Ullman, M. T., & Corkin, S. (2001). Bilateral medial temporal lobe damage does not affect lexical or grammatical processing: Evidence from amnesic patient H. M. *Hippocampus, 11*(4), 347–360.

Kerkhof, A. J. F. M. (2005). Suicide prevention discussed at the WHO European Ministerial Conference on Mental Health. *Crisis, 26*(2), 51–52.

Kernberg, O. F. (1989). Narcissistic personality disorder in childhood. *Psychiatr. Clin. N. Amer., 12*(3), 671–694.

Kernberg, O. F. (1992). *Aggression in personality disorders and its perversions.* New Haven, CT: Yale University Press.

Kernberg, O. F. (1997). Convergences and divergences in contemporary psychoanalytic technique and psychoanalytic psychotherapy. In J. K. Zeig (Ed.), *The evolution of psychotherapy: The third conference.* New York: Brunner/Mazel.

Kernberg, O. F. (2001). The concept of libido in the light of contemporary psychoanalytic theorizing. In P. Hartocollis (Ed.), *Mankind's Oedipal destiny: Libidinal and aggressive aspects of sexuality* (pp. 95–111). Madison, CT: International Universities Press.

Kernberg, O. F. (2005). Object relations theories and technique. In E. S. Person, A. M. Cooper,

& G. O. Gabbard (Eds.), *The American Psychiatric Publishing textbook of psychoanalysis* (pp. 57–75). Washington, DC: American Psychiatric Publishing.

Kernberg, O. F., & Caligor, E. (2005). A psychoanalytic theory of personality disorders. In M. F. Lenzenweger & J. F. Clarkin (Eds.), *Major theories of personality disorder* (2nd ed., pp. 114–156). New York: Guilford Press.

Kernberg, P. F., & Wiener, J. M. (2004). Personality disorders. In J. M. Wiener & M. K. Dulcan (Eds.), *The American Psychiatric Publishing textbook of child and adolescent psychiatry* (3rd ed., pp. 775–793). Washington, DC: American Psychiatric Publishing.

Kerr, J. H., Lindner, K. J., & Blaydon, M. (2007). *Exercise dependence.* London: Routledge.

Kersting, K. (2005). Serious rehabilitation. *Monitor Psychol., 36*(1), 38–41.

Kessing, L. V. (2004). Endogenous: Reactive and neurotic depression—Diagnostic stability and long-term outcome. *Psychopathology, 37*(3), 124–130.

Kessler, D. A., & Pines, W. L. (1990). The federal regulation of prescription drug advertising and promotion. *JAMA, 264*(18), 2409–2415.

Kessler, R. C. (2002). Epidemiology of depression. In I. H. Gotlib & C. L. Hammen (Eds.), *Handbook of depression* (pp. 23–42). New York: Guilford Press.

Kessler, R. C., Adler, L. A., Barkley, R., Biederman, J., Conners, C. K., Demler, O., et al. (2006). The prevalence and correlates of adult ADHD in the United States: Results from the National Comorbidity Survey Replication. *Amer. J. Psychiat., 163*(4), 716–723.

Kessler, R. C., Adler, L. A., Barkley, R., Biederman, J., Conners, C. K., Faraone, S. V., et al. (2005). Patterns and predictors of attention-deficit/hyperactivity disorder persistence into adulthood: Results from the National Comorbidity Survey Replication. *Biol. Psychiat., 57*(11), 1442–1451.

Kessler, R. C., Amminger, G. P., Aguilar-Gaxiola, S., Alongo, J., & Lee, S. (2007). Age of onset of mental disorders: A review of recent literature. *Curr. Opin. Psychiat., 20*(4), 359–364.

Kessler, R. C., Berglund, P. A., Borges, G., Castilla-Puentes, R. C., Glantz, M. D., Jaeger, S. A., Merikangas, K. R., Nock, M. K., Russo, L. J., & Stang, P. E. (2007). Smoking and suicidal behaviors in the National Comorbidity Survey: Replication. *J. Nerv. Ment. Dis., 195*(5), 369–377.

Kessler, R. C., Berglund, P., Demler, O., Jin, R., Koretz, D., Merikangas, K. R., et al. (2003). The epidemiology of major depressive disorder: Results from the National Comorbidity Survey Replication (NCS-R). *JAMA, 289*(23), 3095–3105.

Kessler, R. C., Berglund, P., Demler, O., Jin, R., & Walters, E. E. (2005). Lifetime prevalence and age-of-onset distributions of DSM-IV disorders in the National Comorbidity Survey Replication. *Arch. Gen. Psychiat., 62*, 593–602.

Kessler, R. C., Chiu, W. T., Demler, O., & Walters, E. E. (2005). Prevalence, severity, and comorbidity of 12-month DSM-IV disorders in the National Comorbidity Survey Replication. *Arch. Gen. Psychiat., 62*, 617–627.

Kessler, R. C., Chiu, W. T., Jin, R., Ruscio, A. M., Shear, K., & Walters, E. E. (2006).

The epidemiology of panic attacks, panic disorder, and agoraphobia in the National Comorbidity Survey Replication. *Arch. Gen. Psychiat., 63*, 415–424.

Kessler, R. C., Coccaro, E. F., Fava, M., Jaeger, S., Jin, R., & Walters, E. (2006). The prevalence and correlates of DSM-IV intermittent explosive disorder in the national comorbidity survey replication. *Arch. Gen. Psychiat., 63*(6), 669–678.

Kessler, R. C., DuPont, R. L., Berglund, P., & Wittchen, H. U. (1999). Impairment in pure and comorbid generalized anxiety disorder and major depression at 12 months in two national surveys. *Amer. J. Psychiat., 156*(12), 1915–1923.

Kessler, R. C., Galea, S., Gruber, M. J., Sampson, N. A., Ursano, R. J., & Wessely, S. (2008). Trends in mental illness and suicidality after Hurricane Katrina. *Mol. Psychiat., 13*(4), 374–384.

Kessler, R. C., Haro, J-M., Heeringa, S. G., Pennell, B. E., & Ustun, T. B. (2006). The World Health Organization World Mental Health Survey Initiative. *Epidem.-e-Psichiatr. Soc., 15*(3), 161–166.

Kessler, R. C., McGonagle, K. A., Zhao, S., Nelson, C. B., Hughes, M., Eshleman, S., et al. (1994). Lifetime and 12-month prevalence of DSM-III-R psychiatric disorders among persons aged 15–54 in the United States: Results from the National Comorbidity Survey. *Arch. Gen. Psychiat., 51*(1), 8–19.

Kessler, R. C., Sonnega, A., Bromet, E., Hughes, M., & Nelson, C. B. (1995). Posttraumatic stress disorder in the National Comorbidity Survey. *Arch. Gen. Psychiat., 52*, 1048–1060.

Kessler, R. C., & Stang, P. E. (Eds.). (2006). *Health and work productivity: Making the business case for quality health care.* Chicago, IL: University of Chicago Press.

Kessler, R. C., & Zhao, S. (1999). The prevalence of mental illness. In A.V. Horwitz & T. L. Scheid (Eds.), *A handbook for the study of mental health: Social contexts, theories, and systems.* Cambridge, England: Cambridge University Press.

Kety, S. S. (1988). Schizophrenic illness in the families of schizophrenic adoptees: Findings from the Danish national sample. *Schizophr. Bull., 14*(2), 217–222.

Kety, S. S., Rosenthal, D., Wender, P. H., et al. (1968). The types and prevalence of mental illness in the biological and adoptive families of schizophrenics. *J. Psychiatr. Res., 6*, 345–362.

Kety, S. S., Rosenthal, D., Wender, P. H., et al. (1975). Mental illness in the biological and adoptive families of adopted individuals who became schizophrenic: A preliminary report based on psychiatric interviews. In R. R. Fieve, D. Rosenthal, & H. Brill (Eds.), *Genetic research in psychiatry.* Baltimore, MD: Johns Hopkins University Press.

Kety, S. S., Rosenthal, D., Wender, P. H., Schulsinger, F., & Jacobsen, B. (1978). The biologic and adoptive families of adopted individuals who become schizophrenic: Prevalence of mental illness and other characteristics. In L. C. Wynne, R. L. Cromwell, & S. Matthysse (Eds.), *The nature of schizophrenia: New approaches to research and treatment.* New York: Wiley.

Keyes, C. L. M., & Goodman, S. H. (Eds.). (2006). *Women and depression: A handbook for the social, behavioral, and biomedical sciences.* New York: Cambridge University Press.

Keys, A., Brozek, J., Henschel, A., Mickelson, O., & Taylor, H. L. (1950). *The biology of human starvation.* Minneapolis: University of Minnesota Press.

Khan, S., Murray, R. P., & Barnes, G. E. (2002). A structural equation model of the effect of poverty and unemployment on alcohol abuse. *Addic. Behav., 27*(3), 405–423.

Khandker R. K., & Simoni-Wastila, L. J. (1998). Differences in prescription drug utilization and expenditures between blacks and whites in the Georgia Medicaid population. *Inquiry, 35,* 78–87.

Khawaja, N. G., & Chapman, D. (2007). Cognitive predictors of worry in a non-clinical population. *Clin. Psychologist, 11*(1), 24–32.

Khouzam, H. R., Ghafoori, B., & Hierholzer, R. (2005). Progress in the identification, diagnosis and treatment of posttraumatic stress disorder. In T. A. Corales (Ed.), *Trends in posttraumatic stress disorder research* (pp. 1–28). Hauppauge, NY: Nova Science Publishers.

Kiecolt-Glaser, J. K., & Glaser, R. (1999). Chronic stress and mortality among older adults. *JAMA, 282*(23), 2259–2260.

Kiecolt-Glaser, J. K., & Glaser, R. (1999). Psychoneuroimmunology and immunotoxicology: Implications for carcinogenesis. *Psychosom. Med., 61*(3), 271–272.

Kiecolt-Glaser, J. K., Dura, J. R., Speicher, C. E., Trask, O. J., & Glaser, R. (1991). Spousal caregivers of dementia victims: Longitudinal changes in immunity and health. *Psychosom. Med., 53,* 345–362.

Kiecolt-Glaser, J. K., Garner, W., Speicher, C., Penn, G. M., Holliday, J., & Glaser, R. (1984). Psychosocial modifiers of immunocompetence in medical students. *Psychosom. Med., 46,* 7–14.

Kiecolt-Glaser, J. K., Glaser, R., Gravenstein, S., Malarkey, W. B., & Sheridan, J. (1996). Chronic stress alters the immune response to influenza virus vaccine in older adults. *Proc. Natl. Acad. Sci. USA, 93,* 3043–3047.

Kiecolt-Glaser, J. K., McGuire, L., Robles, T. F., & Glaser, R. (2002). Psychoneuroimmunology: Psychological influences on immune function and health. *J. Cons. Clin. Psychol., 70*(3), 537–547.

Kiecolt-Glaser, J. K., Page, G. G., Marucha, P. T., MacCallum, R. C., & Glaser, R. (1998). Psychological influences on surgical recovery. Perspectives from psychoneuroimmunology. *Amer. Psychologist, 53*(11), 1209–1218.

Kiernan, W. (2000). Where we are now: Perspectives on employment of persons with mental retardation. *Focus Autism Other Dev. Disabil., 15*(2), 90–96.

Kiesler, C. A. (2000). The next wave of change for psychology and mental health services in the health care revolution. *Amer. Psychologist, 55*(5), 481–487.

Kiesler, D. J. (1966). Some myths of psychotherapy research and the search for a paradigm. *Psychol. Bull., 65,* 110–136.

Kiesler, D. J. (1995). Research classic: "Some myths of psychotherapy research and the search for a paradigm": Revisited. *Psychother. Res., 5*(2), 91–101.

Kiev, A. (1989). Suicide in adults. In J. G. Howells (Ed.), *Modern perspectives in the psychiatry of the affective disorders.* New York: Brunner/Mazel.

Kihlström, J. F. (2001). *Dissociative disorders.* New York: Kluwer Academic/Plenum.

Kihlström, J. F. (2002). To honor Kraepelin . . .: From symptoms to pathology in the diagnosis of mental illness. In L. E. Beutler & M. L. Malik (Eds.), *Rethinking the DSM: A psychological perspective. Decade of behavior.* Washington, DC: American Psychological Association.

Kihlström, J. F. (2005). Is hypnosis an altered state of consciousness or what? *Contemp. Hyp., 22,* 34–38.

Kihlström, J. F. (2007). Consciousness in hypnosis. In E. Thompson, P. D. Zelazo, & M. Moscovitch (Eds.), *The Cambridge handbook of consciousness* (pp. 445–479). New York: Cambridge University Press.

Kim, C. H., Jayathilake, K., & Meltzer, H. Y. (2003). Hopelessness, neurocognitive function, and insight in schizophrenia: Relationship to suicidal behavior. *Schizo. Res., 60*(1), 71–80.

Kim, S. W., Grant, J. E., Kim, S. I., Swanson, T. A., Bernstein, G. A., Jaszcz, W. B., et al. (2004). A possible association of recurrent streptococcal infections and acute onset of obsessive-compulsive disorder. *J. Neuropsychiat. Clin Neurosci., 16*(3), 252–260.

Kimball, A. (1993). Nipping and tucking. In Skin deep: Our national obsession with looks. *Psychol. Today, 26*(3), 96.

King, G. A., Polivy, J., & Herman, C. P. (1991). Cognitive aspects of dietary restraint: Effects on person memory. *Inter. J. Eat. Disorders, 10*(3), 313–321.

King, L. (2002, March 19). Interview with Russell Yates. *Larry King Live, CNN.*

King, N. J., Heyne, D., & Ollendick, T. H. (2005). Cognitive-behavioral treatments for anxiety and phobic disorders in children and adolescents: A review. *Behav. Disorders, 30*(3), 241–257.

King, N. J., Muris, P., & Ollendick, T. H. (2004). Specific phobia. In J. S. March & T. L. Morris (Eds.), *Anxiety disorders in children and adolescents* (2nd ed., pp. 263–279). New York: Guilford Press.

King, R. A. (2003). Psychodynamic approaches to youth suicide. In R. A. King & A. Apter (Eds.), *Suicide in children and adolescents* (pp. 150–169). New York: Cambridge University Press.

King, R. A., & Apter, A. (Eds.). (2003). *Suicide in children and adolescents.* New York: Cambridge University Press.

Kinzie, J., Leung, P., Boehnlein, J., & Matsunaga, D. (1992). Psychiatric epidemiology of an Indian village: A 19-year replication study. *J. Nerv. Ment. Dis., 180*(1), 33–39.

Kirby, M. (2000). Psychiatry, psychology, law and homosexuality—Uncomfortable bedfellows. *Psychiatry, Psychol. Law, 7*(2), 139–149.

Kirchmayer, U., Davoli, M., Verster, A. D., Amato, L., Ferri, M., & Perucci, C. A. (2002). A systematic review on the efficacy of naltrexone maintenance treatment in opioid dependence. *Addiction, 97*(10), 1241–1249.

Kirk, S. A., & Kutchins, H. (1992). *The selling of DSM: The rhetoric of science in psychiatry.* New York: Aldine de Gruyter.

Kirmayer, L. J. (2001). Cultural variations in the clinical presentation of depression and anxiety: Implications for diagnosis and treatment. *J. Clin. Psychiat., 62*(Suppl. 13), 22–28.

Kirmayer, L. J. (2002). The refugee's predicament. *Evol. Psychiat., 67*(4), 724–742.

Kirmayer, L. J. (2003). Failures of imagination: The refugee's narrative in psychiatry. *Anthropol. Med., 10*(2), 167–185.

Kirmayer, L. J., & Looper, K. J. (2007). Somatoform disorders. In M. Hersen, S. M. Turner, & D. C. Beidel (Eds.), *Adult psychopathology and diagnosis* (5th ed., pp. 410–472). Hoboken, NJ: Wiley.

Kirschenbaum, H. (2004). Carl Rogers's life and work: An assessment on the 100th anniversary of his birth. *J. Couns. Dev., 82*(1), 116–124.

Kisker, G. W. (1977). *The disorganized personality.* New York: McGraw-Hill.

Kleber, H. D., & Galanter, M. (Eds.). (2008). *The American Psychiatric Publishing textbook of substance abuse treatment* (4th ed.). Arlington, VA: American Psychiatric Publishing.

Klein, D. F. (1964). Delineation of two drug-responsive anxiety syndromes. *Psychopharmacologia, 5,* 397–408.

Klein, D. F., & Fink, M. (1962). Psychiatric reaction patterns to imipramine. *Amer. J. Psychiat., 119,* 432–438.

Klein, D. N., Santiago, N. J., Vivian, D., Blalock, J. A., Kocsis, J. H., Markowitz, J. C., et al. (2004). Cognitive-behavior analysis system of psychotherapy as a maintenance treatment for chronic depression. *J. Cons. Clin. Psychol., 72*(4), 681–688.

Klein, W. C., & Jess, C. (2002). One last pleasure? Alcohol use among elderly people in nursing homes. *Hlth. Soc. Work., 27*(3), 193–203.

Kleinman, A. (1987). Anthropology and psychiatry: The role of culture in cross-cultural research on illness. *Brit. J. Psychiat., 151,* 447–454.

Klerman, G. L., & Weissman, M. M. (1992). Interpersonal psychotherapy. In E. S. Paykel (Ed.), *Handbook of affective disorders.* New York: Guilford Press.

Klerman, G. L., Weissman, M. M., Markowitz, J., Glick, I., Wilner, P. J., Mason, B., et al. (1994). Medication and psychotherapy. In A. E. Bergin & S. L. Garfield (Eds.), *Handbook of psychotherapy and behavior change* (4th ed.). New York: Wiley.

Kline, N. S. (1958). Clinical experience with iproniazid (Marsilid). *J. Clin. Exp. Psychopathol., 19*(1, Suppl.), 72–78.

Kling, K. C., Hyde, J. S., Showers, C. J., & Buswell, B. N. (1999). Gender differences in self-esteem: A meta-analysis. *Psychol. Bull., 125*(4), 470–500.

Klitzman, R. (2008). *When doctors become patients.* New York: Oxford University Press.

Klocek, J. W., Oliver, J. M., & Ross, M. J. (1997). The role of dysfunctional attitudes, negative life events, and social support in the prediction of depressive dysphoria: A prospective longitudinal study. *Soc. Behav. Pers., 25*(2), 123–136.

Klopfer, B., & Davidson, H. (1962). *The Rorschach technique.* New York: Harcourt, Brace.

Kluft, R. P. (1985). Hypnotherapy of childhood multiple personality disorder. *Amer. J. Clin. Hyp., 27*(4), 201–210.

Kluft, R. P. (1987). The simulation and dissimulation of multiple personality disorder. *Amer. J. Clin. Hyp., 30*(2), 104–118.

Kluft, R. P. (1988). The dissociative disorders. In J. Talbott, R. Hales, & S. Yudofsky (Eds.), *Textbook of psychiatry.* Washington, DC: American Psychiatric Press.

Kluft, R. P. (1991). Multiple personality disorder. In A. Tasman & S. M. Goldfinger (Eds.), *Ameri-*

can Psychiatric Press review of psychiatry (Vol. 10). Washington, DC: American Psychiatric Press.

Kluft, R. P. (1992). Discussion: A specialist's perspective on multiple personality disorder. *Psychoanal. Inq., 12*(1), 139–171.

Kluft, R. P. (1993). Basic principles in conducting the psychotherapy of multiple personality disorder. In R. P. Kluft & C. G. Fine (Eds.), *Clinical perspectives on multiple personality disorder.* Washington, DC: American Psychiatric Press.

Kluft, R. P. (1999). An overview of the psychotherapy of dissociative identity disorder. *Amer. J. Psychother., 53*(3), 289–319.

Kluft, R. P. (2000). The psychoanalytic psychotherapy of dissociative identity disorder in the context of trauma therapy. *Psychoanal. Inq., 20*(2), 259–286.

Kluft, R. P. (2001). Dissociative disorders. In H. S. Friedman (Ed.), *Specialty articles from the encyclopedia of mental health.* San Diego: Academic Press.

Kluger, J. (2004, December 6). Blowing a gasket. *Time, 164*(23), pp. 72–80.

Knight, B. G., Kaskie, B., Shurgot, G. R., & Dave, J. (2006). Improving the mental health of older adults. In J. E. Birren & K. W. Schaie (Eds.), *Handbook of the psychology of aging* (6th ed., pp. 408–425). San Diego, CA: Elsevier.

Knight, S. C., Meyer, R. G., & Goldstein, A. M. (2007). Forensic hypnosis. In A. M. Goldstein (Ed.), *Forensic psychology: Emerging topics and expanding roles* (pp. 734–763). Hoboken, NJ: Wiley.

Knudson, R. M. (2006). Anorexia dreaming: A case study. *Dreaming, 16*(1), 43–52.

Knutson, B., Wolkowitz, O. M., Cole, S. W., Chan, T., Moore, E. A., Johnson, R. C., et al. (1998). Selective alteration of personality and social behavior by serotonergic intervention. *Amer. J. Psychiat., 155,* 373–379.

Koch, W. J., & Haring, M. (2008). Posttraumatic stress disorder. In M. Hersen & J. Rosqvist (Eds.), *Handbook of psychological assessment, case conceptualization, and treatment, Vol. 1: Adults* (pp. 263–290). Hoboken, NJ: John Wiley & Sons.

Kocsis, R. N. (2008). *Serial murder and the psychology of violent crimes.* Totowa, NJ: Humana Press.

Koegel, L. K., Koegel, R. L., & Brookman, L. I. (2005). Child-initiated interactions that are pivotal in intervention for children with autism. In E. D. Hibbs & P. S. Jensen (Eds.), *Psychosocial treatments for child and adolescent disorders: Empirically based strategies for clinical practice* (2nd ed., pp. 633–657). Washington, DC: American Psychological Association.

Koenen, K. C., Lyons, M. J., Goldberg, J., Simpson, J., Williams, W. M., Toomey, R., et al. (2003). Co-twin control study of relationships among combat exposure, combat-related PTSD, and other mental disorders. *J. Traum. Stress, 16*(5), 433–438.

Koenig, H. G. (2002). The connection between psychoneuroimmunology and religion. In H. G. Koenig & H. J. Cohen (Eds.), *The link between religion and health: Psychoneuroimmunology and the faith factor.* New York: Oxford University Press.

Koenigsberg, H. W., Buchsbaum, M. S., Buchsbaum, B. R., Schneiderman, J. S., Tang, C. Y., New, A., et al. (2005). Functional MRI of visuospatial working memory in schizotypal personality disorder: A region-of-interest analysis. *Psychol. Med., 35*(7), 1019–1030.

Koenigsberg, H. W., Harvey, P. D., Mitropoulou, V., Schmeidler, J., New, A. S., Good-man, M., et al. (2002). Characterizing affective instability in borderline personality disorder. *Amer. J. Psychiat., 159*(5), 784–788.

Koenigsberg, H., Harvey, P., Mitropoulou, V., New, A. Goodman, M., Silverman, J., et al. (2001). Are the interpersonal and identity disturbances in the borderline personality disorder criteria linked to the traits of affectivity and impulsivity? *J. Pers. Disorders, 15,* 358–370.

Koenigsberg, H. W., Reynolds, D., Goodman, M., New, A. S., Mitropoulou, V., Trestman, R. L., et al. (2003). Risperidone in the treatment of schizotypal personality disorder. *Journal of Clinical Psychiatry, 64*(6), 628–634.

Koerner, B. I. (2007). Drug makers find new markets by publicizing "hidden epidemics" of mental illness. In A. Quigley (Ed.), *Current controversies: Mental health.* Detroit: Greenhaven Press/Thomson Gale.

Koh, K. B., Kim, D. K., Kim, S. Y., & Park, J. K. (2005). The relation between anger expression, depression, and somatic symptoms in depressive disorders and somatoform disorders. *J. Clin. Psychiat., 66*(4), 485–491.

Koh, M., Nishimatsu, Y., & Endo, S. (2000). Dissociative disorder. *J. Inter. Soc. Life Info. Sci., 18*(2), 495–498.

Kohler, F. W., Strain, P. S., & Goldstein, H. (2005). Learning experiences . . . An alternative program for preschoolers and parents: Peer-mediated interventions for young children with autism. In E. D. Hibbs & P. S. Jensen (Eds.), *Psychosocial treatments for child and adolescent disorders: Empirically based strategies for clinical practice* (2nd ed., pp. 659–687). Washington, DC: American Psychological Association.

Kohut, H. (1966). Forms and transformation of narcissism. *J. Amer. Psychoanal. Assoc., 14,* 243–272.

Kohut, H. (1977). *The restoration of the self.* New York: International Universities Press.

Kohut, H. (1984). *How does analysis cure?* Chicago: University of Chicago Press.

Kohut, H. (2001). On empathy. *Eur. J. Psychoanal. Ther. Res., 2*(2), 139–146.

Kohut, H., & Wolf, E. S. (1978). The disorders of the self and their treatment: An outline. *Inter. J. Psychoanal., 59*(4), 413–425.

Kokish, R., Levenson, J. S., & Blasingame, G. D. (2005). Post-conviction sex offender polygraph examination: Client-reported perceptions of utility and accuracy. *Sex. Abuse: J. Res. Treat., 17*(2), 211–221.

Kolff, C. A., & Doan, R. N. (1985). Victims of torture: Two testimonies. In E. Stover & E. O. Nightingale (Eds.), *The breaking of bodies and minds: Torture, psychiatric abuse, and the health professions.* New York: W. H. Freeman.

Kolodny, R., Masters, W. H., & Johnson, J. (1979). *Textbook of sexual medicine.* Boston: Little, Brown.

Komaroff, A. L., Masuda, M., & Holmes, T. H. (1986). The Social Readjustment Rating Scale: A comparative study of Negro, white, and Mexican Americans. *J. Psychosom. Res., 12,* 121–128.

Komaroff, A. L., Masuda, M., & Holmes, T. H. (1989). The Social Readjustment Rating Scale: A comparative study of Black, white, and Mexican Americans. In T. H. Holmes and E. M. David (Eds.), *Life change, life events, and illness.* New York: Praeger.

Kong, D. (1998, November 18). Still no solution in the struggle on safeguards—Doing harm: Research on the mentally ill. *Boston Globe,* p. A1.

Konrad, N., Daigle, M. S., Daniel, A. E., Dear, G. E., Frottier, P., & Hayes, L. M. (2007). Preventing suicide in prisons, Part I: Recommendations from the International Association for Suicide Prevention Task Force in Prisons. *J. Crisis Int. Suic. Prev., 28,* 113–121.

Koob, G. F. (2008). Neurobiology of addiction. In H. D. Kleber & M. Galanter (Eds.), *The American Psychiatric Publishing textbook of substance abuse treatment* (4th ed., pp. 3–16). Arlington, VA: American Psychiatric Publishing.

Koob, G. F., & LeMoal, M. (2008). Addiction and the brain antireward system. In S. Fiske, D. L. Schacter, & R. Sternberg (Eds.), *Annual review of psychology* (Vol. 59). Palo Alto, CA: Annual reviews.

Koocher, G. P., & Keith-Spiegel, P. (2008). *Ethics in psychology and the mental health professions: Standards and cases* (3rd ed.). Oxford, England: Oxford University Press.

Koopman, C., Palesh, O., Marten, B., Thompson, B., Ismailji, T., Holmes, D. D., et al. (2004). Child abuse and adult interpersonal trauma as predictors of posttraumatic stress disorder symptoms among women seeking treatment for intimate partner violence. In T. A. Corales (Ed.), *Focus on posttraumatic stress disorder research* (pp. 1–16). Hauppauge, NY: Nova Science.

Kopelowicz, A., Liberman, R. P., & Zarate, R. (2002). Psychosocial treatments for schizophrenia. In P. E. Nathan & J. M. Gorman (Eds.), *A guide to treatments that work* (2nd ed., pp. 201–228). London: Oxford University Press.

Kopelowicz, A., Liberman, R. P., & Zarate, R. (2007). Psychosocial treatments for schizophrenia. In P. E. Nathan & J. M. Gorman (Eds.), *A guide to treatments that work* (3rd ed., pp. 243–269). New York: Oxford University Press.

Kopelowicz, A., Liberman, R. P., & Zarate, R. (2008). Psychosocial treatments for schizophrenia. In K. T. Mueser & D. V. Jeste (Eds.), *Clinical handbook of schizophrenia* (pp. 243–269). New York: Guilford Press.

Koponen, H., Rantakallio, P., Veijola, J., Jones, P., Jokelainen, J., & Isohanni, M. (2004). Childhood central nervous system infections and risk for schizophrenia. *Eur. Arch. Psychiat. Clin. Neurosci., 254*(1), 9–13.

Korchin, S. J., & Sands, S. H. (1983). Principles common to all psychotherapies. In C. E. Walker (Ed.), *The handbook of clinical psychology.* Homewood, IL: Dow Jones-Irwin.

Kordon, A., Kahl, K. G., Broocks, A., Voderholzer, U., Rasche-Rauchle, H., & Hohagen, F. (2005). Clinical outcome in patients with obsessive-compulsive disorder after discontinuation of SRI treatment: Results from a two-year follow-up. *Eur. Arch. Psychiat. Clin. Neurosci., 255*(1), 48–50.

Koren, D., Norman, D., Cohen, A., Berman, J., & Klein, E. M. (2005). Increased PTSD risk with combat-related injury: A matched comparison study of injured and uninjured soldiers experiencing the same combat events. *Amer. J. Psychiat., 162*(2), 276–282.

Korintheberg, R., Shreck, J., Weser, J., & Lehmkuhl, G. (2004). Posttraumatic syndrome after minor head injury cannot be predicted by neurological investigation. *Brain Development, 26*(2), 113–117.

Koss, M. P. (1993). Rape: Scope, impact, interventions, and public policy responses. *Amer. Psychologist, 48*(10), 1062–1069.

Koss, M. P. (2005). Empirically enhanced reflections on 20 years of rape research. *J. Interpers. Violence, 20*(1), 100–107.

Koss, M. P., & Heslet, L. (1992). Somatic consequences of violence against women. *Arch. Fam. Med., 1*(1), 53–59.

Koss, M. P., Woodruff, W. J., & Koss, P. (1991). Criminal victimization among primary care medical patients: Prevalence, incidence, and physician usage. *Behav. Sci. Law, 9,* 85–96.

Kosten, T. R., George, T. P., & Kleber, H. D. (2005). The neurobiology of substance dependence: Implications for treatment. In R. J. Frances, A. H. Mack, & S. I. Miller (Eds.), *Clinical textbook of addictive disorders* (3rd ed., pp. 3–15). New York: Guilford Press.

Kosten, T. R., Sofuoglu, M., & Gardner, T. J. (2008). Clinical management: Cocaine. In H. D. Kleber & M. Galanter (Eds.), *The American Psychiatric Publishing textbook of substance abuse treatment* (4th ed., pp. 157–168). Arlington, VA: American Psychiatric Publishing.

Kösters, M., Burlingame, G. M., Nachtigall, C., & Strauss, B. (2006). A meta-analytic review of the effectiveness of inpatient group psychotherapy. *Group Dynamics: Theory Res. Prac., 10*(2), 146–163.

Kouri, E. M., & Pope, H. G., Jr. (2000). Abstinence symptoms during withdrawal from chronic marijuana use. *Exp. Clin. Psychopharmacol., 8*(4), 483–492.

Koury, M. A., & Rapaport, M. H. (2007). Quality of life impairment in anxiety disorders. In M. S. Ritsner & A. G. Awad (Eds.), *Quality of life impairment in schizophrenia, mood and anxiety disorders: New perspectives on research and treatment.* The Netherlands: Springer.

Kovacs, M., Goldston, D., & Gatsonis, C. (1993). Suicidal behaviors and childhood-onset depressive disorders: A longitudinal investigation. *J. Amer. Acad. Child Adol. Psychiat., 32,* 8–20.

Kposowa, A. J., McElvain, J. P., & Breault, K. D. (2008). Immigration and suicide: The role of marital status, duration of residence, and social integration. *Arch. Suic. Res., 12*(1), 82–92.

Kraines, S. H., & Thetford, E. S. (1972). *Help for the depressed.* Springfield, IL: Thomas.

Krakauer, S. Y. (2001). *Treating dissociative identity disorder: The power of the collective heart.* Philadelphia: Brunner-Routledge.

Krapohl, D. J. (2002). The polygraph in personnel screening. In M. Kleiner (Ed.), *The handbook of polygraph testing.* San Diego, CA: Academic.

Kratochwill, T. R. (1992). Single-case research design and analysis: An overview. In T. R. Kratochwill & J. R. Levin (Eds.), *Single-case research design and analysis: New directions for psychology and education.* Hillsdale, NJ: Lawrence Erlbaum.

Kravitz, R. L., Epstein, R. M., Feldman, M. D., Franz, C. E., Azari, R., Wilkes, M. S., et al. (2005). Influence of patients' requests for direct-to-consumer advertised antidepressants. *JAMA, 293*(16), 1905–2002.

Kreek, M. J. (2008). Neurobiology of opiates and opioids. In H. D. Kleber & M. Galanter (Eds.), *The American Psychiatric Publishing textbook of substance abuse treatment* (4th ed., pp. 247–264). Arlington, VA: American Psychiatric Publishing.

Krishnan, K. R. R., Swartz, M. S., Larson, M. J., & Santo-Liquido, G. (1984). Funeral mania in recurrent bipolar affective disorders: Reports of three cases. *J. Clin. Psychiat., 45,* 310–311.

Krueger, R. G., & Kaplan, M. S. (2000). Evaluation and treatment of sexual disorders: Frottage. In L. Vandecreed & T. L. Jackson (Eds.), *Innovations in clinical practice: A source book* (Vol. 18, pp. 185–197). Sarasota, FL: Professional Resource Press.

Krueger, R. G., & Kaplan, M. S. (2002). Behavioral and psychopharmacological treatment of the paraphilic and hypersexual disorders. *J. Psychiatr. Prac., 8*(1), 21–32.

Krug, A. W., Ziegler, C. G., & Bornstein, S. R. (2008). DHEA and DHEA-S, and their functions in the brain and adrenal medulla. In A. Weizman & M. S. Ritsner, (Eds.), *Neuroactive steroids in brain function, behavior and neuropsychiatric disorders: Novel strategies for research and treatment* (pp. 227–239). New York: Springer Science + Business Media.

Krug, E. G., Dahlberg, L. L., Mercy, J. A., Zwi, A. B., & Lozano, R. (Eds.). (2002). *World report on violence and health.* Geneva: World Health Organization. Retrieved April 3, 2007, from http://www.who.int/violence_injury_prevention/violence/world_report/en/full_en.pdf

Kruger, S., Young, L. T., & Braunig, P. (2005). Pharmacotherapy of bipolar mixed states. *Bipolar Disord. 7*(3), 205–215.

Ksir, C., Hart, C. L., & Oakley, R. (2008). *Drugs, society, and human behavior* (12th ed.). Boston: McGraw-Hill.

Kubler, A., Murphy, K., & Garavan, H. (2005). Cocaine dependence and attention switching within and between verbal and visuospatial working memory. *Eur. J. Neurosci., 21*(7), 1984–1992.

Kubrin, C., Wadsworth, T., & DiPietro, S. (2006). Deindustrialization, disadvantage and suicide among young Black males. *Soc. Forces, 84,* 1559–1579.

Kuhn, R. (1958). The treatment of depressive states with G-22355 (imipramine hydrochloride). *Amer. J. Psychiat., 115,* 459–464.

Kuhn, T. S. (1962). *The structure of scientific revolutions.* Chicago: University of Chicago Press.

Kulka, R. A., Schlesenger, W. E., Fairbank, J. A., Hough. R. L., Jordan, B. K., Marmar, C. R., et al. (1990). *Trauma and the Vietnam War generation: Report of findings from the National Vietnam Veterans Readjustment Study.* New York: Brunner/Mazel.

Kumari, V., Das, M., Hodgins, S., Zachariah, E., Barkataki, I., Howlett, M., et al. (2005). Association between violent behaviour and impaired prepulse inhibition of the startle response in antisocial personality disorder and schizophrenia. *Behav. Brain Res., 158,* 159–166.

Kung, S., & Mrazek, D. A. (2005). Psychiatric emergency department visits on full-moon nights. *Psychiatr. Serv., 56*(2), 221–222.

Kuo, W., Gallo, J. J., & Eaton, W. W. (2004). Hopelessness, depression, substance disorder, and suicidality. *Soc. Psychiat. Psychiatr. Epidemiol., 39,* 497–501.

Kupfer, D. J. (2005). The increasing medical burden in bipolar disorder. *JAMA, 293*(20), 2528–2530.

Kuriansky, J. B. (1988). Personality style and sexuality. In R. A. Brown & J. R. Field (Eds.), *Treatment of sexual problems in individual and couples therapy.* Costa Mesa, CA: PMA Publishing.

Kurtz, D. L., Stewart, R. B., Zweifel, M., Li, T.-K., & Froehlich, J. C. (1996). Genetic differences in tolerance and sensitization to the sedative/hypnotic effects of alcohol. *Pharmacol. Biochem. Behav., 53*(3), 585–591.

Kutcher, S., & Gardner, D. M. (2008). Use of selective serotonin reuptake inhibitors and youth suicide: Making sense from a confusing story. *Curr. Opin. Psychiat., 21*(1), 65–69.

Kutscher, E. C. (2008). Antipsychotics. In K. T. Mueser & D. V. Jeste (Eds.), *Clinical handbook of schizophrenia* (pp. 159–167). New York: Guilford Press.

Lagnado, L. (2007, December 4). Prescription abuse seen in U.S. nursing homes. *Wall Street Journal Online.* Retrieved January 21, 2008, from http://online.wsj.com/article/SB119672919018312521.html

Lahey, B. B. (2008). Oppositional defiant disorder, conduct disorder, and juvenile delinquency. In S. P. Hinshaw & T. P. Beauchaine (Eds.), *Child and adolescent psychopathology* (pp. 335–369). Hoboken, NJ: Wiley.

Lahey, B. B., & Loeber, R. (1994). Framework for a developmental model of oppositional defiant disorder and conduct disorder. In D. K. Routh (Ed.), *Disruptive behavior disorders in childhood* (pp. 139–180). New York: Plenum.

Lahey, B. B., Loeber, R., Burke, J. D., & Applegate, B. (2005). Predicting future antisocial personality disorder in males from a clinical assessment in childhood. *J. Cons. Clin. Psychol., 73*(3), 389–399.

Laing, R. D. (1959). *The divided self: An existential study in sanity and madness.* London: Tavistock.

Laing, R. D. (1964). *The divided self* (2nd ed.). London: Pelican.

Laing, R. D. (1967). *The politics of experience.* New York: Pantheon.

Lalonde, J. K., Hudson, J. I., Gigante, R. A., & Pope, H. G., Jr. (2001). Canadian and American psychiatrists' attitudes toward dissociative disorders diagnoses. *Canad. J. Psychiat., 46*(5), 407–412.

Lalonde, J. K., Hudson, J. I., & Pope, H. G., Jr. (2002). Canadian and American psychiatrists' attitudes toward dissociative disorder diagnoses: The authors reply. *Canad. J. Psychiat., 47*(3), 1.

Lamb, D. H., Catanzaro, S. J., & Moorman, A. S. (2003). Psychologists reflect on their sexual relationships with clients, supervisees, and students: Occurrence, impact, rationales and collegial intervention. *Profess. Psychol., 34,* 102–107.

Lamb, M. (1998). Cybersex: Research notes on the characteristics of the visitors to online chat rooms. *Deviant Behav.: Interdiscip. J., 19,* 121–135.

Lambert, K., & Kinsley, C. H. (2005). *Clinical neuroscience: The neurobiological foundations of mental health.* New York: Worth Publishers.

Lambert, M. J., & Bergin, A. E. (1994). The effectiveness of psychotherapy. In A. E. Bergin & S. L. Garfield (Eds.), *Handbook of psychotherapy and behavioral change* (4th ed.). New York: Wiley.

Lambert, M. J., Shapiro, D. A., & Bergin, A. E. (1986). The effectiveness of psychotherapy. In S. L. Garfield & A. E. Bergin (Eds.), *Handbook of psychotherapy and behavioral change* (3rd ed.). New York: Wiley.

Lambert, M. J., Weber, F. D., & Sykes, J. D. (1993, April). Psychotherapy versus placebo. Poster presented at the annual meeting of the Western Psychological Association, Phoenix, AZ.

Lambert, M. T. (2003). Suicide risk assessment and management: Focus on personality disorders. *Curr. Opin. Psychiat., 16*(1), 71–76.

Lamprecht, F., Kohnke, C., Lempa, W., Sack, M., Matzke, M., & Munte, T. F. (2004). Event-related potentials and EMDR treatment of posttraumatic stress disorder. *Neuroscience Research, 49*(2), 267–272.

Landrigan, P. (2007). Cited in M. Ritter, Lead linked to aging in older brains. *YAHOO! News.* January, 27, 2008.

Landry, M. J. (1994). *Understanding drugs of abuse: The processes of addiction, treatment, and recovery.* Washington, DC: American Psychiatric Press.

Landsbergis, P. A., Schnall, P. L., Belkic, K. L., Baker, D., Schwartz, J. E., & Pickering T. G. (2003). The workplace and cardiovascular disease: Relevance and potential role for occupational health psychology. In L. E. Tetrick & J. C. Quick (Eds.), *Handbook of occupational health psychology.* Washington, DC: American Psychological Association.

Landsbergis, P. A., Schnall, P. L., Warren, K., Pickering, T. G., & Schwartz, J. E. (1994). Association between ambulatory blood pressure and alternative formulations of job strain. *Scand. J. Work Envir. Hlth., 20,* 349–363.

Lang, A. J. (2004). Treating generalized anxiety disorder with cognitive-behavioral therapy. *J. Clin. Psychiat., 65*(Suppl. 13), 14–19.

Lang, J. (1999, April 16). Local jails dumping grounds for mentally ill. *Detroit News.*

Lange, A., van de Ven, J. P., Schrieken, B., & Smit, M. (2004). "Interapy" burnout: Prevention and therapy of burnout via the Internet. *Verhaltenstherapie, 14*(3), 190–199.

Langenbucher, J., & Nathan, P. E. (2006). Diagnosis and classification. In F. Andrasik (Ed.), *Comprehensive handbook of personality and psychopathology, Vol. II: Adult psychopathology* (pp. 3–20). Hoboken, NJ: Wiley.

Langevin, R., Bain, J., Wortzman, G., Hucker, S., et al. (1988). Sexual sadism: Brain, blood, and behavior. *Ann. N.Y. Acad. Sci., 528,* 163–171.

Langley, J. (2006). *Boys get anorexia too: Coping with male eating disorders in the family.* London: Paul Chapman.

Långström, N., & Seto, M. C. (2006). Exhibitionist and voyeuristic behavior in a Swedish national population survey. *Arch. Sex. Behav., 35,* 427–435.

Långström, N., & Zucker, K. J. (2005). Transvestic fetishism in the general population: Prevalence and correlates. *J. Sex Marital Ther., 31*(2), 87–95.

Lanning, K. V. (2001). *Child molesters: A behavioral analysis* (4th ed.). Washington, DC: National Center for Missing and Exploited Children.

Lanyon, R. I. (2007). Utility of the psychological screening inventory: A review. *J. Clin. Psychol., 63*(3), 283–307.

Lara, M. E., & Klein, D. N. (1999). Psychosocial processes underlying the maintenance and persistence of depression: Implications for understanding chronic depression. *Clin. Psychol. Rev., 19*(5), 553–570.

Large, M. M., Nielssen, O., Ryan, C. J., & Hayes, R. (2008). Mental health laws that require dangerousness for involuntary admission may delay the initial treatment of schizophrenia. *Soc. Psychiat. Psychiatr. Epidemiol., 43*(3), 251–256.

Larsson, B., & Ivarsson, T. (1998). Clinical characteristics of adolescent psychiatric inpatients who have attempted suicide. *Eur. Child Adol. Psychiat., 7*(4), 201–208.

Lask, B., & Bryant-Waugh, R. (Eds.). (2000). *Anorexia nervosa and related eating disorders in childhood and adolescence* (2nd ed.). Hove, England: Psychology Press/Taylor & Francis.

Lasker Foundation. (2000). *Exceptional returns: The economic value of America's investment in biomedical research, 2000.* Retrieved from http://www.laskerfoundation.org/reports/pdf/exceptional.pdf

Latner, J. D., & Wilson, G. T. (2002). Self-monitoring and the assessment of binge eating. *Behav. Ther., 33*(3), 465–477.

Laumann, E. O., Gagnon, J. H., Michael, R. T., & Michaels, S. (1994). *The social organization of sexuality.* Chicago: University of Chicago Press.

Laumann, E. O., Nicolosi, A., Glasser, D. B., Paik, A., Gingell, C., Moreira, E., et al. (2005). Sexual problems among women and men aged 40–80 years: Prevalence and correlates identified in the Global Study of Sexual Attitudes and Behaviors. *International Journal of Impotence Research, 17,* 39–57.

Laumann, E. O., Paik, A., & Rosen, R. C. (1999). Sexual dysfunction in the United States: Prevalence and predictors. *JAMA, 281*(13), 1174.

Lauronen, E., Veijola, J., Isohanni, I., Jones, P. B., Nieminen, P., & Isohanni, M. (2004). Link between creativity and mental disorder. *Psychiatry: Interpers. Biol. Process., 67*(1), 81–98.

Lavretsky, H. (2008). History of schizophrenia as a psychiatric disorder. In K. T. Mueser & D. V. Jeste (Eds.), *Clinical handbook of schizophrenia* (pp. 3–13). New York: Guilford Press.

Lawford, B. R., Young, R. McD., Rowell, J. A., Gibson, J. N., et al. (1997). Association of the D2 dopamine receptor A1 allele with alcoholism: Medical severity of alcoholism and type of controls. *Biol. Psychiat., 41,* 386–393.

Lawlor, B. A., McCarron, M., Wilson, G., & McLoughlin, M. (2001). Temporal lobe-oriented CT scanning and dementia in Down's syndrome. *Inter. J. Ger. Psychiat., 16*(4), 427–429.

Lawson, W. B. (1986). Racial and ethnic factors in psychiatric research. *Hosp. Comm. Psychiat., 37,* 50–54.

Lawson, W. B. (1996). Clinical issues in the pharmacotherapy of African-Americans. *Psychopharmacol. Bull., 32,* 275–281.

Lawson, W. B. (2008). Schizophrenia in African Americans. In K. T. Mueser & D. V. Jeste (Eds.), *Clinical handbook of schizophrenia* (pp. 616–623). New York: Guilford Press.

Lazarov, O., Robinson, J., Tang, Y. P., Hairston, I. S., Korade-Mirnics, Z., Lee, V. M., et al. (2005). Environmental enrichment reduces Abeta levels and amyloid deposition in transgenic mice. *Cell, 120*(5), 572–574.

Lazarus, A. A. (1965). The treatment of a sexually inadequate man. In L. P. Ullman & L. Krasner (Eds.), *Case studies in behavior modification.* New York: Holt, Rinehart & Winston.

Lazarus, R. S., & Folkman, S. (1984). *Stress, appraisal, and coping.* New York: Springer.

le Grange, D., Crosby, R. D., & Lock, J. (2008). Predictors and moderators of outcome in family-based treatment for adolescent bulimia nervosa. *J. Amer. Acad. Child Adol. Psychiat., 47*(4), 464–470.

le Grange, D., Crosby, R. D., Rathouz, P. J., & Leventhal, B. L. (2007). A randomized controlled comparison of family-based treatment and supportive psychotherapy for adolescent bulimia nervosa. *Arch. Gen. Psychiat., 64*(9), 1049–1056.

Le Unes, A. D., Nation, J. R., & Turley, N. M. (1980). Male-female performance in learned helplessness. *J. Psychol., 104,* 255–258.

Leahy, R. L. (2004). Cognitive-behavioral therapy. In R. G. Heimberg, C. J. Turk, & D. S. Mennin (Eds.), *Generalized anxiety disorder: Advances in research and practice.* New York: Guilford Press.

Leahy, R. L. (2005). Special series: Cognitive therapy of bipolar disorder: Introduction. *Cog. Behav. Pract., 12*(1), 64–65.

Leahy, R. L., Beck, J., & Beck, A. T. (2005). Cognitive therapy for the personality disorders. In S. Strack (Ed.), *Handbook of personality and psychopathology* (pp. 442–461). Hoboken, NJ: Wiley.

Leamon, M. H., Feldman, M. D., & Scott, C. L. (2007). Factitious disorders and malingering. In S. C. Yudofsky, J. A. Bourgeois, & R. E. Hales (Eds.), *The American Psychiatric Publishing Board prep and review guide for psychiatry* (pp. 245–249). Washington, DC: American Psychiatric Publishing.

Leane, W., & Shute, R. (1998). Youth suicide: The knowledge and attitudes of Australian teachers and clergy. *Suic. Life-Threat. Behav., 28*(2), 165–173.

Leavitt, F. (2001). Iatrogenic recovered memories: Examining the empirical evidence. *Amer. J. Forens. Psychol., 19*(2), 21–32.

Leavitt, F. (2002). "The reality of repressed memories" revisited and principles of science. *J. Trauma. Dissoc., 3*(1), 19–35.

LeCroy, C. W. (2005). Building an effective primary prevention program for adolescent girls: Empirically based design and evaluation. *Brief Treat. Crisis Intervent., 5*(1), 75–84.

Ledoux, S., Miller, P., Choquet, M., & Plant, M. (2002). Family structure, parent-child relationships, and alcohol and other drug use among teenagers in France and the United Kingdom. *Alcohol Alcoholism, 37*(1), 52–60.

Lee, D. E. (1985). Alternative self-destruction. *Percept. Motor Skills, 61*(3, Part 2), 1065–1066.

Lee, J., & Sue, S. (2001). Clinical psychology and culture. In D. Matsumoto (Ed.), *The handbook of culture and psychology.* New York: Oxford University Press.

Lee, T., & Seeman, P. (1980). Elevation of brain neuroleptic/dopamine receptors in schizophrenia. *Amer. J. Psychiat., 137,* 191–197.

Leenaars, A. A. (1989). *Suicide notes: Predictive clues and patterns.* New York: Human Sciences Press.

Leenaars, A. A. (1991). Suicide in the young adult. In A. A. Leenaars (Ed.), *Life span perspectives of suicide: Time-lines in the suicide process.* New York: Plenum Press.

Leenaars, A. A. (2002). In defense of the idiographic approach: Studies of suicide notes and personal documents. *Arch. Suic. Res., 6*(1), 19–30.

Leenaars, A. A. (2004). Altruistic suicide: A few reflections. *Arch. Suic. Res., 8*(1), 1–7.

Leenaars, A. A. (2007). Gun-control legislation and the impact of suicide. *Crisis: J. Crisis Intervent. Suic. Prev., 28*(Suppl. 1), 50–57.

Leenaars, A. A., Connolly, J., Cantor, C., EchoHawk, M., He, Z.-X., Kokorina, N., et al. (2001). Suicide, assisted suicide and euthanasia: International perspectives. *Irish J. Psychol. Med., 18*(1), 33–37.

Leenaars, A. A., & Lester, D. (2004). The impact of suicide prevention centers on the suicide rate in the Canadian provinces. *Crisis, 25*(2), 65–68.

Leenstra, A. S., Ormel, J., & Giel, R. (1995). Positive life change and recovery from depression and anxiety: A three-stage longitudinal study of primary care attenders. *Brit. J. Psychiat., 166*(3), 333–343.

Legrand, L. N., Iacono, W. G., & McGue, M. (2005). Predicting addiction: Behavioral genetics uses twins and time to decipher the origins of addiction and learn who is most vulnerable. *Amer. Sci., 93*(2), March–April 2005, 140–147.

Lehman, A. F., Kreyenbuhl, J., Buchanan, R. W., Dickerson, F. B., Dixon, L. B., Goldberg, R., et al. (2004). The schizophrenia Patient Outcomes Research Team (PORT): Updated treatment recommendations 2003. *Schizo. Bull., 30,* 193–217.

Lehmann, H. E. (1985). Current perspectives on the biology of schizophrenia. In M. N. Menuck & M. V. Seeman. *New perspectives in schizophrenia.* New York: Macmillan.

Leiblum, S. R. (2004). Gay marriage: Notes from North America. *Sex. Relation. Ther., 19*(4), 361–362.

Leiblum, S. R. (2007). Sex therapy today: Current issues and future perspectives. In S. R. Leiblum (Ed.), *Principles and practice of sex therapy* (4th ed., pp. 3–22). New York: Guilford Press.

Leibowitz, R. Q. (2007). Disclosure of trauma in the medical setting. In E. K. Carll (Ed.), *Trauma psychology: Issues in violence, disaster, health, and illness* (Vol. 2). Westport, CT: Praeger Publishers.

Leichsenring, F. (2001). Comparative effects of short-term psychodynamic psychotherapy and cognitive-behavioral therapy in depression. A meta-analytic approach. *Clin. Psychol. Rev., 21*(3), 401–419.

Leichsenring, F., & Rabung, S. (2008). Effectiveness of long-term psychodynamic psychotherapy: A meta-analysis. *JAMA, 300*(13), 1551–1565.

Lejoyeux, M., Huet, F., Claudon, M., Fichelle, A., Casalino, E., & Lequen, V. (2008). Characteristics of suicide attempts preceded by alcohol consumption. *Arch. Suic. Res., 12*(1), 30–38.

Lekander, M. (2002). Ecological immunology: The role of the immune system in psychology and neuroscience. *Eur. Psychiat., 7*(2), 98–115.

Lemonick, M. D., & Goldstein, A. (2002, April 14). At your own risk. *Time,* 46–57.

Lengua, L. J., Long, A. C., Smith, K. I., & Meltzoff, A. N. (2005). Pre-attack symptomatology and temperament as predictors of children's responses to the September 11 terrorist attacks. *J. Child Psychol. Psychiat., 46*(6), 631–645.

Lenox, R. H., McNamara, R. F., Papke, R. L., & Manji, H. K. (1998). Neurobiology of lithium: An update. *J. Clin. Psychiat., 59*(Suppl. 6), 37–47.

Lenzenweger, M. F., & Clarkin, J. F. (2005). The personality disorders: History, classification, and research issues. In J. F. Lenzenweger & J. F. Clarkin (Eds.), *Major theories of personality disorder* (2nd ed., pp. 1–42). New York: Guilford Press.

Lenzenweger, M. F., Lane, M. C., Loranger, A. W., & Kessler, R. C. (2007). DSM-IV personality disorders in the National Comorbidity Survey Replication. *Biol. Psychiat., 62*(6), 553–564.

Leon, G. R. (1984). *Case histories of deviant behavior* (3rd ed.). Boston: Allyn & Bacon.

Leonard, H., & Wen, X. (2002). The epidemiology of mental retardation: Challenges and opportunities in the new millennium. *Ment. Retard. Disabil. Res. Rev., 8,* 117–134.

Leonardo, E. D., & Hen, R. (2006). Genetics of affective and anxiety disorders. *Annu. Rev. Psychol., 57,* 117–137.

Leong, F. T. L., & Leach, M. M. (Eds.). (2008). *Suicide among racial and ethnic minority groups: Theory, research, and practice.* New York: Routledge/Taylor & Francis Group.

Leong, G. B. (2000). Diminished capacity and insanity in Washington State: The battle shifts to admissibility. *J. Amer. Acad. Psychiat. Law, 28*(1), 77–81.

Leor, J., Poole, W. K., & Kloner, R. A. (1996) Sudden cardiac death triggered by an earthquake. *N. Engl. J. Med., 334*(7), 413–419.

Lepore, S. J., Revenson, T. A., Weinberger, S. L., Weston, P., Frisina, P. G., Robertson, R., et al. (2006). Effects of social stresses on cardiovascular reactivity in black and white woman. *Ann. Behav. Med., 31*(2), 120–127.

Leppamaki, S., Partonen, T., Vakkun, O., Lonnqvist, J., Partinen, M., & Laudon, M. (2003). Effect of controlled-release melatonin on sleep quality, mood, and quality of life in subjects with seasonal or weather-associated changes in mood and behaviour. *Eur. Neuropsychopharmacology, 13*(3), 137–145.

Leroux, J. A. (1986). Suicidal behavior and gifted adolescents. *Roper Rev., 9*(2), 77–79.

Leshner, A. I., et al. (1992). *Outcasts on the main street: Report of the Federal Task Force on Homelessness and Severe Mental Illness.* Washington, DC: Interagency Council on the Homeless.

Lesser, I. M., Castro, D. B., Gaynes, B. N., Gonzalez, J., Rush, A. J., Alpert, J. E., et al. (2007). Ethnicity/race and outcome in the treatment of depression: Results from STAR★D. *Med. Care, 45*(11), 1043–1051.

Lester, D. (1972). Myth of suicide prevention. *Comprehen. Psychiat., 13*(6), 555–560.

Lester, D. (1974). The effects of suicide prevention centers on suicide rates in the United States. *Pub. Hlth. Rep., 89,* 37–39.

Lester, D. (1985). The quality of life in modern America and suicide and homicide rates. *J. Soc. Psychol., 125*(6), 779–780.

Lester, D. (1989). *Can we prevent suicide?* New York: AMS Press.

Lester, D. (1991). The etiology of suicide and homicide in urban and rural America. *J. Rural Commun. Psychol., 12*(1), 15–27.

Lester, D. (2000). *Why people kill themselves: A 2000 summary of research on suicide.* Springfield, IL: Charles C. Thomas.

Lester, D., Innamorati, M., & Pompili, M. (2007). Psychotherapy for preventing suicide. In R. Tatarelli, M. Pompili, & P. Girardi (Eds.), *Suicide in psychiatric disorders.* New York: Nova Science Publishers.

Lester, D., & Saito, Y. (1999). The reasons for suicide in Japan. *Omega: J. Death Dying, 38*(1), 65–68.

Lester, D., Wood, P., Williams, C., & Haines, J. (2004). Motives for suicide: A study of Australian suicide notes. *Crisis, 25*(1), 33–34.

Leutwyler, K. (1996). Paying attention: The controversy over ADHD and the drug Ritalin is obscuring a real look at the disorder and its underpinnings. *Scientif. Amer., 272*(2), 12–13.

Levant, R. F. (2000, February). Interviewed in P. A. McGuire. New hope for people with schizophrenia. *Monitor Psychol., 31*(2), 24–28.

Levenson, E. (1982). Language and healing. In S. Slipp (Ed.), *Curative factors in dynamic psychotherapy* (pp. 91–103). New York: McGraw-Hill.

Levenson, M. R. (1992). Rethinking psychopathy. *Theory Psychol., 2*(1), 51–71.

Levesque, R. J. R. (1996). Regulating the private relations of adults with mental disabilities: Old laws, new policies, hollow hopes. *Behav. Sci. Law, 14,* 83–106.

Levesque, R. J. R. (2002). *Dangerous adolescents, model adolescents: Shaping the role and promise of education.* New York: Kluwer Academic/Plenum Publishers.

Levi, F., LaVecchia, C., Lucchini, F., Negri, E., Saxena, S., Maulik, P. K., et al. (2003). Trends in mortality from suicide, 1965–99. *Acta Psychiatrica Scandinavica, 108*(5), 341–349.

Levin, E. (1983, February 21). A sweet surface hit a troubled soul in the late Karen Carpenter, a victim of anorexia nervosa. *People Weekly* (quoting Cherry Boone O'Neill).

Levine, M. D. (1987). *How schools can help combat student eating disorders: Anorexia nervosa and bulimia.* Washington, DC: National Education Assoc.

Lévi-Strauss, C. (1977). *L'identité.* Paris: Presses Universitaires de France.

Levitan, H. L. (1981). Implications of certain dreams reported by patients in a bulimic phase of anorexia nervosa. *Canad. J. Psychiat., 26*(4), 228–231.

Levy, E., Shefler, G., Loewenthal, U., Umansky, R., Bar, G., & Heresco-Levy, U. (2005). Characteristics of schizophrenia residents and staff rejection in community mental health hostels. *Israel J. Psychiat. Rel. Sci., 42*(1), 23–32.

Levy, K. N., Reynoso, J. S., Wasserman, R. H., & Clarkin, J. F. (2007). Narcissistic personality disorder. In W. O'Donohue, K. A. Fowler, S. O. Lilienfeld (Eds.). *Personality disorders: Toward the DSM-V.* Los Angeles: Sage Publications.

Leweke, F. M., Gerth, C. W., Koethe, D., Klosterkotter, J., Ruslanova, I., Krivogorsky, B., et al. (2004). Antibodies to infectious agents in individuals with recent onset schizophrenia. *Eur. Arch. Psychiat. Clin. Neurosci., 254*(1), 4–8.

Lewin, B. D. (1950). *The psychoanalysis of elation.* New York: Norton.

Lewinsohn, P. M., Antonuccio, D. O., Steinmetz, J. L., & Teri, L. (1984). *The coping with depression course.* Eugene, OR: Castalia.

Lewinsohn, P. M., Clarke, G. N., Hops, H., & Andrews, J. (1990). Cognitive-behavioral treatment for depressed adolescents. *Behav. Ther., 21,* 385–401.

Lewinsohn, P. M., Hoberman, H. M., Rosenbaum, M. (1988). A prospective study of risk factors for unipolar depression. *J Abnorm Psychol.*, *97*(3), 251–264.

Lewinsohn, P. M., Rohde, P., Teri, L., & Tilson, M. (1990, April). Presentation. Western Psychological Association.

Lewinsohn, P. M., Sullivan, J. M., & Grosscup, S. J. (1982). Behavioral therapy: Clinical applications. In A. T. Rush (Ed.), *Short-term psychotherapies for the depressed patient.* New York: Guilford Press.

Lewinsohn, P. M., Youngren, M. A., & Grosscup, S. J. (1979). Reinforcement and depression. In R. A. Depue (Ed.), *The psychobiology of the depressive disorders.* New York: Academic Press.

Lewis, L. (2005). Patient perspectives on the diagnosis, treatment, and management of bipolar disorder. *Bipolar Disord.,* 7(Suppl. 1), 33–37.

Lewis, L., & Hoofnagle, L. (2005). Patient perspectives on provider competence: A view from the Depression and Bipolar Support Alliance. *Admin. Policy Ment. Hlth., 32*(5–6), 497–503.

Lewis, L. J. (2006). Sexuality, race, and ethnicity. In R. D. McAnulty & M. M. Burnette (Eds.). *Sex and sexuality, Vol. 1: Sexuality today: Trends and controversies.* Westport, CT: Praeger Publishers.

Lewis, N. D., & Piotrowski, Z. A. (1954) Clinical diagnosis of manic-depressive psychosis. *Proc. Annu. Meet. Am. Psychopathol. Assoc., 12* (42d Meeting), 25–28.

Lewis, O., & Chatoor, I. (1994). Eating disorders. In J. M. Oldham & M. B. Riba (Eds.), *Review of psychiatry* (Vol. 13). Washington, DC: American Psychiatric Press.

Lewis-Harter, S. (2000). Psychosocial adjustment of adult children of alcoholics: A review of the recent empirical literature. *Clin. Psychol. Rev., 20*(3), 311–337.

Lewy, A. J., Emens, J. S., Bernert, R. A., & Lefler, B. J. (2004). Eventual entrainment of the human circadian pacemaker by melatonin is independent of the circadian phase of treatment initiation: Clinical implications. *J. Biol. Rhythms, 19*(1), 68–75.

Li, R., & El-Mallakh, R. S. (2004). Differential response of bipolar and normal control lymphoblastoid cell sodium pump to ethacrynic acid. *J. Affect. Disorders, 80*(1), 1–17.

Li, T. K. (2000). Pharmacogenetics of responses to alcohol and genes that influence alcohol drinking. *J. Stud. Alc., 61*(1), 5–12.

Liberman, R. P. (1982). Assessment of social skills. *Schizo. Bull., 8*(1), 82–84.

Liberman, R. P., & Raskin, D. E. (1971). Depression: A behavioral formulation. *Arch. Gen. Psychiat., 24,* 515–523.

Libow, J. A. (1995). Munchausen by proxy victims in adulthood: A first look. *Child Abuse Negl., 19*(9), 1131–1142.

Libow, J. A., & Schreirer, H. A. (1998). Factitious disorder by proxy. In R. T. Ammerman & J. V. Campo (Eds.), *Handbook of pediatric psychology and psychiatry, Vol. 1: Psychological and psychiatric issues in the pediatric setting.* Boston: Allyn & Bacon.

Lickey, M. E., & Gordon, B. (1991). *Medicine and mental illness: The use of drugs in psychiatry.* New York: W. H. Freeman.

Lieb, K., Zanarini, C., Schmal, C., Linehan, M. M., & Bohus, M. (2004). Borderline personality disorder. *Lancet, 364,* 453–461.

Lieb, R., Merikangas, K. R., Hoefler, M., Pfister, H., Isensee, B., & Wittchen, H. U. (2002). Parental alcohol use disorders and alcohol use and disorders in offspring: A community study. *Psychol. Med., 32*(1), 63–78.

Lieber, A. L. (1978). Human aggression and the lunar synodic cycle. *J. Clin. Psychiat., 39*(5), 385–392.

Lieberman, J. A., Chakos, M., Wu, H., Alvir, J., Hoffman, E., Robinson, D., et al. (2001). Longitudinal study of brain morphology in first episode schizophrenia. *Biol. Psychiat., 49*(6), 487–499.

Lieberman, J. D., & Sales, B. D. (2007). *Scientific jury selection.* Washington, DC: American Psychological Association.

Liebman, J. I., McKinley-Pace, M. J., Leonard, A. M., Sheesley, L. A., Gallant, C. L., Renkey, M. E., & Lehman, E. B. (2002). Cognitive and psychosocial correlates of adults' eyewitness accuracy and suggestibility. *Pers. Individ. Diff., 33*(1), 49–66.

Liebowitz, M. R., Mangano, R. M., Bradwejn, J., & Asnis, G. (2005). A randomized controlled trial of venlafaxine extended release in generalized social anxiety disorder. *J. Clin. Psychiat., 66*(2), 238–247.

Lifton, R. J. (2005). *Home from the war: Learning from Vietnam veterans: With a new preface by the author on the war in Iraq.* New York: Other Press.

Lightdale, H. A., Mach, A. H., & Frances, R. J. (2008). Psychodynamics. In H. D. Kleber & M. Galanter (Eds.), *The American Psychiatric Publishing textbook of substance abuse treatment* (4th ed., pp. 333–347). Arlington, VA: American Psychiatric Publishing.

Lilienfield, S. O., & Lynn, S. J. (2003). Dissociative identity disorder: Multiple personalities, multiple controversies. In S. O. Lilienfeld, S. J. Lynn, et al. (Eds.), *Science and pseudoscience in clinical psychology.* New York: Guilford Press.

Limosin, F., Rouillon, F., Payan, C., Cohen, J. M., & Strub, N. (2003). Prenatal exposure to influenza as a risk factor for adult schizophrenia. *Acta Psychiatr. Scandin., 107,* 331–335.

Lindahl, V., Pearson, J. L., & Colpe, L. (2005). Prevalence of suicidality during pregnancy and the postpartum. *Arch. Women's Ment. Hlth., 8*(2), 77–87.

Lindau, S. T., Schumm, L. P., Laumann, E. O., Levinson, W., O'Muircheartaigh, C. A., & Waite, L. J. (2007). A study of sexuality and health among older adults in the United States. *N. Engl. J. Med., 357,* 762–774.

Lindberg, N., Tani, P., Virkkunen, M., Porkka-Heiskanen, T., Appelberg, B., Naukkarinen, H., et al. (2005). Quantitative electroencephalographic measures in homicidal men with antisocial personality disorder. *Psychiatr. Res., 136*(1), 7–15.

Linde, K., Berner, M., Egger, M., & Mulrow, C. (2005). St John's wort for depression: Meta-analysis of randomised controlled trials. *Brit. J. Psychiat., 186*(2), 99–107.

Linden, M., Wurzendorf, K., Ploch, M., & Schaefer, M. (2008). Self medication with St. John's wort in depressive disorders: An observational study in community pharmacies. *J. Affect. Disorders, 107*(1–3), 205–210.

Lindholm, C., & Lindholm C. (1981). World's strangest mental illnesses. *Sci. Digest,* 52–58.

Lindner, M. (1968). *Hereditary and environmental influences upon resistance to stress.* Unpublished doctoral dissertation, University of Pennsylvania, Philadelphia.

Lindsay, D. S. (1994). Contextualizing and clarifying criticisms of memory work in psychotherapy. *Consciousness Cog., 3,* 426–437.

Lindsay, D. S. (1996). Contextualizing and clarifying criticisms of memory work in psychotherapy. In K. Pezdek & W. P. Banks (Eds.), *The recovered memory/false memory debate.* San Diego: Academic Press.

Lindsay, J., Sykes, E., McDowell, I., Verreault, R., & Laurin, D. (2004). More than the epidemiology of Alzheimer's disease: Contributions of the Canadian Study of Health and Aging. *Canad. J. Psychiat., 49*(2), 83–91.

Lindsay, R. C. L., Ross, D. F., Read, J. D., & Toglia, M. P. (Eds.). (2007). *The handbook of eyewitness psychology, Vol. 11: Memory for people.* Mahwah, NJ: Lawrence Erlbaum.

Linehan, M. M. (1987). Dialectical behavior therapy for borderline personality disorder: Theory and method. *Bull. Menninger Clin., 51,* 261–276.

Linehan, M. M. (1993). *Cognitive-behavioral treatment of borderline personality disorder.* New York: Guilford Press.

Linehan, M. M. (1993). *Skills training manual for treating borderline personality disorder.* New York: Guilford Press.

Linehan, M. M., Cochran, B. N., & Kehrer, C. A. (2001). Dialectical behavior therapy for borderline personality disorder. In D. H. Barlow (Ed.), *Clinical handbook of psychological disorders* (3rd ed., pp. 470–522). New York: Guilford Press.

Linehan, M. M., Comtois, K. A., Murray, A., Brown, M. Z., Gallop, R. J., Heard, H. L., et al. (2006). Two-year randomized trial + follow-up of dialectical behavior therapy vs. therapy by experts for suicidal behaviors and borderline personality disorder. *Arch. Gen. Psychiat., 63,* 757–766.

Linehan, M. M., & Dexter-Mazza, E. T. (2008). Dialectical behavior therapy for borderline personality disorder. In D. H. Barlow (Ed.), *Clinical handbook of psychological disorders: A step-by-step treatment manual* (4th ed.). New York: Guilford Press.

Link, B. G., & Phelan, J. C. (2006). Fundamental social causes: The ascendancy of social factors as determinants of distributions of mental illnesses in populations. In W. W. Eaton (Ed.), *Medical and psychiatric comorbidity over the course of life.* Washington, DC: American Psychiatric Publishing.

Link, B. G., Struening, E. L., Neese-Todd, S., Asmussen, S., & Phelan, J. C. (2001). Stigma as a barrier to recovery: The consequences of stigma for the self-esteem of people with mental illness. *Psychiatr. Serv., 52*(12), 1621–1626.

Link, B. G., Yang, L. H., Phelan, J. C., & Collins, P. Y. (2004). Measuring mental illness stigma. *Schizo. Bull., 30*(3), 511–541.

Links, J. M., Zubieta, J. K., Meltzer, C. G., Strumpfel, M. J., & Frist, J. J. (1996). Influence of spatially heterogenous background activity on "hot object" quantitation in brain emission computed tomography. *J. Computer Assisted Tomography, 20,* 680–687.

Links, P. S., Stockwell, M., & MacFarlane, M. M. (2004). Is couple therapy indicated for patients with dependent personality disorder? *J. Fam. Psychother., 15*(3), 63–79.

Linz, D., & Imrich, D. (2001). Child pornography. In S. O. White (Ed.), *Handbook of youth and justice* (pp. 79–111). New York: Kluwer Academic/ Plenum Press.

Lion, J. R. (2008). Psychotherapeutic interventions. In K. Tardiff & R. I. Simon (Eds.), *Textbook of violence assessment and management* (pp. 325–338). Arlington, VA: American Psychiatric Publishing.

Liotti, M., Mayberg, H. S., McGinnis, S., Brannan, S. L., & Jerabek, P. (2002). Unmasking disease-specific cerebral blood flow abnormalities: Mood challenge in patients with remitted unipolar depression. *Amer. J. Psychiat., 159,* 1830–1840.

Lipkin, P. H., Cozen, M. A., Thompson, R. E., & Mostofsky, S. H. (2005). Stimulant dosage and age, race, and insurance type in a sample of children with attention-deficit/hyperactivity disorder. *J. Child Adol. Psychopharmacol., 15*(2), 240–248.

Lipton, A. A., & Simon, F. S. (1985). Psychiatric diagnosis in a state hospital: Manhattan State revisited. *Hosp. Comm. Psychiat., 36*(4), 368–373.

Lis, A., Parolin, L., Calvo, V., Zennaro, A., & Meyer, G. (2007). The impact of administration and inquiry on Rorschach Comprehensive System protocols in a national reference sample. *J. Pers. Assess., 89*(Suppl.1), S193–S200.

Lissau, I., Overpeck, M. D., Ruan, W. J., Due, P., Holstein, B. E., & Hediger, M. L. (2004). Body mass index and overweight in adolescents in 13 European countries, Israel, and the United States. *Arch. Pediatr. Adoles. Med., 159*(1), 27–33.

Litman, R. E., & Farberow, N. L. (1994). Pop-rock music as precipitating cause in youth suicide. *J. Forens. Sci., 39,* 494–499.

Litwack, T., Zapf, P. A., Groscup, J. L., & Hart, S. D. (2006). Violence risk assessment: Research, legal, and clinical considerations. In A. K. Hess & I. B. Weiner (Eds.), *Handbook of forensic psychology* (3rd ed., pp. 487–533). New York: Wiley.

Liu, A. (2007). *Gaining: The truth about life after eating disorders.* New York: Warner Books.

Livesley, W. J. (2000). A practical approach to the treatment of patients with borderline personality disorder. *Psychiatr. Clin. N. Amer., 23*(1), 211–232.

Lochman, J. E., Barry, T. D., & Pardini, D. A. (2003). Anger control training for aggressive youth. In A. E. Kazdin & J. R. Weisz (Eds.), *Evidence-based psychotherapies for children and adolescents* (pp. 263–281). New York: Guilford Press.

Lock, J., & le Grange, D. (2005). Family-based treatment of eating disorders. *Inter. J. Eat. Disorders, 37*(Suppl.), S64–S67.

Loebel, J. P., Loebel, J. S., Dager, S. R., & Centerwall, B. S. (1991). Anticipation of nursing home placement may be a precipitant of suicide among the elderly. *J. Amer. Ger. Soc., 39*(4), 407–408.

Loeber, R., & Keenan, K. (1994). Interaction between conduct disorder and its comorbid conditions: Effects of age and gender. *Clinical Psychology Review, 14,* 497–523.

Loewenstein, R. J. (1991). Psychogenic amnesia and psychogenic fugue: A comprehensive review. In A. Tasman & S. M. Goldfinger (Eds.), *American Psychiatric Press review of psychiatry* (Vol. 10). Washington, DC: American Psychiatric Press.

Loewenstein, R. J. (2007). Dissociative identity disorder: Issues in the iatrogenesis controversy. In D. Spiegel, E. Vermetten, & M. Dorahy (Eds.), *Traumatic dissociation: Neurobiology and treatment* (pp. 275–299). Washington, DC: American Psychiatric Publishing.

Loewenthal, K. (2007). *Religion, culture and mental health.* New York: Cambridge University Press.

Loftus, E. F. (1993). The reality of repressed memories. *Amer. Psychologist, 48,* 518–537.

Loftus, E. F. (1997). Repressed memory accusations: Devastated families and devastated patients. *Appl. Cog. Psychol., 11,* 25–30.

Loftus, E. F. (2000). Remembering what never happened. In E. Tulving, et al. (Eds.), *Memory, consciousness, and the brain: The Tallinn Conference.* Philadelphia: Psychology Press/Taylor & Francis.

Loftus, E. F. (2001). Imagining the past. *Psychologist, 14*(11), 584–587.

Loftus, E. F. (2003). Make-believe memories. *Amer. Psychologist, 58*(11), 867–873.

Loftus, E. F. (2003). Our changeable memories: Legal and practical implications. *Nature Reviews: Neuroscience, 4,* 231–234.

Loftus, E. F., & Cahill, L. (2007). Memory distortion: From misinformation to rich false memory. In J. S. Nairne (Ed.), *The foundations of remembering: Essays in honor of Henry L. Roediger, III.* New York: Psychology Press.

Logan, T. K., Walker, R., Jordan, C. E., & Leukefeld, C. G. (2006). *Women and victimization: Contributing factors, interventions, and implications.* Washington, DC: American Psychological Association.

Logue, A. W. (1991). *The psychology of eating and drinking.* New York: W. H. Freeman.

Lohr, K. (2007, October 15). Atlanta shooting suspect to use insanity defense. *NPR Morning Edition.* Retrieved October 2007 from http://www.npr.org/templates/story/story.php?storyId=15276491

Lombardi, E. L., Wilchins, R. A., Priesing, D., & Malouf, D. (2001). Gender violence: Transgender experiences with violence and discrimination. *J. Homosex., 42*(1), 89–101.

Lonigan, C. J., Shannon, M. P., Taylor, C. M., et al. (1994). Children exposed to disaster: II. Risk factors for the development of post-traumatic symptomatology. *J. Amer. Acad. Child Adol. Psychiat., 33,* 94–105.

Lonigan, C. J., Vasey, M. W., Phillips, B. M., & Hazen, R. A. (2004). Temperament, anxiety, and the processing of threat-relevant stimuli. *J. Clin. Child Adol. Psychol., 33*(1), 8–20.

Loomer, H. P., Saunders, J. C., & Kline, N. S. (1957). A clinical and phamacodynamic evaluation of iproniazid as a psychic energizer. *Amer. Psychiat. Assoc. Res. Rep., 8,* 129.

López, S. R., & Guarnaccia, P. J. (2000). Cultural psychopathology: Uncovering the social world of mental illness. *Annu. Rev. Psychol., 51,* 571–598.

López, S. R., & Guarnaccia, P. J. (2005). Cultural dimensions of psychopathology: The social world's impact on mental illness. In B. A. Winstead & J. E. Maddux, *Psychopathology: Foundations for a contemporary understanding* (pp. 19–37). Mahwah, NJ: Lawrence Erlbaum.

LoPiccolo, J. (1985). Advances in diagnosis and treatment of male sexual dysfunction. *J. Sex Marital Ther., 11*(4), 215–232.

LoPiccolo, J. (1991). Post-modern sex therapy for erectile failure. In R. C. Rosen & S. R. Leiblum (Eds.), *Erectile failure: Diagnosis and treatment.* New York: Guilford Press.

LoPiccolo, J. (1992). Paraphilias. *Nord. Sex., 10*(1), 1–14.

LoPiccolo, J. (1995). Sexual disorders and gender identity disorders. In R. J. Comer, *Abnormal psychology* (2nd ed.). New York: W. H. Freeman.

LoPiccolo, J. (1997). Sex therapy: A post-modern model. In S. J. Lynn & J. P. Garske (Eds.), *Contemporary psychotherapies: Models and methods* (2nd ed.). Columbus, OH: Merrill.

LoPiccolo, J. (2002). Postmodern sex therapy. In F. W. Kaslow (Ed.), *Comprehensive handbook of psychotherapy: Integrative/eclectic* (Vol. 4, pp. 411–435). New York: Wiley.

LoPiccolo, J. (2004). Sexual disorders affecting men. In L. J. Haas (Ed.), *Handbook of primary care psychology* (pp. 485–494). New York: Oxford University Press.

LoPiccolo, J., & Stock, W. E. (1987). Sexual function, dysfunction, and counseling in gynecological practice. In Z. Rosenwaks, F. Benjamin, & M. L. Stone (Eds.), *Gynecology.* New York: Macmillan.

LoPiccolo, J., & Van Male, L. M. (2000). Sexual dysfunction. In A. E. Kazdin (Ed.), *Encyclopedia of psychology* (Vol. 7, pp. 246–251). Washington, DC: Oxford University Press/American Psychological Association.

Lorand, S. (1968). Dynamics and therapy of depressive states. In W. Gaylin (Ed.), *The meaning of despair.* New York: Jason Aronson.

Lord, M. (2002). One year after 9/11—A nation changed. *U. S. News World Rep., 133*(7), 33.

Loros, J. J., Woodland-Hastings, J., & Schibler, U. (2004). Adapting to life on a rotating world at the gene expression level. In J. C. Dunlap, J. J. Loros, & P. J. Decoursey (Eds.), *Chronobiology: Biological timekeeping* (pp. 255–290). Sunderland, MA: Sinauer Associates.

Lovaas, O. I. (1987). Behavioral treatment and normal educational/intellectual functioning in young autistic children. *J. Cons. Clin. Psychol., 55,* 3–9.

Lovaas, O. I. (2003). *Teaching individuals with developmental delays: Basic intervention techniques.* Austin, TX: Pro-Ed.

Lovejoy, M. (1982). Expectations and the recovery process. *Schizo. Bull., 8*(4), 605–609.

Lovejoy, M. (2001). Disturbances in the social body: Differences in body image and eating problems among African-American and white women. *Gender Soc., 15*(2), 239–261.

Löwe, B., Mundt, C., Wolfgang, H., Brunner, R., Backenstrass, M., Kronmüller, K., et al. (2008). Validity of current somatoform disorder diagnoses: Perspectives for classification in DSM-V and ICD-11. *Psychopathology, 41*(1), 4–9.

Lu, L. (1999). Personal or environmental causes of happiness: A longitudinal analysis. *J. Soc. Psychol., 139*(1), 79–90.

Luborsky, E. B., O'Reilly-Landry, M., & Arlow, J. A. (2008). Psychoanalysis. In R. J. Corsini & D. Wedding (Eds.), *Current psychotherapies* (8th ed.). Belmont, CA: Thomson Brooks/Cole.

Luborsky, L. (1973). Forgetting and remembering (momentary forgetting) during psychotherapy. In M. Mayman (Ed.), *Psychoanalytic research and psychological issues* (Monograph 30). New York: International Universities Press.

Luborsky, L. (2004). Helen Sargent's 1961 paper: Both a classic and still current. *Psychiat.: Interpers. Biol. Process.*, 67(1), 23–25.

Luborsky, L., Diguer, L., Luborsky, E., & Schmidt, K. A. (1999). The efficacy of dynamic versus other psychotherapies: Is it true that "everyone has won and all must have prizes"?—An update. In D. S. Janowsky (Ed.), *Psychotherapy indications and outcomes.* Washington, DC: American Psychiatric Press.

Luborsky, L., Rosenthal, R., Diguer, L., Andrusyna, T. P., Berman, J. S., Levitt, J. T., Seligman, D. A., & Krause, E. D. (2002). The dodo bird verdict is alive and well—mostly. *Clin. Psychol.: Sci. Prac.*, 9(1), 2–12.

Luborsky, L., Rosenthal, R., Diguer, L., Andrusyna. T. P., Levitt, J. T., Seligman, D. A., Berman, J. S., & Krause, E. D. (2003). Are some psychotherapies much more effective than others? *J. Appl. Psychoanal. Stud.*, 5(4), 455–460.

Luborsky, L., Singer, B., & Luborsky, L. (1975). Comparative studies of psychotherapies. *Arch. Gen. Psychiat.*, 32, 995–1008.

Lucas, G. (2006). Object relations and child psychoanalysis. (French). *Revue Franc. Psychan.*, 70(5), 1435–1473.

Lucas, R. E. (2007). Adaptation and the set-point model of subjective well-being: Does happiness change after major life events? *Curr. Direct. Psychol. Sci.*, 16(2), 75–79.

Ludwig, A. M. (1994). Creative activity and mental illness in female writers. *Amer. J. Psychiat.*, 151, 1650–1656.

Ludwig, A. M. (1995). *The price of greatness: Resolving the creativity and madness controversy.* New York: Guilford Press.

Lukas, C., & Seiden, H. M. (2007). *Silent grief: Living in the wake of suicide* (Rev. ed.). London: Jessica Kingsley Publishers.

Lumley, V. A., & Scotti, J. R. (2001). Supporting the sexuality of adults with mental retardation: Current status and future directions. *J. Positive Behav. Interventions*, 3(2), 109–119.

Lundqvist, D., & Ohman, A. (2005). Emotion regulates attention: The relation between facial configurations, facial emotion, and visual attention. *Visual Cog.*, 12(1), 51–84.

Lundqvist, T. (2005). Cognitive consequences of cannabis use: Comparison with abuse of stimulants and heroin with regard to attention, memory and executive functions. *Pharmacol Biochem Behav.*, 81, 391–330.

Lutgendorf, S. K., Moore, M. B., Bradley, S., Shelton, B. J., & Lutz, C. T. (2005). Distress and expression of natural killer receptors on lymphocytes. *Brain, Behav. Immun.*, 19(3), 185–194.

Lutgendorf, S. K., Russell, D., Ullrich, P., Harris, T. B., & Wallace, R. (2004). Religious participation, interleukin-6, and mortality in older adults. *Hlth. Psychol.*, 23(5), 465–475.

Lyketsos, C. G., Lopez, O., Jones, B., et al. (2002). Prevalence of neuropsychiatric symptoms in dementia and mild cognitive impairment: Results from the cardiovascular health study. *JAMA*, 288, 1475–1483.

Lykken, D. T., & Tellegen, A. (1996). Happiness is a stochastic phenomenon. *Psychol. Sci.*, 7(3), 186–189.

Lyman, B. (1982). The nutritional values and food group characteristics of foods preferred during various emotions. *J. Psychol.*, 112, 121–127.

Lyneham, H. J., Abbott, M. J., & Rapee, R. M. (2007). Interrater reliability of the anxiety disorders interview schedule for DSM-IV: Child and parent version. *J. Amer. Acad. Child Adol. Psychat.*, 46, 731–736.

Lynn, S. J., & Kirsch, I. (2006). Introduction: Definitions and early history. In I. Kirsch & J. Steven, *Essentials of clinical hypnosis: An evidence-based approach* (pp. 3–15). Washington, DC: American Psychological Association.

Lynn, S. J., & Kirsch, I. (2006). Questions and controversies. In I. Kirsch & J. Steven, *Essentials of clinical hypnosis: An evidence-based approach* (pp. 197–213). Washington, DC: American Psychological Association.

Lynn, S. J., Kirsch, I., Knox, J., Fassler, O., & Lilienfeld, S. O. (2007). Hypnosis and neuroscience: Implications for the altered state debate. In G. A. Jamieson (Ed.), *Hypnosis and conscious states: The cognitive neuroscience perspective* (pp. 145–165). New York: Oxford University Press.

Lyon, K. A. (1992). Shattered mirror: A fragment of the treatment of a patient with multiple personality disorder. *Psychoanal. Quarter.*, 12(1), 71–94.

Lysaker, P. H., & Bell, M. (1995). Work and meaning: Disturbance of volition and vocational dysfunction in schizophrenia. *Psychiatry*, 58(4), 392–400.

Lysaker, P. H., & Hermans, H. J. M. (2007). The dialogical self in psychotherapy for persons with schizophrenia: A case study. *J. Clin. Psychol.*, 63(2), 129–139.

MacDonald, M. G. (2007). Suicide intervention trainees' knowledge of myths about suicide. *Psychol. Rep.*, 101(2), 561–564.

MacDonald, M. G. (2007). Undergraduate education majors' knowledge about suicide. *Percept. Motor Skills*, 105(2), 373–378.

MacDonald, W. L. (1998). The difference between blacks' and whites' attitudes toward voluntary euthanasia. *J. Sci. Study Religion*, 37(3), 411–426.

Macias, W., Pashupati, K., & Lewis, L. S. (2007). A wonderful life or diarrhea and dry mouth? Policy issues of direct-to-consumer drug advertising on television. *Hlth Commun.*, 22(3), 241–252.

MacIntyre, D., & Carr, A. (1999). Helping children to the other side of silence: A study of the impact of the stay safe program on Irish children's disclosures of sexual victimization. *Child Abuse Negl.*, 23(12), 1327–1340.

Mack, A., & Joy, J. (2001). *Marijuana as medicine? The science beyond the controversy.* Washington, DC: National Academy Press.

MacLaren, V. V. (2001). A qualitative review of the Guilty Knowledge Test. *J. Appl. Psychol.*, 86(4), 674–683.

Madianos, M. G., & Madianou, D. (1992). The effects of long-term community care on relapse and adjustment of persons with chronic schizophrenia. *Inter. J. Ment. Hlth.*, 21(1), 37–49.

Madill, A., & Holch, P. (2004). A range of memory possibilities: The challenge of the false memory debate for clinicians and researchers. *Clin. Psychol. Psychother.*, 11(5), 299–310.

Maes, M., DeVos, N., VanHunsel, F., VanWest, D., Westenberg, H., Cosyns, P., et al. (2001). Pedophilia is accompanied by increased plasma concentrations of catecholamines, in particular, epinephrine. *Psychiat. Res.*, 103(1), 43–49.

Magee, C. L. (2007). The use of herbal and other dietary supplements and the potential for drug interactions in palliative care. *Pall. Med.*, 21(6), 547–548.

Magee, L., Rodebaugh, T. L., & Heimberg, R. G. (2006). Negative evaluation is the feared consequence of making others uncomfortable: A response to Rector, Kocovski, and Ryder. *J. Soc. Clin. Psychol.*, 25. 929–936.

Magherini, G., & Biotti, V. (1998). Madness in Florence in the 14th–18th centuries: Judicial inquiry and medical diagnosis, care, and custody. *Inter. J. Law and Psychiat.*, 21(4), 355–368.

Maher, B. F. G., Stough, C., Shelmerdine, A., Wesnes, K., & Nathan, P. J. (2002). The acute effects of combined administration of Ginkgo biloba and Bacopa monniera on cognitive function in humans. *Human Psychopharmacol. Clin. Exp.*, 17(3), 163–164.

Maher, W. B., & Maher, B. A. (1985). Psychopathology: I. From ancient times to the eighteenth century. In G. A. Kimble & K. Schlesinger (Eds.), *Topics in the history of psychology* (Vol. 2). Hillsdale, NJ: Lawrence Erlbaum.

Maher, W. B., & Maher, B. A. (2003). Abnormal psychology. In D. K. Freedheim (Ed.), *Handbook of psychology: History of psychology* (Vol. 1, pp. 303–336). New York: Wiley.

Mahlberg, R., Kunz, D., Sutej, I., Kuhl, K. P., & Hellweg, R. (2004). Melatonin treatment of day-night rhythm disturbances and sundowning in Alzheimer disease: An open-label pilot study using actigraphy. *J. Clin. Psychopharmacol.*, 24(4), 456–459.

Mahrer, A. R. (2000). Philosophy of science and the foundations of psychotherapy. *APA*, 55(10), 1117–1125.

Mahrer, A. R. (2003). What are the foundational beliefs in the field of psychotherapy? *Psychol.: J. Hellen. Psychol. Soc.*, 10(1), 1–19.

Mahrer, A. R. (2005). What is psychotherapy for? A plausible alternative to empirically supported therapies, therapy relationships, and practice guidelines. *J. Contemp. Psychother.*, 35(1), 99–115.

Maier, W., Hofgen, B., Zobel, A., & Rietschel, M. (2005). Genetic models of schizophrenia and bipolar disorder: Overlapping inheritance or discrete genotypes? *Eur. Arch. Psychiat. Clin. Neurosci.*, 255(3), 159–166.

Malberg, J. E., & Bonson, K. R. (2001). How MDMA works in the brain. In J. Holland (Ed.), *Ecstasy: The complete guide: A comprehension look at the risks and benefits of MDMA* (pp. 29–38). Rochester, VT: Park Street Press.

Malberg, J. E., & Schechter, L. E. (2005). Increasing hippocampal neurogenesis: A novel mechanism for antidepressant drugs. *Curr. Pharmaceut. Design*, 11, 145–155.

Malcolm, A. H. (1990, June 9). Giving death a hand. *New York Times*, p. A6.

Maldonado, J. R., & Spiegel, D. (2003). Dissociative disorders. In S. C. Yudofsky & R. E. Hales (Eds.), *The American Psychiatric Publishing textbook of clinical psychiatry* (4th ed., pp. 709–742). Washington, DC: American Psychiatric Publishing.

Maldonado, J. R., & Spiegel, D. (2007). Dissociative disorders. In S. C. Yudofsky, J. A. Bourgeois, & R. E. Hales (Eds.), *The American Psychiatric Publishing Board prep and review guide for psychiatry* (pp. 251–258). Washington, DC: American Psychiatric Publishing.

Maletzky, B. M. (2000). Exhibitionism. In M. Hersen & M. Biaggio (Eds.), *Effective brief therapies: A clinician's guide.* San Diego, CA: Academic.

Maletzky, B. M. (2002). The paraphilias: Research and treatment. In P. E. Nathan & J. M. Gorman (Eds.), *A guide to treatments that work* (2nd ed., pp. 525–557). London: Oxford University Press.

Maletzky, B. M. (2003). A serial rapist treated with behavioral and cognitive techniques and followed for 12 years. *Clin. Case Stud., 2*(2), 127–153

Maletzky, B. M., & Steinhauser, C. (2004). Sexual deviations. In M. Hersen (Ed.), *Psychological assessment in clinical practice: A pragmatic guide* (pp. 197–241). New York: Brunner-Routledge.

Malik, M. L., & Beutler, L. E. (2002). The emergence of dissatisfaction with the DSM. In L. E. Beutler & M. L. Malik (Eds.), *Rethinking the DSM: A psychological perspective. Decade of behavior.* Washington, DC: American Psychological Association.

Malik, V., Schulze, M., & Hu, F. (2006). Intake of sugar-sweetened beverages and weight gain: A systematic review. *Amer. J. Clin. Nutrit., 84,* 274–288.

Maller, R. G., & Reiss, S. (1992). Anxiety sensitivity in 1984 and panic attacks in 1987. *J. Anx. Dis., 6*(3), 241–247.

Malone, K. M., Corbitt, E. M., Li, S., & Mann, J. J. (1996). Prolactin response to fenfluramine and suicide attempt lethality in major depression. *Brit. J. Psychiat., 168,* 324–329.

Mammen, O. K., Kolk, D.. J., & Pilkonis, P. A. (2002). Negative affect and parental aggression in child physical abuse. *Child Abuse Negl., 26,* 407–424.

Mamounas, J., Lykouras, E., Oulis, P., & Christodoulou, G. N. (2001). Premorbid adjustment in schizophrenia: Associations with clinical variables. *Psychiatriki, 12*(2), 134–141.

Manji, H. K., Bebchuk, J. M., Moore, G. J., Glitz, D., Hasanat, K. A., & Chen, G. (1999). Modulation of CNS signal transduction pathways and gene expression by mood-stabilizing agents: Therapeutic implications. *J. Clin. Psychiat., 60*(Suppl. 2), 27–39.

Mann, D. (2004). Born to lie? *WebMD,* June 28, 2004.

Mann, J. J., & Currier, D. (2007). Neurobiology of suicidal behavior. In R. Tatarelli, M. Pompili, & P. Girardi (Eds.), *Suicide in psychiatric disorders.* New York: Nova Science Publishers.

Mann, T., Tomiyama, A. J., Westling, E., Lew, A.-M., Samuels, B., & Chatman, J. (2007). Medicare's search for effective obesity treatments: Diets are not the answer. *Amer. Psychol., 62,* 220–233.

Manson, J. E., Skerrett, P. J., & Willett, W. C. (2004). Obesity as a risk factor for major health outcomes. In G. A. Bray & C. Bouchard (Eds.), *Handbook of obesity: Etiology and pathophysiology* (2nd ed.). New York: Marcel Dekker.

Manson, J. E., Willett, W. C., Stampfer, M. J., Colditz, G. A., et al. (1995). Body weight and mortality among women. *N. Engl. J. Med., 333*(11), 677–685.

Manuck, S. B., Cohen, S., Rabin, B. S., Muldoon, M. F., & Bachen, E. A. (1991). Individual differences in cellular immune responses to stress. *Psychol. Sci., 2,* 1–5.

Maraziti, D., Akiskal, H. S., Rossi, A., & Cassano, G. B. (1999). Alteration of the platelet serotonin transporter in romantic love. *Psychol. Med., 29*(3), 741–745.

Marchione, M. (2005, March 8). Experimental diet pill keeping pounds off. *Associated Press (Orlando)/Netscape News with CNN.* .

Marchione, M. (2007, September 10). Thousands of GIs cope with brain damage. *Yahoo! News.* Retrieved September 10, 2008, from http://news.yahoo.com

Marder, S. L., & Kane, J. M. (Eds.). (2005). Optimizing pharmacotherapy to maximize outcome in schizophrenia: Optimizing the long-term effectiveness of antipsychotic therapy. *J. Clin. Psychiat., 66*(1), 122–125.

Marder, S. R., Kramer, M., Ford, L., Eerdekens, E., Lim, P., Eerdekens, M., & Lowy, A. (2007). Efficacy and safety of paliperidone extended-release tablets: Results of a 6-week, randomized, placebo-controlled study. *Biol. Psychiat., 62*(12), 1363–1370.

Margo, J. L. (1985). Anorexia nervosa in adolescents. *Brit. J. Med. Psychol., 58*(2), 193–195.

Margraf, J., Ehlers, A., Roth, W. T., Clark, D. B., et al. (1991). How "blind" are double-blind studies? *J. Cons. Clin. Psychol., 59*(1), 184–187.

Maris, R. W. (2001). Suicide. In H. S. Friedman (Ed.), *Specialty articles from the encyclopedia of mental health.* San Diego: Academic Press.

Mark, R. L., Coffey, R. M., Vandivort-Warren, R., Harwood, H. J., King, E. C., et al. (2005). U.S. spending for mental health and substance treatment, 1991–2001. *Health Affairs* (Web Exclusive), March 29.

Mark, T. L., Dirani, R., Slade, E., & Russo, P. A. (2002). Access to new medications to treat schizophrenia. *J. Behav. Hlth. Serv. Res., 29*(1), 15–29.

Mark, T. L., Harwood, H. J., McKusick, D. C., King, E. D., Vandivort-Warren, R., & Buck, J. A. (2008). Mental health and substance abuse spending by age, 2003. *J. Behav. Hlth. Serv. Res., 35*(3), 279–289.

Mark, T. L., Palmer, L. A., Russo, P. A., & Vasey, J. (2003). Examination of treatment pattern differences by race. *Ment. Hlth. Serv. Res., 5*(4), 241–250.

Markin, R. D., & Kivlighan, D. M., Jr. (2007). Bias in psychotherapist ratings of client transference and insight. *Psychother.: Theory, Res. Pract. Train., 44*(3), 300–315.

Markovitz, P. J. (2001). Pharmacotherapy. In W. J. Livesley (Ed.), *Handbook of personality disorders: Theory, research, and treatment* (pp. 475–494). New York: Guilford Press.

Markovitz, P. J. (2004). Recent trends in the pharmacotherapy of personality disorders. *J. Pers. Disorders, 18*(1), 90–101.

Markowitz, J. C. (2006). The clinical conduct of interpersonal psychotherapy. *Focus, 4,* 179.

Marks, I. M. (1977). Phobias and obsessions: Clinical phenomena in search of a laboratory model. In J. Maser and M. Seligman (Eds.), *Psychopathology: Experimental models.* San Francisco: Freeman.

Marks, I. M. (1987). *Fears, phobias and rituals: Panic, anxiety and their disorders.* New York: Oxford University Press.

Marks, I. M., & Gelder, M. G. (1967). Transvestism and fetishism: Clinical and psychological changes during faradic aversion. *Brit. J. Psychiat., 113,* 711–730.

Marlatt, G. A., Blume, A. W., & Parks, G. A. (2001). Integrating harm reduction therapy and traditional substance abuse treatment. *J. Psychoact. Drugs, 33*(1), 13–21.

Marlatt, G. A., Kosturn, C. F., & Lang, A. R. (1975). Provocation to anger and opportunity for retaliation as determinants of alcohol consumption in social drinkers. *J. Abnorm. Psychol., 84*(6), 652–659.

Maron, E., Kuikka, J. T., Shlik, J., Vasar, V., Vanninen, E., & Tiihonen, J. (2004). Reduced brain serotonin transporter binding in patients with panic disorder. *Psychiat. Res Neuroimaging, 132*(2), 173–181.

Maron, E., Nikopensius, T., Koks, S., Altmae, S., Heinaste, E., Vabrit, K., et al. (2005). Association study of 909 candidate gene polymorphisms in panic disorder. *Psychiat. Genet., 15*(1), 17–24.

Marques, J. K., Wiederanders, M., Day, D. M., Nelson, C., & van Ommeren, A. (2005). Effects of a relapse prevention program on sexual recidivism: Final results from California's Sex Offender Treatment and Evaluation Project (SOTEP). *Sex. Abuse: J. Res. Treat., 17*(1), 79–107.

Marquis, J. N., & Morgan, W. G. (1969). *A guidebook for systematic desensitization.* Palo Alto, CA: Veterans Administration Hospital.

Marshall, J. J. (1997). Personal communication.

Marshall, M. A., & Brown, J. D. (2008). On the psychological benefits of self-enhancement. In E. C. Chang (Ed.), *Self-criticism and self-enhancement: Theory, research, and clinical implications* (pp. 19–35). Washington, DC: American Psychological Association.

Marshall, T., Jones, D. P. H., Ramchandani, P. G., Stein, A., & Bass, C. (2007). Intergenerational transmission of health benefits in somatoform disorders. *Brit. J. Psychiat., 191*(4), 449–450.

Marshall, W. L., & Hucker, S. J. (2006). Severe sexual sadism: Its features and treatment. In R. D. McAnulty & M. M. Burnette (Eds.), *Sex and sexuality, Vol. 3: Sexual deviation and sexual offenses.* Westport, CT: Praeger.

Marshall, W. L., & Kennedy, P. (2003). Sexual sadism in sexual offenders. An elusive diagnosis. *Aggress. Viol. Behav., 8* (1), 1–22.

Marshall, W. L., Serran, G. A., Marshall, L. E., & O'Brien, M. D. (2008). Sexual deviation. In M. Hersen & J. Rosqvist (Eds.), *Handbook of psychological assessment, case conceptualization and treatment, Vol. 1: Adults.* Hoboken, NJ: John Wiley & Sons.

Marston, W. M. (1917). Systolic blood pressure changes in deception. *J. Exp. Physiol., 2,* 117–163.

Mart, E. G. (2004). Factitious disorder by proxy: A call for the abandonment of an outmoded diagnosis. *J. Psychiat. Law, 32*(3), 297–314.

Martens, W. H. J. (2005). Multidimensional model of trauma and correlated antisocial personality disorder. *J. Loss Trauma, 10*(2), 115–129.

Martin, A. R., Nieto, J. M. M., Ruiz, J. P. N., & Jimenez, L. E. (2008). Overweight and obesity:

The role of education, employment and income in Spanish adults. *Appetite, 51*(2), 266–272.

Martin, G., Bergen, H. A., Roeger, L., & Allison, S. (2004). Depression in young adolescents: Investigations using 2 and 3 factor versions of the Parental Bonding Instrument. *J. Nerv. Ment. Dis., 192*(10), 650–657.

Martin, J. K., Kraft, J. M., & Roman, P. M. (1994). Extent and impact of alcohol and drug use problems in the workplace: A review of the empirical evidence. In S. Macdonald & P. Roman (Eds.), *Research advances in alcohol and drug problems, Vol. 11: Drug testing in the workplace.* New York: Plenum Press.

Martin, P. L. (2000). Potency and pregnancy in Japan: Did Viagra push the pill? *Tulsa Law. J., 35,* 651–677.

Martin, R. J. (2007). Stalking: Prevention and intervention. In E. K. Carll (Ed.), *Trauma psychology: Issues in violence, disaster, health, and illness* (Vol. 1). Westport, CT: Praeger Publishers.

Martin, R., & Hull, R. (2007). The case study perspective on psychological research. In D. F. Halpern, R. J. Sternberg, & H. L. Roediger, III (Eds.), *Critical thinking in psychology* (pp. 90–109). New York: Cambridge University Press.

Martin, S. (2002). Easing migraine pain. *Monit. Psychol., 33(4),* 71.

Martineau, C. (2004, March 18). Life: Telling a tale with too many words: Chantal Martineau explores hypergraphia, a rare compulsion to keep writing. *The Guardian* (London).

Maruff, P., Wood, S. J., Velakoulis, D., Smith, D. J., Soulsby, B., Suckling, J., et al. (2005). Reduced volume of parietal and frontal association areas in patients with schizophrenia characterized by passivity delusions. *Psychol. Med., 35*(6), 783–789.

Marx, B. P., & Sloan, D. M. (2005). Peritraumatic dissociation and experimental avoidance as predictors of posttraumatic stress symptomatology. *Behav. Res. Ther., 43*(5), 569–583.

Mascaro, N., Arnette, N. C., Santana, M. C., & Kaslow, N. J. (2007). Longitudinal relations between employment and depressive symptoms in low-income, suicidal African American women. *J. Clin. Psychol., 63*(6), 541–553.

Masdrakis, V. G., & Papakostas, I. G. (2004). The role of challenges in the research for the etiology of panic disorder. *Psychiatriki, 15*(2), 129–142.

Mashour, G. A., Walker, E. E., & Martuza, R. L. (2005). Psychosurgery: Past, present, and future. *Brain Res., 48*(3), 409–419.

Masling, J. (2004). A storied test. *PsycCRITIQUES,* [np].

Maslow, A. H. (1970). *Motivation and personality* (2nd ed.). New York: Harper & Row.

Masters, W. H., & Johnson, V. E. (1966). *Human sexual response.* Boston: Little, Brown.

Masters, W. H., & Johnson, V. E. (1970). *Human sexual inadequacy.* Boston: Little, Brown.

Mathew, J., & McGrath, J. (2002). Readability of consent forms in schizophrenia research. *Austal. New Zeal. J. Psychiat., 36*(4), 564–565.

Mathews, D. M., & Wang, M. (2007). Anesthesia awareness and trauma. In E. K. Carll (Ed.), *Trauma psychology: Issues in violence, disaster, health, and illness* (Vol. 2). Westport, CT: Praeger Publishers.

Matsumoto, D. (1994). *Cultural influence on research methods and statistics.* Pacific Grove, CA: Brooks/Cole.

Matsumoto, D. (Ed.). (2001). *The handbook of culture and psychology.* New York: Oxford University Press.

Matsumoto, D. (2007). Culture, context, and behavior. *J. Pers., 75*(6), 1285–1320.

Matsumoto, D., & Juang, L. (2008). *Culture and psychology* (4th ed.). Australia: Thomson Wadsworth.

Mattia, J. I., & Zimmerman, M. (2001). Epidemiology. In W. J. Livesley (Ed.), *Handbook of personality disorders: Theory, research, and treatment* (pp. 107–123). New York: Guilford Press.

Maugh, T. H., II. (1995, May 31). Researchers hone in on gene that may cause "werewolf" disorder. *Los Angeles Times,* p. A3.

Mauri, M. C., Volonteri, L. S., Colasanti, G., & Panza, G. (2005). Acute, continuation and maintenance phases of antidepressant treatment. *Minerva Psichiatrica, 46*(2), 89–98.

Maurice, W. L. (2007). Sexual desire disorders in men. In S. R. Leiblum (Ed.), *Principles and practice of sex therapy* (4th ed., pp. 181–210). New York: Guilford Press.

May, P. R. A., & Tuma, A. H. (1964). Choice of criteria for the assessment of treatment outcome. *J. Psychiatr. Res., 2*(3), 16–527.

May, P. R. A., Tuma, A. H., & Dixon, W. J. (1981). Schizophrenia: A follow-up study of the results of five forms of treatment. *Arch. Gen. Psychiat., 38,* 776–784.

Mayahara, K., & Ito, H. (2002). Readmission of discharged schizophrenic patients with and without day care in Japan. *Inter. Med. J., 9*(2), 121–123.

Mayberg, H. S. (2003). PET imaging in depression: A neurosystems perspective. *Neuroimaging Clin. N. Amer., 13,* 805–815.

Mayberg, H. S. (2006). Defining neurocircuits in depression. *Psychiatric Annals, 36,* 259–266.

Mayberg, H. S., Brannan, S. K., Mahurin, R. K., Jerabek, P. A., Brickman, J. S., Tekell, J. L., et al. (1997). Cingulate function in depression: A potential predictor of treatment response. *Neuroreport, 8,* 1057–1061.

Mayberg, H. S., Brannan, S. K., Mahurin, R. K., & McGinnis, S. (2000). Regional metabolic effects of fluoxetine in major depression: Serial changes and relationship to clinical response. *Biol. Psychiat., 48,* 830–843.

Mayberg, H. S., Lozano, A. M., Voon, V., McNeely, H. E., Seminowicz, D., Hamani, C., et al. (2005). Deep brain stimulation for treatment-resistant depression. *Neuron, 45,* 651–660.

Mayou, R., Kirmayer, L. J., Simon, G., Kroenke, K., & Sharpe, M. (2005). Somatoform disorders: Time for a new approach in DSM-V. *Amer. J. Psychiat., 162*(5), 847–855.

Mayr, U. (2007). Cited in J. Steenhuysen, Brain gets a thrill from charity: Study. *YAHOO! News,* June 14, 2007.

McAnulty, R. D. (2006). Pedophilia. In R. D. McAnulty & M. M. Burnette (Eds.), *Sex and sexuality, Vol. 3: Sexual deviation and sexual offenses.* Westport, CT: Praeger Publishers.

McAnulty, R. D., & Burnette, M. M. (Eds.). (2006). *Sex and sexuality, Vol. 1: Sexuality today: Trends and controversies.* Westport, CT: Praeger Publishers.

McCabe, R. E., & Antony, M. M. (2005). Panic disorder and agoraphobia. In M. M. Antony, D. R. Ledley, & R. G. Heimberg (Eds.), *Improving outcomes and preventing relapse in cognitive-behavioral therapy* (pp. 1–37). New York: Guilford Press.

McCaghy, C. H., Capron, T. A., Jamieson, J. D., & Carey, S. H. (2006). *Deviant behavior: Crime, conflict, and interest groups* (7th ed.). New York: Pearson/Allyn & Bacon.

McCance-Katz, E. F., & Kosten, T. R. (2005). Psychopharmacological treatments. In R. J. Frances, A. H. Mack, & S. I. Miller (Eds.), *Clinical textbook of addictive disorders* (3rd ed., pp. 688–614). New York: Guilford Press.

McCarroll, J. E., Fullerton, C. S., Ursano, R. J., & Hermsen, J. M. (1996). Posttraumatic stress symptoms following forensic dental identification: Mt. Carmel, Waco, Texas. *Amer. J. Psychiat., 153,* 778–782.

McClelland, S. (1998, September 21). Grief crisis counsellors under fire: Trauma teams were quick to descend on Peggy's Cove. Susan McClelland asks whether they do more harm than good. *Ottawa Citizen,* p. A4.

McCloud, A., Barnaby, B., Omu, N., Drummond, C., & Aboud, A. (2004). Relationship between alcohol use disorders and suicidality in a psychiatric population: In-patient prevalence study. *Brit. J. Psychiat., 184*(5), 439–445.

McClung, H. J., Boyne, L. J., Linsheid, T., Heitlinger, L. A., Murray, R. D., Fyda, J., et al. (1993). Is combination therapy for encopresis nutritionally safe? *Pediatrics, 91,* 591–594.

McClure, E. B., Monk, C. S., Nelson, E. E., Parrish, J. M., Adler, A., Blair, R. J., et al. (2007). Abnormal attention modulation of fear circuit function in pediatric generalized anxiety disorder. *Arch. Gen. Psychiat., 64,* 97–106.

McConaghy, N. (2005). Sexual dysfunctions and disorders. In B. A. Winstead & J. E. Maddux (Eds.), *Psychopathology: Foundations for a contemporary understanding* (pp. 255–280). Mahwah, NJ: Lawrence Erlbaum.

McConnaughey, J. (2007, May 31). NFL study links concussions, depression. *San Francisco Chronicle.* Retrieved May 31, 2007, from http://www.sfgate.com/cgi-bin/article.cgi?f=/n/a/2007/05/31/sports/s135640D10.DTL

McCormick, L. H. (2000). Improving social adjustment in children with attention-deficit/hyperactivity disorder. *Arch. Fam. Med., 9*(2), 191–194.

McCoy, S. A. (1976). Clinical judgments of normal childhood behavior. *J. Cons. Clin. Psychol., 44*(5), 710–714.

McDermott, B. M., & Jaffa, T. (2005). Eating disorders in children and adolescents: An update. *Curr. Opin. Psychiat., 18*(4), 407–410.

McDermut, W., Miller, I. W., & Brown, R. A. (2001). The efficacy of group psychotherapy for depression: A meta-analysis and review of the empirical research. *Clin. Psychol.: Sci. Prac., 8*(1), 98–116.

McDowell, D. (2005). Marijuana, hallucinogens, and club drugs. In R. J. Frances, A. H. Mack, & S. I. Miller (Eds.), *Clinical textbook of addictive disorders* (3rd ed., pp. 157–183). New York: Guilford Press.

McEachin, J. J., Smith, T., & Lovaas, O. I. (1993). Long-term outcome for children with autism who received early intensive behavioral treatment. *Amer. J. Ment. Retard., 97*(4), 359–372.

McEvoy, P. M. (2007). Effectiveness of cognitive behavioural group therapy for social phobia in a community clinic: A benchmarking study. *Behav. Res. Ther., 45*(12), 3030–3040.

McEvoy, P. M., & Richards, D. (2007). Gatekeeping access to community mental health teams: A qualitative study. *Inter. J. Nurs. Stud., 44*(3), 387–395.

McEwen, B. S. (2002). Protective and damaging effects of stress mediators: The good and bad sides of the response to stress. *Metabolism, 51*(Suppl 1), 2–4.

McFarland, L. A., Ryan, A. M., Sacco, J. M., & Kriska, D. (2004). Examination of structured interview ratings across time: The effects of applicant race, rater race, and panel composition. *J. Manag., 30*(4), 435–452.

McFarlane, T., Carter, J., & Olmsted, M. (2005). Eating disorders. In M. M. Antony, D. R. Ledley, & R. G. Heimberg (Eds.), *Improving outcomes and preventing relapse in cognitive-behavioral therapy* (pp. 268–305). New York: Guilford Press.

McGeer, P. L., & McGeer, E. G. (1996). Anti-inflammatory drugs in the fight against Alzheimer's disease. In R. J. Wurtman, S. Corkin, J. H. Growdon, & R. M. Nitsch (Eds.), *The neurobiology of Alzheimer's disease.* New York: New York Academy of Sciences.

McGhie, A., & Chapman, J. S. (1961). Disorders of attention and perception in early schizophrenia. *Brit. J. Med. Psychol., 34,* 103–116.

McGinn, D., & DePasquale, R. (2004, August 23). Taking depression on. *Newsweek,* pp. 59–60.

McGlothlin, J. M. (2008). *Developing clinical skills in suicide assessment, prevention, and treatment.* Alexandria, VA: American Counseling Association.

McGoldrick, M., Loonan, R., & Wohlsifer, D. (2007). Sexuality and culture. In S. R. Leiblum (Ed.), *Principles and practice of sex therapy* (4th ed., pp. 416–441). New York: Guilford Press.

McGowan, S., Lawrence, A. D., Sales, T., Quested, D., & Grasby P. (2004). Presynaptic dopaminergic dysfunction in schizophrenia: A positron emission tomography [^{18}F] fluorodopa study. *Arch. Gen. Psychiat., 61,* 134–142.

McGrath, M., & Torres, A. (2008). Forensic psychology, forensic psychiatry, and criminal profiling: The mental health professional's contribution to criminal profiling. In B. E. Turvey (Ed.), *Criminal profiling: An introduction to behavioral evidence analysis* (3rd ed., pp. 113–132). San Diego, CA: Elsevier.

McGrath, M. L., Mellon, M. W., & Murphy, L. (2000). Empirically supported treatments in pediatric psychology: Constipation and encopresis. *J. Pediatr. Psychol., 25*(4), 225–254.

McGrath, P. A., & Hillier, L. M. (2001). Recurrent headache: Triggers, causes, and contributing factors. In P. A. McGrath & L. M. Hiller (Eds.), *The child with headache: Diagnosis and treatment* (pp. 77–107). Seattle, WA: IASP Press.

McGuffin, P., Katz, R., Watkins, S., & Rutherford, J. (1996). A hospital-based twin register of the heritability of DSM-IV unipolar depression. *Arch. Gen. Psychiat., 53,* 129–136.

McGuire, P. A. (2000, February). New hope for people with schizophrenia. *Monit. Psychol., 31*(2), 24–28.

McGuire, P. K., Shah, G. M. S., & Murray, R. M. (1993). Increased blood flow in Broca's area during auditory hallucinations in schizophrenia. *Lancet, 342,* 703–706.

McGuire, P. K., Silbersweig, D. A., Wright, I., Murray, R. M., et al. (1995). Abnormal monitoring of inner speech: A physiological basis for auditory hallucinations. *Lancet, 346,* 596–600.

McGuire, P. K., Silbersweig, D. A., Wright, I., Murray, R. M., Frackowiak, R. S., & Frith, C. D. (1996). The neural correlates of inner speech and auditory verbal imagery in schizophrenia: Relationship to auditory verbal hallucinations. *Brit. J. Psychiat., 169*(2), 148–159.

McIntosh, J. L., Hubbard, R. W., & Santos, J. F. (1985). Suicide facts and myths: A study of prevalence. *Death Stud., 9,* 267–281.

McIntosh, J. L., & Santos, J. F. (1982). Changing patterns in methods of suicide by race and sex. *Suic. Life-Threat. Behav., 12,* 221–233.

McIntosh, K., & Kleiman, A. M. (2007). "Natural" alternatives to antidepressants: St. John's wort, kava kava, and others. Broomall, PA: Mason Crest Publishers.

McKay, D., Gosselin, J. T., & Gupta, S. (2008). Body dysmorphic disorder. In J. S. Abramowitz, D. McKay, & S. Taylor (Eds.), *Obsessive-compulsive disorder: Subtypes and spectrum conditions.* Oxford, England: Elsevier.

McKee, S. A., Harris, G. T., Rice, M. E., & Silk, L. (2007). Effects of a Snoezelen room on the behavior of three autistic clients. *Res. Dev. Disabl., 28*(3), 304–316.

McKendrick, K., Sullivan, C., Banks, S., & Sacks, S. (2007). Modified therapeutic community treatment for offenders with MICA disorders: Antisocial personality disorder and treatment outcomes. *J. Offender Rehab., 44*(2–3), 133–159.

McKisack, C., & Waller, G. (1997). Factors influencing the outcome of group psychotherapy for bulimia nervosa. *Inter. J. Eat. Disorders, 22,* 1–13.

McLay, R. N., Daylo, A. A., & Hammer, P. S. (2006). No effect of lunar cycle on psychiatric admissions or emergency evaluations. *Military Med., 171*(12), 1239–1242.

McLean, P. D., & Hakstian, A. R. (1979). Clinical depression: Comparative efficacy of outpatient treatments. *J. Cons. Clin. Psychol., 47*(5), 818–836.

McLeod, H. J., Byrne, M. K., & Aitken, R. (2004). Automatism and dissociation: disturbances of consciousness and volition from a psychological perspective. *Inter. J. Law Psychiat., 27*(5), 471–487.

McMahon, R. J., & Frick, P. J. (2005). Evidence-based assessment of conduct problems in children and adolescents. *J. Clin. Child Adol. Psychol., 34,* 477–505.

McMahon, R. J., & Kotler, J. S. (2008). Evidence-based therapies for oppositional behavior in young children. In R. G. Steele, T. D. Elkin, & M. C. Roberts (Eds.), *Handbook of evidence-based therapies for children and adolescents: Bridging science and practice.* New York: Springer.

McNally, R. J. (2001). The cognitive psychology of repressed and recovered memories of childhood sexual abuse: Clinical implications. *Psychiatr. Ann., 31*(8), 509–514.

McNally, R. J. (2001). Vulnerability to anxiety disorders in adulthood. In R. E. Ingram & J. M. Price (Eds.), *Vulnerability to psychopathology: Risk across the lifespan* (pp. 304–321). New York: Guilford Press.

McNally, R. J. (2004, April 1). Psychological debriefing does not prevent posttraumatic stress disorder. *Psychiatr. Times,* p. 71.

McNally, R. J., Bryant, R. A., & Ehlers, A. (2003). Does early psychological intervention promote recovery from posttraumatic stress? *Psychol. Sci. Publ. Interest, 4*(2), 45–79.

McNally, R. J., Clancy, S. A., & Barrett, H. M. (2004). Forgetting trauma? In P. Hertel, & D. Reisberg (Eds.), *Memory and emotion* (pp. 129–154). London: Oxford University Press.

McNally, R. J., Clancy, S. A., Barrett, H. M., & Parker, H. A. (2005). Reality monitoring in adults reporting repressed, recovered, or continuous memories of childhood sexual abuse. *J. Abnorm. Psychol., 114*(1), 147–152.

McNeal, E. T., & Cimbolic, P. (1986). Antidepressants and biochemical theories of depression. *Psychol. Bull., 99*(3), 361–374.

McNeely, H. E., Mayberg, H. S., Lozano, A. M., & Kennedy, S. H. (2008). Neuropsychological impact of Cg25 deep brain stimulation for treatment-resistant depression: Preliminary results over 12 months. *J. Nerv. Ment. Dis., 196*(5), 405–410.

McNeil, E. B. (1967). *The quiet furies.* Englewood Cliffs, NJ: Prentice Hall.

McPherson, M., Smith-Lovin, L., & Brashears, M. (2006). Social isolation in America: Changes in core discussion networks over two decades. *Amer. Sociol. Rev., 71,* 353–375.

McSweeney, S. (2004). Depression in women. In L. Cosgrove & P. J. Caplan (Eds.), *Bias in psychiatric diagnosis* (pp. 183–188). Northvale, NJ: Jason Aronson.

Mealy, M., Stephan, W., & Urrutia, I. C. (2007). The acceptability of lies: A comparison of Ecuadorians and Euro-Americans. *Inter. J. Intercult. Relations, 31*(6), 689–702.

Mechanic, D. (2004). The rise and fall of managed care. *J. Hlth. Soc. Behav., 45*(Suppl.), 76–86.

Medford, N., Brierley, B., Brammer, M., Bullmore, E. T., David, A. S., & Phillips, M. L. (2006). Emotional memory in depersonalization disorder: A functional MRI study. *Psychiat. Res. Neuroimaging, 148*(2–3), 93–102.

Mednick, S. A. (1971). Birth defects and schizophrenia. *Psychol. Today, 4,* 48–50.

Meehl, P. E. (1960). The cognitive activity of the clinician. *Amer. Psychologist, 15,* 19–27.

Meehl, P. E. (1996). *Clinical versus statistical prediction: A theoretical analysis and a review of the evidence.* Northvale, NJ: Jason Aronson.

Meeks, T. W., & Jeste, D. V. (2008). Older individuals. In K. T. Mueser & D.V. Jeste (Eds.), *Clinical handboook of schizophrenia* (pp. 390–397). New York: Guilford Press.

Meichenbaum, D. H. (1975). A self-instructional approach to stress management: A proposal for stress inoculation training. In I. Sarason & C. D. Spielberger (Eds.), *Stress and anxiety* (Vol. 2). New York: Wiley.

Meichenbaum, D. H. (1977). *Cognitive-behavior modification: An integrative approach.* New York: Plenum Press.

Meichenbaum, D. H. (1993). Stress inoculation training: A 20-year update. In P. M. Lehrer & R. L. Woolfolk (Eds.), *Principles and practice of stress management* (2nd ed.). New York: Guilford Press.

Meichenbaum, D. H. (1997). The evolution of a cognitive-behavior therapist. In J. K. Zeig (Ed.), *The evolution of psychotherapy: The third conference.* New York: Brunner/Mazel.

Meiser, B., Mitchell, P. B., Kasparian, N. A., Strong, K., Simpson, J. M., Mireskandari, S., et al. (2007). Attitudes towards childbearing, causal attributes for bipolar disorder and psychological distress: A study of families with multiple cases of bipolar disorder. *Psychol. Med.*, *37*, 1601–1611.

Melamed, B. G., Kaplan, B., & Fogel, J. (2001). Childhood health issues across the life span. In A. Baum, T. A. Revenson, & J. E. Singer (Eds.), *Handbook of health psychology* (pp. 449–458). Mahwah, NJ: Lawrence Erlbaum.

Melfi, C. A., Croghan, T. W., Hanna, M. P., & Robinson, R. L. (2000). Racial variation in antidepressant treatment in a Medicaid population. *J. Clin. Psychiat.*, *61*(1), 16–21.

Melo, J. A., Shendure, J., Pociask, K., & Silver, L. M. (1996, June). Identification of sex-specific quantiative trait loci controlling alcohol preference in C57BL/6 mice. *Nature Genetics*, *13*, 147–153.

Melville, J. (1978). *Phobias and obsessions.* New York: Penguin.

Melville, J. D., & Naimark, D. (2002). Punishing the insane: The verdict of guilty but mentally ill. *J. Amer. Acad. Psychiat. Law*, *30*(4), 553–555.

Mendelowitz, E., & Schneider, K. (2008). Existential psychotherapy. In R. J. Corsini & D. Wedding (Eds.), *Current psychotherapies* (8th ed.). Belmont, CA: Thomson Brooks/Cole.

Mendels, J. (1970). *Concepts of depression.* New York: Wiley.

Mendlewicz, J., Linkowski, P., & Wilmotte, J. (1980). Linkage between glucose-6–phosphate dehydrogenase deficiency in manic depressive psychosis. *Brit. J. Psychiat.*, *137*, 337–342.

Mendlewicz, J., Simon, P., Sevy, S., Charon, F., Brocas, H., Legros, S., et al. (1987). Polymorphic DNA marker on X chromosome and manic depression. *Lancet*, *1*, 1230–1232.

Mennin, D. S. (2004). Emotion regulation therapy for generalized anxiety disorder. *Clin. Psychol. Psychother.*, *11*(1), 17–29.

Mennin, D. S., Heimberg, R. G., Turk, C. L., & Fresco, D. M. (2002). Applying an emotion regulation framework to integrative approaches to generalized anxiety disorder. *Clin. Psycol.: Sci. Pract.*, *9*, 85–90.

Mennin, D. S., Heimberg, R. G., Turk, C. L., & Fresco, D. M. (2005). Preliminary evidence for an emotion dysregulation model of generalized anxiety disorder. *Behav. Res. Ther.*, *43*(10), 1281–1310.

Mennin, D. S., Turk, C. L., Heimberg, R. G., & Carmin, C. (2004). Regulation of emotion in generalized anxiety disorder. In M. A. Reinecke & D. A. Clark (Eds.), *Cognitive therapy over the lifespan: Theory, research, and practice* (pp. 60–89). New York: Wiley.

Menninger, K. (1938). *Man against himself.* New York: Harcourt.

Mercer, C. H., Fenton, K. A., Johnson, A. M., Wellings, K., Macdowall, W., McManus, S., et al. (2003). Sexual function problems and help seeking behaviour in Britain: National probability sample survey. *Brit. Med. J.*, *327*, 426–427.

Merenda, R. R. (2008). The posttraumatic and sociocognitive etiologies of dissociative identity disorder: A survey of clinical psychologists. *Diss. Abstr. Inter.: Sect. B: Sci. Eng.*, *68*(8-B), 55–84.

Mergl, R., Seidscheck, I., Allgaier, A. K., Moller, H. J., Hegerl, U., & Henkel, V. (2007). Depressive, anxiety, and somatoform disorders in primary care: Prevalence and recognition. *Depress. Anx.*, *24*(3), 185–195.

Merikangas, K. R., Akiskal, H. S., Angst, J., Greenberg, P. E., Hirschfeld, R. M. A., Petukhova, M., et al. (2007). Lifetime and 12-month prevalence of bipolar spectrum disorder in the National Comorbidity Survey Replication. *Arch. Gen. Psychiat.*, *64*(5), 543–552.

Merskey, H. (1986). Classification of chronic pain: Descriptions of chronic pain syndromes and definitions of pain terms. *Pain*, *3*, 226.

Merskey, H. (2004). Somatization, hysteria, or incompletely explained symptoms? *Canad. J. Psychiat.*, *49*(10), 649–651.

Merzenich, M. M., Jenkins, W. M., Johnston, P., Schreiner, C., et al. (1996). Temporal processing deficits of language-learning impaired children ameliorated by training. *Science*, *271*, 77–84.

Messas, G., Meira-Lima, I., Turchi, M., Franco, O., Guindalini, C., Castelo, A., et al. (2005). Association study of dopamine D2 and D3 receptor gene polymorphisms with cocaine dependence. *Psychiat. Genet.*, *15*(3), 171–174.

Metz, M. E., & Epstein, N. (2002). Assessing the role of relationship conflict in sexual dysfunction. *J. Sex Marital Ther.*, *28*(2), 139–164.

Metz, M. E., & Pryor, J. L. (2000). Premature ejaculation: A psychophysiological approach for assessment and management. *J. Sex Marital Ther.*, *26*(4), 293–320.

Metzl, J. M. (2004). Voyeur nation? Changing definitions of voyeurism, 1950–2004. *Harvard Rev. Psychiat.*, *12*(q), 127–131.

Meuret, A. E., Ritz, T., Wilhelm, F. H., & Roth, W. T. (2005). Voluntary hyperventilation in the treatment of panic disorder—functions of hyperventilation, their implications for breathing training, and recommendations for standardization. *Clin. Psychol. Rev.*, *25*(3), 285–306.

Meydan, J., Liu, X., & Hasin, D. (2005). Letter to the Editors: Alcohol and drug use in schizophrenia as predictors of functional impairment. *Schizo. Res.*, *77*(1), 105–106.

Meyer, G. J., Finn, S. E., Eyde, L. D., Kay, G. G., Moreland, K. L., Dies, R. R., et al. (2001). Psychological testing and psychological assessment: A review of evidence and issues. *Amer. Psychologist*, *56*(2), 128–165.

Meyer, G. J., Finn, S. E., Eyde, L. D., Kay, G. G., Moreland, K. L., Dies, R. R., et al. (2003). Psychological testing and psychological assessment: A review of evidence and issues. In A. E. Kazdin (Ed.), *Methodological issues and strategies in clinical research* (3rd ed., pp. 265–345). Washington, DC: American Psychological Association.

Meyer, J. S., & Quenzer, L. F. (2005). *Psychopharmacology: Drugs, the brain, and behavior.* Sunderland, MA: Sinauer Associates.

Meyer, R. G. (2002). *Case studies in abnormal behavior* (6th ed.). Needham Heights, MA: Allyn & Bacon.

Meyer, U., Feldon, J., Schedlowski, M., & Yee, B. K. (2005) Towards an immuno-precipitated neurodevelopmental animal model of schizophrenia. *Neurosci. Biobehav. Rev.*, *29*(6), 913–947.

Meyer, U., Nyffeler, M., Schwendener, S., Knuesel, I., Yee, B. K., & Feldon, J. (2008). Relative prenatal and postnatal maternal contributions to schizophrenia-related neurochemical dysfunction after in utero immune challenge. *Neuropsychopharmacology*, *33*(202), 441–456.

Meyerhoff, D. J., Blumenfeld, R., Truran, D., Lindgren, J., Flenniken, D., Cardenas, V., et al. (2004, April). Effects of heavy drinking, binge drinking, and family history of alcoholism on regional brain metabolites. *Alcohol.: Clin. Exp. Res.*, 650–661.

Meyers, L. (2006). Help wanted: Geropsychologists. *Monitor on Psychology*, *37*(8), 28–29.

Meyers, L. (2008). Warding off dementia. *Monitor on Psychology*, *39*(3), 22–23.

Mezzasalma, M. A., Valenca, A. M., Lopes, F. L., Nascimento, I., Zin, W. A., & Nardi, A. E. (2004). Neuroanatomy of panic disorder. *Revista Brasileira de Psiquiatria*, *26*(3), 202–206.

MFA. (2008). Common bacterial. Phoenix, AZ: Meningitis Foundation of America.

MHA (Mental Health America). (2004). *NMHA policy positions: In support of the insanity defense.* National Mental Health Association, March 7, 2004.

MHA (Mental Health America). (2007). The insanity defense is a legitimate legal approach. In A. Quigley (Ed.), *Current controversies: Mental health.* Detroit: Greenhaven Press/Thomson Gale.

MHA (Mental Health America). (2008). *Americans reveal top stressors, how they cope.* Alexandria, VA: Author.

Michael, R. T., Gagnon, J. H., Laumann, E. O., & Kolata, G. (1994). *Sex in America: A definitive survey.* Boston: Little, Brown.

Michael, T., Ehlers, A., Halligan, S. L., & Clark, D. M. (2005). Unwanted memories of assault: What intrusion characteristics are associated with PTSD? *Behav. Res. Ther.*, *43*(5), 613–628.

Michel, A., Ansseau, M., Legros, J.-J., Pitchot, W., & Mormont, C. (2002). The transsexual: What about the future. *Eur. Psychiat.*, *17*(6), 353–362.

Miguel, E. C., Leckman, J. F., Rauch, S., do Rosario-Campos, M. C., Hounie, A. G., Mercadante, M. T., et al. (2005). Obsessive-compulsive disorder phenotypes: Implications for genetic studies. *Mol. Psychiat.*, *10*(3), 258–275.

Miguel, E. C., Rauch, S. L., & Jenike, M. A. (1997). Obsessive-compulsive disorder. *Neuropsychiat. Basal Ganglia*, *20*(4), 863–883.

Millar, H. R., Wardell, F., Vyvyan, J. P., Naji, S. A., Prescott, G. J., & Eagles, J. M. (2005). Anorexia nervosa mortality in northeast Scotland, 1965–1999. *Amer. J. Psychiat.*, *162*(4), 753–757.

Miller, F. G., Emanuel, E. J., Rosenstein, D. L., & Straus, S. E. (2004). Ethical issues concerning research in complementary and alternative medicine. *JAMA*, *291*(5), 599–604.

Miller, M., & Kantrowitz, B. (1999, January 25). Unmasking Sybil: A re-examination of the most famous psychiatric patient in history. *Newsweek*, pp. 66–68.

Miller, M. A., & Rahe, R. H. (1997). Life changes scaling for the 1990s. *J. Psychosom. Res.*, *43*(3), 279–292.

Miller, M. C. (2004). Hypochondria. *Harvard Mental Health Letter*, July 1, 2004.

Miller, M. C. (2005). Falling apart: Dissociation and its disorders. *Harvard Mental Health Letter*, January 1, 2005.

Miller, M. C. (2005). What is body dysmorphic disorder? *Harvard Mental Health Letter*, July 1, 2005.

Miller, M. N., & Pumariega, A. (1999). Culture and eating disorders. *Psychiatr. Times., XVI*(2).

Miller, N. E. (1948). Studies of fear as an acquirable drive: I. Fear as motivation and fear-reduction as reinforcement in the learning of new responses. *J. Exp. Psychol., 38,* 89–101.

Miller, P. M., Ingham, J. G., & Davidson, S. (1976). Life events, symptoms, and social support. *J. Psychiatr. Res., 20*(6), 514–522.

Miller, S. G. (1994). Borderline personality disorder from the patient's perspective. *Hosp. Comm. Psychiat., 45*(12), 1215–1219.

Miller, S. G. (1999). Borderline personality disorder in cultural context: Commentary on Paris. *Psychiatry, 59*(2), 193–195.

Miller, T. W. (2007). Trauma, change, and psychological health in the 21st century. *Amer. Psychologist, 62*(8), 889–898.

Miller, W. R. (1983). Controlled drinking, *Quart. J. Stud. Alcohol., 44,* 68–83.

Miller, W. R. (2000). Rediscovering fire: Small interventions, large effects. *Psychol. Addict. Behav., 14*(1), 6–18.

Miller, W. R., Leckman, A. L., Delaney, H. D., & Tinchom, M. (1992). Long-term follow-up of behavioral self-control training. *J. Stud. Alc., 51,* 108–115.

Miller, W. R., & Seligman, M. E. (1975). Depression and learned helplessness in man. *J. Abnorm. Psychol., 84*(3), 228–238.

Millon, T. (1969). *Modern psychopathology: A biosocial approach to maladaptive learning and functioning.* Philadelphia: Saunders.

Millon, T. (1990). The disorders of personality. In L. A. Pervin (Ed.), *Handbook of personality theory and practice.* New York: Guilford Press.

Millon, T. (1990). *Toward a new personology.* New York: Wiley.

Millon, T. (1999). *Personality-guided therapy.* New York: Wiley.

Millon, T., Davis, R., Millon, C., Escovar, L., & Meagher, S. (2000). *Personality disorders in modern life.* New York: Wiley.

Millon, T., & Grossman, S. (2007). *Moderating severe personality disorders: A personalized psychotherapy approach.* Hoboken, NJ: Wiley.

Milner, B. (1971). Interhemispheric difference in the localization of psychological processes in man. *Brit. Med. Bull., 27,* 272–277.

Mineka, S., & Ohman, A. (2002). Phobias and preparedness: The selective, automatic, and encapsulated nature of fear. *Biol. Psychiat., 51*(9), 927–937.

Mineka, S., & Zinbarg, R. (2006). A contemporary learning theory perspective on the etiology of anxiety disorders: It's not what you thought it was. *Amer. Psychologist, 61,* 10–26.

Minton, H. L. (2002). *Departing from deviance: A history of homosexual rights and emancipatory science in America.* Chicago: University of Chicago Press.

Minuchin, S. (1974). *Families and family therapy.* Cambridge, MA: Harvard University Press.

Minuchin, S. (1987). My many voices. In J. K. Zeig (Ed.), *The evolution of psychotherapy.* New York: Brunner/Mazel.

Minuchin, S. (1997). The leap to complexity: Supervision in family therapy. In J. K. Zeig (Ed.), *The evolution of psychotherapy: The third conference.* New York: Brunner/Mazel.

Minuchin, S., Rosman, B. L., & Baker, L. (1978). *Psychosomatic families: Anorexia nervosa in context.* Cambridge, MA: Harvard University Press.

Mio, J. S., Barker-Hackett, L., & Tumambing, J. (2006). *Multicultural psychology, Understanding our diverse communities.* New York: McGraw-Hill.

Miranda, J., Siddique, J., Belin, T. R., & Kohn-Wood, L. P. (2005). Depression prevalence in disadvantaged young black women: African and Caribbean immigrants compared to US-born African Americans. *Soc. Psychiat. Psychiatr. Epidemiol. 40*(4), 253–258.

Mirin, S. M., & Weiss, R. D. (1991). Substance abuse and mental illness. In R. J. Frances, A. H. Mack, & S. I. Miller (Eds.), *Clinical textbook of addictive disorders.* New York: Guilford Press.

Mirone, V., Longo, N., Fusco, F., Mangiapia, F., Granata, A. M., & Perretti, A. (2001). Can the BC reflex evaluation be useful for the diagnosis primary premature ejaculation? *International Journal of Impotence Research, 13,* S47.

Mirsky, I. A. (1958). Physiologic, psychologic, and social determinants of the etiology of duodenal ulcer. *Amer. J. Digestional Dis., 3,* 285–314.

Mirzaei, S., Gelpi, E., Roddrigues, M., Knoll, P., & Gutierrez-Lobos, K. (2005). Progress in post-traumatic stress disorder research. In T. A. Corales (Ed.), *Focus on posttraumatic stress disorder research* (pp. 157–177). Hauppauge, NY: Nova Science Publishers.

Mishara, B. L. (1999). Conceptions of death and suicide in children ages 6–12 and their implications for suicide prevention. *Suic. Life-Threat. Behav., 29*(2), 105–118.

Mitchell, I. (2001). Treatment and outcome for victims. In G. Adshead & D. Brooke (Eds.), *Munchausen's syndrome by proxy: Current issues in assessment, treatment and research* (pp. 185–196). London: Imperial College Press.

Mitchell, J. E., Devlin, M. J., de Zwaan, M., Crow, S. J., & Peterson, C. B. (2008). *Binge-eating disorder: Clinical foundations and treatment.* New York: Guilford Press.

Mitchell, J. E., Halmi, K., Wilson, G. T., Agras, W. S., Kraemer, H., & Crow, S. (2002). A randomized secondary treatment study of women with bulimia nervosa who fail to respond to CBT. *Inter. J. Eat. Disorders, 32*(3), 271–281.

Mitchell, J. T. (1983). When disaster strikes. . . the critical incident stress debriefing process. *J. Emerg. Med. Serv., 8,* 36–39.

Mitchell, J. T. (2003). Crisis intervention & CISM: A research summary. Retrieved from www.icisf.org/articles/cism_research_summary.pdf

Mitchell, J. T., & Everly, G. S., Jr. (2000). Critical incident stress management and critical incident stress debriefing: Evolutions, effects, and outcomes. In B. Raphael & J. P. Wilson (Eds.), *Psychological debriefing: Theory, practice, and evidence* (pp. 71–90). Cambridge, England: Cambridge University Press.

Mitchell, L. (2004). The great pretenders. *The Age.com.au.* Retrieved July 4, 2005, from global.factiva.com/en/arch/print_results.asp

Mittal, V. A., Kalus, O., Bernstein, D. P., & Siever, L. J. (2007). Schizoid personality disorder. In W. O'Donohue, K. A. Fowler, & S. O. Lilienfeld (Eds.). *Personality disorders: Toward the DSM-V.* Los Angeles: Sage Publications.

Mittendorfer-Rutz, E., Rasmussen, F., & Wasserman, D. (2008). Familial clustering of suicidal behaviour and psychopathology in young suicide attempters: A register-based nested case control study. *Soc. Psychiat. Psychiatr. Epidemiol., 43*(1), 28–36.

Modlin, T. (2002). Sleep disorders and hypnosis: To cope or cure? *Sleep Hyp., 4*(1), 39–46.

Modrow, J. (1992). *How to become a schizophrenic: The case against biological psychiatry.* Everett, WA: Apollyon Press.

Moene, F. C., Spinhoven, P., Hoogduin, K. A. L., & van Dyck, R. (2002). A randomised controlled clinical trial on the additional effect of hypnosis in a comprehensive treatment programme for in-patients with conversion disorder of the motor type. *Psychother. Psychosom., 71*(2), 66–76.

Mohler, H., & Okada, T. (1977). Benzodiazepine receptor: Demonstration in the central nervous system. *Science, 198*(4319), 849–851.

Mohler, H., Richards, J. G., & Wu, J.-Y. (1981). Autoradiographic localization of benzodiazepine receptors in immunocytochemically identified Y-aminobutyric synapses. *Proc. Natl. Acad. Sci., USA, 78,* 1935–1938.

Mohlman, J., Gorenstein, E. E., Kleber, M., de Jesus, M., Gorman, J. M., & Papp, L. A. (2003). Standard and enhanced cognitive-behavior therapy for late-life generalized anxiety disorder: Two pilot investigations. *Amer. J. Ger. Psychiat., 11*(1), 24–32.

Moldavsky, D. (2004, June 1). Transcultural psychiatry for clinical practice. *Psychiatr. Times, XXI*(7), p. 36.

Molina, I. A., Dulmus, C. N., & Sowers, K. M. (2005). Secondary prevention for youth violence: A review of selected school-based programs. *Brief Treat. Crisis Intervent., 5*(1), 1–3.

Molnar, B. E., Buka, S. L., & Kessler, R. C. (2001). Child sexual abuse and subsequent psychopathology: Results from the National Comorbidity Survey. *Amer. J. Pub. Hlth., 91*(5), 753–760.

Monahan, J. (1992). Mental disorder and violent behavior: Perceptions and evidence. *Amer. Psychologist, 47*(4), 511–521.

Monahan, J. (1993). Limiting therapist exposure to *Tarasoff* liability: Guidelines for risk containment. *Amer. Psychologist, 48*(3), 242–250.

Monahan, J. (2001). Major mental disorder and violence: Epidemiology and risk assessment. In G. F. Pinard & L. Pagani (Eds.), *Clinical assessment of dangerousness: Empirical contributions* (pp. 89–102). New York: Cambridge University Press.

Monahan, J. (2008). Limiting therapist exposure to Tarasoff liability: Guidelines for risk containment. In D. N. Bersoff (Ed.), *Ethical conflicts in psychology* (4th ed., pp. 180–186). Washington, DC: American Psychological Association.

Monahan, J., Redlich, A. D., Swanson, J., Robbins, P. C., Appelbaum, P. S., Petrila, J., et al. (2005). Use of leverage to improve adherence to psychiatric treatment in the community. *Psychiat. Serv., 56*(1), 37–44.

Monette, J., du Fort, G. G., Fung, S. H., Massoud, F., Moride, Y., Arsenault, L., & Afilalo, M. (2001). Evaluation of the Confusion Assessment Method (CAM) as a screening tool for delirium in the emergency room. *Gen. Hosp. Psychiat., 23*(1), 20–25.

Monroe, S. M., & Hadjiyannakis, K. (2002). The social environment and depression: Focusing on severe life stress. In I. H. Gotlib & C. L. Hammen (Eds.), *Handbook of depression: Research and treatment* (pp. 314–340). New York: Guilford Press.

Monroe, S. M., Slavich, G. M., Torres, L. D., & Gotlib, I. H. (2007). Severe life events predict specific patterns of change in cognitive biases in major depression. *Psychol. Med., 37*(6), 863–871.

Monson, C. M., Stevens, S. P., & Schnurr, P. P. (2005). Cognitive-behavioral couple's treatment for posttraumatic stress disorder. In T. A. Corales (Ed.), *Focus on posttraumatic stress disorder research* (pp. 245–274). Hauppauge, NY: Nova Science Publishers.

Monti, F., Agostini, F., & Martini, A. (2004). Postpartum depression and mother-infant interaction. *Eta Evolutiva, 78,* 77–84.

Moore, C. L., Flowers, C. R., & Taylor, D. (2000). Vocational rehabilitation services: Indicators of successful rehabilitation for persons with mental retardation. *J. Appl. Rehabil. Counsel., 31*(2), 36–40.

Moore, K., & Walkup, J. (2007). Use of accounts in long term friendships sustained after one friend develops a psychotic illness. In J. E. Pletson (Ed.), *Psychology and schizophrenia.* New York: Nova Science Publishers.

Moore, M. T. (1997, October 30). Maine initiative would give the vote to all mentally ill. *USA Today,* p. 12A.

Moorhead, D. J., Stashwick, C. K., Reinherz, H. Z., Giaconia, R. M., Streigel-Moore, R. M., & Paradis, A. D. (2003). Child and adolescent predictors for eating disorders in a community population of young adult women. *Inter. J. Eat. Disorders, 33*(1), 1–9.

Moos, R. H., & Cronkite, R. C. (1999). Symptom-based predictors of a 10-year chronic course of treated depression. *J. Nerv. Ment. Dis., 187*(6), 360–368.

Moos, R. H., & Timko, C. (2008). Outcome research on 12-step and other self-help programs. In H. D. Kleber & M. Galanter (Eds.), *The American Psychiatric Publishing textbook of substance abuse treatment* (4th ed., pp. 511–521). Arlington, VA: American Psychiatric Publishing.

Moreno, C., Laje, G., Blanco, C., Jiang, H., Schmidt, A. B., & Olfson, M. (2007). National trends in the outpatient diagnosis and treatment of bipolar disorder in youth. *Arch. Gen. Psychiat., 64*(9), 1032–1039.

Morgan, A. B., & Lilienfeld, S. O. (2000). A meta-analytic review of the relation between antisocial behavior and neuropsychological measures of executive function. *Clinical Psychology Review, 20,* 113–136.

Morgan, A. H., & Hilgard, E. R. (1973). Age differences in susceptibility to hypnosis. *Inter. J. Clin. Exp. Hyp., 21,* 78–85.

Morgan, C. D., & Murray, H. A. (1935). A method of investigating fantasies: The Thematic Apperception Test. *Arch. Neurol. Psychiat., 34,* 289–306.

Morgan, J., & Laungani, P. (Eds.). (2002) *Death and bereavement around the world* (Vols. 1–4). Amityville, NY: Baywood.

MORI (Market Opinion Research International). (1999, May 22). Poll on animal experimentation. *New Scientist.*

MORI (Market Opinion Research International). (2005, January). Use of animals in medical research for Coalition for Medical Progress. London: Author.

Morokoff, P. J., & Gillilland, R. (1993). Stress, sexual functioning, and marital satisfaction. *J. Sex Res., 30*(1), 43–53.

Morrison, A. P. (2008). Cognitive-behavioral therapy. In D. V. Jeste & K. T. Mueser (Eds.), *Clinical handbook of schizophrenia* (pp. 226–239). New York: Guilford Press.

Morrissey, J. P., & Cuddeback, G. S. (2008). Jail diversion. In K. T. Mueser & D. V. Jeste (Eds.), *Clinical handbook of schizophrenia* (pp. 524–532). New York: Guilford Press.

Morse, S. (2003, December 13). Homeward hound: A case of dog fugue? *Animal News.*

Morse, S. J. (1982). A preference for liberty: The case against involuntary commitment of the mentally disordered. *Calif. Law Rev., 70,* 55–106.

Mortley, J., Wade, J., & Enderby, P. (2004). Superhighway to promoting a client-therapist partnership: Using the Internet to deliver word-retrieval computer therapy, monitored remotely with minimal speech and language therapy input. *Aphasiology, 18*(3), 193–211.

Mosconi, L., De Santi, S., Li, J., Tsui, W. H., Li, Y., Boppana, M., et al. (2008). Hippocampal hypometabolism predicts cognitive decline from normal aging. *Neurobiol. Aging, 29*(5), 676–692.

Moser, L. L., & Bond, G. R. (2008). Assertive community treatment. In K. T. Mueser & D. V. Jeste (Eds.), *Clinical handbook of schizophrenia* (pp. 329–338). New York: Guilford Press.

Moskowitz, E. S. (2001). *In therapy we trust: America's obsession with self-fulfillment.* Baltimore: Johns Hopkins University Press.

Moskowitz, E. S. (2008). *In therapy we trust: America's obsession with self-fulfillment.* Baltimore, MD: Johns Hopkins University Press.

Moss, D. (2002). Biofeedback. In S. Shannon (Ed.), *Handbook of complementary and alternative therapies in mental health* (pp. 135–158). San Diego, CA: Academic Press.

Mowbray, C. T., Grazier, K. L., & Holter, M. (2002). Managed behavioral health care in the public sector: Will it become the third shame of the States? *Psychiatr. Serv., 53*(2), 157–170.

Mowrer, O. H. (1939). A stimulus-response analysis of anxiety and its role as a reinforcing agent. *Psychol. Rev., 46,* 553–566.

Mowrer, O. H. (1947). On the dual nature of learning: A reinterpretation of "conditioning" and "problem-solving." *Harvard Educ. Rev., 17,* 102–148.

Mowrer, O. H., & Mowrer, W. M. (1938). Enuresis: A method for its study and treatment. *Amer. J. Orthopsychiat., 8,* 436–459.

MTA Cooperative Group. (1999). A 14-month randomized clinical trial of treatment strategies for attention-deficit/hyperactivity disorder. *Arch. Gen. Psychiat., 56,* 1073–1086.

MTA Cooperative Group. (2004). National Institute of Mental Health multimodal treatment study of ADHD follow-up: Changes in effectiveness and growth after the end of treatment. *Pediatrics, 113,* 762–769.

MTC. (2008). *The Methadone treatment directory.* Methadone Treatment Centers.

Mueller, R. A., & Courchesne, E. (2000). Autism's home in the brain: Reply. *Neurology, 54*(1), 270.

Mueller, S. E., Petitjean, S., Boening, J., & Wiesbeck, G. A. (2007). The impact of self-help group attendance on relapse rates after alcohol detoxification in a controlled study. *Alcohol Alcoholism, 42*(2), 108–112.

Mulhern, B. (1990, December 15–18). Everyone's problem, no one's priority. *Capital Times.*

Mulholland, A. M., & Mintz, L. B. (2001). Prevalence of eating disorders among African American women. *J. Couns. Psychol., 48*(1), 111–116.

Munn-Giddings, C., & Borkman, T. (2005). Self-help/mutual aid as a psychosocial phenomenon. In S. Ramon & J. E. Williams (Eds.), *Mental health at the crossroads: The promise of the psychosocial approach* (pp. 137–154). Burlington, VT: Ashgate Publishing.

Munsey, C. (2008). DoD allocates $25 million to study PTSD. *Monitor on Psychology, 39*(7), 16–17.

Muran, E. (2007). Rape trauma. In F. M. Dattilio & A. Freeman (Eds.), *Cognitive-behavioral strategies in crisis intervention* (3rd ed., pp. 476–493). New York: Guilford Press.

Murdock, S. G., O'Neill, R. E., & Cunningham, E. (2005). A comparison of results and acceptability of functional behavioral assessment procedures with a group of middle school students with emotional/behavioral disorders (E/BD). *J. Behav. Educ., 14*(1), 5–18.

Murphy, E., & Carr, A. (2000). Enuresis and encopresis. In A. Carr (Ed.), *What works with children and adolescents? A critical review of psychological interventions with children, adolescents and their families* (pp. 49–64). Florence, KY: Taylor & Frances/Routledge.

Murphy, G. M., Jr., Hollander, S. B., Rodrigues, H. E., Kremer, C., & Schatzberg, A. F. (2004). Effects of the serotonin transporter gene promoter polymorphism on mirtazapie and paroxetine efficacy and adverse events in geriatric major depression. *Arch. Gen. Psychiat., 61*(11), 1163–1169.

Murphy, J. G., McDevitt-Murphy, M. E., & Barnett, N. P. (2005). Drink and be merry? Gender, life satisfaction, and alcohol consumption among college students. *Psychol. Addict. Behav., 19,* 184–191.

Murphy, S. M. (1990). Rape, sexually transmitted diseases and human immunodeficiency virus infection. *Inter. J. STD AIDS, 1,* 79–82.

Murphy, W. D., & Page, I. J. (2006). Exhibitionism. In R. D. McAnulty & M. M. Burnette (Eds.), *Sex and sexuality, Vol. 3: Sexual deviation and sexual offenses.* Westport, CT: Praeger Publishers.

Murphy, W. J. (2001). The Victim Advocacy and Research Group: Serving a growing need to provide rape victims with personal legal representation to protect privacy rights and to fight gender bias in the criminal justice system. *J. Soc. Distress Homeless, 10*(1), 123–138.

Murray, K. (1993, May 9). When the therapist is a computer. *New York Times,* Section 3, p. 25.

Mydans, S. (1996, October 19). New Thai tourist sight: Burmese "giraffe women." *New York Times,* p. C1.

Myers, D. G. (2000). The funds, friends, and faith of happy people. *Amer. Psychologist, 55*(1), 56–67.

Myers, D. G., & Diener, E. (1996, May). The pursuit of happiness. *Scientif. Amer.,* pp. 70–72.

Mylant, M. L., Ide, B., Guevas, E., & Meehan, M. (2002). Adolescent children of alcoholics: Vulnerable or resilient? *J. Amer. Psychiat. Nurs. Assoc., 8*(2), 57–64.

Myrick, H., & Wright, T. (2008). Clinical management of alcohol abuse and dependence. In

H. D. Kleber & M. Galanter (Eds.), *The American Psychiatric Publishing textbook of substance abuse treatment* (4th ed., pp. 129–142). Arlington, VA: American Psychiatric Publishing.

Nace, E. P. (2005). Alcohol. In R. J. Frances, A. H. Mack, & S. I. Miller (Eds.), *Clinical textbook of addictive disorders* (3rd ed., pp. 75–104). New York: Guilford Press.

Nace, E. P. (2008). The history of Alcoholics Anonymous and the experiences of patients. In H. D. Kleber & M. Galanter (Eds.), *The American Psychiatric Publishing textbook of substance abuse treatment* (4th ed., pp. 499–509). Arlington, VA: American Psychiatric Publishing.

Nahas, Z., Marangell, L. B., Husain, M. M., Rush, A. J., Sackeim, H. A., Lisanby, S. H., et al. (2005). Two-year-outcome of vagus nerve stimulation (VNS) for treatment of major depressive episodes. *J. Clin. Psychiat., 66*(9), 1097–1104.

NAHIC (National Adolescent Health Information Center). (2006). *Fact sheet on suicide: Adolescents & young adults.* San Francisco, CA: University of California, San Francisco.

Naimi, T. S., Brewer, R. D., Mokdad, A., Denny, C., Serdula, M. K., & Marks, J. S. (2003). Binge drinking among US adults. *JAMA, 289*(1), 70–75.

Najman, J. M., Andersen, M. J., Bor, W., O'Callaghan, M. J., & Williams, G. M. (2000). Postnatal depression—Myth and reality: Maternal depression before and after the birth of a child. *Soc. Psychiat. Psychiatr. Epidemiol., 35*(1), 19–27.

NAMI (National Alliance for the Mentally Ill). (2002). Retrieved from www.nami.org

NAMI (National Alliance for the Mentally Ill). (2008). Retrieved from www.nami.org

Nantel-Vivier, A., & Pihl, R. O. (2008). Biological vulnerability to depression. In J. R. Z. Abela & B. L. Hankin (Eds.), *Handbook of depression in children and adolescents.* New York: Guilford Press.

Nardi, A. E., Valenca, A. M., Nascimento, I., & Zin, W. A. (2001). Hyperventilation challenge test in panic disorder and depression with panic attacks. *Psychiat. Res., 105,* 57–65.

Narrow, W. E., Rae, D. S., Robins, L. N., & Regier, D. A. (2002). Revised prevalence based estimates of mental disorders in the United States: Using a clinical significance criterion to reconcile 2 surveys' estimates. *Arch. Gen. Psychiat., 59*(2), 115–123.

Nasar, S. (2002, March 18). A majestic person, despite flaws: Some recent reports about mathematician John Nash distort the truth. *Los Angeles Times,* p. B3.

Nash, J. M. (1997). Special report: Fertile minds. *Newsweek, 149*(5), 48–56.

Nash, J. M. (1997, May 5). Addicted. *Time,* pp. 68–76.

Nash, M. R. (2001, July). The truth and the hype of hypnosis. *Scientif. Amer.,* pp. 47–55.

Nash, M. R. (2004). Salient findings: Pivotal reviews and research on hypnosis, soma, and cognition. *Inter. J. Clin. Exp. Hyp., 52*(1), 82–88.

Nash, M. R. (2005). Salient findings: A potentially groundbreaking study on the neuroscience of hypnotizability, a critical review of hypnosis' efficacy, and the neurophysiology of conversion disorder. *Inter. J. Clin. Exp. Hyp., 53*(1), 87–93.

Nash, M. R. (2006). Salient findings: Identifying the building blocks of hypnotizability, and the neural underpinnings of subjective pain. *Inter. J. Clin. Exp. Hyp., 54*(3), 360–365.

Nathan, P. B., & Gorman, J. M. (Eds.). (2007). *A guide to treatments that work* (3rd ed.). New York: Oxford University Press.

Nathan, P. E. (2007). Efficacy, effectiveness, and the clinical utility of psychotherapy research. In J. Weinberger & G. Stefan (Eds.), *The art and science of psychotherapy* (pp. 69–83). New York: Routledge/Taylor & Francis Group.

Nathan, P. E., & Lagenbucher, J. W. (1999). Psychopathology: Description and classification. *Annu. Rev. Psychol., 50,* 79–107.

National Center for PTSD. (2008). Appendix A. Case examples from Operation Iraqi Freedom. *Iraq War Clinician Guide.* Washington, DC: Department of Veteran Affairs.

National Crime Victimization Survey (NCVS). (1993). Highlights from 20 years of surveying crime victims: The National Crime Victimization Survey, 1973–1992. Washington, DC: Bureau of Justice Statistics.

National Crime Victimization Survey (NCVS). (1996). Washington, DC: Bureau of Justice Statistics.

National Crime Victimization Survey (NCVS). (1997). Washington, DC: Bureau of Justice Statistics.

National Crime Victimization Survey (NCVS). (2006). Washington, DC: Bureau of Justice Statistics.

National Task Force on the Prevention and Treatment of Obesity. (2000). Overweight, obesity, and health risk. *Arch. Intern. Med., 160,* 898–904.

Nazarian, M., & Craske, M. G. (2008). Panic and agoraphobia. In M. Hersen & J. Rosqvist (Eds.), *Handbook of psychological assessment, case conceptualization, and treatment, Vol. 1: Adults* (pp. 171–203). Hoboken, NJ: John Wiley & Sons.

Nazemi, H., Kleinknecht, R. A., Dinnel, D. L., Lonner, W. J., Nazemi, S., Shamlo, S., et al. (2003). A study of panic attacks in university students of Iran. *J. Psychopathology Behav. Assess., 25*(3), 191–201.

NCASA (National Center on Addiction and Substance Abuse at Columbia University). (2007, March). *Wasting the best and the brightest: Substance abuse at America's colleges and universities.* Washington, DC: Author.

NCCAM. (2008, January 24). How to apply for a research grant. Retrieved May 31, 2008, from http://nccam.nih.gov/research

NCHS (National Center for Health Statistics). (2005). Asthma prevalence, health care use and mortality, 2002. Hyattsville, MD: Author.

NCHS (National Center for Health Statistics). (2006). *Self-inflicted injury/suicide.* Hyattsville, MD: NCHS. Retrieved August 13, 2008, from www.cdc.gov

Neal, A. M., Lilly, R. S., & Zakis, S. (1993). What are African American children afraid of? *J. Anx. Disorders, 7,* 129–139.

Neckelmann, D., Mykletun, A., & Dahl, A. A. (2007). Chronic insomnia as a risk factor for developing anxiety and depression. *Sleep, 30*(7), 873–880.

Neeleman, J., Wessely, S., & Lewis, G. (1998). Suicide acceptability in African- and white Americans: The role of religion. *J. Nerv. Ment. Dis., 186*(1), 12–16.

Neergaard, L. (2007, August 13). Helping find lost Alzheimer's patients. *Yahoo! News.* Retrieved August 15, 2007, from http://news.yahoo.com

Neisser, U. (2004, September 14). Cited in S. Friess, Historical events can be 'misremembered', *USA Today,* D09.

Neisser, U., Boodoo, G., Bouchard, T. J., Jr., Boykin, A. W., et al. (1996). Intelligence: Knowns and unknowns. *Amer. Psychologist, 51*(2), 77–101.

Nejad, A. G. (2007). Belief in transforming another person into a wolf: Could it be a variant of lycanthropy? *Acta Psychiatr. Scandin., 115*(2), 159–161.

Nelson, T. D. (2006). *The psychology of prejudice* (2nd ed.). New York: Pearson/Allyn & Bacon.

Nelson, T. F., & Wechsler, H. (2001). Alcohol and college athletes. *Med. Sci. Sports Exercise, 33*(1), 43–47.

Nemade, R., Reiss, N. S., & Dombeck, M. (2007). *Depression: Major depression & unipolar varieties.* Retrieved on April 23, 2008, at www.MentalHelp.net

Nemecek, S. (1996, September). Mysterious maladies. *Scientif. Amer.,* 24–26.

Neto, J. A. de S., & Araujo, L. M. (2004). Melatonin and psychiatric disorders. *J. Brasileiro de Psiquiatria, 53*(1), 38–45.

Neugebauer, R. (1978). Treatment of the mentally ill in medieval and early modern England: A reappraisal. *J. Hist. Behav. Sci., 14,* 158–169.

Neugebauer, R. (1979). Medieval and early modern theories of mental illness. *Arch. Gen. Psychiat., 36,* 477–483.

Neuman, P. A., & Halvorson, P. A. (1983). *Anorexia nervosa and bulimia: A handbook for counselors and therapists.* New York: Van Nostrand-Reinhold.

Neumark-Sztainer, D. R., Wall, M. M., Haines, J. I., Story, M. T., Sherwood, N. E., & van den Berg, P. A. (2007). Shared risk and protective factors for overweight and disordered eating in adolescents. *Amer. J. Prev. Med., 33*(5), 359–369.

Neumeister, A., Charney, D. S., & Drevets, W. C. (2005). Hippocampus, VI: Depression and the hippocampus. *Amer. J. Psychiat., 162*(6), 1057.

New York Times. (1993, February 9). West Side man to stay in hospital until hearing. (By Mary B. Tabor).

New, A. S., Hazlett, E. A., Buchsbaum, M. S., Goodman, M., Reynolds, D., Mitropoulou, V., et al. (2002). Blunted prefrontal cortical 18fluorodeoxyglucose positron emission tomography response to meta-chlorophenylpiperazine in impulse aggression. *Arch. Gen. Psychiat., 59,* 621–629.

New, A. S., Trestman, R. F., Mitropoulou, V., Goodman, M., Koenigsberg, H. H., Silverman, J., et al. (2004). Low prolactin response to fenfluramine in impulsive aggression. *J. Psychiatr. Res., 38,* 223–230.

Newcomer, R., Fox, P. J., & Harrington, C. A. (2001). Health and long-term care for people with Alzheimer's disease and related dementias: Policy research issues. *Aging Ment. Hlth., 5*(Suppl. 1), S124–S137.

Newman, C. F., & Fingerhut, R. (2005). Psychotherapy for avoidant personality disorder. In J. Holmes, G. O. Gabbard, & J. S. Beck (Eds.), *Oxford textbook of psychotherapy* (pp. 311–319). New York: Oxford University Press.

Newman, F. L., & Wong, S. E. (2004). Progress and outcomes assessment of individual patient data: Selecting single-subject design and statistical procedures. In M. E. Maruish (Ed.), *The use of psychological testing for treatment planning and outcomes assessment, Vol. 1: General considerations* (3rd ed., pp. 273–289). Mahwah, NJ: Lawrence Erlbaum.

Neylan, T. C., Brunet, A., Pole, N., Best, S. R., Metzler, T. J., Yehuda, R., & Marmar, C. R. (2005). PTSD symptoms predict waking salivary cortisol levels in police officers. *Psychoneuroendocrinology, 30*(4), 373–381.

Neziroglu, F., McKay, D., Todaro, J., & Yaryura-Tobias, J. A. (1996). Effect of cognitive behavior therapy on persons with body dysmorphic disorder and comorbid Axis II diagnoses. *Behav. Ther., 27*, 67–77.

Neziroglu, F., Roberts, M., & Yaryura-Tobias, J. A. (2004). A behavioral model for body dysmorphic disorder. *Psychiatr. Ann., 34*(12), 915–920.

Nezlek, J. B., Hampton, C. P., & Shean, G. D. (2000). Clinical depression and day-to-day social interaction in a community sample. *J. Abnorm. Psychol., 109*(1), 11–19.

Ni, H., & Cohen, D. (2004). Trends in health insurance coverage by race/ethnicity among persons under 65 years of age: United States 1997–2001. National Center for Health Statistics. Retrieved from www.cdc.gov/nchs/products/pubs/pubd/hestats/healthinsur.htm

Ni, X., Chan, K., Bulgin, N., Sicard, T., Bismil, R., McMain, S., et al. (2006). Association between serotonin transporter gene and borderline personality disorder. *J. Psychiat. Res., 40*, 448–453.

Nichols, M., & Shernoff, M. (2007). Therapy with sexual minorities: Queering practice. In S. R. Leiblum (Ed.), *Principles and practice of sex therapy* (4th ed., pp. 379–414). New York: Guilford Press.

Nichols, S. L., & Waschbusch, D. A. (2004). A review of the validity of laboratory cognitive tasks used to assess symptoms of ADHD. *Child Psychiat. Human Dev., 34*, 297–315.

Nichols, W. C. (2004). Integrative marital and family treatment of dependent personality disorders. In M. M. MacFarlane (Ed.), *Family treatment of personality disorders: Advances in clinical practice* (pp. 173–204). Binghamton, NY: Haworth Clinical Practice Press.

Nicolson, P. (1999). Loss, happiness and postpartum depression: The ultimate paradox. *Canad. Psychol., 40*(2), 162–178.

Nield, L. S., & Kamat, D. (2004). Enuresis: How to evaluate and treat. *Clin. Pediatr., 43*(5), 409–415.

Nietzel, M. T., Bernstein, D. A., Milich, R. S., & Kramer, G. (2003). *Introduction to clinical psychology* (6th ed.). Upper Saddle River, NJ: Pearson Education.

Nijinsky, V. (1936). *The diary of Vaslav Nijinsky.* New York: Simon & Schuster.

Ninan, P. T., & Dunlop, B. W. (2005). Neurobiology and ethiology of panic disorder. *J. Clin. Psychiat., 66*(Suppl. 4), 3–7.

NINDS (National Institute of Neurological Disorders and Stroke). (2006). Narcolepsy fact sheet. Bethesda, MD: Author.

Nishina, A., Juvonen, J., & Witkow, M. R. (2005). Sticks and stones may break my bones, but names will make me feel sick: The psychosocial, somatic, and scholastic consequences of peer harassment. *J. Clin. Child Adol. Psychol., 34*(1), 37–48.

Nishino, S., Mignot, E., & Dement, W. C. (1995). Sedative hypnotics. In A. F. Schatzberg & C. B. Nemeroff (Eds.), *The American Psychiatric Press textbook of psychopharmacology.* Washington, DC: American Psychiatric Press.

NMHA (National Mental Health Association). (1999, June 5). Poll. *U.S. Newswire.*

Nobel, J. (2007, March 25). Global warming hits a raw nerve for some: 'Eco-anxiety' latest worry for Americans. *Columbia News Service.*

Nock, M. K., Kazdin, A. E., Hiripi, E., & Kessler, R. C. (2006). Prevalence, subtypes, and correlates of DSM-IV conduct disorder in the National Comorbidity Survey Replication. *Psychol. Med., 36*(5), 699–710.

Nock, M. K., Kazdin, A. E., Hiripi, E., & Kessler, R. C. (2007). Lifetime prevalence, correlates, and persistence of oppositional defiant disorder: Results from the National Comorbidity Survey Replication. *J. Child Psychol. Psychiat., 48*(7), 703–713.

Noeker, M. (2004). Factitious disorder and factitious disorder by proxy. *Praxis der Kinderpsychol. Kinderpsych., 53*(7), 449–467.

Nolan, P. (2002). Object relations as a context for an integrative approach to psychotherapy. In P. Nolan & I. S. Nolan (Eds.), *Object relations and integrative psychotherapy: Tradition and innovation in theory and practice* (pp. 8–27). London: Whurr Publishers.

Nolan, S. A., Strassle, C. G., Roback, H. B., & Binder, J. L. (2004). Negative treatment effects in dyadic psychotherapy: A focus on prevention and intervention strategies. *J. Contemp. Psychother., 34*(4), 311–330.

Nolen-Hoeksema, S. (1987). Sex differences in unipolar depression: Evidence and theory. *Psychol. Bull., 101*(2), 259–282.

Nolen-Hoeksema, S. (1990). *Sex differences in depression.* Stanford, CA: Stanford University Press.

Nolen-Hoeksema, S. (1995). Gender differences in coping with depression across the lifespan. *Depression, 3*, 81–90.

Nolen-Hoeksema, S. (1998). The other end of the continuum: The costs of rumination: *Psychological Inquiry, 9*(3), 216–219.

Nolen-Hoeksema, S. (2000). The role of rumination in depressive disorders and mixed anxiety/depressive symptoms. *J. Abnorm. Psychol., 109*, 504–511.

Nolen-Hoeksema, S. (2002). Gender differences in depression. In I. H. Gotlib & C. L. Hammen (Eds.), *Handbook of depression* (pp. 492–509). New York: Guilford Press.

Nolen-Hoeksema, S., & Corte, C. (2004). Gender and self-regulation. In K. D. Vohs & R. F. Baumeister (Eds.), *Handbook of self-regulation: Research, theory, and applications* (pp. 411–421). New York: Guilford Press.

Nolen-Hoeksema, S., & Girgus, J. (1995). Explanatory style and achievement, depression, and gender differences in childhood and early adolescence. In G. Buchanan & M. Seligman (Eds.), *Explanatory style.* Hillsdale, NJ: Lawrence Erlbaum.

Noll, R., & Turkington, C. (1994). *The encyclopedia of memory and memory disorders.* New York: Facts on File.

Nomura, H., Inoue, S., Kamimura, N., Shimodera, S., Mino, Y., Gregg, L., & Tarrier, N. (2005). A cross-cultural study on expressed emotion in carers of people with dementia and schizophrenia: Japan and England. *Soc. Psychiat. Psychiatr. Epidemiol., 40*(7), 564–570.

Nonacs, R. M. (2002, March 12). Postpartum psychiatric illness. *eMed. J., 3*(3).

Nonacs, R. M. (2007). Postpartum depression. *eMedicine Clinical Reference.* Retrieved July 30, 2008, from http: /www.emedicine.com/med/topic 3408.htm

Noonan, D. (2003, June 16). A healthy heart. *Newsweek, 141*(24), 48–52.

Norcross, J. C., Beutler, L. E., & Levant, R. F. (Eds.). (2006). *Evidence-based practices in mental health: Debate and dialogue on the fundamental questions.* Washington, DC: American Psychological Association.

Norcross, J. C., & Goldfried, M. R. (Eds.). (2005). *Handbook of psychotherapy integration* (2nd ed.). New York: Oxford University Press.

Norcross, J. C., Prochaska, J. O., & Farber, J. A. (1993). Psychologists conducting psychotherapy: New findings and historical comparisons on the psychotherapy division membership. *Psychotherapy, 30*(4), 692–697.

Nordentoft, M., Qin, P., Helweg-Larsen, K., & Juel, K. (2007). Restrictions in means for suicide: An effective tool in preventing suicide: The Danish experience. *Suic. Life-Threat. Behav., 37*(6), 688–697.

Nordhus, I. H., & Nielsen, G. H. (2005). Mental disorders in old age: Clinical syndromes, prevalence and benefits of psychological treatment. *Nordisk Psykologi, 57*(1), 86–103.

Nordstrom, P., Samuelsson, M., & Asberg, M. (1995). Survival analysis of suicide risk after attempted suicide. *Acta Psychiatr. Scandin., 91*(5), 336–340.

Norko, M. A., & Baranoski, M. V. (2008). The prediction of violence; detection of dangerousness. *Brief Treat. Crisis Intervent., 8*(1), 73–91.

Norra, C., Mrazek, M., Tuchtenhagen, F., Gobbele, R., Buchner, H., Sass, H., & Herpertz, S. C. (2003). Enhanced intensity dependence as a marker of low serotonergic neurotransmission in borderline personality disorder. *J. Psychiatr. Res., 37*(1), 23–33.

North, C. S. (2005). Somatoform disorders. In E. H. Rubin & C. F. Zorumski (Eds.), *Adult psychiatry* (2nd ed., pp. 261–274). Oxford, England: Blackwell Publishing.

North, C. S., & Yutzy, S. H. (2005). Dissociative disorders, factitious disorders, and malingering. In E. H. Rubin & C. F. Zorumski (Eds.), *Adult psychiatry* (2nd ed., pp. 275–289). Oxford, England: Blackwell Publishing.

Norton, A. (2007, July 18). Weight bias may harm obese children. *Yahoo! News.* Retrieved July 22, 2007, from http://news.yahoo.com

Novak, B., McDermott, B. E., Scott, C. L., & Guillory, S. (2007). Sex offenders and insanity: An examination of 42 individuals found not guilty by reason of insanity. *J. Amer. Acad. Psychiat. Law, 35*(4), 444–450.

Noveck, J. (2007, October 24). The crying game: Male vs. female tears. Associated Pess.

Noyes, R., Jr. (1999). The relationship of hypochondriasis to anxiety disorders. *Gen. Hosp. Psychiat., 21*(1), 8–17.

Noyes, R., Jr. (2001). Comorbidity in generalized anxiety disorder. *Psychiatr. Clin. N. Amer., 24*(1), 41–55.

Noyes, R., Jr., Stuart, S., Langbehn, D. R., Happel, R. L., Longley, S. L., Muller, B. A., et al. (2003). Test of an interpersonal model of hypochondriasis. *Psychosom. Med., 65*(2), 292–300.

Noyes, R., Jr., Stuart, S., Langbehn, D. R., Happel, R. L., Longley, S. L., & Yagla, S. J. (2002). Childhood antecedents of hypochondriasis. *Psychosomatics: J. Consult. Liaison Psychiat., 43*(4), 282–289.

Noyes, R., Jr., Stuart, S. P., & Watson, D. B. (2008). A reconceptualization of the somatoform disorders. *Psychosom.: J. Cons. Liaison Psychiat., 49*(1), 14–22.

NRC (National Research Council). (2001). *Educating children with autism.* Washington, DC: National Academy Press.

NSDUH. (2005). *National survey on drug use.* Washington, DC: Department of Health and Human Services, Substance Abuse and Mental Health Services Administration, Office of Applied Studies.

NSDUH. (2007). *National survey on drug use.* Washington, DC: Department of Health and Human Services, Substance Abuse and Mental Health Services Administration, Office of Applied Studies.

NSDUH. (2008). *National survey on drug use.* Washington, DC: Department of Health and Human Services, Substance Abuse and Mental Health Services Administration, Office of Applied Studies.

Nussbaum, R. L., & Ellis, C. E. (2003). Alzheimer's disease and Parkinson's disease. *N. Engl. J. Med., 348,* 1356–1364.

Nwokike, J. (2005). Federal insanity acquittees. *J. Amer. Acad. Psychiat. Law, 33*(1), 126–128.

Nydegger, R. V., & Paludi, M. (2006). Obsessive-compulsive disorder: Diagnostic, treatment, gender, and cultural issues. In T. Plante (Ed.) *Mental disorders of the new millennium* (Vol. 3). New York: Praeger.

O'Brien, C., & Kampman, K. M. (2008). Antagonists of opioids. In H. D. Kleber & M. Galanter (Eds.), *The American Psychiatric Publishing textbook of substance abuse treatment* (4th ed., pp. 325–329). Arlington, VA: American Psychiatric Publishing.

O'Brien, C. P., & Lyons, F. (2000). Alcohol and the athlete. *Sports Med., 29,* 295–300.

O'Brien, C. P., & McKay, J. (2002). Pharmacological treatments for substance use disorders. In P. E. Nathan & J. M. Gorman (Eds.), *A guide to treatments that work* (2nd ed.). London: Oxford University Press.

O'Brien, C. P., O'Brien, T. J., Mintz, J., & Brady, J. P. (1975). Conditioning of narcotic abstinence symptoms in human subjects. *Drug. Alc. Dep., 1,* 115–123.

O'Brien, K. M., & Vincent, N. K. (2003). Psychiatric comorbidity in anorexia and bulimia nervosa: Nature, prevalence and causal relationships. *Clin. Psychol. Rev., 23*(1), 57–74.

O'Brien, W. H., & Tabaczynski, T. (2007). Unstructured interviewing. In J. C. Thomas & M. Hersen (Eds.), *Handbook of clinical interviewing with children.* Thousand Oaks, CA: Sage Publications.

O'Connor, B. P. (2008). Other personality disorders. In M. Hersen & J. Rosqvist (Eds.), *Handbook of psychological assessment, case conceptualization and treatment, Vol. 1: Adults* (pp. 438–462). Hoboken, NJ: John Wiley & Sons.

O'Connor, R. C., & Leenaars, A. A. (2004). A thematic comparison of suicide notes drawn from Northern Ireland and the United States. *Curr. Psychol.: Dev., Learn., Personal., Soc., 22*(4), 339–347.

O'Donohue, W., Fowler, K. A., & Lilienfeld, S. O. (Eds.). (2007). *Personality disorders: Toward the DSM-V.* Los Angeles: Sage Publications.

O'Hara, M. W. (2003). Postpartum depression. *Clinician's Research Digest, Supplemental Bulletin 29.*

O'Malley, S. S., Jaffe, A. J., Chang, G., Schottenfeld, R., Meyer, R., & Rounsaville, B. (1992). Naltrexone and coping skills therapy for alcohol dependence. *Arch. Gen. Psychiat., 49,* 881–888.

O'Malley, S. S., Jaffe, A. J., Rode, S., & Rounsaville, B. J. (1996). Experience of a "slip" among alcoholics treated with naltrexone or placebo. *Amer. J. Psychiat., 153,* 281–283.

O'Malley, S. S., Krishnan-Sarin, S., Farren, C., & O'Connor, P. G. (2000). Naltrexone-induced nausea in patients treated for alcohol dependence: Clinical predictors and evidence for opioid-mediated effects. *J. Clin. Psychopharmacol., 20*(1), 69–76.

Oderda, G. M., & Klein-Schwartz, W. (1983). Lunar cycle and poison center calls. *J. Toxicol. Clin. Toxicol., 20*(5), 487–495.

Oesterle, S., Hill, K. G., Hawkins, J. D., Guo, J., Catalano, R. F., & Abbott, R. D. (2004). Adolescent heavy episodic drinking trajectories and health in young adulthood. *J. Stud. Alc., 65,* 204–212.

Oesterreich, L. (2003, November). *Understanding children: Fears.* Ames, IA: Iowa State University Extension.

OFWW. (2004, December 25). Drivers admit to experiencing road rage. *Obesity, Fitness & Wellness Week,* 1209.

Ogden, C. L., Flegal, K. M., Carroll, M. D., & Johnson, C. L. (2002). Prevalence and trends in overweight among US children and adolescents, 1999–2000. *JAMA, 288,* 1728–1732.

Ogden, J., & Ward, E. (1995). Help-seeking behavior in sufferers of vaginismus. *Sex. Marit. Ther., 10*(1), 23–30.

Ogloff, J. R. P., Schweighofer, A., Turnbull, S. D., & Whittemore, K. (1992). Empirical research regarding the insanity defense: How much do we really know? In J. R. P. Ogloff (Ed.), *Law and psychology: The broadening of the discipline* (pp. 171–210). Durham, NC: Carolina Academic Press.

Ohayon, M. M., Lemoine, P., Arnaud-Briant, V., & Dreyfus, M. (2002). Prevalence and consequenstes of sleep disorders in a shift worker population. *J. Psychosom. Res., 53*(1), 577–583.

Ohman, A., Erixon, G., & Lofberg, I. (1975). Phobias and preparedness: Phobic versus neutral pictures as continued stimuli for human autonomic responses. *J. Abnorm. Psychol., 84,* 41–45.

Ohman, A., & Mineka, S. (2003). The malicious serpent: Snakes as a prototypical stimulus for an evolved module of fear. *Curr. Direct. Psychol. Sci., 12*(1), 5–9.

Ohman, A., & Soares, J. J. F. (1993). On the automatic nature of phobic fear: Conditioned electrodermal responses to masked fear-relevant stimuli. *J. Abnorm. Psychol., 102*(1), 121–132.

Okawa, J. B., Gaby, L., & Griffith, J. L. (2003, November). *Dissociation and auditory hallucinations in survivors of torture.* Paper presented at the annual meeting of the International Society for Traumatic Stress Studies, Chicago, IL.

Okawa, J. B., & Hauss, R. B. (2007). The trauma of politically motivated torture. In E. K. Carll (Ed.), *Trauma psychology: Issues in violence, disaster, health, and illness* (Vol. 1). Westport, CT: Praeger Publishers.

Okello, E. S., & Ekblad, S. (2006). Lay concepts of depression among the Baganda of Uganda: A pilot study. *Transcult. Psychiat., 43*(2), 287–313.

Oldham, J. (Ed.). (2007). Launching DSM-V. *J. Psychiatr. Pract., 13*(6), 351.

Olff, M., Langeland, W., Draijer, N., & Gersons, B. (2007). Gender differences in post-traumatic stress disorder. *Psychol. Bull., 133*(2), 183–204.

Olfman, S. (2007). Bipolar children: Cutting-edge controversy. In S. Olfman (Ed.), *Bipolar children: Cutting-edge controversy, insights, and research.* Westport, CT: Praeger Publishers.

Olfson, M., & Klerman, G. L. (1993). Trends in the prescription of antidepressants by office based psychiatrists. *Amer. J. Psychiat., 150*(4), 571–577.

Oliver, R. J., Spilsbury, J. C., Osiecki, S. S., Denihan, W. M., & Zureick. J. L. (2008). Brief report: Preliminary results of a suicide awareness mass media campaign in Cuyahoga County, Ohio. *Suic. Life-Threat. Behav., 38*(2), 245–249.

Ollendick, T. H., King, N. J., & Chorpita, B. F. (2006). Empirically supported treatments for children and adolescents. In P. C. Kendall (Ed.), *Child and adolescent therapy: Cognitive-behavioral procedures* (3rd ed., pp. 492–520). New York: Guilford Press.

Olmos de Paz, T. (1990). Working-through and insight in child psychoanalysis. *Melanie Klein & Object Relations, 8*(1), 99–112.

Olmsted, M. P., Kaplan, A. S., & Rockert, W. (1994). Rate and prediction of relapse in bulimia nervosa. *Amer. J. Psychiat., 151*(5), 738–743.

Olmsted, M. P., Kaplan, A. S., & Rockert, W. (2005). Defining remission and relapse in bulimia nervosa. *Inter. J. Eat. Disorders, 38*(1), 1–6.

Olsen, C. E., Poulsen, H. D., & Lublin, H. K. F. (2005). Drug therapy of dementia in elderly patients: A review. *Nordic J. Psychiat., 59*(2), 71–77.

Olsson, S. E., & Moller, A. R. (2003). On the incidence and sex ratio of transsexualism in Sweden. *Arch. Sex. Behav., 32*(4), 381–386.

ONDCP (Office of National Drug Control Policy). (2000). Methadone. *ONDCP Drug Policy Information Clearinghouse Fact Sheet.*

ONDCP (Office of National Drug Control Policy). (2002). Methadone. *ONDCP Drug Policy Information Clearinghouse Fact Sheet.*

ONDCP (Office of National Drug Control Policy). (2008). *Drug facts.*

Onen, S. H., Onen, F., Mangeon, J. P., Abidi, H., Courpron, P., & Schmidt, J. (2005). Alcohol abuse and dependence in elderly emergency department patients. *Arch. Geront. Geriat., 41*(2), 191–200.

Oquendo, M. A., Brent, D. A., Birmaher, B., Greenhill, L., Kolko, D., Stanley, B., et al. (2005). Posttraumatic stress disorder comorbid with major depression: Factors mediating the association with suicidal behavior. *Amer. J. Psychiat., 162*(3), 580–586.

Oquendo, M. A., Dragatsi, D., Harkavy-Friedman, J., Dervic, K., Currier, D., Burke, A. K., et al. (2005). Protective factors against suicidal behavior in Latinos. *J. Nerv. Ment. Dis., 193*(7), 438–443.

Oquendo, M. A., Lizardi, D., Greenwald. S., Weissman, M. M., & Mann, J. J. (2004). Rates of lifetime suicide attempt and rates of lifetime major depression in different ethnic groups in the United States. *Acta Psychiatr. Scandin., 110*(6), 446–451.

Oquendo, M. A., Placidi, G. P. A., Malone, K. M., Campbell, C., Keilp, J., Brodsky, B., et al. (2003). Positron emission tomography of regional brain metabolic responses to a serotonergic challenge and lethality of suicide attempts in major depression. *Arch. Gen. Psychiat., 60*(1), 14–22.

Oquendo, M. A., Russo, S. A., Underwood, M. D., Kassir, S. A., Ellis, S. P., Mann, J. J., & Arango, V. (2006). Higher post mortem prefrontal 5-HT2A receptor binding correlates with lifetime aggression in suicide. *Biol. Psychiat., 59*, 235–243.

Orbach, I., & Iohan, M. (2007). Stress, distress, emotional regulation and suicide attempts in female adolescents. In R. Tatarelli, M. Pompili, & P. Girardi (Eds.), *Suicide in psychiatric disorders.* New York: Nova Science Publishers.

ORR (United States Department of Health and Human Services, Office of Refugee Resettlement). (2006). Office of Refugee Resettlement (ORR) Services for Survivors of Torture Program: Program description. Retrieved October 5, 2006, from http://www.acf.hhs.gov/programs/orr/programs/services_survivors_torture.htm

Orsillo, S. M., Weathers, F. W., Litz, B. T., Steinberg, H. R., et al. (1996). Current and lifetime psychiatric disorders among veterans with war zone-related posttraumatic stress disorder. *J. Nerv. Ment. Dis., 184*, 307–313.

Ortiz, D. (2001). The survivors' perspective: Voices from the center. In E. Gerrity, T. M. Keane, & F. Tuma (Eds.), *The mental health consequences of torture* (pp. 13–34). New York: Kluwer Academic/Plenum Publishers.

Oshima, I., Mino, Y., & Inomata, Y. (2005). Effects of environmental deprivation on negative symptoms of schizophrenia: A nationwide survey in Japan's psychiatric hospitals. *Psychiat. Res., 136*(2–3), 163–171.

Oslin, D. W. (2006). Addictions. In D.V. Jeste & J. H. Friedman (Eds.), *Psychiatry for neurologists* (pp. 93–104). Totowa, NJ: Humana Press.

Oslin, D. W., & Holden, R. (2002). Recognition and assessment of alcohol and drug dependence in the elderly. In A. M. Gurnack, R. Atkinson, & N. J. Osgood (Eds.), *Treating alcohol and drug abuse in the elderly.* New York: Springer.

Osman, A., Barrios, F. X., Gutierrez, P. M., Williams, J. E., & Bailey, J. (2008). Psychometric properties of the Beck Depression Inventory-II in nonclinical adolescent samples. *J. Clin. Psychol., 64*(10), 83–102.

Osterweil, N. (2003, October 16). Halloween: The truth is out there. Available from MedicineNet.com

Osterweis, M., & Townsend, J. (1988). *Understanding bereavement reactions in adults and children: A booklet for lay people.* Rockville, MD: U.S. Department of Health and Human Services.

Ostrove, N. M. (2001, July 24). Statement before the subcommittee on consumer affairs, foreign commerce, and tourism, Senate committee on commerce, science, and transportation. Retrieved from www.fda.gov

Otten, K. L. (2004). An analysis of a classwide self-monitoring approach to improve the behavior of elementary students with severe emotional and behavioral disorders. *Diss. Abstr. Inter.: Sect. A: Human. Soc. Sci., 65*(3-A), 893.

Otto, M. W., & Deveney, C. (2005). Cognitive-behavioral therapy and the treatment of panic disorder: Efficacy and strategies. *J. Clin. Psychiat., 66*(Suppl. 4), 28–32.

Ouellette, S. C. (1993). Inquiries into hardiness. In L. Goldberger & S. Beznitz (Eds.), *Handbook of stress: Theoretical and clinical aspects* (2nd ed.). New York: Free Press.

Ouellette, S. C., & DiPlacido, J. (2001). Personality's role in the protection and enhancement of health: Where the research has been, where it is stuck, how it might move. In A. Baum, T. A. Revenson, & J. E. Singer (Eds.), *Handbook of health psychology.* Mahwah, NJ: Lawrence Erlbaum.

Overton, D. (1964). State-dependent or "dissociated" learning produced with pentobarbital. *J. Compar. Physiol. Psychol., 57*, 3–12.

Overton, D. (1966). State-dependent learning produced by depressant and atropine-like drugs. *Psychopharmacologia, 10*, 6–31.

Ovsiew, F. (2006). Hysteria in neurological practice: The somatoform and dissociative disorders. In D.V. Jeste & J. H. Friedman (Eds.), *Psychiatry for neurologists* (pp. 67–80). Totowa, NJ: Humana Press.

Owen, F., Crow, T. J., & Poulter, M. (1987). Central dopaminergic mechanisms in schizophrenia. *Acta Psychiatr. Belg., 87*(5), 552–565.

Owen, F., Crow, T. J., Poulter, M., et al. (1978). Increased dopamine receptor sensitivity in schizophrenia. *Lancet, 2*, 223–226.

Owen-Howard, M. (2001). Pharmacological aversion treatment of alcohol dependence. I. Production and prediction of conditioned alcohol aversion. *Amer. J. Drug Alc. Abuse, 27*(3), 561–585.

Owens, M., & McGowan, I. W. (2006). Madness and the moon: The lunar cycle and psychopathology. *German J. Psychiat., 9*(3), 123–127.

Oyama, H., Watanabe, N., Ono, Y., Sakashita, T., Takenoshita, Y., Taguchi, M., et al. (2005). Community-based suicide prevention through group activity for the elderly successfully reduced the high suicide rate for females. *Psychiat. Clin. Neurosci., 59*(3), 337–344.

Oyebode, J. R. (2008). Death, dying and bereavement. In R. Woods & L. Clare (Eds.), *Handbook of the clinical psychology of ageing* (2nd ed., pp. 75–94). New York: Wiley.

Ozer, E. J. (2005). The impact of violence on urban adolescents: Longitudinal effects of perceived school connection and family support. *J. Adol. Res., 20*(2), 167–192.

Ozer, E. J., Best, S. R., Lipsey, T. L., & Weiss, D. S. (2003). Predictors of posttraumatic stress disorder and symptoms in adults: A meta-analysis. *Psychol. Bull., 129*(1), 52–73.

Ozonoff, S., Dawson, G., & McPartland, J. (2002). *A parent's guide to Asperger syndrome and high-functioning autism: How to meet the challenges and help your child thrive.* New York: Guilford Press.

Packer, I. K. (2008). Specialized practice in forensic psychology: Opportunities and obstacles. *Profess. Psychol.: Res. Pract., 39*(2), 245–249.

Padwa, L. (1996). *Everything you pretend to know and are afraid someone will ask.* New York: Penguin.

Pagnin, D., de Queirox, V., Pini, S., & Cassano, G.-B. (2004). Efficacy of ECT in depression: A meta-analytic review. *J. ECT, 20*(1), 13–20.

Painot, D., Jotterand, S., Kammer, A., Fossati, M., & Golay, A. (2001). Simultaneous nutritional cognitive-behavioral therapy in obese patients. *Patient Educ. Counsel., 42*(1), 47–52.

Pajer, K. (1995). New strategies in the treatment of depression in women. *J. Clin. Psychiat., 56*(Suppl. 2), 30–37.

Palermo, G. B., Kocsis, R. N., & Slovenko, R. (Eds.). (2005). *Offender profiling: An introduction to the sociopsychological analysis of violent crime.* Springfield, IL: Charles C. Thomas.

Palmer, A. (2003). Behavioral program helps autistic children make progress. *Monit. Psychol., 34*(9), 15.

Palmer, L., Fiorito, M., & Tagliareni, L. (2007). Mental status examination: A comprehensive multicultural, developmental approach. In M. Hersen & J. C. Thomas (Eds.), *Handbook of clinical interviewing with adults* (pp. 62–76). Thousand Oaks, CA: Sage Publishing.

Palmore, E. B. (2001). The Ageism Survey: First findings. *Gerontologist, 41*(5), 572–575.

Palmore, E. B. (2004). Research note: Ageism in Canada and the United States. *J. Cross-Cult. Ger., 19*(1), 41–46.

Palmore, E. B., Branch, L., & Harris, D. K. (Eds.). (2005). *Encyclopedia of ageism.* Binghamton, NY: Haworth Pastoral Press.

Pamuk, E., Makuc, D., Heck, K., Reuben, C., & Lochner, K. (1998). Socioeconomic status and health chartbook. In National Center for Health Statistics, *Health, United States, 1998.* Hyattsville, MD: National Center for Health Statistics.

Papadimitriou, G. N., Calabrese, J. R., Dikeos, D. G., & Christodoulou, G. N. (2005). Rapid cycling bipolar disorder: Biology and pathogenesis. *Inter. J. Neuropsychopharmacol., 89*(2), 281–292.

Papastavrou, E., Kalokerinou, A., Papacostas, S. S., Tsangari, H., & Sourtzi, P. (2007). Caring for a relative with dementia: Family caregiver burden. *J. Adv. Nurs., 58*(5), 446–457.

Papolos, D., Hennen, J., & Cockerham, M. S. (2005). Factors associated with parent-reported suicide threats by children and adolescents with community-diagnosed bipolar disorder. *J. Affect. Disorders, 86*(2–3), 267–275.

Paris, J. (1991). Personality disorders, parasuicide, and culture. *Transcult. Psychiatr. Res. Rev., 28*(1), 25–39.

Paris, J. (2001). Cultural risk factors in personality disorders. In J. F. Schumaker & T. Ward (Eds.), *Cultural cognition and psychopathology.* Westport, CT: Praeger.

Paris, J. (2001). Psychosocial adversity. In W. J. Livesley (Ed.), *Handbook of personality disorders: Theory, research, and treatment* (pp. 231–241). New York: Guilford Press.

Paris, J. (2005). Borderline personality disorder. *Canad. Med. Assoc. J., 172*(12), 1579–1583.

Parker, A., & Bhugra, D. (2000). Attitudes of British medical students towards male homosexuality. *Sex. Relat. Ther., 15*(2), 141–149.

Parker, G. (1992). Early environment. In E. S. Paykel (Ed.), *Handbook of affective disorders.* New York: Guilford Press.

Parker, G., Hadzi-Pavlovic, D., Greenwald, S., & Weissman, M. (1995). Low parental care as a risk factor to lifetime depression in a community sample. *J. Affect. Disorders, 33*(3), 173–180.

Parker, G. B., & Brotchie, H. L. (2004). From diathesis to dimorphism: The biology of gender differences in depression. *J. Nerv. Ment. Dis., 192*(3), 210–216.

Parker, S., Nichter, M., Vuckovic, N., Sims, C., & Ritenbaugh, C. (1995). Body image and weight concerns among African American and white adolescent females: Differences that make a difference. *Human Organization, 54*(2), 103–114.

Parrott, A. C. (1999). Does cigarette smoking cause stress? *Amer. Psychologist, 54*(10), 817–820.

Parrott, A. C. (2000). Cigarette smoking does cause distress. *Amer. Psychologist, 55*(10), 1159–1160.

Partin, J. C., Hamill, S. K., Fischel, J. E., & Partin, J. S. (1992). Painful defecation and fecal soiling in children. *Pediatrics, 89,* 1007–1009.

Paton, C., & Beer, D. (2001). Caffeine: The forgotten variable. *Inter. J. Psychiat. Clin. Prac., 5*(4), 231–236.

Patrick, C. J. (2007). Antisocial personality disorder and psychopathy. In W. O'Donohue, K. A. Fowler, & S. O. Lilienfeld (Eds.). *Personality disorders: Toward the DSM-V.* Los Angeles: Sage Publications.

Patton, J. R., Polloway, E. A., & Smith, T. E. C. (2000). Educating students with mild mental retardation. *Focus Autism Other Dev. Disabil., 15*(2), 80–89.

Paul, G. L. (1967). The strategy of outcome research in psychotherapy. *J. Couns. Psychol., 31,* 109–118.

Paul, G. L. (2000). Milieu therapy. In A. E. Kazdin (Ed.), *Encyclopedia of psychology* (Vol. 5, pp. 250–252). New York: Oxford University Press.

Paul, G. L., & Lentz, R. (1977). *Psychosocial treatment of the chronic mental patient.* Cambridge, MA: Harvard University Press.

Pauls, C. A., & Stemmler, G. (2003). Repressive and defensive coping during fear and anger. *Emotion, 3*(3), 284–302.

Pawlak, C. R., Magarinos, A. M., Melchor, J., McEwen, B., & Strickland, S. (2003). Tissue plasminogen in the amygdala is critical for stress-induced anxiety-like behavior. *Nature Neurosci., 6*(2), 168–174.

Paykel, E. S. (2003). Life events and affective disorders. *Acta Psychiatr. Scandin., 108*(Suppl. 418), 61–66.

Paykel, E. S. (2003). Life events: Effects and genesis. *Psychol. Med., 33*(7), 1145–1148.

Paykel, E. S. (2006). Editorials: Depression: Major problem for public health. *Epidem.-e-Psichiatr. Soc., 15*(1), 4–10.

Paykel, E. S., & Cooper, Z. (1992). Life events and social stress. In E. S. Paykel (Ed.), *Handbook of affective disorders.* New York: Guilford Press.

Payne, A. F. (1928). *Sentence completion.* New York: New York Guidance Clinics.

Payne, J. L., Potash, J. B., & DePaulo, J. R., Jr. (2005). Recent findings on the genetic basis of bipolar disorder. *Psychiatr. Clin. N. Amer., 28*(2), 481–498.

Pear, R. (2008). House approves bill on mental health parity. *New York Times,* March 6, 2008.

Pearlman, E. (2005). Terror of desire: The etiology of eating disorders from an attachment theory perspective. *Psychoanal. Rev. 92*(2), 223–235.

Pekkanen, J. (2002). Dangerous minds. *Washingtonian,* July, 2002.

Pekkanen, J. (2007). Involuntary commitment is essential. In A. Quigley (Ed.), *Current controversies: Mental health.* Detroit: Greenhaven Press/Thomson Gale.

Pelham, M. F., & Lovell, M. R. (2005). Issues in neuropsychological assessment. In J. M. Silver, T. W. McAllister, & S. C. Yudofsky (Eds.), *Textbook of traumatic brain injury* (pp. 159–172). Washington, DC: American Psychiatric Publishing.

Pendery, M. L., Maltzman, I. M., & West, L. J. (1982). Controlled drinking by alcoholics? New findings and a reevaluation of a major affirmative study. *Science, 217*(4555), 169–175.

Penn, D. L., & Nowlin-Drummond, A. (2001). Politically correct labels and schizophrenia: A rose by any other name? *Schizo. Bull., 27*(2), 197–203.

Pennington, B. F. (2002). *The development of psychopathology: Nature and nurture.* New York: Guilford Press.

Penninx, B. W., Guralnik, J. M., Ferrucci, L., Simonsick, E. M., Deeg, D. J., & Wallace, R. B. (1998). Depressive symptoms and physical decline in community-dwelling older persons. *JAMA, 279*(21), 1720–1726.

Pepe, M. (2002). Cited in Getting past the trauma. *Psychol. Today, 35*(1), 54.

Perelman, M. A. (2005). Psychosocial evaluation and combination treatment of men with erectile dysfunction. *Urologic Clinics of North America, 32,* 441–445.

Perez, A., Leifman, S., & Estrada, A. (2003). Reversing the criminalization of mental illness. *Crime and Delinquency, 49*(1), 62–78.

Perez-Alvarez, M., Garcia-Montes, J. M., Perona-Garcelan, S., Vallina-Fernandez, O. (2008). Changing relationships with voices: New therapeutic perspectives for treating hallucinations. *Clin. Psychol. Psychother., 15,* 75–85.

Perilla, J. L., Norris, F. H., & Lavizzo, E. A. (2002). Ethnicity, culture, and disaster response: Identifying and explaining ethnic differences in PTSD six months after Hurricane Andrew. *J. Soc. Clin. Psychol., 21,* 20–45.

Perkins, H. W. (2002). Surveying the damage: A review of research on consequences of alcohol misuse in college populations. *J. Alcohol Stud.,* Suppl. 14, 91–100.

Perlin, M. L. (2000). *The hidden prejudice: Mental disability on trial.* Washington, DC: American Psychological Association.

Perlin, M. L. (2003). Beyond Dusky and Godinez: Competency before and after trial. *Behav. Sci. Law., 21*(3), 297–310.

Perlin, M. L. (2004). "Salvation" or a "lethal dose"? Attitudes and advocacy in right to refuse treatment cases. *J. Forens. Psychol. Pract., 4*(4), 51–69.

Perls, T. T. (1995, January). The oldest old. *Scientif. Amer.,* pp. 70–75.

Perry, J. D. C., & Perry, J. C. (2004). Conflicts, defenses and the stability of narcissistic personality features. *Psychiatry: Interpers. Biol. Process., 67*(4), 310–330.

Perske, R. (1972). The dignity of risk and the mentally retarded. *Ment. Retard., 10,* 24–27.

Peter, O., Attila, K., Viktor, V., & Sandor, F. (2004). Risk factors of attempted suicide in elderly: The role of cognitive impairment. *Psychiatria Hungarica, 19*(6), 524–530.

Peters, R. H., Sherman, P. B., & Osher, F. C. (2008). Treatment in jails and prisons. In K. T. Mueser & D. V. Jeste (Eds.), *Clinical handbook of schizophrenia* (pp. 354–364). New York: Guilford Press.

Peters, R. M. (2004). Racism and hypertension among African Americans. *Western J. Nurs. Res., 26*(6), 612–631.

Peterson, C. (2006). *A primer in positive psychology.* Oxford, England: Oxford University Press.

Peterson, C., Ruch, W., Beermann, U., Park, N., & Seligman, M. E. P. (2007). Strengths of character, orientations to happiness, and life satisfaction. *J. Positive Psychol., 2*(3), 149–156.

Peterson, L., & Roberts, M. C. (1991). Treatment of children's problems. In C. E. Walker (Ed.), *Clinical psychology: Historical and research foundations.* New York: Plenum Press.

Petherick, W. (2008). Stalking. In B. E. Turvey (Ed.), *Criminal profiling: An introduction to behavioral evidence analysis* (3rd ed., pp. 449–482). San Diego, CA: Elsevier.

Petrie, K. J., Fontanilla, I., Thomas, M. G., Booth, R. J., & Pennebaker, J. W. (2004). Effect of written emotional expression on immune function in patients with human immunodeficiency virus infection: A randomized trial. *Psychosom. Med., 66*(2), 272–275.

Petrocelli, J. V. (2002). Effectiveness of group cognitive-behavioral therapy for general symptomatology: A meta-analysis. *J. Spec. Group Work, 27*(1), 92–115.

Petry, N. M. (2001). Substance abuse, pathological gambling, and impulsiveness. *Drug Alc. Dep., 63*(1), 29–38.

Petry, N. M. (2005). Conclusions. In N. M. Petry (Ed.), *Pathological gambling: Etiology, comorbidity, and treatment* (pp. 279–282). Washington, DC: American Psychological Association.

Pew Research Center for the People and the Press. (1997). *Trust and citizen engagement in metropolitan Philadelphia: A case study.* Washington, DC: Author.

Pezawas, L., Meyer-Lindenberg, A., Drabant, E. M., Verchinski, B. A., Munoz, K. E., Kolachana, B. S., et al. (2005). 5-HTTLPR polymorphism impacts human cingulate-amygdala interactions: a genetic susceptibility mechanism for depression. *Nat. Neurosci., 8,* 828–834.

Pfeffer, C. R. (1986). *The suicidal child.* New York: Guilford Press.

Pfeffer, C. R. (2003). Assessing suicidal behavior in children and adolescents. In R. A. King & A. Apter (Eds.), *Suicide in children and adolescents* (pp. 211–226). Cambridge, England: Cambridge University Press.

Phares, V. (2003). *Understanding abnormal child psychology.* Hoboken, NJ: Wiley.

Phares, V. (2008). *Understanding abnormal child psychology* (2nd ed.). Hoboken, NJ: Wiley.

Phillips, D. P. (1974). The influence of suggestion on suicide: Substantive and theoretical implications of the *Werther* effect. *Amer. Sociol. Rev., 39,* 340–354.

Phillips, D. P., & Ruth, T. E. (1993). Adequacy of official suicide statistics for scientific research and public policy. *Suic. Life-Threat. Behav., 23*(4), 307–319.

Phillips, E. L., Greydanus, D. E., Pratt, H. D., & Patel, D. R. (2003). Treatment of bulimia nervosa: Psychological and psychopharmacologic considerations. *J. Adol. Res., 18*(3), 261–279.

Phillips, K. A. (2005). Olanzapine augmentation of fluoxetine in body dysmorphic disorder. *Amer. J. Psychiat., 162*(5), 1022.

Phillips, K. A. (2005). Placebo-controlled study of pimozide augmentation of fluoxetine in body dysmorphic disorder. *Amer. J. Psychiat., 162*(2), 377–379.

Phillips, K. A., & Castle, D. J. (2002). Body dysmorphic disorder. In D. J. Castle & K. A. Phillips (Eds.), *Disorders of body image.* Petersfield, England: Wrightson Biomedical Publishing, Ltd.

Phillips, K. A., Fallon, B. A., & King, T. (2008). Somatoform and factitious disorders and malingering measures. In A. J. Rush, Jr., M. B. First, & D. Blacker (Eds.), *Handbook of psychiatric measures* (2nd ed., pp. 559–585). Arlington, VA: American Psychiatric Publishing.

Phillips, K. A., Grant, J. E., Siniscalchi, J. M., Stout, R., & Price, L. H. (2005). A retrospective follow-up study of body dysmorphic disorder. *Comprehen. Psychiat., 46,* 315–321.

Phillips, K. A., McElroy, S. L., Keck, P. E., Pope, H. G., et al. (1993). Body dysmorphic disorder: 30 cases of imagined ugliness. *Amer. J. Psychiat., 150*(2), 302–308.

Phillips, K. A., Pagano, M. E., Menard, W., Fay, C., & Stout, R. L. (2005). Predictors of remission from body dysmorphic disorder: A prospective study. *J. Nerv. Ment. Dis., 193*(8), 564–567.

Phillips, M. L., Medford, N., Senior, C., Bullmore, E. T., Suckling, J., Brammer, M. J., Andrew, C., Sierra, M., Williams, S. C. R., & David, A. S. (2001). Depersonalization disorder: Thinking without feeling. *Psychiat. Res.: Neuroimaging, 108*(3), 145–160.

Philogene, G. (Ed.). (2004). *Racial identity in context: The legacy of Kenneth B. Clark.* Washington, DC: American Psychological Association.

Pickel, K. L. (2004). When a lie becomes the truth: The effects of self-generated misinformation on eyewitness memory. *Memory, 12*(1), 14–26.

Pickover, C. A. (1999). *Strange brains and genius: The secret lives of eccentric scientists and madmen.* New York: HarperCollins/Quill.

Piek, J. P., Rigoli, D., Pearsall-Jones, J. G., Martin, N. C., Hay, D. A., Bennett, K. S., et al. (2007). Depressive symptomatology in child and adolescent twins with attention-deficit hyperactivity disorder and/or developmental coordination disorder. *Twin Res. Human Genet., 10*(4), 587–596.

Pierce, K., & Courchesne, E. (2001). Evidence for a cerebellar role in reduced exploration and stereotyped behavior in autism. *Biol. Psychiat., 49*(8), 655–664.

Pierce, K., & Courchesne, E. (2002). "A further support to the hypothesis of a link between serotonin, autism and the cerebellum": Reply. *Biol. Psychiat., 52*(2), 143

Pike, K. M., & Borovoy, A. (2004). The rise of eating disorders in Japan: Issues of culture and limitations of the model of "westernization." *Cult. Med. Psychiat., 28*(4): 493–531.

Pilgrim, D. (2003). Mental disorder and violence: An empirical picture in context. *J. Ment. Hlth., 12*(1), 7–18.

Pillemer, K., & Suitor, J. J. (2002). Peer support for Alzheimer's caregivers: Is it enough to make a difference? *Res. Aging, 24*(2), 171–192.

Pinals, D. A., Packer, I., Fisher, B., & Roy, K. (2004). Relationship between race and ethnicity and forensic clinical triage dispositions. *Psychiatric Services 55,* 873–878.

Pine, D. S. (2005). Editorial: Where have all the clinical trials gone? *J. Child Psychol Psychiat., 46*(5), 449–450.

Pinel, J. P. J., Assanand, S., & Lehman, D. R. (2000). Hunger, eating, and ill health. *Amer. Psychologist, 55*(10), 1105–1116.

Pines, W. L. (1999). A history and perspective on direct-to-consumer promotion. *Food Drug Law J., 54,* 489–518.

Pingitore, D., Snowden, L. R., Sansome, R., & Klikman, M. (2001). Persons with depressive symptoms and the treatments they receive: A comparison of primary care physicians and psychiatrists. *Inter. J. Psychiat. Med., 31,* 41–60.

Pinhas, L., Toner, B. B., Ali, A., Garfinkel, P. E., & Stuckless, N. (1999). The effects of the ideal of female beauty on mood and body satisfaction. *Inter. J. Eat. Disorders, 25*(2), 223–226.

Pinto, A., Eisen, J. L., Mancebo, M. C., & Rasmussen, S. A. (2008). Obsessive-compulsive personality disorder. In J. S. Abramowitz, D. McKay, & S. Taylor (Eds.), *Obsessive-compulsive disorder: Subtypes and spectrum conditions.* Oxford, England: Elsevier.

Piotrowski, C., Belter, R. W., & Keller, J. W. (1998). The impact of "managed care" on the practice of psychological testing: Preliminary findings. *J. Pers. Assess., 70*(3), 441–447.

Piper, A., & Merskey, H. (2004). The persistence of folly: A critical examination of dissociative identity disorder. Part I. The excesses of an improbable concept. *Canad. J. Psychiat., 49*(9), 592–600.

Piper, A., & Merskey, H. (2004). The persistence of folly: Critical examination of dissociative identity disorder. Part II: The defence and decline of multiple personality or dissociative identity disorder. *Canad. J. Psychiat., 49*(10), 678–683.

Piper, W. E., & Joyce, A. S. (2001). Psychosocial treatment outcome. In W. J. Livesley (Ed.), *Handbook of personality disorders: Theory, research, and treatment* (pp. 323–343). New York: Guilford Press.

Plante, T. G. (1999). *Contemporary clinical psychology.* New York: Wiley.

Plante, T. (2006). How can we prevent abnormal behavior from occurring and developing? In T. Plante (Ed.) *Mental disorders of the new millennium.* New York: Praeger.

Pless, M., & Carlsson, M. (2000). Effects of motor skill intervention on developmental coordination disorder: A meta-analysis. *Adap. Phys. Activ. Q., 17*(4), 381–401.

Pole, N., Best, S. R., Metzler, T., & Marmar, C. R. (2005). Why are Hispanics at greater risk for PTSD? *Cult. Div. Ethnic Minority Psychol., 11*(2), 144–161.

Pole, N., Best, S. R., Weiss, D. S., Metzler, T., Liberman, A. J., & Fagan, J. (2001). Effects of gender and ethnicity on duty-related posttraumatic stress symptoms among urban police officers. *J. Nerv. Ment. Dis., 189*(7), 442–448.

Poling, A., Ehrhardt, K., & Porritt, M. (2008). Psychopharmacology as practiced by psychologists. In M. Hersen & A. M. Gross (Eds.), *Handbook of clinical psychology, Vol. 2: Children and adolescents.* Hoboken, NJ: John Wiley & Sons.

Pollack, M. H. (2005). The pharmacotherapy of panic disorder. *J. Clin. Psychiat., 66*(Suppl. 4), 23–27.

Polydorou, S., & Kleber, H. D. (2008). Detoxification of opioids. In H. D. Kleber & M. Galanter (Eds.), *The American Psychiatric Publishing textbook of substance abuse treatment* (4th ed., pp. 265–287). Arlington, VA: American Psychiatric Publishing.

Pomerantz, J. M. (2003). No place to go: The mentally ill in jails and prisons. *Drug Benef. Trends, 15*(5), 29–30.

Pompili, M., & Lester, D. (2007). Suicide risk in schizophrenia. In R. Tatarelli, M. Pompili, & P. Girardi (Eds.), *Suicide in psychiatric disorders.* New York: Nova Science Publishers.

Pompili, M., Lester, D., Grispini, A., Calandro, F., De Pisa, E., & Innamorati, M. (2007). Suicide and attempted suicide in anorexia nervosa, bulimia nervosa, obesity and weight-image concern. In R. Tatarelli, M. Pompili, & P. Girardi (Eds.), *Suicide in psychiatric disorders.* New York: Nova Science Publishers.

Pompili, M., Lester, D., Leenaars, A. A., Tatarelli, R., & Girardi, P. (2008). Psychache and suicide: A preliminary investigation. *Suic. Life-Threat. Behav., 38*(1), 116–121.

Pompili, M., Ruberto, A., Girardi, P., & Tatarelli, R. (2004). Understanding suicide in schizophrenia: A national imperative for prevention. *Psichiatria e Psicoterapia, 23*(4), 275–281.

Pope, H. G., Jr., Olivardia, R., Gruber A., & Borowiecki, J. (1999). Evolving ideals of male body image as seen through action toys. *Inter. J. Eat. Disorders, 26*(1), 65–72.

Pope, H. G., Jr., Poliakoff, M. B., Parker, M. P., Boynes, M., & Hudson, J. I. (2007). Is dissociative amnesia a culture-bound syndrome? Findings from a survey of historical literature: Reply. *Psychol. Med., 37*(7), 1065–1067.

Pope, K. S., & Brown, L. S. (1996). *Recovered memories of abuse: Assessment, therapy, forensics.* Washington, DC: American Psychological Association.

Pope, K. S., Keith-Spiegel, P., & Tabachnick, B. G. (2006). Sexual attraction to clients: The human therapist and the (sometimes) inhuman training system. *Train. Educ. Profess. Psychol., 5*(2), 96–111.

Pope, K. S., & Tabachnick, B. G. (1993). Therapists' anger, hate, fear, and sexual feelings: National survey of therapist responses, client characteristics, critical events, formal complaints, and training. *Profess. Psychol.: Res. Pract., 24*(2), 142–152.

Pope, K. S., & Vasquez, M. J. T. (2007). *Ethics in psychotherapy and counseling.* Hoboken, NJ: Wiley.

Pope, K. S., & Wedding, D. (2008). Contemporary challenges and controversies. In R. J. Corsini & D. Wedding (Eds.), *Current psychotherapies* (8th ed.). Belmont, CA: Thomson Brooks/Cole.

Pope, K. S., Sonne, J. L., & Greene, B. (2006). *What therapists don't talk about and why: Understanding taboos that hurt us and our clients.* Washington, DC: American Psychological Association.

Popper, C. W. (1988). Disorders usually first evident in infancy, childhood, or adolescence. In J. Talbott, R. S. Hales, & S. C. Yudofsky (Eds.), *Textbook of psychiatry.* Washington, DC: American Psychiatric Press.

Porcerelli, J., Dauphin, B., Ablon, J. S., et al. (2007). Psychoanalysis of avoidant personality disorder: A systematic case study. *Psychother.: Theory Res. Prac., 44,* 1–13.

Poretz, M., & Sinrod, B. (1991). *Do you do it with the lights on?* New York: Ballantine Books.

PORT (Patient Outcomes Research Team). (1998). Cited in S. Barlas, Patient outcome research team study on schizophrenia offers grim indictment. *Psychiatr. Times, XV*(6).

Porter, S., & ten-Brinke, L. (2008). Reading between the lies: Identifying concealed and falsified emotions in universal facial expressions. *Psychol. Sci., 19*(5), 508–514.

Portnoy, D. (2008). Relatedness: Where existential and psychoanalytic approaches converge. In K. J. Schneider (Ed.), *Existential-integrative psychotherapy: Guideposts to the core of practice* (pp. 268–281). New York: Routledge/Taylor & Francis Group.

Post, R. M. (2005). The impact of bipolar depression. *J. Clin. Psychiat., 66*(Suppl. 5), 5–10.

Post, R. M., Ballenger, J. C., & Goodwin, F. K. (1980). Cerebrospinal fluid studies of neurotransmitter function in manic and depressive illness. In J. H. Wood (Ed.), *The neurobiology of cerebrospinal fluid* (Vol. 1). New York: Plenum Press.

Post, R. M., Lake, C. R., Jimerson, D. C., Bunney, J. H., Ziegler, M. G., & Goodwin, F. K. (1978). Cerebrospinal fluid norepinephrine in affective illness. *Amer. J. Psychiat., 135*(8), 907–912.

Potvin, S., Stip, E., Lipp, O., Roy, M. A., Demers, M. F., Bouchard, R. H., et al. (2008). Anhedonia and social adaptation predict substance abuse evolution in dual diagnosis schizophrenia. *Amer. J. Drug Alc. Abuse, 34*(1), 75–82.

Poulos, C. X., Le, A. D., & Parker, J. L. (1995). Impulsivity predicts individual susceptibility to high levels of alcohol self-administration. *Behav. Pharmacol., 6*(8), 810–814.

Present, J., Crits-Christoph, P., Gibbons, M. B. C., Hearon, B., Ring-Kurtz, S., Worley, M., et al. (2008). Sudden gains in the treatment of generalized anxiety disorder. *J. Clin. Psychol., 64*(1), 119–126.

Pressler, M. W. (2004). Another cup? Coffee bars just keep spilling across the landscape. *Washington Post,* May 23, 2004.

Preuss, U. W., Zill, P., Koller, G., Bondy, B., & Soyka, M. (2007). D2 dopamine receptor gene haplotypes and their influence on alcohol and tobacco consumption magnitude in alcohol-dependent individuals. *Alcohol Alcoholism, 42*(3), 258–266.

Price, D. D., Finniss, D. G., & Benedetti, F. (2008). A comprehensive review of the placebo effect: Recent advances and current thought. In S. Fiske, D. L. Schacter, & R. Sternberg (Eds.), *Annual review of psychology* (Vol. 59). Palo Alto, CA: Annual reviews.

Priebe, S., & Fakhoury, W. K. H. (2008). Quality of life. In K. T. Mueser & D. V. Jeste (Eds.), *Clinical handbook of schizophrenia* (pp. 581–591). New York: Guilford Press.

Prien, R. F., Caffey, E. M., Jr., & Klett, C. J. (1974). Factors associated with treatment success in lithium carbonate prophylaxis. *Arch. Gen. Psychiat., 31,* 189–192.

Princeton Survey Research Associates. (1996). *Healthy steps for young children: Survey of parents.* Princeton: Author.

Prochaska, J. O., & Norcross, J. C. (1994). *Systems of psychotherapy: A transtheoretical analysis* (3rd ed.). Pacific Grove, CA: Brooks/Cole.

Prochaska, J. O., & Norcross, J. C. (1999). *Systems of psychotherapy: A transtheoretical analysis* (4th ed.). Pacific Grove, CA: Brooks/Cole.

Prochaska, J. O., & Norcross, J. C. (2003). *Systems of psychotherapy: A transtheoretical analysis* (5th ed.). Pacific Grove, CA: Brooks/Cole.

Prochaska, J. O., & Norcross, J. C. (2006). *Systems of psychotherapy: A transtheoretical analysis.* Pacific Grove, CA: Brooks/Cole.

Prochaska, J. O., & Norcross, J. C. (2007). *Systems of psychotherapy: A transtheoretical analysis* (6th ed.). Pacific Grove, CA: Brooks/Cole.

Proctor, R. W., & Capaldi, E. J. (2006). *Why science matters: Understanding the methods of psychological research.* Malden, MA: Blackwell Publishing.

Protopopescu, X., Pan, H., Tuesher, O., Cloitre, M., Goldstein, M., Engelien, W., et al. (2005). Differential time courses and specificity of amygdala activity in posttraumatic stress disorder subjects and normal control subjects. *Biol. Psychiat., 57*(5), 464–473.

Prudic, J., & Sackeim, H. A. (1999). Electroconvulsive therapy and suicide risk. *J. Clin. Psychiat., 60*(Suppl. 2), 104–110.

Prusiner, S. B. (1991). Molecular biology of prion diseases. *Science, 252,* 1515–1522.

Pryce, C. R., Ruedi-Bettschen, D., Dettling, A. C., Weston, A., Russig, H., Ferger, B., et al. (2005). Long-term effects of early-life environmental manipulations in rodents and primates: Potential animal models in depression research. *Neurosci. Biobehav. Rev., 29*(4–5), 649–674.

Pugh, L. A. (2003). *The psychological effects of the September 11th terrorist attacks on individuals with prior exposure to traumatic events.* Princeton Thesis #15387, Mudd Lib.

Pugno, M. (2007). The subjective well-being paradox: A suggested solution based on relational goods. In P. L. Porta & L. Bruni (Eds.), *Handbook on the economics of happiness* (pp. 263–289). Northampton, MA: Edward Elgar Publishing.

Pull, C. B. (2005). Current status of virtual reality exposure therapy in anxiety disorders. *Curr. Opin. Psychiat., 18*(1), 7–14.

Pumariega, A., Gustavson, C. R., Gustavson, J. C., Stone Mkotes, P., & Ayers, S. (1994). Eating attitudes in African-American women: The *Essence* eating disorders survey. *Eat. Disord.: J. Treat. Prev., 2*(1), 5–16.

Putnam, F. W. (1984). The psychophysiologic investigation of multiple personality disorder. *Psychiatr. Clin. N. Amer., 7,* 31–40.

Putnam, F. W. (1985). Multiple personality disorder. *Med. Aspects Human Sex., 19*(6), 59–74.

Putnam, F. W. (1988). The switch process in multiple personality disorder and other state-change disorders.

Putnam, F. W. (1992). Are alter personalities fragments of figments? *Psychoanal. Inq., 12*(1), 95–111.

Putnam, F. W. (2000). Dissociative disorders. In A. J. Sameroff, M. Lewis et al. (Eds.), *Handbook of developmental psychopathology* (2nd ed., pp. 739–754). New York: Kluwer Academic/Plenum Press.

Putnam, F. W., Zahn, T. P., & Post, R. M. (1990). Differential autonomic nervous system activity in multiple personality disorder. *J. Psychiatr. Res., 31*(3), 251–260.

Pyszora, N. M., Barker, A. F., & Kopelman, M. D. (2003). Amnesia for criminal offences: A study of life sentence prisoners. *J. Forens. Psychiat. Psychol., 14,* 475–490.

Quas, J. A., Malloy, L. C., Melinder, A., Goodman, G. S., D-Mello, M., & Schaaf, J. (2007). Developmental differences in the effects of repeated interviews and interviewer bias on young children's event memory and false reports. *Dev. Psychol., 43*(4), 823–837.

Querido, J. G., & Eyberg, S. M. (2005). Parent-child interaction therapy: Maintaining treatment gains of preschoolers with disruptive behavior disorders. In E. D. Hibbs & P. S. Jensen (Eds.), *Psychosocial treatments for child and adolescent disorders: Empirically based strategies for clinical practice* (2nd ed., pp. 575–97). Washington, DC: American Psychological Association.

Raab, K. A. (2007). Manic depression and religious experience: The use of religion in therapy. *Ment. Hlth, Religion Culture, 10*(5), 473–487.

Rabinowitz, J., Levine, S. Z., Brill, N., & Bromet, E. J. (2007). The premorbid adjustment scale structured interview (PAS-SI): Preliminary findings. *Schizophrenia Research, 90*(1–3), 255–257.

Raboch, J., & Raboch, J. (1992). Infrequent orgasm in women. *J. Sex Marital Ther., 18*(2), 114–120.

Rachman, S. (1966). Sexual fetishism: An experimental analog. *Psychol. Rec., 18,* 25–27.

Rachman, S. (1993). Obsessions, responsibility and guilt. *Behav. Res. Ther., 31*(2), 149–154.

Radomsky, A. S., Ashbaugh, A. R., Gelfand, L. A., & Dugas, M. J. (2008). Doubting and compulsive checking. In J. S. Abramowitz, D. McKay, & S. Taylor (Eds.), *Obsessive-compulsive disorder: Subtypes and spectrum conditions.* Oxford, England: Elsevier.

Rahey, L., & Craig, W. M. (2002). Evaluation of an ecological program to reduce bullying in schools. *Canad. J. Couns., 36*(4), 281–296.

Rajkowska, G. (2000). Postmortem studies in mood disorders indicate altered numbers of neurons and glial cells. *Biol. Psychiat., 48,* 766–777.

Ralevski, E., Sanislow, C. A., Grilo, C. M., Skodol, A. E., Gunderson, J. G., Shea, M. T., et al. (2005). Avoidant personality disorder and social phobia: Distinct enough to be separate disorders? *Acta Psychiatr. Scandin., 112*(3), 208–214.

Ralston, P. A. (1991). Senior centers and minority elders: A critical review. *Gerontologist, 31,* 325–331.

Ramaekers, J. G., Kauert, G., van Ruitenbeek, P., Theunissen, E. L., Schneider, E., & Moeller, M. R. (2006). High-potency marijuana impairs executive function and inhibitory motor control. *Neuropsychopharmacology, 31*(10), 2296–2303.

Ramchandani, P., Stein, A., Evans, J., O'Connor, T. G., & ALSPAC Study Team. (2005). Paternal depression in the postnatal period and child development: A prospective population study. *Lancet, 365*(9478), 2201–2205.

Ramey, C. T., & Ramey, S. L. (1992). Effective early intervention. *Ment. Retard., 30*(6), 337–345.

Ramey, C. T., & Ramey, S. L. (1998). Early intervention and early experience. *Amer. Psychologist, 53,* 109–120.

Ramey, C. T., & Ramey, S. L. (2004). Early learning and school readiness: Can early intervention make a difference? *Merrill-Palmer Quart., 50*(4), 471–491.

RAND Corporation. (2008, April 17). 1 in 5 Iraq, Afghanistan vets has PTSD, major depression. *Science Blog.* Retrieved May 19, 2008, from http://www.scienceblog.com/cms/1-5-iraq-afghanistan-vet-has-ptsd-major-depression-rand-15954.html

Rao, D. G. (2005). The wolf in the consulting room. In V. Volkan & S. Akhtar (Eds.), *Mental zoo: Animals in the human mind and its pathology* (pp. 97–124). Madison, CT: International Universities Press.

Rapee, R. M. (2003). The influence of comorbidity on treatment outcome for children and adolescents with anxiety disorders. *Behav. Res. Ther., 41*(1), 105–112.

Raphael, B., & Wilson, J. P. (Eds.). (2000). *Psychological debriefing: Theory, practice and evidence.* Cambridge, England: Cambridge University Press.

Rapoport, J. L. (1989, March). The biology of obsessions and compulsions. *Scientif. Amer.,* pp. 82–89.

Rapp, C. A., & Goscha, R. J. (2008). Strengths-based case management. In K. T. Mueser & D. V. Jeste (Eds.), *Clinical handbook of schizophrenia* (pp. 319–328). New York: Guilford Press.

Rapport, M. D., Kofler, M. J., Alderson, R. M., & Raiker, J. S. (2008). Attention-deficit/hyperactivity disorder. In D. Reitman (Ed.), *Handbook of psychological assessment, case conceptualization, and treatment, Vol. 2: Children and adolescents.* Hoboken, NJ: John Wiley & Sons.

Raskin, D. C., & Honts, C. R. (2002). The comparison question test. In M. Kleiner (Ed.), *The handbook of polygraph testing.* San Diego, CA: Academic.

Raskin, M., Peeke, H. V. S., Dickman, W., & Pinkster, H. (1982). Panic and generalized anxiety disorders: Developmental antecedents and precipitants. *Arch. Gen. Psychiat., 39,* 687–689.

Raskin, N. J., Rogers, C. R., & Witty, M. C. (2008). Client-centered therapy. In R. J. Corsini & D. Wedding (Eds.), *Current psychotherapies* (8th ed.). Belmont, CA: Thomson Brooks/Cole.

Rasmussen, S. A., & Eisen, J. L. (1992). The epidemiology and clinical features of obsessive

compulsive disorder. *Psychiatr. Clin. N. Amer., 15*(4), 743–758.

Rasmussen, S. A., & Eisen, J. L. (1992). The epidemiology and differential diagnosis of obsessive compulsive disorder. *J. Clin. Psychiatr., 53*(4), 4–10.

Rathbone, J. (2001). *Anatomy of masochism.* New York: Kluwer Academic/Plenum.

Rawson, R. A., & Ling, W. (2008). Clinical management: Methamphetamine. In H. D. Kleber & M. Galanter (Eds.), *The American Psychiatric Publishing textbook of substance abuse treatment* (4th ed., pp. 169–179). Arlington, VA: American Psychiatric Publishing.

Raymond, K. B. (1997). The effect of race and gender on the identification of children with attention deficit hyperactivity disorder. *Diss. Abstr. Inter.: Sect. A: Human Soc. Sci., 57*(12-A), 5052.

Read, J., Agar, K., Barker-Collo, S., Davies, E., & Moskowitz, A. (2001). Assessing suicidality in adults: Integrating childhood trauma as a major risk factor. *Profess. Psychol.: Res. Pract., 32*(4), 367–372.

Read, K., & Purse, M. (2007, March 22). Postpartum psychosis: Linked to bipolar disorder. *About.com.* Retrieved July 30, 2008, from http://bipolar.about.com/od/relateddisorders/a/postpartumpsych.htm

Redick, R. W., Witkin, M. J., Atay, J. E., & Manderscheid, R. W. (1992). Specialty mental health system characteristics. In R. W. Manderscheid & M. A. Sonnenschein (Eds.), *Mental health, United States, 1992.* Washington, DC: U.S. Department of Health and Human Services.

Redmond, D. E. (1977). Alterations in the function of the nucleus locus coeruleus: A possible model for studies of anxiety. In I. Hanin & E. Usdin (Eds.), *Animal models in psychiatry and neurology.* New York: Pergamon Press.

Redmond, D. E. (1979). New and old evidence for the involvement of a brain norepinephrine system in anxiety. In W. E. Fann, I. Karacan, A. D. Pokorny, & R. L. Williams (Eds.), *Phemenology and treatment of anxiety.* New York: Spectrum.

Redmond, D. E. (1981). Clonidine and the primate locus coeruleus: Evidence suggesting anxiolytic and anti-withdrawal effects. In H. Lal & S. Fielding (Eds.), *Psychopharmacology of clonidine.* New York: Alan R. Liss.

Redmond, D. E. (1985). Neurochemical basis for anxiety and anxiety disorders: Evidence from drugs which decrease human fear or anxiety. In A. H. Tuma & J. Maser (Eds.), *Anxiety and the anxiety disorders.* Hillsdale, NJ: Lawrence Erlbaum.

Redwine, L., Mills, P. J., Sada, M., Dimsdale, J., Patterson, T., & Grant, I. (2004). Differential immune cell chemotaxis responses to acute psychological stress in Alzheimer caregivers compared to non-caregiver controls. *Psychosom. Med., 66*(5), 770–775.

Reeb, R. N. (2000). Classification and diagnosis of psychopathology: Conceptual foundations. *J. Psychol. Pract., 6*(1), 3–18.

Reed, G. M., & Eisman, E. J. (2006). Uses and misuses of evidence: Managed care, treatment guidelines, and outcomes measurement in professional practice. In C. D. Goodheart, A. E. Kazdin, & R. J. Sternberg (Eds.), *Evidence-based psychotherapy: Where practice and research meet* (pp. 13–35). Washington, DC: American Psychological Association.

Rees, W. D., & Lutkin, S. G. (1967). Mortality of bereavement. *Brit. Med. J., 4,* 13–16.

Reese, L. E., & Vera, E. M. (2007). Culturally relevant prevention: The scientific and practical considerations of community-based programs. *Couns. Psychologist, 36*(6), 763–778.

Regehr, C., Cadell, S., & Jansen, K. (1999). Perceptions of control and long-term recovery from rape. *Amer. J. Orthopsychiat., 69*(1), 110–115.

Regier, D. A., Narrow, W. E., Rae, D. S., Manderscheid, R. W., Locke, B. Z., & Goodwin, F. K. (1993). The de facto U.S. Mental and Addictive Disorders Service System: Epidemiologic Catchment Area prospective 1-year prevalence rates of disorders in services. *Arch. Gen. Psychiat., 50,* 85–94.

Reich, G. (2005). Family relationships and family therapy of eating disorders. *Praxis Kinderpsychol. Kinderpsych. 54*(4), 318–336.

Reid, W. H., & Gacono, C. (2000). Treatment of antisocial personality, psychopathy, and other characterologic antisocial syndromes. *Behav. Sci. Law, 18,* 647–662.

Reinecke, M. A., & Ginsburg, G. S. (2008). In J. R. Z. Abela & B. L. Hankin (Eds.), *Handbook of depression in children and adolescents* (pp. 179–206). New York: Guilford Press.

Reinecke, M. A., Washburn, J. J., & Becker-Weidman, E. (2007). Depression and suicide. In F. M. Dattilio & A. Freeman (Eds.), *Cognitive-behavioral strategies in crisis intervention* (3rd ed., pp. 25–67). New York: Guilford Press.

Reis, B. (2005). The self is alive and well and living in relational psychoanalysis. *Psychoanal. Psychol., 22*(1), 86–95.

Reisch, T., Schuster, U., & Michel, K. (2007). Suicide by jumping and accessibility of bridges: Results from a national survey in Switzerland. *Suic. Life-Threat. Behav., 37*(6), 681–687.

Reissing, E. D., Binik, Y. M., Khalife, S., Cohen, D., & Amsel, R. (2003). Etiological correlates of vaginismus: Sexual and physical abuse, sexual knowledge, sexual self-schema and relationship adjustment. *J. Sex Marital Ther., 29*(1), 47–59.

Reitan, R. M., & Wolfson, D. (1996). Theoretical, methodological, and validational bases of the Halstead-Reitan neuropsychological test battery. In I. Grant & K. M. Adams (Eds.), *Neuropsychological assessment of neuropsychiatric disorders* (2nd ed., pp. 3–42). New York: Oxford University Press.

Reitan, R. M., & Wolfson, D. (2001). The Halstad-Reitan Neuropsychological Test Battery: Research findings and clinical application. In A. S. Kaufman & N. L. Kaufman (Eds.), *Specific learning disabilities and difficulties in children and adolescents: Psychological assessment and evaluation* (pp. 309–346). New York: Cambridge University Press.

Reitan, R. M., & Wolfson, D. (2005). The effect of age and education transformations on neuropsychological test scores of persons with diffuse or bilateral brain damage. *Appl. Neuropsychol., 12*(4), 181–189.

Ren, M., Senatorov, V. V., Chen, R.-W., & Chuang, D.-M. (2003). Postinsult treatment with lithium reduces brain damage and facilitates neurological recovery in a rat ischemia/reperfusion model. *Proc. Natl. Acad. Sci., 100,* 6210–6215.

Renaud, J., Berlim, M. T., McGirr, A., Tousignant, M., & Turecki, G. (2008). Current psychiatric morbidity, aggression/impulsivity, and personality dimensions in child and adolescent suicide: A case-control study. *J. Affect. Disorders, 105*(1–3), 221–228.

Rende, R., Slomkowski, C., McCaffery, J., Lloyd-Richardson, E. E., & Niaura, R. (2005). A twin-sibling study of tobacco use in adolescence: Etiology of individual differences and extreme scores. *Nicotine and Tobacco Res., 7*(3), 413–419.

Rennison, C. M. (2002, August). Rape and sexual assault: Reporting to police and medical attention, 1992–2000 (NCJ 194530). Washington, DC: U.S. Department of Justice Statistics Selected Findings.

Resick, P. A., & Calhoun, K. S. (2001). Posttraumatic stress disorder. In D. H. Barlow (Ed.), *Clinical handbook of psychological disorders: A step-by-step treatment manual* (3rd ed.). New York: Guilford Press.

Resnick, P. H. J., & Harris, M. R. (2002). Retrospective assessment of malingering in insanity defense cases. In R. I. Simon & D. W. Schuman (Eds.), *Retrospective assessment of mental states in litigation: Predicting the past* (pp. 101–134) Washington, DC: American Psychiatric Publishing.

Ressler, K., & Davis, M. (2003). Genetics of childhood disorders: L. Learning and memory, part 3: Fear conditioning. *J. Amer. Acad. Child Adol. Psychiat., 42*(5), 612–615.

Retz, W., Retz-Junginger, P., Supprian, T., Thome, J., & Rosier, M. (2004). Association of serotonin transporter promoter gene polymorphism with violence: Relation with personality disorders, impulsivity, and childhood ADHD psychopathology. *Behav. Sci. Law., 22*(3), 415–425.

Reulbach, U., Biermann, T., Markovic, K., Kornhuber, J., & Bleich, S. (2007). The myth of the birthday blues: A population-based study about the association between birthday and suicide. *Comprehen. Psychiat., 48*(6), 554–557.

Reuters. (2004, September 7). It's a bumper-to-bumper life. *Reuters (Washington)/Yahoo!News).*

Reynolds, C. F., III, Frank, E., Perel, J. M., Imber, S. D., Cornes, C., Miller, M. D., et al. (1999). Nortriptyline and interpersonal psychotherapy as maintenance therapies for recurrent major depression: A randomized controlled trial in patients older than 59 years. *JAMA, 281*(1), 39–45.

Reynolds, L. (1990). Drug-free after 30 years of dependence. *Aging, 361,* 26–27.

Rezayof, A., Alijanpour, S., Zarrindast, M. R., & Rassouli, Y. (2008). Ethanol state-dependent memory: Involvement of dorsal hippocampal muscarinic and nicotinic receptors. *Neurobiol. Learn. Memory, 89*(4), 441–447.

Richard, I. H., & Lyness, J. M. (2006). An overview of depression. In D. V. Jeste & J. H. Friedman (Eds.), *Psychiatry for neurologists* (pp. 33–42). Totowa, NJ: Humana Press.

Richard, M. (2005). Effective treatment of eating disorders in Europe: Treatment outcome and its predictors. *Eur. Eat. Disord. Rev., 13*(3), 169–179.

Richards, P. S., & Bergin, A. E. (Eds.). (2000). Toward religious and spiritual competency for mental health professionals. In P. S. Richards & A. E. Bergin, *Handbook of psychotherapy and religious diversity.* Washington, DC: American Psychological Association.

Richards, P. S., & Bergin, A. E. (Eds.). (2004). *Casebook for a spiritual strategy in counseling and psychotherapy.* Washington, DC: American Psychological Association.

Richards, P. S., & Bergin, A. E. (2005). *A spiritual strategy for counseling and psychotherapy* (2nd ed.). Washington, DC: American Psychological Association.

Richardson, J. T. E. (2002). The aetiology, assessment, and rehabilitation of memory impairment following mild head injury. *Tidsskrift for Norsk Psykologforening, 39*(8), 700–706.

Richman, L. S., Kohn-Wood, L. P., & Williams, D. R. (2007). The role of discrimination and racial identity for mental health service utilization. *J. Soc. Clin. Psychol., 26*(8), 960–981.

Ridgway, P. (2008). Supported housing. In K. T. Mueser & D. V. Jeste (Eds.), *Clinical handbook of schizophrenia* (pp. 287–297). New York: Guilford Press.

Ridout, N., Astell, A. J., Reid, I. C., Glen, T., & O'Carroll, R. E. (2003). Memory bias for emotional facial expressions in major depression. *Cog. Emot., 17*(1), 101–122.

Rieber, R. W. (1999). Hypnosis, false memory and multiple personality: A trinity of affinity. *Hist. Psychiat., 10*(37), 3–11.

Rieber, R. W. (2002). The duality of the brain and the multiplicity of minds: Can you have it both ways? *Hist. Psychiat. 13*(49, pt1), 3–18.

Riesch, S. K., Jacobson, G., Sawdey, L., Anderson, J., & Henriques, J. (2008). Suicide ideation among later elementary school-aged youth. *J. Psychiatr. Ment. Hlth. Nurs., 15*(4), 263–277.

Riess, H. (2002). Integrative time-limited group therapy for bulimia nervosa. *Inter. J. Group Psychother., 52*(1), 1–26.

Rigby, K. (2002). Bullying in childhood. In P. K. Smith & C. H. Hart (Eds.), *Blackwell handbook of childhood social development* (pp. 549–568). Malden, MA: Blackwell.

Rihmer, Z., & Angst, J. (2005). Epidemiology of bipolar disorder. In S. Kasper & R. M. A. Hirschfeld (Eds.), *Handbook of bipolar disorder: Diagnosis and therapeutic approaches* (pp. 21–45). New York: Taylor & Francis.

Rihmer, Z., Rutz, W., & Pihlgren, H. (1995). Depression and suicide on Gotland. An intensive study of all suicides before and after a depression-training programme for general practitioners. *J. Affect. Disorders, 35,* 147–152.

Ringuette, E., & Kennedy, T. (1966). An experimental study of the double bind hypothesis. *J. Abnorm. Psychol., 71,* 136–141.

Riskind, J. H., & Williams, N. L. (2005). The looming cognitive style and generalized anxiety disorder: Distinctive danger schemas and cognitive phenomenology. *Cog. Ther. Res., 29*(1), 7–27.

Ritsner, M. S., & Gibel, A. (2007). Quality of life impairment syndrome in schizophrenia. In M. S. Ritsner & A. G. Awad (Eds.), *Quality of life impairment in schizophrenia, mood and anxiety disorders: New perspectives on research and treatment.* The Netherlands: Springer.

Ritter, M. (2008). Lead linked to aging in older brains. *YAHOO! News.* January, 27, 2008.

Ritvo, J. I., & Causey, H. L., III. (2008). Community-based treatment. In H. D. Kleber & M. Galanter (Eds.), *The American Psychiatric Publishing textbook of substance abuse treatment* (4th ed., pp. 477–490). Arlington, VA: American Psychiatric Publishing.

Rivas, L. A. (2001). Controversial issues in the diagnosis of narcissistic personality disorders: A review of the literature. *Journal of Mental Health Counseling, 23,* 22–35.

Ro, O., Martinsen, E. W., Hoffart, A., Sexton, H., & Rosenvinge, J. H. (2005). Adults with chronic eating disorders: Two-year follow-up after inpatient treatment. *Eur. Eat. Disord. Rev., 13*(4), 255–263.

Roazen, P. (1992). The rise and fall of Bruno Bettelheim. *Psychohist. Rev., 20*(3), 221–250.

Robb, A. S., Silber, T. J., Orrell-Valente, J. K., Valadez-Meltzer, A., Ellis, N., Dadson, M., et al. (2002). Supplemental nocturnal nasogastric refeeding for better short-term outcome in hospitalized adolescent girls with anorexia nervosa. *Amer. J. Psychiat., 159*(8), 1347–1353.

Roberts, M. (2007, December 18). Tests, eBay and the public good. Associated Press.

Robertson, P. K. (2004). The historical effects of depathologizing homosexuality on the practice of counseling. *Fam. J.: Couns. Ther. Couples Fam., 12*(2), 163–169.

Robinson, M. S., & Alloy, L. B. (2003). Negative cognitive styles and stress-reactive rumination interact to predict depression: A prospective study. *Cog. Ther. Res., 27*(3), 275–292.

Robinson, T. N., Borzekowski, D. L. G., Matheson, D. M., & Kraemer, H. C. (2007). Effects of fast food branding on young children's taste preferences. *Arch. Pediatr. Adoles. Med., 161*(8), 792–797.

Roche, B., & Quayle, E. (2007). Sexual disorders. In D. W. Woods & J. W. Kanter (Eds.), *Understanding behavior disorders: A contemporary behavioral perspective.* Reno, NV: Context Press.

Roche, T. (2002, January 20). The Yates odyssey. *TIME.com: Nation.*

Rochlen, A. B., Zack, J. S., & Speyer, C. (2004). Online therapy: Review of relevant definitions, debates, and current empirical support. *J. Clin. Psychol., 60*(3), 269–283.

Rodebaugh, T. L., Holaway, R. M., & Heimberg, R. G. (2004). The treatment of social anxiety disorder. *Clin. Psychol. Rev., 24,* 883–908.

Rodgers, C. S., Norman, S. B., Thorp, S. R., Lang, A. J., & Lebeck, M. M. (2005). Trauma exposure, posttraumatic stress disorder and health behaviors: Impact on special populations. In T. A. Corales (Ed.), *Focus on posttraumatic stress disorder research* (pp. 203–224). Hauppauge, NY: Nova Science Publishers.

Rodgers, J. (2000). Cognitive performance amongst recreational users of "ecstasy". *Psychopharmacology (Berl), 151*(1), 19–24.

Rodier, P. M. (2000, February). The early origins of autism. *Scientif. Amer.,* pp. 56–63.

Rodin, J. (1992). Sick of worrying about the way you look? Read this. *Psychol. Today, 25*(1), 56–60.

Rodriguez, B. F., Weisberg, R. B., Pagano, M. E., Machan, J. T., Culpepper, L., & Keller, M. B. (2004). Frequency and patterns of psychiatric comorbidity in a sample of primary care patients with anxiety disorders. *Comprehen. Psychiat., 45*(2), 129–137.

Roe, D., & Davidson, L. (2008). Recovery. In K. T. Mueser & D. V. Jeste (Eds.), *Clinical handbook of schizophrenia* (pp. 566–574). New York: Guilford Press.

Roelofs, K., Hoogduin, K. A. L., Keijsers, G. P. J., Naering, G. W. B., Moene, F. C., & Sandijck, P. (2002). Hypnotic susceptibility in patients with conversion disorder. *J. Abnorm. Psychol., 111*(2), 390–395.

Roemer, L., Salters, K., Raffa, S. D., & Orsillo, S. M. (2005). Fear and avoidance of internal experiences in GAD: Preliminary tests of a conceptual model. *Cog. Ther. Res., 29*(1), 71–88.

Roesch, R. (1991). *The encyclopedia of depression.* New York: Facts on File.

Roesch, R., Zapf, P. A., Golding, S. L., & Skeem, J. L. (1999). Defining and assessing competence to stand trial. In A. K. Hess, I. B. Weiner, et al. (Eds.), *The handbook of forensic psychology* (2nd ed.). New York: Wiley.

Roe-Sepowitz, D., Bedard, L. E., & Pate, K. (2007). The impact of child abuse on dissociative symptoms: A study of incarcerated women. *J. Trauma Dissociat., 8*(3), 7–26.

Roesler, T. A., & McKenzie, N. (1994). Effects of childhood trauma on psychological functioning of adults sexually abused as children. *J. Nerv. Ment. Dis., 182*(3), 145–150.

Rogers, C. R. (1951). *Client-centered therapy.* Boston: Houghton Mifflin.

Rogers, C. R. (1954). The case of Mrs. Oak: A research analysis. In C. R. Rogers & R. F. Dymond (Eds.), *Psychotherapy and personality change* (pp. 259–269). Chicago: University of Chicago Press.

Rogers, C. R. (1987). Rogers, Kohut, and Erickson: A personal perspective on some similarities and differences. In J. K. Zeig (Ed.), *The evolution of psychotherapy.* New York: Brunner/Mazel.

Rogers, C. R. (2000). Interview with Carl Rogers on the use of the self in therapy. In M. Baldwin (Ed.), *The use of self in therapy* (2nd ed., pp. 29–38). Binghamton, NY: Haworth.

Rogers, M. A., Kasai, K., & Fukuda, M.. (2007). Executive deficits in schizophrenia and mood disorder: Similarities and differences. In J. E. Pletson (Ed.), *Psychology and schizophrenia.* New York: Nova Science Publishers.

Rogers, P. (2005). Caffeine and health. *Psychologist, 18*(1), 9.

Rogers, R. (2004). Diagnostic, explanatory, and detection models of Munchausen by proxy: Extrapolations from malingering and deception. *Child Abuse Negl., 28*(2), 225–238.

Rogers, R. (2008). Insanity evaluations. In R. Jackson (Ed.), *Learning forensic assessment* (pp. 109–128). New York: Routledge/Taylor & Francis Group.

Roggla, H., & Uhl, A. (1995). Depression and relapses in treated chronic alcoholics. *Inter. J. Addic., 30*(3), 337–349.

Rogler, L. H., Malgady, R. G., & Rodriguea, O. (1989). *Hispanics and mental health: A framework for research.* Malabar, FL: Krieger Publishing.

Rohrer, G. E. (2005). The problem of assessment and diagnosis. In G. Rohrer, *Mental health and literature: Literary lunacy and lucidity* (pp. 1–23). Chicago, IL: Lyceum Books.

Roloff, P. (2001). The nurse's role in a pilot program using a modified cognitive-behavioral approach. In B. Kinoy (Ed.), *Eating disorders: New directions in treatment and recovery* (2nd ed., pp. 127–132). New York: Columbia University Press.

Rolon, Y. M., & Jones, J. C. W. (2008). Right to refuse treatment. *J. Amer. Acad. Psychiat. Law, 36*(2), 252–255.

Romano, E., & De Luca, R. V. (2001). Male sexual abuse: A review of effects, abuse characteristics, and links with later psychological functioning. *Aggress. Viol. Behav., 6*(1), 55–78.

Romito, S., Bottanelli, M., Pellegrini, M., Vicentini, S., Rizzuto, N., & Bertolasi, L. (2004). Botulinum toxin for the treatment of genital pain syndromes. *Gynecologic and Obstetric Investigation, 58*(3), 164–167.

Rose, S., Bisson, J. I., & Wessely, S. (2001). Psychological debriefing for preventing post traumatic stress disorder (PTSD) (Cochrane Review). In The Cochrane Library, issue 4. Oxford, England: Update Software.

Rosen, E. F., Anthony, D. L., Booker, K. M., Brown, T. L., et al. (1991). A comparison of eating disorder scores among African American and white college females. *Bull. Psychon. Soc., 29*(1), 65–66.

Rosen, L. (2005). "Online therapy" is excellent e-primer. *Natl. Psychologist, 14*(6), 16.

Rosen, L. W., & Hough, D. O. (1988). Pathogenic weight-control behaviors of female college gymnasts. *Physician Sports Med., 16*(9), 141–144.

Rosen, L. W., McKeag, D. B., Hough, D. O., & Curley, V. (1986). Pathogenic weight-control behavior in female athletes. *Physician Sports Med., 14*(1), 79–86.

Rosen, R. C. (2007). Erectile dysfunction: Integration of medical and psychological approaches. In S. R. Leiblum (Ed.), *Principles and practice of sex therapy* (4th ed., pp. 277–310). New York: Guilford Press.

Rosen, R. C., & Leiblum, S. R. (1995). Hypoactive sexual desire (Special issue: Clinical sexuality). *Psychiatr. Clin. N. Amer., 18*(1), 107–121.

Rosen, R. C., & Rosen, L. R. (1981). *Human sexuality.* New York: Knopf.

Rosenbaum, T. Y. (2007). Physical therapy management and treatment of sexual pain disorders. In S. R. Leiblum (Ed.), *Principles and practice of sex therapy* (4th ed., pp. 157–178). New York: Guilford Press.

Rosenberg, H. (1993). Prediction of controlled drinking by alcoholics and problem drinkers. *Psychol. Bull., 113*(1), 129–139.

Rosenberg, J., & Rosenbereg, S. (Eds.). (2006). *Community mental health: Challenges for the 21st century.* New York: Routledge.

Rosenberg, S. D., & Mueser, K. T. (2008). Trauma and posttraumatic stress syndromes. In K. T. Mueser & D. V. Jeste (Eds.), *Clinical handbook of schizophrenia* (pp. 447–458). New York: Guilford Press.

Rosenberg, T., & Pace, M. (2006). Burnout among mental health professionals: Special considerations for the marriage and family therapist. *J. Marital Fam. Ther., 32*(1), 87–99.

Rosenfeld, B. (2004). Influence of depression and psychosocial factors on physician-assisted suicide. In B. Rosenfeld, *Assisted suicide and the right to die: The interface of social science, public policy, and medical ethics* (pp. 77–93). Washington, DC: American Psychological Association.

Rosenhan, D. L. (1973). On being sane in insane places. *Science, 179*(4070), 250–258.

Rosenheck, R., & Fontana, A. (1996). Race and outcome of treatment for veterans suffering from PTSD. *J. Traum. Stress, 9,* 343–351.

Rosenthal, M. B., Berndt, E. R., Donohue, J. M., Frank, R. G., & Epstein, A. M. (2002). Promotion of prescription drugs to consumers. *N. Engl. J. Med., 346*(7), 498–505.

Rosenthal, N. E., & Blehar, M. C. (Eds.). (1989). *Seasonal affective disorders and phototherapy.* New York: Guilford Press.

Rosenthal, R. (1966). *Experimenter effects in behavioral research.* New York: Appleton–Century–Crofts.

Rosenthal, R., & Jacobson, L. (1968). *Pygmalion in the classroom.* New York: Holt, Rinehart & Winston.

Rosenthal, R. N., & Levounis, P. (2005). Polysubstance use, abuse, and dependence. In R. J. Frances, A. H. Mack, & S. I. Miller (Eds.), *Clinical textbook of addictive disorders* (3rd ed., pp. 245–270). New York: Guilford Press.

Rosenzweig, M. R. (1996). Aspects of the search for neural mechanisms of memory. In J.T. Spence, J. M. Darley, & D. J. Foss (Eds.), *Annual review of psychology* (Vol. 47). Palo Alto, CA: Annual Reviews.

Ross, C. A., & Gahan, P. (1988). Techniques in the treatment of multiple personality disorder. *Amer. J. Psychother., 42*(1), 40–52.

Ross, C. A., Miller, S. D., Bjornson, L., Reagor, P., Fraser, G. A., & Anderson, G. (1991). Abuse histories in 102 cases of multiple personality disorder. *Canad. J. Psychiat., 36,* 97–101.

Rossler, W., Lauber, C., Angst, J., Haker, H., Gamma, A., Eich, D., et al. (2007). The use of complementary and alternative medicine in the general population: Results from a longitudinal community study. *Psychol. Med., 37*(1), 73–84.

Roth, A., & Fonagy, P. (2005). *What works for whom? A critical review of psychotherapy research* (2nd ed.). New York: Guilford Press.

Roth, B. L., Hanizavareh, S. M., & Blum, A. E. (2004). Serotonin receptors represent highly favorable molecular targets for cognitive enhancement in schizophrenia and other disorders. *Psychopharmacology, 174,* 17–24.

Rothbaum, B. O., Foa, E. B., Riggs, D. S., Murdock, T., & Walsh, W. (1992). A prospective examination of posttraumatic stress disorder in rape victims. *J. Traum. Stress, 5*(3), 455–475.

Rowan, P. (2005, July 31). Cited in J. Thompson, "Hungry for love": Why 11 million of us have serious issues with food. *Independent on Sunday.*

Roy, A. (1992). Genetics, biology, and suicide in the family. In R. W. Maris, A. L. Berman, et al. (Eds.), *Assessment and prediction of suicide* (pp. xxii, 697). New York: Guilford Press.

Roy-Byrne, P. P. (2005). The GABA-benzodiazepine receptor complex: Structure, function, and role in anxiety. *J. Clin. Psychiat., 66*(Suppl. 2), 14–20.

Roy-Byrne, P., Arguelles, L., Vitek, M. E., Goldberg, J., Keane, T. M., True, W. R., et al. (2004). Persistence and change of PTSD symptomatology: A longitudinal co-twin control analysis of the Vietnam Era Twin Registry. *Soc. Psychiat. Psychiatr. Epidemiol., 39*(9), 681–685.

Roysamb, E. (2006). Personality and well-being. In M. E. Vollrath (Ed.), *Handbook of personality and health* (pp. 115–134). New York: John Wiley & Sons.

Rozee, P. D. (2005). Resistance: Successes and challenges. In A. Barnes (Ed.), *The handbook of women, psychology, and the law* (pp. 265–279). New York: Wiley.

Rubertsson, C., Waldenstrom, U., Wickberg, B., Radestad, I., & Hildingsson, I. (2005). Depressive mood in early pregnancy and post-partum: Prevalence and women at risk in a national Swedish sample. *J. Reprod. Infant Psychol., 23*(2), 155–166.

Rubin, E. H. (2005). Psychiatry and old age. In E. H. Rubin & C. F. Zorumski (Eds.), *Adult psychiatry* (2nd ed.). Oxford, England: Blackwell Publishing.

Rubinstein, S., & Caballero, B. (2000). Is Miss America an undernourished role model? *JAMA, 283*(12), 1569.

Rudd, M. D., Berman, L., Joiner, T. E., Nock, M., Mandrusiak, M., Van Orden, K., et al. (2006). Warning signs for suicide: Theory, research, and clinical application. *Suicide Life-Threat. Behav., 36*, 255–262.

Rufer, M., Hand, I., Alsleben, H., Braatz, A., Ortmann, J., Katenkamp, B., et al. (2005). Long-term course and outcome of obsessive-compulsive patients after cognitive-behavioral therapy in combination with either fluvoxamine or placebo: A 7-year follow-up of a randomized double-blind trial. *Eur. Arch. Psychiat. Clin. Neurosci., 255*(2), 121–128.

Rurup, M. L., Onwuteaka-Philipsen, B. D., Van Der Wal., G., Van Der Heide, A., & Van Der Mass, P. J. (2005). A "suicide pill" for older people: Attitudes of physicians, the general population, and relatives of patients who died after euthanasia or physician-assisted suicide in The Netherlands. *Death Stud., 29*(6), 519–534.

Ruscio, A. M., Brown, T. A., Chiu, W. T., Sareen, J., Stein, M. B., & Kessler, R. C. (2008). Social fears and social phobia in the USA: Results from the National Comorbidity Survey Replication. *Psychol. Med., 38*(1), 15–28.

Ruscio, A. M., Chiu, W. T., Roy-Byrne, P., Stang, P. E., Stein, D. J., Wittchen, H. U., & Kessler, R. C. (2007). Broadening the definition of generalized anxiety disorder: Effects on prevalence and associations with other disorders in the National Comorbidity Survey Replication. *J. Anx. Disorders, 21*(5), 662–676.

Rush, A. J., & Frances, A. (2000). Expert consensus guideline series: Treatment of psychiatric and behavioral problems in mental retardation. *Amer. J. Ment. Retard., 105*(3), 159–228.

Russell, G. (1979). Bulimia nervosa: An ominous variant of anorexia nervosa. *Psychol. Med., 9*(3), 429–448.

Russell, M. C., Silver, S. M., Rogers, S., & Darnell, J. N. (2007). Responding to an identified need: A joint Department of Defense/Department of Veterans Affairs training program in eye movement desensitization and reprocessing (EMDR) for clinicians providing trauma services. *Inter. J. Stress Manag., 14*, 61–71.

Russell, T. (2007). Reducing stress at work. [Electronic version]. *Human Resources*, May 1, 2007.

Russo, N. F., & Tartaro, J. (2008). Women and mental health. In F. L. Denmark & M. A. Paludi (Eds.), *Psychology of women: A handbook of issues and theories* (2nd ed., pp. 440–483). Westport, CT: Praeger Publishers.

Ruta, N., & Cohen, L. S. (1998). Postpartum mood disorders: Diagnosis and treatment guidelines. *J. Clin. Psychiat., 59*(Suppl 2), 34–40.

Ruuska, J., Kaltiala-Heino, R., Rantanen, P., & Koivisto, A. M. (2005). Psychopathological distress predicts suicidal ideation and self-harm in adolescent eating disorder outpatients. *Eur. Child Adol. Psychiat., 14*(5), 276–281.

Rystedt, I. B., & Bartels, S. J. (2008). Medical comorbidity. In K. T. Mueser & D.V. Jeste (Eds.), *Clinical handbook of schizophrenia* (pp. 424–436). New York: Guilford Press.

Saba, G., Mekaoui, L., Leboyer, M., & Schurhoff, F. (2007). Patients' health literacy in psychotic disorders. *Neuropsychiat. Dis. Treat., 3*(4), 511–517.

Sackett, P. R., Borneman, M. J., & Connelly, B. S. (2008). High-stakes testing in higher education and employment. *Amer. Psychologist, 63*(4), 215–227.

Sacks, O. (2000, May). *An anthropologist on Mars: Some personal perspectives on autism.* Keynote address. Eden Institute Foundation's Sixth Annual Princeton Lecture Series on Autism. Princeton, NJ.

Sadavoy, J. (2004). *Psychotropic drugs and the elderly: Fast facts.* New York: W. W. Norton.

Sadavoy, J., Meier, R., & Ong, A. Y. M. (2004). Barriers to access to mental health services for ethnic seniors: The Toronto Study. *Canad. J. Psychiat., 49*(3), 192–199.

Sadock, B. J., & Sadock, V. A. (2007). *Synopsis of psychiatry: Behavioral sciences/clinical psychiatry* (10th ed.). Philadelphia: Wolters Kluwer/Lippincott Williams & Wilkins.

Safer, D. (1994). The impact of recent lawsuits on methylphenidates sales. *Clin. Pediatr., 33*(3), 166–168.

Safer, D., & Krager, J. (1992). Effect of a media blitz and a threatened lawsuit on stimulant treatment. *JAMA, 268*(8), 1004–1007.

Safren, S. A., Gershuny, B. S., Marzol, P., Otto, M. W., & Pollack, M. H. (2002). History of childhood abuse in panic disorder, social phobia, and generalized anxiety disorder. *J. Nerv. Ment. Dis., 190*(7), 453–456.

Sahoo, F. M., Sahoo, K., & Harichandan, S. (2005). Five big factors of personality and human happiness. *Soc. Sci. Inter., 21*(1), 20–28.

Sajatovic, M., Madhusoodanan, S., & Fuller, M. A. (2008). Clozapine. In K. T. Mueser & D.V. Jeste (Eds.), *Clinical handbook of schizophrenia* (pp. 178–185). New York: Guilford Press.

Sakheim, D. K., Hess, E. P., & Chivas, A. (1988). General principles for short-term inpatient work with multiple personality-disorder patients. *Psychotherapy, 24*, 117–124.

Salekin, R. T., & Rogers, R. (2001). Treating patients found not guilty by reason of insanity. In J. B. Ashford, B. D. Sales, & W. H. Reid (Eds.) *Treating adult and juvenile offenders with special needs* (pp. 171–195). Washington, DC: American Psychological Association.

Sales, B. D., & Shuman, D. W. (2005). *Experts in court: Reconciling law, science, and professional knowledge.* Washington, DC: American Psychological Association.

Sales, E., Baum, M., & Shore, B. (1984). Victim readjustment following assault. *J. Soc. Issues, 40*(1), 117–136.

Salkovskis, P. M. (1985). Obsessional-compulsive problems: A cognitive-behavioural analysis. *Behav. Res. Ther., 23*, 571–584.

Salkovskis, P. M. (1999). Understanding and treating obsessive-compulsive disorder. *Behav. Res. Ther., 37*(Suppl. 1), S29–S52.

Salkovskis, P. M., Thorpe, S. J., Wahl, K., Wroe, A. L., & Forrester, E. (2003). Neutralizing increases discomfort associated with obsessional thoughts: An experimental study with obsessional patients. *J. Abnorm. Psychol., 112*(4), 709–715.

Salkovskis, P. M., & Westbrook, D. (1989). Behaviour therapy and obsessional ruminations: Can failure be turned into success? *Behav. Res. Ther., 27*, 149–160.

Salome, F., Boyer, P., & Fayol, M. (2002). Written but not oral verbal production is preserved in young schizophrenic patients. *Psychiat. Res., 111*(2–3), 137–145.

Salvatore, G., Nicolo, G., & Dimaggio, G. (2005). Impoverished dialogical relationship patterns in paranoid personality disorder. *Amer. J. Psychother., 59*(3), 247–265.

Salzer, M. S., Kaplan, K., & Atay, J. (2006). State psychiatric hospital census after the 1999 Olmstead decision: Evidence of decelerating deinstitutionalization. *Psychiatr. Serv., 57*(10), 1501–1504.

SAMHSA. (2007, January 26). *The NSDUH Report: Methamphetamine use.* Washington DC: Department of Health and Human Services.

SAMHSA. (2007, March 13). *Emergency room visits climb for misuse of prescription and over-the-counter drugs.* Washington DC: Department of Health and Human Services.

SAMHSA. (2008, June 16). *National survey on drug use and health.* Washington DC: Department of Health and Human Services.

SAMHSA. (2008, June 16). *Racial and ethnic groups: Reports and data.* Washington DC: Department of Health and Human Services.

Samnaliev, M., & Clark, R. E. (2008). The economics of schizophrenia. In K. T. Mueser & D.V. Jeste (Eds.), *Clinical handbook of schizophrenia* (pp. 507–515). New York: Guilford Press.

Sampath, G., Shah, A., Kraska, J., & Soni, S. D. (1992). Neuroleptic discontinuation in the very stable schizophrenic patient: Relapse rates and serum neuroleptic levels. *Human Psychopharmacol. Clin. Exp., 7*(4), 255–264.

Sample, I. (2005, November 30). Mental illness link to art and sex. *Guardian.* Retrieved July 6, 2007, from http://www.guardian.co.uk

Samuel, V. J., Curtis, S., Thornell, A., George, P., Taylor, A., Brome, D. R., et al. (1997). The unexplored void of ADHD and African-American research: A review of the literature. *J. Attent. Disorders, 1*(4), 197–207.

Samuels, J., Eaton, W. W., Bienvenu, J., III, Brown, C. H., Costa, P. T., Jr., & Nestadt, G. (2002). Prevalence and correlates of personality disorders in a community sample. *Brit. J. Psychiat., 180*, 536–542.

Sandler, I. N., Wolchik, S. A., & Ayers, T. S. (2008). Resilience rather than recovery: A contextual framework on adaptation following bereavement. *Death Stud., 32*(1), 59–73.

Sandler, M. (1990). Monoamine oxidase inhibitors in depression: History and mythology. *J. Psychopharmacol., 4*(3), 136–139.

Sands, J. M., & Miller, L. E. (1991). Effects of moon phase and other temporal variable on absenteeism. *Psychol. Rep., 69*(3, Pt. 1), 959–962.

Sano, M. (2003). Noncholinergic treatment options for Alzheimer's disease. *J. Clin. Psychiat., 64*(Suppl. 9), 23–28.

Sansone, R. A., Levitt, J. L., & Sansone, L. A. (2005). The prevalence of personality disorders among those with eating disorders. *Eat. Disord.: J. Treat. Prev., 13*(1), 7–21.

Sansone, R. A., Songer, D. A., & Miller, K. A. (2005). Childhood abuse, mental healthcare utilization, self-harm behavior, and multiple psychiatric diagnoses among inpatients with and without a borderline diagnosis. *Comprehen. Psychiat., 46,* 117–120.

Santiseban, D. A., Muir-Malcolm, J. A., Mitrani, V. B., & Szapocznik, J. (2001). Chapter 16: Integrating the study of ethnic culture and family psychology intervention science. In H. A. Liddle, D. A. Santiseban, R. F. Levant, & J. H. Bray (Eds.), *Family psychology: Science-based interventions* (pp. 331–352). Washington, DC: American Psychological Association.

Santtila, P., Sandnabba, N. K., Alison, L., & Nordling, N. (2002). Investigating the underlying structure in sadomasochistically oriented behavior. *Arch. Sex. Behav., 31*(2), 185–196.

Santtila, P., Sandnabba, N. K., & Nordling, N. (2006). Sadomasochism. In R. D. McAnulty & M. M. Burnette (Eds.), *Sex and sexuality, Vol. 3: Sexual deviation and sexual offenses.* Westport, CT: Praeger Publishers.

Sapolsky, R. M. (2000). Glucocorticoids and hippocampal atrophy in neuropsychiatric disorders. *Arch. Gen. Psychiat., 57,* 925–935.

Sapolsky, R. M. (2004). Is impaired neurogenesis relevant to the affective symptoms of depression? *Biol. Psychiat., 56,* 137–139.

Sar, V., Akyuz, G., & Dogan, O. (2007). Prevalence of dissociative disorders among women in the general population. *Psychiat. Res., 149*(1–3), 169–176.

Sar, V., Akyuz, G., Kundakci, T., Kiziltan, E., & Dogan, O. (2004). Childhood trauma, dissociation, and psychiatric comorbidity in patients with conversion disorder. *Amer. J. Psychiat., 161*(12), 2271–2276.

Sareen, J., Enns, M. W., & Cox, B. J. (2004). Potential for misuse of sedatives. *Amer. J. Psychiat., 161,* 1722–1723.

Sarid, O., Anson, O., Yaari, A., & Margalith, M. (2004). Coping styles and changes in humoural reaction during academic stress. *Psychol. Health Med. 9*(1), 85–98.

Sarro, S., & Sarro, V. (2004). Koro syndrome: A case report. *Transcult. Psychiatry, 41,* 558–560.

Sarter, M., Bruno, J. P., & Parikh, V. (2007). Abnormal neurotransmitter release underlying behavioral and cognitive disorders: Toward concepts of dynamic and function-specific dysregulation. *Neuropsychopharmacology, 32*(7), 1452–1461.

Sarwer, D. B., Gibbons, L. M., & Crerand, C. E. (2004). Treating body dysmorphic disorder with cognitive-behavior therapy. *Psychiatr. Ann., 32*(12), 934–941.

Sassi, R. B., & Soares, J. C. (2002). Neural circuitry and signaling in bipolar disorder. In G. B. Kaplan & Hammer, R. P. (Eds.), *Brain circuitry and signaling in psychiatry: Basic science and clinical implications.* Washington, DC: American Psychiatric Publishing.

Satir, V. (1964). *Conjoint family therapy: A guide to therapy and technique.* Palo Alto, CA: Science & Behavior Books.

Satir, V. (1967). *Conjoint family therapy* (Rev. ed.). Palo Alto, CA: Science & Behavior Books.

Satir, V. (1987). Going behind the obvious: The psychotherapeutic journey. In J. K. Zeig (Ed.), *The evolution of psychotherapy.* New York: Brunner/Mazel.

Satterfield, J. M. (2002). Culturally sensitive cognitive-behavioral therapy for depression with low-income and minority clients. In T. Patterson & F. W. Kaslow (Eds.), *Comprehensive handbook of psychotherapy: Cognitive-behavioral approaches* (Vol. 2, pp. 519–545). Hoboken, NJ: Wiley.

Saudino, K. J., Pedersen, N. L., Lichenstein, P., McClearn, G. E., & Plomin, R. (1997). Can personality explain genetic influence on life events? *J. Pers. Soc. Psychol., 72*(1), 196–206.

Saudino, K. J., Wertz, A. E., Gagne, J. R., & Chawla, S. (2004). Night and day: Are siblings as different in temperament as parents say they are? *J. Pers. Soc. Psychol., 87*(5), 698–706.

Savic, I., Berglund, H., Lindström, P., & Gustafsson, J. A. (2005). Brain response to putative pheromones in homosexual men. *PNAS Proceedings of the National Academy of Sciences of the United States of America, 102*(20), 7356–7361.

Savla, G. N., Moore, D. J., & Palmer, B. W. (2008). Cognitive functioning. In K. T. Mueser & D. V. Jeste (Eds.), *Clinical handbook of schizophrenia* (pp. 91–99). New York: Guilford Press.

Sawle, G. A., & Kear, C. J. (2001). Adult attachment style and pedophilia: A developmental perspective. *Inter. J. Offend. Ther. Compar. Crimin., 45*(1), 32–50.

Scelfo, J. (2005, June 13). Bad girls go wild. *Newsweek,* 66–67.

Schacter, D. L. (2001). *The seven sins of memory.* New York and Boston: Houghton Mifflin.

Scher, C. D., Steidtmann, D., Luxton, D., & Ingram, R. E. (2006). Specific phobia: A common problem, rarely treated. In T. G. Plante (Ed.), *Mental disorders of the new millennium, Vol. 1: Behavioral issues.* Westport, CT: Praeger Publishers.

Scheuermann, B., Webber, J., Boutot, E. A., & Goodwin, M. (2003). Problems with personnel preparation in autism spectrum disorders. *Focus Autism Other Dev. Disabil., 18,* 197–206.

Scheuffgen, K., Happe, F., Anderson, M., & Frith, U. (2000). High "intelligence," low "IQ"? Speed of processing and measured IQ in children with autism. *Dev. Psychopathol., 12*(1), 83–90.

Schiffman, J., Abrahamson, A., Cannon, T., LaBrie, J., Parnas, J. Schulsinger, F., et al. (2001). Early rearing factors in schizophrenia. *Inter. J. Ment. Hlth., 30*(1), 3–16.

Schiffman, J., LaBrie, J., Carter, J., Cannon, T., Schulsinger, F., Parnas, J., et al. (2002). Perception of parent-child relationships in high-risk families, and adult schizophrenia outcome of offspring. *J. Psychiatr. Res., 36*(1), 41–47.

Schiffman, J., Maeda, J. A., Hayashi, K., Michelsen, N., Sorensen, H. J., Ekstrom, M., et al. (2006). Premorbid childhood ocular alignment abnormalities and adult schizophrenia-spectrum disorder. *Schizo. Res., 81*(2–3), 253–260.

Schiffman, J., Pestle, S., Mednick, S., Ekstrom, M., Sorensen, H., & Mednick S. (2005). Childhood laterally and adult schizophrenia spectrum disorders: A prospective investigation. *Schizo. Res., 72*(2–3), 151–160.

Schiffman, J., Walker, E., Ekstrom, M., Schulsinger, F., Sorensen, H., & Mednick S. (2004). Childhood videotaped social and neuromotor precursors of schizophrenia: A prospective investigation. *Amer. J. Psychiat., 161*(11), 2021–2027.

Schildkraut, J. J. (1965). The catecholamine hypothesis of affective disorders: A review of supporting evidence. *Amer. J. Psychiat., 122*(5), 509–522.

Schlenger, W. E., Caddell, J. M., Ebert, L., Jordan, B. K., Rourke, K. M., Wilson, D., et al. (2002). Psychological reactions to terrorist attacks. *JAMA, 288*(5), 581–588.

Schlesinger, J., & Ismail, H. (Eds.). (2004). Heroic, not disordered: Creativity and mental illness revisited: Comment. *Brit. J. Psychiat., 184*(4), 363–364.

Schmidtke, A., & Häfner, H. (1988). The Werther effect after television films: New evidence for an old hypothesis. *Psychol. Med., 18,* 665–676.

Schneider, F., Boehner, H., Habel, U., Salloum, J. B., Stierstorfer, A., Hummel, T. C., et al. (2002). Risk factors for postoperative delirium in vascular surgery. *Gen. Hosp. Psychiat., 24*(1), 28–34.

Schneider, K. J. (2003). Existential-humanistic psychotherapies. In A. S. Gurman & S. B. Messer (Eds.), *Essential psychotherapies: Theory and practice* (2nd ed.). New York: Guilford Press.

Schneider, K. J. (2004). *Rediscovery of awe: Splendor, mystery and the fluid center of life.* St. Paul, MN: Paragon House.

Schneider, K. J. (Ed.). (2008). *Existential integrative psychotherapy: Guideposts to the core of practice.* New York: Routledge/Taylor & Francis Group.

Schneider, K. L., & Shenassa, E. (2008). Correlates of suicide ideation in a population-based sample of cancer patients. *J. Psychosoc. Oncology, 26*(2) 49–62.

Schneider, M. F., Kern, R. M., & Curlette, W. L. (2007). Narcissism, imagery, early recollections, and social interest. *J. Individ. Psychol., 63*(2), 123–125.

Schneider, R. M. (2006). Group bereavement support for spouses who are grieving the loss of a partner to cancer. *Soc. Work Groups, 29*(2–3), 259–278.

Schottenfeld, R. S. (2008). Opioid maintenance treatment. In H. D. Kleber & M. Galanter (Eds.), *The American Psychiatric Publishing textbook of substance abuse treatment* (4th ed., pp. 289–308). Arlington, VA: American Psychiatric Publishing.

Schreiber, F. R. (1973). *Sybil.* Chicago: Regnery.

Schreiber, G. B., Robins, M., Striegel-Moore, R., Obarzanek, E., Morrison, J. A., & Wright, D. J. (1996). Weight medication efforts reported by Black and White preadolescent girls: National heart, lung, and blood institute growth and health study, *Pediatrics, 98,* 63–70.

Schreibman, L., & Koegel, R. L. (2005). Training for parents of children with autism: Pivotal responses, generalization, and individualization of interventions. In E. D. Hibbs & P. S. Jensen (Eds.), *Psychosocial treatments for child and adolescent disorders: Empirically based strategies for clinical practice* (2nd ed., pp. 605–631). Washington, DC: American Psychological Association.

Schroder, M., & Carroll, R. (1999). Sexological outcomes of gender reassignment surgery. *J. Sex Educ. Ther., 24*(3), 137–146.

Schuel, H., Burkman, L. J., Lippes, J. Crickard, K., Mahony, M. C., Guiffrida, A., et al. (2002). Evidence that anandamide-signalling regulates human sperm functions required for fertilization. *Molecular Reproduction and Development, 63,* 376–387.

Schulte, A. (2003, August 16). *Prescriptions for antidepressants by psychiatrists and general practitioners: The effect of patient characteristics.* Paper presented at the annual meeting of the American Sociological Association, Atlanta GA. Retrieved August 24, 2008, from www.allacademic.com/meta/p107107_index.html

Schultz, L. T., Heimberg, R. G., & Rodebaugh, T. L. (2008). Social anxiety disorder. In M. Hersen & J. Rosqvist (Eds.), Handbook of psychological assessment, case conceptualization, and treatment, Vol. 1: Adults (pp. 204–236). Hoboken, NJ: John Wiley & Sons.

Schultz, L. T., Heimberg, R. G., Rodebaugh, T. L., Schneier, F. R., Liebowitz, M. R., & Telch, M. J. (2006). The Appraisal of Social Concerns scale: Psychometric validation with a clinical sample of patients with social anxiety disorder. Behav. Ther., 37(4), 393–405.

Schultz, W. (2006). Behavioral theories and the neurophysiology of reward. Annu. Rev. Psychol., 57, 87–115.

Schumaker, J. F. (2001). The age of insanity: Modernity and mental health. Westport, CT: Praeger.

Schuster, M. A., Stein, B. D., Jaycox, L. H., Collins, R. L., Marshall, G. N., Elliot, M. N., et al. (2001). A national survey of stress reactions after the September 11, 2001, terrorist attacks. N. Engl. J. Med., 20, 1507–1512.

Schuurmans, J., Comijs, H. C., Beekman, A. T. F., de Beurs, E., Deeg, D. J. H., Emmelkamp, P. M. G., et al. (2005). The outcome of anxiety disorders in older people at 6-year follow-up: Results from the Longitudinal Aging Study Amsterdam. Acta Psychiatr. Scandin., 111(6), 420–428.

Schwalb, M. (1999). Interviewed in M. S. Baum, Autism: Locked in a solitary world. HealthState, 17(2), 18–22.

Schwartz, B. S., & Stewart, W. F. (2007). Lead and cognitive function in adults: A questions and answers approach to a review of the evidence for cause, treatment, and prevention. Inter. Rev. Psychiat., 19(6), 671–692.

Schwartz, J. B. (2000). Nutraceuticals: Sorting out fact, fiction, and uncertainty. J. Gend. Specif. Med., 3(4), 30–32, 37.

Schwartz, J. M., & Begley, S. (2002). The mind and the brain: Neuroplasticity and the power of mental force. New York: Regan Books/Harper Collins.

Schwartz, S. (1993). Classic studies in abnormal psychology. Mountain View, CA: Mayfield Publishing.

Schwartz, S., & Johnson, J. J. (1985). Psychopathology of childhood. New York: Pergamon Press.

Scott, E. L., Eng, W., & Heimberg, R. G. (2002). Ethnic differences in worry in a nonclinical population. Depress. Anx., 15(2), 79–82.

Scott, H. (2008). The "gentler sex": Patterns in female serial murder. In R. N. Kocsis (Ed.), Serial murder and the psychology of violent crimes (pp. 179–196). Totowa, NJ: Humana Press.

Scott, J., & Colom, F. (2005). Psychosocial treatments for bipolar disorders. Psychiatr. Clin. N. Amer., 28(2), 371–384.

Sedaris, D. (2000). Me talk pretty one day. Boston: Little, Brown.

Sedvall, G. (1990). Monoamines and schizophrenia. International Symposium: Development of a new antipsychotic: Remoxipride. Acta Psychiatr. Scandin., 82(Suppl. 358), 7–13.

Seelinger, G., & Mannel, M. (2007). Drug treatment in juvenile depression—Is St. John's wort a safe and effective alternative? Child Adol. Ment. Hlth., 12(3), 143–149.

Seeman, M. V. (2008). Gender. In K. T. Mueser & D.V. Jeste (Eds.), Clinical handbook of schizophrenia (pp. 575–580). New York: Guilford Press.

Segal, R. (2008). The national association for retarded citizens. Silver Spring, MD: The Arc.

Segraves, T., & Althof, S. (2002). Psychotherapy and pharmacotherapy for sexual dysfunctions. In P. E. Nathan & J. M. Gorman (Eds.), A guide to treatments that work (2nd ed., pp. 497–524). London: Oxford University Press.

Segrin, C. (2000). Social skills deficits associated with depression. Clin. Psychol. Rev., 20(3), 379–403.

Segrin, C. (2001). Interpersonal processes in psychological problems. New York: Guilford Press.

Segrin, C., Powell, H. L., Givertz, M., & Brackin, A. (2003). Symptoms of depression, relational quality, and loneliness in dating relationships. Pers. Relationships, 10(1), 25–36.

Seiden, R. H. (1981). Mellowing with age: Factors influencing the nonwhite suicide rate. Inter. J. Aging Human Dev., 13, 265–284.

Seidman, L. J. (1990). The neuropsychology of schizophrenia: A neurodevelopmental and case study approach. J. Neuropsych. Clin. Neurosci., 2(3), 301–312.

Seidman, S. N., & Rieder, R. O. (1995). Sexual behavior through the life cycle: An empirical approach. In J. M. Oldham & M. B. Riba (Eds.), American Psychiatric Press review of psychiatry (Vol. 14). Washington, DC: American Psychiatric Press.

Seligman, M. E. P. (1971). Phobias and preparedness. Behav. Ther., 2, 307–320.

Seligman, M. E. P. (1975). Helplessness. San Francisco: Freeman.

Seligman, M. E. P. (2007). Coaching and positive psychology. Austral. Psychologist, 42(4), 266–267.

Seligman, M. E. P., & Steen, T. A. (2005). Positive psychology progress: Empirical validation of interventions. Amer. Psychologist, 60(5), 410–421.

Seligman, M. E. P., Castellon, C., Cacciola, J., Schulman, P., et al. (1988). Explanatory style change during cognitive therapy for unipolar depression. J. Abnorm. Psychol., 97(1), 13–18.

Selkoe, D. J. (1991). Amyloid protein and Alzheimer's disease. Scientif. Amer., 265, 68–78.

Selkoe, D. J. (1992). Alzheimer's disease: New insights into an emerging epidemic. J. Geriat. Psychiat., 25(2), 211–227.

Selkoe, D. J. (2000). The origins of Alzheimer's disease: A is for amyloid. JAMA, 283(12), 1615–1617.

Selkoe, D. J. (2002). Alzheimer's disease is a synaptic failure. Science, 298(5594), 789–791.

Selling, L. S. (1940). Men against madness. New York: Greenberg.

Selling, L. S. (1942). The psychiatric aspects of the pathological liar. Nerv. Child, 1, 335–350.

Selman, R. (1980). The growth of interpersonal understanding. New York: Academic Press.

Selye, H. (1974). Stress without distress. Philadelphia: Lippincott.

Selye, H. (1976). Stress in health and disease. Woburn, MA: Butterworth.

Senior, J., Hayes, A. J., Pratt, D., Thomas, S. D., Fahy, T., Leese, M., et al. (2007). The identification and management of suicide risk in local prisons. J. Forens. Psychiat. Psychol., 18(3), 368–380.

Serlin, I. (2005). Spiritual diversity and clinical practice. In J. L. Chin (Ed.), The psychology of prejudice and discrimination: Disability, religion, physique, and other traits (Vol. 4, pp. 27–49). Westport, CT: Praeger Publishers/Greenwood Publishing Group.

Serpell, L., & Treasure, J. (2002). Bulimia nervosa: Friend or foe? The pros and cons of bulimia nervosa. Inter. J. Eat. Disorders, 32(2), 164–170.

Seto, M. C., Maric, A., & Barbaree, H. E. (2001). The role of pornography in the etiology of sexual aggression. Aggress. Viol. Behav., 6(1), 35–53.

Sexton, T. L., & Alexander, J. F. (2002). Family-based empirically supported interventions. J. Couns. Psychol., 30(2), 238–261.

Shadish, W. R., & Baldwin, S. A. (2005). Effects of behavioral marital therapy: A meta-analysis of randomized controlled trials. J. Cons. Clin. Psychol., 73(1), 6–14.

Shafran, R. (2005). Cognitive-behavioral models of OCD. In J. S. Abramowitz & A. C. Houts (Eds.), Concepts and controversies in obsessive-compulsive disorder. New York: Springer Science + Business Media.

Shafran, R., Cooper, Z., & Fairburn, C. G. (2002). Clinical perfectionism: A cognitive-behavioural analysis. Behav. Res. Ther., 40(7), 773–791.

Shafranske, E. P., & Sperry, L. (2005). Addressing the spiritual dimension in psychotherapy: Introduction and overview. In L. Sperry & E. P. Shafranske (Eds.). Spiritually oriented psychotherapy. Washington, DC: American Psychological Association.

Shapiro, E. R. (2004). Discussion of Ernst Prelinger's "Thoughts on hate and aggression." Psychoanal. Study Child, 39, 44–51.

Shapiro, J. L., & Bernadett–Shapiro, S. (2006). Narcissism: Greek tragedy, psychological syndrome, cultural norm. In T. G. Plante (Ed.), Mental disorders of the new millennium, Vol. 1: Behavioral issues. Westport, CT: Praeger Publishers.

Shapiro, S. L., & Gavin, A. (2006). Body dysmorphic disorder: When does concern about appearance become pathological? In T. G. Plante (Ed.), Mental disorders of the new millennium, Vol. 3: Biology and function. Westport, CT: Praeger Publishers.

Sharf, R. S. (2008). Theories of psychotherapy and counseling: Concepts and cases (4th ed.). Belmont: Thomson Brooks Cole.

Sharma, M. (Ed.). (2005). Editorial: Improving interventions for prevention and control of alcohol use in college students. J. Alcohol Drug Educ., 49(2), 3–6.

Sharma, V., Khan, M., & Smith, A. (2005). A closer look at treatment resistant depression: Is it due to a bipolar diathesis? J. Affect. Disorders, 84(2–3), 251–257.

Shastry, B. S. (2005). Bipolar disorder: An update. Neurochem. Inter., 46(4), 273–279.

Shaughnessy, M. F., Main, D., & Madewell, J. (2007). An interview with Irvin Yalom. N. Amer. J. Psychol., 9(3), 511–518.

Shaw, K. (2004). Oddballs and eccentrics. Edison, NJ: Castle Books.

Shcherbatykh, I., & Carpenter, D. O. (2007). The role of metals in the etiology of Alzheimer's disease. J. Alzheimer's Dis., 11, 191–205.

Shear, K., Jin, R., Ruscio. A. M., Walters, E. E., & Kessler, R. C. (2006). Prevalence and correlates of estimated DSM-IV child and adult separation anxiety disorder in the National Comorbidity Survey Replication. *Amer. J. Psychiat.*, 163(6), 1074–1083.

Shedler, J., & Westen, D. (2004). Dimensions of personality pathology: An alternative to the five-factor model. *Amer. J. Psychiat.*, 161, 1743–1754.

Shenefelt, P. D. (2003). Hypnosis-facilitated relaxation using self-guided imagery during dermatologic procedures. *Amer. J. Clin. Hyp.*, 45(3), 225–232.

Shenk, D. (2001). *The forgetting: Alzheimer's: Portrait of an epidemic.* New York: Doubleday.

Sher, L., Oquendo, M. A., Falgalvy, H. C., Grunebaum, M. F., Burke, A. K., Zalsman, G., et al. (2005). The relationship of aggression to suicidal behavior in depressed patients with a history of alcoholism. *Addic. Behav.*, 30(6), 1144–1153.

Sheras, P., & Worchel, S. (1979). *Clinical psychology: A social psychological approach.* New York: Van Nostrand.

Sherlock, R. (1983). Suicide and public policy: A critique of the "new consensus." *Bioethics*, 4, 58–70.

Sherrer, M. V., & O'Hare, T. (2008). Clinical case management. In K. T. Mueser & D. V. Jeste (Eds.), *Clinical handbook of schizophrenia* (pp. 309–318). New York: Guilford Press.

Sherry, A., & Whilde, M. R. (2008). Borderline personality disorder. In M. Hersen & J. Rosqvist (Eds.), *Handbook of psychological assessment, case conceptualization and treatment, Vol. 1: Adults* (pp. 403–437). Hoboken, NJ: John Wiley & Sons.

Sherwood, P. R., Given, C. W., Given, B. A., & Von Eye, A. (2005). Caregiver burden and depressive symptoms: Analysis of common outcomes in caregivers of elderly patients. *J. Aging Hlth.*, 17(2), 125–147.

Shiho, Y., Tohru, T., Shinji, S., Manabu, T., Yuka, T., Eriko, T., et al. (2005). Suicide in Japan: Present condition and prevention measures. *Crisis*, 26(1), 12–19.

Shin, L. M., Wright, C. I., Cannistraro, P. A., Wedig, M. M., McMullin, K. Martis, B., et al. (2005). A functional magnetic resonance imaging study of amygdala and medial prefrontal cortex responses to overtly presented fearful faces in posttraumatic stress disorder. *Arch. Gen. Psychiat.*, 62(3), 273–281.

Shirts, B. H., Kim, J. J., Reich, S., Dickerson, F. B., Yolken, R. H., Devlin, B., & Nimgaonkar, V. L. (2007). Polymorphisms in MICB are associated with human herpes virus seropositivity and schizophrenia risk. *Schizo. Res.*, 94(1–3), 342–353.

Shneidman, E. S. (1963). Orientations toward death: Subintentioned death and indirect suicide. In R. W. White (Ed.), *The study of lives.* New York: Atherton.

Shneidman, E. S. (1973). Suicide notes reconsidered. *Psychiatry*, 36, 379–394.

Shneidman, E. S. (1979). An overview: Personality, motivation, and behavior theories. In L. D. Hankoff & B. Einsidler (Eds.), *Suicide: Theory and clinical aspects.* Littleton, MA: PSG Publishing.

Shneidman, E. S. (1981). Suicide. *Suic. Life-Threat. Behav.*, 11(4), 198–220.

Shneidman, E. S. (1985). *Definition of suicide.* New York: Wiley.

Shneidman, E. S. (1987, March). At the point of no return. *Psychol. Today.*

Shneidman, E. S. (1993). *Suicide as psychache: A clinical approach to self-destructive behavior.* Northvale, NJ: Jason Aronson.

Shneidman, E. S. (2001). *Comprehending suicide: Landmarks in 20th-century suicidology.* Washington, DC: American Psychological Association.

Shneidman, E. S. (2005). Anodyne psychotherapy for suicide: A psychological view of suicide. *Clin. Neuropsychiat.: J. Treat. Eval.*, 2(1), 7–12.

Shneidman, E. S. (2005). How I read. *Suic. Life-Threat. Behav.*, 35(2), 117–120.

Shneidman, E. S. (2005). Prediction of suicide revisited: A brief methodological note. *Suic. Life-Threat. Behav.*, 35(1), 1–2.

Shneidman, E. S., & Mandelkorn, P. (1983, 1967). How to prevent suicide. *Public Affairs Pamphlets,* New York City.

Shore, D. A. (Ed.). (2007). *The trust crisis in healthcare: Causes, consequences, and cures.* New York: Oxford University Press.

Shuttleworth-Edwards, A. B., Kemp, R. D., Rust, A. L., Muirhead, J. G. L., Hartman, N. P., & Radloff, S. E. (2004). Cross-cultural effects on IQ test performance: A review and preliminary normative indicators on WAIS-III test performance. *J. Clin. Exp. Neuropsychol.*, 26(7), 903–920.

Sibinga, E. M. S., Ottolini, M. C., Duggan, A. K., & Wilson, M. H. (2004). Parent-pediatrician communication about complementary and alternative medicine use for children. *Clin. Pediatr.*, 43(45), 367–373.

Siegel, B., & Ficcaglia, M. (2006). Pervasive developmental disorders. In M. Hersen & J. C. Thomas (Series Eds.) & R. T. Ammerman (Vol. Ed.), *Comprehensive handbook of personality and psychopathology, Vol. 3: Child psychopathology* (pp. 254–71). Hoboken, NJ: Wiley.

Siegel, R. K. (1990). In J. Sherlock, Getting high—Animals do it, too. *USA Today,* p. 1A.

Sierra, M., Phillips, M. L., Lambert, M. V., Senior, C., David, A. S., & Krystal, J. H. (2001). Lamotrigine in the treatment of depersonalization disorder. *J. Clin. Psychiat.*, 62(10), 826–827.

Sigerist, H. E. (1943). *Civilization and disease.* Ithaca, NY: Cornell University Press.

Sikstrom, S., & Soderlund, G. (2007). Stimulus-dependent dopamine release in attention-deficit/hyperactivity disorder. *Psychol. Rev.*, 114(4), 1047–1075.

Silbersweig, D. A., Stern, E., Frith, C., Cahill, C., et al. (1995). A functional neuroanatomy of hallucinations in schizophrenia. *Nature*, 378, 176–179.

Silverman, K., Evans, S. M., Strain, E. C., & Griffiths, R. R. (1992). Withdrawal syndrome after the double-blind cessation of caffeine consumption. *N. Engl. J. Med.*, 327(16), 1109–1114.

Silverstein, M. L. (2007). Descriptive psychopathology and theoretical viewpoints: Paranoid, obsessive-compulsive, and borderline personality disorders. In M. L. Silverstein, *Disorders of the self: A personality-guided approach* (pp. 97–113). Washington, DC: American Psychological Association.

Simard, V., Nielsen, T. A., Tremblay, R. E., Boivin, M., & Montplaisir, J. Y. (2008). Longitudinal study of bad dreams in preschool-aged children: Prevalence, demographic correlates, risk and protective factors. *Sleep*, 31(1), 62–70.

Simeon, D., Greenberg, J., Nelson, D., Schmeidler, J., & Hollander, E. (2005). Dissociation and posttraumatic stress 1 year after the World Trade Center disaster: Follow-up of a longitudinal survey. *J. Clin. Psychiat.*, 6692), 231–237.

Simeon, D., Knutelska, M., Nelson, D., & Guralnik, O. (2003). Feeling unreal: A depersonalization disorder update of 117 cases. *J. Clin. Psychiat.*, 64(9), 990–997.

Simmon, J. (1990). Media and market study. In skin deep: Our national obsession with looks. *Psychol. Today*, 26(3), 96.

Simon, N. (2000). Autism's home in the brain. *Neurology*, 54(1), 269.

Simonoff, E. (2001). Genetic influences on conduct disorder. In J. Hill & B. Maughan (Eds.), *Conduct disorders in childhood and adolescence. Cambridge child and adolescent psychiatry* (pp. 202–234). New York: Cambridge University Press.

Simons, J. S., Gaher, R. M., Jacobs, G. A., Meyer, D., & Johnson-Jimenez, E. (2005). Associations between alcohol use and PTSD symptoms among American Red Cross disaster relief workers responding to the 9/11/2001 attacks. *Amer. J. Drug Alc. Abuse*, 31(2), 285–304.

Simpson, S. G. (1996, January 17). Cited in W. Leary, As fellow traveler of other illness, depression often goes in disguise. *New York Times,* p. C9.

Singh, V., Muzina, D. J., & Calabrese, J. R. (2005). Anticonvulsants in bipolar disorder. *Psychiatr. Clin. N. Amer.*, 28(2), 301–323.

Sit, D., Rothschild, A. J., & Wisner, K. L. (2006). A review of postpartum psychosis. *J. Women's Hlth.*, 15(4), 352–368.

Sizemore, C. C. (1991). *A mind of my own: The woman who was known as "Eve" tells the story of her triumph over multiple personality disorder.* William Morrow.

Sizemore, C. C., & Pittillo, E. S. (1977). *I'm Eve.* Garden City, NY: Doubleday.

Sjolie, I. I. (2002). A logotherapist's view of somatization disorder and a protocol. *Int. For. Logo Therapy*, 25(1), 24–29.

Skelton, G. (2004, May 6). The State; George Skelton/CAPITOL JOURNAL; For mentally ill, ballot box budgeting might be the answer. *Los Angeles Times* [Home ed.], part B, p. 8.

Skodol, A. E. (2005). The borderline diagnosis: Concepts, criteria, and controversies. In J. G. Gunderson & P. D. Hoffman (Eds.), *Understanding and treating borderline personality disorder* (pp. 3–19). Washington, DC: American Psychiatric Publishing.

Skodol, A. E., Gunderson, J. G., McGlashan, T. H., Dyck, I. R., Stout, R. L., Bender, D. S., et al. (2002). Functional impairment in patients with schizotypal, borderline, avoidant, or obsessive-compulsive personality disorder. *Amer. J. Psychiat.*, 159(2), 276–283.

Sloan, D. M. (2002). Does warm weather climate affect eating disorder pathology? *Inter. J. Eat. Disorders*, 32, 240–244.

Sloan, D. M., Mizes, J. C., Helbok, C., & Muck, R. (2004). Efficacy of sertraline for bulimia nervosa. *Inter. J. Eat. Disorders*, 36(1), 48–54.

Sloutsky, V. M., & Fisher, A. V. (2004). Induction and categorization in young children: A similarity-based model. *J. Exp. Psychol. Gen.*, 133(2), 166–188.

Slovenko, R. (1992). Is diminished capacity really dead? *Psychiatr. Ann.*, 22(11), 566–570.

Slovenko, R. (2002). *Psychiatry in law/Law in psychiatry.* New York: Brunner-Routledge.

Slovenko, R. (2002). The role of psychiatric diagnosis in the law. *J. Psychiat. Law, 30*(3), 421–444.

Slovenko, R. (2004). A history of the intermix of psychiatry and law. *J. Psychiat. Law, 32*(4), 561–592.

Slovenko, R. (2006). Editorial: Patients who deceive. *Inter. J. Offender Ther. Compar. Criminology, 50*(3), 241–244.

Sluhovsky, M. (2007). *Believe not every spirit: Possession, mysticism, & discernment in early modern Catholicism.* Chicago: University of Chicago Press.

Smith, A. (2006). Cognitive empathy and emotional empathy in human behavior and evolution. *Psychol. Record, 56*(1), 3–21.

Smith, D. B. (2007, March 25). Can you live with the voices in your head? *New York Times.* Retrieved from http://www.nytimes.com

Smith, G. R., Rost, K., & Kashner, T. M. (1995). A trial of the effect of a standardized psychiatric consultation on health outcomes and costs in somatizing patients. *Arch. Gen. Psychiat., 52*(3), 238–243.

Smith, M. L., & Glass, G. V. (1977). Meta-analysis of psychotherapy outcome studies. *Amer. Psychologist, 32*(9), 752–760.

Smith, M. L., Glass, G. V., & Miller, T. I. (1980). *The benefits of psychotherapy.* Baltimore: Johns Hopkins University Press.

Smith, T., Lovaas, N. W., & Lovaas, O. I. (2002). Behaviors of children with high-functioning autism when paired with typically developing versus delayed peers: A preliminary study. *Behav. Intervent., 17*(3), 129–143.

Smoller, J. W., Rosenbaum, J. F., Biederman, J., Kennedy, J., Dai, D., Racette, S. R., et al. (2003). Association of a genetic marker at the corticotropin-releasing hormone locus with behavioral inhibition. *Biol Psychiat., 54*(12), 1376–1381.

Smyth, J. M., & Pennebaker, J. W. (2001). What are the health effects of disclosure? In A. Baum, T. A. Revenson, & J. E. Singer (Eds.), *Handbook of health psychology* (pp. 339–348). Mahwah, NJ: Lawrence Erlbaum.

Snipes, J. B., & Maguire, E. R. (1995). Country music, suicide, and spuriousness. *Soc. Forces, 74,* 327–329.

Snow, E. (1976, December). In the snow. *Tex. Mon. Mag.*

Snyder, D. K., & Castellani, A. M. (2006). Current status and future directions in couple therapy. *Annu. Rev. Psychol., 57,* 317–344.

Snyder, D. K., Castellani, A. M., & Whisman, M. A. (2006). Current status and future directions in couple therapy. *Ann. Rev. Psychol., 57,* 317–344.

Snyder, S. (1980). *Biological aspects of mental disorder.* New York: Oxford University Press.

Snyder, W. V. (1947). *Casebook of non-directive counseling.* Boston: Houghton Mifflin.

Soares, J. C., Mallinger, A. G., Dippold, C. S., Frank, E., & Kupfer, D. J. (1999). Platelet membrane phospholipids in euthymic bipolar disorder patients: Are they affected by lithium treatment? *Biol. Psychiat., 45*(4), 453–457.

Soban, C. (2006). What about the boys? Addressing issues of masculinity within male anorexia nervosa in a feminist therapeutic environment. *Inter. J. Men's Hlth., 5*(3), 251–267.

Sobczak, S., Honig, A., van Duinen, M. A., & Riedel, W. J. (2002). Serotonergic dysregulation in bipolar disorders: A literature review of serotonergic challenge studies. *Bipolar Disord., 4*(6), 347–356.

Sobell, M. B., & Sobell, L. C. (1973). Individualized behavior therapy for alcoholics. *Behav. Ther., 4*(1), 49–72.

Sobell, M. B., & Sobell, L. C. (1984). The aftermath of heresy: A response to Pendery et al.'s (1982) critique of "Individualized Behavior Therapy for Alcoholics." *Behav. Res. Ther., 22*(4), 413–440.

Sobell, M. B., & Sobell, L. C. (1984). Under the microscope yet again: A commentary on Walker and Roach's critique of the Dickens Committee's enquiry into our research. *Brit. J. Addic., 79*(2), 157–168.

Sohn, A., & Grayson, C. (2005). *Parenting your Asperger child.* New York: Perigree

Soliman, M., Santos, A. M., & Lohr, J. B. (2008). Emergency, inpatient, and residential treatment. In K. T. Mueser & D. V. Jeste (Eds.), *Clinical handbook of schizophrenia* (pp. 339–353). New York: Guilford Press.

Soloff, P. H. (2005). Pharmacotherapy in borderline personality disorder. In J. G. Gunderson & P. D. Hoffman (Eds.), *Understanding and treating borderline personality disorder: A guide for professionals and families.* Washington, DC: American Psychiatric Publishing.

Soloff, P. H., Fabio, A., Kelly, T. M., Malone, K. M., & Mann, J. J. (2005). High-lethality status in patients with borderline personality disorder. *J. Pers. Disorders, 19*(4), 386–399.

Solomon, R. L. (1980). The opponent-process theory of acquired motivation: The costs of pleasure and the benefits of pain. *Amer. Psychologist, 35,* 691–712.

Solter, V., Thaller, V., Bagaric, A., Karlovic, D., Crnkovic, D., & Potkonjak, J. (2004). Study of schizophrenia comorbid with alcohol addiction. *Eur. J. Psychiat., 18*(1), 15–22.

Somers, J. M., Goldner, E. M., Waraich, P., & Hsu, L. (2004). Prevalence studies of substance-related disorders: A systematic review of the literature. *Canad. J. Psychiat., 49*(6), [np].

Sommer, B. R., & Schatzberg, A. F. (2002). Ginkgo biloba and related compounds in Alzheimer's disease. *Psychiatr. Ann., 32*(1), 13–18.

Sommers-Flanagan, J., & Sommers-Flanagan, R. (2003). *Clinical interviewing* (3rd ed.). New York: Wiley.

Sommers-Flanagan, J., & Sommers-Flanagan, R. (2007). Our favorite tips for interviewing couples and families. *Psychiatr. Clin. N. Amer., 30*(2), 275–281.

Sorensen, J. L., & Copeland, A. L. (2000). Drug abuse treatment as an HIV prevention strategy: A review. *Drug Alc. Rev., 59*(1) 17–31.

Sorokin, J. E., Giordani, B., Mohs, R. C., Losonczy, M. F., et al. (1988). Memory impairment in schizophrenic patients with tardive dyskinesia. *Biol. Psychiatry, 23*(2), 129–135.

Sorrentino, D., Mucca, A., Merlotti, E., Galderisi, S., & Maj, M. (2005). Modified nutritional counseling to increase motivation to treatment in anorexia nervosa. *Eur. Psychiat., 20*(2), 186–187.

Soukup, J. E. (2006). Alzheimer's disease: New concepts in diagnosis, treatment, and management. In T. G. Plante (Ed.), *Mental disorders of the new millennium, Vol. 3: Biology and function.* Westport, CT: Praeger Publishers.

Spagnolo, A. B., Murphy, A. A., & Librera, L. A. (2008). Reducing stigma by meeting and learning from people with mental illness. *Psychiatr. Rehab. J., 31*(3), 186–193.

Spalter, A. R., Gwirtsman, H. E., Demitrack, M. A., & Gold, P. W. (1993). Thyroid function in bulimia nervosa. *Biol. Psychiat., 33,* 408–414.

Spangler, L., Newton, K. M., Grothaus, L. C., Reed, S. D., Ehrlich, K., & LaCroix, A. Z. (2007). The effects of black cohosh therapies on lipids, fibrinogen, glucose and insulin. *Maturitas, 57*(2), 195–204.

Spaniel, F., Hajek, T., Tintera, J., Harantova, P., Dezortova, M., & Hajek, M. (2003). Differences in fMRI and MRS in a monozygotic twin pair discordant for schizophrenia (case report). *Acta Psychiatr. Scandin.* 107(2), 155–157.

Spanos, N. P., & Coe, W. C. (1992). A social-psychological approach to hypnosis. In E. Fromm & M. R. Nash (Eds.), *Contemporary hypnosis research.* New York: Guilford Press.

Spanton, T. (2008, July 28). UFOs: We believe. *The Sun.* Retrieved August 2008 from http://www.thesun.co.uk/sol/homepage/news/ufos/article1477122.ece

Sparling, J., Dragomir, C., Ramey, S. L., & Florescu, L. (2005). An educational intervention improves developmental progress of young children in a Romanian orphanage. *Infant Ment. Hlth. J., 26*(2), 127–142.

Spence, S. A. (2005). Prefrontal white matter—The tissue of lies? *Brit. J. Psychiat., 187*(4), 326–327.

Speranza, M., Corcos, M., Loas, G., Stephan, P., Guilbaud, O., Perez-Diaz, F., Venisse, J-L., Bizouard, P., Halfon, O., Flament, M., & Jeammet, P. (2005). Depressive personality dimenisons and alexithymia in eating disorders. *Psychiat. Res., 135*(2), 153–163.

Sperling, A. (2005). Housing update: Threats continue to Section 8 program. *NAMI Advocate, 3*(1), 6.

Sperry, L. (2003). *Handbook of diagnosis and treatment of DSM-IV-TR personality disorders* (2nd ed.). New York: Brunner-Routledge.

Sperry, L., Koenigsberg, H., Harvey, P., Mitropoulou, V., New, A. Goodman, M., Silverman, J., et al. (2001). Are the interpersonal and identity disturbances in the borderline personality disorder criteria linked to the traits of affectivity and impulsivity? *J. Pers. Disorders, 15,* 358–370.

Spiegel, A. (2005). The dictionary of disorder. *The New Yorker,* January 3, 2005, 56–63.

Spiegel, D. (1994). Dissociative disorders. In R. E. Hales, S. C. Yudofsky, & J. A. Talbott (Eds.), *The American Psychiatric Press textbook of psychiatry* (2nd ed.). Washington, DC: American Psychiatric Press.

Spiegel, D. (2002). Mesmer minus magic: Hypnosis and modern medicine. *Inter. J. Clin. Exp. Hyp., 50*(4), 397–406.

Spiegel, D., & Fawzy, F. I. (2002). Psychosocial interventions and prognosis in cancer. In H. G. Koenig & H. J. Cohen (Eds.), *The link between religion and health: Psychoneuroimmunology and the faith factor* (pp. 84–100). New York: Oxford University Press.

Spiegler, M. D., & Guevremont, D. C. (2003). *Contemporary behavior therapy.* Belmont, CA: Thomson/Wadsworth.

Spielberger, C. D. (1966). Theory and research on anxiety. In C. D. Spielberger (Ed.), *Anxiety and behavior*. New York: Academic Press.

Spielberger, C. D. (1972). Anxiety as an emotional state. In C. D. Spielberger (Ed.), *Anxiety: Current trends in theory and research* (Vol. 1). New York: Academic Press.

Spielberger, C. D. (1985). Anxiety, cognition, and affect: A state-trait perspective. In A. H. Tuma & J. Maser (Eds.), *Anxiety and the anxiety disorders*. Hillsdale, NJ: Lawrence Erlbaum.

Spielrein, S. (1995). On the psychological content of a case of schizophrenia (dementia praecox). *Evolution Psychiatr., 60*(1), 69–95. [French.]

Spinewine, A., Swine, C., Dhillon, S., Franklin, B. D., Tulkens, P. M., Wilmotte, L., et al. (2005). Appropriateness of use of medicines in elderly inpatients: Qualitative study. *Brit. Med. J., 331*(7522), October, [np].

Spirito, A., & Esposito-Smythers, C. (2008). Evidence-based therapies for adolescent suicidal behavior. In R. G. Steele, T. D. Elkin, & M. C. Roberts (Eds.), *Handbook of evidence-based therapies for children and adolescents: Bridging science and practice*. New York: Springer.

Spitz, R. A. (1945). Hospitalization: An inquiry into the genesis of psychiatric conditions of early childhood. In R. S. Eissler, A. Freud, H. Hartman, & E. Kris (Eds.), *The psychoanalytic study of the child* (Vol. 1). New York: International Universities Press.

Spitz, R. A. (1946). *Anaclitic depression. The psychoanalytic study of the child* (Vol. 2). New York: International Universities Press.

Spitzer, R. L., Gibbon, M., Skodol, A. E., Williams, J. B. W., & First, M. B. (Eds.). (1994). *DSM-IV casebook: A learning companion to the diagnostic and statistical manual of mental disorders* (4th ed.). Washington, DC: American Psychiatric Press.

Spitzer, R. L., Skodol, A., Gibbon, M., & Williams, J. B. W. (1981). *DSM-III case book* (1st ed.). Washington, DC: Aerican Psychiatric Press.

Spitzer, R. L., Skodol, A., Gibbon, M., & Williams, J. B. W. (1983). *Psychopathology: A case book*. New York: McGraw-Hill.

Sprecher, S., & Hatfield, E. (1996). Premarital sexual standards among U. S. college students: Comparison with Russian and Japanese students. *Arch. Sex. Behav., 25*(3), 261–288.

Springman, R. E., Wherry, J. N., & Notaro, P. C. (2006). The effects of interviewer race and child race on sexual abuse disclosures in forensic interviews. *J. Child Sex. Abuse, 15*(3), 99–116.

Squire, L. R. (1977). ECT and memory loss. *Amer. J. Psychiat., 134*, 997–1001.

Squire, L. R., & Slater, P. C. (1983). Electroconvulsive therapy and complaints of memory dysfunction: A prospective three-year follow-up study. *Brit. J. Psychiat., 142*, 1–8.

Sramek, J. J., & Pi, E. H. (1996). Ethnicity and antidepressant response. *Mt. Sinai J. Med., 63*, 320–325.

Sreenivasan, S., Weinberger, L. E., & Garrick, T. (2003). Expert testimony in sexually violent predator commitments: Conceptualizing legal standards of "mental disorder" and "likely to reoffend." *J. Amer. Acad. Psychiat. Law, 31*(4), 471–485.

Stacciarini, J. M. R., O'Keeffe, M., & Mathews, M. (2007). Group therapy as treatment for depressed Latino women: A review

of the literature. *Issues Ment. Hlth. Nurs., 28*(5), 473–488.

Stack, S. (1987). Celebrities and suicide: A taxonomy and analysis, 1948–1983. *Amer. Sociol. Rev., 52*, 401–412.

Stack, S. (1998). The relationship of female labor force participation to suicide: A comparative analysis. *Arch. Suic. Res., 4*(3), 249–261.

Stack, S. (2003). Media coverage as a risk factor in suicide. *J. Epidemiol. Comm. Hlth., 57*(4), 238–240.

Stack, S. (2004). Emile Durkheim and altruistic suicide. *Arch. Suic. Res., 8*(1), 9–22.

Stack, S. (2005). Suicide in the media: A quantitative review of studies based on nonfictional stories. *Suic. Life-Threat. Behav., 35*(2), 121–133.

Stack, S., & Gundlach, J. (1992). The effect of country music on suicide. *Soc. Forces, 71*, 211–218.

Stack, S., Gundlach, J., & Reeves, J. L. (1994). The heavy metal subculture and suicide. *Suic. Life-Threat. Behav., 24*, 15–23.

Stack, S., & Kposowa, A. J. (2008). The association of suicide rates with individual-level suicide attitudes: A cross-national analysis. *Soc. Sci. Quart., 89*(1), 39–59.

Stagnitti, M. N. (2005, May). *Antidepressant use in the U.S. civilian noninstitutionalized population, 2002* (MEPS-HC, Statistical Brief No. 77). Rockville, MD: AHRQ/NCHS.

Staley, J. K., Gottschalk, C., Petrakis, I. L., Gueorguieva, R., O'Malley, S., Baldwin, R., et al. (2005). Cortical gamma-aminobutyric acid type A-benzodiazepine receptors in recovery from alcohol dependence: Relationship to features of alcohol dependence and cigarette smoking. *Arch. Gen. Psychiat., 62*(8), 877–888.

Stanford, M. S. (2007). Demon or disorder: A survey of attitudes toward mental illness in the Christian church. *Ment. Hlth, Religion Culture, 1*(5), 445–449.

Stanley, B., & Brodsky, B. S. (2005). Suicidal and self-injurious behavior in borderline personality disorder: A self-regulation model. In J. G. Gunderson & P. D. Hoffman (Eds.), *Understanding and treating borderline personality disorder: A guide for professionals and families* (pp. 43–63). Washington, DC: American Psychiatric Publishing.

Stanley, B., Molcho, A., Stanley, M., Winchel, R., Gameroff, M. J., Parsons, B., et al. (2000). Association of aggressive behavior with altered serotonergic function in patients who are not suicidal. *Amer. J. Psychiat., 157*(4), 609–614.

Stanley, M., Stanley, B., Traskman-Bendz, L., Mann, J. J., & Meyendorff, E. (1986). Neurochemical findings in suicide completers and suicide attempters. In R. W. Maris (Ed.), *Biology of suicide*. New York: Guilford Press.

Stanley, M., Virgilio, J., & Gershon, S. (1982). Tritiated imipramine binding sites are decreased in the frontal cortex of suicides. *Science, 216*, 1337–1339.

Steadman, H. J., Monahan, J., Robbins, P. C., Appelbaum, P., Grisso, T., Klassen, D., et al. (1993). From dangerousness to risk assessment: Implications for appropriate research strategies. In S. Hodgins (Ed.), *Mental disorder and crime*. New York: Sage.

Stearns, P. N. (2006). Far and contemporary history: A review essay. *J. Soc. Hist., 40*(2), 477–484.

Steege, J. F., & Ling, F. W. (1993). Dyspareunia: A special type of chronic pelvic pain. *Obstet. Gynecol. Clin. North Am., 20*, 779–793.

Steele, R. G., Roberts, M. C., & Elkin, T. D. (2008). Evidence-based therapies for children and adolescents: Problems and prospects. In R. G. Steele, T. D. Elkin, & M. C. Roberts (Eds.), *Handbook of evidence-based therapies for children and adolescents: Bridging science and practice*. New York: Springer.

Steffen, K. J., Roerig, J. L., Mitchell, J. E., & Uppala, S. (2006). Emerging drugs for eating disorder treatment. *Expert Opinion on Emerging Drugs, 11*(2), 315–336.

Stein, D., Kaye, W. H., Matsunaga, H., Orbach, I., Har-Evan, D., Frank, G., et al. (2002). Eating-related concerns, mood, and personality traits in recovered bulimia nervosa subjects: A replication study. *Inter. J. Eat. Disorders, 32*(2), 225–229.

Stein, D. J., & Fineberg, N. A. (2007). *Obsessive-compulsive disorder*. Oxford, England: Oxford University Press.

Stein, J. (2003, August 4). Just say Om. *Time, 162*(5), pp. 48–56.

Stein, Z., Susser, M., Saenger, G., & Marolla, F. (1972). Nutrition and mental performance. *Science, 178*, 708–713.

Steiner, H., Smith, C., Rosenkranz, R. T., & Litt, I. (1991). The early care and feeding of anorexics. *Child Psychiat. Human Dev., 21*(3), 163–167.

Steiner, M., & Tam, W. Y. K. (1999). Postpartum depression in relation to other psychiatric disorders. In L. J. Miller (Ed.), *Postpartum mood disorders*. Washington, DC: American Psychiatric Press.

Steinhausen, H. C. (2002). The outcome of anorexia nervosa in the 20th century. *Amer. J. Psychiat., 159*(8), 1284–1293.

Steinhausen, H. C., Boyadjieva, S., Grigoroiu-Serbanescu, M., Seidel, R., & Winkler-Metzke, C. (2000). A transcultural outcome study of adolescent eating disorders. *Acta Psychiatr. Scandin., 101*(1), 60–66.

Steketee, G., Frost, R., Bhar, S., Bouvard, M., Clamari, J., Carmin, C., et al. (2003). Psychometric validation of the obsessive beliefs questionnaire and the interpretation of intrusions inventory. Part I. *Behav. Res. Ther., 41*(8), 863–878.

Stellrecht, N. E., Joiner, T. E., & Rudd, M. D. (2006). Responding to and treating negative interpersonal processes in suicidal depression. *J. Clin. Psych., 62*, 1129–1140.

Stern. (2004). Survey. *Stern magazine*, July 23, 2004.

Stern, A. (1938): Psychoanalytic investigation and therapy in the borderline group of neuroses. *Psychoanal. Q., 7*, 467–489.

Sternberg, R. J., Grigorenko, E. L., & Bundy, D. A. (2001). The predictive value of IQ. *Merrill-Palmer Q., 47*(1), 1–41.

Stetter, F. (2000). Psychotherapy. In G. Zernig, A. Saria, et al. (Eds.), *Handbook of alcoholism. Pharmacology and toxicology*. Boca Raton, FL: CRC Press.

Stetter, F., & Kupper, S. (2002). Autogenic training: A meta-analysis of clinical outcome studies. *Appl. Psychophysiol. Biofeedback, 27*(1), 45–98.

Stevens, J., Harman, J. S., & Kelleher, K. J. (2005). Race/ethnicity and insurance status as factors associated with ADHD treatment patterns. *J. Child Adol. Psychopharmacol., 15*(1), 88–96.

Stevens, J., & Ward-Estes, J. (2006). Attention-deficit/hyperactivity disorder. In M. Hersen & J. C. Thomas (Series Eds.) & R. T. Ammerman (Vol. Ed.), *Comprehensive handbook of personality and psychopathology, Vol. 3: Child psychopathology* (pp. 316–329). Hoboken, NJ: Wiley.

Stevens, L. M., Lynm, C., & Glass, R. M. (2002). Postpartum depression. *JAMA, 287*(6), 802.

Stevenson, R. W. D., & Elliott, S. L. (2007). Sexuality and illness. In S. R. Leiblum (Ed.), *Principles and practice of sex therapy* (4th ed., pp. 313–349). New York: Guilford Press.

Steverman, S. (2007). *Two more states enact parity laws. NCSL, 28*(483).

Steward, S., & Worley, P. (2002). Local synthesis of proteins at synaptic sites on dendrites: Role in synaptic plasticity and memory consolidation? *Neurobiol. Learn. Memory, 78*(3), 508–527.

Stewart, A. (2004). Prevention of eating disorders. In P. B. Harper & K. N. Dwivedi (Eds.), *Promoting the emotional well-being of children and adolescents and preventing their mental ill health: A handbook* (pp. 173–197). Philadelphia: Jessica Kingsley Publishers.

Stewart, M. E., Ebmeier, K. P., & Deary, I. J. (2005). Personality correlates of happiness and sadness: EPQ-R and TPQ compared. *Pers. Individ. Diff., 38*(5), 1085–1096.

Stewart, R. E., & Chambless, D. L. (2007). Does psychotherapy research inform treatment decisions in private practice: *J. Clin. Psychol., 63*(3), 267–281.

Stewart, S. H., Taylor, S., Jang, K. L., Cox, B. J., Watt, M. C., Fedoroff, I. C., et al. (2001). Causal modeling of relations among learning history, anxiety sensitivity, and panic attacks. *Behav. Res. Ther., 39*(4), 443–456.

Stewart, T. M., & Williamson, D. A. (2008). Bulimia nervosa. In M. Hersen & J. Rosqvist (Eds.), *Handbook of psychological assessment, case conceptualization and treatment, Vol. 1: Adults.* Hoboken, NJ: John Wiley & Sons.

Stewart, T. M., & Williamson, D. A. (2008). Bulimia nervosa. In M. Hersen & J. Rosqvist (Eds.), *Handbook of psychological assessment, case conceptualization, and treatment, Vol. 1: Adults.* Hoboken, NJ: John Wiley & Sons.

Stice, E., Hayward, C., Cameron, R. P., Killen, J. D., & Taylor, C. B. (2000). Body-image and eating disturbances predict onset of depression among female adolescents: A longitudinal study. *J. Abnorm. Psychol., 109*(3), 438–444.

Stief, E. A. (2004). Parental perceptions of attention-deficit/hyperactivity disorder: Etiology, diagnosis, and treatment. *Diss. Abstr. Inter.: Sect. B: Sci. Eng., 64*(10-B), 5236.

Stillion, J. M. (1985). *Death and the sexes: An examination of differential longevity, attitudes, behaviors, and coping skills.* Washington, DC: Hemisphere.

Stoil, M. (2001). Behavioral health's "finest hour." *Behav. Hlth. Manage., 21*(5), 8–10.

Stolberg, R. A., Clark, D. C., & Bongar, B. (2002). Epidemiology, assessment, and management of suicide in depressed patients. In I. H. Gotlib & C. L. Hammen (Eds.), *Handbook of depression* (pp. 581–601). New York: Guilford Press.

Stoll, A. L., Renshaw, P. F., Yurgelun-Todd, D. A., & Cohen, B. M. (2000). Neuroimaging in bipolar disorder. *Bipolar Disord., 2,* 148–164.

Stone, M. H. (1989). Schizoid personality disorder. In *Treatments of psychiatric disorders: A task force report of the American Psychiatric Association.* Washington, DC: American Psychiatric Press.

Stone, T. H., Winslade, W. J., & Klugman, C. M. (2000). Sex offenders, sentencing laws and pharmaceutical treatment: A prescription for failure. *Behav. Sci. Law, 18*(1), 83–110.

Strachan, E. (2008). Civil commitment evaluations. In R. Jackson (Ed.), *Learning forensic assessment* (pp. 509–535). New York: Routledge/Taylor & Francis Group.

Strain, E. C., & Lofwall, M. R. (2008). Buprenorphine maintenance. In H. D. Kleber & M. Galanter (Eds.), *The American Psychiatric Publishing textbook of substance abuse treatment* (4th ed., pp. 309–324). Arlington, VA: American Psychiatric Publishing.

Strate, J. M., Zalman, M., & Hunter, D. J. (2005). Physician-assisted suicide and the politics of problem definition. *Mortality, 10*(1), 23–41.

Stratton, V. N., & Zalanowski, A. H. (1994). Affective impact of music vs. lyrics. *Empir. Stud. Arts, 12*(2), 173–184.

Stratton, V., & Zalanowski, A. (1999). *Study on music and emotion.* Paper presented at annual meeting of Eastern Psychological Association, Providence, RI.

Strauch, I. (2004). Cited in *Newsweek, 144*(6), August 9, 2004, 46.

Strawn, J. R., Keck, P. E., Jr., & Caroff, S. N. (2007). Neuroleptic malignant syndrome. *Amer. J. Psychiat., 164*(6), 870–876.

Street, W. R. (1994). *A chronology of noteworthy events in American psychology.* Washington, DC: American Psychological Association.

Stricker, G., & Trierweiler, S. J. (1995). The local clinical scientist. A bridge between science and practice. *Amer. Psychologist, 50*(12), 995–1002.

Strickland, B. R., Hale, W. D., & Anderson, L. K. (1975). Effect of induced mood states on activity and self-reported affect. *J. Cons. Clin. Psychol., 43*(4), 587.

Strickland, T. L., Ranganath, V., Lin, K. M., Poland, R. E., Mendoza, R., & Smith, M. W. (1991). Psychopharmacologic considerations in the treatment of black American populations. *Psychopharmacol. Bull., 27,* 441–448.

Striegel-Moore, R. H., Fairburn, C. G., Wilfley, D. E., Pike, K. M., Dohm, F-A., & Kraemer, H. C. (2005). Toward an understanding of risk factors for binge-eating disorder in black and white women: A community-based case-control study. *Psychol. Med., 35*(6), 907–917.

Striegel-Moore, R. H., Silberstein, L. R., & Rodin, J. (1993). The social self in bulimia nervosa: Public self-consciousness, social anxiety, and perceived fraudulence. *J. Abnorm. Psychol., 102*(2), 297–303.

Strober, M., Freeman, R., Lampert, C., Diamond, J., & Kaye, W. (2000). Controlled family study of anorexia nervosa and bulimia nervosa: Evidence of shared liability and transmission of partial syndromes. *Amer. J. Psychiat., 157*(3), 393–401.

Strober, M., Freeman, R., Lampert, C., Diamond, J., & Kaye, W. (2001). Males with anorexia nervosa: A controlled study of eating disorders in first-degree relatives. *Inter. J. Eat. Disorders, 29*(3), 264–269.

Stroebe, M., & Schut, H. (2005). To continue or relinquish bonds: A review of consequences for the bereaved. *Death Stud., 29*(6), 477–494.

Stroebe, M., Schut, H., & Stroebe, W. (2005). Attachment in coping with bereavement: A theoretical integration. *Rev. Gen. Psychol., 9*(1), 48–66.

Stroebe, M., Schut, H., & Stroebe, W. (2007). Health outcomes of bereavement. *Lancet, 370*(9603), 1960–1973.

Stroebe, M., van Son, M., Stroebe, W., Kleber, R., Schut, H., & van den Bout, J. (2000). On the classification and diagnosis of pathological grief. *Clin. Psychol. Rev., 20*(1), 57–75.

Strober, M., & Yager, J. (1985). A developmental perspective on the treatment of anorexia nervosa in adolescents. In D. M. Garner & P. E. Garfinkel (Eds.), *Handbook of psychotherapy for anorexia nervosa and bulimia.* New York: Guilford Press.

Stromme, P., & Magnus, P. (2000). Correlations between socioeconomic status, IQ and aetiology in mental retardation: A population-based study of Norwegian children. *Soc. Psychiat. Psychiatr. Epidemiol., 35*(1), 12–18.

Strothers, H. S., Rust, G., Minor, P., et al. (2005). Prescription of pharmacotherapy for depression in elderly people varies with age, race, gender, and length of care. *J. Amer. Ger. Soc., 53,* 456–461.

Strümpfel, U. (2004). Research on gestalt therapy. *International Gestalt Journal, 27*(1), 9–54.

Strümpfel, U. (2006). *Therapie der gefühle: Forschungsbefunde zur gestalttherapie.* Cologne, Germany: Edition Huanistiche Psychologie.

Strümpfel, U., & Goldman, R. (2001). Contacting gestalt therapy. In D. Cain & J. Seeman (Eds.), *Humanistic psychotherapies: Handbook on research and practice.* Washington, DC: American Psychological Association.

Strutin, K. (2007). *Criminal justice resources: Sex offender laws.* Retrieved from http://www.llrx.com/features/sexoffenderlaws.htm

Stuart, S., Noyes, R., Jr., Starcevic, V., & Barsky, A. (2008). An integrative approach to somatoform disorders combining interpersonal and cognitive-behavioral theory and techniques. *J. Contemp. Psychother., 38*(1), 45–53.

Stuart, S., O'Hara, M. W., & Gorman, L. L. (2003). The prevention and psychotherapeutic treatment of postpartum depression. *Arch. Women's Ment. Hlth., 6*(Suppl. 2), s57–s69.

Stunkard, A. J. (1975). From explanation to action in psychosomatic medicine: The case of obesity. *Psychosom. Med., 37,* 195–236.

Stunkard, A. J., Sorenson, T. I. A., Hanis, C., Teasdale, T. W., et al. (1986). An adoption study of human obesity. *N. Engl. J. Med., 314,* 193–198.

Sturgeon, V., & Taylor, J. (1980). Report of a five-year follow-up study of mentally disordered sex offenders released from Atascadero State Hospital in 1973. *Criminal Justice* J. Western S. Univ., San Diego, 4, 31–64.

Sturmey, P. (2008). Adults with intellectual disabilities. In M. Hersen & J. Rosqvist (Eds.), *Handbook of psychological assessment, case conceptualization, and treatment, Vol. 1: Adults.* Hoboken, NJ: John Wiley & Sons.

Styron, W. (1990). *Darkness visible: A memoir of madness.* New York: Random House.

Su, J. C., & Birmingham, C. L. (2002). Zinc supplementation in the treatment of anorexia nervosa. *Eat. Weight Disord., 7*(1), 20–22.

Suarez, E. C. (2004). C-reactive protein is associated with psychological risk factors of cardiovascular disease in apparently healthy adults. *Psychosom. Med., 66*(5), 684–691.

Sudak, H., Maxim, K., & Carpenter, M. (2008). Suicide and stigma: A review of the literature and personal reflections. *Academ. Psychiat., 32*(2), 136–142.

Sudhalter, V., Cohen, I. L., Silverman, W., & Wolf-Schein, E. G. (1990). Conversational analyses of males with fragile X, Down syndrome, and autism: Comparison of the emergence of deviant language. *Amer. J. Ment. Retard., 94,* 431–441.

Sue, D. W., & Sue, D. (2003) *Counseling the culturally diverse: Theory and practice* (4th ed.). New York: Wiley.

Suhail, K., & Nisa, Z. (2002). Prevalence of eating disorders in Pakistan: Relationship with depression and body shape. *Eat. Weight Disord., 7*(2), 131–138.

Suinn, R. M. (2001). The terrible twos—anger and anxiety. *Amer. Psychologist, 56*(1), 27–36.

Sullivan, C. J., McKendrick, K., Sacks, S., & Banks, S. (2007). Modified therapeutic community treatment for offenders with MICA disorders: Substance use outcomes. *Amer. J. Drug Alc. Abuse, 33*(6), 823–832.

Sullivan, H. S. (1953). *The interpersonal theory of psychiatry.* New York: Norton.

Sullivan, H. S. (1962). *Schizophrenia as a human process.* New York: Norton.

Sullivan, P. W., Valuck, R., Saseen, J., & MacFall, H. M. (2004). A comparison of the direct costs and cost effectiveness of serotonin reuptake inhibitors and associated adverse drug reactions. *CNS Drugs, 18*(13), 911–932.

Suls, J., & Rothman, A. (2004). Evolution of the biopsychosocial model: Prospects and challenges for health psychology. *Hlth. Psychol., 23*(2), 119–125.

Sunstein, C. R., & Nussbaum, M. C. (Eds.). (2004). *Animal rights: Current debates and new directions.* PsychINFO Weekly 2005/03 Week 2.

Suppes, T., Baldessarini, R. J., Faedda, G. L., & Tohen, M. (1991). Risk of recurrence following discontinuation of lithium treatment in bipolar disorder. *Arch. Gen. Psychiat., 48*(12), 1082–1088.

Suppes, T., Kelly, D. I., & Perla, J. M. (2005). Challenges in the management of bipolar depression. *J. Clin. Psychiat., 66*(Suppl. 5), 11–16.

Susser, E., Neugebauer, R., Hoek, H. W., Brown, A. S., Lin, S., Labovitz, D., et al. (1996). Schizophrenia after prenatal famine. *Arch. Gen. Psychiat., 53*(1), 25–31.

Suzuki, K., Takei, N., Kawai, M., Minabe, Y., & Mori, N. (2003). Is Taijin Kyofusho a culture-bound syndrome? *Amer. J. Psychiat., 160*(7), p. 1358.

Svartberg, M., & Stiles, T. C. (1991). Comparative effects of short-term psychodynamic psychotherapy: A meta-analysis. *J. Cons. Clin. Psychol., 59,* 704–714.

Svartberg, M., Stiles, T. C., & Seltzer, M. H. (2004). Randomized, controlled trial of the effectiveness of short-term dynamic psychotherapy and cognitive therapy for Cluster C personality disorders. *American Journal of Psychiatry, 161,* 810–817.

Swaab, D. F. (2005). The role of hypothalamus and endocrine system in sexuality. In J. S. Hyde (Ed.), *Biological substrates of human sexuality.* Washington, DC: American Psychological Association.

Swallow, M., Yutzy, S. H., & Dinwiddie, S. H. (2005). Forensic issues. In E. H. Rubin & C. F. Zorumski (Eds.), *Adult psychiatry* (2nd ed., pp. 420–428). Oxford, England: Blackwell Publishing.

Swann, A. C. (2005). Long-term treatment in bipolar disorder. *J. Clin. Psychiat., 66*(Suppl. 1), 7–12.

Swanson, J., Holzer, C., Ganju, V., & Jono, R. (1990). Violence and psychiatric disorder in the community: Evidence from the Epidemiological Catchment Area Surveys. *Hosp. Comm. Psychiat., 41,* 761–770.

Swartz, M. S., Wagner, H. R., Swanson, J. W., Hiday, V. A., & Burns, B. J. (2002). The perceived coerciveness of involuntary outpatient commitment: Findings from an experimental study. *J. Amer. Acad. Psychiat. Law, 30*(2), 207–217.

Swayze, V. W. (1995). Frontal leukotomy and related psychosurgical procedures in the era before antipsychotics (1935–1954): A historical overview. *Amer. J. Psychiat., 152*(4), 505–515.

Swendsen, J. D., & Mazure, C. M. (2000). Life stress as a risk factor for postpartum depression: Current research and methodology. *Clin. Psychol.: Sci. Prac., 7*(1), 17–31.

Swonger, A. K., & Constantine, L. L. (1983). *Drugs and therapy: A handbook of psychotropic drugs* (2nd ed.). Boston: Little, Brown.

Szabo, M., & Lovibond, P. F. (2004). The cognitive content of thought-listed worry episodes in clinic-referred anxious and nonreferred children. *J. Clin. Child Adol. Psychol., 33*(3), 613–622.

Szasz, T. S. (1960). The myth of mental illness. *Amer. Psychologist, 15,* 113–118.

Szasz, T. S. (1963). *The manufacture of madness.* New York: Harper & Row.

Szasz, T. S. (1977). *Psychiatric slavery.* New York: Free Press.

Szasz, T. S. (1997). *The manufacture of madness: A comprehensive study of the Inquisition and the mental health movement.* Syracuse, NY: Syracuse University Press.

Szasz, T. S. (2005). "Knowing What Ain't So": R. D. Laing and Thomas Szasz. *Exist. Anal., 16*(1), 13–126.

Szasz, T. S. (2006). The pretense of psychology as science: The myth of mental illness in statu nascendi. *Curr. Psych.: Devel. Learn. Pers. Soc., 25*(1), 42–49.

Szasz, T. S. (2007). *Coercion as cure: A critical history of psychiatry.* New Brunswick, NJ: Transaction.

Szegedy-Maszak, M. (2005). The worst of all bets. *U. S. News & World Report, 138*(19), 53–54.

Szeszko, P. R., Ardekani, B. A., Ashtari, M., Malhotra, A. K., Robinson, D. G., Bilder, R. M., et al. (2005). White matter abnormalities in obsessive-compulsive disorder: A diffusion tensor imaging study. *Arch. Gen Psychiat. 62,* 782–790.

Szymanski, S., Cannon, T. D., Gallacher, F., Erwin, R. J., & Gur, R. E. (1996). Course of treatment response in first-episode and chronic schizophrenia. *Amer. J. Psychiat., 153*(4), 519–525.

Szymanski, S., Lieberman, J., Alvir, J. M., Mayerhoff, D., et al. (1995). Gender differences in onset of illness, treatment response, course, and biologic indexes in first-episode schizophrenic patients. *Am. J. Psychiatry, 152*(5), 698–703.

Szymanski, S., Lieberman, J., Pollack, S., Kane, J. M., Safferman, A., Munne, R., et al. (1996). Gender differences in neuroleptic nonresponsive clozapine-treated schizophrenics. *Biol. Psychiat., 39,* 249–254.

Tacon, A., & Caldera, Y. (2001). Behavior modification. In R. McComb & J. Jacalyn (Eds.), *Eating disorders in women and children: Prevention, stress management, and treatment* (pp. 263–272). Boca Raton, FL: CRC Press.

TADS (Treatment for Adolescents with Depression Study Team, U.S.). (2004). Fluoxetine, cognitive behavioral therapy, and their combination for adolescents with depression: Treatment for Adolescents with Depression Study (TADS) randomized controlled trial. *JAMA, 292*(7), 807–820.

TADS (Treatment for Adolescents with Depression Study Team, U.S.). (2005). The Treatment for Adolescents with Depression Study (TADS): Demographic and clinical characteristics. *J. Amer. Acad. Child Adol. Psychiat., 44*(1), 28–40.

TADS (Treatment for Adolescents with Depression Study Team, U.S.). (2007). The Treatment for Adolescents with Depression Study (TADS): Long-term effectiveness and safety outcomes. *Arch. Gen. Psychiat., 64*(10), 1132–1144.

Tafet, G. E., Feder, D. J., Abulafia, D. P., & Roffman, S. S. (2005). Regulation of hypothalamic-pituitary-adrenal activity in response to cognitive therapy in patients with generalized anxiety disorder. *Cog. Affect. Behav. Neurosci., 5*(1), 37–40.

Talavera, J. A., Sáz-Ruiz, J., & Garcia-Toro, M. (1994) Quantitative measurement of depression through speech analysis. *Eur. Psychiat., 9*(4), 185–193.

Talbott, J. A. (2004). Deinstitutionalization: Avoiding the disasters of the past. *Psychiatr. Serv., 55*(10), 1112–1115.

Tallis, F., Davey, G., & Capuzzo, N. (1994). The phenomenology of non-pathological worry: A preliminary investigation. In G. Davey & F. Tallis (Eds.), *Worrying: Perspectives on theory, assessment and treatment* (pp. 61–89). Chichester, England: John Wiley.

Tamblyn, R., Abrahamowicz, M., du Berger, R., McLeon, P., & Bartlett, G. (2005). A 5-year prospective assessment of the risk associated with individual benzodiazepines and doses in new elderly users. *J. Amer. Ger. Soc., 53*(2), 233–241.

Tamminga, C. A., Shad, M. U., & Ghose, S. (2008). Neuropsychiatric aspects of schizophrenia. In S. C. Yudofsky & R. E. Hales (Eds.), *The American Psychiatric Publishing textbook of neuropsychiatry and behavioral neurosciences* (5th ed.). Washington, DC: American Psychiatric Publishing.

Tang, C. S-K. (2006). Positive and negative post-disaster psychological adjustment among adult survivors of the Southeast Asian earthquake-tsunami. *J. Psychosom. Res., 61*(5), 699–705.

Tang, C. S-K. (2007). Trajectory of traumatic stress symptoms in the aftermath of extreme natural disaster: A study of adult Thai survivors of the 2004 Southeast Asian earthquake and tsunami. *J. Nerv. Ment. Dis., 195*(1), 54–59.

Tanner, L. (2008, May 8). Medical know-how raises suicide risk for doctors. *Yahoo! News.* Retrieved May 8, 2008, from http://news.yahoo.com

Tantam, D. (2006). The machine as psycho-therapist: Impersonal communication with a machine. *Adv. Psychiatr. Treat., 12,* 416–426.

Tarrier, N. (2008). Schizophrenia and other psychotic disorders. In D. H. Barlow (Ed.), *Clinical handbook of psychological disorders: A step-by-step treatment manual* (4th ed.). New York: Guilford Press.

Tarrier, N., Taylor, K., & Gooding, P. (2008). Cognitive-behavioral interventions to reduce suicide behavior: A systematic review and meta-analysis. *Behav. Mod., 32*(1), 77–108.

Tartaro, C., & Lester, D. (2005). An application of Durkheim's theory of suicide to prison suicide rates in the United States. *Death Stud., 29*(5), 413–422.

Tatarelli, R., Pompili, M., & Girardi, P. (Eds.). (2007). *Suicide in psychiatric disorders.* New York: Nova Science Publishers.

Tate, D. C., Reppucci, N. D., & Mulvey, E. P. (1995). Violent juvenile delinquents. *Amer. Psychologist, 50*(9), 777–781.

Taube-Schiff, M., & Lau, M. A. (2008). Major depressive disorder. In M. Hersen & J. Rosqvist (Eds.), *Handbook of psychological assessment, case conceptualization, and treatment, Vol. 1: Adults* (pp. 319–351). Hoboken, NJ: John Wiley & Sons.

Tavris, C. (1993). Beware the incest-survivor machine. *New York Times Book Review.*

Taylor, C. B., Farquhar, J. W., Nelson, E., & Agras, S. (1977). Relaxation therapy and high blood pressure. *Arch. Gen. Psychiat., 34,* 339–342.

Taylor, D. J., McCrae, C. M., Gehrman, P., Dautovich, N., & Lichtein, K. L. (2008). Insomnia. In M. Hersen & J. Rosqvist (Eds.), *Handbook of psychological assessment, case conceptualization and treatment, Vol 1: Adults.* Hoboken, NJ: Wiley.

Taylor, G. M., & Ste. Marie, D. M. (2001). Eating disorders symptoms in Canadian female pair and dance figure skaters. *Int. J. Sport Psychol., 32*(1), 21–28.

Taylor, H. A. (2007). Moving beyond compliance: Measuring ethical quality to enhance the oversight of human subjects research. *IRB: Ethics Human Res., 29*(5), 9–14.

Taylor, R. (1975). *Electroconvulsive treatment (ECT): The control of therapeutic power.* Exchange.

Taylor, S., Thordarson, D. S., Fedoroff, I. C., Maxfield, L., Lovell, K., & Ogrodniczuk, J. (2003). Comparative efficacy, speed, and adverse effects of three PTSD treatments: Exposure therapy, EMDR, and relaxation training. *J. Cons. Clin. Psychol., 71,* 330–338.

Taylor, S., Wald, J., & Asmundson, G. J. G. (2005). Current status and future directions in the cognitive-behavioral treatment of PTSD. In T. A. Corales (Ed.), *Trends in posttraumatic stress disorder research* (pp. 263–284). Hauppauge, NY: Nova Science Publishers.

Taylor, S. E. (2004). The accidental neuroscientist: Positive resources, stress responses, and course of illness. In G. G. Berntson & J. T. Cacioppo (Eds.), *Essays in social neuroscience* (pp. 133–141). Cambridge, MA: The MIT Press.

Taylor, S. E. (2006). *Health psychology* (6th ed.). New York: McGraw Hill.

Teicher, M. H., Andersen, S. L., Navalta, C. P., Tomoda, A., Polcari, A., & Kim, D. (2008). Neuropsychiatric disorders of childhood and adolescence. In S. C. Yudofsky & R. E. Hales (Eds.), *The American Psychiatric Publishing textbook of neuropsychiatry and behavioral neurosciences* (5th ed.). Washington, DC: American Psychiatric Publishing.

Telch, C. F., & Agras, W. S. (1993). The effects of a very low calorie diet on binge eating. *Behav. Ther., 24,* 177–193.

Telner, J. I., Lapierre, Y. D., Horn, E., & Browne, M. (1986). Rapid reduction of mania by means of reserpine therapy. *Amer. J. Psychiat., 143*(8), 1058.

Teng, C. T., Akerman, D., Cordas, T. A., Kasper, S., et al. (1995). Seasonal affective disorder in a tropical country: A case report. *Psychiatr. Res., 56*(1), 11–15.

Tenhula, W. N., & Bellack, A. S. (2008). Social skills training. In K. T. Mueser & D. V. Jeste (Eds.), *Clinical handbook of schizophrenia* (pp. 240–248). New York: Guilford Press.

Teplin, L. A., Abram, K. M., & McClelland, G. M. (1994). Does psychiatric disorder predict violent crime among released jail detainees? *Amer. Psychologist, 49*(4), 335–342.

Teri, L., & Lewinsohn, P. M. (1986). Individual and group treatment of unipolar depression: Comparison of treatment outcome and identification of predictors of successful treatment outcome. *Behav. Ther., 17*(3), 215–228.

Thakker, J., & Ward, T. (1998). Culture and classification: The cross-cultural application of the DSM-IV. *Clin. Psych. Rev., 18,* 501–529.

Thakur, C. P., & Sharma, D. (1984). Full moon and crime. *Brit. Med. J. (Clin. Res. Ed.), 289*(6460), 1789–1791.

Thase, M. E. (2005). Correlates and consequences of chronic insomnia. *Gen. Hosp. Psychiat., 27*(2), 100–112.

Thase, M. E. (2006). The failure of evidence-based medicine to guide treatment of antidepressant nonresponders. *J. Clin. Psychiat., 67*(12), 1833–1835.

Thase, M. E., Buysse, D. J., Frank, E., Cherry, C. R., Cornes, C. L., Mallinger, A. G., et al. (1997). Which depressed patients will respond to interpersonal psychotherapy? The role of abnormal EEG sleep profiles. *Amer. J. Psychiatry, 154*(4), 502–509.

Thase, M. E., Frank, E., Kornstein, S., & Yonkers, K. A. (2000). Gender differences in response to treatments of depression. In E. Frank (Ed.), *Gender and its effects on psychopathology* (pp. 103–129). Washington, DC: American Psychiatric Press.

Thase, M. E., Jindal, R., & Howland, R. H. (2002). Biological aspects of depression. In I. H. Gotlib & C. L. Hammen (Eds.), *Handbook of depression* (pp. 192–218). New York: Guilford Press.

Thase, M. E., Trivedi, M. H., & Rush, A. J. (1995). MAOIs in the contemporary treatment of depression. *Neuropsychopharmacology, 12*(3), 185–219.

Theodorou, S., & Haber, P. S. (2005). The medical complications of heroin use. *Curr. Opin. Psychiat., 18*(3), 257–263.

Thienemann, M. (2004). Introducing a structured interview into a clinical setting. *J. Amer. Acad. Child Adol. Psychiat., 43*(8), 1057–1060.

Thigpen, C. H., & Cleckley, H. M. (1957). *The three faces of Eve.* New York: McGraw-Hill.

Thio, A. (2006). *Deviant behavior* (8th ed.). New York: Pearson/Allyn & Bacon.

Thomas, J. (2004). Firewall needed between marketing and science. *The National Psychologist, 13*(5), pp. 1, 5.

Thomas, J. (2005). Expansion of Tarasoff "duty to warn" headed to trial in California. *The National Psychologist, 14*(1), pp. 1, 3.

Thompson, A. H., Stuart, H., Bland, R. C., Arboleda-Florez, J., Warner, R., & Dickson, R. A. (2002). Attitudes about schizophrenia from the pilot site of the WPA worldwide campaign against the stigma of schizophrenia. *Soc. Psychiat. Psychiatr. Epidemiol., 37*(10), 475–482.

Thompson, L. W., Tang, P. C. Y., Mario, J. D., Cusing, M., & Gallagher-Thompson, D. (2007). Bereavement and adjustment disorders. In D. G. Blazer, D. C. Steffens, & E. W. Busse (Eds.), *Essentials of geriatric psychiatry* (pp. 219–239). Washington, DC: American Psychiatric Publishing.

Thompson, R., & Keene, K. (2004). The pros and cons of caffeine. *The Psychologist, 17*(12), [np].

Thoresen, C. E., & Plante, T. G. (2005). Spirituality, religion, and health: What we know and what should you know? *Clinician's Res. Dig., Suppl. Bull. 32,* 1–2.

Thurston, C. (2008, April). Dietary supplements: The latest trends and issues. *Nutraceuticals World.* Retrieved May 2008 from http://www.nutraceuticalsworld.com/articles/2008/04/dietary-supplements-the-latest-trends-issues

Tierney, A. J. (2000). Egas Moniz and the origins of psychosurgery: A review commemorating the 50th anniversary of Moniz's Nobel Prize. *J. Hist. Neurosci., 9*(1), 22–36.

Time Poll. (2002). Kid poll: Young people's views on 9/11 anniversary conducted by Nickelodeon and *Time.*

Time. (1982, October 25). p. 70.

Time. (1983, September 5). Child abuse: The ultimate betrayal. (By Ed Magnuson).

Tjaden, P., & Thoennes, N. (2000). Prevalence and consequences of male-to-female and female-to-male intimate partner violence as measured by the National Violence Against Women Survey. *Violence Against Women, 6*(2), 142–161.

Tolan, P., Gorman-Smith, D., & Henry, D. (2006). Family violence. *Annu. Rev. Psychol., 57,* 557–583.

Tolin, D. F., & Meunier, S. A. (2008). Contamination and decontamination. In J. S. Abramowitz, D. McKay, & S. Taylor (Eds.), *Obsessive-compulsive disorder: Subtypes and spectrum conditions.* Oxford, England: Elsevier.

Tonigan, J. S., & Connors, G. J. (2008). Psychological mechanisms in Alcoholics Anonymous. In H. D. Kleber & M. Galanter (Eds.), *The American Psychiatric Publishing textbook of substance abuse treatment* (4th ed., pp. 491–498). Arlington, VA: American Psychiatric Publishing.

Torgersen, S. (1983). Genetic factors in anxiety disorders. *Arch. Gen. Psychiat., 40,* 1085–1089.

Torgersen, S. (1983). Genetics of neurosis: The effects of sampling variation upon the twin concordance ratio. *Brit. J. Psychiat., 142,* 126–132.

Torgersen, S. (1984). Genetic and nosological aspects of schizotypal and borderline personality disorders: A twin study. *Arch. Gen. Psychiat., 41,* 546–554.

Torgersen, S. (1990). Comorbidity of major depression and anxiety disorders in twin pairs. *Amer. J. Psychiat., 147,* 1199–1202.

Torgersen, S. (2000). Genetics of patients with borderline personality disorder. *Psychiatr. Clin. N. Amer., 23*(1), 1–9.

Toro, J., Cervera, M., Feliu, M. H., Garriga, N., Jou, M., Martinez, E., & Toro, E. (2003). Cue exposure in the treatment of resistant bulimia nervosa. *Inter. J. Eat. Disorders, 34*(2), 227–234.

Toro, J., Gila, A., Castro, J., Pombo, C., & Guete, O. (2005). Body image, risk factors for eating disorders and sociocultural influences in Spanish adolescents. *Eat. Weight Disord., 10*(2), 91–97.

Torrey, E. F. (1991). A viral-anatomical explanation of schizophrenia. *Schizo. Bull., 17*(1), 15–18.

Torrey, E. F. (1999, April 16). Interviewed in J. Lang, Local jails dumping grounds for mentally ill: 700,000 acutely ill held yearly. *Detroit News.*

Torrey, E. F. (2001). *Surviving schizophrenia: A manual for families, consumers, and providers* (4th ed.). New York: HarperCollins.

Torrey, E. F. (2002). Studies of individuals with schizophrenia never treated with antipsychotic medications: A review. *Schizo. Res., 58*(2–3), 101–115.

Torrey, E. F. (2006). *Surviving schizophrenia: A manual for families, patients and providers.* New York: HarperCollins.

Torrey, E. F., Bowler, A. E., Taylor, E. H., & Gottesman, I. I. (1994). *Schizophrenia and manic-depressive disorder.* New York: Basic Books.

Tosone, C. (2006). Living everyday lies: The experience of self. *Clin. Soc. Work J., 34*(3), 335–348.

Tozzi, F., Thornton, L. M., Klump, K. L., Fichter, M. M., Halmi, K. A., Kaplan, A. S., et al. (2005). Symptom fluctuation in eating disorders: Correlates of diagnostic crossover. *Am. J. Psychiat., 162,* 732–740.

Tractenberg, R. E., Singer, C. M., & Kaye, J. A. (2005). Symptoms of sleep disturbance in persons with Alzheimer's disease and normal elderly. *J. Sleep Res., 14*(2), 177–185.

Tramontin, M., & Halpern, J. (2007). The psychological aftermath of terrorism: The 2001 World Trade Center attack. In E. K. Carll (Ed.), *Trauma psychology: Issues in violence, disaster, health, and illness* (Vol. 1). Westport, CT: Praeger Publishers.

Travis, C. B. (2005). Heart disease and gender inequity. *Psychol. Women Quart., 29,* 15–23.

Travis, C. B., & Meltzer, A. L. (2008). Women's health: Biological and social systems. In F. L. Denmark & M. A. Paludi (Eds.), *Psychology of women: A handbook of issues and theories* (2nd ed., pp. 353–399). Westport, CT: Praeger Publishers.

Treaster, J. B. (1992, September 20). After hurricane, Floridians show symptoms seen in war. *New York Times.*

Treasure, J., Todd, G., & Szmukler, G. (1995). The inpatient treatment of anorexia nervosa.

In G. Szmukler, C. Dare, & J. Treasure (Eds.), *Handbook of eating disorders: Theory, treatment and research.* Chichester, England: Wiley.

Treatment Advocacy Center. (2007). *Briefing paper: Criminalization of individuals with severe psychiatric disorders.* Retrieved from www.Treatmentadvocacycenter.org

Trierweiler, S. J., Neighbors, H. W., Munday, C., Thompson, S. E., Binion, V. J., & Gomez, J. P. (2000). Clinician attribution associated with diagnosis of schizophrenia in African American and non-African American patients. *J. Cons. Clin. Psychol., 68,* 171–175.

Triggs, W. J., McCoy, K. J., Greer, R., Rossi, F., Bowers, D., Kortenkamp, S., et al. (1999). Effects of left frontal transcranial magnetic stimulation on depressed mood, cognition, and corticomotor threshold. *Biol. Psychiat., 45,* 1440–1446.

Troiano, R. P., Frongillo, E. A., Sobal, J., & Levitsky, D. A. (1996). The relationship between body weight and mortality: A quantitative analysis of combined information from existing studies. *Inter. J. Obesity, 20,* 63–75.

Trull, T. J., Sher, K. J., Minks-Brown, C., Durbin, J., & Burr, R. (2000). Borderline personality disorder and substance use disorders: A review and integration. *Clin. Psychol. Rev., 20*(2), 235–253.

Trull, T. J., Stepp, S. D., & Durrett, C. A. (2003). Research on borderline personality disorder: An update. *Curr. Opin. Psychiat., 16*(1), 77–82.

Trull, T. J., & Widiger, T. A. (2003). Personality disorders. In G. Stricker, T. A. Widiger, & I. B. Wiener (Eds.), *Handbook of psychology: Clinical psychology.* New York: Wiley.

Tryon, G. (1987). Abuse of therapist by patient. *Profess. Psychologist, 17,* 357–363.

Trzepacz, P. T., & Meagher, D. J. (2008). Neuropsychiatric aspects of delirium. In S. C. Yudofsky & R. E. Hales (Eds.), *The American psychiatric publishing textbook of neuropsychiatry and behavioral neurosciences* (5th ed.). Washington, DC: American Psychiatric Publishing.

Tsai, J. L., & Chentsova-Dutton, Y. (2002). Understanding depression across cultures. In I. H. Gotlib & C. L. Hammen (Eds.), *Handbook of depression* (pp. 467–491). New York: Guilford Press.

Tsai, J. L., Ying, Y. W., & Lee, P. A. (2001). Cultural predictors of self-esteem: A study of Chinese American female and male young adults. *Cult. Div. Ethnic Minority Psychol., 7,* 284–297.

Tsuang, M. T., Bar, J. L., Harley, R. M., & Lyons, M. J. (2001). The Harvard twin study of substance abuse: What we have learned. *Harv. Rev. Psychiat., 9*(6), 267–279.

Tsuang, M., Domschke, K., Jerkey, B. A., & Lyons, M. J. (2004). Agoraphobic behavior and panic attack: A study of male twins. *J. Anx. Disord., 18*(6), 799–807.

Tsuchiya, K. J., Agerbo, E., & Mortensen, P. B. (2005). Parental death and bipolar disorder: A robust association was found in early maternal suicide. *J. Affect. Disorders, 86*(2–3), 151–159.

Tucker, E. (2007, April 22). Advocates for mentally ill say restrictions on voting unfair. *Boston.com.* Retrieved August 19, 2008, from http://www.boston.com

Tucker, J. A., Foushee, H. R., Black, B. C., & Roth, D. L. (2007). Agreement between

prospective interactive voice response self-monitoring and structured retrospective reports of drinking and contextual variables during natural resolution attempts. *J. Stud. Alc. Drugs, 68*(4), 538–542.

Turk, C. L., Heimberg, R. G., & Hope, D. A. (2001). Social anxiety disorder. In D. H. Barlow (Ed.), *Clinical handbook of psychological disorders: A step-by-step treatment manual* (3rd ed.). New York: Guilford Press.

Turk, C. L., Heimberg, R. G., Luterek, J. A., Mennin, D. S., & Fresco, D. M. (2005). Emotion dysregulation in generalized anxiety disorder: A comparison with social anxiety disorder. *Cog. Ther. Res., 29*(1), 89–106.

Turkat, I. D., Keane, S. P., & Thompson-Pope, S. K. (1990). Social processing errors among paranoid personalities. *J. Psychopathol. Behav. Assess., 12*(3), 263–269.

Turkington, C., & Harris, J. R. (2001). *The encyclopedia of memory and memory disorders* (2nd ed.). New York: Facts on File.

Turner, E. H., Matthews, A. M., Linardatos, E., Tell, R. A., & Rosenthal, R. (2008). Selective publication of antidepressant trials and its influence on apparent efficacy. *N. Engl. J. Med., 358,* 252–260.

Turner, J., Batik, M., Palmer, L. J., Forbes, D., & McDermott, B. M. (2000). Detection and importance of laxative use in adolescents with anorexia nervosa. *J. Amer. Acad. Child Adol. Psychiat., 39*(3), 378–385.

Turner, S. M., Beidel, D. C., & Frueh, B. C. (2005). Multicomponent behavioral treatment of chronic combat-related posttraumatic stress disorder: Trauma management therapy. *Behav. Mod., 29*(1), 39–69.

Turton, M. D., O'Shea, D., Gunn, I., Beak, S. A., et al. (1996, January 4). A role for glucagon-like peptide-1 in the central regulation of feeding. *Nature, 379,* 69–72.

Turvey, B. E. (2008). A history of criminal profiling. In B. E. Turvey (Ed.), *Criminal profiling: An introduction to behavioral evidence analysis* (3rd ed., pp. 1–42). San Diego, CA: Elsevier.

Turvey, B. E. (2008). Ethics and the criminal profiler. In B. E. Turvey (Ed.), *Criminal profiling: An introduction to behavioral evidence analysis* (3rd ed., pp. 717–744). San Diego, CA: Elsevier.

Turvey, B. E., & McGrath, M. (2006). Criminal profilers and the media: Profiling the Beltway snipers. In W. Petherick (Ed.), *Serial crime: Theoretical and practical issues in behavioral profiling.* San Diego, CA: Elsevier.

Twain, M. (1884). *The adventures of Huckleberry Finn.*

Twemlow, S. W., Fonagy, P., & Sacco, F. C. (2003). Modifying social aggression in schools. *J. Appl. Psychoanal. Stud., 5*(2), 211–222.

Tyre, P. (2005, December 5). Fighting anorexia: No one to blame. *Newsweek, 146*(23), 50–59.

Tyrer, P., Mitchard, S., Methuen, C., & Ranger, M. (2003). Treatment rejecting and treatment seeking personality disorders: Type R and type S. *J. Pers. Disorders, 17*(3), 263–268.

Tyrer, P., & Simmonds, S. (2003). Treatment models for those with severe mental illness and comorbid personality disorder. *Brit. J. Psychiat., 182*(Suppl. 44), s15–s18.

Tyson, A. S. (2006, December 20). Repeat Iraq tours raise risk of PTSD, Army finds. *Washington Post.* Retrieved July 6, 2007, from www.washingtonpost.com

U.S. Census Bureau. (1990). *Statistical abstract of the United States.* Washington, DC: U.S. Government Printing Office.

U.S. Census Bureau. (1994). *Statistical abstract of the United States.* Washington, DC: U.S. Government Printing Office.

U.S. Census Bureau. (2000). *Statistical abstract of the United States.* Washington, DC: U.S. Government Printing Office.

U.S. Census Bureau. (2004). *Statistical abstract of the United States, 2005* (124th ed.). Washington, DC: Government Printing Office.

U.S. Census Bureau. (2005). *Statistical abstract of the United States, 2006* (125th ed.). Washington, DC: Government Printing Office.

U.S. Census Bureau. (2006). Table H101. Health insurance coverage status and type of coverage by selected characteristics: 2005 all races. *Annu. Demogr. Survey. March supplement.* Retrieved January 21, 2007, from http://pubdb3.census.gov/macro/032006/health/h01_001.htm

U.S. Census Bureau. (2008). *Statistical abstract of the United States: 2008* Retrieved June 17, 2008, from http://www.census.gov/statab/www

U.S. Department of Justice. (1994). *Violence between inmates: Domestic violence.* Annapolis Junction, MD: Bureau of Justice Statistics Clearinghouse.

U.S. Department of Justice. (2000). Report. Washington, DC: Author.

U.S. Department of Justice. (2006, September 10). *Teens and young adults experience the highest rates of violent crime.* Bureau of Justice Statistics. Retrieved August 11, 2008, from http://ojp.usdoj.gov/ bjs/glance/vage.html

Uchoa, D. D. (1985). Narcissistic transference? *Rev. Bras. Psicanal., 19*(1), 87–96.

Ueda, K., & Matsumoto, Y. (2003). National strategy for suicide prevention in Japan. *Lancet, 361*(9360), 882.

Uher, R., & Treasure, J. (2005). Brain lesions and eating disorders. *J. Neurol, Neurosurg, Psychiat., 76*(6), 852–857.

Ullmann, L. P., & Krasner, L. (1975). *A psychological approach to abnormal behavior* (2nd ed.). Englewood Cliffs, NJ: Prentice Hall.

Ulrich, R. S. (1984). View from a window may influence recovery from surgery. *Science, 224,* 420–421.

Underwood, M. K. (2003). *Social aggression among girls.* New York: Guilford Press.

Ungar, W. J., Mirabelli, C., Cousins, M., & Boydell, K. M. (2006). A qualitative analysis of a dyad approach to health-related quality of life measurement in children with asthma. *Soc. Sci. Med., 63*(9), 2354–2366.

UNINCB (United Nations International— Narcotics Control Board) Report. (1996). Cited in J. Roberts, Behavioral disorders are overdiagnosed in U.S. *Brit. Med. J., 312,* 657.

Urcuyo, K. R., Boyers, A. E., Carver, C. S., & Antoni, M. H. (2005). Finding benefit in breast cancer: Relations with personality, coping, and concurrent well-being. *Psychol. Hlth., 20*(2), 175–192.

Uretsky, S. (1999, June 25). *Clear as mud: They call it informed consent.* HeathScott.

Ursano, R. J., Boydstun, J. A., & Wheatley, R. D. (1981). Psychiatric illness in U.S. Air Force Vietnam prisoners of war: A five-year follow-up. *Amer. J. Psychiat., 138*(3), 310–314.

Ursano, R. J., Fullerton, C. S., Epstein, R. S., Crowley, B., Kao, T. C., Vance, K., et al. (1999). Acute and chronic posttraumatic stress disorder in motor vehicle accident victims. *Amer. J. Psychiat., 156*(4), 589–595.

Ursano, R. J., McCarroll, J. E., & Fullerton, C. S. (2003). Traumatic death in terrorism and disasters: The effects of posttraumatic stress and behavior. In R. J. Ursano, C. S. Fullerton, & A. E. Norwood (Eds.), *Terrorism and disaster: Individual and community mental health interventions* (pp. 308–332). New York: Cambridge University Press.

Utsey, S. O., Payne, Y. A., Jackson, E. S., & Jones, A. M. (2002). Race-related stress, quality of life indicators, and life satisfaction among elderly African Americans. *Cult. Div. Ethnic Minority Psychol., 8*(3), 224–233.

Utsey, S. O., Stanard, P., & Hook, J. N. (2008). Understanding the role of cultural factors in relation to suicide among African Americans: Implications for research and practice. In M. M. Leach & F. T. L. Leong (Eds.), *Suicide among racial and ethnic minority groups: Theory, research, and practice* (pp. 57–79). New York: Routledge/Taylor & Francis Group.

Vahia, I. V., & Cohen, C. I. (2008). Psychopathology. In K. T. Mueser & D.V. Jeste (Eds.), *Clinical handbook of schizophrenia* (pp. 82–90). New York: Guilford Press.

Vahia, V. N., & Vahia, I. V. (2008). Schizophrenia in developing countries. In K. T. Mueser & D.V. Jeste (Eds.), *Clinical handbook of schizophrenia* (pp. 549–555). New York: Guilford Press.

Vaillant, G. E. (1993). *The wisdom of the ego.* Cambridge, MA: Harvard University Press.

Vakili, A., Tayebi, K., Jafari, M. R., Zarrindast, M. R., & Djahanguiri, B. (2004). Effect of ethanol on morphine state-dependent learning in the mouse: Involvement of GABAergic, opioidergic and cholinergic systems. *Alcohol Alcoholism, 39*(5), 427–432.

Valbak, K. (2001). Good outcome for bulimic patients in long-term group analysis: A single-group study. *Eur. Eat. Disord. Rev., 9*(1), 19–32.

Valdiserri, E.V., Carroll, K. R., & Hartl, A. J. (1986). A study of offenses committed by psychotic inmates in a county jail. *Hosp. Comm. Psychiat., 37,* 163–165.

Valenstein, E. S. (1986). *Great and desperate cures.* New York: Basic Books.

van der Flier, W. M., van der Vlies, A. E., Weverling-Rijnsburger, A. W. E., de Boer, N. L., Admiraal-Behloul, F., Bollen, E. L. E. M., et al. (2005). MRI measures and progression of cognitive decline in nondemented elderly attending a memory clinic. *Inter. J. Ger. Psychiat., 20*(11), 1060–1066.

van Egmond, J. J. (2003). The multiple meanings of secondary gain. *Amer. J. Psychoanal., 63*(2), 137–147.

van Emmerik, A. A., Kamphuis, J. H., Hulsbosch, A. M., & Emmelkamp, P. M. (2002). Single session debriefing after psychological trauma: A meta-analysis. *Lancet, 360*(9335), 766–771.

van Griensven, F., Chakkraband,, M. L.-Somchai, Thienkrua, W., Pengjuntr, W., Cardozo, B. L., Tantipiwatanaskul, P., et al. (2006). Mental health problems among adults in tsunami-affected areas in southern Thailand. *JAMA, 296*(5), 537–548.

van Hout, W. J. P. J., & Emmelkamp, P. M. G. (2002). Exposure in vivo therapy in anxiety disorders: Procedure and efficacy. *Gedragstherapie, 35*(1), 7–23.

Van Koppen, P. J. (2007). Misapplication of psychology in court. In D. Carson, R. Milne, F. Pakes, K. Shalev, & A. Shawyer (Eds.), *Applying psychology to criminal justice.* Hoboken, NJ: John Wiley & Sons.

Van Orden, K. A., Witte, T. K., Selby, E. A., Bender, T. W., & Joiner, T. E., Jr. (2008). Suicidal behavior in youth. In J. R. Z. Abela & B. L. Hankin (Eds.), *Handbook of depression in children and adolescents.* New York: Guilford Press.

van Os, J., Faòanas, L., Cannon, M., Macdonald, A., & Murray, R. (1997). Dermatoglyphic abnormalities in psychosis: A twin study. *Biol. Psychiat., 41,* 624–626.

Van Praag, H. M. (1983). CSF 5–HIAA and suicide in non-depressed schizophrenics. *Lancet, 2,* 977–978.

Van Rossen & Associates (2002). Modeling advice. Retrieved January 2006 from www.modelingadvice.com

Van Wagner, K. (2007). Phobia list: An A to Z list of phobias. *About.com.* Retrieved July 22, 2008, from http://psychology.about.com/od/.phobias/a/phobialist.htm

van Walsum, K. L. (2004). Nos Malades: Three examples of Christian influences in care for the insane in pre-revolutionary France and Belgium. *J. Psychol. Christianity 23*(3), 219–233.

VandeCreek, L. (Ed.). *Innovations in clinical practice: Focus on adults.* Sarasota, FL: Professional Resource Press.

Vannoy, S. D., Duberstein, P., Cukrowicz, K., Lin, E., Fan, M. Y., & Unutzer, J. (2007). The relationship between suicide ideation and late-life depression. *Amer. J. Ger. Psychiat., 15*(12), 1024–1033.

Vartanian, L. R., Polivy, J., & Herman, C. P. (2004). Implicit cognitions and eating disorders: Their application in research and treatment. *Cog. Behav. Prac., 11,* 160–167.

Vasiliadis, H. M., Lesage, A., Adair, C., Wang, P. S., & Kessler, R. C. (2007). Do Canada and the United States differ in prevalence of depression and utilization of services? *Psychiatr. Serv., 58*(1), 63–71.

Veale, D. (2004). Body dysmorphic disorder. *Postgrad. Med. J., 80,* 67–71.

Vedantam, S. (2005, June 26). Patients' diversity is often discounted: Alternatives to mainstream medical treatment call for recognizing ethic, social differences. *Washington Post,* p. A01.

Vedantam, S. (2007, April 3). Criteria for depression are too broad, researchers say. *Washington Post,* p. A02.

Veiga-Martinez, C., Perez-Alvarez, M., & Garcia-Montes, J. M. (2008). Acceptance and commitment therapy applied to treatment of auditory hallucinations. *Clin. Case Stud., 7,* 118–135.

Venditti, E., Wing, R., Jakicic, J., Butler, B., & Marcus, M. (1996). Weight cycling, psychological health, and binge eating in obese women. *J. Cons. Clin. Psychol., 64*(2), 400–405.

Venneri, A., Bartolo, A., McCrimmon, S., & St. Clair, D. (2002). Memory and dating of past events in schizophrenia. *J. Inter. Neuropsychol. Soc., 8*(6), 861–866.

Verhaeghe, P., Vanheule, S., & De Rick, A. (2007). Actual neurosis as the underlying psychic structure of panic disorder, somatization, and somatoform disorder: An integration of

Freudian and attachment perspectives. *Psychoanal. Quart., 76*(4), 1317–1350.

Vernberg, E. M., La Greca, A. M., Silverman, W. K., & Prinstein, M. J. (1996). Prediction of posttraumatic stress symptoms in children after Hurricane Andrew. *J. Abnorm. Psychol., 105*(2), 237–248.

Verschuere, B., Crombez, G., Koster, E. H. W., & Uzieblo, K. (2006). Psychopathy and physiological detection of concealed information: A review. *Psycholica Belgica, 46*(1–2), 99–116.

Vetter, H. J. (1969). *Language behavior and psychopathology.* Chicago: Rand McNally.

Vidovic, V., Juresa, V., Begovac, I., Mahnik, M., & Tocilj, G. (2005). Perceived family cohesion, adaptability and communication in eating disorders. *Eur. Eat. Disord. Rev., 13*(1), 19–28.

Vieta, E. (2005). The package of care for patients with bipolar depression. *J. Clin. Psychiat., 66*(Suppl. 5), 34–39.

Vieta, E., & Phillips, M. L. (2007). Deconstructing bipolar disorder: A critical review of its diagnostic validity and a proposal for DSM-V and ICD-11. *Schiz. Bull., 33*(4), 886–892.

Viney, W. (2000). Dix, Dorothea Lynde. In A. E. Kazdin (Ed.), *Encyclopedia of psychology* (Vol. 3, pp. 65–66). Washington, DC: Oxford University Press/American Psychological Association.

Visser, M. (2003). Gregory Bateson on deuterolearning and double bind: A brief conceptual history. *J. Hist. Behav. Sci., 39*(3), 269–278.

Vitaliano, P. P., Persson, R., Kiyak, A., Saini, H., & Echeverria, D. (2005). Caregiving and gingival symptom reports: Psychophysiologic mediators. *Psychosom. Med., 67*(6), 930–938.

Vitousek, K. M., & Gray, J. A. (2006). Outpatient management of anorexia nervosa. In P. J. Cooper & A. Stein (Eds.), *Childhood feeding problems and adolescent eating disorders.* London: Routledge (Taylor & Francis Group).

Volkmar, F. R. (2001). Pharmacological interventions in autism: Theoretical and practical issues. *J. Clin. Child Psychol., 30*(1), 80–87.

Volkow, N. D., Fowler, J. S., & Wang, G. J. (2004). The addicted human brain viewed in the light of imaging studies: Brain circuits and treatment strategies. *Neuropharmacology, 47*(Suppl. 1), 3–13.

Volkow, N. D., Fowler, J. S., Wang., G. J., & Swanson, J. M. (2004). Dopamine in drug abuse and addiction: Results from imaging studies and treatment implications. *Mol. Psychiat., 9*(6), 557–569.

Volkow, N. D., Wang, G. J., Fowler, J. S., Logan, J., Gatley, S. J., Wong, C., et al. (1999). Reinforcing effects of psychostimulants in humans are associated with increases in brain dopamine and occupancy of D_2 receptors. *J. Pharmacol. Exp. Ther., 291*(1), 409–415.

Vonnegut, M. (1974, April). Why I want to bite R. D. Laing. *Harper's, 248*(1478), 80–92.

Vrij, A. (2004). The polygraph and lie detection. *Howard J. Criminal Justice, 43*(1), 108–110.

Vrij, A. (2008). *Detecting lies and deceit: Pitfalls and opportunities* (2nd ed.). New York: Wiley.

Wagstaff, G. F., MacVeigh, J., Boston, R., Scott, L., Brunas-Wagstaff, J., & Cole, J. (2003). Can laboratory findings on eyewitness testimony be generalized to the real world? An archival analysis of the influence of violence,

weapon presence, and age on eyewitness accuracy. *J. Psychol.: Interdisc. Appl., 137*(1), 17–28.

Walcott, D. D., Pratt, H. D., & Patel, D. R. (2003). Adolescents and eating disorders: Gender, racial, ethnic, sociocultural and socioeconomic issues. *J. Adol. Res., 18*(3), 223–243.

Waldinger, M., Berendsen, H., Blok, B., Olivier, B., & Holstege, B. (1998). Premature ejaculation and serotonergic antidepressants-induced delayed ejaculation: The involvement of the serotonergic system. *Behavior, Brain and Research, 92*(2), 111–118.

Walker, A. C. (2008). Grieving in the Muscogee Creek tribe. *Death Stud., 32*(2), 123–141.

Walker, C. E. (2003). Elimination disorders: Enuresis and encopresis. In M. C. Roberts (Ed.), *Handbook of pediatric psychology* (3rd ed., pp. 544–560). New York: Guilford Press.

Walker, R. L., Townley, G. E., & Asiamah, D. D. (2008). Suicide prevention in U.S. ethnic minority populations. In M. M. Leach & F. T. L. Leong (Eds.), *Suicide among racial and ethnic minority groups: Theory, research, and practice* (pp. 203–227). New York: Routledge/Taylor & Francis Group.

Wall, T. L., Shea, S. H., Chan, K. K., & Carr, L. G. (2001). A genetic association with the development of alcohol and other substance use behavior in Asian Americans. *J. Abnorm. Psychol., 110*(1), 173–178.

Wallace, M. (2002). Nash: Film no whitewash. *60 Minutes* interview, March 17, 2002.

Wallace, S. E. (1981). The right to live and the right to die. In S. E. Wallace & A. Eser (Eds.), *Suicide and euthanasia: The rights of personhood.* Knoxville: University of Tennessee Press.

Wallace, T. L., Stellitano, K. E., Neve, R. L., & Duman, R. S. (2004). Effects of cyclic adnosine monophosphate response element binding protein overexpression in the basolateral amygdala on behavioral models of depression and anxiety. *Biol. Psychiat., 56*(3), 151–160.

Wallis, C. (2005, February 28). The right (and wrong) way to treat pain. *Time, 165*(9), 46–57.

Wallis, C. (2005, January 17). The new science of happiness. *Time, 165*(3), A2–A9.

Walsh, E., Moran, P., Scott, C., McKenzie, K., Burns, T., Creed, F., Tyrer, P., Murray, R. M., & Fahy, T. (2003). Prevalence of violent victimisation in severe mental illness. *Brit. J. Psychiat., 183*(3), 233–238.

Walsh, T., McClellan, J. M., McCarthy, S. E., Addington, A. M., Pierce, S. B., Cooper, G. M., et al. (2008). Rare structural variants disrupt multiple genes in neurodevelopmental pathways in schizophrenia. *Science, 320*(5875), 539–543.

Walters, G. D. (2000). Behavioral self-control training for problem drinkers: A metal-analysis of randomized control studies. *Behav. Ther., 31*(1), 135–149.

Walters, G. D. (2002). The heritability of alcohol abuse and dependence: A meta-analysis of behavior genetic research. *Amer. J. Drug Alc. Abuse, 28*(3), 557–584.

Wampold, B. E. (2006). Designing a research study. In F. T. Leong & J. T. Austin, *The psychology research handbook, a guide for graduate students and research assistants* (2nd ed., pp. 93–103). Thousand Oaks, CA: Sage.

Wampold, B. E. (2007). Psychotherapy: The humanistic (and effective) treatment. *Amer. Psychologist, 62*(8), 857–873.

Wang Ping. (2000). *Aching for beauty: Footbinding in China.* Minneapolis, MN: University of Minnesota Press.

Wang, G., Pratt, M., Macera, C. A., Zheng, Z-J., & Heath, G. (2004). Physical activity, cardiovascular disease, and medical expenditures in U.S. adults. *Ann. Behav. Med., 28*(2), 88–94.

Wang, H. Y., Markowitz, P., Levinson, D., Undie, A. S., & Friedman, E. (1999). Increased membrane-associated protein kinase C activity and translocation in blood platelets from bipolar affective disorder patients. *J. Psychiatr. Res., 33*(2), 171–179.

Wang, M., & Jiang, G-R. (2007). Psychopathological mechanisms and clinical assessment of dissociative identity disorder. *Chinese J. Clin. Psychol., 15*(4), 426–429.

Wang, P. S., Aguilar-Gaxiola, S., Alonso, J., Angermeyer, M. C., Borges, G., Bromet, E. J., et al. (2007). Use of mental health services for anxiety, mood, and substance disorders in 17 countries in the WHO world mental health surveys. *Lancet, 370*(9590), 841–850.

Wang, P. S., Berglund, P., Olfson, M., Pincus, H. A., Wells, K. B., & Kessler, R. C. (2005). Failure and delay in initial treatment contact after first onset of mental disorders in the National Comorbidity Survey Replication. *Arch. Gen. Psychiat., 62,* 603–613.

Wang, P. S., Demler, O., & Kessler, R. C. (2002). Adequacy of treatment for serious mental illness in the United States. *Amer. J. Pub. Hlth., 92*(1), 92–98.

Wang, P. S., Demler, O., Olfson, M., Pincus, H. A., Wells, K. B., & Kessler, R. C. (2006). Changing profiles of service sectors used for mental health care in the United States. *Amer. J. Psychiat., 163*(7), 1187–1198.

Wang, P. S., Lane, M., Olfson, M., Pincus, H. A., Wells, K. B., & Kessler, R. C. (2005). Twelve-month use of mental health services in the United States. *Arch. Gen. Psychiat., 62,* 629–640.

Wang, S. S. (2007, September 25). Depression care: The business case. *Wall Street Journal Online.* Retrieved October 19, 2007, from http://blogs.wsj.com/health

Wang, S. S. (2007, December 4). The graying of shock therapy. *Wall Street Journal Online.* Retrieved August 14, 2008, from http://online.wsg.com/public/article_print/SB119673737406312767.html

Ward, E. C. (2007). Examining differential treatment effects for depression in racial and ethnic minority women: A qualitative systematic review. *JAMA, 99*(3), 265–274.

Waring, M., & Ricks, D. (1965). Family patterns of children who become adult schizophrenics. *J. Nerv. Ment. Dis., 140*(5), 351–364.

Warner, J. (2004). How Americans rank at spotting a liar. *WebMD,* April 2, 2004.

Warner, J. (2004, June 25). Alien abduction tales offer clues on memory: Study: Distress doesn't necessarily validate traumatic memories. *WebMD Health,* June 25, 2004.

Warren, R. (1997). REBT and generalized anxiety disorder. In J. Yankura, & W. Dryden (Eds.), *Using REBT with common psychological problems: A therapist's casebook.* New York: Springer.

Waschbusch, D. A. (2002). A meta-analytic examination of comorbid hyperactive-impulsive-attention problems and conduct problems. *Psychol. Bull., 128,* 118–150.

Wass, H., Miller, M. D., & Redditt, C. A. (1991). Adolescents and destructive themes in rock music: A follow-up. *Omega: J. Death Dying, 23,* 199–206.

Wasserman, I. M., & Stack, S. (2000). The relationship between occupation and suicide among African American males: Ohio, 1989–1991. In R. W. Maris, S. S. Canetto, J. L. McIntosh, & M. M. Silverman (Eds.), *Review of suicidology, 2000.* New York: Guilford Press.

Waters, A. M., & Craske, M. G. (2005). Generalized anxiety disorder. In M. M. Antony, D. R. Ledley, & R. G. Heimberg (Eds.), *Improving outcomes and preventing relapse in cognitive-behavioral therapy* (pp. 77–126). New York: Guilford Press

Waters, F. A. V., Badcock, J. C., & Maybery, M. T. (2007). Hearing voices: What are they telling us? In J. E. Pletson (Ed.), *Psychology and schizophrenia.* New York: Nova Science Publishers.

Watson, J. B. (1930). *Behaviorism* (Rev. ed.). Chicago: University of Chicago Press.

Watson, J. B., & Rayner, R. (1920). Conditioned emotional reaction. *J. Exp. Psychol., 3,* 1–14.

Watson, P. J., & Shalev, A. Y. (2005). Assessment and treatment of adult acute responses to traumatic stress following mass traumatic events. *CNS Spectrums, 10*(2), 123–131.

Watson, S. J., Benson, J. A., Jr., & Joy, J. E. (2000). Marijuana and medicine: Assessing the science base: A summary of the 1999 Institute of Medicine Report. *Arch. Gen. Psychiat., 57*(6), 547–552.

Watson, T. S., Watson, T. S., & Ret, J. (2008). Learning, motor, and communication disorders. In D. Reitman (Ed.), *Handbook of psychological assessment, case conceptualization, and treatment, Vol. 2: Children and adolescents.* Hoboken, NJ: John Wiley & Sons.

Watt, T. T. (2002). Marital and cohabiting relationships of adult children of alcoholics: Evidence from the National Survey of Family and Households. *J. Fam. Issues, 23*(2), 246–265.

Way, B. M., Miraglia, R., Sawyer, D. A., Beer, R., & Eddy, J. (2005). Factors related to suicide in New York State prisons. *Inter. J. Law Psychiat., 28*(3), 207–221.

Weaver, M. F., & Schnoll, S. H. (2008). Hallucinogens and club drugs. In H. D. Kleber & M. Galanter (Eds.), *The American Psychiatric Publishing textbook of substance abuse treatment* (4th ed., pp. 191–200). Arlington, VA: American Psychiatric Publishing.

Webster-Stratton, C. (2005). Early intervention with videotype modeling: Programs for families of children with oppositional defiant disorder or conduct disorder. In E. D. Hibbs & P. S. Jensen (Eds.), *Psychosocial treatments for child and adolescent disorders: Empirically based strategies for clinical practice* (2nd ed., pp. 507–555). Washington, DC: American Psychological Association.

Wechsler, H., Davenport, A., Dowdall, G., Moeykens, B., & Castillo, S. (1994). Health and behavioral consequences of binge drinking in college. *JAMA, 272*(21), 1672–1677.

Wechsler, H., Dowdell, G. W., Davenport, A., & Castillo, S. (1995). Correlates of college student binge drinking. *Amer. J. Pub. Hlth., 85*(7), 921–926.

Wechsler, H., Lee, J. E., Kuo, M., & Lee, H. (2000). College binge drinking in the 1990s: A continuing problem: Results of the Harvard School of Public Health 1999 College Alcohol Study. *J. Amer. Coll. Hlth., 48*(5), 199–210.

Wechsler, H., Lee, J. E., Kuo, M., Seibring, M., Nelson, T. F., & Lee, H. (2002). Trends in alcohol use, related problems and experience of prevention efforts among US college students 1993 to 2001: Results from the 2001 Harvard School of Public Health college alcohol study. *J. Amer. Coll. Hlth., 50,* 203–217.

Wechsler, H., & Nelson, T. F. (2008). What we have learned from the Harvard School of Public Health College Alcohol Study: Focusing attention on college student alcohol consumption and the environmental conditions that promote it. *J. Stud. Alc. Drugs, 69,* 481–490.

Wechsler, H., Seibring, M., Liu, I. C., & Ahl, M. (2004). Colleges respond to student binge drinking: Reducing student demand or limiting access. *J. Amer. Coll. Hlth., 52*(4), 159–168.

Wechsler, H., & Wuethrich, B. (2002). *Dying to drink: Confronting binge drinking on college campuses.* Emmaus, PA: Rodale Press.

Weder, N. D., Muralee, S., Penland, H., & Tampi, R. R. (2008). Catatonia: A review. *Ann. Clin. Psychiat., 20*(2), 97–107.

Weeks, D., & James, J. (1995). *Eccentrics: A study of sanity and strangeness.* New York: Villard.

Weeks, L., & Knox, R. (2008). Q& A: Behind the anthrax investigations. *NPR Archives.* Washington, DC: NPR.

Weggen, S., Eriksen, J. L., Sagi, S. A., et al. (2003). Evidence that nonsteroidal anti-inflammatory drugs decrease amyloid beta 42 production by direct modulation of gamma-secretase activity. *J. Biol. Chem., 278,* 31831–31837.

Weiden, P. J., & Kane, J. M. (Eds.). (2005). Optimizing pharmacotherapy to maximize outcome in schizophrenia: What is effectiveness with antipsychotic medications? *J. Clin. Psychiat., 66*(1), 122–128.

Weil, M. (2005, January 8). Rosemary Kennedy, 86: President's disabled sister. *Washington Post,* p. B06.

Weinberg, I., & Maltsberger, J. T. (2007). Suicidal behaviors in borderline personality disorder. In R. Tatarelli, M. Pompili, & P. Girardi (Eds.), *Suicide in psychiatric disorders.* New York: Nova Science Publishers.

Weinberg, M. K., Tronick, E. Z., Beeghly, M., Olson, K. L., Kernan, H., & Riley, J. M. (2001). Subsyndromal depressive symptoms and major depression in postpartum women. *Amer. J. Orthopsychiat., 71*(1), 87–97.

Weinberger, J., & Rasco, C. (2007). Empirically supported common factors. In J. Weinberger & S. G. Hofmann (Eds.), *The art and science of psychotherapy* (pp. 103–129). New York: Routledge/ Taylor & Francis Group.

Weiner, H. (1977). *Psychobiology and human disease.* New York: Elsevier.

Weiner, I. B., & Greene, R. L. (2008). *Handbook of personality assessment.* Hoboken, NJ: John Wiley & Sons.

Weinstein, D. D. (2007). Review of pathological gambling: A clinical guide to treatment. *J. Clin. Psychiat., 68*(5), 807.

Weis, R., & Smenner, L. (2007). Construct validity of the Behavior Assessment system for Children (BASC) Self-Report of Personality: Evidence from adolescents referred to residential treatment. *J. Psychoeduc. Assess., 25*(2), 111–126.

Weisman, R. L. (Ed.). (2004). Introduction to the special section on integrating community mental health and the criminal justice systems for adults with severe mental illness: Bridges and barriers. *Psychiatr. Quart., 75*(2), 105–106.

Weiss, B., & Feldman, R. S. (2006). Looking good and lying to do it: Deception as an impression management strategy in job interviews. *J. Appl. Soc. Psychol., 36*(4), 1070–1086.

Weiss, B., & Garber, J. (2003). Developmental differences in the phenomenology of depression. *Dev. Psychopathol., 15,* 403–430.

Weiss, D. E. (1991). *The great divide.* New York: Poseidon Press/Simon & Schuster.

Weiss, D. S., Marmar, C. R., Schlenger, W. E., Fairbank, J. A., Jordan, B. K., Hough, R. L., et al. (1992). The prevalence of lifetime and partial posttraumatic stress disorder in Vietnam theater veterans. *J. Traum. Stress, 5*(3), 365–376.

Weiss, J., Diamond, T., Demark, J., & Lovald, B. (2003). Involvement in Special Olympics and its relations to self-concept and actual competency in participants with developmental disabilities. *Res. Dev. Disabil., 24,* 281–305.

Weiss, R. D., Potter, J. S., & Iannucci, R. A. (2008). Inpatient treatment. In H. D. Kleber & M. Galanter (Eds.), *The American Psychiatric Publishing textbook of substance abuse treatment* (4th ed., pp. 445–458). Arlington, VA: American Psychiatric Publishing.

Weissberg, R. P. (2000). Improving the lives of millions of school children. *Amer. Psychologist, 55,* 1360–1372.

Weissman, M. M., et al. (1992). The changing rate of major depression: Cross-national comparisons. Cross-national collaborative group. *JAMA, 268*(21), 3098–3105.

Weissman, M. M. (2000). Social functioning and the treatment of depression. *J. Clin. Psychiat., 61*(Suppl.), 33–38.

Weissman, M. M., Livingston, B. M., Leaf, P. J., Florio, L. P., & Holzer, C., III. (1991). Affective disorders. In L. N. Robins & D. A. Regier (Eds.), *Psychiatric disorders in America: The Epidemiologic Catchment Area Study.* New York: Free Press.

Weissman, M. M., & Markowitz, J. C. (2002). Interpersonal psychotherapy for depression. In I. H. Gotlib & C. L. Hammen (Eds.), *Handbook of depression* (pp. 404–421). New York: Guilford Press.

Weissman, S. W. (2000). America's psychiatric work force. *Psychiatr. Times, 17*(11).

Weisz, J. R., McCarty, C. A., & Valeri, S. M. (2006). Effects of psychotherapy for depression in children and adolescents: A meta-analysis. *Psychol. Bull., 132*(1), 132–149.

Weizenbaum, J. (1966). ELIZA—a computer program for the study of natural language communication between man and machine. *Computational Linguistics, 9,* 36–41.

Wekerle, C., MacMillan, H. L., Leung, E., & Jamieson, E. (2007). Child maltreatment. In M. Hersen & A. M. Gross (Eds.), *Handbook of clinical psychology* (Vol. 2). Hoboken, NJ: John Wiley & Sons.

Welburn, K. R., Fraser, G. A., Jordan, S. A., Cameron, C., Webb, L. M., & Raine, D. (2003). Discriminating dissociative identity disorder from schizophrenia and feigned dissociation on psychological tests and structured interview. *J. Traum. Dissoc., 4*(2), 109–130.

Welch, W. M. (2007). Post-traumatic stress disorder is a serious problem for Iraq War veterans. In A. Quigley (Ed.), *Current controversies: Mental health*. Detroit: Greenhaven Press/Thomson Gale.

Wells, A. (2005). The metacognitive model of GAD: Assessment of meta-worry and relationship with DSM-IV generalized anxiety disorder. *Cog. Ther. Res., 29*(1), 107–121.

Wells, A., & Carter, K. (1999). Preliminary tests of a cognitive model of generalised anxiety disorder. *Behav. Res. Ther., 37*, 585–594.

Wells, A., & Papageorgiou, C. (1998). Relationships between worry, obsessive-compulsive symptoms and meta-cognitive beliefs. *Behav Res Ther., 36*, 899–913.

Wells, G. L. (2008). Field experiments on eyewitness identification: Towards a better understanding of pitfalls and prospects. *Law Human Behav., 32*(1), 6–10.

Wells, G. L., & Loftus, E. F. (2003). Eyewitness memory for people and events. In A. M. Goldstein (Ed.), *Handbook of psychology, Vol. 11: Forensic psychology* (pp. 149–160). Hoboken, NJ: Wiley.

Wells, G. L., & Olsen, E. A. (2003). Eyewitness testimony. *Annu. Rev. Psychol., 54*, 277–295.

Wells, R., et al. (2007, July 15). Canine and feline emergency room visits and the lunar cycle: 11,940 cases (1992–2002). *Journal of the American Veterinary Medical Association*.

Welsh, C. J., & Liberto, J. (2001). The use of medication for relapse prevention in substance dependence disorders. *J. Psychiatr. Prac., 7*(1), 15–31.

Wender, P. H., Kety, S. S., Rosenthal, D., Schulsinger, F., Ortmann, J., & Lunde, I. (1986). Psychiatric disorders in the biological and adoptive families of adopted individuals with affective disorders. *Arch. Gen. Psychiat., 43*, 923–929.

Weng, X., Odouli, R., & Li, D. K. (2008). Maternal caffeine consumption during pregnancy and the risk of miscarriage: A prospective cohort study. *Amer. J. Obstet. Gynecol., 198*(3), 297.e1–8.

Wenzel, T. (2002). Forensic evaluation of sequels to torture. *Curr. Opin. Psychiat., 15*, 611–615.

Werth, J. L., Jr. (1996). *Rational suicide? Implications for mental health professionals*. Washington, DC: Taylor & Francis.

Werth, J. L., Jr. (Ed.). (1999). *Contemporary perspectives on rational suicide*. Philadelphia, PA: Brunner/Mazel.

Werth, J. L., Jr. (2000). Recent developments in the debate over physician-assisted death. In R. W. Maris, S. S. Canetto, J. L. McIntosh, & M. M. Silverman (Eds.), *Review of suicidology, 2000*. New York: Guilford Press.

Werth, J. L., Jr. (2001). Policy and psychosocial considerations associated with non-physician assisted suicide: A commentary on Ogden. *Death Stud., 25*(5), 403–411.

Werth, J. L., Jr. (2004). The relationships among clinical depression, suicide, and other actions that may hasten death. *Behav. Sci. Law, 22*(5), 627–649.

Wertheimer, A. (2001). *A special scar: The experiences of people bereaved by suicide* (2nd ed.). East Sussex, England: Brunner-Routledge.

Westen, D., & Muderrisoglu, S. (2006). Clinical assessment of pathological personality traits. *Amer. J. Psychiat*.

Westen, D., Dutra, L., & Shedler, J. (2005). Assessing adolescent personality pathology: Quantifying clinical judgment. *Brit. J. Psychiat., 186*(3), 227–238.

Westen, D., Feit, A., & Zittel, C. (1999). Focus chapter: Methodological issues in research using projective methods. In P. C. Kendall, J. N. Butcher, & G. N. Holmbeck (Eds.), *Handbook of research methods in clinical psychology* (2nd ed.). New York: Wiley.

Westermeyer, J. (1993). Substance use disorders among young minority refugees: Common themes in a clinical sample. *NIDA Res. Monogr. 130*, 308–320.

Westermeyer, J. (2001). Alcoholism and co-morbid psychiatric disorders among American Indians. *Amer. Indian Alsk. Native Ment. Health Res. 10*, 27–51.

Westermeyer, J. (2004). Acculturation: Advances in theory, measurement, and applied research. *J. Nerv. Ment. Dis., 192*(5), 391–392.

Westermeyer, J., & Dickerson, D. (2008). Minorities. In H. D. Kleber & M. Galanter (Eds.), *The American Psychiatric Publishing textbook of substance abuse treatment* (4th ed., pp. 639–650). Arlington, VA: American Psychiatric Publishing.

Westermeyer, J., & Thuras, P. (2005). Association of antisocial personality disorder and substance disorder morbidity in a clinical sample. *Amer. J. Drug Alc. Abuse, 31*(1), 93–110.

Westheimer, R. K., & Lopater, S. (2005). *Human sexuality: A psychosocial perspective* (2nd ed.). Baltimore, MD: Lippincott Williams & Wilkins.

Wetherell, J. L., Lang, A. J., & Stein, M. B. (2006). Anxiety disorders. In D.V. Jeste & J. H. Friedman (Eds.), *Psychiatry for neurologists* (pp. 43–58). Totowa, NJ: Humana Press.

Wetterberg, L. (1999). Melatonin and clinical application. *Reprod. Nutr. Dev., 39*(3), 367–382.

Wetterling, T. (2005). Somatic diseases in elderly patients with delirium. *Zeitschrift Gerontopsychol. Psychiat., 18*(1), 3–7.

Wetzel, R. D., & Murphy, G. E. (2005). Suicide. In E. H. Rubin & C. F. Zorumski (Eds.), *Adult psychiatry* (2nd ed., pp. 409–419). Oxford, England: Blackwell Publishing.

Weyandt, L. L. (2006). The physiological basis of cognitive and behavioral disorders. Mahwah, NJ: Lawrence Erlbaum.

Wheatley, D. (2004). Triple-blind, placebo-controlled trial of ginkgo biloba in sexual dysfunction due to antidepressant drugs. *Human Psychopharmacol. Clin. Exp., 19*(8), 545–548.

Wheeler, B. W., Gunnell, D., Metcalfe, C., Stephens, P., & Martin, R. M. (2008). The population impact on incidence of suicide and non-fatal self harm of regulatory action against the use of selective serotonin reuptake inhibitors in under 18s in the United Kingdom: Ecological study. *Brit. Med. J., 336*(7643), 542.

Whiffen, V. E., & Demidenko, N. (2006). Mood disturbance across the life span. In J. Worell & C. D. Goodheart (Eds.), *Handbook of girls' and women's psychological health* (pp. 51–59). New York: Oxford University Press.

Whisman, M. A. (2001). The association between depression and marital dissatisfaction. In S. R. H. Beach (Ed.), *Marital and family processes in depression: A scientific foundation for clinical practice* (pp. 3–24). Washington, DC: American Psychological Association.

Whisman, M. A., & Bruce, M. L. (1999). Marital dissatisfaction and incidence of major depressive episode in a community sample. *J. Abnorm. Psychol., 108*(4), 674–678.

Whisman, M. A., & McGarvey, A. L. (1995). Attachment, depressotypic cognitions, and dysphoria. *Cog. Ther. Res., 19*(6), 633–650.

Whitaker, L. C. (2007). Forces pushing prescription psychotropic drugs in college mental health. *J. Coll. Student Psychother., 21*(3–4), 1–25.

Whitaker, R. (2002). *Mad in America: Bad science, bad medicine, and the enduring mistreatment of the mentally ill*. Cambridge, MA: Perseus.

Whitehead, W. E., Crowell, M. D., Heller, B. R., Robinson, J. C., et al. (1994). Modeling and reinforcement of the sick role during childhood predicts adult illness behavior. *Psychosom. Med., 56*, 541–550.

Whiteside, M. (1983, September 12). A bedeviling new hysteria. *Newsweek*.

Whitford, T. J., Farrow, T. F. D., Gomes, L., Brennan, J., Harris, A. W. F., & Williams, L. M. (2005). Grey matter deficits and symptom profile in first episode schizophrenia. *Psychiat. Res.: Neuroimaging, 139*(3), 229–238.

Whiting, J. W., et al. (1966). *I. Field guide for a study of socialization. Six cultures series*. New York: Wiley.

Whitman, T. A., & Akutagawa, D. (2004). Riddles in serial murder: A synthesis. *Aggress. Viol. Behav., 9*(6), 693–703.

Whittle, S. (2002). *Respect and equality: Transsexual and transgender rights*. London: Cavendish Publishing.

Whitty, M. T., & Carville, S. E. (2008). Would I lie to you? Self-serving lies and other-oriented lies told across different media. *Computers Human Behav., 24*(3), 1021–1031.

WHO (World Health Organization). (1983). *Depressive disorders in different cultures: Report of the WHO collaborative study of standardized assessment of depressive disorders*. Geneva: World Health Organization.

WHO (World Health Organization). (2000, June). *Female genital mutilation fact sheet*. Retrieved April 3, 2007, from http://www.who.int/mediacentre/factsheets/fs241/en

WHO (World Health Organization). (2004). Prevalence, severity, and unmet need for treatment of mental disorders in the World Health Organization World Mental Health Surveys. *JAMA, 291*(21), 2581–2590.

WHO (World Health Organization). (2006). *Depression*. Retrieved from http://www.who.int/mental_health/management/depression/definition/en

Wichniak, A., Riemann, D., Kiemen, A., Voderholzer, U., & Jernajczyk, W. (2000). Comparison between eye movement latency and REM sleep parameters in major depression. *Eur. Arch. Psychiat. Clin. Neurosci., 250*(1), 48–52.

Wicker, B. (2008). New insights from neuroimaging into the emotional brain in autism. In E. McGregor, M. Núñez, K. Cebula, & J. C. Gómez (Eds.), *Autism: An integrated view from neurocognitive, clinical, and intervention research*. Malden, MA: Blackwell Publishing.

Wickwire, E. M., Jr., Roland, M. M. S., Elkin, T. D., & Schumacher, J. A. (2008). Sleep disorders. In D. Reitman (Ed.), *Handbook of psychological assessment, case conceptualization, and treatment, Vol. 2: Children and adolescents*. Hoboken, NJ: Wiley.

Widiger, T. A. (2006). Understanding personality disorders. In S. K. Huprich, (Ed.), *Rorschach assessment of the personality disorders.* Mahwah, NJ: Lawrence Erlbaum.

Widiger, T. A. (2007). Alternatives to DSM-IV: Axis II. In S. O. Lilienfeld, W. O'Donohue, & K. A. Fowler (Eds.), *Personality disorders: Toward the DSM-V* (pp. 21–40). Thousand Oaks, CA: Sage Publications.

Widiger, T. A. (2007). Current controversies in nosology and diagnosis of personality disorders. *Psychiatr. Ann., 37*(2), 93–99.

Widiger, T. A., & Simonsen, E. (2005). Alternative dimensional models of personality disorder: Finding a common ground. *J. Pers. Disorders., 19*(2), 110–130.

Widiger, T. A., & Simonsen, E. (2005). Introduction to the special section: The American Psychiatric Association's research agenda for the DSM-V. *J. Pers. Disorders., 19*(2), 103–109.

Widloecher, D. (2001). The treatment of affects: An interdisciplinary issue. *Psychoanal. Q., 70*(1), 243–264.

Widom, C. S. (2001). Child abuse and neglect. In S. O. White (Ed.), *Handbook of youth and justice* (pp. 31–47). New York: Kluwer Academic/Plenum Press.

Widom, C. S., DuMont, K., & Szaja, S. J. (2007). A prospective investigation of major depressive disorder and comorbidity in abused and neglected children grown up. *Arch. Gen. Psychiat., 64*(1), 49–56.

Wiederhold, B. K., & Wiederhold, M. D. (2005). Posttraumatic stress disorder. In M. D. Wiederhold & B. K. Wiederhold (Eds.), *Virtual reality therapy for anxiety disorders: Advances in evaluation and treatment* (pp. 117–124). Washington, DC: American Psychological Association.

Wiederhold, B. K., & Wiederhold, M. D. (2005). Specific phobias and social phobia. In M. D. Wiederhold & B. K. Weiderhold, *Virtual reality therapy for anxiety disorders: Advances in evaluation and treatment* (pp. 125–138). Washington, DC: American Psychological Association.

Wiederman, M. W. (2001). "Don't look now": The role of self-focus in sexual dysfunction. *Fam. J. Counsel. Ther. Couples Fam., 9*(2), 210–214.

Wiegand, T., Thai, D., & Benowitz, N. (2008). Medical consequences of the use of hallucinogens: LSD, mescaline, PCP, and MDM ("ecstasy"). In J. Brick (Ed.), *Handbook of the medical consequences of alcohol and drug abuse* (2nd ed., pp. 461–490). New York: Haworth Press/Taylor & Francis Group.

Wiens, A. N., Mueller, E. A., & Bryan, J. E. (2001). Assessment strategies. In M. Hersen & V. B. Van Hasselt (Eds.), *Advanced abnormal psychology* (2nd ed., pp. 23–41). New York: Kluwer Academic/Plenum Press.

Wikan, U. (1991). *Managing turbulent hearts.* Chicago: University of Chicago Press.

Wilber, D. Q. (2008, June 7). Doctors request increase in freedom, driver's license for Hinckley. *Washington Post.* Retrieved August 19, 2008, from http://www.washingtonpost.com

Wilder-Smith, O. H. G. (2005). Opioid use in the elderly. *Eur. J. Pain, 9*(2), 137–140.

Wiley-Exley, E. (2007). Evaluations of community mental health care in low- and middle-income countries: A 10-year review of the literature. *Soc. Sci. Med., 64*(6), 1231–1241.

Wilkes, M. S., Bell, R. A., & Kravitz, R. L. (2000). Direct-to-consumer prescription drug advertising: Trends, impact, and implications. *Hlth. Affairs, 19*(2), 110–128.

Will, O. A. (1961). Paranoid development and the concept of self: Psychotherapeutic intervention. *Psychiatry, 24*(2), 516–530.

Will, O. A. (1967). Psychological treatment of schizophrenia. In A. M. Freedman & H. I. Kaplan (Eds.), *Comprehensive textbook of psychiatry.* Baltimore: Williams & Wilkins.

Williams, C. C. (1983). The mental foxhole: The Viet Nam veterans' search for meaning. *Amer. J. Orthopsychiat., 53*(1), 4–17.

Williams, P. G. (2004). The psychopathology of self-assessed health: A cognitive approach to health anxiety and hypochondriasis. *Cog. Ther. Res., 28,* 629–644.

Williams, T. M. (2008). *Black pain: It just looks like we're not hurting.* New York: Scribner.

Williams, T. O., Jr., Eaves, R. C., Woods-Groves, S., & Mariano, G. (2007). Stability of scores for the Slosson Full-Range Intelligence Test. *Psychol. Rep., 101*(1), 135–140.

Williamson, D. A., White, M. A., York-Crowe, E., & Stewart, T. M. (2004). Cognitive-behavioral theories of eating disorders. *Behavior Modification, 28*(6), 711–738.

Willick, M. S. (2001). Psychoanalysis and schizophrenia: A cautionary tale. *J. Amer. Psychoanal. Assoc., 49*(1), 27–56.

Willick, M. S., Milrod, D., & Karush, R. K. (1998). Psychoanalysis and the psychoses. In M. Furer, E. Nersessian, & C. Perri (Eds.), *Controversies in contemporary psychoanalysis: Lectures from the faculty of the New York Psychoanalytic Institute.* Madison, CT: International Universities Press.

Willis, S. L., Tennstedt, S. L., Marsiske, M., Ball, K., Elias, J., Koepke, K. M., et al. (2006). Long-term effects of cognitive training on everyday functional outcomes in older adults. *JAMA, 296*(23), 2805–2814.

Wilson, G. T. (2005). Psychological treatment of eating disorders. *Ann. Rev. Clin. Psychol., 1*(1), 439–465.

Wilson, G. T. (2008). Behavior therapy. In R. J. Corsini & D. Wedding (Eds.), *Current psychotherapies* (8th ed.). Belmont, CA: Thomson Brooks/Cole.

Wilson, G. T., Becker, C. B., & Heffernan, K. (2003). Eating disorders. In E. J. Mash & R. A. Barkley (Eds.), *Child psychopathology* (2nd ed., pp. 687–715). New York: Guilford Press.

Wilson, G. T., Heffernan, K., & Black, C. M. D. (1996). Eating disorders. In E. J. Mash & R. A. Barkley (Eds.), *Developmental psychopathology.* New York: Guilford Press.

Wilson, K. A., Chambless, D. L., & de Beurs, E. (2004). Beck anxiety inventory. In M. E. Maruish (Ed.), *The use of psychological testing for treatment planning and outcomes assessment, Vol. 3: Instruments for adults* (3rd ed., pp.399–419). Mahwah, NJ: Lawrence Erlbaum.

Wilson, K. A., & Hayward, C. (2005). A prospective evaluation of agoraphobia and depression symptoms following panic attacks in a community sample of adolescents. *J. Anx. Dis., 19*(1), 87–103.

Wilson, R. S., Scherr, P. A., Schneider, J. A., Tang, Y., & Bennett, D. A. (2007). Relation of cognitive activity to risk of developing Alzheimer disease. *Neurology, 69*(20), 1911–1920.

Wincze, J. P., Bach, A. K., & Barlow, D. H. (2008). Sexual dysfunction. In D. H. Barlow (Ed.), *Clinical handbook of psychological disorders: A step-by-step treatment manual* (4th ed.). New York: Guilford Press.

Winerman, L. (2005). A virtual cure. *Monitor Psychol., 36*(7), 87–89.

Wing, L. (1976). *Early childhood autism.* Oxford, England: Pergamon Press.

Wing, L., & Potter, D. (2002). The epidemiology of autistic spectrum disorders: Is prevalence rising? *Ment. Retard. Disabil. Res. Rev. Special Issue: The Epidemiology of Neurodevelopmental Disorders, 8,* 151–161.

Winick, B. J. (2008). A therapeutic jurisprudence approach to dealing with coercion in the mental health system. *Psychiat, Psychol. Law, 15*(1), 25–39.

Wink, P. (1996). Narcissism. In C. G. Costello (Ed.), *Personality characteristics of the personality disordered.* New York: Wiley.

Winn, B. D., Skinner, C. H., Allin, J. D., & Hawkins, J. A. (2004). Practicing school consultants can empirically validate interventions: A description and demonstration of the non-concurrent multiple-baseline design. *J. Appl. School Psychol., 20*(2), 109–128.

Winslade, W. J., & Ross, J. (1983). *The insanity plea.* New York: Scribner's.

Winstead, B. A., & Sanchez, J. (2005). Gender and psychopathology. In B. A. Winstead & J. E. Maddux (Eds.), *Psychopathology: Foundations for a contemporary understanding* (pp. 39–61). Mahwah, NJ: Lawrence Erlbaum.

Winston, A. S. (Ed.). (2004). *Defining difference: Race and racism in the history of psychology.* Washington, DC: American Psychological Association.

Winterman, D. (2006). A tan to die for. *BBC News.* Retrieved July 6, 2007, from http://news.bbc.co.uk/go/pr/fr/-/2/hi/uk_news/magazine/6101740.stm

Wirz-Justice, A., Graw, P., Kräuchi, K., Sarrafzadeh, A., et al. (1996). "Natural" light treatment of seasonal affective disorder. *J. Affect. Disord., 37,* 109–120.

Wisner, K. L., Perel, J. M., Peindl, K. S., Hanusa, B. H., Findling, R. L., & Rapport, D. (2001). Prevention of recurrent postpartum depression: A randomized clinical trial. *J. Clin. Psychiat., 62*(2), 82–86.

Witkiewitz, K. A., & Marlatt, G. A. (2004). Relapse prevention for alcohol and drug problems: That was zen, this is tao. *Amer. Psychologist, 59*(4), 224–235.

Witkiewitz, K. A., & Marlatt, G. A. (Eds.). (2007). *Therapist's guide to evidence-based relapse prevention.* San Diego, CA: Elsevier.

Witte, T. K., Merrill, K. A., Stellrecht, N. E., Bernert, R. A., Hollar, D. L., Schatschneider, C., et al. (2008). "Impulsive" youth suicide attempters are not necessarily all that impulsive. *J. Affect. Disorders, 107*(1–3), 107–116.

Wittstein, I. S., Thiemann, D. R., Lima, J. A. C., Baughman, K. L., Schulman, S. P., Gerstenblith, G., et al. (2005). Neurohumoral features of myocardial stunning due to sudden emotional stress. *N. Engl. J. Med., 352*(6), 539–548.

Witztum, E., Maragalit, H., & Van-der-Hart, O. (2002). Combat-induced dissociative amnesia: Review and case example of generalized dissociative amnesia. *J. Trauma Dissociat., 3*(2), 35–55.

Wolberg, L. R. (1967). *The technique of psychotherapy.* New York: Grune & Stratton.

Wolchik, S. A., West, S. G., Sandler, I. N., Tein, J. Y., Coatsworth, D., Lengua, L., et al. (2000). An experimental evaluation of theory-based mother and mother-child programs for children of divorce. *J. Cons. Clin. Psychol.,* 68, 843–856.

Wolfe, B. E. (2005). The application of the integrative model to specific anxiety disorders. In B. E. Wolfe, *Understanding and treating anxiety disorders: An integrative approach to healing the wounded self* (pp. 125–153). Washington, DC: American Psychological Association.

Wolfe, D. A., Edwards, B., Manion, I., & Koverola, C. (1988). Early intervention for parents at risk for child abuse and neglect: A preliminary investigation. *J. Cons. Clin. Psychol.,* 56, 40–47.

Wolff, S. (1991). Schizoid personality in childhood and adult life I: The vagaries of diagnostic labeling. *Br. J. Psychiatry, 159,* 615–620.

Wolff, S. (2000). Schizoid personality in childhood and Asperger syndrome. In S. S. Sparrow, A. Klin, & F. R. Volkmar (Eds.), *Asperger syndrome* (pp. 278–305). New York: Guilford Press.

Wolkowitz, O. M., & Reus, V. I. (2002). De hydroepiandrosterone as a neurohormone in the treatment of depression and dementia. In D. Mischoulon & J. F. Rosenbaum (Eds.), *Natural medications for psychiatric disorders: Considering the alternatives* (pp. 62–82). Philadelphia: Lippincott, Williams & Wilkins.

Wolpe, J. (1969). *The practice of behavior therapy.* Oxford, England: Pergamon Press.

Wolpe, J. (1987). The promotion of scientific psychotherapy: A long voyage. In J. K. Zeig (Ed.), *The evolution of psychotherapy.* New York: Brunner/Mazel.

Wolpe, J. (1990). *The practice of behavior therapy* (4th ed.). Elmsford, NY: Pergamon Press.

Wolpe, J. (1995). Reciprocal inhibition: Major agent of behavior change. In W. T. O'Donohue & L. Krasner (Eds.), *Theories of behavior therapy: Exploring behavior change.* Washington, DC: American Psychological Association.

Wolpe, J. (1997). From psychoanalytic to behavioral methods in anxiety disorders: A continuing evolution. In J. K. Zeig (Ed.), *The evolution of psychotherapy: The third conference.* New York: Brunner/Mazel.

Wolpe, J. (1997). Thirty years of behavior therapy. *Behav. Ther.,* 28(4), 633–635.

Wong, J. P. S., Stewart, S. M., Claassen, C., Lee, P. W. H., Rao, U., & Lam, T. H. (2008). Repeat suicide attempts in Hong Kong community adolescents. *Soc. Sci. Med.,* 66(2), 232–241.

Wong, Y., & Huang, Y. (2000). Obesity concerns, weight satisfaction and characteristics of female dieters: A study on female Taiwanese college students. *J. Amer. Coll. Nutr.,* 18(2), 194–199.

Wood, J. M., Garb, H. N., Lilienfeld, S. O., & Nezworski, M. T. (2002). Clinical assessment. *Annu. Rev. Psychol.,* 53, 519–543.

Woodruff, P. (2004). Auditory hallucinations: Insights and questions from neuroimaging. *Cog. Neuropsychiat.,* 9(1/2), 73–91.

Woods, B. (2008). Suicide and attempted suicide in later life. In R. Woods & L. Clare (Eds.), *Handbook of the clinical psychology of ageing* (2nd ed., pp. 111–119). New York: Wiley.

Woods, S. J. (2005). Intimate partner violence and post-traumatic stress disorder symptoms in women: What we know and need to know. *J. Interpers. Violence,* 20(4), 394–402.

Woodside, D. B., Bulid, C. M., Halmi, K. A., Fichter, M. M., Kaplan, A., Berrettini, W. H., et al. (2002). Personality, perfectionism, and attitudes towards eating in parent of individuals with eating disorders. *Inter. J. Eat. Disorders,* 31(3), 290–299.

Woodson, J. C., & Gorski, R. A. (2000). Structural sex differences in the mammalian brain: Reconsidering the male/female dichotomy. In A. Matsumoto (Ed.), *Sexual differentiation of the brain* (pp. 229–255). Boca Raton, FL: CRC Press.

Woodward, J. (2008, June 12). Bullies blamed after suicide of "Emo" music fan. *The Independent.* Retrieved June 14, 2008, from www.Independent.co.uk

Wortman, C. M., Wolff, K., & Bonanno, G. A. (2004). Loss of an intimate partner through death. In D. J. Mashek & A. Aron (Eds.), *Handbook of closeness and intimacy* (pp. 305–320). Mahwah, NJ: Lawrence Erlbaum.

Wright, J. (1984). EAP: An important supervisory tool. *Supervisory Management,* 29(12), 16–17.

Wright, L. W., Jr., & Hatcher, A. P. (2006). Treatment of sex offenders. In R. D. McAnulty & M. M. Burnette (Eds.), *Sex and sexuality, Vol. 3: Sexual deviation and sexual offenses.* Westport, CT: Praeger Publishers.

Wright, L. W., Jr., Hatcher, A. P., & Willerick, M. S. (2006). Violent sex crimes. In R. D. McAnulty & M. M. Burnette (Eds.), *Sex and sexuality, Vol. 3: Sexual deviation and sexual offenses.* Westport, CT: Praeger Publishers.

Wright, N. R., & Thompson, C. (2002). Withdrawal from alcohol using monitored alcohol consumption: A case report. *Alcohol Alcoholism,* 37(4), 344–346.

Wright, S., & Truax, P. (2008). Behavioral conceptualization. In M. Hersen & J. Rosqvist (Eds.), *Handbook of psychological assessment, case conceptualization, and treatment, Vol. 1: Adults* (pp. 53–75). Hoboken, NJ: John Wiley & Sons.

Wroble, M. C., & Baum, A. (2002). Toxic waste spills and nuclear accidents. In A. M. La Greca, W. K. Silverman, E. M. Vernberg, & M. C. Roberts (Eds.), *Helping children cope with disasters and terrorism* (pp. 207–221). Washington, DC: American Psychological Association.

Wu, D. M., Lu, J., Zheng, Y. L., Zhou, Z., Shan, Q., & Ma, D. F. (2008). Purple sweet potato color repairs D-galactose-induced spatial learning and memory impairment by regulating the expression of synaptic proteins. *Neurobiol. Learn. Memory,* 90(1), 19–27.

Wu, G., & Shi, J. (2005). The problem of AIM and countermeasure for improvement in interviews. *Psychol. Sci. (China),* 28(4), 952–955.

Wu, J., Kramer, G. L., Kram, M., Steciuk, M., Crawford, I. L., & Petty, F. (1999). Serotonin and learned helplessness: A regional study of 5–HT-sub(1A), 5–HT-sub(2A) receptors and the serotonin transport site in rat brain. *J. Psychiatr. Res.,* 33(1), 17–22.

Wu, L. T., Pilowsky, D. J., & Schlenger, W. E. (2005). High prevalence of substance use disorders among adolescents who use marijuana and inhalants. *Drug Alc. Dep.,* 78(1), 23–32.

Wunderlich, U., Bronisch, T., & Wittchen, H. U. (1998). Comorbidity patterns in adolescents and young adults with suicide attempts. *Eur. Arch. Psychiat. Clin. Neurosci.,* 248(2), 87–95.

Wurman, R. S., Leifer, L., & Sume, D. (2000). *Information anxiety 2.* Indianapolis, IN: Que.

Wyatt, G. W., & Parham, W. D. (2007). The inclusion of culturally sensitive course materials in graduate school and training programs. *Psychother.: Theory, Res. Pract. Train.,* 22(2, Suppl.) Sum 1985, 461–468.

Yalom, I. D. (1960). Aggression and forbiddenness in voyeurism. *Arch. Gen. Psychiat., 3,* 305–319.

Yalom, I. D., & Leszcz, M. (Col.). (2005). *The theory and practice of group psychotherapy* (5th ed.). New York: Basic Books.

Yamasaki, A., Chinami, M., Morgenthaler, S., Kaneko, Y., Nakashima, K., & Shirakawa, T. (2004). Enterprise failures correlate positively with suicide rate for both sexes in Japan. *Psychol. Rep., 95*(3, Part 1), 917–920.

Yamasaki, A., Sakai, R., & Shirakawa, T. (2005). Low income, unemployment, and suicide morality rates for middle-age persons in Japan. *Psychol. Rep., 96*(2), 337–348.

Yang, Y., Raine, A., Narr, K. L., Lencz, T., LaCasse, L., Colletti, P., et al. (2007). Localisation of increased prefrontal white matter in pathological liars. *Brit. J. Psychiat., 190*(2), 174–175.

Yehuda, R., & Bierer, L. M. (2007). Transgenerational transmission of cortisol and PTSD risk. *Prog. Brain Res., 167,* 121–135.

Yen, C. F., Kuo, C. Y., Tsai, P. T., Ko, C. H., Yen, J. Y., & Chen, T. T. (2007). Correlations of quality of life with adverse effects of medication, social support, course of illness. *Depress. Anx., 24*(8), 563–570.

Yen, S., Sr., Shea, M. T., Battle, C. L., Johnson, D. M., Zlotnick, C., Dolan-Sewell, R., et al. (2002). Traumatic exposure and posttraumatic stress disorder in borderline, schizotypal, avoidant and obsessive-compulsive personality disorders: Findings from the Collaborative Longitudinal Personality Disorders Study. *J. Nerv. Ment. Dis., 190*(8), 510–518.

Yewchuk, C. (1999). Savant syndrome: Intuitive excellence amidst general deficit. *Dev. Disabil. Bull., 27*(1), 58–76.

Yi, H. Y., et al. (2005). *Trends in alcohol-related traffic fatalities in the United States, 1977–2003.* (NIAAA Surveillance Report No. 71). Bethesda, MD: USPHS.

Yoder, K. A., Hoyt, D. R., & Whitbeck, L. B. (1998). Suicidal behavior among homeless and runaway adolescents. *J. Youth Adolescence, 27*(6), 753–771.

Yontef, G., & Jacobs, L. (2008). Gestalt therapy. In R. J. Corsini & D. Wedding (Eds.), *Current psychotherapies* (8th ed.). Belmont, CA: Thomson Brooks/Cole.

Yoshimasu, K., Kiyohara, C., & Ohkuma, K. (2002). Efficacy of day care treatment against readmission in patients with schizophrenia: A comparison between out-patients with and without day care treatment. *Psychiat. Clin. Neurosci., 56*(4), 397–401.

Young, J. (2002). Morals, suicide, and psychiatry: A view from Japan. *Bioethics, 16*(5), 412–424.

Young, K. S. (2005). Classifying sub-types, consequences, and causes of Internet addiction. *Psicol. Cond. Rev. Inter. Psicol. Clin. Salud* (Spanish), 13(3), 463–480.

Young, K. S. (2007). Cognitive behavior therapy with Internet addicts: Treatment outcomes and implications. *CyberPsychol. Behav., 10*(5), 671–679.

Young, M., Benjamin, B., & Wallis, C. (1963). Mortality of widowers. *Lancet, 2,* 454–456.

Yu, D. L., & Seligman, M. E. P. (2002). Preventing depressive symptoms in Chinese children. *Prev. Treat., 5,* [np].

Yusko, D. (2008). At home, but locked in war. Retrieved from: *Times-Union (Albany) Online.*

Yutzy, S. H. (2007). Somatoform disorders. In S. C. Yudofsky, J. A. Bourgeois, & R. E. Hales (Eds.), *The American Psychiatric Publishing Board prep and review guide for psychiatry* (pp. 235–243). Washington, DC: American Psychiatric Publishing.

Zakzanis, K. K., Campbell, Z., & Jovanovski, D. (2007). The neuropsychology of ecstasy (MDMA) use: A quantitative review. *Human Psychopharmacol.: Clin. Exp., 22*(7), 427–435.

Zanarini, M. C., Frankenburg, F. R., Hennen, J., Reich, D. B., & Silk, K. R. (2005). Psychosocial functioning of borderline patients and Axis II comparison subjects followed prospectively for six years. *J. Pers. Disorders, 19,* 19–29.

Zapf, P. A., & Roesch, R. (2006). Competency to stand trial: A guide for evaluators. In A. K. Hess & I. B. Weiner (Eds.), *Handbook of forensic psychology* (3rd ed., pp. 305–331). New York: Wiley.

Zec, R. F., Zellers, D., Belman, J., Miller, J., Matthews, J., Ferneau-Belman, D., & Robbs, R. (2001). Long-term consequences of severe closed-head injury on episodic memory. *J. Clin. Exp. Neuropsychol., 23*(5), 671–691.

Zec, R. F., Zellers, D., Belman, J., Miller, J., Matthews, J., Ferneau-Belman, D., & Robbs, R. (2002). "Long-term consequences of severe closed-head injury on episodic memory": Erratum. *J. Clin. Exp. Neuropsychol., 24*(1), 130.

Zelkowitz, P., Paris, J., Guzder, J., & Feldman, R. (2001). Diathesis and stressors in borderline pathology of childhood: The role of neuropsychological risk and trauma. *J. Amer. Acad. Child Adol. Psychiat., 40,* 100–105.

Zerbe, K. J. (1993). *The body betrayed: Women, eating disorders, and treatment.* Washington, DC: American Psychiatric Press.

Zerbe, K. J. (2008). *Integrated treatment of eating disorders beyond the body betrayed.* New York: W. W. Norton.

Zettle, R. D. (2007). *ACT for depression: A clinician's guide to using acceptance and commitment therapy in treating depression.* Oakland, CA: New Harbinger.

Zhang, J., & Lester, D. (2008). Psychological tensions found in suicide notes: A test for the strain theory of suicide. *Arch. Suic. Res., 12*(1), 67–73.

Zhou, J.-N., Hofman, M. A., Gooren, L. J. G., & Swaab, D. F. (1995). A sex difference in the human brain and its relation to transsexuality. *Nature, 378,* 68–70.

Zhou, J.-N., Hofman, M. A., Gooren, L. J. G., & Swaab, D. F. (1997). A sex difference in the human brain and its relation to transsexuality. *Nature, 378,* 68–70.

Zhou, S., Chan, E., Pan, S. Q., Huang, M., & Lee, E. J. D. (2004). Pharmacokinetic interactions of drugs with St John's wort. *J. Psychopharmacol., 18*(2), 262–276.

Ziedonis, D., Williams, J., Corrigan, P., & Smelson, D. (2000). Management of substance abuse in schizophrenia. *Psychiatr. Ann., 30*(1), 67–75.

Zilboorg, G., & Henry, G. W. (1941). *A history of medical psychology.* New York: Norton.

Zimbardo, P. (1976). Rational paths to madness. Presentation at Princeton University, Princeton, NJ.

Zipp, F., & Aktas, O. (2006). The brain as a target of inflammation: Common pathways link inflammatory and neurodegenerative diseases. *Trends Neurosci., 29*(9), 518–527.

Zito, J. M., Safer, D. J., dos Reis, S., Gardner, J. F., Boles, M., & Lynch, F. (2000). Trends in prescribing of psychotropic medications to preschoolers. *JAMA, 283*(8), 1025–1030.

Zivin, J. (2000, April). Understanding clinical trials. *Scientif. Amer.,* p. 69.

Zoellner, T. (2000, November). "Don't get even, get mad." *Men's Health, 15*(9), 56.

Zohar, J., & Pato, M. T. (1991). Diagnostic considerations. In M. T. Pato & J. Zohar (Eds.), *Current treatments of obsessive-compulsive disorder.* Washington, DC: American Psychiatric Press.

Zonana, H., Roth, J. A., & Coric, V. (2004). Forensic assessment of sex offenders. In R. I. Simon & L. H. Gold (Eds.), *The American Psychiatric Publishing textbook of forensic psychiatry* (pp. 349–376). Washington, DC: American Psychiatric Publishing.

Zucker, K. J. (2005). Gender identity disorder in children and adolescents. *Ann. Rev. Clin. Psychol., 1*(1), 467–492.

Zucker, K. J., & Bradley, S. J. (1995). *Gender identity disorder and psychosexual problems in children and adolescents.* New York: Guilford Press.

Journal Abbreviations

Academ. Med. *Academic Medicine*
Academ. Psychiat. *Academic Psychiatry*
Accid. Anal. Prev. *Accident Analysis and Prevention*
Acta Psychiatr. Scandin. *Acta Psychiatrica Scandinavica*
Addic. Behav. *Addictive Behaviors*
Addic. Disord. Treat. *Addictive Disorders and Their Treatment*
Addiction *Addiction*
Admin. Policy Ment. Hlth. *Administration and Policy in Mental Health*
Adol. Psychiat. *Adolescent Psychiatry*
Adolescence *Adolescence*
Adv. Behav. Res. Ther. *Advances in Behavior Research and Therapy*
Adv. Drug React. Toxicol. Rev. *Advanced Drug Reaction and Toxicology Review*
Adv. Mind-Body Med. *Advances in Mind-Body Medicine*
Adv. Nurs. Sci. *Advances in Nursing Science*
Aggress. Viol. Behav. *Aggression and Violent Behavior*
Aging *Aging*
Aging Ment. Hlth. *Aging and Mental Health*
Aging Neuropsychol. Cog. *Aging, Neuropsychology, and Cognition*
Alcohol Alcoholism *Alcohol and Alcoholism*
Alcoholism Treat. Quart. *Alcoholism Treatment Quarterly*
Alz. Disease Assoc. Disord. *Alzheimer's Disease and Associated Disorders*
Amer. Behav. Sci. *American Behavioral Scientist*
Amer. Hlth. *American Health*
Amer. J. Addict. *American Journal on Addiction*
Amer. J. Alz. Disease Other Dement. *American Journal of Alzheimer's Disease and Other Dementias*

Amer. J. Cardiol. *American Journal of Cardiology*
Amer. J. Clin. Hyp. *American Journal of Clinical Hypnosis*
Amer. J. Clin. Hypnother. *American Journal of Clinical Hypnotherapy*
Amer. J. Clin. Nutr. *American Journal of Clinical Nutrition*
Amer. J. Comm. Psychol. *American Journal of Community Psychology*
Amer. J. Criminal Justice *American Journal of Criminal Justice*
Amer. J. Drug Alc. Abuse *American Journal of Drug and Alcohol Abuse*
Amer. J. Fam. Ther. *American Journal of Family Therapy*
Amer. J. Forens. Psychol. *American Journal of Forensic Psychology*
Amer. J. Ger. Pharmacother. *American Journal of Geriatric Pharmacotherapy*
Amer. J. Ger. Psychiat. *American Journal of Geriatric Psychiatry*
Amer. J. Hlth. Sys. Pharmacol. *American Journal of Health Systems and Pharmacology*
Amer. J. Hospice Pall. Care *American Journal of Hospice and Palliative Care*
Amer. J. Hospice Pall. Med. *American Journal of Hospice and Palliative Medicine*
Amer. J. Med. Genet. *American Journal of Medical Genetics*
Amer. J. Ment. Def. *American Journal of Mental Deficiency*
Amer. J. Ment. Retard. *American Journal of Mental Retardation*
Amer. J. Obstet. Gynecol. *American Journal of Obstetrics and Gynecology*
Amer. J. Orthopsychiat. *American Journal of Orthopsychiatry*
Amer. J. Prev. Med. *American Journal of Preventive Medicine*
Amer. J. Psychiat. *American Journal of Psychiatry*
Amer. J. Psychoanal. *American Journal of Psychoanalysis*
Amer. J. Psychother. *American Journal of Psychotherapy*
Amer. J. Publ. Hlth. *American Journal of Public Health*
Amer. Psychologist *American Psychologist*
Amer. Sci. *American Scientist*
Amer. Sociol. Rev. *American Sociological Review*
Animal Behav. *Animal Behavior*
Animal Welfare *Animal Welfare*
Ann. Amer. Psychother. Assn. *Annals of the American Psychotherapy Association*
Ann. Behav. Med. *Annals of Behavioral Medicine*
Ann. Clin. Psychiat. *Annals of Clinical Psychiatry*
Ann. Internal Med. *Annals of Internal Medicine*
Ann. Med. *Annals of Medicine*
Ann. Neurol. *Annals of Neurology*
Ann. Pharmacother. *Annals of Pharmacotherapy*
Annales Medico Psychologiques *Annales Medico Psychologiques*
Annu. Rev. Clin. Psychol. *Annual Review of Clinical Psychology*
Annu. Rev. Neurosci. *Annual Review of Neuroscience*
Annu. Rev. Psychol. *Annual Review of Psychology*
Anthropol. Med. *Anthropology and Medicine*
Anx. Disorders *Anxiety Disorders*
Anx., Stress, Coping: Inter. J. *Anxiety, Stress, and Coping: An International Journal*
Aphasiology *Aphasiology*
Appetite *Appetite*
Appl. Cog. Psychol. *Applied Cognitive Psychology*
Appl. Dev. Sci. *Applied Developmental Science*
Appl. Hlth. Econ. Policy *Applied Health Economics and Health Policy*
Appl. Neuropsychol. *Applied Neuropsychology*

Appl. Prev. Psychol. *Applied Preventive Psychology*
Appl. Psychol. Measure. *Applied Psychological Measurement*
Appl. Psychophysiol. Biofeedback *Applied Psychophysiology and Biofeedback*
Arch. Fam. Med. *Archives of Family Medicine*
Arch. Gen. Psychiat. *Archives of General Psychiatry*
Arch. Geront. Geriat. *Archives of Gerontology and Geriatrics*
Arch. Internal Med. *Archives of Internal Medicine*
Arch. Neurol. *Archives of Neurology*
Arch. Pediatr. Adoles. Med. *Archives of Pediatric Adolescent Medicine*
Arch. Psychiat. Psychother. *Archives of Psychiatry and Psychotherapy*
Arch. Psychiatr. Nursing *Archives of Psychiatric Nursing*
Arch. Sex. Behav. *Archives of Sexual Behavior*
Arch. Suic. Res. *Archives of Suicide Research*
Arch. Women's Ment. Hlth. *Archives of Women's Mental Health*
Assessment *Assessment*
Austral. J. Clin. Exp. Hyp. *Australian Journal of Clinical and Experimental Hypnosis*
Austral. J. Psychol. *Australian Journal of Psychology*
Austral. New Zeal. J. Psychiat. *Australian and New Zealand Journal of Psychiatry*
Austral. Psychol. Soc. *Australian Psychological Society*
Austral. Psychologist *Australian Psychologist*
Autism *Autism*

Bagimlik Dergisi *Bagimlik Dergisi*
Basic Appl. Soc. Psychol. *Basic and Applied Social Psychology*
Behav. Brain Res. *Behavioral Brain Research*
Behav. Change *Behaviour-Change*
Behav. Cog. Psychother. *Behavioural and Cognitive Psychotherapy*
Behav. Genet. *Behavioral Genetics*
Behav. Intervent. *Behavioral Interventions*
Behav. Med. *Behavioral Medicine*
Behav. Mod. *Behavior Modification*
Behav. Neurosci. *Behavioral Neuroscience*
Behav. Pharmacol. *Behavioral Pharmacology*
Behav. Psychother. *Behavioiral Psychotherapy*
Behav. Res. Meth. Instru. Computers *Behavioral Research Methods, Instruments and Computers*
Behav. Res. Ther. *Behavioral Research and Therapy*
Behav. Sci. *Behavioral Science*
Behav. Sci. Law *Behavioral Sciences and the Law*
Behav. Ther. *Behavior Therapy*
Behav. Ther. Exp. Psychiat. *Behaviour Therapy and Experimental Psychiatry*
Behav. Therapist *Behavior Therapist*
Bioethics *Bioethics*
Biofeed. Self-Reg.. *Biofeedback Self Regulation*
Biol. Psychiat. *Biological Psychiatry*
Biol. Psychol. *Biological Psychology*
Biol. Rhythm Res. *Biological Rhythm Research*
Bipolar Disord. *Bipolar Disorders*
Body Image *Body Image*
Brain Behav. Immun,. *Brain, Behavior, and Immunity*
Brain Inj. *Brain Injury*
Brain Res. Reviews *Brain Research*
Brief Treat. Crisis Intervent. *Brief Treatment and Crisis Intervention*
Brit. J. Clin. Psychol.. *British Journal of Clinical Psychology*
Brit. J. Cog. Psychother. *British Journal of Cognitive Psychotherapy*
Brit. J. Criminol. *British Journal of Criminology*
Brit. J. Dev. Psychol. *British Journal of Developmental Psychology*

Brit. J. Forensic Prac. *British Journal of Forensic Practice*
Brit. J. Guid. Couns. *British Journal of Guidance and Counseling*
Brit. J. Med. Psychol. *British Journal of Medical Psychology*
Brit. J. Psychiat. *British Journal of Psychiatry*
Brit. J. Psychol. *British Journal of Psychology*
Brit. J. Urol. *British Journal of Urology*
Brit. Med. J. *British Medical Journal*
Bull. Amer. Acad. Psychiat. Law *Bulletin of the American Academy of Psychiatry Law*
Bull. Menninger Clin. *Bulletin of the Menninger Clinic*
Bull. Psychol. *Bulletin de Psychologie*
Bull. Psychosom. Soc. *Bulletin of the Psychosomatic Society*

Canad. J. Neurol. Sci. *Canadian Journal of Neurological Science*
Canad. J. Psychiat. *Canadian Journal of Psychiatry*
Canad. J. Psychoanal. *Canadian Journal of Psychoanalysis*
Canad. Med. Assoc. J., *Canadian Medical Association Journal*
Canad. Psychol. *Canadian Psychology*
Cell *Cell*
Cephalalgia *Cephalalgia*
Child Abuse Negl. *Child Abuse and Neglect*
Child Adol. Ment. Hlth. *Child and Adolescent Mental Health*
Child Adol. Psychiat. Clin. N. Amer. *Child and Adolescent Psychiatric Clinics of North America*
Child Dev. *Child Development*
Child Fam. Behav. Ther. *Child and Family Behavior Therapy*
Child Maltreat: J. Amer. Profess. Soc. Abuse Child. *Child Maltreatment: Journal of the American Professional Society on the Abuse of Children*
Child Psychiat. Human Dev. *Child Psychiatry and Human Development*
Chinese J. Clin. Psychol. *Chinese Journal of Clinical Psychology*
Chinese Ment. Hlth. J. *Chinese Mental Health Journal*
Circulation *Circulation*
Clin. Case Stud. *Clinical Case Studies*
Clin. Child Fam. Psychol. Rev. *Clinical Child and Family Psychology Review*
Clin. Child Psychol. Psychiat. *Clinical Child Psychology and Psychiatry*
Clin. Electroencephalogr. *Clinical Electroencephalography*
Clin. J. Pain *Clinical Journal of Pain*
Clin. Neuropharmacol. *Clinical Neuropharmacology*
Clin. Neuropsychiat.: J. Treat. Eval. *Clinical Neuropsychiatry: Journal of Treatment Evaluation*
Clin. Pediatr. *Clinical Pediatrics*
Clin. Psychol. Psychother. *Clinical Psychology and Psychotherapy*
Clin. Psychol. Psychother. *Clinical Psychology and Psychotherapy*
Clin. Psychol. Rev. *Clinical Psychology Review*
Clin. Psychol.: Sci. Prac. *Clinical Psychology: Science and Practice*
Clin. Soc. Work J. *Clinical Social Work Journal*
Clin. Ther.: Inter. J. Drug Ther. *Clinical Therapeutics: The International Journal of Drug Therapy*
Clinica-y-Salud *Clinica-y-Salud*
Clinician's Res. Dig. *Clinician's Research Digest*
CNS Drug Rev. *CNS Drug Reviews*
CNS Drugs *CNS Drugs*
CNS Spectrums *CNS Spectrums*
Cog. Behav. Pract. *Cognitive and Behavioral Practice*

Cog. Brain Res. *Cognitive Brain Research*
Cog. Emot. *Cognition and Emotion*
Cog. Ther. Res. *Cognitive Therapy and Research*
Coll. Student J. *College Student Journal*
Communic. Res. *Communication Research*
Comprehen. Psychiat. *Comprehensive Psychiatry*
Comprehen. Ther. *Comprehensive Therapy*
Computers Human Behav. *Computers in Human Behavior*
Contemp. Fam. Ther.: Inter. J. *Contemporary Family Therapy: An International Journal*
Contemp. Hyp. *Contemporary Hypnosis*
Couns. Psychologist *Counseling Psychologist*
Criminal Behav. Ment. Hlth. *Criminal Behaviour and Mental Health*
Criminal Justice Behav. *Criminal Justice and Behavior*
Crisis *Crisis*
Crisis: J. Crisis Intervent. Suic. Prev. *Crisis: Journal of Crisis Intervention and Suicide Prevention*
Crit. Rev. Neurobiol. *Critical Review of Neurobiology*
Cult. Div. Ethnic Minority Psychol. *Cultural Diversity and Ethnic Minority Psychology*
Cult. Med. Psychiat. *Culture, Medicine and Psychiatry*
Cult. Psychiat. *Cultural Psychiatry*
Curr. Alz. Res. *Current Alzheimer Research*
Curr. Direct. Psychol. Sci. *Current Directions in Psychological Science*
Curr. Opin. Psychiat. *Current Opinions in Psychiatry*
Curr. Probl. Pediatr., *Current Problems in Pediatrics*
Curr. Psychol.: Dev. Learn. Personal. Soc. *Current Psychology: Developmental, Learning, Personality, Social*
CyberPsychol. Behav. *CyberPsychology and Behavior*

Death Stud. *Death Studies*
Dement. Ger. Cogn. Disord. *Dementia and Geriatric Cognitive Disorders*
Depress. Anx. *Depression and Anxiety*
Dermatol. Surg. *Dermatologic Surgery*
Dev. Psychol. *Developmental Psychology*
Dev. Psychopathology. *Development and Psychopathology*
Direct. Psychiat. *Directions in Psychiatry*
Diss. Abstr. Inter.: Sect. A: Human Soc. Sci. *Dissertation Abstracts International: Section A: Humanities and Social Sciences*
Diss. Abstr. Inter.: Sect. B: Sci. Eng. *Dissertation Abstracts International: Section B: The Sciences and Engineering*
Dissociat.: Prog. Dissociat. Disorders *Dissociation: Progress in the Dissociative Disorders*
Dreaming *Dreaming*
Drug Alc. Dep. *Drug and Alcohol Dependence*
Drug Benef. Trends *Drug Benefit Trends*
Drugs *Drugs*
Dyslexia: Inter. J. Res. Pract. *Dyslexia: An International Journal of Research and Practice*

Early Intervent. Psychiat. *Early Intervention in Psychiatry*
Eat. Behav. *Eating Behaviors*
Eat. Disord.: J. Treat. Prev. *Eating disorders: The Journal of Treatment and Prevention*
Eat. Weight Disord. *Eating and Weight Disorders*
Educ. Train. Dev. Disabil. *Education and Training in Developmental Disabilities*
Emotion *Emotion*
Empir. Stud. Arts *Empirical Studies of the Arts.*
Epidem. e Psichiatr. Soc. *Epidemiologia e Psichiatria Sociale*
Encephale *Encephale*

Eta Evolutiva *Eta Evolutiva*
Ethical Human Psychol. Psychiat. *Ethical Human Psychology and Psychiatry*
Ethnicity Dis. *Ethnicity and Disease*
Ethics Behav. *Ethics and Behavior*
Eur. Arch. Psychiat. Clin. Neurosci. *European Archives of Psychiatry and Clinical Neuroscience*
Eur. Child Adol. Psychiat. *European Child and Adolescent Psychiatry*
Eur. Eat. Disord. Rev. *European Eating Disorders Review*
Eur. J. Med. Res. *European Journal of Medical Research*
Eur. J. Pain *European Journal of Pain*
Eur. J. Pers. *European Journal of Personality*
Eur. J. Psychiat. *European Journal of Psychiatry*
Eur. J. Psychoanal. Ther. Res. *European Journal for Psychoanalytic Therapy and Research*
Eur. J. Psychol. Assess. *European Journal of Psychological Assessment*
Eur. Neurol. *European Neurology*
Eur. Neuropsychopharmacology *European Neuropsychopharmacology*
Eur. Psychiat. *European Psychiatry*
Eur. Urol. *European Urology*
Evol. Psychiat. *Evolution Psychiatrique*
Exist. Anal. *Existential Analysis*
Exp. Clin. Psychopharmacol. *Experimental and Clinical Psychopharmacology*

Fam. J.: Couns. Ther. Couples Fam. *Family Journal: Counseling and Therapy for Couples and Families*
Fam. Pract. News *Family Practice News*
Fam. Rel.: Interdiscip. J. Appl. Fam. Stud. *Family Relations: Interdisciplinary Journal Applied Family Studies*
Fam. Ther. *Family Therapy*
Focus Autism Other Dev. Disabil. *Focus on Autism and Other Developmental Disabilities*

G. Ital. Suic. *Giornale Italiano di Suicidologia*
Gen. Hosp. Psychiat. *General Hospital Psychiatry*
Gender Soc. *Gender and Society*
German J. Psychiat. *German Journal of Psychiatry*
Gerontologist *Gerontologist*

Harvard Rev. Psychiat. *Harvard Review of Psychiatry*
Headache *Headache*
Hlth. Commun. *Health Communication*
Hlth. Econ. *Health Economics*
Hippocampus *Hippocampus*
Hist. Psychiat. *History of Psychiatry*
Hlth. Psychol. *Health Psychology*
Homeostasis Hlth. Dis. *Homeostasis Health and Disease*
Homicide Stud.: Interdisc. Internat. J. *Homicide Studies: An Interdisciplinary and International Journal*
Hong Kong J. Psychiat. *Hong Kong Journal of Psychiatry*
Hosp. Comm. Psychiat. *Hospital Community Psychiatry*
Howard J. Criminal Justice *Howard Journal of Criminal Justice*
Human Mutat. *Human Mutation*
Human Psychopharmacol.: Clin. Exp. *Human Psychopharmacology: Clinical and Experimental*

Imag. Cog. Pers. *Imagination, Cognition and Personality*
Indian J. Clin. Psychol. *Indian Journal of Clinical Psychology*
Infancy *Infancy*
Infant Ment. Hlth. J. *Infant Mental Health Journal*
Injury Prev. *Injury Prevention*

Inquiry *Inquiry*
Inter. Clin. Psychopharmacology *International Clinical Psychopharmacology*
Inter. J. Aging Human Dev. *International Journal of Aging and Human Development*
Inter. J. Behav. Dev. *International Journal of Behavioral Development*
Inter. J. Behav. Med. *International Journal of Behavioral Medicine*
Inter. J. Clin. Exp. Hyp. *International Journal of Clinical and Experimental Hypnosis*
Inter. J. Compar. Psychol. *International Journal of Comparative Psychology*
Inter. J. Eat. Disorders *International Journal of Eating Disorders*
Inter. J. Emerg. Mental Hlth. *International Journal of Emergency Mental Health*
Inter. J. Epidemiol. *International Journal of Epidemiology*
Inter. J. Forens. Ment. Hlth. *International Journal of Forensic Mental Health*
Inter. J. Ger. Psychiat. *International Journal of Geriatric Psychiatry*
Inter. J. Intercult. Relations *International Journal of Intercultural Relations*
Inter. J. Law Psychiat. *International Journal of Law and Psychiatry*
Inter. J. Men's Hlth. *Inter. J. Men's Hlth.*
Inter. J. Ment. Hlth. Promot. *International Journal of Mental Health Promotion*
Inter. J. Methods Psychiatr. Res. *Inter. J. Methods. Psychiatr. Res.*
Inter. J. Neuropsychopharmacol. *International Journal of Neuropsychopharmacology*
Inter. J. Neurosci. *International Journal of Neuroscience*
Inter. J. Nurs. Stud. *International Journal of Nursing Studies*
Inter. J. Offender Ther. Compar. Criminology *International Journal of Offender Therapy and Comparative Criminology*
Inter. J. Psychiat. Clin. Prac. *International Journal of Psychiatry in Clinical Practice*
Inter. J. Psychiat. Med. *International Journal of Psychiatry in Medicine*
Inter. J. Psychol. Religion *International Journal for the Psychology of Religion*
Inter. J. Psychopharmacol. *International Journal of Psychopharmacology*
Inter. J. Psychophysiol. *International Journal of Psychophysiology*
Inter. J. Soc. Psychiat. *International Journal of Social Psychiatry*
Inter. J. Stress Manag. *International Journal of Stress Management*
Inter. J. Transgenderism *International Journal of Transgenderism*
Inter. Med. J. *International Medical Journal*
Inter. Psychoger. *International Psychogeriatrics*
Inter. Rev. Psychiat. *International Review of Psychiatry*
IRB: Ethics Human Res. *IRB: Ethics and Human Research*
Irish J. Psychol. Med. *Irish Journal of Psychological Medicine*
Israel J. Psychiat. Rel. Sci. *Israel Journal of Psychiatry and Related Sciences*
Issues Ment. Hlth. Nurs. *Issues in Mental Health Nursing*
Issues Psychoanal. Psychol. *Issues in Psychoanalytic Psychology*
Ital. J. Neurol. Sci. *Italian Journal of Neurological Sciences*

J. Abnorm. Child Psychol. *Journal of Abnormal Child Psychology*
J. Abnorm. Psychol. *Journal of Abnormal Psychology*
J. Addic. Diseases *Journal of Addictive Diseases*
J. Adol. Hlth. *Journal of Adolescent Health*
J. Adol. *Journal of Adolescence*
J. Adol. Res. *Journal of Adolescent Research*
J. Adv. Nurs. *Journal of Advanced Nursing*
J. Advert. Res. *Journal of Advertising Research*
J. Affect. Disorders *Journal of Affective Disorders*
J. Aggress. Maltreat. Trauma *Journal of Aggression, Maltreatment and Trauma*
J. Aging Hlth. *Journal of Aging and Health*
J. Alcohol Drug Educ. *Journal of Alcohol and Drug Education*
J. Alcohol Stud. *Journal of Alcohol Studies*
J. Alzheimer Dis., *Journal of Alzheimer's Disease*
J. Amer. Acad. Child Adol. Psychiat. *Journal of the American Academy of Child and Adolescent Psychiatry*
J. Amer. Acad. Psychiat. Law *Journal of the American Academy of Psychiatry and the Law*
J. Amer. Acad. Psychoanal. Dynamic Psychiat. *Journal of the American Academy of Psychoanalysis and Dynamic Psychiatry*
J. Amer. Board Fam. Pract. *Journal of American Board of Family Practitioners*
J. Amer. Coll. Hlth. *Journal of American College Health*
J. Amer. Ger. Soc. *Journal of the American Geriatrics Society*
J. Amer. Osteopath. Assoc. *Journal of American Osteopath Associates*
J. Amer. Psychiat. Nurs. Assoc. *Journal of the American Psychiatric Nurses Association*
J. Amer. Psychoanal. Assoc. *Journal of the American Psychoanalytical Association*
J. Anx. Disorders *Journal of Anxiety Disorders*
J. Appl. Behav. Anal. *Journal of Applied Behavior Analysis*
J. Appl. Physiol. *Journal of Applied Physiology*
J. Appl. Psychoanal. Stud. *Journal of Applied Psychoanalytic Studies*
J. Appl. School Psychol. *Journal of Applied School Psychology*
J. Appl. Soc. Psychol. *Journal of Applied Social Psychology*
J. Asthma *Journal of Asthma*
J. Attent. Disorders *Journal of Attention Disorders*
J. Behav. Decis. Making *Journal of Behavioral Decision Making*
J. Behav. Educ. *Journal of Behavioral Education*
J. Behav. Hlth. Serv. Res. *Journal of Behavioral Health Services & Research*
J. Behav. Ther. Exp. Psychiat., *Journal of Behavioral Therapy and Experimental Psychiatry*
J. Biol. Rhythms *Journal of Biological Rhythms*
J. Cardiovasc. Pharmacol. Ther. *Journal of Cardiovascular Pharmacology and Therapy*
J. Child Adol. Psychiatr. Nurs. *Journal of Child and Adolescent Psychiatric Nursing*
J. Child Adol. Psychopharmacol. *Journal of Child and Adolescent Psychopharmacology*
J. Child Psychol. Psychiat. *Journal of Child Psychology and Psychiatry*
J. Child Sex. Abuse *Journal of Child Sexual Abuse*
J. Clin. Child Psychol. *Journal of Clinical Child Psychology*
J. Clin. Exp. Neuropsychol. *Journal of Clinical and Experimental Neuropsychology*
J. Clin. Geropsychol. *Journal of Clinical Geropsychology*
J. Clin. Psychiat. *Journal of Clinical Psychiatry*
J. Clin. Psychoanal. *Journal of Clinical Psychoanalysis*

J. Clin. Psychol. *Journal of Clinical Psychology*
J. Clin. Psychol. Med. Settings *Journal of Clinical Psychology in Medical Settings*
J. Clin. Psychopharmacol. *Journal of Clinical Psychopharmacology*
J. Cog. Psychother. *Journal of Cognitive Psychotherapy*
J. Coll. Student Psychother. *Journal of College Student Psychotherapy*
J. Comm. Psychol. *Journal of Community Psychology*
J. Cons. Clin. Psychol. *Journal of Consulting and Clinical Psychology*
J. Contemp. Psychother. *Journal of Contemporary Psychotherapy*
J. Couns. Dev. *Journal of Counseling & Development*
J. Couns. Psychol. *Journal of Counseling Psychology*
J. Cross-Cult. Ger. *Journal of Cross-Cultural Gerontology*
J. Cross-Cult. Psychol. *Journal of Cross-Cultural Psychology*
J. Dev. Behav. Pediatr. *Journal of Developmental and Behavioral Pediatrics*
J. Dev. Phys. Disabil. *Journal of Developmental and Physical Disabilities*
J. ECT *Journal of ECT*
J. Epidemiol. Comm. Hlth. *Journal of Epidemiology and Community Health*
J. Exp. Psychol. Gen. *Journal of Experimental Psychology General*
J. Exp. Soc. Psychol. *Journal of Experimental Social Psychology*
J. Fam. Pract. *Journal of Family Practice*
J. Fam. Psychol. *Journal of Family Psychology*
J. Fam. Psychother. *Journal of Family Psychotherapy*
J. Forens. Psychiat. Psychol. *Journal of Forensic Psychiatry and Psychology*
J. Forens. Psychol. Pract. *Journal of Forensic Psychology Practice*
J. Forens. Sci. *Journal of Forensic Sciences*
J. Gay Lesbian Psychother. *Journal of Gay and Lesbian Psychotherapy*
J. Gen. Internal Med. *Journal of General Internal Medicine*
J. Gen. Psychol. *Journal of Genetic Psychology*
J. Ger. A Biol. Sci. Med. Sci. *Journal of Gerontology, A: Biological Science and Medical Science*
J. Ger. B Psychol. Sci. Soc. Sci. *Journal of Gerontology, B: Psychological Science and Social Science*
J. Hist. Behav. Sci. *Journal of the History of the Behavioral Sciences*
J. Hist. Neurosci. *Journal of the History of the Neurosciences*
J. Hlth. Care Poor Underserved. *Journal of Health Care for the Poor and Underserved*
J. Hlth. Soc. Behav. *Journal of Health and Social Behavior*
J. Homosexuality *Journal of Homosexuality*
J. Human. Psychol. *Journal of Humanistic Psychology*
J. Individ. Psychol. *Journal of Individual Psychology*
J. Intell. Dev. Disabl. *Journal of Intellectual and Developmental Disability*
J. Intell. Disab. Res. *Journal of Intellectual Disability Research*
J. Interpers. Violence *Journal of Interpersonal Violence*
J. Learn. Disabil. *Journal of Learning Disabilities*
J. Loss Trauma *Journal of Loss and Trauma*
J. Manage. *Journal of Management*
J. Marital Fam. Ther. *Journal of Marital and Family Therapy*
J. Marr. Fam. *Journal of Marriage and Family*
J. Med. Ethics *Journal of Medical Ethics*
J. Med. Genet. *Journal of Medical Genetics*
J. Med. Internet Res. *Journal of Medical Internet Research*

J. Ment. Hlth. UK *Journal of Mental Health UK*
J. Ment. Hlth. Policy Econ. *Journal of Mental Health Policy and Economics*
J. Mind Behav. *Journal of Mind and Behavior*
J. Music Ther. *Journal of Music Therapy*
J. Nerv. Ment. Dis. *Journal of Nervous and Mental Disease*
J. Neuroimmun. *Journal of Neuroimmunology*
J. Neurol. Neurosurg. Psychiat. *Journal of Neurology and Neurosurgical Psychiatry*
J. Neuropsychiat. Clin. Neurosci. *Journal of Neuropsychiatry and Clinical Neurosciences*
J. Neurosci. *Journal of Neuroscience*
J. Neurotrauma *Journal of Neurotrauma*
J. Nurs. Scholarship *Journal of Nursing Scholarship*
J. Occup. Hlth. Psychol. *Journal of Occupational Health Psychology*
J. Offender Rehab. *Journal of Offender Rehabilitation*
J. Pain Sympt. Manag. *Journal of Pain and Symptom Management*
J. Perinat. Med. *Journal of Perinatal Medicine*
J. Pers. Assess. *Journal of Personality Assessment*
J. Pers. Disorders *Journal of Personality Disorders*
J. Pers. *Journal of Personality*
J. Pers. Soc. Psychol. *Journal of Personality and Social Psychology*
J. Positive Psychol. *Journal of Positive Psychology*
J. Primary Prev. *Journal of Primary Prevention*
J. Psychiat. Law *Journal of Psychiatry and Law*
J. Psychiatr. Ment. Hlth. Nurs. *Journal of Psychiatric and Mental Health Nursing*
J. Psychiatr. Pract. *Journal of Psychiatric Practice*
J. Psychiatr. Res. *Journal of Psychiatric Research*
J. Psychoeduc. Assess. *Journal of Psychoeducational Assessment*
J. Psychol. Christianity *Journal of Psychology and Christianity*
J. Psychol. *Journal of Psychology*
J. Psychol.: Interdiscip. Appl. *Journal of Psychology: Interdisciplinary and Applied*
J. Psychopharmacol. *Journal of Psychopharmacology*
J. Psychosoc. Oncology *Journal of Psychosocial Oncology*
J. Psychosom. Res. *Journal of Psychosomatic Research*
J. Psychother. Prac. Res. *Journal of Psychotherapy Practice and Research*
J. Reprod. Infant Psychol. *Journal of Reproductive and Infant Psychology*
J. Sci. Study Religion *Journal for the Scientific Study of Religion*
J. Sex Marital Ther. *Journal of Sex and Marital Therapy*
J. Sex Res. *Journal of Sex Research*
J. Sex. Aggress. *Journal of Sexual Aggression*
J. Sleep Res. *Journal of Sleep Research*
J. Soc. Clin. Psychol. *Journal of Social and Clinical Psychology*
J. Soc. Distress Homeless *Journal of Social Distress and the Homeless*
J. Soc. Hist. *Journal of Social History*
J. Soc. Issues *Journal of Social Issues*
J. Soc. Pers. Relationships *Journal of Social and Personal Relationships*
J. Soc. Psychol. *Journal of Social Psychology*
J. Sociol. Soc. Welfare *Journal of Sociology and Social Welfare*
J. Stud. Alc. *Journal of Studies on Alcohol*
J. Stud. Alc. Drugs *Journal of Studies on Alcohol and Drugs*
J. Substance Abuse Treat. *Journal of Substance Abuse Treatment*
J. Traum. Stress *Journal of Traumatic Stress*
J. Trauma Dissociat., *Journal of Trauma and Dissociation*

J. Women's Hlth. *Journal of Women's Health*
J. Workplace Behav. Hlth. *Journal of Workplace Behavioral Health*
J. Youth Adolescence *Journal of Youth and Adolescence*
JAMA *Journal of the American Medical Association*
Jap. J. Hyp. *Japanese Journal of Hypnosis*

Kindheit Entwicklung *Kindheit und Entwicklung*

Lancet *Lancet*
Law Human Behav. *Law and Human Behavior*
Learn. Memory *Learning and Memory*

Maturitas *Maturitas*
Med. J. Austral. *Medical Journal of Australia*
Med. Sci. Sports Exercise *Medicine and Science in Sports and Exercise*
Medica Psicosomatica *Medica Psicosomatica*
Med. Care *Medical Care*
Memory *Memory*
Ment. Hlth. Aspects Dev. Disabil. *Mental Health Aspects of Developmental Disabilities*
Ment. Hlth. Religion Culture *Mental Health, Religion and Culture*
Ment. Hlth. Serv. Res. *Mental Health Services Research*
Ment. Phys. Disabil. Law Reporter *Mental and Physical Disability Law Reporter*
Ment. Retard. *Mental Retardation*
MEPS *Medical Expenditure Panel Survey*
Merrill-Palmer Quart. *Merrill-Palmer Quarterly*
Michigan Sociol. Rev. *Michigan Sociological Review*
Military Med. *Military Medicine*
Minerva Psichiatrica *Minerva Psichiatrica*
MMW Fortschr Med. [German]
MMWR CDC *MMWR CDC*
Mol. Psychiat. *Molecular Psychiatry.*
Monitor Psychol. *Monitor on Psychology*
Mortality *Mortality*
Mt. Sinai J. Med. *Mt. Sinai Journal of Medicine*

N. Engl. J. Med. *New England Journal of Medicine*
NAMI Advocate *NAMI Advocate*
Natl. Psychologist *National Psychologist*
Natl. Vital Statistics Rep. *National Vital Statistics Reports*
Nature *Nature*
Ned Tidjschr Geneeskd *Nederlands Tijdschrift voor Geneeskunde*
Nerv. Child *Nervous Child*
Neurobiol. Aging *Neurobiology of Aging*
Neurobiol. Learn. Memory *Neurobiology of Learning and Memory*
Neurochem. Inter. *Neurochemistry International*
Neurol. Clin. *Neurologic Clinics*
Neurology *Neurology*
Neuropathology *Neuropathology*
Neuropsychiat. Basal Ganglia *Neuropsychiatry of the Basal Ganglia*
Neuropsychiat. Dis. Treat. *Neuropsychiatric Disease and Treatment*
Neuropsychiat. Neuropsychol. Behav. Neurol. *Neuropsychiatry, Neuropsychology, and Behavioral Neurology*
Neuropsychobiology *Neuropsychobiology*
Neuropsychol. *Neuropsychology*
Neuropsychopharmacology *Neuropsychopharmacology*
Neurorep. Rapid Communic. Neurosci. Res. *Neuroreport for Rapid Communication of Neuroscience Research*
Neurosci. Biobehav. Rev. *Neuroscience and Biobehavioral Reviews*

Neurotoxicol. Teratol. *Neurotoxicology and Teratology*
New Zeal. Med. J. *New Zealand Medical Journal*
Nicotine Tobacco Res. *Nicotine Tobacco Research*
Nordic J. Psychiat. *Nordic Journal of Psychiatry*
Nordisk Psykologi *Nordisk Psykologi*

Omega: J. Death Dying *Omega: Journal of Death and Dying*

Pain *Pain*
Pall. Med. *Palliative Medicine*
Patient Educ. Couns. *Patient Education and Counseling*
Pediatr. Clin. N. Amer. *Pediatric Clinics of North America*
Pediatrics *Pediatrics*
Paediatrics Child Hlth. *Paediatrics and Child Health*
Percept. Motor Skills *Perceptual and Motor Skills*
Pers. Individ. Diff. *Personality and Individual Differences*
Pers. Relationships *Personal Relationships*
Pers. Soc. Psychol. Bull. *Personality and Social Psychology Bulletin*
Perspect. Biol. Med. *Perspectives in Biology and Medicine*
Pharma Marketletter *Pharma Marketletter*
Pharmacol. Biochem. Behav. *Pharmacology, Biochemistry and Behavior*
Pharmacopsychiatry *Pharmacopsychiatry*
Philos. Psychiat. Psychol. *Philosophy, Psychiatry, and Psychology*
Physiol. Behav. *Physiology and Behavior*
Postgrad. Med. J. *Postgraduate Medical Journal*
Pragmat. Case Stud. Psychother. *Pragmatic Case Studies in Psychotherapy*
Praxis Kinderpsychol. Kinderpsych. *Praxis der Kinderpsychologie und Kinderpsychiatrie*
Prev. Med.: Inter. J. Devoted to Pract. Theory *Preventive Medicine: An International Journal Devoted to Practice and Theory*
Prev. Treat. *Prevention and Treatment*
Primary Psychiat. *Primary Psychiatry*
Proc. Natl. Acad. Sci. USA *Proceedings of the National Academy of Science*
Profess. Psychol.: Res. Pract. *Professional Psychology: Research and Practice*
Profess. School Couns. *Professional School Counseling*
Prog. Neuropsychopharmacol. Biol. Psychiat. *Progressive Neuropsychopharmacological Biological Psychiatry*
Psichiatria e Psicoterapia *Psichiatria e Psicoterapia*
Psicol. Cond.: Rev. Inter. Psicol. Clin. Salud *Psicologia Conductual: Revista Internacional de Psicologia Clinica de las Salud*
Psiquiatria *Psiquiatria*
PsycCRITIQUES, *PsycCRITIQUES*
Psychiat. Clin. Neurosci. *Psychiatry and Clinical Neurosciences*
Psychiat. Genet. *Psychiatry and Genetics*
Psychiatry: Interpers. Biol. Process. *Psychiatry: Interpersonal and Biological Processes*
Psychiatr. Quart. *Psychiatric Quarterly*
Psychiat. Psychol. Law *Psychiatry, Psychology and Law*
Psychiat. Res. Neuroimaging *Psychiatry Research: Neuroimaging*
Psychiat. Res. *Psychiatry Research*
Psychiatr. Ann. *Psychiatric Annals*
Psychiatr. Bull. *Psychiatric Bulletin*
Psychiatr. Clin. N. Amer. *Psychiatric Clinics of North America*
Psychiatr. Rehab. J. *Psychiatric Rehabilitation Journal*
Psychiatr. Serv. *Psychiatric Services*

Psychiatr. Times *Psychiatric Times*
Psychiatria Fennica *Psychiatria Fennica*
Psychiatria Hungarica *Psychiatria Hungarica*
Psychiatriki *Psychiatriki*
Psychoanal Child Study *Psychological Child Study*
Psychoanal. Quart. *Psychoanalytical Quarterly*
Psychoanal. Psychol. *Psychoanalytic Psychology*
Psychoanal. Rev. *Psychoanalytic Review*
Psychodyn. Pract.: Indiv. Groups Org. *Psychodynamic Practice: Individuals, Groups and Organisations*
Psychogeriatrics *Psychogeriatrics*
Psychol. Aging *Psychology and Aging*
Psychol. Assess. *Psychological Assessment*
Psychol. Bull. *Psychological Bulletin*
Psychol. Hlth. Med. *Psychology, Health and Medicine*
Psychol. Hlth. *Psychology and Health*
Psychol. Med. *Psychological Medicine*
Psychol. Publ. Policy Law *Psychology, Public Policy, and Law*
Psychol. Record *Psychological Record*
Psychol. Rep. *Psychological Reports*
Psychol. Rev. *Psychological Review*
Psychol. Schools *Psychology in the Schools*
Psychol. Sci. *Psychological Science*
Psychol. Sci. Publ. Interest *Psychological Science in the Public Interest*
Psychol. Serv. *Psychological Services*
Psychol.: J. Hellen. Psychol. Soc. *Psychology: The Journal of the Hellenic Psychological Society*
Psychogeriatrics *Psychogeriatrics*
Psychologica Belgica *Psychologica Belgica*
Psychologist *Psychologist*
Psycholoog *Psycholoog*
Psychoneuroendocrinology *Psychoneuroendocrinology*
Psycho-Oncology *Psycho-Oncology*
Psychopathology *Psychopathology*
Psychopharmacol. Bull. *Psychopharmacology Bulletin*
Psychopharmacology (Berl) *Psychopharmacology (Berlin)*
Psychopharmacology *Psychopharmacology*
Psychophysiology *Psychophysiology*
Psychosoc. Rehab. J. *Psychosocial Rehabilitation Journal*
Psychosom. Med. *Psychosomatic Medicine*
Psychosomatics *Psychosomatics*
Psychosom.: J. Con. Liaison Psychiat. *Psychosomatics: Journal of Consultation Liaison Psychiatry*
Psychother. Forum *Psychotherapie Forum*
Psychother. Psychosomat. *Psychotherapy and Psychosomatics*
Psychother. Res. *Psychotherapy Research*
Psychotherapy *Psychotherapy*
Psychother.: Theory, Res. Pract. Train. *Psychotherapy: Theory, Research, Practice, Training*
Public Pers. Manag. *Public Personnel Management*

Q. Rev. Biol. *The Quarterly Review of Biology*

Rehab. Couns. Bull. *Rehabilitation Counseling Bulletin*
Rehab. Nursing *Rehabilitation Nursing*
Rehab. Psychol. *Rehabilitation Psychology*
Remed. Spec. Educ. *Remedial and Special Education*
Reprod. Nutr. Dev. *Reproductive and Nutritional Development*
Res. Dev. Disabl. *Research in Developmental Disabilities*
Res. Nursing Hlth. *Research in Nursing and Health*
Res. Soc. Work Prac. *Research on Social Work Practice*
Rev. Gen. Psychol. *Review of General Psychology*
Revista Argentina de Clinica Psicologica *Revista Argentina de Clinica Psicologica*

Revista Brasileira de Psiquiatria *Revista Brasileira de Psiquiatria*
Revue Franc. Psychan. *Revue Française de Psychanalyse*
Ricerche di Psicologia *Ricerche di Psicologia*

S. Afr. J. Psychol. *South African Journal of Psychology*
S. Afr. Psychiat. Rev. *South African Psychiatry Review*
Salud Mental *Salud Mental*
Scand. J. Psychol. *Scandinavian Journal of Psychology*
Scand. J. Work Envir. Hlth. *Scandinavian Journal of Work, Environment and Health*
Schizo. Bull. *Schizophrenia Bulletin*
Schizo. Res. *Schizophrenia Research*
Science *Science*
Scientif. Amer. *Scientific American*
Sex. Abuse J. Res. Treat. *Sexual Abuse Journal of Research and Treatment*
Sex. Relationship Ther. *Sexual Relationship Therapy*
Sexualities, Evol. Gender *Sexualities, Evolution and Gender*
Sleep: J. Sleep Sleep Disord. Res. *Sleep: Journal Sleep and Sleep Disorders Research*
Sleep Hyp. *Sleep and Hypnosis*
Soc. Behav. Pers. *Social Behavior and Personality*
Soc. Forces *Social Forces*
Soc. Psychiat. Psychiatr. Epidemiol. *Social Psychiatry and Psychiatric Epidemiology*
Soc. Sci. Inter. *Social Science International*
Soc. Sci. Med. *Social Science and Medicine*
Soc. Sci. Quart. *Social Science Quarterly*
Soc. Sci. Res. *Social Science Research*
Soc. Study Addict. *Society for the Study of Addiction*
Soc. Work *Social Work*
Soc. Work Hlth. Care *Social Work Health Care*
Soc. Work Groups *Social Work with Groups*
Sports Med. *Sports Medicine*
Steroids *Steroids*
Stress Hlth: J. Inter. Soc. Invest. Stress *Stress and Health: Journal of the International Society for the Investigation of Stress*
Stress, Trauma, Crisis: Inter. J. *Stress, Trauma, and Crisis: An International Journal*
Stress: Inter. J. Biol. Stress *Stress: The International Journal of the Biology of Stress*
Substance Use Misuse *Substance Use and Misuse*
Suic. Life-Threat. Behav. *Suicide and Life-Threatening Behavior*

Teach. Psychol., *Teaching of Psychology*
Theory Psychol. *Theory and Psychology*
Ther. Comm. *Therapeutic Communities*
Trauma, Violence, Abuse *Trauma, Violence, Abuse*
Train. Educ. Profess. Psychol. *Training and Education in Professional Psychology*
Trends Cell Biol. *Trends in Cell Biology*
Trends Neurosci. *Trends in Neuroscience*
Twin Res. Human Genet. *Twin Research and Human Genetics*

Verhaltenstherapie *Verhaltenstherapie*
Violence Against Women *Violence Against Women*
Visual Cog. *Visual Cognition*

Western J. Nurs. Res. *Western Journal of Nursing Research*
Women Ther. *Women and Therapy*

Zeitschrift Gerontopsychol. Psychiat. *Zeitschrift für Gerontopsychologie und Psychiatrie*

name index

Sykes, J. D., 116
Sylvester, D., 134
Szabo, M., 550
Szasz, T. S., 7, 478, 632
Szegedy-Maszak, M., 520
Szeszko, P. R., 157
Szymanski, S., 487, 488

Tabachnick, B. G., 630, 645
Tabaczynski, T., 92
Tacon, A., 363
Tafet, G. E., 129, 130
Tager-Flusberg, H., 575
Tagliareni, L., 92
Takahashi, Y., 326
Talavera, J. A., 85, 117, 260, 554
Talbott, J. A., 19
Tallis, F., 126
Tam, W. Y. K., 248
Tamblyn, R., 598
Tamminga, C. A., 454, 459, 464, 465, 466, 467, 468, 470, 477
Tang, C. S.-K., 44
Tanner, L., 316
Tantam, D., 72
Tarkan, L., 611
Tarloff, D., 630
Tarrier, N., 44, 333, 472, 492, 493
Tartaro, C., 324
Tartaro, J., 164, 169, 171, 176, 261, 262, 355, 357
Tatarelli, R., 318
Tate, D. C., 563
Taube-Schiff, M., 242, 244, 246, 247, 252, 258, 259, 260, 283, 289, 292, 296, 297
Tavris, C., 223
Taylor, C. B., 194
Taylor, D. J., 589, 596
Taylor, G. M., 355
Taylor, H. A., 42, 43
Taylor, J., 627
Taylor, J. E., 492
Taylor, R., 286
Taylor, S., 42, 43, 150, 179, 180, 184, 210, 211, 216
Taylor, S. E., 159, 176, 185, 186, 187, 191, 193, 194, 579, 586, 596
Teicher, M. H., 565, 572, 577, 582, 584, 585
Telch, C. F., 349
Tellegen, A., 21, 192
Telner, J. I., 267
ten-Brinke, L., 533
Teng, C. T., 253
Tenhula, W. N., 462
Teplin, L. A., 521, 633
Teri, L., 280
Thakker, J., 97
Thakur, C. P., 14
Thase, M. E., 185, 249, 252, 290, 292, 295, 303
Theodorou, S., 383
Thetford, E. S., 244
Thienemann, M., 92
Thigpen, C. H., 33, 225
Thio, A., 314, 316
Thirsk, J., 310
Thoennes, N., 170

Thomas, C., 145
Thomas, J., 643
Thomas, J. C., 93
Thompson, A. H., 496
Thompson, C., 405
Thompson, H. S., 317
Thompson, J. C., 257
Thompson, L. W., 282, 599, 614
Thompson, R., 388
Thoresen, C. E., 193
Thorne, B. M., 12
Thornicroft, G., 629, 635
Thornton, W. B., 137
Thruman, U., 629
Thuras, P., 521
Thurston, C., 286
Tierney, A. J., 483
Tiffany, S. T., 399
Timberlake, J., 137
Timko, C., 407, 409
Tjaden, P., 170
Todd, R. D., 242, 249
Tolan, P., 560, 561
Tolin, D. F., 150
Tolstoy, L., 87
Tomes, N., 112, 268, 434, 632
Tondo, L., 333
Tonigan, J. S., 409
Tooby, J., 512
Torgersen, S., 147, 526
Toro, J., 361, 367
Torre, J., 245
Torres, A., 620
Torrey, E. F., 19, 20, 454, 470, 471, 481, 498, 499, 500, 501, 502, 503, 504, 505, 635
Tosone, C., 532
Townsend, J., 282
Tozzi, F., 342
Tractenberg, R. E., 603
Tramontin, M., 172, 174, 175, 178, 181, 182
Travis, C. B., 185, 186, 188, 193, 352, 356, 357
Travolta, J., 438
Treaster, J. B., 170
Treasure, J., 354, 366, 369
Trierweiler, S. J., 33, 473
Triggs, W. J., 294
Trivedi, M. H., 290
Troiano, R. P., 356
Truax, P., 92, 98, 104, 105
Trull, T. J., 524, 531
Tryon, G., 630
Trzepacz, P. T., 601, 602
Tsai, J. L., 97, 262
Tsuang, M. T., 147, 400
Tsuchiya, K. J., 267
Tucker, E., 636
Tucker, J. A., 104
Tuke, W., 15, 26
Tulsky, J., A., 197
Tuma, A. H., 487
Tuma, J., 172
Turk, C. L., 129, 142
Turkat, I. D., 513
Turkington, C., 226, 227, 228, 608
Turley, N. M., 261
Turner, E. H., 290

Turner, J., 351
Turner, J. E., Jr., 257
Turner, S. M., 180
Turner, S. M., 180, 550, 552
Turton, M. D., 354
Turvey, B. E., 639
Twain, M. (S. Clemens), 379, 597, 546
Twemlow, S. W., 559
Twenge, J. M., 534
Tyler, C., 356, 357
Tyre, P., 345, 363, 569
Tyrer, P., 510, 531
Tyson, A. S., 169

Uchoa, D. D., 535
Ueda, K., 326
Uher, R., 354
Uhl, A., 399
Ullman, M. T., 607
Ullmann, L. P., 472
Ulrich, R. S., 198
Underwood, M. K., 558
Ungar, W. J., 93, 198
Urcuyo, K. R., 193
Uretsky, S., 41
Ursano, R. J., 178, 182, 193
Useda, J. D., 513, 514
Utsey, S. O., 332
Utsey, S. O., 332, 614

Vahia, I. V., 474
Vahia, V. N., 457, 474
Vail, D. A., 356, 357
Vaillant, G. E., 399
Vakili, A., 229
Valbak, K., 368
Valdiserri, E. V., 634
Valenstein, E. S., 483
van der Flier, W. M., 605
van der Ploeg, H. M., 177
van der Riet Wooley, R., 27
van Egmond, J. J., 213
van Emmerik, A. A., 182
van Gogh, V., 270, 315, 471
van Griensven, F., 44
van Hout, W. J. P. J., 151, 213
Van Koppen, P. J., 648
Van Male, L. M., 426
Van Nuys, D., 641
Van Orden, K. A., 317, 320, 327, 328, 333, 336, 337
van Os, J., 471
Van Praag, H. M., 325
Van Wagner, K., 138
van Walsum, K. L., 13, 15
VandeCreek, L., 185
Vanheule, S., 213
Vannoy, S. D., 138, 331, 596
Vartanian, L. R., 344, 353
Vasiliadis, H. M., 242
Vasquez, M. J. T., 642
Vazquez, A. M. M., 179
Veale, D., 210
Vecina, M. L., 172
Vedantam, S., 298, 514
Veiga-Martinez, C., 210, 493
Venditti, E., 356
Venneri, A., 462

Vera, E. M., 20
Verhaeghe, P., 213, 601
Vernberg, E. M., 170
Vernon, P. A., 514
Verschuere, B., 99
Vetter, H. J., 459
Victoria, Queen of England, 241
Videbech, T., 324
Vidovic, V., 358
Vieta, E., 90, 109, 110, 303
Vincent, N. K., 344
Viney, W., 15
Visser, M., 475
Vitaliano, P. P., 192
Vitousek, K. M., 363
Volkmar, F. R., 577
Volkow, N. D., 385, 401
Vollmayr, B., 247, 259
Voltaire, 486
von Krafft-Ebing, R., 16
von Meduna, J., 288
Vonnegut, M., 477
Voruganti, L. N. P., 117, 492
Vrij, A., 99, 100, 533

Wadden, T. A., 357
Wagner, P. S., 21
Wagstaff, G. F., 639
Wain, L., 93
Wakefield, J. C., 296
Walch, S. E., 185
Walcott, D. D., 360
Waldinger, M. D., 423, 424, 433
Waldman, S., 245
Wales, H. W., 633
Walker, A. C., 282
Walker, C. E., 571
Walker, E. A., 278
Walker, E. F., 513, 517, 518
Walker, R. L., 315
Walkup, J., 462
Wall, J. R., 101
Wall, T. L., 377
Wallace, M., 275, 457
Wallace, S. E., 313
Wallace, T. L., 250
Waller, G., 368
Wallis, C., 21, 276
Walsh, E., 21, 636
Walsh, T., 466, 472
Walters, B., 245
Walters, G. D., 400
Wampold, B. E., 34, 40, 44, 75
Wang, G., 186
Wang, G., 186
Wang, H.Y., 270
Wang, M., 227, 228
Wang, P., 212
Wang, P. S., 20, 24, 83, 123, 135, 136, 140, 144, 169, 276, 301, 375, 502
Wang, S. S., 289, 597, 643, 644
Ward, E. C., 82, 284
Ward, E., 434
Ward, T., 97, 631
Ward-Estes, J., 564, 568
Waring, M., 472
Warner, J., 231, 533
Warren, R., 127

subject index

Page numbers followed by f indicate illustrations; those followed by t indicate tables.

AAMR Adaptive Behavior Scales, 581
ABAB design, 44
Abilify (aripiprazole), 490
Abnormal psychology. *See also* Psychological abnormality
  definition of, 2
  idiographic understanding of, 28
  leading theories of, 21–22
  nomothetic understanding of, 28
  psychogenic perspective in, 15–16
  somatogenic perspective in, 14–15
Absentmindedness, 228
Abstinence
  sexual, 417
  vs. controlled substance use, 405
Abuse. *See* Child abuse; Domestic violence; Sexual abuse
Acceptance and Commitment Therapy (ACT)
  for depression, 69, 283
  for hallucinations, 493–495
Acculturation, 361
Acetylcholine
  in Alzheimer's disease, 610
  in memory, 606
Acquired immunodeficiency syndrome, in substance abusers, 407
ACTH, in stress reaction, 166, 166f
Acute stress disorder, 167–184
  definition of, 168. *See also* Stress disorders, psychological
Addiction
  gambling, 520
  Internet, 555
  sexual, 435
  substance, 374. *See also* Substance abuse
Addington v. Texas, 630
Adjustment disorders, 177
Adolescents. *See also* Children; College students
  binge drinking by, 375
  bipolar disorder in, 556–557
  common problems of, 550
  delinquent, 560
  depression in, 297, 553–556
  eating disorders in. *See* Anorexia nervosa; Bulimia nervosa
  obesity in, 357, 357f
  sexual behavior of, 419
  substance abuse by, 375, 391f, 394f
  suicide by, 327–330
Adoption studies
  of depression, 249
  of schizophrenia, 465–466
Adrenal glands, 52
  in stress reaction, 166, 166f, 192–193
Adrenocorticotropic hormone (ACTH), in stress reaction, 166, 166f
Advertising, drug, 298, 299
Affect, in schizophrenia, 461
Affective inventories, 98–99, 99t
Affectual awareness, 431

African Americans. *See also* Cultural factors; Racial/ethnic groups
  alcohol abuse by, 377
  antidepressant prescribing for, 293
  antipsychotic prescribing for, 491
  attention-deficit/hyperactivity disorder in, 568–569
  depression in, 262, 263
  eating disorders in, 360–361
  generalized anxiety disorder in, 124
  phobias in, 135, 136
  schizophrenia in, 473, 474f
  suicide by, 314f, 315, 330, 332
Aftercare
  in community approach, 499
  right to, 635
Age. *See also* Adolescents; Children; Elderly
  antidepressant use and, 293
  dementia and, 602f
  hypnotic susceptibility and, 230, 230f
  suicide and, 314, 314f, 325–332
Aggression. *See also* Criminal behavior; Violence
  bullying and, 559
  in conduct disorder, 558–559. *See also* Conduct disorder
  cultural aspects of, 522, 523f
  mental disorders and, 631
  modeling of, 64, 521
  relational, 62, 558
  serotonin and, 325
  suicide and, 325
  against therapists, 630
Agoraphobia, 134, 144
Agranulocytosis, 491
Agreeableness, 544
AIDS, in substance abusers, 407
Al-Anon, 409
Alateen, 409
Alcohol, physical effects of, 375–376
Alcohol abuse/dependence, 375–380. *See also* Substance abuse
  by adolescents, 378, 394f
  binge drinking in, 375, 378
  biochemical factors in, 400–401
  blood alcohol level in, 376–377, 376t
  by college students, 378
  controlled use vs. abstinence in, 405
  cultural aspects of, 82, 377
  delirium tremens in, 379
  dependence in, 379, 382t
  in elderly, 598–599
  fetal alcohol syndrome in, 380
  gender differences in, 376, 376t
  genetic factors in, 400
  health effects of, 380, 382t
  intoxication in, 382t
  Korsakoff's syndrome in, 380, 606
  patterns of, 378–379
  personal/social impact of, 379–380, 382t
  physical effects of, 375–376
  in pregnancy, 380
  rates of, 375, 376
  suicide and, 317–320
  tolerance in, 374, 400–401

  treatment of, 402–410. *See also* Substance abuse, treatment of
    antagonist drugs in, 405–406
  withdrawal in, 379, 400–401
Alcohol dehydrogenase, 376
Alcohol withdrawal delirium, 379
Alcoholics Anonymous (AA), 407–409
Alexithymism, in eating disorders, 352
Alogia, in schizophrenia, 462
Alprazolam (Xanax), for panic disorder, 147, 149
Alternate personalities, 224
Altruistic lying, 532
Altruistic suicide, 323
Alzheimer's disease, 594, 602–614
  abnormal proteins in, 606–607
  age at onset of, 602
  antipsychotics for, 611
  autoimmune response in, 608
  beta-amyloid protein in, 604, 609, 609f
  brain abnormalities in, 604
  caregiver stress in, 612, 612f
  causes of, 604–608
  course of, 603
  day care for, 612, 612f
  diagnosis of, 603t, 604, 609
  in Down syndrome, 584
  familial, 604
  genetic factors in, 604
  history of, 602–603
  lead exposure and, 608
  living situations in, 612–614
  memory impairment in, 604–608
  neurofibrillary tangles in, 604
  prevalence of, 603
  prevention of, 610
  risk factors for, 609
  senile plaques in, 604
  symptoms of, 603–604
  treatment of, 610
  viral infections and, 608
  zinc and, 608
Amenorrhea, in anorexia nervosa, 346, 366
American Law Institute test, 621–622
American Psychological Association, 449, 637
  code of ethics, 641–643
Amnesia
  anterograde, 606
  circumscribed, 220
  continuous, 220–221
  dissociative, 219–221
  generalized, 220
  hypnotic, 230
  localized, 220
  music therapy for, 613
  retrograde, 606
  selective, 220
Amnestic disorders, 606–607
Amnestic episode, 220
Amok, 106
Amphetamine abuse, 387–388. *See also* Substance abuse
Amphetamine psychosis, 467
Amygdala, 51, 51f
  age-related changes in, 605f
  in anxiety, 146–147, 147f
  in depression, 250f, 251
  in fear reaction, 146, 146f
  in memory, 605

Psychosis
  amphetamine, 467
  cocaine-induced, 384, 466t
  definition of, 453
  due to medical condition, 466t
  postpartum, 468–469, 625
  schizophrenia as, 453. *See also* Schizophrenia
  substance-induced, 384, 466t
  treatment of, 55. *See also* Antipsychotics
  types of, 466t
Psychosomatic disorders. *See* Stress disorders, psychophysiological
Psychosurgery, 55
  for epilepsy, 607
  lobotomy in, 27–28, 55, 482–483
  memory loss after, 606–607
  right to refuse, 635
  trephination in, 8, 8f, 55
Psychotherapy, 18. *See also* Treatment *and specific types*
Psychotic symptoms, in depression, 246
Psychotropic drugs, 17, 54–55. *See also* Treatment *and specific drugs and disorders*
  clinical studies of, 41
  development of, 56f
  marketing of, 298, 299
  prescribing privileges for, 637–638
  regulation of, 298–299
  right to refuse, 635, 636
Pyromania, 520

Quasi-experimental studies, 42
Quetiapine (Seroquel), 490

Racial/ethnic groups, 81–82. See also under Cultural; Culture
  acculturation in, 361
  depression in, 262–263
  disorders of elderly in, 614–615, 615f
  eating disorders in, 360–361
  generalized anxiety disorder in, 123t, 124
  hate crimes against, 521t
  phobias in, 135
  stress disorders in, 188–189
  substance abuse in, 375, 375f, 377, 409
  suicide in, 314f, 315
Random assignment, 40
Rap groups, for posttraumatic stress disorder, 180
Rape. *See also* Sexual abuse
  stress disorders and, 170–172
Rapid ejaculation, 422–423, 424t
  treatment of, 433
Rapid eye movement (REM) sleep, 252, 596
Rapprochement movement, 116
Rational-emotive therapy, 129, 280
Rationalization, 58t
Reaction formation, 58t, 152
Reading disorder, 582
Realistic anxiety, 124
Reality principle, 57
Receptors, 52, 52f
Reference, delusions of, 458
Regression, 58t
  anal, 540–541
  in depression, 251–252
  in schizophrenia, 471
Rehearsal, in social skills training, 143

Reinforcement
  in social skills training, 143
  for somatoform disorders, 218
Relapse-prevention training
  for pedophilia, 441
  for substance abuse, 404
Relational aggression, in conduct disorder, 558
Relational psychoanalytic therapy, 62
  for borderline personality disorder, 528
Relaxation training, 132–133, 194
  for phobias, 140
Reliability
  of clinical observation, 103
  of *DSM-IV-TR,* 109–110
  interrater, 90
  of interviews, 96
  of IQ tests, 102–103
  test-retest, 90
Religious beliefs, 73
  suicide and, 312–314, 326
Religious shrines, 11
REM sleep, 252, 596
Reminyl (galantamine), for Alzheimer's disease, 610
Renaissance, mental illness in, 10–12
Replication, 32
Reporting compulsions, 153
Repression, 57, 58t, 125
  in dissociative disorders, 227
Research. *See* Clinical research
Residency, psychiatric, 22
Residential crisis centers, 499
Residual schizophrenia, 462, 463
Resiliency, 176
Resistance, in psychodynamic therapy, 60
Response inventories, 98–99, 99t
Reticular formation, 381
Retrograde amnesia, 606
Retrospective analysis, of suicide, 312
Rett's disorder, 572
Reversal design, 44
Reverse anorexia nervosa, 362–363
Reward centers, in substance abuse, 401, 401f, 406
Reward-deficiency syndrome, 401
Rey Complex Figure Test, 103
Risperidone (Risperdal), 490
Ritalin (methylphenidate), 566–567, 567f, 568
Rituals, 150, 151
Rivastigmine (Exelon), for Alzheimer's disease, 610
RNA, in memory, 606
Robinson v. California, 633
Roger's humanistic theory, 70–71. *See also* Humanistic-existential model
Rohypnol, 392
Role disputes, 284
Role playing, 73
  in social skills training, 143
Roles, social, 76
Rome, Ancient, 8–10
Rorschach Comprehensive System, 96
Rorschach test, 94, 94f, 96
Rosenthal effect, 40
Routines, normal, 149f
Rule boys, 574–575

Rumination, in depression, 262

Sadism, sexual, 442–443
St. John's-wort, 286, 287
St. Vitus dance, 10
Samaritans, 333
SAM-e, 287
Savant skills, 576
Scales of Independent Behavior Revised, 581
Schizoaffective disorder, 466t
Schizoid personality disorder, 511f, 515–516, 524t
Schizophrenia, 453–479
  active phase of, 463
  ambivalence in, 462
  anhedonia in, 462
  avolition in, 462
  behavioral view of, 472
  biochemical abnormalities in, 446–467
  biology of, 467–470, 470f
  blunted affect in, 462
  brain abnormalities in, 469–470, 470f
  catatonic, 463–464
  causes of, 464–477
  clinical picture of, 454–455
  cognitive view of, 472–473
  as constructive process, 476–477
  course of, 463
  cultural aspects of, 473–474, 474f
  definition of, 27
  delusions in, 457–458
  derailment in, 458–459
  diagnosis of, 463–464, 463t
  diasthesis-stress model of, 477–478
  disorganized, 463
  dopamine hypothesis for, 467–468
  double-bind hypothesis for, 475–476
  downward drift theory of, 454
  early theories of, 27–28
  in elderly, 600–601
  expressed emotion and, 476, 496
  family issues in, 474–476, 496–497
  fingerprints in, 471
  flat affect in, 462
  genetic factors in, 464–466, 465f
  hallucinations in, 460, 472–473, 492–495
  heightened perceptions in, 459
  homelessness and, 503f, 504
  inappropriate affect in, 461
  Laing's view of, 476–477
  living situations in, 503–504, 503f
  loose associations in, 458–459
  media depictions of, 454, 456–457
  overview of, 453–454, 477–478, 505
  paranoid, 464
  poverty of speech in, 462
  prevalence of, 453, 454f
  prodromal phase of, 463
  psychodynamic view of, 471–472
  psychological views of, 471–473
  as psychosis, 453, 466t
  research on, 27
  residual, 463, 464
  social labeling and, 474–475
  social withdrawal in, 462
  sociocultural views of, 473–477
  socioeconomic status and, 454, 473
  speech abnormalities in, 459, 462

DSM-IV-TR classification

Diagnostic and Statistical Manual of Mental Disorders, Fourth Edition, Text Revision, and *Diagnostic and Statistical Manual of Mental Disorders, Fourth Edition*, Washington, DC, American Psychiatric Association, 2000, 1994. Reprinted by permission.

(All categories are on Axis I except those indicated otherwise.)

Disorders Usually First Diagnosed in Infancy, Childhood, or Adolescence

Mental Retardation

Note: These are coded on Axis II.
Mild mental retardation
Moderate mental retardation
Severe mental retardation
Profound mental retardation
Mental retardation, severity unspecified

Learning Disorders

Reading disorder
Mathematics disorder
Disorder of written expression
Learning disorder NOS*

Motor Skills Disorder

Developmental coordination disorder

Communication Disorders

Expressive language disorder
Mixed receptive-expressive language disorder
Phonological disorder
Stuttering
Communication disorder NOS*

Pervasive Developmental Disorders

Autistic disorder
Rett's disorder
Childhood disintegrative disorder
Asperger's disorder
Pervasive development disorder NOS*

Attention-Deficit and Disruptive Behavior Disorders

Attention-deficit/hyperactivity disorder
    Combined type
    Predominantly inattentive type
    Predominantly hyperactive-impulsive type
Attention-deficit/hyperactivity disorder NOS*
Conduct disorder
Oppositional defiant disorder
Disruptive behavior disorder NOS*

Feeding and Eating Disorders of Infancy or Early Childhood

Pica
Rumination disorder
Feeding disorder of infancy or early childhood

Tic Disorders

Tourette's disorder
Chronic motor or vocal tic disorder
Transient tic disorder
Tic disorder NOS*

*NOS = Not otherwise specified

Elimination Disorders

Encopresis
    With constipation and overflow incontinence
    Without constipation and overflow incontinence
Enuresis (not due to a general medical condition)

Other Disorders of Infancy, Childhood, or Adolescence

Separation anxiety disorder
Selective mutism
Reactive attachment disorder of infancy or early childhood
Stereotypic movement disorder
Disorder of infancy, childhood, or adolescence NOS*

Delirium, Dementia, and Amnestic and Other Cognitive Disorders

Delirium

Delirium due to . . . *(indicate the general medical condition)*
Substance intoxication delirium
Substance withdrawal delirium
Delirium due to multiple etiologies
Delirium NOS*

Dementia

Dementia of the Alzheimer's type, with early onset
Dementia of the Alzheimer's type, with late onset
Vascular dementia

Dementia Due to Other General Medical Conditions

Dementia due to HIV disease
Dementia due to head trauma
Dementia due to Parkinson's disease
Dementia due to Huntington's disease
Dementia due to Pick's disease
Dementia due to Creutzfeldt-Jakob disease
Dementia due to . . . *(indicate the general medical condition not listed above)*
Substance-induced persisting dementia
Dementia due to multiple etiologies
Dementia NOS*

Amnestic Disorders

Amnestic disorders due to . . . *(indicate the general medical condition)*
Substance-induced persisting amnestic disorder
Amnestic disorder NOS*

Other Cognitive Disorders

Cognitive disorder NOS*

Mental Disorders Due to a General Medical Condition Not Elsewhere Classified

Catatonic disorder due to . . . *(indicate the general medical condition)*
Personality change due to . . . *(indicate the general medical condition)*
Mental disorder NOS* due to . . . *(indicate the general medical condition)*

Substance-Related Disorders

(Alcohol; Amphetamine; Caffeine; Cannabis; Cocaine; Hallucinogen; Inhalant; Nicotine; Opioid; Phencyclidine; Sedative, Hypnotic, or Anxiolytic; Polysubstance; Other)

Substance Use Disorders

Substance dependence
Substance abuse

Substance-Induced Disorders

Substance intoxication
Substance withdrawal
Substance intoxication delirium
Substance withdrawal delirium
Substance-induced persisting dementia
Substance-induced persisting amnestic disorder
Substance-induced psychotic disorder
Substance-induced mood disorder
Substance-induced anxiety disorder
Substance-induced sexual dysfunction
Substance-induced sleep disorder
Substance-related disorder NOS*

Schizophrenia and Other Psychotic Disorders

Schizophrenia
    Paranoid type
    Disorganized type
    Catatonic type
    Undifferentiated type
    Residual type
Schizophreniform disorder
Schizoaffective disorder
Delusional disorder
Brief psychotic disorder
Shared psychotic disorder
Psychotic disorder due to . . . *(indicate the general medical condition)*
Substance-induced psychotic disorder
Psychotic disorder NOS*

Mood Disorders

Depressive Disorders

Major depressive disorder
Dysthymic disorder
Depressive disorder NOS*

Bipolar Disorders

Bipolar I disorder
Bipolar II disorder
Cyclothymic disorder
Bipolar disorder NOS*
Mood disorder due to . . . *(indicate the general medical condition)*
Substance-induced mood disorder
Mood disorder NOS*

Anxiety Disorders

Panic disorder without agoraphobia
Panic disorder with agoraphobia
Agoraphobia without history of panic disorder
Specific phobia
Social phobia
Obsessive-compulsive disorder
Posttraumatic stress disorder